More Than Just a Textbook

*Log on to **tx.msmath2.com** to...*

Access your book from home

- Online Student Edition
- Student Workbooks

See mathematical concepts come to life

- Personal Tutor
- Concepts in Motion: BrainPOP® Movies
- Concepts in Motion: Interactive Labs
- Concepts in Motion: Animations

Practice what you've learned

- Chapter Readiness
- Extra Examples
- Self-Check Quizzes
- Reading in the Content Area
- Graphing Calculator Keystrokes
- Vocabulary Review
- Chapter Tests
- Texas Test Practice

Try these other fun activities

- Cross-Curricular Projects
- Real-World Careers
- GameZone Games

Glencoe Mathematics

TEXAS Mathematics

Course 2

Authors

Day • Frey • Howard • Hutchens

Luchin • McClain • Molix-Bailey

Ott • Pelfrey • Price

Vielhaber • Willard

McGraw Hill Glencoe

New York, New York Columbus, Ohio Chicago, Illinois Peoria, Illinois Woodland Hills, California

About the Cover

The Texas Prairies and Lakes region offers a wide range of attractions. Among them is the State Fair of Texas. Located in Dallas, it boasts the 212-foot Texas Star-the tallest Ferris wheel in North America. As with all circles, the ratio of the circumference of the Texas Star to its diameter is a constant, π. You'll learn more about ratios in Chapter 7 and circumference in Chapter 12.

About the Graphics

Kaleidoscopic dodecagon. Created with *Mathematica.*
A random collection of colored polygons in the plane is formed. A wedge of opening angle 2Pi/24 is cut out and a symmetric kaleidoscopic graphics is constructed by reflection and rotation of the polygons of the wedge. For more information, and for programs to construct such graphics, see: www.wolfram.com/r/textbook.

Glencoe

The McGraw-Hill Companies

Send all inquiries to:
Glencoe/McGraw-Hill
8787 Orion Place
Columbus, OH 43240-4027

ISBN-13: 978-0-07-874047-3
ISBN-10: 0-07-874047-9

5 6 7 8 9 10 043/027 15 14 13 12 11 10 09 08

Contents in Brief

Authors

Rhonda J. Molix-Bailey
Mathematics Consultant
Mathematics by Design
DeSoto, Texas

Roger Day, Ph.D.
Associate Professor of Mathematics
Department of Mathematics
Illinois State University
Normal, Illinois

Patricia Frey, Ed.D.
Math Coordinator at Westminster Community Charter School
Buffalo, New York

Arthur C. Howard
Mathematics Teacher
Houston Christian High School
Houston, Texas

Deborah A. Hutchens, Ed.D.
Principal
Chesapeake, Virginia

Beatrice Luchin
Mathematics Consultant
League City, Texas

Kay McClain, Ed.D.
Assistant Professor
Vanderbilt University
Nashville, Tennessee

Jack M. Ott, Ph.D.
Distinguished Professor of Secondary Education Emeritus
University of South Carolina
Columbia, South Carolina

Ronald Pelfrey, Ed.D.
Mathematics Specialist
Appalachian Rural Systemic Initiative and Mathematics Consultant
Lexington, Kentucky

Jack Price, Ed.D.
Professor Emeritus
California State Polytechnic University
Pomona, California

Kathleen Vielhaber
Mathematics Consultant
St. Louis, Missouri

Teri Willard, Ed.D.
Assistant Professor
Department of Mathematics
Central Washington University
Ellensburg, Washington

Contributing Author

FOLDABLES™ **Dinah Zike**
Educational Consultant, Dinah-Might Activities, Inc.
San Antonio, Texas

Texas Mathematics Advisory Board

Glencoe wishes to thank the following professionals for their invaluable feedback during the development of the program. They reviewed the table of contents, the prototype of the Teacher Wraparound Edition, and the Get Ready for the Texas Test chapter.

Louisa Acosta
Mathematics Teacher/Dept. Chair
Pflugerville Middle School
Pflugerville, Texas

Teresa Gillioz
Mathematics Teacher/Dept. Chair
Deepwater Jr. High/ Deer Park ISD
Pasadena, Texas

Susan Kocher
7th Grade Mathematics Teacher/Mathematics Dept. Chair
Katy ISD
Katy, Texas

Gail Brown
Teacher, Sixth Grade Mathematics
Mann Middle School
Abilene, Texas

Rita Hines
Advanced Placement Mathematics Teacher
Townview's Science and Engineering Magnet
Dallas, Texas

Sharon L. Kotarski
IB/AP Teacher
Coronado High School
El Paso, Texas

Leslie Denise Cerqueira
Mathematics Dept. Co-Chair & Teacher
South Houston Intermediate School
South Houston, Texas

John W. Kaatz
Mathematics Teacher/Dept. Chair
Westwood High School
Austin, Texas

Gary Lamoureaux
6th Grade Mathematics Teacher
Running Brushy Middle School
Leander, Texas

Maryann S. McDaniel
Mathematics Coordinator
Waller Independent School District
Waller, Texas

Antoinette Norris-Woodson
Mathematics & Kumon Instructor
Lake Jackson Kumon/
Angleton High School
Angleton, Texas

CaLandra Pervis
Secondary Mathematics Consultant
Project GRAD-Houston
Houston, Texas

Monique M. Smith
Mathematics Department Chairperson
Patrick Henry Middle School
Houston, Texas

Kimberly Moos
7th Grade Mathematics Teacher
Francis R. Scobee Jr. High School
San Antonio, Texas

Lizabeth Pool Peters, M. Ed.
Mathematics Dept. Chair & Educator
Hal Peterson Middle School
Kerrville, Texas

Damian J. Pillatzke
Secondary Mathematics Teacher
El Paso High School
El Paso, Texas

Nancy Trent
Mathematics Teacher
The Woodlands High School
The Woodlands, Texas

Mayen S. Nelson
Mathematics Dept. Chair
Woodson K-8
Houston, Texas

Dori Peterson
Mathematics Coordinator
John Paul Stevens High School
San Antonio, Texas

Cyndi Smith
Instructional Specialist
Mann Middle School
Abilene, Texas

Nancy Waldrum
Instructional Services Coordinator
Paris High School
Paris, Texas

Consultants

Glencoe/McGraw-Hill wishes to thank the following professionals for their feedback. They were instrumental in providing valuable input toward the development of this program in these specific areas.

Differentiated Instruction

Nancy Frey, Ph.D.
Associate Professor of Literacy
San Diego State University
San Diego, California

English Language Learners

Mary Avalos, Ph.D.
Assistant Chair, Teaching and Learning
Assistant Research Professor
University of Miami, School of Education
Coral Gables, Florida

Jana Echevarria, Ph.D.
Professor, College of Education
California State University, Long Beach
Long Beach, California

Josefina V. Tinajero, Ph.D.
Dean, College of Education
The University of Texas at El Paso
El Paso, Texas

Gifted and Talented

Ed Zaccaro
Author
Mathematics and science books for gifted children
Bellevue, Iowa

Graphing Calculator

Ruth M. Casey
Mathematics Teacher
Department Chair
Anderson County High School
Lawrenceburg, Kentucky

Jerry Cummins
Former President
National Council of Supervisors of Mathematics
Western Springs, Illinois

Learning Disabilities

Kate Garnett, Ph.D.
Chairperson, Coordinator
Learning Disabilities
School of Education
Department of Special Education
Hunter College, CUNY
New York, New York

Mathematical Fluency

Jason Mutford
Mathematics Instructor
Coxsackie-Athens Central School District
Coxsackie, New York

Pre-AP

Dixie Ross
AP Calculus Teacher
Pflugerville High School
Pflugerville, Texas

Reading and Vocabulary

Douglas Fisher, Ph.D.
Director of Professional Development and Professor
City Heights Educational Collaborative
San Diego State University
San Diego, California

Lynn T. Havens
Director of Project CRISS
Kalispell School District
Kalispell, Montana

Texas Reviewers

Each Texas Reviewer reviewed at least two chapters of the Student Edition, giving feedback and suggestions for improving the effectiveness of the mathematics instruction.

Louisa Acosta
Mathematics Teacher/Dept. Chair
Pflugerville Middle School
Pflugerville, Texas

Gail Brown
Teacher, Sixth Grade Mathematics
Mann Middle School
Abilene, Texas

Sondra E. Cano
Mathematics/Algebra Teacher
Jackson Intermediate School
Pasadena, Texas

Leslie Denise Cerqueira
Mathematics Dept. Co-Chair & Teacher
South Houston Intermediate School
South Houston, Texas

Karen Gailey
7th Grade Mathematics Teacher
Canutillo Middle School
Canutillo, Texas

Teresa Gillioz
Mathematics Teacher/Dept. Chair
Deepwater Jr. High/Deer Park ISD
Pasadena, Texas

Debbie Jacobs
Mathematics Department Head
Thompson Intermediate
Houston, Texas

Susan Kocher
7th Grade Mathematics Teacher/Math Dept. Chair
Katy ISD
Katy, Texas

Gary Lamoureaux
6th Grade Mathematics Teacher
Running Brushy Middle School
Leander, Texas

Barbara A. Leach
Retired
Crowley ISD
Crowley, Texas

Robin Lewis
Grade 7 Teacher/Mathematics Dept. Chair
Fairmont Jr. High
Deer Park, Texas

Tammie Manley-Gurley
Teacher
Forestwood Middle School
Lewisville, Texas

Carol McKeever, M. Ed.
Mathematics Teacher/Instructional Specialist for Mathematics
Central Middle School
Nederland, Texas

Lauralee Monsées
7th Grade Mathematics
Lamar Middle School
Austin, Texas

Mark S. Montgomery
7th Grade Mathematics
Tennyson Middle School
Waco, Texas

Kimberly Moos
7th Grade Mathematics Teacher
Francis R. Scobee Jr. High School
San Antonio, Texas

Jennifer Myers
Teacher
Cross Timbers Intermediate School
Arlington, Texas

Mayen S. Nelson
Mathematics Dept. Chair
Woodson K–8
Houston, Texas

Antoinette Norris-Woodson
Mathematics & Kumon Instructor
Lake Jackson Kumon/Angleton High School
Angleton, Texas

Charlotte L. Parker
Mathematics/6 Instructor
Donna Shepard Intermediate
Mansfield, Texas

Sandra Parrish
Mathematics Teacher
Levelland Middle School
Levelland, Texas

S. L. Pease
Mathematics Department Chair
San Angelo Central High School
San Angelo, Texas

Lizabeth Pool Peters, M. Ed.
Mathematics Dept. Chair & Educator
Hal Peterson Middle School
Kerrville, Texas

Lou Ann Peterson
Mathematics Teacher
Grisham Middle School
Austin, Texas

Emily Potts
Mathematics Teacher
Robinson Middle School
Plano, Texas

Sherrie Raines
Peer Facilitator; Mathematics Dept. Head
San Jacinto Intermediate
Pasadena, Texas

Margaret E. Reed
8th Grade Mathematics/Algebra Teacher
Lake Jackson Intermediate
Lake Jackson, Texas

Cyndi Smith
Instructional Specialist
Mann Middle School
Abilene, Texas

Monique M. Smith
Mathematics Department Chairperson
Patrick Henry Middle School
Houston, Texas

Joe Valentino
Mathematics Teacher
Clint Small Middle School
Austin, Texas

Unit 1

Number and Operations: Integers and Decimals

CHAPTER 1 Introduction to Algebra and Functions

Student Toolbox

Prerequisite Skills

- Get Ready for Chapter 1 23
- Get Ready for the Next Lesson 29, 33, 37, 41, 47, 52, 56, 61

Reading and Writing Mathematics

- Reading in the Content Area 38
- Reading Math 30, 35, 69
- Reading Word Problems 24
- Vocabulary Link 31, 53
- Writing in Math 29, 33, 37, 41, 42, 47, 52, 56, 61, 67

Texas Test Practice

- Griddable 52, 67
- Multiple Choice 29, 33, 37, 41, 47, 51, 52, 56, 61, 67
- Worked Out Example 50

Higher Order Thinking H.O.T. Problems

- Challenge 29, 33, 37, 41, 47, 52, 56, 61, 67
- Find the Error 41, 52
- Number Sense 56
- Open Ended 29, 33, 37, 41, 47, 56, 61, 67
- Select the Operation 43
- Select a Tool 61
- Which One Doesn't Belong? 33

Cross-Curricular Project 21

FOLDABLES™ 22, 70

Lesson 1-10, p. 66

CHAPTER 2 Integers

Lesson 2-7, p. 111

Student Toolbox

Table of Contents

CHAPTER 3 Applying Decimals

ASSESSMENT

Student Toolbox

Prerequisite Skills

Reading and Writing Mathematics

Texas Test Practice

Higher Order Thinking H.O.T. Problems

Lesson 3-2, p. 135

CHAPTER 4 Algebra: Linear Equations and Functions

Lesson 4-1, p. 177

Student Toolbox

Unit 2

Number and Operations: Fractions

CHAPTER 5 Fractions, Decimals, and Percents

Student Toolbox

Prerequisite Skills

- Get Ready for Chapter 5 227
- Get Ready for the Next Lesson 232, 237, 243, 248, 253, 258, 262

Reading and Writing Mathematics

- Reading Word Problems 233
- Vocabulary Link 245, 259
- Writing in Math 232, 237, 238, 243, 248, 253, 258, 262, 268

Texas Test Practice

- Griddable 237, 268
- Multiple Choice 232, 237, 243, 248, 253, 258, 262, 268
- Worked Out Example 265

Higher Order Thinking H.O.T. Problems

- Challenge 232, 237, 243, 248, 253, 258, 262, 268
- Find the Error 243, 258
- Number Sense 232, 239
- Open Ended 232, 242, 248, 258, 262
- Reasoning 261
- Select the Operation 239
- Select a Technique 262
- Which One Doesn't Belong? 253, 268

Cross-Curricular Project 225

FOLDABLES™ 226, 269

Lesson 5-1, p. 231

CHAPTER 6 Applying Fractions

Lesson 6-5, p. 302

Student Toolbox

Prerequisite Skills

Reading and Writing Mathematics

Texas Test Practice

Higher Order Thinking H.O.T. Problems

Unit 3

Patterns, Relationships, and Algebraic Thinking

Chapter 7 Ratios and Proportions

Lesson 7-1, p. 333

Student Toolbox

CHAPTER 8

Applying Percents

Lesson 8-7, p. 416

Student Toolbox

Prerequisite Skills

Reading and Writing Mathematics

Texas Test Practice

Higher Order Thinking H.O.T. Problems

Table of Contents

Unit 4

Statistics and Probability

Chapter 9 Statistics: Analyzing Data

Student Toolbox

Prerequisite Skills

Reading and Writing Mathematics

Texas Test Practice

Higher Order Thinking H.O.T. Problems

Lesson 9-3, p. 456

CHAPTER 10

Probability

Lesson 10-4, p. 520

Student Toolbox

Prerequisite Skills

Reading and Writing Mathematics

Texas Test Practice

Higher Order Thinking H.O.T. Problems

Unit 5

Geometry and Measurement

Chapter 11 Geometry: Polygons

Student Toolbox

Prerequisite Skills

Reading and Writing Mathematics

Texas Test Practice

Higher Order Thinking H.O.T. Problems

Lesson 11-9, p. 599

CHAPTER 12

Measurement: Two- and Three-Dimensional Figures

ASSESSMENT

Get Ready for the Texas Test

Student Toolbox

Prerequisite Skills

Reading and Writing Mathematics

Texas Test Practice

Higher Order Thinking H.O.T. Problems

CHAPTER 13 Extending Algebra and Geometry

Student Toolbox

Prerequisite Skills

Reading and Writing Mathematics

Texas Test Practice

Higher Order Thinking H.O.T. Problems

Student Handbook

Built-In Workbooks

Reference

Lesson 13-2, p. 679

Texas Essential Knowledge and Skills for Mathematics Grade 7

Knowledge and Skills		Student Expectation
NUMBER, OPERATION, AND QUANTITATIVE REASONING		
(7.1)	The student represents and uses numbers in a variety of equivalent forms.	The student is expected to: **(A)** compare and order integers and positive rational numbers; **(B)** convert between fractions, decimals, whole numbers, and percents mentally, on paper, or with a calculator; and **(C)** represent squares and square roots using geometric models.
(7.2)	The student adds, subtracts, multiplies, or divides to solve problems and justify solutions.	The student is expected to: **(A)** represent multiplication and division situations involving fractions and decimals with models, including concrete objects, pictures, words, and numbers; **(B)** use addition, subtraction, multiplication, and division to solve problems involving fractions and decimals; **(C)** use models, such as concrete objects, pictorial models, and number lines, to add, subtract, multiply, and divide integers and connect the actions to algorithms; **(D)** use division to find unit rates and ratios in proportional relationships such as speed, density, price, recipes, and student-teacher ratio; **(E)** simplify numerical expressions involving order of operations and exponents; **(F)** select and use appropriate operations to solve problems and justify the selections; and **(G)** determine the reasonableness of a solution to a problem.
PATTERNS, RELATIONSHIPS, AND ALGEBRAIC THINKING		
(7.3)	The student solves problems involving direct proportional relationships.	The student is expected to: **(A)** estimate and find solutions to application problems involving percent; and **(B)** estimate and find solutions to application problems involving proportional relationships such as similarity, scaling, unit costs, and related measurement units.
(7.4)	The student represents a relationship in numerical, geometric, verbal, and symbolic form.	The student is expected to: **(A)** generate formulas involving unit conversions, perimeter, area, circumference, volume, and scaling; **(B)** graph data to demonstrate relationships in familiar concepts such as conversions, perimeter, area, circumference, volume, and scaling; and **(C)** use words and symbols to describe the relationship between the terms in an arithmetic sequence (with a constant rate of change) and their positions in the sequence.

Knowledge and Skills		Student Expectation
(7.5)	The student uses equations to solve problems.	The student is expected to: **(A)** use concrete and pictorial models to solve equations and use symbols to record the actions; and **(B)** formulate problem situations when given a simple equation and formulate an equation when given a problem situation.
GEOMETRY AND SPATIAL REASONING		
(7.6)	The student compares and classifies two- and three-dimensional figures using geometric vocabulary and properties.	The student is expected to: **(A)** use angle measurements to classify pairs of angles as complementary or supplementary; **(B)** use properties to classify triangles and quadrilaterals; **(C)** use properties to classify three-dimensional figures, including pyramids, cones, prisms, and cylinders; and **(D)** use critical attributes to define similarity.
(7.7)	The student uses coordinate geometry to describe location on a plane.	The student is expected to: **(A)** locate and name points on a coordinate plane using ordered pairs of integers; and **(B)** graph reflections across the horizontal or vertical axis and graph translations on a coordinate plane.
(7.8)	The student uses geometry to model and describe the physical world.	The student is expected to: **(A)** sketch three-dimensional figures when given the top, side, and front views; **(B)** make a net (two-dimensional model) of the surface area of a three-dimensional figure; and **(C)** use geometric concepts and properties to solve problems in fields such as art and architecture.
MEASUREMENT		
(7.9)	The student solves application problems involving estimation and measurement.	The student is expected to: **(A)** estimate measurements and solve application problems involving length (including perimeter and circumference) and area of polygons and other shapes; **(B)** connect models for volume of prisms (triangular and rectangular) and cylinders to formulas of prisms (triangular and rectangular) and cylinders; and **(C)** estimate measurements and solve application problems involving volume of prisms (rectangular and triangular) and cylinders.

Knowledge and Skills		Student Expectation
PROBABILITY AND STATISTICS		
(7.10)	The student recognizes that a physical or mathematical model can be used to describe the experimental and theoretical probability of real-life events.	The student is expected to: **(A)** construct sample spaces for simple or composite experiments; and **(B)** find the probability of independent events.
(7.11)	The student understands that the way a set of data is displayed influences its interpretation.	The student is expected to: **(A)** select and use an appropriate representation for presenting and displaying relationships among collected data, including line plot, line graph, bar graph, stem and leaf plot, circle graph, and Venn diagrams, and justify the selection; and **(B)** make inferences and convincing arguments based on an analysis of given or collected data.
(7.12)	The student uses measures of central tendency and range to describe a set of data.	The student is expected to: **(A)** describe a set of data using mean, median, mode, and range; and **(B)** choose among mean, median, mode, or range to describe a set of data and justify the choice for a particular situation.

The Alamo, San Antonio

Knowledge and Skills		Student Expectation
UNDERLYING PROCESSES AND MATHEMATICAL TOOLS		
(7.13)	The student applies Grade 7 mathematics to solve problems connected to everyday experiences, investigations in other disciplines, and activities in and outside of school.	The student is expected to: **(A)** identify and apply mathematics to everyday experiences, to activities in and outside of school, with other disciplines, and with other mathematical topics; **(B)** use a problem-solving model that incorporates understanding the problem, making a plan, carrying out the plan, and evaluating the solution for reasonableness; **(C)** select or develop an appropriate problem-solving strategy from a variety of different types, including drawing a picture, looking for a pattern, systematic guessing and checking, acting it out, making a table, working a simpler problem, or working backwards to solve a problem; and **(D)** select tools such as real objects, manipulatives, paper/pencil, and technology or techniques such as mental math, estimation, and number sense to solve problems.
(7.14)	The student communicates about Grade 7 mathematics through informal and mathematical language, representations, and models.	The student is expected to: **(A)** communicate mathematical ideas using language, efficient tools, appropriate units, and graphical, numerical, physical, or algebraic mathematical models; and **(B)** evaluate the effectiveness of different representations to communicate ideas.
(7.15)	The student uses logical reasoning to make conjectures and verify conclusions.	The student is expected to: **(A)** make conjectures from patterns or sets of examples and nonexamples; and **(B)** validate his/her conclusions using mathematical properties and relationships.

State Mammal: Nine-banded Armadillo

Start Smart!

As you gear up to study mathematics, you are probably wondering, "What will I learn this year?" There are three focal points this year:

- Use direct proportional relationships in percent, geometry, measurement, and probability,
- Apply operations with decimals, fractions, and integers, and
- Use statistical measures to describe data.

Along the way, you'll learn more about problem solving, how to use the tools and language of mathematics, and how to THINK mathematically.

Let's Get Started!

Get Ready To Solve Problems

A Plan for Problem Solving

Real-World Problem Solving In 2001, Eric Weihenmayer made history as one of a few adventurous people who have made it to the summit of Mt. Everest, the highest peak in the world. What makes Eric's feat so incredible is that he is blind. He and his team had to plan the journey carefully and come up with unique solutions along the way when things didn't go just as they planned. Eric, who was a former mathematics teacher, and his team are expert problem solvers.

You may not face a challenge as big as Mt. Everest this year. But, when you do encounter a new problem situation, there is a series of steps that will help you to attack the problem efficiently. It's called the *four-step plan.*

Real-World EXAMPLE

MOUNTAIN CLIMBING **The Seven Summits are the highest mountains on each continent. The ages of two of the youngest climbers of the Seven Summits are 23 years 9 days and 22 years 175 days. What is the age difference between the two climbers?**

1 EXPLORE *What are you trying to find? Restate the problem in your own words. Use as few words as possible.*
You need to find the age difference between the climbers.

Do you think you'll need any additional information such as a formula or measurement conversion?
You may need to know the number of days in one year.
1 year = 365 days

2 PLAN *Are there any key words in the problem?*
The problem asks you to find the difference between the ages.
To find the difference, subtract.

Estimate the answer.

Think 23 years 9 days − 22 years 175 days
$\approx$ 23 years − 22.5 years
$\approx$ 0.5 year

3 SOLVE Before you can subtract, convert 1 year to days.

$$\begin{array}{r} 23\text{ yr} + 9\text{ d} \\ \underline{-\ 22\text{ yr} + 175\text{ d}} \end{array} \rightarrow \begin{array}{r} 22\text{ yr} + 365 + 9\text{ d} \\ \underline{-\ 22\text{ yr} + 175\text{ d}} \end{array} \rightarrow \begin{array}{r} 22\text{ yr} + 374\text{ d} \\ \underline{-\ 22\text{ yr} + 175\text{ d}} \\ 199\text{ d} \end{array}$$

The age difference between the climbers is 199 days.

4 CHECK ***Is the answer reasonable?***
Compare your answer to the estimate. Since 199 days is a little more than one half year, the answer is reasonable.

Practice

Use the four-step plan to solve each problem.

1. As the length of a gift box increases by $2\frac{1}{4}$ inches, the price of the gift box increases by \$1.50. There are five different sizes of gift boxes. The box shown at the right is the middle-sized gift box. It costs \$4.65. What are the lengths of the remaining gift boxes? What do they cost?

2. The counselors at Hembrick Middle School are assigning students to math classes for the coming year. There can be no more than 28 students in any class. The counselors decided to add or remove the same number of students from each class. How many students should be moved? What are the new class sizes?

Mr. Leonard	Ms. Jackowski	Coach Broussard	Mrs. Almedia	Mr. Chan	Miss Banks
31	24	26	30	23	25

3. The Academic Boosters expect 500 people at the annual awards banquet. If each table seats 8 people, how many tables are needed?

4. Samantha was making treat bags for her classmates. She has already made 2 dozen bags. If she wants to have a treat bag for each of the 33 students in her class, how many more should she make?

5. Mrs. Bentley spent \$125 to rent a popcorn machine for the school carnival and \$80 to buy popcorn, oil, and other supplies. If she sold 256 bags of popcorn for \$2 each, how much money did she make after paying for the machine and the supplies?

Problem-Solving Strategies

Real-World Problem Solving The artistry of stained glass windows has been around since about 313 A.D. Sometimes the designer uses repeated patterns, like tessellations, to create the window.

There are many different types of problems that you encounter in your life. In mathematics, one of the most common problem-solving strategies is the *look for a pattern* strategy. You can use problem-solving strategies to solve a variety of problems.

Real-World EXAMPLE

SCHOOL Steven is trying to determine the maximum number of students that can sit in the small auditorium at his school. The first row has 28 seats. He notices that the second row has two more seats than the first row, and the third row has two more seats than the second row. If there are 8 rows of seats in the auditorium, how many students can be seated at one time?

1 EXPLORE *What are you trying to find? Restate the problem in your own words. Use as few words as possible.*
You need to find the total number of students that can be seated in the auditorium.

What information do you need to solve the problem?
You need the number of seats in each row.

2 PLAN Make a table showing the number of seats in each row. Then find the total number of seats in the auditorium.

3 SOLVE You could add to find the total. But, if you look closely, you'll notice another pattern in the table—pairs of numbers add up to 70.

Row Number	1	2	3	4	5	6	7	8
Number of Seats	28	30	32	34	36	38	40	42

There are 4 groups of 70. So, there are 4(70) or 280 seats in the auditorium.

4 CHECK ***Is the answer reasonable?***
Four of the numbers round to 30, and four round to 40.
$4 \times 30 = 120$ and $4 \times 40 = 160$. $120 + 160 = 280$ ✔

Practice

Use the *look for a pattern* strategy to solve each problem.

1. Caton and Jordan are playing a game called Mancala. They have been keeping score by placing a ✔ beside the winner's name. If the pattern continues, how many wins will Caton have after 20 games?

Game	1	2	3	4	5	6	7	8
Caton	✔	✔		✔		✔	✔	
Jordan			✔		✔			✔

2. The table shows the amount of money in Jennifer's savings and checking accounts for the last several months. If the trend continues, in which month will Jennifer's savings account be greater than her checking account? How much money will she have in each account?

Month	Savings (dollars)	Checking (dollars)
1	346.25	735.75
2	388.75	693.25
3	431.25	650.75
4	473.75	608.25
…	…	…

3. Blaise Pascal was a famous mathematician who lived in the 1600s. Pascal is well known for a pattern known as Pascal's Triangle. What patterns do you see in Pascal's Triangle?

1
1 1
1 2 1
1 3 3 1
1 4 6 4 1
1 5 10 10 5 1
1 6 15 20 15 6 1
1 7 21 35 35 21 7 1

Multi-Step Problems

Real-World Problem Solving Reliant Stadium, home of the Houston Texans, went into sports history books in September, 2002, as the first NFL stadium with a retractable roof. The roof is made up of two sections that meet at the 50-yard line. Imagine the problem-solving situations the engineers, architects, and contractors encountered when designing and building this stadium! How do you suppose they solved them?

You encounter mathematics everyday. But usually it's not written as a problem like 10×25. Often the mathematics you encounter takes more than one step to solve. We call these problems *multi-step problems*. How do you solve a multi-step problem?—one step at a time.

Real-World EXAMPLE

FOOD The Fort Couch Middle School Cafeteria has a special lunch every Thursday. How much will you save by buying the special on Thursday instead of each item separately on any other day?

Entreé		Sides	
Chili	\$1.49	Salad	\$1.19
Chicken Fingers	\$1.39	Fruit	\$0.99
Hamburger	\$1.99	Tortilla Chips	\$1.29
All Drinks	\$0.99	**Thursday Special**	
		Chili, Salad, and Drink	\$3.49

1 EXPLORE *What are you trying to find?*
You need to find how much you'll save by buying the special instead of buying the items separately. So, you need to find the difference between the two costs.

What information do you need to find the difference?
You need the cost of the special and the total cost of the items.

2 PLAN

What steps do you need to solve the problem?

Step 1 Find the total cost of the items by adding.

Step 2 Find the difference between the cost of the special and the total of the items.

3 SOLVE

Step 1

\$1.49	cost of chili
1.19	cost of salad
+ 0.99	cost of drink
\$3.67	total cost

Step 2

\$3.67	total cost
− 3.49	cost of special
\$0.18	difference

So, you will save \$0.18 by buying the special on Thursday instead of each item separately on any other day.

4 CHECK

Use estimation to check. The three items together cost about \$1.50 + \$1.20 + \$1.00 or about \$3.70. The special costs about \$3.50. So the difference is about \$0.20. ✔

Practice

1. **CIRCUS** The table displays the ticket prices for the circus. For one show, 180 adult tickets, 360 child tickets, 70 student tickets, and 50 senior tickets were sold. Find the total income from tickets for the one show.

Ticket Prices	
Adult	\$5
Student	\$4
Child	\$2
Senior	\$3

2. **EARNINGS** Dolores earns \$9 an hour and worked a total of 75 hours this month. Dexter earns \$7 an hour and worked a total of 94 hours this month. How much more did Dolores earn this month than Dexter?

3. **GEOMETRY** The courtyard at Eastmoor Middle School is shaped like a rectangle that is 18.8 feet long. If the width of the courtyard is 4.8 feet less than the length, what is the total distance around the courtyard?

4. **TIME** Nathan has 3 hours before he has to be at field hockey practice. He spends 45 minutes working on homework, 25 minutes eating dinner, and 35 minutes watching television. How much time does he have left before he has to be at hockey practice?

5. **MOVIES** The table shows the concession stand prices including tax at Movie Central. Paula ordered 2 medium drinks and a large popcorn. If she gave the cashier \$10, how much change should she receive?

Movie Central Menu

Drinks		Popcorn	
Small	\$1.99	Small	\$2.49
Medium	\$2.75	Medium	\$3.50
Large	\$3.50	Large	\$3.95

Tools for Problem Solving

The Graphing Calculator

This year, you may use an exciting tool to help you solve problems—a graphing calculator. Graphing Calculator Labs have been included in your textbook so you can use technology to explore concepts. These labs use the TI-83 Plus or TI-84 Plus calculator. A graphing calculator does more than just graph. You can also use it to calculate.

[Y=] is used to enter equations.

Press [2nd] to access the additional functions listed above each key.

The [x^2] key is used to find the second power of a number or expression.

Press [ON] to turn on your calculator. Press [2nd] [OFF] to turn off your calculator.

[(–)] is used to indicate a negative or opposite value.

Press [2nd] [TABLE] to display a table of values for equations entered using the [Y=] key.

Press [CLEAR] once to clear an entry. Press [CLEAR] twice to clear the screen.

Use the operation keys to add, subtract, multiply or divide. Multiplication is shown as * on the screen and division is displayed as /.

The [ENTER] key acts like an equals button to evaluate an expression. It is also used to select menu items.

EXAMPLE Entering Expressions

1 Evaluate each expression.

a. **$6 + 4 \times 5 - 9$**

Keystrokes: 6 [+] 4 [×] 5 [−] 9 [ENTER]

b. **$3 + 2 \times 10 - 12 \div 4$**

Keystrokes: 3 [+] 2 [×] 10 [−] 12 [÷] 4 [ENTER]

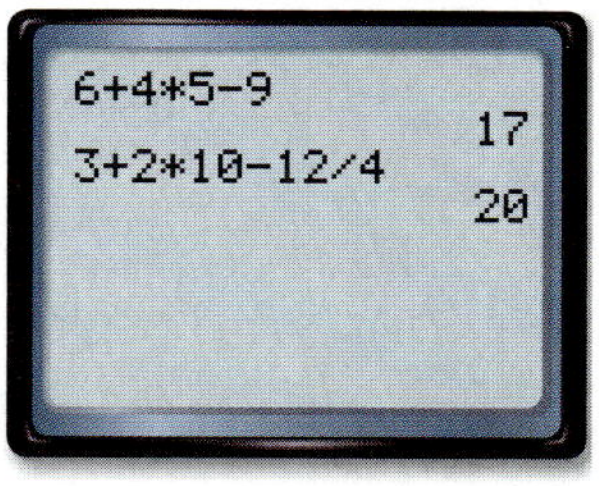

Evaluate each expression.

1. $20 \div 2 \times 10$
2. $14 + 28 \div 7$
3. $25 + 10 - 5 \div 5$
4. $200 - 10 \times 10 \times 2$
5. $12 \div 4 \times 2 + 8$
6. $114 + 10 - 9 \times 9$

EXAMPLE Using Parentheses

2 Evaluate each expression.

a. **$4 \times (3 + 2) \div (12 - 10)$**

Keystrokes: 4 [×] [(] 3 [+] 2 [)] [÷] [(] 12 [−] **10** [)] [ENTER]

b. **$3(12 - 5) + (7 + 4)$**

Keystroke: 3 [(] 12 [−] 5 [)] [+] [(] 7 [+] 4 [)] [ENTER]

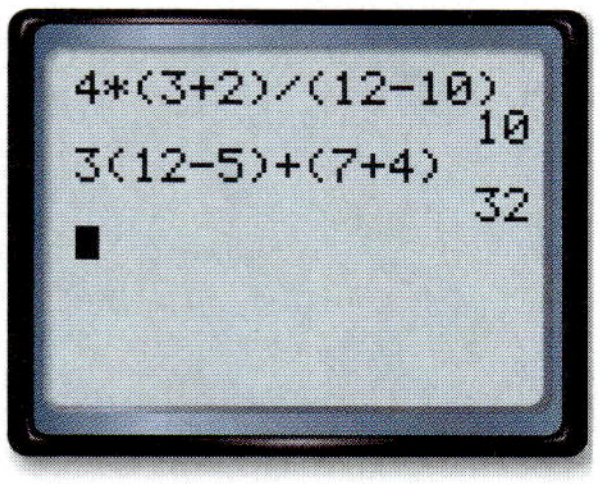

Evaluate each expression.

7. $6 \times (8 + 4) \div 2$
8. $2 \times (3 + 9) \times 2$
9. $(8 + 12) \times (8 \div 4)$
10. $(13 - 6) \times (2 + 1)$
11. $(30 - 14) \times (2 + 8)$
12. $(26 - 2) \div (15 - 3)$

EXAMPLE Evaluating with Integers

3 Evaluate each expression.

a. **$6 + (-4)$**

Keystrokes: 6 [+] [(] [(−)] 4 [)] [ENTER]

b. **$-8(-3)$**

Keystrokes: [(−)] 8 [(] [(−)] 3 [)] [ENTER]

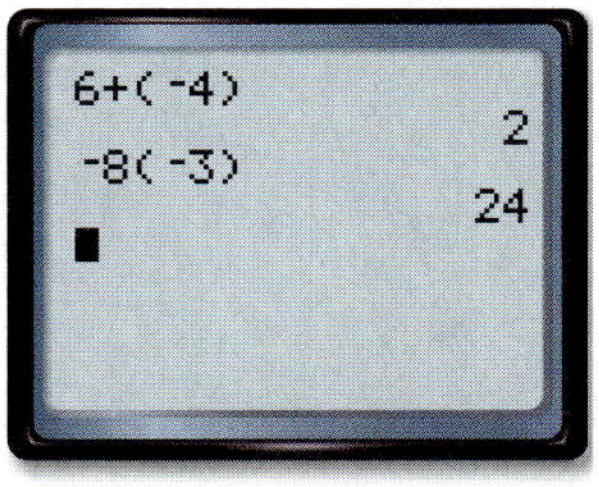

Evaluate each expression.

13. $-4 + 8$
14. $14 + (-16)$
15. $-36 - 40$
16. $18 - (-32)$
17. $5(-12)$
18. $-6(-11)$

Techniques for Problem Solving

Choose the Best Method of Computation

Solving problems is more than using paper and pencil. Follow the path to choose the best method of computation.

Practice

Choose the best method of computation to solve each problem. Then solve.

1. A restaurant prepared 1,987 lunches last week. *About* how many lunches were prepared each day?
2. Eduardo purchased a bag of pretzels, a mechanical pencil, and a package of baseball cards. The total bill is $9.12. He gives the cashier a $20 bill. How much change should he receive?

For Exercises 3–5, use the information in the table.

Animal	Heart Rates (beats per minute)
Cat	120
Elephant	30
Horse	44
Mouse	700
Rabbit	205

Source: *Merck Veterinary Manual*

3. On average, how many times does an elephant's heart beat in 1 hour?
4. On average, how many times does a horse's heart beat in 1 hour?
5. On average, how many more times does a mouse's heart beat in 1 hour than a rabbit's heart?
6. The number of students at Blendon Middle School is half the number it was twenty years ago. If there were 826 students twenty years ago, how many students are there now?
7. Enrique has two samples of the same chemical. He wants to store both samples in a 0.5-liter container. One sample is 0.38 liter. The other sample is 0.21 liter. Can he store both samples in the container?
8. The table below shows the average number of pounds of various meat consumed per person in the United States.

2004 Per Capita Meat Consumption (pounds)	
Chicken	85.1
Beef	66.1
Pork	51.3
Turkey	17.1
Lamb & Mutton	1.1

Source: National Turkey federation

About how many more pounds of beef than turkey is consumed on average by each person per year?

9. Pluto, normally the farthest planet from the Sun, is also the slowest. Its average speed around the Sun is 10,604 miles per hour. Earth, by contrast, travels 6.28 times as fast. What is the average speed of Earth?
10. Emilio is taking karate lessons. The instructor charges $25 for each lesson. If Emilio has 8 lessons in one month, how much does he owe the instructor?

How to Use Your Math Book

Reading Your Math Book

Why do I need my math book? Have you ever been in class and not understood all of what was presented? Or, you understood everything in class, but at home, got stuck on how to solve a couple of problems? Maybe you just wondered when you were ever going to use this stuff?

These next few pages are designed to help you understand everything your math book can be used for ... besides homework problems!

Before you read, have a goal.

- What information are you trying to find?
- Why is this information important to you?
- How will you use the information?

Have a plan when you read.

- Read the Main IDEA at the beginning of the lesson.
- Look over photos, tables, graphs, and opening activities.
- Locate words highlighted in yellow and read their definitions.
- Find Key Concept and Concept Summary boxes for a preview of what's important.
- Skim the example problems.

Keep a positive attitude.

- Expect mathematics reading to take time.
- It is normal to *not* understand some concepts the first time.
- If you don't understand something you read, it is likely that others don't understand it either.

Doing Your Homework

Regardless of how well you paid attention in class, by the time you arrive at home, your notes may no longer make any sense and your homework seems impossible. It's during these times that your book can be most useful.

- Each lesson has example problems, solved step-by-step, so you can review the day's lesson material.
- Math Online has extra examples at tx.msmath2.com to coach you through solving those difficult problems.
- Each exercise set has HOMEWORK HELP boxes that show you which examples may help with your homework problems.
- Answers to the odd-numbered problems are in the back of the book. Use them to see if you are solving the problems correctly. If you have difficulty on an even problem, do the odd problem next to it. That should give you a hint about how to proceed with the even problem.

Studying for a Test

You may think there is no way to study for a math test. However, there *are* ways to review before a test. Your book can help!

- Review all of the new vocabulary words and be sure you understand their definitions. These can be found on the first page of each lesson or highlighted in yellow in the text.
- Review the notes you've taken on your FOLDABLES Study Organizer and write down any questions that you still need answered.
- Practice all of the concepts presented in the chapter by using the chapter Study Guide and Review. It has additional problems for you to try as well as more examples to help you understand. You can also take the Chapter Practice Test.
- Take the Self-Check Quizzes at tx.msmath2.com.

Scavenger Hunt

Let's Get Started

Use the Scavenger Hunt below to learn where things are located in each chapter.

1. What is the title of Chapter 1?
2. How can you tell what you'll learn in Lesson 1-1?
3. Sometimes you may ask "When am I ever going to use this". Name a situation that uses the concepts from Lesson 1-2.
4. In the margin of Lesson 1-2, there is a Vocabulary Link. What can you learn from that feature?
5. What is the key concept presented in Lesson 1-3?
6. How many examples are presented in Lesson 1-3?
7. What is the title of the feature in Lesson 1-3 that tells you how to read square roots?
8. What is the web address where you could find extra examples?
9. Suppose you're doing your homework on page 40 and you get stuck on Exercise 18. Where could you find help?
10. What problem-solving strategy is presented in the Problem-Solving Investigation in Lesson 1-5?
11. List the new vocabulary words that are presented in Lesson 1-7.
12. What is the web address that would allow you to take a self-check quiz to be sure you understand the lesson?
13. There is a Real-World Career mentioned in Lesson 1-10. What is it?
14. On what pages will you find the Study Guide and Review for Chapter 1?
15. Suppose you can't figure out how to do Exercise 25 in the Study Guide and Review on page 72. Where could you find help?

TEXAS Data File

The following pages contain data about Texas that you'll use throughout the book.

TEXAS STADIUM

Texas Stadium

Season	Attendance
2004	510,892
2003	511,224
2002	504,717
2001	505,501
2000	504,360
1999	513,295
1998	510,438
1997	511,767
1996	513,794
1995	518,167

Source: football.ballparks.com

SAN ANTONIO SPURS

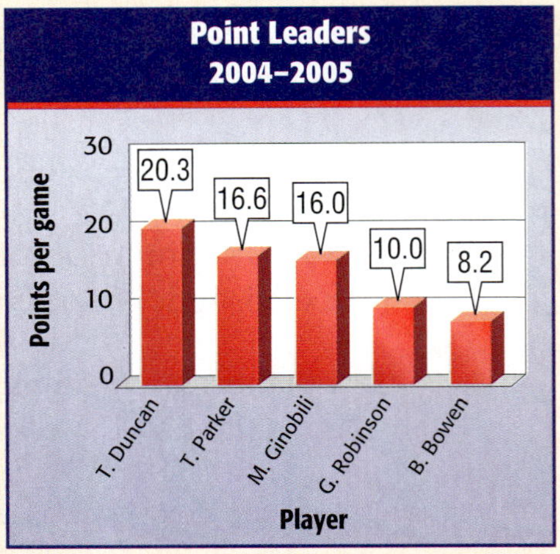

Source: nba.com

BOOMERANG ROLLER COASTER

Amusement Park: Six Flags Fiesta Texas
Dimensions: $288\frac{3}{4}$ feet × $98\frac{5}{12}$ feet
Capacity: 760 riders per hour
Length: 935 feet
Height: $116\frac{1}{2}$ feet
Speed: 47 miles per hour
Duration: 1 minute 48 seconds
G-Force: 5.2
Source: rcdb.com

TEMPERATURE

Record Temperatures in Texas					
Record	°F	°C	Date	Location	Elevation (feet)
High	120	49	August 12, 1936	Seymour	1,291
Low	−23	−31	February 8, 1933	Seminole	3,275

Source: infoplease.com

KIDDIE PARK SAN ANTONIO

Source: kiddiepark.com

HOUSTON

EGG ROLLS Houston produces 80% of the egg rolls sold in grocery stores. A skilled wrapper can produce 4,000 egg rolls in an 8-hour period.

Source: texancultures.utsa.edu

STONEHENGE II

The Original Stonehenge is an ancient monument located in England. The outer rim is composed of 18-foot high stones, arranged in a circle with a diameter of 108 feet. Stonehenge II, located in Hunt, Texas is 90% as wide and 60% as tall as the orginal monument.

Source: roadsideamerica.com/attract

MOUNTAIN LION

Habitat: Usually found throughout the Trans-Pecos, as well as the brushlands of south Texas and portions of the Hill Country
Body length: $2\frac{1}{2}$–3 ft
Height at shoulder: 25–30 in.
Source: tpwd.state.tx.us

ROSEATE SPOONBILL

Habitat: Usually found in the bays, marshes, and estuaries along the Gulf Coast
Height: 32 in. (81 cm)
Average wingspan: 50 in. (127 cm)
Source: tpwd.state.tx.us

SPACE CENTER HOUSTON

Space Center Houston
Admission Fees

Adults	$17.95
Children (4-11)	$13.95
Seniors	$16.95
Parking	$4.00

Source: spacecenter.org

ROUTE 66 FACTS

- There were originally 178 miles in Texas, from Texola to Glenrio.
- About 91% of the route is still in use.
- The route is on the south side of I-40 from Oklahoma to Amarillo, except for McLean; is on the north side of I-40 from Amarillo to New Mexico.

Source: historic66.com

JALAPEÑO CORNBREAD

Recipe for: Jalapeño Cornbread

$\frac{3}{4}$ cup yellow cornmeal	1 cup buttermilk
$\frac{3}{4}$ cup flour	3 eggs, slightly beaten
1 tablespoon sugar	3 tablespoons butter, melted
1 teaspoon salt	$\frac{1}{3}$ cup Jalapeño peppers, finely chopped
1 tablespoon baking powder	$\frac{1}{2}$ cup cheddar cheese, shredded
$\frac{1}{2}$ teaspoon baking soda	$\frac{1}{4}$ cup onion, chopped

TRANSPORTATION

Licensed Drivers		
Year	**Texas**	**United States**
2000	14,024,305	190,625,023
1995	12,369,243	176,628,482
1990	11,136,694	167,015,250
1985	10,809,078	156,868,277
1980	9,287,286	145,295,036
1975	7,509,497	129,790,666
1970	6,380,057	111,542,787
1965	5,413,887	98,502,152
1960	4,352,168	87,252,563
1955	3,874,834	74,685,949
1950	2,687,349	59,322,278

Source: texasalmanac.com

TEXAS CITRUS PRODUCTION

Texas Citrus Production

Year	Oranges (million boxes)	Grapefruit (million boxes)
2004	1.77*	6.60
2005	1.53	5.40

*1.53 million boxes are early and mid-season oranges, and 0.23 million boxes were Valencia oranges

Source: nass.usda.gov/tx

THE ALAMO

TEXAS STATE FAIR

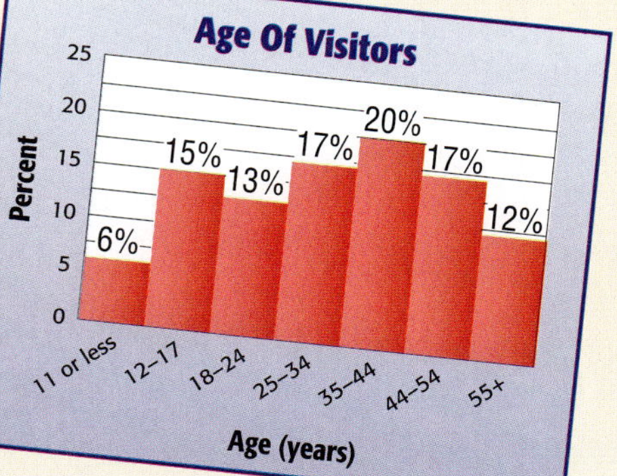

Source: bigtex.com

GALVESTON, TEXAS

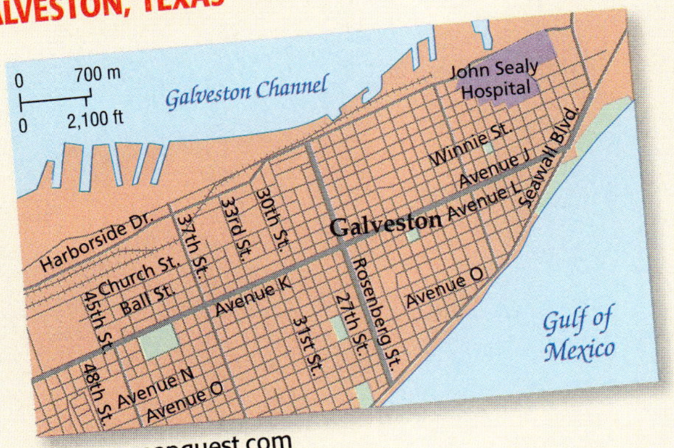

Source: mapquest.com

Unit 1

Number and Operations: Integers and Decimals

Focal Point

Apply addition, subtraction, multiplication, and division of decimals and integers to solve problems and equations.

CHAPTER 1
Introduction to Algebra and Functions

BIG Idea Represent relationships in numerical, geometric, verbal, and symbolic form.

CHAPTER 2
Integers

BIG Idea Represent and use numbers in a variety of equivalent forms.

BIG Idea Add, subtract, multiply, and divide to solve problems and justify solutions.

CHAPTER 3
Applying Decimals

BIG Idea Add, subtract, multiply, and divide to solve problems and justify solutions.

CHAPTER 4
Algebra: Linear Equations and Functions

BIG Idea Use equations to solve problems.

Cross-Curricular Project

Math and Geography

The Wide World of Soccer Soccer fans, get up on your feet! You've been selected to join us on a world-wide soccer adventure. Along the way, you'll gather data about the geography of countries where soccer is the favorite sport. You'll also make some predictions about the future of soccer in the United States. We will be leaving on our adventure shortly, so pack your math tools and your thinking cap. This is one adventure you don't want to miss!

Math Online Log on to tx.msmath2.com to begin.

CHAPTER 1

Introduction to Algebra and Functions

Knowledge and Skills

- Add, subtract, multiply, or divide to solve problems and justify solutions. **TEKS 7.2**
- Represent relationships in numerical, geometric, verbal, and symbolic form. **TEKS 7.4**

Key Vocabulary

algebra (p. 44)

defining the variable (p. 50)

evaluate (p. 31)

numerical expression (p. 38)

Real-World Link

TIME Tours of the Texas Capitol are approximately 45 minutes in length. You can use the four-step problem-solving plan to determine about how many tours are given daily between 8:30 A.M. and 4:30 P.M.

FOLDABLES™ Study Organizer

Introduction to Algebra and Functions Make this Foldable to help you organize your notes. Begin with eleven sheets of notebook paper.

1. **Staple** the eleven sheets together to form a booklet.

2. **Cut** tabs. Make each one 2 lines longer than the one before it.

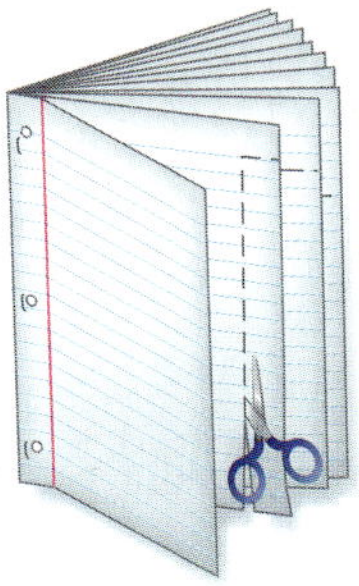

3. **Write** the chapter title on the cover and label each tab with the lesson number.

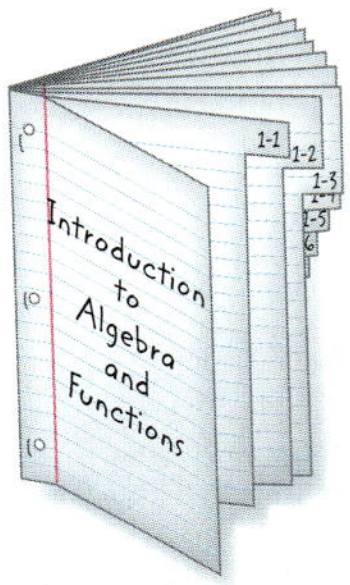

GET READY for Chapter 1

Diagnose Readiness You have two options for checking Prerequisite Skills.

Option 2

Math Online Take the Online Readiness Quiz at tx.msmath2.com.

Option 1

Take the Quick Quiz below. Refer to the Quick Review for help.

QUICK Quiz

Add. (Used in Lessons 1-1, 1-4 through 1-10)

1. 89.3 + 16.5
2. 7.9 + 32.45
3. 54.25 + 6.39
4. 10.8 + 2.6
5. **TECHNOLOGY** Patrick bought a personal electronic organizer for \$59.99 and a carrying case for \$12.95. What was his total cost, not including tax?

Subtract. (Used in Lessons 1-1, 1-4 through 1-10)

6. 24.6 − 13.3
7. 9.1 − 6.6
8. 30.55 − 2.86
9. 17.4 − 11.2

Multiply. (Used in Lessons 1-1 through 1-10)

10. 4 × 7.7
11. 9.8 × 3
12. 2.7 × 6.3
13. 8.5 × 1.2

Divide. Round to the nearest hundredth, if necessary. (Used in Lessons 1-1, 1-4 through 1-10)

14. 37.49 ÷ 4.6
15. 14.31 ÷ 2.7
16. 5.94 ÷ 6.16
17. 11.15 ÷ 2.5
18. **PIZZA** Four friends decided to split the cost of a pizza evenly. The total cost was \$25.48. How much does each friend need to pay?

QUICK Review

Example 1 Find 17.89 + 43.2.

$$\begin{array}{r} 17.89 \\ +\ 43.20 \\ \hline 61.09 \end{array}$$

Line up the decimal points.
Annex a zero.

Example 2 Find 37.45 − 8.52.

$$\begin{array}{r} 37.45 \\ -\ 8.52 \\ \hline 28.93 \end{array}$$

Line up the decimal points.

Example 3 Find 1.7 × 3.5.

1.7 ← 1 decimal place
× 3.5 ← + 1 decimal place
5.95 ← 2 decimal places

Example 4 Find 24.6 ÷ 2.5.

$2.5\overline{)24.6} \rightarrow 25.\overline{)246.}$ Multiply both numbers by the same power of 10.

$$\begin{array}{r} 9.84 \\ 25\overline{)246.00} \\ -225 \\ \hline 21\ 0 \\ -20\ 0 \\ \hline 1\ 00 \\ -1\ 00 \\ \hline 0 \end{array}$$

Annex zeros.

Divide as with whole numbers.

READING Word Problems

Making Sense

When you solve a word problem, the first thing to do is to read the problem carefully. The last thing to do is to see whether your answer makes sense. Sometimes a picture can help.

> Kelly lives 5 miles from school. This is 4 times as far as Miguel lives from school. How far does Miguel live from school?

If you look just at the key words in the problem, it might seem that 4 *times* 5 would give the solution.

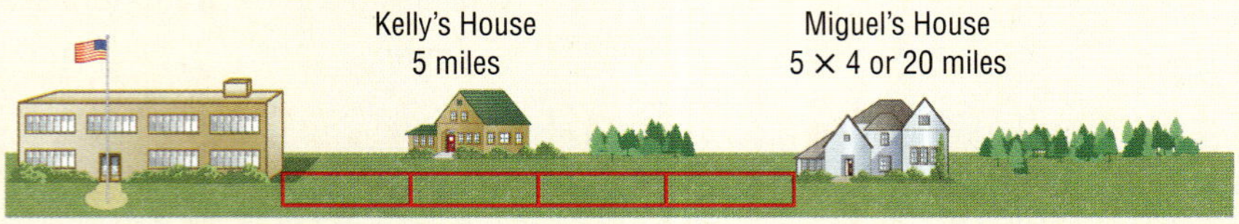

But the important question is, "Does this solution make sense?" In this case, the solution does *not* make sense because Kelly lives farther away. This problem is solved by dividing.

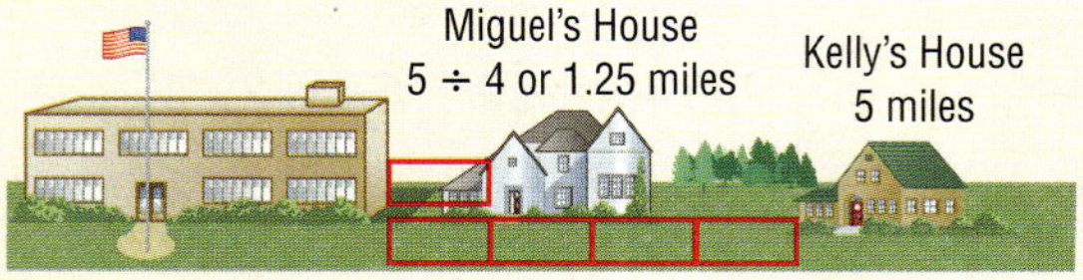

So, Miguel lives 1.25 miles away from school.

PRACTICE

For Exercises 1 and 2, choose the model that illustrates each problem. Explain your reasoning. Then solve.

1. Jennifer has saved $210 to purchase an MP3 player. She needs $299 to buy it. How much more money does she need?

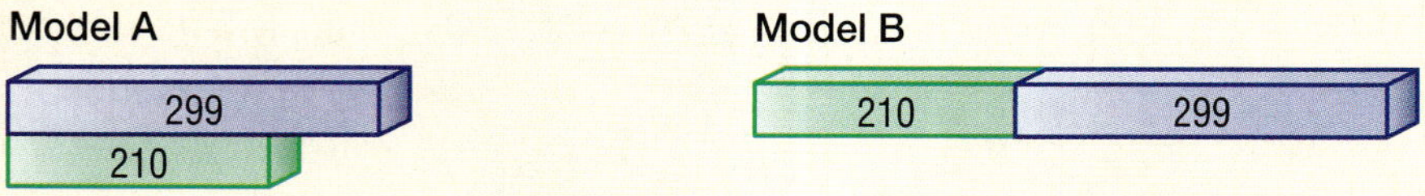

2. The school cafeteria sold 465 lunches on Thursday. They expect to sell 75 more lunches on Friday because they serve pizza that day. How many lunches do they expect to sell on Friday?

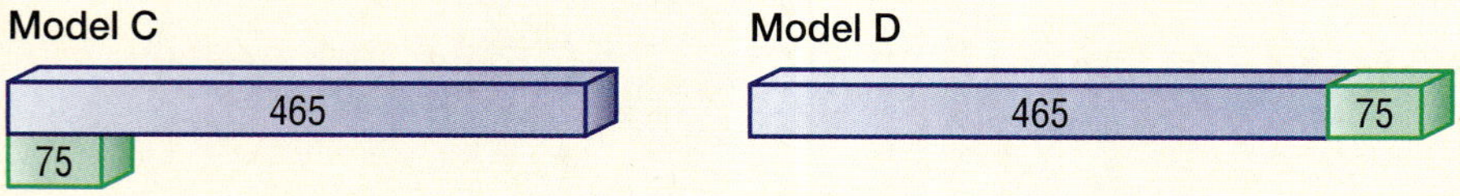

1-1 A Plan for Problem Solving

Main IDEA

Solve problems using the four-step plan.

Targeted TEKS
7.13 The student applies Grade 7 mathematics to solve problems connected to everyday experiences, investigations in other disciplines, and activities in and outside of school.
(B) use a problem-solving model that incorporates understanding the problem, making a plan, carrying out the plan, and evaluating the solution for reasonableness.
Also addresses TEKS 7.13(A).

GET READY for the Lesson

ANALYZE GRAPHS The bar graph shows the countries with the most world championship motocross wins. What is the total number of wins for these five countries?

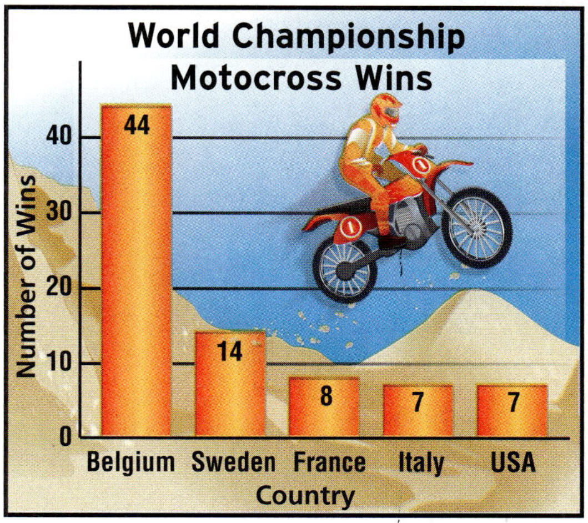

Source: Motocross.com

1. Do you have all of the information necessary to solve this problem?
2. Explain how you would solve this problem. Then solve it.
3. Does your answer make sense? Explain.
4. What can you do if your first attempt at solving the problem does not work?

In mathematics, there is a *four-step plan* you can use to help you solve any problem.

1. **Explore**
   - Read the problem carefully.
   - What information is given?
   - What do you need to find out?
   - Is enough information given?
   - Is there any extra information?

2. **Plan**
   - How do the facts relate to each other?
   - Select a strategy for solving the problem. There may be several that you can use.
   - Estimate the answer.

3. **Solve**
   - Use your plan to solve the problem.
   - If your plan does not work, revise it or make a new plan.
   - What is the solution?

4. **Check**
   - Does your answer fit the facts given in the problem?
   - Is your answer reasonable compared to your estimate?
   - If not, make a new plan and start again.

STUDY TIP

Four-Step Plan
No matter what strategy you use, you can always use the four-step plan to solve a problem.

Real-World Link In a recent year, worldwide consumers purchased 8.8 million LCD (Liquid Crystal Display) TVs.
Source: *Display Search*

EXAMPLE Use the Four-Step Plan

1 **TELEVISION** **There were about 260 million TVs in the U.S. in 2005. This amount increases by 4 million each year after 2005. In what year will there be at least 300 million TVs?**

Explore *What are you trying to find?*
In what year will there be at least 300 million TVs in the U.S.?

What information do you need to solve the problem?
You know how many TVs there were in 2005.
Also, the number increases by 4 million each year.

Plan Find the number of TVs needed to reach 300 million. Then divide this number by 4 to find the number of years that will pass before the total reaches 300 million TVs.

Solve The change in the number of TVs from 260 million to 300 million is 300 − 260 or 40 million TVs. Dividing the difference by 4, you get 40 ÷ 4 or 10.

You can also use the *make a table* strategy.

Year	'05	'06	'07	'08	'09	'10	'11	'12	'13	'14	'15
Number (millions)	260	264	268	272	276	280	284	288	292	296	300

+4 +4 +4 +4 +4 +4 +4 +4 +4 +4

So, there will be at least 300 million TVs in the U.S. in the year 2015.

Check 10 years × 4 million = 40 million
260 million + 40 million = 300 million ✔

CHECK Your Progress

a. **WHALES** A baby blue whale gains about 200 pounds each day. About how many pounds does a baby blue whale gain per hour?

Problems can be solved using different operations or strategies.

KEY CONCEPT — Problem-Solving Strategies

guess and check	use a graph
look for a pattern	work backward
make an organized list	eliminate possibilities
draw a diagram	estimate reasonable answers
act it out	use logical reasoning
solve a simpler problem	make a model

EXAMPLE Use a Strategy in the Four-Step Plan

2 **SPORTS** **In a basketball tournament, 128 teams play in the first round. Then there are 64 teams left to play in the second round, 32 teams left to play in the third round, and so on. How many rounds does it take to determine a winner?**

Explore You know the number of teams at the start of the tournament.

Plan You can look for a pattern by organizing the information in a table. Then continue the pattern until two teams are left.

Solve

Round	1	2	3	4	5	6	7
Number of Teams	128	64	32	16	8	4	2

÷2 ÷2

So, a winner is determined after 7 rounds.

Check Complete the diagram to show that the answer is correct.

Round 1 → 128 teams: 64 teams win, 64 teams lose

Round 2 → 64 teams: 32 teams win, 32 teams lose

Round 3 → 32 teams: 16 teams win, 16 teams lose

CHECK Your Progress

Solve using the four-step plan.

b. **SPORTS** How many rounds would it take to determine a winner if 512 teams participated in the tournament?

Online Personal Tutor at tx.msmath2.com

CHECK Your Understanding

Use the four-step plan to solve each problem.

Example 1 (p. 26)

1. **ANALYZE TABLES** There are more than 100 lakes in Texas. The table lists the sizes of six of these lakes. About how many times larger is Lake Livingston than Ray Roberts Lake?

Example 2 (p. 27)

2. **E-MAIL** If Isaac receives an e-mail every 20 minutes during the workday, how many e-mails would he expect to receive between 8:00 A.M. and noon?

Texas Lake	Size (acres)
Lake Arrowhead	14,390
Cooper Lake	19,280
Ray Roberts Lake	29,350
Lake Whitney	23,560
Lake Livingston	90,000
Lake Tawakoni	36,700

Source: *Texas Parks and Wildlife*

Exercises

HOMEWORK HELP	
For Exercises	**See Examples**
3–6	1
7–10	2

Use the four-step plan to solve each problem.

3. **BIRDS** Most hummingbirds flap their wings about 50 times a second. How many times can a hummingbird flap its wings in one minute?

4. **PLANETS** Jupiter is about 3 times the size of Neptune. If the diameter of Jupiter is 88,736 miles, what is the approximate diameter of Neptune?

5. **MONEY** To attend the class picnic, each student will have to pay $5 for transportation and $6 for food. If there are 379 students in the class, how much money will be collected for the picnic?

6. **DVD RENTALS** A video store took in $5,400 in DVD rentals during July. January sales are expected to be double that amount. If DVDs rent for $4, how many DVD rentals are expected in January?

7. **GEOMETRY** What are the next two figures in the pattern?

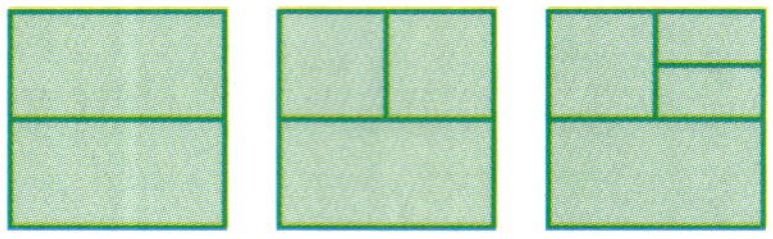

8. **NUMBERS** What are the next two numbers in the pattern?

9, 27, 81, 243, 729, ■, ■

ANALYZE TABLES For Exercises 9 and 10, use the commuter train schedule shown.

A commuter train departs from a train station and travels to the city each day. The schedule shows the first five departure and arrival times.

Commuter Train Schedule	
Departure	**Arrival**
6:30 A.M.	6:50 A.M.
7:15 A.M.	7:35 A.M.
8:00 A.M.	8:20 A.M.
8:45 A.M.	9:05 A.M.
9:30 A.M.	9:50 A.M.

9. How often does the commuter train arrive in the city?

10. What is the latest time that passengers can depart from the train station if they need to arrive in the city no later than noon?

11. **COOKING** Mr. Sanders is serving fried turkey at 3:00 P.M. The 15-pound turkey has to cook 3 minutes for every pound and then cool for at least 45 minutes. What is the latest time he can start frying?

12. **COLLECTIONS** In 2002, Adam starting collecting 6 die-cast cars every year. In 2004, his sister Lydia started collecting 9 cars per year. In what year did Adam and Lydia have the same number of cars?

13. **FIND THE DATA** Refer to the Texas Data File on pages 16–19 of your book. Choose some data and write a real-world problem in which you would use the four-step plan to solve the problem.

14. **ANALYZE TABLES** The sizes of Earth's oceans in millions of square kilometers are shown in the table. If the combined size of Earth's oceans is 367 million square kilometers, what is the size of the Pacific Ocean?

Earth's Oceans

Ocean	Size (million km^2)
Arctic	45
Atlantic	77
Indian	69
Pacific	■
Southern	20

Source: *The World Factbook*

EXTRA PRACTICE
See pages 717, 755.

Math Online
Self-Check Quiz at tx.msmath2.com

15. **MONEY** Kishi wants to buy a DVD player that costs $250 with tax. So far, she has saved $145. If she saves $5 every week, in how many weeks will she be able to purchase the DVD player?

H.O.T. Problems

16. **CHALLENGE** Use the digits 1, 2, 3, 4, and 5 to form a two-digit number and a three-digit number so that their product is as small as possible. Use each digit only once.

17. **OPEN ENDED** Create a real-world problem that can be solved by adding 79 and 42 and then multiplying the result by 3.

18. **WRITING IN MATH** Explain why it is important to plan before solving a problem.

TEST PRACTICE

19. Jeannie has $72 to spend on birthday gifts for her mother. Which three items from the table could Jeannie purchase, not including tax?

Item	Cost
sweater	$29.50
gloves	$22.75
purse	$32.00
chocolates	$15.00
movie passes	$27.75

A gloves, movie passes, sweater

B movie passes, sweater, purse

C sweater, gloves, chocolates

D sweater, gloves, purse

20. Mr. Brooks went on a business trip. The trip was 380 miles, and the average price of gasoline was $3.15 per gallon. What information is needed to find the amount Mr. Brooks spent on gasoline for the trip?

F Number of times Mr. Brooks stopped to fill his tank with gasoline

G Number of miles the car can travel using one gallon of gasoline

H Number of hours the trip took

J Average number of miles Mr. Brooks drove per day

GET READY for the Next Lesson

PREREQUISITE SKILL **Multiply.**

21. 10×10

22. $3 \times 3 \times 3$

23. $5 \times 5 \times 5 \times 5$

24. $2 \times 2 \times 2 \times 2 \times 2$

1-2 Powers and Exponents

Main IDEA

Use powers and exponents.

Targeted TEKS 7.2 The student adds, subtracts, multiplies, or divides to solve problems and justify solutions. **(E) simplify numerical expressions involving** order of operations and **exponents.**

NEW Vocabulary

factors
exponent
base
powers
squared
cubed
evaluate
standard form
exponential form

GET READY for the Lesson

TECHNOLOGY The amount of available storage space on a computer chip doubles every year.

1. How is doubling shown in the table?
2. If the pattern continues, how much space will be available by year 6?
3. What is the relationship between the number of 2s and the year?

Year	Amount of Storage Space (units)
1	$2 = 2$
2	$2 \times 2 = 4$
3	$2 \times 2 \times 2 = 8$
4	$2 \times 2 \times 2 \times 2 = 16$

Two or more numbers that are multiplied together to form a product are called **factors**. When the same factor is used, you may use an exponent to simplify the notation.

The centered dots indicate multiplication.

The **exponent** tells how many times the base is used as a factor.

$$16 = \underbrace{2 \cdot 2 \cdot 2 \cdot 2}_{\text{common factors}} = 2^4$$

common factors

The **base** is the common factor.

Numbers expressed using exponents are called **powers**.

Powers	Words
5^2	five to the second power or five **squared**
4^3	four to the third power or four **cubed**
2^4	two to the fourth power

EXAMPLES Write Powers as Products

Write each power as a product of the same factor.

1 7^5

Seven is used as a factor five times.

$7^5 = 7 \cdot 7 \cdot 7 \cdot 7 \cdot 7$

2 3^2

Three is used as a factor twice.

$3^2 = 3 \cdot 3$

READING Math

First Power When a number does not have an exponent, the exponent is understood to be 1. For example, $8 = 8^1$.

CHECK Your Progress

Write each power as a product of the same factor.

a. 6^4 b. 1^3 c. 9^5

You can **evaluate**, or find the value of, powers by multiplying the factors. Numbers written without exponents are in **standard form**.

EXAMPLES Write Powers in Standard Form

Vocabulary Link
Evaluate
Everyday Use to find what something is worth
Math Use find the value of

Evaluate each expression.

3 2^5

$2^5 = 2 \cdot 2 \cdot 2 \cdot 2 \cdot 2$ — 2 is used as a factor 5 times.
$= 32$ — Multiply.

4 4^3

$4^3 = 4 \cdot 4 \cdot 4$ — 4 is used as a factor 3 times.
$= 64$ — Multiply.

CHECK Your Progress

Evaluate each expression.

d. 10^2 **e.** 7^3 **f.** 5^4

Math Online Personal Tutor at tx.msmath2.com

Numbers written with exponents are in **exponential form**.

EXAMPLE Write Numbers in Exponential Form

5 **Write $3 \cdot 3 \cdot 3 \cdot 3$ in exponential form.**

3 is the base. It is used as a factor 4 times. So, the exponent is 4.

$3 \cdot 3 \cdot 3 \cdot 3 = 3^4$

CHECK Your Progress

Write each product in exponential form.

g. $5 \cdot 5 \cdot 5$ **h.** $12 \cdot 12 \cdot 12 \cdot 12 \cdot 12 \cdot 12$

CHECK Your Understanding

Examples 1, 2 (p. 30)

Write each power as a product of the same factor.

1. 9^3
2. 3^4
3. 8^5

Examples 3, 4 (p. 31)

Evaluate each expression.

4. 2^4
5. 7^2
6. 10^3
7. **POPULATION** There are approximately 7^{10} people living in the United States. About how many people is this?

Example 5 (p. 31)

Write each product in exponential form.

8. $5 \cdot 5 \cdot 5 \cdot 5 \cdot 5 \cdot 5$
9. $1 \cdot 1 \cdot 1 \cdot 1$
10. $4 \cdot 4 \cdot 4 \cdot 4 \cdot 4$

Exercises

HOMEWORK HELP	
For Exercises	See Examples
11–16	1, 2
17–24	3, 4
25–28	5

Write each power as a product of the same factor.

11. 1^5
12. 4^2
13. 3^8
14. 8^6
15. 9^3
16. 10^4

Evaluate each expression.

17. 2^6
18. 4^3
19. 7^4
20. 4^6
21. 1^{10}
22. 10^1

23. **BIKING** In a recent year, the number of 12- to 17-year-olds that went off-road biking was 10^6. Write this number in standard form.

24. **TRAINS** The Maglev train in China is the fastest passenger train in the world. Its average speed is 3^5 miles per hour. Write this speed in standard form.

Write each product in exponential form.

25. $3 \cdot 3$
26. $7 \cdot 7 \cdot 7 \cdot 7$
27. $1 \cdot 1 \cdot 1 \cdot 1 \cdot 1 \cdot 1 \cdot 1 \cdot 1$
28. $6 \cdot 6 \cdot 6 \cdot 6 \cdot 6$

Write each power as a product of the same factor.

29. *four to the fifth power*
30. *nine squared*

Evaluate each expression.

31. *six to the fourth power*
32. *6 cubed*

GEOMETRY For Exercises 33 and 34, use the figures shown below.

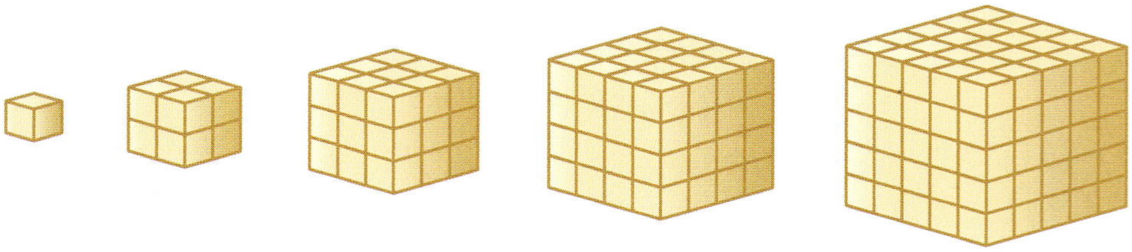

33. Find the number of unit cubes that make up each cube. Write your answers using exponents.
34. Why do you think the expression 2^3 is sometimes read as *2 cubed*?

35. **NUMBERS** Write $5 \cdot 5 \cdot 5 \cdot 5 \cdot 4 \cdot 4 \cdot 4$ in exponential form.

36. **COMPUTERS** A gigabyte is a measure of computer data storage capacity. One gigabyte stores 2^{30} bytes of data. Use a calculator to find the number in standard form that represents two gigabytes.

EXTRA PRACTICE
See pages 717, 755.
Math Online
Self-Check Quiz at tx.msmath2.com

Order the following powers from least to greatest.

37. $6^5, 1^{14}, 4^{10}, 17^3$
38. $2^8, 15^2, 6^3, 3^5$
39. $5^3, 4^6, 2^{11}, 7^2$

H.O.T. Problems

40. **CHALLENGE** Write two different powers that have the same value.

41. **Which One Doesn't Belong?** Identify the number that does not belong with the other three. Explain your reasoning.

4	9	16	50

42. **OPEN ENDED** Select a number between 1,000 and 2,000 that can be expressed as a power.

43. **WRITING IN MATH** Analyze the number pattern shown at the right. Then write a convincing argument as to the value of 2^0. Based on your argument, what do you think will be the value of 2^{-1}?

$2^4 = 16$
$2^3 = 8$
$2^2 = 4$
$2^1 = 2$
$2^0 = ?$

TEST PRACTICE

44. Which model represents 6^3?

A
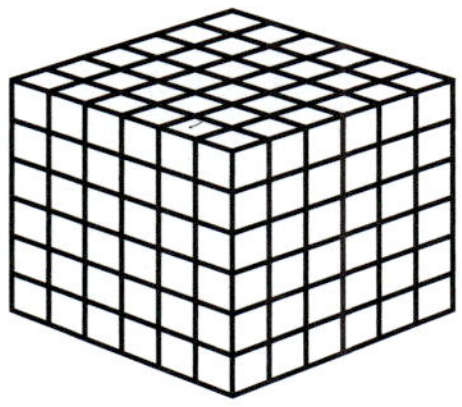

B
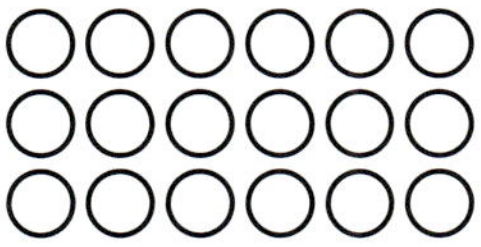

C
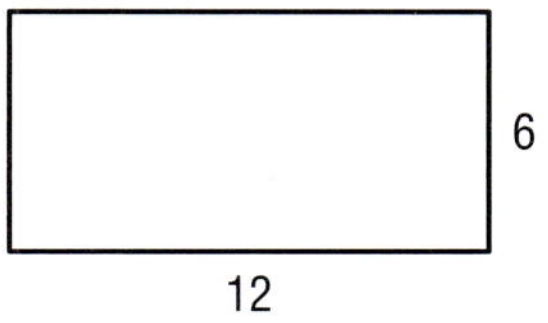

D
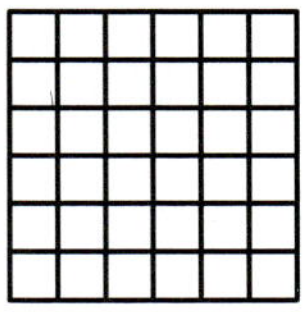

Spiral Review

45. **RACING** The graph shows which numbered cars have the most wins at the Indianapolis 500. How many more times did the number 3 car win than the number 14 car? (Lesson 1-1)

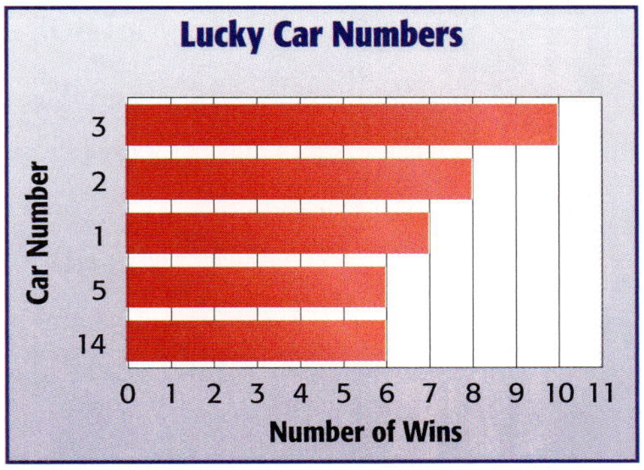

Source: indy500.com

46. **PRODUCTION** A machine on a production line fills 8 soft drink cans per minute. How many cans does it fill in 8 hours? (Lesson 1-1)

GET READY for the Next Lesson

PREREQUISITE SKILL Multiply.

47. 2 • 2
48. 3 • 3
49. 5 • 5
50. 7 • 7

1-3 Squares and Square Roots

Main IDEA

Find squares of numbers and square roots of perfect squares.

Targeted TEKS 7.1 The student represents and uses numbers in a variety of equivalent forms. **(C) represent squares and square roots using geometric models.** *Also addresses TEKS 7.14(A).*

NEW Vocabulary

square
perfect squares
square root
radical sign

MINI Lab

A square with an area of 36 square units is shown.

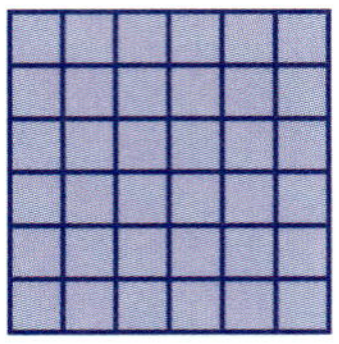

1. Using tiles, try to construct squares with areas of 4, 9, and 16 square units.
2. Try to construct squares with areas 12, 18, and 20 square units.
3. Which of the areas form squares?
4. What is the relationship between the lengths of the sides and the areas of these squares?
5. Using your square tiles, create a square that has an area of 49 square units. What are the lengths of the sides of the square?

The area of the square at the right is 5 • 5 or 25 square units. The product of a number and itself is the **square** of the number. So, the square of 5 is 25.

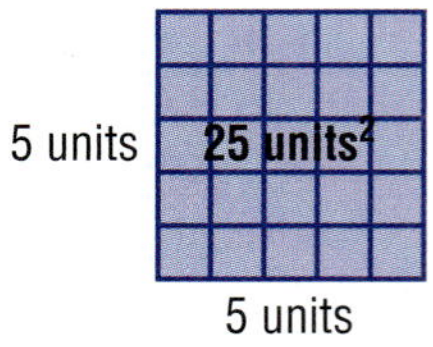

EXAMPLES Find Squares of Numbers

1 Find the square of 3.

$3 \cdot 3 = 9$ Multiply 3 by itself.

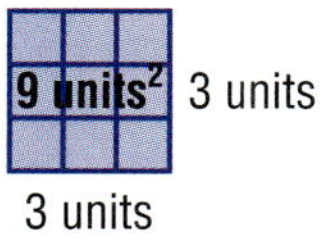

2 Find the square of 15.

METHOD 1 Use paper and pencil.

$15 \cdot 15 = 225$ Multiply 15 by itself.

METHOD 2 Use a calculator.

15 [x^2] [ENTER] 225

CHOOSE Your Method

Find the square of each number.

a. 8 **b.** 12 **c.** 23

READING Math

Square Roots Read $\sqrt{16} = 4$ as *the square root of 16 is 4.*

Numbers like 9, 16, and 225 are called square numbers or **perfect squares** because they are squares of whole numbers. The factors multiplied to form perfect squares are called **square roots**. A **radical sign**, $\sqrt{\ }$, is the symbol used to indicate the square root of a number.

KEY CONCEPT — Square Root

Words A square root of a number is one of its two equal factors.

Examples

Numbers	Algebra
$4 \cdot 4 = 16$, so $\sqrt{16} = 4$.	If $x \cdot x$ or $x^2 = y$, then $\sqrt{y} = x$.

EXAMPLES Find Square Roots

3 **Find $\sqrt{81}$.**

$9 \cdot 9 = 81$, so $\sqrt{81} = 9$. What number times itself is 81?

4 **Find $\sqrt{196}$.**

2nd [x^2] 196 ENTER 14 Use a calculator.

So, $\sqrt{196} = 14$.

CHECK Your Progress

Find each square root.

d. $\sqrt{64}$

e. $\sqrt{289}$

Real-World EXAMPLE

5 **SPORTS The infield of a baseball field is a square with an area of 8,100 square feet. What are the dimensions of the infield?**

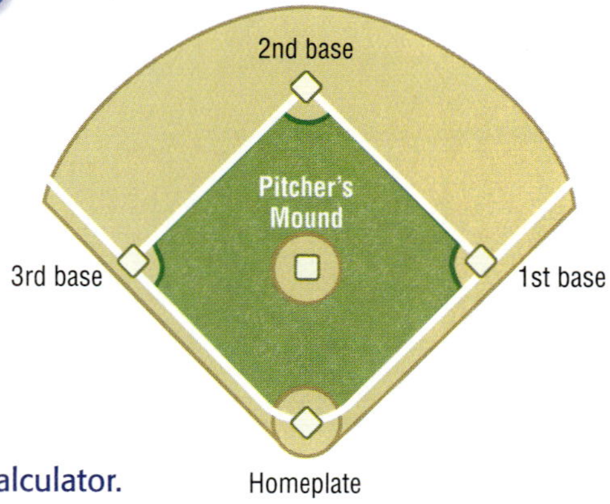

The infield is a square. By finding the square root of the area, 8,100, you find the length of one side of the infield.

2nd [$\sqrt{\ }$] 8,100 ENTER 90 Use a calculator.

The length of one side of the infield is 90 feet. So, the dimensions of the infield are 90 feet by 90 feet.

Real-World Link The average lifespan of a major league baseball is 7 pitches.
Source: superkids.com

CHECK Your Progress

f. **SPORTS** The largest ring in amateur boxing is a square with an area of 400 square feet. What are the dimensions of the ring?

Math Online Personal Tutor at tx.msmath2.com

CHECK Your Understanding

Examples 1, 2 (p. 34)

Find the square of each number.

1. 6
2. 10
3. 17
4. 30

Examples 3, 4 (p. 35)

Find each square root.

5. $\sqrt{9}$
6. $\sqrt{36}$
7. $\sqrt{121}$
8. $\sqrt{169}$

Example 5 (p. 35)

9. **ROAD SIGNS** Historic Route 66 from Chicago to Los Angeles is known as the Main Street of America. If the area of a Route 66 sign measures 576 square inches and the sign is a square, what are the dimensions of the sign?

Exercises

HOMEWORK HELP

For Exercises	See Examples
10–17	1, 2
18–25	3, 4
26–27	5

Find the square of each number.

10. 4
11. 1
12. 7
13. 11
14. 16
15. 20
16. 18
17. 34

Find each square root.

18. $\sqrt{4}$
19. $\sqrt{16}$
20. $\sqrt{49}$
21. $\sqrt{100}$
22. $\sqrt{144}$
23. $\sqrt{256}$
24. $\sqrt{529}$
25. $\sqrt{625}$

26. **ROOMS** Emma's bedroom is shaped like a square. What are the dimensions of the room if the area of the floor is 196 square feet?

27. **SPORTS** For the floor exercise, gymnasts perform their tumbling skills on a mat that has an area of 1,600 square feet. How much room does a gymnast have to run along one side of the mat?

28. What is the square of 12?

29. Find the square of 19.

30. **GARDENING** A square garden has an area of 225 square feet. How much fencing will a gardener need to buy in order to place fencing around the garden?

EXTRA PRACTICE

See pages 717, 755.

Math Online
Self-Check Quiz at tx.msmath2.com

GEOGRAPHY For Exercises 31–33, refer to the squares in the diagram. They represent the approximate areas of Texas, Michigan, and Florida.

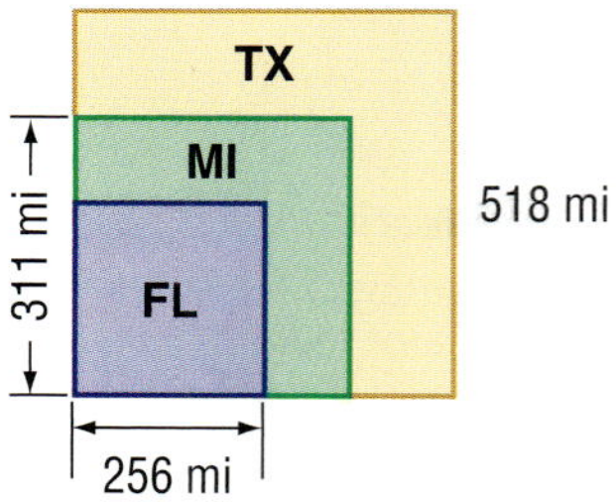

31. What is the area of Michigan in square miles?

32. How much larger is Texas than Florida?

33. The water areas of Texas, Michigan, and Florida are about 6,724 square miles, 40,000 square miles, and 11,664 square miles, respectively. Make a similar diagram comparing the water areas of these states. Label the squares.

34. **GAMES** A chessboard has an area of 324 square inches. There is a 1-inch border around the 64 squares on the board. What is the length of one side of the region containing the small squares?

H.O.T. Problems

35. **CHALLENGE** The area of a square that is 8 meters by 8 meters is how much greater than the area of a square containing 9 square meters? Explain.

36. **OPEN ENDED** Write a number whose square is between 200 and 300.

CHALLENGE For Exercises 37 and 38, use the diagram shown.

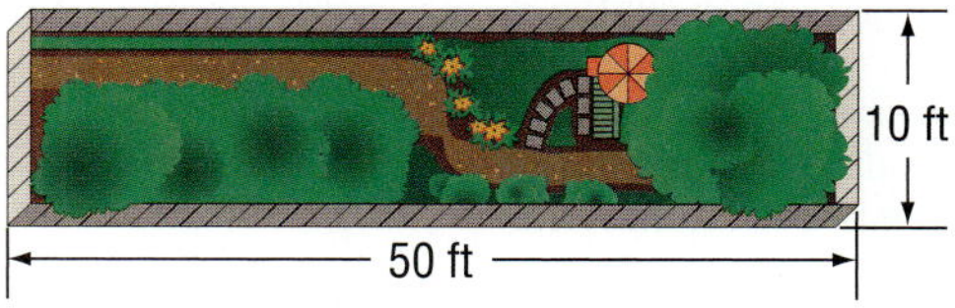

37. Could the garden area be made larger using the same amount of fencing? Explain.

38. Describe the largest garden area possible using the same amount of fencing. How do the perimeter and area compare to the original garden?

39. **WRITING IN MATH** Explain why raising a number to the second power is called *squaring* the number.

TEST PRACTICE

40. Which model represents the square of 4?

A 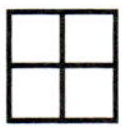

C 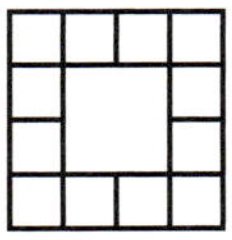

B 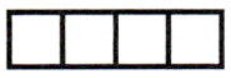

D 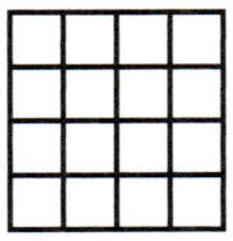

41. Which measure can be the area of a square if the measure of the side length is a whole number?

F 836 sq ft

G 949 sq ft

H 1,100 sq ft

J 1,225 sq ft

Spiral Review

Write each power as a product of the same factor. (Lesson 1-2)

42. 3^4 43. 8^5 44. 7^2 45. 2^6

46. **SHIPPING** Jocelyn spent a total of $24 to ship 4 packages. If the packages are equal in size and weight, how much did it cost to ship each package? (Lesson 1-1)

GET READY for the Next Lesson

PREREQUISITE SKILL Add, subtract, multiply, or divide.

47. $13 + 8$ 48. $10 - 6$ 49. 5×6 50. $36 \div 4$

1-4 Order of Operations

Main IDEA

Evaluate expressions using the order of operations.

Targeted TEKS **7.2** The student adds, subtracts, multiplies, or divides to solve problems and justify solutions. **(E) simplify numerical expressions involving order of operations and exponents.**

NEW Vocabulary

numerical expression
order of operations

GET READY for the Lesson

SPORTS The Kent City football team made one 6-point touchdown and four 3-point field goals in its last game. Kaitlyn and Percy each use an expression to find the total number of points the team scored.

Kaitlyn	Percy
$6 + 4 \cdot 3 = 6 + 12$	$(6 + 4) \cdot 3 = 10 \cdot 3$
$= 18$	$= 30$
The team scored 18 points.	The team scored 30 points.

1. List the differences between their calculations.
2. Whose calculations are correct?
3. Make a conjecture about what should be the first step in simplifying $6 + 4 \cdot 3$.

The expression $6 + 4 \cdot 3$ is a **numerical expression**. To evaluate expressions, use the **order of operations**. These rules ensure that numerical expressions have only one value.

KEY CONCEPT — Order of Operations

1. Evaluate the expressions inside grouping symbols.
2. Evaluate all powers.
3. Multiply and divide in order from left to right.
4. Add and subtract in order from left to right.

EXAMPLES Use Order of Operations

1 **Evaluate $5 + (12 - 3)$.**

$5 + (12 - 3) = 5 + 9$ — Subtract first, since 12 − 3 is in parentheses.

$= 14$ — Add 5 and 9.

2 **Evaluate $8 - 3 \cdot 2 + 7$.**

$8 - 3 \cdot 2 + 7 = 8 - 6 + 7$ — Multiply 3 and 2.

$= 2 + 7$ — Subtract 6 from 8.

$= 9$ — Add 2 and 7.

CHECK Your Progress

Evaluate each expression.

a. $39 \div (9 + 4)$

b. $10 + 8 \div 2 - 6$

READING in the Content Area

For strategies in reading this lesson, visit tx.msmath2.com.

Math Online **Extra Examples at** tx.msmath2.com

EXAMPLE Use Order of Operations

3 **Evaluate $5 \cdot 3^2 - 7$.**

$5 \cdot 3^2 - 7 = 5 \cdot 9 - 7$ Find the value of 3^2.

$= 45 - 7$ Multiply 5 and 9.

$= 38$ Subtract 7 from 45.

CHECK Your Progress Evaluate each expression.

c. 3×10^4

d. $(5 - 1)^3 \div 4$

In addition to using the symbols × and •, multiplication can be indicated by using parentheses. For example, $2(3 + 5)$ means $2 \times (3 + 5)$.

EXAMPLE Use Order of Operations

4 **Evaluate $14 + 3(7 - 2)$.**

$14 + 3(7 - 2) = 14 + 3(5)$ Subtract 2 from 7.

$= 14 + 15$ Multiply 3 and 5.

$= 29$ Add 14 and 15.

CHECK Your Progress Evaluate each expression.

e. $20 - 2(4 - 1) \cdot 3$

f. $6 + 8 \div 2 + 2(3 - 1)$

Real-World EXAMPLE

5 **VIDEO GAMES** Evita is buying a video game station, three extra controllers, and four new video games. What is the total cost?

Item	Quantity	Unit Cost
game station	1	$180
controller	3	$24
game	4	$35

Words	cost of 1 game station	+	cost of 3 controllers	+	cost of 4 games
Expression	$180	+	3 × 24	+	4 × 35

$180 + 3 \times 24 + 4 \times 35 = 180 + 72 + 140$ Multiply from left to right.

$= 392$ Add.

The total cost is $392.

Real-World Link
A team of 500 engineers and technicians built the first video game console in 1966.

CHECK Your Progress

g. What is the total cost of a video game station, four extra controllers, and three new video games?

Online Personal Tutor at tx.msmath2.com

CHECK Your Understanding

Evaluate each expression.

Examples 1, 2 (p. 38)

1. $8 + (5 - 2)$
2. $25 \div (9 - 4)$
3. $14 - 2 \cdot 6 + 9$
4. $8 \cdot 5 - 4 \cdot 3$

Examples 3, 4 (p. 39)

5. 4×10^2
6. $45 \div (4 - 1)^2$
7. $17 + 2(6 - 3) - 3 \times 4$
8. $22 - 3(8 - 2) + 12 \div 4$

Example 5 (p. 39)

9. **COINS** Isabelle has 3 nickels, 2 quarters, 2 dimes, and 7 pennies. Write an expression that can be used to find how much money Isabelle has altogether. How much money does Isabelle have?

Exercises

HOMEWORK HELP

For Exercises	See Examples
10–17	1, 2
18–23	3
24–27	4
28, 29	5

Evaluate each expression.

10. $(1 + 8) \times 3$
11. $10 - (3 + 4)$
12. $(25 \div 5) + 8$
13. $(11 - 2) \div 9$
14. $3 \cdot 2 + 14 \div 7$
15. $4 \div 2 - 1 + 7$
16. $12 + 6 \div 3 - 4$
17. $18 - 3 \cdot 6 + 5$
18. 6×10^2
19. 3×10^4
20. $5 \times 4^3 + 2$
21. $8 \times 7^2 - 6$
22. $8 \div 2 \times 6 + 6^2$
23. $9^2 - 14 \div 7 \cdot 3$
24. $(17 + 3) \div (4 + 1)$
25. $(6 + 5) \cdot (8 - 6)$
26. $6 + 2(4 - 1) + 4 \times 9$
27. $3(4 + 7) - 5 \cdot 4 \div 2$

For Exercises 28 and 29, write an expression for each situation. Then evaluate to find the solution.

Item	Cost
box of favors	\$7
box of balloons	\$5
roll of crepe paper	\$2

28. **MONEY** Julian orders nine rolls of crepe paper, four boxes of balloons, and two boxes of favors for the school dance. What is the total cost?

29. **TRAINING** On Mondays, Wednesdays, and Fridays, Jacob trains for a marathon for 2 hours a day. On Tuesdays and Thursdays, he trains for 3 hours a day, and on Saturdays, he trains for 4 hours. On Sundays, he does not train. How many hours does Jacob train per week?

Evaluate each expression.

30. $(2 + 10)^2 \div 4$
31. $9 \div 3 \cdot 4(10 - 8) + 16$
32. $3 \cdot 4(5.2 + 3.8) + 2.7$
33. $7 \times 9 - (4 - 3.2) + 1.8$

EXTRA PRACTICE
See pages 718, 755.
Math Online
Self-Check Quiz at tx.msmath2.com

For Exercises 34 and 35, write an expression for each situation. Then evaluate to find the solution.

34. **GEOMETRY** Kimi wants to place wooden molding around the perimeter of the front of the bird house she built. How many inches of molding will she need?

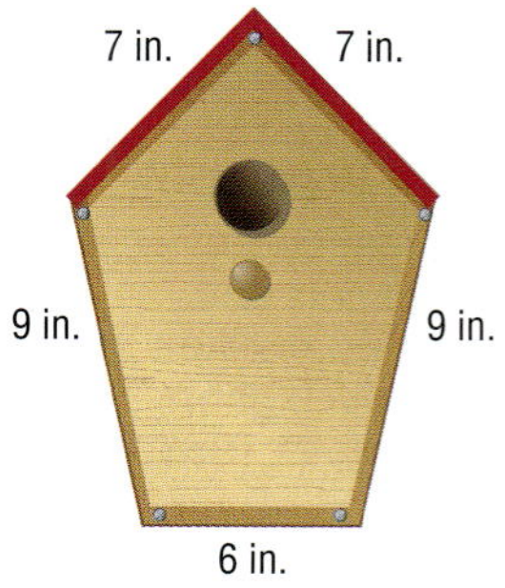

35. **MONEY** Suppose that your family orders 2 pizzas, 2 orders of garlic bread, and 1 order of BBQ wings from Mario's Pizza Shop. How much change will you receive from $30?

Mario's Pizza Shop

Item	Cost
14" pizza	$8
garlic bread	$2
BBQ wings	$4

H.O.T. Problems

36. **OPEN ENDED** Write an expression containing five numbers that is evaluated by first multiplying.

37. **FIND THE ERROR** Yutaka and Cynthia are evaluating $16 - 24 \div 6 \cdot 2$. Who is correct? Explain your reasoning.

38. **CHALLENGE** Insert parentheses to make $72 \div 9 + 27 - 2 = 0$ a true statement.

39. **WRITING IN MATH** Write a real-world problem in which you would need to use the order of operations to solve it.

TEST PRACTICE

40. Simplify $10 - 3 \cdot 2 + 4(15 - 5)$.

A 19

B 38

C 44

D 80

41. Alana has 2 boxes that contain 24 straws each and 3 boxes that contain 15 cups each. Which expression CANNOT be used to find the total number of items she has?

F $2(24) + 3(15)$

G $3 \times 15 + 2 \times 24$

H $5 \times (24 + 15)$

J $15 + 15 + 15 + 24 + 24$

Spiral Review

Find each square root. (Lesson 1-3)

42. $\sqrt{64}$

43. $\sqrt{2{,}025}$

44. $\sqrt{784}$

45. **INTERNET** Each day, Internet users perform 2^5 million searches using a popular search engine. How many searches is this? (Lesson 1-2)

GET READY for the Next Lesson

46. **PREREQUISITE SKILL** A Chinese checkerboard has 121 holes. How many holes can be found on eight Chinese checkerboards? (Lesson 1-1)

1-5 Problem-Solving Investigation

MAIN IDEA: Solve problems using the guess and check strategy.

Targeted TEKS 7.13 The student applies Grade 7 mathematics to solve problems connected to everyday experiences, investigations in other disciplines, and activities in and outside of school. **(C) select or develop an appropriate problem-solving strategy from a variety of different types, including...systematic guessing and checking...to solve a problem.** *Also addresses TEKS 7.13(B).*

P.S.I. TEAM +

e-Mail: GUESS AND CHECK

Your MISSION: Use guess and check to solve the problem.

THE PROBLEM: How many adult and student tickets were sold?

Justin: The total ticket sales for the school play were $255. Adult tickets cost $7 and student tickets cost $4. Also, twice as many students bought tickets as adults.

EXPLORE	You know adult tickets are \$7, student tickets are \$4, and twice as many students bought tickets than did adults.	
PLAN	Make a guess and check it. Adjust the guess until you get the correct answer.	
SOLVE	Make a guess.	
	10 adults, 20 students $7(10) + 4(20) = \$150$ >>>>>> Adjust the guess upward.	too low
	20 adults, 40 students $7(20) + 4(40) = \$300$ >>>>>>> Adjust the guess downward slightly.	too high
	18 adults, 36 students $7(18) + 4(36) = \$270$ >>>>>>> Adjust the guess downward again.	too high
	17 adults, 34 students $7(17) + 4(34) = \$255$ >>>>>>> So, there were 17 adult and 34 student tickets sold.	correct
CHECK	Seventeen adult tickets cost \$119, and 34 student tickets cost \$136. Since \$119 + \$136 = \$255 and 34 tickets are twice as many as 17 tickets, the guess is correct.	

Analyze The Strategy

1. Explain why you must keep a caful record of each of your guesses and their results in the *solve* step of the problem-solving plan.
2. **WRITING IN MATH** Write a problem that could be solved by guess and check. Then write the steps you would take to find the solution to your problem.

Mixed Problem Solving

Use the *guess and check* strategy to solve Exercises 3–6.

3. **MONEY** A band sponsored a car wash to help pay for their uniforms. They charged $4 for a car and $6 for an SUV. During the first hour, they washed 16 vehicles and earned $78. How many of each type of vehicle did they wash?

4. **NUMBERS** A number is multiplied by 6. Then 4 is added to the product. The result is 82. What is the number?

5. **ANALYZE TABLES** Flor is burning a CD. Suppose the CD holds 30 minutes of music. Which songs should she select from the list below to record the maximum time on the CD without going over?

SONG	TIME
A	3 min 30 s
B	6 min 0 s
C	4 min 45 s
D	5 min 30 s
E	5 min 6 s
F	4 min 15 s
G	4 min 30 s
H	3 min 48 s

6. **MONEY** Kelly has $2.80 in change in her purse. If she has an equal number of nickels, dimes, and quarters, how many of each does she have?

Use any strategy to solve Exercises 7–10. Some strategies are shown below.

PROBLEM-SOLVING STRATEGIES
- Use the four-step plan.
- Guess and check.

7. **BRIDGES** The total length of wire used in the cables supporting the Golden Gate Bridge in San Francisco is about 80,000 miles. This is 5,300 miles longer than three times the distance around Earth at the Equator. What is the distance around Earth at the Equator?

8. **GEOMETRY** What are the next two figures in the pattern?

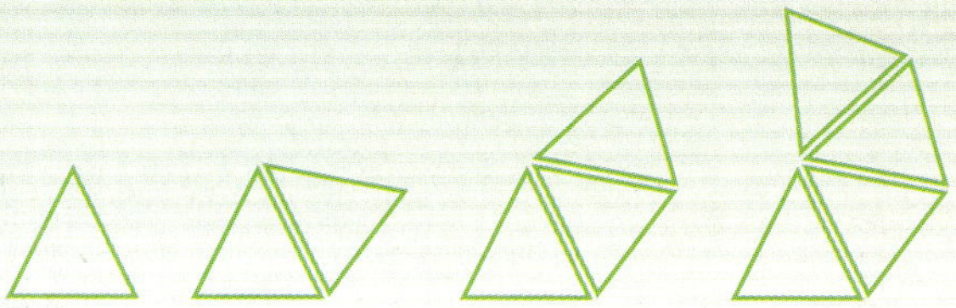

9. **NUMBERS** What are the next two numbers in the pattern?

   16, 32, 64, 128, 256, ■, ■

10. **SOUVENIRS** A souvenir shop sells standard-sized postcards in packages of 5 and large-sized postcards in packages of 3. If Juan bought 16 postcards, how many packages of each did he buy?

Select the Operation

For Exercises 11 and 12, select the appropriate operation(s) to solve the problem. Justify your selection(s) and solve the problem.

11. **ANALYZE TABLES** The table gives the average snowfall, in inches, for Valdez, Alaska, for the months October through April.

Month	Snowfall
October	11.6
November	40.3
December	73.0
January	65.8
February	59.4
March	52.0
April	22.7

Source: ncdc.noaa.gov

How many inches total of snowfall could a resident of Valdez expect to receive from October to April?

12. **ROLLER COASTERS** The Wicked Twister roller coaster can accommodate 1,056 passengers per hour. The coaster has 8 vehicles. If each vehicle carries 4 passengers, how many runs are made in one hour?

1-6 Algebra: Variables and Expressions

Main IDEA

Evaluate simple algebraic expressions.

Targeted TEKS 7.2 The student adds, subtracts, multiplies, or divides to solve problems and justify solutions. **(E) simplify numerical expressions involving order of operations and exponents.** *Also addresses TEKS 7.2(B).*

NEW Vocabulary

variable
algebra
algebraic expression
coefficient

REVIEW Vocabulary

evaluate find the value (Lesson 1-2)

MINI Lab

The pattern is made up of triangles, each with side lengths of 1.

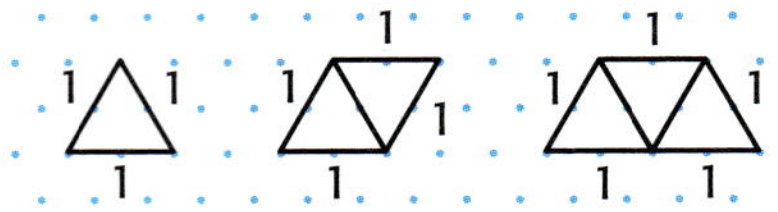

1. Draw the next three figures in the pattern.
2. Find the perimeter of each figure and record your data in a table like the one shown below. The first three are completed for you.

Number of Triangles	1	2	3	4	5	6
Perimeter	3	4	5	■	■	■

3. Without drawing the figure, determine the perimeter of a figure made up of 10 triangles. Check by making a drawing.
4. Find a relationship between the number of triangles and the perimeter at each stage of the pattern.

In the Mini Lab, you found that the perimeter of the figure is two more than the number of triangles. You can use a placeholder, or **variable**, to represent the number of triangles. A variable is a symbol that represents an unknown quantity.

number of triangles → $n + 2$ → perimeter of figure

The branch of mathematics that involves expressions with variables is called **algebra**. The expression $n + 2$ is called an **algebraic expression** because it contains variables, numbers, and at least one operation.

EXAMPLE Evaluate an Algebraic Expression

1 Evaluate $n + 3$ if $n = 4$.

$n + 3 = 4 + 3$ Replace n with 4.

$= 7$ Add 4 and 3.

CHECK Your Progress

Evaluate each expression if $c = 8$ and $d = 5$.

a. $c - 3$ b. $15 - c$ c. $c + d$

Concepts in Motion
Interactive Lab tx.msmath2.com

In algebra, the multiplication sign is often omitted.

$6d$	$9st$	mn
6 times d	9 times s times t	m times n

The numerical factor of a multiplication expression that contains a variable is called a **coefficient**. So, 6 is the coefficient of $6d$.

EXAMPLES Evaluate Expressions

2 Evaluate $8w - 2v$ if $w = 5$ and $v = 3$.

$8w - 2v = 8(5) - 2(3)$ Replace w with 5 and v with 3.

$= 40 - 6$ Do all multiplications first.

$= 34$ Subtract 6 from 40.

3 Evaluate $4y^2 + 2$ if $y = 3$.

$4y^2 + 2 = 4(3)^2 + 2$ Replace y with 3.

$= 4(9) + 2$ Evaluate the power.

$= 38$ Multiply, then add.

CHECK Your Progress

Evaluate each expression if $a = 4$ and $b = 3$.

d. $9a - 6b$

e. $\frac{ab}{2}$

f. $2a^2 + 5$

Real-World Link Athletic trainers use the formula $\frac{3(220 - a)}{5}$, where a is a person's age, to find their minimum training heart rate.
Source: CMPMedica Ltd.

The fraction bar is a grouping symbol. Evaluate the expressions in the numerator and denominator separately before dividing.

Real-World EXAMPLE

4 HEALTH Use the formula at the left to find Kaylee's minimum training heart rate if she is 15 years old.

$\frac{3(220 - a)}{5} = \frac{3(220 - 15)}{5}$ Replace a with 15.

$= \frac{3(205)}{5}$ Subtract 15 from 220.

$= \frac{615}{5}$ Multiply 3 and 205.

$= 123$ Divide 615 by 5.

Kaylee's minimum training heart rate is 123 beats per minute.

CHECK Your Progress

g. **GEOMETRY** To find the area of a triangle, you can use the formula $\frac{bh}{2}$, where h is the height and b is the base. What is the area in square inches of a triangle with a height of 6 inches and base of 8 inches?

CHECK Your Understanding

Example 1 (p. 44)

Evaluate each expression if $a = 3$ and $b = 5$.

1. $a + 7$
2. $8 - b$
3. $b - a$

4. **HEALTH** The standard formula for finding your maximum heart rate is $220 - a$, where a represents a person's age in years. What is your maximum heart rate?

Examples 2–4 (p. 45)

Evaluate each expression if $m = 2$, $n = 6$, and $p = 4$.

5. $6n - p$
6. $7m - 2n$
7. $3m + 4p$
8. $n^2 + 5$
9. $15 - m^3$
10. $3p^2 - n$
11. $\frac{mn}{4}$
12. $\frac{3n}{9}$
13. $\frac{5n + m}{8}$

Exercises

HOMEWORK HELP

For Exercises	See Examples
14–29	1–3
30–31	4

Evaluate each expression if $d = 8$, $e = 3$, $f = 4$, and $g = 1$.

14. $d + 9$
15. $10 - e$
16. $4f + 1$
17. $8g - 3$
18. $f - e$
19. $d + f$
20. $10g - 6$
21. $8 + 5d$
22. $\frac{d}{5}$
23. $\frac{16}{f}$
24. $\frac{5d - 25}{5}$
25. $\frac{(5 + g)^2}{2}$
26. $6f^2$
27. $4e^2$
28. $d^2 + 7$
29. $e^2 - 4$

30. **BOWLING** The expression $5n + 2$ can be used to find the total cost in dollars of bowling where n is the number of games bowled. How much will it cost Vincent to bowl 3 games?

31. **HEALTH** A nurse can use the expression $110 + \frac{A}{2}$, where A is a person's age, to estimate a person's normal systolic blood pressure. Estimate the normal systolic blood pressure for a 16-year old.

Evaluate each expression if $x = 3.2$, $y = 6.1$, and $z = 0.2$.

32. $x + y - z$
33. $8 - y + x$
34. $y - z + 5$

Complete each table.

35.

Quarts (q)	Gallons ($\frac{q}{4}$)
4	1
6	1.5
8	■
10	■
12	■

36.

Dollars (d)	Quarters ($4d$)
1	4
2	8
3	■
4	■
5	■

37. **SCIENCE** The expression $\frac{32t^2}{2}$ gives the falling distance of an object in feet after t seconds. How far would a bungee jumper fall 2 seconds after jumping?

EXTRA PRACTICE
See pages 718, 755.
Math Online
Self-Check Quiz at
tx.msmath2.com

38. **GEOMETRY** To find the total number of diagonals for any given polygon, you can use the expression $\frac{n(n-3)}{2}$, where n is the number of sides of the polygon. What is the total number of diagonals for a 10-sided polygon?

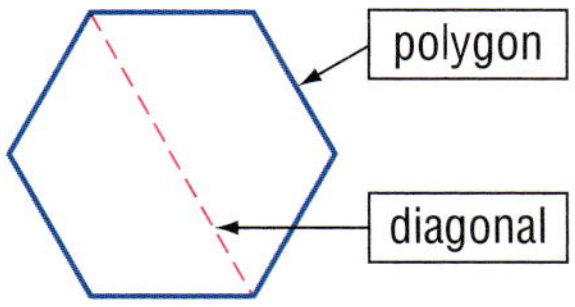

H.O.T. Problems

39. **OPEN ENDED** Write an algebraic expression with the variable x that has a value of 3 when evaluated.

40. **CHALLENGE** Name values of x and y so that the value of $7x + 2$ is greater than the value of $3y + 23$.

41. **WRITING IN MATH** Tell whether the statement below is *sometimes*, *always*, or *never* true. Justify your reasoning.

The expressions $x - 3$ and $y - 3$ represent the same value.

TEST PRACTICE

42. Which expression could be used to find the cost of buying b baseball bats at \$75 each and g baseball gloves at \$98 each?

A $75b + 98g$

B $b + g$

C $75 + 98$

D $75b \cdot 98g$

43. Juan opened a bank account with \$40 and deposited \$15 each month after the first one. He saved \$100 by December. In which month did he open the account?

F July

G August

H September

J October

Spiral Review

44. **SHOPPING** A grocery store sells hot dog buns in packages of 8 and 12. How many 8-packs and 12-packs could you buy if you needed 44 hot dog buns? Use the *guess and check* strategy. (Lesson 1-5)

Evaluate each expression. (Lesson 1-4)

45. $6(5) - 2$

46. $9 + 9 \div 3$

47. $4 \cdot 2(8 - 1)$

48. $(17 + 3) \div 5$

49. Find $\sqrt{361}$. (Lesson 1-3)

GET READY for the Next Lesson

PREREQUISITE SKILL **Determine whether each sentence is *true* or *false*.** (Lesson 1-4)

50. $15 - 2(3) = 9$

51. $20 \div 5 \times 4 = 1$

52. $4^2 + 6 \cdot 7 = 154$

CHAPTER 1 Mid-Chapter Quiz

Lessons 1-1 through 1-6

1. **TEST PRACTICE** A cycling club is planning a 1,800-mile trip. The cyclers average 15 miles per hour. What additional information is needed to determine the number of days it will take them to complete the trip? (Lesson 1-1)

   A The number of cyclists in the club

   B The number of miles of rough terrain

   C The number of hours they plan to cycle each day

   D Their average speed per minute

Write each power as a product of the same factor. (Lesson 1-2)

2. 4^5
3. 9^6

4. **OCEANS** The world's largest ocean, the Pacific Ocean, covers approximately 4^3 million square miles. Write this area in standard form. (Lesson 1-2)

5. **ZOOS** The Lincoln Park Zoo in Illinois is $2 \cdot 2 \cdot 2 \cdot 2 \cdot 2 \cdot 2 \cdot 2$ years old. Write this age in exponential form. (Lesson 1-2)

6. **TEST PRACTICE** The model below represents $\sqrt{49} = 7$.

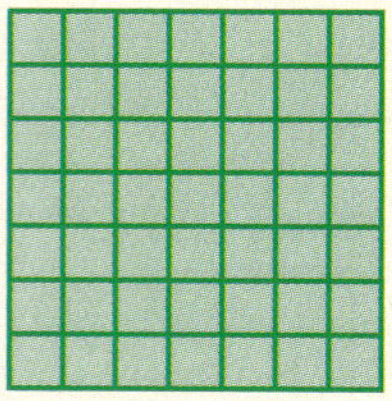

Which arrangement of small squares can be used to model a large square that represents $\sqrt{324}$? (Lesson 1-3)

   F 9 rows of 36 squares

   G 18 rows of 18 squares

   H 12 rows of 27 squares

   J 6 rows of 54 squares

Find the square of each number. (Lesson 1-3)

7. 4
8. 12

Find each square root. (Lesson 1-3)

9. $\sqrt{64}$
10. $\sqrt{289}$

11. **LANDSCAPING** A bag of lawn fertilizer covers 2,500 square feet. Describe the largest square that one bag of fertilizer could cover. (Lesson 1-3)

Evaluate each expression. (Lesson 1-4)

12. $25 - (3^2 + 2 \times 5)$
13. $\frac{2(7-3)}{2^2}$

14. **GEOMETRY** The perimeter of a rectangle is 42 inches and its area is 104 square inches. Find the dimensions of the rectangle. Use the *guess and check* strategy. (Lesson 1-5)

15. **TEST PRACTICE** Ana buys some baseball bats at $35 each and some baseball gloves at $48 each. Which expression could be used to find the total cost of the sports items? (Lesson 1-6)

   A $35b \cdot 48g$

   B $\frac{35b}{48g}$

   C $35b + 48g$

   D $48g - 35b$

Evaluate each expression if $x = 12$, $y = 4$, and $z = 8$. (Lesson 1-6)

16. $x - 5$
17. $3y + 10z$
18. $\frac{yz}{2}$
19. $\frac{(y+8)^2}{x}$

20. **HEALTH** The expression $\frac{w}{30}$, where w is a person's weight in pounds, is used to find the approximate number of quarts of blood in the person's body. How many quarts of blood does a 120-pound person have? (Lesson 1-6)

1-7 Algebra: Equations

Main IDEA

Solve equations using mental math.

Targeted TEKS **7.5** The student uses equations to solve problems. **(B)** formulate problem situations when given a simple equation and **formulate an equation when given a problem situation**.

NEW Vocabulary

equation
solution
solving an equation
defining the variable

GET READY for the Lesson

BASKETBALL The table shows the number of wins for six WNBA teams after playing 34 games each.

1. How many losses did each team have?
2. Write a rule to describe how you found the number of losses.
3. Let w represent the number of wins and ℓ represent the number of losses. Rewrite your rule using numbers, variables, and an equals sign.

Women's National Basketball Association, 2005

Team	Wins	Losses
Sacramento	25	?
Los Angeles	17	?
Houston	19	?
Seattle	20	?
Minnesota	14	?
Phoenix	16	?

Source: wnba.com

An **equation** is a sentence that contains an equals sign, =. The equals sign tells you that the expression on the left is equivalent to the expression on the right.

$$7 = 8 - 1 \qquad 3(4) = 12 \qquad 17 = 13 + 2 + 2$$

An equation that contains a variable is neither true nor false until the variable is replaced with a number. A **solution** of an equation is a numerical value for the variable that makes the sentence true.

The process of finding a solution is called **solving an equation**. Some equations can be solved using mental math.

EXAMPLE Solve an Equation Mentally

1 Solve $18 = 14 + t$ mentally.

$18 = 14 + t$ Write the equation.

$18 = 14 + 4$ You know that $14 + 4$ is 18.

$18 = 18$ Simplify.

So, $t = 4$. The solution is 4.

CHECK Your Progress

Solve each equation mentally.

a. $p - 5 = 20$ b. $8 = y \div 3$ c. $7h = 56$

TEST EXAMPLE

2 **Each day, Sierra cycles 3 miles on a bicycle trail. The equation $3d = 36$ represents how many days it will take her to cycle 36 miles. How many days d will it take her to cycle 36 miles?**

A 10 **B** 12 **C** 15 **D** 20

Test-Taking Tip

Backsolving To find which answer choice is the solution, you can also substitute each value for x to see which answer choice makes the left side of the equation equal to the right side.

Read the Test Item

Solve $3d = 36$ to find how many days it will take to cycle 36 miles.

Solve the Test Item

$3d = 36$ Write the equation.

$3 \cdot 12 = 36$ You know that $3 \cdot 12$ is 36. Therefore, $d = 12$.

It will take Sierra 12 days to cycle 36 miles. The answer is B.

CHECK Your Progress

d. Jordan has 16 video games. This is 3 less than the number Casey has. To find how many video games Casey has, the equation $v - 3 = 16$ can be used. How many video games v does Casey have?

F 13 **G** 15 **H** 18 **J** 19

Online Personal Tutor at tx.msmath2.com

When you choose a variable to represent one of the unknowns, this is called **defining the variable**.

Real-World EXAMPLE

3 **FOOD** **The total cost of a hamburger, and a soft drink is \$5.50. If the drink costs \$2.50, what is the cost of the hamburger?**

Words	cost of a hamburger	plus	cost of a soft drink	is	\$5.50.
Variable	Let h represent the cost in dollars of the hamburger.				
Equation	$h + 2.50 = 5.50$				

$h + 2.50 = 5.50$ Write the equation.

$3 + 2.50 = 5.50$ Replace h with 3 to make the equation true. So, $h = 3$.

The number 3 is the solution. The cost of the hamburger is \$3.00.

STUDY TIP

Defining the Variable Although any symbol can be used, it is a good idea to use the first letter of the word you are defining as a variable. For example: h stands for the cost of a hamburger.

CHECK Your Progress

e. Aaron buys a movie rental, popcorn, and a soft drink for a total cost of \$6.25. What is the cost of the popcorn if the movie rental and soft drink cost \$4.70 together?

CHECK Your Understanding

Example 1 (p. 49)

Solve each equation mentally.

1. $75 = w + 72$
2. $y - 18 = 20$
3. $\frac{r}{9} = 6$

Example 2 (p. 50)

4. **TEST PRACTICE** David scored 7 points in a football game. Together, he and Jason scored 28 points. Solve the equation $7 + p = 28$ to find how many points p Jason scored.

   A 14 **B** 21 **C** 23 **D** 35

Example 3 (p. 50)

5. **MONEY** Jessica buys a notebook and a pack of pencils for a total of \$3.50. What is the cost of the notebook if the pack of pencils costs \$1.25?

Exercises

HOMEWORK HELP

For Exercises	See Examples
6–17	1
18–19, 33–34	2
20–21	3

Solve each equation mentally.

6. $b + 7 = 13$
7. $8 + x = 15$
8. $y - 14 = 20$
9. $a - 18 = 10$
10. $25 - n = 19$
11. $x + 17 = 63$
12. $77 = 7t$
13. $3d = 99$
14. $n = \frac{30}{6}$
15. $16 = \frac{u}{4}$
16. $20 = y \div 5$
17. $84 \div z = 12$

18. **MONEY** Maria charges \$9 per hour of baby-sitting. Solve the equation $9h = 63$ to find how many hours h Maria needs to baby-sit to earn \$63.

19. **SNACKS** A box initially contained 25 snack bars. If there are 14 snack bars remaining, solve the equation $25 - x = 14$ to find how many snack bars x were eaten.

For Exercises 20 and 21, define a variable. Then write and solve an equation.

20. **BASKETBALL** During one game of his rookie year, LeBron James scored 41 of the Cleveland Cavaliers' 107 points. How many points did the rest of the team score?

21. **EXERCISE** On Monday and Tuesday, Derrick walked a total of 6.3 miles. If he walked 2.5 miles on Tuesday, how many miles did he walk on Monday?

Solve each equation mentally.

22. $1.5 + j = 10.0$
23. $1.2 = m - 4.2$
24. $n - 1.4 = 3.5$
25. $13.4 - h = 9.0$
26. $9.9 + r = 24.2$
27. $w + 15.8 = 17.0$

EXTRA PRACTICE
See pages 719, 755.
Math Online
Self-Check Quiz at tx.msmath2.com

28. **PENGUINS** The table shows the average height of Emperor and Adelie penguins. Write and solve an addition equation to find how much taller Emperor penguins are than Adelie penguins.

Type of Penguin	Height (in.)
Emperor	51
Adelie	18

29. **WHALES** Each winter, Humpback whales migrate 1,500 miles to the Indian Ocean. However, scientists tracked one whale that migrated 5,000 miles in one season. Write and solve an equation that can be used to find how many miles farther than normal the whale traveled.

H.O.T. Problems

30. **CHALLENGE** Find the values of a and b if $0 \cdot a = b$. Explain your reasoning.

31. **FIND THE ERROR** Joshua and Ivan each solved $w - 25 = 50$. Whose solution is correct? Explain your reasoning.

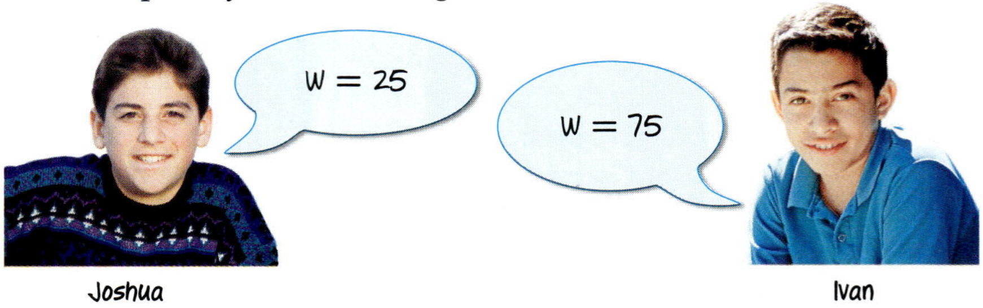

32. **WRITING IN MATH** Explain what it means to solve an equation.

TEST PRACTICE

33. The diagram shows the distance from Madison to Hudson and from Lawrence to Hudson. Which equation can be used to find how many miles x Lawrence is from Hudson than Madison?

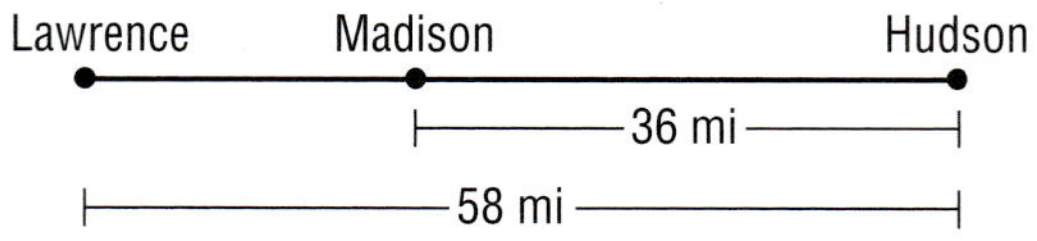

A $58 = x + 36$

B $58 = \frac{x}{36}$

C $36 \cdot 58 = x$

D $x - 36 = 58$

34. **GRIDDABLE** A teacher has 48 pencils to divide among a group of students. Use the equation $\frac{48}{p} = 6$ to find p, the number of students in the group if each student gets 6 pencils.

Spiral Review

35. **ALGEBRA** Evaluate $3a + b^2$ if $a = 2$ and $b = 3$. (Lesson 1-6)

Evaluate each expression. (Lesson 1-4)

36. $11 \cdot 6 \div 3 + 9$

37. $5 \cdot 13 - 6^2$

38. $1 + 2(8 - 5)^2$

39. **DINING** Four hundred sixty people are scheduled to attend a banquet. If each table seats 8 people, how many tables are needed? (Lesson 1-1)

GET READY for the Next Lesson

PREREQUISITE SKILL Multiply. (Lesson 1-4)

40. $2 \cdot (4 + 10)$

41. $(9 \cdot 1) \cdot 8$

42. $(5 \cdot 3)(5 \cdot 2)$

43. $(6 + 8) \cdot 12$

1-8 Algebra: Properties

Main IDEA

Use Commutative, Associative, Identity, and Distributive properties to solve problems.

Targeted TEKS 7.15 The student uses logical reasoning to make conjectures and verify conclusions. **(B)** **validate his/her conclusions using mathematical properties and relationships.**

NEW Vocabulary

equivalent expressions
properties

Vocabulary Link

Distribute
Everyday Use to divide among several, as in distribute a deck of cards

Distributive
Math Use property that allows you to multiply a sum by a number

GET READY for the Lesson

RESTAURANTS Land-Ho! Fish Market is having a special.

1. Find the total cost for a 5-member family, without tax and tip, if each one orders a fish-bake dinner and cheesecake.
2. Describe the method you used to find the total cost.

Here are two ways to find the total cost of the dinner:

number of people → $5(\$9 + \$2)$ ← 1 dinner and 1 cheesecake

cost of 5 dinners → $5(\$9) + 5(\$2)$ ← cost of 5 cheesecakes

The expressions $5(\$9 + \$2)$ and $5(\$9) + 5(\$2)$ are **equivalent expressions** because they have the same value, $55. This shows how the **Distributive Property** combines addition and multiplication.

KEY CONCEPT — Distributive Property

Words To multiply a sum by a number, multiply each addend of the sum by the number outside the parentheses.

Examples

Numbers	Algebra
$3(4 + 6) = 3(4) + 3(6)$	$a(b + c) = a(b) + a(c)$

EXAMPLES Write Sentences as Equations

Use the Distributive Property to evaluate each expression.

1 $5(3 + 2)$

$5(3 + 2) = 5(3) + 5(2)$
$= 15 + 10$ Multiply.
$= 25$ Add.

2 $(7 + 4)3$

$(7 + 4)3 = 7(3) + 4(3)$
$= 21 + 12$ Multiply.
$= 33$ Add.

CHECK Your Progress

a. $6(1 + 4)$

b. $(9 + 3)6$

You can use the Distributive Property to solve problems mentally.

Real-World EXAMPLE

3 **HISTORY The Pony Express riders carried mail from Missouri to California in eight days. On average, the riders covered 250 miles each day. About how far did the riders travel?**

Use the Distributive Property to multiply 8(250) mentally.

$8(250) = 8(200 + 50)$	Rewrite 250 as 200 + 50.
$= 8(200) + 8(50)$	Distributive Property
$= 1{,}600 + 400$	Multiply.
$= 2{,}000$	Add.

The riders traveled about 2,000 miles.

CHECK Your Progress

c. Jennifer saved $120 each month for five months. How much did she save in all? Use the Distributive Property to multiply mentally.

Online Personal Tutor at tx.msmath2.com

STUDY TIP

Properties The *Commutative Property* shows how the terms move and change places.

The *Associative Property* shows how the parentheses move and change places.

Properties are statements that are true for all numbers.

CONCEPT Summary — Real Number Properties

Commutative Properties	The order in which two numbers are added or multiplied does not change their sum or product.
Associative Properties	The way in which three numbers are grouped when they are added or multiplied does not change their sum or product.
Identity Properties	The sum of an addend and 0 is the addend. The product of a factor and 1 is the factor.

EXAMPLES Identify Properties

Name the property shown by each statement.

4 $6 + (2 + 7) = (6 + 2) + 7$ — Associative Property of Addition

5 $15 \cdot 10 = 10 \cdot 15$ — Commutative Property of Multiplication

CHECK Your Progress

Name the property shown by each statement.

d. $4(6 + 8) = 4(6) + 4(8)$

e. $a + 0 = a$

CHECK Your Understanding

Examples 1, 2 (p. 53)

Use the Distributive Property to evaluate each expression.

1. $7(4 + 3)$
2. $5(6 + 2)$
3. $(2 + 5)3$
4. $(10 + 8)2$

Example 3 (p. 54)

5. **MENTAL MATH** Admission to watch the Texas Rangers costs \$12 to sit in the bleachers and \$5 for a hot dog. Use the Distributive Property to mentally find the total cost for 4 tickets and 4 hot dogs.

6. **MENTAL MATH** A cheetah can run 65 miles per hour at maximum speed. At this rate, how far could a cheetah run in 2 hours? Use the Distributive Property to multiply mentally.

Examples 4, 5 (p. 54)

Name the property shown by each statement.

7. $5 + 4 = 4 + 5$
8. $6(9 + 3) = 6(9) + 6(3)$

Exercises

HOMEWORK HELP

For Exercises	See Examples
9–12	1, 2
13–22	4, 5
23, 24	3

Use the Distributive Property to evaluate each expression.

9. $2(6 + 7)$
10. $5(8 + 9)$
11. $(3 + 8)4$
12. $(11 + 3)8$

Name the property shown by each statement.

13. $1 \cdot (5 \cdot 9) = (1 \cdot 5) \cdot 9$
14. $8 + 9 = 9 + 8$
15. $7 \cdot 1 = 7$
16. $8 + 0 = 8$
17. $4 + b = b + 4$
18. $mn = nm$
19. $(1 + r) + s = 1 + (r + s)$
20. $(2 + 7)n = 2n + 7n$
21. $x(y + z) = xy + xz$
22. $k \cdot 1 = k$

MENTAL MATH For Exercises 23 and 24, use the Distributive Property to multiply mentally.

23. **TRAVEL** Each year about 27 million people visit Paris, France. About how many people will visit Paris over a five-year period?

24. **ROLLER COASTERS** One ride on the Flashback coaster at Six Flags over Texas lasts 108 seconds. How long will it take to ride this coaster three times?

The Distributive Property also can be applied to subtraction. Use the Distributive Property to evaluate each expression.

25. $2(5 - 4)$
26. $7(8 - 6)$
27. $(7 - 3)9$
28. $6(12 - 5)$

ALGEBRA Use one or more properties to rewrite each expression as an equivalent expression that does not use parentheses.

29. $(y + 1) + 4$
30. $2 + (x + 4)$
31. $4(8b)$
32. $(3a)2$
33. $2(x + 3)$
34. $4(2 + b)$
35. $6(c + 1)$
36. $3(f + 4) + 2f$

EXTRA PRACTICE

See pages 719, 755.

Math Online

Self-Check Quiz at tx.msmath2.com

MILEAGE For Exercises 37 and 38, use the table that shows the driving distance between certain cities in Texas.

From	To	Driving Distance (mi)
Amarillo	Houston	610
Houston	San Antonio	195

37. Write a sentence that compares the mileage from Amarillo to Houston to San Antonio and the mileage from San Antonio to Houston to Amarillo.

38. Name the property that is illustrated by this sentence.

H.O.T. Problems

39. **OPEN ENDED** Write an equation that illustrates the Associative Property of Addition.

40. **NUMBER SENSE** Analyze the statement $(11 + 18)5 = 11 + 18(5)$. Then tell whether the statement is *true* or *false*. Explain your reasoning.

41. **CHALLENGE** A *counterexample* is an example showing that a statement is not true. Provide a counterexample to the following statement.

Division of whole numbers is associative.

42. **WRITING IN MATH** Write about a real-world situation that can be solved using the Distributive Property. Then use it to solve the problem.

TEST PRACTICE

43. Which expression can be written as $6(9 + 8)$?

A $8 \cdot 6 + 8 \cdot 9$

B $6 \cdot 9 + 6 \cdot 8$

C $6 \cdot 9 \cdot 6 \cdot 8$

D $6 + 9 \cdot 6 + 8$

44. Jared deposited \$5 into his savings account. Six months later, his account balance had doubled. If his old balance was b dollars, which of the following would be equivalent to his new balance of $2(b + 5)$ dollars?

F $2b + 5$

G $2b + 7$

H $b + 10$

J $2b + 10$

Spiral Review

Name the number that is the solution of the given equation. (Lesson 1-7)

45. $7.3 = t - 4$; 10.3, 11.3, 12.3

46. $35.5 = 5n$; 5.1, 7.1, 9.1

47. **PETS** It is believed that a dog ages 7 human years for every calendar year. This situation can be represented by the expression $7y$ where y is the age of the dog in calendar years. Find the human age of a dog that has lived for 12 calendar years. (Lesson 1-6)

48. Evaluate $(14 - 9)^4$. (Lesson 1-4)

GET READY for the Next Lesson

PREREQUISITE SKILL Find the next number in each pattern.

49. 2, 4, 6, 8, ■

50. 10, 21, 32, 43, ■

51. 1.4, 2.2, 3.0, 3.8, ■

1-9 Algebra: Arithmetic Sequences

Main IDEA

Describe the relationships and extend terms in arithmetic sequences.

Targeted TEKS 7.4 The student represents a relationship in numerical, geometric, verbal, and symbolic form. **(C) use words and symbols to describe the relationship between the terms in an arithmetic sequence (with a constant rate of change) and their positions in the sequence.** *Also addresses TEKS 7.13(D).*

NEW Vocabulary

sequence
term
arithmetic sequence

MINI Lab

Use centimeter cubes to make the three figures shown.

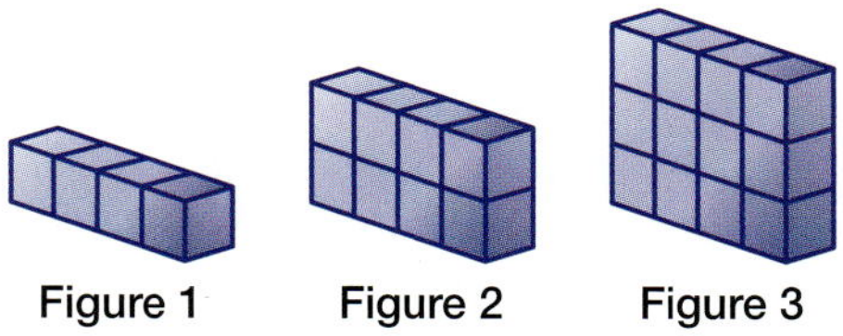

1. How many centimeter cubes are used to make each figure?
2. What pattern do you see? Describe it in words.
3. Suppose this pattern continues. Copy and complete the table to find the number of cubes needed to make each figure.

Figure	1	2	3	4	5	6	7	8
Cubes Needed	4	8	12					

4. How many cubes would you need to make the 10th figure? Explain your reasoning.

A **sequence** is an ordered list of numbers. Each number in a sequence is called a **term**. In an **arithmetic sequence**, each term is found by adding the same number to the previous term. An example of an arithmetic sequence is shown.

8, 11, 14, 17, 20, ...
+3 +3 +3 +3

In this sequence, each term is found by adding 3 to the previous term.

EXAMPLE Describe and Extend Sequences

1 **Describe the relationship between the terms in the arithmetic sequence 8, 13, 18, 23, ... Then write the next three terms in the sequence.**

8, 13, 18, 23, ...
+5 +5 +5

Each term is found by adding 5 to the previous term. Continue the pattern to find the next three terms.

$23 + 5 = 28$ $\qquad 28 + 5 = 33$ $\qquad 33 + 5 = 38$

The next three terms are 28, 33, and 38.

CHECK Your Progress

Describe the relationship between the terms in each arithmetic sequence. Then write the next three terms in the sequence.

a. 0, 13, 26, 39, ...

b. 4, 7, 10, 13 ...

Arithmetic sequences can also involve decimals.

EXAMPLE Describe and Extend Sequences

2 **Describe the relationship between the terms in the arithmetic sequence 0.4, 0.6, 0.8, 1.0, … Then write the next three terms in the sequence.**

0.4, 0.6, 0.8, 1.0, …
+0.2 +0.2 +0.2

Each term is found by adding 0.2 to the previous term. Continue the pattern to find the next three terms.

$1.0 + 0.2 = 1.2$ $1.2 + 0.2 = 1.4$ $1.4 + 0.2 = 1.6$

The next three terms are 1.2, 1.4, and 1.6.

CHECK Your Progress

Describe the relationship between the terms in each arithmetic sequence. Then write the next three terms in the sequence.

c. 1.0, 1.3, 1.6, 1.9, …

d. 2.5, 3.0, 3.5, 4.0, …

Online **Personal Tutor at** tx.msmath2.com

Concepts in Motion
Animation tx.msmath2.com

In a sequence, each term has a specific position within the sequence. Consider the sequence 2, 4, 6, 8, 10, …

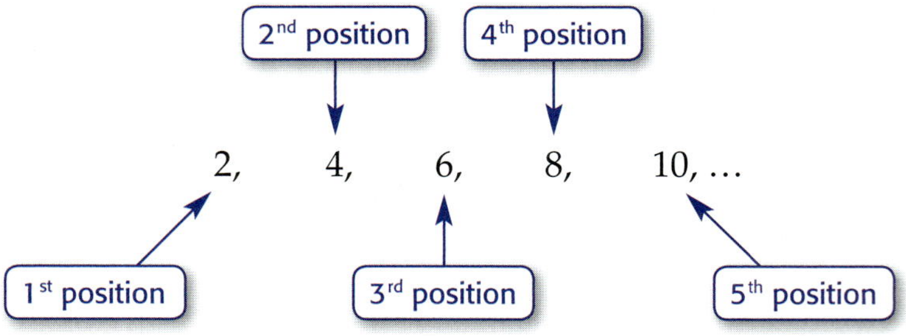

The table below shows the position of each term in this sequence. Notice that as the position number increases by 1, the value of the term increases by 2.

Position	Operation	Value of Term
1	$1 \cdot 2 = 2$	2
2	$2 \cdot 2 = 4$	4
3	$3 \cdot 2 = 6$	6
4	$4 \cdot 2 = 8$	8
5	$5 \cdot 2 = 10$	10

(+1 between successive positions; +2 between successive values of term)

You can also write an algebraic expression to represent the relationship between any term in a sequence and its position in the sequence. In this case, if n represents the position in the sequence, the value of the term is $2n$.

Real-World EXAMPLE

STUDY TIP

Arithmetic Sequences When looking for a pattern between the position number and each term in the sequence, it is often helpful to make a table.

3 GREETING CARDS The homemade greeting cards that Meredith makes are sold in boxes at a local gift store. Each week, the store sells five more boxes than the previous week.

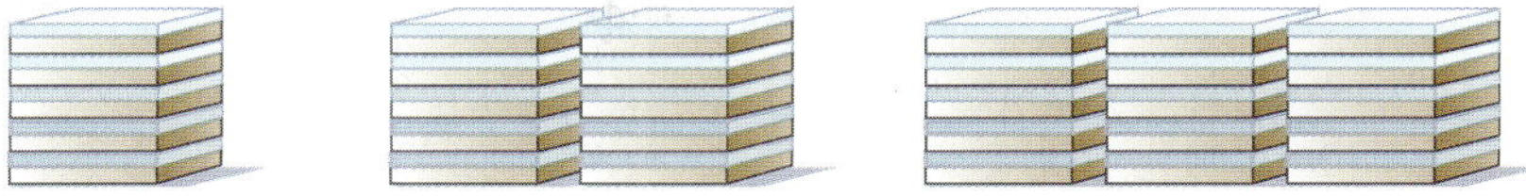

Week 1 Week 2 Week 3

If this pattern continues, what algebraic expression can be used to help her find the total number of boxes sold at the end of the 100th week? Use the expression to find the total.

Make a table to display the sequence.

Position	Operation	Value of Term
1	$1 \cdot 5$	5
2	$2 \cdot 5$	10
3	$3 \cdot 5$	15
n	$n \cdot 5$	$5n$

Each term is 5 times its position number. So, the expression is $5n$.

$5n$ Write the expression.

$5(100) = 500$ Replace n with 100.

So, at the end of 100 weeks, 500 boxes will have been sold.

CHECK Your Progress

e. **GEOMETRY** If the pattern continues, what algebraic expression can be used to find the number of circles used in the 50th figure? How many circles will be in the 50th figure?

Figure 1 Figure 2 Figure 3

CHECK Your Understanding

Examples 1–2 (pp. 57–58)

Describe the relationship between the terms in each arithmetic sequence. Then write the next three terms in each sequence.

1. 0, 9, 18, 27, …
2. 4, 9, 14, 19, …
3. 1, 1.1, 1.2, 1.3, …
4. 5, 5.4, 5.8, 6.2, …

Example 3 (p. 59)

5. **PLANTS** The table shows the height of a certain plant each month after being planted. If this pattern continues, what algebraic expression can be used to find the height of the plant at the end of twelve months? Find the plant's height after 12 months.

Month	Height (in.)
1	3
2	6
3	9
4	12

Exercises

HOMEWORK HELP	
For Exercises	See Examples
6–11	1
12–17	2
18, 19	3

Describe the relationship between the terms in each arithmetic sequence. Then write the next three terms in each sequence.

6. 0, 7, 14, 21, …
7. 1, 7, 13, 19, …
8. 26, 34, 42, 50, …
9. 19, 31, 43, 55, …
10. 6, 16, 26, 36, …
11. 33, 38, 43, 48, …
12. 0.1, 0.4, 0.7, 1.0, …
13. 2.4, 3.2, 4.0, 4.8, …
14. 2.0, 3.1, 4.2, 5.3, …
15. 4.5, 6.0, 7.5, 9.0, …
16. 1.2, 3.2, 5.2, 7.2, …
17. 4.6, 8.6, 12.6, 16.6, …

18. **COLLECTIONS** Hannah is starting a doll collection. Each year, she buys 6 dolls. Suppose she continues this pattern. What algebraic expression can be used to find the number of dolls in her collection after any number of years? How many dolls will Hannah have after 25 years?

19. **EXERCISE** The table shows the number of laps that Jorge swims each week. Jorge's goal is to continue this pace. What algebraic expression can be used to find the total number of laps he will swim after any given number of weeks? How many laps will Jorge swim after 6 weeks?

Week	Number of Laps
1	7
2	14
3	21
4	28

Describe the relationship between the terms in each arithmetic sequence. Then write the next three terms in each sequence.

20. 18, 33, 48, 63, …
21. 20, 45, 70, 95, …
22. 38, 61, 84, 107, …

In a *geometric sequence*, each term is found by multiplying the previous term by the same number. Write the next three terms of each geometric sequence.

23. 1, 4, 16, 64, …
24. 2, 6, 18, 54, …
25. 4, 12, 36, 108, …

26. **DISPLAYS** Kendra is stacking boxes of tissues for a store display. Each minute, she stacks another layer of boxes. If the pattern continues, how many boxes will be displayed after 45 minutes?

NUMBER SENSE **Find the 100th number in each sequence.**

27. 12, 24, 36, 48, …
28. 14, 28, 42, 56, …
29. 0, 50, 100, 150, …
30. 0, 75, 150, 225, …

31. **RESEARCH** The Fibonacci sequence is one of the most well-known sequences in mathematics. Use the Internet or another source to write a paragraph about the Fibonacci sequence.

EXTRA PRACTICE
See pages 719, 755.
Math Online
Self-Check Quiz at
tx.msmath2.com

H.O.T. Problems

CHALLENGE **Not all sequences are arithmetic. But, there is still a pattern. Describe the relationship between the terms in each sequence. Then write the next three terms in the sequence.**

32. 1, 2, 4, 7, 11, …

33. 0, 2, 6, 12, 20, …

34. **OPEN ENDED** Write five terms of an arithmetic sequence and describe the rule for finding the terms.

35. **SELECT A TOOL** Suppose you want to begin saving $15 each month. Which of the following tools would you use to determine the amount you will have saved after 2 years? Justify your selection(s). Then use the tool(s) to solve the problem.

paper/pencil | real object | technology

36. **WRITING IN MATH** Janice earns $6.50 per hour running errands for her neighbor. Explain how the hourly earnings form an arithmetic sequence.

TEST PRACTICE

37. Which sequence follows the rule $3n - 2$, where n represents the position of a term in the sequence?

A 21, 18, 15, 12, 9, …

B 3, 6, 9, 12, 15, …

C 1, 7, 10, 13, 16, …

D 1, 4, 7, 10, 13, …

38. Which expression can be used to find the nth term in this sequence?

Position	1	2	3	4	5	n^{th}
Value of Term	2	5	10	17	26	

F $n^2 + 1$

G $2n + 1$

H $n + 1$

J $2n^2 + 2$

Spiral Review

Name the property shown by each statement. (Lesson 1-8)

39. $8 + 4.1 = 4.1 + 8$

40. $3(n + 6) = 3n + 3(6)$

Solve each equation mentally. (Lesson 1-7)

41. $f - 26 = 3$

42. $\frac{a}{4} = 8$

43. $30 + y = 50$

44. **SCIENCE** At normal temperatures, sound travels through water at a rate of $5 \cdot 10^3$ feet per second. Write this rate in standard form. (Lesson 1-2)

GET READY for the Next Lesson

PREREQUISITE SKILL **Find the value of each expression.** (Lesson 1-6)

45. $2x$ if $x = 4$

46. $d - 5$ if $d = 8$

47. $3m - 3$ if $m = 2$

Extend 1-9

Algebra Lab
Exploring Sequences

Main IDEA

Explore patterns in sequences of geometric figures.

Targeted TEKS 7.4 Patterns, relationships, and algebraic thinking. The student represents a relationship in numerical, geometric, verbal, and symbolic form. **(C) use words and symbols to describe the relationship between the terms in an arithmetic sequence (with a constant rate of change) and their positions in the sequence.** *Also addresses TEKS 7.14(A).*

ACTIVITY

STEP 1 Use toothpicks to build the figures below.

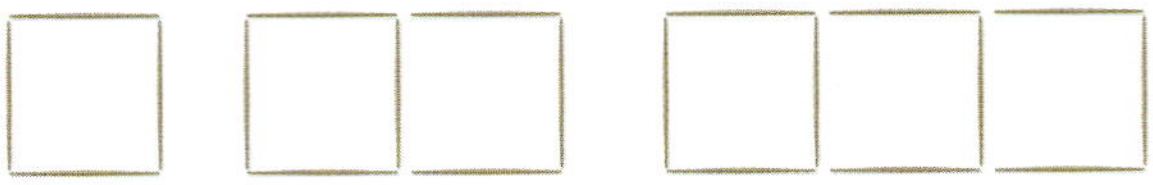

Figure 1 Figure 2 Figure 3

STEP 2 Make a table like the one shown and record the figure number and number of toothpicks used in each figure.

Figure Number	Number of Toothpicks
1	4
2	
3	
⋮	

STEP 3 Construct the next figure in this pattern. Record your results.

STEP 4 Repeat Step 3 until you have found the next four figures in the pattern.

Analyze the Results

1. How many additional toothpicks were used each time to form the next figure in the pattern? Where is this pattern found in the table?
2. Based on your answer to Exercise 1, how many toothpicks would be in Figure 0 of this pattern?
3. Remove one toothpick from your pattern so that Figure 1 is made up of just three toothpicks as shown. Then create a table showing the number of toothpicks that would be in the first 7 figures by continuing the same pattern as above.

Figure 1

4. How many toothpicks would there be in Figure n of this new pattern?
5. How could you adapt the expression you wrote in Exercise 4 to find the number of toothpicks in Figure n of the original pattern?
6. **MAKE A PREDICTION** How many toothpicks would there be in Figure 10 of the original pattern? Explain your reasoning. Then check your answer by constructing the figure.
7. Find the number of toothpicks in Figure n of the pattern below, and predict the number of toothpicks in Figure 12. Justify your answer.

Figure 1 Figure 2 Figure 3

1-10 Algebra: Equations and Functions

Main IDEA

Make function tables and write equations.

Targeted TEKS
7.5 The student uses equations to solve problems. **(B) formulate problem situations when given a simple equation and formulate an equation when given a problem situation.** *Also addresses TEKS 7.14(A).*

NEW Vocabulary

function
function rule
function table
domain
range

GET READY for the Lesson

FAST FOOD Suppose you can buy hamburgers for $2 each.

1. Copy and complete the table to find the cost of 2, 3, and 4 hamburgers.
2. Describe the pattern in the table between the cost and the number of hamburgers.

Hamburgers		
Number	Multiply by 2	Cost ($)
1	2 × 1	2
2		
3		
4		

A relationship that assigns exactly one *output* value for each *input* value is called a **function**. In a function, you start with an input number, perform one or more operations on it, and get an output number. The operation performed on the input is given by the **function rule**.

You can organize the input numbers, output numbers, and the function rule in a **function table**. The set of input values is called the **domain**, and the set of output values is called the **range**. The symbols { and }, which are called braces, are used to list the elements in a set.

EXAMPLE Make a Function Table

1 **MONEY MATTERS** **Suppose you earn $5 each week. Make a function table that shows your total earnings after 1, 2, 3, and 4 weeks. Then identify the domain and range.**

Input	Function Rule	Output
Number of Weeks	Multiply by 5	Total Earnings ($)
1	5 × 1	5
2	5 × 2	10
3	5 × 3	15
4	5 × 4	20

The domain is {1, 2, 3, 4}, and the range is {5, 10, 15, 20}.

CHECK Your Progress

a. Suppose a student movie ticket costs $3. Make a function table that shows the total cost for 1, 2, 3, and 4 tickets. Then identify the domain and range.

Concepts in MOtion
Interactive Lab tx.msmath2.com

STUDY TIP

Input and Output When x and y are used in an equation, x usually represents the input, and y usually represents the output.

Functions are often written as equations with two variables—one to represent the input and one to represent the output. Here's an equation for the situation in Example 1.

Input: number of weeks.

$$5x = y$$

Output: total earnings

Function rule: multiply by 5

Real-World EXAMPLES

2 **ANIMALS An armadillo sleeps 19 hours each day. Write an equation using two variables to show the relationship between the number of hours h an armadillo sleeps in d days.**

Input	Function Rule	Output
Number of Days (d)	Multiply by 19	Number of Hours Slept (h)
1	1×19	19
2	2×19	38
3	3×19	57
d	$d \times 19$	$19d$

Words Number of hours slept equals number of days times 19 hours each day.

Variable Let d represent the number of days. Let h represent the number of hours.

Equation $h = 19d$

3 **How many hours does an armadillo sleep in 4 days?**

$h = 19d$ Write the equation.

$h = 19(4)$ Replace d with 4.

$h = 76$ Multiply.

An armadillo sleeps 76 hours in 4 days.

Real-World Career

How Does a Botanist Use Math? A botanist gathers and studies plant statistics to solve problems and draw conclusions about various plants.

Math Online For more information, go to tx.msmath2.com.

CHECK Your Progress

BOTANIST A botanist discovers that a certain species of bamboo grows 4 inches each hour.

b. Write an equation using two variables to show the relationship between the growth g in inches of this bamboo plant in h hours.

c. How much will the species of bamboo grow after 6 hours?

Online Personal Tutor at tx.msmath2.com

CHECK Your Understanding

Example 1 (p. 63)

Copy and complete each function table. Then identify the domain and range.

1. $y = 3x$

x	$3x$	y
1	3 • 1	3
2	3 • 2	
3	3 • 3	
4		

2. $y = 4x$

x	$4x$	y
0	4 • 0	
1	4 • 1	
2		
3		

3. **MUSIC** Jonas downloads 8 songs each month onto his digital music player. Make a function table that shows the total number of songs downloaded after 1, 2, 3, and 4 months. Then identify the domain and range.

Examples 2, 3 (p. 64)

SPORTS For Exercises 4 and 5, use the following information.

The top speed reached by a standing skateboarder is 80 feet per second.

4. Write an equation using two variables to show the relationship between the distance d that a skateboarder can travel in time t.
5. How far will the skateboarder travel in 4 seconds?

Exercises

HOMEWORK HELP

For Exercises	See Examples
6–10	1
11–14	2, 3

Copy and complete each function table. Then identify the domain and range.

6. $y = 2x$

x	$2x$	y
0	2 • 0	0
1	2 • 1	
2		
3		

7. $y = 6x$

x	$6x$	y
1		
2		
3		
4		

8. $y = 9x$

x	$9x$	y
1		
2		
3		
4		

Make a function table for each situation. Then identify the domain and range.

9. **PIZZA** A pizza shops sells 25 pizzas each hour. Find the number of pizzas sold after 1, 2, 3, and 4 hours.

10. **TYPING** Suppose you can type 60 words per minute. What is the total number of words typed after 5, 10, 15, and 20 minutes?

INTERNET For Exercises 11 and 12, use the following information.

An Internet provider charges a customer $20 each month of service.

11. Write an equation using two variables to show the relationship between the total amount charged c, after m months of Internet service.
12. What is the total cost for 6 months of Internet service?

Real-World Link Crickets are among the 800,000 different types of insects in the world.
Source: kidsport.com

INSECTS **For Exercises 13 and 14, use the following information.**

A cricket will chirp approximately 35 times per minute when the outside temperature is 72°F.

13. Write an equation using two variables to show the relationship between the total number of times a cricket will chirp t, after m minutes at this temperature.

14. How many times will a cricket have chirped after 15 minutes at this temperature?

Copy and complete each function table. Then identify the domain and range.

15. $y = x - 1$

x	$x - 1$	y
1		
2		
3		
4		

16. $y = x + 5$

x	$x + 5$	y
1		
2		
3		
4		

17. $y = x + 0.25$

x	$x + 0.25$	y
0		
1		
2		
3		

18. $y = x - 1.5$

x	$x - 1.5$	y
2		
3		
4		
5		

GEOMETRY **For Exercises 19 and 20, use the following information.**

The formula for the area of a rectangle whose length is 6 units is $A = 6w$.

19. Make a function table that shows the area in square units of a rectangle whose width is 2, 3, 4, and 5 units.

20. Study the pattern in your table. Explain how the area of a rectangle whose length is 6 units changes when the width is increased by 1 unit.

ANALYZE TABLES **For Exercises 21–23, use the table that shows the approximate velocity of certain planets as they orbit the Sun.**

Orbital Velocity Around Sun

Planet	Velocity (mi/s)
Mercury	30
Earth	19
Jupiter	8
Saturn	6
Neptune	5

21. Write an equation to show the relationship between the total number of miles m Jupiter travels in s seconds as it orbits the Sun.

22. What equation can be used to show the total number of miles Earth travels?

23. How many miles does Jupiter travel in 1 minute? Earth?

EXTRA PRACTICE
See pages 720, 755.
Math Online
Self-Check Quiz at tx.msmath2.com

H.O.T. Problems

CHALLENGE Write an equation for the function shown in each table.

24.

x	y
1	3
2	4
3	5
4	6

25.

x	y
2	6
4	12
6	18
8	24

26.

x	y
1	3
2	5
3	7
4	9

27. **OPEN ENDED** Write about a real-world situation that can be represented by the equation $y = 3x$.

28. **WRITING IN MATH** Explain the relationship among an *input*, an *output*, and a *function rule*.

TEST PRACTICE

29. The table shows the number of hand-painted T-shirts Mi-Ling can make after a given number of days.

Number of Days (x)	Total Number of T-Shirts (y)
1	6
2	12
3	18
4	24

Which function rule represents the data?

A $y = 4x$

B $y = 5x$

C $y = 6x$

D $y = 12x$

30. **GRIDDABLE** Refer to Exercise 29. How many T-shirts can Mi-Ling make in 6 days?

31. Cristina needs to have 50 posters printed to advertise a community book fair. The printing company charges $3 to print each poster. Which table represents this situation?

F

posters	cost ($)
3	3
6	6
9	9
p	p

H

posters	cost ($)
1	3
2	6
3	9
p	$3 + p$

G

posters	cost ($)
1	3
2	6
3	9
p	$3p$

J

posters	cost ($)
3	1
6	2
9	3
p	$p \div 3$

Spiral Review

32. **PATTERNS** Write the next three terms of the sequence 27, 36, 45, 54, … (Lesson 1-9)

Use the Distributive Property to evaluate each expression. (Lesson 1-8)

33. $5(9 + 7)$

34. $(12 + 4)4$

35. $8(7 - 2)$

36. $(6 - 5)10$

ALGEBRA Evaluate each expression if $a = 2$ and $b = 5$. (Lesson 1-6)

37. $8 + a$

38. $a + b$

39. $2b - a$

40. $3a^2 - b$

41. **ALLOWANCE** If Karen receives a weekly allowance of $8, about how much money in all will she receive in two years? (Lesson 1-1)

Extend 1-10

Graphing Calculator Lab
Functions and Tables

Main IDEA

Use technology to represent and compare functions.

Targeted TEKS **7.15** The student uses logical reasoning to make conjectures and verify conclusions. **(A)** **make conjectures from patterns or sets of examples** and non-examples. *Also addresses TEKS 7.14(A).*

You can use a TI-83/84 Plus graphing calculator to represent functions.

ACTIVITY

1 **GROCERIES** **A grocery store has 12-ounce bottles of sports drink on sale for \$1.80 each, with no limit on how many you can buy. In addition, you can use a coupon for \$1 off one bottle. Make a table showing the cost for 3, 4, 5, 6, and 7 bottles of this drink.**

STEP 1 Write an equation to show the relationship between the number of bottles purchased x and their cost y.

Cost is \$1.80 per bottle less \$1.

$$y = 1.80x - 1$$

STEP 2 Press [Y=] on your calculator. Then enter the function into Y_1 by pressing 1.80 [X,T,θ,n] [−] 1 [ENTER].

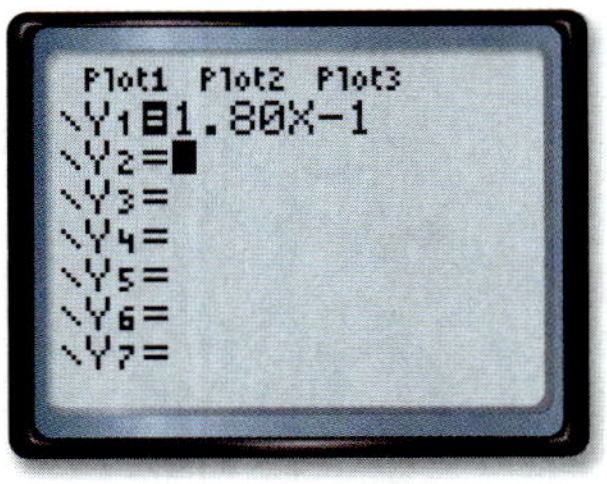

STEP 3 Next, set up a table of x- and y-values. Press [2nd] [TBLSET] to display the table setup screen. Then press [↓] [↓] [→] [ENTER] to highlight Indpnt: Ask.

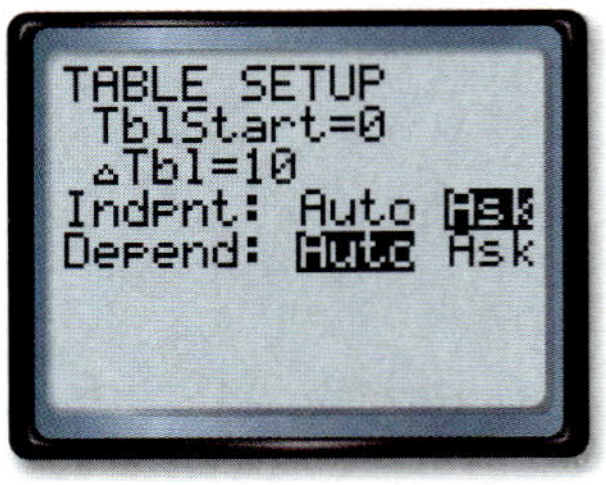

STEP 4 Access the table by pressing [2nd] [TABLE]. Then key in each number of bottles, pressing [ENTER] after each entry.

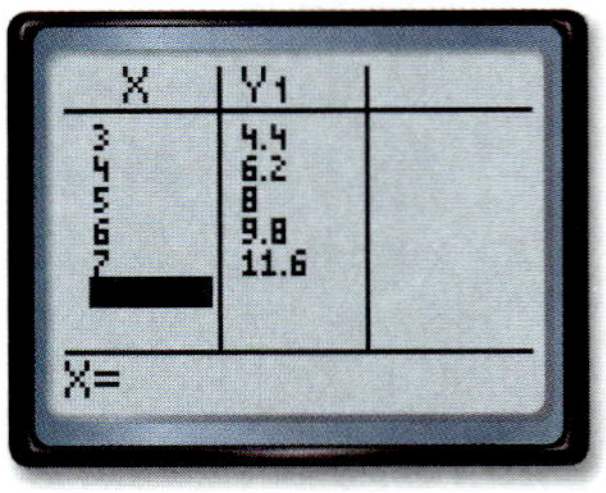

Analyze the Results

1. Analyze the table to determine how many bottles you can buy for \$10. Explain your reasoning.

2. **MAKE A CONJECTURE** Notice that you can purchase 5 bottles for the whole dollar amount of \$8. How many bottles will you be able to purchase the next whole dollar amount? Use the calculator to test your conjecture.

ACTIVITY

2 **CAMPING** **Out-There Campground charges each group a camping fee of \$20 plus \$4.25 per person per night. Roughing-It Campground charges \$6.25 per person per night. Make a table showing the one-night fee for 2, 3, 4, 5, and 6 people to camp at each campground.**

STEP 1 Write an equation to show the relationship between the number of people *x* and the one-night fee *y* for them to camp at each campground.

Out-There Campground

Fee is \$20 plus \$4.25 per person.

$$y = 20 + 4.25x$$

Roughing-It Campground

Fee is \$6.25 per person.

$$y = 6.25x$$

READING Math

The phrase *\$4.25 per person* means *\$4.25 for each person.*

STEP 2 Enter the function for the Out-There Campground into Y_1 and the function for the Roughing-It Campground into Y_2.

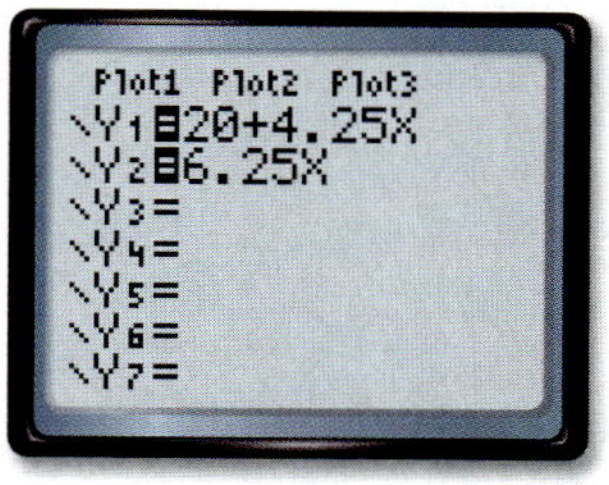

STEP 3 Next, set up a table of *x*- and *y*-values as in Activity 1.

STEP 4 Then access the table and key in each number of people

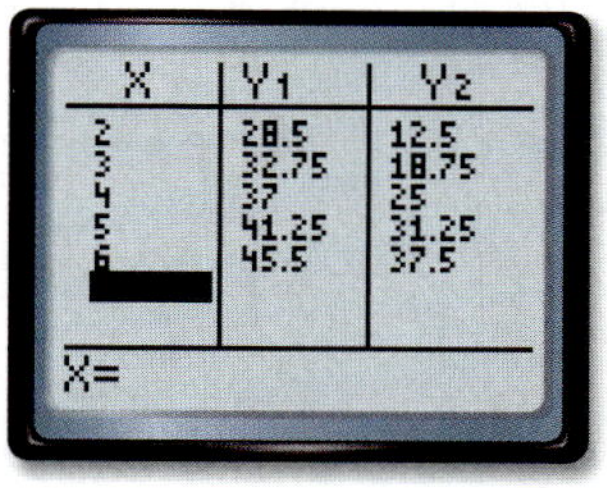

ANALYZE THE RESULTS

3. For 2, 3, 4, 5, and 6 people, which campground charges the greater total nightly cost to camp?

4. **MAKE A CONJECTURE** Will the nightly total cost to camp at each campground ever be the same? If so, for what number of people?

5. Use the graphing calculator to test your conjecture from Exercise 4. Were you correct? If not, use the graphing calculator to guess and check until you find the correct number of people.

6. If all other aspects of these two campgrounds are equal, write a recommendation as to which campground a group of *n* people should choose based on your cost analysis.

CHAPTER 1

Study Guide and Review

STUDY TO GO Download Vocabulary Review from tx.msmath2.com

FOLDABLES™ Study Organizer

GET READY to Study

Be sure the following Key Concepts are noted in your Foldable.

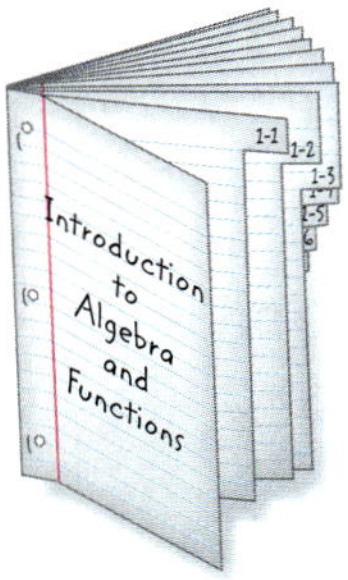

Key Concepts

Squares and Square Roots (Lesson 1-3)

- The square of a number is the product of a number and itself.
- A square root of a number is one of its two equal factors.

Order of Operations (Lesson 1-4)

- Do all operations within grouping symbols first. Evaluate all powers before other operations. Multiply and divide in order from left to right. Add and subtract in order from left to right.

Properties (Lesson 1-8)

- Distributive Property
  $5(2 + 4) = 5 \cdot 2 + 5 \cdot 4$
  $(3 + 2)4 = 3 \cdot 4 + 2 \cdot 4$
- Commutative Property
  $3 + 2 = 2 + 3$
  $7 \cdot 4 = 4 \cdot 7$
- Associative Property
  $6 + (3 + 8) = (6 + 3) + 8$
  $5 \cdot (2 \cdot 3) = (5 \cdot 2) \cdot 3$
- Identity Property
  $4 + 0 = 4$
  $4 \cdot 1 = 4$

Functions (Lesson 1-10)

- A function is a relationship that assigns exactly one *output* value for each *input* value.
- In a function, the function rule gives the operation to perform on the input.

Key Vocabulary

algebra (p. 44)
algebraic expression (p. 44)
arithmetic sequence (p. 57)
base (p. 30)
coefficient (p. 45)
defining the variable (p. 50)
domain (p. 63)
equation (p. 49)
equivalent expressions (p. 53)
evaluate (p. 31)
exponent (p. 30)
factors (p. 30)
function (p. 63)
function rule (p. 63)
numerical expression (p. 38)
order of operations (p. 38)
perfect square (p. 35)
powers (p. 30)
radical sign (p. 35)
range (p. 63)
sequence (p. 57)
solution (p. 49)
square (p. 34)
square root (p. 35)
term (p. 57)
variable (p. 44)

Vocabulary Check

State whether each sentence is *true* or *false*. If *false*, replace the underlined word or number to make a true sentence.

1. <u>Numerical expressions</u> have the same value.
2. Two or more numbers that are multiplied together are called <u>powers</u>.
3. The <u>range</u> of a function is the set of input values.
4. A function assigns exactly <u>two</u> *output* values for each *input* value.
5. An <u>equation</u> is a sentence that contains an equals sign.
6. A <u>sequence</u> is an ordered list of numbers.
7. The product of a number and itself is the <u>square root</u> of the number.

Math Online Vocabulary Review at tx.msmath2.com

Lesson-by-Lesson Review

1-1 A Plan for Problem Solving (pp. 25–29)

Use the four-step plan to solve each problem.

8. **CELLULAR PHONES** Sherita's service charges a monthly fee of \$20.00 plus \$0.15 per minute. One monthly bill is \$31.25. How many minutes did Sherita use during the month?
9. **CAR RENTAL** ABC Car Rental charges \$25 per day to rent a mid-sized car plus \$0.20 per mile driven. Mr. Ruiz rents a mid-sized car for 3 days and drives a total of 72 miles. Find the amount of Mr. Ruiz's bill.
10. **DOGS** There are more than 5 million puppies born in the United States each year. About how many puppies will be born after 4 years?

Example 1 **A bag of mulch covers 25 square feet of garden space. Taylor uses 7 bags of mulch to cover her garden. How large is Taylor's garden?**

Explore Taylor used 7 bags of mulch, each covering 25 square feet.

Plan Multiply 25 by 7.

Solve $25 \cdot 7 = 175$

Taylor's garden is 175 square feet.

Check $175 \div 7 = 25$, so the answer is reasonable.

1-2 Powers and Exponents (pp. 30–33)

Write each power as a product of the same factor.

11. 3^4
12. 9^6
13. 5^1
14. 7^5
15. Write *5 to the fourth power* as a product of the same factor.

Evaluate each expression.

16. 3^5
17. 7^9
18. 2^8
19. 18^2
20. 10^4
21. 100^1
22. Write $15 \cdot 15 \cdot 15$ in exponential form.
23. **PATHS** At the edge of a forest, there are two paths. At the end of each path, there are two additional paths. If at the end of each of those paths there are two more paths, how many paths are there at the end?

Example 2 **Write 2^3 as a product of the same factor.**

The base is 2. The exponent 3 means that 2 is used as a factor 3 times.

$2^3 = 2 \cdot 2 \cdot 2$

Example 3 **Evaluate 4^5.**

The base is 4. The exponent 5 means that 4 is used as a factor 5 times.

$4^5 = 4 \cdot 4 \cdot 4 \cdot 4 \cdot 4$

$= 1{,}024$

Study Guide and Review

1-3 Squares and Square Roots (pp. 34–37)

Find the square of each number.

24. 4 **25.** 13

Find each square root.

26. $\sqrt{81}$ **27.** $\sqrt{324}$

28. TILE The area of a certain kind of ceramic tile is 25 square inches. What is the length of one side?

Example 4 **Find the square of 15.**

$15 \cdot 15 = 225$ Multiply 15 by itself.

Example 5 **Find the square root of 441.**

$21 \cdot 21 = 441$, so $\sqrt{441} = 21$.

1-4 Order of Operations (pp. 38–41)

Evaluate each expression.

29. $24 - 8 + 3^2$ **30.** $48 \div 6 + 2 \cdot 5$

31. $9 + 3(7 - 5)^3$ **32.** $15 + 9 \div 3 - 7$

33. SEATING In planning for a ceremony, 36 guests need to be seated with 4 guests per table. An additional 12 guests need to be seated with 3 guests per table. Write an expression to determine how many tables are needed. Then evaluate the expression.

Example 6 **Evaluate $24 - (8 \div 4)^4$.**

$24 - (8 \div 4)^4 = 24 - 2^4$ Divide 8 by 4.

$= 24 - 16$ Find the value of 2^4.

$= 8$ Subtract.

1-5 PSI: Guess and Check (pp. 42–43)

Solve. Use the *guess and check* strategy.

34. TRAVEL Lucinda is driving away from Houston at 50 miles per hour. When she is 100 miles away, Tom leaves Houston, driving at 60 miles per hour in the same direction. After how many hours will Tom pass Lucinda?

35. FARMING A farmer sells a bushel of soybeans for \$5 and a bushel of corn for \$3. If he hopes to earn \$164 and plans to sell 40 bushels in all, how many bushels of soybeans does he need to sell?

Example 7 **Find two numbers whose product is 30 and whose difference is 13.**

Make a guess and check to see if it is correct. Then adjust the guess until it is correct.

5 and 6 — $5 \cdot 6 = 30$ and $6 - 5 = 1$ incorrect

3 and 10 — $3 \cdot 10 = 30$ and $10 - 3 = 7$ incorrect

2 and 15 — $2 \cdot 15 = 30$ and $15 - 2 = 13$ correct

The two numbers are 2 and 15.

Mixed Problem Solving
For mixed problem-solving practice, see page 755.

1-6 Algebra: Variables and Expressions (pp. 44–47)

Evaluate each expression if $a = 10$, $b = 4$, and $c = 8$.

36. $(a - b)^2$
37. $ab \div c$
38. $3b^2 + c$
39. $\frac{(b + c)^2}{3}$
40. **PRODUCTION** The cost of producing T-shirts is given by the expression $350 + 0.82x$, where x is the number of T-shirts produced. Find the cost of producing 750 T-shirts.

Example 8 **Evaluate $2m^2 - 5n$ if $m = 4$ and $n = 3$.**

$2m^2 - 5n = 2(4)^2 - 5(3)$	Replace m with 4 and n with 3.
$= 2(16) - 5(3)$	Find the value of 4^2.
$= 32 - 15$	Multiply.
$= 17$	Subtract.

1-7 Algebra: Equations (pp. 49–52)

Solve each equation mentally.

41. $h + 9 = 17$
42. $31 - y = 8$
43. $\frac{t}{9} = 12$
44. $100 = 20g$
45. **COUNTY FAIRS** Five friends wish to ride the Ferris wheel which requires 3 tickets per person. The group has a total of 9 tickets. Write and solve an equation to find the number of additional tickets needed for everyone to ride the Ferris wheel.

Example 9 **Solve $14 = 5 + x$ mentally.**

$14 = 5 + x$	Write the equation.
$14 = 5 + 9$	You know that $5 + 9 = 14$.
$14 = 14$	Simplify.

The solution is 9.

1-8 Algebra: Properties (pp. 53–56)

Name the property shown by each statement.

46. $3 + 8 = 8 + 3$
47. $6(1 + 4) = 6(1) + 6(4)$
48. $29 \cdot 1 = 29$
49. **SALES** Pat and Wesley sold roses at 7 houses for $2 a piece, and 3 people in each house bought a rose. To figure out how much money they earned, Wesley multiplied 2 by 7 and then by 3. Pat multiplied 3 by 2 and then by 7. Name the property that is shown.

Example 10 **Name the property shown by the statement $12 + (8 + 2) = (12 + 8) + 2$.**

This statement shows that the way in which three numbers are grouped when they are added does not change their sum. This is an example of the Associative Property of Addition.

1-9 Algebra: Arithmetic Sequences (pp. 57–61)

Describe the relationship between the terms in each arithmetic sequence. Then find the next three terms in each sequence.

50. 3, 9, 15, 21, 27, ...

51. 2.6, 3.4, 4.2, 5, 5.8, ...

52. 0, 7, 14, 21, 28, ...

MONEY For Exercises 53 and 54, use the following information.

Tanya collected $4.50 for the first car washed at a band fundraiser. After the second and third car were washed, the donations totaled $9 and $13.50, respectively.

53. If this donation pattern continues, what algebraic expression can be used to find the amount of money earned for any number of cars washed?

54. How much money will be collected after a total of 8 cars have been washed?

Example 11 At the end of day 1, Sierra read 25 pages of a novel. By the end of days 2 and 3, she read a total of 50 and 75 pages, respectively. If the pattern continues, what expression will give the total number of pages read after any number of days?

Make a table to display the sequence.

Position	Operation	Value of Term
1	1 • 25	25
2	2 • 25	50
3	3 • 25	75
n	n • 25	$25n$

Each term is 25 times its position number. So, the expression is $25n$.

1-10 Algebra: Equations and Functions (pp. 63–67)

Copy and complete the function table. Then identify the domain and range.

55. $y = 4x$

x	$4x$	y
5		
6		
7		
8		

56. **NAME TAGS** Charmaine can make 32 name tags per hour. Make a function table that shows the number of name tags she can make in 3, 4, 5, and 6 hours.

Example 12 Create and complete a function table for $y = 3x$. Then identify the domain and range.

Select any four values for the input x.

x	$3x$	y
3	3(3)	9
4	3(4)	12
5	3(5)	15
6	3(6)	18

The domain is {3, 4, 5, 6}.

The range is {9, 12, 15, 18}.

CHAPTER 1 Practice Test

1. **PIZZA** Ms. Carter manages a pizza parlor. The average daily costs are \$40, plus \$52 to pay each employee. It also costs \$2 to make each pizza. If 42 pizzas were made one day, requiring the work of 7 employees, what were her total costs that day?

Write each power as a product of the same factor. Then evaluate the expression.

2. 3^5
3. 15^4

4. **HOME REPAIR** Gregory wants to stain the 15-foot-by-15-foot deck in his backyard. One can of stain covers 200 square feet of surface. Is one can of stain enough to cover his entire deck? Explain your reasoning.

Find each square root.

5. $\sqrt{121}$
6. $\sqrt{900}$

7. **STANDARDS PRACTICE** What is the value of $8 + (12 \div 3)^3 - 5 \times 9$?

   A 603 **C** 27
   B 135 **D** 19

8. **ANIMALS** Irene has 6 pets, some dogs and some birds. Her animals have a total of 16 legs. How many of each pet does Irene have?

Evaluate each expression if $x = 12$, $y = 5$, and $z = 3$.

9. $x - 9$
10. $8y$
11. $(y - z)^3$
12. $\frac{xz}{y + 13}$

Solve each equation mentally.

13. $9 + m = 16$
14. $d - 14 = 37$
15. $32 = \frac{96}{t}$
16. $6x = 126$

17. **SAVINGS** Deb is saving \$54 per month to buy a new camera. Use the Distributive Property to mentally find how much she has saved after 7 months. Explain.

Name the property shown by each statement.

18. $2 + (3 + 7) = (2 + 3) + 7$
19. $5(w + 2) = 5w + 5(2)$

20. **STANDARDS PRACTICE** The table shows the number of hours Teodoro spent studying for his biology test over four days. If the pattern continues, how many hours will Teodoro study on Sunday?

Day	Study Time (hours)
Monday	0.5
Tuesday	0.75
Wednesday	1.0
Thursday	1.25

   F 1.5 hours **H** 2.0 hours
   G 1.75 hours **J** 2.5 hours

Describe the relationship between the terms in each arithmetic sequence. Then write the next three terms in the sequence.

21. 7, 16, 25, 34, …
22. 59, 72, 85, 98, …

23. **TRAVEL** Beth drove at the rate of 65 miles per hour for several hours. Make a function table that shows her distance traveled after 2, 3, 4, and 5 hours. Then identify the domain and range.

MONEY For Exercises 24 and 25, use the following information.

Anthony earns extra money after school doing yard work for his neighbors. He charges \$12 for each lawn he mows.

24. Write an equation using two variables to show the relationship between the number of lawns mowed m and number of dollars earned d.
25. Then find the number of dollars earned if he mows 14 lawns.

Texas Test Practice

Chapter 1

Read each question. Then fill in the correct answer on the answer document provided by your teacher or on a sheet of paper.

1. A store owner bought some paperback books and then sold them for $4.50 each. He sold 35 books on Monday and 52 books on Tuesday. What piece of information is needed to find the amount of profit made from sales on Monday and Tuesday?

   A Number of books sold on Wednesday

   B Number of hardback books sold on Monday and Tuesday

   C Total number of paperback books sold

   D How much the owner paid for each of the paperback books

2. The table shows the number of milkshakes sold at an ice cream shop each day last week.

Day of Week	Number of Milkshakes
Sunday	31
Monday	9
Tuesday	11
Wednesday	15
Thursday	18
Friday	24
Saturday	28

   Which statement is NOT supported by these data?

   F There were almost three times as many milkshakes sold on Sunday as on Tuesday.

   G There were half as many milkshakes sold on Monday as on Thursday.

   H There were 11 more milkshakes sold on Tuesday than on Saturday.

   J The total number of milkshakes sold during the week was 136.

3. Which description shows the relationship between a term and n, its position in the sequence?

Position	1	2	3	4	5	n
Value of Term	3	6	9	12	15	

   A Add 2 to n

   B Divide n by 3

   C Multiply n by 3

   D Subtract n from 2

4. **GRIDDABLE** Andrew spent $\frac{1}{2}$ of his Saturday earnings on a pair of jeans and $\frac{1}{2}$ of the remaining amount on a DVD. After he spent $7.40 on lunch, he had $6.10 left. How much in dollars did Andrew earn on Saturday?

TEST-TAKING TIP

Question 5 When you shade the answer bubbles on the answer sheet, be sure your shading covers the bubble completely.

5. Which model represents 9^2?

   F
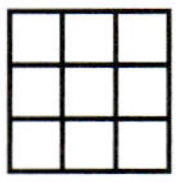

   G
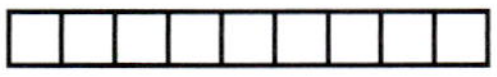

   H
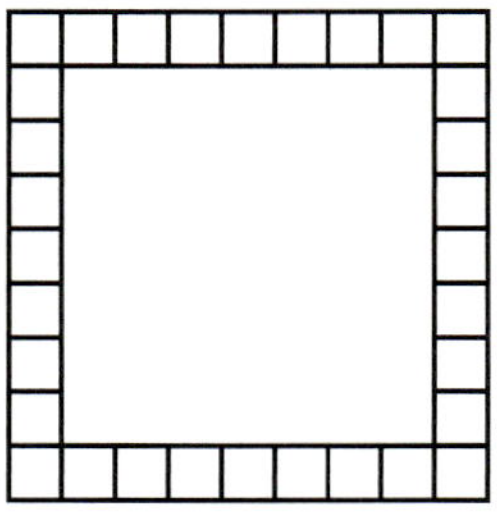

   J
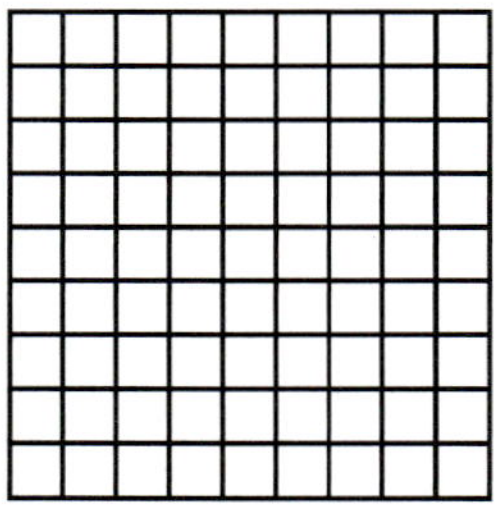

Get Ready for the Texas Test
For test-taking strategies and more practice, see pages TX1–TX23.

6. Mrs. Albert drove 850 miles and the average price of gasoline was \$2.50 per gallon. What information is needed to find the amount Mrs. Albert spent on gasoline for the trip?
   - **A** Number of hours the trip took
   - **B** Number of miles per hour traveled
   - **C** Average number of miles the car traveled per gallon of gasoline
   - **D** Average number of miles Mrs. Albert drove per day

7. Mr. Thompson wants to estimate the total amount he spends on insurance and fuel for his car each month. Insurance costs about \$300 per month, and he expects to drive an average of 150 miles per week. What else does he need to estimate his monthly expenses?
   - **F** The cost of fuel and the one-way distance to work
   - **G** The cost of fuel and the number of miles per gallon his car gets
   - **H** The cost of fuel and his weekly pay
   - **J** The gallons of fuel needed per week

8. Jeremy bought 3 hamburgers at \$1.99 each, 2 orders of onion rings at \$0.89 each, and 4 soft drinks at \$1.25 each. He paid 6.75% tax on the whole order. What other information is necessary to find Jeremy's correct change?
   - **A** Total cost of the order
   - **B** Amount he paid in tax
   - **C** Reason for buying the food
   - **D** Amount he gave the cashier

9. Emily bought 2.5 pounds of salami for \$1.99 per pound. About how much did she pay?
   - **F** Less than \$4.00
   - **G** Between \$4 and \$4.50
   - **H** Between \$4.50 and \$5.50
   - **J** More than \$5.50

10. To hold a wedding reception, a restaurant charges \$45 per hour for use of a private room plus \$19.50 per person. Which expression can be used to find the total cost of a 4-hour wedding reception for 75 people?
    - **A** $4 \times 45 + 19.50 + 75$
    - **B** $4 \times 75 + 45 + 19.50$
    - **C** $4 \times 19.50 + 75 \times 45$
    - **D** $4 \times 45 + 75 \times 19.50$

Pre-AP

Record your answers on a sheet of paper. Show your work.

11. Figures 1, 2, and 3 are made of equal-size squares.

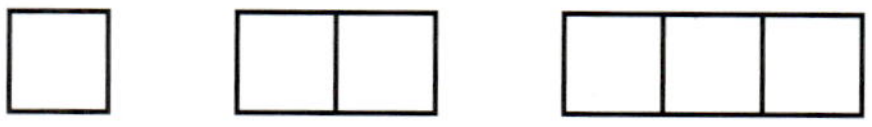

Figure 1 Figure 2 Figure 3

Each side in Figure 1 is 2 units in length. The table shows the perimeter of the first 2 figures.

Figure	1	2	3	4	5	6
Perimeter	8	12				

   a. Extend the pattern to find the perimeters of Figures 3–6.

   b. Is the sequence of perimeters arithmetic? Explain.

NEED EXTRA HELP?											
If You Missed Question...	1	2	3	4	5	6	7	8	9	10	11
Go to Lesson...	1-1	1-1	1-9	1-1	1-3	1-1	1-1	1-1	1-1	1-4	1-9
For Help with Test Objective...	6	1	6	2	1	1	2	6	6	2	1

CHAPTER 2

Integers

Knowledge and Skills

- Represent and use numbers in a variety of equivalent forms. **TEKS 7.1**
- Add, subtract, multiply, or divide to solve problems and justify solutions. **TEKS 7.2**

Key Vocabulary

graph (p. 80)

integer (p. 80)

negative integer (p. 80)

positive integer (p. 80)

Real-World Link

Sports In miniature golf, a score above par can be written as a positive integer and a score below par can be written as a negative integer.

FOLDABLES™ Study Organizer

Integers Make this Foldable to help you organize your notes. Begin with two sheets of $8\frac{1}{2}''$ by $11''$ paper.

1. **Fold** one sheet in half from top to bottom. Cut along fold from edges to margin.

2. **Fold** the other sheet in half from top to bottom. Cut along fold between margins.

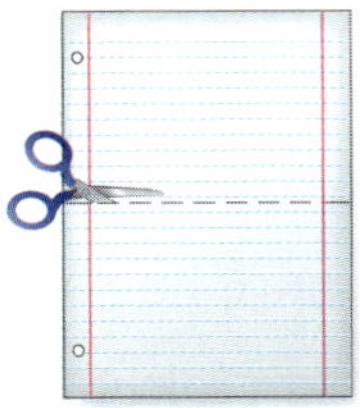

3. **Insert** first sheet through second sheet and align folds.

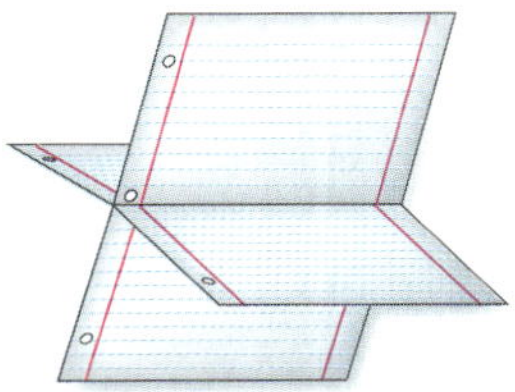

4. **Label** each inside page with a lesson number and title.

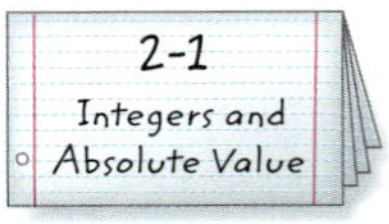

GET READY for Chapter 2

Diagnose Readiness You have two options for checking Prerequisite Skills.

Option 2

Math Online Take the Online Readiness Quiz at tx.msmath2.com.

Option 1

Take the Quick Quiz below. Refer to the Quick Review for help.

QUICK Quiz

Replace each ● with < or > to make a true sentence. (Used in Lesson 2-2)

1. 1,458 ● 1,548
2. 36 ● 34
3. 1.02 ● 1.20
4. 76.7 ● 77.6
5. **COINS** Philippe has \$5.17 in coins and Garrett has \$5.71 in coins. Who has the greater amount?

Evaluate each expression if $a = 7$, $b = 2$, and $c = 11$. (Used in Lessons 2-4 and 2-5)

6. $a + 8$
7. $a + b + c$
8. $c - b$
9. $a - b + 4$
10. **TEMPERATURE** At 8 A.M., it was 63°F. By noon, the temperature had risen 9 degrees Fahrenheit. What was the temperature at noon?

Evaluate each expression if $m = 9$ and $n = 4$. (Used in Lessons 2-7 and 2-8)

11. $6mn$
12. $n \div 2 - 1$
13. $m + 5 \times n$
14. $m^2 \div (n + 5)$
15. **PLANES** The distance in miles that an airplane travels is given by rt where r is the rate of travel and t is the time. Find the distance an airplane traveled if $t = 4$ hours and $r = 475$ miles per hour.

QUICK Review

Example 1

Replace the ● with < or > to make a true sentence.

3.14 ● 3.41

3.14
3.41
↑

Line up the decimal points. Starting at the left, compare the digits in each place-value position.

The digits in the tenths place are not the

Example 2

Evaluate the expression $11 - a + b$ if $a = 2$ and $b = 8$.

$11 - a + b = 11 - 2 + 8$	Replace *a* with 2 and *b* with 8.
$= 9 + 8$	Subtract 2 from 11.
$= 17$	Add 9 and 8.

Example 3

Evaluate the expression $n^2 \div 16 + m$ if $m = 3$ and $n = 8$.

$n^2 \div 16 + m = 8^2 \div 16 + 3$	Replace *m* with 3 and *n* with 8.
$= 64 \div 16 + 3$	Evaluate 8^2.
$= 4 + 3$	Divide 64 by 16.
$= 7$	Add 4 and 3.

2-1 Integers and Absolute Value

Main IDEA

Read and write integers, and find the absolute value of a number.

Reinforcement of TEKS 6.1 The student represents and uses rational numbers in a variety of equivalent forms. **(C) use integers to represent real-life situations.**

GET READY for the Lesson

FOOTBALL The graph shows the number of yards the Bears gained or lost on the first four downs. A value of −3 represents a 3-yard loss.

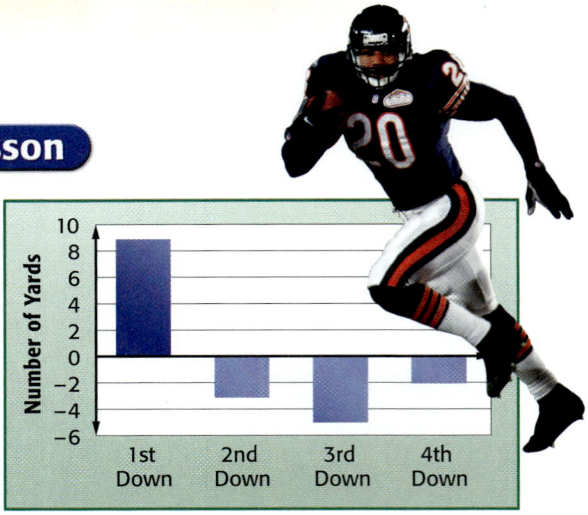

1. What does a value of −2 represent?
2. On which down did they lose the most yards?
3. How can you represent a gain of 9 yards?

NEW Vocabulary

integer
negative integer
positive integer
graph
absolute value

Numbers like 9 and −2 are called integers. An **integer** is any number from the set {…, −4, −3, −2, −1, 0, 1, 2, 3, 4, …} where … means *continues without end*.

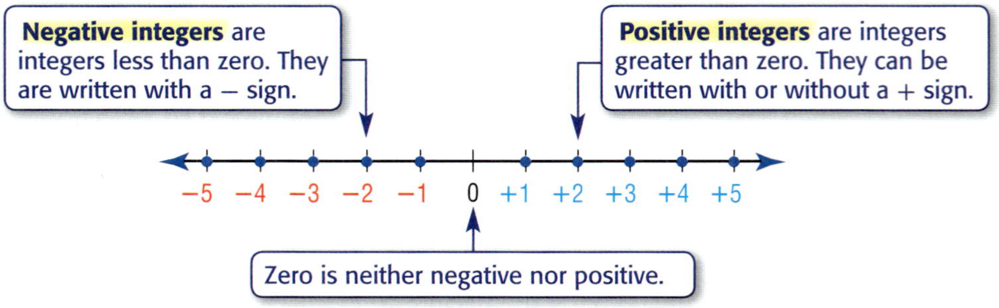

READING Math

Integers and Absolute Value

+ 3	*positive three*
− 3	*negative three*
|3|	*absolute value of three*

Real-World EXAMPLES

WEATHER **Write an integer for each situation.**

1 **an average temperature of 5 degrees below normal**

Because it represents *below* normal, the integer is −5.

2 **an average rainfall of 5 inches above normal**

Because it represents *above* normal, the integer is +5 or 5

CHECK Your Progress **Write an integer for each situation.**

a. 6 degrees above normal

b. 2 inches below normal

Integers can be graphed on a number line. To **graph** a point on the number line, draw a point on the line at its location.

EXAMPLE Graph Integers

3 **Graph the set of integers {4, −6, 0} on a number line.**

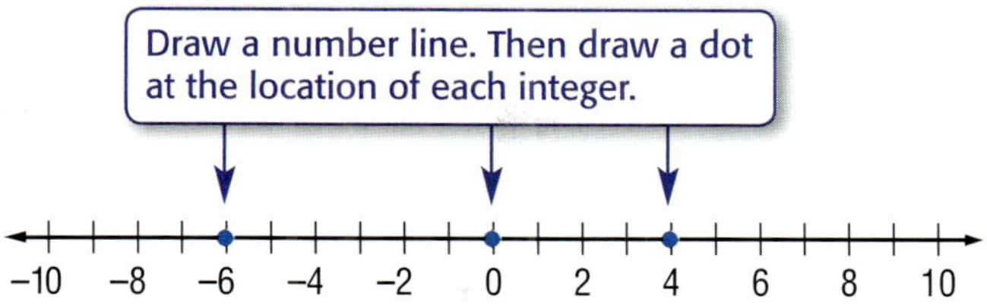

CHECK Your Progress

Graph each set of integers on a number line.

c. {−2, 8, −7}

d. {−4, 10, −3, 7}

Online Personal Tutor at tx.msmath2.com

On the number line below, notice that −5 and 5 are each 5 units from 0, even though they are on opposite sides of 0. Numbers that are the same distance from zero on a number line have the same **absolute value**.

KEY CONCEPT — Absolute Value

Words The absolute value of a number is the distance the number is from zero on a number line.

Examples $|-5| = 5$ $|5| = 5$

EXAMPLES Evaluate Expressions

Evaluate each expression.

4 $|-4|$

On the number line, the graph of −4 is 4 units from 0. So, $|-4| = 4$.

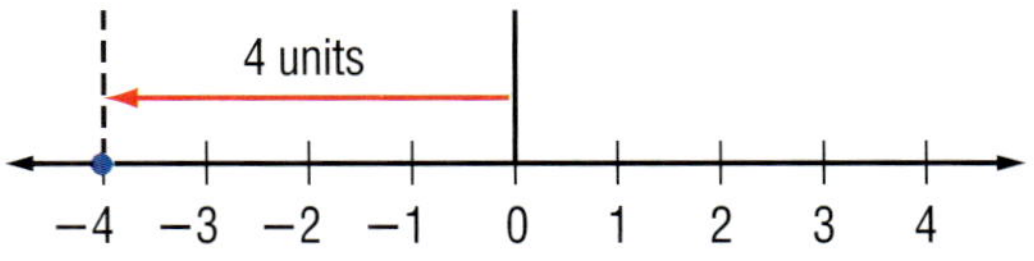

5 $|-5| - |2|$

$|-5| - |2| = 5 - 2$ $|-5| = 5, |2| = 2$

$= 3$ Subtract.

STUDY TIP

Order of Operations When evaluating $|-5| - |2|$, evaluate the absolute values before subtracting.

CHECK Your Progress

Evaluate each expression.

e. $|8|$

f. $2 + |-3|$

g. $|-6| - 5$

CHECK Your Understanding

Examples 1, 2 (p. 80)

Write an integer for each situation.

1. a loss of 11 yards
2. 6°F below zero
3. a deposit of \$16
4. 250 meters above sea level
5. **STOCK MARKET** The price of a company's stock fell 21 points in one week. Write an integer to represent the amount the stock price fell.

Example 3 (p. 81)

Graph each set of integers on a number line.

6. $\{11, -5, -8\}$
7. $\{2, -1, -9, 1\}$

Examples 4, 5 (p. 81)

Evaluate each expression.

8. $|-9|$
9. $1 + |7|$
10. $|-6| - |1|$

Exercises

HOMEWORK HELP

For Exercises	See Examples
11–20	1, 2
21–24	3
25–30	4, 5

Write an integer for each situation.

11. a profit of \$9
12. a bank withdrawl of \$50
13. 53°C below zero
14. 7 inches more than normal
15. 2 feet below flood level
16. 160 feet above sea level
17. an elevator goes up 12 floors
18. no gain on first down
19. **GOLF** In golf, scores are often written in relationship to *par,* the average score for a round at a certain course. Write an integer to represent a score that is 7 under par.
20. **PETS** Javier's pet guinea pig gained 8 ounces in one month. Write an integer to describe the amount of weight his pet gained.

Graph each set of integers on a number line.

21. $\{0, 1, -3\}$
22. $\{3, -7, 6\}$
23. $\{-5, -1, 10, -9\}$
24. $\{-2, -4, -6, -8\}$

Evaluate each expression.

25. $|10|$
26. $|-12|$
27. $|-7| - 5$
28. $7 + |4|$
29. $|-9| + |-5|$
30. $|8| - |-2|$
31. $|-10| \div 2 \times |5|$
32. $12 - |-8| + 7$
33. $|27| \div 3 - |-4|$

EXTRA PRACTICE
See pages 720, 756.
Math Online
Self-Check Quiz at tx.msmath2.com

34. **WEATHER** A meteorologist reports a 20° change in the temperature from yesterday to today. Explain what this could mean.
35. **SCIENCE** Suppose you rub a balloon through your hair to make the balloon stick to a wall. There are 17 positive charges on the wall and 25 negative charges on the balloon. Write an integer for each charge.

H.O.T. Problems

36. **REASONING** If $|x| = 3$, what is the value of x?

37. **CHALLENGE** Determine whether the following statement is *true* or *false*. If *false*, give a counterexample.

The absolute value of every integer is positive.

38. **WRITING IN MATH** Write about a real-world situation that uses negative integers. Explain what the negative integer means in that situation.

TEST PRACTICE

39. Which point is located at −3 on the number line?

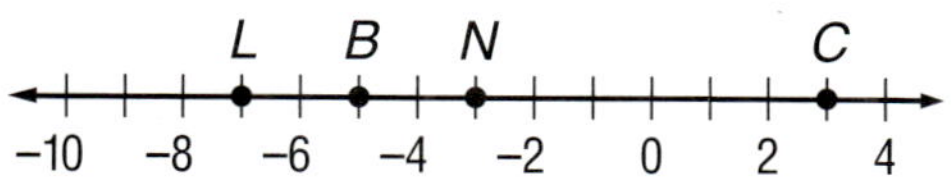

A Point *B*

B Point *C*

C Point *L*

D Point *N*

40. Which statement about these real-world situations is NOT true?

F A \$100 check deposited in a bank can be represented by +100.

G A loss of 15 yards in a football game can be represented by −15.

H A temperature of 20 below zero can be represented by −20.

J A submarine diving 300 feet under water can be represented by +300.

Spiral Review

Copy and complete each function table. Identify the domain and range. (Lesson 1-10)

41. $y = x - 4$

x	$x - 4$	y
4		
5		
6		
7		

42. $y = 9x$

x	$9x$	y
0		
1		
2		
3		

43. $y = 5x + 1$

x	$5x + 1$	y
1		
2		
3		
4		

44. **GEOMETRY** The table shows the side length and perimeter of several equilateral triangles. Write an expression that describes the perimeter if x represents the side length. (Lesson 1-9)

Side Length (in.)	2	3	4	5	6
Perimeter (in.)	6	9	12	15	18

GET READY for the Next Lesson

PREREQUISITE SKILL **Replace each ● with < or > to make a true sentence.**

45. 16 ● 6

46. 101 ● 111

47. 87.3 ● 83.7

48. 1,051 ● 1,015

2-2 Comparing and Ordering Integers

Main IDEA

Compare and order integers.

Targeted TEKS 7.1 The student represents and uses numbers in a variety of equivalent forms. **(A) compare and order integers** and positive rational numbers.

GET READY for the Lesson

WEATHER The wind chill table shows how cold air feels on human skin.

WIND CHILL					
Wind (mph)	Temperature (°F)				
	15	10	5	0	−5
5	7	1	−5	−11	−16
10	3	−4	−10	−16	−22
15	0	−7	−13	−19	−26
20	−2	−9	−15	−22	−29

1. What is the wind chill if there is a wind at 20 miles per hour and the temperature is 5°?
2. Which feels colder, a temperature of 15° with a 20 mile-per-hour wind or a temperature of 10° with a 10 mile-per-hour wind?
3. Graph both wind chills in Exercise 2 on a number line.

When two numbers are graphed on a number line, the number to the left is always less than the number to the right. The number to the right is always greater than the number to the left.

Concepts in Motion
Interactive Lab tx.msmath2.com

KEY CONCEPT — Compare Integers

Model

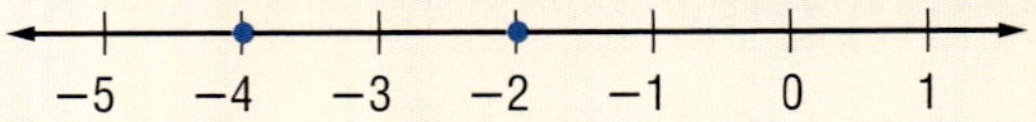

Words −4 is less than −2. −2 is greater than −4.

Examples $-4 < -2$ $-2 > -4$

EXAMPLE Compare Two Integers

1 **Replace the ● with < or > to make −5 ● −3 a true sentence.**

Graph each integer on a number line.

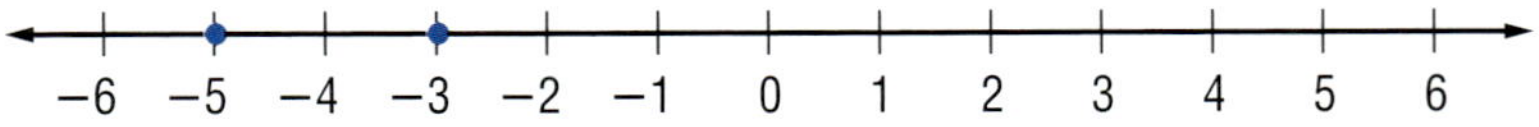

Since −5 is to the left of −3, $-5 < -3$.

CHECK Your Progress

Replace each ● with < or > to make a true sentence.

a. −8 ● −4 b. 5 ● −1 c. −10 ● −13

READING in the Content Area

For strategies in reading this lesson, visit tx.msmath2.com.

TEST EXAMPLE

2 **The lowest temperatures in Alaska, Florida, Hawaii, and Montana are listed in the table. Which list shows these temperatures in order from coldest to warmest?**

State	Record Low Temperature (°F)
Alaska	−80
Florida	−2
Hawaii	12
Montana	−70

Source: *The World Almanac and Book of Facts*

A −80, −70, 12, −2

B −80, −70, −2, 12

C 12, −2, −70, −80

D −2, 12, −70, −80

Test-Taking Tip

Eliminating Answer Choices
If you are unsure of the correct answer, eliminate the choices you know are incorrect. Then consider the remaining choices. You can eliminate choice C since the list begins with a positive number.

Read the Test Item

To order the integers, graph them on a number line.

Solve the Test Item

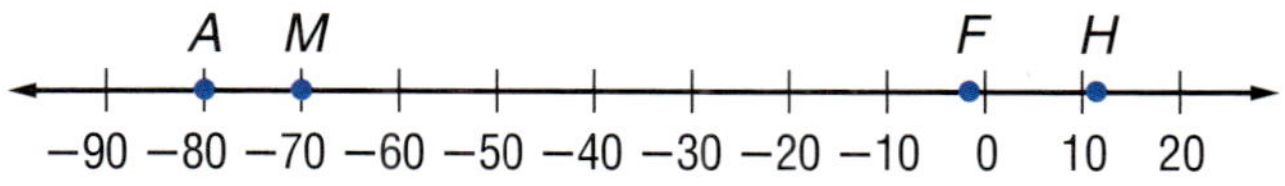

Order the integers from coldest to warmest by reading from left to right: −80, −70, −2, 12. So, the answer is B.

CHECK Your Progress

d. A newspaper reporter lists the third round scores of the top five finishers in a golf tournament. Which list shows these scores from least to greatest?

F 5, 2, 0, −1, −3

G −1, −3, 0, 2, 5

H −3, −1, 0, 2, 5

J 0, −1, 2, −3, 5

Online **Personal Tutor at** tx.msmath2.com

CHECK Your Understanding

Example 1 (p. 84)

Replace each ● with < or > to make a true sentence.

1. −4 ● −6
2. −2 ● 8
3. 0 ● −10

Example 2 (p. 85)

Order the integers in each set from least to greatest.

4. {−13, 9, −2, 0, 4}
5. {12, −16, −10, 19, −18}

6. **TEST PRACTICE** The elevations, in feet, for the lowest points in California, Oklahoma, Lousiana, and Kentucky are listed. Which list shows the elevations in order from highest to lowest?

A 289, −282, 257, −8

B −8, 257, −282, 289

C −282, −8, 257, 289

D 289, 257, −8, −282

Exercises

HOMEWORK HELP

For Exercises	See Examples
7–14	1
15–20	2
35–36	2

Replace each ● with < or > to make a true sentence.

7. −7 ● −3
8. −21 ● −12
9. −6 ● −11
10. −15 ● −33
11. 17 ● −20
12. 4 ● −4
13. −5 ● 17
14. −12 ● 8

Order the integers in each set from least to greatest.

15. {−8, 11, 6, −5, −3}
16. {7, −2, 14, −9, 2}
17. {5, −6, −7, −4, 1, 3}
18. {−12, 15, 8, −15, −23, 10}

19. **ANALYZE TABLES** The ocean floor is divided into five zones according to how deep sunlight penetrates. Order the zones from closest to the surface to nearest to the ocean floor.

Zone	Beginning Ocean Depth
Abyssal	−4,000 m
Hadal	−6,000 m
Midnight	−1,000 m
Sunlight	0 m
Twilight	−200 m

20. **STOCK MARKET** Kevin's dad owns stock in five companies. The change in the stock value for each company was as follows: Company A, +12; Company B, −5; Company C, −25; Company D, +18; Company E, −10. Order the companies from the worst performing to best performing.

Real-World Link About 20 million bicycles are sold each year in the U.S.
Source: bicyclinginfo.org

Replace each ● with <, >, or = to make a true sentence.

21. −13 ● |−14|
22. |36| ● −37
23. −12 ● |12|
24. |−29| ● |92|

ANALYZE TABLES For Exercises 25 and 26, use the information in the table. It shows the low temperatures in Albuquerque, New Mexico, for January 3–9 of a recent year.

Day	Jan. 3	Jan. 4	Jan. 5	Jan. 6	Jan. 7	Jan. 8	Jan. 9
Temperature (°F)	3	−4	−15	−12	−17	−8	2

Source: weather.com

25. Order the dates from the coldest temperature to the warmest.
26. Which temperature is the middle, or *median*, temperature?
27. **MONEY** Marva is saving money for a new bike and has already saved $21. She keeps track of her money in a log. Write the integers she should use to represent each entry.

Determine whether each sentence is *true* or *false*. If *false*, change one number to make the sentence true.

28. −8 > 5
29. −7 < 0
30. |5| < −6
31. 10 > |−8|

EXTRA PRACTICE
See pages 720, 756.
Math Online
Self-Check Quiz at tx.msmath2.com

H.O.T. Problems

32. **NUMBER SENSE** If 0 is the greatest integer in a set of five integers, what can you conclude about the other four integers?

33. **CHALLENGE** What is the greatest integer value of n such that $n < 0$?

34. **WRITING IN MATH** Develop a method for ordering a set of negative integers from least to greatest without the aid of a number line. Explain your method and use it to order the set $\{-5, -8, -1, -3\}$.

TEST PRACTICE

35. On a certain game show, contestants receive positive numbers of points for correct responses and negative numbers of points for incorrect responses. Which list gives the points a contestant received during one round of the game in order from highest to lowest?

    A −200, −400, −1000, 200, 600

    B 600, −1000, −400, −200, 200

    C 600, 200, −200, −400, −1000

    D −1000, −400, −200, 600, 200

36. Which statement about the values shown is NOT true?

State	Low Temperature (°F)
AR	−29
GA	−17
MS	−19
VA	−30
TX	−23

Source: *The World Almanac*

   F Virginia's record low is less than the record low for Arkansas.

   G Arkansas' record low is less than the record low for Georgia.

   H Mississippi's record low is greater than the record low for Texas.

   J Texas' record low is less than the record low for Arkansas.

Spiral Review

Write an integer for each situation. (Lesson 2-1)

37. 9°C below zero

38. a gain of 20 feet

HOBBIES For Exercises 39 and 40, use the following information. (Lesson 1-10)

Sophia estimates that she knits 6 rows of an afghan each hour.

39. Write an equation using two variables to represent the total number of rows r completed by Sophia after time t.

40. How many rows will Sophia have completed after 4 hours?

GET READY for the Next Lesson

PREREQUISITE SKILL Graph each point on a vertical number line that goes from −10 on the bottom to 10 at the top. (Lesson 2-1)

41. −3

42. 0

43. 4

44. −7

2-3 The Coordinate Plane

Main IDEA

Graph points on a coordinate plane.

Targeted TEKS 7.7 The student uses coordinate geometry to describe location on a plane. **(A) locate and name points on a coordinate plane using ordered pairs of integers.** *Also addresses 7.14(A).*

NEW Vocabulary

coordinate plane
x-axis
y-axis
origin
quadrant
ordered pair
x-coordinate
y-coordinate

GET READY for the Lesson

MAPS A map of Terrell's neighborhood is shown.

1. Suppose Terrell starts at the corner of Russel and Main and walks 2 blocks east and 1 block north. Name the intersection of his location.
2. Using the words *north, south, west,* and *east,* write directions to go from the corner of School and Highland to the corner of Main and Oak.

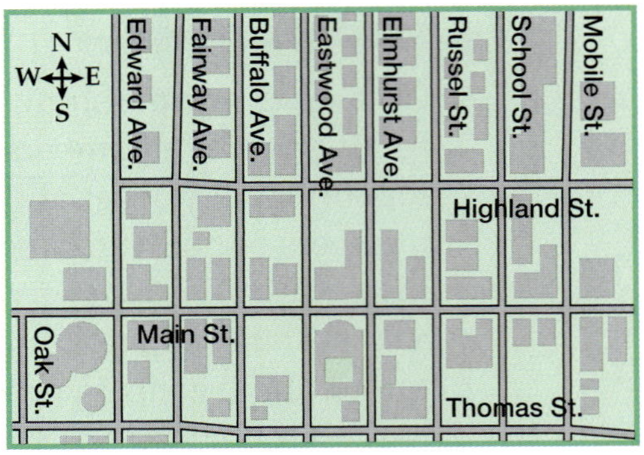

On city maps, towns and streets are often located on a grid. In mathematics, we use a grid called a **coordinate plane**, to locate points.

KEY CONCEPT — Compare Integers

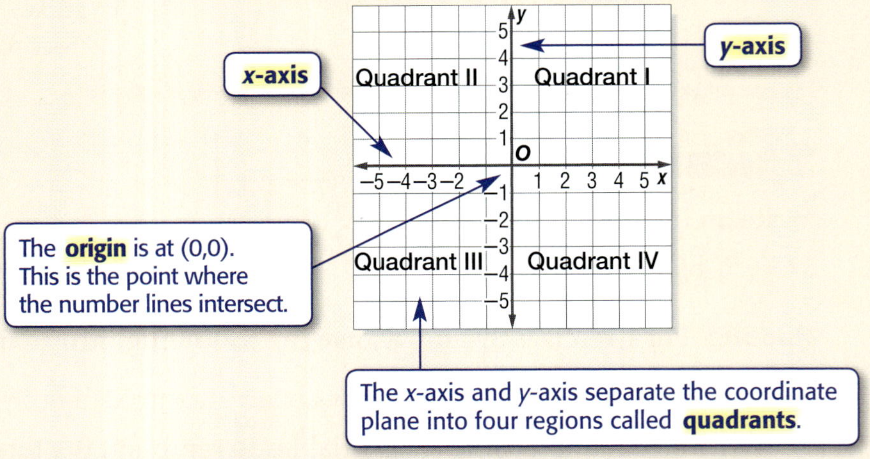

An **ordered pair** is a pair of numbers, such as (5, −4), used to locate a point in the coordinate plane.

(5, −4)

The first number is the ***x*-coordinate** and corresponds to a number on the *x*-axis.

The second number is the ***y*-coordinate** and corresponds to a number on the *y*-axis.

When naming an ordered pair, moving *right* or *up* on a coordinate plane is in the *positive* direction. Moving *left* or *down* is in the *negative* direction.

EXAMPLE Naming Points Using Ordered Pairs

1 **Write the ordered pair that names point *D*. Then name the quadrant in which the point is located.**

- Start at the origin.
- Move left on the *x*-axis to find the *x*-coordinate of point *D*, which is −4.
- Move up to find the *y*-coordinate, which is 2.

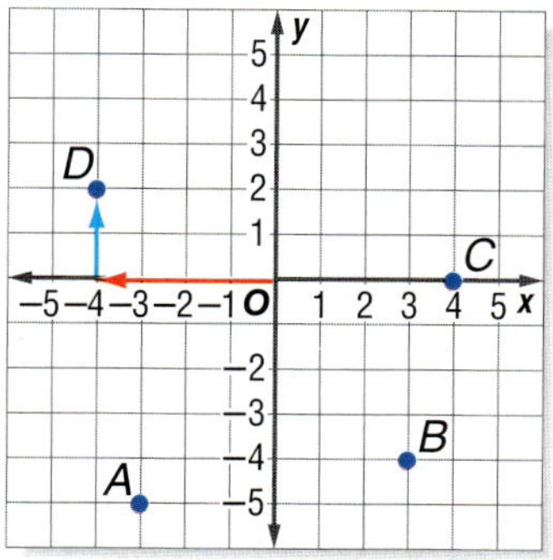

So, point *D* is named by the ordered pair (−4, 2). Point *D* is located in Quadrant II.

CHECK Your Progress

Write the ordered pair that names each point. Then name the quadrant or axis on which the point is located.

a. *A* **b.** *B* **c.** *C*

EXAMPLE Graph an Ordered Pair

2 **Graph and label point *K* at (2, −5).**

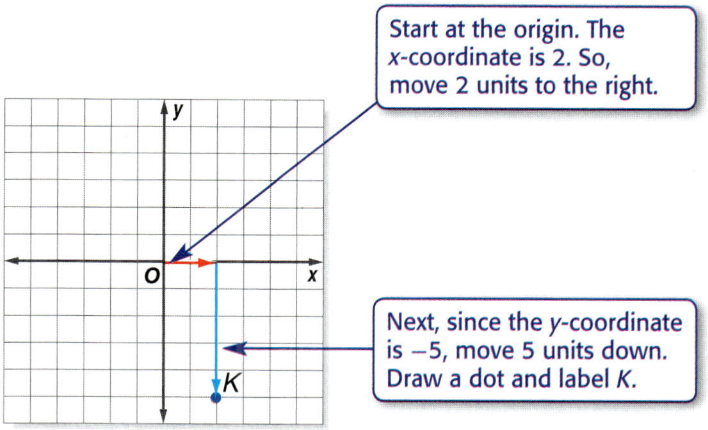

READING Math

Scale When no numbers are shown on the *x*- or *y*-axis, you can assume that each square is 1 unit long on each side.

CHECK Your Progress

On graph paper, draw a coordinate plane. Then graph and label each point.

d. $L(-4, 2)$ **e.** $M(-5, -3)$ **f.** $N(0, 1)$

Math Online Personal Tutor at tx.msmath2.com

How Does a Cartographer Use Math? Cartographers use coordinates to prepare geographic, political, and cultural maps of large areas.

Math Online
For more information, go to tx.msmath2.com.

Real-World EXAMPLES

3 GEOGRAPHY The world map can be divided into a coordinate plane where (x, y) represents (degrees longitude, degrees latitude). In what country is the point (−120° longitude, 55° latitude) located?

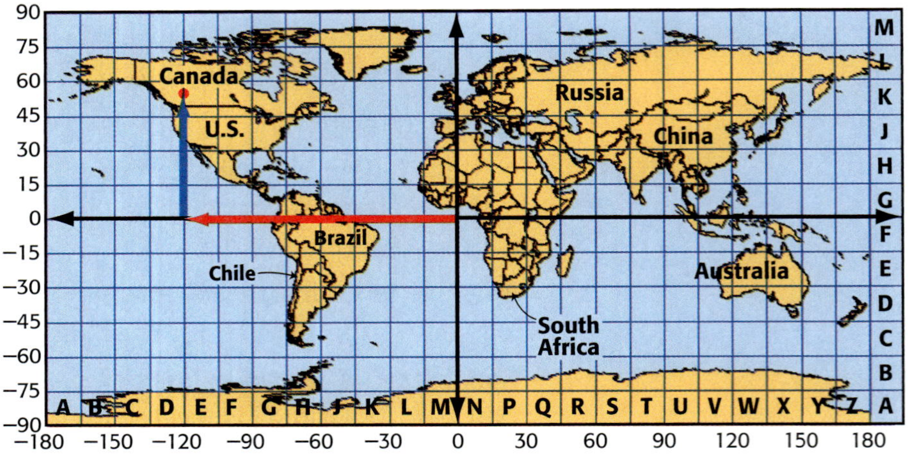

Source: www.colorado.edu

Start at the origin. Move −120° left and then 55° up. This point is located in Canada.

4 Name the country that is located entirely in quadrant III.
Quadrant III is the bottom-left quadrant. Of the countries labeled, Chile is the only country located entirely in Quadrant III.

CHECK Your Progress **For Exercises g and h, use the map above.**

g. In what country is the point (20° longitude, −35° latitude) located?

h. Name a country from the map that is located in Quadrant I.

CHECK Your Understanding

Example 1 (p. 89)

Write the ordered pair for each point graphed at the right. Then name the quadrant or axis on which each point is located.

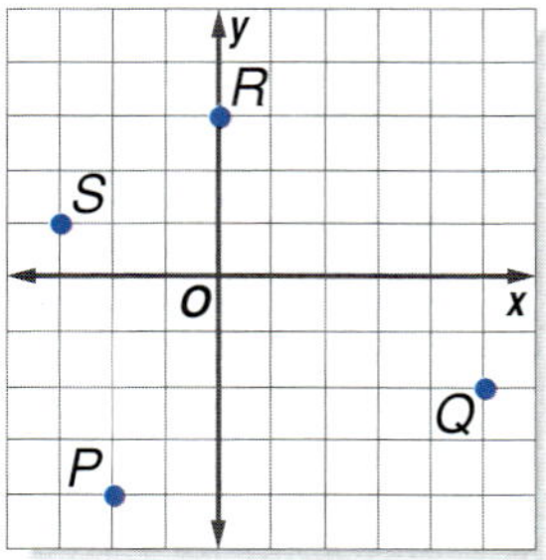

1. P
2. Q
3. R
4. S

Example 2 (p. 89)

On graph paper, draw a coordinate plane. Then graph and label each point.

5. $T(2, 3)$
6. $U(-4, 6)$
7. $V(-5, 0)$
8. $W(1, -2)$

Examples 3, 4 (p. 90)

GEOGRAPHY For Exercises 9 and 10, use the map in Example 3 above.

9. In what country is the point (105° longitude, 30° latitude) located?
10. In which quadrant is Australia located?

Exercises

HOMEWORK HELP	
For Exercises	See Examples
11–22, 37	1
23–34, 38	2
35–36	3

Write the ordered pair for each point graphed at the right. Then name the quadrant or axis on which each point is located.

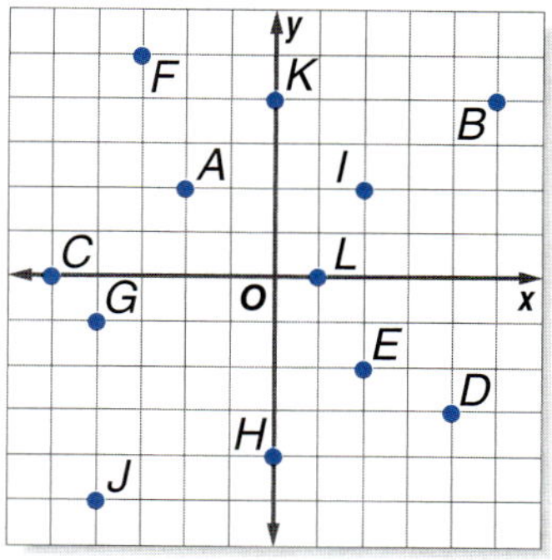

11. A 12. B 13. C
14. D 15. E 16. F
17. G 18. H 19. I
20. J 21. K 22. L

On graph paper, draw a coordinate plane. Then graph and label each point.

23. $M(5, 6)$ 24. $N(-2, 10)$ 25. $P(7, -8)$ 26. $Q(3, 0)$
27. $R(-1, -7)$ 28. $S(8, 1)$ 29. $T(-3, 7)$ 30. $U(5, -2)$
31. $V(0, 6)$ 32. $W(-5, -7)$ 33. $X(-4, 0)$ 34. $Y(0, -5)$

ZOOS For Exercises 35–38, use the map of the Brookfield Zoo.

Brookfield Zoo, Brookfield, IL

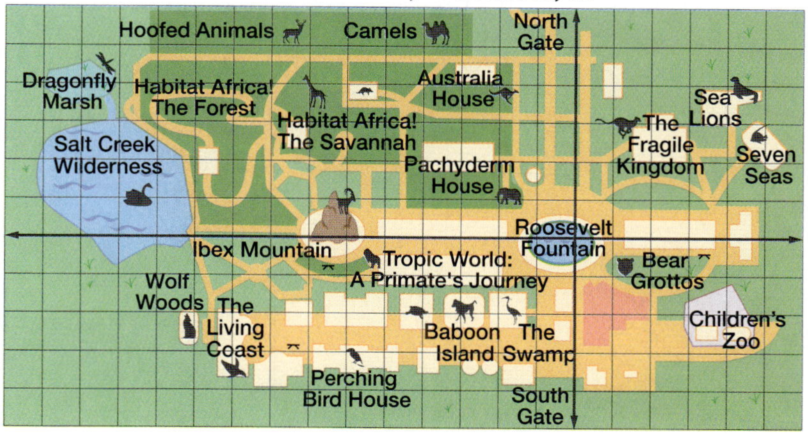

Real-World Link Polar bears are just one of the more than 400 species at the Brookfield Zoo.
Source: brookfieldzoo.org

35. What exhibit is located at $(4, -2)$?
36. In which quadrant is the Dragonfly Marsh exhibit located?
37. Find the ordered pair that represents the location of Baboon Island.
38. What is located at the origin?

On graph paper, draw a coordinate plane. Then graph and label each point.

39. $X(1.5, 3.5)$ 40. $Y\left(3\frac{1}{4}, 2\frac{1}{2}\right)$ 41. $Z\left(2, 1\frac{2}{3}\right)$

42. **GEOMETRY** Graph the points $A(-3, 2)$, $B(2, 2)$, $C(2, -4)$, and $D(-3, -4)$ on the same coordinate plane. Connect points A and B, B and C, C and D, and D and A. Name the figure.

43. **RESEARCH** Use the Internet or other resources to explain why the coordinate plane is sometimes called the Cartesian plane and the myth behind its invention.

EXTRA PRACTICE
See pages 721, 756.
Math Online
Self-Check Quiz at tx.msmath2.com

Determine whether each statement is *sometimes*, *always*, or *never* true. Explain or give a counterexample to support your answer.

44. Both x- and y-coordinates of a point in quadrant I are negative.
45. The x-coordinate of a point that lies on the x-axis is negative.
46. The y-coordinate of a point in quadrant IV is negative.

H.O.T. Problems

47. **OPEN ENDED** Create a display that shows how to determine in what quadrant a point is located without graphing. Then provide an example that demonstrates how your graphic is used.

48. **CHALLENGE** Find the possible locations for any ordered pair whose x- and y-coordinates are always the same integer. Explain.

49. **WRITING IN MATH** Explain why the location of point $A(1, -2)$ is different than the location of point $B(-2, 1)$.

TEST PRACTICE

50. Which of the following points lie within the triangle graphed at the right?

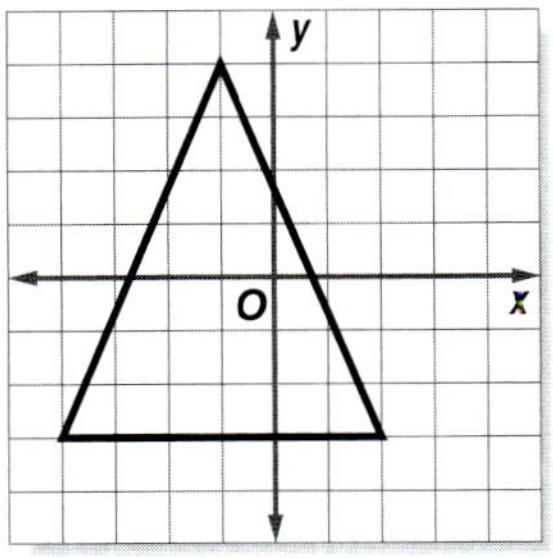

A $A(-4, -1)$
B $B(1, 3)$
C $C(-1, 2)$
D $D(2, -2)$

51. What are the coordinates of the point that shows the location of the hotel on the map?

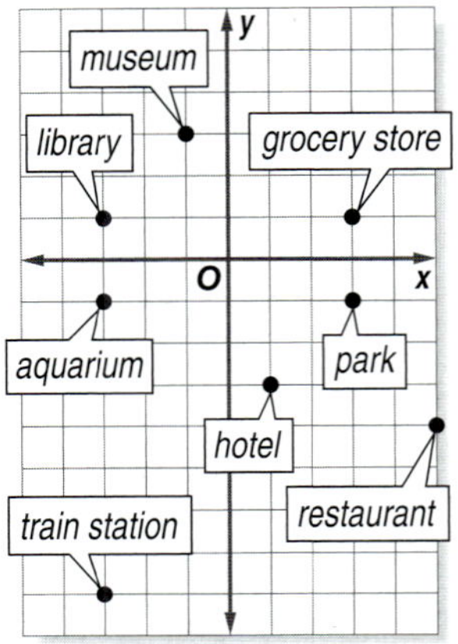

F $(-1, -3)$
G $(1, -3)$
H $(-1, 3)$
J $(1, 3)$

Spiral Review

Replace each ● with <, >, or = to make a true sentence. (Lesson 2-2)

52. -8 ● -3
53. 26 ● -30
54. 14 ● $|-15|$
55. -40 ● $|40|$

56. Find the absolute value of -101. (Lesson 2-1)

57. **SPORTS** A triathlon competition consists of swimming 3 miles, running 10 miles, and bicycling 35 miles. How many miles does an athlete travel during the competition? (Lesson 1-1)

GET READY for the Next Lesson

PREREQUISITE SKILL **Add.**

58. $138 + 246$
59. $814 + 512$
60. $2{,}653 + 4{,}817$
61. $6{,}003 + 5{,}734$

Explore 2-4

Algebra Lab
Adding Integers

Main IDEA

Use counters to model the addition of integers.

Targeted TEKS 7.2 The student adds, subtracts, multiplies, or divides to solve problems and justify solutions. **(C) use models, such as concrete objects, pictorial models, and number lines, to add,** subtract, multiply, and divide **integers and connect the actions to algorithms.** *Also addresses 7.14(A).*

You can use positive and negative counters to model the addition of integers. The counter ⊕ represents 1, and the counter ⊖ represents −1. Remember that addition means *combining* two sets.

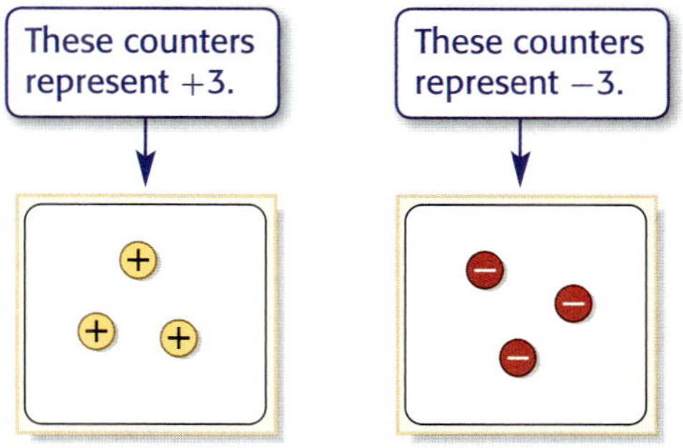

ACTIVITY

1 Use counters to find −2 + (−4).

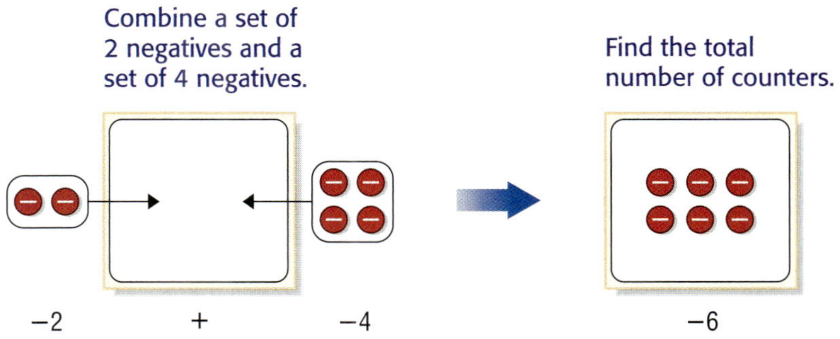

So, −2 + (−4) = −6.

CHECK Your Progress

Use counters or a drawing to find each sum.

a. 5 + 6   b. −3 + (−5)   c. −5 + (−4)

d. 7 + 3   e. −2 + (−5)   f. −8 + (−6)

READING Math

Addends and Sums The numbers you add are called *addends*. The result is called the *sum*.

The following two properties are important when modeling operations with integers.

- When one positive counter is paired with one negative counter, the result is called a **zero pair.** The value of a zero pair is 0.
- You can add or remove zero pairs from a mat because adding or removing zero does not change the value of the counters on the mat.

Concepts in Motion
Animation tx.msmath2.com

STUDY TIP

Adding Integers
If there are more negatives than positives, the sum is negative.

ACTIVITIES

Use counters to find each sum.

2 $-5 + 3$

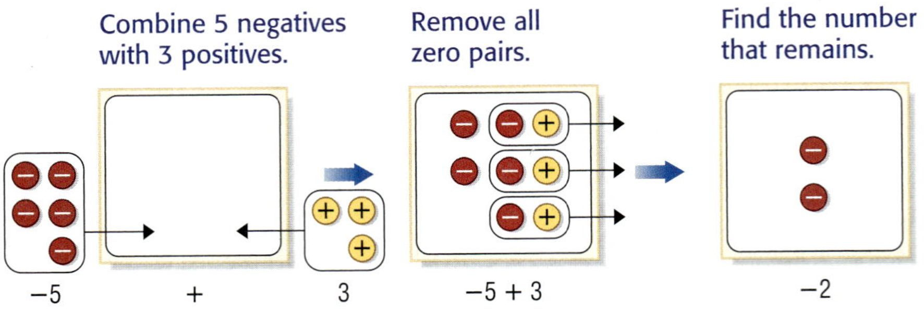

So, $-5 + 3 = -2$.

3 $4 + (-1)$

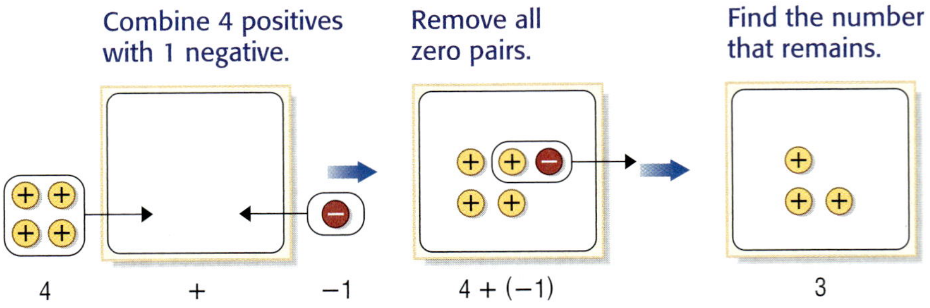

So, $4 + (-1) = 3$.

CHECK Your Progress

Use counters or a drawing to find each sum.

g. $-6 + 5$ **h.** $3 + (-6)$ **i.** $-2 + 7$

j. $8 + (-3)$ **k.** $-9 + 1$ **l.** $-4 + 10$

ANALYZE THE RESULTS

1. Write two addition sentences where the sum is positive. In each sentence, one addend should be positive and the other negative.
2. Write two addition sentences where the sum is negative. In each sentence, one addend should be positive and the other negative.
3. **MAKE A CONJECTURE** Write a rule that will help you determine how to find the sum of any two integers.

2-4 Adding Integers

Main IDEA

Add integers.

Targeted TEKS 7.2 The student adds, subtracts, multiplies, or divides to solve problems and justify solutions. **(C) use models, such as concrete objects, pictorial models, and number lines, to add,** subtract, multiply, and divide **integers and connect the actions to algorithms.**

NEW Vocabulary

opposites
additive inverse

GET READY for the Lesson

EARTH SCIENCE Thunderstorms are made of both positive and negative electrical charges. There are extra negative charges (electrons) at the bottom of a thundercloud, and extra positive charges (protons) at the top.

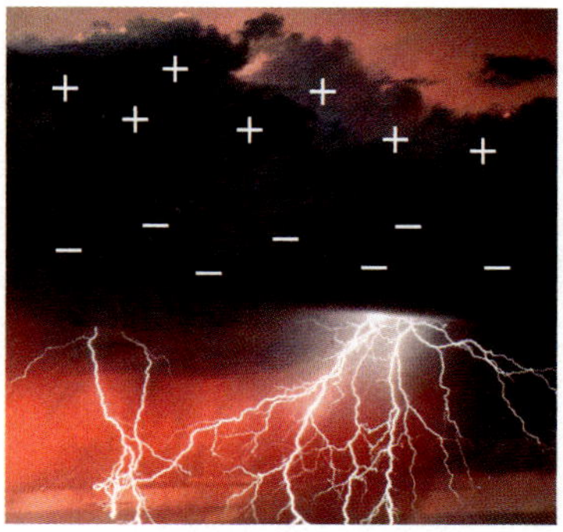

1. What is the charge at the top of a cloud where there are more protons than electrons?
2. What is the charge at the bottom of a cloud where there are more electrons than protons?

Combining positive and negative electrical charges in a thunderstorm is similar to adding integers.

EXAMPLE Add Integers with the Same Sign

1 Find $-3 + (-2)$.

Use a number line.

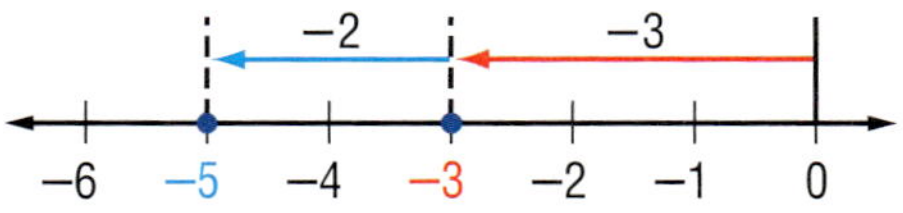

- Start at 0.
- Move 3 units left to show -3.
- From there, move 2 units left to show -2.

So, $-3 + (-2) = -5$.

CHECK Your Progress **Add.**

a. $-5 + (-7)$

b. $-10 + (-4)$

STUDY TIP

Adding Integers You can also use counters to add integers.

These and other examples suggest the following rule.

KEY CONCEPT **Add Integers with the Same Sign**

Words To add integers with the same sign, add their absolute values. The sum is:

- positive if both integers are positive.
- negative if both integers are negative.

Examples $7 + 4 = 11$ $\quad -7 + (-4) = -11$

EXAMPLE Add Integers with the Same Sign

2 **Find $-26 + (-17)$.**

$-26 + (-17) = -43$ Both integers are negative, so the sum is negative.

CHECK Your Progress **Add.**

c. $-14 + (-16)$

d. $23 + 38$

The integers 5 and -5 are called **opposites** because they are the same distance from 0, but on opposite sides of 0. Two integers that are opposites are also called **additive inverses**.

Vocabulary Link
Opposite
Everyday Use something that is across from or is facing the other way, as in running the opposite way.

Math Use two numbers that are the same distance from 0, but on opposite sides of 0.

KEY CONCEPT — Additive Inverse Property

Words The sum of any number and its additive inverse is 0.

Examples $5 + (-5) = 0$

Models can also help you add integers with different signs.

EXAMPLES Add Integers with Different Signs

3 **Find $5 + (-3)$.**

Use a number line.

- Start at zero.
- Move 5 units right.
- Then move 3 units left.

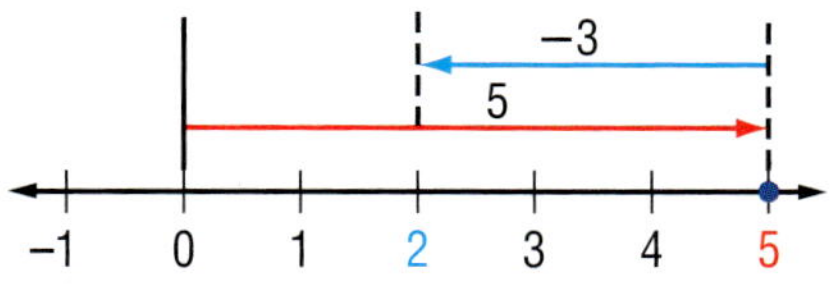

So, $5 + (-3) = 2$.

4 **Find $-3 + 2$.**

Use a number line.

- Start at zero.
- Move 3 units left.
- Then move 2 units right.

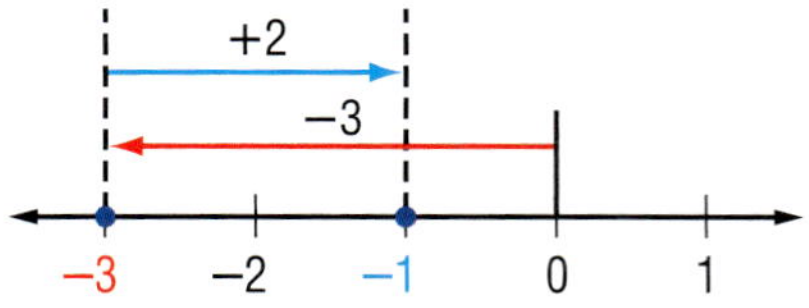

So, $-3 + 2 = -1$.

CHECK Your Progress **Add.**

e. $6 + (-7)$

f. $-15 + 19$

STUDY TIP
Look Back You can review **absolute value** in Lesson 2-1.

KEY CONCEPT — Add Integers with Different Signs

Words To add integers with different signs, subtract their absolute values. The sum is:

- positive if the positive integer's absolute value is greater.
- negative if the negative integer's absolute value is greater.

Examples $9 + (-4) = 5$ $-9 + 4 = -5$

EXAMPLES Add Integers with Different Signs

5 **Find 7 + (−1).**

$7 + (-1) = 6$ Subtract absolute values; 7 − 1 = 6. Since 7 has the greater absolute value, the sum is positive.

6 **Find −8 + 3.**

$-8 + 3 = -5$ Subtract absolute values; 8 − 3 = 5. Since −8 has the greater absolute value, the sum is negative.

CHECK Your Progress **Add.**

g. $10 + (-12)$

h. $-13 + 18$

You can use this and other properties to add more than two integers.

EXAMPLE Use the Additive Inverse Property

7 **Find 2 + (−15) + (−2).**

$2 + (-15) + (-2) = 2 + (-2) + (-15)$	Commutative Property (+)
$= 0 + (-15)$	Additive Inverse Property
$= -15$	Identity Property of Addition

CHECK Your Progress **Add.**

i. $(-14) + (-6) + 6$

j. $-23 + 17 + 23$

Math Online Personal Tutor at tx.msmath2.com

Real-World Link The Great Barrier Reef off the coast of Australia is home to 1,500 species of fish.
Source: deh.gov.au

Real-World EXAMPLE

8 **OCEANOGRAPHY** **Anna was scuba diving 16 meters below the surface of the water near the Great Barrier Reef. She rose 7 meters to swim next to a dolphin that was above her. Write an addition sentence to describe this situation. Then find the sum and explain its meaning.**

Anna is 16 meters under water, and rises 7 meters. So, her new depth can be represented by the sentence $-16 + 7$.

$-16 + 7 = -9$ Subtract absolute values; since −16 has the greater absolute value, the sum is negative.

The dolphin is 9 meters below the surface of the water.

CHECK Your Progress

k. **WEATHER** The temperature is −3°F. An hour later, it has dropped 6°. Write an addition sentence to describe this situation. Then find the sum and explain its meaning.

CHECK Your Understanding

Examples 1–6 (pp. 95–97)

Add.

1. $-6 + (-8)$
2. $4 + 5$
3. $-3 + 10$
4. $-15 + 8$
5. $7 + (-11)$
6. $14 + (-6)$

Example 7 (p. 97)

7. $-27 + 27$
8. $15 + 9 + (-9)$

Example 8 (p. 97)

9. **MONEY** Camilia owes her brother \$25, so she gives her brother the \$18 she earned dog-sitting for the neighbors. Write an addition sentence to describe this situation. Then find the sum and explain its meaning.

Exercises

HOMEWORK HELP

For Exercises	See Examples
10–13	1, 2
14–21	3–6
22–27	7
28–31	8

Add.

10. $-22 + (-16)$
11. $-10 + (-15)$
12. $6 + 10$
13. $17 + 11$
14. $18 + (-5)$
15. $13 + (-19)$
16. $13 + (-7)$
17. $7 + (-20)$
18. $-19 + 24$
19. $-12 + 10$
20. $-30 + 16$
21. $-9 + 11$
22. $21 + (-21)$
23. $-8 + 8$
24. $-34 + 25 + (-25)$
25. $-16 + 16 + 22$
26. $25 + 3 + (-25)$
27. $7 + (-19) + (-7)$

Write an addition expression to describe each situation. Then find each sum and explain its meaning.

28. **SUBMARINE** A submarine dives 106 feet below the water. Then it rises 63 feet.

29. **SKATEBOARDING** Hakeem starts at the top of a half pipe 8 feet above street level. He descends 14 feet to the lowest point in his run.

30. **BANKING** Stephanie has \$152 in the bank. She withdraws \$20.

31. **FOOTBALL** A quarterback is sacked for a loss of 5 yards. On the next play, his team receives a penalty and loses 15 more yards.

ALGEBRA Evaluate each expression if $x = -10$, $y = 7$, and $z = -8$.

32. $x + 14$
33. $z + (-5)$
34. $x + y$
35. $x + z$

36. **ANALYZE TABLES** In golf, the person with the lowest total score is the winner. The table lists the scores for each round in reference to par of the top two finishers in the 2005 Open Championship.

Player	Round 1	Round 2	Round 3	Round 4
Tiger Woods	−6	−5	−1	−2
Colin Montgomerie	−1	−6	−2	0

Who had the better score, Woods or Montgomerie? Justify your answer.

EXTRA PRACTICE

See pages 721, 756.

Math Online

Self-Check Quiz at tx.msmath2.com

37. **FIND THE DATA** Refer to Texas Data File on pages 16–19 of your book. Choose some data and write a real-world problem in which you would add a positive and a negative integer. Then find the sum and explain its meaning.

H.O.T. Problems

38. **FIND THE ERROR** Brooke and Jordan are finding $-12 + 13$. Who is correct? Explain your reasoning.

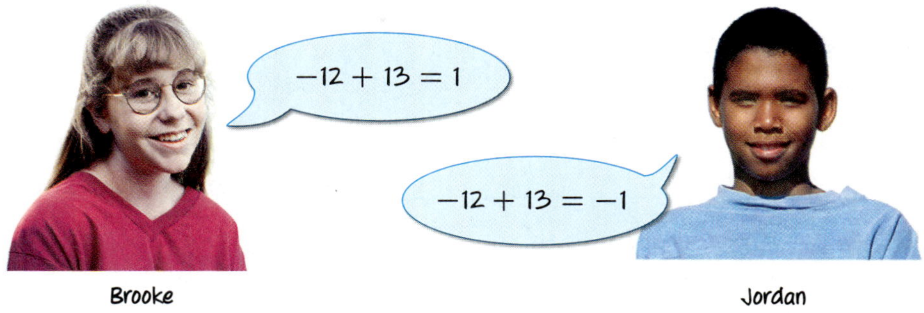

CHALLENGE **Simplify.**

39. $8 + (-8) + a$ 40. $x + (-5) + 1$ 41. $-9 + m + (-6)$ 42. $-1 + n + 7$

43. **WRITING IN MATH** Explain how you know whether a sum is positive, negative, or zero without actually adding.

TEST PRACTICE

44. Which expression does the model represent?

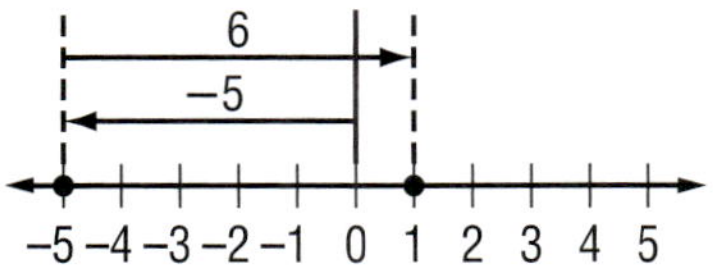

A $-5 + 1$ C $-5 + 4$

B $-5 + 3$ D $-5 + 6$

45. **GRIDDABLE** In the first round of questions on a quiz show, Consula earned 500 points, lost 200 points, lost 100 points, and earned 1,000 points. What was Consula's score at the end of the first round?

Spiral Review

Write the ordered pair for each point graphed at the right. Then name the quadrant or axis on which each point is located. (Lesson 2-3)

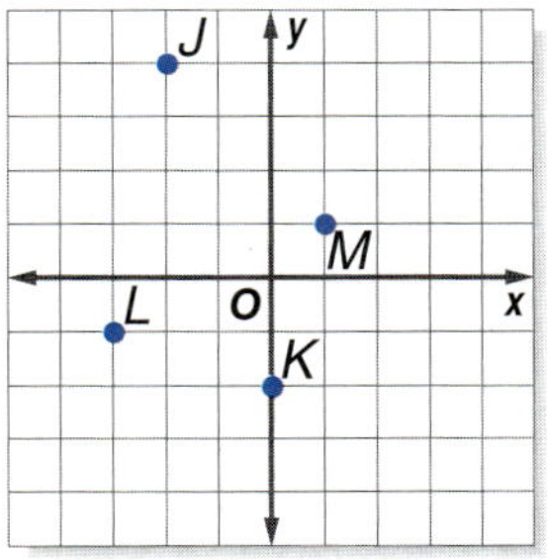

46. J 47. K 48. L 49. M

50. Order 6, −3, 0, 4, −8, 1, and −4 from least to greatest. (Lesson 2-2)

GET READY for the Next Lesson

PREREQUISITE SKILL **Subtract.**

51. 287 − 125 52. 420 − 317 53. 5,684 − 2,419 54. 7,000 − 3,891

CHAPTER 2 Mid-Chapter Quiz

Lessons 2-1 through 2-4

Write an integer for each situation. (Lesson 2-1)

1. dropped 45 feet
2. a bank deposit of $100
3. gained 8 pounds
4. lost a $5 bill

5. **OCEANS** The deepest point in the world is the Mariana Trench in the Western Pacific Ocean at a depth of 35,840 feet below sea level. Write this depth as an integer. (Lesson 2-1)

Evaluate each expression. (Lesson 2-1)

6. $|-16|$
7. $|24|$
8. $|-9| - |3|$
9. $|-13| + |-1|$

10. **ANALYZE TABLES** The table shows two temperature changes over the course of 15 minutes.

Location	Year	Temperature Change
Rapid City, SD	1911	−47°F
Ft. Assiniboine, MT	1892	+42°F

Source: infoplease.com

Which location had the greater change in temperature? (Lesson 2-1)

11. **TEST PRACTICE** The local news records the following changes in average daily temperature for the past week: 4°, −7°, −3°, 2°, 9°, −8°, 1°. Which list shows the temperatures from least to greatest? (Lesson 2-2)

A 9°, 4°, 2°, 1°, −3°, −7°, −8°
B −7°, −8°, 1°, −3°, 2°, 4°, 9°
C −8°, −7°, −3°, 1°, 2°, 4°, 9°
D −8°, −7°, 1°, 2°, 3°, 4°, 9°

Replace each ● with <, >, or = to make a true sentence. (Lesson 2-2)

12. -4 ● 4
13. -8 ● -11
14. $|-14|$ ● $|3|$
15. $|-12|$ ● $|12|$

On graph paper, draw a coordinate plane. Then graph and label each point. (Lesson 2-3)

16. $D(4, -3)$
17. $E(-1, 2)$
18. $F(0, -5)$
19. $G(-3, 0)$

20. **TEST PRACTICE** Which line contains the ordered pair $(-1, 4)$? (Lesson 2-3)

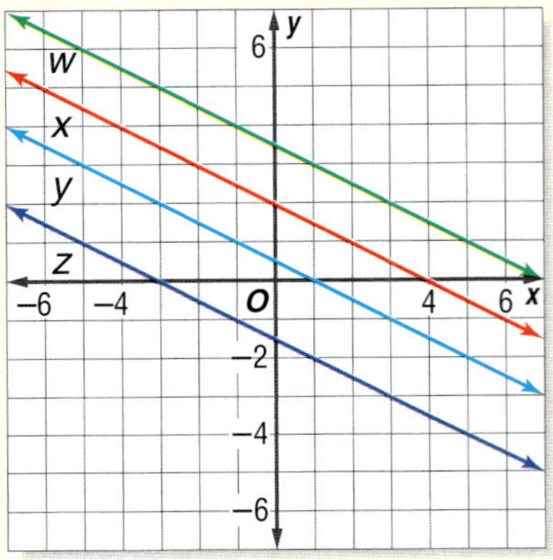

F line w
G line x
H line y
J line z

Add. (Lesson 2-4)

21. $3 + 4 + (-3)$
22. $7 + (-11)$
23. $-5 + (-6)$
24. $8 + (-1) + 1$
25. $-19 + 19$
26. $6 + 4 + (-6)$

27. **TEST PRACTICE** Identify the expression that is represented by the model below. (Lesson 2-4)

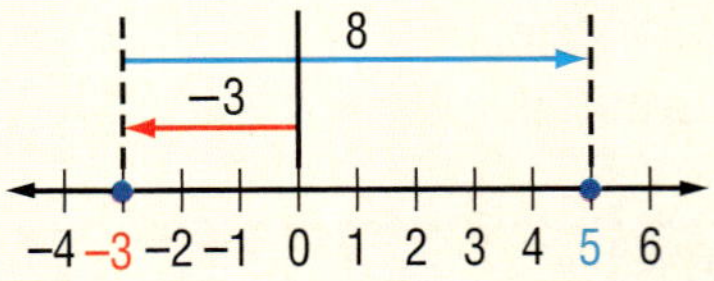

A $-3 + 5$
B $-5 + 3$
C $-3 + 8$
D $5 + -3$

Explore 2-5

Algebra Lab
Subtracting Integers

Main IDEA

Use counters to model the subtraction of integers.

Targeted TEKS 7.2 The student adds, subtracts, multiplies, or divides to solve problems and justify solutions. **(C) use models, such as concrete objects, pictorial models, and number lines, to** add, **subtract,** multiply, and divide **integers and connect the actions to algorithms.**

You can also use counters to model subtraction of integers. Remember one meaning of subtraction is to *take away*.

ACTIVITIES

Use counters to find each difference.

1 **6 − 4**

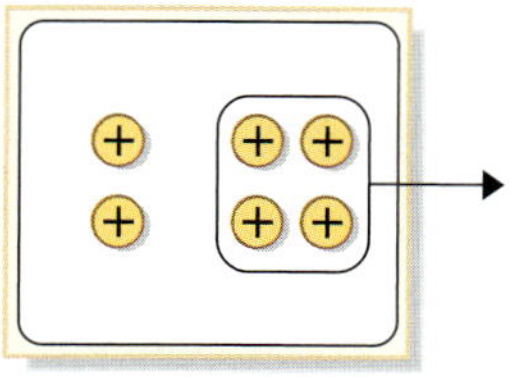

Place 6 positive counters on the mat. Remove 4 positive counters.

So, 6 − 4 = 2.

2 **3 − (−2)**

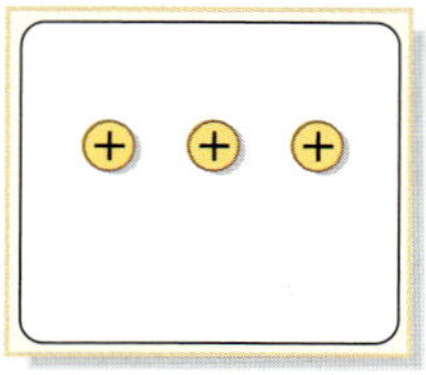

Place 3 positive counters on the mat. Remove 2 negative counters. However, there are 0 negative counters.

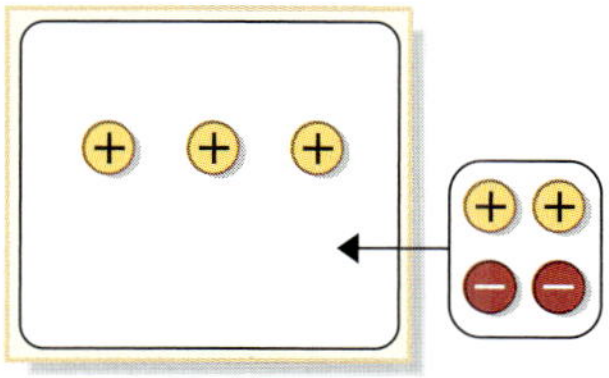

Add 2 zero pairs to the set.

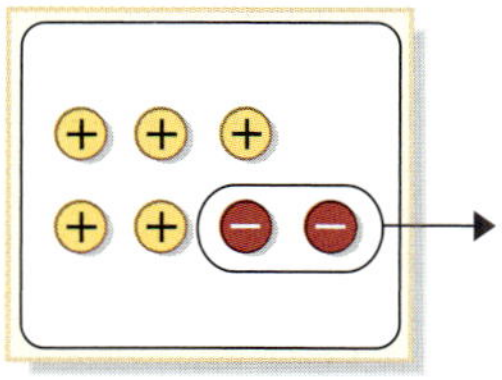

Now you can remove 2 negative counters. Find the remaining number of counters.

So, 3 − (−2) = 5.

CHECK Your Progress

Use counters or a drawing to find each difference.

a. 7 − 6 **b.** 5 − (−3) **c.** 6 − (−3) **d.** 5 − 8

ACTIVITIES

Use counters to find each difference.

3 $-5 - (-2)$

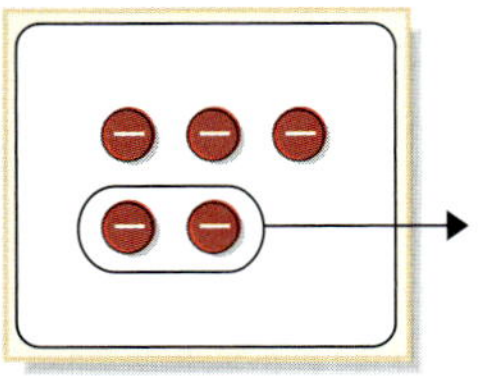

Place 5 negative counters on the mat. Remove 2 negative counters.

So, $-5 - (-2) = -3$.

4 $-4 - 3$

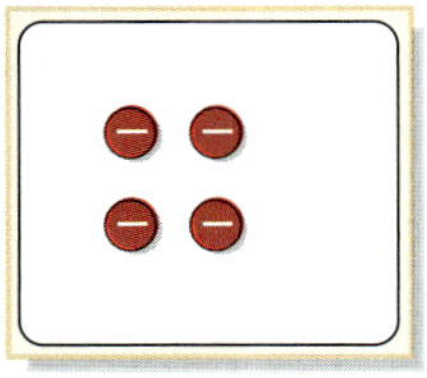

Place 4 negative counters on the mat. Remove 3 positive counters. However, there are 0 positive counters.

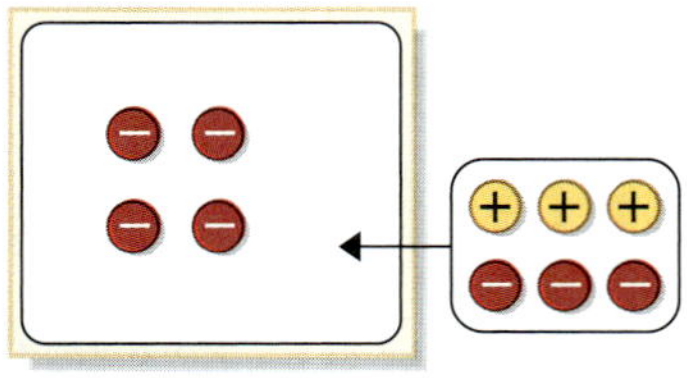

Add 3 zero pairs to the set.

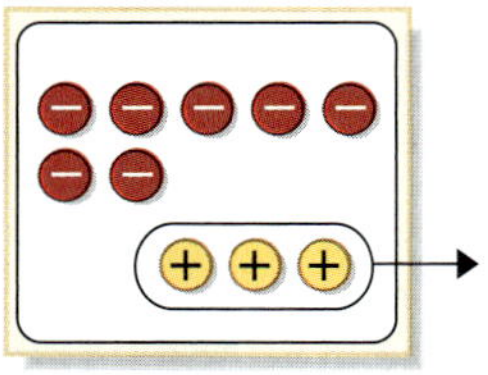

Now you can remove 3 positive counters. Find the remaining number of counters.

So, $-4 - 3 = -7$.

READING Math

Minuends, Subtrahends, and Differences In the subtraction sentence $-4 - 3 = -7$, -4 is the *minuend*, 3 is the *subtrahend*, and -7 is the *difference*.

CHECK Your Progress

Use counters or a drawing to find each difference.

e. $-6 - (-3)$ f. $-7 - 3$ g. $-5 - (-7)$

ANALYZE THE RESULTS

1. Write two subtraction sentences where the difference is positive. Use a combination of positive and negative integers.
2. Write two subtraction sentences where the difference is negative. Use a combination of positive and negative integers.
3. **MAKE A CONJECTURE** Write a rule that will help you determine the sign of the difference of two integers.

2-5 Subtracting Integers

Main IDEA

Subtract integers.

Targeted TEKS 7.2 The student adds, subtracts, multiplies, or divides to solve problems and justify solutions. **(C) use models, such as concrete objects, pictorial models, and number lines, to** add, **subtract,** multiply, and divide **integers and connect the actions to algorithms.**

MINI Lab

You can use number lines to model subtraction problems.

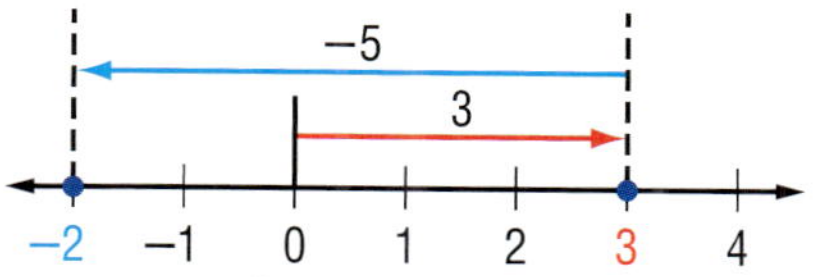

$3 - 5 = -2$

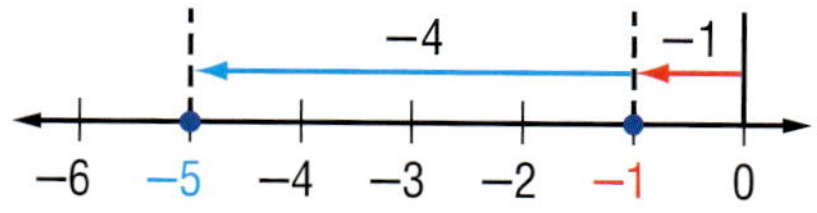

$-1 - 4 = -5$

1. Write a related addition sentence for each subtraction sentence.

Use a number line to find each difference. Write an equivalent addition sentence for each.

2. $1 - 5$ 3. $-2 - 1$ 4. $-3 - 4$ 5. $0 - 5$

When you subtract 5, the result is the same as adding its opposite, −5. When you subtract 4, the result is the same as adding its opposite, −4.

opposite

$3 - 5 = -2$ $3 + (-5) = -2$

same result

opposite

$-1 - 4 = -5$ $-1 + (-4) = -5$

same result

Concepts in Motion
Interactive Lab tx.msmath2.com

KEY CONCEPT — Subtract Integers

Words To subtract an integer, add its opposite.

Examples $4 - 9 = 4 + (-9) = -5$

EXAMPLES Subtract Positive Integers

1 Find 8 − 13.

$8 - 13 = 8 + (-13)$ To subtract 13, add −13.

$= -5$ Simplify.

2 Find −10 − 7.

$-10 - 7 = -10 + (-7)$ To subtract 7, add −7.

$= -17$ Simplify.

STUDY TIP

Technology Use the [−] key to subtract a number. Use the [(−)] key to enter a negative number.

CHECK Your Progress **Subtract.**

a. $6 - 12$ b. $-20 - 15$ c. $-22 - 26$

EXAMPLES Subtract Negative Integers

3 **Find $1 - (-2)$.**

$1 - (-2) = 1 + 2$ To subtract -2, add 2.

$= 3$ Simplify.

4 **Find $-10 - (-7)$.**

$-10 - (-7) = -10 + 7$ To subtract -7, add 7.

$= -3$ Simplify.

CHECK Your Progress **Subtract.**

d. $4 - (-12)$ e. $-15 - (-5)$ f. $18 - (-6)$

EXAMPLE Evaluate an Expression

5 **ALGEBRA** **Evaluate $x - y$ if $x = -6$ and $y = -5$.**

$x - y = -6 - (-5)$ Replace x with -6 and y with -5.

$= -6 + (5)$ To subtract -5, add 5.

$= -1$ Simplify.

CHECK Your Progress

Evaluate each expression if $a = 5$, $b = -8$, and $c = -9$.

g. $b - 10$ h. $a - b$ i. $c - a$

Online Personal Tutor at tx.msmath2.com

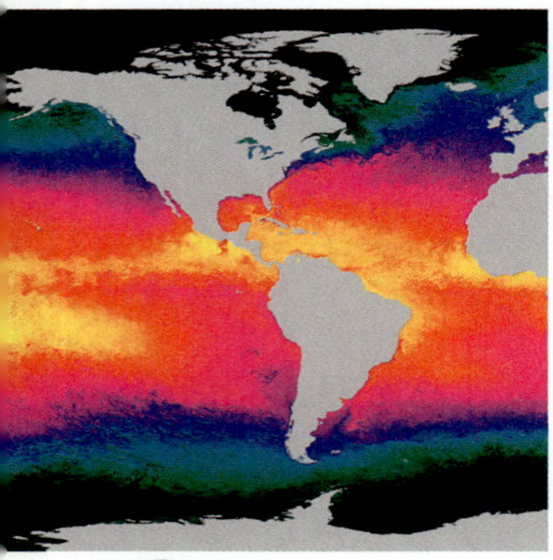

Real-World Link A sea-surface temperature map shows the minimum temperature at -2°C and the maximum temperature at 31°C.

Real-World EXAMPLE

6 **EARTH SCIENCE** **Refer to the information at the left. What is the difference between the maximum and the minimum temperatures on the map?**

To find the difference in temperatures, subtract the lower temperature from the higher temperature.

$31 - (-2) = 31 + 2$ To subtract -2, add 2.

$= 33$ Simplify.

So, the difference between the temperatures is 33°C.

CHECK Your Progress

j. **GEOGRAPHY** The Dead Sea's deepest part is 799 meters below sea level. A plateau to the east of the Dead Sea rises to about 1,340 meters above sea level. What is the difference between the top of the plateau and the deepest part of the Dead Sea?

CHECK Your Understanding

Examples 1, 2 (p. 103)

Subtract.

1. $14 - 17$
2. $10 - 30$
3. $-4 - 8$
4. $-2 - 23$

Examples 3, 4 (p. 104)

5. $14 - (-10)$
6. $5 - (-16)$
7. $-3 - (-1)$
8. $-11 - (-9)$

Example 5 (p. 104)

ALGEBRA **Evaluate each expression if $p = 8$, $q = -14$, and $r = -6$.**

9. $r - 15$
10. $q - r$
11. $p - q$

Example 6 (p. 104)

12. **SPACE** The temperatures on the moon vary from $-173°C$ to $127°C$. Find the difference in temperatures.

Exercises

HOMEWORK HELP

For Exercises	See Examples
13–16, 21–24	1, 2
17–20, 25–28	3, 4
29–36	5
37–40	6

Subtract.

13. $0 - 10$
14. $13 - 17$
15. $-9 - 5$
16. $-8 - 9$
17. $4 - (-19)$
18. $27 - (-8)$
19. $-11 - (-42)$
20. $-27 - (-19)$
21. $12 - 26$
22. $31 - 48$
23. $-25 - 5$
24. $-44 - 41$
25. $52 - (-52)$
26. $15 - (-14)$
27. $-27 - (-33)$
28. $-18 - (-20)$

ALGEBRA **Evaluate each expression if $f = -6$, $g = 7$, and $h = 9$.**

29. $g - 7$
30. $f - 6$
31. $-h - (-9)$
32. $f - g$
33. $h - f$
34. $g - h$
35. $5 - f$
36. $4 - (-g)$

ANALYZE TABLES **For Exercises 37–40, use the information below.**

State	California	Georgia	Louisiana	New Mexico	Texas
Lowest Elevation (ft)	−282	0	−8	2,842	0
Highest Elevation (ft)	14,494	4,784	535	13,161	8,749

37. What is the difference between the highest elevation in Texas and the lowest elevation in Louisiana?
38. Find the difference between the lowest elevation in New Mexico and the lowest elevation in California.
39. Find the difference between the highest elevation in Georgia and the lowest elevation in California.
40. What is the difference between the lowest elevations in Texas and Louisiana?

EXTRA PRACTICE

See pages 721, 756.

Math Online
Self-Check Quiz at tx.msmath2.com

ALGEBRA **Evaluate each expression if $h = -12$, $j = 4$, and $k = 15$.**

41. $-j + h - k$
42. $|h - j|$
43. $k - j - h$

H.O.T. Problems

44. **OPEN ENDED** Write a subtraction sentence using integers. Then, write the equivalent addition sentence, and explain how to find the sum.

45. **FIND THE ERROR** Alicia and Mitsu are finding $-16 - (-19)$. Who is correct? Explain your reasoning.

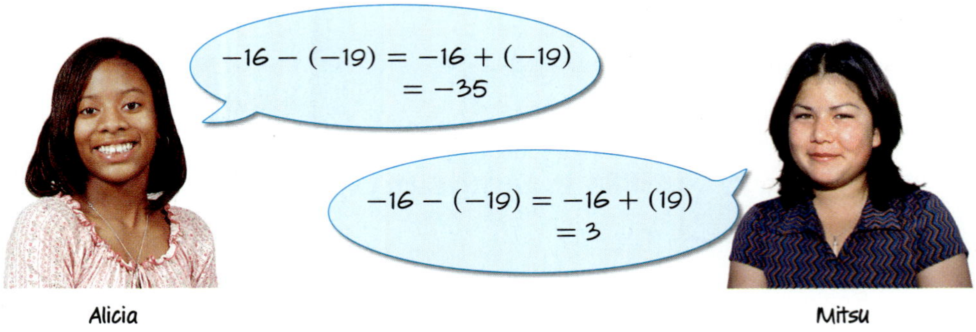

46. **CHALLENGE** *True* or *False*? When n is a negative integer, $n - n = 0$.

47. **WRITING IN MATH** Explain how additive inverses are used in subtraction.

TEST PRACTICE

48. Which sentence about integers is NOT always true?

A positive − positive = positive
B positive + positive = positive
C negative + negative = negative
D positive − negative = positive

49. Which subtraction sentence is modeled on the number line?

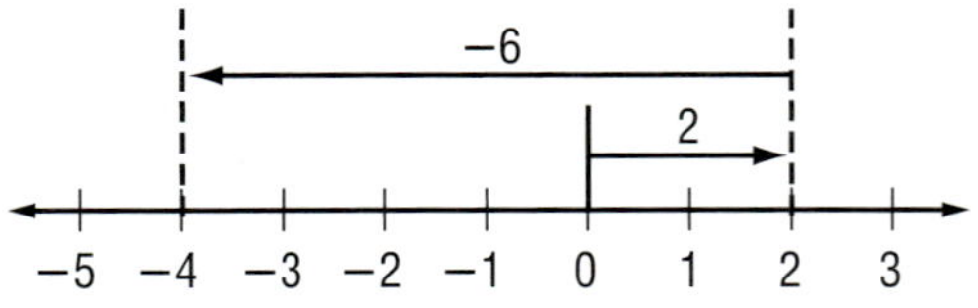

F $2 - (-6) = -4$ **H** $-2 - 4 = -6$
G $-6 - 2 = -4$ **J** $2 - 6 = -4$

Spiral Review

Add. (Lesson 2-4)

50. $10 + (-3)$ 51. $-2 + (-9)$ 52. $-7 + (-6)$ 53. $-18 + 4$

54. In which quadrant does the ordered pair $(5, -6)$ lie? (Lesson 2-3)

55. **NUMBERS** A number times 2 is added to 7. The result is 23. What is the number? Use the *guess and check* strategy. (Lesson 1-5)

GET READY for the Next Lesson

56. **PREREQUISITE SKILL** An electronics store sells one brand of a cellular telephone for \$129.99 and another for \$79.99. What is the approximate difference in the costs? (Lesson 1-1)

2-6 Problem-Solving Investigation

MAIN IDEA: Solve problems by looking for a pattern.

Targeted TEKS 7.13 The student applies Grade 7 mathematics to solve problems connected to everyday experiences, investigations in other disciplines, and activities in and outside of school. **(C) select or develop an appropriate problem-solving strategy from a variety of diffrent types, including...looking for a pattern...to solve a problem.** *Also addresses 7.13(B).*

P.S.I. TEAM +

I-M: LOOK FOR A PATTERN

Your MISSION: Look for a pattern to solve the problem.

THE PROBLEM: How long will it take Antonia to save enough money to buy a digital music player that costs $330?

ERIC: Hi, Antonia! I hear that you are saving to buy a digital music player?

ANTONIA: After one month, I had saved $50. After 2 months, I had $85. After three months, I had $120. After four months, I had $155. I plan to keep saving at this rate.

EXPLORE	She began with $50 and added more money to her savings every month. You need to find the number of months when she will have $330.
PLAN	Look for a pattern. Then extend the pattern to find the solution.
SOLVE	After the initial $50, she saved $35 each month. Extend the pattern. $50, $85, $120, $155, $190, $225, $260, $295 $330 (each step +$35) She will have enough money saved in 9 months.
CHECK	She saved 8 × $35 or $280 in 8 months. So, 9 months is a reasonable answer.

Analyze The Strategy

1. Explain when you would use the look for a pattern strategy to solve a problem.
2. Describe how to solve a problem using the *look for a pattern* strategy.
3. **WRITING IN MATH** Write a problem that could be solved by looking for a pattern.

Mixed Problem Solving

Use the *look for a pattern* strategy to solve Exercises 4–6.

4. **DISPLAYS** A display of cereal boxes is stacked as shown below.

If the display contains 7 rows of boxes and the top three rows are shown, how many boxes are in the display?

5. **SPORTS** Laura makes 3 free throws out of every 5 she attempts. Find the number of free throws she will make after 15, 20, and 30 attempts.

6. **INSECTS** The table shows about how many times a firefly flashes at different temperatures. About how many times will a firefly flash when the temperature is 36°C?

Outside Temperature (°C)	Flashes per Minute
16	8
20	9
24	11
28	14

Use any strategy to solve Exercises 7–10. Some strategies are shown below.

PROBLEM-SOLVING STRATEGIES
- Use the four-step plan.
- Guess and check.
- Look for a pattern.

7. **COINS** Olivia has seven coins that total \$1.32. What are the coins?

8. **MONEY** Tonya is going to a used bookstore to buy a desk lamp for \$8.50 and several books. Each book costs \$3.50. What is the greatest number of books she can buy if she has \$30 to spend?

9. **MONEY** While on vacation, Francisco sent postcards and letters to his friends. He spent \$3.08 on postage. A stamp for a letter costs 39¢, and a stamp for a postcard costs 24¢. How many postcards and letters did he send?

10. **GEOMETRY** What is the next figure in the pattern shown?

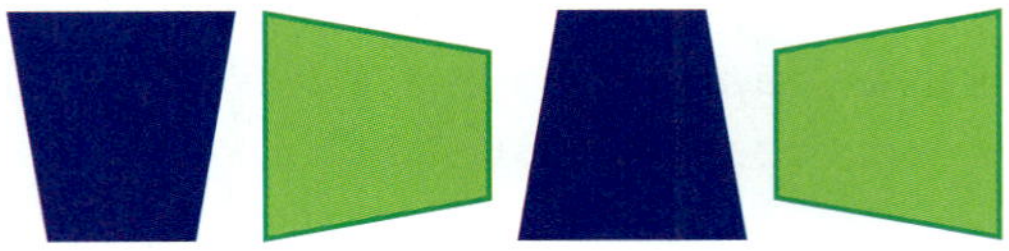

Select the Operation

For Exercises 11–13, select the appropriate operation(s) to solve the problem. Justify your selection(s) and solve the problem.

11. **POPULATION** The total land area of North Carolina is about 48,711 square miles. If an average of 175 persons were living in each square mile of North Carolina in 2004, what was the population of North Carolina in 2004?

12. **NUTRITION** The table shows the calories in Allie's breakfast. About how many total calories are there in all?

Food	Calories
Whole-wheat bagel	156
Skim milk	9
Nonfat strawberry yogurt	11
Fresh fruit salad	14

13. **SCIENCE** Hydrothermal vents are similar to geysers, but are found on the ocean floor. A hydrothermal vent chimney can grow at an average rate of 9 meters in 18 months. What is the average rate of growth per month?

2-7 Multiplying Integers

Main IDEA

Multiply integers.

Targeted TEKS 7.2 The student adds, subtracts, multiplies, or divides to solve problems and justify solutions. **(C)** **use models, such as concrete objects, pictorial models, and number lines, to** add, subtract, **multiply** and divide **integers and connect the actions to algorithms.** *Also addresses TEKS 7.13(D).*

MINI Lab

Counters can be used to multiply integers.

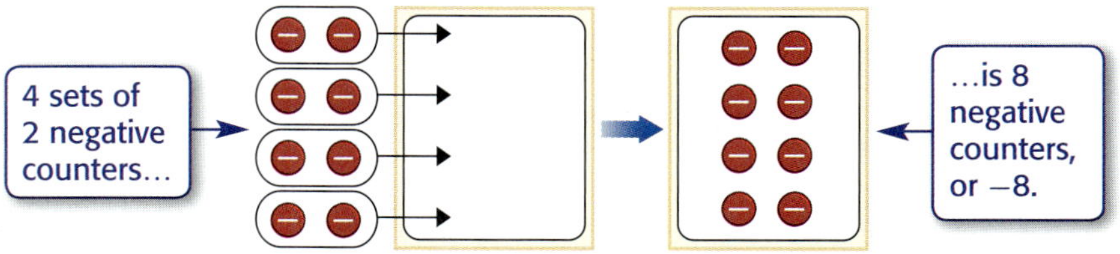

1. Write a multiplication sentence that describes the model above.

Find each product using counters or a drawing.

2. $3(-2)$ 3. $4(-3)$ 4. $1(-7)$ 5. $5(-2)$

Remember that multiplication is the same as repeated addition. The multiplication expression $4(-2)$ in the Mini Lab means that -2 is used as an addend four times.

$$4(-2) = (-2) + (-2) + (-2) + (-2)$$
$$= -8$$

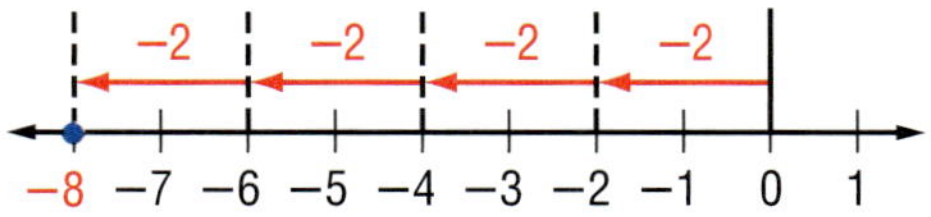

By the Commutative Property of Multiplication, $4(-2) = -2(4)$. When two integers have different signs, the following rule applies.

KEY CONCEPT **Multiply Integers with Different Signs**

Words	The product of two integers with different signs is negative.
Examples	$6(-4) = -24$ $-5(7) = -35$

EXAMPLES Multiply Integers with Different Signs

1 Find 3(−5).

$3(-5) = -15$ The integers have different signs. The product is negative.

2 Find −6(8).

$-6(8) = -48$ The integers have different signs. The product is negative.

CHECK Your Progress

Multiply.

a. $9\ (-2)$ b. $-7(4)$

STUDY TIP

Multiplying by Zero The Multiplicative Property of Zero states that when any number is multiplied by zero, the product is zero.

The product of two positive integers is positive. You can use a pattern to find the sign of the product of two negative integers.

positive × negative = negative

$(2)(-3) = -6$

$(1)(-3) = -3$

$(0)(-3) = 0$

$(-1)(-3) = 3$

$(-2)(-3) = 6$

negative × negative = positive

(+3 between each successive product)

Each product is 3 more than the previous product. This pattern can also be shown on a number line.

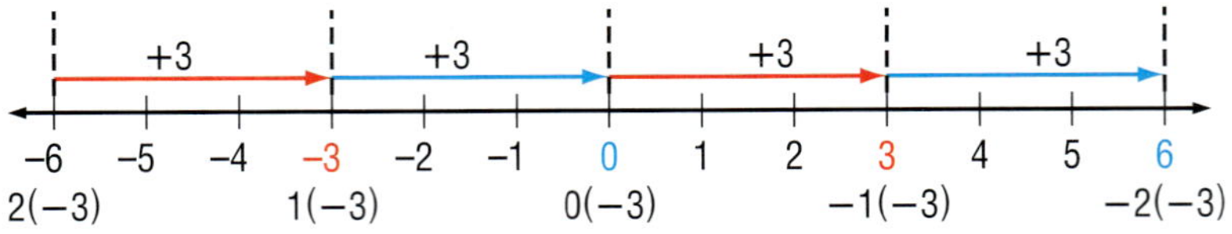

These and other examples suggest the following rule.

KEY CONCEPT — Multiply Integers with Same Sign

Words The product of two integers with the same sign is positive.

Examples $2(6) = 12$ $-10(-6) = 60$

EXAMPLES Multiply Integers with the Same Sign

3 **Find −11(−9).**

$-11(-9) = 99$ The integers have the same sign. The product is positive.

STUDY TIP

Look Back You can review **exponents** in Lesson 1-2.

4 **Find $(-4)^2$.**

$(-4)^2 = (-4)(-4)$ There are two factors of −4.

$= 16$ The product is positive.

5 **Find −3(−4)(−2).**

$-3(-4)(-2) = [-3(-4)](-2)$ Associative Property

$= 12(-2)$ $-3(-4) = 12$

$= -24$ $12(-2) = -24$

CHECK Your Progress

Multiply.

c. $-12(-4)$ d. $(-5)^2$ e. $-7(-5)(-3)$

Online Personal Tutor at tx.msmath2.com

Real-World Link The MIR submersible that explored the Titanic shipwreck was able to descend to −20,000 feet.
Source: spaceadventures.com

Real-World EXAMPLE

6 **SUBMERSIBLES** **A submersible is diving from the surface of the water at a rate of 90 feet per minute. What is the depth of the submersible after 7 minutes?**

If the submersible descends 90 feet per minute, then after 7 minutes, the vessel will be $-90(7)$ or 630 feet below the surface. Thus, the submersible will descend to -630 feet.

CHECK Your Progress

f. **MONEY** Mr. Simon's bank automatically deducts a $4 monthly maintenance fee from his savings account. What integer represents a change in his savings account from one year of fees?

Negative numbers are often used when evaluating algebraic expressions.

EXAMPLE Evaluate Expressions

7 **ALGEBRA** **Evaluate pqr if $p = -3$, $q = 4$, and $r = -1$.**

$pqr = -3(4)(-1)$	Replace p with -3, q with 4, and r with -1.
$= (-12)(-1)$	Multiply -3 and 4.
$= 12$	Multiply -12 and -1.

CHECK Your Progress

g. Evaluate xyz if $x = -7$, $y = -4$, and $z = 2$.

CHECK Your Understanding

Examples 1, 2 (p. 109)

Multiply.

1. $6(-10)$
2. $11(-4)$
3. $-2(14)$
4. $-8(5)$

Examples 3–5 (p. 110)

Multiply.

5. $-15(-3)$
6. $-7(-9)$
7. $(-8)^2$
8. $(-3)^3$
9. $-1(-3)(-4)$
10. $2(4)(5)$

Example 6 (p. 111)

11. **MONEY** Monifa owns 100 shares of a certain stock. Suppose the price of the stock drops by $3 per share. Write a multiplication expression to find the change in Monifa's investment. Explain the answer.

Example 7 (p. 111)

ALGEBRA **Evaluate each expression if $f = -1$, $g = 7$, and $h = -10$.**

12. $5f$
13. fgh

Exercises

HOMEWORK HELP

For Exercises	See Examples
14–19, 28	1, 2
20–27, 29	3–5
30–37	7
38–39	6

Multiply.

14. $8(-12)$
15. $11(-20)$
16. $-15(4)$
17. $-7(10)$
18. $-7(11)$
19. $25(-2)$
20. $-20(-8)$
21. $-16(-5)$
22. $(-6)^2$
23. $(-5)^3$
24. $(-4)^3$
25. $(-9)^2$
26. $-4(-2)(-8)$
27. $-9(-1)(-5)$
28. Find the product of 10 and -10.
29. Find -7 squared.

ALGEBRA Evaluate each expression if $w = 4$, $x = -8$, $y = 5$, and $z = -3$.

30. $-4w$
31. $3x$
32. xy
33. xz
34. $7wz$
35. $-2wx$
36. xyz
37. wyx

Write a multiplication expression to represent each situation. Then find each product and explain its meaning.

38. **ECOLOGY** Wave erosion causes a certain coastline to recede at a rate of 3 centimeters each year. This occurs uninterrupted for a period of 8 years.

39. **EXERCISE** Ethan burns 650 Calories when he runs for 1 hour. Suppose he runs 5 hours in one week.

ALGEBRA Evaluate each expression if $a = -6$, $b = -4$, $c = 3$, and $d = 9$.

40. $-3a^2$
41. $-cd^2$
42. $-2a + b$
43. $b^2 - 4ac$

44. **BANKING** Tamika's aunt writes a check for $150 each month for her car loan. She writes another check for $300 twice a year to pay for car insurance. Write an expression involving multiplication and addition to describe how these expenses affect her checking account balance on a yearly basis. Then evaluate the expression and explain its meaning.

45. **FIND THE DATA** Refer to the Texas Data File on pages 16–19 of your book. Choose some data and write a real-world problem in which you would multiply integers.

GEOMETRY For Exercises 46–48, use the graph at the right.

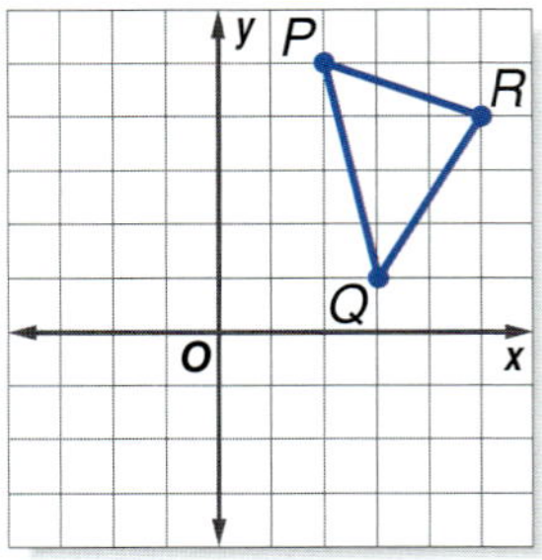

46. Name the ordered pairs for P, Q, and R. Multiply each x- and y-coordinate by -1 to get three new ordered pairs.

47. Graph the ordered pairs and connect them to form a new triangle. Describe its position with respect to the original triangle.

48. In which quadrant does a triangle lie if only the y-coordinates of the original triangle are multiplied by -2?

EXTRA PRACTICE

See pages 722, 756.

Math Online
Self-Check Quiz at tx.msmath2.com

H.O.T. Problems

49. **OPEN ENDED** Write a multiplication sentence whose product is -18.

50. **NUMBER SENSE** Explain how to evaluate $(-9)(-6)(15)(-7 + 7)$ as simply as possible.

51. **CHALLENGE** Evaluate $(-1)^{50}$. Explain your reasoning.

52. **SELECT A TECHNIQUE** Luis is trying to determine whether the product of three negative integers is negative or positive. Which of the following techniques might he use to determine the answer? Justify your selections. Then provide an example that illustrates the answer.

mental math | number sense | estimation

53. **WRITING IN MATH** Explain when the product of three integers is positive.

TEST PRACTICE

54. An oil rig is drilling into the ground at a rate of 7 feet per minute. What integer represents the position of the drill after 42 minutes?

A -294

B -35

C 35

D 294

55. Which of the following numbers is the 7th number in the sequence shown?

$$1, -2, 4, -8, 16, \ldots$$

F -64

G -32

H 32

J 64

Spiral Review

56. **NUMBERS** What are the next three numbers in the pattern $1, -3, 9, -27, 81, \ldots$? (Lesson 2-6)

Subtract. (Lesson 2-5)

57. $-25 - (-33)$
58. $-6 - 14$
59. $9 - 30$
60. $13 - (-12)$

ALGEBRA Evaluate each expression if $x = -4$, $y = 6$, and $z = 1$. (Lesson 2-4)

61. $x + (-2)$
62. $-1 + z$
63. $-15 + y$
64. $x + y$

65. **SCIENCE** The low temperatures in degrees Fahrenheit for ten cities one day were $-3, 27, 13, -6, -14, 36, 47, 52, -2$, and 0. Order these temperatures from greatest to least. (Lesson 2-2)

GET READY for the Next Lesson

PREREQUISITE SKILL Divide.

66. $72 \div 9$
67. $120 \div 6$
68. $84 \div 21$
69. $215 \div 43$

2-8 Dividing Integers

Main IDEA

Divide integers.

Targeted TEKS 7.2 The student adds, subtracts, multiplies, or divides to solve problems and justify solutions. **(C) use models, such as concrete objects, pictorial models, and number lines, to** add, subtract, multiply and **divide integers and connect the actions to algorithms.**

MINI Lab

You can use counters to model division of integers. Follow these steps to find $-10 \div 5$.

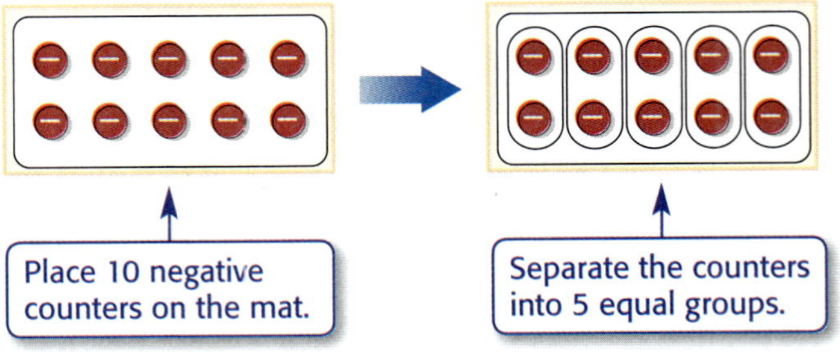

There are 2 negative counters in each group. So, $-10 \div 5 = -2$.

Find each quotient using counters or a drawing.

1. $-6 \div 2$

2. $-12 \div 3$

Division of numbers is related to multiplication. When finding the quotient of two integers, you can use a related multiplication sentence.

READING Math

Division Sentence In the division sentence $80 \div (-10) = -8$, 80 is called the *dividend*, -10 is called the *divisor*, and -8 is called the *quotient*.

The factor in the multiplication sentence ...

$2(6) = 12 \rightarrow 12 \div 2 = 6$

$4(5) = 20 \rightarrow 20 \div 4 = 5$

... is the quotient in the division sentence.

Since multiplication and division sentences are related, you can use them to find the quotient of integers with different signs.

different signs

$2(-6) = -12 \rightarrow -12 \div 2 = -6$

$-2(-6) = 12 \rightarrow 12 \div (-2) = -6$

negative quotient

These related sentences lead to the following rule.

KEY CONCEPT — Dividing Integers with Different Signs

Words The quotient of two integers with different signs is negative.

Examples $33 \div (-11) = -3$ $\quad -64 \div 8 = -8$

EXAMPLES Dividing Integers with Different Signs

1 **Find $80 \div (-10)$.** The integers have different signs.

$80 \div (-10) = -8$ The quotient is negative.

2 **Find $\frac{-55}{11}$.** The integers have different signs.

$\frac{-55}{11} = -5$ The quotient is negative.

CHECK Your Progress **Divide.**

a. $20 \div (-4)$ b. $\frac{-81}{9}$ c. $-45 \div 9$

STUDY TIP

Dividing Integers Dividing integers with the same or different signs follow the same rules as multiplication.

You can also use multiplication and division sentences to find the quotient of integers with the same sign.

same signs

$4(5) = 20 \rightarrow 20 \div 4 = 5$

$-4(5) = -20 \rightarrow -20 \div (-4) = 5$

positive quotient

These related sentences lead to the following rule.

KEY CONCEPT Divide Integers with the Same Sign

Words The quotient of two integers with the same sign is positive.

Examples $15 \div 5 = 3$ $-64 \div (-8) = 8$

EXAMPLES Dividing Integers with the Same Sign

3 **Find $-14 \div (-7)$.** The integers have the same sign.

$-14 \div (-7) = 2$ The quotient is positive.

4 **ALGEBRA** **Evaluate $-16 \div x$ if $x = -4$.**

$-16 \div x = -16 \div (-4)$ Replace x with -4.

$= +4$ Divide. The quotient is positive.

CHECK Your Progress **Divide.**

d. $-24 \div (-4)$ e. $-9 \div (-3)$ f. $\frac{-28}{-7}$

g. **ALGEBRA** Evaluate $a \div b$ if $a = -9$ and $b = -3$.

Online Personal Tutor at tx.msmath2.com

Real-World Link In January 2004, Mars Exploration Rover successfully sent signals to Earth after landing on Mars.
Source: nasa.gov

Real-World EXAMPLE

5 **ASTRONOMY** The average surface temperature on Mars is −81°F. Use the expression $\frac{5(F-32)}{9}$, where F represents the number of degrees Fahrenheit, to find the temperature on Mars in degrees Celsius.

$$\frac{5(F-32)}{9} = \frac{5(-81-32)}{9} \quad \text{Replace } F \text{ with } -81.$$

$$= \frac{5(-113)}{9} \quad \text{Subtract inside the parentheses first.}$$

$$= \frac{-565}{9} \quad \text{Multiply 5 and } -113.$$

$$\approx -62.8 \quad \text{Divide.}$$

The average temperature on the surface of Mars is about −63°C.

CHECK Your Progress

h. **WEATHER** The average temperature in January for North Pole, Alaska, is −24.4°C. Use the expression $\frac{9C+160}{5}$, where C represents the number of degrees Celsius, to find this temperature in degrees Fahrenheit.

CONCEPT Summary — Operations with Integers

Operation	Rule
Add	**Same Sign:** Add absolute values. The sum has the same sign as the integers. **Different Signs:** Subtract absolute values. The sum has the sign of the integer with greater absolute value.
Subtract	To subtract an integer, add its opposite.
Multiply and Divide	**Same Signs:** The product or quotient is positive. **Different Signs:** The product or quotient is negative.

CHECK Your Understanding

Examples 1–3 (p. 115)

Divide.

1. $32 \div (-8)$
2. $-16 \div 2$
3. $\frac{42}{-7}$
4. $-30 \div (-5)$
5. $55 \div 11$
6. $\frac{-16}{-4}$

Example 4 (p. 115)

ALGEBRA **Evaluate each expression if $x = 8$ and $y = -5$.**

7. $15 \div y$
8. $xy \div (-10)$

Example 5 (p. 116)

9. **HISTORY** The lowest recorded temperature in California is −45°F on January 20, 1937. Use the expression in Example 5 to find this temperature in degrees Celsius. Round to the nearest tenth.

Exercises

HOMEWORK HELP

For Exercises	See Examples
10–13, 16–19	1, 2
14–15, 20–23	3
24–31	4
32–33	5

Divide.

10. $50 \div (-5)$
11. $56 \div (-8)$
12. $-18 \div 9$
13. $-36 \div 4$
14. $-15 \div (-3)$
15. $-100 \div (-10)$
16. $\frac{22}{-2}$
17. $\frac{84}{-12}$
18. $\frac{-26}{13}$
19. $\frac{-27}{3}$
20. $\frac{-21}{-7}$
21. $\frac{-54}{-6}$
22. Divide -200 by -100.
23. Find the quotient of -65 and -13.

ALGEBRA **Evaluate each expression if $r = 12$, $s = -4$, and $t = -6$.**

24. $-12 \div r$
25. $72 \div t$
26. $r \div s$
27. $rs \div 16$
28. $\frac{t - r}{3}$
29. $\frac{8 - r}{-2}$
30. $\frac{s + t}{5}$
31. $\frac{t + 9}{-3}$

32. **MONEY** Last year, Mr. Engle's total income was \$52,000, while his total expenses were \$53,800. Use the expression, $\frac{I - E}{12}$ where I represents total income and E represents total expenses, to find the average difference between his income and expenses each month.

33. **SCIENCE** The boiling point of water is affected by changes in elevation. Use the expression $\frac{-2A}{1{,}000}$, where A represents the altitude in feet, to find the number of degrees Fahrenheit the boiling point of water changes at an altitude of 5,000 feet.

Real-World Link An adult koala is 25–30 inches long and weighs 15–30 pounds.
Source: koalaexpress.com

ALGEBRA **Evaluate each expression if $d = -9$, $f = 36$, and $g = -6$.**

34. $\frac{-f}{d}$
35. $\frac{12 - (-f)}{-g}$
36. $\frac{f^2}{d^2}$
37. $g^2 \div f$

38. **ANIMALS** Ten years ago, the estimated Australian koala population was 1,000,000. Today, there are about 100,000 koalas. Use the expression $\frac{N - P}{10}$, where N represents the new population and P the previous population to find the average change in the koala population per year for the 10 year period.

39. **ANALYZE GRAPHS** The *mean* of a set of data is the sum of the data divided by the number of items in the data set. The graph shows the profit made by five magazines that experienced poor sales in a recent year. What is the mean profit for these five magazines?

No Profit at the Newsstand

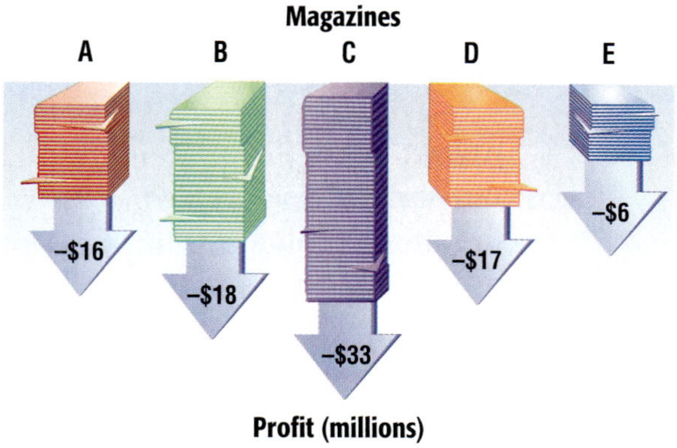

EXTRA PRACTICE
See pages 722, 756.
Math Online
Self-Check Quiz at tx.msmath2.com

H.O.T. Problems

40. **OPEN ENDED** Write a division sentence with a quotient of −12.

41. **Which One Doesn't Belong?** Identify the expression that does not belong with the other three. Explain your reasoning.

$-24 \div 6$	$-18 \div (-9)$	$28 \div (-7)$	$-22 \div 11$

42. **PATTERNS** Find the next two numbers in the pattern 729, −243, 81, −27, 9, … . Explain your reasoning.

43. **CHALLENGE** Order from least to greatest all of the numbers by which −20 is divisible.

44. **WRITING IN MATH** Explain how knowing the rules for multiplying integers can help you remember the rules for dividing integers.

TEST PRACTICE

45. Which division expression is represented by the model?

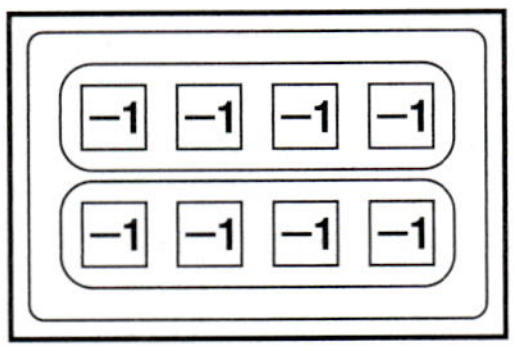

A $-8 \div 2$

B $-4 \div 2$

C $-8 \div (-4)$

D $-4 \div (-1)$

46. The width of a beach at 8:00 P.M. is 107 feet. At 3:00 A.M., the width of the beach narrows to 23 feet due to the high tide. What is the average change in the width of the beach per hour?

F −15 ft/h

G −13 ft/h

H −12 ft/h

J −10 ft/h

Spiral Review

Multiply. (Lesson 2-7)

47. $14(-2)$

48. $-20(-3)$

49. $-5(7)$

50. $(-9)^2$

51. **GEOMETRY** What is the next figure in the pattern shown at the right? (Lesson 2-6)

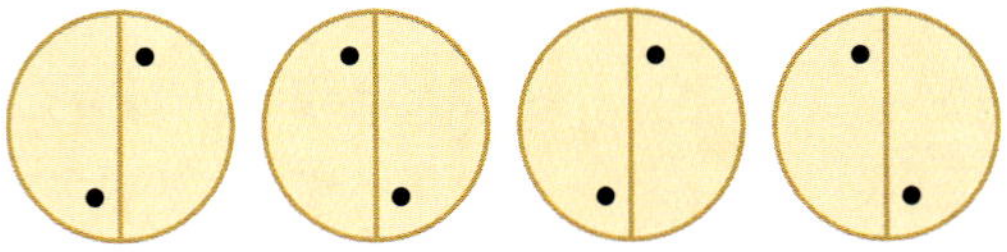

52. Find $6 - (-12)$. (Lesson 2-5)

53. **DIVING** Valentina jumped into 12 feet of water and touched the bottom of the pool before she surfaced. Write an integer to describe where Valentina was in relation to the surface of the water when she touched the bottom of the pool. (Lesson 2-1)

Find each square root. (Lesson 1-3)

54. $\sqrt{324}$

55. $\sqrt{900}$

56. $\sqrt{576}$

CHAPTER 2 Study Guide and Review

STUDY TO GO Download Vocabulary Review from tx.msmath2.com

FOLDABLES™ Study Organizer GET READY to Study

Be sure the following Key Concepts are noted in your Foldable.

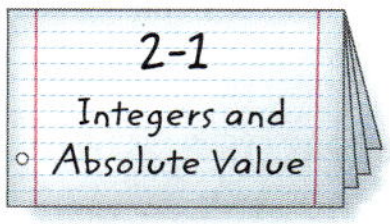

Key Concepts

Absolute Value (Lesson 2-1)

- The absolute value of a number is the distance the number is from zero on a number line.

Comparing and Ordering Integers (Lesson 2-2)

- When two numbers are graphed on a number line, the number to the left is always less than the number to the right.

Graphing Points (Lesson 2-3)

- On a coordinate plane, the vertical number line is the y-axis and the horizontal number line is the x-axis. The origin is at (0, 0) and is the point where the number lines intersect. The x-axis and y-axis separate the plane into four quadrants.

Integer Operations (Lessons 2-4, 2-5, 2-7, 2-8)

- To add integers with the same sign, add their absolute value. The sum is positive if both integers are positive and negative if both integers are negative.
- The sum of any number and its additive inverse is 0.
- To add integers with different signs, subtract their absolute values. The sum is positive if the positive integer's absolute value is greater and negative if the negative integer's absolute value is greater.
- To subtract an integer, add its opposite.
- The product or quotient of two integers with different signs is negative.
- The product or quotient of two integers with the same sign is positive.

Key Vocabulary

absolute value (p. 81)
additive inverse (p. 96)
coordinate plane (p. 88)
graph (p. 80)
integer (p. 80)
negative integer (p. 80)
opposites (p. 96)
ordered pair (p. 88)
origin (p. 88)
positive integer (p. 80)
quadrant (p. 88)
x-axis (p. 88)
x-coordinate (p. 88)
y-axis (p. 88)
y-coordinate (p. 88)

Vocabulary Check

State whether each sentence is *true* or *false*. If *false*, replace the underlined word or number to make a true sentence.

1. Integers less than zero are <u>positive</u> integers.
2. The <u>origin</u> is the point where the x-axis and y-axis intersect.
3. The <u>absolute value</u> of 7 is −7.
4. The sum of two negative integers is <u>positive</u>.
5. The <u>x-coordinate</u> of the ordered pair (2, −3) is −3.
6. Two integers that are opposites are also called <u>additive inverses</u>.
7. The product of a positive and a negative integer is <u>negative</u>.
8. The x-axis and the y-axis separate the plane into four <u>coordinates</u>.
9. The quotient of two negative integers is <u>negative</u>.

CHAPTER 2

Study Guide and Review

Lesson-by-Lesson Review

2-1 Integers and Absolute Value (pp. 80–83)

Write an integer for each situation.

10. a loss of \$150
11. 350 feet above sea level
12. a gain of 8 yards
13. 12°F below 0

Evaluate each expression.

14. $|100|$
15. $|-32|$
16. $|-16| + |9|$

17. **JUICE** Mavis drank 48 milliliters of apple juice before replacing the carton in the refrigerator. Write an integer that shows the change in the volume of juice.

Example 1 **Write an integer for 8 feet below sea level.**

Since this situation represents an elevation *below* sea level, −8 represents the situation.

Example 2 **Evaluate $|-10|$.**

On the number line, the graph of −10 is 10 units from 0.

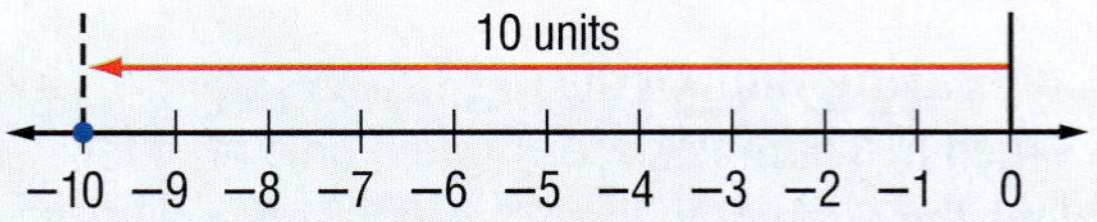

2-2 Comparing and Ordering Integers (pp. 84–87)

Replace each ● with < or > to make a true sentence.

18. −3 ● −9
19. 8 ● −12
20. −3 ● 3
21. $|-10|$ ● $|-13|$
22. 25 ● $|8|$
23. 0 ● $|-4|$

Order each set of integers from least to greatest.

24. $\{-3, 8, -10, 0, 5, -12, 9\}$
25. $\{-21, 19, -23, 14, -32, 25\}$
26. $\{-17, -18, 18, 15, -16, 16\}$

27. **EARTH SCIENCE** The predicted low temperatures for Monday through Friday are 3°, −1°, −2°, 0°, and 1°. Order the temperatures from greatest to least.

Example 3 **Replace ● with < or > to make −4 ● −7 a true sentence.**

Graph each integer on a number line.

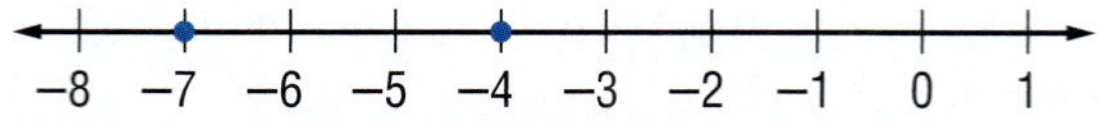

Since −4 is to the right of −7, −4 > −7.

Example 4 **Order the integers −4, −3, 5, 3, 0, −2 from least to greatest.**

Graph the integers on a number line.

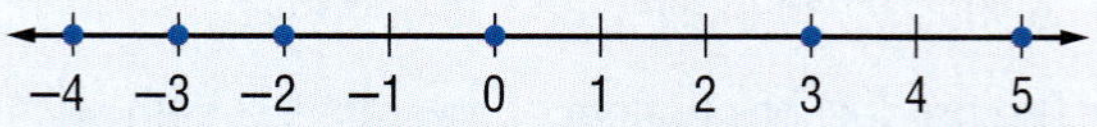

Order the integers by reading from left to right: −4, −3, −2, 0, 3, 5.

Mixed Problem Solving
For mixed problem-solving practice, see page 756.

2-3 The Coordinate Plane (pp. 88–92)

On graph paper, draw a coordinate plane. Then graph and label each point.

28. $E(1, -4)$
29. $F(-5, 2)$
30. $G(-2, -3)$
31. $H(4, 0)$

32. **ROUTES** Starting at the school, Pilar walked 1 block east and 3 blocks south. From there, she walked 5 blocks west and 4 blocks north to the park. If the school represents the origin, what is the ordered pair for the park?

Example 5 Graph and label the point $S(3, -1)$.

Draw a coordinate plane. Move 3 units to the right. Then move 1 unit down. Draw a dot and label it $S(3, -1)$.

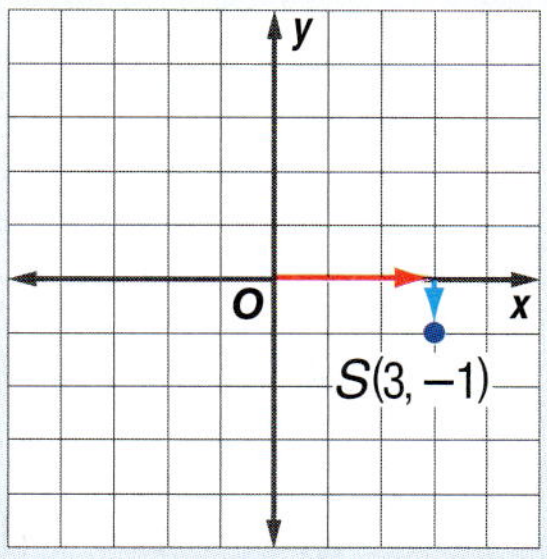

2-4 Adding Integers (pp. 95–99)

Add.

33. $-6 + 8$
34. $-4 + (-9)$
35. $7 + (-12)$
36. $-18 + 18$

37. **FOOTBALL** On the first play of the game, the Bulldogs lost 8 yards. On the second and third plays, they gained 5 yards and then lost 2 yards. Find the result of the first three plays.

Example 6

Find $-4 + 3$.

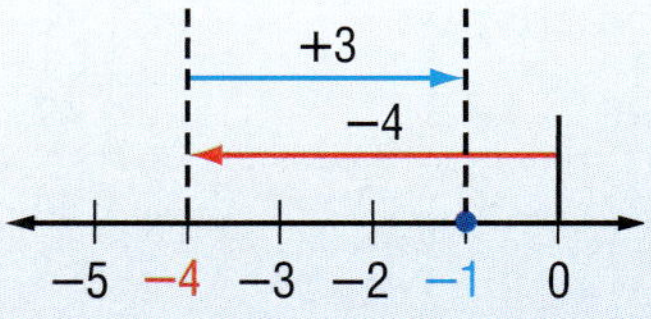

So, $-4 + 3 = -1$.

2-5 Subtracting Integers (pp. 103–106)

Subtract.

38. $-5 - 8$
39. $3 - 6$
40. $5 - (-2)$
41. $-4 - (-8)$

42. **GOLF** Owen shot 2 under par while his friend Nathan shot 3 above par. By how many shots was Owen's score better than Nathan's?

Example 7 Find $-3 - 9$.

$-3 - 9 = -3 + (-9)$ To subtract 9, add −9.
$= -12$ Simplify.

Study Guide and Review

2-6 PSI: Look For a Pattern (pp. 107–108)

Solve. Look for a pattern.

43. HEALTH The average person blinks 12 times per minute. At this rate, how many times does the average person blink in one day?

44. SALARY Suki gets a job that pays \$31,000 per year. She is promised a \$2,200 raise each year. At this rate, what will her salary be in 7 years?

45. DOGS A kennel determined that they need 144 feet of fencing to board 2 dogs, 216 feet to board 3 dogs, and 288 feet to board 4 dogs. If this pattern continues, how many feet of fencing is needed to board 8 dogs?

Example 8 **A theater has 18 seats in the first row, 24 seats in the second row, 30 seats in the third row, and so on. If this pattern continues, how many seats are in the sixth row?**

Begin with 18 seats and add 6 seats for each additional row.

So, there are 48 seats in the ninth row.

Row	Number of Seats
1	18
2	24
3	30
4	36
5	42
6	48

2-7 Multiplying Integers (pp. 109–113)

Multiply.

46. $-4(3)$ **47.** $8(-6)$

48. $-5(-7)$ **49.** $-2(40)$

ALGEBRA **Evaluate each expression if $a = -4$, $b = -7$, and $c = 5$.**

50. ab **51.** $-3c$

52. bc **53.** abc

Example 9 **Find $-4(3)$.**

$-4(3) = -12$ The integers have different signs. The product is negative.

Example 10 **Evaluate xyz if $x = -6$, $y = 11$, and $z = -10$.**

xyz

$= (-6)(11)(-10)$ $x = -6, y = 11, z = -10.$

$= (-66)(-10)$ Multiply -6 and 11.

$= 660$ Multiply -66 and -10.

2-8 Dividing Integers (pp. 114–118)

Divide.

54. $-45 \div (-9)$ **55.** $36 \div (-12)$

56. $-12 \div 6$ **57.** $-81 \div (-9)$

Example 11 **Find $-72 \div (-9)$.**

$-72 \div (-9) = 8$ The integers have the same sign. The quotient is positive.

Chapter 2 Practice Test

1. **WEATHER** Adam is recording the change in the outside air temperature for a science project. At 8:00 A.M., the high temperature was 42°F. By noon, the outside temperature had fallen 11°F. By mid-afternoon, the outside air temperature had fallen 12°F and by evening, it had fallen an additional 5°F. Write an integer that describes the final change in temperature.

Evaluate each expression.

2. $|-3|$
3. $|-18| - |6|$

Replace each ● with <, >, or = to make a true sentence.

4. -3 ● -9
5. $|9|$ ● $|-12|$

6. The Texas Longhorns recorded the following yardage in six plays: 9, −2, 5, 0, 12, and −7. Order these integers from least to greatest.

7. **TEST PRACTICE** Which of the following coordinates lie within the rectangle graphed below?

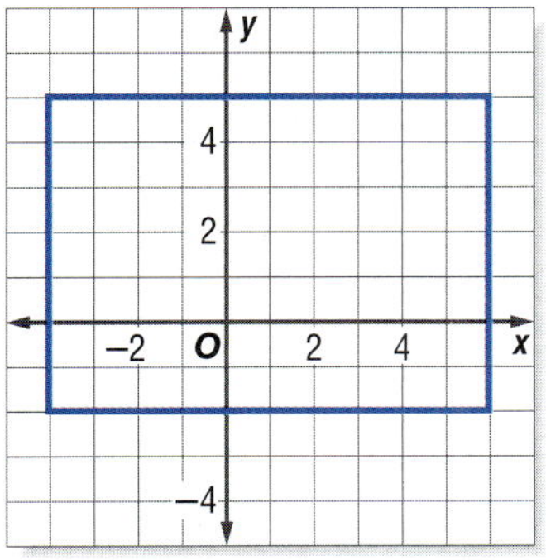

A (5, 6)
B (0, −3)
C (−5, 1)
D (−3, 0)

8. **DEBT** Amanda owes her brother $24. If she plans to pay him back an equal amount from her piggy bank each day for six days, describe the change in the amount of money in her piggy bank each day.

Write the ordered pair for each point graphed. Then name the quadrant in which each point is located.

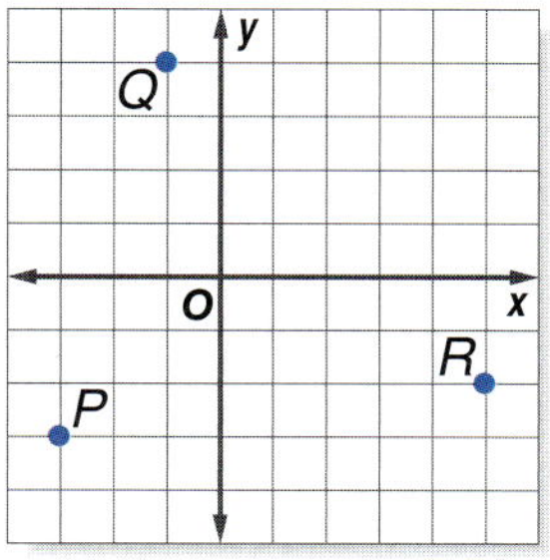

9. *P*
10. *Q*
11. *R*

Add, subtract, multiply, or divide.

12. $12 + (-9)$
13. $-3 - 4$
14. $-7 - (-20)$
15. $-7(-3)$
16. $5(-11)$
17. $-36 \div (-9)$
18. $-15 + (-7)$
19. $8 + (-6) + (-4)$
20. $-9 - 7$
21. $-13 + 7$

22. **TEST PRACTICE** Kendrick created a 6-week schedule for practicing the piano. If the pattern continues, how many hours will he practice during the sixth week?

The table shows the number of hours he practiced in the first three weeks.

Week	1	2	3
Hours	4	7	10

F 15 hours
G 18 hours
H 19 hours
J 22 hours

Evaluate each expression if $a = -5$, $b = 4$, and $c = -12$.

23. $ac \div b$
24. $\frac{a - b}{3}$

25. **STOCK MARKET** The value of a stock went down $3 each week for a period of seven weeks. Describe the change in the value of the stock at the end of the seven week period.

CHAPTER 2

Texas Test Practice
Cumulative, Chapters 1–2

Read each question. Then fill in the correct answer on the answer document provided by your teacher or on a sheet of paper.

1. The daily low temperatures for Cleveland, Ohio, over the last five days were 15°F, −2°F, 8°F, −6°F, and 5°F. Which expression can be used to find the average daily low temperature during the last five days?

A $(15 + 2 + 8 + 6 + 5) \div 5$

B $15 + 2 + 8 + 6 + 5 \div 5$

C $[15 + (-2) + 8 + (-6) + 5] \div 5$

D $15 + (-2) + 8 + (-6) + 5 \div 5$

TEST-TAKING TIP

Question 1 Check every answer choice of a multiple-choice question. Each time you find an incorrect answer, cross it off so you remember that you've eliminated it.

2. If point *B* is moved 5 units to the left and 3 units up, what will be the new coordinates of point *B*?

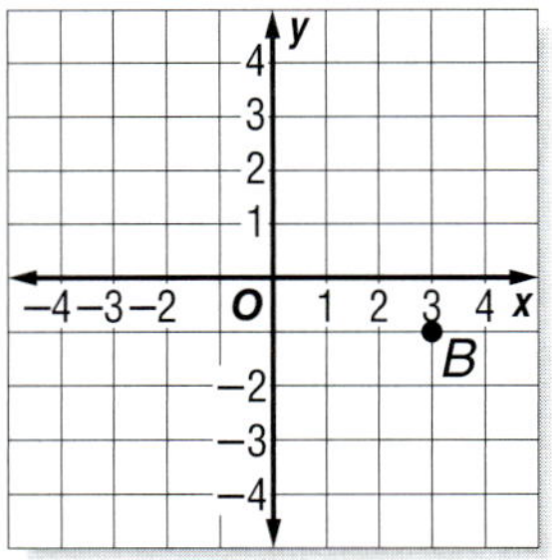

F $(-5, 3)$

G $(0, 0)$

H $(8, -4)$

J $(-2, 2)$

3. **GRIDDABLE** Simplify the expression below.

$$3 + 6(10 - 7) - 3^2$$

4. Manuel is planning to swim every day this week. On the first day, he swam 1 mile. On the second day, he swam $1\frac{1}{2}$ miles and on the third day he swam 2 miles. If the pattern continues, how far will he swim on the sixth day?

A 3 mi

B $3\frac{1}{2}$ mi

C 4 mi

D $4\frac{1}{2}$ mi

5. Sue typically spends between \$175 and \$250 each month on clothes. Which of the following is the best estimate for the amount she spends in 6 months?

F From \$600 to \$1,200

G From \$900 to \$1,300

H From \$1,050 to \$1,500

J From \$1,200 to \$1,500

6. Which expression is represented by the model below?

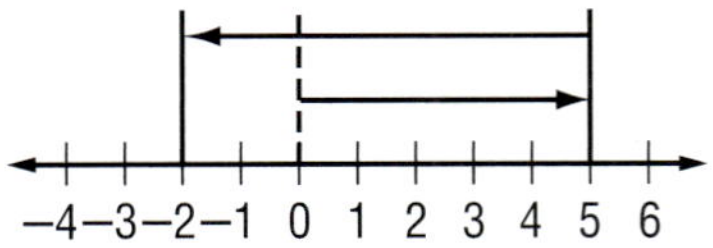

A $5 - 0$

B $-5 - 7$

C $7 - 5$

D $5 - 7$

7. The top four runners of a race were Alicia, Kyle, Drew, and Juanita. Drew finished before Juanita. Alicia finished after both boys, but before Juanita. What information is needed to determine the order of the runners from first to fourth?

F Did Kyle finish before or after Drew?

G Did Alicia finish before or after Juanita?

H Did Drew finish before or after Alicia?

J Did Kyle finish before or after Alicia?

Math Online Texas Test Practice at tx.msmath2.com

Get Ready for the Texas Test
For test-taking strategies and more practice, see pages TX1–TX23.

8. Which expression is represented by the model below?

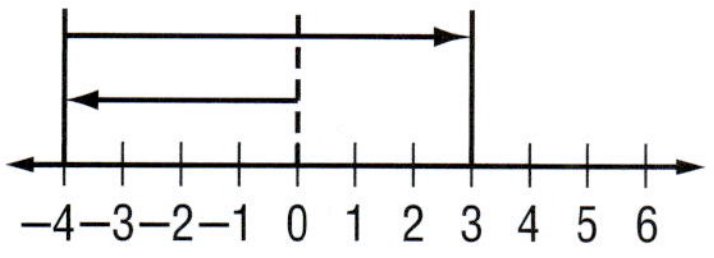

A $-4 + 0$ C $-4 + 7$
B $-4 + 3$ D $-4 + 2$

9. Which of the following relationships is best represented by the data in the table?

x	y
1	36
2	72
3	108
4	144
5	180

F Conversion of feet to inches
G Conversion of inches to yards
H Conversion of feet to yards
J Conversion of yards to inches

10. If point A is moved 2 units to the right and 4 units down, what will be point A's new coordinates?

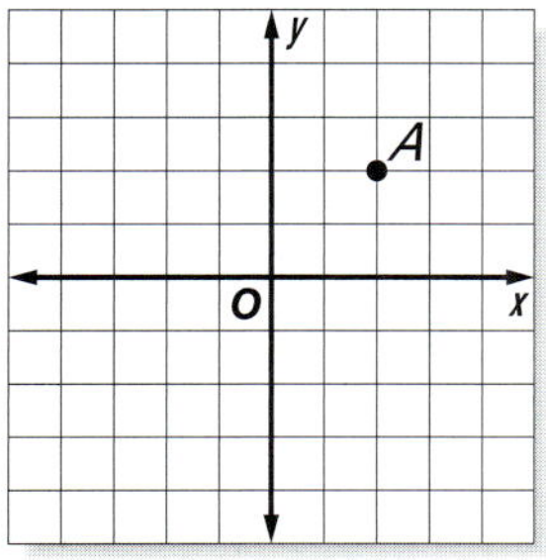

A $(0, -2)$ C $(0, 6)$
B $(4, -2)$ D $(4, 6)$

11. Nick spends a total of 75 hours per week at work and at the gym. He goes to the gym from 6:45 A.M. to 8:45 A.M., Monday through Friday. Which equation can be used to find t, the maximum number of hours Nick works at his job each week?

F $t = 75 - (5 \times 2)$
G $t = 75 + 5 + 2$
H $t = 75 - 2 + 2 + 2 + 2 + 2$
J $t = 5 \times 2 - 75$

Pre-AP

Record your answers on a sheet of paper. Show your work.

12. Use the table of ordered pairs to answer the questions below.

x	y
−2	1
3	2
−1	−4

a. Plot the ordered pairs in the table on a coordinate plane. Then connect the points on the graph.

b. In which quadrant is a point on the graph not represented?

c. What shape is formed in the graph above?

d. How could you increase the size of the figure you drew above?

e. Add four more columns to the table. Label the columns $x + y$, $x - y$, xy, and $x \div y$. Complete the table.

NEED EXTRA HELP?												
If You Missed Question...	1	2	3	4	5	6	7	8	9	10	11	12
Go to Lesson...	1-6	2-3	1-4	2-6	1-1	2-5	1-1	2-4	2-6	2-3	1-7	2-3
For Help with Test Objective...	1	3	1	6	1	1	6	1	2	3	6	2

CHAPTER 3

Applying Decimals

Knowledge and Skills

- Add, subtract, multiply, or divide to solve problems and justify solutions. **TEKS 7.2**

Key Vocabulary

compatible numbers (p. 129)
metric system (p. 157)
scientific notation (p. 162)

Real-World Link

Fruit Texas Red Grapefruit, grown in the Rio Grande Valley, is a good source of fiber. One serving has 6 grams of fiber. You can multiply 6 by 1,000 to convert grams to milligrams.

FOLDABLES™ Study Organizer

Applying Decimals Make this Foldable to help you organize your notes. Begin with a sheet of 11″ by 17″ paper.

1. **Fold** the paper into fourths widthwise.

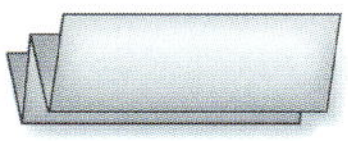

2. **Fold** this folded paper in half again and open to find eight equal rows.

3. **Fold** a 2″ tab along the long side.

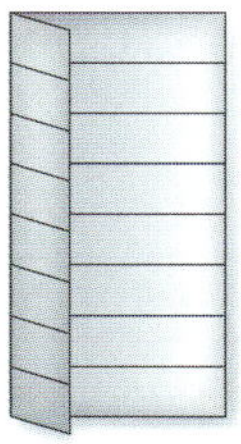

4. **Trace** along the fold lines and label each lesson number and title.

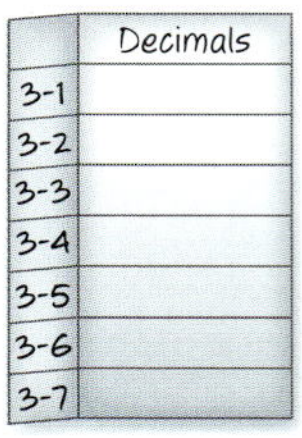

GET READY for Chapter 3

Diagnose Readiness You have two options for checking Prerequisite Skills.

Option 2

Math Online Take the Online Readiness Quiz at tx.msmath2.com.

Option 1

Take the Quick Quiz below. Refer to the Quick Review for help.

QUICK Quiz

Round each decimal to the nearest whole number. (Used in Lesson 3-1)

1. 45.68
2. 89.5
3. 17.3
4. 34.26
5. **BICYCLES** A new bicycle costs \$378.61. What is the cost to the nearest dollar?

Multiply. (Used in Lesson 3-2)

6. 13×4
7. 27×36
8. 15×12
9. 145×7
10. **CDs** Each package of CDs contains 24 CDs. If you have 12 packages of CDs, how many are there?

Divide. (Used in Lesson 3-4)

11. $45 \div 5$
12. $858 \div 26$
13. $504 \div 36$
14. $1{,}445 \div 17$
15. **SAVINGS** Cheryl saved a total of \$294 over the past six months. On average, how much did she save each month?

Evaluate each power of 10. (Used in Lessons 3-3, 3-6, and 3-7)

16. 10^2
17. 10^5
18. 10^3
19. 10^4

QUICK Review

Example 1

Round the decimal 22.48 to the nearest whole number.

$22.48 \rightarrow 22$ $\quad 22.48 < 22.5$
22.48 rounds down to 22.

Example 2

Find 65 × 19.

$$\begin{array}{r} 65 \\ \times\ 19 \\ \hline 585 \\ +\ 650 \\ \hline 1235 \end{array}$$

Annex a zero.

Example 3

Find 1,296 ÷ 48.

$$\begin{array}{r} 27 \\ 48\overline{)1296} \\ -\ 96 \\ \hline 336 \\ -\ 336 \\ \hline 0 \end{array}$$

Example 4

Evaluate 10^6.

$$\begin{aligned} 10^6 &= 10 \cdot 10 \cdot 10 \cdot 10 \cdot 10 \cdot 10 \\ &= 1{,}000{,}000 \end{aligned}$$

3-1 Estimating with Decimals

Main IDEA

Estimate with decimals.

Targeted TEKS 7.13 The student applies Grade 7 mathematics to solve problems connected to everyday experiences, investigations in other disciplines, and activities in and outside of school. **(D) select** tools such as real objects, manipulatives, paper/pencil, and technology or **techniques such as mental math, estimation, and number sense to solve problems.** *Also addresses TEKS 6.2(D).*

NEW Vocabulary

compatible numbers

READING in the Content Area

For strategies in reading this lesson, visit tx.msmath2.com.

GET READY for the Lesson

ANALYZE GRAPHS The majority of the world's farm-raised catfish supply comes from the United States. The table shows the number of farm-raised catfish in five states.

1. Round each amount to the nearest hundred million.
2. About how many times more farm-raised catfish are there in Mississippi than Louisiana?

Farm-Raised Catfish

State	Catfish (millions)
Mississippi	792.5
Arkansas	495.2
Alabama	348.6
Louisiana	153.1
Texas	89.6

Source: *Scholastic Book of World Records*

To estimate products and quotients of decimals, use the same methods you used to estimate sums and differences of decimals.

EXAMPLE Estimate a Product

1 **Estimate 8.7 × 2.8.**

8.7	→	9	Round 8.7 to 9.
× 2.8	→	× 3	Round 2.8 to 3.
		27	

The product is about 27.

CHECK Your Progress **Estimate each product.**

a. 9.6 × 1.8

b. 68.4 × 21.3

Real-World EXAMPLE

2 **DOGS** **A greyhound can travel 39.3 miles per hour. At this speed, about how far could a greyhound travel in 6.5 hours?**

39.3	→	40	Round 39.3 to 40.
× 6.5	→	× 7	Round 6.5 to 7.
		280	

The greyhound could travel about 280 miles.

CHECK Your Progress

c. **MONEY** Suppose one U.S. dollar is equal to 5.8 Egyptian pounds. About how many Egyptian pounds would you receive for $48.50?

Online Personal Tutor at tx.msmath2.com

Compatible numbers are numbers that are easy to divide mentally. You can use compatible numbers when estimating quotients.

EXAMPLE Estimate a Quotient

3 **Estimate 32.8 ÷ 3.9.**

$3.9\overline{)32.8} \rightarrow \overset{8}{4\overline{)32}}$

Round 32.8 to 32 since 32 and 4 are compatible numbers.

The quotient is *about* 8. Use your calculator to find the actual quotient. How close is your estimate?

CHECK Your Progress **Estimate each quotient.**

d. 49.3 ÷ 7.6

e. $24.2\overline{)98.1}$

Real-World Link The shell of a leatherback turtle can reach a length of 1.7 meters.

Source: leatherback.org

Real-World EXAMPLE

4 **TURTLES** **A Pacific Leatherback turtle can weigh up to 704.4 kilograms. An Olive Ridley turtle can weigh up to 49.9 kilograms. About how many times heavier is the Pacific Leatherback turtle?**

$49.9\overline{)704.4} \rightarrow \overset{14}{50\overline{)700}}$

Divide mentally. You know that 100 ÷ 50 = 2. So, it follows that 700 ÷ 50 = 7(2) or 14.

The Pacific Leatherback is about 14 times heavier than the Olive Ridley turtle.

CHECK Your Progress

f. **CARS** There are approximately 147.8 million cars in the United States. If Italy has approximately 33.4 million cars, about how many times more cars does the U.S. have than Italy?

CHECK Your Understanding

Example 1 (p. 128)

Estimate each product.

1. 5.8 × 4.4
2. 27.3 × 9.8
3. 57.1 × 32.9

Example 2 (p. 128)

4. **MONEY** A grocery store sells American cheese for $3.89 per pound. About how much would 1.89 pounds of the cheese cost?

Example 3 (p. 129)

Estimate each quotient.

5. 24.2 ÷ 4.7
6. 40.79 ÷ 6.8
7. $38.1\overline{)984.76}$

Example 4 (p. 129)

8. **WEATHER** The average yearly precipitation for the Dallas-Fort Worth area is 34.73 inches. About how much precipitation does the area receive each month?

Exercises

HOMEWORK HELP

For Exercises	See Examples
9–14	1
15–16	2
17–22	3
23–24	4

Estimate each product.

9. 9.7×3.3
10. 3.4×5.6
11. 17.5×8.4
12. 26.3×9.7
13. $\begin{array}{r} 33.6 \\ \times\ 82.1 \\ \hline \end{array}$
14. $\begin{array}{r} 99.1 \\ \times\ 11.2 \\ \hline \end{array}$

15. **FRUIT** On average, America produces 36.5 million tons of fruit each year. About how much fruit do they produce in 2.25 years?

16. **SCIENCE** A single year on Saturn is equal to 29.4 years on Earth. About how many Earth years are equal to 3.2 Saturn years?

Estimate each quotient.

17. $32.4 \div 2.8$
18. $57.2 \div 9.4$
19. $76.2 \div 18.4$
20. $45.8 \div 23.6$
21. $11.4\overline{)35.7}$
22. $23.3\overline{)119}$

23. **SEWING** Mauricio bought 6.75 yards of fabric for a total of \$47.50. About how much was the cost per yard?

24. **MONEY** Emily spent a total of \$38.04 on four CDs. If each CD cost the same amount, what is a reasonable amount for the cost of each CD?

Use estimation to determine whether each answer is reasonable. If the answer is reasonable, write *yes*. If not, write *no* and provide a reasonable estimate.

25. $22.8 \times 4.7 = 107.16$
26. $36.75 \div 7.5 = 4.9$
27. $2.1 \times 4.9 \times 7.2 = 105.84$
28. $7.8 \times 1.1 \times 4.2 = 50$
29. $74.5 \div 23.8 = 7.26$
30. $108.9 \div 19.8 = 5.5$

Estimate.

31. 83.4×44.4
32. 103.8×90.5
33. 67.35×68.5
34. $645.49 \div 373.4$
35. $299.50 \div 121.7$
36. $48.67 \div 99.89$

37. **TRAVEL** About how far would you run in 1 minute if you run 12.5 feet per second?

38. **MONEY** Hannah's hourly wage working at an ice cream shop is \$5.85. The table gives her hours worked for five days. She estimates her earnings to be \$120. Without calculating her actual earnings, determine if her estimate is more or less than her actual earnings. Explain your reasoning.

Day	Hours Worked
Monday	3.5
Tuesday	4.25
Wednesday	3.75
Thursday	2.5
Friday	4.75

39. **FIND THE DATA** Refer to the Texas Data File on pages 16–19. Choose some data and write a real-world problem in which you would estimate the product or quotient of decimals.

EXTRA PRACTICE

See pages 723, 757.

Math Online
Self-Check Quiz at tx.msmath2.com

H.O.T. Problems

40. **CHALLENGE** A scooter can travel between 22 and 28 miles on each gallon of gasoline. If one gallon of gasoline costs between $2.45 and $2.75 per gallon, about how much will it cost to travel 75 miles?

41. **OPEN ENDED** Apply what you know about estimation to write three decimals whose product is about 40.

42. **SELECT A TECHNIQUE** Jonah is buying 8 items that cost $2.50 each. Which of the following techniques might Jonah use to determine whether $20 will be enough to pay for the items, not including tax? Justify your selection(s). Then use the technique(s) to solve the problem.

mental math	number sense	estimation

43. **WRITING IN MATH** Create a division expression involving decimals in which you could use compatible numbers to estimate the quotient. Then describe how you would estimate the quotient using compatible numbers.

TEST PRACTICE

44. Green peppers are on sale for $2.89 per pound. Mrs. Moseley bought 1.75 pounds of peppers. About how much did she pay for the peppers?

 A Less than $4

 B Between $5 and $6

 C Between $6 and $7

 D More than $7

45. Both Mario and Andrew mow yards during the summer to earn money.

Mario	Andrew
$8.25/hr	$5.85/hr

Suppose Mario and Andrew each work 20 hours. About how much more money will Mario earn?

 F $30 **H** $60

 G $40 **J** $70

Spiral Review

Divide. (Lesson 2-8)

46. $-36 \div 4$ 47. $64 \div (-8)$ 48. $-24 \div (-6)$ 49. $\frac{-121}{11}$

Multiply. (Lesson 2-7)

50. $5(-3)$ 51. $-2(-8)$ 52. $(-8)^2$ 53. $-6(9)$

54. **ALGEBRA** Khalid collects coins. He has 5 more than Tyler has. Write an expression that represents the amount of coins Khalid has in his collection. Let t represent the amount of coins Tyler has. (Lesson 1-6)

GET READY for the Next Lesson

PREREQUISITE SKILL **Find each product.**

55. 4×6 56. 3×5 57. 8×9 58. 9×3

Explore 3-2

Math Lab
Multiplication with Decimal Models

Main IDEA

Multiply decimals using decimal models.

Targeted TEKS 7.2 The student adds, subtracts, multiplies, or divides to solve problems and justify solutions. **(A) represent multiplication** and division **situations involving** fractions and **decimals with models, including concrete objects, pictures,** words, **and numbers.**

Concepts in Motion
Animation tx.msmath2.com

You can use decimal models to multiply a decimal by a whole number. Recall that a 10-by-10 grid represents the whole number 1.

ACTIVITY

1 Find 0.4 × 3 using decimal models.

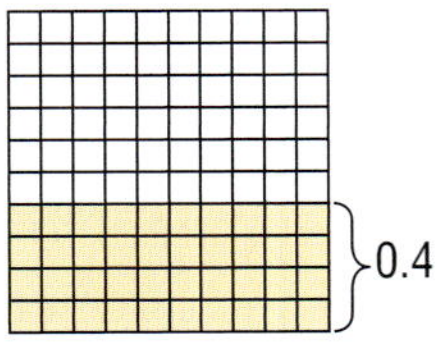

Draw a decimal model. Shade 4 rows yellow to represent 0.4. Recall that each row or column represents 0.1.

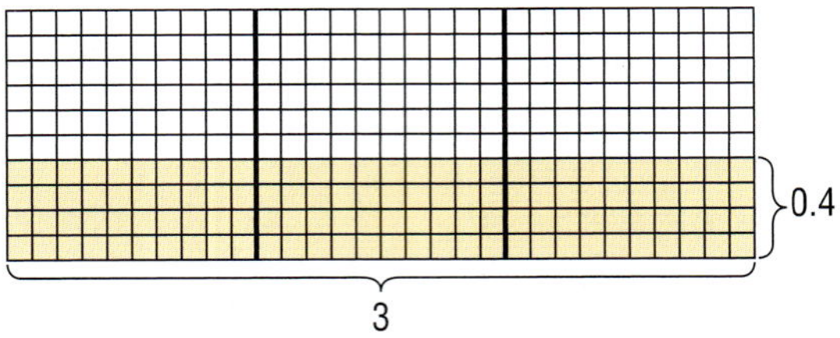

To represent 3, draw two more models identical to your first for a total of 3 models of 0.4.

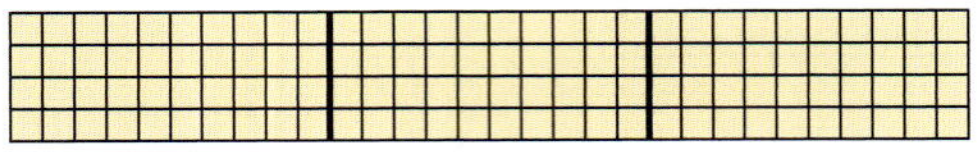

Cut off the shaded rows.

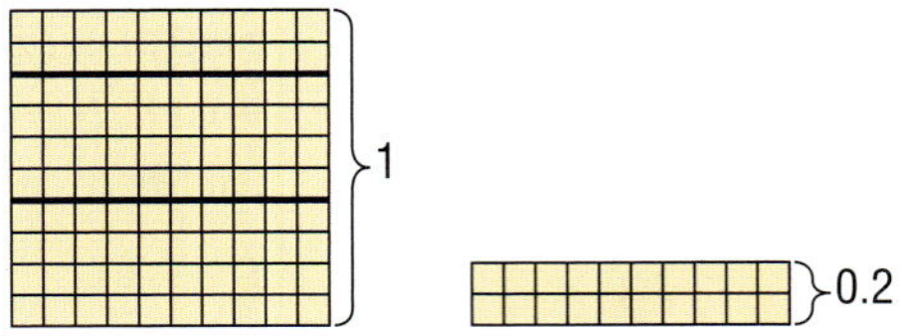

Rearrange these rows to form as many 10-by-10 models as possible.

The product is *1 and 2 tenths.*

So, 0.4 × 3 = 1.2.

CHECK Your Progress

Find each product using decimal models.

a. 0.8 × 3 **b.** 0.3 × 2 **c.** 0.2 × 4 **d.** 1.3 × 2

Analyze the Results

1. The decimal factors in Exercises a–c are numbers between 0 and 1. Write a sentence comparing the whole number factors in these Exercises to the products found.
2. **MAKE A CONJECTURE** Is the product of a decimal between 0 and 1 and a whole number greater than or less than the whole number? Test your conjecture on 0.5 × 4. Check your answer by making a model.
3. **MAKE A PREDICTION** Examine the factors and product of Exercise d. Use your observations to predict whether 2.4 × 3 will be greater than or less than 3. Check your prediction by modeling the product.

You can use similar decimal models to multiply a decimal by a decimal.

STUDY TIP

Decimal Models Recall that each small square of a decimal model represents 0.01.

ACTIVITIES

2 **Find 0.3 × 0.6 using decimal models.**

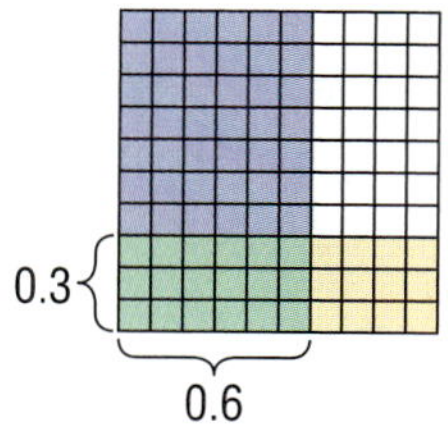

Draw a decimal model, and shade 3 rows yellow to represent 0.3.

Then shade 6 columns blue to represent 0.6.

There are *18 hundredths* in the overlapping green region.

So, 0.3 × 0.6 = 0.18.

3 **Find 0.9 × 1.2 using decimal models.**

Since 1.2 is greater than 1 but less than 2, use two decimal models.

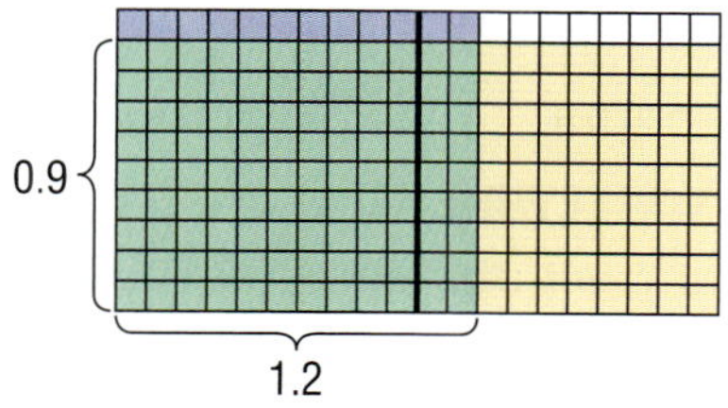

Shade 9 rows of each model yellow to represent 0.9.

Then shade all of one model and 2 columns of the other model blue to represent 1.2.

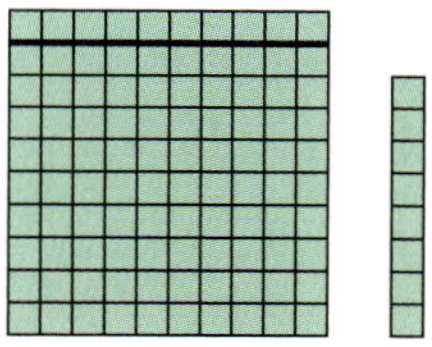

Cut off the squares that are shaded green. Then rearrange them to form 10-by-10 grids.

There are *1 and 8 hundredths* in the overlapping green region.

So, 0.9 × 1.2 = 1.08.

STUDY TIP

Estimation You can use estimation to check if your answer is reasonable.

0.9 × 1.2 → 1 × 1 or 1

CHECK Your Progress

Use decimal models to find each product.

e. 0.4 × 0.4 **f.** 0.5 × 0.7 **g.** 0.8 × 2.4 **h.** 0.5 × 1.7

ANALYZE THE RESULTS

4. **MAKE A CONJECTURE** Analyze Exercises e–h. How are the number of decimal places in the factors and in the product related? Use this pattern to find 0.2 × 0.8. Then check your conjecture by modeling the product.

5. **MAKE A PREDICTION** Predict whether the products 0.4 × 0.2 and 0.4 × 1.5 are each greater than or less than 0.4. Explain your reasoning. Check your answers by modeling each product.

3-2 Multiplying Decimals

Main IDEA

Multiply decimals.

Targeted TEKS 7.2 The student adds, subtracts, multiplies, or divides to solve problems and justify solutions. **(A) represent multiplication** and division **situations involving** fractions and **decimals with models,** including concrete objects, pictures, **words and numbers.** *Also addresses TEKS 7.2(B), 7.13(D).*

GET READY for the Lesson

INSECTS The speeds of three insects are shown.

1. Use the addition sentence 13.3 + 13.3 to find the distance a hornet can travel in 2 hours.
2. Write the multiplication sentence that could be used to find this distance.
3. How are the answers for Exercises 1 and 2 related?

Repeat the steps in Exercises 1–3 for each insect and number of hours.

4. hornet, 3 hours
5. dragonfly, 2 hours
6. hawk moth, 4 hours
7. **MAKE A CONJECTURE** How are the number of decimal places in each product and set of factors related?

How Fast Do Insects Fly?

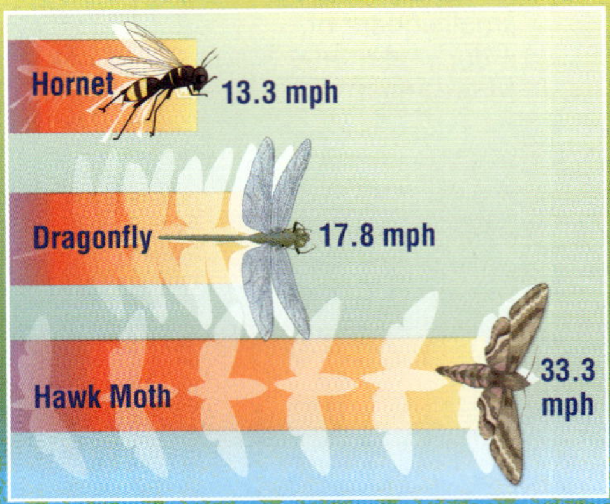

Source: *Scholastic Book of World Records*

When multiplying a decimal by a whole number, multiply as with whole numbers. To place the decimal point in each product, use estimation or count decimal places.

STUDY TIP

Symbols
The symbol ≈ means *approximately equal to.*

EXAMPLE Multiply a Decimal by a Whole Number

1 **Find 1.82 × 3.**

METHOD 1 **Use estimation.**

$$\begin{array}{r} 1.82 \\ \times\ \ 3 \\ \hline 5.46 \end{array}$$

Estimate $1.82 \times 3 \approx 2 \times 3$ or 6

Since the estimate is 6, place the decimal point after the 5.

METHOD 2 **Count decimal places.**

1.82 ← 2 decimal places
× 3
5.46 ← 2 decimal places

CHOOSE Your Method **Multiply.**

a. 0.7 × 4
b. 1.63 × 7
c. 6 × 1.324

Real-World EXAMPLE

2 **ANIMALS** Use the information at the left to find the distance a kangaroo travels after it jumps 4 times.

$$\begin{array}{r} 0.006 \\ \times \quad 4 \\ \hline 0.024 \end{array}$$

There are 3 decimal places.

Remember to annex a zero.

After 4 jumps, a kangaroo travels 0.024 mile.

CHECK Your Progress

d. **MEASUREMENT** Human hair grows 0.003 centimeter each day. How many centimeters does human hair grow in a week?

Real-World Link
With every jump, a large kangaroo travels about 0.006 mile.
Source: *Corsinet Trivia*

To place the decimal point in the product of two decimals, use estimation or find the sum of the decimal places in each factor.

EXAMPLES Multiply Decimals

3 Find 0.9 × 0.8.

METHOD 1 **Use estimation.**

$$\begin{array}{r} 0.9 \\ \times \ 0.8 \\ \hline 0.72 \end{array}$$

Estimate $0.9 \times 0.8 \approx 1 \times 1$ or 1

Since the estimate is 1, place the decimal point before the 7. Place a zero before the decimal point.

METHOD 2 **Count decimal places.**

0.9	←	1 decimal place
× 0.8	←	+ 1 decimal place
0.72	←	2 decimal places

4 Find 4.07 × 3.1. **Estimate** $4.07 \times 3.1 \approx 4 \times 3$ or 12

4.07	←	2 decimal places
× 3.1	←	+ 1 decimal place
407		
+ 1221		
12.617	←	3 decimal places

Check for Reasonableness $12.617 \approx 12$ ✔

CHOOSE Your Method

Multiply.

e. 0.5 × 0.9

f. 1.04 × 2.3

g. 0.06 × 2.48

Math Online Personal Tutor at tx.msmath2.com

Real-World EXAMPLE

5 **ANALYZE TABLES** **The prices of fruit and nut mixes are shown. To the nearest cent, what is the total cost of 1.55 pounds of trail mix and 3.3 pounds of sweet and salty mix?**

Fruit & Nut Mixes	
Type of Mix	**Price ($/lb)**
Trail	2.37
Yogurt Nut	2.62
Sweet & Salty	2.69

First, find the total cost of each mix.

Trail Mix

Estimate

$\$2.37 \times 1.55 \approx \$2 \times 2$ or $4

$$\begin{array}{rl} 2.37 & \leftarrow \text{ 2 decimal places} \\ \times\ 1.55 & \leftarrow \text{ + 2 decimal places} \\ \hline 1185 & \\ 1185 & \\ +\ 237 & \\ \hline 3.6735 & \leftarrow \text{ 4 decimal places} \end{array}$$

Check for Reasonableness

$\$3.6735 \approx \$4$ ✔

Sweet & Salty Mix

Estimate

$\$2.69 \times 3.3 \approx \$3 \times 3$ or $9

$$\begin{array}{rl} 2.69 & \leftarrow \text{ 2 decimal places} \\ \times\ 3.3 & \leftarrow \text{ + 1 decimal place} \\ \hline 807 & \\ +\ 807 & \\ \hline 8.877 & \leftarrow \text{ 3 decimal places} \end{array}$$

Check for Reasonableness

$\$8.877 \approx \$9$ ✔

To the nearest cent, the trail mix costs $3.67. The sweet and salty mix costs $8.88. The total cost is $3.67 + $8.88 or $12.55.

CHECK Your Progress

h. Use the table above. How much more does 2.5 pounds of yogurt nut mix cost than 1.25 pounds of trail mix?

STUDY TIP

Using Estimation You can use estimation to place the decimal point and check the reasonableness of the answer.

CHECK Your Understanding

Example 1 (p. 134)

Multiply.

1. $\begin{array}{r} 0.3 \\ \times\ 9 \\ \hline \end{array}$ **2.** 1.4×2 **3.** 0.005×3 **4.** $\begin{array}{r} 0.012 \\ \times\ 7 \\ \hline \end{array}$

Example 2 (p. 135)

5. **INSECTS** An average worker bee produces 0.083 teaspoon of honey in its lifetime. How much honey would 5 worker bees produce in their lifetimes?

Examples 3, 4 (p. 135)

Multiply.

6. 0.7×0.9 **7.** $\begin{array}{r} 1.5 \\ \times\ 2.7 \\ \hline \end{array}$ **8.** $\begin{array}{r} 1.02 \\ \times\ 4.8 \\ \hline \end{array}$ **9.** 3.04×0.26

Example 5 (p. 136)

10. **COINS** A quarter has a mass of 5.67 grams and a dime has a mass of 2.268 grams. How much more mass do 4 quarters have than 4 dimes?

Exercises

HOMEWORK HELP	
For Exercises	See Examples
11–24	1, 2
25–36	3, 4
37–38	5

Multiply.

11. 0.5×7
12. 0.8×2
13. 2.4×6
14. 4.1×7
15. 2.13×6
16. 1.22×8
17. 3.01×4
18. 5.06×7
19. 0.03×2
20. 0.004×5
21. 0.011×6
22. 0.026×3

23. **MEASUREMENT** Erika needs 1.8 yards of ribbon to make a bow. How many yards of ribbon will she need to make 6 bows?

24. **MONEY** Suppose you buy 5 cheeseburgers at $1.52 each. What is the total cost of the cheeseburgers before tax is added?

Multiply.

25. 0.6×0.7
26. 0.1×0.4
27. 0.8×1.7
28. 0.9×2.3
29. 0.3×6.1
30. 1.7×2.3
31. 1.08×0.2
32. 2.38×0.4
33. 7.68×1.6
34. 6.05×3.4
35. 3.45×1.25
36. 4.56×3.21

Real-World Link The Turkey Creek hiking trail in Austin, Texas, is 2.5 miles long.
Source: austinexplorer.com

37. **DISTANCE** Curtis hikes for 1.25 hours at an average speed of 2.6 miles per hour. How many miles does Curtis hike?

38. **RECYCLING** A seventh grade class collected 267.75 pounds of aluminum to recycle. If a recycling company pays $0.65 per pound of aluminum, how much will the students earn? Round to the nearest cent.

Multiply.

39. thirteen thousandths times two and five tenths
40. twenty-eight times forty-five ten thousandths

For Exercises 41 and 42, write a multiplication expression for each model. Then find the product.

41. 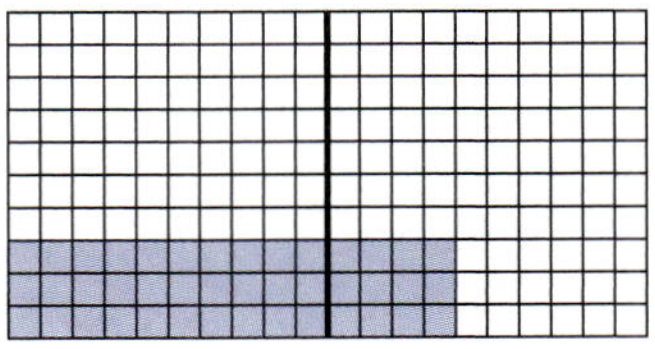

42. 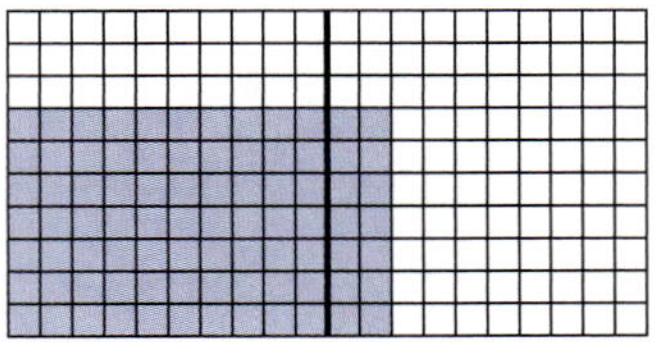

43. **TRAVEL** If one United States dollar could be exchanged for 138.96 Japanese yen, how many yen would a tourist receive for 25 U.S. dollars?

Evaluate.

44. $7 + 1.8 \times 0.5 - 4$
45. $2.3(8 - 3) \times 2$
46. $(1.5)^2 + 6$
47. $(2.3)^2 + (1.1)^2$
48. $8 + (2.4)^2 - 5$
49. $(5.6 + 3.2)^2 - 10$

50. **ANALYZE TABLES** Rogelio buys two 3-ring binders and a ruler. If he pays using a $10 bill, how much change will he receive?

School Supplies	
Item	**Cost**
package of paper	$0.99
3-ring binder	$1.95
package of pens	$1.19
ruler	$0.75

51. **MONEY** Venus' hourly wage is $15.75 per hour. The number of hours she worked is shown on her paycheck. For each hour of overtime she is paid for one and a half hours. How much did Venus earn last week?

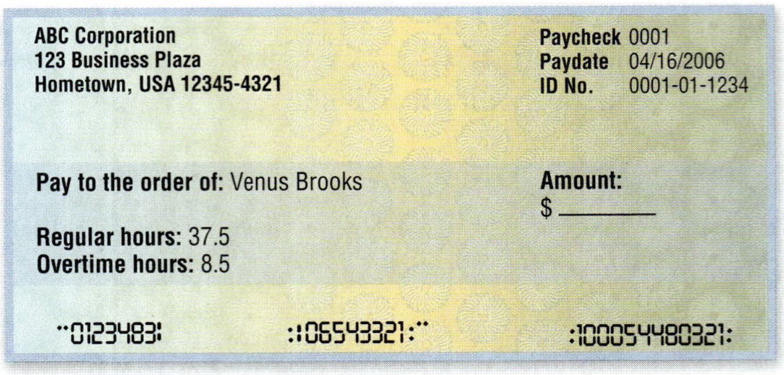
ABC Corporation
123 Business Plaza
Hometown, USA 12345-4321

Paycheck 0001
Paydate 04/16/2006
ID No. 0001-01-1234

Pay to the order of: Venus Brooks

Amount:
$ ______

Regular hours: 37.5
Overtime hours: 8.5

ANALYZE TABLES **For Exercises 52 and 53, use the table to the right.**

Coin	Thicknesses (mm)
penny	1.55
nickel	1.95
dime	1.35
quarter	1.75

52. Suppose 6 coins are stacked in one pile and have a thickness of 11.1 millimeters. If you have only two types of coins, what coins do you have?

53. How many of each coin do you have?

ALGEBRA **Evaluate each expression if $a = 0.45$, $b = 2.6$, and $c = 7.2$.**

54. $9 + ab$

55. $5b^2 + 2$

56. $3.5c - 4b$

PATTERNS **Find the next number in each sequence. Justify your answer.**

57. 1.2, 3.6, 10.8, 32.4, …

58. 1, 0.2, 0.04, 0.008, …

EXTRA PRACTICE
See pages 723, 757.
Math Online
Self-Check Quiz at tx.msmath2.com

59. **COOKING** A casserole calls for 1.5 pounds of ground beef. Ground beef is on sale for $1.98 per pound. Estimate the cost of the ground beef needed to make 3 casseroles. Then find the actual cost. Is your estimate reasonable? Explain your reasoning.

H.O.T. Problems

CHALLENGE **Find each square root.**

60. $\sqrt{0.16}$

61. $\sqrt{0.25}$

62. $\sqrt{2.25}$

63. $\sqrt{1.44}$

REASONING **Tell whether each statement is *sometimes*, *always*, or *never* true. Give an example or counterexample for each.**

64. When two decimals, both less than 1, are multiplied, the product is less than 1.

65. When two decimals, both greater than 1, are multiplied, the product is less than both of the factors.

66. **OPEN ENDED** Write a multiplication expression where both factors are decimals and the product is between 3 and 4.

67. **SELECT A TECHNIQUE** Julia is trying to determine whether 125×0.9 is greater than, less than, or equal to 125. Which of the following techniques might Julia use to determine the answer? Justify your selection(s). Then use the technique(s) to solve the problem.

mental math | number sense | estimation

68. **WRITING IN MATH** Write about a real-world situation that can be solved by multiplying decimals.

TEST PRACTICE

69. **GRIDDABLE** The table shows the average number of hours of sleep per day for three mammals.

Animal	Time Asleep (h/day)
Lion	20.0
Opossum	19.4
Giant Armadillo	18.1

Source: *Top Ten of Everything*

How many more hours will an opossum sleep in a year than a giant armadillo?

70. Which expression does the decimal model represent?

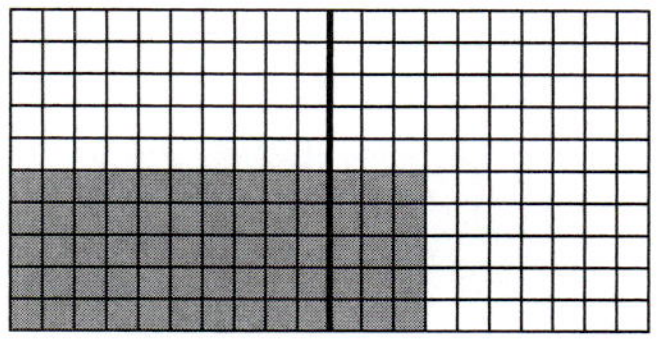

A 0.5×1.3

B 1.5×0.3

C 0.05×1.3

D 5×13

Spiral Review

Estimate. (Lesson 3-1)

71. 47.2×1.8

72. $17.2 \div 3.3$

73. $73.5 \div 24.1$

Divide. (Lesson 2-8)

74. $-48 \div (-3)$

75. $-63 \div 9$

76. $72 \div (-4)$

77. **ALGEBRA** Jennifer has 2 rolls of film with 36 exposures and 3 rolls of film with 24 exposures. Write a numerical expression that you could use to find the total number of photos Jennifer can take. (Lesson 1-6)

GET READY for the Next Lesson

PREREQUISITE SKILL **Evaluate.** (Lesson 1-2)

78. 10^1

79. 10^3

80. 10^5

3-3 Multiplying by Powers of Ten

Main IDEA

Multiply decimals mentally by powers of ten.

Targeted TEKS 7.2 The student adds, subtracts, multiplies, or divides to solve problems and justify solutions. **(A) represent multiplication** and division **situations involving** fractions and **decimals with models including** concrete objects, pictures, **words and numbers.** *Also addresses TEKS 7.2(B).*

MINI Lab

Numbers like 10, 100, and 1,000 are called *powers of 10* because they can be obtained by raising 10 to a whole number power.

1. Copy and complete the table shown.

Decimal		Power of 10		Product
1.24	×	1	=	1.24
1.24	×	10	=	12.4
1.24	×	100	=	■
1.24	×	1,000	=	■
1.24	×	10,000	=	■

2. Look for a pattern in the products. Write one or two sentences that describe this pattern.
3. How can you find the product of a number and a power of 10 without using paper or pencil or a calculator?

Multiplying a decimal by a power of 10 moves the decimal point to the right the same number of places as the number of zeros in the power of 10.

EXAMPLES Multiply by Power of Ten Greater than 1

Find each product.

1 **0.35 × 100**

$0.35 \times 100 = 0.35$ — 100 has 2 zeros, so move the decimal point 2 places to the right.

$= 35$ — Since 35 is a whole number, remove the leading zero and decimal point.

2 **8.5 × 1,000**

$8.5 \times 1{,}000 = 8.500$ — 1,000 has 3 zeros, so move the decimal point 3 places to the right. Annex zeros as needed.

$= 8{,}500$ — Remove the decimal point and add a comma.

STUDY TIP

Check for Reasonableness The product of a number and a power of ten that is *greater than* 1 will always be greater than the original number.

CHECK Your Progress

Find each product.

a. 2.72 × 1,000

b. 5.98 × 10,000

Real-World EXAMPLE

REVIEW Vocabulary

standard form a number written without exponents; *Example*: 4,800 (Lesson 1-2)

3 VIDEO GAMES In a recent year, a football video game sold 3.2 million copies. Write this number in standard form.

3.2 million = 3.2 × 1,000,000 — The word *million* means 1,000,000.

= 3.200000 — 1,000,000 has 6 zeros. So, move the decimal point 6 places to the right. Annex zeros as needed.

= 3,200,000 — Remove the decimal point and add commas.

So, 3,200,000 copies of the video game were sold.

CHECK Your Progress

c. **ROADS** There are about 3.9 million miles of roads in the United States. Write the amount of roads in standard form.

d. **SUN** The diameter of the Sun is about 1.39 million kilometers. Write this diameter in standard form.

Online **Personal Tutor at** tx.msmath2.com

A similar pattern is found when multiplying a decimal by powers of 10 like 0.1 and 0.01 that are less than one. In these numbers, $0.1 = \frac{1}{10}$ and $0.01 = \frac{1}{100}$.

STUDY TIP

Check for Reasonableness The product of a number and a decimal between 0 and 1 is always *less than* the original number.

Decimal		Power of 10		Product
12.4	×	0.1	=	1.24
12.4	×	0.01	=	0.124
12.4	×	0.001	=	0.0124

The table above suggests that multiplying a decimal by a power of 10 less than one moves the decimal point to the *left* the same number of places as there are after the decimal point.

EXAMPLE Multiply by a Power of Ten Less than One

4 Find 5.4 × 0.01.

5.4 × 0.01 = 05.4 — There are 2 places after the decimal point, so move the decimal point 2 places to the left.

= 0.054 — Annex zeros as needed.

CHECK Your Progress

Find each product.

e. 93.6 × 0.1

f. 7.84 × 0.001

Real-World Link
The original Goddess of Liberty statue was about $\frac{1}{10}$ the height of the Statue of Liberty.
Source: *Texas Senate Media Services*

Real-World EXAMPLE

5 **STATUES** **The height of the Statue of Liberty from base to torch is about 152 feet. Use this information and the information at the left to find the height of the original Goddess of Liberty statue that once stood atop the Texas capitol.**

The fraction $\frac{1}{10}$ can be written as 0.1.

Words	Goddess of Liberty's height	was	$\frac{1}{10}$	of	Statue of Liberty's height
Variable	Let h represent the height of the Goddess of Liberty.				
Equation	h	=	0.1	×	152

$h = 0.1 \times 152$ — Write the equation.

$h = 152.$ — There is 1 place after the decimal point. So, move the decimal point 1 place to the left.

$h = 15.2$

The height of the original Goddess of Liberty statue was about 15.2 feet.

CHECK Your Progress

g. **SCHOOL** There are 730 students enrolled at Harrison Middle School. Next school year, enrollment is expected to increase by $\frac{1}{10}$. By how many students will enrollment increase?

CHECK Your Understanding

Examples 1, 2 (p. 140)

Find each product.

1. 0.67×10
2. 1.6×100
3. $8.95 \times 1{,}000$

Example 3 (p. 141)

4. **SPORTS** The seasonal attendance at a baseball stadium was 3.45 million people. Write the number of people in standard form.

Example 4 (p. 141)

Find each product.

5. 0.45×0.1
6. 0.8×0.01
7. 3.2×0.001

Example 5 (p. 142)

8. **PETS** The number of registered Aby cats in the U.S. is about $\frac{1}{100}$ the number of registered Labrador retriever dogs. If there are about 140,000 Labs registered in the U.S., about how many Aby cats are registered? (*Hint*: $\frac{1}{100} = 0.01$)

Exercises

HOMEWORK HELP	
For Exercises	See Examples
9–20	1, 2
21–22	3
23–34	4
35–36	5

Find each product.

9. 0.25×100 **10.** 6.55×100 **11.** 0.9×10

12. 3.48×10 **13.** $7.62 \times 1{,}000$ **14.** $0.5 \times 1{,}000$

15. 0.67×10 **16.** 3.8×10 **17.** $9.53 \times 10{,}000$

18. $8.125 \times 10{,}000$ **19.** $17.201 \times 1{,}000$ **20.** $18.50 \times 1{,}000$

Write each number in standard form.

21. **SCIENCE** The planet Mercury is 28.6 million miles from the Sun.

22. **ART** The most expensive painting by a female artist sold for 5.6 million dollars.

Find each product.

23. 0.3×0.01 **24.** 4.63×0.01 **25.** 8.7×0.1

26. 16.89×0.1 **27.** 0.346×0.01 **28.** 5.872×0.01

29. 0.02×0.1 **30.** 0.007×0.1 **31.** 0.45×0.001

32. 23.5×0.001 **33.** 0.03×0.001 **34.** 345.69×0.001

35. **MONEY** If a jar of mushrooms costs $0.89, what will be the total cost of 100 jars of mushrooms?

36. **SPACE** The diameter of the Sun is about 864,000 miles. Which planet has a diameter that is about 0.1 the diameter of the Sun?

Planet	Diameter (mi)
Venus	7,521
Jupiter	88,732
Earth	7,926
Saturn	74,975

Source: *The World Almanac*

Find each product.

37. 0.78×10^2 **38.** 3.651×10^4 **39.** $0.75 \times \frac{1}{10^2}$

40. 23.89×10^3 **41.** $34.1 \times \frac{1}{10^3}$ **42.** 54.02×0.001

ALGEBRA **Evaluate each expression if $a = 0.1$, $b = 0.01$, and $c = 10$.**

43. $3.2a$ **44.** $1.47 \times c^3$ **45.** $12 \times b$ **46.** $c^4 \times 8.4$

47. **MONEY** The soccer ball shown is on sale for one tenth off the original price. What will be the sale price?

48. **MOVIES** One week, a movie theater sold 6,500 tickets. The next week, the number of tickets sold decreased by one-hundredth. How many tickets were sold in the second week?

EXTRA PRACTICE
See pages 723, 757.
Math Online
Self-Check Quiz at tx.msmath2.com

H.O.T. Problems

49. **CHALLENGE** Explain how you could find the product of 0.3 and a number mentally. Then use your method to find 0.3×25.

50. **FIND THE ERROR** Dario and Olivia are finding 0.60×10^3 mentally. Who is correct? Explain.

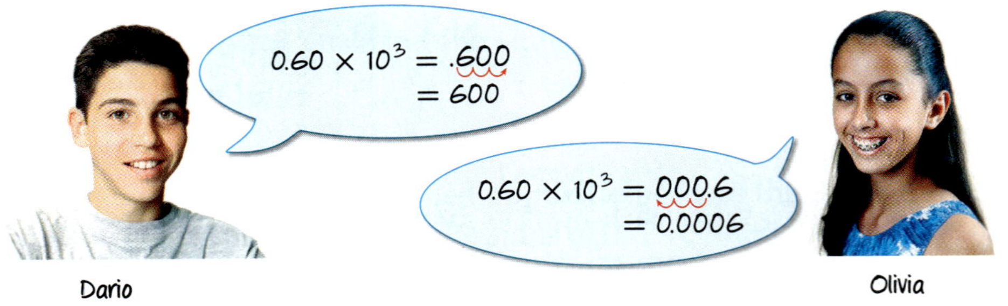

51. **WRITING IN MATH** Suppose you plan to purchase 10 items that each cost \$4.95. Explain how you can mentally find the cost of the 10 items.

TEST PRACTICE

52. Which item listed costs about one hundred times more than a snack bar?

Item	Price ($)
Television	498.95
Lunch Combo	5.25
6-pack Soft Drink	3.25
Snack Bar	0.50
Pair of Shoes	49.98

A 6-pack soft drink
B pair of shoes
C lunch combo
D television

53. The length of a blue whale is approximately 10 times the length of a polar bear. What is the approximate length of a blue whale?

F 0.75 feet
G 7.5 feet
H 75 feet
J 750 feet

Spiral Review

Multiply. (Lesson 3-2)

54. 0.8×7
55. 5.1×4.3
56. 5.82×4.9
57. 0.083×0.24

Estimate. (Lesson 3-1)

58. 2.8×9
59. 32.1×7.8
60. $46.8 \div 1.8$
61. $4.6\overline{)43.1}$

62. **NUMBERS** The number one trillion is written as 1,000,000,000,000. Write this number in exponential form as a power of 10. (Lesson 1-2)

GET READY for the Next Lesson

PREREQUISITE SKILL **Divide.**

63. $16 \div 5$
64. $74 \div 8$
65. $110 \div 4$
66. $257 \div 8$

Explore 3-4

Math Lab
Division with Decimal Models

Main IDEA

Divide decimals using decimal models.

Targeted TEKS 7.2 The student adds, subtracts, multiplies, or divides to solve problems and justify solutions **(A) represent** multiplication and **division situations involving** fractions and **decimals with models, including concrete objects, pictures,** words, **and numbers.**

Concepts in Motion
Animation tx.msmath2.com

You can use decimal models to divide decimals.

ACTIVITY

1 **Find 2.6 ÷ 2 using decimal models.**

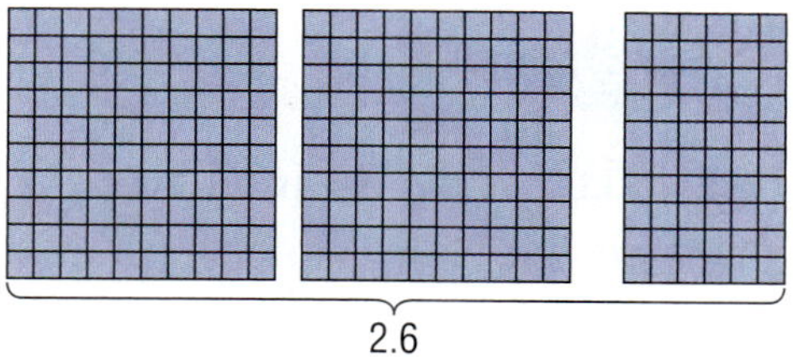

Use two decimal models and 6 tenths to represent 2.6.

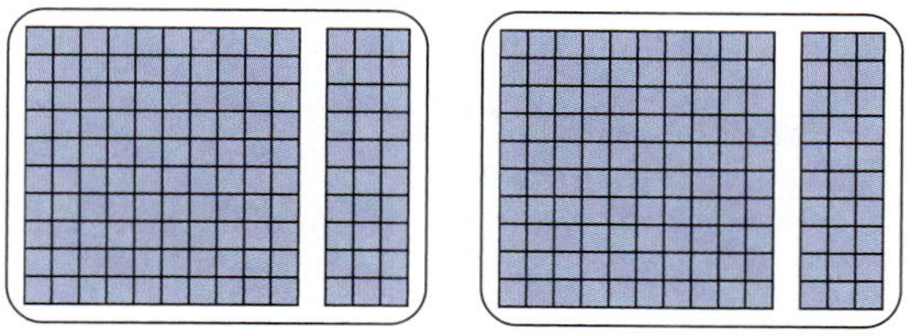

Separate the models into two equal groups.

Each group contains one whole and 3 tenths. So, 2.6 ÷ 2 = 1.3.

CHECK Your Progress

Use decimal models to find each quotient.

a. 4.8 ÷ 2 **b.** 3.9 ÷ 3 **c.** 1.2 ÷ 4 **d.** 0.54 ÷ 3

ACTIVITY

2 **Find 1.8 ÷ 0.3 using decimal models.**

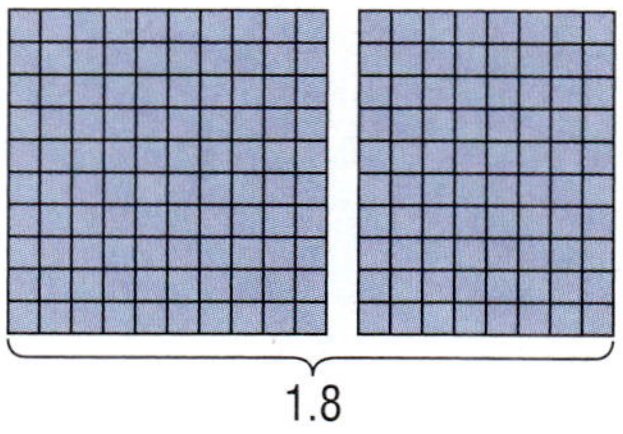

Draw one decimal model and 8 tenths to represent 1.8.

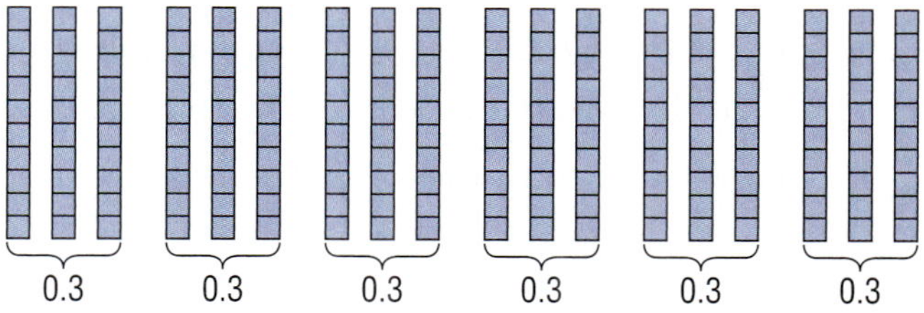

Replace the whole decimal model with tenths. Then separate the tenths into groups of three tenths to represent dividing by 0.3.

There are six groups of three tenths. So, 1.8 ÷ 0.3 = 6.

CHECK Your Progress

Use decimal models to find each quotient.

e. $1.6 \div 0.4$ **f.** $1.5 \div 0.3$ **g.** $2.4 \div 0.8$ **h.** $2.7 \div 0.9$

ACTIVITY

3 **Find 0.2 ÷ 0.05 using decimal models.**

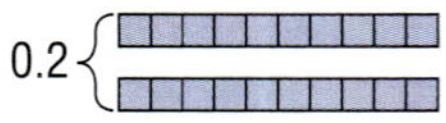

Use two tenths to represent 0.2.

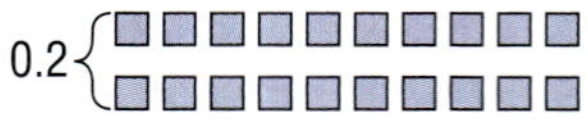

Replace the tenths with hundredths since you are dividing by hundredths.

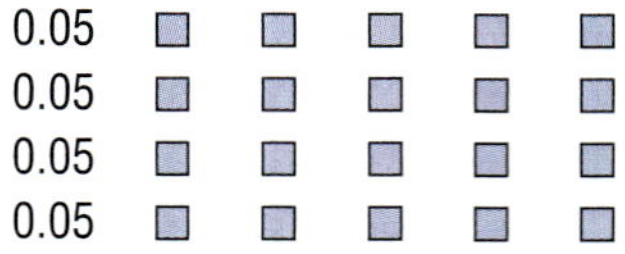

Separate the hundredths into groups of five hundredths to represent dividing by 0.05.

There are four groups of five hundredths in 0.2. So, $0.2 \div 0.05 = 4$.

CHECK Your Progress

Use decimal models to find each quotient.

i. $0.4 \div 0.08$ **j.** $0.3 \div 0.03$ **k.** $0.8 \div 0.04$ **l.** $0.6 \div 0.05$

Analyze the Results

1. Use decimal models to find $2.8 \div 4$. What is $28 \div 4$? How do the quotients compare?
2. **MAKE A CONJECTURE** Use the result from Exercise 1 and Exercises a–d to devise a rule for how to divide a decimal by a whole number.
3. Refer to Activities 2 and 3. Tell why the decimal model representing the dividend needs to be separated into the smallest place value of the divisor.
4. Explain why the quotient $0.6 \div 0.03$ is a whole number. What does the quotient represent?
5. Find the missing divisor in $0.4 \div$ ■ $= 2$. Explain your reasoning.

3-4 Dividing Decimals

Main IDEA

Divide decimals.

Targeted TEKS 7.2 The student adds, subtracts, multiplies, or divides to solve problems and justify solutions. **(A) represent** multiplication and **division situations involving** fractions and **decimals with models, including concrete objects, pictures, words, and numbers.** *Also addresses TEKS 7.2(B), 7.2(G).*

GET READY for the Lesson

MEASUREMENT Luis has two plastic straws that each need to be cut into 3 pieces of equal length. The problems below show how Luis used division to find the lengths of the cut pieces.

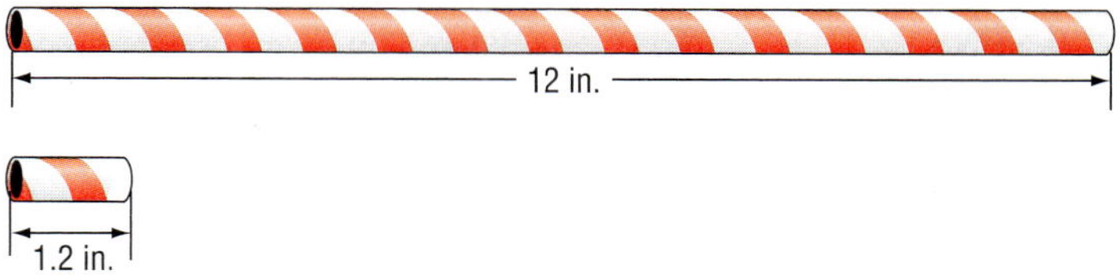

12-inch straw

$$\begin{array}{r} 4 \\ 3\overline{)12} \\ -12 \\ \hline 0 \end{array}$$

Each piece will be 4 inches long.

1.2-inch straw

$$\begin{array}{r} 0.4 \\ 3\overline{)1.2} \\ -12 \\ \hline 0 \end{array}$$

Each piece will be 0.4 inches long.

1. Compare the digits in the division problems.
2. What do you notice about the steps of the division process?
3. Describe the place value of the quotient. Explain your answer.

Dividing a decimal by a whole number is similar to dividing whole numbers.

EXAMPLE Divide Decimal by a Whole Number

1 **Find 7.6 ÷ 4.** **Estimate** $7.6 \div 4 \approx 8 \div 4$ or 2

$$\begin{array}{r} 1.9 \\ 4\overline{)\,7.6} \\ -\,4 \\ \hline 36 \\ -\,36 \\ \hline 0 \end{array}$$

Place the decimal point directly above the decimal point in the dividend.

Divide as with whole numbers.

$7.6 \div 4 = 1.9$ **Check for Reasonableness** $1.9 \approx 2$ ✔

STUDY TIP

Check for Accuracy To check that the answer is correct, multiply the quotient by the divisor. In Example 1, $1.9 \times 4 = 7.6$.

CHECK Your Progress

Divide.

a. $5.4 \div 3$ b. $12.9 \div 6$ c. $6.3 \div 6$

Real-World Link Hockey skates are fitted with a 0.06-inch wide blade whereas figure skates have a 0.125-inch blade.

Real-World EXAMPLE

2 **SKATING** **The charge for 5 adult admission tickets to an ice rink is \$26.25. What is the cost for each ticket?**

Estimate $26.25 \div 5 \approx 25 \div 5$ or 5

$$\begin{array}{r} 5.25 \\ 5\overline{)26.25} \\ -25 \\ \hline 12 \\ -10 \\ \hline 25 \\ -25 \\ \hline 0 \end{array}$$

The cost for each ticket was \$5.25.

Check for Reasonableness $5.25 \approx 5$ ✔

CHECK Your Progress

d. **MEASUREMENT** You have 16.8 ounces of juice to divide into 4 equal servings. How many ounces will each serving be?

To divide by a decimal, change the divisor to a whole number. To do this, multiply both the divisor and dividend by the same power of ten. Then divide as with whole numbers.

divisor → $0.5\overline{)4.5}$ ← dividend

EXAMPLE Divide a Decimal by a Decimal

3 **Find 6.49 ÷ 2.2.** **Estimate** $6.49 \div 2.2 \approx 6 \div 2$ or 3

To change to a whole number, multiply by 10.

$2.2\overline{)6.49}$ →

$$\begin{array}{r} 2.95 \\ 22\overline{)64.90} \\ -44 \\ \hline 209 \\ -198 \\ \hline 110 \\ -110 \\ \hline 0 \end{array}$$

Place the decimal point. Divide as with whole numbers.

Multiply by the same number, 10.

Annex a zero and continue.

So, $6.49 \div 2.2$ is 2.95. **Check for Reasonableness** $2.95 \approx 3$ ✔

CHECK Your Progress

Divide.

e. $22.1 \div 3.4$

f. $7.82 \div 4.6$

EXAMPLE Zeros in the Quotient and Dividend

4 **Find 128.8 ÷ 0.92.** **Estimate** $128.8 \div 0.92 \approx 130 \div 1$ or 130

To change to a whole number, multiply by 10^2 or 100.

$0.92\overline{)128.80}$ →

$$\begin{array}{r} 140. \\ 92\overline{)12880.} \\ -92 \\ \hline 368 \\ -368 \\ \hline 00 \end{array}$$

Multiply by the same number, 100.

Place the decimal point. Divide as with whole numbers.

Write a zero in the ones place of the quotient since $0 \div 92 = 0$.

So, $128.8 \div 0.92$ is 140.

Check for Reasonableness $140 \approx 130$ ✔

CHECK Your Progress **Divide.**

g. $199.68 \div 9.6$

h. $74.9\overline{)5.992}$

TEST EXAMPLE

5 **GRIDDABLE** The Thompson family purchased 8.8 gallons of gasoline for $18.04. How much did they pay per gallon?

Read the Test Item

To find the price per gallon, divide the total cost by the number of gallons purchased. Round to the nearest cent, or hundredths place, if necessary.

Solve the Test Item

$8.8\overline{)18.04}$ →

$$\begin{array}{r} 2.05 \\ 88.\overline{)180.40} \\ -176 \\ \hline 44 \\ -0 \\ \hline 440 \\ -440 \\ \hline 0 \end{array}$$

Multiply each by 10.

Fill in the Grid

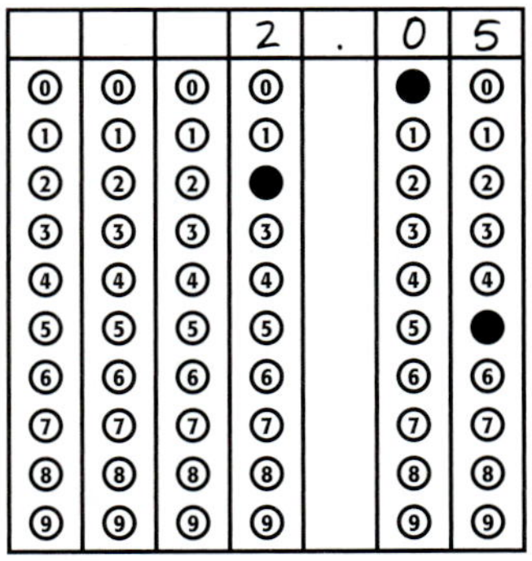

Test-Taking Tip

Fill in the Grid Write 2.05 in the answer boxes at the top of the grid. Then be sure to grid in 2 and 05 with respect to the given decimal point.

CHECK Your Progress

i. **GRIDDABLE** Mrs. Myers bought 2.5 pounds of hamburger for $5.20. How much did she pay in dollars per pound?

Online Personal Tutor at tx.msmath2.com

CHECK Your Understanding

Example 1 (p. 147)

Divide.

1. $8.7 \div 3$
2. $5.8 \div 4$
3. $4.36 \div 4$

Example 2 (p. 148)

4. **MONEY** Melissa bought 3 yards of fabric for a total of $11.37. How much did she pay for each yard of fabric?

Examples 3, 4 (pp. 148–149)

Divide.

5. $9.81 \div 0.3$
6. $5.76 \div 3.2$
7. $0.003\overline{)2.475}$
8. $14.4 \div 0.12$
9. $0.22\overline{)0.0132}$
10. $0.5\overline{)85}$

Example 5 (p. 149)

11. **TEST PRACTICE** Kenji walked 3.4 miles in 69.6 minutes. At this rate, how many minutes did it take Kenji to walk each mile? Round to the nearest tenth if necessary.

Exercises

HOMEWORK HELP

For Exercises	See Examples
12–23	1
24–25	2
26–39	3, 4
58–60	5

Divide.

12. $6.4 \div 2$
13. $4\overline{)7.2}$
14. $12.8 \div 8$
15. $25.2 \div 7$
16. $6.24 \div 4$
17. $7\overline{)7.56}$
18. $6\overline{)2.7}$
19. $4.4 \div 5$
20. $4.05 \div 3$
21. $6.09 \div 5$
22. $5\overline{)0.028}$
23. $0.045 \div 6$

24. **MONEY** Karen bought 4 picture frames for a total of $23.96. If each picture frame cost the same, how much did each picture frame cost?

25. **NUTRITION** There are 74.4 grams of sugar in 3 servings of grapes. How many grams of sugar are in a single serving of grapes?

Divide.

26. $0.34 \div 0.2$
27. $0.2\overline{)8.24}$
28. $1.6\overline{)0.768}$
29. $0.238 \div 1.7$
30. $1.45\overline{)130.5}$
31. $8.23\overline{)82.3}$
32. $3.18\overline{)63.6}$
33. $0.82 \div 0.4$
34. $90.175 \div 2.5$
35. $1.9\overline{)38.57}$
36. $20.24 \div 2.3$
37. $13.8\overline{)131.1}$

38. **TRAVEL** Zu-Wang traveled 67.5 miles in 1.5 hours. Find the speed at which she traveled if her speed stayed the same without stopping.

39. **MONEY** Justin spent $1.62 on 3.3 pounds of bananas. To the nearest cent, what was the cost of the bananas per pound?

Evaluate each expression.

40. $(4.2 \times 9) \div 3.5$
41. $22 - 12.6 \div 4$
42. $24.75 \div (1.5 + 4)$

Evaluate each expression if $g = 0.25$, $h =$ one and eight-tenths, and $j = 6$.

43. $h \div g$ 44. $h \div j$ 45. $3j \div h$

Real-World Link The game of bocce is played with eight large bocce balls and one small target ball called the pallino. **Source:** bocce.com

46. **SPORTS** The approximate size of a bocce court and a shuffleboard court is shown. To the nearest tenth, how many times larger is a bocce court than a shuffleboard court?

Bocce	Shuffleboard
109.9 square meters	21.7 square meters

47. **TRACK** Lindsay is on her school track team. At the last track meet, she ran the 400-meter event in 50.26 seconds. To the nearest tenth, find her speed in meters per second.

48. **SPACE** The table shows how many Earth years it takes four of the planets to revolve around the Sun. How many times longer does it take Pluto than Jupiter to revolve around the Sun? Round to the nearest tenth.

Planet	Revolution
Pluto	248.5
Jupiter	11.9
Saturn	29.5
Neptune	164.8

Source: *Time for Kids Almanac*

49. **GEOGRAPHY** Potter County in Texas has an area of 921.98 square miles. Rockwall County in Texas has an area of 148.7 square miles. How many times larger is Potter County than Rockwall County?

ANALYZE TABLES For Exercises 50 and 51, refer to the table that shows the size and cost of two different packages of fruit chews.

Fruit Chews		
Bag	**Cost**	**Size of Bags**
Large-sized	\$4.89	13 ounce
Regular-sized	\$2.59	6.5 ounce

50. Which package costs less per ounce?

51. Would it make sense to buy one large package or two regular packages? Explain your reasoning.

EXTRA PRACTICE
See pages 724, 757.
Math Online
Self-Check Quiz at tx.msmath2.com

52. **FIND THE DATA** Refer to the Texas Data File on pages 16–19. Choose some data and write a real-world problem in which you would divide decimals.

H.O.T. Problems

53. **CHALLENGE** Provide a counterexample to the following statement.

Division of decimals is commutative.

54. **OPEN ENDED** Give an example of a division problem in which it is necessary to annex one or more zeros to the dividend.

55. **Which One Doesn't Belong?** Without actually dividing, identify the quotient that is NOT greater than 1. Explain your reasoning.

$2.4 \div 6$ $2.4 \div 0.06$ $2.4 \div 0.6$ $2.4 \div 0.006$

56. **CHALLENGE** One rectangle has an area of 3.42 square feet. Another rectangle has an area of 2.36 square feet. Which rectangle is wider if the length of both rectangles is 0.4 feet? Explain your answer. (*Hint*: Area = length × width)

57. **WRITING IN MATH** Explain how you can use estimation to place the decimal point in the quotient.

TEST PRACTICE

58. The table shows the cost of four different-sized jars of peanut butter. Which jar costs the least per ounce?

Size	Price
12-ounce	1.99
16-ounce	2.85
28-ounce	3.79
32-ounce	4.49

A 12-ounce **C** 28-ounce

B 16-ounce **D** 32-ounce

59. **GRIDDABLE** Suppose you have 6.5 feet of ribbon that you need to cut into 0.25-foot lengths. How many pieces of ribbon will you have?

60. **GRIDDABLE** How many 0.75 pound bags of cashews can be made from 4.5 pounds of cashews?

Spiral Review

Multiply mentally. (Lesson 3-3)

61. 0.85 × 10 62. 4.68 × 0.001 63. 0.572 × 0.1

64. **DISTANCE** The round trip from Terrance's home to the park is 1.2 miles. If he walks to the park every day for 4 days, how far does he walk? (Lesson 3-2)

Estimate. (Lesson 3-1)

65. 6.8 + 21.1 66. 67.4 − 29.4 67. 11.3 × 57.4 68. 23.5 ÷ 7.6

69. **TEMPERATURE** The daily temperatures for Boise, Idaho for one week in July were 88°F, 85°F, 87°F, 84°F, 86°F, 83°F, and 85°F. Look for a pattern. If this pattern continues, what will the daily temperatures be for the next three days? (Lesson 2-6)

Order each set of integers from least to greatest. (Lesson 2-2)

70. 4, 0, −5, −7, 3 71. −8, 8, 7, −2, −5 72. −12, 1, 6, 8, 0, −4, −3

GET READY for the Next Lesson

73. **PREREQUISITE SKILL** Four added to the product of a decimal and 3 is 9.1. What is the number? Use the *guess and check* strategy. (Lesson 1-5)

CHAPTER 3

Mid-Chapter Quiz

Lessons 3-1 through 3-4

1. **TEST PRACTICE** A pound of peanuts costs $0.88. If Shelby bought 4.5 pounds of peanuts, about how much did she pay for them? (Lesson 3-1)
   - **A** Less than $1.00
   - **B** Between $1.00 and $3.00
   - **C** Between $3.00 and $5.00
   - **D** More than $5.00

Estimate each product or quotient. (Lesson 3-1)

2. 5.3×7.8
3. 42.3×18.9
4. $41.6 \div 7.7$
5. $3.9\overline{)57.8}$

6. **RECREATION** Mr. Ramirez bought 2 adult tickets and 3 children's tickets for his family to attend a popular theme park. The table below lists the prices of admission to the park.

Ticket	Price
Children under 4	Free
Children (ages 4–12)	$22.98
Adult	$37.40
Senior Citizen	$17.85

How much did Mr. Ramirez spend on admission to the park? (Lesson 3-2)

Multiply. (Lesson 3-2)

7. 0.013×4
8. 5.62×3.7

9. **RENTALS** A car rental company charges $19.50 per day to rent a car plus $0.10 for each mile traveled. Find the total cost of renting a car for 3 days if you drive 875 miles. (Lessons 3-2 and 3-3)

Find each product. (Lesson 3-3)

10. $7.15 \times 1{,}000$
11. 21.304×0.1
12. 0.062×0.001
13. $0.009 \times 10{,}000$

14. **SCIENCE** Earth is about 93 million miles away from the Sun. Write this distance in standard form. (Lesson 3-3)

Divide. (Lesson 3-4)

15. $62.65 \div 7$
16. $3.4\overline{)26.35}$
17. $0.01\overline{)19}$
18. $0.6344 \div 0.13$

19. **WEATHER** The normal average precipitation for Orange on the Gulf Coast of Texas is 58.3 inches, while El Paso in West Texas averages only 8.8 inches annually. How many times greater is the normal average precipitation for Orange than for El Paso? (Lesson 3-4)

20. **TEST PRACTICE** The prices of three different packages of ground hamburger are given in the table.

Type	Weight (pounds)	Price
Sirloin	5	$14.90
Chuck	3	$7.92
Ground Round	6	$15.84

Which of the following costs the least per pound? (Lesson 3-4)

- **F** The sirloin and ground chuck
- **G** The ground chuck only
- **H** The ground round only
- **J** The ground chuck and ground round

3-5 Problem-Solving Investigation

MAIN IDEA: Choose the best method of computation.

Targeted TEKS 7.2 The student adds, subtracts, multiplies, and divides to solve problems and justify solutions **(F) select and use appropriate operations to solve problems and justify the selections.** *Also addresses TEKS 7.13(B).*

P.S.I. TEAM +

e-Mail: CHOOSE THE BEST METHOD OF COMPUTATION

YOUR MISSION: Choose mental math, estimation, paper or pencil, or a calculator to solve the problem.

THE PROBLEM: About how much more will my older brother spend if he buys an MP3 player?

> Winona: My older brother wants to buy either a DVD player for his room or an MP3 player. The DVD player costs \$105.99. The MP3 player costs \$249.99.

EXPLORE	You know the cost of the DVD player and the cost of the MP3 player. You need to find *about* how much more the MP3 player costs than the DVD player.
PLAN	Since an exact answer is not needed, estimate.
SOLVE	\$249.99 → \$250 Round \$249.99 to \$250. − \$105.99 → − \$100 Round \$105.99 to \$100. \$150 So, the MP3 player costs about \$150 more than the DVD player.
CHECK	You know that subtraction and addition are inverse operations. Since \$150 + \$100 = \$250, the answer is correct.

Analyze The Strategy

1. Explain when you should use a calculator to solve a problem.
2. Explain when paper and pencil would be the most appropriate method to use.
3. **WRITING IN MATH** Write a problem that can be solved by using mental math. Then explain how to solve it.

Mixed Problem Solving

For Exercises 4–7, choose the best method of computation. Then use the method to solve the problem.

4. **HOBBIES** Yago has exactly \$36.12 to spend on scrapbooking supplies. If each package of stickers costs \$3.95, about how many packages can she buy?

5. **MEASUREMENT** A furlong is a unit of length exactly equal to 201.168 meters and is often used in the length of horse races. If a race is 5.75 furlongs, how long is the race in meters?

6. **BANKING** About how many automated teller machine (ATM) transactions were made in the U.S. in the five-year period?

U.S. ATM Transactions	
Year	**Number (billion)**
2000	12.8
2001	13.6
2002	10.5
2003	10.8
2004	11.0

Source: *Financial Services Fact Book*

7. **PIZZA** The total cost of pizza was shared equally among 6 friends. If the pizza cost \$18.60, how much did each friend pay?

Use any strategy to solve Exercises 8–11. Some strategies are shown below.

PROBLEM-SOLVING STRATEGIES
- Use the four-step plan.
- Guess and check.

8. **NUMBERS** A number is multiplied by 27. Then 2 is added to the product. The result is 947. What is the number?

9. **SCIENCE** Earth travels at about 67×10^3 miles per hour around the Sun. It takes 365.25 days for Earth to travel around the Sun. How long is Earth's orbit?

10. **HURRICANES** As hurricanes gain strength, their central pressure decreases. The table below lists several hurricanes and their central pressure, in pounds per square inch.

Year	Hurricane	Pressure
1967	Beulah	27.17
1980	Allen	26.55
1988	Gilbert	26.23
1999	Brett	29.32

Source: noaa.gov

Which two hurricanes have central pressures that differ by 2.77 inches?

11. **HIGHWAYS** In a recent year, there were 6,393,603 kilometers of roadways in the U.S. If about 4,180,000 kilometers of roadways were paved, about how many roadways were unpaved?

Select the Operation

For Exercises 12 and 13, select the appropriate operation(s) to solve the problem. Justify your selection(s) and solve the problem.

12. **ANALYZE TABLES** The table gives the average annual consumption, in pounds per person, of several foods in the U.S.

Year	Red Meat	Poultry	Fish & Shellfish
1910	125.9	16.0	11.2
1940	124.3	14.6	11.0
1970	145.1	40.1	11.7
2000	120.2	77.4	15.2
2002	120.5	81.0	15.6

Source: *The World Almanac*

How many more pounds per year did the average person eat in 2002 than in 1910?

13. **SKATEBOARD** In April, Mia had saved \$44.80 towards the purchase of a new skateboard. Over the next four months, she saved the same amount each month and had a total of \$173.20 saved. How much money did she save each month?

READING Word Problems

Use a Definition Map

The key to understanding word problems is to understand the definition of new vocabulary words. A *definition map* can help you visualize the parts of a good definition. Ask yourself these questions about the vocabulary terms.

- What is it? (Category)
- What can it be compared to? (Comparisons)
- What is it like? (Properties)
- What are some examples? (Illustrations)

Here's a definition map for *millimeter*. You'll learn about millimeters in the next lesson.

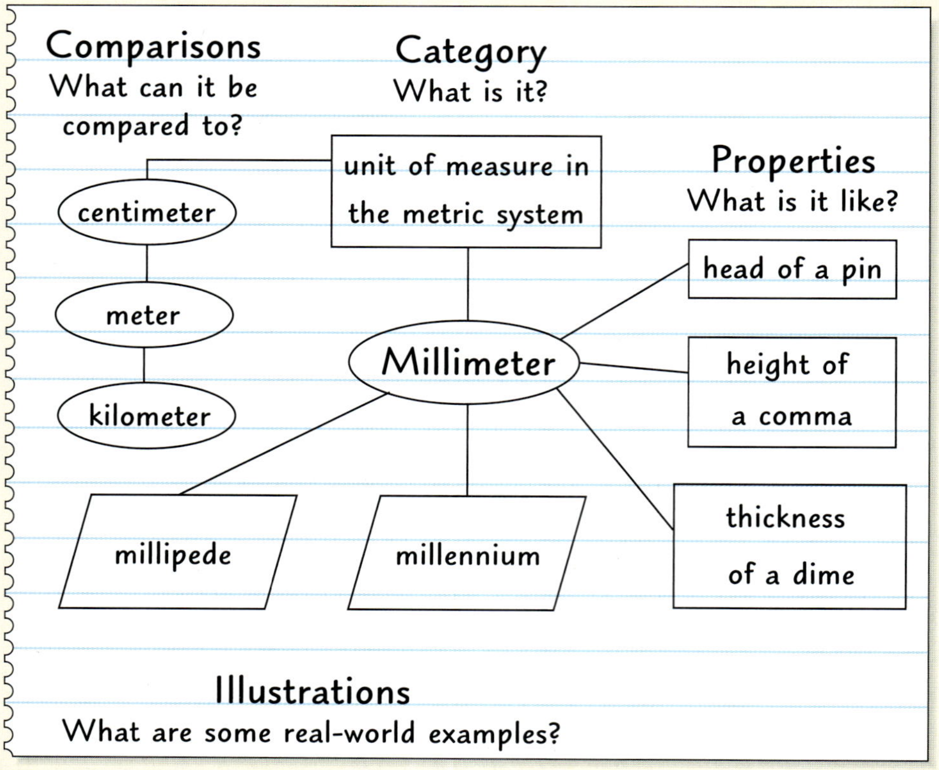

PRACTICE

Make a definition map for each term.

1. centimeter (page 157)
2. gram (page 157)
3. integer (page 80)
4. sequence (page 57)

3-6 Measurement: The Metric System

Main IDEA

Change metric units of length, capacity, and mass.

Reinforcement of TEKS 6.8 The student solves application problems involving estimation and measurement of length, area, time, temperature, volume, weight, and angles. **(D) convert measures within the same measurement system** (customary and **metric**) **based on relationships between units.** *Also addresses TEKS 7.3(B), 7.4(A).*

NEW Vocabulary

metric system
meter
liter
gram
kilogram

MINI Lab

The lengths of two objects are shown below.

Object	Length (millimeters)	Length (centimeters)
paper clip	45	4.5
CD case	144	14.4

1. Select three other objects. Find and record the width of all five objects to the nearest millimeter and tenth of a centimeter.
2. Compare the measurements of the objects, and write a rule that describes how to convert from millimeters to centimeters.
3. Measure the length of your classroom in meters. Make a conjecture about how to convert this measure to centimeters. Explain.

The **metric system** is a decimal system of measures. The prefixes commonly used in this system are kilo-, centi-, and milli-.

Prefix	Meaning In Words	Meaning In Numbers
kilo-	thousands	1,000
centi-	hundredths	0.01
milli-	thousandths	0.001

In the metric system, the base unit of *length* is the **meter** (m). Using the prefixes, the names of other units of length are formed. Notice that the prefixes tell you how the units relate to the meter.

Unit	Symbol	Relationship to Meter	
kilometer	km	1 km = 1,000 m	1 m = 0.001 km
meter	m	1 m = 1 m	
centimeter	cm	1 cm = 0.01 m	1 m = 100 cm
millimeter	mm	1 mm = 0.001 m	1 m = 1,000 mm

The **liter** (L) is the base unit of *capacity*, the amount of dry or liquid material an object can hold. The **gram** (g) measures *mass*, the amount of matter in an object. The prefixes can also be applied to these units. Whereas the meter and liter are the base units of length and capacity, the base unit of mass is the **kilogram** (kg).

To change a metric measure of length, mass, or capacity from one unit to another, you can use the relationship between the two units and multiplication by a power of 10.

EXAMPLES Convert Units in the Metric System

STUDY TIP

Metric Conversions When converting from a larger unit to a smaller unit, the power of ten being multiplied will be greater than 1.

When converting from a smaller unit to a larger unit, the power of ten will be less than 1.

1 Complete 4.5 L = ▒ mL.

You need to convert liters to milliliters. Use the relationship 1 L = 1,000 mL.

1 L = 1,000 mL	Write the relationship.
4.5 × 1 L = 4.5 × 1,000 mL	Multiply each side by 4.5 since you have 4.5 L.
4.5 L = 4,500 mL	To multiply 4.5 by 1,000, move the decimal point 3 places to the right.

2 Complete 500 mg = ▒ g.

You need to convert milligrams to grams. Use the relationship 1 mg = 0.001 g.

1 mg = 0.001 g	Write the relationship.
500 × 1 mg = 500 × 0.001 g	Multiply each side by 500 since you have 500 mg.
500 mg = 0.5 g.	To multiply 500 by 0.001, move the decimal point 3 places to the left.

CHECK Your Progress

Complete.

a. 25.4 g = ▒ kg

b. 158 mm = ▒ m

Real-World EXAMPLE

Real-World Link The mascot of the State Fair of Texas is a 15.9-meter tall cowboy named Big Tex.
Source: bigtex.com

3 MASCOTS At the State Fair of Texas, Big Tex greets visitors with a great big "Howdy, folks!" Use the information at the left to find the height of Big Tex in kilometers.

You are converting meters to kilometers. Since Big Tex is 15.9 meters tall, use the relationship 1 m = 0.001 km.

1 m = 0.001 km	Write the relationship.
15.9 × 1 m = 15.9 × 0.001	Multiply each side by 15.9 since you have 15.9 m.
15.9 m = 0.0159 km	To multiply 15.9 by 0.001, move the decimal point 3 places to the left.

So, the height of Big Tex is 0.0159 kilometer.

CHECK Your Progress

c. **FOOD** A bottle contains 1.75 liters of juice. How many milliliters of juice does the bottle contain?

Online Personal Tutor at tx.msmath2.com

CHECK Your Understanding

Examples 1, 2 (p. 158)

Complete.

1. 3.7 m = ■ cm
2. 550 m = ■ km
3. 45 g = ■ mg
4. 3,800 mg = ■ g
5. 1,460 mL = ■ L
6. 2.34 kL = ■ L

Example 3 (p. 158)

7. **SPORTS** How many kilometers does a team of athletes run in a 1,600-meter relay race?

Exercises

HOMEWORK HELP

For Exercises	See Examples
8–23	1, 2
24–27	3

Complete.

8. 720 cm = ■ m
9. 983 mm = ■ m
10. 3.2 m = ■ cm
11. 0.03 m = ■ mm
12. 64 kg = ■ g
13. 7.5 g = ■ mg
14. 925 mg = ■ g
15. 73.2 g = ■ mg
16. 997 g = ■ kg
17. 82.1 g = ■ kg
18. 345 mL = ■ L
19. 9.1 L = ■ mL
20. 43 L = ■ kL
21. 130.5 kL = ■ L
22. 0.046 kL = ■ L
23. 57,000 mL = ■ L

24. **WATERFALLS** At 979 meters tall, Angel Falls in Venezuela is the highest waterfall in the world. How many kilometers tall is the waterfall?

25. **FOOD** An 18-ounce jar contains 510 grams of grape jelly. How many kilograms of grape jelly does the jar contain?

26. **BUILDINGS** The Taipei Financial Center in Taipei, Taiwan, is about 0.508 kilometers tall. What is the approximate height of the building in meters?

27. **BIRDS** The world's largest bird is the ostrich whose mass can be as much as 156.5 kilograms. What is this weight in grams?

Complete.

28. 0.85 cm = ■ mm
29. 0.22 mm = ■ cm
30. 0.05 km = ■ mm
31. 0.93 km = ■ cm
32. 23,000 mg = ■ kg
33. 40,000 mL = ■ kL
34. Which is greater, 654 milliliters or 0.5 liter?
35. Which is less, 23 meters or 200 centimeters?

Real-World Link The length of the largest avocado seed measured 76 millimeters.
Source: *Book of World Records*

FOOD **For Exercise 36, use the information at the left.**

36. How many centimeters long was the largest avocado seed?

37. The mass of avocado fruits ranges from 0.1 kilogram to more than 1.2 kilograms in mass. What is the range of the mass of avocado fruits in grams?

38. **RESEARCH** Use the Internet or another source to investigate relationships between metric units of mass and capacity. Explain the relationships and give examples of how they are used in the real world.

Order each set of measures from least to greatest.

39. 0.02 km, 50 m, 3,000 cm

40. 660 mL, 0.06 L, 6.6 kL

41. 0.32 kg, 345 g, 35,100 mg

42. 2,650 mm, 130 cm, 5 m

43. **ANALYZE TABLES** The table shows the lengths of bridges in the United States. Which bridges are about 1 kilometer in length? Justify your answer.

Bridge	Length (m)
Mackinac, MI	1,158
George Washington, NY	1,067
Tacoma Narrows II, WA	853
Oakland Bay, CA	704
Pennybacker, TX	345
Sunshine Skyway, FL	8,712
Golden Gate, CA	2,780

44. **CARPENTRY** Jacinta needs a 2.5-meter pole for a birdfeeder that she is building. How many centimeters will she need to cut off a 3-meter pole in order to use it for the birdfeeder?

EXTRA PRACTICE
See pages 724, 757.
Math Online
Self-Check Quiz at tx.msmath2.com

45. **BAKING** A bakery uses 900 grams of peaches per cobbler. How many cobblers can be made using 4.5 kilograms of peaches?

46. **MONUMENTS** Washington Monument is 169 meters. A replica of the monument is 13 centimeters tall. How many times greater is the height of the actual monument than the replica?

H.O.T. Problems

47. **FIND THE ERROR** Hunter and Arturo are converting 45.7 milligrams to grams. Who is correct? Explain your reasoning.

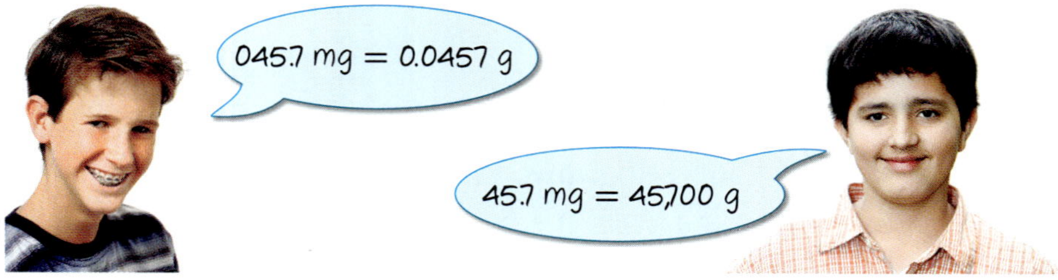

48. **CHALLENGE** The metric prefix *giga* refers to something one billion times larger than the base unit. How many meters are in 3.9 gigameters?

49. **OPEN ENDED** Construct a problem in which you would multiply by 0.001 to convert units and obtain a decimal number of units.

50. **WRITING IN MATH** Explain why it makes sense to multiply by a power of 10 that is greater than 1 when changing from a larger unit to a smaller unit.

TEST PRACTICE

51. The table shows the mass of four wireless telephones. Find the approximate total mass of the telephones in kilograms.

Telephone Owner	Mass (g)
Elena	100.4
Kevin	70.8
Marissa	95.6
Corey	120.4

A 3.9 kilograms

B 0.39 kilogram

C 39.0 kilograms

D 390.0 kilograms

52. Which relationship between the given units of measure is correct?

F One gram is $\frac{1}{100}$ of a centigram.

G One meter is $\frac{1}{100}$ of a centimeter.

H One gram is $\frac{1}{1,000}$ of a kilogram.

J One milliliter is $\frac{1}{100}$ of a liter.

53. **GRIDDABLE** The height of a flagpole is 17.24 meters. Write the flagpole's height in centimeters.

Spiral Review

For Exercises 54 and 55, choose the best method of computation. Then use the method to solve the problem. (Lesson 3-5)

54. **ANIMALS** The average cow produces 40 glasses of milk each day. How many glasses of milk will an average cow produce in a year?

55. **INSECTS** Honey bees fly about 20 miles per hour. How far can a honey bee travel in 3 hours?

Divide. (Lesson 3-4)

56. $4.8 \div 1.5$

57. $0.091 \div 0.26$

58. $6\overline{)5.04}$

59. Evaluate $16.4 \times a^4$ if $a = 10$. (Lesson 3-3)

60. **TEMPERATURE** The daily high temperatures, in degrees Fahrenheit, for a city over the course of 5 days were 66°, 68°, 65°, 67° and 64°. If this pattern continues, find the temperature on the sixth day. Use the *look for a pattern* strategy. (Lesson 2-6)

Find each sum. (Lesson 2-4)

61. $5 + (-2) + 6$

62. $-4 + (-5) + 3$

63. $-4 + (-9) + (-5)$

GET READY for the Next Lesson

PREREQUISITE SKILL **Evaluate each expression.** (Lesson 1-2)

64. 10^3

65. 10^5

66. 10^7

67. 10^4

3-7 Scientific Notation

Main IDEA

Write numbers greater than 100 in scientific notation and in standard form.

Preparation for TEKS 8.1 The student understands that different forms of numbers are appropriate for different situations. **(D) express numbers in scientific notation,** including negative exponents, **in appropriate problem situations using a calculator.**

GET READY for the Lesson

ASTRONOMY Astronomers often deal with measures that are very large.

Astronomy Fact	Approximate Measure
Speed of Light	300,000,000 m/s
Light-Year	950,000,000,000,000 km
Mass of Sun	1,000,000,000,000,000,000,000,000,000,000 kg

Use paper, pencil, and the information above to solve each problem.

1. The distance from Earth to the nearest star, Proxima Centauri, is approximately 4 light-years. What is this distance in kilometers?
2. Black holes can be 15 times as massive as the Sun. What is the mass of one black hole in kilograms?
3. About how long does it take for light from the Sun to reach Earth, 150,000,000,000 meters away?

NEW Vocabulary

scientific notation

Very large numbers can be difficult to read and work with. For this reason, these numbers are often written using **scientific notation**.

KEY CONCEPT — Scientific Notation

Words A number is expressed in scientific notation when it is written as the product of a factor and a power of ten. The factor must be greater than or equal to 1 and less than 10.

Examples 3.5×10^6

- 3.5: factor greater than or equal to 1, but less than 10
- 10^6: power of 10 written in exponential form

To write a large number in scientific notation, move the decimal to the right of the first digit in the number. Then find the power of ten.

EXAMPLES Write a Number in Scientific Notation

1 **Write 23,500,000 in scientific notation.**

$23{,}500{,}000 = 2.35 \times 10{,}000{,}000$ — The decimal point moved 7 places, so the power of 10 has 7 zeros.

$= 2.35 \times 10^7$ — $10{,}000{,}000 = 10^7$

2 **Write 1,400,000 in scientific notation.**

$1,400,000 = 1.4 \times 1,000,000$ — The decimal point moved 6 places. So the power of 10 has 6 zeros.

$= 1.4 \times 10^6$ — $1,000,000 = 10^6$

CHECK Your Progress

Write each number in scientific notation.

a. 38,000,000 b. 19,800 c. 8,610,000

Online Personal Tutor at tx.msmath2.com

Real-World EXAMPLE

3 **SCIENCE** **A light-year, the distance light travels in one year, is about 5,880,000,000,000 miles. How many miles is 50 light years?**

One light-year in scientific notation is 5.88×10^{12} miles. To find the number of miles in 50 light years, use a calculator to multiply 5.88×10^{12} by 50.

5.88 [×] [2nd] [EE] 12 [×] 50 [ENTER] 2.94 E14

The E represents the exponent of the power of 10.

So, there are 2.94×10^{14} miles in 50 light years.

STUDY TIP

Alternative Keystrokes
You can also enter the number in Example 3 by pressing 5.88 [2nd] $[10^x]$ 12.

CHECK Your Progress

d. **FOOD** If consumers spend about $1,800,000,000 on hot dogs each year, find the amount spent in 15 years.

To write a number written in scientific notation in standard form, you can use the order of operations.

EXAMPLES Write Scientific Notation in Standard Form

4 **Write 5.2×10^5 in standard form.**

$5.2 \times 10^5 = 5.2 \times 100,000$ — $10^5 = 100,000$

$= 520000.$ — Move the decimal point 5 places to the right.

$= 520,000$ — Remove the decimal point. Add comma.

STUDY TIP

Look Back
To evaluate 5.2×10^5 using the order of operations, see Lesson 1-4.

5 **Write 1.6×10^3 in standard form.**

$1.6 \times 10^3 = 1.6 \times 1,000$ — $10^3 = 1,000$

$= 1600.$ — Move the decimal point 3 places to the right.

$= 1,600$ — Remove the decimal point. Add comma.

CHECK Your Progress

Write each number in standard form.

e. 7.2×10^4 f. 3.8×10^9 g. 1.0×10^8

Real-World EXAMPLE

6 **INTERNET** **The table shows the number of Internet users in four different countries. How many times more Internet users are there in the U.S. than in Japan?**

Internet Users	
Country	**Users**
U.S.	1.686×10^8
Sweden	9.04×10^6
Japan	5.6×10^7
China	4.58×10^7

Source: internetworldstats.com

To find how many times more Internet users there are in the U.S. than in Japan, divide 1.686×10^8 by 5.6×10^7. Since the numbers are large, use a calculator.

1.686 [2nd] [EE] 8 [÷] 5.6 [2nd] [EE] 7 [ENTER]

So, there are about 3 times more Internet users in the U.S. than in Japan.

STUDY TIP

Technology
To show all numbers in scientific notation on the TI-83/84 Plus, press [MODE] [▶] [ENTER] [2nd] [QUIT].

CHECK Your Progress

h. **INTERNET** Use the information in the table above to determine how many times more Internet users there are in China than in Sweden.

CHECK Your Understanding

Examples 1, 2 (pp. 162–163)

Write each number in scientific notation.

1. 410,000
2. 80,000
3. 15,800,000
4. 6,800,000
5. 2.6 million
6. 5.43 million

Example 3 (p. 163)

7. **FOOD** Americans consume more than 10,000,000,000 bowls of soup each year. How many bowls of soup will Americans consume over 15 years? Express this amount in scientific notation.

Examples 4, 5 (p. 163)

Write each number in standard form.

8. 2.0×10^5
9. 7.05×10^6
10. 3.1×10^4

Example 6 (p. 164)

11. **LANGUAGES** The table shows the number of people in the world who speak certain languages. How many times more people speak Chinese than French?

12. **LANGUAGES** How many times more people speak Spanish than Turkish?

World Languages Spoken	
Language	**Number of People**
Chinese	1.1×10^9
English	5.14×10^8
Spanish	4.25×10^8
French	1.29×10^8
Turkish	6.0×10^7

Source: *Time Almanac for Kids*

Exercises

HOMEWORK HELP

For Exercises	See Examples
13–24	1, 2
25–26	3
27–34	4, 5
35–36	6

Write each number in scientific notation.

13. 36,000
14. 29,700
15. 154,000
16. 502,000
17. 8,406,000
18. 2,130,000
19. 24,800,000
20. 35,900,000
21. 4 million
22. 1.7 million
23. 30 billion
24. 50.3 billion

For Exercises 25 and 26, express the results in scientific notation.

25. **SUBWAYS** Each year, about 2,840,000,000 people ride on the subway system in Tokyo. What is the approximate number of passengers that ride on the subway in 5 years?

26. **BUSINESS** The number 15,400,000,000 gives the yearly earnings of a fast-food company. If the company earns the same amount each year for the next 15 years, what will be the total earnings?

Write each number in standard form.

27. 4.9×10^3
28. 6.3×10^4
29. 5.4×10^6
30. 1.9×10^8
31. 2.48×10^5
32. 7.96×10^6
33. 9.80×10^8
34. 4.73×10^{10}

35. **ANIMALS** Anteaters can eat about 1.08×10^7 insects in one year. How many insects will an anteater eat in its lifetime if its lifespan is 14 years?

36. **TOYS** In 2003, the people of Japan spent about $\$8.8 \times 10^9$ on toys. About how much did the people of Japan spend on toys each month?

Real-World Link The popular puzzle cube shown has 1,929,770,126,028,800 possible color combinations.
Source: *Book of World Records*

Replace each ● with <, >, or = to make a true sentence.

37. 5,000 ● 5.0×10^3
38. 600 ● 6.0×10^1
39. 81,900 ● 8.19×10^5
40. 1 million ● 1.1×10^6

41. Order the numbers 63,400, 6.98×10^6, 6.03×10^5, and 5,980,100 from least to greatest.

42. **GEOGRAPHY** The world's oceans hold about 1.37×10^9 cubic kilometers of water. Lake Mead in Nevada holds about 3.42×10^1 cubic kilometers of water. How many times more cubic kilometers of water does the world's oceans hold compared to Lake Mead?

43. **ANALYZE TABLES** The table shows the distance Mercury and Pluto are from the Sun.

Celestial Body	Distance from the Sun (mi)
Mercury	3.6×10^7
Pluto	3.666×10^9

How much farther is Pluto from the Sun than Mercury?

EXTRA PRACTICE
See pages 725, 757.
Math Online
Self-Check Quiz at tx.msmath2.com

H.O.T. Problems

CHALLENGE **Powers of 10 that are between 0 and 1 can be expressed using negative exponents. Use the table at the right to write each expression in standard form.**

Decimal	Power of 10
0.1	10^{-1}
0.01	10^{-2}
0.001	10^{-3}
0.0001	10^{-4}

44. 4.5×10^{-2} **45.** 1.8×10^{-1}

46. 8.9×10^{-4} **47.** 7.2×10^{-3}

48. Write a rule you can use to multiply a number by a negative power of 10.

49. **OPEN ENDED** Differentiate between standard form and scientific notation. Be sure to include examples of each.

50. **NUMBER SENSE** Which number describes the population of Texas, 2.2×10^7 or 2.2×10^4? Explain your reasoning.

51. **WRITING IN MATH** Determine whether the number 36.42×10^5 is written in scientific notation. Explain your reasoning.

TEST PRACTICE

52. Asia has an area of about 44,600,000 square kilometers. Which expression represents this number in scientific notation?

A 4.46×10^6 **C** 4.46×10^8

B 4.46×10^7 **D** 4.46×10^9

53. The annual number of people visiting Grand Canyon can be represented by the expression 4×10^6. Which number represents this amount?

F 40,000 **H** 4,000,000

G 400,000 **J** 400,000,000

Spiral Review

Complete. (Lesson 3-6)

54. 1.01 kg = ■ g **55.** 36 mL = ■ L **56.** 2.33 km = ■ m

57. **RACING** The Indianapolis Motor Speedway has 3,200,000 bricks that lie beneath the 2.5 miles of track. How many bricks lie beneath one mile of track at the race track? (Lesson 3-5)

Name the ordered pair for each point graphed. Then identify the quadrant in which each point lies. (Lesson 2-3)

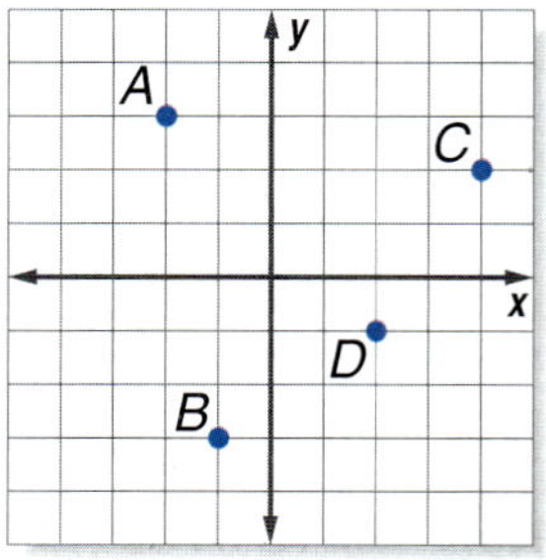

58. *A* **59.** *B*

60. *C* **61.** *D*

Describe the relationship between the terms in each arithmetic sequence. Then write the next three terms in each sequence. (Lesson 1-9)

62. 13, 17, 21, 25, 29, . . . **63.** 5.4, 6.1, 6.8, 7.5, 8.2, . . . **64.** 156, 162, 168, 174, 180, . . .

Study Guide and Review

STUDY TO GO Download Vocabulary Review from tx.msmath2.com

FOLDABLES™ Study Organizer

GET READY to Study

Be sure the following Key Concepts are noted in your Foldable.

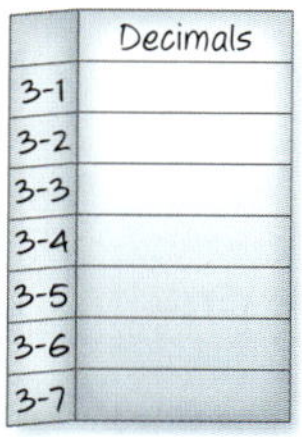

Key Concepts

Multiplying Decimals (Lesson 3-2)

- The number of decimal places in the product of two decimals is the sum of the number of decimal places in the factors.

Multiplying by Powers of 10 (Lesson 3-3)

- To multiply a decimal by a power of ten that is greater than 1, move the decimal point to the right the same number of places as the number of zeros in the power of 10.
- To multiply a decimal by a power of ten that is less than 1, move the decimal point to the left the same number of places as there are after the decimal point.

Dividing Decimals (Lesson 3-4)

- To divide by a decimal, change the divisor to a whole number by multiplying both the divisor and dividend by the same power of ten. Then divide as with whole numbers.

Scientific Notation (Lesson 3-7)

- A number is expressed in scientific notation when it is written as the product of a factor and a power of ten. The factor must be greater than or equal to 1 and less than 10.

Key Vocabulary

compatible numbers (p. 129)
gram (p. 157)
kilogram (p. 157)
liter (p. 157)
meter (p. 157)
metric system (p. 157)
scientific notation (p. 162)

Vocabulary Check

State whether each sentence is *true* or *false*. If *false*, replace the underlined word or number to make a true sentence.

1. The meter measure mass.
2. Compatible numbers can be used to estimate the quotient of $40.8 \div 6.8$ by rounding 40.8 to 42 and 6.8 to 7 and then dividing.
3. The base unit of length in the metric system is the liter.
4. The number 58,200 is written in scientific notation as 58.2×10^3.
5. The base unit of mass in the metric system is the kilogram.
6. The prefix *milli* means millionths.
7. The number 4.6×10^7 has 7 zeros.
8. One gram has a mass that is smaller than one kilogram.
9. To write 29,500,000 in scientific notation, move the decimal 7 places to the right.
10. The prefix *centi* means hundredths.

CHAPTER 3

Study Guide and Review

Lesson-by-Lesson Review

3-1 Estimating with Decimals (pp. 128–131)

Estimate each product.

11. 8.9×3.2
12. 7.2×2.7
13. 17.9×22.1

Estimate each quotient.

14. $32.6 \div 5.4$
15. $97.7 \div 4.65$
16. $\$63.25 \div \$19.99$

17. **PARTY PLANNING** Alana wants to buy pretzels that cost $1.89 a bag. If she has exactly $14.34 in her pocket, about how many bags of pretzels can she buy for a party?

Example 1 Estimate 27.5 × 7.3.

$$\begin{array}{r} 27.5 \\ \underline{\times\ 7.3} \end{array} \rightarrow \begin{array}{r} 30 \\ \underline{\times\ 7} \\ 210 \end{array}$$

Round 27.5 to 30.
Round 7.3 to 7.

The product is *about* 210.

Example 2 Estimate 43.8 ÷ 8.9.

$$8.9\overline{)43.8} \rightarrow \begin{array}{r} 5 \\ 9\overline{)45} \end{array}$$

Round 43.8 to 45 and 8.9 to 9 since 45 and 9 are compatible numbers.

The quotient is *about* 5.

3-2 Multiplying Decimals (pp. 134–139)

Multiply.

18. 0.6×4
19. 0.007×3
20. 4.9×5
21. 1.24×0.4
22. 6.5×2.9
23. 5.83×1.47

24. **MONEY** In a recent year, the average hourly wage for an employee of an internet service provider in Texas was $12.51. The average weekly hours worked was 37.2. To the nearest penny, what were the average weekly earnings?

Example 3 Find 3.7 × 8.

Estimate 4 × 8 or 32

3.7	←	1 decimal place
× 8	←	+ 0 decimal places
29.6	←	1 decimal place

Check for Reasonableness $29.6 \approx 32$ ✔

Example 4 Find 13.6 × 1.81.

Estimate 13.6 × 1.81 → 14 × 2 or 28

13.6	←	1 decimal place
× 1.81	←	+ 2 decimal places
136		
1088		
+ 136		
24.616	←	3 decimal places

Check for Reasonableness $24.616 \approx 28$ ✔

Mixed Problem Solving
For mixed problem-solving practice, see page 757.

3-3 Powers of Ten (pp. 140–144)

Find each product.

25. 0.81×100
26. 62.3×0.1
27. 17.5×0.01
28. $0.94 \times 1{,}000$
29. **PHYSICS** The speed of light is 1.86×10^5 miles per second. Write this number in standard notation.

Example 5 **Find 0.98 × 1,000.**

$0.98 \times 1{,}000 = 0980.$ 1,000 has 3 zeros, so move the decimal point 3 places to the right.

$= 980$

Example 6 **Find 623.45 × 0.01.**

$623.45 \times 0.01 = 6.2345$ There are 2 places after the decimal point, so move the decimal point 2 places to the left.

$= 6.2345$

3-4 Dividing Decimals (pp. 147–152)

Divide.

30. $88.02 \div 5.4$
31. $0.01\overline{)5.77}$
32. $60.12 \div 8.35$
33. $2.5\overline{)13.68}$
34. **WEATHER** The record for the greatest annual rainfall for the state of Texas is 109.38 inches. At this rate, find the average monthly rainfall.

Example 7 **Divide 109.22 by 17.2.**

$17.2\overline{)109.22} \rightarrow 172\overline{)1092.2}$ Multiply both numbers by 10.

$$\begin{array}{r} 6.35 \\ 172\overline{)1092.2} \\ \underline{-1032} \\ 602 \\ \underline{-516} \\ 860 \\ \underline{-860} \\ 0 \end{array}$$

Place the decimal point and divide as with whole numbers.

Annex a zero and continue.

3-5 PSI: Choose the Best Method of Computation (pp. 154–155)

Choose the best method of computation. Then use the method to solve the problem.

35. **SCHOOL** Lauren's classmates collected 100 aluminum cans each weighing 14.5 grams. What was the total weight of the cans?
36. **MONEY** In one year, Nate earned \$546 for doing his chores. If he earned the same amount each week, what was his weekly allowance?

Example 8 **If each jar of pasta sauce costs \$1.89, about how much will you pay for 8 jars of pasta sauce?**

Since an exact answer is not needed, you can use estimation.

$\$1.89 \times 8 \approx \$2 \times 8$ or $\$16$

So, you will pay about \$16.

CHAPTER 3

Study Guide and Review

3-6 Measurement: The Metric System (pp. 157–161)

Complete.

37. 76.5 kL = ■ L

38. 22,650 m = ■ km

39. 118 mg = ■ g

40. 0.36 cL = ■ mL

41. **ANIMALS** The roadrunner can run as fast as 24.14 kilometers in one hour. How many meters can a roadrunner run in one hour?

42. **MUSEUMS** The National Yo-Yo Museum in Chico, California has the world's largest working wooden yo-yo, Big Yo. Big Yo has a mass of about 116,132 grams. What is the mass in kilograms of Big Yo?

Example 9 **Complete 0.95 kg = ■ g.**

You need to convert kilograms to grams. Use the relationship 1 kg = 1,000 g. Multiply each side by 0.95 since you have 0.95 kg. To multiply 0.95 × 1,000, move the decimal point 3 places to the right.

$1 \text{ kg} = 1{,}000 \text{ g}$

$0.95 \times 1 \text{ kg} = 0.95 \times 1{,}000 \text{ g}$

$0.95 \text{ kg} = 950 \text{ g}$

Example 10 **Complete 4.23 cm = ■ m.**

You need to convert centimeters to meters. Use the relationship 1 cm = 0.01 m. Multiply each side by 4.23 since you have 4.23 cm. To multiply 4.23 by 0.01, move the decimal point 2 places to the left.

$1 \text{ cm} = 0.01 \text{ m}$

$4.23 \times 1 \text{ cm} = 4.23 \times 0.01 \text{ m}$

$4.23 \text{ cm} = 0.0423 \text{ m}$

3-7 Scientific Notation (pp. 162–166)

Write each number in scientific notation.

43. 2,314,900

44. 78,000

45. 20 billion

46. 216,000,000

Write each number in standard form.

47. 6.94×10^4

48. 1.3×10^7

49. **POPULATION** The population of the U.S. was about 2.96×10^8 people. If the population of the world was about 6.5×10^9 people, how many times greater was the world's population than that of the United States?

Example 11 **Write 8,900,000 in scientific notation.**

8,900,000

= 8,900,000 — The decimal point moved 6 places, so the power of 10 has 6 zeros.

$= 8.9 \times 1{,}000{,}000$

$= 8.9 \times 10^6$ — $1{,}000{,}000 = 10^6$

Example 12 **Write 5.49×10^6 in standard form.**

5.49×10^5

$= 5.49 \times 100{,}000$ — $10^5 = 100{,}000$

= 549000 — Move the decimal point 5 places to the right.

= 549,000 — Remove the decimal point. Add comma.

CHAPTER 3

Practice Test

Estimate each product or quotient.

1. 6.7×3.12
2. $78.9 \div 8.44$

3. **POPULATION** The table shows the population density in persons per square mile of several states.

State	Population Density
Alaska	1.1
Texas	79.6
California	217.2
Rhode Island	1,003.2

Source: census.gov

About how many times greater is the population density of Rhode Island than of Alaska?

Multiply.

4. 17.1×5.3
5. 11.2×0.08
6. 25.7×0.6
7. 103.5×1.02

8. **MONEY** The table gives the rates for several ranges of weights of packages sent by mail.

Weight (pounds)	Rate
not over 1.0	$3.85
not over 2.0	$3.95
not over 3.0	$4.75
not over 4.0	$5.30
not over 5.0	$5.85

What will be the total cost if Mrs. Collins needs to mail two packages, each weighing 3.8 pounds, and one package weighing 1.1 pounds?

Find each product.

9. 43.89×0.01
10. $0.07 \times 1{,}000$

Divide.

11. $53.46 \div 6$
12. $1.2\overline{)0.78}$
13. $3.05\overline{)7.93}$
14. $2.64 \div 0.04$

15. **TEST PRACTICE** Tanya has 170.4 centimeters of string from which she needs to cut into pieces that are 28.4 centimeters long. Which expression can be used to find the maximum number of pieces of string that she can cut?

A 170.4×28.4
B $28.4 \div 170.4$
C $28.4 + 170.4$
D $170.4 \div 28.4$

Complete.

16. 6.21 mm = ■ cm
17. 48.7 kL = ■ L
18. 2.45 kg = ■ g
19. 1,970 m = ■ km

20. **NUTRITION** An ounce of chocolate contains about 20 milligrams of caffeine. How many grams of caffeine are in an ounce of chocolate?

Write each number in scientific notation.

21. 49,000
22. 718

Write each number in standard form.

23. 1.4×10^3
24. 5.82×10^6

25. **TEST PRACTICE** Saturn is approximately 840.44×10^6 miles from the Sun. Which of the following is NOT equivalent to the distance from Saturn to the Sun?

F 84,044,000 miles
G 8.4044×10^8 miles
H 840,440,000 miles
J $84{,}044 \times 10{,}000$ miles

CHAPTER 3

Texas Test Practice

Cumulative, Chapters 1–3

Read each question. Then fill in the correct answer on the answer document provided by your teacher or on a sheet of paper.

1. A baseball stadium increased ticket prices. The table shows the old price, t, and the new price, n, of the tickets. Which formula can be used to calculate the new ticket price?

Ticket	Old Price (t)	New Price (n)
Child	\$4.50	\$6.00
Student	\$6.00	\$8.00
Senior	\$7.50	\$10.00
Adult	\$9.00	\$12.00

A $n = t \times 1.5$

B $n = t \div 0.75$

C $n = t \div 1.5$

D $n = t \times 0.75$

2. Jacob has \$5.50 to spend on pencils. If each pencil costs \$0.30, which expression can be used to find the maximum number of pencils Jacob can buy?

F 0.3×5.5

G $5.5 \div 0.3$

H $0.3 + 5.5$

J $5.5 - 0.3$

3. If point A is moved 3 units to the right and 2 units up, what will be the new coordinates of point A?

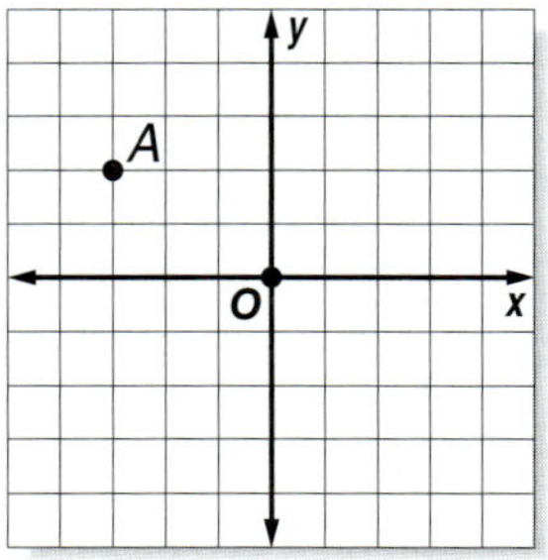

A $(-5, 3)$

B $(0, 4)$

C $(8, -4)$

D $(-2, 2)$

4. Which problem situation matches the equation below?

$$25x = 300$$

F Laura made \$300 mowing lawns. What is x, the average number of minutes that it took to mow each lawn?

G Katrina has \$300 in her bank account. She writes a check to the grocery store for \$25. What is x, the amount left in her checking account?

H Alan needs 300 volunteers to staff a special event. He already has 25 names. What is x, the number of volunteers Alan still needs?

J Jeff collected 300 baseball cards. He wants to divide them evenly into 25 piles. What is x, the number of cards in each pile?

5. **GRIDDABLE** You can drive your car 19.5 miles with one gallon of gasoline. How many miles can you drive with 11.9 gallons of gasoline?

6. Which sequence follows the rule $2n + 4$, where n represents the position of a term in the sequence?

A 3, 5, 7, 9, 11, . . .

B 6, 8, 10, 12, 14, . . .

C 1, 3, 5, 7, 9, . . .

D 8, 12, 16, 20, 24, . . .

7. What is the value of the expression $(4 + 4)^2 \div 2 - 3 \times 5$?

F 145

G 65

H 17

J 1

Math Online Texas Test Practice at tx.msmath2.com

Get Ready for the Texas Test
For test-taking strategies and more practice, see pages TX1–TX23.

8. The table shows the profit of a company over 5 years. Which of the following statements is supported by the information in the table?

Year	Profit (millions of dollars)
2001	8.6
2002	10.2
2003	15.3
2004	13.7
2005	11.9

A The profit in 2002 was five times greater than the net profit in 2001.

B The greatest increase in profit for two consecutive years occurred from 2001 to 2002.

C The greatest decrease in profit for two consecutive years occurred from 2004 to 2005.

D The sum of the profits for 2002 and 2003 was greater than the sum of the profits for 2004 and 2005.

9. **GRIDDABLE** If point D is moved 6 units to the right and 2 units down, what will be the y-coordinate of point D's new coordinates?

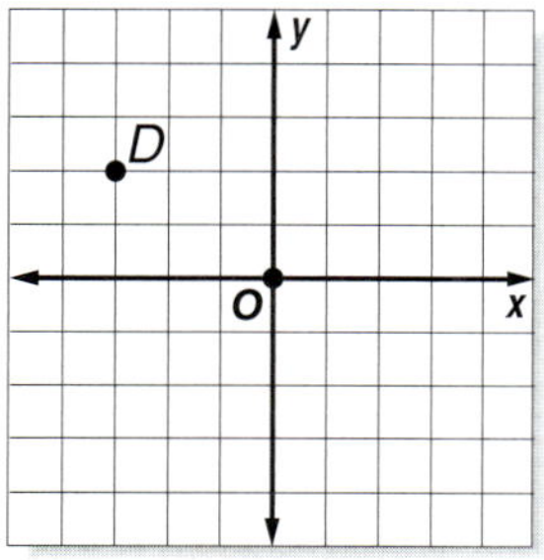

10. Which of the following is the perimeter of the rectangle?

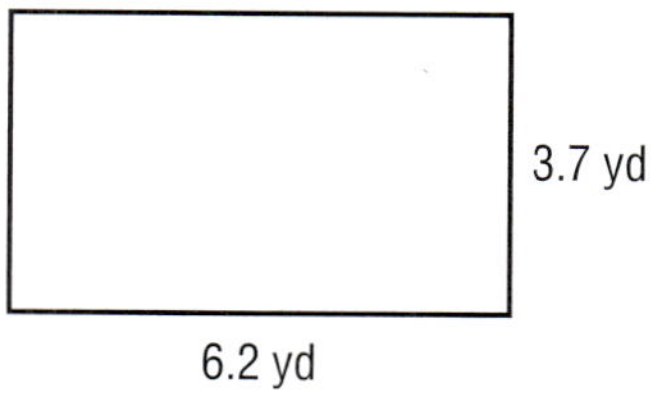

F 6.5 yd

G 9.4 yd

H 12.2 yd

J 19.8 yd

TEST-TAKING TIP

Question 10 Use estimation to eliminate any unreasonable answers. For example, eliminate answer F because one of the sides by itself is almost 6.5 yards.

Pre-AP

Record your answers on a sheet of paper. Show your work.

11. The dimensions of the rectangle are given below.

a. What is the area of the rectangle?

b. What is the perimeter of the rectangle?

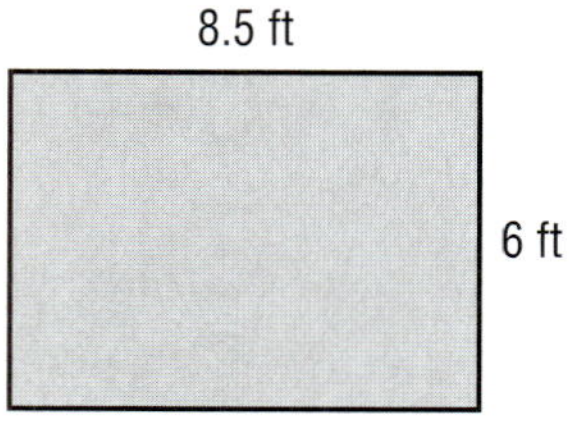

c. How does the perimeter and area change if each dimension is doubled? Explain.

NEED EXTRA HELP?											
If You Missed Question...	1	2	3	4	5	6	7	8	9	10	11
Go to Lesson...	3-2	3-4	2-3	1-7	3-2	1-9	1-4	1-1	2-3	3-5	3-2
For Help with Test Objective...	2	1	3	2	1	2	4	5	3	1	1

CHAPTER 4

Algebra: Linear Equations and Functions

Knowledge and Skills

- Use equations to solve problems. **TEKS 7.5**
- Solve application problems involving estimation and measurement. **TEKS 7.9**

Key Vocabulary

formula (p. 192)
linear equation (p. 212)
two-step equation (p. 199)
work backward strategy (p. 196)

Real-World Link

Airplanes You can use the linear equation $d = rt$ to determine the distance d that an airplane travels at a certain rate r for time t.

FOLDABLES™ Study Organizer

Algebra: Linear Equations and Functions Make this Foldable to help you organize your notes. Begin with a sheet of 11″ by 17″ paper.

1. **Fold** the short sides toward the middle.

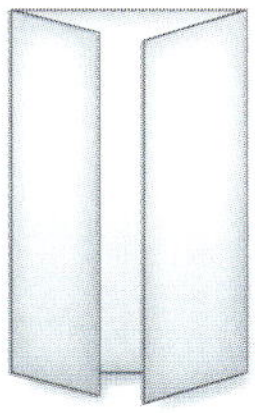

2. **Fold** the top to the bottom.

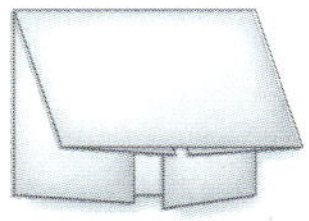

3. **Open.** Cut along the second fold to make four tabs.

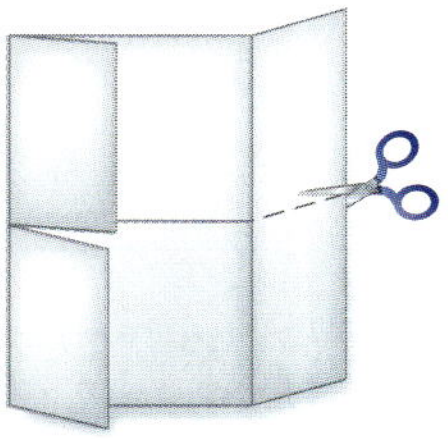

4. **Label** each of the tabs as shown.

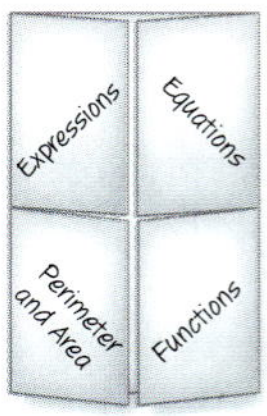

GET READY for Chapter 4

Diagnose Readiness You have two options for checking Prerequisite Skills.

Option 2

Math Online Take the Online Readiness Quiz at tx.msmath2.com.

Option 1

Take the Quick Quiz below. Refer to the Quick Review for help.

QUICK Quiz

Name the number that is the solution of the given equation. (Used in Lessons 4-2, 4-3, and 4-5)

1. $a + 15 = 19$; 4, 5, 6
2. $11k = 77$; 6, 7, 8
3. $x + 9 = -2$; 7, −11, 11

Graph each point on a coordinate plane. (Used in Lesson 4-7)

4. $(-4, 3)$
5. $(-2, -1)$
6. **HIKING** Keith hiked 4 miles north and 2 miles west from the campground before he rested. If the origin represents the campground, graph Keith's resting point.

Add. (Used in Lessons 4-2 and 4-5)

7. $-3 + (-5)$
8. $-8 + 3$
9. $9 + (-5)$
10. $-10 + 15$

Subtract. (Used in Lessons 4-2 through 4-5)

11. $-5 - 6$
12. $8 - 10$
13. $8 - (-6)$
14. $-3 - (-1)$

Divide. (Used in Lessons 4-3 and 4-5)

15. $-6 \div (-3)$
16. $-12 \div 3$
17. $10 \div (-5)$
18. $-24 \div (-4)$

QUICK Review

Example 1 **Name the number that is the solution of $24 \div a = 3$; 7, 8, or 9.**

$24 \div a = 3$	Write the equation.
$24 \div 7 = 3$? No.	Substitute $a = 7$.
$24 \div 8 = 3$? Yes.	Substitute $a = 8$.
$24 \div 9 = 3$? No.	Substitute $a = 9$.

The solution is 8.

Example 2 **Graph the point $(-1, 3)$ on a coordinate plane.**

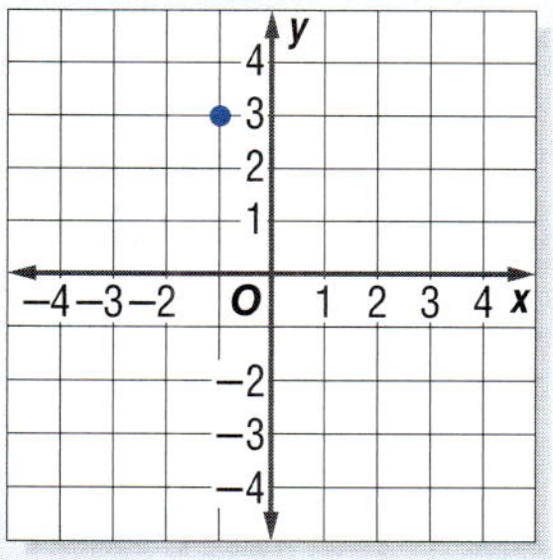

The first number in an ordered pair tells you to move left or right from the origin. The second number tells you to move up or down.

Example 3 **Find $-4 + (-2)$.**

$-4 + (-2) = -6$ — Since −4 and −2 are both negative, add their absolute values. The sum is negative also.

Example 4 **Find $9 - (-7)$.**

$9 - (-7) = 9 + (7)$	Subtracting −7 is the same as adding 7.
$= 16$	Add.

Example 5 **Find $-16 \div 2$.**

$-16 \div 2 = -8$ — Since −16 and 2 have opposite signs, their quotient is negative.

4-1 Writing Expressions and Equations

Main IDEA

Write verbal phrases and sentences as simple algebraic expressions and equations.

Targeted TEKS 7.5 The student uses equations to solve problems. **(B) formulate problem situations when given a simple equation and formulate an equation when given a problem situation.** *Also addresses TEKS 7.14(A).*

GET READY for the Lesson

PLANETS Earth has only one moon, but other planets have many moons. For example, Uranus has 21 moons, and Saturn has 10 more moons than Uranus.

1. What operation would you use to find how many moons Saturn has? Explain.
2. Jupiter has about three times as many moons as Uranus. What operation would you use to find how many moons Jupiter has?

Words and phrases in problems often suggest addition, subtraction, multiplication, and division. Here are some examples.

Addition and Subtraction		Multiplication and Division	
sum	difference	each	divide
more than	less than	product	quotient
increased by	less	multiplied	per
in all	decreased by	twice	separate

REVIEW Vocabulary

algebraic expression a combination of variables, numbers, and at least one operation; Example: $d + 5$ (Lesson 1-4)

EXAMPLE Write a Phrase as an Expression

1 **Write the phrase *five dollars more than Jennifer earned* as an algebraic expression.**

Words	five dollars more than Jennifer earned.
Variable	Let d represent the number of dollars Jennifer earned.
Expression	$d + 5$

CHECK Your Progress

Write the phrase as an algebraic expression.

a. 3 more runs than the Pirates scored

Remember, an equation is a sentence in mathematics that contains an equals sign. When you write a verbal sentence as an equation, you can use the equals sign (=) for the words *equals* or *is*.

EXAMPLES Write Sentences as Equations

Write each sentence as an algebraic equation.

2 Six less than a number is 20.

Six less than a number is 20.

Let n represent the number.

$n - 6 = 20$

3 Three times Jack's age equals 12.

Three times Jack's age equals 12.

Let a represent Jack's age.

$3a = 12$

READING Math

Less Than You can write *six more than a number* as either $6 + n$ or $n + 6$. But *six less than a number* can only be written as $n - 6$.

CHECK Your Progress

Write each sentence as an algebraic equation.

b. Seven more than a number is 15.

c. Five times the number of students is 250.

Real-World EXAMPLE

4 AMUSEMENT PARKS The *Texas Star* Ferris wheel is 69 feet taller than the *Texas Giant* roller coaster. If the *Texas Star* is 212 feet tall, how tall is the *Texas Giant*? Write an equation that models this situation.

Words	The *Texas Star* is 69 feet taller than the *Texas Giant*.
Variable	Let g represent the height of the *Texas Giant*.
Equation	$212 \quad = \quad 69 \quad + \quad g$

The equation is $212 = 69 + g$.

Real-World Link The *Texas Star*, located at the State Fair of Texas, is 212 feet tall.
Source: bigtex.com

CHECK Your Progress

d. **ANIMALS** North American cougars are about 1.5 times as long as cougars found in the tropical jungles of Central America. If North American cougars are about 75 inches long, how long is the tropical cougar? Write an equation that models this situation.

TEST EXAMPLE

5 Which problem situation matches the equation $x - 5.83 = 3.17$?

A Tyler ran 3.17 kilometers. His friend ran the same distance 5.83 seconds faster than Tyler. What is x, the time in seconds that Tyler ran?

B Lynn and Heather measured the length of worms in science class. Lynn's worm was 5.83 centimeters long, and Heather's worm was 3.17 centimeters long. What is x, the average length of the worms?

C Keisha's lunch cost \$5.83. She received \$3.17 in change when she paid the bill. What is x, the amount of money she gave the cashier?

D Mr. Carlos paid \$3.17 for a notebook that originally cost \$5.83. What is x, the amount of money that Mr. Carlos saved?

Test-Taking Tip

Vocabulary Terms Before taking a standardized test, review the meaning of vocabulary terms such as *average*.

Read the Test Item

You need to find which problem situation matches the equation $x - 5.83 = 3.17$.

Solve the Test Item

- You can eliminate A because you cannot add or subtract different units of measure.
- You can eliminate B because to find an average you add and then divide.
- Act out C. If you gave the cashier x dollars and your lunch cost \$5.83, you would subtract to find your change, \$3.17. This is the correct answer.
- Check D, just to be sure. To find the amount Mrs. Carlos saved, you would calculate $5.83 - 3.17$, not $x - 5.83$.

The solution is C.

CHECK Your Progress

e. **Which problem situation matches the equation $4y = 6.76$?**

F Mrs. Thomas bought 4 gallons of gas. Her total cost was \$6.76. What is y, the cost of one gallon of gas?

G Jordan bought 4 CDs that were on sale for \$6.76 each. What is y, the total cost of the CDs?

H The width of a rectangle is 4 meters. The length is 6.76 meters more than the width. What is y, the length of the rectangle?

J The average yearly rainfall is 6.76 inches. What is y, the amount of rainfall you might expect in 4 years?

Online Personal Tutor at tx.msmath2.com

CHECK Your Understanding

Example 1 (p. 176)

Write each phrase as an algebraic expression.

1. a number increased by eight
2. ten dollars more than Grace has

Examples 2, 3 (p. 177)

Write each sentence as an algebraic equation.

3. Nine less than a number equals 24.
4. Two points less than his score is 4.
5. Twice the number of miles is 18.
6. One half the regular price is $13.

Example 4 (p. 177)

7. **GEOGRAPHY** The median age of people living in Texas is three years younger than the median age of the entire United States. Use this information and the information at the right to write an equation to find the median age in the United States.

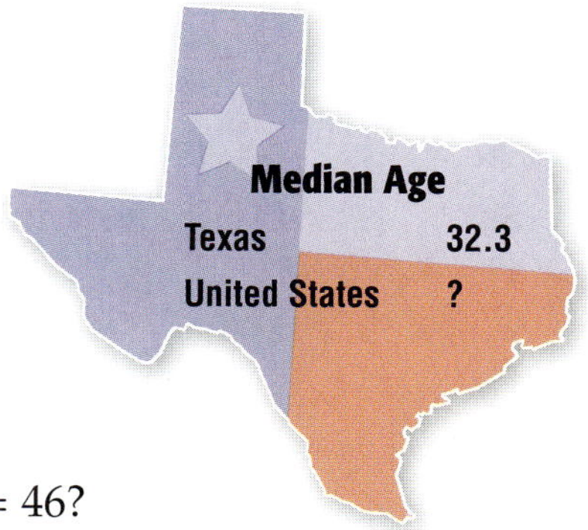

Example 5 (p. 178)

8. **TEST PRACTICE** Which problem situation matches the equation $x - 15 = 46$?

A The original price of a jacket is $46. The sale price is $15 less. What is x, the sale price of the jacket?

B Mark had several baseball cards. He sold 15 of the cards and had 46 left. What is x, the amount of cards Mark had to start with?

C Sonja scored 46 points in last week's basketball game. Talisa scored 15 points less. What is x, the amount of points Talisa scored?

D Katie earned $15 baby-sitting this week. Last week she earned $46. What is x, her average earnings for the two weeks?

Exercises

HOMEWORK HELP

For Exercises	See Examples
9–16	1
17–22	2, 3
23–24	4
41	5

Write each phrase as an algebraic expression.

9. fifteen increased by t
10. five years older than Luis
11. a number decreased by ten
12. three feet less than the length
13. the product of r and 8
14. twice as many oranges
15. Emily's age divided by 3
16. the quotient of a number and −12

Write each sentence as an algebraic equation.

17. The sum of a number and four is equal to −8.
18. Two more than the number of frogs is 4.
19. The product of a number and five is −20.
20. Ten times the number of students is 280.
21. Ten inches less than her height is 26.
22. Five less than a number is 31.

Real-World Link A giraffe's heart can pump 16 gallons of blood in one minute. **Source:** zoo.org

For Exercises 23 and 24, write an equation that models each situation.

23. **ANIMALS** A giraffe is 3.5 meters taller than a camel. If a giraffe is 5.5 meters tall, how tall is a camel?

24. **FOOTBALL** Brett Favre led the National Football League with 32 touchdown passes in 2003. This was twice as many touchdown passes as Donovan McNabb had. Find the number of touchdown passes for McNabb.

GEOMETRY For Exercises 25–28, describe the relationship that exists between the length and width of each rectangle.

25. The width is x, and the length is $4x$.
26. The length is $x + 3$, and the width is x.
27. The length is x, and the width is $x - 5$.
28. The length is x, and the width is $0.5x$.

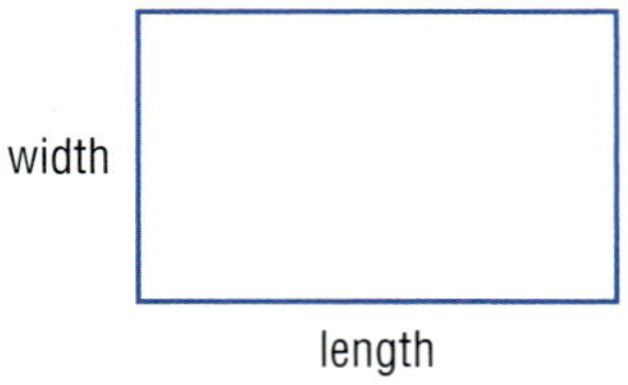

Write each phrase as an algebraic expression.

29. nine dollars less than Felipe has
30. 2 more than twice as many bikes
31. 2 inches taller than her sister
32. the width decreased by 12 inches
33. \$300 more than the car cost
34. hours worked at \$5 for each hour

EXTRA PRACTICE See pages 725, 758.
Math Online Self-Check Quiz at tx.msmath2.com

ANALYZE TABLES For Exercises 35 and 36, use the table.

The table shows the average lifespan of several kinds of paper currency in the United States. Let y represent the average lifespan of a \$5 bill.

U.S. Currency

Kind	Lifespan (years)
\$1	1.5
\$5	2
\$10	3
\$20	4
\$50	9
\$100	9

Source: Federal Reserve System

35. Which lifespan can be represented by $2y$?

36. Write an expression to represent the lifespan of a \$50 bill.

H.O.T. Problems

37. **OPEN ENDED** Write a verbal sentence that translates into the equation $n + 5 = 8$.

38. **FIND THE ERROR** Antonio and Candace are writing an algebraic expression for the phrase *2 less than a number*. Who is correct? Explain.

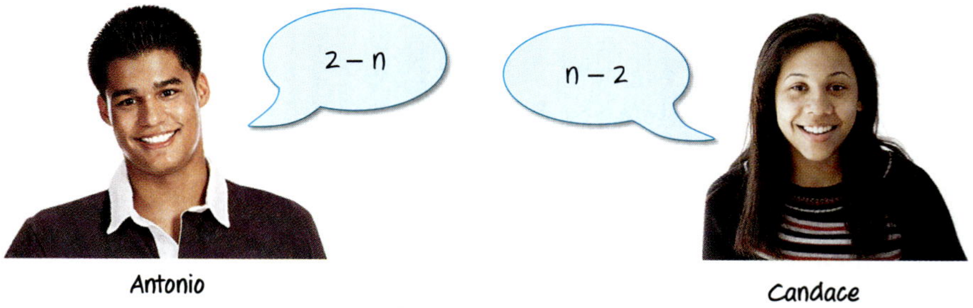

39. **CHALLENGE** If x is an odd number, how would you represent the odd number immediately following it? preceding it?

40. **WRITING IN MATH** Analyze the meaning of the expressions $a + 5$, $a - 3$, $2a$, and $\frac{a}{2}$ if a represents someone's age.

TEST PRACTICE

41. Which problem situation matches the equation below?

$$\frac{(80 + 95 + 86 + 100 + x)}{5} = 90$$

A The weights of four packages are 80 ounces, 95 ounces, 86 ounces, and 100 ounces. Find x, the sum of the weights of the four packages.

B Juan talked 80 minutes, 95 minutes, 86 minutes, and 100 minutes on his cell phone. Find x, the average time Juan talked on his phone.

C Courtney's first four quiz grades were 80, 95, 86, and 100. Find x, the grade Courtney needs on her fifth quiz to have an average of 90.

D The heights of four trees in a park are 80 feet, 95 feet, 86 feet, and 100 feet. Find x, the average height of the trees.

42. The table lists prices for a movie.

Ticket	Price
Adult	\$8
Student	\$$s$
Senior	\$6

Which equation could be used to find the cost of admission for a student s, if the total cost of admission for two adults, one senior, and one student is \$27?

F $s = 16 + 6$

G $27 = 22 \cdot s$

H $27 = s + 22$

J $27 + 16 + 6 = s$

Spiral Review

Write each number in standard form. (Lesson 3-7)

43. 2.7×10^3 **44.** 3.8×10^5 **45.** 9.36×10^6

46. How many centimeters are in 8 meters? (Lesson 3-6)

ANALYZE DATA For Exercises 47 and 48, use the table which shows the cost of two different plans for downloading music. (Lesson 3-4)

Music Downloads	
Plan A	\$0.99 per song
Plan B	\$15.99 per month for unlimited downloads

47. Suppose you download 12 songs in one month. Find the cost per song using Plan B.

48. When is it less expensive to use Plan B instead of Plan A?

Evaluate each expression. (Lesson 1-4)

49. $3 + 7 \cdot 4 - 6$ **50.** $8(16 - 5) - 6$

51. $12 - 18 \div 9$ **52.** $75 \div 3 + 6(5 - 1)$

GET READY for the Next Lesson

PREREQUISITE SKILL Find each sum. (Lesson 2-4)

53. $-8 + (-3)$ **54.** $-10 + 9$ **55.** $12 + (-20)$ **56.** $-15 + 15$

Explore 4-2

Algebra Lab
Solving Equations Using Models

Main IDEA

Solve equations using models.

Targeted TEKS 7.5 The student uses equations to solve problems. **(A)** **use concrete and pictorial models to solve equations and use symbols to record the actions.** *Also addresses TEKS 7.14(A).*

Concepts in Motion **Animation** tx.msmath2.com

In Chapter 2, you used counters to add, subtract, multiply, and divide integers. Integers can also be modeled using algebra tiles. The table shows how these two types of models are related.

Type of Model	Variable x	Integer 1	Integer −1
Cups and Counters			
Algebra Tiles	x	1	−1

You can use either type of model to solve equations.

ACTIVITY

1 **Solve $x + 2 = 5$ using cups and counters or a drawing.**

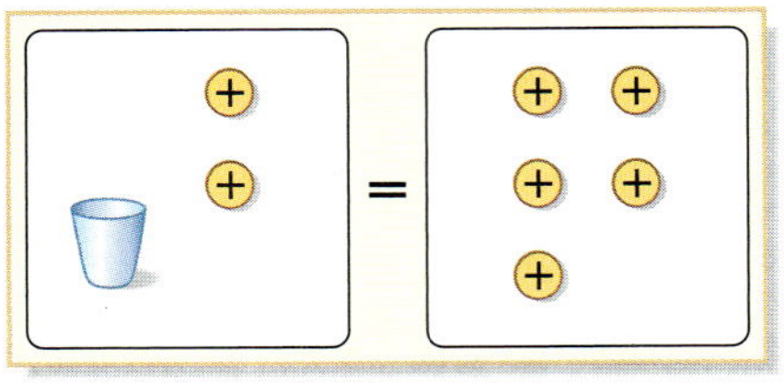

$x + 2 = 5$

Model the equation.

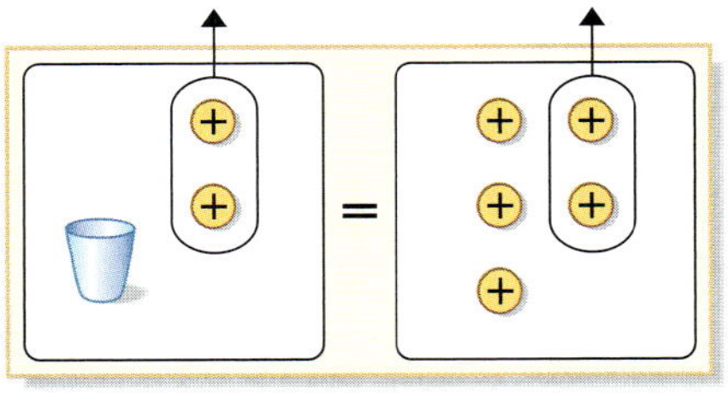

$x + 2 - 2 = 5 - 2$

Remove the same number of counters from each side of the mat until the cup is by itself on one side.

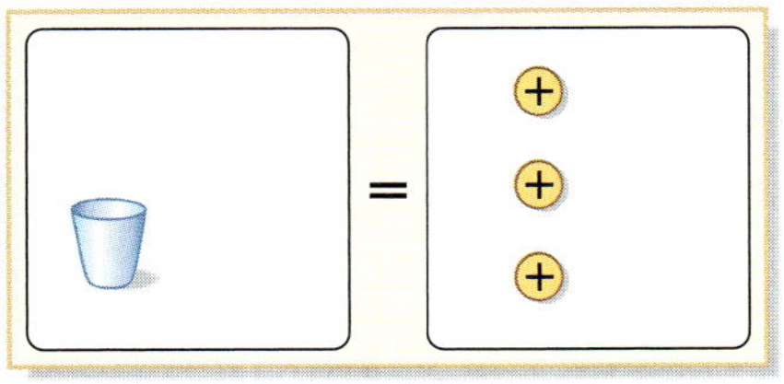

$x = 3$

The number of counters remaining on the right side of the mat represents the value of x.

Therefore, $x = 3$. Since $3 + 2 = 5$, the solution is correct.

CHECK Your Progress

Solve each equation using cups and counters or a drawing.

a. $x + 4 = 4$ **b.** $5 = x + 4$ **c.** $4 = 1 + x$ **d.** $2 = 2 + x$

REVIEW Vocabulary

zero pair a number paired with its opposite; *Example*: 2 and −2. (Explore 2-4)

You can add or subtract a zero pair from either side of an equation without changing its value, because the value of a zero pair is zero.

ACTIVITY

2 **Solve $x + 2 = -1$ using models.**

$x + 2 \quad = \quad -1$

Model the equation.

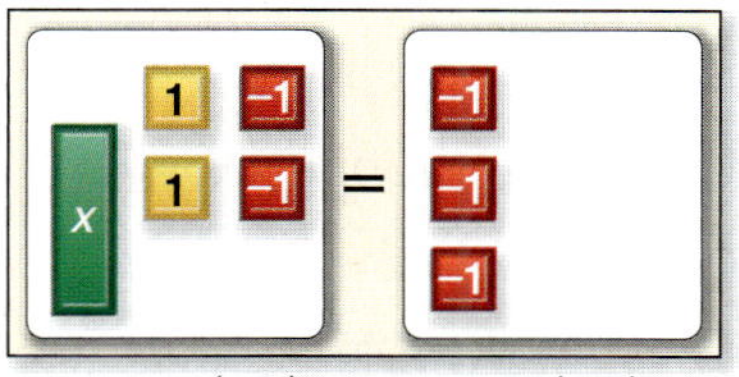

$x + 2 + (-2) \quad = \quad 1 + (-2)$

Add 2 negative tiles to the left side of the mat and add 2 negative tiles to the right side of the mat.

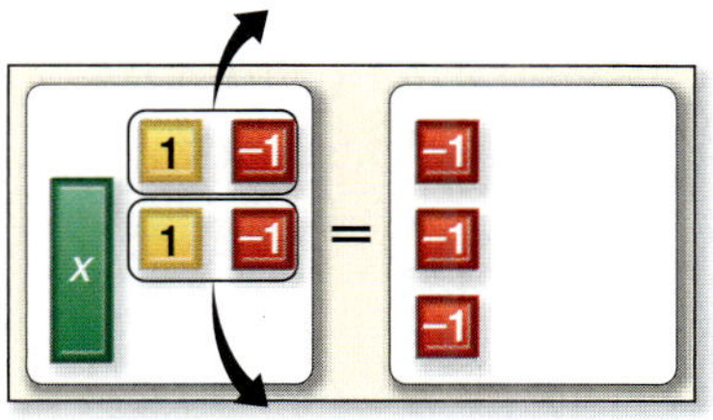

$x \quad = \quad -3$

Remove all of the zero pairs from the left side. There are 3 negative tiles on the right side of the mat.

Therefore, $x = -3$. Since $-3 + 2 = -1$, the solution is correct.

CHECK Your Progress

Solve each equation using models or a drawing.

e. $-2 = x + 1$ **f.** $x - 3 = -2$ **g.** $x - 1 = -3$ **h.** $4 = x - 2$

ANALYZE THE RESULTS

Explain how to solve each equation using models or a drawing.

1.

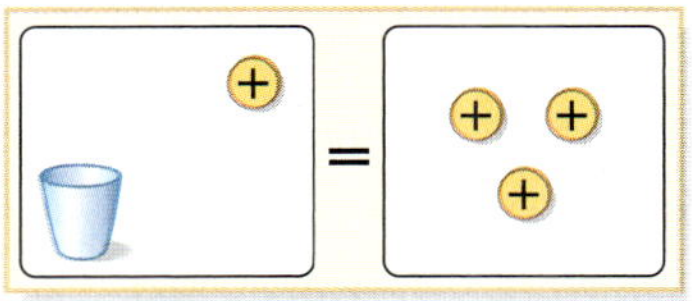

$x + 1 \quad = \quad 3$

2.

$x + 3 \quad = \quad -2$

3. **MAKE A CONJECTURE** Write a rule that you can use to solve an equation like $x + 3 = 2$ without using models or a drawing.

4-2 Solving Addition and Subtraction Equations

Main IDEA

Solve addition and subtraction equations.

Targeted TEKS 7.5 The student uses equations to solve problems. **(A) use concrete and pictorial models to solve equations and use symbols to record the actions.** *Also addresses TEKS 7.14(A).*

NEW Vocabulary

inverse operations

GET READY for the Lesson

VIDEO GAMES Max had some video games, and then he bought two more games. Now he has six games.

1. What does x represent in the figure?
2. What addition equation is shown in the figure?
3. Explain how to solve the equation.
4. How many games did Max have in the beginning?

You can use inverse operations to solve equations. **Inverse operations** "undo" each other. To undo the addition of 2 in the equation $x + 2 = 6$, subtract 2 from each side of the equation. The variable is now by itself on one side of the equation.

Use Models

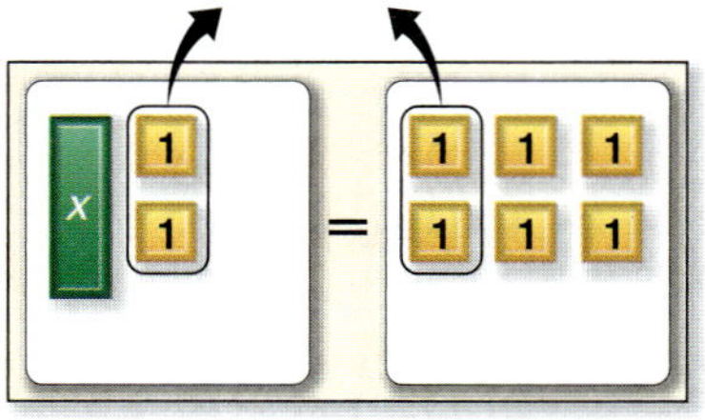

Use Symbols

$$\begin{aligned} x + 2 &= 6 \\ -2 &= -2 \\ \hline x &= 4 \end{aligned}$$

Subtracting 2 from each side of an equation illustrates the Subtraction Property of Equality.

KEY CONCEPT — Subtraction Property of Equality

Words If you subtract the same number from each side of an equation, the two sides remain equal.

Symbols If $a = b$, then $a - c = b - c$.

Examples

Numbers	Algebra
$6 = 6$	$x + 2 = 6$
$-2 = -2$	$-2 = -2$
$4 = 4$	$x = 4$

READING in the Content Area

For strategies in reading this lesson, visit tx.msmath2.com.

REVIEW Vocabulary

solve finding a number that makes the equation true (Lesson 1-6)

EXAMPLES Solve Addition Equations

1 Solve $x + 5 = 8$. Check your solution.

$x + 5 = 8$	Write the equation.
$-5 = -5$	Subtract 5 from each side.
$x = 3$	Simplify.

Check	$x + 5 = 8$	Write the original equation.
	$3 + 5 \stackrel{?}{=} 8$	Replace *x* with 3.
	$8 = 8$ ✓	The sentence is true.

The solution is 3.

2 Solve $x + 6 = 4$.

$x + 6 = 4$	Write the equation.
$-6 = -6$	Subtract 6 from each side.
$x = -2$	Simplify.
The solution is -2.	Check the solution.

CHECK Your Progress

Solve each equation.

a. $y + 6 = 9$ b. $x + 3 = 1$ c. $-3 = a + 4$

Real-World EXAMPLE

Real-World Career . . .
How Does a Marine Biologist use Math?
A marine biologist uses math to analyze data about marine animals.

Math Online For more information, go to tx.msmath2.com.

3 MARINE BIOLOGY **Bottle-nosed dolphins and killer whales are the best-known species of the dolphin family. A killer whale, which can grow to a length of 9 meters, is 4 meters longer than a bottle-nosed dolphin. How long is a bottle-nosed dolphin?**

Words	A whale	is	4 meters longer than		a dolphin.
Variable	Let *x* represent the length of the dolphin.				
Equation	9	=	4	+	*x*

$9 = 4 + x$	Write the equation.
$-4 = -4$	Subtract 4 from each side.
$5 = x$	Simplify.

The bottle-nosed dolphin is 5 meters long.

CHECK Your Progress

d. **WEATHER** The highest recorded temperature in El Paso, Texas, is 114°F. This is 122° greater than the lowest recorded temperature. Write and solve an equation to find the lowest recorded temperature.

Online Personal Tutor at tx.msmath2.com

Similarly, you can use inverse operations and the Addition Property of Equality to solve equations like $x - 2 = 1$.

KEY CONCEPT — Addition Property of Equality

Words If you add the same number to each side of an equation, the two sides remain equal.

Symbols If $a = b$, then $a + c = b + c$.

Examples

Numbers	Algebra
$5 = 5$	$x - 2 = 4$
$+3 = +3$	$+2 = +2$
$8 = 8$	$x = 6$

EXAMPLE Solve a Subtraction Equation

4 **Solve $x - 2 = 1$.**

$x - 2 = 1$	Write the equation.
$+2 = +2$	Add 2 to each side.
$x = 3$	Simplify.
The solution is 3.	Check the solution.

CHECK Your Progress

Solve each equation.

e. $y - 3 = 4$ f. $r - 4 = -2$ g. $q - 8 = -9$

Real-World EXAMPLE

5 **SHOPPING** **A pair of shoes costs \$25. This is \$14 less than the cost of a pair of jeans. Find the cost of the jeans.**

Words	Shoes	are	\$14 less than	jeans
Variable	Let x represent the cost of jeans.			
Equation	25	=	$x - 14$	

$25 = x - 14$	Write the equation.
$+14 = +14$	Add 14 to each side.
$39 = x$	Simplify.

The cost of the jeans is \$39.

STUDY TIP

Check for reasonableness Ask yourself which costs more: the shoes or the jeans. Then check your answer. Does it show that the jeans cost more than the shoes?

CHECK Your Progress

h. **ANIMALS** The average lifespan of a tiger is 22 years. This is 13 years less than a lion. Write and solve an equation to find the lifespan of a lion.

CHECK Your Understanding

Examples 1, 2 (p. 185)

Solve each equation. Check your solution.

1. $n + 6 = 8$
2. $7 = y + 2$
3. $m + 5 = 3$
4. $-2 = a + 6$

Example 3 (p. 185)

5. **FLYING** Orville and Wilbur Wright made the first airplane flights in 1903. Wilbur's flight was 364 feet. This was 120 feet longer than Orville's flight. Write and solve an equation to find the length of Orville's flight.

Example 4 (p. 186)

Solve each equation. Check your solution.

6. $x - 5 = 6$
7. $-1 = c - 6$

Example 5 (p. 186)

8. **PRESIDENTS** John F. Kennedy was the youngest president to be inaugurated. He was 43 years old. This was 26 years younger than the oldest president to be inaugurated—Ronald Reagan. Write and solve an equation to find how old Reagan was when he was inaugurated.

Exercises

HOMEWORK HELP

For Exercises	See Examples
9–12	1
13–16	2
17–20	4
21–24	3, 5

Solve each equation. Check your solution.

9. $a + 3 = 10$
10. $y + 5 = 11$
11. $9 = r + 2$
12. $14 = s + 7$
13. $x + 8 = 5$
14. $y + 15 = 11$
15. $r + 6 = -3$
16. $k + 3 = -9$
17. $s - 8 = 9$
18. $w - 7 = 11$
19. $-1 = q - 8$
20. $-2 = p - 13$

For Exercises 21–24, write an equation. Then solve the equation.

21. **MUSIC** Last week Tiffany practiced her bassoon a total of 7 hours. This was 2 hours more than she practiced the previous week. How many hours did Tiffany practice the previous week?

22. **CIVICS** In the 2004 presidential election, Ohio had 20 electoral votes. This is 14 votes less than Texas had. How many electoral votes did Texas have in 2004?

23. **AGES** Zack is 15 years old. This is 3 years younger than his brother Tyler. How old is Tyler?

24. **BASKETBALL** The Mavericks scored 122 points in their last game. This was 5 points less than they scored in the previous game. How many points did they score in their previous game?

Solve each equation. Check your solution.

25. $34 + r = 95$
26. $64 + y = 84$
27. $-23 = x - 18$
28. $-59 = m - 11$
29. $-18 + c = -30$
30. $-34 = t + 9$
31. $a - 3.5 = 14.9$
32. $x - 2.8 = 9.5$
33. $r - 8.5 = -2.1$
34. $z - 9.4 = -3.6$
35. $n + 1.4 = 0.72$
36. $b + 2.25 = 1$

For Exercises 37–42, write an equation. Then solve the equation.

37. **MONEY** Suppose you have d dollars. After you pay your sister the \$5 you owe her, you have \$18 left. How much money did you have at the beginning?

38. **MONEY** Suppose you have saved \$38. How much more do you need to save to buy a small television that costs \$65?

39. **GEOMETRY** The sum of the measures of the angles of a triangle is 180°. Find the missing measure.

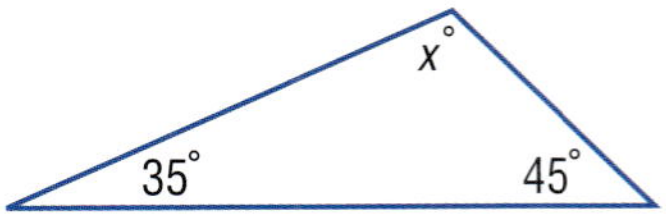

40. **VOLCANOES** Alaska, Hawaii, and Washington have active volcanoes. Alaska has 43, Hawaii has 5, and Washington has v. If they have 52 active volcanoes in all, how many volcanoes does Washington have?

41. **GOLF** The table shows Michelle Wie's scores for four rounds of a recent LPGA Championship. Her total score was 0 (even par). What was her score for the third round?

Round	Score
First	0
Second	+2
Third	s
Fourth	+4

42. **BUSINESS** At the end of the day, the closing price of XYZ Stock was \$62.87 per share. This was \$0.62 less than the opening price. Find the opening price.

Real-World Link
At age 13, Michelle Wie became the youngest player to win any adult USGA event.
Source: thegolfchannel.com

ANALYZE TABLES **For Exercises 43–45, use the table.**

Tallest Steel Roller Coasters in North America	Height (feet)	Drop (feet)	Speed (mph)
Superman The Escape	415	328	s
Millennium Force	h	300	93
Titan	245	d	85
Goliath	235	255	85
Nitro	230	215	80

Source: rcdb.com

43. *Superman The Escape* is 105 feet taller than *Millennium Force*. Write and solve an addition equation to find the height of *Millennium Force*.

44. *Nitro* has a drop that is 40 feet less than *Titan*'s. Write and solve a subtraction equation to find *Titan*'s drop.

45. The difference in the speeds of *Superman The Escape* and *Millennium Force* is 7 miles per hour. If *Superman The Escape* has the greater speed, write and solve a subtraction equation to find its speed.

EXTRA PRACTICE
See pages 725, 758.
Math Online
Self-Check Quiz at tx.msmath2.com

H.O.T. Problems

46. **Which One Doesn't Belong?** Identify the equation that does not have the same solution as the other three. Explain your reasoning.

$x - 1 = -3$	$b + 5 = -7$	$10 + y = 8$	$-6 + a = -8$

47. **CHALLENGE** Suppose $x + y = 10$ and the value of x increases by 3. If their sum remains the same, what must happen to the value of y?

48. **WRITING IN MATH** Write a problem about a real-world situation that can be represented by the equation $p - 25 = 50$.

TEST PRACTICE

49. The Sears Tower in Chicago is 1,454 feet tall. It is 204 feet taller than the Empire State Building in New York City. Which equation can be used to find the height h of the Empire State Building?

A $1{,}454 = h - 204$

B $h = 1{,}454 + 204$

C $1{,}454 = h + 204$

D $204 - h = 1{,}454$

50. The model represents the equation $x + 3 = 7$.

How can you find the value of x?

F Add 3 beans to each side.

G Subtract 7 beans from each side.

H Subtract 3 beans from each side.

J Add 7 beans to each side.

Spiral Review

51. **SCIENCE** The boiling point of water is 180° higher than its freezing point. If p represents the freezing point, write an expression that represents the boiling point of water. (Lesson 4-1)

52. Write 458,000 in scientific notation. (Lesson 3-7)

53. **ANALYZE TABLES** The table shows the lengths of long bridges located in the United States. If all four bridges were laid end to end, what would be the total length in kilometers? (Lesson 3-6)

Bridge	Length (m)
Mackinac, MI	1,158
George Washington, NY	1,067
Tacoma Narrows II, WA	853
Oakland Bay, CA	704

GET READY for the Next Lesson

PREREQUISITE SKILL **Find each quotient.** (Lesson 3-4)

54. $15.6 \div 13$

55. $8.84 \div 3.4$

56. $75.25 \div 0.25$

57. $0.76 \div 0.5$

4-3 Solving Multiplication Equations

Main IDEA

Solve multiplication equations.

Targeted TEKS 7.5 The student uses equations to solve problems. **(A) use concrete and pictorial models to solve equations and use symbols to record the actions.**

NEW Vocabulary

formula

REVIEW Vocabulary

coefficient the numerical factor for a multiplication expression; *Example:* the coefficient of $4x$ is 4. (Lesson 1-4)

MINI Lab

Concepts in Motion BrainPOP® tx.msmath2.com

MONEY Suppose three friends order an appetizer of nachos that costs \$6. They agree to split the cost equally. The figure below illustrates the multiplication equation $3x = 6$, where x represents the amount each friend pays.

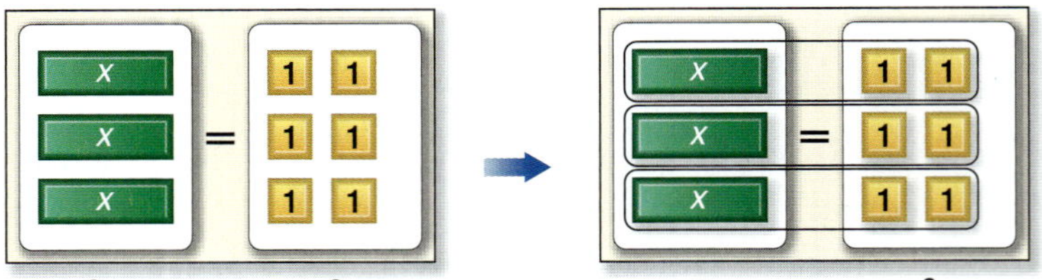

$3x = 6$ → $x = 2$

Each x is matched with \$2.

Each friend pays \$2. The solution of $3x = 6$ is 2.

Solve each equation using models or a drawing.

1. 

$3x = 12$

2. 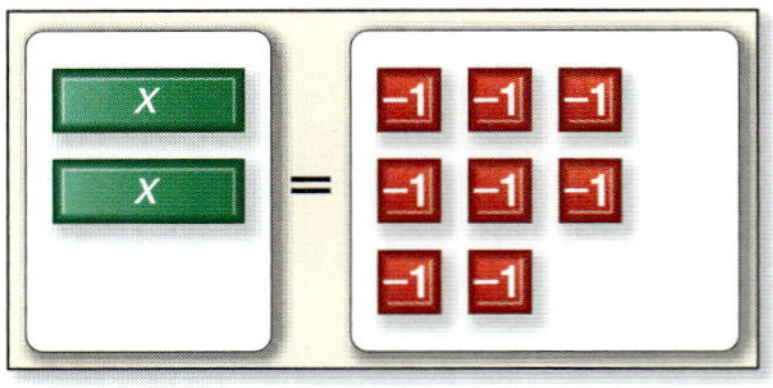

$2x = -8$

3. $4x = 20$

4. $8 = 2x$

5. $3x = -9$

6. What operation did you use to find each solution?

7. How can you use the coefficient of x to solve $8x = 40$?

Equations like $3x = 6$ are called multiplication equations because the expression $3x$ means 3 *times the value of* x. Division and multiplication are inverse operations. So, you can use the Division Property of Equality to solve multiplication equations.

KEY CONCEPT — Division Property of Equality

Words If you divide each side of an equation by the same nonzero number, the two sides remain equal.

Symbols If $a = b$ and $c \neq 0$, then $\frac{a}{c} = \frac{b}{c}$.

Examples

Numbers	Algebra
$8 = 8$	$2x = -6$
$\frac{8}{2} = \frac{8}{2}$	$\frac{2x}{2} = \frac{-6}{2}$
$4 = 4$	$x = -3$

EXAMPLES Solve Multiplication Equations

1 **Solve $20 = 4x$. Check your solution.**

$20 = 4x$	Write the equation.
$\frac{20}{4} = \frac{4x}{4}$	Divide each side of the equation by 4.
$5 = x$	$20 \div 4 = 5$
The solution is 5.	Check the solution.

2 **Solve $-8y = 24$.**

$-8y = 24$	Write the equation.
$\frac{-8y}{-8} = \frac{24}{-8}$	Divide each side by -8.
$y = -3$	$24 \div (-8) = -3$
The solution is -3.	Check the solution.

CHECK Your Progress

Solve each equation.

a. $30 = 6x$ b. $-6a = 36$ c. $-9d = -72$

Many real-world situations increase at a constant rate. These can be represented by multiplication equations.

Real-World EXAMPLE

3 **TEXT MESSAGING** **It costs $0.10 to send a text message. You can spend a total of $5.00. How many text messages can you send?**

Words	Total	is equal to	cost of each message	times	number of messages.
Variable	Let m represent the number of messages you can send.				
Equation	5.00	=	0.10	•	m

$5.00 = 0.10m$	Write the equation.
$\frac{5.00}{0.10} = \frac{0.10m}{0.10}$	Divide each side by 0.10.
$50 = m$	$5.00 \div 0.10 = 50$

At $0.10 per message, you can send 50 text messages for $5.00.

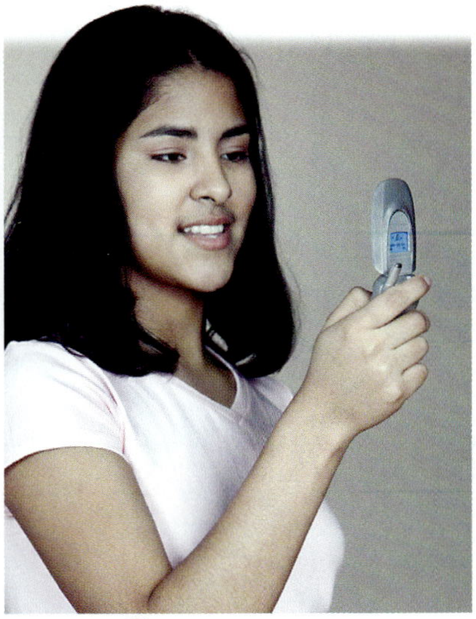

Real-World Link
Over 60% of teenagers' text messages are sent from their homes—even when a landline is available.
Source: xerox.com

CHECK Your Progress

d. **TRAVEL** Mrs. Acosta's car can travel an average of 24 miles on each gallon of gasoline. Write and solve an equation to find how many gallons of gasoline she will need for a trip of 348 miles.

A **formula** is an equation that shows the relationship among certain quantities. One of the most common formulas is the equation $d = rt$, which gives the relationship among distance d, rate r, and time t.

Real-World EXAMPLE

READING Math

Speed Another name for *rate* is *speed*.

4 **ANIMALS** **The tortoise is one of the slowest land animals, reaching an average top speed of about 0.25 mile per hour. At this speed, how long will it take a tortoise to travel 1.5 miles?**

You are asked to find the time t it will take to travel a distance d of 1.5 miles at a rate r of 0.25 mile per hour.

METHOD 1 **Substitute, then solve.**

$d = rt$	Write the equation.
$1.5 = 0.25t$	Replace d with 1.5 and r with 0.25.
$\frac{1.5}{0.25} = \frac{0.25t}{0.25}$	Divide each side by 0.25.
$6 = t$	$1.5 \div 0.25 = 6$

METHOD 2 **Solve, then substitute.**

$d = rt$	Write the equation.
$\frac{d}{r} = \frac{rt}{r}$	Divide each side by r to solve the equation for t.
$\frac{d}{r} = t$	Simplify.
$\frac{1.5}{0.25} = t$	Replace d with 1.5 and r with 0.25.
$6 = t$	$1.5 \div 0.25 = 6$

It would take a tortoise 6 hours to travel 1.5 miles.

CHOOSE Your Method

e. **SCIENCE** A sound wave travels a distance of 700 meters in 2.5 seconds. Find the average speed of the sound wave.

Online **Personal Tutor at** tx.msmath2.com

CHECK Your Understanding

Examples 1, 2 (p. 191)

Solve each equation. Check your solution.

1. $6c = 18$
2. $15 = 3z$
3. $-8x = 24$
4. $-9r = -36$

Example 3 (p. 191)

5. **BABY-SITTING** Gracia earns \$5 per hour when she baby-sits. How many hours does she need to work to earn \$75?

Example 4 (p. 192)

6. **SWIMMING** A shark can swim at an average speed of about 25 miles per hour. At this rate, how long will it take a shark to swim 60 miles?

Exercises

HOMEWORK HELP

For Exercises	See Examples
7–12	1
13–18	2
19–20	3
21–22	4

Solve each equation. Check your solution.

7. $7a = 49$
8. $9e = 27$
9. $2x = -6$
10. $3y = -21$
11. $35 = 5v$
12. $72 = 12r$
13. $-4j = 36$
14. $-12y = 60$
15. $-4s = -16$
16. $-6z = -36$
17. $48 = -6r$
18. $-28 = -7f$

For Exercises 19–22, write an equation. Then solve the equation.

19. **MONEY** Brandy wants to buy a digital camera that costs $300. If she saves $15 each week, in how many weeks will she have enough money for the camera?

20. **KITES** In a simple kite, the length of the longer stick should be 1.5 times the length of the shorter stick. Find the length of the shorter stick for the kite shown at the right.

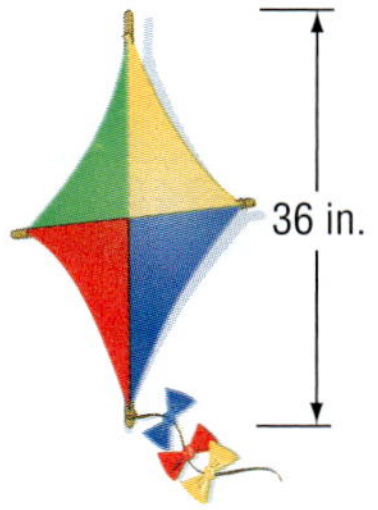

21. **TRAVEL** A Boeing 747 aircraft has an average cruising speed of about 600 miles per hour. At that rate, how long will it take to travel 1,500 miles?

22. **INSECTS** A dragonfly, the fastest insect, can fly a distance of 50 feet in about 2 seconds. Find a dragonfly's average speed in feet per second.

Solve each equation. Check your solution.

23. $0.4x = 9.2$
24. $0.9y = 13.5$
25. $5.4 = 0.3p$
26. $9.72 = 1.8a$
27. $3.9y = 18.33$
28. $2.6b = 2.08$

ANALYZE TABLES For Exercises 29 and 30, use the table.

Name	Track Length (ft)	Time of Ride
Blue Streak	2,558	1 min 45 s
Corkscrew	2,050	2 min
Magnum	5,106	2 min
Mean Streak	5,427	2 min 45 s

Source: rcdb.com

29. Without calculating, explain whether the *Blue Streak* or *Magnum* has the greater average speed.

30. Find the average speed of each roller coaster in feet per second.

31. **EARTHQUAKES** Scientists determine the epicenter of an earthquake by measuring the time it takes for surface waves to travel between two places. Surface waves travel about 6 kilometers per second through Earth's crust. The distance from Los Angeles to Phoenix is 600 kilometers. Write and solve a multiplication equation to find how long it would take surface waves to travel from Los Angeles to Phoenix.

32. **WATER** A case of water bottles costs $9.48. If there are 12 water bottles in the case, find the cost per bottle. Then find the decrease in cost per bottle if the cost of a case is reduced to $8.64.

EXTRA PRACTICE

See pages 726, 758.

Math Online
Self-Check Quiz at tx.msmath2.com

H.O.T. Problems

33. **FIND THE ERROR** Jesse and Haley are solving $-5x = 30$. Who is correct? Explain.

34. **CHALLENGE** Solve $3|x| = 12$. Explain your reasoning.

WRITING IN MATH Write a real-world problem that could be represented by each equation.

35. $2x = 16$

36. $3x = 75$

37. $4x = -8$

TEST PRACTICE

38. A football player can run 20 yards in 3.4 seconds. Which equation could be used to find y, the number of yards the football player can run in a second?

 A $20y = 3.4$

 B $3.4 - y = 20$

 C $3.4y = 20$

 D $20 + y = 3.4$

39. **GRIDDABLE** A car is traveling at a speed of 75 feet per second. How many yards will the car travel in 90 seconds if it maintains the same speed?

40. Use the formula $A = bh$ to find the height of a parallelogram with a base of 34 millimeters and an area of 612 square millimeters.

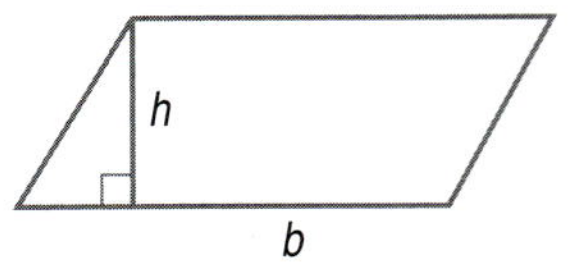

 F 20,800 mm

 G 646 mm

 H 578 mm

 J 18 mm

Spiral Review

ALGEBRA Solve each equation. Check your solution. (Lesson 4-2)

41. $y + 8 = -2$

42. $x - 7 = -2$

43. $20 = z + 23$

44. **ALGEBRA** Write an algebraic expression for the phrase *the product of −3 and y.* (Lesson 4-1)

45. **MONTHS** A lunar month, the time from one new moon to the next is 29.5 days. How many days longer is our calendar year of 365 days than 12 lunar months? (Lesson 3–2)

GET READY for the Next Lesson

PREREQUISITE SKILL Draw the next two figures in the pattern. (Lesson 2-6)

46.

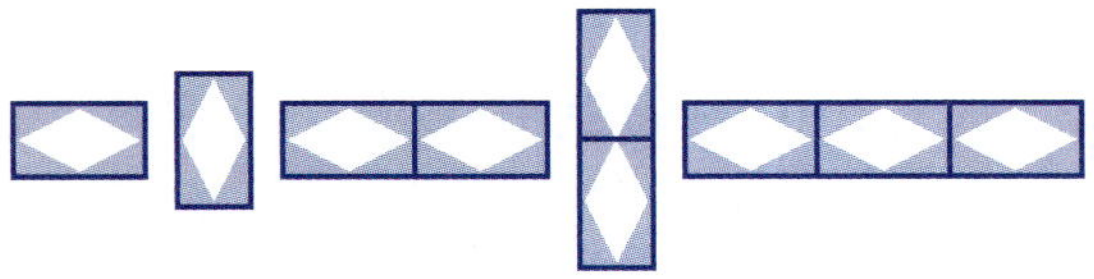

CHAPTER 4 Mid-Chapter Quiz

Lessons 4-1 through 4-3

Write each sentence as an algebraic equation. (Lesson 4-1)

1. The product of a number and 3 is -16.
2. 10 less than a number is 45.

3. **FLYING** An airplane is flying at an altitude of t feet before it increases its altitude by 1,000 feet. Write an expression for its new altitude. (Lesson 4-1)

4. **TEST PRACTICE** Kim's time for the 5K race was 4 minutes less than Tanya's time. If Tanya's time is t, which expression represents Kim's time? (Lesson 4-1)

   A $4 - t$ **C** $t + 4$

   B $t - 4$ **D** $4t$

Solve each equation. Check your solution. (Lesson 4-2)

5. $21 + m = 33$
6. $a - 5 = -12$

7. **GEOMETRY** The sum of the measures of the angles of a triangle is 180°. Write and solve an equation to find the missing measure m. (Lesson 4-2)

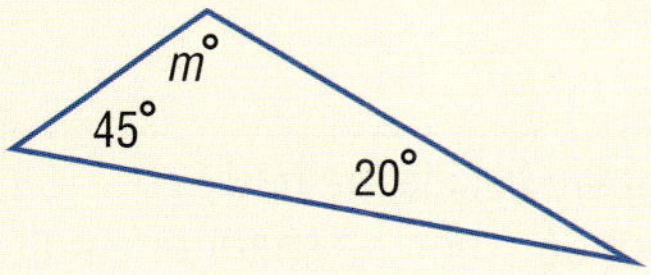

8. **TEST PRACTICE** Trevor's test score was 5 points lower than Ursalina's test score. If Ursalina scored 85 on the test, which equation would give Trevor's score d when solved? (Lesson 4-2)

   F $85 = d + 5$

   G $d - 5 = 85$

   H $80 = d + 5$

   J $d - 5 = 80$

9. **PETS** Cameron has 11 goldfish. This is 7 fewer goldfish than his friend Julia has. Write and solve a subtraction equation to determine the number of goldfish g that Julia has. (Lesson 4-2)

10. **MEASUREMENT** The Grand Canyon has a maximum depth of almost 5,280 feet. An average four-story apartment building has a height of 66 feet. Write and solve a multiplication equation to determine the number of apartment buildings b, stacked on top of each other, that would fill the Grand Canyon. (Lesson 4-3)

Solve each equation. Check your solution. (Lesson 4-3)

11. $5f = -75$
12. $-1.6w = 4.8$
13. $63 = 7y$
14. $-28 = -2d$

15. **TEST PRACTICE** The model represents the equation $3s = -18$.

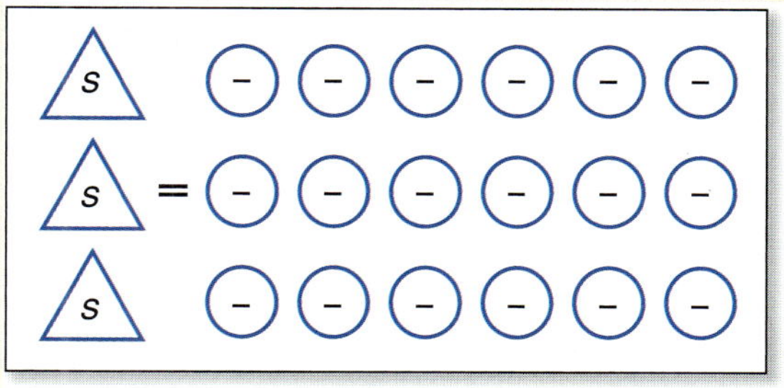

What is the value of s? (Lesson 4-3)

   A 6 **C** 21

   B -6 **D** -21

16. **LAWN SERVICE** Trey estimates he will earn \$470 next summer cutting lawns in his neighborhood. This amount is 2.5 times the amount a he earned this summer. Write and solve a multiplication equation to find how much Trey earned this summer. (Lesson 4-3)

4-4 Problem-Solving Investigation

MAIN IDEA: Solve problems using the work backward strategy.

Targeted TEKS 7.13 The student applies Grade 7 mathematics to solve problems connected to everyday experiences,... and activities in and outside of school. **(C) select or develop an appropriate problem-solving strategy from a variety of different types, including... working backwards to solve a problem.** *Also addresses TEKS 7.13(B).*

P.S.I. TEAM +

e-Mail: WORK BACKWARD

YOUR MISSION: Work backward to solve the problem.

THE PROBLEM: How much money did Carlos take to the movies today?

> Carlos: Well, I spent $9 on movie tickets. Then I spent $5 on candy, and one half of what was left on popcorn. I have $3 left.

EXPLORE	You know he has $3 left and the amounts spent. You need to find the initial amount he had.	
PLAN	Start with the end result and work backward.	
SOLVE	He has $3 left.	3
	Undo the half spent on popcorn. >>>>>>>>>>>>>>>>>>>>>>>>>	× 2 6
	Undo the $5 spent on candy. >>>>>>>>>>>>>>>>>>>>>>>>>>>>	+ 5 11
	Undo the $9 spent on movie tickets. >>>>>>>>>>>>>>>>>>>>>>>>	+ 9 20
	So, Carlos initially had $20.	
CHECK	Assume that he started with $20. After buying movie tickets, he had $20 − $9 or $11. He spent $5 on candy, so he had $11 − $5 or $6. Then he spent one half of the rest on popcorn, so he had $6 ÷ 2 or $3. So, our answer of $20 is correct.	

Analyze The Strategy

1. Explain when you would use the work backward strategy to solve a problem.
2. Describe how to solve a problem by working backward.
3. **WRITING IN MATH** Write a problem that could be solved by working backward. Then write the steps you would take to find the solution to your problem.

Mixed Problem Solving

Use the *work backward* strategy to solve Exercises 4–7.

4. **MONEY** Mia spent \$4.50 at the bakery and then spent four times that amount at the grocery. She had \$12.80 left. How much did she have initially?

5. **NUMBER THEORY** A number is multiplied by 4. Then 6 is subtracted from the product. After adding 5, the result is 15. What is the number?

6. **TIME** A portion of a shuttle bus schedule is shown. What is the earliest time after 9 A.M. when the bus departs?

Departs	Arrives
8:55 A.M.	9:20 A.M.
?	10:08 A.M.
10:31 A.M.	10:56 A.M.
11:19 A.M.	11:44 A.M.

7. **VIDEOS** Jack rented 2 times as many DVDs as Paloma last month. Paloma rented 4 fewer than Greg, but 4 more than Grace. Greg rented 9 DVDs. How many DVDs did each person rent?

Use any strategy to solve Exercises 8–12. Some strategies are shown below.

PROBLEM-SOLVING STRATEGIES
- Use the four-step plan.
- Guess and check.
- Look for a pattern.
- Work backward.

8. **GEOGRAPHY** The land area of Texas is 267,277 square miles. This is about 5 times the land area of Arkansas. Estimate the land area of Arkansas.

9. **AGE** Maya is two years older than her sister Jenna. Jenna is 5 years older than their brother Terry, who is 9 years younger than their brother Trent. Trent is 17 years old. How old is Maya?

10. **FOOD** At the grocery store, Mateo buys a ham for \$24.98 and a vegetable tray for \$17.49. There is no tax. He gives the cashier one bill and receives less than \$10 in change. What was the denomination of the bill Mateo gave the cashier?

11. **PATTERNS** Draw the sixth figure in the pattern shown.

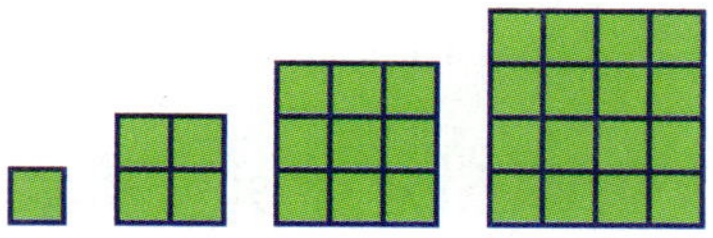

12. **WATERFALLS** The Angel waterfall in Venezuela, the highest waterfall in the world, is 3,212 feet high. It is 87 feet higher than 2.5 times the height of the Empire State Building. Find the height of the Empire State Building.

Select the Operation

For Exercises 13 and 14, select the appropriate operation(s) to solve the problem. Justify your selection(s) and solve the problem.

13. **AIRCRAFT** An aircraft carrier travels about 6 inches per gallon of fuel. Raquel's car travels about 28 miles per gallon of fuel. If there are 5,280 feet in one mile, how many more inches per gallon would Raquel's car get than an aircraft carrier?

14. **SCHOOL SUPPLIES** Alexandra wishes to buy 5 pens, 1 ruler, and 7 folders to start the school year. The prices are shown in the table.

Item	Cost
Pens	\$2.09
Ruler	\$0.99
Folder	\$1.19

If there is no tax, is \$20 enough to pay for Alexandra's school supplies? Explain your reasoning.

READING Word Problems

Simplify the Problem

Have you ever tried to solve a long word problem and didn't know where to start? Try to rewrite the problem using only the most important words. Here's an example.

STEP 1 Read the problem and identify the important words and numbers.

SHOPPING Television shopping networks are a popular way to shop. In addition to the cost of the items, you usually pay a shipping fee. Kylie wants to order several pairs of running shorts that cost \$12 each. The shipping fee is \$7. How many shorts can she order with \$55?

STEP 2 Simplify the problem. Keep all of the important words and numbers, but use fewer of them.

The total cost for some shorts that cost \$12 each plus a shipping fee of \$7 is \$55. How many can she buy?

STEP 3 Simplify it again. Use a variable for the unknown.

The total cost of x shorts at \$12 each plus \$7 is \$55.

PRACTICE

Use the method above to simplify each problem.

1. **MONEY** Akira is saving money to buy a scooter that costs \$125. He has already saved \$80 and plans to save an additional \$5 each week. In how many weeks will he have enough money for the scooter?
2. **TRAVEL** A taxi company charges \$1.50 per mile plus a \$10 fee. Suppose Olivia can afford to spend \$19 for a taxi ride from her apartment to the mall. How far can she travel by taxi with \$19?
3. **TEMPERATURE** The current temperature is 40°. It is expected to rise 5° each hour for the next several hours. In how many hours will the temperature be 60°?
4. **MONEY** Joaquin wants to buy some DVDs that are each on sale for \$10 plus a CD that costs \$15. How many DVDs can he buy if he has \$75 to spend?

4-5 Solving Two-Step Equations

Main IDEA

Solve two-step equations.

Targeted TEKS 7.5 The student uses equations to solve problems. **(A) use concrete and pictorial models to solve equations and use symbols to record the actions.** *Also addresses TEKS 7.13(D).*

NEW Vocabulary

two-step equation

MINI Lab

Concepts in Motion BrainPOP® tx.msmath2.com

MONEY A florist charges \$2 for each balloon in an arrangement and a \$3 delivery fee. You have \$9 to spend. The model illustrates the equation $2x + 3 = 9$, where x represents the number of balloons.

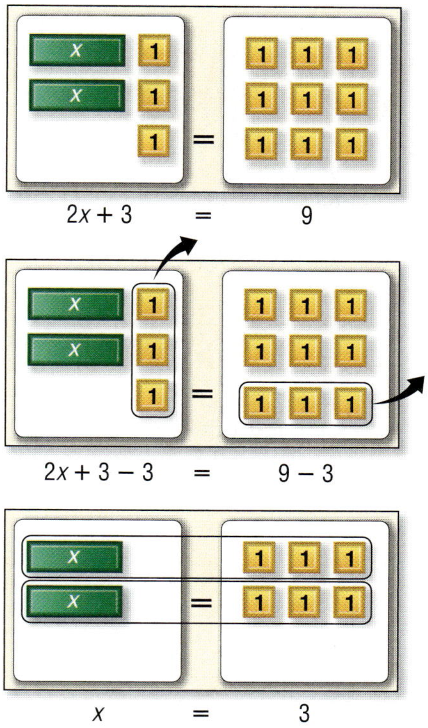

To solve $2x + 3 = 9$, remove three 1-tiles from each side of the mat. Then divide the remaining tiles into two equal groups. The solution of $2x + 3 = 9$ is 3.

Solve each equation by using models or a drawing.

1. $2x + 1 = 5$
2. $3x + 2 = 8$
3. $2 = 5x + 2$

A **two-step equation** has two different operations. To solve a two-step equation, undo the operations in reverse order of the order of operations.

EXAMPLE Solve a Two-Step Equation

1 Solve $2x + 3 = 9$.

$2x + 3 = 9$	Write the equation.
$-3 = -3$	Subtract 3 from each side.
$2x = 6$	
$\frac{2x}{2} = \frac{6}{2}$	Divide each side by 2.
$x = 3$	Simplify.

The solution is 3.

STUDY TIP

Work Backward In $2x + 3 = 9$, x is first multiplied by 2 and then 3 is added. So, you should "undo" the addition first and then the multiplication.

CHECK Your Progress

Solve each equation.

a. $2x + 4 = 10$ b. $3x + 1 = 7$ c. $5 = 2 + 3x$

EXAMPLES Solve Two-Step Equations

2 **Solve $3x + 2 = 23$. Check your solution.**

$3x + 2 = 23$	Write the equation.
$-2 = -2$	Subtract 2 from each side.
$3x = 21$	
$\frac{3x}{3} = \frac{21}{3}$	Divide each side by 3.
$x = 7$	Simplify.

Check $3x + 2 = 23$	Write the original equation.
$3(7) + 2 \stackrel{?}{=} 23$	Replace *x* with 7.
$21 + 2 \stackrel{?}{=} 23$	Simplify.
$23 = 23$ ✓	The sentence is true.

The solution is 7.

STUDY TIP

Checking Solutions You can often use arithmetic facts to check the solutions of simple equations.

3 **Solve $-2y - 7 = 3$.**

$-2y - 7 = 3$	Write the equation.
$+7 = +7$	Add 7 to each side.
$-2y = 10$	
$\frac{-2y}{-2} = \frac{10}{-2}$	Divide each side by −2.
$y = -5$	Simplify.
The solution is −5.	Check the solution.

4 **Solve $4 + 5r = -11$.**

$4 + 5r = -11$	Write the equation.
$-4 \quad = -4$	Subtract 4 from each side.
$5r = -15$	
$\frac{5r}{5} = -\frac{15}{5}$	Divide each side by 5.
$r = -3$	Simplify.
The solution is −3.	Check the solution.

CHECK Your Progress

Solve each equation.

d. $4x + 5 = 13$ **e.** $8y + 15 = 71$ **f.** $-3n - 8 = 7$

g. $-5s + 8 = -2$ **h.** $1 + 2y = -3$ **i.** $-2 + 6w = 10$

Online **Personal Tutor at** tx.msmath2.com

CONCEPT Summary — Solving Two-Step Equations

To solve a two-step equation:

Step 1 Undo the addition or subtraction first.

Step 2 Then undo the multiplication or division.

Some real-world situations start with a given amount and increase at a certain rate.

Real-World Link Over 6.7 million teenagers bowl at least once a year.
Source: census.gov

Real-World EXAMPLE

5 **BOWLING** **Suppose you spend $6 to rent bowling shoes at The Bowling Alley. Each game costs $3.50. How many games can you bowl if you have $20 to spend?**

Words	cost of shoes	plus	cost of one game	times	number of games	equals $20.	
Variable	Let n represent the number of games.						
Equation	6	+	3.50	·	n	=	20

$$6 + 3.50n = 20$$ Write the equation.

$$-6 \qquad = -6$$ Subtract 6 from each side.

$$3.50n = 14$$

$$\frac{3.50n}{3.50} = \frac{14}{3.50}$$ Divide each side by 3.50.

$$n = 4$$ $14 \div 3.50 = 4$

Check

$$6 + 3.50n = 20$$ Write the original equation.

$$6 + 3.50(4) \stackrel{?}{=} 20$$ Replace n with 4.

$$6 + 14 \stackrel{?}{=} 20$$ Simplify.

$$20 = 20 \checkmark$$ The sentence is true.

You can bowl 4 games. Is this answer reasonable?

CHECK Your Progress

j. **FITNESS** A fitness club is having a special offer where you pay $22 to join plus a $16 monthly fee. You have $150 to spend. Write and solve an equation to find how many months you can use the fitness club.

CHECK Your Understanding

Examples 1–4 (pp. 199–200)

Solve each equation. Check your solution.

1. $3x + 1 = 7$
2. $4h - 6 = 22$
3. $-6r + 1 = -17$
4. $-3y - 5 = 10$
5. $13 = 1 + 4s$
6. $-7 = 1 + 2n$

Example 5 (p. 201)

7. **MONEY** Syreeta wants to buy some CDs, each costing $14, and a DVD that cost $23. She has $65 to spend. Write and solve an equation to find how many CDs she can buy.

Exercises

HOMEWORK HELP

For Exercises	See Examples
8–11	1, 2
12–15	3
16–19	4
20–21	5

Solve each equation. Check your solution.

8. $3x + 1 = 10$ **9.** $5x + 4 = 19$ **10.** $2t + 7 = -1$

11. $6m + 1 = -23$ **12.** $-4w - 4 = 8$ **13.** $-7y + 3 = -25$

14. $-8s + 1 = 33$ **15.** $-2x + 5 = -13$ **16.** $3 + 8n = -5$

17. $5 + 4d = 37$ **18.** $14 + 2p = 8$ **19.** $25 + 2y = 47$

For Exercises 20 and 21, write an equation. Then solve the equation.

20. **WEATHER** The temperature is 20°F. It is expected to rise at a rate of 4° each hour for the next several hours. In how many hours will it be 32°?

21. **MONEY** Raimundo has saved $74 toward a new sound system that costs $149. He plans on saving an additional $15 each week. How many weeks will it take Raimundo to save enough money to buy the sound system?

Solve each equation. Check your solution.

22. $2r - 3.1 = 1.7$ **23.** $4t + 3.5 = 12.5$ **24.** $16b - 6.5 = 9.5$

25. $5w + 9.2 = 19.7$ **26.** $16 = 0.5r - 8$ **27.** $0.2n + 3 = 8.6$

For Exercises 28 and 29, write an equation. Then solve the equation.

28. **CELL PHONES** A cell phone company charges a monthly fee of $39.99 for unlimited *off-peak* minutes on the nights and weekends but $0.45 for each *peak* minute during the weekday. If Brad's monthly cell phone bill was $62.49, for how many *peak* minutes did he get charged?

29. **PLANTS** In ideal conditions, bamboo can grow 47.6 inches each day. At this rate, how many days will it take a bamboo shoot that is 8 inches tall to reach a height of 80 feet?

TEMPERATURE For Exercises 30 and 31, use the following information and the graph.

Temperature is usually measured on the Fahrenheit scale (°F) or the Celsius scale (°C). Use the formula $F = 1.8C + 32$ to convert from one scale to the other.

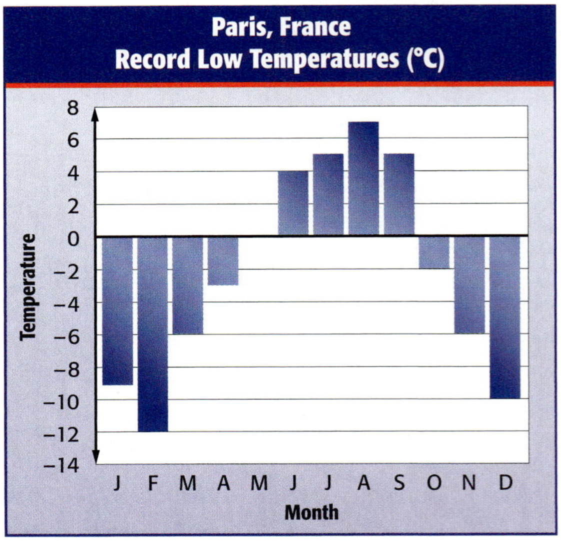

Source: www.usatoday.com/weather

30. The highest temperature ever recorded in Virginia Beach, Virginia, was 104°F. Find this temperature in degrees Celsius.

31. The lowest temperature ever recorded in Virginia Beach was −3°F. Is this temperature greater or less than the lowest temperature ever recorded in Paris, France?

EXTRA PRACTICE

See pages 726, 758.

Math Online
Self-Check Quiz at
tx.msmath2.com

H.O.T. Problems

32. **CHALLENGE** Refer to Exercises 30 and 31. Is there a temperature at which the number of Celsius degrees is the same as the number of Fahrenheit degrees? If so, find it. If not, explain why not.

33. **CHALLENGE** Suppose your school is selling magazine subscriptions. Each subscription costs \$20. The company pays the school half of the total sales in dollars. The school must also pay a one-time fee of \$18. What is the fewest number of subscriptions that can be sold to earn a profit of \$200?

34. **SELECT A TECHNIQUE** Bianca rented a car for a flat fee of \$19.99 plus \$0.26 per mile. Which of the following techniques might she use to determine the approximate number of miles she can drive for \$50. Justify your selection(s). Then use the technique(s) to solve the problem.

Mental Math | Number Sense | Estimation

35. **WRITING IN MATH** Write a real-world problem that would be represented by the equation $2x + 5 = 15$.

TEST PRACTICE

36. A taxi driver charges \$2.00 plus \$0.80 for each mile traveled. Which expression could be used to find the cost of a taxi ride of m miles?

A $2.80m$

B $2m + 0.80$

C $2 + 0.80m$

D $2m + 0.80m$

37. **GRIDDABLE** In 2006, the first-class postage rates were \$0.39 for the first ounce plus an additional cost for each ounce.

Weight (oz)	1	2	3	4
Postage (dollars)	0.39	0.62	0.85	1.08

What is the cost, in dollars, for a 12-ounce letter?

Spiral Review

38. **SCHEDULES** Jaime needs to be at the bus stop by 7:10 A.M. If it takes her 7 minutes to walk to the bus stop and 40 minutes to get ready in the morning, what is the latest time that she can set her alarm in order to be at the bus stop 5 minutes earlier than she needs to be? Use the *work backward* strategy. (Lesson 4-4)

ALGEBRA Solve each equation. Check your solution. (Lessons 4-2 and 4-3)

39. $4f = 28$

40. $-3y = -15$

41. $p - 14 = 27$

42. $-11 = n + 2$

43. **SCUBA DIVING** Find the vertical distance between two divers if one diver is 27 feet below sea level and the other diver is 13 feet below sea level. (Lesson 2-5)

GET READY for the Next Lesson

PREREQUISITE SKILL Multiply or divide. (Lessons 3-2 and 3-4)

44. 2.5×20

45. 3.5×4

46. $4{,}200 \div 2.1$

47. $104 \div 6.5$

4-6 Geometry: Perimeter and Area

Main IDEA

Find the perimeters and areas of figures.

Targeted TEKS 7.9 The student solves application problems involving estimation and measurement. **(A) estimate measurements and solve application problems involving length (including perimeter** and circumference) and **area of polygons** and other shapes. *Also addresses TEKS 7.4(A), 7.13(A), 7.14(A).*

NEW Vocabulary

perimeter
area

Concepts in Motion
Interactive Lab tx.msmath2.com

GET READY for the Lesson

PARKS Central Park in New York City contains a running track, walking paths, playgrounds, and even a carousel.

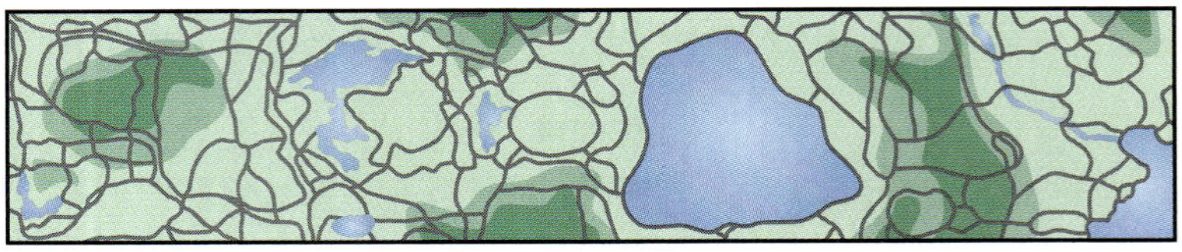

1. If you walked around the outer edge of the entire park, how far would you walk? Describe how you found the distance.
2. Explain how you can use both multiplication and addition to find the distance.

The distance around a geometric figure is called the **perimeter**. To find the perimeter of a rectangle, you can use addition or a formula.

KEY CONCEPT — Perimeter of a Rectangle

Words The perimeter P of a rectangle is twice the sum of the length ℓ and width w.

Symbols $P = \ell + \ell + w + w$

$P = 2\ell + 2w$ or $2(\ell + w)$

Model

EXAMPLE Find the Perimeter of a Rectangle

1 **Find the perimeter of the rectangle shown at the right.**

$P = 2\ell + 2w$ — Perimeter of a rectangle
$P = 2(15) + 2(4)$ — Replace ℓ with 15 and w with 4.
$P = 30 + 8$ — Multiply.
$P = 38$ — Add.

The perimeter is 38 centimeters.

CHECK Your Progress

a. Find the perimeter of a rectangle whose length is 14.5 inches and width is 12.5 inches.

If you know the perimeter of a rectangle and the measure of one of the sides, you can solve an equation to find the remaining side.

Real-World EXAMPLE

2 **GARDENS** **Elan is designing a rectangular garden. He wants the length to be 12 feet. He also wants the put a fence around the garden. If he has 40 feet of fencing, what is the greatest width the garden can be?**

$P = 2\ell + 2w$	Perimeter of a rectangle
$40 = 2(12) + 2w$	Replace P with 40 and ℓ with 12.
$40 = 24 + 2w$	Multiply.
$40 - 24 = 24 + 2w - 24$	Subtract 24 from each side.
$16 = 2w$	Simplify.
$8 = w$	Divide each side by 2.

The greatest width the garden can be is 8 feet wide.

CHECK Your Progress

b. **FRAMES** Angela bought a frame for a photo of her friends. The width of the frame is 8 inches. If the distance around the frame is 36 inches, what is the length of the frame?

The distance *around* a rectangle is its perimeter. The measure of the surface *enclosed* by a rectangle is its **area**.

KEY CONCEPT — Area of a Rectangle

Words The area A of a rectangle is the product of the length ℓ and width w.

Symbols $A = \ell \cdot w$

Model

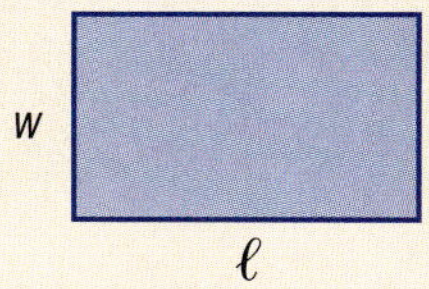

EXAMPLE Find the Area of a Rectangle

3 **VOLLEYBALL** **Find the area of the volleyball court shown at the right.**

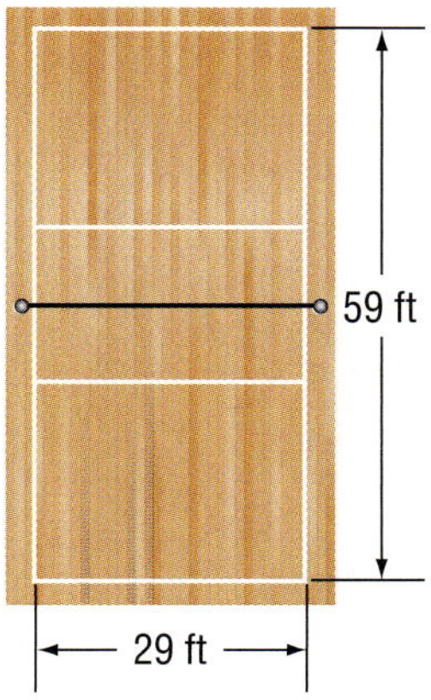

$A = \ell \cdot w$	Area of a rectangle
$A = 59 \cdot 29$	Replace ℓ with 59 and w with 29.
$A = 1{,}711$	Multiply.

The area is 1,711 square feet.

CHECK Your Progress

c. **VIDEO GAMES** Find the perimeter and area of the top of a video game console that measures 18 inches long and 15 inches wide.

STUDY TIP

Area Units When finding area, the units are also multiplied. So, area is given in *square units*. Consider a rectangle 2 ft by 3 ft.

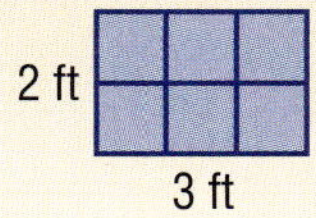

$A = 2 \text{ ft} \cdot 3 \text{ ft}$

$A = (2 \cdot 3)(\text{ft} \cdot \text{ft})$

$A = 6 \text{ ft}^2$

EXAMPLE Use Area to Find a Missing Side

4 **The area of a rectangle is 53.94 square feet. If the width is 8.7 feet, find the length.**

METHOD 1 **Substitute, then solve.**

$A = \ell w$	Write the equation.
$53.94 = \ell(8.7)$	Replace *A* with 53.94 and *w* with 8.7.
$\frac{53.94}{8.7} = \frac{\ell(8.7)}{8.7}$	Divide each side by 8.7.
$\ell = 6.2$	Simplify.

METHOD 2 **Solve, then substitute.**

$A = \ell w$	Write the equation.
$\frac{A}{w} = \frac{\ell w}{w}$	Divide each side by *w*.
$\frac{A}{w} = \ell$	Simplify.
$\frac{53.94}{8.7} = \ell$	Replace *A* with 53.94 and *w* with 8.7.
$\ell = 6.2$	Simplify.

So, the length of the rectangle is 6.2 feet.

STUDY TIP

Check for Reasonableness You know that $53.94 \approx 54$ and that $8.7 \approx 9$. Since $54 \div 9 = 6$, the answer is reasonable.

CHOOSE Your Method

d. What is the width of a rectangle that has an area of 135 square meters and a length of 9 meters?

Online Personal Tutor at tx.msmath2.com

CHECK Your Understanding

Example 1 (p. 204) **Find the perimeter of each rectangle.**

1. 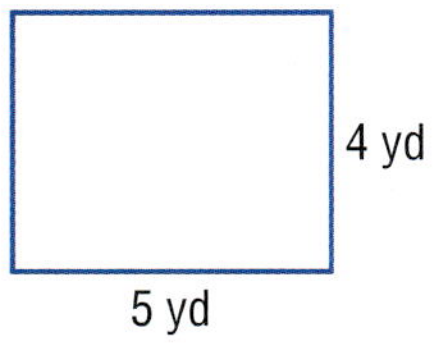

2. 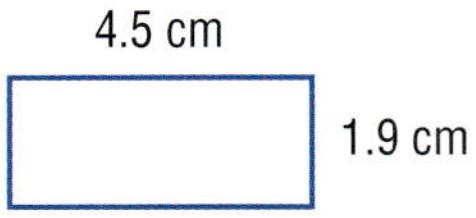

Example 2 (p. 205)

3. **PHOTOGRAPHY** A photograph is 5 inches wide. The perimeter of the photograph is 24 inches. What is the length of the photograph?

Example 3 (p. 205) **Find the area of each rectangle.**

4. 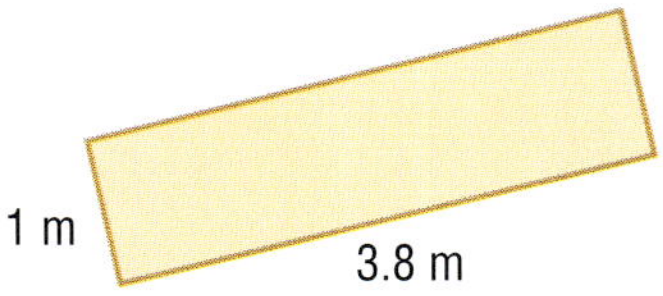

5. 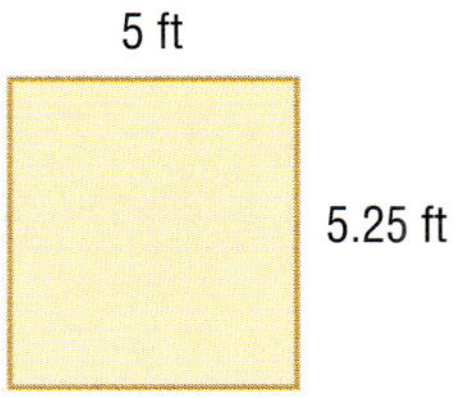

Example 4 (p. 206)

6. **ALGEBRA** The area and length of a rectangle are 30 square feet and 6 feet, respectively. What is the width of the rectangle?

Exercises

For Exercises	See Examples
7–12	1
13–14	2
15–20	3
21–22	4

HOMEWORK HELP

Find the perimeter of each rectangle.

7. 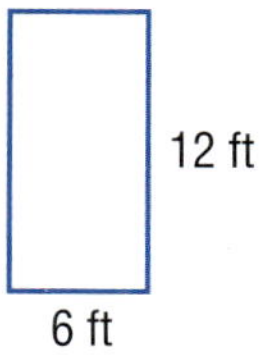

8. 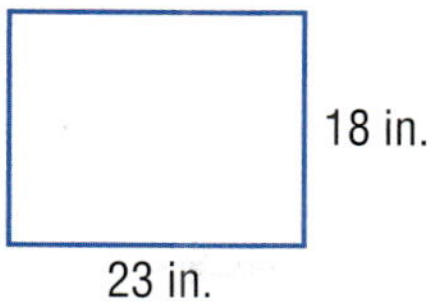

9. 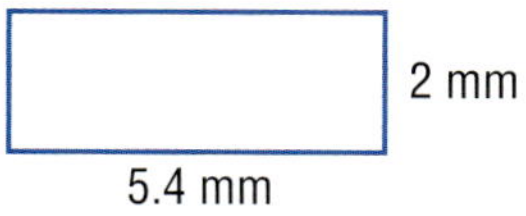

10. 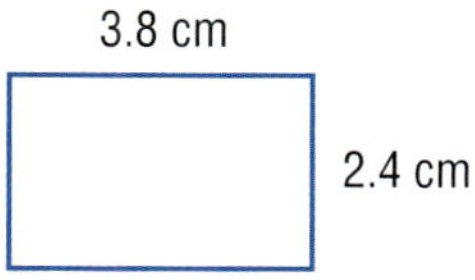

11. $\ell = 1.5$ ft, $w = 4$ ft

12. $\ell = 5.75$ ft, $w = 8$ ft

13. **SEWING** The fringe used to outline a placemat is 60 inches. If the width of the placemat is 12 inches, what is the measure of its length?

14. **GAMES** Orlando marks off a rectangular section of grass to use as a playing field. He knows that he needs to mark off 111 feet around the border of the playing field. If the field is 25.5 feet long, what is its width?

Find the area of each rectangle.

15. 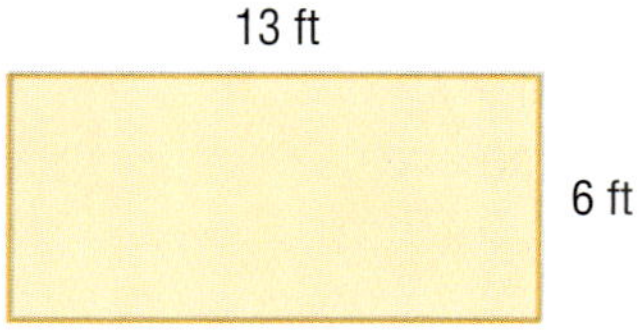

16. 

17. 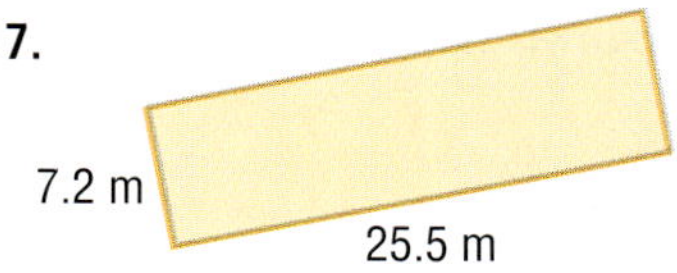

18. 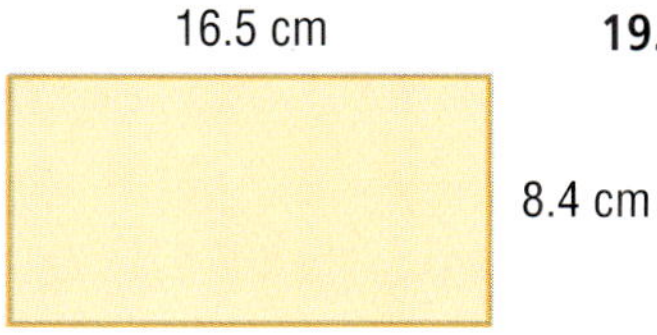

19. $\ell = 3.25$ in., $w = 2$ in.

20. $\ell = 4.5$ ft, $w = 10.6$ ft

21. **QUILTING** Daniela's grandmother is making a quilt that is 7 squares wide. If she needs 35 squares total, how many squares long is the length?

22. **PAINTING** A rectangular mural is painted on a wall. If the mural is 12 feet wide and covers 86.4 square feet, what is the height of the mural?

Find the missing measure.

23. $P = 115.6$ ft, $w = 24.8$ ft

24. $A = 189.28\ \text{cm}^2$, $w = 16.9$ cm

ANALYZE TABLES **For Exercises 25 and 26, use the table shown.**

Football Field	Length (ft)	Width (ft)
American	300	160
Canadian	330	197

25. How much greater is the area of a Canadian football field than an American football field?

26. An *acre* equals 43,560 square feet. How many acres are there in a Canadian football field? Round to the nearest tenth of an acre and explain the method you used to solve the problem.

For Exercises 27–30, determine whether the problem involves perimeter or area. Then solve.

27. **HIKING** Ramón walked along a rectangular hiking path. Initially, he walked 3 miles north before he turned east. If he walked a total of 14 miles, how many miles did he walk east before he turned south?

28. **BORDERS** Kaitlyn's bedroom is shaped like a rectangle. She is putting a wallpaper border along the top of each rectangular wall. If the length of the room is 13 feet and the width is 9.8 feet, about how many feet of border does she need?

29. **DECKS** Armando built a rectangular deck in his backyard. The deck takes up 168.75 square feet of space. If the deck's width is 12.8 feet, what is its approximate length?

30. **FLOORING** Jasmine plans to use 1-foot square tiles to tile her kitchen floor, which measures 18.5 feet by 14 feet. If there are 40 tiles per box, how many boxes must she buy?

Real-World Link
Regulation volleyball courts are 18 meters long by 9 meters wide, not including the free zone.
Source: usavolleyball.org

31. **VOLLEYBALL** For safety, regulation courts have a "free zone" added to the width of each side of the court. If the free zone on each side is 3 meters wide, use the information to the left to find the area of the entire volleyball court including the free zone.

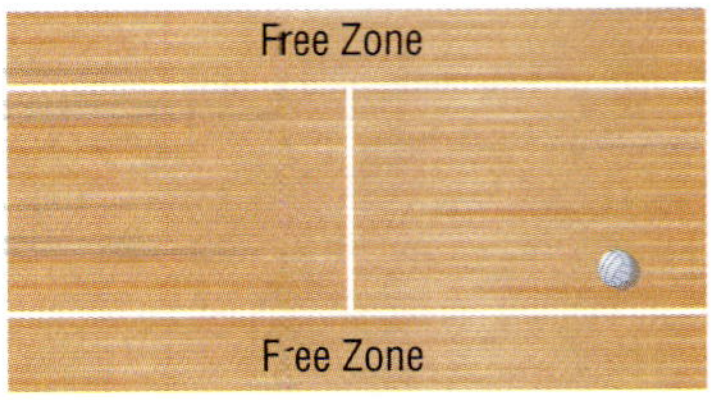

32. **GEOMETRY** Use the diagram at the right to write formulas for the perimeter P and area A of a square.

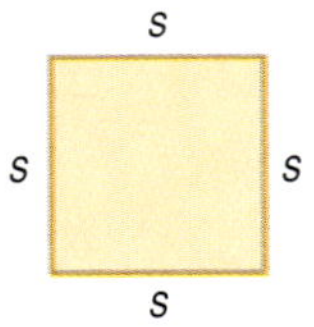

33. **FIND THE DATA** Refer to the Texas Data File on pages 16–19. Choose some data and write a real-world problem in which you would find the perimeter and area of a rectangle.

EXTRA PRACTICE
See pages 727, 758.
Math Online
Self-Check Quiz at tx.msmath2.com

H.O.T. Problems

34. **OPEN ENDED** Draw and label three different rectangles that have an area of 24 square centimeters.

CHALLENGE For Exercises 35–38, find each equivalent measurement. Provide a diagram to justify your answers. The diagram for Exercise 35 is shown.

35. $1 \text{ yd}^2 = \blacksquare \text{ ft}^2$
36. $4 \text{ yd}^2 = \blacksquare \text{ ft}^2$
37. $1 \text{ ft}^2 = \blacksquare \text{ in}^2$
38. $2 \text{ ft}^2 = \blacksquare \text{ in}^2$

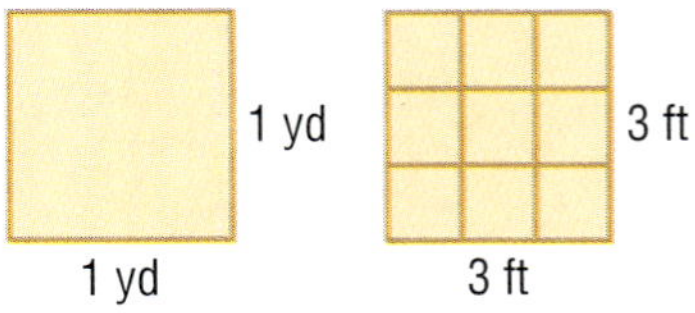

NUMBER SENSE For Exercises 39 and 40, describe the effect on the perimeter and area in each of the following situations.

39. The width of a rectangle is doubled.
40. The length of a side of a square is doubled.

41. **CHALLENGE** A rectangle has width w. Its length is one unit more than 3 times its width. Write an expression that represents the perimeter of the rectangle.

42. **WRITING IN MATH** Decide whether the statement is *true* or *false*. Explain your reasoning and provide examples.

Of all rectangles with a perimeter of 24 square inches, the one with the greatest area is a square.

TEST PRACTICE

43. Oakland Garden Center created a design plan for the Nelson family's rock garden. The shaded areas will hold flowers and the rest of the garden will be rock.

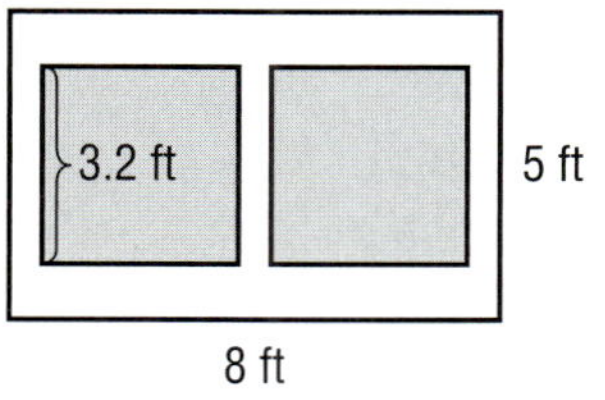

If each shaded area is a square, what is the area of the garden that will be rock?

A 19.52 ft^2 C 40 ft^2

B 29.76 ft^2 D 60.48 ft^2

44. The rectangle below has width 4.75 feet and perimeter P feet.

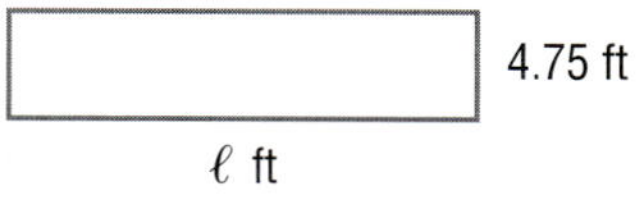

Which of the following could be used to find the length of the rectangle?

F $P = 4.75 + \frac{\ell}{2}$

G $P = 4.75 - \ell$

H $P = 9.5 + 2\ell$

J $P = 9.5 - 2\ell$

Spiral Review

Solve each equation. Check your solution. (Lesson 4-5)

45. $5d + 12 = 2$ 46. $13 - f = 7$ 47. $10 = 2g + 3$ 48. $6 = 3 - 3h$

49. **MONEY** Anna was charged $11.25 for returning a DVD 5 days late. Write and solve an equation to find how much the video store charges per day for late fees. (Lesson 4-3)

Replace each ● with a <, >, or = to make a true sentence. (Lesson 3-7)

50. $4{,}500$ ● 4.5×10^3 51. $10{,}000$ ● 1×10^5 52. $1{,}400{,}000$ ● 1.4×10^5

53. **AGE** The sum of Denise's and Javier's ages is 26 years. If Denise is 4 years older than Javier, find Javier's age. Use the *guess and check* strategy. (Lesson 1-5)

GET READY for the Next Lesson

PREREQUISITE SKILL Graph and label each point on a coordinate plane. (Lesson 2-3)

54. $(-4, 2)$ 55. $(3, -1)$ 56. $(-3, -4)$ 57. $(2, 0)$

Explore 4-7

Math Lab
Representing Relationships

Main IDEA

Graph data to demonstrate the relationship between the dimensions and the perimeter of a rectangle.

Targeted TEKS 7.4 The student represents a relationship in numerical, geometric, verbal, and symbolic form. **(B) graph data to demonstrate relationships in familiar concepts such as** conversions, **perimeter**, area, circumference, volume, and scaling.

In this lab, you will investigate the relationships between the dimensions and the perimeter of a rectangle.

ACTIVITY

STEP 1 Use 10 chenille stems, 24 centimeters in length, to form 10 rectangles with different dimensions.

STEP 2 Measure and record the width and length of each rectangle to the nearest centimeter in a table like the one at the right.

Width (cm)	Length (cm)

Analyze the Results

1. What rectangle measure does 24 centimeters represent?
2. Find the sum of the width and length for each of your rectangles. Write a sentence that describes the relationship between this sum and the measure of the length of the stem for each rectangle. Then write a rule that describes this relationship for a rectangle with a width w and length ℓ.
3. In this activity, if a rectangle has a length of 4.5 centimeters, what is its width? Explain your reasoning. Write a rule that can be used to find w when ℓ is known for any rectangle in this Activity.
4. **GRAPH THE DATA** Graph the data in your table on a coordinate plane like the one at the right.

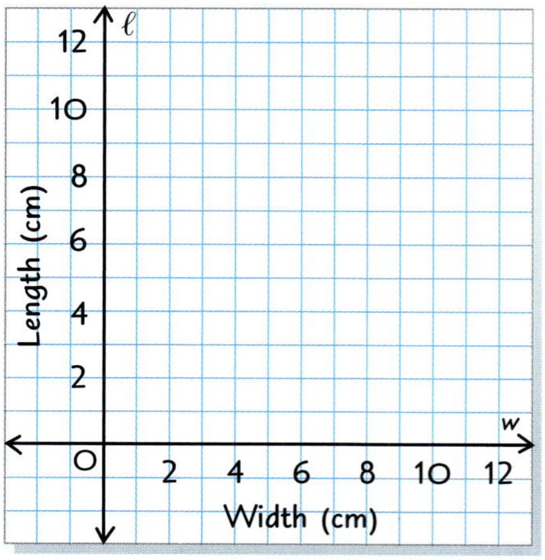

5. Describe what the ordered pair (w, ℓ) represents. Describe how these points appear on the graph.
6. Use your graph to find the width. of a rectangle whose length is 7 centimeters. Explain your method.
7. **MAKE A CONJECTURE** If the length of each chenille stem was 20 centimeters, how would this affect the data in your table? the rule you wrote in Exercise 3? the appearance of your graph?

4-7 Functions and Graphs

Main IDEA

Graph data to demonstrate relationships.

Targeted TEKS 7.4 The student represents a relationship in numerical, geometric, verbal, and symbolic form. **(B) graph data to demonstrate relationships in familiar concepts such as conversions, perimeter,** area, circumference, volume, and scaling.

NEW Vocabulary

linear equation

REVIEW Vocabulary

function a relation in which each element of the input is paired with exactly one element of the output according to a specified rule (Lesson 1-10)

GET READY for the Lesson

MONEY The Westerville Marching Band is going on a year-end trip to an amusement park. Each band member must pay an admission price of \$15. In the table, this is represented by $15m$.

Total Cost of Admission

Number of Members	$15m$	Total Cost (\$)
1	15(1)	15
2	15(2)	30
3	15(3)	
4		
5		
6		

1. Copy and complete the function table for the total cost of admission.
2. Graph the ordered pairs (number of members, total cost).
3. Describe how the points appear on the graph.

Ordered pairs in the form (input, output), or (x, y), can be used to represent a function. These ordered pairs can then be graphed on a coordinate plane as part of the graph of the function.

Real-World EXAMPLE

1 **SCIENCE** **The table shows temperatures in Celsius and the corresponding temperatures in Fahrenheit. Make a graph of the data to show the relationship between Celsius and Fahrenheit.**

Celsius	Fahrenheit
5	41
10	50
15	59
20	68
25	77
30	86

The ordered pairs (5, 41), (10, 50), (15, 59), (20, 68), (25, 77), and (30, 86) represent this function. Graph the ordered pairs.

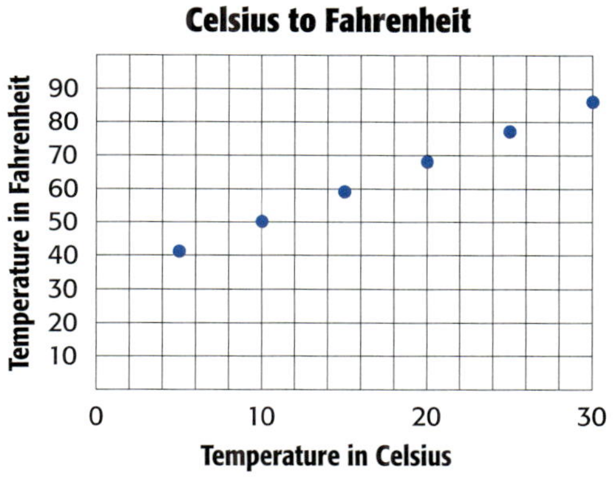

The graph shows the relationship between Celsius and Fahrenheit.

CHECK Your Progress

a. **MUSIC** The table shows the money remaining on a \$75 gift certificate after a certain number of CDs are bought. Make a graph to show how the number of CDs bought and the remaining balance are related.

\$75 Music Gift Certificate	
Number of CDs	**Balance (\$)**
1	63
2	51
3	39
4	27
5	15

The solution of an equation with two variables consists of two numbers, one for each variable, that make the equation true. The solution is usually written as an ordered pair (x, y), which can be graphed.

EXAMPLE Graph Solutions of Linear Equations

2 **Graph $y = 2x + 1$.**

Select any four values for the input x. We chose 2, 1, 0, and -1. Substitute these values for x to find the output y.

x	$2x + 1$	y	(x, y)
2	$2(2) + 1$	5	(2, 5)
1	$2(1) + 1$	3	(1, 3)
0	$2(0) + 1$	1	(0, 1)
-1	$2(-1) + 1$	-1	$(-1, -1)$

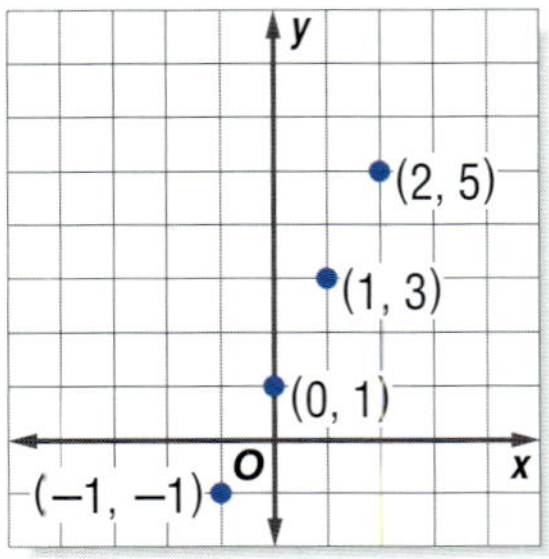

Four solutions are (2, 5), (1, 3), (0, 1), and $(-1, -1)$. Graph the solutions to show the graph of $y = 2x + 1$.

CHECK Your Progress

Graph each equation.

b. $y = x - 3$ c. $y = -3x$ d. $y = -3x + 2$

Online Personal Tutor at tx.msmath2.com

STUDY TIP

Graphing Equations Only two points are needed to graph the line. However, graph more points to check accuracy.

Notice that all four points in the graph lie on a line. Draw a line through the points to graph *all* solutions of the equation $y = 2x + 1$. The graph of (3, 7) is also on the line.

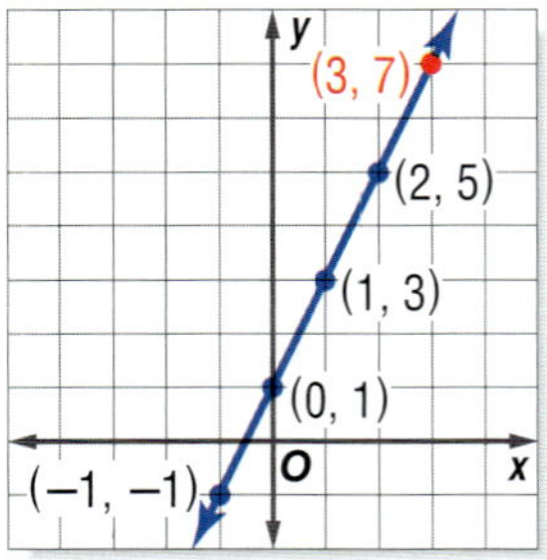

$y = 2x + 1$	Write the equation.
$7 \stackrel{?}{=} 2(3) + 1$	Replace x with 3 and y with 7.
$7 = 7$ ✓	This sentence is true.

So, (3, 7) is also a solution of $y = 2x + 1$.

An equation like $y = 2x + 1$ is called a **linear equation** because its graph is a straight line.

Real-World EXAMPLE

Real-World Link About one fourth of all skateboarding purchases are made by teenagers from 14 to 17 years old.

Source: *Statistical Abstract of the United States*

3 **SKATEBOARDING** **The top speed reached by a standing skateboarder is 80 feet per second. The equation $d = 80t$ describes the distance d that a skateboarder can travel in time t. Represent the function with a graph.**

Step 1 Select any four values for t. Select only positive numbers because t represents time. Make a function table.

t	$80t$	d	(t, d)
1	80(1)	80	(1, 80)
2	80(2)	160	(2, 160)
3	80(3)	240	(3, 240)
4	80(4)	320	(4, 320)

Step 2 Graph the ordered pairs and draw a line through the points.

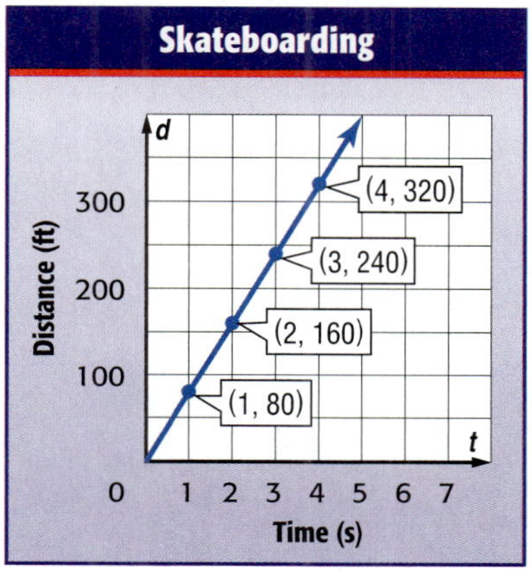

CHECK Your Progress

e. **JOBS** Sandi makes \$6 an hour baby-sitting. The equation $m = 6h$ describes how much money m she earns baby-sitting for h hours. Represent this function with a graph.

CONCEPT Summary — Representing Functions

Words There are 12 inches in one foot.

Table

Feet	Inches
1	12
2	24
3	36
4	48

Equation $f = 12n$, where f represents the number of feet and n represents the number of inches

Graph

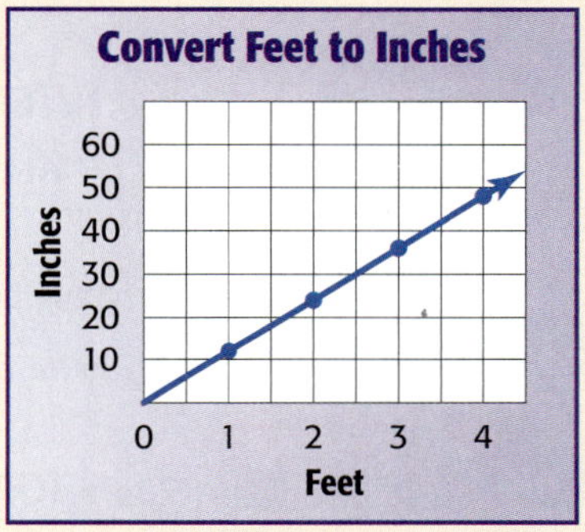

CHECK Your Understanding

Example 1 (p. 211)

Graph the function represented by each table.

1.

Total Cost of Baseballs	
Baseball	**Total Cost ($)**
1	4
2	8
3	12
4	16

2.

Convert Minutes to Seconds	
Minutes	**Seconds**
1	60
2	120
3	180
4	240

Example 2 (p. 212)

Graph each equation.

3. $y = x - 1$
4. $y = -1x$
5. $y = -2x + 3$

Example 3 (p. 213)

6. **GEOMETRY** The perimeter of a square is 4 times greater than the length of one of its sides. The equation $p = 4s$ describes the perimeter p of a square with sides s units long. Represent this function with a graph.

Exercises

HOMEWORK HELP	
For Exercises	**See Examples**
7–8	1
9–14	2
15–16	3

Graph the function represented by each table.

7.

Total Phone Bill	
Time (min)	**Total (¢)**
1	8
2	16
3	24
4	32

8.

Calories in Fruit Cups	
Servings	**Total Calories**
1	70
3	210
5	350
7	490

Graph each equation.

9. $y = x + 1$
10. $y = x + 3$
11. $y = x$
12. $y = -2x$
13. $y = 2x + 3$
14. $y = 3x - 1$

For Exercises 15 and 16, represent each function with a graph.

15. **CARS** A car averages 36 miles per gallon of gasoline. The function $m = 36g$ represents the miles m driven using g gallons of gasoline.

16. **INTERNET** An Internet provider charges $20 a month for service. The equation $c = 20m$ describes the total charge c for m months of Internet access.

Graph each equation.

17. $y = 0.25x$
18. $y = x + 0.5$
19. $y = 0.5x - 1$

20. **SHOPPING** You buy a DVD for $14 and CDs for $9 each. The equation $t = 14 + 9c$ represents the total amount t that you spend if you buy 1 DVD and c CDs. Represent this function with a graph.

EXTRA PRACTICE

See pages 727, 758.

Math Online
Self-Check Quiz at tx.msmath2.com

H.O.T. Problems

21. **OPEN ENDED** Draw the graph of a linear function. Name three ordered pairs in the function.

CHALLENGE For Exercises 22 and 23, let x represent the first number and let y represent the second number. Draw a graph of each function.

22. The second number is three more than the first number.

23. The second number is the product of -3 and the first number.

24. **WRITING IN MATH** Describe how you use a function table to create the graph of a function.

TEST PRACTICE

25. The graph shows the relationship between the number of hours Jennifer spent jogging and the total number of miles she jogged. Which table best represents the data in the graph?

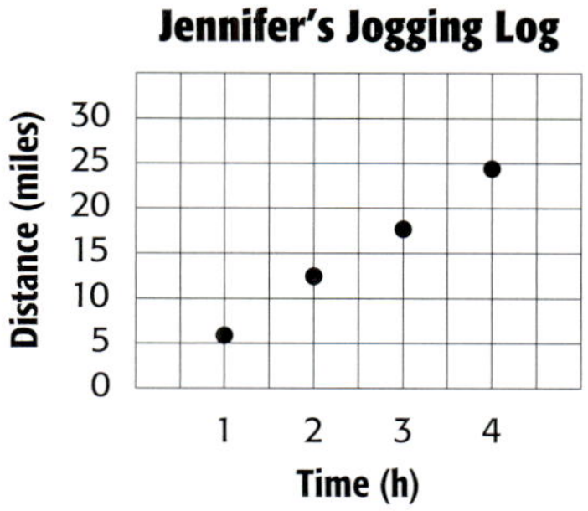

A

Time (h)	Distance (mi)
6	4
12	3
18	2
24	1

B

Time (h)	Distance (mi)
2	6
3	12
4	18
5	24

C

Time (h)	Distance (mi)
1	6
2	12
3	18
4	24

D

Time (h)	Distance (mi)
4	6
3	6
2	6
1	6

Spiral Review

26. **RUGS** The area and width of a rug are 323 square inches and 17 inches respectively. What is the perimeter of the rug? (Lesson 4-6)

Solve each equation. Check your solution. (Lesson 4-5)

27. $4y + 19 = 7$

28. $10x + 2 = 32$

29. $48 - 8j = 16$

30. $14 = 2 - 6d$

31. Evaluate $|5| + |-10|$. (Lesson 2-1)

Cross-Curricular Project

Math and Geography

The Wide World of Soccer It is time to complete your project. Use the information and data you have gathered about countries where soccer is a favorite sport to prepare a Web page or poster. Be sure to include a graph with your project.

Math Online **Cross-Curricular Project at** tx.msmath2.com

Extend 4-7

Graphing Calculator Lab
Graphing Relationships

Main IDEA

Use technology to graph relationships involving conversions of measurement.

Targeted TEKS 7.4 The student represents a relationship in numerical, geometric, verbal, and symbolic form. **(B) graph data to demonstrate relationships in familiar concepts such as conversions,** perimeter, area, circumference, volume, and scaling. *Also addresses TEKS 7.15(A).*

You can use a TI-83/84 Plus graphing calculator to graph relationships.

ACTIVITY

1 MEASUREMENT Use the table at the right to write a function that relates the number of yards x to the number of feet y. Then graph your function.

Yards (x)	Feet (y)
1	3
2	6
3	9
4	12

STEP 1 By examining the table, you can see that the number of feet is 3 times the number of yards. Write a function.

The number of feet	is	3 times	the number of yards.
y	$=$	3	x

STEP 2 Press [Y=] and enter the function $y = 3x$ into Y_1.

STEP 3 Adjust your viewing window. Press [WINDOW] and change the values to reflect the range of values in the table.

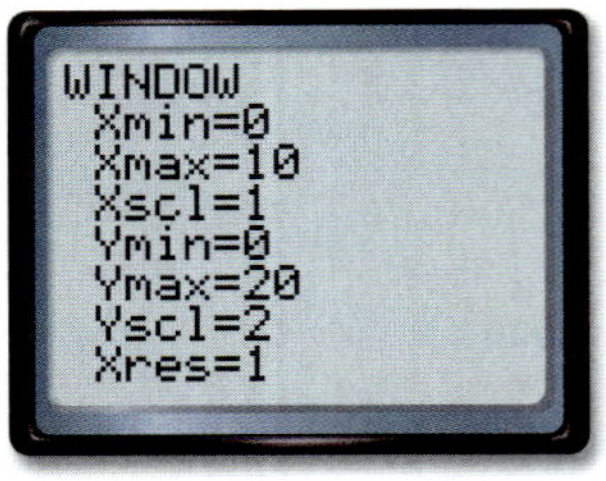

STEP 4 Finally, graph the function by pressing [GRAPH].

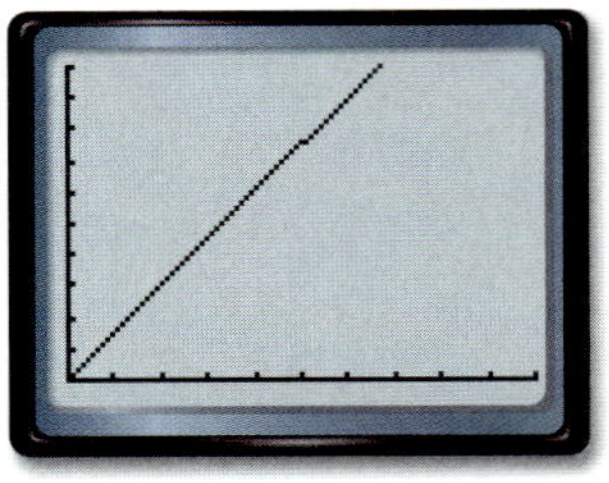

ANALYZE THE RESULTS

1. Test the function above using one of the values from the table and the CALC feature on your calculator. Press [2nd] [CALC] 1 and then enter an x-value of 3. What y-value is displayed? What do each of these values represent and how are they represented on the graph?
2. Use your graph to convert 7 yards into feet. Explain your method.
3. **MAKE A CONJECTURE** Write a function that could be used to convert feet into yards. What is an appropriate window for a graph of this function? Graph and test your function.
4. Use your function from Exercise 3 to convert 16 feet into yards.
5. Write a function that could be used to convert 36 ounces to pounds. Indicate an appropriate window, then use a graph of the function to convert 36 ounces to pounds. (*Hint*: 1 pound = 16 ounces)

Math Online Other Calculator Keystrokes at tx.msmath2.com

CHAPTER 4

Study Guide and Review

STUDY TO GO Download Vocabulary Review from tx.msmath2.com

FOLDABLES™ Study Organizer

GET READY to Study

Be sure the following Key Concepts are noted in your Foldable.

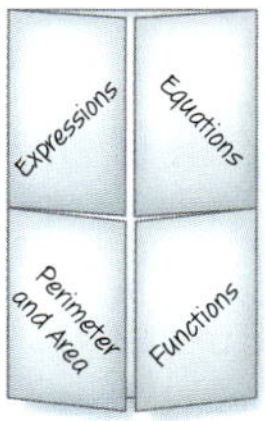

Key Concepts

Solving Equations (Lessons 4-2, 4-3, and 4-5)

- If you add or subtract the same number from each side of an equation, the two sides remain equal.
- If you divide each side of an equation by the same nonzero number, the two sides remain equal.
- To solve a two-step equation:

  Step 1 Undo the addition or subtraction first.

  Step 2 Then undo the multiplication or division.

Perimeter and Area Formulas (Lesson 4-6)

- The perimeter *P* of a rectangle is twice the sum of the length ℓ and width *w*.
- The area *A* of a rectangle is the product of the length ℓ and width *w*.

Linear Functions (Lesson 4-7)

- The graph of a linear function is a straight line. Ordered pairs in the form (*x*, *y*) can be used to represent a function and graphed on the coordinate plane as part of the graph of the function.

Key Vocabulary

formula (p. 192)
inverse operations (p. 184)
linear equation (p. 212)
two-step equation (p. 199)
work backward strategy (p. 196)

Vocabulary Check

State whether each sentence is *true* or *false*. If *false*, replace the underlined word or number to make a true sentence.

1. Inverse operations *undo* each other.
2. The words *more than* sometimes suggest the operation of multiplication.
3. The formula $d = rt$ gives the distance d traveled at a rate of r for t units of time.
4. The algebraic expression representing the words *six less than m* is $6 - m$.
5. Use the work backward strategy when you are given a final result and asked to find an earlier amount.
6. The word *each* sometimes suggests the operation of division.
7. In solving the equation $4x + 3 = 15$, first divide each side by 4.
8. The solution to the equation $p + 4.4 = 11.6$ is $p = 7.2$.
9. The process of solving a two-step equation uses the work backward strategy.
10. The expression $5x$ means 5 more than x.
11. To find the distance around a rectangle, use the formula for its area.
12. The word *per* sometimes suggests the operation of subtraction.

Lesson-by-Lesson Review

4-1 Writing Expressions and Equations (pp. 176–181)

Write each phrase as an algebraic expression.

13. the sum of a number and 5
14. six inches less than her height
15. twice as many apples

Write each sentence as an algebraic equation.

16. Ten years older than Theresa's age is 23.
17. Four less than a number is 19.
18. The quotient of 56 and a number is 14.
19. **AMUSEMENT PARKS** This year, admission to a popular amusement park is \$8.75 more than the previous year's admission fee. Write an expression describing the cost of this year's admission.

Example 1 **Write the phrase as an algebraic expression.**

four times the price

Let p represent the price.

The algebraic expression is $4p$.

Example 2 **Write the sentence as an algebraic equation.**

Six less than the number of cookies is 24.

Let c represent the number of cookies.

The equation is $c - 6 = 24$.

4-2 Solving Addition and Subtraction Equations (pp. 184–189)

Solve each equation. Check your solution.

20. $x + 5 = 8$
21. $r + 8 = 2$
22. $p + 9 = -4$
23. $s - 8 = 15$
24. $n - 1 = -3$
25. $w - 9 = 28$
26. **COOKIES** Marjorie baked some chocolate chip cookies for her and her sister. Her sister ate 6 of these cookies. If there were 18 cookies left, write and solve an equation to find how many cookies c Marjorie baked.

Example 3 **Solve $x + 6 = 4$.**

$$\begin{aligned} x + 6 &= 4 \\ -6 &= -6 \quad \text{Subtract 6 from each side.} \\ x &= -2 \end{aligned}$$

Example 4 **Solve $y - 3 = -2$.**

$$\begin{aligned} y - 3 &= -2 \\ +3 &= +3 \quad \text{Add 3 to each side.} \\ y &= 1 \end{aligned}$$

Mixed Problem Solving
For mixed problem-solving practice, see page 758.

4-3 Solving Multiplication Equations (pp. 190–194)

Solve each equation. Check your solution.

27. $7c = 28$
28. $-8w = 72$
29. $10y = -90$
30. $-12r = -36$

31. **MONEY** Matt borrowed $98 from his father. He plans to repay his father at $14 per week. Write and solve an equation to find the number of weeks *w* required to pay back his father.

Example 5 **Solve $-4b = 32$.**

$-4b = 32$

$\frac{-4b}{-4} = \frac{32}{-4}$ Divide each side by −4.

$b = -8$

4-4 PSI: Work Backward (pp. 196–197)

Solve. Use the *work backward* strategy.

32. **BASEBALL** Last baseball season, Nelson had four less than twice the number of hits Marcus had. Nelson had 48 hits. How many hits did Marcus have last season?

33. **CREDIT CARDS** Alicia paid off $119 of her credit card balance and made an additional $62.75 in purchases. If she now owes $90.45, what was her starting balance?

Example 6 **A number is divided by 2. Then 4 is added to the quotient. After subtracting 3, the result is 18. What is the number?**

Start with the final value and work backward with each resulting value until you arrive at the starting value.

$18 + 3 = 21$ Undo subtracting 3.

$21 - 4 = 17$ Undo adding 4.

$17 \cdot 2 = 34$ Undo dividing by 2.

The number is 34.

4-5 Solving Two-Step Equations (pp. 199–203)

Solve each equation. Check your solution.

34. $3y - 12 = 6$
35. $6x - 4 = 20$
36. $2x + 5 = 3$
37. $5m + 6 = -4$
38. $10c - 8 = 90$
39. $3r - 20 = -5$

40. **NUMBERS** Ten more than five times a number is 25. Find the number.

Example 7 **Solve $3p - 4 = 8$.**

$3p - 4 = 8$

$\underline{+4 = +4}$ Add 4 to each side.

$3p = 12$

$\frac{3p}{3} = \frac{12}{3}$ Divide each side by 3.

$p = 4$

4-6 Geometry: Perimeter and Area (p. 204–209)

Find the perimeter and area of each rectangle.

41. 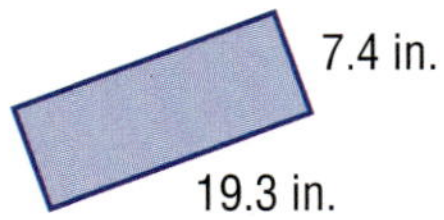

42. 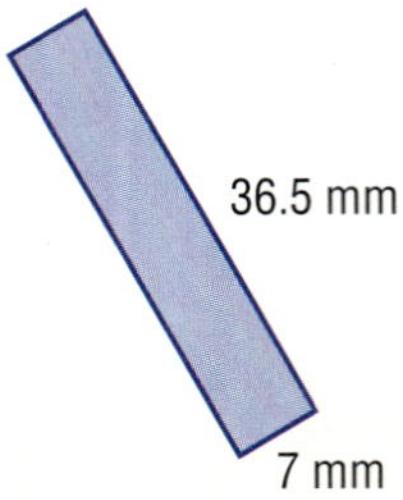

Find the missing measure.

43. $P = 56$ mi, $\ell = 21$ mi

44. $A = 10.26$ ft^2, $w = 2.7$ ft

45. $A = 272$ yd^2, $\ell = 17$ yd

46. $P = 14.2$ cm, $w = 2.6$ cm

47. **CARPET** In order to carpet her rectangular living room, Flora needs 192 square feet of carpet. If the length of her living room is 16 feet, find the width.

Example 8 **The perimeter of a rectangle is 38 meters. If the length is 7 meters, find the width.**

$P = 2\ell + 2w$	Perimeter formula
$38 = 2(7) + 2w$	Replace *P* with 38 and ℓ with 7.
$38 = 14 + 2w$	Simplify.
$24 = 2w$	Subtract 14 from each side.
$\frac{24}{2} = \frac{2w}{2}$	Divide each side by 2.
$12 = w$	Simplify.

The width is 12 meters.

Example 9 **The area of a rectangle is 285 square inches. If the width is 15 inches, find the length.**

$A = \ell w$	Area formula
$285 = \ell(15)$	Replace *A* with 285 and *w* with 15.
$\frac{285}{15} = \frac{15\ell}{15}$	Divide each side by 15.
$19 = \ell$	Simplify.

The length is 19 inches.

4-7 Functions and Graphs (p. 211–215)

Graph each equation.

48. $y = x + 5$

49. $y = x - 4$

50. $y = 2x$

51. $y = -1x$

52. $y = 3x + 2$

53. $y = -2x + 3$

MONEY MATTERS **For Exercises 54–56, use the following infomation.**

Angel earns \$6 per hour working at the Ice Cream Shop.

54. Make a table that shows her total earnings for working 3, 5, 7, and 9 hours.

55. Write an equation in which x represents the number of hours and y represents Angel's total earnings.

56. Graph the equation.

Example 10 **Graph $y = x + 3$.**

Select four values for x. Substitute these values for x to find values for y.

x	$x + 3$	y
-1	$-1 + 3$	2
0	$0 + 3$	3
1	$1 + 3$	4
2	$2 + 3$	5

Four solutions are $(-1, 2)$, $(0, 3)$, $(1, 4)$, and $(2, 5)$. The graph is shown below.

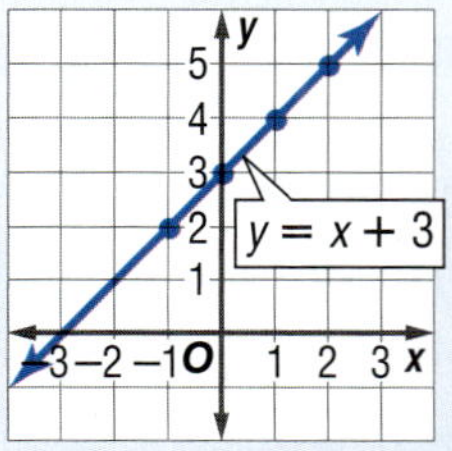

CHAPTER 4

Practice Test

Write each phrase as an algebraic expression or equation.

1. \$5 less than Tomasita has
2. 4 years older than Hana
3. 56 inches is 9 inches shorter than Jacob's height.
4. Twice the distance from the park to the post office is 5 miles.

5. **FLOWERS** The number of tulips in Paula's garden is 8 less than the number of marigolds. If there are 16 tulips, write and solve an equation to determine the number of marigolds m.

6. **TEST PRACTICE** Between 1 A.M. and 2 A.M., the temperature fell 14°F. This was half the total amount the temperature fell during the night. Which equation would give the total change in temperature during the night?

   A $0.5t = 14$
   B $0.5t = -14$
   C $2t = 14$
   D $2t = -14$

ANALYZE TABLES **For Exercises 7–9, use the table below. It shows how Jared's age and his sister Emily's are related.**

Jared's age (yr)	1	2	3	4	5
Emily's age (yr)	7	8	9	10	11

7. Write an equation in which x represents Jared's age, and y represents Emily's age.
8. Graph the equation.
9. Predict how old Emily will be when Jared is 10 years old.

10. **TOURISM** The Statue of Liberty is 151 feet tall. It is 835 feet shorter than the Eiffel Tower. Write and solve an equation to find the height of the Eiffel Tower.

Solve each equation. Check your solution.

11. $x + 5 = -8$
12. $y - 11 = 15$
13. $9z = -81$
14. $-6k + 4 = -38$
15. $3z - 7 = 17$
16. $2g - 9 = -5$

17. **PIZZA** Chris and Joe shared a pizza. Chris ate two more than twice as many pieces as Joe, who ate 3 pieces. If there were 3 pieces left, how many pieces were there initially? Use the *work backward* strategy.

18. **TEST PRACTICE** A giant cake decorated as an American flag was 60 feet in length. If it took A square feet of icing to cover the top of the cake, which of the following would represent the cake's perimeter?

   F $P = 120 + 2 \cdot \frac{A}{60}$
   G $P = 120 + 2A$
   H $P = 60 + \frac{A}{60}$
   J $P = 60 + 2A$

Find the perimeter and area of each rectangle.

19.
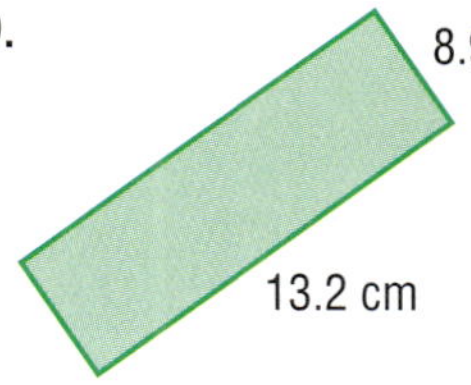

20.

Graph each equation.

21. $y = x + 1$
22. $y = 2x$
23. $y = 2x - 3$
24. $y = -x + 1$

25. **MOVIES** A student ticket to the movies costs \$6. The equation $c = 6t$ describes the total cost c for t tickets. Make a function table that shows the total cost for 1, 2, 3, and 4 tickets and then graph the equation.

CHAPTER 4 Texas Test Practice

Cumulative, Chapters 1–4

Read each question. Then fill in the correct answer on the answer document provided by your teacher or on a sheet of paper.

1. The model below represents the two-step equation $2x + 4 = 14$. What is the first step you should perform to find the value of x?

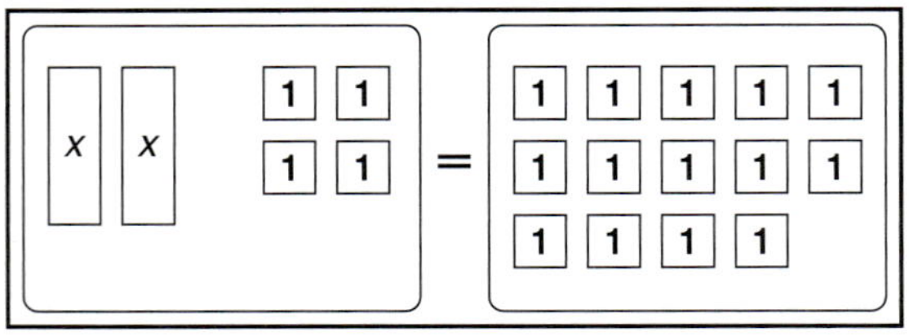

A Add 14 algebra tiles to each side of the model.

B Divide the algebra tiles equally between the 2 x-tiles.

C Add 4 algebra tiles to each side of the model.

D Subtract 4 algebra tiles from each side of the model.

2. Which line contains the ordered pair $(-2, 4)$?

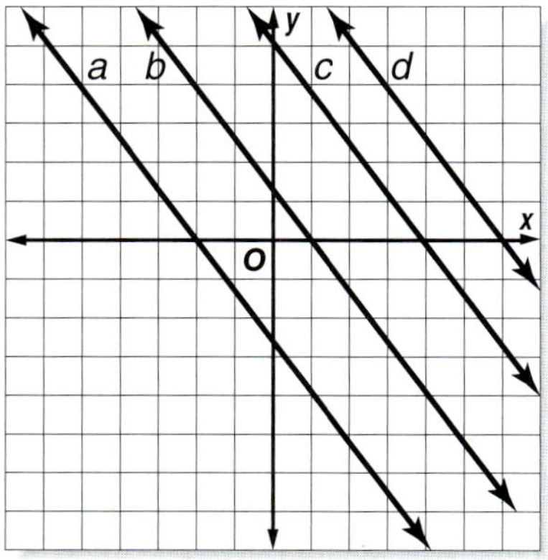

F line a

G line c

H line b

J line d

3. Which description shows the relationship between a term and n, its position in the sequence?

Position	3	4	5	6	7	n
Value of Term	13	17	21	25	29	

A Add 4 to n.

B Multiply n by 5 and add 1.

C Multiply n by 3 and add 2.

D Multiply n by 4 and add 1.

4. **GRIDDABLE** What is the y value of the ordered pair that is represented by point A?

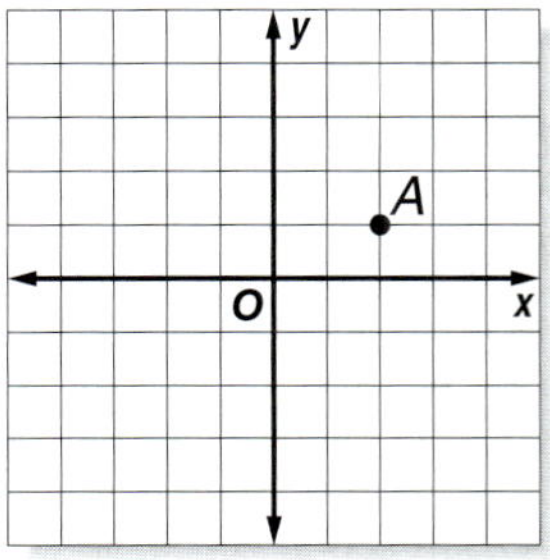

5. Which problem situation matches the equation below?

$$x - 9 = 15$$

F Allison is nine years younger than her sister Pam. Allison is 15 years old. What is x, Pam's age?

G David's portion of the restaurant bill is \$9 more than Sam's portion of the bill. If Sam pays \$9, find the amount x, that David pays.

H The sum of two numbers is 15. One of the numbers is 9. What is x, the other number?

J Elizabeth hiked 9 miles on her first day of a hiking trip. If she hiked a total of 15 miles, what is x, the distance she traveled on the second day?

Math Online Texas Test Practice at tx.msmath2.com

Get Ready for the Texas Test
For test-taking strategies and more practice, see pages TX1–TX23.

6. Which model represents 5^2?

A 

B 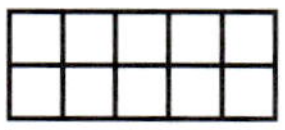

C 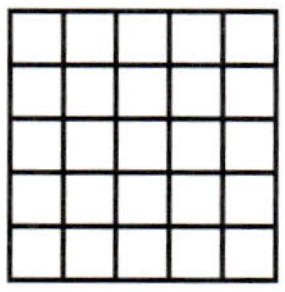

D 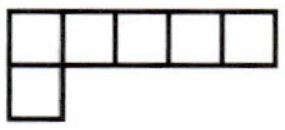

TEST-TAKING TIP

Question 6 Read the question carefully to check that you answered the question that was asked. In question 6, you are asked to pick which model represents 5^2, not to evaluate it.

7. Which of the following coordinates lies within the triangle graphed below?

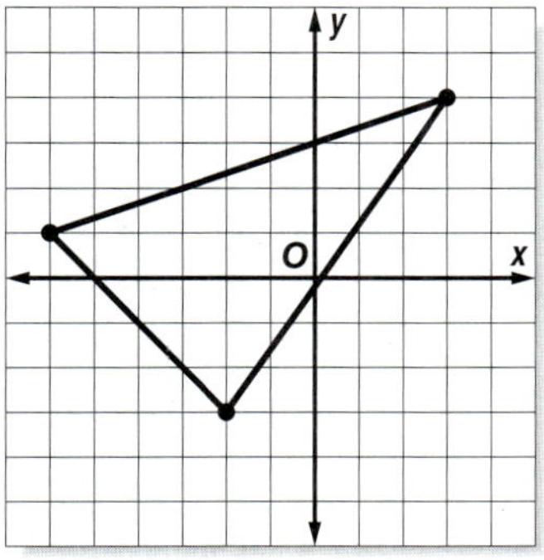

F (5, −2) H (−3, 6)
G (2, 0) J (−1, −1)

8. Which expression can be used to find the maximum number of 0.2-meter pieces of lumber than can be cut from a 3.2-meter length of lumber?

A 0.2×3.2 C $0.2 + 3.2$
B $3.2 \div 0.2$ D $3.2 - 0.2$

9. An art teacher bought 25.5 pounds of sand. Each pound of sand costs \$0.40. How much did the art teacher spend on the sand?

F \$12.50 H \$10.00
G \$10.20 J \$9.50

Pre-AP

Record your answers on a sheet of paper. Show your work.

10. The distances traveled by a bicycle rider are given in the table.

Time (hours)	Distance (miles)
1	10
2	20
3	30
4	40
5	50

a. Graph the ordered pairs to compare the time spent traveling and the distance traveled.

b. Write an equation that relates the time t to the distance d.

c. Use your equation to predict the distance traveled in 3.5 hours.

NEED EXTRA HELP?										
If You Missed Question...	1	2	3	4	5	6	7	8	9	10
Go to Lesson...	4-5	4-7	1-9	2-3	4-1	1-2	2-3	3-4	3-2	4-7
For Help with Test Objective...	2	3	2	3	2	1	3	1	1	3

Unit 2

Number and Operations: Fractions

Focal Point

Represent and use numbers in a variety of equivalent forms and apply addition, subtraction, multiplication, and division of fractions.

CHAPTER 5
Fractions, Decimals, and Percents

BIG Idea Represent and use numbers in a variety of forms.

CHAPTER 6
Applying Fractions

BIG Idea Add, subtract, multiply, and divide to solve problems and justify solutions.

Cross-Curricular Project

Math and Health

A Well-Balanced Diet You are what you eat! So are you ice cream or broccoli? You're on a mission to find out! Along the way, you collect and analyze data about what you eat over a period of five days. You'll also take on the role of a nutritionist, reasearching the Food Pyramid and creating a healthy meal plan. So bring a hearty appetite and your math tool kit. This adventure will tantalize your taste buds!

Math Online Log on to tx.msmath2.com to begin.

CHAPTER 5

Fractions, Decimals, and Percents

Knowledge and Skills

- Represent and use numbers in a variety of forms. **TEKS 7.1**

Key Vocabulary

equivalent fractions (p. 240)

percent (p. 250)

ratio (p. 250)

simplest form (p. 240)

Real-World Link

Insects Monarch butterflies have a wingspan of $3\frac{3}{8}$ inches to $4\frac{7}{8}$ inches. You can write these fractions as 3.375 and 4.875, respectively.

FOLDABLES™ Study Organizer

Fractions, Decimals, and Percents Make this Foldable to help you organize your notes. Begin with five sheets of $8\frac{1}{2}'' \times 11''$ paper.

1. **Stack** five sheets of paper $\frac{3}{4}$ inch apart.

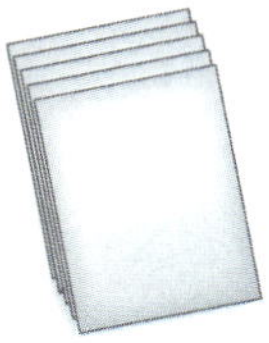

2. **Roll** up bottom edges so that all tabs are the same size.

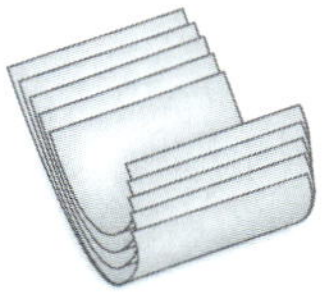

3. **Crease** and staple along the fold.

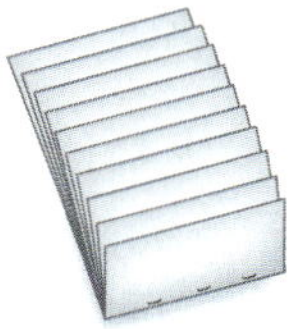

4. **Write** the chapter title on the front. Label each tab with a lesson number and title.

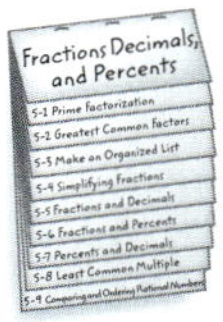

GET READY for Chapter 5

Diagnose Readiness You have two options for checking Prerequisite Skills.

Option 2

Math Online Take the Online Readiness Quiz at tx.msmath2.com.

Option 1

Take the Quick Quiz below. Refer to the Quick Review for help.

QUICK Quiz

State which decimal is greater.
(Used in Lesson 5-9)

1. 0.6, 0.61 **2.** 1.25, 1.52

3. 0.33, 0.13 **4.** 1.08, 10.8

5. **LUNCH** Kirsten spent $4.21 on lunch while Almanzo spent $4.12. Who spent the greater amount?

Use divisibility rules to determine whether each number is divisible by 2, 3, 5, 6, or 10.
(Used in Lessons 5-1 and 5-2)

6. 125 **7.** 78 **8.** 37

9. **MUFFINS** Without calculating, determine whether 51 banana nut muffins can be evenly distributed among 3 persons. Explain.

Divide. (Used in Lessons 5-4, 5-5, 5-6, and 5-7)

10. $12 \div 6$ **11.** $18 \div 3$

12. $2 \div 5$ **13.** $3 \div 4$

Write each power as a product of the same factor. (Used in Lesson 5-1)

14. 2^3 **15.** 5^5

16. 7^2 **17.** 9^4

QUICK Review

Example 1

State which decimal is greater, 7.4 or 7.04.

7.4
7.04
↑
7.4 is greater.

Line up the decimal points and compare place value. The 4 in the tenths place is greater than the 0 in the tenths place.

Example 2

Use divisibility rules to determine whether 84 is divisible by 2, 3, 5, 6, or 10.

2: Yes, the ones digit, 4, is divisible by 2.
3: Yes, the sum of the digits, 12, is divisible by 3.
5: No, the ones digit is neither 0 nor 5.
6. Yes, the number is divisible by both 2 and 3.
10: No, the ones digit is not 0.

Example 3

Find $1 \div 5$.

$$\begin{array}{r} 0.2 \\ 5\overline{)1.0} \\ -10 \\ \hline 0 \end{array}$$

Divide 1 by 5 until there is a remainder of 0 or a repeating pattern.

Example 4

Write 4^3 as a product of the same factor.

$4^3 = 4 \times 4 \times 4$

Explore 5-1

Math Lab
Exploring Factors

Main IDEA

Discover factors of whole numbers.

Reinforcement of TEKS 6.1 The student represents and uses rational numbers in a variety of equivalent forms. **(E) identify factors of a positive integer, common factors, and the greatest common factor of a set of positive integers.**

ACTIVITY

STEP 1 Number each index card consecutively with the numbers 1 through 30.

STEP 2 Pass out the index cards in order, giving each student one index card. Have each student stand up and write the number 1 on the back of his or her card.

STEP 3 Begin with the student holding the "2" card. Have this student and every second student sit down and write the number 2 on the back of his or her card. The other students remain standing.

STEP 4 Next, start with the student holding the "3" card. Have this student and every third student stand up or sit down (depending on whether the student is already sitting or standing) and write the number 3 on the back of his or her card.

STEP 5 Continue this process for each of the remaining numbers up to 30. The thirtieth student ends the activity by standing or sitting, and writing the number 30 on the back of his or her card.

ANALYZE THE RESULTS

1. How many students are standing at the end of the activity? Which cards are they holding?

2. **LOOK FOR A PATTERN** Suppose there were 100 students holding index cards. Extend the pattern in Exercise 1 to predict the numbers that would be held by students standing at the end of the activity.

3. Explain the relationship between the numbers on the front and the back of the cards.

4. Separate the cards into two groups: one group with exactly two numbers on the back of the card and one group with more than two numbers. Describe any special characteristics of each group.

5-1 Prime Factorization

Main IDEA

Find the prime factorization of a composite number.

Reinforcement of TEKS 6.1 The student represents and uses rational numbers in a variety of equivalent forms. **(D) write prime factorizations using exponents.**

NEW Vocabulary

prime number
composite number
prime factorization
factor tree

REVIEW Vocabulary

factor two or more numbers that are multiplied together to form a product; *Example*: 2 and 3 are factors of 6.
(Lesson 1-2)

MINI Lab

Concepts in Motion
BrainPOP® tx.msmath2.com

There is only one way that 2 can be expressed as the product of whole numbers. The figure shows that there is only one way that two squares can form a rectangle.

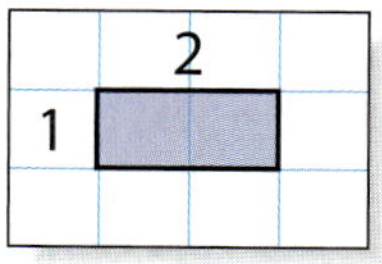

1. Using your grid paper, draw as many different rectangles as possible containing 3, 4, 5, 6, 7, 8, 9, and 10 squares.
2. Which numbers of squares can be drawn in only one rectangle? In more than one rectangle?

The numbers of squares that can only be drawn in exactly one rectangle are prime numbers. The numbers that can be drawn in more than one rectangle are composite numbers.

A **prime number** is a whole number greater than 1 that has exactly two factors, 1 and itself.

A **composite number** is a whole number greater than 1 that has more than two factors.

Whole Numbers	Factors
2	1, 2
3	1, 3
5	1, 5
7	1, 7
4	1, 2, 4
6	1, 2, 3, 6
8	1, 2, 4, 8
9	1, 3, 9
10	1, 2, 5, 10
0	many
1	1

The numbers 0 and 1 are neither prime nor composite.

EXAMPLES Identify Numbers as Prime or Composite

Determine whether each number is *prime* or *composite*.

1 **17**

The number 17 has only two factors, 1 and 17, so it is prime.

2 **12**

The number 12 has six factors: 1, 2, 3, 4, 6, and 12. So, it is composite.

CHECK Your Progress

Determine whether each number is *prime* or *composite*.

a. 11 **b.** 15 **c.** 24

Commutative Property Multiplication is commutative, so the order of the factors does not matter. Both trees give the prime factorization of 60, but in different orders.

Every composite number can be written as a product of prime numbers. The product is the **prime factorization** of the number. You can use a **factor tree** to find the prime factorization.

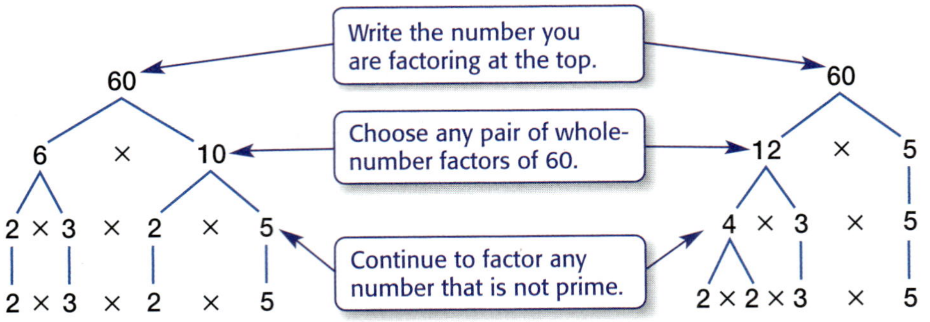

The prime factorization of 60 is $2 \times 2 \times 3 \times 5$, or $2^2 \times 3 \times 5$.

EXAMPLE Find the Prime Factorization

3 **Find the prime factorization of 24.**

METHOD 1

Use a factor tree.

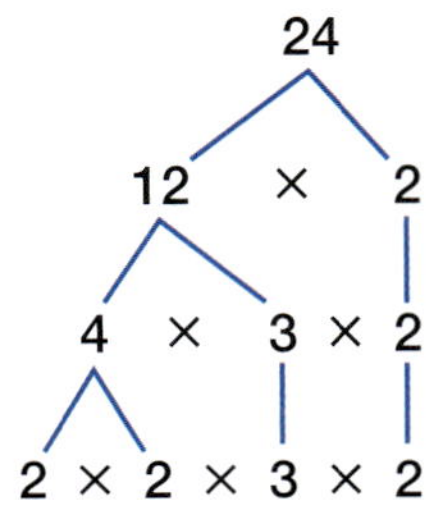

METHOD 2

Divide by prime numbers.

$$\begin{array}{r} 2 \\ 2\overline{)4} \\ 3\overline{)12} \\ 2\overline{)24} \end{array}$$

Start here.

The divisors are 2, 2, 3, and 2.

The prime factorization of 24 is $2 \times 2 \times 3 \times 2$ or $2^3 \times 3$.

CHOOSE Your Method **Find the prime factorization.**

d. 18 **e.** 28 **f.** 16

Online Personal Tutor at tx.msmath2.com

Algebraic expressions like $6ab$ can also be factored as the product of prime numbers and variables.

EXAMPLE Factor an Algebraic Expression

4 **ALGEBRA** **Factor $6ab$.**

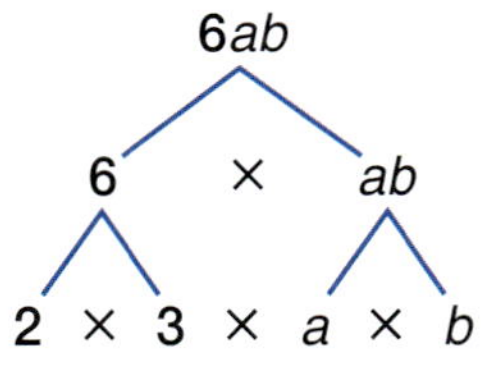

$6ab = 2 \cdot 3 \cdot a \cdot b$

CHECK Your Progress

g. **ALGEBRA** Factor $18xy$.

CHECK Your Understanding

Examples 1, 2 (p. 229)

Determine whether each number is *prime* or *composite*.

1. 7
2. 50
3. 67
4. **GARDENING** Louisa has 72 flowers to plant in rows in a flower bed. How many different ways can she plant the flowers? Justify your answer.

Example 3 (p. 230)

Find the prime factorization of each number.

5. 34
6. 30
7. 12

Example 4 (p. 230)

ALGEBRA Factor each expression.

8. $10ac$
9. $16x^2$
10. $11g^3$

Exercises

HOMEWORK HELP

For Exercises	See Examples
11–18	1, 2
19–28	3
29–34	4

Determine whether each number is *prime* or *composite*.

11. 22
12. 44
13. 13
14. 39
15. 81
16. 31
17. 97
18. 43

Find the prime factorization of each number.

19. 96
20. 42
21. 99
22. 64
23. 210
24. 180
25. 126
26. 375
27. **LOBSTERS** Lobsters can live up to 50 years. What is this amount expressed as a product of primes?

28. **DOGS** Greyhounds can jump a distance of 27 feet. Write this distance as a product of primes.

ALGEBRA Factor each expression.

29. $15mn$
30. $20pq$
31. $34jkm$
32. $49y^2$
33. $52gh^2$
34. $48a^2b^2$

Replace each ■ with prime factors to make a true sentence.

35. $2^3 \cdot$ ■ $\cdot\ 11 = 616$
36. $2 \cdot$ ■ $\cdot\ 5^2 = 450$
37. $3 \cdot 2^4 \cdot$ ■ $= 1{,}200$
38. $2^2 \cdot$ ■ $\cdot\ 3 = 1{,}500$
39. **RIVERS** The Brazos River in Texas is 1,280 miles long. What expression written as a product of primes represents this length?

ALGEBRA For Exercises 40 and 41, determine whether the value of each expression is *prime* or *composite* if $a = 1$ and $b = 5$.

40. $3a + 6b$
41. $7b - 4a$

EXTRA PRACTICE See pages 727, 759.

Math Online Self-Check Quiz at tx.msmath2.com

LANDSCAPING **For Exercises 42–45, use the following information.**

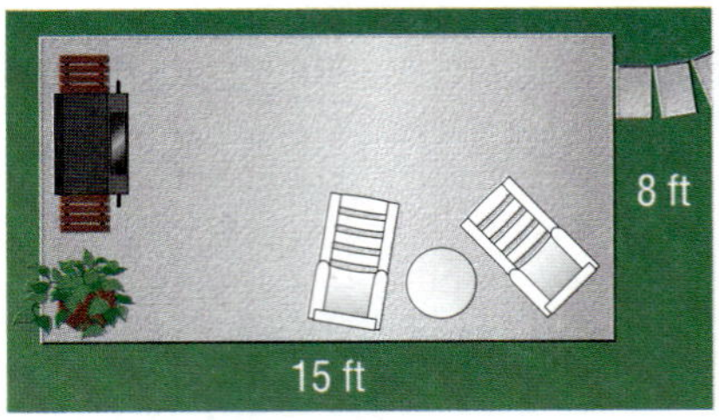

Mrs. Franks is building a patio that covers an area measuring 8 feet by 15 feet. She will use rectangular concrete tiles for the patio.

42. What is the area of the patio?

43. Find the prime factorization of the area.

44. If she can only buy tiles with dimensions that are prime numbers, name the dimensions of the concrete tiles available for her patio.

45. How many tiles will she need to cover the patio?

H.O.T. Problems

46. **NUMBER SENSE** *True* or *False*? All prime numbers are odd. If false, give a counterexample.

47. **CHALLENGE** This whole number is between 30 and 40. It has only two prime factors whose sum is 5. What is the number?

48. **OPEN ENDED** Primes that differ by two are called *twin primes*. For example, 59 and 61 are twin primes. Give three examples of twin primes that are less than 50.

49. **WRITING IN MATH** Suppose n represents a whole number. Is $2n$ prime or composite? Explain.

TEST PRACTICE

50. What is the prime factorization of 126?

A $2^2 \cdot 3 \cdot 7$ C $2 \cdot 3 \cdot 7^2$

B $2 \cdot 3^2 \cdot 7$ D $2^2 \cdot 3^2 \cdot 7^2$

51. Which of the following numbers is NOT a prime number?

F 2 H 16

G 11 J 31

Spiral Review

52. **ALGEBRA** Graph $y = 3x$. (Lesson 4-7)

53. **GEOMETRY** Find the perimeter and area of a rectangle with a length of 13 feet and width of 5 feet. (Lesson 4-6)

Add. (Lesson 2-4)

54. $6 + (-4)$ 55. $-13 + 9$ 56. $25 + (-26)$ 57. $-5 + 5$

GET READY for the Next Lesson

PREREQUISITE SKILL **State whether each number is divisible by 2, 3, 5, 6, 9, or 10.** (Page 708)

58. 24 59. 70 60. 120 61. 99

READING Word Problems

Everyday Meaning

The key to understanding word problems is to understand the meaning of the mathematical terms in the problem. Many words used in mathematics are also used in everyday language.

For example, you will use the terms *factor* and *multiple* in this chapter. Here are two sentences that show their everyday meanings.

- Weather was a *factor* in their decision to postpone the picnic.
- The star quarterback won *multiple* post-season awards.

The table below shows how the everyday meaning is connected to the mathematical meaning.

Term	Everyday Meaning	Mathematical Meaning	Connection
factor from the Latin *factor*, meaning doer	something that actively contributes to a decision or result	2 and 3 are *factors* of 6.	A *factor* helps to make a decision, and in mathematics, factors "make up" a product.
multiple from the Latin *multi-*, meaning many, and *plex*, meaning fold	consisting of more than one or shared by many	The *multiples* of 2 are 0, 2, 4, 6, … .	*Multiple* means many, and in mathematics, a number has infinitely many multiples.

PRACTICE

1. Make a list of other words that have the prefixes *fact-* or *multi-*. Determine what the words in each list have in common.
2. **WRITING IN MATH** Write your own rule for remembering the difference between *factor* and *multiple*.

RESEARCH Use a dictionary to find the everyday meanings of *least*, *greatest*, and *common*. Then use the definitions to determine how to find each number. Do not solve.

3. the greatest common factor of 10 and 15
4. the least common multiple of 2 and 3.

5-2 Greatest Common Factor

Main IDEA

Find the greatest common factor of two or more numbers.

Reinforcement of TEKS 6.1 The student represents and uses rational numbers in a variety of equivalent forms. **(E) identify factors of a positive integer, common factors, and the greatest common factor of a set of positive integers.**

GET READY for the Lesson

INTERNET Some friends spent time in two Internet chat rooms. The Venn diagram shows the chat rooms Ruben, Sydney, Ian, Kamilah, and Christine visited. The friends were able to stay in one chat room or go to the other one.

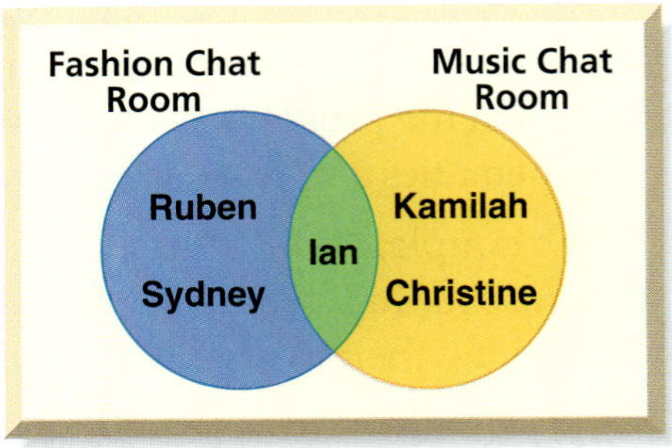

1. Who visited the Fashion Chat Room? the Music Chat Room?
2. Who visited both chat rooms?

As shown above, **Venn diagrams** use overlapping circles to show how common elements among sets of numbers or objects are related. They can also show common factors. The greatest of the common factors of two or more numbers is the **greatest common factor, or GCF**.

NEW Vocabulary

Venn diagram
greatest common factor (GCF)

EXAMPLE Find the Greatest Common Factor

1 Find the GCF of 18 and 48.

METHOD 1 List the factors of the numbers.

factors of 18: 1, 2, 3, 6, 9, 18

factors of 48: 1, 2, 3, 4, 6, 8, 12, 16, 24, 48

List the factors of 18 and 48.

The common factors of 18 and 48 are 1, 2, 3, and 6.
So, the greatest common factor or GCF is 6.

METHOD 2 Use prime factorization.

Write the prime factorization. Then circle the common factors.

$18 = 2 \times 3 \times 3$

$48 = 2 \times 2 \times 2 \times 2 \times 3$

Write the prime factorization of 18 and 48.

The greatest common factor or GCF is 2×3 or 6.

READING in the Content Area

For strategies in reading this lesson, visit tx.msmath2.com.

CHOOSE Your Method

Find the GCF of each pair of numbers.

a. 8, 10 b. 6, 12 c. 10, 17

Math Online Extra Examples at tx.msmath2.com

STUDY TIP

Greatest Common Factor When listing the factors of 12, 24, and 60, it may be helpful to circle the common factors. Then find the largest common factor.

EXAMPLE Find the GCF of Three Numbers

2 **Find the GCF of 12, 24, and 60.**

METHOD 1 List the factors of the numbers.

factors of 12: 1, 2, 3, 4, 6, 12

factors of 24: 1, 2, 3, 4, 6, 8, 12, 24

factors of 60: 1, 2, 3, 4, 5, 6, 10, 12, 15, 20, 30, 60

List the factors of 12, 24, and 60.

The common factors of 12, 24, and 60 are 1, 2, 3, 4, 6, and 12.
So, the greatest common factor or GCF is 12.

METHOD 2 Use prime factorization.

Write the prime factorization. Then circle the common factors.

$12 = 2 \times 2 \times 3$

$24 = 2 \times 2 \times 2 \times 3$

$60 = 2 \times 2 \times 3 \times 5$

Write the prime factorization of 12, 24, and 60.

The common prime factors are 2, 2, and 3. So, the GCF is $2 \times 2 \times 3$, or 12.

CHOOSE Your Method **Find the GCF of each set of numbers.**

d. 30, 45, 75

e. 42, 70, 84

Real-World EXAMPLE

3 **PARADES** **In a parade, 64 eighth-graders are to march in front of 88 seventh-graders. Both groups should have the same number of students in each row. Find the greatest number of students in each row.**

The greatest number of students in each row is the GCF of the number of students in each group.

$64 = 2 \times 2 \times 2 \times 2 \times 2 \times 2 = 2^6$

$88 = 2 \times 2 \times 2 \times 11 = 2^3 \times 11$

The GCF of 64 and 88 is 2^3, or 8.

So, there should be 8 students in each row.

STUDY TIP

Prime Numbers The GCF of prime numbers is 1.

CHECK Your Progress

f. **CARPENTRY** Mr. Glover wants to make shelves for his garage using an 18-foot board and a 36-foot board. He will cut the boards to make shelves of the same length and wants to use all of both boards. Find the longest possible length of each shelf.

Online **Personal Tutor at** tx.msmath2.com

CHECK Your Understanding

Examples 1, 2 (pp. 234–235)

Find the GCF of each set of numbers.

1. 18, 30
2. 45, 60
3. 20, 50
4. 6, 8, 12
5. 8, 20, 40
6. 18, 42, 60

Example 3 (p. 235)

7. **JOBS** A store manager wants to display the inventory of three styles of bicycle helmets in rows with the same number of each style in each row. Find the greatest number of helmets that can be placed in each row.

Bike Helmets	
Style	**Inventory**
Sport	36
Road	72
Mountain	45

Exercises

HOMEWORK HELP	
For Exercises	See Examples
8–15	1
16–19	2
20–21	3

Find the GCF of each set of numbers.

8. 12, 78
9. 40, 50
10. 20, 45
11. 32, 48
12. 24, 48
13. 45, 75
14. 56, 96
15. 40, 125
16. 18, 24, 30
17. 36, 60, 84
18. 35, 49, 84
19. 36, 50, 130

20. **BAKE SALE** Esteban plans to sell the items shown at a bake sale. He arranges the items in groups. Each group has the same number of each item. Find the greatest number of items in each group.

21. **FOOD** The track-and-field coaches threw a party at the end of the season and bought a 12-inch, a 20-inch, and a 32-inch submarine sandwich. The sandwiches are cut into equal-sized pieces. What is the length of the longest piece that can be cut?

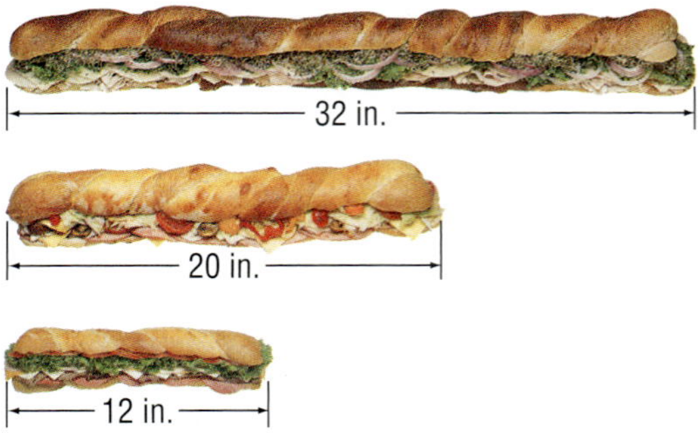

Find the GCF of each set of numbers.

22. 25¢, \$1.50, 75¢, \$3.00
23. 6 feet, 15 feet, 21 feet, 9 feet

ALGEBRA **Find the GCF of each set of expressions.**

24. $24a$, $6a$
25. $30mn$, $40mn$
26. $15xy$, $55y$

Find two numbers whose GCF is the given number.

27. 9
28. 12
29. 15
30. 30

EXTRA PRACTICE
See pages 728, 759.
Math Online
Self-Check Quiz at tx.msmath2.com

CLASS TRIPS For Exercises 31 and 32, use the following information and the table shown.

Class Trip Money ($)	
Monday	56
Tuesday	28
Wednesday	42
Thursday	98

On Friday, Mr. Russo's class is going to the Dallas Museum of Natural History. The amount of money he collected from his students is shown. Each student paid the same amount.

31. What is the greatest cost of the field trip per student?
32. How many students will be going on the class trip?

H.O.T. Problems

CHALLENGE Determine whether each statement is *sometimes*, *always*, or *never* true.

33. The GCF of two numbers is greater than both numbers.
34. If two numbers have no common prime factors, the GCF is 1.
35. The GCF of two numbers is one of the numbers.
36. **WRITING IN MATH** Using the words *factor* and *greatest common factor*, explain the relationship between the numbers 4, 12, and 24.

TEST PRACTICE

37. **GRIDDABLE** The amount of money students raised selling juice is shown.

Type of Juice	Amount Earned ($)
Apple	26
Mixed Fruit	32
Pineapple	28

If all juice drinks cost the same, what is the greatest possible price in dollars per juice drink?

38. Find the greatest common factor of 15, 30, and 45.

A 5

B 9

C 15

D 45

Spiral Review

39. What is the prime factorization of 75? (Lesson 5-1)

Graph each equation. (Lesson 4-7)

40. $y = -x$
41. $y = x + 3$
42. $y = 2x - 1$

43. Estimate $80.2 + 72.1 + 68.5 + 60.7$. (Lesson 3-1)

GET READY for the Next Lesson

44. **PREREQUISITE SKILL** Serena received a gift card to download music from the Internet. She downloaded 3 songs on Monday, 5 songs on Tuesday, and one half of what was left on Wednesday. She has 6 songs left. How many songs were initially on the gift card? Use the *work backward* strategy. (Lesson 4-4)

5-3 Problem-Solving Investigation

MAIN IDEA: Solve problems by making an organized list.

Targeted TEKS 7.13 The student applies Grade 7 mathematics to solve problems connected to everyday experiences, ..., ... and activities in and outside of school. **(C) select or develop an appropriate problem-solving strategy from a variety of different types, including ... making a table ... to solve a problem.** *Also addresses TEKS 7.13(B).*

P.S.I. TEAM +

e-Mail: MAKE AN ORGANIZED LIST

YOUR MISSION: Solve the problem by making an organized list of all the possibilities.

THE PROBLEM: How many different ways can a woodwind trio be made?

Miranda: The first position needs to be either a bass clarinet or a bassoon. The other two positions should be filled by a clarinet, oboe, or flute.

EXPLORE	You know that either a bass clarinet or a bassoon must fill the first position. The other two positions are to be filled with two out of the three remaining instruments. You need to find all possible ways the trio can be made.
PLAN	Make an organized list.
SOLVE	(see table below) There are six possibilities.
CHECK	Draw a tree diagram to check the result.

	Trio 1	Trio 2	Trio 3	Trio 4	Trio 5	Trio 6
Position 1	bass clarinet	bass clarinet	bass clarinet	bassoon	bassoon	bassoon
Position 2	clarinet	oboe	flute	clarinet	oboe	flute
Position 3	oboe	flute	clarinet	oboe	flute	clarinet

There are six possibilities.

Analyze The Strategy

1. Explain why making an organized list was a useful strategy in solving this problem.
2. **WRITING IN MATH** Write a problem that can be solved by making an organized list. Then explain how to solve the problem using this strategy.

Mixed Problem Solving

For Exercises 3–6, solve each problem by making an organized list.

3. **FOOD** Daniel is making a peanut butter and jelly sandwich. His choices are creamy or crunchy peanut butter, white or wheat bread, and grape, apple, or strawberry jelly. How many different types of sandwiches can Daniel make?

4. **GAMES** On the game board, you plan to move two spaces away from square A. You can move horizontally, vertically, or diagonally. How many different moves can you make from square A? List them.

A	B	C
D	E	F
G	H	I

5. **SCIENCE FAIR** A photographer for the school newspaper is taking a picture of Mr. Teasley with the first, second, and third place winners of the science fair. If Mr. Teasley always stands on the far left, how many different ways can the students arrange themselves for the picture?

6. **TELEPHONES** How many phone numbers are possible for one area code if the first three numbers are 268, in that order, and the last four numbers are 0, 9, 7, 1 in any order?

Use any strategy to solve Exercises 7–11. Some strategies are shown below.

PROBLEM-SOLVING STRATEGIES
- Use the four-step plan.
- Guess and check.
- Work backward.
- Make an organized list.

7. **NUMBER SENSE** Consecutive odd numbers are numbers like 1, 3, 5, and 7. Find two consecutive odd numbers whose sum is 56 and whose product is 783.

8. **NUMBER SENSE** Gabriel has to make deliveries to three neighbors. He lives at house *b* on the map. Find the shortest route to make the deliveries and return home.

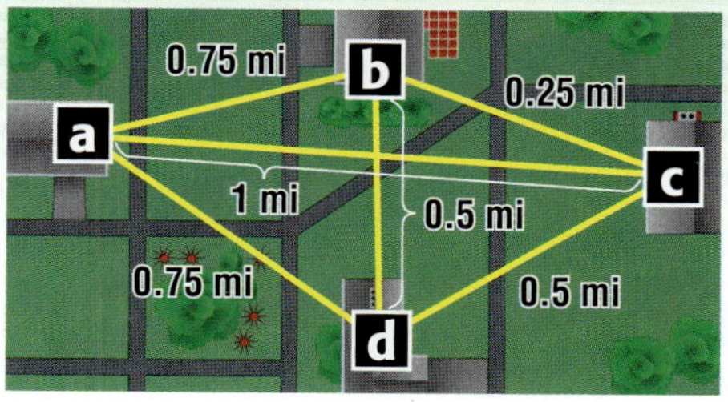

9. **COOKIES** Terez took a bag of cookies to play rehearsal. He gave one half of the cookies to the musicians and then gave five to the director of the play. Terez was left with 15 cookies. How many cookies did he take to rehearsal?

10. **CLOTHES** Jeffrey owns 3 shirts, 2 pairs of pants, and 2 pairs of shoes. How many different outfits can he create?

11. **SNOWFALL** A total of 17 inches of snow fell in a 72-hour period. In the last 24 hours, 6 inches fell, and in the previous 24 hours, 4 inches fell. How many inches fell in the first 24 hours?

Select the Operation

For Exercises 12 and 13, select the appropriate operation(s) to solve the problem. Justify your selection(s) and solve the problem.

12. **EARTH SCIENCE** Giant kelp seaweed is found in the Pacific Ocean. One plant grows 3 feet the first two days. If it continues to grow at the same rate, what would be the length of the seaweed at the end of 80 days?

13. **SCHOOL** Members of student council are raising money to attend a conference. The total costs of the conference are shown in the table. If 24 students attend the conference, how much does each student have to raise?

Transportation	$1,200
Registration	$288
Luncheon	$360

5-4 Simplifying Fractions

Main IDEA

Write fractions in simplest form.

Reinforcement of TEKS 6.1 The student represents and uses rational numbers in a variety of equivalent forms. **(B) generate equivalent forms of rational numbers including whole numbers, fractions, and decimals.** *Also addresses TEKS 7.14(B).*

NEW Vocabulary

equivalent fractions
simplest form

MINI Lab

On grid paper, draw the two figures shown. Shade 4 out of the 10 squares in one figure. Shade 2 out of the 5 rectangles in the other.

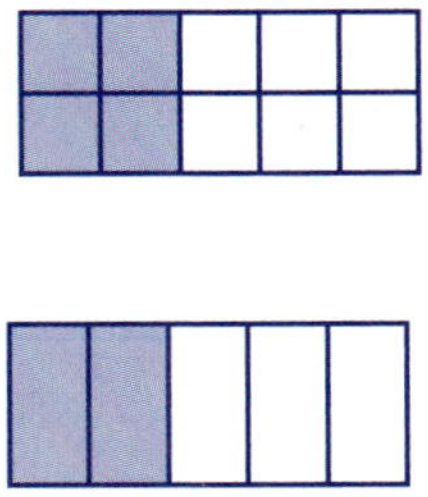

1. Write a fraction to describe each figure: $\frac{\text{number of shaded parts}}{\text{total number of parts}}$.
2. Based on the figures, what can you conclude about the fractions?

Equivalent fractions have the same value. A fraction is in **simplest form** when the GCF of the numerator and denominator is 1.

EXAMPLES Write a Fraction in Simplest Form

1 **Write $\frac{6}{24}$ in simplest form.**

METHOD 1 **Divide by common factors.**

$\frac{6}{24} = \frac{6 \div 2}{24 \div 2} = \frac{3}{12}$ 2 is a common factor of 6 and 24, so divide by 2.

$\frac{3}{12} = \frac{3 \div 3}{12 \div 3} = \frac{1}{4}$ 3 is a common factor of 3 and 12, so divide by 3.

The fraction $\frac{1}{4}$ is in simplest form since 1 and 4 have no common factors greater than 1.

METHOD 2 **Divide by the GCF.**

First, find the GCF of the numerator and denominator.

factors of 6: 1, 2, 3, 6
factors of 24: 1, 2, 3, 4, 6, 8, 12, 24

The GCF of 6 and 24 is 6.

Then, divide the numerator and denominator by the GCF, 6.

$\frac{6}{24} = \frac{6 \div 6}{24 \div 6} = \frac{1}{4}$ Divide the numerator and denominator by the GCF, 6.

So, $\frac{6}{24}$ written in simplest form is $\frac{1}{4}$.

STUDY TIP

Checking Results To check if you simplified correctly, multiply the numerator and denominator of the answer by the GCF. The result should be the original fraction.

STUDY TIP

More Than One Way To write in simplest form, you can also divide by common factors.

$\frac{36}{45} = \frac{36 \div 3}{45 \div 3} = \frac{12}{15}$

$\frac{12}{15} = \frac{12 \div 3}{15 \div 3} = \frac{4}{5}$

So, $\frac{36}{45} = \frac{4}{5}$.

2 **Write $\frac{36}{45}$ in simplest form.**

First, find the GCF of the numerator and denominator.

factors of 36: 1, 2, 3, 4, 6, 9, 12, 18, 36

factors of 45: 1, 3, 5, 9, 15, 45

The GCF of 36 and 45 is 9.

Then, divide the numerator and denominator by the GCF, 9.

$\frac{36}{45} = \frac{36 \div 9}{45 \div 9} = \frac{4}{5}$ — Divide the numerator and denominator by the GCF, 9.

So, $\frac{36}{45}$ written in simplest form is $\frac{4}{5}$.

CHOOSE Your Method

Write each fraction in simplest form.

a. $\frac{7}{28}$ b. $\frac{8}{20}$ c. $\frac{27}{36}$

Real-World EXAMPLE

Real-World Career...
How Does a Music Composer Use Math?
Music composers write notes that can vary in length. There are whole notes, half notes, quarter notes, eighth notes, and sixteenth notes.

Math Online For more information about a career as a music composer, visit: tx.msmath2.com.

3 **MUSIC** **If the fraction of the frequencies of two notes can be simplified, the two notes are harmonious. Use the graphic to find the simplified fraction of the frequency of notes C and E.**

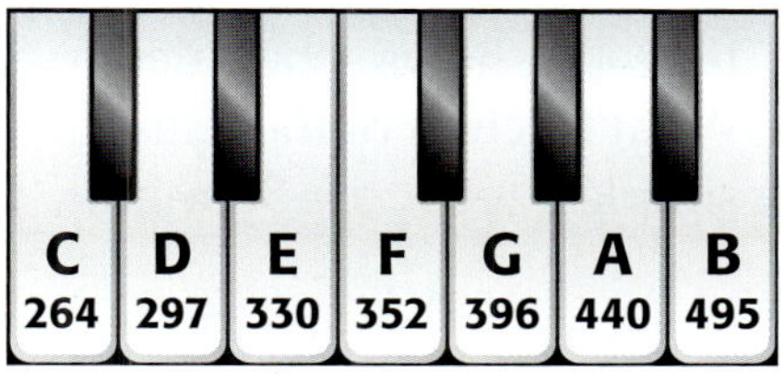

Frequency Chart (Hertz)

$$\frac{\text{frequency of note C}}{\text{frequency of note E}} = \frac{264}{330}$$

$$= \frac{\overset{1}{\cancel{2}} \cdot 2 \cdot 2 \cdot \overset{1}{\cancel{3}} \cdot \overset{1}{\cancel{11}}}{\underset{1}{\cancel{2}} \cdot \underset{1}{\cancel{3}} \cdot 5 \cdot \underset{1}{\cancel{11}}}$$

$$= \frac{4}{5}$$

The slashes mean that part of the numerator and part of the denominator are both divided by the same number. For example, $3 \div 3 = 1$.

The fraction of the frequency of notes C and E is $\frac{4}{5}$.

CHECK Your Progress

d. **MUSIC** Use the graphic above to find the simplified fraction of the frequency of notes D and G. Notes E and F?

e. **MUSIC** Use the graphic above to determine if the notes D and B are harmonious. Justify your answer.

Online Personal Tutor at tx.msmath2.com

CHECK Your Understanding

Examples 1, 2 (pp. 240–241)

Write each fraction in simplest form.

1. $\frac{3}{9}$
2. $\frac{4}{18}$
3. $\frac{10}{25}$
4. $\frac{36}{40}$

Example 3 (p. 241)

5. **ALLOWANCE** Mary received $15 for her weekly allowance. She spent $10 at the movie theater with her friends. What fraction of the money, in simplest form, was spent at the theater?

Exercises

HOMEWORK HELP

For Exercises	See Examples
6–17	1,2
18–19	3

Write each fraction in simplest form.

6. $\frac{9}{12}$
7. $\frac{25}{35}$
8. $\frac{16}{32}$
9. $\frac{14}{20}$
10. $\frac{10}{20}$
11. $\frac{12}{21}$
12. $\frac{15}{25}$
13. $\frac{24}{28}$
14. $\frac{48}{64}$
15. $\frac{32}{32}$
16. $\frac{20}{80}$
17. $\frac{45}{54}$

18. **PRESIDENTS** Of the 43 U.S. presidents, 15 were elected to serve two terms. What fraction of the U.S. presidents, in simplest form, was elected to serve two terms?

19. **TV SHOWS** A television station has 28 prime time TV shows scheduled to air this week. What fraction of the television shows, in simplest form, are 30-minute programs?

WYTB Programming

30-minute	60-minute
20	8

Write each fraction in simplest form.

20. $\frac{45}{100}$
21. $\frac{60}{150}$
22. $\frac{16}{120}$
23. $\frac{35}{175}$

24. **TIME** Fifteen minutes is what part of one hour?

25. **MEASUREMENT** Nine inches is what part of one foot?

26. **CALENDAR** Four days is what part of the month of April?

27. **SLEEP** Marcel spends 8 hours each day sleeping. What fraction of a week, written in simplest form, does Marcel spend sleeping?

28. **MONEY** Each week, Lorenzo receives a $10 allowance. What fraction of his yearly allowance, in simplest form, does he receive each week?

29. **FIND THE DATA** Refer to the Texas Data File on pages 16–19 of your book. Choose some data and write a real-world problem in which you would simplify fractions.

30. **OPEN ENDED** Select a fraction that is *not* in simplest form. Then, simplify it.

EXTRA PRACTICE

See pages 728, 759.

Math Online

Self-Check Quiz at tx.msmath2.com

H.O.T. Problems

31. **CHALLENGE** Both the numerator and denominator of a fraction are even. Is the fraction in simplest form? Explain your reasoning.

32. **FIND THE ERROR** Seki and Luther both wrote $\frac{16}{36}$ in simplest form. Who is correct? Explain.

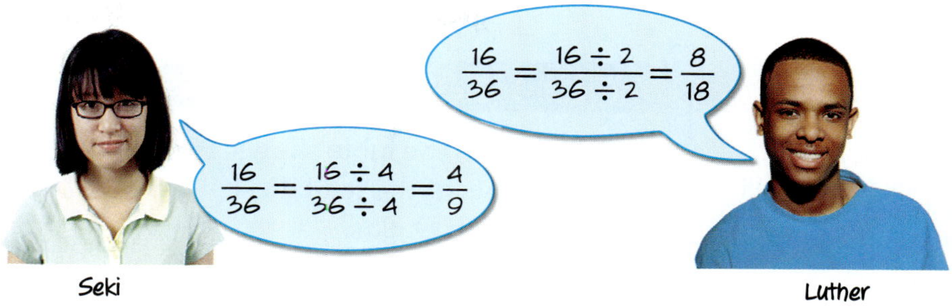

33. **WRITING IN MATH** Explain how to determine whether a fraction is in simplest form.

TEST PRACTICE

34. It takes Benito 12 minutes to walk to school. What fraction represents the part of an hour it takes Benito to walk to school?

A $\frac{12}{1}$

B $\frac{4}{15}$

C $\frac{5}{30}$

D $\frac{1}{5}$

35. What fraction of a foot is 2 inches?

F $\frac{1}{6}$

G $\frac{1}{4}$

H $\frac{1}{3}$

J $\frac{1}{2}$

Spiral Review

36. **SANDWICHES** A deli offers sandwiches with ham, turkey, or roast beef with American, provolone, Swiss, or mozzarella cheese. How many different types of sandwiches can be made if you choose one meat and one cheese? Use the *make an organized list* strategy. (Lesson 5-3)

Find the GCF of each set of numbers. (Lesson 5-2)

37. 27, 36

38. 16, 28

39. 20, 50, 65

40. **ANALYZE GRAPHS** Refer to the graph. At these rates, about how much longer would it take a blue shark to swim 280 miles than it would a sailfish? Use the formula $d = rt$. Justify your answer. (Lesson 4-3)

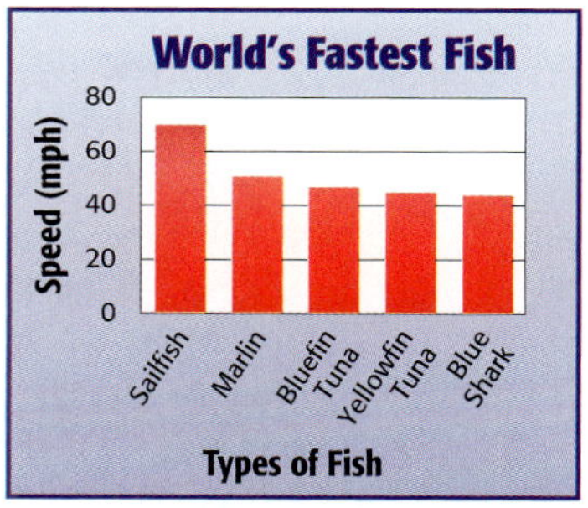

Source: *Top Ten of Everything*

GET READY for the Next Lesson

PREREQUISITE SKILL **Divide.** (Lessons 3-4)

41. $2\overline{)1.0}$

42. $4\overline{)1.00}$

43. $10\overline{)7.0}$

44. $8\overline{)3.000}$

5-5 Fractions and Decimals

Main IDEA

Write fractions as terminating or repeating decimals and write decimals as fractions.

Targeted TEKS **7.1** The student represents and uses numbers in a variety of equivalent forms. **(B) convert between fractions, decimals, whole numbers, and percents mentally, on paper, or with a calculator.** *Also addresses TEKS 7.14(A).*

NEW Vocabulary

terminating decimals
repeating decimals
bar notation

GET READY for the Lesson

BUILDINGS The table shows the heights of the ten tallest buildings in Dallas.

1. What fraction of the buildings are between 600 and 900 feet tall?
2. Express this fraction using words and then as a decimal.
3. What fraction of the buildings are between 710 and 850 feet tall? Express this fraction using words and then as a decimal.

Dallas' Tallest Buildings

Building	Height (ft)
Bank of America Plaza	921
Renaissance Tower	886
Bank One Center	787
JP Morgan Chase Tower	738
Fountain Place	721
Trammell Crow Center	686
1700 Pacific Avenue	655
Thanksgiving Tower	645
Energy Plaza	629
Elm Place	625

Source: dallassky.com

When the denominator of a fraction is a power of 10, you can use place value to write the fraction as a decimal.

Words	Model	Fraction	Decimal
seven tenths	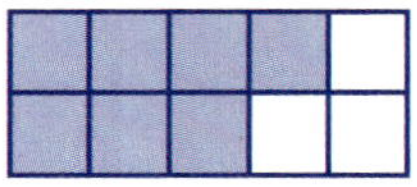	$\frac{7}{10}$	0.7

When the denominator of a fraction is a *factor* of 10, 100, 1000 you can use mental math.

EXAMPLES Use Mental Math

Write each fraction or mixed number as a decimal.

1 $\frac{7}{20}$

THINK $\frac{7}{20} = \frac{35}{100}$ (× 5 numerator and denominator)

So, $\frac{7}{20} = 0.35$.

2 $5\frac{3}{4}$

$5\frac{3}{4} = 5 + \frac{3}{4}$ Think of it as a sum.

$= 5 + 0.75$ You know that $\frac{3}{4} = 0.75$.

$= 5.75$ Add mentally.

So, $5\frac{3}{4} = 5.75$.

CHECK Your Progress

Write each fraction or mixed number as a decimal.

a. $\frac{3}{10}$ b. $\frac{3}{25}$ c. $6\frac{1}{2}$

Any fraction can be written as a decimal by dividing its numerator by its denominator. Division ends when the remainder is zero.

STUDY TIP

Mental Math It will be helpful to memorize the following fraction-decimal equivalencies.

$\frac{1}{2} = 0.5$

$\frac{1}{3} = 0.\overline{3}$ $\quad \frac{2}{3} = 0.\overline{6}$

$\frac{1}{4} = 0.25$ $\quad \frac{3}{4} = 0.75$

$\frac{1}{5} = 0.2$ $\quad \frac{1}{10} = 0.1$

$\frac{1}{8} = 0.125$

EXAMPLE Use Paper and Pencil or a Calculator

3 Write $\frac{3}{8}$ as a decimal.

METHOD 1 **Use paper and pencil.**

$$\begin{array}{r} 0.375 \\ 8\overline{)3.000} \\ -\underline{24} \\ 60 \\ -\underline{56} \\ 40 \\ -\underline{40} \\ 0 \end{array}$$

Divide 3 by 8.

Division ends when the remainder is 0.

METHOD 2 **Use a calculator.**

3 [÷] 8 [ENTER] 0.375

So, $\frac{3}{8} = 0.375$.

CHOOSE Your Method

Write each fraction or mixed number as a decimal.

d. $\frac{7}{8}$ **e.** $2\frac{1}{8}$

Vocabulary Link
Terminate

Everyday Use coming to an end, as in terminate a game.

Math Use a decimal whose digits end.

In Examples 1–3, the decimals 0.35, 5.75, and 0.375 are called terminating decimals. A **terminating decimal** is a decimal whose digits end. Every terminating decimal can be written as a fraction with a denominator of 10, 100, 1,000, and so on.

Repeating decimals have a pattern in the digits that repeats forever. Consider $\frac{1}{3}$.

$$\begin{array}{r} 0.333\ldots \\ 3\overline{)1.000} \\ -\underline{9} \\ 10 \\ -\underline{9} \\ 10 \\ -\underline{9} \\ 1 \end{array}$$

The number 3 repeats. It is represented by three dots.

The remainder after each step is 1.

You can use **bar notation** to indicate that a number repeats forever. A bar is written over the digits that repeat.

$0.33333\ldots = 0.\overline{3}$ $\quad 0.121212\ldots = 0.\overline{12}$ $\quad 11.3858585\ldots = 11.3\overline{85}$

EXAMPLE Write Fractions as Repeating Decimals

4 Write $\frac{7}{9}$ as a decimal.

METHOD 1 **Use paper and pencil.**

$$\begin{array}{r} 0.777\ldots \\ 9\overline{)7.000} \\ -\underline{63} \\ 70 \\ -\underline{63} \\ 70 \\ -\underline{63} \\ 7 \end{array}$$

Notice that the remainder will never be zero. That is, the division does not stop.

METHOD 2 **Use a calculator.**

7 [÷] 9 [ENTER] 0.7777777778

When a calculator displays a repeating decimal, the last digit displayed is rounded.

So, $\frac{7}{9} = 0.777\ldots$ or $0.\overline{7}$.

CHOOSE Your Method

Write each fraction or mixed number as a decimal. Use bar notation if the decimal is a repeating decimal.

f. $\frac{2}{3}$ **g.** $\frac{3}{11}$ **h.** $8\frac{1}{3}$

You can use a power of 10 to write a terminating decimal as a fraction. Place the digits that come after the decimal point in the numerator. Use the place value of the final digit as the denominator.

Real-World Link

Fish	Amount
Guppy	0.25
Angel Fish	0.4
Goldfish	0.15
Molly	0.2

The recommended water temperature for goldfish is 65–72°F.
Source: animal-world.com

Real-World EXAMPLE Use a Power of 10

5 **FISH** **Use the information at the left to find what fraction of the fish in an aquarium are goldfish. Write in simplest form.**

$0.15 = \frac{15}{100}$ The final digit, 5, is in the hundredths place.

$= \frac{3}{20}$ Simplify.

So, $\frac{3}{20}$ of the fish are goldfish.

CHECK Your Progress

Determine the fraction of the aquarium made up by each fish. Write the answer in simplest form.

i. molly **j.** guppy **k.** angel fish

Online Personal Tutor at tx.msmath2.com

CHECK Your Understanding

Examples 1–4 (pp. 244–246)

Write each fraction or mixed number as a decimal. Use bar notation if the decimal is a repeating decimal.

1. $\frac{2}{5}$
2. $\frac{9}{10}$
3. $7\frac{1}{2}$
4. $4\frac{3}{20}$
5. $\frac{1}{8}$
6. $3\frac{5}{8}$
7. $\frac{5}{9}$
8. $1\frac{5}{6}$

Example 5 (p. 246)

Write each decimal as a fraction or mixed number in simplest form.

9. 0.22
10. 0.1
11. 4.6

12. **HOCKEY** During a hockey game, an ice resurfacer travels 0.75 mile during each ice resurfacing. What fraction represents this distance?

Exercises

HOMEWORK HELP

For Exercises	See Examples
13–16	1, 2
17–22	3
23–28	4
29–36	5

Write each fraction or mixed number as a decimal. Use bar notation if the decimal is a repeating decimal.

13. $\frac{4}{5}$
14. $\frac{1}{2}$
15. $4\frac{4}{25}$
16. $7\frac{1}{20}$
17. $\frac{5}{16}$
18. $\frac{3}{16}$
19. $\frac{33}{50}$
20. $\frac{17}{40}$
21. $5\frac{7}{8}$
22. $9\frac{3}{8}$
23. $\frac{4}{9}$
24. $\frac{8}{9}$
25. $\frac{1}{6}$
26. $\frac{8}{11}$
27. $5\frac{1}{3}$
28. $2\frac{6}{11}$

Write each decimal as a fraction or mixed number in simplest form.

29. 0.2
30. 0.9
31. 0.55
32. 0.34
33. 5.96
34. 2.66

35. **INSECTS** The maximum length of a praying mantis is 30.5 centimeters. What mixed number represents this length?

36. **GROCERIES** Suppose you buy the package of deli ham shown. What fraction of a pound did you buy?

37. **FIND THE DATA** Refer to the Texas Data File on page 16–19 of your book. Choose some data and write a real-world problem in which you would write a percent as a decimal.

EXTRA PRACTICE
See pages 729, 759.
Math Online
Self-Check Quiz at tx.msmath2.com

Write each fraction or mixed number as a decimal. Use bar notation if the decimal is a repeating decimal.

38. $\frac{5}{32}$
39. $\frac{13}{24}$
40. $2\frac{5}{7}$
41. $8\frac{1}{33}$

42. **MUSIC** Nicolás practiced playing the cello for 2 hours and 18 minutes. Write the time Nicolás spent practicing as a decimal.

43. **SOFTBALL** The batting average of a softball player is the number of hits divided by the number of at-bats. If Felisa had 50 hits in 175 at-bats and Harmony had 42 hits in 160 at-bats, who had the better batting average? Justify your answer

H.O.T. Problems

44. **OPEN ENDED** Select a fraction that is equivalent to a terminating decimal and one that is equivalent to a repeating decimal.

45. **CHALLENGE** The value of pi (π) is 3.1415926… . The mathematician Archimedes believed that π was between $3\frac{1}{7}$ and $3\frac{10}{71}$. Was Archimedes correct? Explain your reasoning.

46. **WRITING IN MATH** Fractions with denominators of 2, 4, 8, 16, and 32 produce terminating decimals. Fractions with denominators of 6, 12, 18, and 24 produce repeating decimals. What causes the difference? Explain.

TEST PRACTICE

47. Which decimal represents the shaded region of the model?

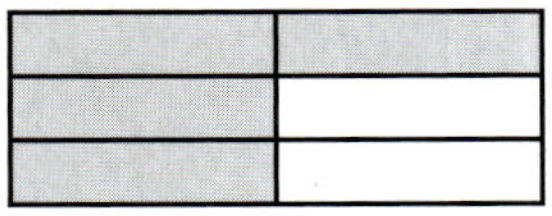

A 0.666

B $0.\overline{6}$

C 0.667

D $0.66\overline{7}$

48. Based on the information given in the table, what fraction represents $0.\overline{8}$?

F $\frac{4}{5}$

G $\frac{80}{99}$

H $\frac{5}{6}$

J $\frac{8}{9}$

Decimal	Fraction
$0.\overline{3}$	$\frac{3}{9}$
$0.\overline{4}$	$\frac{4}{9}$
$0.\overline{5}$	$\frac{5}{9}$
$0.\overline{6}$	$\frac{6}{9}$

Spiral Review

Write each fraction in simplest form. (Lesson 5-4)

49. $\frac{10}{24}$

50. $\frac{39}{81}$

51. $\frac{28}{98}$

52. $\frac{51}{68}$

53. **PIZZA** How many different pizzas can Alfonso order if he can choose thick, thin, or deep dish crust and one topping from either pepperoni, sausage, or mushrooms? Use the *make an organized list* strategy. (Lesson 5-3)

GET READY for the Next Lesson

PREREQUISITE SKILL **Write a fraction for the number of shaded squares to the total number of squares.**

54. 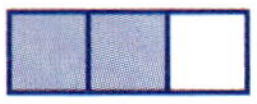

55. 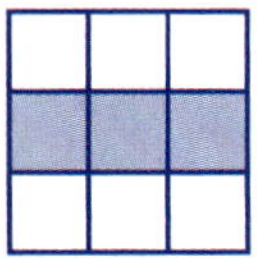

56. 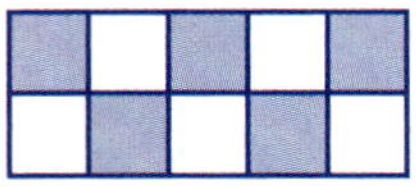

57. 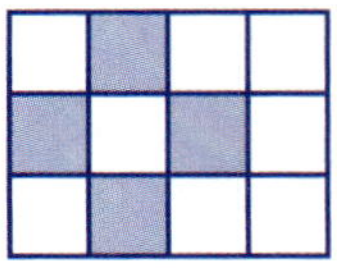

CHAPTER 5

Mid-Chapter Quiz

Lessons 5-1 through 5-5

Determine whether each number is *prime* or *composite*. (Lesson 5-1)

1. 24
2. 61
3. 2

4. **AGE** Kevin just turned 13 years old. How old will he be the next time his age is a prime number?

Find the prime factorization of each number. (Lesson 5-1)

5. 30
6. 120

Factor each expression. (Lesson 5-1)

7. $14x^2y$
8. $50mn$

Find the GCF of each set of numbers. (Lesson 5-2)

9. 16, 40
10. 65, 100

11. **TEST PRACTICE** What is the greatest number of crayons in each row of an 8-, a 64-, and a 96-crayon box if all rows have the same number? (Lesson 5-2)

A 12

B 8

C 4

D 2

12. **TEST PRACTICE** Lynne cannot remember her password to check the messages on her cell phone. She knows that it is a three-digit number consisting of the numbers 1, 4, and 7, but she cannot remember the order. Which list shows all the different possibilities for her password? (Lesson 5-3)

F 147, 174, 417, 714, 741

G 147, 174, 417, 471, 714, 741

H 417, 471, 714, 741

J 147, 174, 74, 417, 17, 471, 714, 741

13. **PIANO** Evelina spends 35 minutes practicing the piano each afternoon after school. What part of one hour does she spend practicing? Write as a fraction in simplest form. (Lesson 5-4)

Write each fraction in simplest form. (Lesson 5-4)

14. $\frac{20}{36}$

15. $\frac{45}{60}$

16. $\frac{63}{108}$

17. $\frac{60}{72}$

18. **CYCLING** A *gear ratio* of a bike is the comparison of the number of teeth on a chainwheel to the number on a freewheel. The gear ratio for Alexis' 10-speed bike is $\frac{22}{30}$. Write this fraction in simplest form. (Lesson 5-4)

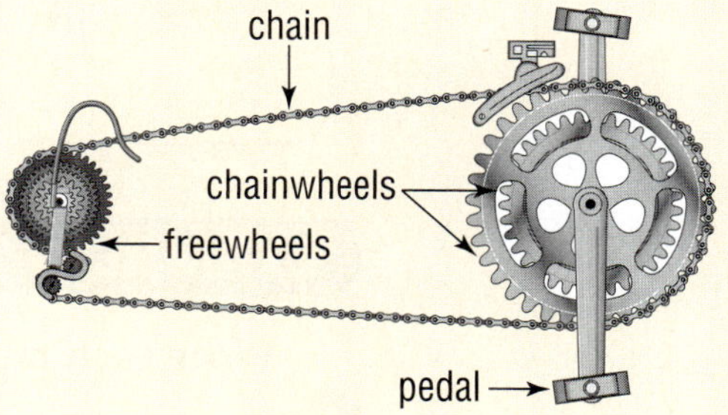

Write each fraction or mixed number as a decimal. Use bar notation if the decimal is a repeating decimal. (Lesson 5-5)

19. $\frac{7}{8}$
20. $\frac{2}{9}$
21. $3\frac{13}{20}$

Write each decimal as a fraction in simplest form. (Lesson 5-5)

22. 0.6
23. 0.48
24. 7.02

25. **ANIMALS** The maximum height of an Asian elephant is 9.8 feet. What mixed number represents this height? (Lesson 5-5)

5-6 Fractions and Percents

Main IDEA

Write fractions as percents and percents as fractions.

Targeted TEKS **7.1** The student represents and uses numbers in a variety of equivalent forms. **(B)** **convert between fractions,** decimals, **whole numbers, and percents mentally, on paper, or with a calculator.**

NEW Vocabulary

ratio
percent

GET READY for the Lesson

Some students were asked to choose methods that make learning subjects more interesting. The results are shown.

Method	Number of Students
Internet	17 out of 50
Teacher	29 out of 100
TV program	1 out of 4
Textbook	3 out of 25

Source: *Opinion Research Corporation*

1. For each method, shade a 10 × 10 grid that represents the number of students that chose the method.
2. What fraction of the students chose the Internet?

A **ratio** is a comparison of two quantities by division. Ratios, like 34 out of 100 can also be written as 34:100 or $\frac{34}{100}$. When a ratio compares a number to 100, it can be written as a **percent**.

KEY CONCEPT — Percent

Words A percent is a part to whole ratio that compares a number to 100.

Symbols $\frac{n}{100} = n\%$

Example

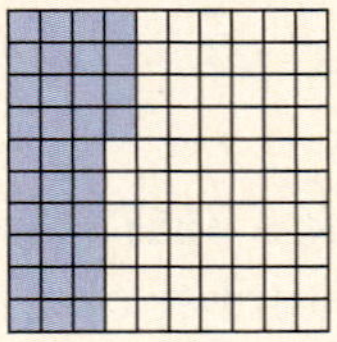

34 out of 100 = 34%

EXAMPLES Write Ratios as Percents

Write each ratio as a percent.

1 Annie answered 90 out of 100 questions correctly.

$\frac{90}{100} = 90\%$

Annie answered 90% of the questions correctly.

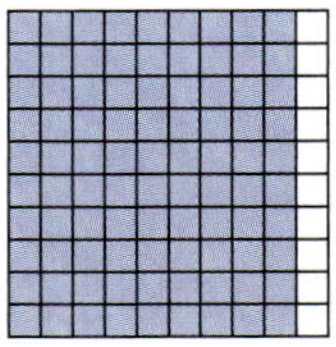

90%

2 On average, 50.5 out of 100 students own a pet.

$\frac{50.5}{100} = 50.5\%$

On average, 50.5% of the students own a pet.

CHECK Your Progress **Write each ratio as a percent.**

a. 45 out of 100 cars sold

b. \$3.30 : \$100 spent on soft drinks

READING Math

Percent *Percent* means per *hundred* or *hundredths*. The symbol % means percent.

Fractions and percents are ratios that can represent the same number. You can write a fraction as a percent by finding an equivalent fraction with a denominator of 100.

EXAMPLE Write a Fraction as a Percent

3 **Write $\frac{3}{20}$ as a percent.**

First, find an equivalent fraction with a denominator of 100. Then write the fraction as a percent.

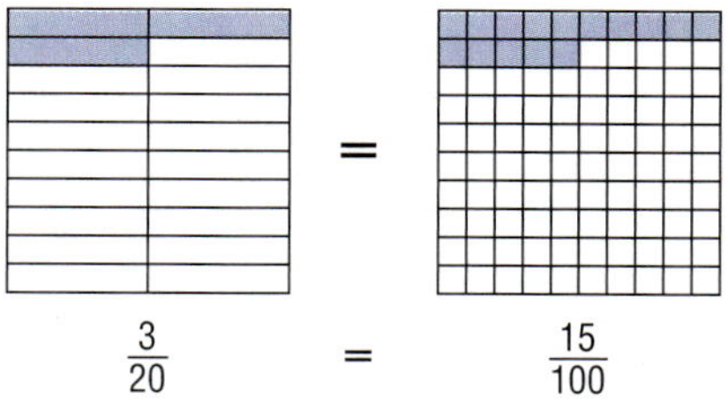

$\frac{3}{20} = \frac{3 \times 5}{20 \times 5} = \frac{15}{100}$ or 15%

So, $\frac{3}{20} = 15\%$.

CHECK Your Progress **Write each fraction as a percent.**

c. $\frac{17}{20}$ d. $\frac{3}{5}$ e. $\frac{2}{25}$

Real-World EXAMPLE

Real-World Link Each state quarter has a diameter of 24.26 millimeters, a thickness of 1.75 millimeters, and weighs 5.670 grams.
Source: usmint.gov

4 **COINS** **The 50 State Quarters® Program allows the United States Mint to release a new quarter every ten weeks from 1999 through 2008 commemorating the 50 states. By the end of 2005, 35 state coins were released. What percent of the coins is this?**

By the end of 2005, 35 out of 50 state coins were released.

$\frac{35}{50} = \frac{70}{100}$ Write an equivalent fraction with a denominator of 100.

$= 70\%$ $\frac{70}{100} = 70\%$

So, 70% of the state coins were released by the end of 2005.

CHECK Your Progress

f. **COINS** What percent of the coins in the 50 State Quarters Program are being released after 2005?

Online Personal Tutor at tx.msmath2.com

EXAMPLE Write a Percent as a Fraction

5 **Write 48% as a fraction in simplest form.**

$48\% = \frac{48}{100}$ Definition of percent

$= \frac{12}{25}$ Simplify.

CHECK Your Progress

Write each percent as a fraction in simplest form.

g. 40% h. 6% i. 24%

CHECK Your Understanding

Examples 1, 2 (p. 250)

Write each ratio as a percent.

1. 57:100 insects are spiders
2. \$29.20 per \$100

Example 3 (p. 251)

Write each fraction as a percent.

3. $\frac{1}{4}$
4. $\frac{6}{10}$
5. $\frac{17}{20}$

Example 4 (p. 251)

6. **TECHNOLOGY** Tansy used $\frac{2}{5}$ of the memory available on her flash drive. What percent of the memory did she use?

Example 5 (p. 251)

Write each percent as a fraction in simplest form.

7. 90%
8. 75%
9. 22%

Exercises

HOMEWORK HELP	
For Exercises	See Examples
10–15	1, 2
16–23	3
24–25	4
26–33	5

Write each ratio as a percent.

10. 87 out of 100 books read
11. 42 per 100 teenagers
12. 12.2 out of 100 points earned
13. 99.9:100 miles driven
14. $11\frac{3}{4}$ out of 100 feet
15. $66\frac{2}{3}$:100 yards run

Write each fraction as a percent.

16. $\frac{7}{10}$
17. $\frac{16}{20}$
18. $\frac{15}{25}$
19. $\frac{13}{50}$
20. $\frac{1}{5}$
21. $\frac{3}{5}$
22. $\frac{19}{20}$
23. $\frac{10}{10}$

24. **PETS** Twenty out of every 25 households own one dog. What percent of households own one dog?

25. **SPORTS** If 15 out of every 50 teens like to ski, what percent of teens like to ski?

Write each percent as a fraction in simplest form.

26. 45%
27. 30%
28. 62%
29. 88%
30. 68%
31. 13%
32. 2%
33. 300%

Replace each ● with >, <, or =.

34. $\frac{1}{4}$ ● 25%
35. $\frac{9}{20}$ ● 55%
36. 78% ● $\frac{3}{5}$
37. 38% ● $\frac{19}{50}$
38. 12% ● $1\frac{1}{5}$
39. $2\frac{2}{5}$ ● 24%

40. **VOLUNTEERING** A Girl Scouts event is expecting 40 out of 50 people to volunteer at a charity auction. So far 30 volunteers have arrived at the auction. What percent of the volunteers have not yet arrived?

EXTRA PRACTICE

See pages 729, 759.

Math Online
Self-Check Quiz at tx.msmath2.com

H.O.T. Problems

41. **GEOMETRY** What percent of the larger rectangle shown is *not* shaded?

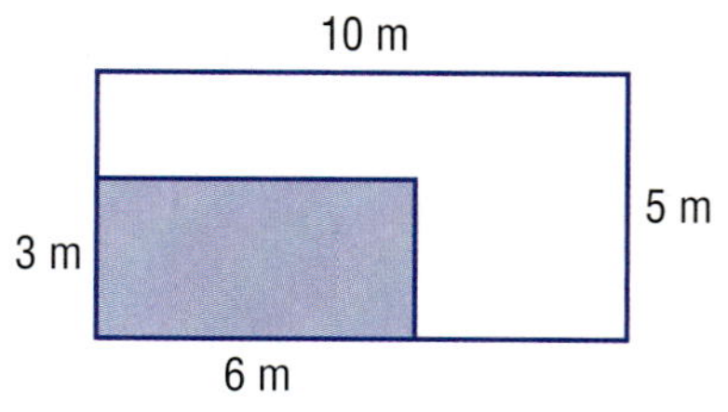

42. **CHALLENGE** Apply what you know about percents, fractions, and decimals to write $12\frac{1}{2}\%$ as a fraction. Justify your answer.

43. **Which One Doesn't Belong?** Identify the ratio that does not have the same value as the other three. Explain your reasoning.

$\frac{10}{100}$	1%	$\frac{1}{10}$	100 out of 1,000

44. **WRITING IN MATH** Explain how you know which model represents 36%. Then explain why that model also represents $\frac{9}{25}$.

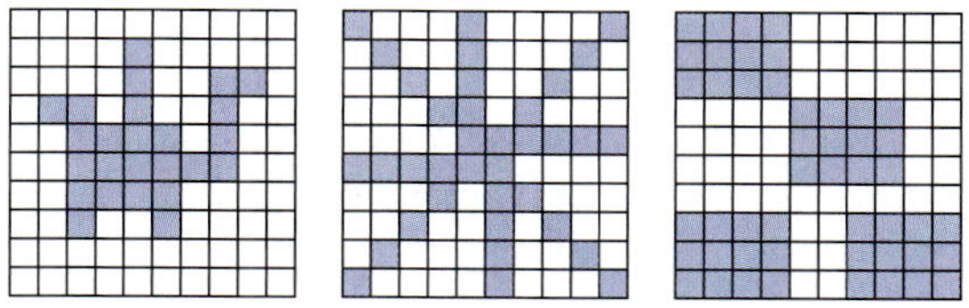

Model 1 Model 2 Model 3

TEST PRACTICE

45. What percent of the model is shaded?

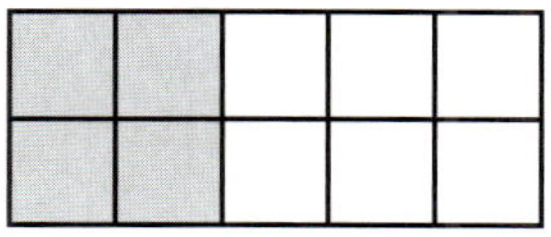

A 25% **C** 40%

B 30% **D** 60%

46. Cats spend about $\frac{3}{10}$ of their time awake grooming themselves. Which number is equivalent to $\frac{3}{10}$?

F 3% **H** 33.3%

G 30% **J** 300%

Spiral Review

Write each decimal as a fraction or mixed number in simplest form. (Lesson 5-5)

47. 0.6 48. 0.15 49. 2.8

50. **TIME** The drive to a football game took 56 minutes. Twenty-four minutes of the time was spent stopped in traffic. What fraction of the drive, in simplest form, was spent in stopped traffic? (Lesson 5-4)

Solve each equation. (Lesson 4-2)

51. $x + 7 = 10$ 52. $m - 2 = 8$ 53. $12 + a = 16$

GET READY for the Next Lesson

PREREQUISITE SKILL **Multiply or divide.** (Lessons 3-2 and 3-4)

54. 16.2×10 55. 0.71×100 56. $14.4 \div 100$ 57. $791 \div 1{,}000$

5-7 Percents and Decimals

Main IDEA

Write percents as decimals and decimals as percents.

Targeted TEKS 7.1 The student represents and uses numbers in a variety of equivalent forms. **(B) convert between** fractions, **decimals, whole numbers, and percents mentally, on paper,** or with a calculator.

GET READY for the Lesson

READING The graphic shows the reasons that students in 6th through 12th grades read.

1. Write the percent of students who read for fun as a fraction.
2. Write the fraction as a decimal.
3. Compare the decimal in Question 2 with its percent form. Identify any similarities or differences.

Source: National Education Association, *American Demographics*

In Lesson 5-5, you learned that any fraction can be written as a decimal. You can use this fact to write percents as decimals.

EXAMPLE Write Percents as Decimals

1 Write 7% as a decimal.

METHOD 1 Write the percent as a fraction.

$7\% = \frac{7}{100}$ Write the percent as a fraction.

$= 0.07$ Write the fraction as a decimal.

METHOD 2 Divide mentally.

The % symbol means to divide by 100. So, remove the % symbol and divide by 100.

$7\% = .07$ Remove the % symbol and divide by 100. Add placeholder zero.

$= 0.07$ Add leading zero.

So, $7\% = 0.07$.

STUDY TIP

Division
When dividing by 100, the decimal point moves two places left.

CHOOSE Your Method

Write each percent as a decimal.

a. 8% b. 54% c. 85.2%

Real-World EXAMPLE

Concepts in Motion
Interactive Lab tx.msmath2.com

2 **GEOGRAPHY** Alaska is the largest state, making up about $16\frac{1}{10}\%$ of the land area of the United States. Write this amount as a decimal.

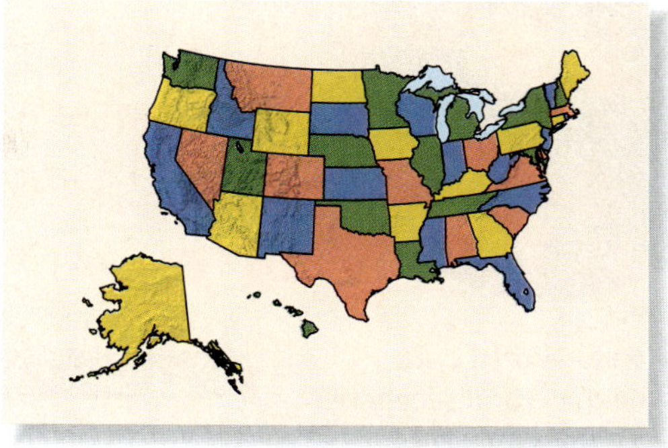

$16\frac{1}{10}\% = 16.1\%$ — Write $\frac{1}{10}$ as 0.1.

$= 16.1$ — Remove the % symbol and divide by 100.

$= 0.161$ — Add leading zero.

So, $16\frac{1}{10}\% = 0.161$.

CHECK Your Progress

d. **GEOGRAPHY** About $6\frac{4}{5}\%$ of the total area of the United States is water. What decimal represents this amount?

e. **GEOGRAPHY** The total area of Australia is about $38\frac{11}{20}\%$ of the total area of North America. Write the amount as a decimal.

EXAMPLE Write Decimals as Percents

3 Write 0.4 as a percent.

STUDY TIP

Division
When multiplying by 100, the decimal point moves two places right.

METHOD 1 **Write the decimal as fraction.**

$0.4 = \frac{4}{10}$ or $\frac{40}{100}$ — Write the decimal as a fraction.

$= 40\%$ — Write the fraction as a percent.

METHOD 2 **Multiply mentally.**

Multiply by 100 and add the % symbol.

$0.4 = 0.40$ — Multiply by 100. Add a placeholder zero.

$= 40\%$ — Add the % symbol.

So, $0.4 = 40\%$.

CHOOSE Your Method Write each decimal as a percent.

f. 0.5 g. 0.34 h. 0.98

Online Personal Tutor at tx.msmath2.com

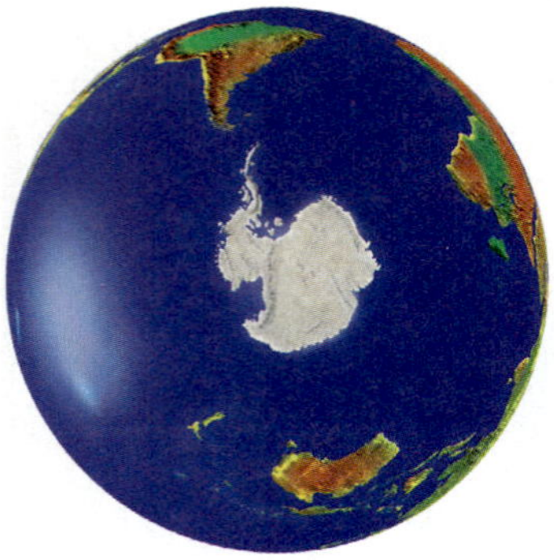

Real-World Link
Of the world's icebergs, 93% are found surrounding the Antarctic.
Source: JPL Polar Oceanography Group

Real-World EXAMPLE

4 **SCIENCE** **About 0.875 of an iceberg's mass is underwater. What percent of an iceberg's mass is underwater?**

$0.875 = 0.875$ Multiply by 100.

$= 87.5\%$ Add the % symbol.

So, 87.5% of an iceberg's mass is underwater.

CHECK Your Progress

i. **EXERCISE** Each day, Rico and his dog walk 0.625-mile. What percent of a mile do they walk?

CONCEPT Summary

Percent as a Decimal

To write a percent as a decimal, divide the percent by 100 and remove the percent symbol.

$25\% = .25$ or 0.25

Decimal as a Percent

To write a decimal as a percent, multiply the percent by 100 and add the percent symbol.

$0.58 = 0.58 = 58\%$

CHECK Your Understanding

Example 1 (p. 254)

Write each percent as a decimal.

1. 68%
2. 5%
3. 27.6%

Example 2 (p. 255)

4. **SPENDING** A family spends about $33\frac{2}{5}\%$ of their annual income on housing. What decimal represents the amount spent on housing?

Example 3 (p. 255)

Write each decimal as a percent.

5. 0.09
6. 0.3
7. 0.73

Example 4 (p. 256)

8. **BASKETBALL** The table shows the top five WNBA players with the highest free-throw averages for the 2005 regular season. What percent of the time does Katie Smith make a free-throw?

Player	Average
Anna DeForge	0.85
Kelly Miller	0.848
Allison Feaster	0.846
Katie Smith	0.782
Vickie Johnson	0.774

Source: nba.com

Exercises

HOMEWORK HELP

For Exercises	See Examples
9–20	1
21–22	2
23–34	3
35–37	4

Write each percent as a decimal.

9. 27%
10. 70%
11. 6%
12. 4%
13. 18.5%
14. 56.4%
15. 2.2%
16. 3.8%
17. $27\frac{7}{10}\%$
18. $15\frac{1}{2}\%$
19. $30\frac{1}{4}\%$
20. $46\frac{2}{5}\%$

21. **BONES** An adult human body has $68\frac{3}{5}\%$ of the number of bones it had at birth. What decimal represents this amount?

22. **VIDEO GAMES** Brian reaches the sixth level of a video game $92\frac{3}{4}\%$ of the time he plays. What decimal represents this percent?

Write each decimal as a percent.

23. 0.7
24. 0.6
25. 5.8
26. 8.2
27. 0.95
28. 0.08
29. 0.17
30. 0.78
31. 0.675
32. 0.145
33. 0.012
34. 0.7025

LACROSSE **For Exercises 35–37, use the table shown. What percent of the games played did each team win?**

35. Cedar Park
36. Cypress-Fairbanks
37. Which team won 11 out of 16 games?

Texas Lacrosse, 2004 Season

School Name	Portion of Games Won
Memorial, Houston	0.6875
Cedar Park	0.727
Cypress-Fairbanks	1.0
Hockaday School	0.8

Replace each ● with >, <, or = to make a true sentence.

38. 0.25% ● 0.125
39. 0.76 ● 76.5%
40. 500% ● 50
41. 99% ● 0.985
42. 0.325 ● 30%
43. 56% ● 0.5625

44. **SPORTS** A tennis player won 0.805 of the matches she played. What percent of the matches did she lose?

ANALYZE TABLES **For Exercises 45–48, use the table and the information given.**

Five scales can be used to build a model train based on the life-size original. For example, a G-scale train is about 4% of the size of the original. So, the model of a train that measures 75 feet would measure 36 inches.

45. Find the decimal equivalents for each scale.
46. Which scale is the smallest?
47. Find the approximate length of an actual 75-foot train in the N scale.
48. Which scale is used if a model of a 75-foot train is about 18.75 inches?

Scale	Percent Equivalent
G	4.4%
O	2.083%
HO	1.15%
N	0.625%
Z	0.45%

Source: internettrains.com

EXTRA PRACTICE

See pages 729, 759.

Math Online
Self-Check Quiz at tx.msmath2.com

H.O.T. Problems

49. OPEN ENDED Write any decimal between 0 and 1. Then write it as a fraction in simplest form and as a percent.

50. FIND THE ERROR Janelle and Gregorio both wrote 0.881 as a percent. Who is correct? Explain.

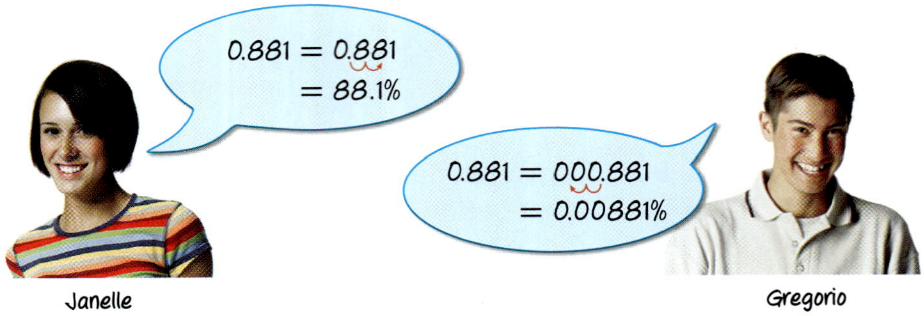

CHALLENGE Write each fraction as a percent.

51. $\frac{3}{8}$ **52.** $\frac{1}{40}$ **53.** $\frac{1}{32}$

54. WRITING IN MATH Write a word problem about a real-world situation in which you would change a decimal to a percent.

TEST PRACTICE

55. It is estimated that 13.9% of the population of Texas was born outside the United States. Which number is NOT equivalent to 13.9%?

A $\frac{139}{1{,}000}$ **C** 0.139

B $\frac{13.9}{100}$ **D** 1.39

56. Which of the following is ordered from least to greatest?

F 0.42, $\frac{2}{5}$, 50%, $\frac{3}{4}$

G $\frac{2}{5}$, 0.42, 50%, $\frac{3}{4}$

H $\frac{3}{4}$, $\frac{2}{5}$, 0.42%, 50%

J $\frac{3}{4}$, 0.42, $\frac{2}{5}$, 50%

Spiral Review

Write each ratio as a percent. (Lesson 5-6)

57. 72 out of 100 animals **58.** \$9.90:\$100 **59.** 3.1 out of 100 households

60. Write $9\frac{3}{8}$ as a decimal. (Lesson 5-5)

61. MONEY Marina earned \$187.50 by working 30 hours. If she works 35 hours at this rate, how much will she earn? (Lessons 3-2 and 3-4)

62. BALLOONS Write an integer that represents a hot-air balloon descending 83 feet. (Lesson 2-1)

GET READY for the Next Lesson

PREREQUISITE SKILL Write the prime factorization of each number. (Lesson 5-1)

63. 50 **64.** 32 **65.** 76 **66.** 105

5-8 Least Common Multiple

Main IDEA

Find the least common multiple of two or more numbers.

Reinforcement of TEKS 6.1 The student represents and uses rational numbers in a variety of equivalent forms. **(E) identify factors of a positive integer, common factors, and the greatest common factor of a set of positive integers.** *Also addresses TEKS 7.13(D).*

NEW Vocabulary

multiple
least common multiple (LCM)

Vocabulary Link

Multiply
Everyday Use to find the product

Multiple
Math Use the product of a number and any whole number

MINI Lab

Model the first floors of Building 1 and Building 2, as shown.

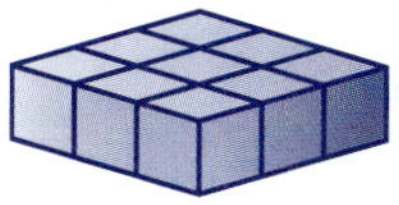

Building 1

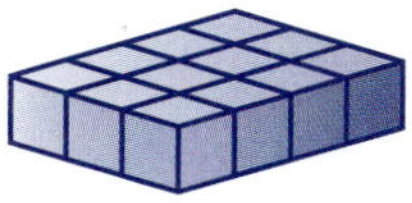

Building 2

1. Add a second floor to each building. Record the total number of cubes used in a table like the one shown below.

Number of Floors	1	2	3	4	5
Number of Cubes in Building 1	9	■	■	■	■
Number of Cubes in Building 2	12	■	■	■	■

2. Add floors until each building has five floors.
3. Describe two buildings that have the same number of cubes.
4. If you keep adding floors, will the two buildings have the same number of cubes again? Explain.

A **multiple** is the product of a number and any whole number. The **least common multiple**, or **LCM**, of two or more numbers is the least of their common multiples, excluding zero.

EXAMPLES Find the LCM

1 Find the LCM of 6 and 10.

METHOD 1 List the nonzero multiples.

multiples of 6: 6, 12, 18, 24, 30, 36, 42, 48, 54, 60, …

multiples of 10: 10, 20, 30, 40, 50, 60, 70, 80, …

Notice that 30 and 60 are common multiples. The least of these is 30, so the LCM of 6 and 10 is 30.

METHOD 2 Use prime factorization.

$6 = 2 \cdot 3$

$10 = 2 \cdot 5$

The prime factors of 6 and 10 are 2, 3, and 5.

The LCM is the least product that contains the prime factors of each number. So, multiply the greatest power of 2, 3, and 5. The LCM of 6 and 10 is $2 \cdot 3 \cdot 5$ or 30.

So, the LCM of 6 and 10 is 30.

2 **Find the LCM of 45 and 75.**

Use Method 2. Find the prime factorization of each number.

$45 = 3 \cdot 3 \cdot 5$ or $3^2 \cdot 5$

$75 = 3 \cdot 5 \cdot 5$ or $3 \cdot 5^2$

The prime factors of 45 and 75 are 3 and 5. Write the prime factorization using exponents.

Multiply the greatest power of 3 and 5.
The LCM of 45 and 75 is $3^2 \cdot 5^2$ or $9 \cdot 25$, which is 225.

CHOOSE Your Method

Find the LCM of each set of numbers.

a. 3, 12 **b.** 10, 12 **c.** 25, 30

Real-World EXAMPLE

3 **PARTY Ling needs to buy paper plates, napkins, and cups for a party. Plates come in packages of 12, napkins come in packages of 16, and cups come in packages of 8. If she wants to have the same number of plates, napkins, and cups, what is the least number of packages she will have to buy?**

First find the LCM of 8, 12, and 16.

$8 = 2 \cdot 2 \cdot 2$ or 2^3

$12 = 2 \cdot 2 \cdot 3$ or $2^2 \cdot 3$

$16 = 2 \cdot 2 \cdot 2 \cdot 2$ or 2^4

The prime factors of 8, 12, and 16 are 2 and 3. Write the prime factorization using exponents.

The LCM of 8, 12, and 16 is $2^4 \cdot 3$ or $16 \cdot 3$, which is 48.

To find the number of packages of each Ling needs to buy, divide 48 by the amount in each package.

cups: $48 \div 8$ or 6 packages

plates: $48 \div 12$ or 4 packages

napkins: $48 \div 16$ or 3 packages

So, Ling will need to buy 6 packages of cups, 4 packages of plates, and 3 packages of napkins.

Real-World Link
Each day, about 700,000 people in the U.S. celebrate their birthday.
Source: hallmark.com

CHECK Your Progress

d. VEHICLES Mr. Hernandez changes his car's oil every 3 months, rotates the tires every 6 months, and replaces the air filter once a year. If he completed all three tasks in April, what will be the next month he again completes all three tasks?

Online Personal Tutor at tx.msmath2.com

CHECK Your Understanding

Examples 1–3 (pp. 259–260)

Find the LCM of each set of numbers.

1. 4, 14
2. 6, 7
3. 12, 15
4. 21, 35
5. 3, 5, 12
6. 6, 14, 21

Example 3 (p. 260)

7. **GOVERNMENT** The number of years per term for a U.S. President, senator, and representative is shown. Suppose a senator was elected in the presidential election year 2004. In what year will he or she campaign again during a presidential election year?

Elected Office	Term (yr)
President	4
Senator	6
Representative	2

Exercises

HOMEWORK HELP

For Exercises	See Examples
8–13, 20	1, 2
14–19, 21	3

Find the LCM for each set of numbers.

8. 6, 8
9. 8, 18
10. 12, 16
11. 24, 36
12. 11, 12
13. 45, 63
14. 2, 3, 5
15. 6, 8, 9
16. 8, 12, 16
17. 12, 15, 28
18. 22, 33, 44
19. 12, 16, 36

20. **CHORES** Hernando walks his dog every two days. He gives his dog a bath once a week. Today, Hernando walked his dog and then gave her a bath. How many days will pass before he does both chores on the same day?

21. **TEXT MESSAGING** Three friends use text messaging to notify their parents of their whereabouts. If all three contact their parents at 3:00 P.M., at what time will all three contact their parents again at the same time?

Friend	Time Interval
Linda	every 30 min
Brandon	every 45 min
Edward	every 60 min

Find the LCM of each set.

22. \$3.00, \$14.00
23. 10¢, 25¢, 5¢
24. 9 inches, 2 feet

Write two numbers whose LCM is the given number.

25. 35
26. 56
27. 70
28. 30

29. **SNACKS** Alvin's mom needs to buy snacks for soccer practice. Juice boxes come in packages of 10. Oatmeal snack bars come in packages of 8. She wants to have the same number of juice boxes and snack bars, what is the least number of packages of each snack that she will have to buy?

30. **REASONING** The LCM of two consecutive positive numbers is greater than 200 and is a multiple of 7. What are the least possible numbers?

EXTRA PRACTICE
See pages 730, 759.
Math Online
Self-Check Quiz at tx.msmath2.com

H.O.T. Problems

31. **CHALLENGE** Two numbers have an LCM of $2^2 \cdot 3 \cdot 5^2$. Their GCF is $2 \cdot 5$. If one of the numbers is $2 \cdot 3 \cdot 5$, what is the other number?

32. **SELECT A TECHNIQUE** The schedule for each of three trains is shown. Suppose a train from each line leaves Clark Street at 11:35 A.M. Which of the following technique(s) might you use to determine the next time all three trains will be leaving at the same time? Justify your selection(s). Then use the technique to solve the problem.

Clark Street Train Station	
Train	**Leaves Station**
Red-line	every 14 minutes
Blue-line	every 16 minutes
Brown-line	every 8 minutes

mental math | number sense | estimation

33. **OPEN ENDED** Write three numbers that have an LCM of 30.

34. **WRITING IN MATH** Describe the relationship between 12, 4, and 3 using the words *multiple* and *factor*.

TEST PRACTICE

35. Which rule describes the common multiples of 12 and 18, where n represents the counting numbers?

A $12n$

B $18n$

C $36n$

D $216n$

36. Which of the following is the least common multiple of 24 and 60?

F 72

G 96

H 120

J 1,140

Spiral Review

Write each percent as a decimal. (Lesson 5-7)

37. 55%

38. 26.4%

39. $\frac{1}{4}$%

40. 2%

41. **DIAMONDS** Sixty-eight percent of engagement rings have a diamond that is round in shape. Write this percent as a fraction in simplest form. (Lesson 5-6)

42. **ALGEBRA** Solve $3x = 18$. (Lesson 4-3)

43. **PLANETS** The planet Jupiter is 480,000,000 miles from the Sun. Write this distance in scientific notation. (Lesson 3-7)

GET READY for the Next Lesson

PREREQUISITE SKILL **Replace each ● with <, > or = to make a true sentence.** (Page 710)

44. 6.85 ● 5.68

45. 2.34 ● 2.43

46. 6.9 ● 5.99

5-9 Comparing and Ordering Rational Numbers

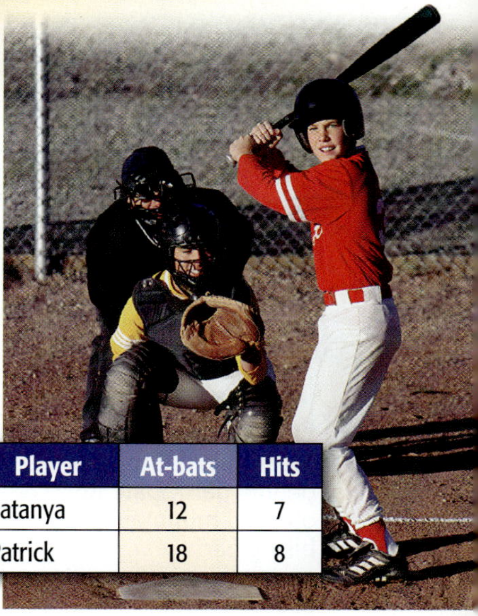

Main IDEA

Compare and order fractions, decimals, and percents.

Targeted TEKS 7.1 The student represents and uses numbers in a variety of equivalent forms. **(A) compare and order** integers and **positive rational numbers.** *Also addresses TEKS 7.14(A).*

NEW Vocabulary

common denominator
least common denominator (LCD)
rational numbers

GET READY for the Lesson

SOFTBALL The table shows how Latanya and Patrick did during the first month of the softball season.

1. A batting average is the ratio of hits to at-bats. Write each player's batting average as a fraction in simplest form.
2. Which player has the better batting average? Justify your answer using fraction models.

Player	At-bats	Hits
Latanya	12	7
Patrick	18	8

A **common denominator** is a common multiple of the denominators of two or more fractions. The **least common denominator or LCD** is the LCM of the denominators. To compare and order fractions, rename each fraction using their LCD or write each fraction as a decimal.

Real-World EXAMPLE

1 **Who has the better batting average, Latanya or Patrick?**

METHOD 1 **Rename using the LCD.**

The LCD of the denominators, 12 and 18, is 36.

Latanya: $\frac{7}{12} = \frac{7 \cdot 3}{12 \cdot 3} = \frac{21}{36}$ Patrick: $\frac{8}{18} = \frac{8 \cdot 2}{18 \cdot 2} = \frac{16}{36}$

Since $\frac{21}{36} > \frac{16}{36}$, then $\frac{7}{12} > \frac{8}{18}$. Latanya has the better average.

METHOD 2 **Write each fraction as a decimal.**

Use a calculator.

Latanya: 7 [÷] 12 or $0.58\overline{3}$ [ENTER] 0.583333333

Patrick: 8 [÷] 18 or $0.\overline{4}$ [ENTER] 0.444444444

Since $0.58\overline{3} > 0.\overline{4}$, then $\frac{7}{12} > \frac{8}{18}$. Latanya has the better average.

CHOOSE Your Method

Replace each ● with <, >, or = to make a true sentence.

a. $\frac{5}{6}$ ● $\frac{7}{9}$ b. $\frac{1}{5}$ ● $\frac{7}{50}$ c. $\frac{9}{16}$ ● $\frac{7}{10}$

Real-World EXAMPLE

Real-World Link More than 8.2 million people participate in off-road mountain biking each year.
Source: *National Sporting Goods Association*

2 **MOUNTAIN BIKING** **In Coach Ito's first period class, 19 out of 32 students own a mountain bike. In his seventh period class, 16 out of 28 students own a mountain bike. Do a greater fraction of students own a mountain bike in the first period class or the seventh period class?**

Since the denominators are large, write $\frac{19}{32}$ and $\frac{16}{28}$ as decimals and then compare.

$19 \div 32 \approx 0.5938$ $\quad$ $16 \div 28 \approx 0.5714$ $\quad$ Use a calculator.

Since $0.5938 > 0.5714$, then $\frac{19}{32} > \frac{16}{28}$. So, a greater fraction of students in the first period class own a mountain bike.

CHECK Your Progress

d. **BOWLING** Twelve out of 32 students in second period class like to bowl. In fifth period class, 12 out of 29 students like to bowl. In which class do a greater fraction of the students like to bowl?

Fractions, decimals, and percents are all related. It is a good idea to memorize these common fraction-decimal-percent equivalents.

CONCEPT Summary — Fractions-Decimals-Percents

$\frac{1}{4} = 0.25 = 25\%$	$\frac{1}{5} = 0.2 = 20\%$	$\frac{1}{8} = 0.125 = 12.5\%$	$\frac{1}{10} = 0.1 = 10\%$
$\frac{1}{2} = 0.5 = 50\%$	$\frac{2}{5} = 0.4 = 40\%$	$\frac{3}{8} = 0.375 = 37.5\%$	$\frac{3}{10} = 0.3 = 30\%$
$\frac{3}{4} = 0.75 = 75\%$	$\frac{3}{5} = 0.6 = 60\%$	$\frac{5}{8} = 0.625 = 62.5\%$	$\frac{7}{10} = 0.7 = 70\%$
$1 = 1.00 = 100\%$	$\frac{4}{5} = 0.8 = 80\%$	$\frac{7}{8} = 0.875 = 87.5\%$	$\frac{9}{10} = 0.9 = 90\%$

Fractions, terminating and repeating decimals, percents, and integers are all examples of rational numbers.

KEY CONCEPT — Rational Numbers

Words A **rational number** is a number that can be expressed as a fraction.

Symbols $\frac{a}{b}$, where a and b are integers and $b \neq 0$

Model

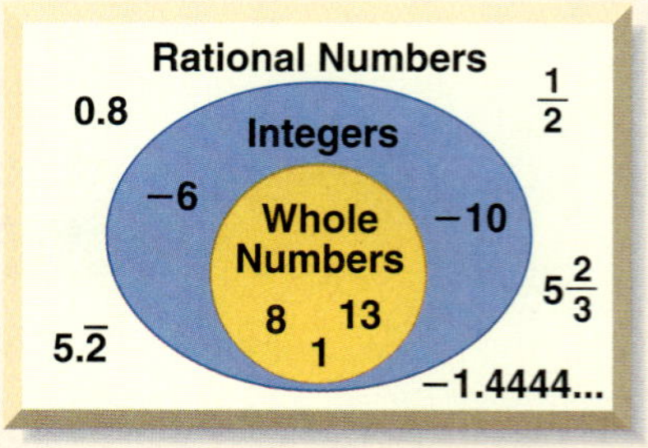

EXAMPLES Identify Rational Numbers

Determine whether each number is rational. Explain your reasoning.

3 **−5**

Since −5 can be written as $\frac{-5}{1}$ or $\frac{5}{-1}$, it is rational.

4 **2.010010001...**

The number 2.010010001...neither terminates nor repeats. Therefore, it is not rational.

CHECK Your Progress

Determine whether each number is rational. Write *yes* or *no*. Explain your reasoning.

e. 36% f. 0.121121112... g. 0.777...

TEST EXAMPLE

5 Emma's quiz scores for the grading period are $\frac{14}{20}$, 0.68, 80%, and $\frac{5}{10}$.

Which list shows the scores from least to greatest?

A 80%, $\frac{14}{20}$, 0.68, $\frac{5}{10}$

B $\frac{5}{10}$, $\frac{14}{20}$, 0.68, 80%

C 80%, 0.68, $\frac{14}{20}$, $\frac{5}{10}$

D $\frac{5}{10}$, 0.68, $\frac{14}{20}$, 80%

Test-Taking Tip

Eliminate Possibilities Eliminate the possibilities that you know are incorrect. Then consider the choices that remain. In Example 5, you can eliminate Choices A and C since 80% > 0.68.

Read the Test Item

To order the scores, you need to compare the scores. First write each number as a decimal. Then compare.

Solve the Test Item

$\frac{14}{20} = 0.7$ 0.68 $80\% = 0.8$ $\frac{5}{10} = 0.5$

Since $0.5 < 0.68 < 0.7 < 0.8$, you can write $\frac{5}{10} < 0.68 < \frac{14}{20} < 80\%$.

So, the answer is D.

CHECK Your Progress

h. The amount of rain received on four consecutive days was 0.3-inch, $\frac{3}{5}$-inch, 0.75-inch, and $\frac{2}{3}$-inch. Which list shows the amounts from least to greatest?

F 0.3-in, $\frac{2}{3}$-in., $\frac{3}{5}$-in., 0.75-in.

G 0.3-in, $\frac{3}{5}$-in., $\frac{2}{3}$-in., 0.75-in.

H 0.75-in., $\frac{2}{3}$-in., $\frac{3}{5}$-in., 0.3-in.

J $\frac{3}{5}$-in., $\frac{2}{3}$-in., 0.3-in., 0.75-in.

Online Personal Tutor at tx.msmath2.com

CHECK Your Understanding

Example 1 (p. 263)

Replace each ● with <, >, or = to make a true sentence.

1. $\frac{6}{15}$ ● $\frac{3}{8}$
2. $\frac{1}{6}$ ● $\frac{3}{18}$
3. $2\frac{4}{5}$ ● $2\frac{7}{8}$

Example 2 (p. 264)

4. **SOCCER** The table shows the average saves for two soccer goalies. Who has the better average, Elliot or Shanna? Explain.

Name	Average
Elliot	3 saves out of 4
Shanna	7 saves out of 11

Examples 3, 4 (p. 265)

Determine whether each number is rational. Write *yes* or *no*. Explain your reasoning.

5. $\frac{1}{11}$
6. 0.023024025…

Example 5 (p. 265)

7. **TEST PRACTICE** The lengths of four insects are 0.02-inch, $\frac{1}{8}$-inch, 0.1-inch, and $\frac{2}{3}$-inch. Which list shows the lengths in inches from least to greatest?

   A 0.1, 0.02, $\frac{1}{8}$, $\frac{2}{3}$

   B $\frac{1}{8}$, 0.02, 0.1, $\frac{2}{3}$

   C 0.02, 0.1, $\frac{1}{8}$, $\frac{2}{3}$

   D $\frac{2}{3}$, 0.02, 0.1, $\frac{1}{8}$

Exercises

HOMEWORK HELP

For Exercises	See Examples
8–19	1
20–25, 49	2
26–31	3, 4
32–37, 48	5

Replace each ● with <, >, or = to make a true sentence.

8. $\frac{7}{10}$ ● $\frac{2}{3}$
9. $\frac{5}{14}$ ● $\frac{3}{7}$
10. $\frac{4}{7}$ ● $\frac{5}{8}$
11. $\frac{2}{3}$ ● $\frac{10}{15}$
12. $\frac{16}{20}$ ● $\frac{40}{50}$
13. $\frac{17}{24}$ ● $\frac{11}{12}$
14. $\frac{9}{13}$ ● $\frac{14}{20}$
15. $\frac{11}{15}$ ● $\frac{5}{9}$
16. $2\frac{3}{4}$ ● $2\frac{2}{3}$
17. $6\frac{2}{3}$ ● $6\frac{1}{2}$
18. $5\frac{5}{7}$ ● $5\frac{11}{14}$
19. $3\frac{11}{16}$ ● $3\frac{7}{8}$
20. 40% ● 112 out of 25
21. 3 out of 5 ● 59%
22. 0.82 ● 5 out of 6
23. 9 out of 20 ● 0.45
24. **WEATHER** The table shows about how much rain falls in Albuquerque and Denver. Which city has the greater fraction of inches of rain per day? Explain.

City	Amount of Rain (in.)	Number of Days
Albuquerque, NM	9	60
Denver, CO	15	90

Source: weather.com

25. **GAMES** Rocío and Cecil played darts. Rocío hit the bull's-eye 5 out of 18 times. Cecil *missed* the bull's-eye 4 out of 15 times. Who hit the bull's-eye a greater fraction of the time?

Determine whether each number is rational. Write *yes* or *no*. Explain your reasoning.

26. $\frac{1}{9}$
27. 1.141141114...
28. 3.4567891011...
29. 2.232425262...
30. $-3\frac{4}{5}$
31. $5.\overline{23}$

Order each set of numbers from least to greatest.

32. 0.23, 19%, $\frac{1}{5}$
33. $\frac{8}{10}$, 81%, 0.805
34. 0.615, $\frac{5}{8}$, 62%
35. 1.4, $1\frac{1}{25}$, 1.25
36. 0.49, $\frac{49}{50}$, 0.5
37. $\frac{4}{7}$, 44%, 0.47

Real-World Link The Olympic gold medals are actually made out of 92.5% silver, with the gold medal covered in 6 grams of pure gold.
Source: about.com

Replace each ● with <, >, or = to make a true sentence.

38. $\frac{5}{8}$ yard ● $\frac{1}{16}$ yard
39. 0.25 pound ● $\frac{2}{9}$ pound

ANIMALS **For Exercises 40–42, use the table that shows the lengths of the smallest mammals.**

Animal	Length (ft)
Eastern Chipmunk	$\frac{1}{3}$
Kitti's Hog-nosed Bat	$0.8\overline{3}$
European Mole	$\frac{5}{12}$
Masked Shrew	$\frac{1}{6}$
Spiny Pocket Mouse	0.25

Source: *Scholastic Book of World Records*

40. Which animal is the smallest mammal?
41. Which animal is smaller than the European mole but larger than the spiny pocket mouse?
42. Order the animals from greatest to least size.

SOFTBALL **For Exercises 43 and 44, use the following information and the table shown.**
At the 2004 Olympics, the U.S. Women's softball team won the gold medal with a 9-0 record. The table shows the at-bats, hits, and home run statistics for four players on the team.

Player	At-Bats	Hits	Home Runs
Crystal Bustos	26	9	5
Kelly Krestschman	21	7	1
Stacey Nuveman	16	5	2
Natasha Watley	30	12	0

Source: olympics.org

EXTRA PRACTICE

See pages 730, 759.

Math Online
Self-Check Quiz at tx.msmath2.com

43. Write the ratio of hits to at-bats as a decimal for each player. Who had the greatest batting average during the Olympic games?
44. Write the ratio of home runs to at-bats as a decimal for each player. Who had the greatest home run average during the Olympic games?

H.O.T. Problems

45. **Which One Doesn't Belong?** Identify the ratio that does not have the same value as the other three. Explain your reasoning.

9 out of 15	0.06	60%	$\frac{3}{5}$

46. **CHALLENGE** Explain how you know which number, $1\frac{15}{16}$, $\frac{17}{8}$, or $\frac{63}{32}$, is nearest to 2.

47. **WRITING IN MATH** Write a word problem about a real-world situation in which you would compare rational numbers. Then solve the problem.

TEST PRACTICE

48. Which list shows the percent of work completed on each project from least to greatest?

Project	Work Completed
Master Bath	$\frac{3}{4}$
Kitchen	$\frac{1}{4}$
Family Room	$\frac{1}{2}$
Home Office	$\frac{1}{3}$

A 25%, 33%, 50%, 75%

B 0.25%, 0.33%, 0.5%, 0.75%

C 3.3%, 2.5%, 5.0%, 7.5%

D 75%, 50%, 33%, 25%

49. Which of the following statements is true?

F $26\% < \frac{14}{50}$

G $\frac{5}{8} > \frac{2}{3}$

H $0.71\% < \frac{7}{10}$

J $\frac{6}{5} > 1\frac{3}{10}$

50. **GRIDDABLE** In the set of numbers 44%, $\frac{4}{5}$, 0.4, which number is the greatest? Write this number as a decimal.

Spiral Review

Find the LCM of each set of numbers. (Lesson 5-8)

51. 14, 21
52. 3, 13
53. 12, 16

FOOD **The graph shows the results of a survey for favorite pizza toppings. Write the percent of people who chose each topping as a decimal.** (Lesson 5-7)

54. onions
55. vegetables
56. mushrooms

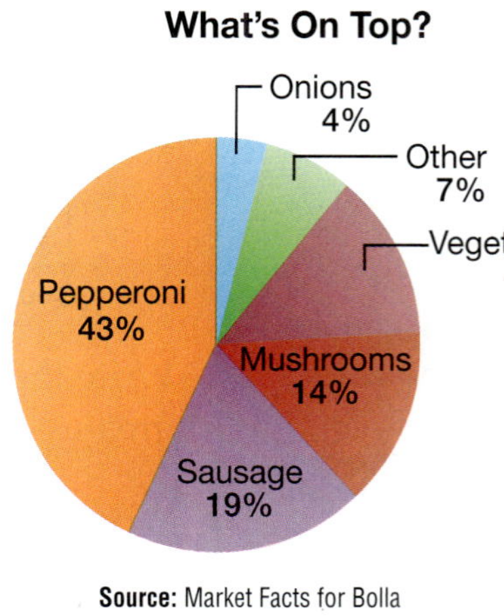

57. Find the GCF of 18 and 72. (Lesson 5-2)

Solve each equation. (Lesson 4-5)

58. $4x + 3 = 15$
59. $2n - 5 = 19$
60. $-8 = -3d + 1$

Study Guide and Review

STUDY TO GO Download Vocabulary Review from tx.msmath2.com

FOLDABLES™ Study Organizer

GET READY to Study

Be sure the following Key Concepts are noted in your Foldable.

Key Concept

Greatest Common Factor (Lesson 5-2)

- The greatest common factor or GCF is the greatest of the common factors of two or more numbers.

Fractions, Decimals, and Percents (Lesson 5-4 to 5-7)

- A fraction is in simplest form when the GCF of the numerator and denominator is 1.
- A terminating decimal is a decimal whose digits end. Repeating decimals have a pattern in the digits that repeats forever.
- A percent is a part to whole ratio that compares a number to 100.
- To write a percent as a decimal, divide the percent by 100 and remove the percent symbol.
- To write a decimal as a percent, multiply the percent by 100 and add the percent symbol.

Least Common Multiple (Lesson 5-8)

- The least common multiple or LCM of two or more numbers is the least of their common multiples.

Rational Numbers (Lesson 5-9)

- A rational number is one that can be expressed as a fraction.

Key Vocabulary

bar notation (p. 245)
common denominator (p. 263)
composite number (p. 229)
equivalent fractions (p. 240)
factor tree (p. 230)
greatest common factor (GCF) (p. 234)
least common denominator (p. 263)
least common multiple (LCM) (p. 259)
multiple (p. 259)
percent (p. 250)
prime factorization (p. 230)
prime number (p. 229)
ratio (p. 250)
rational number (p. 264)
repeating decimal (p. 245)
simplest form (p. 240)
terminating decimal (p. 245)

Vocabulary Check

State whether each sentence is *true* or *false*. If *false*, replace the underlined word or number to make a true sentence.

1. A ratio is a comparison of two numbers by multiplication.
2. A rational number is a whole number greater than 1 that has exactly two factors, 1 and itself.
3. 1.875 is an example of a terminating decimal.
4. A common denominator for the fractions $\frac{2}{3}$ and $\frac{1}{4}$ is 12.
5. The greatest common factor of 3 and 5 is 15.
6. A ratio that compares a number to 100 is a percent.
7. The fractions $\frac{9}{21}$ and $\frac{3}{7}$ are equivalent fractions.

CHAPTER 5

Study Guide and Review

Lesson-by-Lesson Review

5-1 Prime Factorization (pp. 229–232)

Find the prime factorization of each number.

8. 54 **9.** 128 **10.** 68 **11.** 95

12. **ALGEBRA** Factor $36x^2yz^3$.

13. **PLANTS** The palm tree *raffia* has leaves up to 65 feet long. Write this length as a product of primes.

Example 1 **Find the prime factorization of 18.**

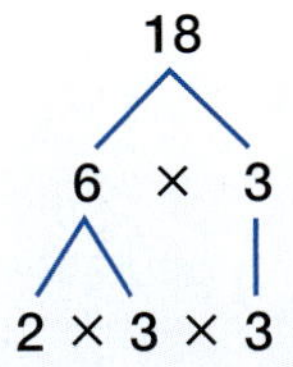

Use a factor tree

The prime factorization of 18 is 2×3^2.

5-2 Greatest Common Factor (p. 234–237)

Find the GCF of each set of numbers.

14. 18, 27 **15.** 30, 72

16. 28, 70, 98 **17.** 42, 63, 105

18. **ALGEBRA** Find the GCF of $18w$ and $54w^2y$.

19. **CLOTHING** Maria spent a total of \$24 on earrings, \$36 on shirts, and \$48 on shorts. If each item cost the same amount, what is the greatest possible price per item?

Example 2 **Find the GCF of 24 and 56.**

First, make a list of all the factors of 24 and 56.

factors of 24: **1**, **2**, 3, **4**, 6, **8**, 12, 24

factors of 56: **1**, **2**, **4**, 7, **8**, 14, 28, 56

common factors: 1, 2, 4, 8

The GCF of 24 and 56 is 8.

5-3 PSI: Make an Organized List (pp. 238–239)

Solve by making an organized list.

20. **SEATING** In how many ways can four friends sit in a row at the movies?

21. **TELEPHONES** A phone company offers 5 different types of long-distance plans and 3 different caller features (call waiting, caller ID, and call forward). How many different kinds of plans can be set up that include a long-distance service and a caller feature?

Example 3 **In how many ways can the letters A, B, and C be arranged?**

The possible outcomes are written below.

ABC ACB
BAC BCA
CAB CBA

There are 6 different ways to arrange the letters.

Mixed Problem Solving
For mixed problem-solving practice, see page 759.

5-4 Simplifying Fractions (p. 240–243)

Write each fraction in simplest form.

22. $\frac{12}{15}$ 23. $\frac{35}{60}$ 24. $\frac{11}{121}$

25. $\frac{14}{63}$ 26. $\frac{37}{45}$ 27. $\frac{55}{110}$

28. **CATS** The average household cat sleeps 18 hours a day. Write a fraction in simplest form comparing the number of hours a household cat sleeps to the number of hours in a day.

Example 4 Write $\frac{24}{32}$ in simplest form.

Find the GCF of the numerator and denominator.

24 = 1, 2, 3, 4, 6, 8, 12, 24

32 = 1, 2, 4, 8, 16, 32

$\frac{24}{32} = \frac{24 \div 8}{32 \div 8} = \frac{3}{4}$ Divide the numerator and denominator by the GCF.

5-5 Fractions and Decimals (pp. 244–248)

Write each fraction or mixed number as a decimal. Use bar notation if the decimal is a repeating decimal.

29. $\frac{3}{4}$ 30. $\frac{7}{8}$ 31. $\frac{5}{9}$

32. $4\frac{1}{3}$ 33. $6\frac{2}{5}$ 34. $1\frac{6}{7}$

Write each decimal as a fraction in simplest form.

35. 0.7 36. 0.44 37. 0.05

38. 0.18 39. 0.54 40. 0.08

41. **RUNNING** Jeremy ran a mile in 5 minutes and 8 seconds. Write this time in minutes as a decimal.

Example 5 Write $\frac{3}{8}$ as a decimal.

$$\begin{array}{r} 0.375 \\ 8\overline{)3.000} \\ -\underline{24} \\ 60 \\ -\underline{56} \\ 40 \\ -\underline{40} \\ 0 \end{array}$$

So, $\frac{3}{8} = 0.375$.

Example 6 Write 0.64 as a fraction.

$0.64 = \frac{64}{100}$ Write as a fraction with a denominator of 100.

$= \frac{16}{25}$ Simplify.

5-6 Fractions and Percents (pp. 250–253)

Write each fraction as a percent.

42. $\frac{32}{100}$ 43. $\frac{11}{25}$ 44. $\frac{47}{50}$ 45. $\frac{8}{20}$

Write each percent as a fraction in simplest form.

46. 68% 47. 95% 48. 42% 49. 16%

50. **FOOD** A survey showed that 58% of school children like peanut butter and jelly sandwiches. Write this percent as a fraction in simplest form.

Example 7 Write $\frac{27}{50}$ as a percent.

$\frac{27}{50} = \frac{54}{100}$ Write an equivalent fraction with a denominator of 100.

$= 54\%$ Definition of percent

Example 8 Write 96% as a fraction.

$96\% = \frac{96}{100}$ Definition of percent

$= \frac{24}{25}$ Simplify.

Study Guide and Review

5-7 Percents and Decimals (pp. 254–258)

Write each percent as a decimal.

51. 48%

52. 7%

53. 12.5%

54. $75\frac{1}{4}\%$

Write each decimal as a percent.

55. 0.61 **56.** 0.055 **57.** 0.19 **58.** 0.999

59. WEATHER Twenty-three percent of the days last month were rainy. Write this percent as a decimal.

Example 9 Write 35% as a decimal.

$35\% = \frac{35}{100}$ Write the percent as a fraction.

$= 0.35$ Write the fraction as a decimal.

Example 10 Write 0.625 as a percent.

$0.625 = 0.625$ Multiply by 100.

$= 62.5\%$ Add the % symbol.

5-8 Least Common Multiple (pp. 259–262)

Find the LCM of each set of numbers.

60. 9, 15

61. 4, 8

62. 16, 24

63. 3, 8, 12

64. 4, 9, 12

65. 15, 24, 30

66. BREAKFAST At a bakery, muffins come in dozens and individual serving containers of orange juice come in packs of 8. If Avery needs to have the same amount of muffins as orange juice containers, what is the least possible number of sets of each he needs to buy?

Example 11 Find the LCM of 8 and 36.

Write each prime factorization.

$8 = 2 \times 2 \times 2 = 2^3$

$36 = 2 \times 2 \times 3 \times 3 = 2^2 \times 3^2$

LCM: $2^3 \times 3^2 = 72$

The LCM of 8 and 36 is 72.

5-9 Comparing and Ordering Rational Numbers (pp. 263–268)

Replace each ● with <, >, or = to make a true sentence.

67. $\frac{3}{8}$ ● $\frac{2}{3}$

68. 0.45 ● $\frac{9}{20}$

69. $\frac{8}{9}$ ● 85%

70. $3\frac{3}{4}$ ● $3\frac{5}{8}$

71. SCHOOL Michael received a $\frac{26}{30}$ on his English quiz and received 81% on his Biology test. In which class did he receive the higher score?

Example 12 Replace ● with <, >, or = to make $\frac{3}{5}$ ● $\frac{5}{8}$ a true sentence.

Find equivalent fractions. The LCD is 40.

$\frac{3}{5} = \frac{3 \times 8}{5 \times 8} = \frac{24}{40}$ $\frac{5}{8} = \frac{5 \times 5}{8 \times 5} = \frac{25}{40}$

Since $\frac{24}{40} < \frac{25}{40}$, then $\frac{3}{5} < \frac{5}{8}$.

Chapter 5 Practice Test

1. Find the prime factorization of 72.
2. Find the GCF of 24 and 40.

3. **SCHEDULES** Farijah registered for French, Pre–Algebra, Life Science, English, and Social Studies. French is only offered first period, Pre–Algebra is only offered fifth period, and she must have lunch fourth period. How many different schedules can she create out of a six period day? Use the make an organized list strategy.

Write each fraction in simplest form.

4. $\frac{24}{60}$ 5. $\frac{64}{72}$

Write each fraction, mixed number, or percent as a decimal. Use bar notation if the decimal is a repeating decimal.

6. $\frac{7}{9}$ 7. $4\frac{5}{8}$ 8. 91%

9. **PRESIDENTS** Calvin Coolidge was the thirtieth president of the United States. He slept an average of 10 hours a day, the most of any United States president. What percent of time each day did President Coolidge sleep?

Write each decimal or percent as a fraction in simplest form.

10. 0.84 11. 0.006 12. 42%

13. **TEST PRACTICE** In a TV commercial, 4 out of 5 dentists recommend a particular brand of toothpaste. Which best represents the percent of dentists that do NOT recommend this brand of toothpaste?

    A 10%
    B 20%
    C 40%
    D 80%

Write each fraction or decimal as a percent.

14. $\frac{15}{25}$ 15. 0.26 16. 0.135

17. **PAINTING** Adrian has already painted 46 square feet of a wall measuring 10 feet by 10 feet. What percent of the wall has he painted?

18. **TEST PRACTICE** If $\frac{3}{5}$ of the figure below is shaded, what percent is unshaded?

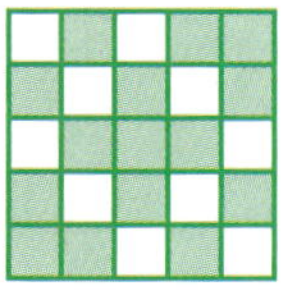

    F 15%
    G 30%
    H 40%
    J 60%

Find the LCM of each set of numbers.

19. 18, 42 20. 4, 5, 12

21. **INSECTS** One type of cicada emerges from hibernation every 17 years. Another type of cicada emerges every 13 years. If both come out of hibernation in the same year, after how many years will this happen again?

Replace each ● with $<$, $>$, or $=$ to make a true sentence.

22. $\frac{3}{5}$ ● $\frac{5}{9}$ 23. $\frac{7}{12}$ ● $\frac{6}{8}$ 24. $\frac{13}{20}$ ● 65%

25. **BASKETBALL** To make it past the first round of tryouts for the basketball team, Paul must make at least 35% of his free-throw attempts. During the first round of tryouts he makes 17 out of 40 attempts. Did Paul make it to the next round of tryouts? Explain your reasoning.

CHAPTER 5

Texas Test Practice

Cumulative, Chapters 1–5

Read each question. Then fill in the correct answer on the answer document provided by your teacher or on a sheet of paper.

1. A large school system estimates that 70.6% of its students will take the bus to school throughout the school year. Which number is NOT equivalent to 70.6%?

   A $\frac{706}{1,000}$

   B $\frac{70.6}{100}$

   C 7.06

   D 0.706

2. Debra is working on three different art projects. She has completed $\frac{1}{4}$, $\frac{3}{8}$, and $\frac{1}{2}$ of these projects, respectively. Which list shows the percent of work completed on these projects from least to greatest?

   F 37.5%, 50%, 25%

   G 50%, 37.5%, 25%

   H 25%, 37.5%, 50%

   J 25%, 50%, 87.5%

3. James guesses that $\frac{4}{5}$ of his class completed their homework last night. What percent of the class completed their homework?

   A 45%

   B 54%

   C 75%

   D 80%

TEST-TAKING TIP

Question 3 Eliminate the possibilities that you know are incorrect. For example, $\frac{4}{5} > \frac{1}{2}$. So, 45% is incorrect because it is less than 50% or $\frac{1}{2}$. Then consider the choices that are left.

4. The model represents the equation $x + 7 = -3$. What is the value of x?

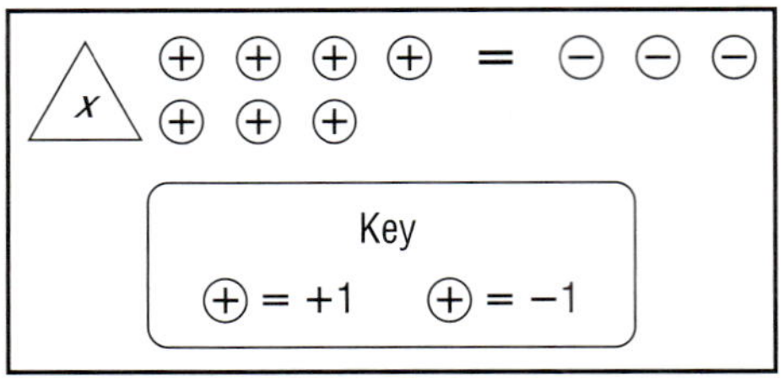

   F 4

   G 3

   H −4

   J −10

5. **GRIDDABLE** Pansies are on sale for $2.95 per flat. If Mr. Hollern spent $23.60 on pansies, how many flats did he buy?

6. Which problem situation matches the equation below?

$$x + 12 = 35$$

   A The difference between two numbers is 35. One of the numbers is 12. What is x, the other number?

   B Laura is 12 years younger than her brother. If Laura is 35 years old, find her brother's age x.

   C The sum of two numbers is 35. One of the numbers is 12. What is x, the other number?

   D Karen had $35. If she received $12, what is x, the total amount of money she now has?

7. **GRIDDABLE** According to the results of a class survey, $\frac{23}{25}$ of the students studied for their history test. Write this fraction as a decimal.

Math Online Texas Test Practice at tx.msmath2.com

Get Ready for the Texas Test
For test-taking strategies and more practice, see pages TX1–TX23.

8. Which sequence follows the rule $2n + 5$, where n represents the position of a term in the sequence?

F 3, 5, 7, 9, 11, ...
H 7, 9, 11, 13, 15, ...
G 6, 8, 10, 12, 14, ...
J 8, 12, 16, 20, 24, ...

9. Nicholas has a comic book collection containing 75 books. He decided to sell $\frac{3}{8}$ of his collection at a garage sale. What percent of his comic books did Nicholas NOT sell?

A $62\frac{1}{2}\%$
C $37\frac{1}{2}\%$
B 38%
D $33\frac{1}{3}\%$

10. Which of the following relationships is represented by the data in the table?

x	*y*
1	5,280
2	10,560
3	15,840
4	21,120
5	26,400

F Conversion of miles to feet
G Conversion of inches to yards
H Conversion of feet to miles
J Conversion of yards to inches

11. Of those students in Lisa's class, $87\frac{1}{2}\%$ have a pet. What fraction of the students in Lisa's class have a pet?

A $\frac{7}{8}$
C $\frac{1}{4}$
B $\frac{2}{3}$
D $\frac{5}{6}$

12. If point B is moved 3 units to the right and 5 units down, what will be point B's new coordinates?

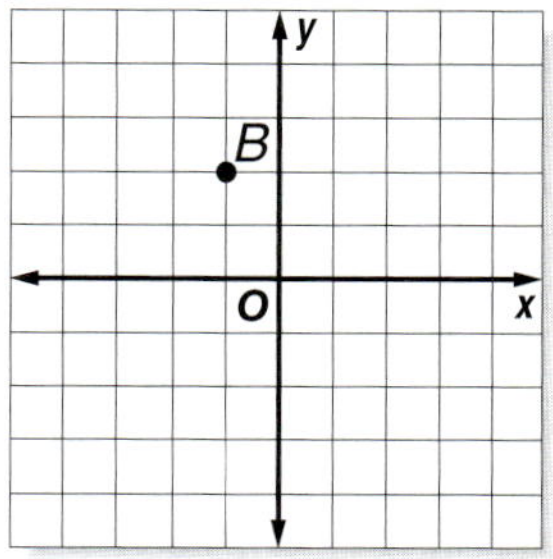

F $(-4, -5)$
H $(2, 7)$
G $(2, -3)$
J $(-4, 7)$

Pre-AP

Record your answers on a sheet of paper. Show your work.

13. The table shows the number of students who volunteered at the food bank.

Classroom	Number of Students Volunteering	Total Number of Students
A	7	24
B	3	8
C	6	18

a. Model the fraction of the number of students volunteering to the total number of students for each classroom on grid paper.

b. Which classroom had the greatest number of students volunteering?

c. Which classroom had the greatest fraction of students volunteering?

d. Write each ratio as a fraction in simplest form, as a decimal, and as a percent.

NEED EXTRA HELP?													
If You Missed Question...	1	2	3	4	5	6	7	8	9	10	11	12	13
Go to Lesson...	5-7	5-9	5-6	4-2	3-4	4-1	5-5	1-9	5-6	2-6	5-6	2-3	5-9
For Help with Test Objective...	1	1	1	2	1	2	1	2	1	2	1	3	1

CHAPTER 6

Applying Fractions

Knowledge and Skills

- Add, subtract, multiply, or divide to solve problems and justify solutions. **TEKS 7.2**

Key Vocabulary

compatible numbers (p. 280)
like fractions (p. 284)
reciprocal (p. 306)
unlike fractions (p. 285)

Real-World Link

Baking The measurements found on measuring cups and spoons are written as fractions. You will use fractions to find how much of each ingredient is needed when you make part of a whole recipe.

FOLDABLES™ Study Organizer

Applying Fractions Make this Foldable to help you organize your notes. Begin with a plain sheet of 11″ by 17″ paper, four index cards, and glue.

1. **Fold** the paper in half widthwise.

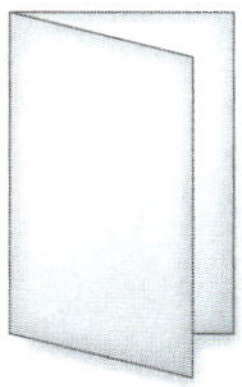

2. **Open** and fold along the length about $2\frac{1}{2}$″ from the bottom.

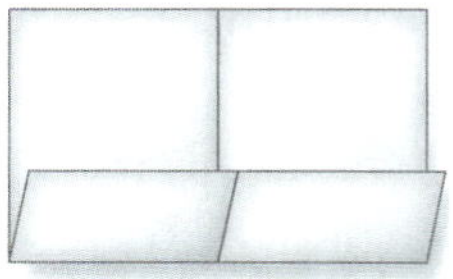

3. **Glue** the edge on each side to form two pockets.

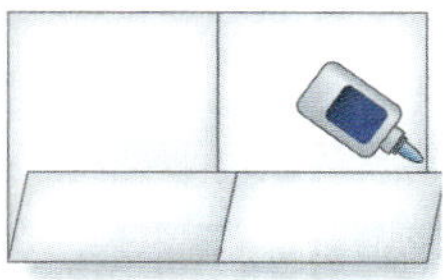

4. **Label** the pockets *Fractions* and *Mixed Numbers*, respectively. Place two index cards in each pocket.

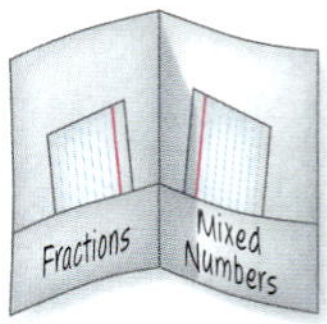

GET READY for Chapter 6

Diagnose Readiness You have two options for checking Prerequisite Skills.

Option 2

Math Online Take the Online Readiness Quiz at tx.msmath2.com.

Option 1

Take the Quick Quiz below. Refer to the Quick Review for help.

QUICK Quiz

Find the LCD of each pair of fractions. (Used in Lessons 6-2 and 6-3)

1. $\frac{5}{7}, \frac{3}{5}$
2. $\frac{1}{2}, \frac{4}{9}$
3. $\frac{8}{15}, \frac{1}{6}$
4. $\frac{3}{4}, \frac{7}{10}$

Multiply or divide. (Used in Lessons 6-5 and 6-7)

5. 1.8×12
6. $99 \div 12$
7. $83 \div 100$
8. 4.6×0.3
9. **ROPE** How many 1.6-meter sections of rope can be cut from a length of rope 6.4 meters?
10. **COINS** Manuel owes each of 8 friends \$0.35. How much does he owe in all?

Complete to show equivalent mixed numbers. (Used in Lessons 6-3 and 6-7)

11. $3\frac{1}{5} = 2\frac{■}{5}$
12. $9\frac{2}{3} = ■\frac{5}{3}$
13. $6\frac{1}{4} = 5\frac{■}{4}$
14. $8\frac{6}{7} = 7\frac{■}{7}$
15. **RECIPES** A recipe calls for $4\frac{2}{3}$ cups of flour. This is equivalent to 3 cups of flour plus an additional how many cups of flour?

QUICK Review

Example 1

Find the LCD of $\frac{5}{6}$ and $\frac{3}{10}$.

The LCD is the LCM of the denominators, 6 and 10, or 30.

Example 2

Find $7.8 \div 0.25$.

$$\begin{array}{r} 31.2 \\ 0.25\overline{)7.80\,0} \\ -7\,5 \\ \hline 30 \\ -25 \\ \hline 50 \\ -50 \\ \hline 0 \end{array}$$

Move the decimal point 2 places to the right and divide as with whole numbers.

Example 3

Complete $4\frac{2}{9} = ■\frac{11}{9}$ to show equivalent mixed numbers.

$$\begin{aligned} 4\frac{2}{9} &= 3 + 1\frac{2}{9} \\ &= 3 + \frac{9}{9} + \frac{2}{9} \\ &= 3 + \frac{11}{9} \\ &= 3\frac{11}{9} \end{aligned}$$

6-1 Estimating with Fractions

Main IDEA

Estimate sums, differences, products, and quotients of fractions and mixed numbers.

Reinforcement of TEKS 6.2 The student adds, subtracts, multiplies, and divides to solve problems and justify solutions. **(D) estimate and round to approximate reasonable results and to solve problems where exact answers are not required.** *Also addresses TEKS 7.13(D).*

NEW Vocabulary

compatible numbers

GET READY for the Lesson

KITES For a kite to have balance while flying, the left and right sides of the horizontal support must each be $\frac{2}{3}$ as long as the bottom of the vertical support. Also, the top must be $\frac{1}{3}$ as long as the bottom portion.

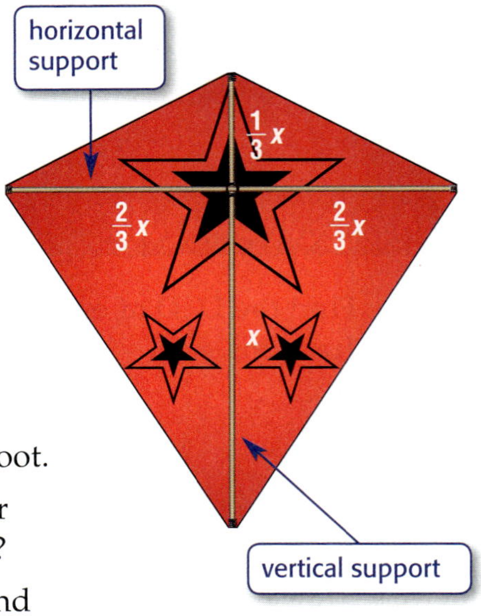

1. Suppose the bottom portion of the vertical support is $2\frac{3}{4}$ feet. Round this length to the nearest foot.
2. About how long should the upper portion of the vertical support be?
3. About how long should the left and right sides of the horizontal support be?

To estimate the sum, difference, product, or quotient of mixed numbers, round the mixed numbers to the nearest whole number.

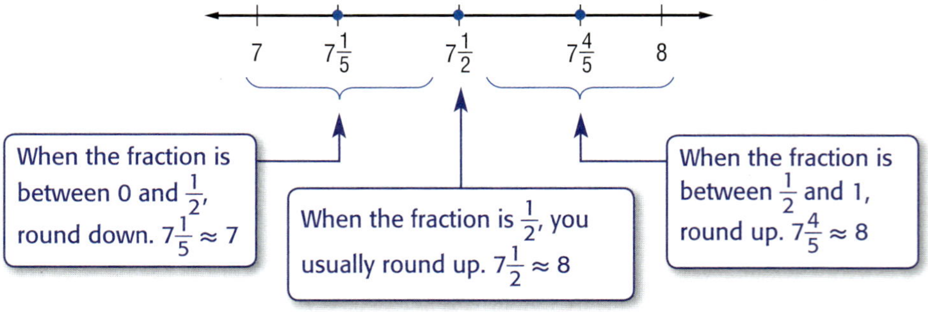

EXAMPLES Estimate with Mixed Numbers

1 Estimate $3\frac{2}{3} + 5\frac{1}{6}$.

$3\frac{2}{3} + 5\frac{1}{6} \approx 4 + 5$ or 9

The sum is *about* 9.

2 Estimate $6\frac{2}{5} \times 1\frac{7}{8}$.

$6\frac{2}{5} \times 1\frac{7}{8} \approx 6 \times 2$ or 12

The product is *about* 12.

CHECK Your Progress

Estimate.

a. $2\frac{1}{5} + 3\frac{1}{2}$

b. $4\frac{3}{8} \times 5\frac{1}{4}$

c. $8\frac{7}{9} \div 2\frac{3}{4}$

To estimate the sum, difference, product, or quotient of fractions, round each fraction to 0, $\frac{1}{2}$, or 1, whichever is closest. Number lines and fraction models, like the ones shown below, can help you decide how to round.

Fractions Close to 0	Fractions Close to $\frac{1}{2}$	Fractions Close to 1
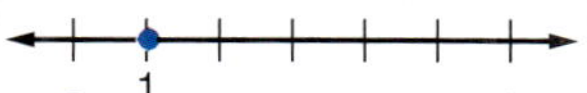	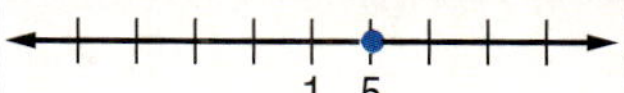	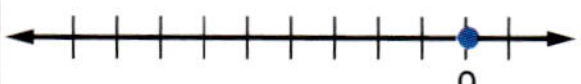
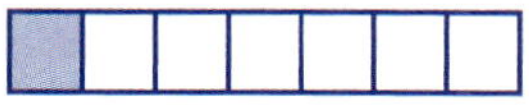 $\frac{1}{7}$	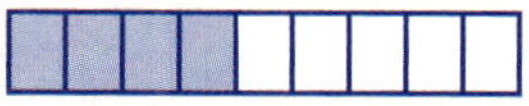 $\frac{4}{9}$	 $\frac{5}{6}$
The numerator is much smaller than the denominator.	The numerator is about half of the denominator.	The numerator is almost as large as the denominator.

EXAMPLES Estimate with Fractions

3 Estimate $\frac{1}{8} + \frac{2}{3}$.

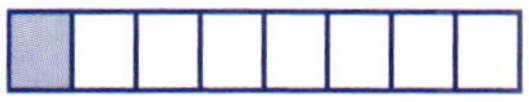

1 is much smaller than 8, so $\frac{1}{8} \approx 0$.

2 is close to half of 3, so $\frac{2}{3} \approx \frac{1}{2}$.

$\frac{1}{8} + \frac{2}{3} \approx 0 + \frac{1}{2} = \frac{1}{2}$ The sum is *about* $\frac{1}{2}$.

STUDY TIP

Estimating with Fractions When one of the fractions is a mixed number, such as $3\frac{5}{8} + \frac{2}{3}$, round the mixed number to the nearest whole number and the fraction to the nearest half.

$3\frac{5}{8} + \frac{2}{3} \approx 4 + \frac{1}{2}$ or about $4\frac{1}{2}$.

4 Estimate $\frac{6}{7} - \frac{7}{10}$.

6 is almost as large as 7, so $\frac{6}{7} \approx 1$.

7 is about half of 10, so $\frac{7}{10} \approx \frac{1}{2}$.

$\frac{6}{7} - \frac{7}{10} \approx 1 - \frac{1}{2} = \frac{1}{2}$ The difference is *about* $\frac{1}{2}$.

5 Estimate $\frac{8}{9} \div \frac{5}{6}$.

$\frac{8}{9} \div \frac{5}{6} \approx 1 \div 1 = 1$ $\frac{8}{9} \approx 1$ and $\frac{5}{6} \approx 1$.

The quotient is *about* 1.

CHECK Your Progress

Estimate.

d. $\frac{4}{5} + \frac{2}{7}$ e. $\frac{5}{8} - \frac{3}{7}$ f. $\frac{3}{5} \times \frac{11}{12}$ g. $\frac{7}{8} \div \frac{2}{5}$

Compatible numbers, or numbers that are easy to compute mentally, can also be used to estimate.

EXAMPLES Use Compatible Numbers

Estimate using compatible numbers.

6 $\frac{1}{3} \cdot 14$ THINK What is $\frac{1}{3}$ of 14?

$\frac{1}{3} \cdot 14 \approx \frac{1}{3} \cdot 15$ or 5 Round 14 to 15, since 15 is divisible by 3. $\frac{1}{3}$ of 15 is $15 \div 3 = 5$.

7 $9\frac{7}{8} \div 4\frac{1}{5}$

$9\frac{7}{8} \div 4\frac{1}{5} \approx 10 \div 4\frac{1}{5}$ Round $9\frac{7}{8}$ to 10.

$\approx 10 \div 5$ or 2 Round $4\frac{1}{5}$ to 5, since 10 is divisible by 5.

STUDY TIP

Compatible Numbers When dividing mixed numbers, round so that the dividend is a multiple of the divisor.

CHECK Your Progress

Estimate using compatible numbers.

h. $\frac{1}{4} \cdot 21$ i. $\frac{1}{3} \cdot 17$ j. $12 \div 6\frac{2}{3}$

Real-World EXAMPLE

8 **MONSTER TRUCKS** The height of the wheels on the monster truck at the left is about $\frac{2}{3}$ of the total height of the truck. Estimate the height of the wheels.

Words	Wheel height is $\frac{2}{3}$ of the truck height.
Variable	Let x represent the wheel height.
Equation	$x = \frac{2}{3} \cdot 15\frac{1}{2}$

$x \approx \frac{2}{3} \cdot 15$ Round $15\frac{1}{2}$ to 15, since 15 is divisible by 3.

$x \approx 10$ $\frac{1}{3}$ of 15 is 5, so $\frac{2}{3}$ of 15 is $2 \cdot 5$ or 10.

The wheels are about 10 feet high.

Real-World Link The monster truck shown is $15\frac{1}{2}$ feet tall and weighs 28,000 pounds.
Source: monstertrucks-uk.com

CHECK Your Progress

k. **GEOMETRY** The area of a rectangle is $19\frac{3}{4}$ square feet. The width of the rectangle is $5\frac{1}{4}$ feet. What is the approximate length of the rectangle?

Online Personal Tutor at tx.msmath2.com

CHECK Your Understanding

Examples 1–5
(p. 278–279)

Estimate.

1. $8\frac{3}{8} + 1\frac{4}{5}$
2. $2\frac{5}{6} - 1\frac{1}{8}$
3. $5\frac{5}{7} \cdot 2\frac{7}{8}$
4. $9\frac{2}{7} \div 2\frac{2}{3}$
5. $\frac{1}{6} + \frac{2}{5}$
6. $\frac{6}{7} - \frac{1}{5}$
7. $\frac{5}{8} \cdot \frac{8}{9}$
8. $\frac{4}{5} \div \frac{6}{7}$

Examples 6, 7
(p. 280)

Estimate using compatible numbers.

9. $\frac{1}{4} \cdot 15$
10. $21\frac{5}{6} \div 9\frac{3}{4}$

Example 8
(p. 280)

11. **CARPENTRY** About how many bookcase shelves like this one shown at the right can a carpenter cut from a board that is 1 foot wide and 12 feet long?

Exercises

HOMEWORK HELP	
For Exercises	See Examples
12–19	1, 2
20–29	3–5
30–35	6–8

Estimate.

12. $3\frac{3}{4} + 4\frac{5}{6}$
13. $1\frac{1}{8} + 5\frac{11}{12}$
14. $5\frac{1}{3} - 3\frac{1}{6}$
15. $4\frac{2}{5} - 1\frac{1}{2}$
16. $2\frac{2}{3} \cdot 6\frac{1}{3}$
17. $1\frac{4}{5} \cdot 3\frac{1}{4}$
18. $6\frac{1}{8} \div 1\frac{2}{3}$
19. $8\frac{1}{2} \div 2\frac{5}{8}$
20. $\frac{3}{4} + \frac{3}{8}$
21. $\frac{5}{8} + \frac{3}{7}$
22. $\frac{5}{9} - \frac{1}{6}$
23. $\frac{3}{4} - \frac{3}{5}$
24. $\frac{1}{8} \cdot \frac{3}{4}$
25. $\frac{4}{9} \cdot \frac{11}{12}$
26. $\frac{4}{5} \div \frac{7}{8}$
27. $\frac{1}{10} \div \frac{5}{6}$

28. **BAKING** Amado wants to make the recipe at the right, but he has only $1\frac{1}{3}$ cups of flour. About how much more flour does he need?

29. **SEWING** Isabella is sewing a trim that is $1\frac{1}{8}$ inches wide on the bottom of a skirt that is $15\frac{7}{8}$ inches long. Approximately how long will the skirt be?

Estimate using compatible numbers.

30. $\frac{1}{4} \cdot 39$
31. $\frac{1}{6} \cdot 37$
32. $23\frac{2}{9} \div 3$
33. $25\frac{3}{10} \div 5\frac{2}{3}$

34. **MONEY** Arleta has \$22. She uses $\frac{1}{3}$ of her money to buy a pair of earrings. About how much money did she spend on the earrings?

35. **SNACKS** A cereal company has 24 pounds of granola to package in bags that contain $1\frac{3}{4}$ pounds of granola. About how many bags will they have?

36. **FIND THE DATA** Refer to the Texas Data File on pages 16–19. Choose some data and write a real-world problem in which you would estimate with fractions.

37. **SPORTS** Paquito and Jeff are on a basketball team. The table shows the approximate fraction of the team's points that each of them scored in a game. If the team scored a total of 72 points, about how many did Paquito and Jeff score together?

Player's Names	Fraction of Total Points Scored
Paquito	$\frac{3}{8}$
Jeff	$\frac{1}{6}$

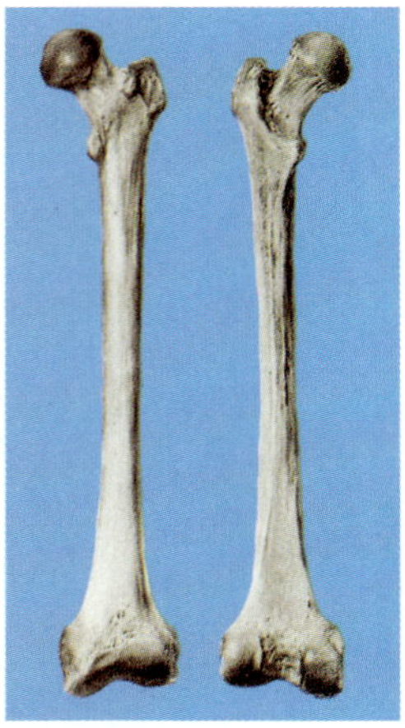

Real-World Link The femur or thigh bone is the longest in length, largest in volume, and strongest bone of the human body.
Source: orthopedics.about.com

38. **RESEARCH** Research the statistics of any basketball team. How can you use fractions to analyze the statistics?

39. **COOKING** Kathryn baked the sheet of brownies shown. She wants to cut it into brownies that are about 2 inches square. How many brownies will there be?

ANALYZE TABLES For Exercises 40–43, use the following information and the table shown.

The adult human skeleton is made up of 206 bones. The table shows the approximate fraction of the bones that each body part(s) makes up.

Body Part(s)	Fraction of Total Bones
Feet	$\frac{1}{4}$
Hands & Feet	$\frac{1}{2}$

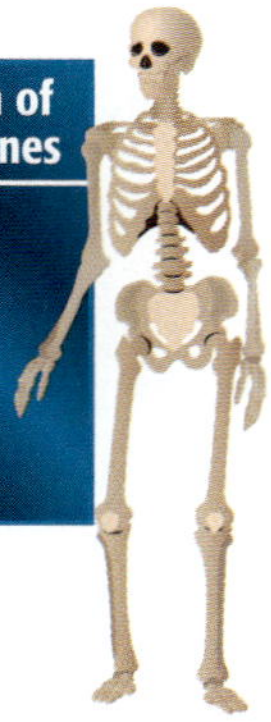

40. About how many bones are in the feet?
41. About how many bones are in both hands and feet?
42. About how many bones are in one hand?
43. The length of your thighbone is equal to $\frac{1}{4}$ of your height. About how many inches long is your thighbone?

EXTRA PRACTICE
See pages 730, 760.
Math Online
Self-Check Quiz at tx.msmath2.com

H.O.T. Problems

44. **CHALLENGE** If a number being divided is rounded up and the divisor is rounded down, what is the effect on the new quotient?

45. **OPEN ENDED** Select two fractions whose estimated difference and product is $\frac{1}{2}$. Justify your selection.

46. **NUMBER SENSE** Determine which of the following has a sum that is greater than 1. Write *yes* or *no* and explain.

a. $\frac{1}{2} + \frac{4}{7}$
b. $\frac{3}{4} + \frac{5}{8}$
c. $\frac{2}{5} + \frac{1}{6}$
d. $\frac{2}{3} + \frac{4}{7}$

47. **SELECT A TECHNIQUE** To make the crust for a peach cobbler, Dion needs $3\frac{1}{4}$ cups of flour, $1\frac{2}{3}$ cups of sugar, and $1\frac{2}{3}$ cups of hot water. He needs to mix all of these in a large bowl. The largest bowl he can find holds 6 cups. Which of the following techniques might Dion use to determine whether he can use this bowl to mix the ingredients? Justify your selection(s). Then use the technique(s) to solve the problem.

mental math | number sense | estimation

48. **WRITING IN MATH** Describe when estimation is a better method for solving a problem rather than using a pencil and paper, a calculator, or a computer. Then give a real-world example.

TEST PRACTICE

49. A chef has $15\frac{2}{3}$ cups of penne pasta and $22\frac{1}{4}$ cups of rigatoni pasta. About how much pasta is there altogether?

A 7 cups

B 35 cups

C 38 cups

D 42 cups

50. On a full tank of gasoline, a certain car can travel 360 miles. The needle on its gasoline gauge is shown. Without refueling, which is the best estimate of how far the car can travel?

F 150 miles

G 180 miles

H 240 miles

J 329 miles

Spiral Review

Replace each ● with <, >, or = to make a true sentence. (Lesson 5-9)

51. $\frac{7}{8}$ ● 0.75

52. $\frac{4}{5}$ ● $\frac{5}{7}$

53. $\frac{1}{3}$ ● $\frac{7}{3}$

54. $\frac{6}{11}$ ● $\frac{9}{14}$

55. **SHOPPING** A store sells a 3-pack of beaded necklaces and a 5-pack of beaded bracelets. How many packages of each must you buy so that you have the same number of necklaces and bracelets? (Lesson 5-8)

Write each decimal as a percent. (Lesson 5-7)

56. 0.56

57. 0.375

58. 0.07

59. 0.019

GET READY for the Next Lesson

PREREQUISITE SKILL **Find the LCD of each pair of fractions.** (Lesson 5-9)

60. $\frac{3}{4}, \frac{5}{12}$

61. $\frac{1}{2}, \frac{7}{10}$

62. $\frac{1}{6}, \frac{1}{8}$

63. $\frac{4}{5}, \frac{2}{3}$

6-2 Adding and Subtracting Fractions

Main IDEA

Add and subtract fractions.

Targeted TEKS 7.2 The student adds, subtracts, multiplies, or divides to solve problems and justify solutions. **(B) use addition, subtraction,** multiplication, and division **to solve problems involving fractions** and decimals. *Also addresses TEKS 7.14(B).*

NEW Vocabulary

like fractions
unlike fractions

READING in the Content Area

For strategies in reading this lesson, visit tx.msmath2.com.

MINI Lab

Concepts in Motion
BrainPOP® tx.msmath2.com

1. Find $\frac{3}{8}$ inch on a ruler. From that point, add $\frac{4}{8}$ inch. What is the result?
2. Use a ruler to add $\frac{1}{4}$ inch and $\frac{2}{4}$ inch.

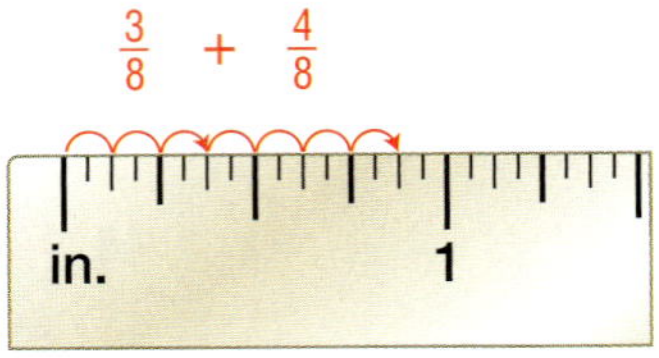

Find each sum. Check using a ruler.

3. $\frac{5}{8} + \frac{7}{8}$
4. $\frac{3}{16} + \frac{1}{16}$
5. $\frac{1}{2} + \frac{3}{4}$

Fractions that have the same denominators are called **like fractions**.

KEY CONCEPT — Add and Subtract Like Fractions

Words To add or subtract like fractions, add or subtract the numerators and write the result over the denominator.

Examples

Numbers	Algebra
$\frac{1}{5} + \frac{3}{5} = \frac{1+3}{5}$ or $\frac{4}{5}$	$\frac{a}{c} + \frac{b}{c} = \frac{a+b}{c}$, where $c \neq 0$
$\frac{11}{12} - \frac{4}{12} = \frac{11-4}{12}$ or $\frac{7}{12}$	$\frac{a}{c} - \frac{b}{c} = \frac{a-b}{c}$, where $c \neq 0$

EXAMPLES Add and Subtract Like Fractions

1 **Add $\frac{5}{9} + \frac{2}{9}$. Write in simplest form.**

$\frac{5}{9} + \frac{2}{9} = \frac{5+2}{9}$ Add the numerators.

$= \frac{7}{9}$ Write the sum over the denominator.

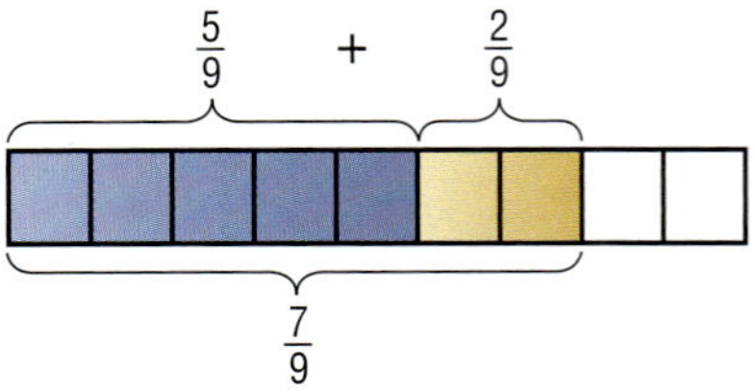

2 **Subtract $\frac{9}{10} - \frac{1}{10}$. Write in simplest form.**

$\frac{9}{10} - \frac{1}{10} = \frac{9-1}{10}$ Subtract the numerators.

$= \frac{8}{10}$ Write the difference over the denominator.

$= \frac{4}{5}$ Simplify.

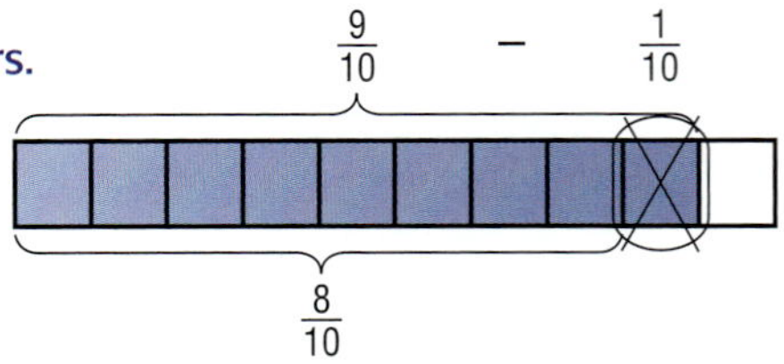

CHECK Your Progress Add or subtract. Write in simplest form.

a. $\frac{1}{6} + \frac{3}{6}$

b. $\frac{3}{7} - \frac{1}{7}$

REVIEW Vocabulary

LCD the least common multiple of the denominators of two or more fractions; *Example*: the LCD of $\frac{1}{4}$ and $\frac{2}{3}$ is 12. (Lesson 5-9)

To add or subtract **unlike fractions**, or fractions with different denominators, rename the fractions using the LCD. Then add or subtract as with like fractions.

EXAMPLES Add and Subtract Unlike Fractions

3 **Add $\frac{1}{2} + \frac{1}{6}$. Write in simplest form.** **Estimate** $\frac{1}{2} + 0 = \frac{1}{2}$

METHOD 1 **Use a model.**

$$\begin{array}{r} \frac{1}{2} \\ +\frac{1}{6} \\ \hline \frac{4}{6} \text{ or } \frac{2}{3} \end{array}$$

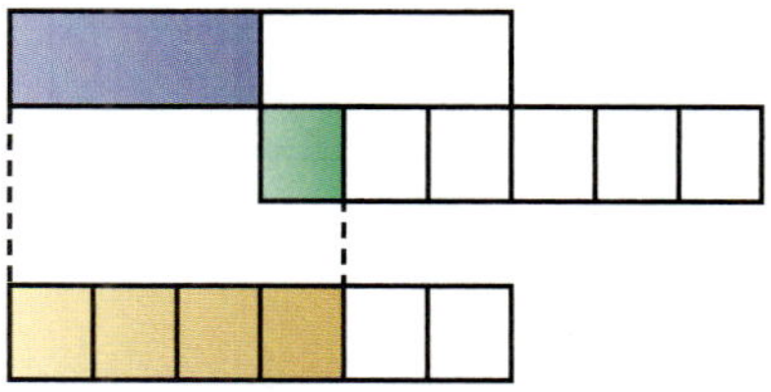

METHOD 2 **Use the LCD.**

The least common denominator (LCD) of $\frac{1}{2}$ and $\frac{1}{6}$ is 6.

Rename using the LCD, 6. Add.

$$\begin{array}{rcccccr} \frac{1}{2} & \rightarrow & \frac{1 \times 3}{2 \times 3} & = & \frac{3}{6} & \rightarrow & \frac{3}{6} \\ +\frac{1}{6} & \rightarrow & \frac{1 \times 1}{6 \times 1} & = & +\frac{1}{6} & \rightarrow & +\frac{1}{6} \\ \hline & & & & & & \frac{4}{6} \text{ or } \frac{2}{3} \end{array}$$

So, $\frac{1}{2} + \frac{1}{6} = \frac{2}{3}$. **Check for Reasonableness** $\frac{2}{3} \approx \frac{1}{2}$ ✔

4 **Subtract $\frac{7}{8} - \frac{3}{4}$. Write in simplest form.** **Estimate** $1 - 1 = 0$

The least common denominator (LCD) of $\frac{7}{8}$ and $\frac{3}{4}$ is 8.

Rename using the LCD, 8. Subtract.

$$\begin{array}{rcccccr} \frac{7}{8} & \rightarrow & \frac{7 \times 1}{8 \times 1} & = & \frac{7}{8} & \rightarrow & \frac{7}{8} \\ -\frac{3}{4} & \rightarrow & -\frac{3 \times 2}{4 \times 2} & = & -\frac{6}{8} & \rightarrow & -\frac{6}{8} \\ \hline & & & & & & \frac{1}{8} \end{array}$$

Check for Reasonableness $\frac{1}{8} \approx 0$ ✔

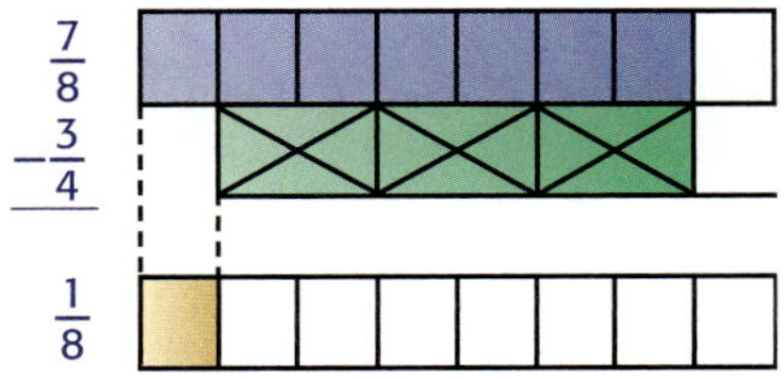

CHOOSE Your Method

c. $\frac{8}{9} - \frac{2}{3}$

d. $\frac{5}{6} - \frac{3}{8}$

e. $\frac{7}{8} + \frac{3}{4}$

Online Personal Tutor at tx.msmath2.com

Real-World EXAMPLES

WEATHER **The average precipitation for November and December in Grand Junction, Colorado, is $\frac{7}{10}$ inch and $\frac{3}{5}$ inch, respectively.**

Real-World Link The average precipitation for April and October in Phoenix, Arizona, is $\frac{3}{10}$ inches and $\frac{4}{5}$ inches, respectively.
Source: *The World Almanac*

5 **On average, how much more precipitation fell in November than in December?**

The phrase *how much more* suggests subtraction, so find $\frac{7}{10} - \frac{3}{5}$.

$\frac{7}{10} - \frac{3}{5} = \frac{7}{10} - \frac{3 \times 2}{5 \times 2}$ The LCD of $\frac{7}{10}$ and $\frac{3}{5}$ is 10.

$= \frac{7}{10} - \frac{6}{10}$ Rename the fractions using the LCD.

$= \frac{1}{10}$ Subtract the numerators.

On average, $\frac{1}{10}$ inch more precipitation fell in November.

6 **Find the average precipitation for both months combined.**

The phrase *combined* suggests addition, so find $\frac{7}{10} + \frac{3}{5}$.

$\frac{7}{10} + \frac{3}{5} = \frac{7}{10} + \frac{6}{10}$ Rename.

$= \frac{13}{10}$ Add.

$= 1\frac{3}{10}$ Write $\frac{13}{10}$ as a mixed number.

The average precipitation was $1\frac{3}{10}$ inches.

CHECK Your Progress

f. **WEATHER** Using the information at the left, find the difference of the average precipitation for Phoenix for April and October.

CHECK Your Understanding

Examples 1–4 (pp. 284–285)

Add or subtract. Write in simplest form.

1. $\frac{4}{9} + \frac{2}{9}$
2. $\frac{5}{6} + \frac{4}{9}$
3. $\frac{3}{8} - \frac{1}{8}$
4. $\frac{4}{5} - \frac{2}{5}$
5. $\frac{1}{6} + \frac{3}{8}$
6. $\frac{2}{3} + \frac{5}{6}$
7. $\frac{5}{6} - \frac{7}{12}$
8. $\frac{3}{4} - \frac{1}{3}$

Examples 5, 6 (p. 286)

For Exercises 9 and 10, choose an operation to solve each problem. Then solve the problem.

9. **FRAMING** Cassandra cuts $\frac{5}{16}$ inch off the top of a photo and $\frac{3}{8}$ inch off the bottom. How much smaller is the total height of the photo now?

10. **CHORES** A bucket was $\frac{7}{8}$ full with soapy water. After washing the car, the bucket was only $\frac{1}{4}$ full. What part of the water was used?

Math Online Extra Examples at tx.msmath2.com

Exercises

HOMEWORK HELP

For Exercises	See Examples
11–14	1, 2
15–22	3, 4
23–26	5, 6

Add or subtract. Write in simplest form.

11. $\frac{3}{7} + \frac{1}{7}$
12. $\frac{5}{8} + \frac{7}{8}$
13. $\frac{5}{6} - \frac{1}{6}$
14. $\frac{7}{10} - \frac{3}{10}$
15. $\frac{1}{15} + \frac{3}{5}$
16. $\frac{7}{12} + \frac{7}{10}$
17. $\frac{5}{8} + \frac{11}{12}$
18. $\frac{7}{9} + \frac{5}{6}$
19. $\frac{7}{9} - \frac{1}{3}$
20. $\frac{4}{5} - \frac{1}{6}$
21. $\frac{4}{9} - \frac{2}{15}$
22. $\frac{3}{10} - \frac{1}{4}$

23. **BUILDING** Ebony is building a shelf to hold the two boxes shown. What is the smallest width she should make the shelf?

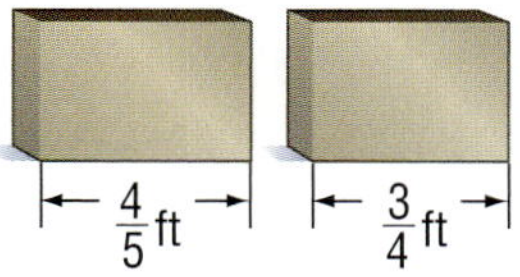

24. **PRESIDENTS** As of 2005, $\frac{5}{14}$ of the U.S. presidents were born in either Virginia or Ohio, and $\frac{1}{6}$ were born in either New York or Massachusetts. What fraction of presidents were born in these four states?

25. **FOOD** Makayla bought $\frac{1}{4}$ pound of ham and $\frac{5}{8}$ pound of turkey. How much more turkey did she buy?

26. **ANIMALS** The three-toed sloth can travel $\frac{3}{20}$ miles per hour while a giant tortoise can travel $\frac{17}{100}$ miles per hour. How much faster, in miles per hour, is the giant tortoise?

Real-World Link Thomas Jefferson, the third President of the United States, was born in Virginia. He served in office from 1801 to 1809.
Source: whitehouse.gov

Simplify.

27. $\frac{1}{7} + \frac{1}{2} + \frac{5}{28}$
28. $\frac{1}{4} + \frac{5}{6} + \frac{7}{12}$
29. $\frac{1}{6} + \left(\frac{2}{3} - \frac{1}{4}\right)$
30. $\frac{5}{6} - \left(\frac{1}{2} + \frac{1}{3}\right)$
31. $1 + \frac{1}{4}$
32. $1 - \frac{5}{8}$
33. $2 + \frac{2}{3}$
34. $3 - \frac{1}{6}$

35. **SPORTS** After 1 hour, Jon had finished $\frac{5}{6}$ of a long-distance race, and Cheng had finished $\frac{7}{9}$ of it. At that time, who had finished a greater fraction of the race, and by how much?

36. **ANALYZE TABLES** Lolita and Salvador each receives an equal allowance. The table shows the fraction of their allowance they each deposit into savings and the fraction they spend at the mall. Determine who has the greater amount of money left and by how much. Explain your reasoning.

Where Money Goes	Fraction of Allowance	
	Lolita	Salvador
savings account	$\frac{1}{2}$	$\frac{1}{3}$
spent at mall	$\frac{1}{4}$	$\frac{3}{5}$
left over	■	■

37. **BOOK REPORTS** Four students were scheduled to give book reports in a 1 hour class period. After the first report, $\frac{2}{3}$ hour remained. If the next two students' reports took $\frac{1}{6}$ hour and $\frac{1}{4}$ hour, respectively, what fraction of the hour remained after the final students' report? Justify your answer.

ALGEBRA **Evaluate each expression if $a = \frac{3}{4}$ and $b = \frac{5}{6}$.**

38. $\frac{1}{2} + a$

39. $b - \frac{7}{10}$

40. $b - a$

41. $a + b$

42. **BIKING** Mrs. Escalante was riding a bicycle on a bike path. After riding $\frac{2}{3}$ of a mile, she discovered that she still needed to travel $\frac{3}{4}$ of a mile to reach the end of the path. How long is the bike path?

43. **CELL PHONES** Out of 160 cell phone owners, $\frac{3}{8}$ use their phone for text messaging, $\frac{1}{4}$ prefer playing games, and the remaining owners prefer taking pictures. What fraction of owners prefers using their cell phone for text messaging or taking pictures?

EXTRA PRACTICE
See pages 731, 760.
Math Online
Self-Check Quiz at
tx.msmath2.com

44. **TRACK** LaTasha and Eric are jogging on a track. LaTasha jogs $\frac{1}{4}$ of a mile and then stops. Eric jogs $\frac{5}{8}$ of a mile, stops and then turns around and jogs $\frac{1}{2}$ of a mile. Who is farther ahead on the track? How much farther? Explain.

H.O.T. Problems

45. **CHALLENGE** Fractions, such as $\frac{1}{2}$ or $\frac{1}{3}$, whose numerators are 1, are called *unit fractions*. Describe a method you can use to add two unit fractions mentally. Explain your reasoning and use your method to find $\frac{1}{99} + \frac{1}{100}$.

46. **OPEN ENDED** Provide a counterexample to the following statement.

The sum of three fractions with odd numerators is never $\frac{1}{2}$.

47. **FIND THE ERROR** Meagan and Lourdes are finding $\frac{5}{9} + \frac{1}{6}$. Who is correct? Explain.

Meagan

Lourdes

48. **WRITING IN MATH** To make a cake, Felicia needs 1 cup of flour but she only has a $\frac{2}{3}$-measuring cup and a $\frac{3}{4}$-measuring cup. Which method will bring her closest to having the amount of flour she needs? Explain.

   a. Fill the $\frac{2}{3}$ measuring cup twice.
   b. Fill the $\frac{2}{3}$ measuring cup once.
   c. Fill the $\frac{3}{4}$ measuring cup twice.
   d. Fill the $\frac{3}{4}$ measuring cup once.
   e. Fill the $\frac{2}{3}$ and $\frac{3}{4}$ measuring cups each once.

TEST PRACTICE

49. The table gives the number of hours Orlando spent at football practice for one week.

Day	Time (hours)
Monday	$1\frac{1}{2}$
Tuesday	2
Wednesday	$2\frac{1}{3}$
Thursday	$1\frac{5}{6}$
Friday	$2\frac{1}{2}$
Saturday	$1\frac{3}{4}$

How many more hours did he practice over the last three days than he did over the first three days?

A $\frac{1}{4}$ h

B $\frac{1}{2}$ h

C $\frac{2}{3}$ h

D $\frac{3}{4}$ h

50. Which model best represents $\frac{3}{8} + \frac{1}{4}$?

F

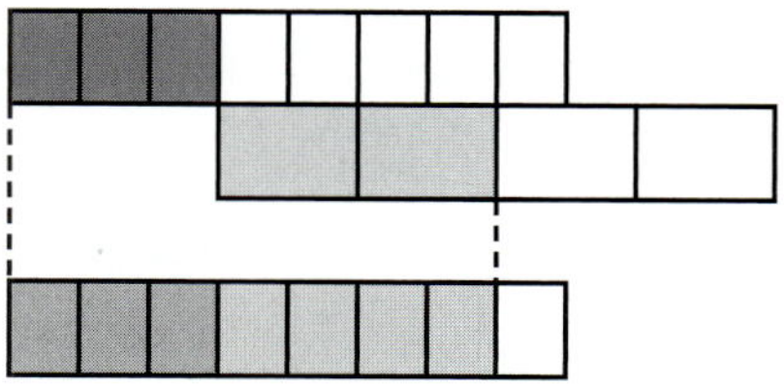

G

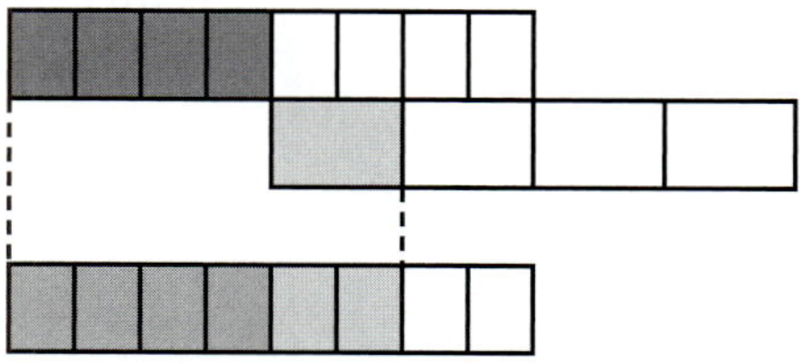

H

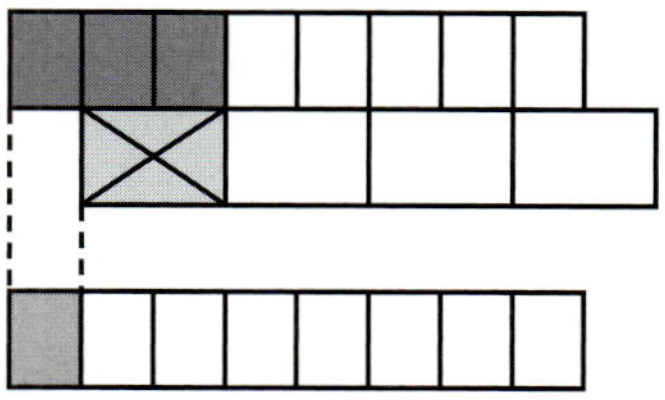

J

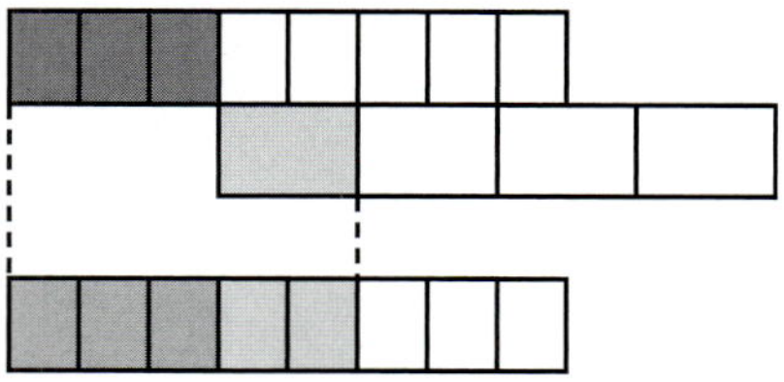

Spiral Review

Estimate (Lesson 6-1)

51. $\frac{6}{7} - \frac{5}{12}$ **52.** $4\frac{1}{9} + 3\frac{3}{4}$ **53.** $16\frac{2}{3} \div 8\frac{1}{5}$ **54.** $5\frac{4}{5} \cdot 3\frac{1}{3}$

55. PETS The table shows where pet owners get their pets. Where do most pet owners get their pets? (Lesson 5-9)

Source	Fraction of Pet Owners
Animal Shelter	$\frac{3}{20}$
Friend/Family	$\frac{21}{50}$
Pet Store	0.07
Find as a stray	0.14

Source: *Yankelovich Partners*

56. Write 0.248 as a percent. (Lesson 5-7)

ALGEBRA **Find each sum if $a = -3$ and $b = 2$.** (Lessons 2-4 and 2-5)

57. $a + b$ **58.** $a - b$ **59.** $b - a$

GET READY for the Next Lesson

PREREQUISITE SKILL **Complete.**

60. $5\frac{2}{3} = 5 + \blacksquare$ **61.** $1 = \frac{\blacksquare}{9}$ **62.** $1 = \frac{\blacksquare}{5}$ **63.** $\blacksquare = 4 + \frac{3}{8}$

6-3 Adding and Subtracting Mixed Numbers

Main IDEA

Add and subtract mixed numbers.

Targeted TEKS 7.2 The student adds, subtracts, multiplies, and divides to solve problems and justify solutions. **(B) use addition, subtraction,** multiplication, and division **to solve problems involving fractions** and decimals. *Also addresses TEKS 7.13(D).*

GET READY for the Lesson

ASTRONOMY Astronomers use *astronomical units* (AU) to represent large distances in space. One AU is the average distance from Earth to the Sun. Mercury is about $\frac{2}{5}$ AU from the Sun.

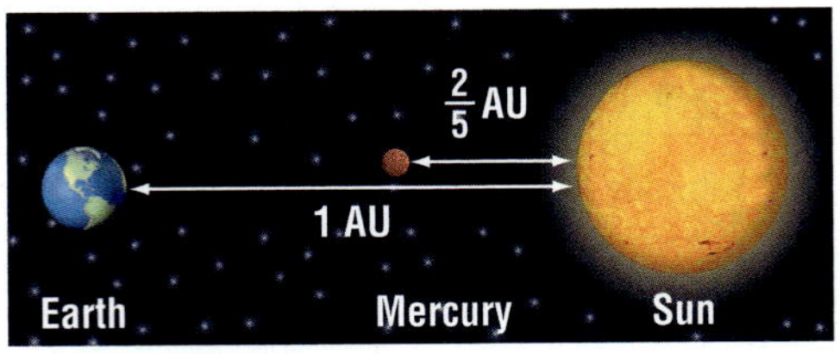

Diagram is not drawn to scale.

1. Jupiter is $5\frac{2}{5}$ AU from the Sun and Saturn's distance is $9\frac{1}{2}$ AU. Write an expression to find how much closer to the Sun Jupiter is than Saturn.
2. Find the difference of the fractional parts of the mixed numbers.
3. Find the difference of the whole numbers.
4. **MAKE A CONJECTURE** Explain how to find $9\frac{1}{2} - 5\frac{2}{5}$. Then use your conjecture to find the difference.

To add or subtract mixed numbers, first add or subtract the fractions. If necessary, rename them using the LCD. Then add or subtract the whole numbers and simplify if necessary.

EXAMPLES Add and Subtract Mixed Numbers

1 **Find $7\frac{4}{9} + 10\frac{2}{9}$. Write in simplest form.**

Estimate $7 + 10 = 17$

$$7\frac{4}{9} + 10\frac{2}{9}$$ Add the whole numbers and fractions separately.

$$17\frac{6}{9} \text{ or } 17\frac{2}{3}$$ Simplify.

Check for Reasonableness $17\frac{2}{3} \approx 17$ ✔

CHECK Your Progress

Add. Write in simplest form.

a. $6\frac{1}{8} + 2\frac{5}{8}$

b. $5\frac{1}{5} + 2\frac{3}{10}$

c. $1\frac{5}{9} + 4\frac{1}{6}$

2 Find $8\frac{5}{6} - 2\frac{1}{3}$. Write in simplest form.

Estimate $9 - 2 = 7$

$$
\begin{array}{rcr}
8\frac{5}{6} & \rightarrow & 8\frac{5}{6} \\
-2\frac{1}{3} & \rightarrow & -2\frac{2}{6} \\
\hline
 & & 6\frac{3}{6} \text{ or } 6\frac{1}{2}
\end{array}
$$

Rename the fraction using the LCD. Then subtract.

Simplify.

Check for Reasonableness $6\frac{1}{2} \approx 7$ ✔

CHECK Your Progress

Subtract. Write in simplest form.

d. $5\frac{4}{5} - 1\frac{3}{10}$ **e.** $13\frac{7}{8} - 9\frac{3}{4}$ **f.** $8\frac{2}{3} - 2\frac{1}{2}$

g. $7\frac{3}{4} - 4\frac{1}{3}$ **h.** $11\frac{5}{6} - 3\frac{1}{8}$ **i.** $9\frac{4}{7} - 5\frac{1}{2}$

Sometimes when you subtract mixed numbers, the fraction in the first mixed number is less than the fraction in the second mixed number. In this case, rename the first fraction as an improper fraction in order to subtract.

STUDY TIP

Improper Fractions An improper fraction has a numerator that is greater than or equal to the denominator. Examples of improper fractions are $\frac{5}{4}$ and $2\frac{6}{5}$.

EXAMPLES Rename Mixed Numbers to Subtract

3 Find $2\frac{1}{3} - 1\frac{2}{3}$.

Estimate $2 - 1\frac{1}{2} = \frac{1}{2}$

Since $\frac{1}{3}$ is less than $\frac{2}{3}$, rename $2\frac{1}{3}$ before subtracting.

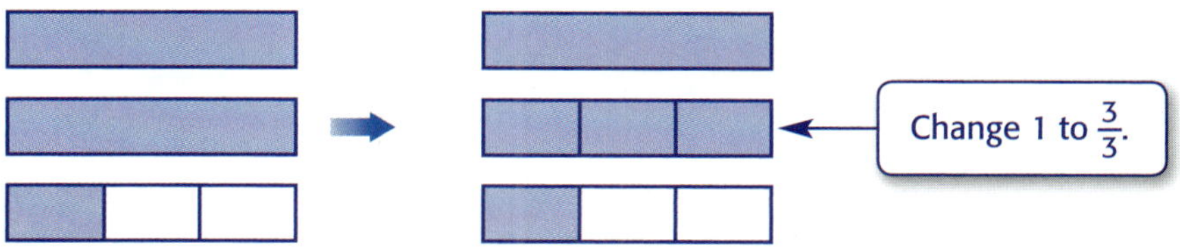

$2\frac{1}{3} = 1\frac{3}{3} + \frac{1}{3}$ or $1\frac{4}{3}$

$$
\begin{array}{rcr}
2\frac{1}{3} & \rightarrow & 1\frac{4}{3} \\
-1\frac{2}{3} & \rightarrow & -1\frac{2}{3} \\
\hline
 & & \frac{2}{3}
\end{array}
$$

Rename $2\frac{1}{3}$ as $1\frac{4}{3}$.

Subtract the whole numbers and then the fractions.

Check for Reasonableness $\frac{2}{3} \approx \frac{1}{2}$ ✔

4 Find $8 - 3\frac{3}{4}$. **Estimate** $8 - 4 = 4$

Using the denominator of the second fraction, $8 = 8\frac{0}{4}$.

Since $\frac{0}{4}$ is less than $\frac{3}{4}$, rename 8 before subtracting.

$$\begin{array}{rcr} 8 & \rightarrow & 7\frac{4}{4} \\ -3\frac{3}{4} & \rightarrow & -3\frac{3}{4} \\ \hline & & 4\frac{1}{4} \end{array}$$

Rename 8 as $7 + \frac{4}{4}$ or $7\frac{4}{4}$.

Subtract.

Check for Reasonableness $4\frac{1}{4} \approx 4$ ✔

CHECK Your Progress Subtract. Write in simplest form.

j. $11\frac{2}{5} - 2\frac{3}{5}$ k. $5\frac{3}{8} - 4\frac{11}{12}$ l. $7 - 1\frac{1}{2}$

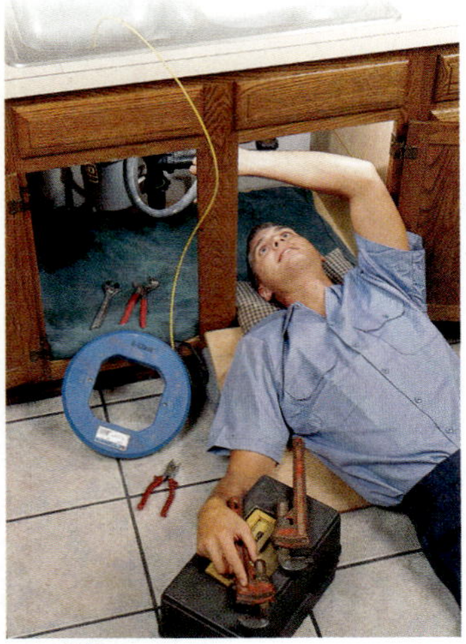

Real-World Career

How Does a Plumber Use Math?

Plumbers add and subtract mixed numbers when calculating the dimensions for installing house fixtures such as shower stalls and sinks.

Math Online For more information, go to tx.msmath2.com.

Real-World EXAMPLE

5 **BUILDING** There should be $2\frac{2}{3}$ feet of clearance space in front of a bathtub. What is the total width of the bathtub and clearance space shown at the right?

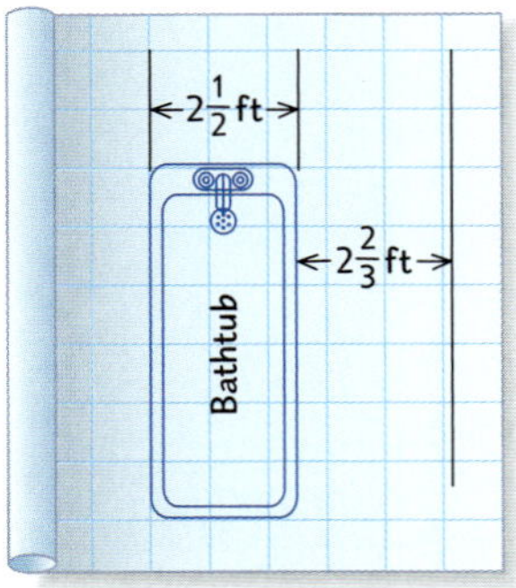

$2\frac{1}{2} + 2\frac{2}{3} = 2\frac{3}{6} + 2\frac{4}{6}$ Rename the fractions.

$= 4 + \frac{7}{6}$ Add the whole numbers and add the fractions.

$= 4 + 1\frac{1}{6}$ Rename $\frac{7}{6}$ as $1\frac{1}{6}$.

$= 5\frac{1}{6}$ Simplify.

The total width is $5\frac{1}{6}$ feet.

CHECK Your Progress

m. **EXERCISE** Jermaine walked $1\frac{5}{8}$ miles on Saturday and $2\frac{1}{2}$ miles on Sunday. How many more miles did he walk on Sunday?

Online Personal Tutor at tx.msmath2.com

CHECK Your Understanding

Examples 1–4 (pp. 290–292)

Add or subtract. Write in simplest form.

1. $1\frac{5}{7} + 8\frac{1}{7}$
2. $8\frac{1}{2} + 3\frac{4}{5}$
3. $7\frac{5}{6} - 3\frac{1}{6}$
4. $9\frac{4}{5} - 2\frac{3}{4}$
5. $3\frac{1}{4} - 1\frac{3}{4}$
6. $5\frac{2}{3} - 2\frac{3}{5}$
7. $11 - 6\frac{3}{8}$
8. $16 - 5\frac{5}{6}$

Example 5 (p. 292)

9. **AQUARIUMS** A fish tank that can hold $18\frac{2}{3}$ gallons of water contains $10\frac{1}{2}$ gallons of water. How much more water is needed to fill the tank?

Exercises

HOMEWORK HELP

For Exercises	See Examples
10–17	1, 2
18–23	3
24–25	4
26–29	5

Add or subtract. Write in simplest form.

10. $2\frac{1}{9} + 7\frac{4}{9}$ **11.** $3\frac{2}{7} + 4\frac{3}{7}$ **12.** $10\frac{4}{5} - 2\frac{1}{5}$ **13.** $8\frac{6}{7} - 6\frac{5}{7}$

14. $9\frac{4}{5} - 2\frac{3}{10}$ **15.** $11\frac{3}{4} - 4\frac{1}{3}$ **16.** $8\frac{5}{12} + 11\frac{1}{4}$ **17.** $8\frac{3}{8} + 10\frac{1}{3}$

18. $9\frac{1}{5} - 2\frac{3}{5}$ **19.** $6\frac{1}{4} - 2\frac{3}{4}$ **20.** $6\frac{3}{5} - 1\frac{2}{3}$ **21.** $4\frac{3}{10} - 1\frac{3}{4}$

22. $14\frac{1}{6} - 7\frac{1}{3}$ **23.** $12\frac{1}{2} - 6\frac{5}{8}$ **24.** $8 - 3\frac{2}{3}$ **25.** $13 - 5\frac{5}{6}$

26. HIKING If Sara and Maggie hiked both of the trails listed in the table, how far did they hike altogether?

Trail	Length (mi)
Woodland Park	$3\frac{2}{3}$
Mill Creek Way	$2\frac{5}{6}$

27. MONUMENTS The diagram shows the heights of the San Jacinto Monument near Houston, Texas, and the Washington Monument. How tall is the San Jacinto Monument?

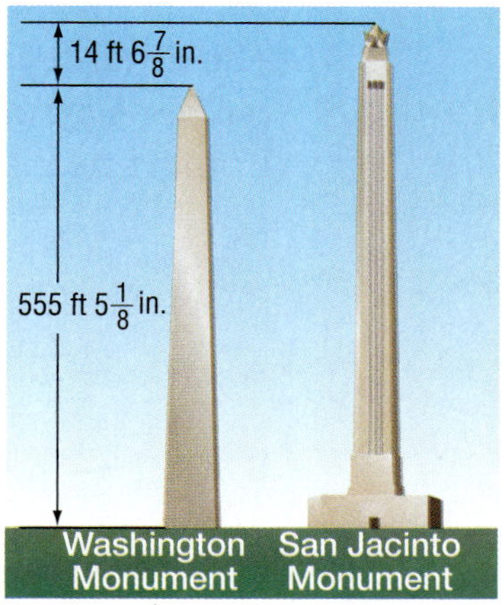

28. GARDENS The length of Kasey's garden is $4\frac{5}{8}$ feet. Find the width of Kasey's garden if it is $2\frac{7}{8}$ feet shorter than the length.

29. HAIRSTYLES Before Alameda got her haircut, the length of her hair was $9\frac{3}{4}$ inches. After her haircut, the length was $6\frac{1}{2}$ inches. How many inches did she have cut?

Add or subtract. Write in simplest form.

30. $10 - 3\frac{5}{11}$ **31.** $24 - 8\frac{3}{4}$ **32.** $6\frac{1}{6} + 1\frac{2}{3} + 5\frac{5}{9}$ **33.** $3\frac{1}{4} + 2\frac{5}{6} - 4\frac{1}{3}$

34. TIME Karen wakes up at 6:00 A.M. It takes her $1\frac{1}{4}$ hours to shower, get dressed, and comb her hair. It takes her $\frac{1}{2}$ hour to eat breakfast, brush her teeth, and make her bed. At what time will she be ready for school?

GEOMETRY Find the perimeter of each figure.

35.

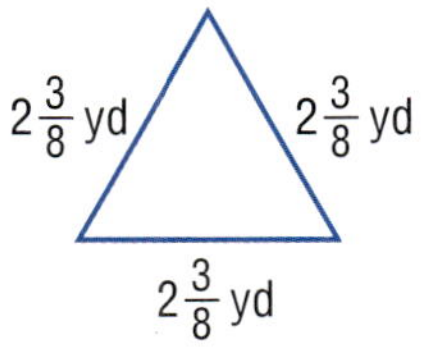

36.

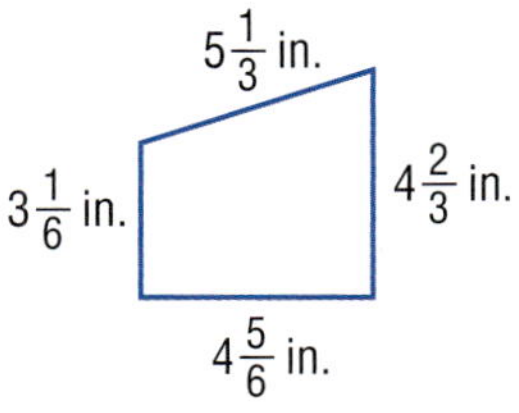

EXTRA PRACTICE

See pages 731, 760.

Math Online
Self-Check Quiz at tx.msmath2.com

H.O.T. Problems

37. OPEN ENDED Select two mixed numbers whose sum or difference is less than $3\frac{1}{9}$.

38. **SELECT A TECHNIQUE** Which of the following techniques could be used to determine whether $6\frac{3}{4} + \frac{4}{5}$ is *greater than, less than,* or *equal to* $2\frac{1}{9} + 6\frac{7}{8}$? Justify your selection(s). Then use the technique(s) to solve the problem.

number sense | mental math | estimation

39. **CHALLENGE** A string is cut in half. One of the halves is thrown away. One-fifth of the remaining half is cut away and the piece left is 8 feet long. How long was the string initially? Justify your answer.

40. **WRITING IN MATH** Create a problem about a real-world situation that involves adding or subtracting two mixed numbers.

TEST PRACTICE

41. The distance from home plate to the pitcher's mound is 60 feet 6 inches and from home plate to second base is 127 feet $3\frac{3}{8}$ inches. Find the distance from the pitcher's mound to second base.

A 68 ft $3\frac{1}{4}$ in.

B 67 ft $8\frac{3}{4}$ in.

C 67 ft $2\frac{5}{8}$ in.

D 66 ft $9\frac{3}{8}$ in.

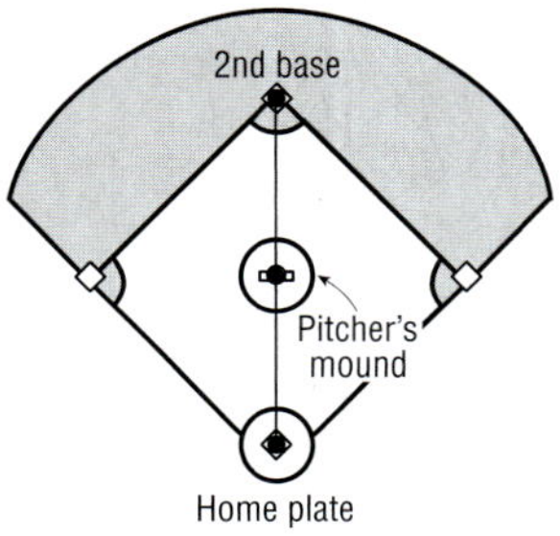

42. A recipe for party mix calls for $4\frac{3}{4}$ cups of cereal. The amount of peanuts needed is $1\frac{2}{3}$ cups less than the amount of cereal needed. How many cups of peanuts and cereal are needed?

F $3\frac{1}{12}$ cups

G $6\frac{1}{2}$ cups

H $7\frac{5}{6}$ cups

J $8\frac{1}{2}$ cups

Spiral Review

43. **SCHOOL** Kai did $\frac{1}{5}$ of her homework in class and $\frac{1}{3}$ more of it on the bus. What fraction of homework does she still need to do? (Lesson 6-2)

Estimate. (Lesson 6–1)

44. $\frac{8}{9} \div \frac{9}{10}$

45. $3\frac{1}{2} + 6\frac{2}{3}$

46. $8\frac{4}{5} \times 7\frac{1}{9}$

47. $4\frac{2}{9} - 1\frac{1}{4}$

48. **CARPET** To carpet a living room whose length is 17 feet, 255 square feet of carpet is needed. Find the width of the living room. (Lesson 4-6)

GET READY for the Next Lesson

49. **PREREQUISITE SKILL** Andre needs to be at the train station by 5:30 P.M. It takes him $\frac{1}{3}$ hour to pack and $1\frac{1}{4}$ hours to get to the station. Find the latest time he should begin packing. Use the *work backward* strategy. (Lesson 4-4)

6-4 Problem-Solving Investigation

MAIN IDEA: Solve problems by eliminating possibilities.

Targeted TEKS 7.13 The student applies Grade 7 mathematics to solve problems connected to everyday experiences, investigations in other disciplines, and activities in and outside of school. **(B) use a problem-solving model that incorporates understanding the problem, making a plan, carrying out the plan, and evaluating the solution for reasonableness.**

P.S.I. TEAM +

e-Mail: ELIMINATE POSSIBILITIES

YOUR MISSION: Eliminate possibilities to solve the problem.

THE PROBLEM: What is the most that Madison can record on the rest of a tape?

MADISON: I recorded $3\frac{1}{4}$ hours of a miniseries on a videotape that can record 6 hours total. What is the most that I can record on the rest of the tape—2, $2\frac{1}{2}$, or 3 hours?

EXPLORE	You know the combined hours of programming must be less than or equal to 6 hours.
PLAN	Eliminate answers that are not reasonable.
SOLVE	You couldn't record 3 more hours on the tape because $3\frac{1}{4} + 3 = 6\frac{1}{4}$. So, eliminate that choice. Now check the choice of $2\frac{1}{2}$ hours. $3\frac{1}{4} + 2\frac{1}{2} = 5\frac{3}{4}$ Since this is less than 6 hours, this choice is correct. You could record $2\frac{1}{2}$ more hours on the tape.
CHECK	Recording 2 more hours would give $3\frac{1}{4} + 2$ or $5\frac{1}{4}$ hours. This is less than the 6-hour maximum, but not the most that you could record.

Analyze The Strategy

1. Describe different ways that you can eliminate possibilities when solving problems.
2. Explain how the strategy of eliminating possibilities is useful for taking multiple choice tests.
3. **WRITING IN MATH** Write a problem that could be solved by eliminating possibilities.

Mixed Problem Solving

Eliminate possibilities to solve Exercises 4–6.

4. **JUICE** Guillermo has a 3-gallon cooler with $1\frac{3}{4}$ gallons of juice in it. If he wants the cooler full for his soccer game, how much juice should he add?

   A 4 gallons **C** $1\frac{1}{4}$ gallons

   B $3\frac{1}{4}$ gallons **D** $\frac{1}{4}$ gallon

5. **ELEPHANTS** An elephant in a zoo eats 58 cabbages in a week. About how many cabbages does an elephant eat in one year?

   F 7 **H** 1,500

   G 700 **J** 3,000

6. **TRAVEL** Mr. Rollins drove 780 miles on a 5-day trip. He rented a car for $23 per day plus $0.15 per mile after 500 free miles. About how much did the rental car cost?

   A $100 **C** $160

   B $130 **D** $180

Use any strategy to solve Exercises 7–11. Some strategies are shown below.

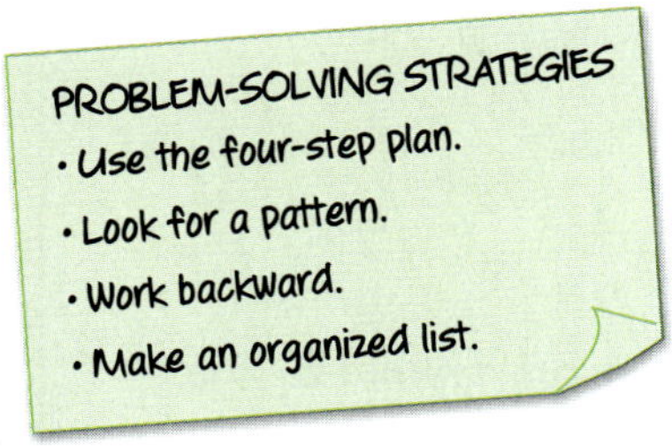

7. **SHELVING** The diagram shows a shelf that holds CDs. Each shelf is $\frac{1}{8}$ inch thick, and the distance between shelves is as shown. How much space is available on each layer of the shelf for a CD?

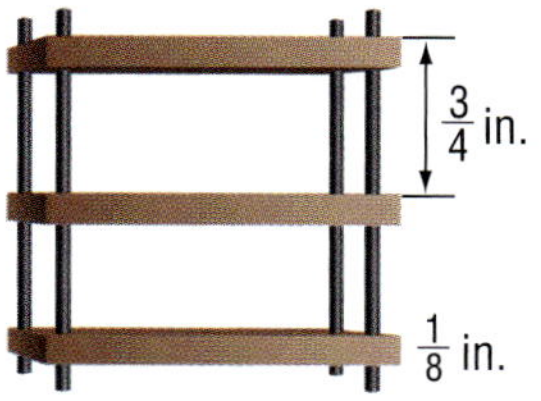

8. **ELEVATORS** An elevator can hold a maximum weight of 3,500 pounds. If the average adult weighs 170 pounds, about how many adults can the elevator hold?

9. **GEOMETRY** Draw the next two figures in the pattern.

10. **SLEEP** A nine month old infant needs about 14 hours of sleep each day while a teenager needs about 10 hours of sleep each day. How much more sleep does a nine month old need than a teenager? Write as a fraction of a day.

11. **WEATHER** In some areas of the rain forest, 325 inches of rain may fall in a year. Is $\frac{1}{3}$ inch, 1 inch, 5 inches, or 33 inches the best estimate for the average rainfall per day in such an area?

Select the Operation

For Exercises 12–14, select the appropriate operation(s) to solve the problem. Justify your selection(s) and solve the problem.

12. **SUPPLIES** Vanessa has $55 to buy school supplies. She bought a backpack for $23.50, a combination lock for $6.25, and 4 binders that are $3.99 each. If mechanical pencils are $2.50 per pack, how many packs can she buy?

13. **PIZZA** Sebastian ate $\frac{2}{5}$ of a pizza while his sister ate $\frac{1}{3}$ of the same pizza. The remainder was stored in the refrigerator. What fraction of the pizza was stored in the refrigerator?

14. **COOKING** A recipe calls for $2\frac{2}{3}$ cups of flour and $1\frac{1}{4}$ cups of sugar. How many more cups of flour are called for than sugar?

CHAPTER 6

Mid-Chapter Quiz

Lessons 6-1 through 6-4

1. **SAVINGS** Tonisha saves $\frac{1}{3}$ of the money she earns baby-sitting. If she earns $25 one evening, estimate the amount she saves. (Lesson 6-1)

Estimate. (Lesson 6-1)

2. $5\frac{1}{9} + 1\frac{7}{8}$
3. $13\frac{1}{2} \div 7\frac{2}{9}$
4. $\frac{11}{20} - \frac{5}{8}$
5. $4\frac{2}{3} \times 1\frac{3}{4}$
6. $7\frac{3}{4} \div 1\frac{4}{5}$
7. $\frac{8}{9} + 2\frac{13}{15}$

8. **TEST PRACTICE** The school cafeteria makes 8 batches of cookies each day. Each batch uses $2\frac{1}{2}$ cups of flour and $1\frac{2}{3}$ cups of sugar. Which is the best estimate of the total amount of flour and sugar used each day for cookies? (Lesson 6-1)

A less than 30 cups

B between 30 cups and 45 cups

C between 45 cups and 55 cups

D more than 55 cups

Add or subtract. Write in simplest form.
(Lesson 6-2)

9. $\frac{11}{15} - \frac{1}{15}$
10. $\frac{4}{7} - \frac{3}{14}$
11. $\frac{1}{2} + \frac{2}{9}$
12. $\frac{5}{8} + \frac{3}{4}$

13. **SCIENCE** $\frac{39}{50}$ of Earth's atmosphere is made up of nitrogen while only $\frac{21}{100}$ is made up of oxygen. What fraction of Earth's atmosphere is either nitrogen or oxygen? (Lesson 6-2)

Add or subtract. Write in simplest form.
(Lesson 6-3)

14. $8\frac{3}{4} - 2\frac{5}{12}$
15. $5\frac{1}{6} - 1\frac{1}{3}$
16. $2\frac{5}{9} + 1\frac{2}{3}$
17. $2\frac{3}{5} + 6\frac{13}{15}$

18. **TEST PRACTICE** The table shows the weight of a newborn infant for the first year. (Lesson 6-3)

Month	Weight (lb)
0	$7\frac{1}{4}$
3	$12\frac{1}{2}$
6	$16\frac{5}{8}$
9	$19\frac{4}{5}$
12	$23\frac{3}{20}$

During which three month period was the infant's weight gain the greatest?

F 0–3 months

G 3–6 months

H 6–9 months

J 9–12 months

19. **PACKING** How much does a $12\frac{3}{4}$-pound package weigh after a $3\frac{5}{8}$-pound book is taken out of it? (Lesson 6-3)

20. **TEST PRACTICE** The table gives the average lifespan of certain animals in fractions of a century. (Lesson 6-4)

Animal	Lifespan (century)
Alligator	$\frac{1}{2}$
Horse	$\frac{1}{5}$
Black Bear	$\frac{9}{50}$
Giraffe	$\frac{1}{10}$
Deer	$\frac{2}{25}$

Source: *World Almanac For Kids*

Which two animals have lifespans that add up to a Black Bear's lifespan?

A alligator and horse

B horse and giraffe

C horse and deer

D deer and giraffe

Explore 6-5

Math Lab
Multiplying Fractions

Main IDEA

Use area models to multiply fractions and mixed numbers.

Targeted TEKS 7.2 The student adds, subtracts, multiplies, or divides to solve problems and justify solutions. **(A) represent multiplication** and division **situations involving fractions** and decimals **with models, including concrete objects, picture, words, and numbers.**

Area models can be used to multiply fractions.

ACTIVITY

Concepts in Motion **Animation** tx.msmath2.com

1 **Find $\frac{3}{4} \times \frac{2}{3}$ using a geoboard.**

The first factor is 3 *fourths* and the second factor is 2 *thirds*.

STEP 1 Use one geoband to show fourths and another to show thirds on the geoboard.

STEP 2 Use geobands to form a rectangle. Place one geoband on the peg to show 3 fourths and another on the peg to show 2 thirds.

STEP 3 Connect the geobands to show a small rectangle.

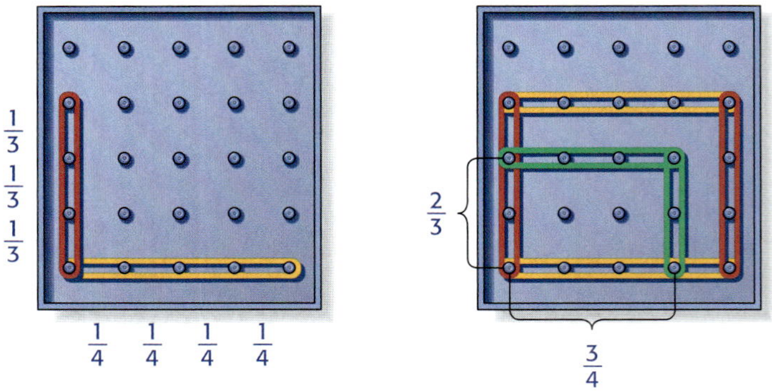

The area of the small rectangle is 6 square units. The area of the large rectangle is 12 square units. So, $\frac{3}{4} \times \frac{2}{3} = \frac{6}{12}$ or $\frac{1}{2}$.

CHECK Your Progress **Find each product using a geoboard.**

a. $\frac{1}{4} \times \frac{1}{3}$ b. $\frac{1}{2} \times \frac{1}{2}$ c. $\frac{3}{4} \times \frac{1}{2}$ d. $\frac{2}{3} \times \frac{1}{4}$

Area models can be used to multiply a mixed number and a fraction.

ACTIVITY

2 **Find $2 \times \frac{1}{4}$ using an area model.**

STEP 1 To represent 2 or $\frac{2}{1}$ draw 2 large rectangles, side by side. Divide each rectangle horizontally into fourths. Color both large rectangles blue.

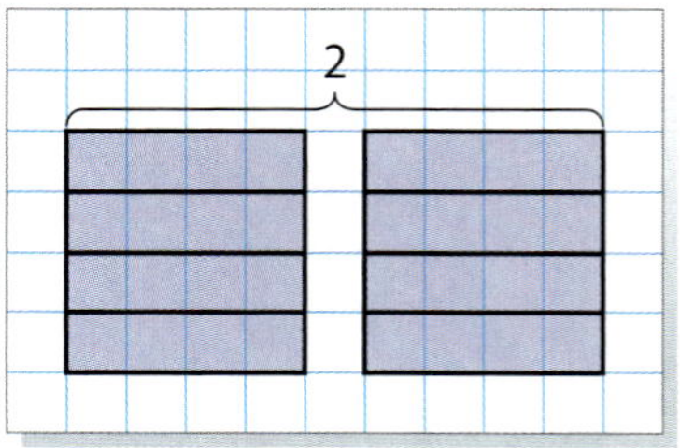

STUDY TIP

Shading
Yellow and blue make green. So, the green sections have been shaded twice and represent the product.

STEP 2 Color 1 fourth of each large rectangle yellow.

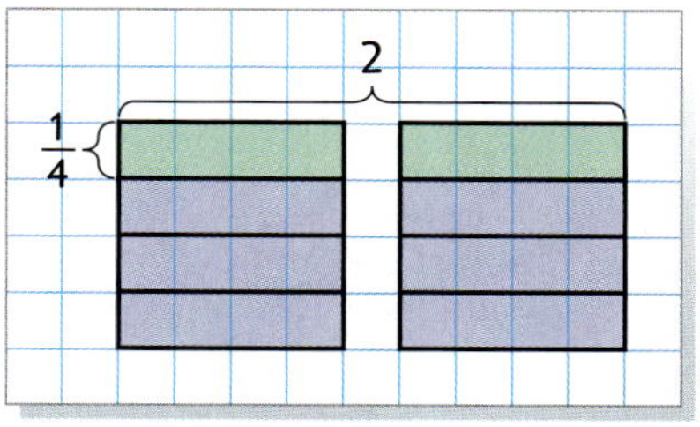

There are two sections shaded green. The fraction of one large rectangle shaded green is $\frac{2}{4}$ or $\frac{1}{2}$.

So, $2 \times \frac{1}{4} = \frac{1}{2}$.

CHECK Your Progress **Find each product using a model.**

e. $3 \times \frac{2}{3}$ f. $2 \times \frac{2}{5}$ g. $4 \times \frac{1}{2}$ h. $3 \times \frac{3}{4}$

ACTIVITY

3 **Find $1\frac{2}{3} \times \frac{1}{2}$ using a model.**

STEP 1 Draw 2 rectangles divided vertically into thirds and horizontally into halves. Color $1\frac{2}{3}$ of the squares blue.

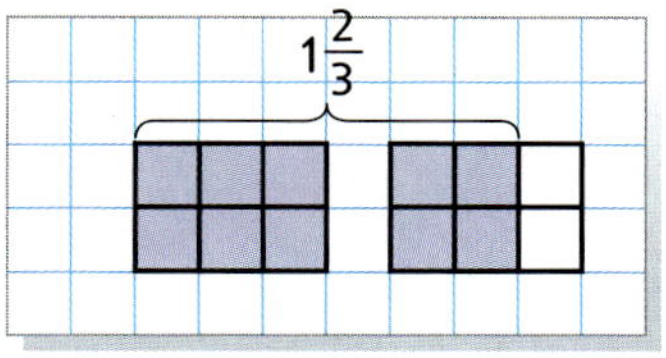

STEP 2 Color $\frac{1}{2}$ of the squares yellow. Then count the small squares that are green.

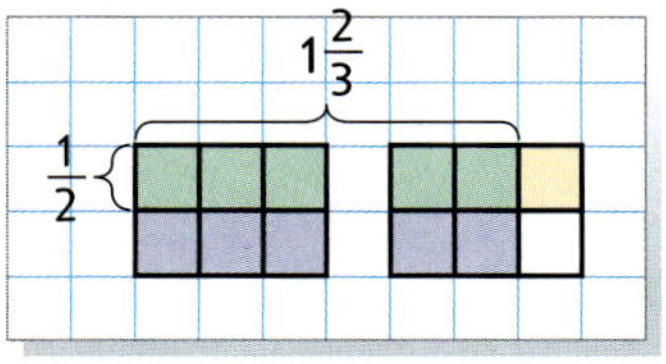

Since the green area is $\frac{3}{6}$ of the first rectangle and $\frac{2}{6}$ of the second rectangle, the total area shaded green is $\frac{3}{6} + \frac{2}{6}$ or $\frac{5}{6}$. So, $1\frac{2}{3} \times \frac{1}{2} = \frac{5}{6}$.

CHECK Your Progress **Find each product using a model.**

i. $1\frac{1}{4} \times \frac{1}{5}$ j. $2\frac{1}{2} \times \frac{3}{4}$ k. $1\frac{2}{3} \times \frac{1}{3}$

ANALYZE THE RESULTS

1. Analyze Exercises a–k. What is the relationship between the numerators of the factors and of the product? Between the denominators of the factors and of the product?

2. **MAKE A CONJECTURE** Write a rule you can use to multiply two fractions.

6-5 Multiplying Fractions and Mixed Numbers

Main IDEA

Multiply fractions and mixed numbers.

Targeted TEKS 7.2 The student adds, subtracts, multiplies, or divides to solve problems and justify solutions. **(A) represent multiplication and division situations involving fractions** and decimals **with models, including** concrete objects, **pictures, words, and numbers.** *Also addresses TEKS 7.2(B), 7.14(A).*

GET READY for the Lesson

FORESTS About $\frac{1}{3}$ of the land in the United States is forests. About $\frac{2}{5}$ of U.S. forests are publicly owned.

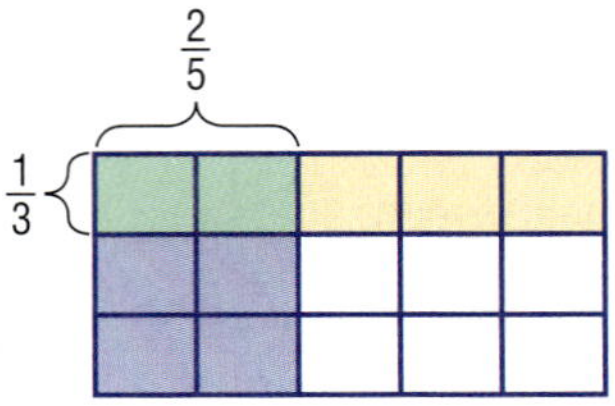

1. What part of the rectangle represents $\frac{1}{3}$?
2. What part of the rectangle represents $\frac{2}{5}$ of $\frac{1}{3}$?
3. **MAKE A CONJECTURE** About what fraction of U.S. land is publicly owned forests?

KEY CONCEPT — Multiply Fractions

Words To multiply fractions, multiply the numerators and multiply the denominators.

Examples

Numbers	Algebra
$\frac{1}{3} \times \frac{2}{5} = \frac{1 \times 2}{3 \times 5}$ or $\frac{2}{15}$	$\frac{a}{b} \cdot \frac{c}{d} = \frac{a \cdot c}{b \cdot d}$ or $\frac{ac}{bd}$, where $b, d \neq 0$

EXAMPLES Multiply Fractions

Multiply. Write in simplest form.

1 $\frac{1}{2} \times \frac{1}{3}$

$\frac{1}{2} \times \frac{1}{3} = \frac{1 \times 1}{2 \times 3}$ ← Multiply the numerators. ← Multiply the denominators.

$= \frac{1}{6}$ Simplify.

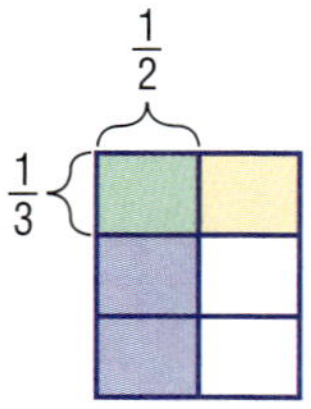

$\frac{1}{6}$ shaded green

2 $2 \times \frac{3}{4}$

$2 \times \frac{3}{4} = \frac{2}{1} \times \frac{3}{4}$ Write 2 as $\frac{2}{1}$.

$= \frac{2 \times 3}{1 \times 4}$ ← Multiply the numerators. ← Multiply the denominators.

$= \frac{6}{4}$ or $1\frac{1}{2}$ Simplify.

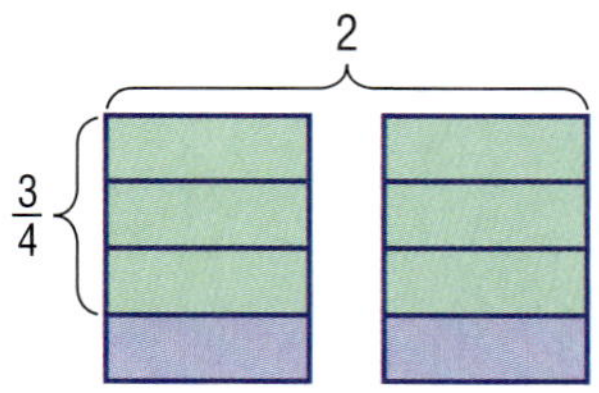

$\frac{6}{4}$ or $1\frac{1}{2}$ shaded green

STUDY TIP

Whole Numbers When multiplying a fraction by a whole number, write the whole number as a fraction with a denominator of 1.

CHECK Your Progress

Multiply. Write in simplest form.

a. $\frac{3}{5} \times \frac{1}{2}$

b. $\frac{1}{3} \times \frac{3}{4}$

c. $\frac{2}{3} \times 4$

If the numerator and denominator of either fraction have common factors, you can simplify before multiplying.

EXAMPLE Simplify Before Multiplying

REVIEW Vocabulary

GCF the greatest of the common factors of two or more numbers; *Example:* the GCF of 8 and 12 is 4. (Lesson 5-2)

3 Find $\frac{2}{7} \times \frac{3}{8}$. Write in simplest form.

$\frac{2}{7} \times \frac{3}{8} = \frac{\overset{1}{\cancel{2}}}{7} \times \frac{3}{\underset{4}{\cancel{8}}}$ Divide 2 and 8 by their GCF, 2.

$= \frac{1 \times 3}{7 \times 4}$ or $\frac{3}{28}$ Multiply.

CHECK Your Progress

Multiply. Write in simplest form.

d. $\frac{1}{3} \times \frac{3}{7}$ e. $\frac{4}{9} \times \frac{1}{8}$ f. $\frac{5}{6} \times \frac{3}{5}$

EXAMPLE Multiply Mixed Numbers

4 Find $\frac{1}{2} \times 4\frac{2}{5}$. Write in simplest form. Estimate $\frac{1}{2} \times 4 = 2$

STUDY TIP

Simplifying
If you forget to simplify before multiplying, you can always simplify the final answer. However, it is usually easier to simplify before multiplying.

METHOD 1 **Rename the mixed number.**

$\frac{1}{2} \times 4\frac{2}{5} = \frac{1}{\underset{1}{\cancel{2}}} \times \frac{\overset{11}{\cancel{22}}}{5}$ Rename $4\frac{2}{5}$ as an improper fraction, $\frac{22}{5}$. Divide 2 and 22 by their GCF, 2.

$= \frac{1 \times 11}{1 \times 5}$ Multiply.

$= \frac{11}{5}$ or $2\frac{1}{5}$ Simplify.

METHOD 2 **Use mental math.**

The mixed number $4\frac{2}{5}$ is equal to $4 + \frac{2}{5}$.

So, $\frac{1}{2} \times 4\frac{2}{5} = \frac{1}{2}\left(4 + \frac{2}{5}\right)$. Use the Distributive Property to multiply, then add mentally.

$\frac{1}{2}\left(4 + \frac{2}{5}\right) = 2 + \frac{1}{5}$ **THINK** Half of 4 is 2 and half of 2 fifths is 1 fifth.

$= 2\frac{1}{5}$ Rewrite sum as mixed number.

So, $\frac{1}{2} \times 4\frac{2}{5} = 2\frac{1}{5}$. **Check for Reasonableness** $2\frac{1}{5} \approx 2$ ✔

CHOOSE Your Method

Multiply. Write in simplest form.

g. $\frac{1}{4} \times 8\frac{4}{9}$ h. $5\frac{1}{3} \times 3$ i. $1\frac{7}{8} \times 2\frac{2}{5}$

Real-World EXAMPLES

5 SLEEP Humans sleep about $\frac{1}{3}$ of each day. If each year is equal to $365\frac{1}{4}$ days, determine the number of days in a year the average human sleeps.

Words	Humans sleep about $\frac{1}{3}$ of $365\frac{1}{4}$ days.
Variable	Let d represent the number of days a human sleeps.
Equation	$d = \frac{1}{3} \cdot 365\frac{1}{4}$

$d = \frac{1}{3} \cdot 365\frac{1}{4}$ Write the equation.

$d = \frac{1}{3} \cdot \frac{1{,}461}{4}$ Rename the mixed number as an improper fraction.

$d = \frac{1}{\cancel{3}_1} \cdot \frac{\cancel{1{,}461}^{487}}{4}$ Divide 3 and 1,461 by their GCF, 3.

$d = \frac{487}{4}$ or $121\frac{3}{4}$ Multiply. Then rename as a mixed number.

The average human sleeps $121\frac{3}{4}$ days each year.

Real-World Link The average group of lions, called a pride, consists of about 15 lions with about $\frac{2}{3}$ of the pride being female.
Source: *African Wildlife Foundation*

6 ANIMALS The house cat has an average lifespan that is $\frac{4}{5}$ of a lion's. If a lion's lifespan is 15 years, find the average lifespan of a house cat.

Words	The lifespan of a house cat is $\frac{4}{5}$ of that of the lion.
Variable	Let c represent the lifespan of a house cat.
Equation	$c = \frac{4}{5} \cdot 15$

$c = \frac{4}{5} \cdot 15$ Write the equation.

$c = \frac{4}{5} \cdot \frac{15}{1}$ Write the whole number 15 as an improper fraction.

$c = \frac{4}{\cancel{5}_1} \cdot \frac{\cancel{15}^{3}}{1}$ Divide 5 and 15 by their GCF, 5.

$c = \frac{12}{1}$ or 12 Multiply, then simplify.

The average lifespan of a house cat is 12 years.

CHECK Your Progress

j. **COOKING** Sofia wishes to make $\frac{1}{2}$ of a recipe. If the original recipe calls for $3\frac{3}{4}$ cups of flour, how many cups should she use?

Online **Personal Tutor at** tx.msmath2.com

CHECK Your Understanding

Examples 1–4 (pp. 300–301)

Multiply. Write in simplest form.

1. $\frac{2}{3} \times \frac{1}{3}$
2. $2 \times \frac{2}{5}$
3. $\frac{1}{6} \times 4$
4. $\frac{1}{4} \times \frac{8}{9}$
5. $2\frac{1}{4} \times \frac{2}{3}$
6. $1\frac{5}{6} \times 3\frac{3}{5}$

Examples 5, 6 (p. 302)

7. **FOOD** An average slice of American cheese is about $\frac{1}{8}$ inch thick. What is the height of a package containing 20 slices?

Exercises

HOMEWORK HELP

For Exercises	See Examples
8–11	1, 2
12–19	3, 4
20–23	5, 6

Multiply. Write in simplest form.

8. $\frac{3}{4} \times \frac{1}{8}$
9. $\frac{2}{5} \times \frac{2}{3}$
10. $9 \times \frac{1}{2}$
11. $\frac{4}{5} \times 6$
12. $\frac{1}{5} \times \frac{5}{6}$
13. $\frac{4}{9} \times \frac{1}{4}$
14. $\frac{2}{3} \times \frac{1}{4}$
15. $\frac{1}{12} \times \frac{3}{5}$
16. $\frac{4}{7} \times \frac{7}{8}$
17. $\frac{2}{5} \times \frac{15}{16}$
18. $\frac{3}{8} \times \frac{10}{27}$
19. $\frac{9}{10} \times \frac{5}{6}$

20. **DVDs** Each DVD storage case is about $\frac{1}{5}$-inch thick. What will be the height of 12 cases sold together in plastic wrapping?

21. **PIZZA** Mark left $\frac{3}{8}$ of a pizza in the refrigerator. On Friday, he ate $\frac{1}{2}$ of what was left of the pizza. What fraction of the entire pizza did he eat on Friday?

22. **GARDENS** The width of a vegetable garden is $\frac{1}{3}$ times its length. If the length of the garden is $7\frac{3}{4}$ feet, what is the width?

23. **RECIPES** A recipe to make one batch of blueberry muffins calls for $4\frac{2}{3}$ cups of flour. How many cups of flour are needed to make 3 batches of blueberry muffins?

Multiply. Write in simplest form.

24. $4\frac{2}{3} \times \frac{4}{7}$
25. $\frac{5}{8} \times 2\frac{1}{2}$
26. $14 \times 1\frac{1}{7}$
27. $3\frac{3}{4} \times 8$
28. $9 \times 4\frac{2}{3}$
29. $4 \times 7\frac{5}{6}$
30. $3\frac{1}{4} \times 2\frac{2}{3}$
31. $5\frac{1}{3} \times 3\frac{3}{4}$

32. **FLAGS** The length of an official United States flag must be $1\frac{9}{10}$ times its width. What is the length of the flag shown at the right?

33. **BICYCLING** Philip rode his bicycle at $9\frac{2}{5}$ miles per hour. If he rode for $\frac{3}{4}$ of an hour, how many miles did he cover?

Evaluate each verbal expression.

34. one-half of five-eighths

35. four-sevenths of two-thirds

36. nine-tenths of one-fourth

37. one-third of eleven-sixteenths

GEOMETRY Find the perimeter and area of each rectangle.

38.

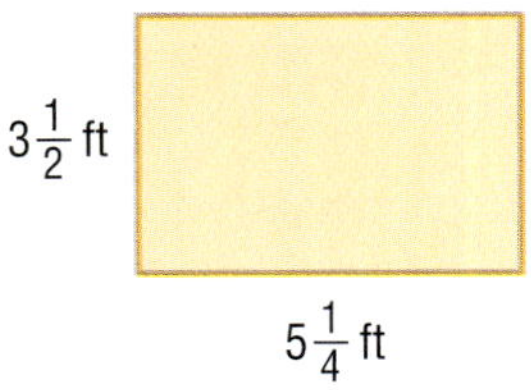

39.

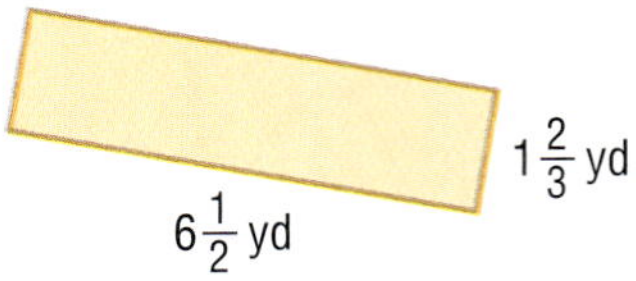

Real-World Link There are an estimated 5 million in-ground swimming pools in the U.S.
Source: *Pool & Spa Service Industry News*

40. **POOLS** The swimming pool at a community center is $90\frac{2}{5}$ feet long and $55\frac{1}{2}$ feet wide. If Natalie swims the perimeter of the pool four times, what is the total number of feet she will swim? Explain how you solved the problem.

MEASUREMENT For Exercises 41–44, use measurement conversions.

41. Find $\frac{1}{2}$ of $\frac{1}{4}$ of a gallon.

42. What is $\frac{1}{60}$ of $\frac{1}{24}$ of a day?

43. Find $\frac{1}{100}$ of $\frac{1}{1{,}000}$ of a kilometer.

44. What is $\frac{1}{12}$ of $\frac{1}{3}$ of a yard?

ALGEBRA Evaluate each expression if $a = 4$, $b = 2\frac{1}{2}$, and $c = 5\frac{3}{4}$.

45. $a \times b + c$

46. $b \times c - a$

47. $2bc$

48. **TELEVISION** One evening, $\frac{2}{3}$ of the students in Rick's class watched television, and $\frac{3}{8}$ of those students watched a reality show, of which $\frac{1}{4}$ taped the show. What fraction of the students in Rick's class watched and taped a reality TV show?

49. **FOOD** Nicolás wants to make one and a half recipes of the pasta salad recipe shown at the right. How much of each ingredient will Nicolás need? Explain how you solved the problem.

Pasta Salad Recipe	
Ingredient	**Amount**
broccoli	$1\frac{1}{4}$ c
cooked pasta	$3\frac{3}{4}$ c
salad dressing	$\frac{2}{3}$ c
cheese	$1\frac{1}{3}$ c

50. **FIND THE DATA** Refer to the Texas Data File on pages 16–19. Choose some data and write a real-world problem in which you would multiply fractions.

Write a multiplication expression to represent each model. Then evaluate the expression.

51.

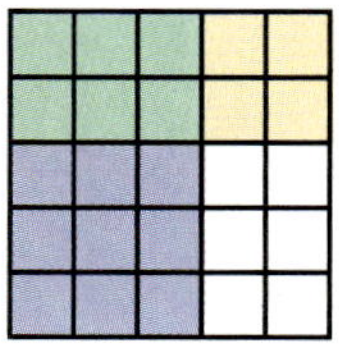

52.

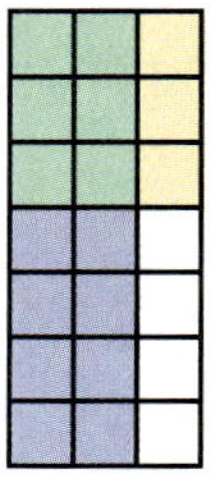

EXTRA PRACTICE
See pages 732, 760.
Math Online
Self-Check Quiz at tx.msmath2.com

H.O.T. Problems

53. **CHALLENGE** Two fractions that are *not* improper are multiplied. Is the product *sometimes*, *always*, or *never* less than 1? Explain your reasoning.

54. **OPEN ENDED** Write two mixed numbers with a product of $7\frac{7}{15}$.

55. **WRITING IN MATH** Explain why $3\frac{2}{5} \times 4\frac{5}{12} \neq (3 \times 4) + \left(\frac{2}{5} \times \frac{5}{12}\right)$.

TEST PRACTICE

56. Which expression is best represented by the model?

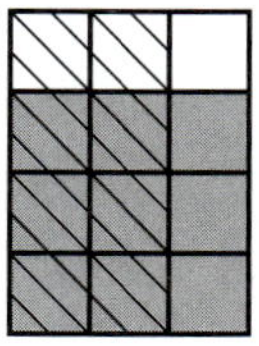

A $\frac{1}{2} \times \frac{2}{3}$

B $\frac{3}{4} \times \frac{1}{3}$

C $\frac{3}{4} \times \frac{2}{3}$

D $\frac{3}{4} \times \frac{1}{3}$

57. Which description gives the relationship between a term and n, its position in the sequence?

Position	1	2	3	4	5	n
Value of Term	$\frac{1}{4}$	$\frac{1}{2}$	$\frac{3}{4}$	1	$1\frac{1}{4}$	

F Subtract 4 from n.

G Add $\frac{1}{4}$ to n.

H Multiply n by $\frac{1}{4}$.

J Divide n by $\frac{1}{4}$.

Spiral Review

58. **GEOMETRY** Find which room dimensions would give an area of $125\frac{3}{8}$ square feet. Use the *eliminate possibilities* strategy. (Lesson 6-4)

A $11\frac{1}{2}$ feet by $10\frac{3}{8}$ feet

B $10\frac{7}{8}$ feet by $12\frac{1}{4}$ feet

C $13\frac{5}{8}$ feet by 9 feet

D $14\frac{3}{4}$ feet by $8\frac{1}{2}$ feet

59. **MEASUREMENT** How much longer is a $2\frac{1}{2}$-inch long piece of string than a $\frac{2}{5}$-inch long piece of string? (Lesson 6-3)

Replace each ● with <, >, or = to make a true sentence. (Lesson 5-9)

60. $\frac{5}{12}$ ● $\frac{2}{5}$

61. $\frac{3}{16}$ ● $\frac{1}{8}$

62. $3\frac{7}{6}$ ● $3\frac{6}{5}$

63. What is the greatest common factor of 12, 30, and 48? (Lesson 5-2)

64. **PHONES** A long-distance telephone company charges a flat monthly fee of \$4.95 and \$0.06 per minute on all long-distance calls. Write and solve an equation to find the number of monthly minutes spent talking long-distance if the bill total was \$22.95. (Lesson 4-5)

GET READY for the Next Lesson

PREREQUISITE SKILL **Solve each equation mentally.** (Lesson 1-7)

65. $x + 2 = 8$

66. $9 + m = 12$

67. $7 - w = 2$

6-6 Algebra: Solving Equations

Main IDEA

Solve equations with rational number solutions.

Targeted TEKS 7.5 The student adds, subtracts, multiplies, or divides to solve problems and justify solutions. **(B) formulate problem situations when given a simple equation and formulate an equation when given a problem situation.** *Also addresses TEKS 7.2(B).*

NEW Vocabulary

multiplicative inverse
reciprocal

Vocabulary Link

Inverse
Everyday Use reversal of order

Multiplicative Inverse
Math Use reversal of order of the numerator and denominator of a fraction

MINI Lab

1. The model shows $\frac{1}{2} \cdot 2$. What is the product?

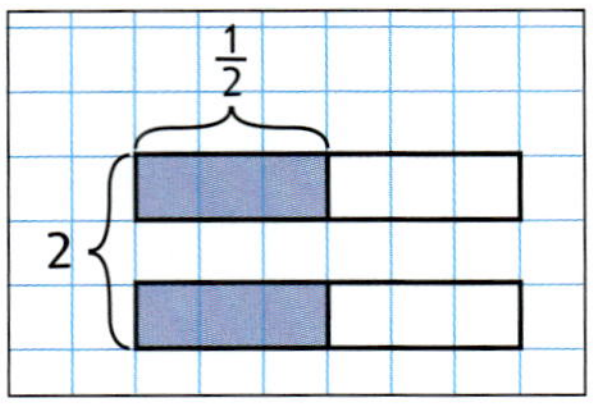

2. Use grid paper to model $\frac{1}{3} \cdot 3$. What is the product?
3. Copy and complete the table below.

$\frac{1}{2} \times 2 =$ ■	$\frac{2}{3} \times \frac{3}{2} =$ ■	$\frac{5}{6} \times$ ■ $= 1$	$\frac{11}{12} \times \frac{12}{11} =$ ■
$\frac{1}{3} \times 3 =$ ■	$\frac{3}{5} \times \frac{5}{3} =$ ■	$\frac{9}{20} \times$ ■ $= 1$	■ $\times \frac{17}{8} = 1$

4. What is true about the numerators and denominators in the fractions in Exercise 3?

Two numbers with a product of 1 are called **multiplicative inverses**, or **reciprocals**.

KEY CONCEPT — Inverse Property of Multiplication

Words The product of a number and its multiplicative inverse is 1.

Examples

Numbers	Algebra
$\frac{3}{4} \times \frac{4}{3} = 1$	$\frac{a}{b} \cdot \frac{b}{a} = 1$, for $a, b \neq 0$

EXAMPLES Find Multiplicative Inverses

1 Find the multiplicative inverse of $\frac{2}{5}$.

$\frac{2}{5} \cdot \frac{5}{2} = 1$ Multiply $\frac{2}{5}$ by $\frac{5}{2}$ to get the product 1.

The multiplicative inverse of $\frac{2}{5}$ is $\frac{5}{2}$, or $2\frac{1}{2}$.

2 Find the multiplicative inverse of $2\frac{1}{3}$.

$2\frac{1}{3} = \frac{7}{3}$ Rename the mixed number as an improper fraction.

$\frac{7}{3} \cdot \frac{3}{7} = 1$ Multiply $\frac{7}{3}$ by $\frac{3}{7}$ to get the product 1.

The multiplicative inverse of $2\frac{1}{3}$ is $\frac{3}{7}$.

CHECK Your Progress

Find the multiplicative inverse of each number.

a. $\frac{5}{6}$ b. $1\frac{1}{2}$ c. 8 d. $\frac{4}{3}$

In Chapter 4, you learned to solve equations using the Addition, Subtraction, and Division Properties of Equality. You can also solve equations by multiplying each side by the same number. This is called the **Multiplication Property of Equality**.

STUDY TIP

Fractions The fraction bar indicates division. So, $\frac{x}{2}$ means x *divided by 2.*

KEY CONCEPT — Multiplication Property of Equality

Words If you multiply each side of an equation by the same nonzero number, the two sides remain equal.

Examples

Numbers	Algebra	
$5 = 5$	$\frac{x}{2} = -3$	$\frac{2}{3}x = 4$
$5 \cdot 2 = 5 \cdot 2$	$\frac{x}{2}(2) = -3(2)$	$\frac{3}{2} \cdot \frac{2}{3}x = \frac{3}{2} \cdot 4$
$10 = 10$	$x = -6$	$x = 6$

EXAMPLES Solve a Division Equation

3 **Solve $7 = \frac{n}{4}$. Check your solution.**

$7 = \frac{n}{4}$ Write the equation.

$7 \cdot 4 = \frac{n}{4} \cdot 4$ Multiply each side of the equation by 4.

$28 = n$ Simplify.

Check $7 = \frac{n}{4}$ Write the original equation.

$7 \stackrel{?}{=} \frac{28}{4}$ Replace n with 28.

$7 = 7$ ✔ Is this sentence true?

4 **Solve $\frac{d}{3.5} = 4.2$.**

$\frac{d}{3.5} = 4.2$ Write the equation.

$\frac{d}{3.5} \cdot 3.5 = 4.2 \cdot 3.5$ Multiply each side by 3.5.

$d = 14.7$ Simplify.

The solution is 14.7.

Check $\frac{d}{3.5} = 4.2$ Write the original equation.

$\frac{14.7}{3.5} \stackrel{?}{=} 4.2$ Replace d with 14.7.

$4.2 = 4.2$ ✔ Is this sentence true?

CHECK Your Progress

Solve each equation. Check your solution.

e. $6 = \frac{m}{8}$ f. $\frac{p}{2.8} = 1.5$ g. $\frac{k}{4.7} = 2.3$

EXAMPLE Solve a Multiplication Equation

5 **Solve $\frac{5}{6}x = 15$. Check your solution.**

$\frac{5}{6}x = 15$	Write the equation.
$\left(\frac{6}{5}\right) \cdot \frac{5}{6}x = \left(\frac{6}{5}\right) \cdot 15$	Multiply each side by the reciprocal of $\frac{5}{6}$, $\frac{6}{5}$.
$\frac{\cancel{6}^{1}}{\cancel{5}_{1}} \cdot \frac{\cancel{5}^{1}}{\cancel{6}_{1}}x = \frac{6}{\cancel{5}_{1}} \cdot \cancel{15}^{3}$	Divide by common factors.
$x = 18$	Simplify.
Check $\frac{5}{6}x = 15$	Write the original equation.
$\frac{5}{6}(18) \stackrel{?}{=} 15$	Replace x with 18.
$15 = 15$ ✔	Is this sentence true?

STUDY TIP

Fractions as Coefficients
The expression $\frac{5}{6}x$ can be read as $\frac{5}{6}$ of x, $\frac{5}{6}$ multiplied by x, $5x$ divided by 6, or $\frac{x}{6}$ multiplied by 5.

CHECK Your Progress

Solve each equation. Check your solution.

h. $\frac{1}{2}x = 8$

i. $\frac{3}{4}x = 9$

j. $\frac{7}{8}x = 21$

TEST EXAMPLE

6 **GRIDDABLE** **Valerie needs $\frac{2}{3}$ yard of fabric to make each hat for the school play. How many hats can she make with 6 yards of fabric?**

Read the Test Item

Each hat needs $\frac{2}{3}$ yard of fabric. Given the number of hats, you would multiply by $\frac{2}{3}$ to find the number of yards of fabric needed.

Solve the Test Item

Write and solve a multiplication equation.

$\frac{2}{3}n = 6$	Write the equation.
$\left(\frac{3}{2}\right) \cdot \frac{2}{3}n = \left(\frac{3}{2}\right) \cdot 6$	Multiply each side by $\frac{3}{2}$.
$n = 9$	Simplify.

Fill in the Grid

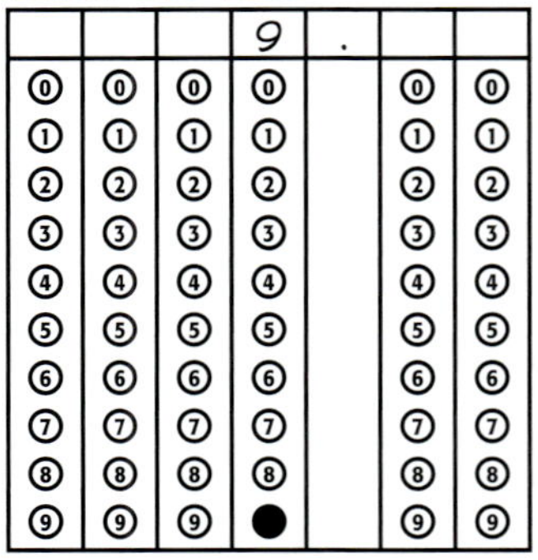

Test-Taking Tip

Griddable Be sure to check your answer. Then, at the top of the grid, write 9 in the answer boxes with respect to the given decimal point. Answers of 9.0 and 9.00 are also acceptable.

CHECK Your Progress

k. **GRIDDABLE** Wilson has 9 pounds of trail mix. How many $\frac{3}{4}$-pound bags of trail mix can he make?

Online Personal Tutor at tx.msmath2.com

CHECK Your Understanding

Examples 1, 2 (p. 306)

Find the multiplicative inverse of each number.

1. $\frac{8}{5}$
2. $\frac{2}{9}$
3. $5\frac{4}{5}$
4. 9

Examples 3–5 (p. 307–308)

Solve each equation. Check your solution.

5. $\frac{k}{16} = 2$
6. $4 = \frac{y}{3}$
7. $\frac{b}{8.2} = 2.5$
8. $0.5 = \frac{h}{3.6}$
9. $\frac{3}{8}a = 12$
10. $6 = \frac{4}{7}x$

Example 5 (p. 308)

11. **FRUIT** If three-fourths of the fruit in a refrigerator are apples and there are 24 apples, the number of pieces of fruit in the refrigerator is given by the equation $\frac{3}{4}f = 24$. How many pieces of fruit are in the refrigerator?

Example 6 (p. 308)

12. **TEST PRACTICE** Dillon deposited $\frac{3}{4}$ of the money he received on his birthday into the bank. If the deposit slip shows how much Dillon deposited, how much money in dollars did he receive for his birthday?

Exercises

HOMEWORK HELP

For Exercises	See Examples
13–20	1, 2
21–26 33–34	3, 4
27–32	5
51–52	6

Find the multiplicative inverse of each number.

13. $\frac{5}{6}$
14. $\frac{11}{2}$
15. $\frac{1}{6}$
16. $\frac{1}{10}$
17. 3
18. 14
19. $5\frac{1}{8}$
20. $6\frac{2}{3}$

Solve each equation. Check your solution.

21. $\frac{x}{12} = 3$
22. $28 = \frac{d}{4}$
23. $\frac{b}{2.4} = 6$
24. $5 = \frac{w}{4.9}$
25. $0.8 = \frac{h}{3.6}$
26. $\frac{m}{4.6} = 2.8$
27. $\frac{2}{5}t = 12$
28. $24 = \frac{3}{4}a$
29. $\frac{7}{8}k = \frac{5}{6}$
30. $\frac{2}{3} = \frac{8}{3}b$
31. $\frac{1}{2}g = 3\frac{1}{3}$
32. $\frac{3}{5}c = 6\frac{1}{4}$

33. **DISTANCE** The distance d Olimpia travels in her car while driving 55 miles per hour for 2.5 hours is given by the equation $\frac{d}{2.5} = 55$. How far did she travel?

34. **ANIMALS** An adult Fitch ferret weighs about 1.8 kilograms. To find its weight in pounds p, you can use the equation $\frac{p}{1.8} = 2.2$. How many pounds does an adult Fitch ferret weigh?

Solve each equation. Check your solution.

35. $\frac{a}{-5} = 15$

36. $-8 = \frac{r}{-2}$

37. $34.5 = \frac{5}{6}m$

38. $\frac{5}{7}x = -1.5$

39. $\frac{1}{4}t = \frac{3}{8}$

40. $\frac{3}{8}m = 1\frac{1}{2}$

Real-World Link The state bird of Texas is the Northern Mockingbird. Adult birds may learn and reproduce up to 200 songs.
Source: dlia.org

For Exercises 41–46, define a variable and write an equation. Then solve.

41. **BIRDS** Texas has 540 species of birds. This is about $\frac{3}{4}$ of all species found in the U.S. How many species of birds are found in the U.S.?

42. **MUSEUMS** Twenty-four students brought their permission slips to attend the class field trip to the local art museum. If this represented $\frac{4}{5}$ of the class, how many students are in the class?

43. **MEASUREMENT** If one serving of cooked rice is $\frac{3}{4}$ cup, how many servings will $16\frac{1}{2}$ cups of rice yield?

44. **SNOWFALL** At noon, snow began falling at the rate of $\frac{1}{2}$ inch an hour. If it continued falling at this rate, when was there a total of $2\frac{3}{4}$ inches of snow on the ground?

45. **SLEEP** The average person spends $\frac{1}{3}$ of their life asleep. According to this, if a person has spent 26 years asleep, how old are they?

EXTRA PRACTICE
See pages 732, 760.
Math Online
Self-Check Quiz at
tx.msmath2.com

46. **ANALYZE TABLES** Tierra recorded the distance she ran each day last week. If she ran $\frac{5}{6}$ of her weekly running goal, what was her running goal?

Distance Ran in One Week

Day	Distance (mi)
Monday	$1\frac{3}{4}$
Wednesday	2
Friday	$1\frac{1}{2}$
Saturday	$2\frac{1}{4}$

H.O.T. Problems

47. **REASONING** Complete the statement: If $8 = \frac{m}{4}$, then $m - 12 = $ ■. Explain your reasoning.

48. **Which One Doesn't Belong?** Identify the pair of numbers that does not belong with the other three. Explain.

$\frac{7}{8}, \frac{8}{7}$	$5, \frac{1}{5}$	$\frac{2}{3}, 3$	$\frac{10}{3}, \frac{3}{10}$

49. **CHALLENGE** The formula for the area A of a triangle is $A = \frac{1}{2}bh$, where b is the base of the triangle and h is the height. Find the value of b in terms of A and h. Justify your answer using the properties of equality.

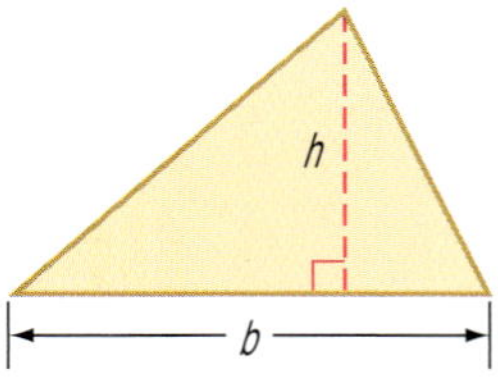

50. **WRITING IN MATH** Explain the Multiplication Property of Equality. Then give an example of an equation in which you would use this property to solve the equation.

TEST PRACTICE

51. Audrey drove 200 miles in 3.5 hours. Which equation can you use to find the rate r at which Audrey was traveling?

A $200 = 3.5r$

B $200 \bullet 3.5 = r$

C $\frac{r}{3.5} = 200$

D $200r = 3.5$

52. **GRIDDABLE** The table shows the results of a survey.

Music Preference	
Type	**Fraction of Students**
pop	$\frac{1}{8}$
country	$\frac{1}{3}$
jazz	$\frac{1}{6}$
rap	$\frac{3}{8}$

If there are 420 students in the school, how many students like to listen to country music?

Spiral Review

Multiply. Write in simplest form. (Lesson 6-5)

53. $\frac{3}{8} \times \frac{4}{9}$

54. $1\frac{1}{2} \times 6$

55. $2\frac{2}{5} \times \frac{1}{6}$

56. $1\frac{1}{2} \times 1\frac{7}{9}$

57. **COOKING** Lawana had $4\frac{2}{3}$ cups of chopped walnuts. She used $1\frac{1}{4}$ cups in a recipe. How many cups of chopped walnuts are left? (Lesson 6-3)

Write each percent as a decimal. (Lesson 5-7)

58. 25%

59. 8%

60. 25.6%

61. 123%

62. **FARMING** A farmer has a rectangular pumpkin field with a perimeter of 3,800 feet. If the width of the pumpkin field is 800 feet, what is the length of the field? (Lesson 4-6)

Write each number in standard form. (Lesson 3-7)

63. 4.72×10^3

64. 8.1×10^5

65. 1.17×10^4

66. **TIME** The table below shows the time needed to complete 4 art projects. If the pattern continues, how much time is needed to complete the fifth art project? (Lesson 2-6)

Project	1	2	3	4	5
Time (min)	8	25	42	59	■

GET READY for the Next Lesson

PREREQUISITE SKILL **Estimate.** (Lesson 6-1)

67. $18\frac{1}{6} \div 3$

68. $24\frac{3}{8} \div 11\frac{7}{9}$

69. $\frac{2}{11} \div \frac{11}{12}$

70. $\frac{9}{10} \div \frac{6}{7}$

READING Word Problems

Meaning of Division

You know that one meaning of division is to *put objects into equal groups*. But there are other meanings too. Look for these meanings when you're solving a word problem.

To share

Zach and his friend are going to share 3 apples equally. How many apples will each boy have?

To take away equal amounts

Isabel is making bookmarks from a piece of ribbon. Each bookmark is 6.5 centimeters long. How many bookmarks can she make from a piece of ribbon that is 26 centimeters long?

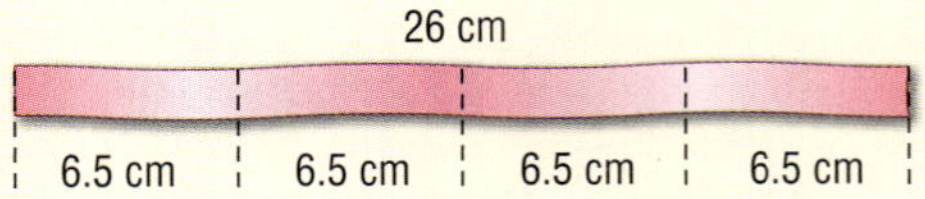

To find how many times greater

The Nile River, the longest river on Earth, is 4,160 miles long. The Rio Grande River is 1,900 miles long. About how many times longer is the Nile than the Rio Grande?

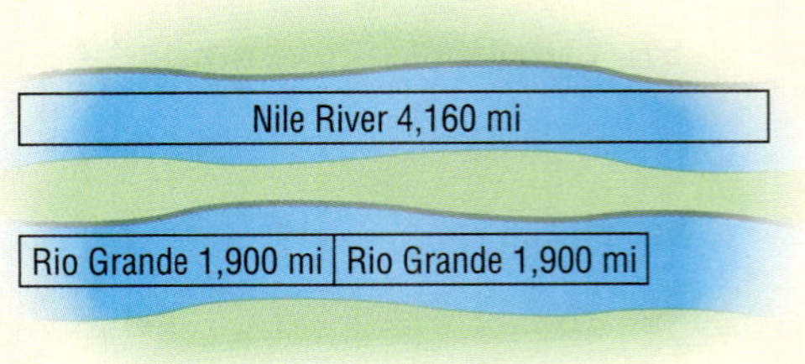

PRACTICE

1. Solve each problem above.

Identify the meaning of division shown in each problem. Then solve the problem.

2. A landscape architect wants to make a border along one side of a garden using bricks that are 0.25 meter long. If the garden is 11.25 meters long, how many bricks does she need?
3. The Jackson family wants to buy a flat-screen television that costs $1,200. They plan to pay in six equal payments. What will be the amount of each payment?
4. A full-grown blue whale can weigh 150 tons. An adult African elephant weighs about 5 tons. How many times greater does a blue whale weigh than an African elephant?
5. Each story in an office building is about 4 meters tall. The Eiffel Tower in Paris, France, is 300 meters tall. How many stories tall is the Eiffel Tower?

6-7 Dividing Fractions and Mixed Numbers

Main IDEA

Divide fractions and mixed numbers.

Targeted TEKS 7.2 The student adds, subtracts, multiplies, or divides to solve problems and justify solutions. **(A) represent** multiplication and **division situations involving fractions** and decimals **with models, including concrete objects, pictures, words, and numbers.** *Also addresses TEKS 7.2(B), 7.13(D).*

MINI Lab

Cut two paper plates into four equal pieces each to show $2 \div \frac{1}{4}$.

1. How many $\frac{1}{4}$'s are in 2 plates?
2. What is $2 \div \frac{1}{4}$?
3. How would you model $3 \div \frac{1}{2}$?
4. What is $3 \div \frac{1}{2}$?
5. What is true about $3 \div \frac{1}{2}$ and 3×2?
6. Write a rule for dividing by a fraction.

You already know that dividing 8 by 2 gives the same result as multiplying 8 by $\frac{1}{2}$, which is the reciprocal of 2.

reciprocals

$$8 \div 2 = 4 \qquad 8 \cdot \frac{1}{2} = 4$$

In the same way, dividing 4 by $\frac{1}{3}$ is the same as multiplying 4 by the reciprocal of $\frac{1}{3}$, or 3. This pattern is true for any fraction.

KEY CONCEPT — Divide by Fractions

Words To divide by a fraction, multiply by its multiplicative inverse, or reciprocal.

Examples

Numbers $\frac{7}{8} \div \frac{3}{4} = \frac{7}{8} \cdot \frac{4}{3}$

Algebra $\frac{a}{b} \div \frac{c}{d} = \frac{a}{b} \cdot \frac{d}{c}$, where $b, c, d \neq 0$

Concepts in Motion
BrainPOP® tx.msmath2.com

EXAMPLE Divide by a Fraction

1 **Find $\frac{3}{4} \div \frac{1}{2}$. Write in simplest form.**

$\frac{3}{4} \div \frac{1}{2} = \frac{3}{4} \cdot \frac{2}{1}$ Multiply by the reciprocal of $\frac{1}{2}$, which is $\frac{2}{1}$.

$= \frac{3}{\cancel{4}_2} \cdot \frac{\cancel{2}^1}{1}$ Divide 4 and 2 by their GCF, 2.

$= \frac{3}{2}$ or $1\frac{1}{2}$ Multiply.

CHECK Your Progress **Divide. Write in simplest form.**

a. $\frac{3}{4} \div \frac{1}{4}$ b. $\frac{4}{5} \div \frac{8}{9}$ c. $\frac{5}{6} \div \frac{2}{3}$

To divide by a mixed number, rename the mixed number as an improper fraction.

EXAMPLES Divide by Mixed Numbers

Real-World Link
A surveyor can survey a line for nine miles before having to use spherical geometry and trigonometry to correct for Earth's curved surface.
Source: *Kansas Society of Land Surveyors*

2 **SURVEYING** **Twelve acres of land are to be divided into $1\frac{1}{2}$-acre lots. How many lots will there be?**

Words	12 acres are divided into $1\frac{1}{2}$- acre lots		
Expression	12	÷	$1\frac{1}{2}$

$12 \div 1\frac{1}{2} = 12 \div \frac{3}{2}$ Rename $1\frac{1}{2}$ as an improper fraction.

$= 12 \cdot \frac{2}{3}$ Multiply by the reciprocal of $\frac{3}{2}$, which is $\frac{2}{3}$.

$= \frac{\overset{4}{\cancel{12}}}{1} \cdot \frac{2}{\underset{1}{\cancel{3}}}$ Divide out common factors.

$= 8$ Multiply.

Check
The model shows 12 acres divided into $1\frac{1}{2}$-acre lots.

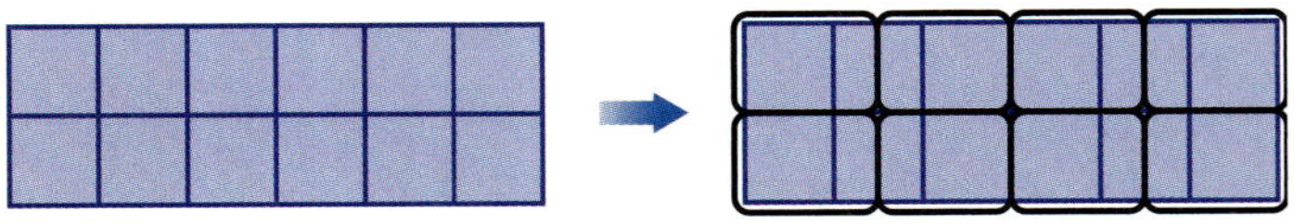

$12 \div 1\frac{1}{2} = 8$

So, there will be 8 lots. ✔

3 **Find $\frac{2}{3} \div 3\frac{1}{3}$. Write in simplest form.**

Estimate $\frac{1}{2} \div 3 = \frac{1}{2} \times \frac{1}{3}$ or $\frac{1}{6}$

$\frac{2}{3} \div 3\frac{1}{3} = \frac{2}{3} \div \frac{10}{3}$ Rename $3\frac{1}{3}$ as an improper fraction.

$= \frac{2}{3} \cdot \frac{3}{10}$ Multiply by the reciprocal of $\frac{10}{3}$, which is $\frac{3}{10}$.

$= \frac{\overset{1}{\cancel{2}}}{\underset{1}{\cancel{3}}} \cdot \frac{\overset{1}{\cancel{3}}}{\underset{5}{\cancel{10}}}$ Divide out common factors.

$= \frac{1}{5}$ Multiply.

Check for Reasonableness $\frac{1}{5}$ is close to $\frac{1}{6}$ ✔

CHECK Your Progress

Divide. Write in simplest form.

d. $5 \div 1\frac{1}{3}$ **e.** $-\frac{3}{4} \div 1\frac{1}{2}$ **f.** $2\frac{1}{3} \div 5$

g. **NUTS** $5\frac{1}{4}$ pounds of cashews will be divided into $\frac{3}{4}$ pound bags. How many such bags can be made?

Real-World EXAMPLE

4 **WOODWORKING** Students in a woodworking class are making butterfly houses. The side pieces of the house need to be $8\frac{1}{4}$ inches long. How many side pieces can be cut from a board measuring $49\frac{1}{2}$ inches long?

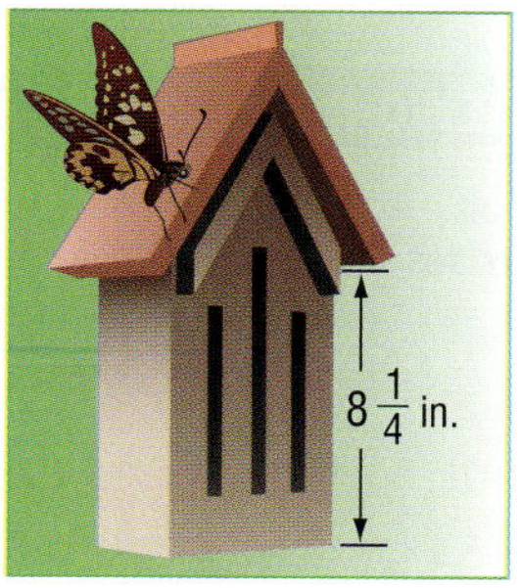

To find how many side pieces can be cut, divide $49\frac{1}{2}$ by $8\frac{1}{4}$.

Estimate Use compatible numbers. $48 \div 8 = 6$

$$49\frac{1}{2} \div 8\frac{1}{4} = \frac{99}{2} \div \frac{33}{4}$$ Rename the mixed numbers as improper fractions.

$$= \frac{99}{2} \cdot \frac{4}{33}$$ Multiply by the reciprocal of $\frac{33}{4}$, which is $\frac{4}{33}$.

$$= \frac{\overset{3}{\cancel{99}}}{\underset{1}{\cancel{2}}} \cdot \frac{\overset{2}{\cancel{4}}}{\underset{1}{\cancel{33}}}$$ Divide out common factors.

$$= \frac{6}{1} \text{ or } 6$$ Multiply.

So, 6 side pieces can be cut.

Check for Reasonableness The answer matches the estimate. ✔

CHECK Your Progress

h. **FOOD** Suppose a small box of cereal contains $12\frac{2}{3}$ cups of cereal. How many $1\frac{1}{3}$-cup servings are in the box?

i. **FLOOR PLANS** The area of a rectangular bedroom is $108\frac{15}{32}$ square feet. If the width of the bedroom is $9\frac{3}{4}$ feet, find the length.

Online Personal Tutor at tx.msmath2.com

CHECK Your Understanding

Examples 1–4 (pp. 313–315)

Divide. Write in simplest form.

1. $\frac{1}{8} \div \frac{1}{3}$
2. $\frac{3}{5} \div \frac{1}{4}$
3. $3 \div \frac{6}{7}$
4. $\frac{3}{4} \div 6$
5. $\frac{1}{2} \div 7\frac{1}{2}$
6. $\frac{4}{7} \div 1\frac{2}{7}$
7. $5\frac{3}{5} \div 4\frac{2}{3}$
8. $6\frac{1}{2} \div 3\frac{5}{7}$

Example 2 (p. 314)

9. **CRAFTS** Damon is making bookmarks like the one shown from a 15-yard spool of ribbon. How many bookmarks can he make?

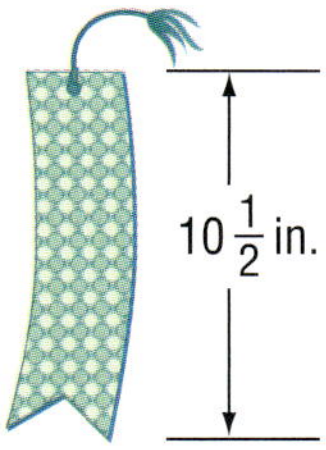

Example 4 (p. 315)

10. **WALKING** On Saturday, Lindsay walked $3\frac{1}{2}$ miles in $1\frac{2}{5}$ hours. What was her walking pace, in miles per hour?

Exercises

HOMEWORK HELP	
For Exercises	See Examples
11–14	1
15–20	2
21–28	3
29–32	4

Divide. Write in simplest form.

11. $\frac{3}{8} \div \frac{6}{7}$
12. $\frac{5}{9} \div \frac{5}{6}$
13. $\frac{2}{3} \div \frac{1}{2}$
14. $\frac{7}{8} \div \frac{3}{4}$
15. $6 \div \frac{1}{2}$
16. $\frac{4}{9} \div 2$
17. $2\frac{2}{3} \div 4$
18. $5 \div 1\frac{1}{3}$

19. **FOOD** Mason has 8 cups of popcorn kernels to divide into $\frac{2}{3}$-cup portions. How many portions will there be?

20. **MOVIES** Cheryl is organizing her movie collection. If each movie case is $\frac{3}{4}$ inch wide, how many movies can fit on a shelf 5 feet wide?

Divide. Write in simplest form.

21. $\frac{2}{3} \div 2\frac{1}{2}$
22. $\frac{8}{9} \div 5\frac{1}{3}$
23. $4\frac{1}{2} \div 6\frac{3}{4}$
24. $5\frac{2}{7} \div 2\frac{1}{7}$
25. $3\frac{4}{5} \div 1\frac{1}{3}$
26. $9\frac{1}{2} \div 2\frac{5}{6}$
27. $5\frac{1}{5} \div \frac{2}{3}$
28. $6\frac{7}{8} \div \frac{3}{4}$

29. **ICE CREAM** Vinh bought $4\frac{1}{2}$ gallons of ice cream to serve at his birthday party. If a pint is $\frac{1}{8}$ of a gallon, how many pint-sized servings can be made?

30. **BEVERAGES** William has $8\frac{1}{4}$ cups of fruit juice. If he divides the juice into $\frac{3}{4}$-cup servings, how many servings will he have?

Real-World Link The swamp rabbit, weighing 1.5 to 3.0 kilograms, is commonly found in eastern Texas.
Source: *The Mammals of Texas-Onlne Edition*

MAMMALS For Exercises 31 and 32, use the table that shows the maximum weights of three mammals common to Texas.

Mammal	Maximum Weight (lb)
Black-tailed Jackrabbit	$8\frac{4}{5}$
Bobcat	$19\frac{4}{5}$
Swamp Rabbit	$6\frac{3}{5}$

Source: *The Mammals of Texas*

31. How many times heavier is the Bobcat than the Swamp Rabbit?
32. How many times heavier is the Black-tailed Jackrabbit than the Swamp Rabbit?

Evaluate each verbal expression.

33. one-half divided by two-fifths
34. five-eighths divided by one-fourth
35. three-fifths divided by two
36. two and one-sixth divided by two-thirds

37. **PIZZA** A concession stand sells three types of pizza. The diagram shows how much pizza of each type is left after the concession stand was open for one hour. If the pizza is sold in slices that are $\frac{1}{8}$ of a whole pizza, how many more slices can be sold?

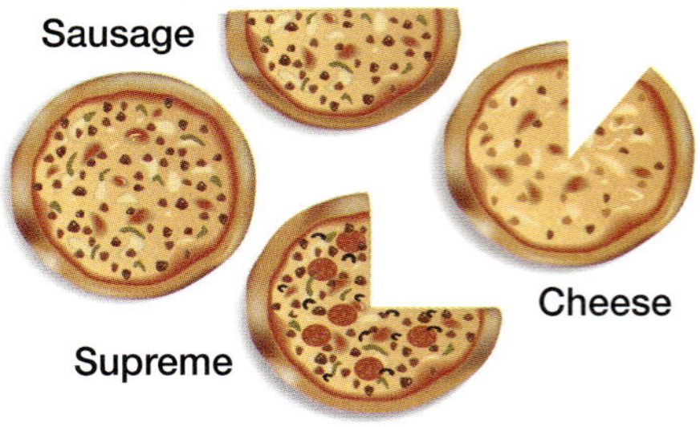

ALGEBRA **Evaluate each expression if $g = \frac{1}{6}$, $h = \frac{1}{2}$, and $j = 3\frac{2}{3}$.**

38. $j \div h$
39. $g \div j$
40. $3g \div h$
41. $h \div \left(\frac{1}{2}j\right)$

42. **SHOPPING** A supermarket sells pretzels in $\frac{3}{4}$-ounce snack-sized bags or $12\frac{1}{2}$-ounce regular-sized bags. How many times larger is the regular-sized bag than the snack-sized bag?

43. **RECIPE** A recipe calls for $2\frac{2}{3}$ cups of brown sugar and $\frac{2}{3}$ cup of confectioner's sugar. How many times greater is the number of cups of brown sugar in the recipe than of confectioner's sugar?

SCHOOL **For Exercises 44 and 45, use the table that shows the number of hours students spend studying each week during the school year.**

Weekly Study Hours

Hours	Fraction of Students
none	$\frac{1}{50}$
1–2	$\frac{2}{25}$
3–5	$\frac{11}{50}$
6–7	$\frac{17}{100}$
8–10	$\frac{1}{5}$
Over 10	$\frac{1}{5}$
Not sure	$\frac{3}{25}$

Source: *Time Magazine*

44. How many times greater was the number of students who spent over 10 hours each week studying than those who spent only 1–2 hours each week studying?

45. How many times greater was the number of students who spent 3 or more hours each week studying than those who spent less than 3 hours each week studying?

46. **SCHOOL SUPPLIES** Tara bought a dozen folders. She took $\frac{1}{3}$ of the dozen and then divided the remaining folders equally among her four friends. What fraction of the dozen did each of her four friends receive and how many folders was this per person?

EXTRA PRACTICE
See pages 732, 760.
Math Online
Self-Check Quiz at tx.msmath2.com

47. **WEATHER** A meteorologist has issued a thunderstorm warning. So far, the storm has traveled 35 miles in $\frac{1}{2}$ hour. If it is currently 5:00 P.M., and the storm is 105 miles away from you, at what time will the storm reach you? Explain how you solved the problem.

H.O.T. Problems

48. **CHALLENGE** Will the quotient $7\frac{1}{6} \div 3\frac{2}{3}$ be a fraction less than 1 or greater than 1? Explain your reasoning.

49. **SELECT A TOOL** Reynaldo cut a rope to make the running knot shown. The rope used to make the knot was $1\frac{1}{2}$ feet long and was $\frac{3}{4}$ of the original rope length. Which of the following tools could be used to determine the rope's original length? Justify your selection(s). Then use your tool(s) to find the length.

paper and pencil | model | calculator | real object

50. **FIND THE ERROR** Evan and José are finding $\frac{3}{4} \div \frac{7}{8}$. Who is correct? Explain your reasoning.

Evan

José

51. **WRITING IN MATH** If you divide a proper fraction by another proper fraction, is it possible to get a mixed number as an answer? Explain your reasoning.

TEST PRACTICE

52. The Corbett family owns 300 acres of land that they plan to rent to people for their horses. How many $7\frac{1}{2}$-acre lots can they make using the 300 acres?

A 21 **C** $40\frac{1}{2}$

B 40 **D** $292\frac{1}{2}$

53. How many $1\frac{1}{8}$-pound boxes of peanuts can be made using $6\frac{3}{4}$ pounds of peanuts?

F 4 **H** 6

G 5 **J** 7

Spiral Review

Find the multiplicative inverse of each number. (Lesson 6-6)

54. $\frac{6}{7}$ 55. $\frac{4}{13}$ 56. 8 57. $5\frac{1}{4}$

58. Find $\frac{1}{10} \times \frac{5}{8}$. Write in simplest form. (Lesson 6-5)

59. **GEOMETRY** Find the length of a rectangular flower bed if the perimeter is 12 feet and the width is 1.5 feet. (Lesson 4-6)

60. **ANIMALS** An elephant herd can move 50 miles in a day. At this rate, about how many miles can an elephant herd move each hour? (Lesson 1-1)

Cross-Curricular Project

Math and Health

A Well-Balanced Diet It's time to complete your project. Use the data you have gathered about the food you eat and about the Food Pyramid to prepare a Web page or poster. Be sure to include a chart and calculations with your project.

Math Online **Cross-Curricular Project at** tx.msmath2.com

CHAPTER 6

Study Guide and Review

STUDY TO GO Download Vocabulary Review from tx.msmath2.com

FOLDABLES Study Organizer — GET READY to Study

Be sure the following Key Concepts are noted in your Foldable.

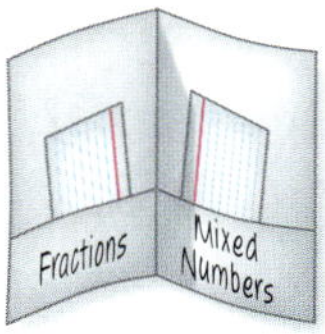

Key Concepts

Estimating with Fractions (Lesson 6-1)

- When the numerator is much smaller than the denominator, round the fraction to 0.
- When the numerator is about half of the denominator, round the fraction to $\frac{1}{2}$.
- When the numerator is almost as large as the denominator, round the fraction to 1.

Adding and Subtracting Fractions

(Lessons 6-2 and 6-3)

- To add or subtract like fractions, add or subtract the numerators and write the result over the denominator.
- To add or subtract unlike fractions, rename the fractions using the LCD. Then add or subtract as with like fractions.
- To add or subtract mixed numbers, first add or subtract the fractions. If necessary, rename them using the LCD. Then add or subtract the whole numbers and simplify if necessary.

Multiplying and Dividing Fractions

(Lessons 6-5 and 6-7)

- To multiply fractions, multiply the numerators and multiply the denominators.
- The product of a number and its multiplicative inverse is 1.
- To divide by a fraction, multiply by its multiplicative inverse, or reciprocal.

Solving Equations (Lesson 6-6)

If you multiply each side of an equation by the same nonzero number, the two sides remain equal.

Key Vocabulary

compatible numbers (p. 280)
like fractions (p. 284)
multiplicative inverse (p. 306)
reciprocal (p. 306)
unlike fractions (p. 285)

Vocabulary Check

Choose the correct term or number to complete each sentence.

1. To add like fractions, add the (numerators, denominators).
2. The symbol $\approx$ means is (*approximately*, *exactly*) *equal to*.
3. When dividing by a fraction, multiply by its (value, reciprocal).
4. When estimating, if the numerator of a fraction is much smaller than the denominator, round the fraction to $\left(0, \frac{1}{2}\right)$.
5. Fractions with different denominators are called (like, unlike) fractions.
6. The multiplicative inverse of $\frac{5}{6}$ is $\left(\frac{6}{5}, -\frac{5}{6}\right)$.
7. The mixed number $2\frac{4}{7}$ can be renamed as $\left(2\frac{7}{7}, 1\frac{11}{7}\right)$.
8. When multiplying fractions, multiply the numerators and (multiply, keep) the denominators.
9. The reciprocal of $\frac{1}{3}$ is $(-3, 3)$.
10. The fractions $\frac{4}{16}$ and $\frac{2}{4}$ are (like, unlike) fractions.
11. Another word for multiplicative inverse is (reciprocal, denominator).
12. The fraction $\frac{x}{2}$ can be read *x multiplied by* $\left(2, \frac{1}{2}\right)$.

Chapter 6 Study Guide and Review

Lesson-by-Lesson Review

6-1 Estimating with Fractions (pp. 278–283)

Estimate.

13. $2\frac{9}{10} \div 1\frac{1}{8}$
14. $6\frac{2}{9} - 5\frac{1}{7}$
15. $\frac{13}{15} \times \frac{1}{5}$
16. $\frac{1}{2} + \frac{3}{8}$
17. $\frac{1}{2} \cdot 25$
18. $15\frac{6}{7} \div 7\frac{1}{3}$
19. **CARPET** Gina wishes to carpet her living room. It has a length of $18\frac{5}{8}$ feet and the width of her living room is $9\frac{1}{2}$ feet. About how many square feet of carpet would be needed for her living room?
20. **FOOTBALL** Jamil practiced football for $1\frac{3}{4}$ hours on Saturday and $2\frac{2}{3}$ hours on Sunday. About how many more hours did he practice on Sunday than on Saturday?

Example 1 Estimate $5\frac{1}{12} + 2\frac{5}{6}$.

1 is much smaller than 12, so $5\frac{1}{2} \approx 5$.

5 is almost as large as 6, so $2\frac{5}{6} \approx 3$.

$5\frac{1}{12} + 2\frac{5}{6} \approx 5 + 3$ or 8

The sum is *about* 8.

Example 2 Estimate $\frac{7}{8} - \frac{4}{7}$.

7 is almost as large as 8, so $\frac{7}{8} \approx 1$.

4 is about half of 7, so $\frac{4}{7} \approx \frac{1}{2}$.

$\frac{7}{8} - \frac{4}{7} \approx 1 - \frac{1}{2}$ or $\frac{1}{2}$

The difference is *about* $\frac{1}{2}$.

6-2 Adding and Subtracting Fractions (pp. 284–289)

Add or subtract. Write in simplest form.

21. $\frac{2}{6} - \frac{1}{6}$
22. $\frac{3}{7} + \frac{9}{14}$
23. $\frac{1}{9} + \frac{5}{9}$
24. $\frac{9}{10} - \frac{3}{10}$
25. $\frac{5}{8} - \frac{5}{12}$
26. $\frac{3}{4} + \frac{7}{20}$
27. **RAIN** At 8 A.M., Della's rain gauge read $\frac{1}{8}$ inch. By 4 P.M., the gauge read $\frac{3}{4}$ inch. How much rain fell between 8 A.M. and 4 P.M.?
28. **PIZZA** Owen ate $\frac{1}{8}$ of a pizza Tuesday night. The next day, he ate an additional $\frac{1}{2}$ of the pizza. What fraction of the pizza has he eaten?

Example 3 Find $\frac{1}{6} + \frac{2}{3}$.

Use a model.

$\frac{1}{6}$

$+\frac{2}{3}$

$\frac{5}{6}$

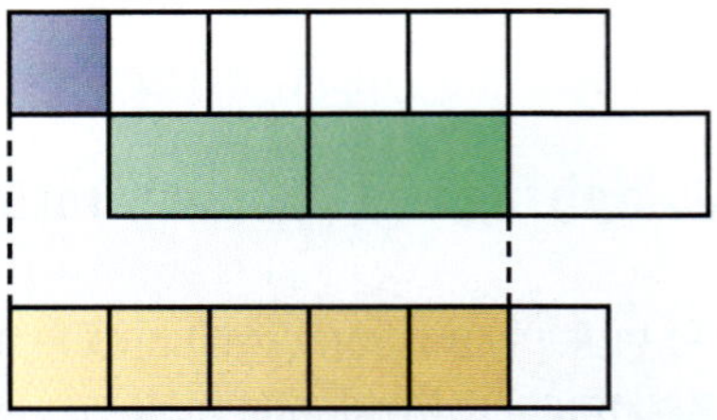

Example 4 Find $\frac{3}{10} - \frac{1}{4}$.

$\frac{3}{10} - \frac{1}{4} = \frac{6}{20} - \frac{5}{20}$ Rename the fractions using the LCD, 20.

$= \frac{1}{20}$ Subtract the numerators.

Mixed Problem Solving
For mixed problem-solving practice, see page 760.

6-3 Adding and Subtracting Mixed Numbers (pp. 290–294)

Add or subtract. Write in simplest form.

29. $3\frac{2}{15} + 6\frac{9}{15}$
30. $4\frac{1}{3} - 2\frac{2}{3}$
31. $8\frac{2}{7} + 1\frac{6}{7}$
32. $7\frac{11}{12} - 4\frac{3}{12}$
33. $7\frac{3}{5} - 5\frac{1}{3}$
34. $5\frac{3}{4} + 1\frac{1}{6}$
35. $3\frac{5}{8} + 11\frac{1}{2}$
36. $4\frac{3}{10} - 2\frac{4}{5}$
37. **BABY-SITTING** Lucas watched his little sister for $2\frac{1}{2}$ hours on Friday, $3\frac{2}{3}$ hours on Saturday, and $1\frac{3}{4}$ hours on Sunday. How many hours did Lucas watch his little sister?

Example 5 Find $5\frac{2}{3} + 3\frac{1}{2}$.

$5\frac{2}{3} + 3\frac{1}{2} = 5\frac{4}{6} + 3\frac{3}{6}$ Rename the fractions.

$= 8\frac{7}{6}$ Add the whole numbers and add the fractions.

$= 9\frac{1}{6}$ $8\frac{7}{6} = 8 + 1\frac{1}{6}$ or $9\frac{1}{6}$

Example 6 Find $4\frac{1}{5} - 2\frac{3}{5}$.

$4\frac{1}{5} - 2\frac{3}{5} = 3\frac{6}{5} - 2\frac{3}{5}$ Rename $4\frac{1}{5}$ as $3\frac{6}{5}$.

$= 1\frac{3}{5}$ Subtract the whole numbers and subtract the fractions.

6-4 PSI: Eliminate Possibilities (pp. 295–296)

Solve by eliminating possibilities.

38. **SCHOOL** It takes Beth 15 minutes to walk to school, $\frac{1}{2}$ mile away. What is her walking pace?
    - A 2 miles per hour
    - B 1 mile per hour
    - C 7.5 miles per hour
    - D 30 miles per hour
39. **COOKING** Which of the following would yield a larger batch of bagels?
    - F Multiply a recipe by $\frac{1}{2}$.
    - G Divide a recipe by $\frac{1}{2}$.
    - H Multiply a recipe by $\frac{3}{4}$.
    - J Divide a recipe by 3.

Example 7 **A group of friends went to a theme park. Six of the friends rode the Ferris wheel. If this was $\frac{2}{3}$ of the group, how many friends were in the group?**

- A 3
- B 6
- C 9
- D 12

Since 6 friends rode the Ferris wheel and this was $\frac{2}{3}$ of the total number of friends in the group, the number of friends in the group must be greater than 6. So, eliminate choices A and B.

If there were 12 friends in the group, the 6 that rode the Ferris wheel would represent $\frac{1}{2}$ of the group. So, eliminate choice D.

Choice C is the only remaining possibility. Since 6 out of 9 is $\frac{6}{9}$ or $\frac{2}{3}$, C is correct.

Study Guide and Review

6-5 Multiplying Fractions and Mixed Numbers (pp. 300–305)

Multiply. Write in simplest form.

40. $\frac{3}{5} \times \frac{2}{7}$
41. $\frac{5}{12} \times \frac{4}{9}$
42. $\frac{3}{5} \times \frac{10}{21}$
43. $4 \times \frac{13}{20}$
44. $2\frac{1}{3} \times \frac{3}{4}$
45. $4\frac{1}{2} \times 2\frac{1}{12}$
46. **TRACK AND FIELD** One lap around the high school track is $\frac{1}{4}$ of a mile. If Mika runs $4\frac{1}{2}$ laps, how far does she run?

Example 8 Find $\frac{5}{9} \times \frac{2}{3}$.

$\frac{5}{9} \times \frac{2}{3} = \frac{5 \times 2}{9 \times 3}$ Multiply the numerators and multiply the denominators.

$= \frac{10}{27}$ Simplify.

Example 9 Find $3\frac{1}{2} \times 2\frac{3}{4}$.

$3\frac{1}{2} \times 2\frac{3}{4} = \frac{7}{2} \times \frac{11}{4}$ Rename $3\frac{1}{2}$ and $2\frac{3}{4}$.

$= \frac{7 \times 11}{2 \times 4}$ Multiply the numerators and multiply the denominators.

$= \frac{77}{8}$ or $9\frac{5}{8}$ Simplify.

6-6 Algebra: Solving Equations (pp. 306–311)

Find the multiplicative inverse of each number.

47. $\frac{7}{12}$
48. 5
49. $3\frac{1}{3}$

Solve each equation. Check your solution.

50. $8 = \frac{w}{2}$
51. $\frac{4}{5}b = 12$
52. $-7.6 = \frac{n}{3}$
53. $\frac{x}{0.3} = 2.5$
54. **BOOKS** Of the books on a shelf, $\frac{2}{3}$ are mysteries. If there are 10 mystery books, how many books are on the shelf?

Example 10 Find the multiplicative inverse of $\frac{9}{5}$.

$\frac{9}{5} \cdot \frac{5}{9} = 1$ The product of $\frac{9}{5}$ and $\frac{5}{9}$ is 1.

The multiplicative inverse of $\frac{9}{5}$ is $\frac{5}{9}$.

Example 11 Solve $\frac{3}{4}g = 2$.

$\frac{3}{4}g = 2$ Write the equation.

$\frac{4}{3} \cdot \frac{3}{4}g = \frac{4}{3} \cdot 2$ Multiply each side by the reciprocal of $\frac{3}{4}$.

$g = \frac{8}{3}$ or $2\frac{2}{3}$ Simplify.

6-7 Dividing Fractions and Mixed Numbers (pp. 313–318)

Divide. Write in simplest form.

55. $\frac{3}{5} \div \frac{6}{7}$
56. $4 \div \frac{2}{3}$
57. $2\frac{3}{4} \div \frac{5}{6}$
58. $-\frac{2}{5} \div 3$
59. $4\frac{3}{10} \div 2\frac{1}{5}$
60. $-\frac{2}{7} \div \frac{8}{21}$
61. **MEASUREMENT** How many $\frac{1}{8}$-inch lengths are in $6\frac{3}{4}$ inches?

Example 12 Find $2\frac{4}{5} \div \frac{7}{10}$.

$2\frac{4}{5} \div \frac{7}{10} = \frac{14}{5} \div \frac{7}{10}$ Rename $2\frac{4}{5}$.

$= \frac{\overset{2}{\cancel{14}}}{\underset{1}{\cancel{5}}} \cdot \frac{\overset{2}{\cancel{10}}}{\underset{1}{\cancel{7}}}$ Multiply by the reciprocal of $\frac{7}{10}$.

$= \frac{4}{1}$ or 4 Simplify.

Chapter 6 Practice Test

Estimate.

1. $5\frac{7}{9} - 1\frac{2}{13}$
2. $3\frac{1}{12} + 6\frac{5}{7}$
3. $\frac{3}{7} \times \frac{13}{15}$
4. $5\frac{2}{3} \div 1\frac{4}{5}$

5. **BAKING** A restaurant uses $2\frac{3}{4}$ pounds of flour to make a batch of dinner rolls. About how many pounds of flour are needed if 3 batches of dinner rolls are to be made?

Add, subtract, multiply, or divide. Write in simplest form.

6. $\frac{4}{15} + \frac{8}{15}$
7. $\frac{7}{10} - \frac{1}{6}$
8. $\frac{5}{8} \times \frac{2}{5}$
9. $6 \times \frac{8}{21}$
10. $4\frac{5}{12} - 2\frac{1}{12}$
11. $6\frac{7}{9} + 3\frac{5}{12}$
12. $8\frac{4}{7} - 1\frac{5}{14}$
13. $4\frac{5}{6} \times 1\frac{2}{3}$
14. $\frac{8}{9} \div 5\frac{1}{3}$
15. $\frac{1}{6} \div 5$

16. **TEST PRACTICE** Seth drove $5\frac{3}{4}$ miles to the bank, $6\frac{1}{3}$ miles to the post office, and $4\frac{5}{6}$ miles to the park. What is the total distance Seth drove?

   A $15\frac{9}{13}$ miles

   B $\frac{7}{12}$ miles

   C $\frac{11}{12}$ miles

   D $16\frac{11}{12}$ miles

17. **SPORTS** Tyler's football practice lasted $2\frac{1}{2}$ hours. If $\frac{1}{4}$ of the time was spent catching passes, how many hours were spent catching passes?

18. **MOVING** The floor of a moving van is $11\frac{1}{3}$ feet long and $7\frac{5}{12}$ feet wide. Find the area of the moving van floor.

19. **TEST PRACTICE** Which model best represents $\frac{1}{3} \times \frac{1}{2}$?

   F

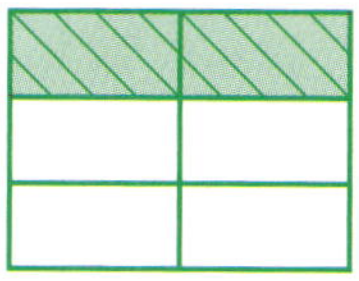

   G

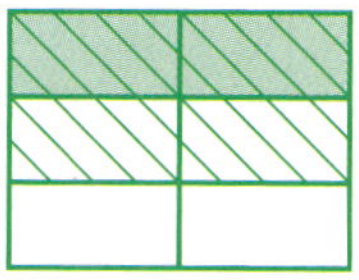

   H

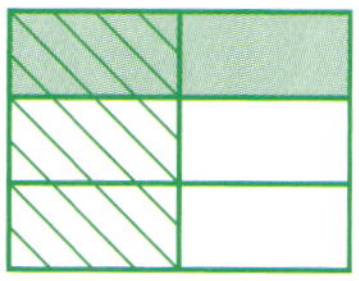

   J

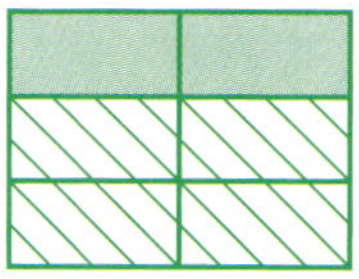

20. **MEASUREMENT** An ounce is $\frac{1}{16}$ of a pound. How many ounces are in $8\frac{3}{4}$ pounds?

ALGEBRA Solve each equation. Check your solution.

21. $\frac{y}{3.7} = 8.1$
22. $6 = \frac{2}{5}m$
23. $\frac{3}{4} = \frac{5}{8}x$
24. $3\frac{1}{6} = \frac{2}{3}p$

25. **TEST PRACTICE** Maria is making a mural that is $9\frac{2}{3}$ feet long. She wants to divide the mural into sections that are each $\frac{5}{8}$ foot. Which equation can be used to find n, the number of sections in Maria's mural?

   A $\frac{5}{8}n = 9\frac{2}{3}$

   B $9\frac{2}{3}n = \frac{5}{8}$

   C $\frac{5}{8} + n = 9\frac{2}{3}$

   D $n - \frac{5}{8} = 9\frac{2}{3}$

CHAPTER 6

Texas Test Practice

Cumulative, Chapters 1–6

Read each question. Then fill in the correct answer on the answer document provided by your teacher or on a sheet of paper.

1. Mrs. Brown needs to make two different desserts for a dinner party. The first recipe requires $2\frac{1}{4}$ cups of flour, and the second recipe requires $\frac{3}{4}$ cup less than the first. Which equation can be used to find n, the number of cups of flour needed for the second recipe?

   A $n = 2\frac{1}{4} - \frac{3}{4}$

   B $n = 2\frac{1}{4} \cdot \frac{3}{4}$

   C $n = 2\frac{1}{4} + \frac{3}{4}$

   D $n = 2\frac{1}{4} \div \frac{3}{4}$

2. Which model best represents the expression $\frac{1}{3} \times \frac{3}{4}$?

   F
   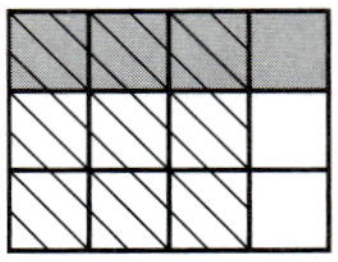

   H
   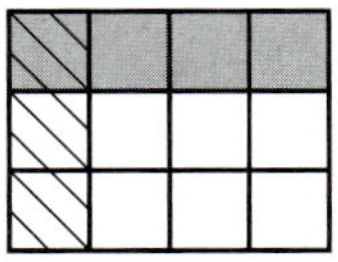

   G
   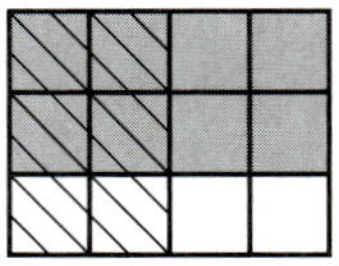

   J
   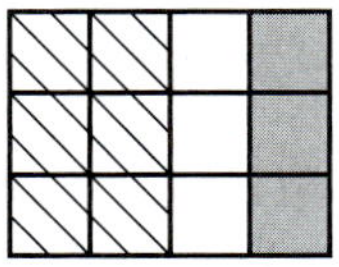

3. Kyle's hockey team has 6 members who are sixth graders, 9 members who are seventh graders, and 5 members who are eighth graders. What percent of the team members are eighth graders?

   A 5%

   B 20%

   C 25%

   D 30%

4. The fraction $\frac{5}{6}$ is found between which pair of fractions on a number line?

   F $\frac{1}{4}$ and $\frac{5}{8}$

   G $\frac{1}{3}$ and $\frac{4}{9}$

   H $\frac{11}{12}$ and $\frac{31}{36}$

   J $\frac{7}{12}$ and $\frac{17}{18}$

5. **GRIDDABLE** The table shows the distance Kelly swam each day last week. What was the total distance, in miles, Kelly swam last week?

Kelly's Swimming

Day	Distance (miles)
Monday	1.5
Tuesday	$2\frac{3}{4}$
Wednesday	2.3
Thursday	3.1
Friday	$1\frac{1}{4}$
Saturday	2.9
Sunday	$3\frac{1}{2}$

6. Lolita spent $74.94 on three sweaters. If each sweater cost the same amount, what was the price of one sweater?

   A $24.98

   B $37.47

   C $21.32

   D $23.89

Get Ready for the Texas Test
For test-taking strategies and more practice, see pages TX1–TX23.

7. What is the value of the expression $(3+4)^2 \div 7 - 2 \times 6$?

F -9 H 30

G -5 J 1

8. Which line contains the ordered pair $(-1, 2)$?

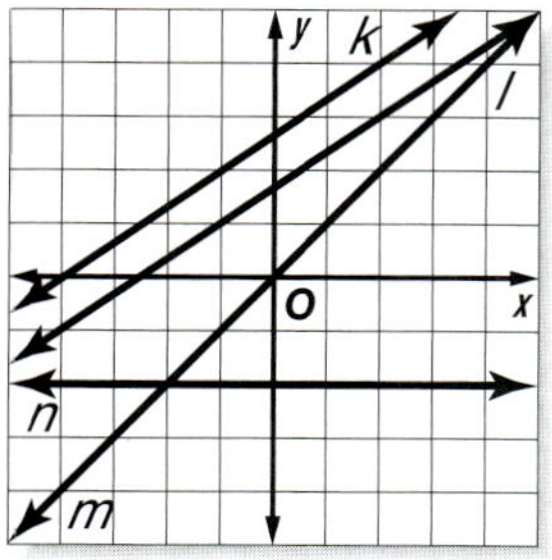

A Line k

B Line l

C Line m

D Line n

9. A pizza shop tried 45 new types of pizza during the past year and 20% of them became popular. Which best represents the fraction of pizzas that did NOT become popular?

F $\frac{1}{5}$ H $\frac{3}{5}$

G $\frac{4}{9}$ J $\frac{4}{5}$

TEST-TAKING TIP

Question 9 Be sure to pay attention to emphasized words, or words that are capitalized. In Question 9, you are asked to find which answer is *not* correct.

10. Which description shows the relationship between a term and n, its position in the sequence?

Position	1	2	3	4	5	n
Value of Term	5	9	13	17	21	

A Add 4 to n.

B Multiply n by 4 and add 1.

C Add 12 to n.

D Multiply n by 1 and add 4.

11. Nicholas has a comic book collection containing 72 books. He decided to sell 54 of his books at a garage sale. What percent of his collection did he sell?

F 80%

G 75%

H 72%

J 54%

Pre-AP

Record your answers on a sheet of paper. Show your work.

12. A box of laundry detergent contains 35 cups. It takes $1\frac{1}{4}$ cups per load of laundry.

a. Write an equation to represent how many loads you can wash with one box.

b. How many loads can you wash with one box?

c. How many loads can you wash with 3 boxes?

NEED EXTRA HELP?												
If You Missed Question...	1	2	3	4	5	6	7	8	9	10	11	12
Go to Lesson...	6-2	6-5	5-6	5-9	5-5	5-5	1-4	4-7	5-6	1-10	5-6	6-7
For Help with Test Objective...	6	1	2	1	1	1	1	3	2	2	2	1

Unit 3

Patterns, Relationships, and Algebraic Thinking

Focal Point

Solve problems involving direct proportional relationships involving number, geometry, and measurement.

CHAPTER 7
Ratios and Proportions

BIG Idea Solve problems involving direct proportional relationships.

BIG Idea Represent relationships in numerical, geometric, verbal, and symbolic form.

CHAPTER 8
Applying Percents

BIG Idea Solve problems involving direct proportional relationships.

BIG Idea Estimate and find solutions to application problems involving percent.

Cross-Curricular Project

Math and Science

Lions, Tigers, and Bears, Oh My! Are you ready to join a team of animal experts? As part of your application to be a zoo's new coordinator, you must complete several challenging tasks. You'll make decisions about what animals to purchase for the zoo. You'll gather data about animals you choose, including their weight and expected lifespan. Finally, you'll present your findings to the hiring committee. So pack up your gear and don't forget your algebra tool kit. This adventure is going to be wild!

Math Online **Log on to tx.msmath2.com to begin.**

CHAPTER 7

Ratios and Proportions

Knowledge and Skills

- Solve problems involving direct proportional relationships. **TEKS 7.3**
- Represent relationships in numerical, geometric, verbal, and symbolic form. **TEKS 7.4**

Key Vocabulary

rate (p. 335)

ratio (p. 330)

proportional (p. 348)

Real-World Link

Statues A bronze replica of the Statue of Liberty can be found in Paris, France. The replica has the ratio 1 : 4 with the Statue of Liberty that stands in New York Harbor.

FOLDABLES™ Study Organizer

Ratios and Proportions Make this Foldable to help you organize your notes. Begin with a sheet of notebook paper.

1. **Fold** lengthwise to the holes.

2. **Cut** along the top line and then make equal cuts to form 6 tabs.

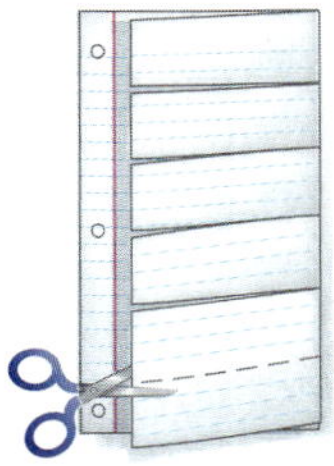

3. **Label** the major topics as shown.

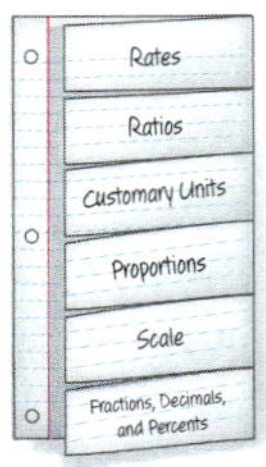

GET READY for Chapter 7

Diagnose Readiness You have two options for checking Prerequisite Skills.

Option 2

Math Online Take the Online Readiness Quiz at tx.msmath2.com.

Option 1

Take the Quick Quiz below. Refer to the Quick Review for help.

QUICK Quiz

Evaluate each expression. Round to the nearest tenth if necessary.
(Used in Lessons 7-2, 7-4, and 7-6)

1. $100 \times 25 \div 52$
2. $10 \div 4 \times 31$
3. $\frac{63 \times 4}{34}$
4. $\frac{2 \times 100}{68}$

Write each fraction in simplest form.
(Used in Lessons 7-1 through 7-4, 7-6, and 7-7)

5. $\frac{9}{45}$
6. $\frac{16}{24}$
7. $\frac{38}{46}$

8. **AGES** Mikhail is 14 years old. His father is 49 years old. What fraction, in simplest form, of his father's age is Mikhail?

Write each decimal as a fraction in simplest form. (Used in Lesson 7-7)

9. 0.78
10. 0.320
11. 0.06

12. **SAVINGS** Belinda has saved 0.92 of the cost of a new bicycle. What fraction, in simplest form, represents her savings?

Complete. (Used in Lesson 7-3)

13. 2 yd = ■ ft
14. 48 oz = ■ lb
15. $4\frac{1}{2}$ ft = ■ yd
16. $3\frac{1}{4}$ h = ■ min

QUICK Review

Example 1

Evaluate $15 \times 32 \div 40$.

$15 \times 32 \div 40 = 480 \div 40$ — Multiply 15 by 32.

$= 12$ — Divide.

Example 2

Write $\frac{16}{44}$ in simplest form.

$\frac{16}{44} = \frac{4}{11}$ (÷ 4 numerator and denominator) — Divide the numerator and denominator by their GCF, 4.

Example 3

Write 0.62 as a fraction in simplest form.

$0.62 = \frac{62}{100}$ — 0.62 is sixty-two hundredths.

$= \frac{31}{50}$ — Divide the numerator and denominator by their GCF, 2.

Example 4

Complete 22 lb = ■ oz.

There are 16 ounces in 1 pound. So, there are 16×22, or 352 ounces in 22 pounds.

7-1 Ratios

Main IDEA

Write ratios as fractions in simplest form and determine whether two ratios are equivalent.

Targeted TEKS **7.2** The student adds, subtracts, multiplies, or divides to solve problems and justify solutions. **(D) use division to find unit rates and ratios in proportional relationships such as speed, density, price, recipes, and student-teacher ratio.** *Also addresses TEKS 7.14(B).*

NEW Vocabulary

ratio
equivalent ratios

READING in the Content Area

For strategies in reading this lesson, visit tx.msmath2.com.

GET READY for the Lesson

SCHOOL The student-teacher ratio of a school compares the total number of students to the total number of teachers.

Middle School	Students	Teachers
Prairie Lake	396	22
Green Brier	510	30

1. Write the student-teacher ratio of Prairie Lake Middle School as a fraction. Then write this fraction with a denominator of 1.
2. Can you determine which school has the lower student-teacher ratio by examining just the number of teachers at each school? just the number of students at each school? Explain.

KEY CONCEPT — Ratios

Words A **ratio** is a comparison of two quantities by division.

Examples

Numbers 3 to 4 3:4 $\frac{3}{4}$

Algebra a to b $a:b$ $\frac{a}{b}$

Ratios can express part to part, part to whole, or whole to part relationships and are often written as fractions in simplest form.

EXAMPLE Write Ratios in Simplest Form

1 **GRILLING Seasonings are often added to meat prior to grilling. Using the recipe, write a ratio comparing the amount of garlic powder to the amount of dried oregano as a fraction in simplest form.**

$$\frac{\text{garlic powder}}{\text{dried oregano}} \quad \frac{4 \text{ tsp}}{6 \text{ tsp}} = \frac{\overset{2}{\cancel{4 \text{ tsp}}}}{\underset{3}{\cancel{6 \text{ tsp}}}} \text{ or } \frac{2}{3}$$

The ratio of garlic powder to dried oregano is $\frac{2}{3}$, 2:3, or 2 to 3. That is, for every 2 units of garlic powder there are 3 units of dried oregano.

CHECK Your Progress

Use the recipe to write each ratio as a fraction in simplest form.

a. pepper : garlic powder

b. oregano : pepper

Ratios that express the same relationship between two quantities are called **equivalent ratios**. Equivalent ratios have the same value.

EXAMPLE Identify Equivalent Ratios

STUDY TIP

Writing Ratios Ratios greater than 1 are expressed as improper fractions and not as mixed numbers.

2 **Determine whether the ratios 250 miles in 4 hours and 500 miles in 8 hours are equivalent.**

METHOD 1 **Compare the ratios written in simplest form.**

250 miles : 4 hours $= \frac{250 \div 2}{4 \div 2}$ or $\frac{125}{2}$ Divide the numerator and denominator by the GCF, 2

500 miles : 8 hours $= \frac{500 \div 4}{8 \div 4}$ or $\frac{125}{2}$ Divide the numerator and denominator by the GCF, 4

The ratios simplify to the same fraction. They are equivalent.

METHOD 2 **Look for a common multiplier relating the two ratios.**

$$\frac{250}{4} = \frac{500}{8} \quad (\times 2 \text{ numerator}, \times 2 \text{ denominator})$$

The numerator and denominator of the ratios are related by the same multiplier, 2. The ratios of miles to hours are equivalent

CHOOSE Your Method

Determine whether the ratios are equivalent.

c. 20 nails for every 5 shingles, 12 nails for every 3 shingles

d. 2 cups flour to 8 cups sugar, 8 cups flour to 14 cups sugar

Online Personal Tutor at tx.msmath2.com

Real-World EXAMPLE

Real-World Link The recommended number of water lilies for a 9-square foot pond is 1.

Source: sustland.umn.edu

3 **PONDS** **For every 9 square feet of surface, a pond should have 2 fish. A pond that has a surface of 45 square feet contains 6 fish. Are these ratios equivalent? Justify your answer.**

Recommended Ratio

$9:2 = \frac{9}{2}$ square feet to fish

Actual Ratio

$45:6 = \frac{45}{6}$ or $\frac{15}{2}$ square feet to fish

Since $\frac{9}{2} \neq \frac{15}{2}$, the ratios are not equivalent. So, the number of fish is not correct for the pond.

CHECK Your Progress

e. **SWIMMING** A community pool requires there to be at least 3 lifeguards for every 20 swimmers. There are 60 swimmers and 9 lifeguards at the pool. Is this the correct number of lifeguards based on the above requirement? Justify your answer.

CHECK Your Understanding

Example 1 (p. 330)

FIELD TRIPS **Use the information in the table to write each ratio as a fraction in simplest form.**

Field Trip Statistics	
Students	180
Adults	24
Buses	4

1. adults : students
2. students : buses
3. buses : people
4. adults : people

Example 2 (p. 331)

Determine whether the ratios are equivalent. Explain.

5. 12 out of 20 doctors agree
   6 out of 10 doctors agree
6. 2 DVDs to 7 CDs
   10 DVDs to 15 CDs

Example 3 (p. 331)

7. **SHOPPING** A grocery store has a brand-name cereal on sale 2 boxes for $5. You buy 6 boxes and are charged $20. Based on the price ratio indicated, were you charged the correct amount? Justify your answer.

Exercises

HOMEWORK HELP	
For Exercises	See Examples
8–17	1
18–21	2
22–23	3

SOCCER **Use the Madison Mavericks team statistics to write each ratio as a fraction in simplest form.**

Madison Mavericks Team Statistics	
Wins	10
Losses	12
Ties	8

8. wins : losses
9. losses : ties
10. losses : games played
11. wins : games played

CARNIVALS **Use the following information to write each ratio as a fraction in simplest form.**

At its annual carnival, Brighton Middle School had 6 food booths and 15 games booths. A total of 66 adults and 165 children attended. The carnival raised a total of $1,600. Of this money, $550 came from ticket sales.

12. children : adults
13. food booths : games booths
14. children : games booths
15. booths : money raised
16. people : children
17. non-ticket sale money : total money

Determine whether the ratios are equivalent. Explain.

18. 20 female lions to 8 male lions,
    34 female lions to 10 male lions
19. $4 for every 16 ounces,
    $10 for every 40 ounces
20. 27 students to 6 microscopes,
    18 students to 4 microscopes
21. 8 roses to 6 babies breath,
    12 roses to 10 babies breath

22. **BAKING** It is recommended that a ham be baked 1 hour for every 2 pounds of meat. Latrell baked a 9-pound ham for 4.5 hours. Did he follow the above recommendation? Justify your answer.

23. **FISHING** Kamala catches two similar looking fish. The larger fish is 12 inches long and 3 inches wide. The smaller fish is 6 inches long and 1 inch wide. Do these fish have an equivalent length to width ratio? Justify your answer.

PHOTOGRAPHY The *aspect ratio* of a photograph is a ratio comparing the length and width. A 35 mm negative has an aspect ratio of 1 : 1.5. Photo sizes with the same aspect ratio can be printed full frame without cropping. Determine which size photos can be printed full frame from a 35 mm negative. Justify your answers.

24. 8″ × 10″ **25.** 5″ × 7.5″ **26.** 10″ × 15″

Real-World Link An orca whale, also called a killer whale, is not really a whale, but a dolphin. Its average birth weight is 300 pounds.
Source: coolantarctica.com

MAMMALS For Exercises 27 and 28, use the information below.

Mammal	Average Brain Weight (lb)	Average Body Weight (lb)
Adult Human	3	150
Adult Orca Whale	12	5,500

27. How much greater is the average weight of an adult orca whale's brain than the average weight of an adult human's brain?

28. Find the brain to body weight ratio for each mammal. Are these ratios equivalent? If not, which mammal has the greater brain to body weight ratio? Justify your answer and explain its meaning.

29. **GEARS** A *gear ratio* is a comparison of the number of teeth of a larger gear to the number of teeth of a smaller gear. What is the gear ratio of the two gears shown? How many times does the smaller gear turn for every turn of the larger gear?

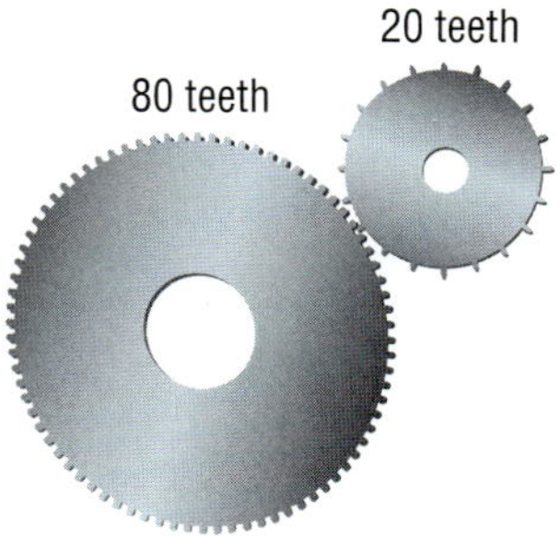

30. **MONEY** A debt to income ratio compares the amount of money owed (debt) to the amount of money earned (income). What is the debt to income ratio for someone earning $2,000 a month who is making payments of $400 a month on their debts?

ANALYZE TABLES For Exercises 31–33, use the table below that shows the logging statistics for three areas of forest.

Area	Estimated Number of Trees Left to Grow	Estimated Number of Trees Removed for Timber
A	440	1,200
B	1,625	3,750
C	352	960

31. For which two areas was the growth-to-removal ratio the same? Explain.

32. Which area had the greatest growth-to-removal ratio? Justify your answer.

33. Find the additional number of trees that should be planted and left to grow in area A so that its growth-to-removal ratio is the same as area B's. Justify your answer.

EXTRA PRACTICE
See pages 733, 761.
Math Online
Self-Check Quiz at tx.msmath2.com

H.O.T. Problems

34. **FIND THE ERROR** Cleveland and Lacey are determining whether the ratios $\frac{6}{4}$ and $\frac{18}{16}$ are equivalent. Who is correct? Explain.

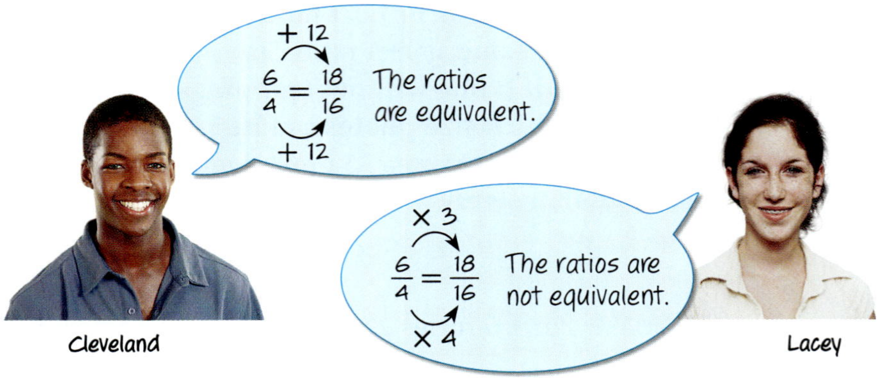

35. **CHALLENGE** Find the missing number in the following pattern. Explain your reasoning. (*Hint*: Look at the ratios of successive numbers.)

480, 240, 80, 20, ■.

36. **WRITING IN MATH** Refer to the application in Exercises 31–33. What would a growth-to-removal ratio greater than 1 indicate?

TEST PRACTICE

37. Which of the following ratios does NOT describe a relationship between the marbles in the jar?

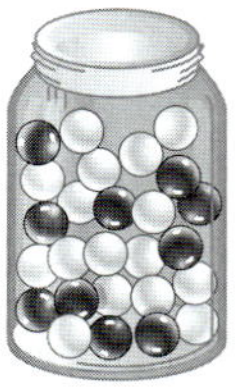

A 8 white : 5 black

B 2 white : 5 black

C 5 black : 13 total

D 8 white : 13 total

38. A class of 24 students has 15 boys. What fraction represents the ratio of girls to boys in the class?

F $\frac{3}{5}$

G $\frac{5}{8}$

H $\frac{3}{8}$

J $\frac{5}{3}$

Spiral Review

39. Find $1\frac{4}{7} \div 1\frac{5}{6}$. Write in simplest form. (Lesson 6-7)

Solve each equation. Check your solution. (Lesson 6-6)

40. $\frac{y}{4} = 7$

41. $\frac{1}{3}x = \frac{5}{9}$

42. $4 = \frac{p}{2.7}$

43. $2\frac{5}{6} = \frac{1}{2}a$

44. **MONEY** Grant and his brother put together their money to buy a present for their mom. If they had a total of \$18 and Grant contributed \$10, how much did his brother contribute? (Lesson 4-2)

GET READY for the Next Lesson

PREREQUISITE SKILL **Divide.** (Lesson 3-4)

45. $9.8 \div 2$

46. $\$4.30 \div 5$

47. $\$12.40 \div 40$

48. $27.36 \div 3.2$

7-2 Rates

Main IDEA

Determine unit rates.

Targeted TEKS **7.2** The student adds, subtracts, multiplies, or divides to solve problems and justify solutions. **(D) use division to find unit rates and ratios in proportional relationships such as speed, density, price, recipes, and student-teacher ratio.** *Also addresses TEKS 7.3(B).*

NEW Vocabulary

rate
unit rate

MINI Lab

Choose a page in a textbook and take turns reading as much as possible in 2 minutes.

1. Count the number of words that each of you read.
2. Write the ratio *number of words to number of minutes* as a fraction.
3. Simplify the fractions by dividing the numerator and the denominator by 2.

A ratio that compares two quantities with different kinds of units is called a **rate**.

$\frac{100 \text{ words}}{2 \text{ minutes}}$ — The units *words* and *minutes* are different.

When a rate is simplified so that it has a denominator of 1 unit, it is called a **unit rate**.

$\frac{50 \text{ words}}{1 \text{ minute}}$ — The denominator is 1 unit.

The unit rate $\frac{50 \text{ words}}{1 \text{ minute}}$ can be read as *50 words per minute.*

The table below shows some common unit rates.

Rate	Unit Rate	Abbreviation	Name
$\frac{\text{number of miles}}{\text{1 hour}}$	miles per hour	mi/h or mph	average speed
$\frac{\text{number of miles}}{\text{1 gallon}}$	miles per gallon	mi/gal or mpg	gas mileage
$\frac{\text{number of dollars}}{\text{1 pound}}$	price per pound	dollars/lb	unit price
$\frac{\text{number of dollars}}{\text{1 hour}}$	dollars per hour	dollars/h	hourly wage

EXAMPLES Find Unit Rates

1 **RUNNING** **Alethia ran 24 miles in 3 hours. What was her average speed in miles per hour?**

Write the rate as a fraction. Then find an equivalent rate with a denominator of 1.

$24 \text{ miles in } 3 \text{ hours} = \frac{24 \text{ mi}}{3 \text{ h}}$ Write the rate as a fraction.

$= \frac{24 \text{ mi} \div 3}{3 \text{ h} \div 3}$ Divide the numerator and the denominator by 3.

$= \frac{8 \text{ mi}}{1 \text{ h}}$ Simplify.

Alethia's average speed, or unit rate, was 8 miles per hour.

STUDY TIP

Mental Math
To find a unit rate mentally, divide the first quantity in the rate by the second quantity.
24 miles in 3 hours
$= \frac{24}{3}$ mi/h
$= 8$ mi/h

2 **GROCERIES** **Find the unit price if it costs $2 for six oranges. Round to the nearest cent if necessary.**

$$\$2 \text{ for six oranges} = \frac{\$2}{6 \text{ oranges}}$$ Write the rate as a fraction.

$$= \frac{\$2 \div 6}{6 \text{ oranges} \div 6}$$ Divide the numerator and the denominator by 6.

$$\approx \frac{\$0.33}{1 \text{ orange}}$$ Simplify.

The unit price is about $0.33 per orange.

CHECK Your Progress

Find each unit rate. Round to the nearest hundredth if necessary.

a. $300 for 6 hours

b. 220 miles on 8 gallons

c. **ESTIMATION** Estimate the unit rate if a 4-pack of mixed fruit sells for $2.12.

Online Personal Tutor at tx.msmath2.com

Unit rates are useful when you want to make comparisons.

TEST EXAMPLE Compare Using Unit Rates

3 The prices of 3 different bags of dog food are given in the table. Which size bag has the lowest price per pound?

A The 40-lb bag only

B The 20-lb bag only

C The 8-lb bag only

D All three bag sizes have the same price per pound.

Dog Food Prices	
Bag Size (pounds)	**Price**
40	$49.00
20	$23.44
8	$9.88

Test-Taking Tip

Alternative Method
One 40-lb bag is equivalent to two 20-lb bags or five 8-lb bags. The cost for one 40-lb bag is $49, the cost for two 20-lb bags is about 2 × $23 or $46, and the cost for five 8-lb bags is about 5 × $10 or $50. So the 20-lb bag has the lowest price per pound.

Read the Test Item

To determine the lowest price per pound, find and compare the unit price for each size bag.

Solve the Test Item

40-pound bag	$49.00 ÷ 40 pounds = $1.225 per pound
20-pound bag	$23.44 ÷ 20 pounds = $1.172 per pound
8-pound bag	$9.88 ÷ 8 pounds = $1.235 per pound

At $1.172 per pound, the 20-pound bag sells for the lowest price per pound. The answer is B.

CHECK Your Progress

d. Tito wants to buy some peanut butter to donate to the local food pantry. If Tito wants to save as much money as possible, which brand should he buy?

Peanut Butter Sales	
Brand	**Sale Price**
Nutty	12 ounces for \$2.19
Grandma's	18 ounces for \$2.79
Bee's	28 ounces for \$4.69
Save-A-Lot	40 ounces for \$6.60

F Nutty, because the quality of the peanut butter is better

G Grandma's, because the price per ounce is about \$0.16

H Bee's, because the price per ounce is about \$0.14

J Save-A-Lot, because he wants to buy 40 ounces

Online Personal Tutor at tx.msmath2.com

Real-World Link Face paint can be made from 1 teaspoon cornstarch and $\frac{1}{2}$ teaspoon each of water and cold cream.
Source: painting.about.com

Real-World EXAMPLE Use a Unit Rate

4 **FACE PAINTING** Lexi painted 3 faces in 12 minutes at the Arts and Crafts fair. At this rate, how many faces can she paint in 40 minutes?

Find the unit rate. Then multiply this unit rate by 40 to find the number of faces she can paint in 40 minutes.

3 faces in 12 minutes $= \frac{3 \text{ faces} \div 12}{12 \text{ min} \div 12} = \frac{0.25 \text{ faces}}{1 \text{ min}}$ Find the unit rate.

$\frac{0.25 \text{ faces}}{1 \cancel{\text{min}}} \cdot 40 \cancel{\text{min}} = 10 \text{ faces}$ Divide out the common units.

Lexi can paint 10 faces in 40 minutes or $\frac{4 \text{ minutes}}{1 \text{ face}}$.

CHECK Your Progress

e. **SCHOOL SUPPLIES** Kimbel bought 4 notebooks for \$6.32. At this same unit price, how much would he pay for 5 notebooks?

CHECK Your Understanding

Examples 1, 2 (pp. 335–336)

Find each unit rate. Round to the nearest hundredth if necessary.

1. 90 miles on 15 gallons
2. 1,680 kilobytes in 4 minutes
3. 5 pounds for \$2.49
4. 152 feet in 16 seconds

Example 3 (pp. 336–337)

5. **TEST PRACTICE** Four stores offer customers bulk CD rates. Which store offers the best buy?

A CD Express C Music Place

B CD Rack D Music Shop

Bulk CD Offers	
Store	**Offer**
CD Express	4 CDs for \$60
Music Place	6 CDs for \$75
CD Rack	5 CDs for \$70
Music Shop	3 CDs for \$40

Example 4 (p. 337)

6. **TRAVEL** After 3.5 hours, Pasha had traveled 217 miles. At this same speed, how far will she have traveled after 4 hours?

Exercises

HOMEWORK HELP	
For Exercises	**See Examples**
7–16	1, 2
17–20	3
21–24	4

Find each unit rate. Round to the nearest hundredth if necessary.

7. 360 miles in 6 hours
8. 6,840 customers in 45 days
9. 152 people for 5 classes
10. 815 Calories in 4 servings
11. 45.5 meters in 13 seconds
12. $7.40 for 5 pounds
13. $1.12 for 8.2 ounces
14. 144 miles in 4.5 gallons

15. **ESTIMATION** Estimate the unit rate if 12 pairs of socks sell for $5.79.

16. **ESTIMATION** Estimate the unit rate if a 26 mile marathon was completed in 5 hours.

17. **SPORTS** The results of a swim meet are shown. Who swam the fastest? Explain your reasoning.

Name	Event	Time (s)
Tawni	50-m Freestyle	40.8
Pepita	100-m Butterfly	60.2
Susana	200-m Medley	112.4

18. **MONEY** A grocery store sells three different packages of bottled water. Which package costs the least per bottle? Explain your reasoning.

6-pack for $3.79

9-pack for $4.50

12-pack for $6.89

NUTRITION **For Exercises 19 and 20, use the table at the right.**

Soft Drink Nutritional Information			
Soft Drink	Serving Size (oz)	Sodium (mg)	Sugar (g)
A	12	40	22
B	8	24	15
C	7	42	30

19. Which soft drink has about twice the amount of sodium per ounce than the other two? Explain.

20. Which soft drink has the least amount of sugar per ounce? Explain.

Real-World Link North Carolina has approximately 8.2 million people in approximately 48,718 square miles.
Source: quickfacts.census.gov

21. **WORD PROCESSING** Ben can type 153 words in 3 minutes. At this rate, how many words can he type in 10 minutes?

22. **FABRIC** Marcus buys 3 yards of fabric for $7.47. Later he realizes that he needs 2 more yards. How much will he pay for the extra fabric?

23. **ESTIMATION** A player scores 87 points in 6 games. At this rate, about how many points would she score in the next 4 games?

24. **JOBS** Dalila earns $94.20 for working 15 hours as a holiday helper wrapping gifts. If she works 18 hours the next week, how much money will she earn?

25. **POPULATION** Use the information at the left. What is the *population density* or number of people per square mile in North Carolina?

ESTIMATION Estimate the unit price for each item. Justify your answers.

26. 

$2.49

27. 

$1.89

28. 

$1.13

29. **RECIPES** A recipe that makes 10 mini-loaves of banana bread calls for $1\frac{1}{4}$ cups flour. How much flour is needed to make 2 dozen mini-loaves using this recipe?

Real-World Link . . . . The winning time for the men's wheelchair division of the 2005 Boston Marathon in Massachusetts was 1 hour, 24 minutes, and 11 seconds. **Source:** boston.com

SPORTS For Exercises 30 and 31, use the information at the left.

30. The wheelchair division for the Boston Marathon is 26.2 miles long. What was the average speed of the winner of the wheelchair division in 2005? Round to the nearest hundredth.

31. At this rate, about how long would it take this competitor to complete a 30 mile race?

32. **GROCERIES** Salami is on sale for $4.48 per pound. If its regular price is $5.28 per pound, how much do you save on a 2.5-pound package of this salami? Justify your answer using two different methods.

ANIMALS For Exercises 33–37, use the graph that shows the average number of heartbeats for an active adult brown bear and a hibernating brown bear.

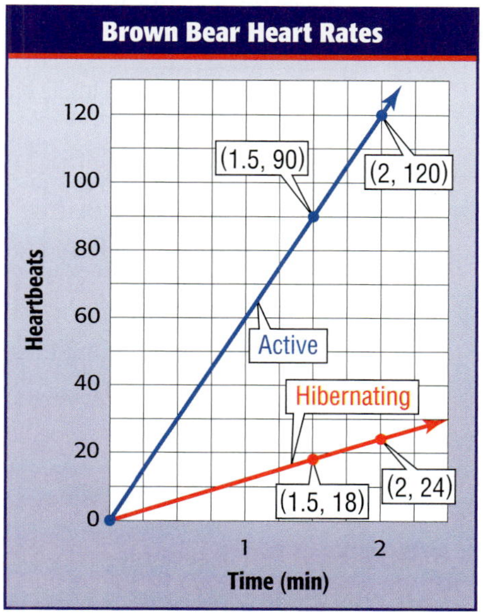

33. What does the point (2, 120) represent on the graph?

34. What does the point (1.5, 18) represent on the graph?

35. What does the ratio of the y-coordinate to the x-coordinate for each pair of points on the graph represent?

36. Use the graph to find the bear's average heart rate when it is active and when it is hibernating.

37. When is the bear's heart rate greater, when it is active or when it is hibernating? How can you tell this from the graph?

38. **TIRES** At Tire Depot, a set of 2 brand new tires sells for $216. The manager's special advertises the same tires selling at a rate of $380 for 4 tires. How much do you save per tire if you purchase the manager's special?

39. **FIND THE DATA** Refer to the Texas Data File on pages 16–19. Choose some data and write a real-world problem in which you would compare unit rates or ratios.

EXTRA PRACTICE
See pages 733, 761.
Math Online
Self-Check Quiz at tx.msmath2.com

H.O.T. Problems

CHALLENGE **Determine whether each statement is *sometimes, always,* or *never* true. Give an example or a counterexample.**

40. A ratio is a rate.

41. A rate is a ratio.

42. **OPEN ENDED** Create a rate and then convert it to a unit rate.

43. **NUMBER SENSE** In which situation will the rate $\frac{x \text{ feet}}{y \text{ minutes}}$ increase? Give an example to explain your reasoning.

a. x increases, y is unchanged

b. x is unchanged, y increases

44. **WRITING IN MATH** Explain how you can use multiplication to check your answer when finding the unit rate for 5.2 miles in 4 hours.

TEST PRACTICE

45. Mrs. Ross needs to buy dish soap. There are four different size containers at a store.

Dish Soap Prices	
Brand	**Price**
Lots of Suds	$0.98 for 8 ounces
Bright Wash	$1.29 for 12 ounces
Spotless Soap	$3.14 for 30 ounces
Lemon Bright	$3.45 for 32 ounces

Mrs. Ross wants to buy the one that costs the least per ounce. Which brand should she buy?

A Lots of Suds

B Bright Wash

C Spotless Soap

D Lemon Bright

46. The table shows the total distance traveled by a car driving at a constant rate of speed.

Time (h)	Distance (mi)
2	130
3.5	227.5
4	260
7	455

Based on this information, how far will the car have traveled after 10 hours?

F 520 miles

G 585 miles

H 650 miles

J 715 miles

Spiral Review

FLOWERS **For Exercises 47–50, use the information in the table to write each ratio as a fraction in simplest form.** (Lesson 7-1)

Flower Arrangement	
Lilies	4
Roses	18
Snapdragons	6

47. lilies : roses

48. snapdragons : lilies

49. roses : flowers

50. flowers : snapdragons

51. **SANDWICHES** Lawanda is making subs. She puts $1\frac{1}{2}$ slices of cheese on each sub. If she has 12 slices of cheese, how many subs can she make? (Lesson 6-6)

GET READY for the Next Lesson

PREREQUISITE SKILL **Solve.** (Lessons 3-2 and 3-4)

52. 2.5×20

53. 3.5×4

54. $104 \div 16$

55. $4{,}200 \div 2{,}000$

Extend 7-2

Math Lab
Rate of Change

Main IDEA

Investigate rate of change.

Targeted TEKS **7.2** The student adds, subtracts, multiplies or divides to solve problems and justify solutions. **(D)** **use division to find unit rates and ratios in proportional relationships such as speed, density, price, recipes, and student-teacher ratio.** *Also addresses TEKS 7.14(A).*

A *rate of change* is a ratio that shows a change in one quantity with respect to a change in another quantity. In this lab, you will use tables and graphs to investigate constant rates of change.

ACTIVITY

STEP 1 Use tiles to build the figures shown below. Then continue the pattern to build the fourth and fifth figures.

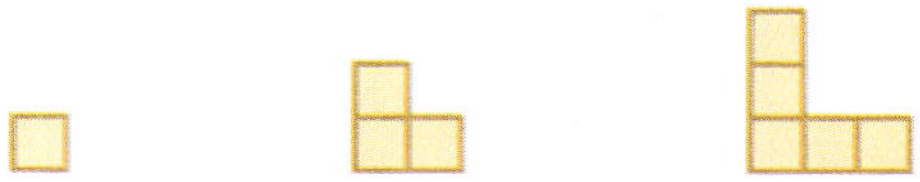

1 2 3

STEP 2 For each figure, record the number of tiles and the perimeter of the figure in a table like the one shown at the right.

Figures	Number of Tiles (x)	Perimeter (y)
1	1	
2	3	
3	5	
4		
5		

STEP 3 Draw a coordinate plane on grid paper and graph the ordered pairs (x, y).

Analyze the Results

1. What do you notice about the points on the graph?
2. Find the ratio $\frac{\text{change in perimeter}}{\text{change in tiles}}$ between the second and third points, the third and fourth points, and the fourth and fifth points. Each ratio is a rate of change. Describe what you observe.
3. Complete: As the number of tiles increases by 2 units, the perimeter of the models increases by ■ units.
4. **MAKE A PREDICTION** Refer to the table at the right. Find the ratio $\frac{\text{change in earnings}}{\text{change in hours worked}}$ for Greg and Monica. Which person's earnings when graphed will form the steeper line? Explain your reasoning.

Hours Worked	Earnings ($)	
	Greg	Monica
1	4	5
2	8	10
3	12	15
4	16	20

5. Graph the ordered pairs (hours worked, earnings) for each person and connect to form a line. The graph of which relationship has the steeper line?

7-3 Measurement: Changing Customary Units

Main IDEA

Change units in the customary system.

Reinforcement of TEKS 6.8 The student solves application problems involving estimation and measurement of length, area, time, temperature, volume, weight, and angles. **(D) convert measures within the same measurement system (customary** and metric) **based on relationships between units**. *Also addresses TEKS 7.3(B), 7.14(A).*

NEW Vocabulary

unit ratio

GET READY for the Lesson

ANIMALS The table shows the approximate weights in tons of several large land animals. One ton is equivalent to 2,000 pounds.

Animal	Weight (T)
Grizzly Bear	1
White Rhinoceros	4
Hippopotamus	5
African Elephant	8

You can use a *ratio table*, whose columns are filled with ratios that have the same value, to convert each weight from tons to pounds.

1. Copy and complete the ratio table. The first two ratios are done for you.

×4

Tons	1	4	5	8
Pounds	2,000	8,000	■	■

×4

To produce equivalent ratios, multiply the quantities in each row by the same number.

2. Then graph the ordered pairs (tons, pounds) from the table. Label the horizontal axis *Weight in Tons* and the vertical axis *Weight in Pounds*. Connect the points. What do you notice about the graph of these data?

The relationships among the most commonly used customary units of length, weight, and capacity are shown in the table below.

KEY CONCEPT — Equality Relationships for Customary Units

Type of Measure	Larger Unit	→	Smaller Unit
Length	1 foot (ft)	=	12 inches (in.)
	1 yard (yd)	=	3 feet
	1 mile (mi)	=	5,280 feet
Weight	1 pound (lb)	=	16 ounces (oz)
	1 ton (T)	=	2,000 pounds
Capacity	1 cup (c)	=	8 fluid ounces (fl oz)
	1 pint (pt)	=	2 cups
	1 quart (qt)	=	2 pints
	1 gallon (gal)	=	4 quarts

Each of the relationships above can be written as a unit ratio. Like a unit rate, a **unit ratio** is one in which the denominator is 1 unit.

$$\frac{3\text{ ft}}{1\text{ yd}} \qquad \frac{2{,}000\text{ lb}}{1\text{ T}} \qquad \frac{4\text{ qt}}{1\text{ gal}}$$

Notice that the numerator and denominator of each fraction above are equivalent, so the value of each ratio is 1. You can multiply by a unit ratio of this type to *convert* or change from larger units to smaller units.

STUDY TIP

Multiplying by 1 Although the number and units changed in Example 1, because the measure is multiplied by 1, the *value* of the converted measure is the same as the original.

EXAMPLES Convert Larger Units to Smaller Units

1 Convert 20 feet into inches.

Since 1 foot = 12 inches, the unit ratio is $\frac{12\text{ in.}}{1\text{ ft}}$.

$20\text{ ft} = 20\text{ ft} \cdot \frac{12\text{ in.}}{1\text{ ft}}$ — Multiply by $\frac{12\text{ in.}}{1\text{ ft}}$.

$= 20\not{\text{ft}} \cdot \frac{12\text{ in.}}{1\not{\text{ft}}}$ — Divide out common units, leaving the desired unit, inches.

$= 20 \cdot 12\text{ in. or }240\text{ in.}$ — Multiply.

So, 20 feet = 240 inches.

2 GARDENING Clarence mixes $\frac{1}{4}$ cup of fertilizer with soil before planting each bulb. How many ounces of fertilizer does he use per bulb?

$\frac{1}{4}\text{ c} = \frac{1}{4}\not{\text{c}} \cdot \frac{8\text{ fl oz}}{1\not{\text{c}}}$ — Since 1 cup = 8 fluid ounces, multiply by $\frac{8\text{ fl oz}}{1\text{ c}}$. Then, divide out common units.

$= \frac{1}{4} \cdot 8\text{ fl oz or }2\text{ fl oz}$ — Multiply.

So, 2 fluid ounces of fertilizer are used per bulb.

CHECK Your Progress

Complete.

a. 36 yd = ■ ft

b. $\frac{3}{4}$ T = ■ lb

c. $1\frac{1}{2}$ qt = ■ pt

REVIEW Vocabulary

reciprocal The product of a number and its reciprocal is 1; *Example*: The reciprocal of $\frac{3}{5}$ is $\frac{5}{3}$. (Lesson 6-7)

To convert from smaller units to larger units, multiply by the reciprocal of the appropriate unit ratio.

EXAMPLES Convert Smaller Units to Larger Units

3 Convert 15 quarts into gallons.

Since 1 gallon = 4 quarts, the unit ratio is $\frac{4\text{ qt}}{1\text{ gal}}$, and its reciprocal is $\frac{1\text{ gal}}{4\text{ qt}}$.

$15\text{ qt} = 15\text{ qt} \cdot \frac{1\text{ gal}}{4\text{ qt}}$ — Multiply by $\frac{1\text{ gal}}{4\text{ qt}}$.

$= 15\not{\text{qt}} \cdot \frac{1\text{ gal}}{4\not{\text{qt}}}$ — Divide out common units, leaving the desired unit, gallons

$= 15 \cdot \frac{1}{4}\text{ gal or }3.75\text{ gal}$ — Multiplying 15 by $\frac{1}{4}$ is the same as dividing 15 by 4.

4 **COSTUMES** **Umeka needs $4\frac{1}{2}$ feet of fabric to make a costume for a play. How many yards of fabric does she need?**

$4\frac{1}{2}$ ft $= 4\frac{1}{2}$ ft $\cdot \frac{1 \text{ yd}}{3 \text{ ft}}$ — Since 1 yard = 3 feet, multiply by $\frac{1 \text{ yd}}{3 \text{ ft}}$. Then, divide out common units.

$= \frac{9}{2} \cdot \frac{1}{3}$ yd — Write $4\frac{1}{2}$ as an improper fraction. Then divide out common factors.

$= \frac{3}{2}$ yd or $1\frac{1}{2}$ yd — Multiply.

So Umeka needs $1\frac{1}{2}$ yards of fabric.

CHECK Your Progress

Complete.

d. 2,640 ft = ▢ mi

e. 5 pt = ▢ qt

f. 100 oz = ▢ lb

g. 76c = ▢ gal

Real-World EXAMPLE

5 **FOOD** **The pork loin roast shown is cut into 10 smaller pork chops of equal weight. How many ounces does each pork chop weigh? Justify your answer.**

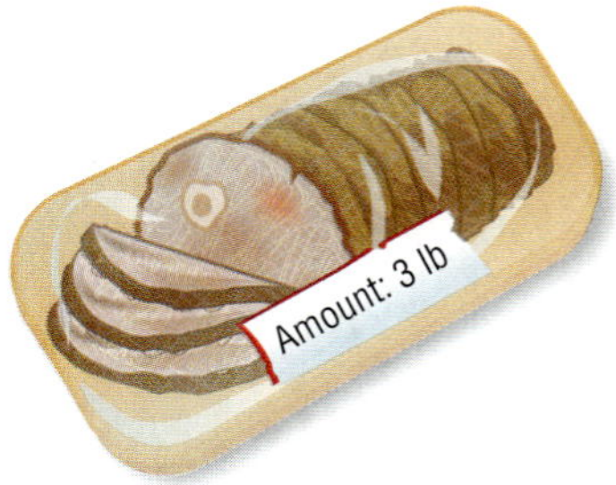

Begin by converting 3 pounds to ounces.

3 lb = 3 lb $\cdot \frac{16 \text{ oz}}{1 \text{ lb}}$ — Since 1 pound = 16 ounces, multiply by $\frac{16 \text{ oz}}{1 \text{ lb}}$. Then, divide out common units.

= 3 • 16 oz or 48 oz — Multiply.

Find the unit rate which gives the number of ounces per pork chop.

$\frac{\text{ounces}}{\text{pork chops}} = \frac{48 \text{ oz}}{10 \text{ pork chops}}$ or 4.8 ounces per pork chop

So, each pork chop weighs 4.8 ounces.

> **STUDY TIP**
>
> **Alternative Method**
> For Example 5, you could also begin by finding the number of pounds per pork chop.
> $\frac{3 \text{ lb}}{10 \text{ pork chops}}$ or
> $\frac{3}{10}$ lb per pork chop
> Then convert the number of pounds per pork chop to ounces.
> $\frac{\frac{3}{10} \text{ lb}}{1 \text{ pork chop}} \cdot \frac{16 \text{ oz}}{1 \text{ lb}}$
> $= \frac{4.8 \text{ oz}}{1 \text{ pork chop}}$

CHECK Your Progress

h. **RECIPES** A recipe calls for 5 cups of strawberries. Are 2 pints of strawberries enough? Justify your answer.

i. **TRUCKS** The height of a semi-truck is $4\frac{1}{2}$ yards. Will the truck fit under an overpass that is $14\frac{1}{2}$ feet tall? Justify your answer.

Online Personal Tutor at tx.msmath2.com

CHECK Your Understanding

Examples 1, 2 (p. 343)

Complete.

1. 3 lb = ▒ oz
2. $5\frac{1}{3}$ yd = ▒ ft
3. 6.5 c = ▒ fl oz

4. **FISH** Grouper are members of the sea bass family. A large grouper can weigh $\frac{1}{3}$ ton. About how much does a large grouper weigh to the nearest pound?

Examples 3, 4 (pp. 343–344)

Complete.

5. 12 qt = ▒ gal
6. 28 in. = ▒ ft
7. 15 pt = ▒ qt

8. **VEHICLES** The world's narrowest electric vehicle is about 35 inches wide and is designed to move down narrow aisles in warehouses. About how wide is this vehicle to the nearest foot?

Example 5 (p. 344)

9. **BIRDS** How many times greater is the weight of an ostrich egg that weighs about 4 pounds than a hummingbird egg that weighs about 0.05 ounce? Justify your answer.

Exercises

HOMEWORK HELP

For Exercises	See Examples
10–21	1–4
22–23	2
24–25	4
26–29	5

Complete.

10. 18 ft = ▒ yd
11. 72 oz = ▒ lb
12. 2 lb = ▒ oz
13. 4 gal = ▒ qt
14. $4\frac{1}{2}$ pt = ▒ c
15. 3 c = ▒ fl oz
16. 2 mi = ▒ ft
17. $1\frac{1}{4}$ mi = ▒ ft
18. 5,000 lb = ▒ T
19. 13 c = ▒ pt
20. $2\frac{3}{4}$ qt = ▒ pt
21. $3\frac{3}{8}$ T = ▒ lb

22. **PUMPKINS** One of the largest pumpkins ever grown weighed about $\frac{1}{2}$ ton. How many pounds did the pumpkin weigh?

23. **SKIING** Speed skiing takes place on a course that is $\frac{2}{3}$ mile long. How many feet long is the course?

24. **BOATING** A 40-foot power boat is for sale by owner. About how long is this boat to the nearest yard?

25. **BLOOD** A total of 35 pints of blood were collected at a local blood drive. How many quarts of blood is this?

26. **CAR REPAIR** A car repair shop changes the oil of 50 cars. They recover $3\frac{1}{2}$ quarts of oil from each car. How many gallons of oil did they recover? Justify your answer.

27. **ESTIMATION** One bushel of apples weighs about 40 pounds. About how many bushels of apples would weigh 1 ton?

28. **PUNCH** Will a 2-quart pitcher hold the entire recipe of citrus punch given at the right? Explain your reasoning.

29. **WEATHER** On Monday, it snowed a total of 15 inches. On Tuesday and Wednesday, it snowed an additional $4\frac{1}{2}$ inches and $6\frac{3}{4}$ inches, respectively. A weather forecaster says that over the last three days, it snowed about $2\frac{1}{2}$ feet. Is this a valid claim? Justify your answer.

Complete.

30. $1\frac{1}{4}$ gal = ■ c
31. 880 yd = ■ mi
32. 24 fl oz = ■ qt
33. 9 c = ■ qt
34. 2.3 yd = ■ in.
35. $3\frac{1}{2}$ T = ■ oz

36. **ESTIMATION** Cristos is a member of the swim team and trains by swimming an average of 3,000 yards a day. About how many miles would he swim by training at this rate for 5 days, to the nearest half-mile?

ANALYZE GRAPHS For Exercises 37–40, use the graph at the right.

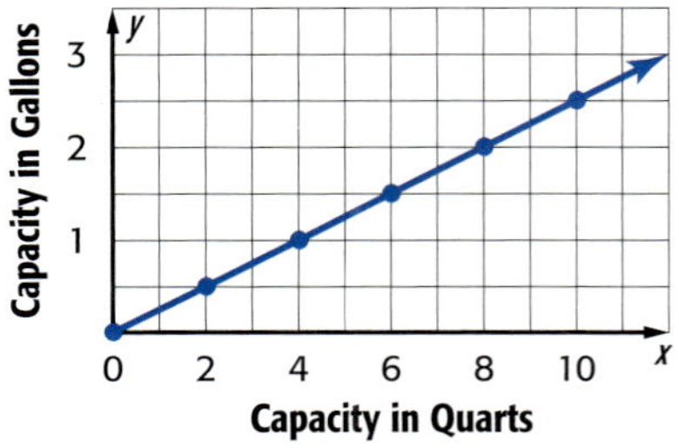

37. What does an ordered pair from this graph represent?

38. Write two sentences that describe the graph.

39. Use the graph to find the capacity in quarts of a 2.5 gallon container. Explain your reasoning.

40. Use the graph to predict the capacity in gallons of a 12 quart container. Explain your reasoning.

EXTRA PRACTICE
See pages 733, 761.
Math Online
Self-Check Quiz at tx.msmath2.com

H.O.T. Problems

41. **OPEN ENDED** Write a problem about a real-world situation in which you would need to convert pints to cups.

REASONING Replace each ● with <, >, or = to make a true sentence. Justify your answers.

42. 16 in. ● $1\frac{1}{2}$ ft
43. $8\frac{3}{4}$ gal ● 32 qt
44. 2.7 T ● 86,400 oz

45. **CHALLENGE** To whiten fabrics, a certain Web site recommends that you soak them in a mixture of $\frac{3}{4}$ cup vinegar, 2 quarts water, and some salt. Does a mixture that contains 1.5 ounces vinegar and 16 ounces water have the same vinegar to water ratio as the recommended mixture? Explain your reasoning.

46. **WRITING IN MATH** Use multiplication by unit ratios of equivalent measures to convert 5 square feet to square inches. Justify your answer.

TEST PRACTICE

47. Which situation is represented by the graph?

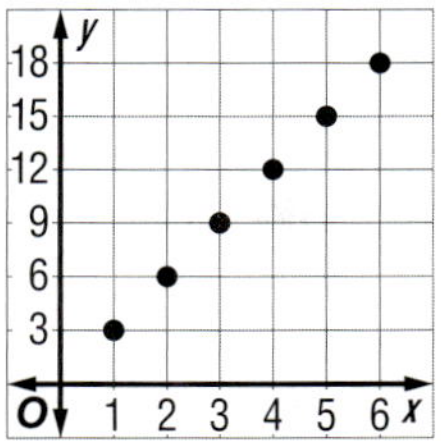

A Conversion of inches to yards

B Conversion of feet to inches

C Conversion of miles to feet

D Conversion of yards to feet

48. How many cups of milk are shown below?

F $\frac{3}{4}$ c

G $1\frac{1}{4}$ c

H $2\frac{1}{2}$ c

J 10 c

Spiral Review

49. **GROCERIES** Three pounds of pears cost $3.57. At this rate, how much would 10 pounds cost? (Lesson 7-2)

Write each ratio as a fraction in simplest form. (Lesson 7-1)

50. 9 feet in 21 minutes

51. 36 calls in 2 hours

52. 14 SUVs out of 56 vehicles

53. $85 for 5 hours

54. 16 cats out of 44 animals

55. 3,048 people per 32 square miles

56. **ICE SKATING** By doubling just the length of the rectangular ice skating rink in Will's backyard from 16 to 32 feet, he increased its area from 128 square feet to 256 square feet. Find the width of both rinks. (Lesson 4-6)

EARNINGS For Exercises 57–59, use the pay stub at the right. (Lesson 4-3)

57. Write and solve an equation to find the regular hourly wage.

58. Write and solve an equation to find the overtime hourly wage.

59. Write and solve an equation to find how many times greater Grace's overtime hourly wage is than her regular hourly wage.

Martin, Grace		Employee #: 4211
Description:	**Hours:**	**Earnings ($):**
Regular hours:	40	300.00
Overtime hours:	2	22.50

GET READY for the Next Lesson

PREREQUISITE SKILL Solve each equation. (Lesson 4-3)

60. $5 \cdot 4 = x \cdot 2$

61. $9 \cdot 24 = 27 \cdot x$

62. $x \cdot 15 = 12 \cdot 4$

63. $8\frac{1}{2} \cdot x = 11 \cdot 17$

7-4 Algebra: Solving Proportions

Main IDEA

Solve proportions.

Targeted TEKS **7.3** The student solves problems involving direct proportional relationships. **(B) estimate and find solutions to application problems involving proportional relationships such as similarity, scaling, unit costs, and related measurement units.** *Also addresses TEKS 7.2(D), 7.5(B), 7.13(D).*

NEW Vocabulary

proportional
cross product

GET READY for the Lesson

NUTRITION The table shows the amount of vitamin C in different serving sizes of a certain cereal.

1. Write the rate $\frac{\text{vitamin C}}{\text{serving size}}$ for each serving size of cereal.
2. Find the number of milligrams per cup for each serving size. What do you notice?

Vitamin C (mg)	Serving Size (c)
15	0.5
60	2

Two quantities are **proportional** if they have a constant rate or ratio. In the example above, notice that the serving size and amount of vitamin C change or *vary* in the same way.

$$\frac{15 \text{ mg}}{0.5 \text{ c}} \overset{\times 4}{=} \frac{60 \text{ mg}}{2 \text{ c}}$$

When the serving size quadruples, the number of milligrams of vitamin C also quadruples.

The unit rates for these different-sized servings are the same, a constant 30 milligrams per cup. So, the amount of vitamin C is proportional to the serving size. Another way of expressing this relationship is by writing a proportion.

$$\frac{15 \text{ mg}}{0.5 \text{ c}} \overset{\times 4}{=} \frac{60 \text{ mg}}{2 \text{ c}} \overset{\div 2}{=} \frac{30 \text{ mg}}{1 \text{ c}}$$

KEY CONCEPT — Proportion

Words A **proportion** is an equation stating that two ratios or rates are equivalent.

Symbols

Numbers $\frac{1}{2} = \frac{3}{6}$, $\frac{8 \text{ ft}}{10 \text{ s}} = \frac{4 \text{ ft}}{5 \text{ s}}$

Algebra $\frac{a}{b} = \frac{c}{d}$, where $b, d \neq 0$

Consider the following proportion.

$$\frac{a}{b} = \frac{c}{d}$$

$$\frac{a}{b} \cdot bd = \frac{c}{d} \cdot bd \quad \text{Multiply each side by } bd.$$

$$ad = bc \quad \text{Simplify.}$$

The products *ad* and *bc* are called the **cross products** of this proportion. The cross products of any proportion are equal. You can compare unit rates or cross products to identify proportional relationships.

EXAMPLE Identify Proportional Relationships

1 **RECREATION** **A carousel makes 4 complete turns after 64 seconds and 5 complete turns after 76 seconds. Based on this information, is the number of turns made by this carousel proportional to the time in seconds? Explain.**

METHOD 1 **Compare unit rates.**

$$\frac{\text{seconds}}{\text{complete turns}} \rightarrow \frac{64\text{ s}}{4\text{ turns}} = \frac{16\text{ s}}{1\text{ turn}} \qquad \frac{76\text{ s}}{5\text{ turns}} = \frac{15.2\text{ s}}{1\text{ turn}}$$

Since the unit rates are not equal, the number of turns is not proportional to the time in seconds.

METHOD 2 **Compare ratios by comparing cross products.**

seconds → $\frac{64}{4} \stackrel{?}{=} \frac{76}{5}$ ← seconds
complete turns → ← complete turns

$64 \cdot 5 \stackrel{?}{=} 4 \cdot 76$ Find the cross products.

$320 \neq 304$ Multiply.

Since the cross products are not equal, the number of turns is not proportional to the time in seconds.

CHOOSE Your Method

Determine if the quantities in each pair of ratios are proportional. Explain.

a. 60 voted out of 100 registered and 84 voted out of 140 registered

b. \$12 for 16 yards of fabric and \$9 for 24 yards fabric

Online Personal Tutor at tx.msmath2.com

You can also use cross products to find a missing value in a proportion. This is known as *solving the proportion*.

STUDY TIP

Mental Math
Some proportions can be solved using mental math.

$$\frac{2.5}{10} = \frac{x}{30}$$

×3

$$\frac{2.5}{10} = \frac{7.5}{30}$$

×3

EXAMPLES Solve a Proportion

2 **Solve** $\frac{21}{5} = \frac{c}{7}$.

$\frac{21}{5} = \frac{c}{7}$ Write the proportion.

$21 \cdot 7 = 5 \cdot c$ Find the cross products.

$147 = 5c$ Multiply.

$\frac{147}{5} = \frac{5c}{5}$ Divide each side by 5.

$29.4 = c$ Simplify.

Check for Reasonableness Since $\frac{21}{5} \approx \frac{20}{5}$ or $\frac{4}{1}$ and $\frac{29.4}{7} \approx \frac{28}{7}$ or $\frac{4}{1}$, the answer is reasonable. ✔

Concepts in Motion
BrainPOP® tx.msmath2.com

3 Solve $\frac{2.6}{13} = \frac{8}{n}$.

$\frac{2.6}{13} = \frac{8}{n}$	Write the proportion.
$2.6 \cdot n = 13 \cdot 8$	Find the cross products.
$2.6n = 104$	Multiply.
$\frac{2.6n}{2.6} = \frac{104}{2.6}$	Divide each side by 2.6.
$n = 40$	Simplify.

CHECK Your Progress Solve each proportion.

c. $\frac{16}{k} = \frac{2}{3}$ d. $\frac{2}{6} = \frac{5}{h}$ e. $\frac{10}{k} = \frac{2.5}{4}$

Real-World Career
How Does a Paleontologist use Math?
In 2001, paleontologists discovered a 6-foot skull of a prehistoric crocodile called *SuperCroc*. By using proportions, they estimated its total length as 40 feet.

Math Online
For more information, go to tx.msmath2.com.

Real-World EXAMPLE

4 **SCIENCE** In one species, a 6-foot crocodile has a 2-foot skull. If skull length is proportional to body length, what is the length of a crocodile of that same species with a 3.5-foot skull?

METHOD 1 Write and solve a proportion.

Let b represent the length of the crocodile with a 3.5-foot skull.

body length →
skull length → $\frac{6 \text{ ft}}{2 \text{ ft}} = \frac{b \text{ ft}}{3.5 \text{ ft}}$ Write a proportion.

$6 \cdot 3.5 = 2 \cdot b$	Find the cross products.
$21 = 2b$	Multiply.
$10.5 = b$	Divide each side by 2.

METHOD 2 Find and use a unit rate or ratio.

body length →
skull length → $\frac{6 \text{ ft} \div 2}{2 \text{ ft} \div 2} = \frac{3}{1}$ There ratio of body length to skull length is 3 : 1.

Words	The body length is 3 times the skull length.
Variable	Let b represent the length of the crocodile with a 3.5 foot skull.
Equation	$b = 3 \cdot 3.5$

$b = 3 \cdot 3.5$ or 10.5 Multiply.

So, a crocodile with a 3.5-foot skull is about 10.5 feet long.

CHOOSE Your Method

f. **RUNNING** How long will it take Salvador to run a 300-meter race if he can run 120 meters in 24 seconds?

CHECK Your Understanding

Example 1 (p. 349)

Determine if the quantities in each pair of ratios are proportional. Explain.

1. 2 adults for 10 children and 3 adults for 12 children
2. 12 inches by 8 inches and 18 inches by 12 inches
3. 8 feet in 21 seconds and 12 feet in 31.5 seconds
4. \$5.60 for 5 pairs of socks and \$7.12 for 8 pairs of socks

Examples 2, 3 (pp. 349–350)

Solve each proportion.

5. $\frac{5}{6} = \frac{t}{18}$
6. $\frac{6}{k} = \frac{24}{28}$
7. $\frac{21}{5} = \frac{c}{7}$
8. $\frac{15}{w} = \frac{2}{5}$
9. $\frac{3}{n} = \frac{2.7}{18}$
10. $\frac{0.2}{3} = \frac{3}{d}$

Example 4 (p. 350)

11. **GROCERIES** Orange juice is on sale 3 half-gallons for \$5. At this rate, find the cost of 5 half-gallons of orange juice to the nearest cent.

12. **TRAVEL** Franco drove 203 miles in 3.5 hours. At this rate, how long will it take him to drive another 29 miles to the next town?

Exercises

HOMEWORK HELP

For Exercises	See Examples
13–20	1
21–32	2, 3
33–40	4

Determine if the quantities in each pair of ratios are proportional. Explain.

13. 20 children from 6 families to 16 children from 5 families
14. 5 pounds of dry ice melts in 30 hours and 4 pounds melts in 24 hours
15. 16 winners out of 200 entries and 28 winners out of 350 entries
16. 5 meters in 7 minutes and 25 meters in 49 minutes
17. 1.4 tons produced every 18 days and 10.5 tons every 60 days
18. 3 inches for every 4 miles and 7.5 inches for every 10 miles

19. **READING** Leslie reads 25 pages in 45 minutes. After 60 minutes, she has read a total of 30 pages. Is her time proportional to the number of pages she reads? Explain.

20. **PETS** A store sells 2 hamsters for \$11 and 6 hamsters for \$33. Is the cost proportional to the number of hamsters sold? Explain.

Solve each proportion.

21. $\frac{3}{8} = \frac{b}{40}$
22. $\frac{x}{12} = \frac{12}{4}$
23. $\frac{c}{7} = \frac{18}{42}$
24. $\frac{5}{k} = \frac{10}{22}$
25. $\frac{3}{8} = \frac{n}{4}$
26. $\frac{15}{4} = \frac{3}{g}$
27. $\frac{45}{5} = \frac{d}{7}$
28. $\frac{30}{a} = \frac{8}{20}$
29. $\frac{1.6}{m} = \frac{2}{3}$
30. $\frac{4.5}{5} = \frac{t}{7}$
31. $\frac{2.5}{4.5} = \frac{7.5}{x}$
32. $\frac{3.8}{5.2} = \frac{7.6}{z}$

33. **SCHOOL** If 4 notebooks weigh 2.8 pounds, how much do 6 of the same notebooks weigh?

34. **COOKING** There are 6 teaspoons in 2 tablespoons. How many teaspoons are in 1.5 tablespoons?

ANALYZE TABLES For Exercises 35–38, use the table.

35. How many stalks of celery yield $3\frac{1}{2}$ cups of celery slices?
36. How many cups of broccoli florets would 1 pound of broccoli produce?
37. About how many ounces of carrots yields 2 cups sliced?
38. How many cups of sliced celery would $7\frac{1}{2}$ stalks of celery yield?

39. **SCIENCE** The ratio of salt to water in a certain solution is 4 to 15. If the solution contains 6 ounces of water, how many ounces of salt does it contain?

Real-World Link Film for an IMAX projection system passes through the projector at the rate of 330 feet per minute or 5.5 feet per second.
Source: hfmgv.org

40. **CONCERTS** Alethia purchased 7 advanced tickets for herself and her friends to a concert and paid $164.50. If the total cost of tickets to the concert is proportional to the number purchased, how many tickets to the same concert did Serefina purchase if she paid a total of $94?

41. **SAVINGS** Pao spent $140 of his paycheck and put the remaining $20 in his savings account. If the number of dollars he spends is proportional to the number he saves, how much of a $156-paycheck will he put into savings?

42. **MOVIES** After 30 seconds, 720 frames of film have passed through a movie projector. At this rate, what is the approximate running time in minutes of a movie made up of 57,000 frames of film?

EXTRA PRACTICE
See pages 734, 761.
Math Online
Self-Check Quiz at tx.msmath2.com

43. **SCHOOL** There are 325 students and 13 teachers at a school. Next school year, the enrollment is expected to increase by 100 students. Write and solve a proportion to find the number of teachers that must be hired so the student-teacher ratio remains the same.

44. **FIND THE DATA** Refer to the Texas Data File on pages 16–19. Choose some data and write a real-world problem in which you would solve a proportion.

H.O.T. Problems

45. **Which One Doesn't Belong?** Identify the rate that is not proportional to the other three. Explain your reasoning.

$4.50 for 5 lb	$2.88 for 3.2 lb	$5.70 for 6 lb	$4.86 for 5.4 lb

46. **CHALLENGE** A box contains juice boxes, bottles of water, and cans of soft drinks. If the ratio of water to juice is 1:6 and the ratio of juice to soft drinks is 3:5, what is the ratio of water to soft drinks? Explain your reasoning.

47. **SELECT A TECHNIQUE** Sweet corn is on sale at \$2.50 for a dozen at a farmer's market. Select one or more of the following technique(s) to determine how many ears you can buy for \$10. Then use this technique to solve the problem.

mental math | estimation | number sense

48. **WRITING IN MATH** Marshall walks 3 large dogs and 2 small dogs for a dog-walking service. If he is hired to walk 2 more large dogs and 2 more small dogs, will the ratio of large dogs to small dogs stay the same? Explain your reasoning.

TEST PRACTICE

49. Mirma gives away 84 flyers over a 3-hour period. If the number of flyers she is able to give away per hour remains the same, which proportion can be used to find x, the number of flyers that she would give away over a 5-hour period?

A $\frac{3}{84} = \frac{x}{5}$

B $\frac{84}{3} = \frac{x}{5}$

C $\frac{5}{3} = \frac{84}{x}$

D $\frac{3}{84} = \frac{x}{8}$

50. A recipe that makes 16 muffins calls for $\frac{1}{2}$ cup of flour. How much flour is needed to make 3 dozen muffins using this recipe?

F $1\frac{1}{8}$ c

G 1 c

H $1\frac{1}{4}$ c

J $1\frac{1}{2}$ c

Spiral Review

MEASUREMENT **Complete.** (Lesson 7-3)

51. 5 qt = ▪ pt

52. $3\frac{1}{2}$ lb = ▪ oz

53. 28 c = ▪ qt

54. **GROCERIES** Which is a better buy: 5 pounds of onions for \$2.99 or 3 pounds of onions for \$1.59? (Lesson 7-2)

Multiply. Write in simplest form. (Lesson 6-5)

55. $3\frac{1}{2} \times 5\frac{7}{8}$

56. $1\frac{2}{3} \times 5\frac{4}{5}$

57. $2\frac{1}{4} \times 7\frac{5}{8}$

GET READY for the Next Lesson

58. **PREREQUISITE SKILL** Mr. Andres is filling up his car with gas that costs \$2.50 per gallon. His car's gas gauge before filling up is shown at the right. If his car's gas tank holds 16 gallons, about how much will Mr. Andres pay to fill up his tank? Use the *eliminate possibilities* strategy. (Lesson 6-4)

A \$15.00

B \$25.00

C \$27.00

D \$35.00

Extend 7-4

Math Lab
Wildlife Sampling

Main IDEA

Use proportions to estimate populations.

Targeted TEKS 7.3 The student solves problems involving direct proportional relationships. (B) **estimate and find solutions to application problems involving proportional relationships such as similarity, scaling, unit costs, and related measurement units.**

Naturalists can estimate the population in a wildlife preserve by using the capture-recapture technique. In this lab, you will model this technique using dried beans in a bowl to represent deer in a forest.

ACTIVITY

STEP 1 Fill a small bowl with dried beans.

STEP 2 Use the paper cup to scoop out some of the beans. These represent the original *captured* deer. Record the number in a table like the one shown at the right. Mark each bean with an × on both sides. Then return these beans to the bowl and mix well.

Original Number Captured			
Trial	Sample	Recaptured	*P*
A			
B			
C			
⋮			
J			
Total			

STEP 3 Scoop another cup of beans from the bowl and count them. This is the *sample* for Trial A. Count the beans with the ×'s. These are the *recaptured* deer. Record both numbers.

STEP 4 Use the proportion below to estimate the total number of beans in the bowl. This represents the total population *P*. Record the value of *P* in the table.

$$\frac{\text{captured}}{\text{total population } (P)} = \frac{\text{recaptured}}{\text{sample}}$$

STEP 5 Return all of the beans to the bowl.

STEP 6 Repeat Steps 3–5 nine times.

Analyze the Results

1. **ESTIMATION** Find the average of the estimates in column *P*. Is this a good estimate of the number of beans in the bowl? Explain your reasoning.
2. Count the actual number of beans in the bowl. How does this number compare to your estimate?

CHAPTER 7 Mid-Chapter Quiz

Lessons 7-1 through 7-4

RECIPE For Exercises 1–3, use the information in the table to write each ratio as a fraction in simplest form. (Lesson 7-1)

Cherry Punch Recipe	
Cherry Juice	4 cups
Apple Juice	2 cups
Ginger Ale	16 cups

1. cherry juice : apple juice
2. apple juice : ginger ale
3. cherry juice : ginger ale

Determine whether the ratios are equivalent. Explain. (Lesson 7-1)

4. 6 out of 9 words spelled correctly
   2 out of 3 words spelled correctly
5. 150 athletes to 15 coaches
   3 athletes to 1 coach
6. 24 points in 4 games
   72 points in 8 games

Find each unit rate. Round to the nearest hundredth if necessary. (Lesson 7-2)

7. 200 miles in 4 hours
8. \$6.20 for 5 pounds
9. 98 carbohydrates in 8 servings

10. **TEST PRACTICE** Celeste's favorite type of chocolate comes in four different amounts. Which amount of chocolate shown in the table has the best unit price? (Lesson 7-2)

Weight (oz)	Cost (\$)
12	2.50
18	3.69
24	4.95
30	6.25

A 12 oz C 24 oz
B 18 oz D 36 oz

Complete. (Lesson 7-3)

11. 42 ft = ▒ yd
12. 9 pt = ▒ qt
13. 7,600 lb = ▒ T
14. $7\frac{1}{2}$ gal = ▒ qt

15. **TEST PRACTICE** Which situation is best represented by the graph? (Lesson 7-3)

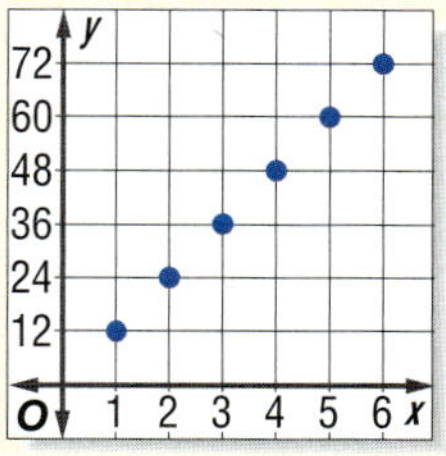

F Conversion of inches to yards
G Conversion of feet to inches
H Conversion of inches to miles
J Conversion of yards to feet

Determine if the quantities in each pair of ratios are proportional. Explain. (Lesson 7-4)

16. 8 pages in 5 minutes and 40 pages in 25 minutes
17. 40 blank CDs for \$9.60 and 24 blank CDs for \$4.80
18. 45 pounds in 30 bags and 72 pounds in 48 bags

Solve each proportion. (Lesson 7-4)

19. $\frac{3}{d} = \frac{12}{20}$
20. $\frac{7}{8} = \frac{m}{48}$
21. $\frac{w}{8} = \frac{1}{3}$
22. $\frac{1}{4} = \frac{3}{t}$

23. **TEST PRACTICE** It took 45 minutes to fill a circular pool of uniform depth to a level of 17 inches. At this rate, which of the following represents the approximate length of time will it take to fill the pool to a level of 35 inches? (Lesson 7-4)

A 138 min C 93 min
B 63 min D 22 min

7-5 Problem-Solving Investigation

MAIN IDEA: Solve problems by drawing a diagram.

Targeted TEKS 7.13 The student applies Grade 7 mathematics to solve problems connected to everyday experiences, investigations in other disciplines, and activities in and outside of school. **(C) select or develop an appropriate problem-solving strategy from a variety of different types, including drawing a picture,... to solve a problem.** *Also addresses TEKS 7.13(B).*

P.S.I. TEAM +

I-M: DRAW A DIAGRAM

YOUR MISSION: Draw a diagram to solve the problem.

THE PROBLEM: How much farther do we have to drive?

Frieda: We've gone about 90 miles, which is about $\frac{2}{3}$ of the way to the campsite. So, how much farther do we have to go?

<table>
<tr><td>EXPLORE</td><td>You know that 90 miles is about $\frac{2}{3}$ of the total distance.</td></tr>
<tr><td>PLAN</td><td>Draw a diagram showing the fractional part of the distance.</td></tr>
<tr><td>SOLVE</td><td>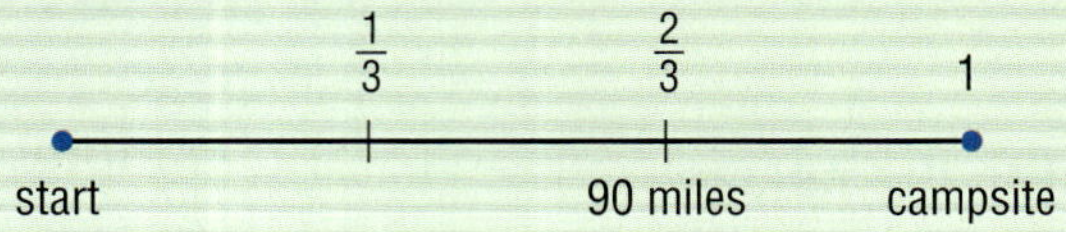

If $\frac{2}{3}$ of the distance is 90 miles, then $\frac{1}{3}$ of the distance would be 45 miles. So, the missing third must be another 45 miles.
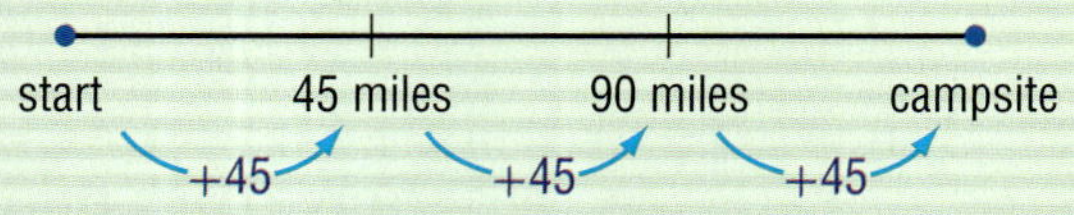

The total distance is 90 + 45 or 135 miles.</td></tr>
<tr><td>CHECK</td><td>Since $\frac{2}{3}$ of the total distance is 90 miles, and $\frac{2}{3}(135) = 90$, the solution checks.</td></tr>
</table>

Analyze The Strategy

1. Determine how far the trip would have been if the 90 miles were only $\frac{1}{3}$ of the total distance. Draw a new diagram for this situation.
2. **WRITING IN MATH** Write a problem that could be solved by drawing a diagram. Exchange your problem with a classmate and solve.

Mixed Problem Solving

Solve Exercises 3–5. Use the *draw a diagram* strategy.

3. **PHYSICAL SCIENCE** A ball is dropped from a height of 10 feet. It hits the ground and bounces up half as high as it fell. This is true for each successive bounce. What height does the ball reach on the fourth bounce?

4. **FAMILY** At Nelia's family reunion, 80% of the people are 18 years of age or older. Half of the remaining people are under 12 years old. If 20 children are under 12 years old, how many people are at the reunion?

5. **VOLUME** A swimming pool is being filled with water. After 25 minutes, $\frac{1}{6}$ of the swimming pool is filled. How much longer will it take to completely fill the pool, assuming the water rate is constant?

Use any strategy to solve Exercises 6–8. Some strategies are shown below.

PROBLEM-SOLVING STRATEGIES
- Use the four-step plan.
- Work backward.
- Eliminate possibilities.
- Draw a diagram.

6. **GEOMETRY** Jamila is adding 3 feet to the length and width of her rectangular garden, as shown.

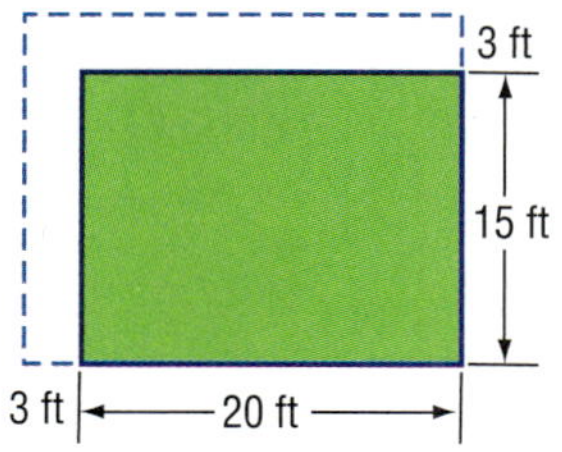

Which expression represents the area of land to be added to the original garden?

A $(15 + 3)(20 + 3)$

B $(15 + 3)(20 + 3) - (15)(20)$

C $(15 - 3)(20 - 3)$

D $(15 - 3)(20 - 3) - (15)(20)$

7. **GAMES** Six members of a video game club are having a tournament. In the first round, every player will play a video game against every other player. How many games will be in the first round of the tournament?

8. **MONEY** Mr. Li has $240 in his checking account after writing checks for $15.70, $43.20, and $18. What was his balance before he wrote the three checks?

Select the Operation

For Exercises 9 and 10, select the appropriate operation(s) to solve the problem. Justify your selection(s) and solve the problem.

9. **BUSINESS** The graph shows the annual spending by five industries in the United States.

Source: *The Top Ten of Everything*

Estimate how much more the automotive industry spends than the retail industry.

10. **TESTS** The scores on a test are found by adding or subtracting points as shown below. If Salazar's score on a 15-question test was 86 points, how many of his answers were correct, incorrect, and blank?

Answer	Points
Correct	+8
Incorrect	−4
No answer	−2

7-6 Scale Drawings

Main IDEA

Solve problems involving scale drawings.

Targeted TEKS 7.3 The student solves problems involving direct proportional relationships. **(B) estimate and find solutions to application problems involving proportional relationships such as similarity, scaling, unit costs, and related measurement units.** *Also addresses TEKS 7.5(B).*

NEW Vocabulary

scale drawing
scale model
scale
scale factor

MINI Lab

Concepts in MOtion Interactive Lab tx.msmath2.com

- Measure the length of each wall, door, window, and chalkboard in your classroom.
- Record each length to the nearest $\frac{1}{2}$ foot.

1. Let 1 unit on the grid paper represent 1 foot. So, 6 units = 6 feet. Convert all of your measurements to units.
2. On grid paper, make a drawing of your classroom like the one shown at the right.

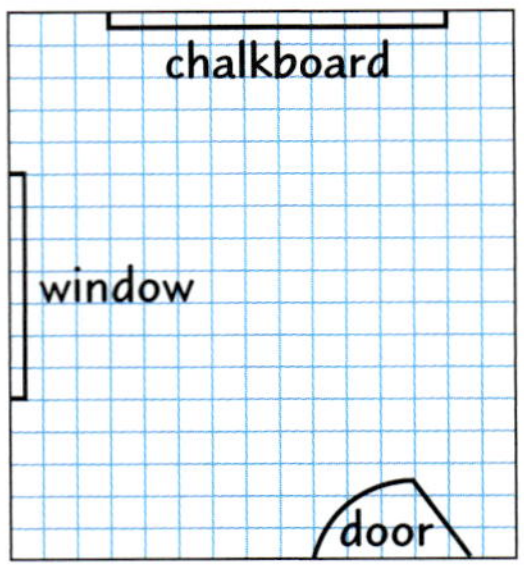

A map is an example of a scale drawing. **Scale drawings** and **scale models** are used to represent objects that are too large or too small to be drawn or built at actual size. The **scale** gives the ratio that compares the measurements on the drawing or model to the measurements of the real object. The measurements on a drawing or model are proportional to measurements of the actual object.

EXAMPLE Use a Map Scale

1 **MAPS** **What is the actual distance between Corpus Christi and Austwell?**

Step 1 Use a centimeter ruler to find the map distance between the two cities. The map distance is about 4.4 centimeters.

Step 2 Write and solve a proportion using the scale. Let d represent the actual distance between the cities.

	Scale		Corpus Christi to Austwell	
map → actual →	$\frac{1 \text{ centimeter}}{20 \text{ kilometers}}$	=	$\frac{4.4 \text{ centimeters}}{d \text{ kilometers}}$	← map ← actual

$1 \times d = 20 \times 4.4$ Cross products

$d = 88$ Simplify.

The distance between the cities is about 88 kilometers.

STUDY TIP

Scale A map scale can be written in different ways, including the following:

1 cm = 20 km

1 cm : 20 km

$\frac{1 \text{ cm}}{20 \text{ km}}$

CHECK Your Progress

a. **MAPS** On the map of Arkansas shown, find the distance between Clarksville and Little Rock. Use a ruler to measure.

A blueprint is another example of a scale drawing.

STUDY TIP

Alternate Method You could also set up and solve the proportion below.

$$\frac{\frac{1}{4}\text{ in.}}{2\text{ ft}} = \frac{\frac{7}{4}\text{ in.}}{w\text{ ft}} \quad (\times 7)$$

So, $w = 14$ ft.

EXAMPLE Use a Blueprint Scale

2 POOLS On the blueprint of the pool, each square has a side length of $\frac{1}{4}$ inch. What is the actual width of the pool?

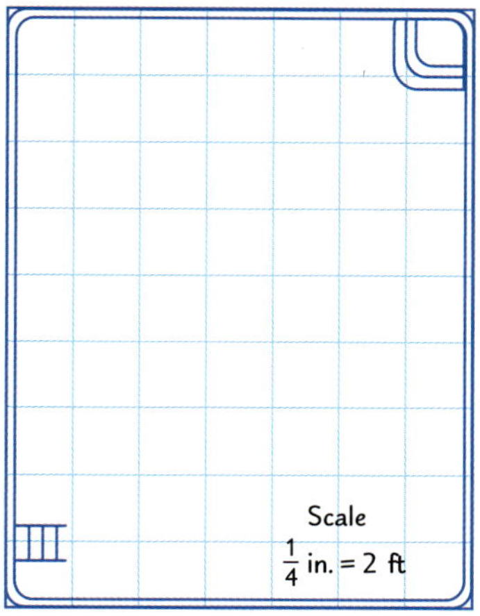

The pool on the blueprint is $1\frac{3}{4}$ inches wide. Write and solve a proportion using the scale. Let w represent the actual width of the pool.

	Scale		Width of Pool	
blueprint →	$\frac{1}{4}$ inch	=	$1\frac{3}{4}$ inches	← blueprint
actual →	2 feet		w feet	← actual

$$\frac{\frac{1}{4}\text{ inch}}{2\text{ feet}} = \frac{1\frac{3}{4}\text{ inches}}{w\text{ feet}}$$

$\frac{1}{4} \cdot w = 2 \cdot 1\frac{3}{4}$ — Cross products

$\frac{1}{4}w = \frac{14}{4}$ — Multiply.

$w = 14$ — Simplify. Multiply each side by 4.

The actual width of the pool is 14 feet.

CHECK Your Progress

b. **INTERIOR DESIGN** On the blueprint of the living room, each square has a side length of $\frac{1}{4}$ inch. What are the actual dimensions of the living room?

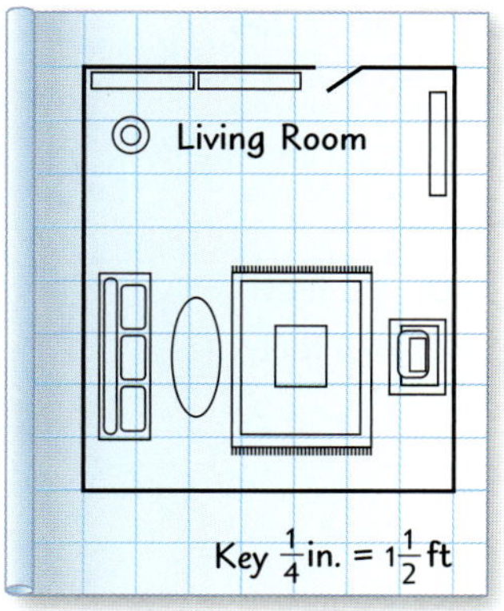

STUDY TIP

Scale The scale is the ratio of the drawing/model measure to the actual measure. It is not always the ratio of a smaller measure to a larger measure.

EXAMPLE Use a Scale Model

3 **COMPUTERS** **Designers are creating a larger model of the computer memory board. If they use a scale of 20 inches = 1 inch, what is the length of the model?**

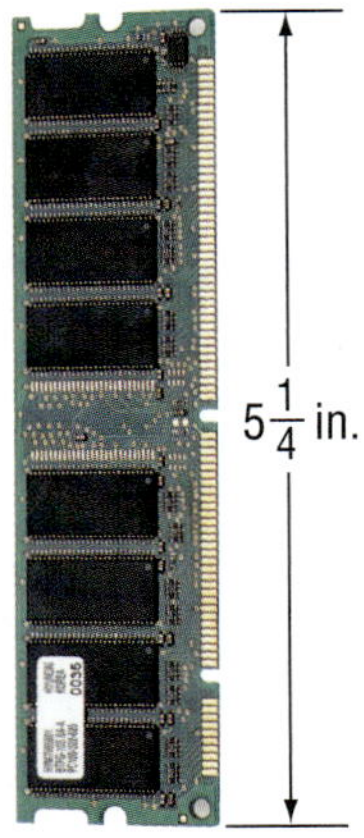

Write a proportion using the scale.
Let m represent the length of the model.

	Scale		Length	
model → actual →	$\frac{20 \text{ inches}}{1 \text{ inch}}$	=	$\frac{m \text{ inches}}{5\frac{1}{4} \text{ inches}}$	← model ← actual

$20 \cdot 5\frac{1}{4} = 1 \cdot m$ Cross products

$105 = m$ Multiply.

The scale model is 105 inches long.

CHECK Your Progress

c. **SCOOTERS** A scooter is $3\frac{1}{2}$ feet long. Find the length of a scale model of the scooter if the scale is 1 inch = $\frac{3}{4}$ feet.

Online Personal Tutor at tx.msmath2.com

In Lesson 7–3, you used ratios to convert units. You can use a similar method to simplify a scale. A scale written as a ratio without units in simplest form is called the **scale factor**.

scale → $\frac{\frac{1}{4} \text{ inch}}{2 \text{ feet}} = \frac{\frac{1}{4} \text{ inch}}{24 \text{ inches}}$ Convert 2 feet to inches.

$= \frac{4}{4} \cdot \frac{\frac{1}{4} \text{ inch}}{24 \text{ inches}}$ Mutiply by $\frac{4}{4}$ to eliminate the fraction in the numerator.

$= \frac{1}{96}$ ← scale factor

STUDY TIP

Equivalent Scales The scales below are equivalent because their scale factors are equal, $\frac{1}{72}$.

- 1 inch = 6 feet
- $\frac{1}{2}$ inch = 3 feet

EXAMPLE Find a Scale Factor

4 **SAILBOATS** **Find the scale factor of a model sailboat if the scale is 1 inch = 6 feet.**

$\frac{1 \text{ inch}}{6 \text{ feet}} = \frac{1 \text{ inch}}{72 \text{ inches}}$ Convert 6 feet to inches.

$= \frac{1}{72}$ Divide out the common units.

The scale factor is $\frac{1}{72}$. That is, each measure on the model is $\frac{1}{72}$ of the actual measure.

CHECK Your Progress

d. **CARS** What is the scale factor of a model car if the scale is 1 inch = 2 feet?

CHECK Your Understanding

Example 1 (pp. 358–359)

GEOGRAPHY **Find the actual distance between each pair of cities in New Mexico. Use a ruler to measure.**

1. Carlsbad and Artesia
2. Hobbs and Eunice
3. Artesia and Eunice
4. Lovington and Carlsbad

Example 2 (p. 359)

BLUEPRINTS **For Exercises 5 and 6, use the blueprint. Each square has a side length of $\frac{1}{2}$ inch.**

5. Find the actual length ℓ of the kitchen.
6. Estimate the walking distance from the range to the refrigerator.

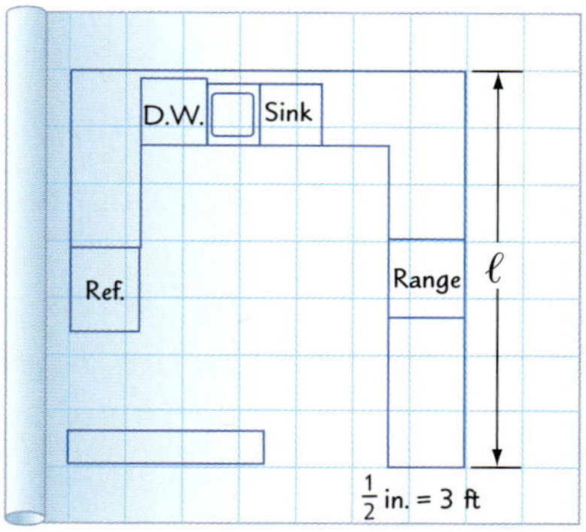

Example 3 (p. 360)

BRIDGES **For Exercises 7 and 8, use the following information.**

A engineer makes a model of the bridge using a scale of 1 inch = 3 yards.

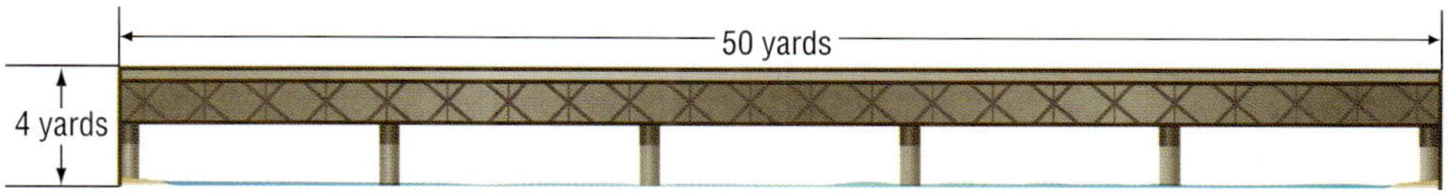

7. What is the length of the model?
8. What is the height of the model?

Example 4 (p. 360)

Find the scale factor of each scale drawing or model.

9.

1 inch = 4 feet

10.

1 centimeter = 15 millimeters

11. **CITY PLANNING** In the aerial view of a city block at the right, the length of Main Street is 2 inches. If Main Street's actual length is 2 miles, find the scale factor of the drawing.

Exercises

HOMEWORK HELP

For Exercises	See Examples
12–15	1
16–17	2
18–24	3, 4

GEOGRAPHY **Find the actual distance between each pair of locations in South Carolina. Use a ruler to measure.**

12. Columbia and Charleston
13. Hollywood and Sumter
14. Congaree Swamp and Charleston
15. Sumter and Columbia

For Exercises 16–18, use the blueprint of an apartment at the right. Each square has a side length of $\frac{1}{4}$ inch.

16. What is the actual length of the living room?
17. Find the actual dimensions of the master bedroom.
18. Find the scale factor for this blueprint.

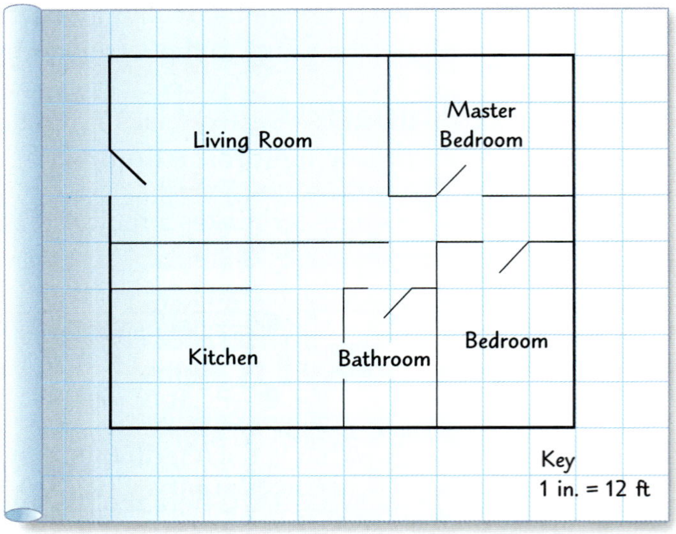

Find the length of each model. Then find the scale factor.

19.

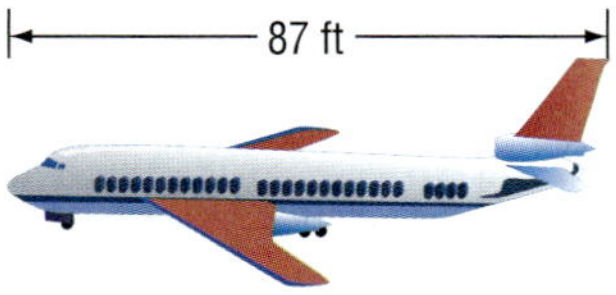

2 in. = 15 ft

20.

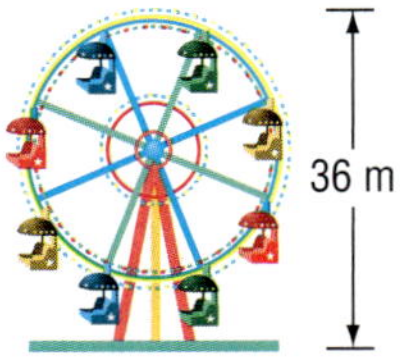

0.5 cm = 1.5 m

21.

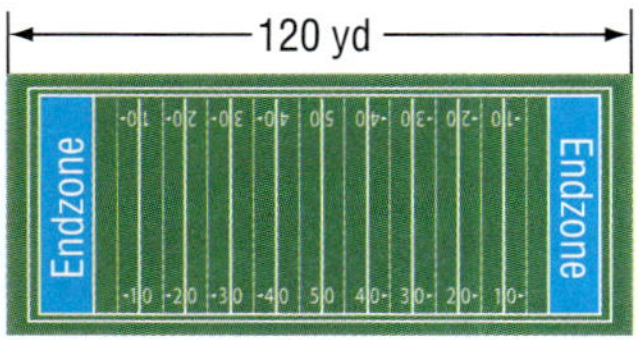

1 in. = 20 yd

22.

1 in. = 0.5 in.

EXTRA PRACTICE

See pages 734, 761.

Math Online
Self-Check Quiz at
tx.msmath2.com

Real-World Link Mount Rushmore is a sculpture that was carved using a model with a scale of 1 inch : 1 foot.

23. **GEOGRAPHY** A map of Bakersfield, California, has a scale of 1 inch to 5 miles. If the city is $5\frac{1}{5}$ inches across on the map, what is the actual distance across the actual city? Use estimation to check your answer.

24. **TREES** A model of a tree is made using a scale of 1 inch : 25 feet. What is the height of the actual tree if the height of the model is $4\frac{3}{8}$ inches?

25. **SCULPTURES** Refer to the information at the left. Find the scale factor and the actual height of George Washington's face on the sculpture if the height of the model's face is 5 feet.

26. **GEOGRAPHY** Lexington and Elizabethtown, Kentucky, are 79 miles apart. If the distance on the map is $2\frac{1}{2}$ inches, find the scale of the map.

27. **RESEARCH** Find the dimensions of any U.S. presidential monument. Give an appropriate scale that can be used to make a scale model of the monument. State the dimensions of the model using your scale.

28. **IGLOOS** The diameter of the circular floor of an igloo is 10 feet. If you were to make a model of the igloo with sugar cubes, which might be an appropriate scale: 1 in. = 1 ft or 1 in. = 50 ft? Explain your reasoning.

29. **LIFE SCIENCE** A scale drawing of a red blood cell is shown below. If the blood cell's actual diameter is 0.008 millimeter, use a ruler to find the scale factor of the drawing.

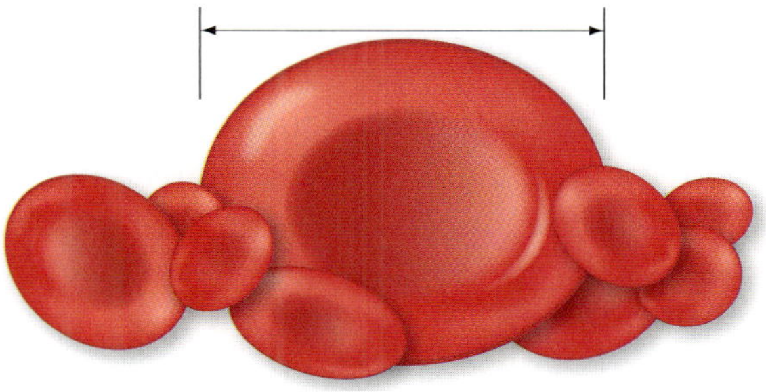

H.O.T. Problems

30. **OPEN ENDED** On grid paper, create a scale drawing of a room in your home. Include the scale that you used.

31. **CHALLENGE** Montoya constructed three models, A, B, and C, of the same figure, with scales of 0.5 cm = 1 mm, 1.5 mm = 4 cm, and 0.25 cm = 2.5 mm, respectively.

    a. Which model is larger than the actual figure? Justify your answer.

    b. Which model is smaller than the actual figure? Justify your answer.

    c. Which model is the same size as the actual figure? Justify your answer.

32. **REASONING** Compare and contrast the terms *scale* and *scale factor*. Include an example in your comparison.

33. **WRITING IN MATH** Explain how you could use estimation to find the actual distance between San Diego, California, and Seattle, Washington, on a map.

TEST PRACTICE

34. A scale drawing of a doctor's office is shown.

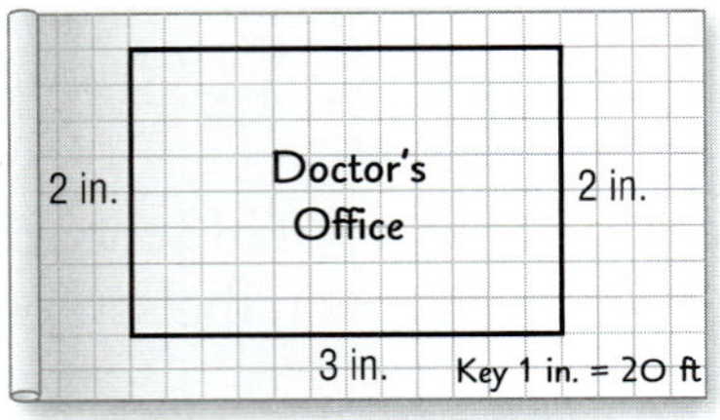

What are the actual dimensions of the doctor's office?

A 24 feet by 48 feet

B 30 feet by 52 feet

C 40 feet by 60 feet

D 37.5 feet by 65 feet

35. **GRIDDABLE** A scale model of a new office building is shown. If the scale is 5 inches = 18 feet, how tall is the actual building in feet?

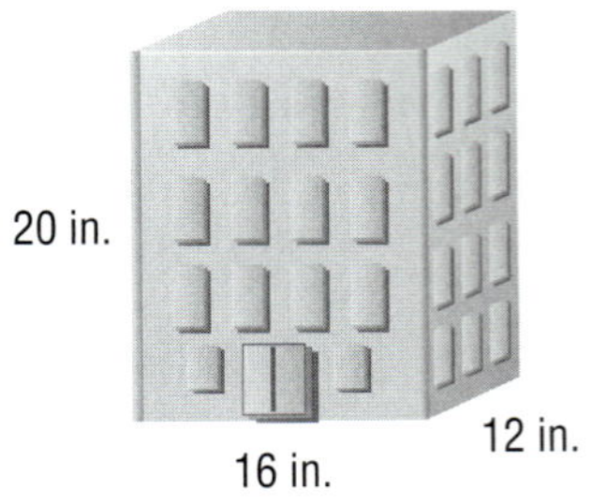

36. Ernesto drew a map of his school. He used a scale in which 1 inch equals 50 feet. What distance on Ernesto's map should represent the 625 feet between the cafeteria and the science lab?

F 8 in. **H** 12.5 in.

G 10.5 in. **J** 15 in.

Spiral Review

37. **BIRDS** In a certain pair of binoculars, objects 35 feet away appear to be only 1 foot away. If a goldfinch is 368 feet away, what will the distance appear to be in the binoculars? Round to the nearest tenth. (Lesson 7-4)

Find each unit rate. (Lesson 7-2)

38. 200 miles in 5 hours 39. 99¢ for 30 ounces 40. 150 meters in 12 seconds

41. **JOGGING** The table shows the number of miles Tonya jogged each week for the past several weeks. Estimate the total number of miles she jogged. (Lesson 6-1)

Week	Miles
1	$7\frac{1}{6}$
2	$8\frac{3}{4}$
3	10
4	$12\frac{1}{4}$
5	$6\frac{2}{3}$

Find each product. (Lesson 3-3)

42. $4.5 \times 1{,}000$

43. 0.361×100

44. $17.89 \times 10{,}000$

45. $0.08 \times 100{,}000$

46. $1.17 \times 1{,}000$

47. 53×100

GET READY for the Next Lesson

PREREQUISITE SKILL **Divide. Write in simplest form.** (Lesson 6-7)

48. $2\frac{3}{4} \div 10$ 49. $4\frac{1}{3} \div 10$ 50. $30\frac{2}{3} \div 100$ 51. $87\frac{1}{2} \div 100$

Extend 7-6

Spreadsheet Lab
Scale Drawings

Main IDEA

Use a spreadsheet to calculate measurements for scale drawings.

Targeted TEKS 7.3 The student solves problems involving direct proportional relationships. **(B) estimate and find solutions to application problems involving proportional relationships such as similarity, scaling, unit costs, and related measurement units.**

A computer spreadsheet is a useful tool for calculating measures for scale drawings. You can change the scale factors and the dimensions, and the spreadsheet will automatically calculate the new values.

ACTIVITY

Suppose you want to make a scale drawing of your school. Set up a spreadsheet like the one shown below. In this spreadsheet, the actual measures are in feet, and the scale drawing measures are in inches.

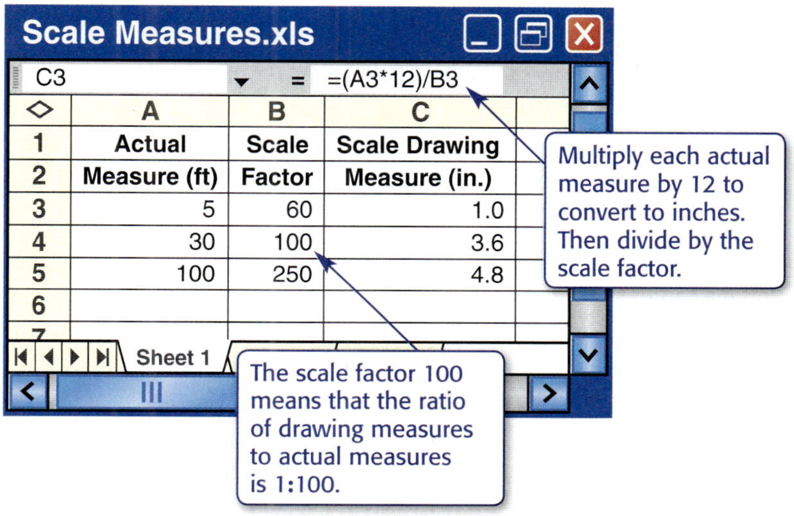
Scale Measures.xls

C3 = =(A3*12)/B3

	A	B	C
1	Actual	Scale	Scale Drawing
2	Measure (ft)	Factor	Measure (in.)
3	5	60	1.0
4	30	100	3.6
5	100	250	4.8
6			

Analyze the Results

1. The length of one side of the school building is 100 feet. If you use a scale factor of 1:250, what is the length on your scale drawing?
2. The length of a classroom is 30 feet. What is the scale factor if the length of the classroom on a scale drawing is 3.6 inches?
3. Calculate the length of a 30-foot classroom on a scale drawing if the scale factor is 1:10.
4. The width of a hallway is 20 feet. What is the scale factor if the width of the hallway on a scale drawing is 2.5 inches?
5. Suppose the actual measures of your school are given in meters. Describe how you could use a spreadsheet to calculate the scale drawing measures in centimeters using a scale factor of 1:50.
6. Choose three rooms in your home and use a spreadsheet to make scale drawings. First, choose an appropriate scale and calculate the scale factor. Include a sketch of the furniture drawn to scale in each room.

7-7 Fractions, Decimals, and Percents

Main IDEA

Write percents as fractions, and decimals and vice versa.

Targeted TEKS 7.1 The student represents and uses numbers in a variety of equivalent forms. **(B) convert between fractions, decimals, whole numbers, and percents mentally, on paper, or with a calculator.** *Also addresses TEKS 7.1(A).*

GET READY for the Lesson

SURVEYS The graph shows the results of a survey in which teens were asked to name the most important invention of the 20th century.

1. What percent of the teens said that the personal computer was the most important invention?
2. How is this percent written as a ratio?
3. Simplify the ratio.

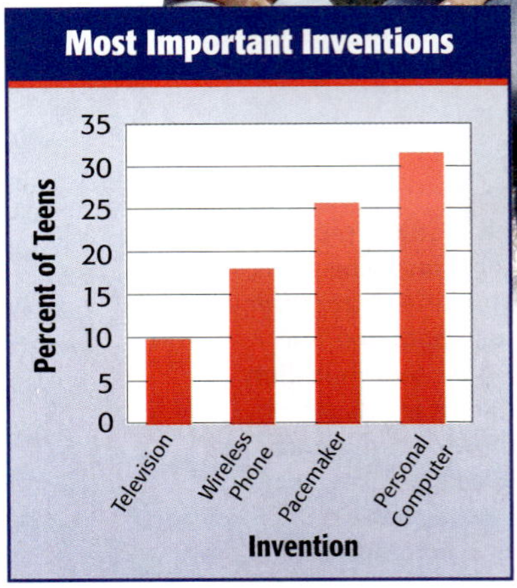

Source: Lemelson-MIT Program

REVIEW Vocabulary

percent a ratio that compares a number to 100 (Lesson 5-6)

In Lesson 5-6, you wrote percents like 32% as fractions by writing fractions with denominators of 100 and then simplifying. You can use the same method to write percents like 16.8% and $8\frac{1}{3}\%$ as fractions.

EXAMPLES Percents as Fractions

1 HOCKEY In men's college hockey, 16.8% of the players are from Ontario, Canada. What fraction is this? Write in simplest form.

$16.8\% = \frac{16.8}{100}$ Write a fraction with a denominator of 100.

$= \frac{16.8}{100} \cdot \frac{10}{10}$ Multiply by $\frac{10}{10}$ to eliminate the decimal in the numerator.

$= \frac{168}{1,000}$ or $\frac{21}{125}$ Simplify.

So, out of every 125 players, 21 are from Ontario.

2 Write $8\frac{1}{3}\%$ as a fraction in simplest form.

$8\frac{1}{3}\% = \frac{8\frac{1}{3}}{100}$ Write a fraction.

$= 8\frac{1}{3} \div 100$ Divide.

$= \frac{25}{3} \div 100$ Write $8\frac{1}{3}$ as an improper fraction.

$= \frac{25}{3} \cdot \frac{1}{100}$ Multiply by the reciprocal of 100, which is $\frac{1}{100}$.

$= \frac{25}{300}$ or $\frac{1}{12}$ Simplify.

Math Online Extra Examples at tx.msmath2.com

CHECK Your Progress

Write each percent as a fraction in simplest form.

a. 15% b. $17\frac{1}{2}\%$ c. $33\frac{1}{3}\%$

To write a fraction like $\frac{8}{25}$ as a percent, multiply the numerator and the denominator by a number so that the denominator is 100. If the denominator is not a factor of 100, you can write fractions as percents by using a proportion.

EXAMPLES Fractions as Percents

3 TESTS On a math test, Amalia got 7 questions correct out of 8. Find her grade as a percent.

To find Amalia's grade, write $\frac{7}{8}$ as a percent.

Estimate $\frac{6}{8} = \frac{3}{4}$ or 75%.

So, $\frac{7}{8}$ is greater than 75%.

$\frac{7}{8} = \frac{n}{100}$ Write a proportion.

$700 = 8n$ Find the cross products.

$\frac{700}{8} = \frac{8n}{8}$ Divide each side by 8.

$87\frac{1}{2} = n$ Simplify.

So, $\frac{7}{8} = 87\frac{1}{2}\%$ or 87.5%.

Check for Reasonableness 87.5% > 75% ✔

STUDY TIP

Choose the Method
To write a fraction as a percent,

- use *multiplication* when a fraction has a denominator that is a factor of 100,
- use a *proportion* for any type of fraction.

4 Write $\frac{4}{15}$ as a percent. Round to the nearest hundredth.

Estimate $\frac{4}{15}$ is about $\frac{4}{16}$, which equals $\frac{1}{4}$ or 25%.

$\frac{4}{15} = \frac{n}{100}$ Write a proportion.

$400 = 15n$ Find the cross products.

$\frac{400}{15} = \frac{15n}{15}$ Divide each side by 15.

400 [÷] 15 [ENTER] 26.66666667 Use a calculator to simplify.

So, $\frac{4}{15}$ is about 26.67%.

Check for Reasonableness 26.67% ≈ 25% ✔

CHECK Your Progress

Write each fraction as a percent. Round to the nearest hundredth if necessary.

d. $\frac{2}{15}$ e. $\frac{7}{16}$ f. $\frac{17}{25}$

Online Personal Tutor at tx.msmath2.com

STUDY TIP

Look Back You can review **writing fractions as decimals** in Lesson 5-3.

In this lesson, you have written percents as fractions and fractions as percents. In Chapter 5, you wrote percents and fractions as decimals. You can also write a fraction as a percent by first writing the fraction as a decimal and then writing the decimal as a percent.

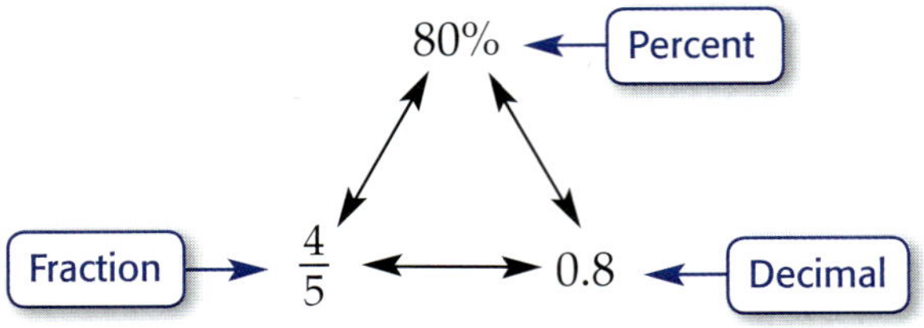

Percents, fractions, and decimals are all different names that represent the same number.

EXAMPLES Fractions as Percents

5 **Write $\frac{5}{6}$ as a percent. Round to the nearest hundredth.**

$\frac{5}{6} = 0.833333333...$ Write $\frac{5}{6}$ as a decimal.

$\approx 83.33\%$ Multiply by 100 and add the %.

6 **BOOKS** **Bryce has read $\frac{3}{5}$ of a book. What percent of the book has he read?**

$\frac{3}{5} = 0.6$ Write the fraction as a decimal.

$= 60\%$ Multiply by 100 and add the %.

So, Bryce has read 60% of the book.

CHECK Your Progress

Write each fraction as a percent. Round to the nearest hundredth if necessary.

g. $\frac{5}{16}$ h. $\frac{7}{12}$ i. $\frac{2}{9}$

j. **LAWNS** Mika is mowing lawns to earn extra money. She has mowed 6 out of 13 lawns. What percent of the lawns has she mowed?

Some fractions whose denominators are not factors of 100 are used often in everyday situations. It is helpful to memorize these fractions and their equivalent decimals and percents. These common equivalents are shown below.

KEY CONCEPT Common Equivalents

Fraction	Decimal	Percent	Fraction	Decimal	Percent
$\frac{1}{3}$	$0.\overline{3}$	$33\frac{1}{3}\%$	$\frac{3}{8}$	0.375	$37\frac{1}{2}\%$
$\frac{2}{3}$	$0.\overline{6}$	$66\frac{2}{3}\%$	$\frac{5}{8}$	0.625	$62\frac{1}{2}\%$
$\frac{1}{8}$	0.125	$12\frac{1}{2}\%$	$\frac{7}{8}$	0.875	$87\frac{1}{2}\%$

CHECK Your Understanding

Examples 1, 2
(pp. 366–367)

Write each percent as a fraction in simplest form.

1. 13.5%
2. 18.75%
3. $7\frac{1}{2}\%$
4. $66\frac{2}{3}\%$
5. **FOOD** Steven and Rebecca ate 62.5% of a pizza. What fraction of the pizza did they eat?

Examples 3–5
(pp. 367–368)

Write each fraction as a percent. Round to the nearest hundredth if necessary.

6. $\frac{3}{4}$
7. $\frac{4}{25}$
8. $\frac{4}{11}$
9. $\frac{1}{9}$

Example 6
(p. 368)

10. **SCHOOL** Moses has finished 11 out of 15 homework questions. To the nearest hundredth, what percent of the homework is complete?

Exercises

HOMEWORK HELP

For Exercises	See Examples
11–14, 19	1
15–18, 20	2
21–32	3–6
33–34	3

Write each percent as a fraction in simplest form.

11. 62.5%
12. 6.2%
13. 28.75%
14. 56.25%
15. $33\frac{1}{3}\%$
16. $16\frac{2}{3}\%$
17. $93\frac{3}{4}\%$
18. $78\frac{3}{4}\%$
19. **POPULATION** According to a recent census, 6.6% of all people living in Florida are 10–14 years old. What fraction of Florida's population is this?
20. **ATTENDANCE** At last year's spring dance, $78\frac{1}{3}\%$ of the student body attended. What fraction of the student body is this?

Write each fraction as a percent. Round to the nearest hundredth if necessary.

21. $\frac{11}{20}$
22. $\frac{18}{25}$
23. $\frac{3}{8}$
24. $\frac{21}{40}$
25. $\frac{29}{30}$
26. $\frac{8}{9}$
27. $\frac{5}{7}$
28. $\frac{1}{16}$
29. $\frac{1}{80}$
30. $\frac{57}{200}$
31. $\frac{5}{12}$
32. $\frac{7}{15}$
33. **LANGUAGES** In Virginia, 1 person out of every 40 speaks an Asian language at home. What percent of people in Virgina is this?
34. **PETS** In a class, 28 out of 32 students had a pet. What percent is this?

Replace each ● with >, <, or = to make a true statement.

35. $0.86 \bullet \frac{7}{8}$
36. $\frac{9}{20} \bullet 45\%$
37. $5\% \bullet 0.004$

Order each set of numbers from least to greatest.

38. $\frac{1}{4}$, 22%, 0.3, 0.02
39. 0.48, $\frac{1}{2}\%$, 0.5, $\frac{2}{5}$

Real-World Link
Out of the 50 states, 23 states border an ocean or the Gulf of Mexico.
Source: theus50.com

40. **GEOGRAPHY** Use the information at the left. What percent of the states in the United States do *not* border an ocean or the Gulf of Mexico?

EXTRA PRACTICE
See pages 735, 761.

Math Online
Self-Check Quiz at
tx.msmath2.com

41. **FIND THE DATA** Refer to the Texas Data File on pages 16–19. Choose some data and write a real-world problem in which you would write a fraction as a percent.

CARS For Exercises 42 and 43, use the table, which shows the percent of people in a recent survey who kept the listed items in their car.

Items in Car	Percent of People
Pen/Pencil	73.0%
Cassette Tapes/CDs	66.1%
First-aid Kit	38.2%
Sports Equipment	28.9%

42. What fraction of people kept a first-aid kit in their car?

43. Approximately 26 out of 125 people surveyed kept a hairbrush in their car. Is this greater or less than the percent who kept sports equipment? Explain.

H.O.T. Problems

44. **CHALLENGE** For what value of x does $\frac{1}{x} = x\%$?

45. **WRITING IN MATH** Describe two ways to write a fraction as a percent.

TEST PRACTICE

46. Ms. Gallagher made 64 ounces of punch. The punch contained 17 ounces of apple juice. Which equation can be used to find x, the percent of apple juice in the punch?

A $\frac{x}{100} = \frac{64}{17}$

B $\frac{x}{17} = \frac{64}{100}$

C $\frac{x}{64} = \frac{17}{100}$

D $\frac{x}{100} = \frac{17}{64}$

47. A group of 150 students were asked if they own a pet. The results are shown.

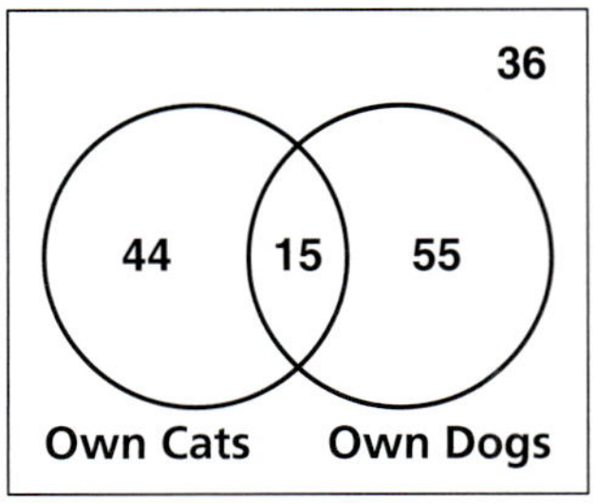

What percent of those surveyed own dogs?

F 50%
G 46.7%
H 36.7%
J 30%

Spiral Review

48. **MODELS** On a scale model of a building, 2 in. = 15 ft. If the model is 9 inches tall, how tall is the actual building? (Lesson 7-6)

Solve each proportion. (Lesson 7-4)

49. $\frac{6}{9} = \frac{4}{x}$

50. $\frac{3}{t} = \frac{9}{5}$

51. $\frac{n}{5} = \frac{2.8}{7}$

52. $\frac{7}{12} = \frac{r}{30}$

GET READY for the Next Lesson

PREREQUISITE SKILL Write each fraction in simplest form. (Lesson 5-4)

53. $\frac{8}{10}$

54. $\frac{45}{100}$

55. $\frac{450}{100}$

56. $\frac{175}{100}$

7-8 Percents Greater Than 100% and Percents Less Than 1%

Main IDEA

Write percents greater than 100% and percents less than 1% as fractions and as decimals, and vice versa.

Targeted TEKS **7.1** The student represents and uses numbers in a variety of equivalent forms. **(B)** **convert between fractions, decimals, whole numbers, and percents mentally, on paper, or with a calculator.**

MINI Lab

- Draw three 10 × 10 squares on a piece of grid paper. Each large square represents 100%. Each small square represents 1%.
- For the first model, use two grids to shade 120 small squares.
- For the second model, shade half of one small square on a grid.

Model 1

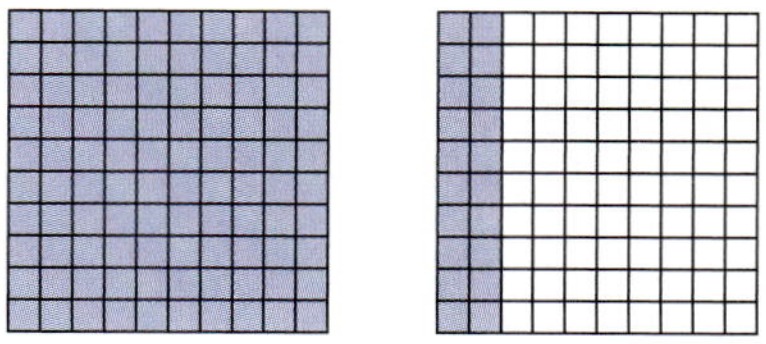

Model 2

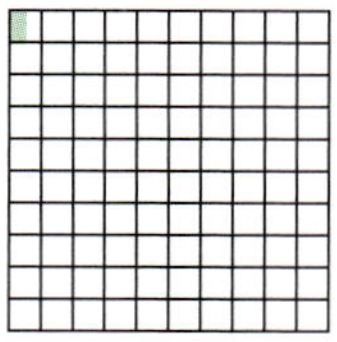

1. What percent does Model 1 represent? Model 2?

Shade grids to represent each percent.

2. 150% 3. 215% 4. $\frac{1}{4}\%$

Percents greater than 100% or less than 1% can be written as decimals. They can also be written as mixed numbers or fractions.

EXAMPLES Percents as Decimals or Fractions

1 **Write 0.2% as a decimal and as a fraction in simplest form.**

$0.2\% = 00.2$ — Divide by 100 and remove % symbol.

$= 0.002$ — Decimal form

$= \frac{2}{1,000}$ or $\frac{1}{500}$ — Fraction form

A percent less than 1% equals a number less than 0.01 or $\frac{1}{100}$.

2 **GEOGRAPHY** **The Amazon River is about 170% as long as the Mississippi River. Write 170% as a mixed number and as a decimal in simplest form.**

$170\% = \frac{170}{100}$ — Definition of percent

$= 1\frac{70}{100}$ or $1\frac{7}{10}$ — Mixed number form

$= 1.7$ — Decimal form

A percent greater than 100% equals a number greater than 1.

So, the Amazon is 1.7 times as long as the Mississippi River.

READING Math

Percents For percents less than 1%, interpret using fractional form. For example, 0.05% of the students means $\frac{1}{2,000}$ or 1 out of every 2,000 students.

CHECK Your Progress

Write each percent as a decimal and as a mixed number or fraction in simplest form.

a. 0.25% b. 300% c. 530%

Online Personal Tutor at tx.msmath2.com

Since you divide by 100 and remove the % symbol to write a percent as a decimal, to write decimals as percents, do the opposite. So, to write decimals less than 0.01 and decimals greater than 1 as percents, multiply by 100 and add a % symbol. Recall that you can multiply by 100 mentally by moving the decimal point two places to the right.

EXAMPLES Decimals as Percents

Write each decimal as a percent.

3 **1.68**

$1.68 = 1.68$ Multiply by 100.

$= 168\%$ Add % symbol.

4 **0.0075**

$0.0075 = 0.0075$ Multiply by 100.

$= 0.75\%$ Add % symbol.

5 **BASEBALL A baseball player's batting average is defined as the total number of hits divided by the total number of at bats. If a baseball player's batting average is 0.285, what percent of the player's at bats were hits?**

$0.285 = 0.285$ Multiply by 100.

$= 28.5\%$ Add % symbol.

The baseball player hit 28.5% of the at bats.

CHECK Your Progress **Write each decimal as a percent.**

d. 2.5 e. 0.004 f. 0.0016

g. **BASEBALL** Find the percent of at bats that were hit by a baseball player if his or her batting average was 0.179.

CHECK Your Understanding

Examples 1, 2 (p. 371)

Write each percent as a decimal and as a mixed number or fraction in simplest form.

1. 325% 2. 200% 3. 480%
4. 0.7% 5. 0.15% 6. 0.5%

Example 1 (p. 371)

7. **MONEY** A company had a 0.9% increase in sales last month. Write 0.9% as a decimal and as a mixed number in simplest form.

Examples 3, 4 (p. 372)

Write each decimal as a percent.

8. 1.8 9. 0.0015 10. 0.0025
11. 2.75 12. 0.0005 13. 3.25

Example 5 (p. 372)

14. **MANUFACTURING** A manufacturer of light bulbs finds that 0.0019 of the light bulbs they manufacture are defective. Write this as a percent.

Exercises

HOMEWORK HELP

For Exercises	See Examples
19–22, 23	1
15–18, 24	2
25–32	3, 4
33, 34	5

Write each percent as a decimal and as a mixed number or fraction in simplest form.

15. 350% **16.** 475% **17.** 600% **18.** 400%

19. 0.6% **20.** 0.05% **21.** 0.55% **22.** 0.04%

23. ENVIRONMENT Freshwater from lakes only accounts for 0.1% of the world's water supply. Write this percent as a decimal and as a mixed number or fraction in simplest form.

24. TOYS A collectible action figure sold for 193% of its original price. Write this percent as a decimal and as a mixed number or fraction in simplest form.

Real-World Link Each year, consumers spend about \$1 billion on action figures and accessories.

Source: *Toy Industry Association, Inc*

Write each decimal as a percent.

25. 8.5 **26.** 35 **27.** 2.64 **28.** 1.07

29. 0.009 **30.** 0.003 **31.** 0.0034 **32.** 0.0077

33. FOOD The size of a large milk shake is 1.4 times of the size of the medium milk shake. Write 1.4 as a percent.

34. CARS A car's tire pressure decreased by 0.098 of its original pressure. Write 0.098 as a percent.

Write each mixed number or fraction as a percent.

35. $3\frac{1}{2}$ **36.** $9\frac{3}{4}$ **37.** $\frac{2}{500}$ **38.** $\frac{1}{400}$

Write each percent as a decimal.

39. $\frac{1}{8}\%$ **40.** $\frac{3}{4}\%$ **41.** $\frac{3}{25}\%$ **42.** $\frac{11}{20}\%$

43. POPULATION The U.S. Census Bureau reported that 0.3% of the population in the United States in 2000 was Japanese. Write this percent as a decimal and as a fraction. Then interpret its meaning as a ratio of the United States population.

44. SCHOOL Adrienne answered all 21 multiple choice questions correctly on her science test. If her teacher decided to let one of the questions count as a bonus, worth the same number of points as the other problems on the test, what was Adrienne's test score? Write your answer as a decimal and as a percent.

LIFE SCIENCE For Exercises 45–46, refer to the table at the right.

45. Write the percent of magnesium found in the human body as a decimal.

46. Which element makes up $\frac{1}{400}$ of the human body?

Elements in the Human Body

Element	Percent
Magnesium	0.05
Potassium	0.35
Sodium	0.15
Sulfur	0.25

Source: chemistry.about.com

EXTRA PRACTICE

See pages 735, 761.

Math Online

Self-Check Quiz at tx.msmath2.com

47. **TIME** One hour is what percent of one week?

48. **PHOTOGRAPHY** A photograph developed from 35 mm film is 428% larger than the negative. Express this percent as a decimal and as a mixed number or fraction in simplest form. Then interpret its meaning.

H.O.T. Problems

49. **FIND THE ERROR** Mikasi and Julie are writing $\frac{3}{2{,}000}$ as a percent. Who is correct? Explain your reasoning.

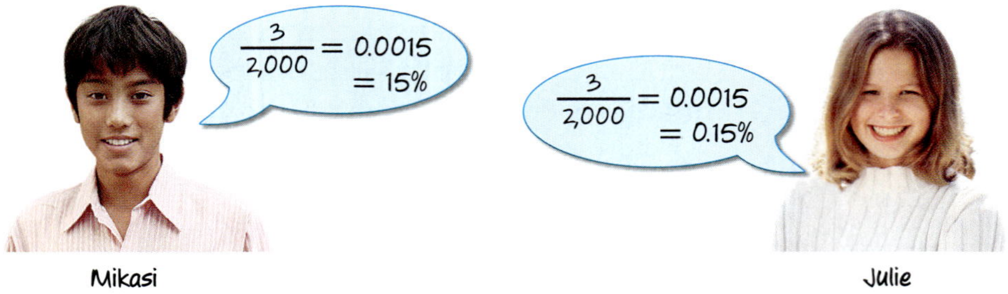

50. **CHALLENGE** The speed of a giraffe is 250% of the speed of a squirrel. If a squirrel speed is 12 miles per hour, find the speed of a giraffe.

51. **WRITING IN MATH** Write a real-world problem involving a percent greater than 100%. Then solve the problem.

TEST PRACTICE

52. What percent of one 10 by 10 grid is modeled below?

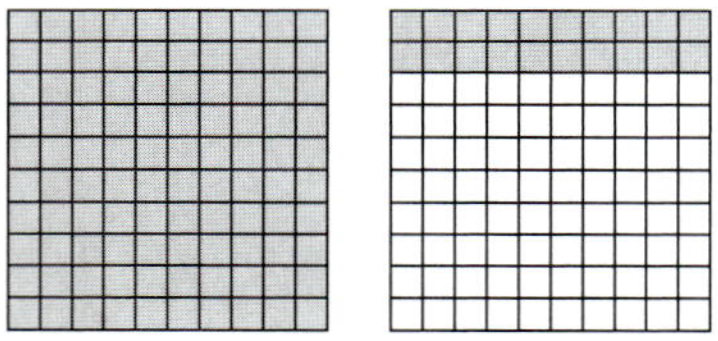

A 80%
B 100%
C 120%
D 130%

53. A certain stock increased its value by 467% over 10 years. Which number is NOT equivalent to 467%?

F 4.67

G 0.467

H $4\frac{67}{100}$

J $\frac{467}{100}$

Spiral Review

Write each percent as a fraction in simplest form. (Lesson 7-7)

54. 7.5%
55. 1.2%
56. $6\frac{1}{4}\%$
57. $92\frac{1}{2}\%$

58. **ANALYZE DRAWINGS** A garage door is 18 feet wide. A scale drawing of this door is shown. Find the scale of the drawing. (Lesson 7-6)

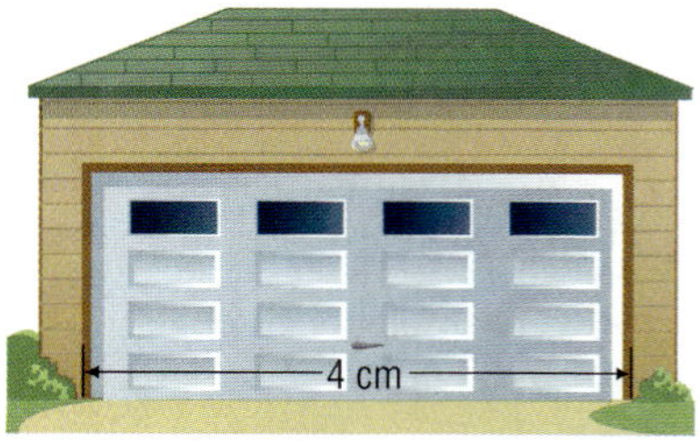

GET READY for the Next Lesson

PREREQUISITE SKILL **Write each percent as a decimal.** (Lesson 5-7)

59. 85%
60. 6.5%
61. 36.9%
62. 12.3%

CHAPTER 7 Study Guide and Review

STUDY TO GO Download Vocabulary Review from tx.msmath2.com

FOLDABLES™ Study Organizer

GET READY to Study

Be sure the following Key Concepts are noted in your Foldable.

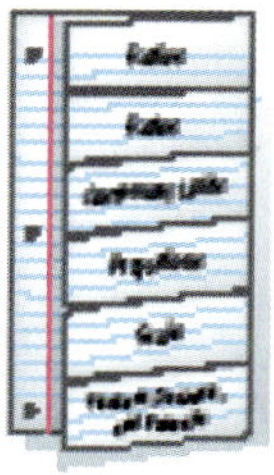

Key Concepts

Ratios and Rates (Lessons 7-1 and 7-2)

- A ratio is a comparison of two quantities by division.
- A rate is a ratio comparing two quantities with different kinds of units.

Changing Customary Units (Lesson 7-3)

- To convert from larger units to smaller units, multiply by the appropriate unit ratio.
- To convert from smaller units to larger units, multiply by the reciprocal of the appropriate unit ratio.

Proportions (Lesson 7-4)

- Proportions are equations that state two ratios or rates are equivalent.

Scale Drawings (Lesson 7-6)

- Scale drawings represent something that is too large or too small to be drawn at actual size.

Fractions, Decimals, and Percents (Lesson 7-7)

- Common equivalents:

Fraction	Decimal	Percent
$\frac{1}{3}$	$0.\overline{3}$	$33\frac{1}{3}\%$
$\frac{2}{3}$	$0.\overline{6}$	$66\frac{2}{3}\%$
$\frac{1}{8}$	0.125	$12\frac{1}{2}\%$
$\frac{3}{8}$	0.375	$37\frac{1}{2}\%$
$\frac{5}{8}$	0.625	$62\frac{1}{2}\%$
$\frac{7}{8}$	0.875	$87\frac{1}{2}\%$

Key Vocabulary

cross products (p. 348)
equivalent ratios (p. 331)
proportion (p. 348)
proportional (p. 348)
rate (p. 335)
ratio (p. 330)
scale (p. 358)
scale drawing (p. 358)
scale factor (p. 360)
scale model (p. 358)
unit rate (p. 335)
unit ratio (p. 343)

Vocabulary Check

Choose the term from the list above that best matches each phrase.

1. a comparison of two quantities by division
2. two ratios that have the same value
3. a ratio of two measurements with different units
4. an equation that shows that two ratios or rates are equivalent
5. used to represent something that is too large or too small for an actual-size drawing
6. the ratio of the distance on a map to the actual distance
7. a scale written as a ratio in simplest form
8. product of the numerator of one ratio in a proportion and the denominator of the other ratio
9. a rate that is simplified so that it has a denominator of 1
10. two quantities that have a constant rate or ratio

Lesson-by-Lesson Review

7-1 Ratios (pp. 330–334)

Write each ratio as a fraction in simplest form.

11. 16 dogs : 12 cats
12. 5 ft : 25 ft
13. 50 boys : 75 girls
14. 36 ft : 6 ft

Determine whether the ratios are equivalent. Explain.

15. 18 out of 24 people agree
    5 out of 20 people agree
16. 27 goldfish to 15 frogs
    9 goldfish to 5 frogs
17. **MUSEUM** A museum requires two tour guides for every 28 visitors. There are 168 visitors and 12 tour guides at the museum. Is this the correct number of tour guides based on the requirement? Justify your answer.

Example 1 **Write the ratio 32 to 18 as a fraction in simplest form.**

$32 \text{ to } 18 = \frac{32}{18}$ Write the ratio as a fraction.

$= \frac{16}{9}$ Simplify.

Example 2 **Determine whether 5 : 6 and 15 : 18 are equivalent.**

$5:6 = \frac{5}{6}$ $\qquad 15:18 = \frac{15}{18}$ or $\frac{5}{6}$

The ratios in simplest form both equal $\frac{5}{6}$. So, 5 : 6 and 15 : 18 are equivalent.

7-2 Rates (pp. 335–340)

Find each unit rate.

18. \$23.75 for 5 pounds
19. 810 miles in 9 days
20. 14 laps in 4 minutes
21. **SHOPPING** Which bottle of laundry detergent shown at right costs the least per ounce?

Bottle	Price
12 oz	\$2.16
32 oz	\$5.60
64 oz	\$10.24

Example 3 **Find the unit price of a 16-ounce box of pasta that is on sale for 96 cents.**

$$\text{16-ounce box for 96 cents} = \frac{96 \text{ cents}}{16 \text{ ounces}}$$

$$= \frac{96 \text{ cents} \div 16}{16 \text{ ounces} \div 16}$$

$$= \frac{6 \text{ cents}}{1 \text{ ounce}}$$

The unit price is 6 cents per ounce.

Mixed Problem Solving
For mixed problem-solving practice, see page 761.

7-3 Measurement: Changing Customary Units (pp. 342–347)

Complete.

22. 4 qt = ■ pt
23. 6 gal = ■ qt
24. 48 oz = ■ lb
25. 9 c = ■ pt
26. **SCARF** Kaneko's scarf is 48 inches long. How many feet long is the scarf?

Example 4 Complete: 32 qt = ■ gal

Since 1 gallon = 4 quarts, the unit ratio is $\frac{1 \text{ gal}}{4 \text{ qt}}$.

$32 \text{ qt} = 32 \text{ qt} \cdot \frac{1 \text{ gal}}{4 \text{ qt}}$ Multiply by $\frac{1 \text{ gal}}{4 \text{ qt}}$.

$= \overset{8}{\cancel{32}} \cancel{\text{qt}} \cdot \frac{1 \text{ gal}}{\underset{1}{\cancel{4}} \cancel{\text{qt}}}$ Divide out common factors and units.

$= 8 \text{ gal}$ Multiply.

7-4 Algebra: Solving Proportions (p. 348–353)

Solve each proportion.

27. $\frac{x}{10} = \frac{3}{5}$
28. $\frac{4}{9} = \frac{24}{m}$
29. $\frac{2}{t} = \frac{8}{50}$
30. $\frac{15}{w} = \frac{35}{21}$
31. $\frac{12}{8} = \frac{a}{6}$
32. $\frac{7}{18} = \frac{d}{6}$
33. **WEIGHT** If 3 televisions weigh 240.6 pounds, how much do 9 of the same televisions weigh?

Example 5 Solve $\frac{6}{9} = \frac{n}{12}$.

$\frac{6}{9} = \frac{n}{12}$ Write the proportion.

$6 \cdot 12 = 9 \cdot n$ Find the cross products.

$72 = 9n$ Multiply.

$\frac{72}{9} = \frac{9n}{9}$ Divide each side by 9.

$8 = n$ Simplify.

7-5 PSI: Draw A Diagram (pp. 356–357)

Solve each problem by drawing a diagram.

34. **PAINTING** Marian is painting a fence that is 72 feet long. She has already painted $\frac{5}{8}$ of the fence. How many feet of fence does she have left to paint?
35. **COOKIES** A cookie jar contains three types of cookies: oatmeal, chocolate chip, and sugar. 60 percent are chocolate chip. Half of the remaining cookies are oatmeal. If there are 9 oatmeal cookies, how many cookies are in the jar?

Example 6 Ramiro has filled $\frac{1}{3}$ or 50 gallons of his fish tank. Find the total capacity of the fish tank.

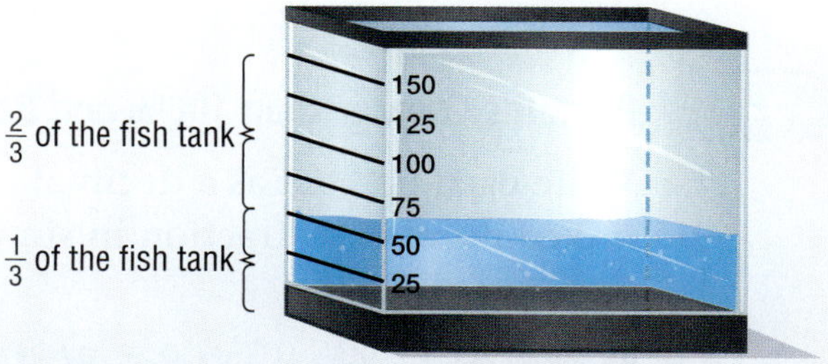

If $\frac{1}{3}$ of the fish tank is 50 gallons, then $\frac{2}{3}$ of the fish tank is 100 gallons. So, the missing two-thirds must be 100 gallons. The total capacity of the fish tank is 50 + 100, or 150 gallons.

Study Guide and Review

7-6 Scale Drawings (pp. 358–364)

36. **MAPS** Washington, D.C, and Baltimore, Maryland, are 2 inches apart on a map. If the scale is $\frac{1}{2}$ inch:6 miles, what is the actual distance between the cities?

37. **MODELS** A Boeing 747 jet is 70.5 meters long and has a wingspan of 60 meters. A model of the 747 has a wingspan of 80 centimeters. What is the length of the model?

Example 7 On a map, the distance between two cities is 10.9 centimeters. If the scale is 1 centimeter = 250 kilometers, what is the actual distance?

Scale / Distance

map → $\frac{1 \text{ cm}}{250 \text{ km}} = \frac{10.9 \text{ cm}}{n \text{ km}}$ ← map
actual → ← actual

$1 \cdot n = 250 \cdot 10.9$

$n = 2{,}725$

The actual distance is 2,725 kilometers.

7-7 Fractions, Decimals, and Percents (pp. 366–370)

Write each percent as a fraction in simplest form.

38. 27.5% 39. 5.4% 40. $45\frac{1}{4}\%$

Write each fraction as a percent. Round to the nearest hundredth if necessary.

41. $\frac{1}{8}$ 42. $\frac{5}{6}$ 43. $\frac{7}{40}$

44. **COINS** A quarter is made of $\frac{1}{12}$ nickel, and the rest is copper. Write the portion of a quarter that is copper as a percent. Round to the nearest hundredth if necessary.

Example 8 Write 82.5% as a fraction in simplest form.

$82.5\% = \frac{82.5}{100}$ Write a fraction with a denominator of 100.

$= \frac{825}{1{,}000}$ Multiply 82.5 and 100 by 10 to eliminate the decimal.

$= \frac{33}{40}$ Simplify.

Example 9 Write $\frac{14}{15}$ as a percent. Round to the nearest hundredth if necessary.

$\frac{14}{15} = 0.933\ldots$ Write $\frac{14}{15}$ as a decimal.

$\approx 93.33\%$ Multiply by 100 and add the %.

7-8 Percents Greater than 100% and Percents Less than 1% (pp. 371–374)

Write each percent as a decimal and as a mixed number or fraction in simplest form.

45. 125% 46. 0.75% 47. 0.5%

Write each decimal as a percent.

48. 0.002 49. 4.75 50. 0.0095

51. **MUSEUM** A museum's attendance increased by 135%. Write 135% as a decimal and as a mixed number in simplest form.

Example 10 Write 248% as a decimal and as a mixed number in simplest form.

$248\% = \frac{248}{100}$ Definition of percent

$= 2.48$ Write as a decimal.

$= 2\frac{48}{100}$ Write as a mixed number.

$= 2\frac{12}{25}$ Simplify.

Example 11 Write 0.008 as a percent.

0.008×100 Multiply by 100.

$= 0.8\%$

CHAPTER 7 Practice Test

LAWN CARE For Exercises 1 and 2, use the following information to write each ratio as a fraction in simplest form.

A bag of fertilizer nutrients contains 18 pounds of nitrogen, 6 pounds of phosphorus, and 12 pounds of potassium.

1. nitrogen : potassium
2. phosphorus : nitrogen

Find each unit rate. Round to the nearest hundredth if necessary.

3. 24 greeting cards for \$4.80
4. 330 miles on 15 gallons of gasoline
5. **TEST PRACTICE** The population of bacteria in 4 different-sized lab dishes are given. Which dish has the lowest density of bacteria or bacteria per square inch?

Dish	Bacteria	Dish Area
1	100	205 sq in.
2	50	125 sq in.
3	35	75 sq in.
4	180	300 sq in.

A Dish 1 **C** Dish 3
B Dish 2 **D** Dish 4

6. **TYPING** Peggy can word process 12 words in 15 seconds. At this rate, how many words can she word process in 3 minutes?

Complete.

7. 9 yd = ▪ ft
8. 11,000 lb = ▪ T
9. 4 lb = ▪ oz
10. 15 qt = ▪ gal
11. **GROCERIES** If 1 can of tomato paste contains 6 ounces, how many pounds do 10 cans contain?

Solve each proportion.

12. $\frac{2}{3} = \frac{x}{42}$
13. $\frac{t}{21} = \frac{15}{14}$
14. **NUTRITION** If an 8-ounce glass of orange juice has 72 milligrams of vitamin C, how much vitamin C is in a 7-ounce glass?
15. **SWIMMING** Solana swims 3 laps in 12 minutes. At this same rate, how many laps will she swim in 30 minutes?

BLUEPRINTS For Exercises 16–18, use the following blueprint of a room.

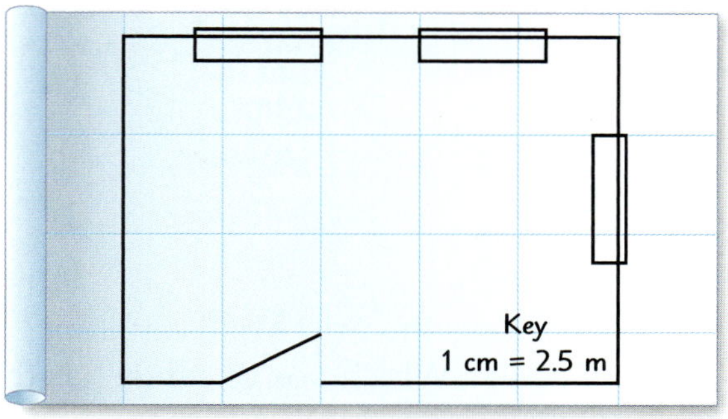

16. Use a centimeter ruler to find the length of the wall with 2 windows.
17. How wide would a 1.4-meter wide dresser appear on this drawing?
18. Find the scale factor of the drawing.

Write each fraction as a percent. Round to the nearest hundredth if necessary.

19. $\frac{5}{8}$
20. $\frac{7}{15}$
21. **TEST PRACTICE** A company test marketed 7 new flavors of gum last year. Only 2 of these received favorable ratings. Which represents the percent of flavors that did NOT receive favorable ratings?

F 71% **H** 5%
G 29% **J** 2%

Write each percent as a fraction or mixed number in simplest form.

22. $83\frac{1}{3}\%$
23. 0.45%
24. 135%
25. Write 0.0095 as a percent.

CHAPTER 7 Texas Test Practice

Cumulative, Chapters 1–7

Read each question. Then fill in the correct answer on the answer document provided by your teacher or on a sheet of paper.

1. Mrs. Stewart painted the door to her deck. The door is a rectangle with length 8 feet and width 4 feet. In the middle of the door, there is a rectangular panel of glass that measures 5 feet by 2 feet. Find the painted area of the door in square feet.

   A 10 ft^2

   B 22 ft^2

   C 24 ft^2

   D 32 ft^2

2. The table shows the prices of 3 different boxes of cereal. Which box of cereal has the highest price per ounce?

Cereal Box Size (ounces)	Price ($)
48	5.45
32	3.95
20	3.10

   F The 20-ounce box

   G The 32-ounce box

   H The 48-ounce box

   J All three boxes have the same price per ounce.

3. A bakery sells 6 bagels for for a total of $2.99 and 4 muffins for a total of $3.29. If you bought 4 dozen bagels and 16 muffins, what is the total cost of the bagels and muffins, not including tax?

   A $64.60

   B $37.08

   C $31.10

   D $26.50

4. Mrs. Black is making 2 pasta salads for a picnic. The first pasta salad requires $4\frac{2}{3}$ cups of pasta, and the second pasta salad requires $\frac{1}{3}$ cup more than the first. Which of the following equations can be used to find n, the number of cups of pasta needed for the second recipe?

   F $n = 4\frac{2}{3} \div \frac{1}{3}$

   G $n = 4\frac{2}{3} + \frac{1}{3}$

   H $n = 4\frac{2}{3} - \frac{1}{3}$

   J $n = 4\frac{2}{3} \times \frac{1}{3}$

5. **GRIDDABLE** Simplify the expression below.

$$8 + 3(15 - 5) - 3^2$$

6. A shoe store had to increase prices. The table shows the regular price, r, and the new price, n, of several shoes. Which of the following formulas can be used to calculate the new price?

Shoe	Regular Price (r)	New Price (n)
A	$25.00	$27.80
B	$30.00	$32.80
C	$35.00	$37.80
D	$40.00	$42.80

   A $n = r - 2.80$

   B $n = r + 2.80$

   C $n = r \times 0.1$

   D $n = r \div 0.1$

7. Annika can run 2 miles in 15 minutes. At this rate, about how long will it take her to run $3\frac{1}{2}$ miles?

   F 26 minutes

   G 32 minutes

   H 36 minutes

   J 45 minutes

Get Ready for the Texas Test
For test-taking strategies and more practice, see pages TX1–TX23.

8. A TV station estimates that 59.2% of its viewers will watch TV at 8:00 P.M. Which number is NOT equivalent to 59.2%?

   A $\frac{592}{1000}$

   B 0.592

   C 0.00592×10^2

   D 5.92

9. You can drive your car 21.75 miles with one gallon of gasoline. How many miles can you drive with 13.2 gallons of gasoline?

   F 13.2

   G 21.75

   H 150.2

   J 287.1

10. The table shows the number of yards of material Leah used each day last week. What was the total number of yards Leah used last week?

Day	Material (yd)
Monday	2.3
Tuesday	$1\frac{3}{4}$
Wednesday	2.8
Thursday	3.1
Friday	$3\frac{1}{4}$
Saturday	1.7
Sunday	$4\frac{1}{2}$

   A 19.4 yd

   B 17 yd

   C 16 yd

   D 16.5 yd

11. JoAnne has a doll collection containing 192 dolls. She decided to give $\frac{5}{8}$ of her collection to her little sister. What percent of her dolls did JoAnne give to her sister?

   F $12\frac{1}{2}\%$

   G $62\frac{1}{2}\%$

   H 63%

   J $63\frac{1}{3}\%$

TEST-TAKING TIP

Question 12 When a question involves information from a previous part of a question, make sure to check that information before you move on.

Pre-AP

Record your answers on a sheet of paper. Show your work.

12. Jessie built a model of her town using items from her family's recycling bin.

   a. One centimeter in Jessie's model equals 10 kilometers in the real town. If Lansdowne Road is 12 centimeters long, on the model, how long is the actual Lansdowne Road?

   b. Jessie cut up milk cartons to construct $\frac{4}{5}$ of her model town. What percent of the model town was constructed using milk cartons?

   c. Jessie used a total of 70 recycled items to build her model town. Explain how to find the number of items that were milk cartons. Then find the number of items that were milk cartons.

NEED EXTRA HELP?

If You Missed Question...	1	2	3	4	5	6	7	8	9	10	11	12
Go to Lesson...	4-6	7-2	3-5	6-2	1-4	1-10	7-2	5-7	3-2	6-2	5-6	7-7
For Help with Test Objective...	2	2	1	6	1	2	1	1	1	1	1	1

CHAPTER 8

Applying Percents

Knowledge and Skills

- Solve problems involving direct proportional relationships. **TEKS 7.3**
- Estimate and find solutions to application problems involving percent. **TEKS 7.3**

Key Vocabulary

percent equation (p. 405)
percent of change (p. 415)
percent proportion (p. 392)
random sample (p. 411)

Real-World Link

Population In a three-year period, the population of Dallas increased from 1,188,580 to 1,208,318. You can use ratios to find the percent of change.

FOLDABLES™ Study Organizer

Applying Percents Make this Foldable to help you organize your notes. Begin with a piece of 11″ by 17″ paper.

1. **Fold** the paper into thirds.

2. **Open** and refold the paper into thirds along the opposite axis.

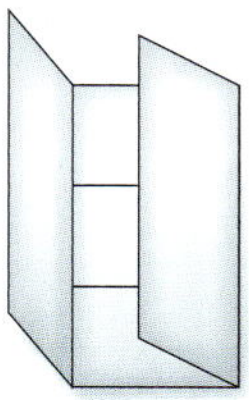

3. **Trace** along the fold lines and label each section with a lesson title or number.

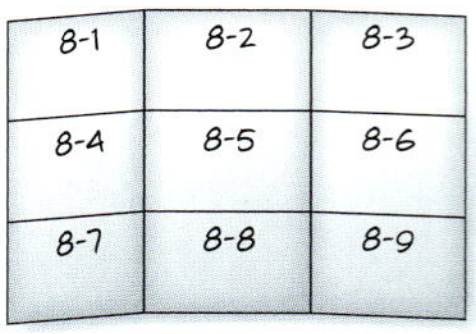

GET READY for Chapter 8

Diagnose Readiness You have two options for checking Prerequisite Skills.

Option 2

Math Online Take the Online Readiness Quiz at tx.msmath2.com.

Option 1

Take the Quick Quiz below. Refer to the Quick Review for help.

QUICK Quiz

Multiply. (Used in Lesson 8-9)

1. $300 \times 0.02 \times 8$
2. $85 \times 0.25 \times 3$
3. $560 \times 0.6 \times 4.5$
4. $154 \times 0.12 \times 5$
5. **MONEY** If Nicole saves \$0.05 every day, how much money will she have in 3 years?

Simplify. Write as a decimal. (Used in Lessons 8-7 and 8-8)

6. $\frac{22-8}{8}$
7. $\frac{50-33}{50}$
8. $\frac{35-7}{35}$
9. **BASEBALL CARDS** Tim has 56 baseball cards. He gives 14 of them away. What decimal represents the portion he has left?

Solve. Round to the nearest tenth if necessary. (Used in Lessons 8-2 and 8-5)

10. $0.4m = 52$
11. $21 = 0.28a$
12. $13 = 0.06s$
13. $0.95z = 37$

Write each percent as a decimal. (Used in Lesson 8-5)

14. 40%
15. 17%
16. 110%
17. 157%
18. 3.25%
19. 7.5%
20. **FOOD** Approximately 92% of a watermelon is water. What decimal represents this amount?

QUICK Review

Example 1

Evaluate $240 \times 0.03 \times 5$.

$240 \times 0.03 \times 5$

$= 7.2 \times 5$ Multiply 240 by 0.03.

$= 36$ Simplify.

Example 2

Simplify $\frac{17-8}{8}$. Write as a decimal.

$\frac{17-8}{8} = \frac{9}{8}$ Subtract 8 from 17.

$= 1.125$ Divide 9 by 8.

Example 3

Solve $0.6k = 7.8$

$0.6k = 7.8$ Write the equation.

$k = 13$ Divide each side by 0.6.

Example 4

Write 9.8% as a decimal.

$9.8\% = 0.098$ Move the decimal point two places to the left and remove the percent symbol.

Explore 8-1

Math Lab
Percent of a Number

Main IDEA

Use a model to find the percent of a number.

Targeted TEKS **7.3** The student solves problems involving direct proportional relationships. **(A)** estimate and **find solutions to application problems involving percent.** *Also addresses TEKS 7.14(A).*

Do you enjoy shopping? If so, you may have seen sales or other discounts represented as percents. For example, consider the following situation. A backpack is on sale for 30% off the original price. If the original price of the backpack is $50, how much will you save?

In this situation, you know the percent. You need to find what part of the original price you will save. In this lab, you will use a model to find the percent of a number or *part* of a whole.

ACTIVITY

1 Find 30% of $50 using a model.

STEP 1 Draw a 1-by-10 rectangle as shown on grid paper. Label the units on the right from 0% to 100% as shown.

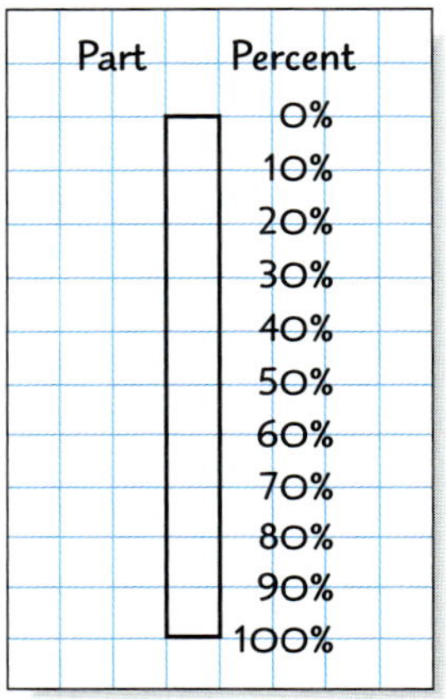

STEP 2 Since $50 represents the original price, mark equal units from $0 to $50 on the left side of the model as shown.

STEP 3 Draw a line from 30% on the right side to the left side of the model as shown and shade the portion of the rectangle above this line.

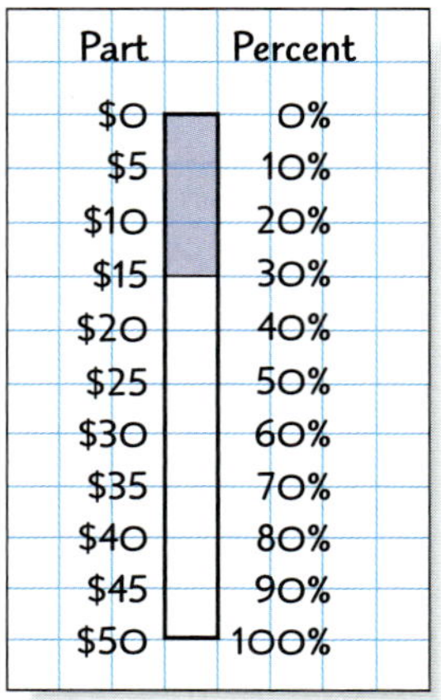

The model shows that 30% of $50 is $15. So, you will save $15.

STUDY TIP

Equal Units
To determine equal units, you can use division. Since $\$50 \div 10 = \$5$, use an interval of $5.

CHECK Your Progress

Draw a model to find the percent of each number.

a. 20% of 120 **b.** 60% of 70 **c.** 90% of 400

Suppose a bicycle is on sale for 35% off the original price. How much will you save if the original price of the bicycle is $180?

ACTIVITY

2 Find 35% of $180 using a model.

STEP 1 Draw a 1-by-10 rectangle as shown on grid paper. Label the units on the right from 0% to 100% as shown.

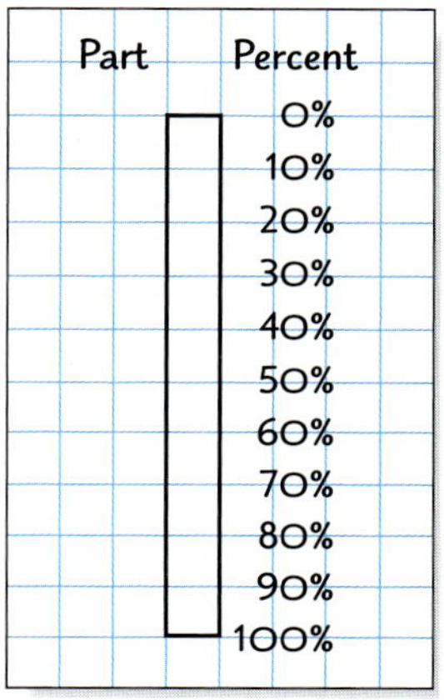

STUDY TIP

Equal Units
For the model at the right, use an interval of $18 since $180 ÷ 10 = $18.

STEP 2 The original price is $180. So, mark equal units from $0 to $180 on the left side of the model as shown.

STEP 3 Draw a line from 35% on the right side to the left side of the model.

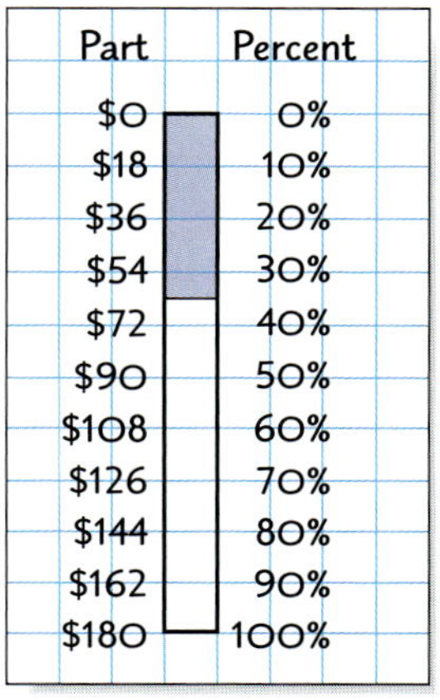

The model shows that 35% of $180 is halfway between $54 and $72, or $63.

So, you will save $63.

CHECK Your Progress

Draw a model to find the percent of each number. If it is not possible to find an exact answer from the model, estimate.

d. 25% of 140 **e.** 7% of 50 **f.** 0.5% of 20

ANALYZE THE RESULTS

1. Tell how to determine the units that get labeled on the left side of a percent model.
2. Explain how to find 40% of 30 using a model.
3. **REASONING** How does knowing 10% of a number help you find the percent of the number when the percent is a multiple of 10%?

8-1 Percent of a Number

Main IDEA

Find the percent of a number.

Targeted TEKS 7.3 The student solves problems involving direct proportional relationships. **(A) estimate and find solutions to application problems involving percent.** *Also addresses TEKS 7.13(D).*

GET READY for the Lesson

FUND-RAISING A group of students are collecting money for a local pet shelter. The model shows that the students have raised 60% of their $2,000 goal or $1,200.

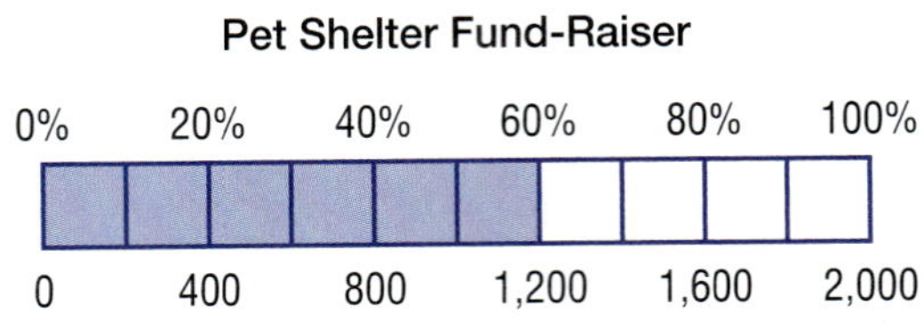

1. Sketch the model and label using decimals instead of percents.
2. Sketch the model using fractions instead of percents.
3. Use these models to write two multiplication sentences that are equivalent to 60% of 2,000 = 1,200.

To find the percent of a number such as 60% of 2,000, you can use one of the following methods.

- Write the percent as a fraction and then multiply, or
- Write the percent as a decimal and then multiply.

EXAMPLE Find the Percent of a Number

1 Find 5% of 300.

To find 5% of 300, you can use either method.

METHOD 1 Write the percent as a fraction.

$5\% = \frac{5}{100}$ or $\frac{1}{20}$

$\frac{1}{20}$ of $300 = \frac{1}{20} \times 300$ or 15

METHOD 2 Write the percent as a decimal.

$5\% = \frac{5}{100}$ or 0.05

0.05 of 300 = 0.05×300 or 15

So, 5% of 300 is 15.

CHOOSE Your Method **Find the percent of each number.**

a. 40% of 70 b. 15% of 100 c. 55% of 160

EXAMPLE Use Percents Greater Than 100%

2 **Find 120% of 75.**

METHOD 1 **Write the percent as a fraction.**

$120\% = \frac{120}{100}$ or $1\frac{1}{5}$

$1\frac{1}{5}$ of $75 = 1\frac{1}{5} \times 75$

$= \frac{6}{5} \times 75$

$= \frac{6}{5} \times \frac{75}{1}$ or 90

METHOD 2 **Write the percent as a decimal.**

$120\% = \frac{120}{100}$ or 1.2

1.2 of $75 = 1.2 \times 75$ or 90

So, 120% of 75 is 90. Use a model to check the answer.

CHOOSE Your Method

d. Find 150% of 20.

e. Find 160% of 35.

STUDY TIP

Check for Reasonableness
120% is a little more than 100%. So, the answer should be a little more than 100% of 75 or a little more than 75.

Real-World EXAMPLE

3 **ANALYZE GRAPHS** **Refer to the graph. If a college has 350 students majoring in medicine, how many can be expected to have stuffed animals in their dorm room?**

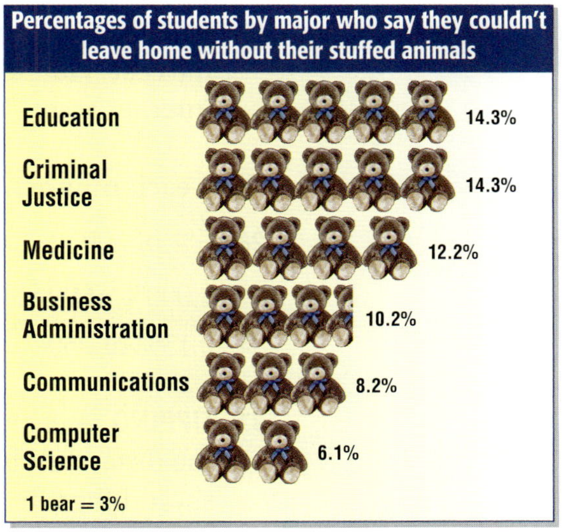

Source: IKEA poll

To find 12.2% of 350, write the percent as a decimal. Then multiply.

12.2% of $350 = 12.2\% \cdot 350$

$= 0.122 \cdot 350$

$= 42.7$

So, about 43 students can be expected to have stuffed animals in their dorm room.

CHECK Your Progress

f. **ANALYZE GRAPHS** Refer to the graph above. Suppose there are 550 students majoring in education. How many can be expected to have stuffed animals in their dorm room?

Online Personal Tutor at tx.msmath2.com

STUDY TIP

Percent of a Number
A scientific calculator can also be used to find the percent of a number. For example, to find 12.2% of 350, push 12.2 [2nd] [%] [×] 350 [ENTER]. The result is 42.7.

CHECK Your Understanding

Find each number. Round to the nearest tenth if necessary.

Examples 1–2 (pp. 386–387)

1. 8% of 50
2. 95% of 40
3. 42% of 263
4. 110% of 70
5. 115% of 20
6. 130% of 78

Example 3 (p. 387)

7. **TAXES** Mackenzie wants to buy a new backpack that costs $50. If the tax rate is 6.5%, how much tax will she pay when she buys the backpack?

Exercises

HOMEWORK HELP

For Exercises	See Examples
8–13, 20–25	1
14–19	2
26–27	3

Find each number. Round to the nearest tenth if necessary.

8. 65% of 186
9. 45% of $432
10. 23% of $640
11. 54% of 85
12. 12% of $230
13. 98% of 15
14. 130% of 20
15. 175% of 10
16. 150% of 128
17. 250% of 25
18. 108% of $50
19. 116% of $250
20. 3.2% of 40
21. 5.4% of 65
22. 23.5% of 128
23. 75.2% of 130
24. 67.5% of 76
25. 18.5% of 500

26. **BASEBALL** Tomás got on base 60% of the times he was up to bat. If he was up to bat 5 times, how many times did he get on base?

27. **INTERNET** A family pays $19 each month for Internet access. Next month, the cost will increase 5%. After this increase, what will be the cost for the Internet access?

Find each number. Round to the nearest hundredth if necessary.

28. $\frac{4}{5}$% of 500
29. $5\frac{1}{2}$% of 60
30. $20\frac{1}{4}$% of 3
31. 1,000% of 99
32. 100% of 79
33. 520% of 100
34. 0.15% of 250
35. 0.3% of 80
36. 0.28% of 50

37. **TIPPING** A customer wants to tip 15% of the restaurant bill. How much change should there be after the tip if the customer pays with a $50 bill?

Sal's Bistro

Herbed Salmon	$16.25
Chicken Pasta	15.25
Iced Tea	1.75
Iced Tea	1.75
Total	$35.00

38. **ESTIMATION** A mountain bike costs $288 plus a 4.8% delivery charge. What is the approximate cost of the bike including the delivery charge?

39. **BUSINESS** A store sells a certain brand of a lawn mower for $275. Next year, the cost of the lawn mower will increase by 8%. What will be the cost of the lawn mower next year?

ANALYZE GRAPHS For Exercises 40–42, use the graph below that shows the results of a poll of 1,746 college students.

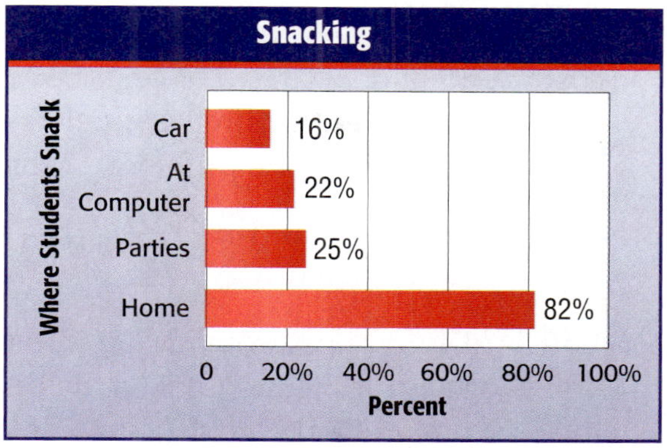

40. How many students can be expected to snack at their computer?
41. How many students can be expected to snack at home?
42. Determine how many more students can be expected to snack at parties than in a car.

Use mental math to find each percent. Justify your answer.

43. 53% of 60
44. 24% of 48
45. 75% of 19

ANALYZE GRAPHS For Exercises 46–49, use the graph that shows the results of a favorite fruit survey.

46. How many people were surveyed?
47. Of those surveyed, how many people prefer peaches?
48. Which type of fruit did more than 100 people prefer?
49. Of those surveyed, how many people did *not* prefer cherries? Explain how you arrived at the answer.

Real-World Link
California, the largest producer of peaches produces about 60% of all the peaches grown in the U.S.
Source: California Tree Fruit Agreement

50. **SHOPPING** The Leather Depot sells a certain leather coat for $179.99. If sales tax is 6.25%, what will be the approximate total cost of the coat?
51. **SCHOOL** Suppose there are 20 questions on a multiple-choice test. If 25% of the answers are choice B, how many of the answers are *not* choice B?
52. **COMMISSION** In addition to her salary, Ms. Sierra earns a 3% *commission*, or fee paid based on a percent of her sales, on every vacation package that she sells. One day, she sold the three vacation packages shown. What was her total commission?

Package #1	Package #2	Package #3
$2,375	$3,950	$1,725

EXTRA PRACTICE
See pages 735, 762.
Math Online
Self-Check Quiz at tx.msmath2.com

H.O.T. Problems

53. **OPEN ENDED** Give two examples of real-world situations in your life in which you would find the percent of a number.

54. **SELECT A TECHNIQUE** Maggie uses a $50 gift card to buy a pair of shoes that cost $24.99 and a purse that costs $19.99. If the tax rate is 7%, will the gift card cover the entire purchase? Select and use one or more of the following techniques to solve the problem. Justify your selection(s).

mental math	number sense	estimation

55. **CHALLENGE** Suppose you add 10% of a number to the number, and then you subtract 10% of the total. Is the result *greater than*, *less than*, or *equal to* the original number? Explain your reasoning.

56. **WRITING IN MATH** Explain which method you prefer to use to find the percent of a number: write the percent as a fraction or write the percent as a decimal. Explain your reasoning.

TEST PRACTICE

57. A football player has made about 80% of the field goals he has attempted in his career. If he attempts 45 field goals in a season, how many would he be expected to make?

A 40

B 36

C 30

D 25

58. Tanner has 200 baseball cards. Of those, 42% are in mint condition. How many of the cards are NOT in mint condition?

F 72

G 84

H 110

J 116

Spiral Review

Write each percent as a decimal. (Lesson 7-8)

59. 750%
60. 900%
61. 0.04%
62. 0.18%

63. **PETS** In Rebecca's class, 17 out of 24 students have pets. What percent of the students have pets? Round to the nearest percent. (Lesson 7-7)

Write each number in scientific notation. (Lesson 3-7)

64. 26,000
65. 345,000
66. 2,009,000

67. **PATTERNS** What are the next three numbers in the pattern 3, 10, 17, 24, …? (Lesson 1-9)

GET READY for the Next Lesson

PREREQUISITE SKILL **Solve each equation.** (Lesson 4-3)

68. $12b = 144$
69. $9x = 630$
70. $8{,}100 = 100k$

READING Word Problems

Meaning of Percent

When you solve percent problems, look for three parts: the *part*, the *whole*, and the *percent*. Consider this example.

The table at the right shows the results of a survey about favorite flavor of sugarless gum.

Favorite Flavor of Sugarless Gum	
Flavor	**Number**
Cinnamon	10
Peppermint	18
Watermelon	12
Total	40

Part

Ten students chose cinnamon as their favorite.

Whole

Forty students were surveyed.

Percent

25% of the students who were surveyed (10 out of 40) chose cinnamon as their favorite.

Using all three parts, 25% of 40 is 10.

PRACTICE

Identify each statement as the *part*, the *whole*, or the *percent*. Then write a sentence using all three parts.

1. The table at the right shows the results of a survey about which "bugs" people dislike most.
   a. Fifty people were surveyed.
   b. 60% disliked spiders the most.
   c. Thirty people disliked spiders.

Least Favorite "Bug"	
Kind	**Number**
Centipede	2
Cockroach	18
Spider	30
Total	50

2. Suppose you find a sale at the mall.
   a. Everything was 20% off.
   b. The original price of a jacket was $30.
   c. You saved $6.

3. You and your family are eating at a restaurant.
   a. The meal cost $34.
   b. You want to leave a tip of 15%.
   c. The tip is $5.10

4. Your sister plays basketball.
   a. She usually makes 75% of her free-throws.
   b. In the last game, she made 6 free-throws.
   c. She had 8 free-throws.

8-2 The Percent Proportion

Main IDEA

Solve problems using the percent proportion.

Targeted TEKS 7.3 The student solves problems involving direct proportional relationships. **(A)** estimate and **find solutions to application problems involving percent.** *Also addresses TEKS 7.14(A).*

NEW Vocabulary

percent proportion

GET READY for the Lesson

SPACE The engine on the space shuttle weighs approximately 19,700 pounds. The entire space shuttle weighs 178,000 pounds.

1. Write the ratio of engine weight to total weight as a fraction.
2. Use a calculator to write the fraction as a decimal to the nearest hundredth.
3. About what percent of the space shuttle's weight is the engine?

In a **percent proportion**, one ratio or fraction compares part of a quantity to the whole quantity, also called the *base*. The other ratio is the equivalent percent written as a fraction with a denominator of 100.

4 out of 5 is 80%.

$$\frac{\text{part} \rightarrow 4}{\text{whole} \rightarrow 5} = \frac{80}{100} \Big\} \text{ percent}$$

When given two of these pieces of information—part, whole, or percent—you can use the proportion to find the missing information.

EXAMPLE Find the Percent

1 What percent of \$15 is \$9?

The number 15 comes after the word *of*, so the whole is 15. You are asked to find the percent, so the part is the remaining number, 9.

Words	What percent of \$15 is \$9?
Variable	Let $n\%$ represent the percent.
Proportion	$\frac{\text{part} \rightarrow 9}{\text{whole} \rightarrow 15} = \frac{n}{100} \Big\} \text{ percent}$

$\frac{9}{15} = \frac{n}{100}$	Write the proportion.
$9 \cdot 100 = 15 \cdot n$	Find the cross products.
$900 = 15n$	Simplify.
$\frac{900}{15} = \frac{15n}{15}$	Divide each side by 15.
$60 = n$	

So, \$9 is 60% of \$15.

CHECK Your Progress

Find each number. Round to the nearest tenth if necessary.

a. What percent of 25 is 20?

b. \$12.75 is what percent of \$50?

EXAMPLE Find the Part

2 What number is 40% of 120?

The percent is 40%. Since the number 120 comes after the word *of*, the whole is 120. You are asked to find the part.

Words	What number is 40% of 120?
Variable	Let p represent the part.
Proportion	part → / whole → $\frac{p}{120} = \frac{40}{100}$ } percent

$\frac{p}{120} = \frac{40}{100}$ Write the proportion.

$p \cdot 100 = 120 \cdot 40$ Find the cross products.

$100p = 4{,}800$ Simplify.

$\frac{100p}{100} = \frac{4{,}800}{100}$ Divide each side by 100.

$p = 48$

So, 48 is 40% of 120.

STUDY TIP

The Percent Proportion
The part usually comes before or after the word *is* and the whole usually comes before or after the word *of*.

CHECK Your Progress

Find each number. Round to the nearest tenth if necessary.

c. What number is 5% of 60?

d. 12% of 85 is what number?

EXAMPLE Find the Whole

3 18 is 25% of what number?

The percent is 25%. The words *what number* come after the word *of*. So, you are asked to find the whole. Thus, 18 is the part.

Words	18 is 25% of what number?
Variable	Let w represent the whole.
Proportion	part → / whole → $\frac{18}{w} = \frac{25}{100}$ } percent

(continued on the next page)

$$\frac{18}{w} = \frac{25}{100}$$ Write the proportion.

$$18 \cdot 100 = w \cdot 25$$ Find the cross products.

$$1{,}800 = 25w$$ Simplify.

$$\frac{1{,}800}{25} = \frac{25w}{25}$$ Divide each side by 25.

$$72 = w$$

So, 18 is 25% of 72.

CHECK Your Progress

Find each number. Round to the nearest tenth if necessary.

e. 40% of what number is 26?

f. 80 is 75% of what number?

Real-World EXAMPLE

4 ANIMALS The average adult male Western Lowland gorilla eats about 33.5 pounds of fruit each day. How much food does the average adult male gorilla eat each day?

Western Lowland Gorilla's Diet	
Food	**Percent**
Fruit	67%
Seeds, Leaves, Stems, and Pith	17%
Insects/ Insect Larvae	16%

You know that 33.5 pounds of fruit is 67% of the total amount eaten daily. So, the problem asks 33.5 is 67% of what number. Thus, you need to find the whole.

$$\frac{33.5}{w} = \frac{67}{100}$$ Write the proportion.

$$33.5 \cdot 100 = w \cdot 67$$ Find the cross products.

$$3{,}350 = 67w$$ Simplify.

$$\frac{3{,}350}{67} = \frac{67w}{67}$$ Divide each side by 67.

$$50 = w$$

So, the average adult male gorilla eats 50 pounds of food each day.

Real-World Link Male Western Lowland gorillas weigh about 350–400 pounds. Females weigh about 160–200 pounds.
Source: colszoo.org

CHECK Your Progress

g. **ZOO** If 200 of the 550 reptiles in a zoo are on display, what percent of the reptiles are on display? Round the nearest whole number.

Online Personal Tutor at tx.msmath2.com

CONCEPT Summary — Types of Percent Problems

Type	Example	Proportion
Find the Percent	What percent of 6 is 3?	$\frac{3}{6} = \frac{n}{100}$
Find the Part	What number is 50% of 6?	$\frac{p}{6} = \frac{50}{100}$
Find the Whole	3 is 50% of what number?	$\frac{3}{w} = \frac{50}{100}$

CHECK Your Understanding

Examples 1–3
(pp. 392–394)

Find each number. Round to the nearest tenth if necessary.

1. What percent of 50 is 18?
2. What percent of \$90 is \$9?
3. What number is 2% of 35?
4. What number is 25% of 180?
5. 9 is 12% of which number?
6. 62 is 90.5% of what number?

Example 4
(p. 394)

7. **PACKAGING** If a box of Brand A cereal contains 10 cups of cereal, how many more cups of cereal are in a box of Brand B cereal?

Exercises

HOMEWORK HELP

For Exercises	See Examples
8–9	1
10–11	2
12–13	3
14–17	4

Find each number. Round to the nearest tenth if necessary.

8. What percent of 60 is 15?
9. \$3 is what percent of \$40?
10. What number is 15% of 60?
11. 12% of 72 is what number?
12. 9 is 45% of what number?
13. 75 is 20% of what number?

14. **SCHOOL** Roman has 2 red pencils in his backpack. If this is 25% of the total number of pencils, how many pencils are in his backpack?

15. **SHOPPING** A paperback book is on sale for \$7.50. This is 60% of the original price. What was the original price of the book?

16. **MOVIES** Sarah and Monique have \$40. They spent 35% of their money on movie tickets. How much money did they spend on movie tickets?

17. **BOOKS** Of the 60 books on a bookshelf, 24 are non-fiction. What percent of the books are non-fiction?

Find each number. Round to the nearest hundredth if necessary.

18. What percent of 25 is 30?
19. What number is 8.2% of 50?
20. 40 is 50% of what number?
21. 12.5% of what number is 24?
22. What number is 0.5% of 8?
23. What percent of 300 is 0.6?

24. **BUSINESS** The first week of June there were 404 customers at an ice cream parlor. Eight weeks later, the number of customers was 175% of this amount. How many customers were there eight weeks later?

25. **MONEY** Ajamu saves 40% of his allowance each week. If he saves \$16 in 5 weeks, how much allowance does Ajamu receive each week?

26. **POPULATION** In 2000, the population of Galveston, Texas, was about 250,000 people. If the population grew by about 6.6% from 2000 to 2003, what was the approximate population of Galveston in 2003?

EXTRA PRACTICE
See pages 736, 762.
Math Online
Self-Check Quiz at tx.msmath2.com

ASTRONOMY For Exercises 27–29, use the table shown.

Planet	Radius (km)
Mercury	2,440
Mars	3,397
Jupiter	71,492

27. Mercury's radius is what percent of Jupiter's radius?
28. If the radius of Mars is about 13.7% of Neptune's radius, what is the radius of Neptune?
29. Earth's radius is about 261.4% of Mercury's radius. What is the radius of Earth?

H.O.T. Problems

30. **OPEN ENDED** Write a proportion that can be used to find the percent scored on a science quiz that has 10 questions.
31. **CHALLENGE** Without calculating, arrange the following from greatest to least value. Justify your reasoning.

    20% of 100, 20% of 500, 5% of 100

32. **WRITING IN MATH** Create a problem involving a percent that can be solved by using the proportion $\frac{3}{b} = \frac{15}{100}$.

TEST PRACTICE

33. Of the 273 students in a school, 95 volunteered to work the book sale. About what percent of the students did NOT volunteer?
    - A 55%
    - B 65%
    - C 70%
    - D 75%

34. A customer at a restaurant leaves a tip of $2.70. This amount is 15% of the total bill. Which equation can be used to find x, the total amount of the food bill?
    - F $\frac{2.70}{15} = \frac{15}{100}$
    - G $\frac{2.70}{x} = \frac{15}{100}$
    - H $\frac{15}{2.70} = \frac{x}{100}$
    - J $\frac{x}{2.70} = \frac{15}{100}$

Spiral Review

Find each number. Round to the nearest tenth if necessary. (Lesson 8-1)

35. What is 25% of 120?
36. Find 45% of 70.

37. **PLANTS** A plant was 275% taller than the month before. What decimal represents this percent? (Lesson 7-8)

MEASUREMENT **Complete.** (Lesson 7-3)

38. 3,000 lb = ■ T
39. 36 in. = ■ ft
40. $4\frac{1}{2}$ lb = ■ oz

GET READY for the Next Lesson

PREREQUISITE SKILL **Multiply.** (Lesson 6-5)

41. $\frac{1}{2} \cdot 60$
42. $\frac{3}{4} \cdot 28$
43. $\frac{2}{5} \cdot 45$

8-3 Percent and Estimation

Main IDEA

Estimate percents by using fractions and decimals.

Targeted TEKS 7.3 The student solves problems involving direct proportional relationships. (A) **estimate** and find **solutions to application problems involving percent.**

GET READY for the Lesson

GRILLING The graph shows the results of a survey in which 80 people were asked which holiday was their favorite for grilling outdoors.

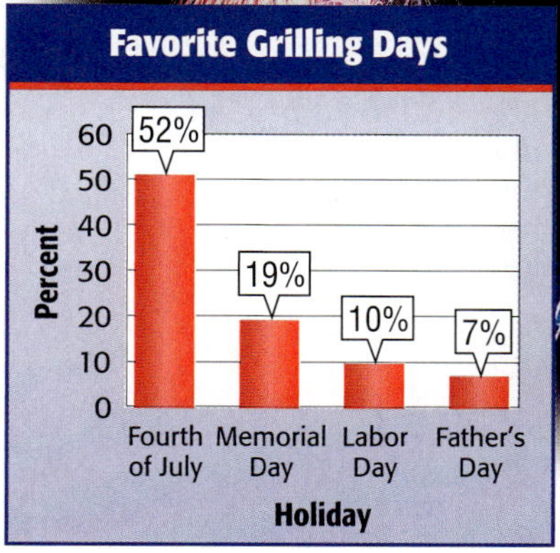

Source: Market Facts for Butterball Turkey

1. What fraction of people surveyed chose Labor Day as their favorite grilling day? How many of the 80 people surveyed is this?
2. Explain how you could use a fraction to estimate the numbers of people who chose the Fourth of July as their favorite grilling day. Then estimate.
3. Use a fraction to estimate the number of people surveyed who chose Memorial Day as their favorite grilling day.

Sometimes an exact answer is not needed when using percents. One way to estimate the percent of a number is to use a fraction.

Real-World EXAMPLE

1 **SPORTS** **Ricardo is the quarterback for the Johnstown Junior High Eagles. He completes 53% of the passes he throws. If he throws 159 passes in a season, about how many will he complete?**

You need to estimate 53% of 159.

53% is about 50% and 159 is about 160.

$53\% \text{ of } 159 \approx \frac{1}{2} \cdot 160$ — $53\% \approx \frac{1}{2}$ and $159 \approx 160$

≈ 80 — Multiply.

So, Ricardo will complete about 80 out of 159 passes in a season.

CHECK Your Progress

a. **REPTILES** Box turtles have been known to live for 120 years. American alligators have been known to live 42% as long as box turtles. About how long can an American alligator live?

Real-World Link . . . . About 30 to 60 percent of urban fresh water in the United States is used for watering lawns.

Another method for estimating the percent of a number is to first find 10% of the number and then multiply. For example, $70\% = 7 \cdot 10\%$. So, 70% of a number equals 7 times 10% of the number.

Real-World EXAMPLE

2 **MONEY** **Dante works after school for a landscaping company and plans to put 80% of each paycheck into a savings account. His paycheck this week was \$295. About how much money will he put into his savings account?**

You need to estimate 80% of \$295.

METHOD 1 **Use a fraction to estimate.**

80% is $\frac{8}{10}$ or $\frac{4}{5}$.

$80\% \text{ of } \$295 \approx \frac{4}{5} \cdot \$300$ — $80\% = \frac{4}{5}$ and round \$295 to \$300.

$\approx \$240$ — Multiply.

METHOD 2 **Use 10% of a number to estimate.**

Step 1 Find 10% of the number.
\$295 is about \$300.
$10\% \text{ of } \$300 = 0.1 \cdot \$300$ — To multiply by 10%, move the decimal point one place to the left.
$= \$30$

Step 2 Multiply.
80% of \$300 is 8 times 10% of \$300.
$8 \cdot \$30 = \$240$

So, Dante will put about \$240 into his savings account.

CHOOSE Your Method

b. **TIPS** Marita wants to leave a 20% tip on a restaurant bill of \$8.74. About how much money should she tip the restaurant server?

Online Personal Tutor at tx.msmath2.com

You can also estimate percents of numbers when the percent is greater than 100 or the percent is less than 1.

STUDY TIP

Check for Reasonableness
When estimating the percent of a number and the percent is greater than 100, the estimate will always be greater than the number.

EXAMPLES Percents Greater Than 100 or Less Than 1

3 **Estimate 122% of 50.**

122% is about 120%.

$120\% \text{ of } 50 = (100\% \text{ of } 50) + (20\% \text{ of } 50)$ — $120\% = 100\% + 20\%$

$= (1 \cdot 50) + \left(\frac{1}{5} \cdot 50\right)$ — $100\% = 1$ and $20\% = \frac{1}{5}$

$= 50 + 10 \text{ or } 60$ — Simplify.

So, 122% of 50 is about 60.

4 **Estimate $\frac{1}{4}$% of 589.**

$\frac{1}{4}$% is one fourth of 1%. 589 is about 600.

$1\% \text{ of } 600 = 0.01 \cdot 600$ — Write 1% as 0.01.

$= 6$ — To multiply by 1%, move the decimal point two places to the left.

One fourth of 6 is $\frac{1}{4} \cdot 6$ or 1.5.

So, $\frac{1}{4}$% of 589 is about 1.5.

CHECK Your Progress

c. 174% of 200 d. 298% of 45 e. 0.25% of 789

Real-World EXAMPLE

5 **POPULATION** **About 0.5% of the people in Laredo, Texas, are of Asian descent. If Laredo has a population of 176,576, estimate the number of people who are of Asian descent.**

0.5% is half of 1%.

$1\% \text{ of } 180{,}000 = 0.01 \cdot 180{,}000$ — 176,576 is about 180,000.

$= 1{,}800$

So, 0.5% of 176,576 is about $\frac{1}{2}$ of 1,800 or 900.

So, about 900 people in Laredo, Texas, are of Asian descent.

CHECK Your Progress

f. **ATTENDANCE** Last year, 639 students attended a summer camp. Of those that attended this year, 0.9% also attended last year. About how many people attended the camp two years in a row?

CHECK Your Understanding

Examples 1–4 (pp. 397–399)

Estimate.

1. 52% of 10
2. 7% of 20
3. 38% of 62
4. 79% of 489
5. 151% of 70
6. $\frac{1}{2}$% of 82

Example 1 (p. 397)

7. **BUSINESS** A bicycle store increases its prices by 23%. About how much more will a customer pay for a bicycle that originally costs $200?

Example 2 (p. 398)

8. **BIRTHDAYS** Of the 78 teenagers at a youth camp, 63% have birthdays in the spring. About how many have birthdays in the spring?

Example 5 (p. 399)

9. **GEOGRAPHY** About 0.8% of the land in Maine is federally owned. If Maine is 19,847,680 acres, about how many acres are federally owned?

Exercises

HOMEWORK HELP

For Exercises	See Examples
10–21	1, 3
22–23	2
24–25	3
26–27, 30	4
28–29, 31	5

Estimate.

10. 47% of 70
11. 21% of 90
12. 39% of 120
13. 76% of 180
14. 57% of 29
15. 92% of 104
16. 24% of 48
17. 28% of 121
18. 88% of 207
19. 62% of 152
20. 65% of 152
21. 72% of 238

22. **MONEY** Jessica spent $42 at the hair salon. About how much money should she tip the hair stylist if she wants to leave a 15% tip?

23. **HEALTH** You use 43 muscles to frown. When you smile, you use 32% of these same muscles. About how many muscles do you use when you smile?

Estimate.

24. 132% of 54
25. 224% of 320
26. $\frac{1}{2}$% of 412
27. $\frac{3}{4}$% of 168
28. 0.4% of 510
29. 0.9% of 74

30. **GEOGRAPHY** The United States has 12,383 miles of coastline. If $\frac{4}{5}$% of the U.S. coastline is located in Georgia, about how many miles of coastline are in Georgia?

31. **BIRDS** During migration, 450,000 sandhill cranes stop to rest in Nebraska. About 0.6% of these cranes stop to rest in Oregon. About how many sandhill cranes stop in Oregon during migration?

Real-World Link About 75% of the entire world sandhill crane population stop to rest in Nebraska during migration.
Source: *World Book of Records*

Estimate.

32. 67% of 8.7
33. 54% of 76.8
34. 32% of 89.9
35. 10.5% of 238
36. 22.2% of 114
37. 98.5% of 45

ANALYZE GRAPHS For Exercises 38–40, use the graph shown.

Amanda's Day

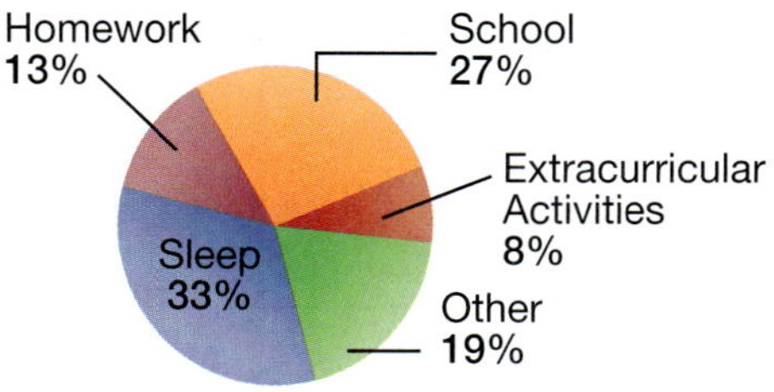

38. About how many hours does Amanda spend doing her homework each day?
39. About how many more hours does Amanda spend sleeping than doing the activities in the "other" category? Justify your answer.
40. What is the approximate number of minutes Amanda spends each day on extracurricular activities?

41. **ANALYZE GRAPHS** In a survey, 1,031 people were asked to choose the greatest athlete of the 20th century. The top five choices are shown. About how many more people chose Michael Jordan than Muhammad Ali?

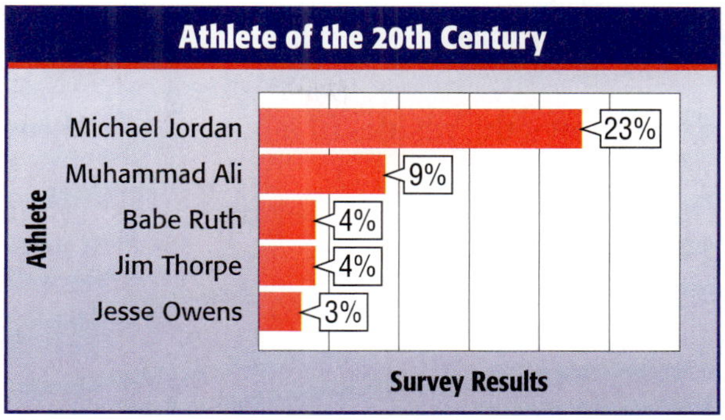

Source: Gallup Poll

42. **ANIMALS** The average white rhinoceros gives birth to a single calf that weighs about 3.8% as much as its mother. If the mother rhinoceros weighs 3.75 tons, about how many pounds does its calf weigh?

43. **POPULATION** According to the 2000 U.S. Census, about 9.4% of the people in Texas live in Houston. If the population of Texas is about 20,852,000, estimate the population of Houston.

EXTRA PRACTICE
See pages 736, 762.

Math Online
Self-Check Quiz at
tx.msmath2.com

GEOLOGY For Exercises 44 and 45, use the following information.

Granite, a stone found in New Hampshire and Vermont, is 0.8% water.

44. About how many pounds of water are there in 3,000 pounds of granite?

45. About how much water is contained in a piece of granite that is $\frac{3}{4}$-inch thick and weighs 15 pounds?

H.O.T. Problems

46. **OPEN ENDED** Write a real-world problem in which the answer can be found by estimating 12% of 50.

47. **CHALLENGE** Explain how you could find $\frac{3}{8}\%$ of \$800.

48. **FIND THE ERROR** Rob and Bethany are estimating 1.5% of 420. Who is correct? Explain.

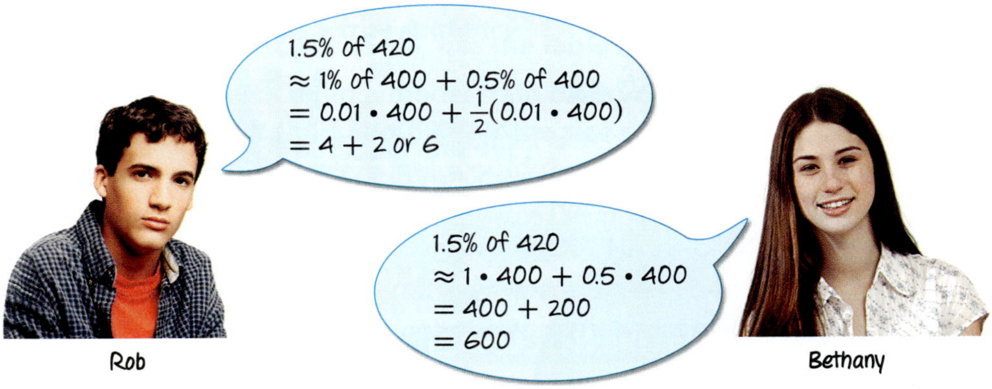

49. **NUMBER SENSE** Is an estimate for the percent of a number *always*, *sometimes*, or *never* greater than the actual percent of the number? Give an example or a counterexample to support your answer.

50. **WRITING IN MATH** Estimate 22% of 136 using two different methods. Justify the steps used in each method.

TEST PRACTICE

51. The graph shows the results of a survey of 510 students.

Pet Preferences

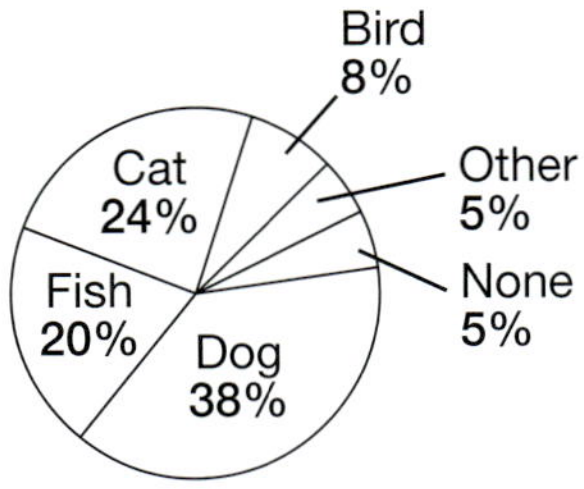

Which is the best estimate for the number of students who prefer cats?

A 75 **C** 225

B 125 **D** 450

52. Megan is buying an entertainment system for $1,789.43. The speakers are 39.7% of the total cost. Which is the best estimate for the cost of the speakers?

F $540

G $630

H $720

J $810

Spiral Review

Find each number. Round to the nearest tenth if necessary. (Lesson 8-2)

53. 6 is what percent of 15?

54. Find 72% of 90.

55. What number is 120% of 60?

56. 35% of what number is 55?

57. **HEALTH** Adults have 32 teeth. Kids have 62.5% the number of teeth of adults. How many teeth do kids have? (Lesson 8-1)

58. **TREES** Japanese Cedar trees can grow to a height that is 43% of the height of a California Redwood. Write this percent as a fraction in simplest form. (Lesson 7-7)

Estimate. (Lesson 6-1)

59. $\frac{8}{9} + \frac{1}{12}$

60. $\frac{4}{7} + \frac{7}{16}$

61. $\frac{7}{8} - \frac{7}{16}$

62. $\frac{4}{5} - \frac{9}{10}$

Solve. Round to the nearest tenth if necessary. (Lesson 4-3)

63. $40 = 0.8x$

64. $10r = 61$

65. $0.07t = 25$

66. $56 = 0.32n$

GET READY for the Next Lesson

67. **PREREQUISITE SKILL** To estimate the age of a dog in human years, count the first year as 15 human years, the second year as 10 human years, and all of the following years as 3 human years. How old in human years is a 6-year old dog? (Lesson 1-1)

8-4 Problem-Solving Investigation

MAIN IDEA: Solve problems by determining reasonable answers.

Targeted TEKS 7.2 The student adds, subtracts, multiplies, or divides to solve problems and justify solutions. **(G) determine the reasonableness of a solution to a problem.** *Also addresses TEKS 7.13(B).*

P.S.I. TEAM +

e-Mail: DETERMINE REASONABLE ANSWERS

YOUR MISSION: Determine reasonable answers to problems.

THE PROBLEM: How much money should Chase leave if he wants to give the server a 15% tip?

Chase: The cost of our meal is \$38.95. I think I should leave a tip of \$4. I'll estimate to determine if this is reasonable.

EXPLORE	The total cost of the meal is \$38.95. Chase wants to leave a 15% tip.
PLAN	Round \$38.95 to \$40. Then use mental math to find 15% of 40.
SOLVE	Round \$38.95 to \$40. 10% of 40 = $0.1 \cdot 40$ or 4 Use mental math. 10% = 0.1 5% of 40 = $\frac{1}{2} \cdot 4$ or 2 15% of 40 = (10% of 40) + (5% of 40) = 4 + 2 or 6 So, \$6 would be a better amount to leave for a tip.
CHECK	Use a calculator to check. 0.15 [×] 38.95 [ENTER] The result is 5.8425, so the answer, 6, is reasonable.

Analyze The Strategy

1. Describe other problem-solving strategies that you could use to determine whether answers are reasonable.
2. **WRITING IN MATH** Write a problem that has an unreasonable answer and ask a classmate to explain why the answer is unreasonable.

Mixed Problem Solving

Determine reasonable answers for Exercises 3–6.

3. **COMMUNICATION** Mykia makes a long distance phone call to her sister and talks for 45 minutes. If the phone company charges \$0.08 per minute, how much would the call cost: about \$1, \$4, or \$6?

4. **SCHOOL** Of 423 students, 57.6% live within 5 miles of the school. What is a reasonable estimate for the number of students living within 5 miles of the school? Explain.

5. **MUSIC** A survey showed that 71% of teens who use computers listen to music at the same time. Suppose there are 410 teens in your school who use computers. Would the number of students who listen to music while on the computer be about 120, 280, or 380? Justify your answer.

6. **ANALYZE GRAPHS** Refer to the graph. Is 30% a reasonable estimate of how much time a family spent at the amusement park during their vacation? Explain.

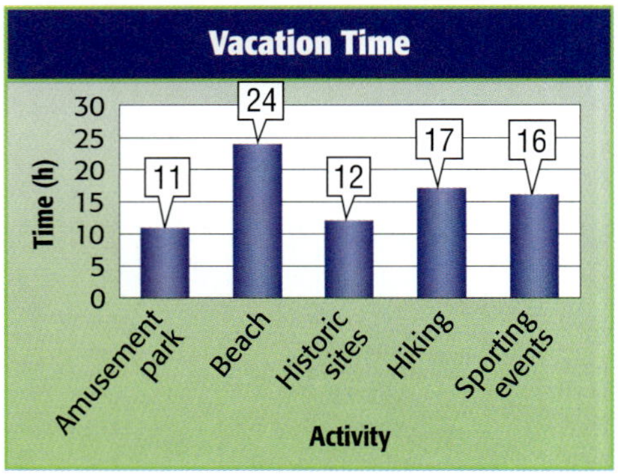

Use any strategy to solve Exercises 7–11. Some strategies are shown below.

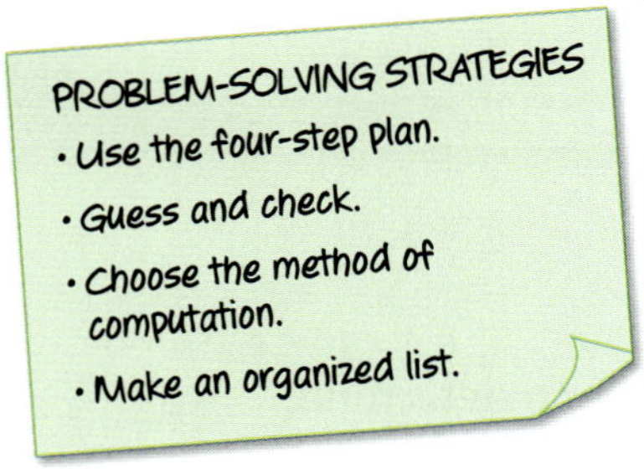

7. **COINS** John has 10 coins that total \$0.83. What are the coins?

8. **ANALYZE GRAPHS** Refer to the graph. Is 95% a reasonable estimation for the percent of drivers who will wear seat belts in 2010?

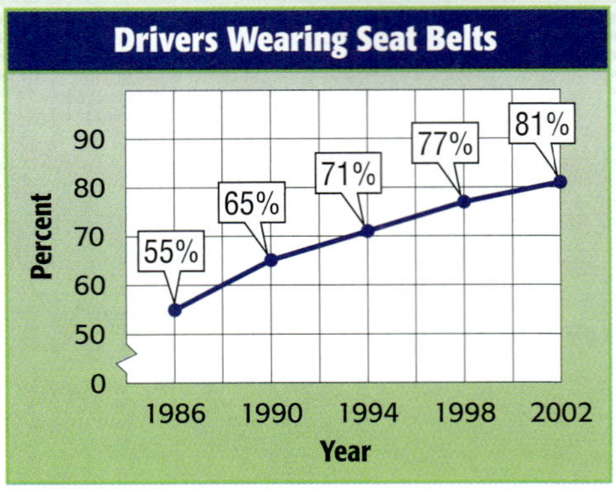

Source: Harris Interactive

9. **CHORES** Leo uses a 2.5-liter container to fill a tank that holds 24 liters of water. How many times will he need to fill the container?

10. **BASKETBALL** Sandra made 18 points in one basketball game. How many possible shot combinations of 2- and 3-pointers could she have made assuming she made no free-throw shots?

11. **NUMBERS** A number is multiplied by 22. Then 8 is added to the product. The result is 184. What is the number?

Select the Operation

For Exercises 12 and 13, select the appropriate operation(s) to solve the problem. Justify your selection(s) and solve the problem.

12. **FUND-RAISER** During a popcorn sale for a fund-raiser, the soccer team gets to keep 25% of the sales. One box of popcorn sells for \$1.50, and the team has sold 510 boxes so far. Has the team raised a total of \$175?

13. **CARPETING** How many square yards of carpet are needed to carpet the two rooms described below?

Room	Dimensions
living room	15 ft by 18 ft
TV room	18 ft by 20 ft

8-5 Algebra: The Percent Equation

Main IDEA

Solve problems by using the percent equation.

Targeted TEKS **7.3** The student solves problems involving direct proportional relationships. **(A)** estimate and **find solutions to application problems involving percent.** *Also addresses TEKS 7.5(B).*

NEW Vocabulary

percent equation

GET READY for the Lesson

AGRICULTURE In a recent year, Texas planted crops on 18.5 million acres of land. The graph shows how the crops were distributed.

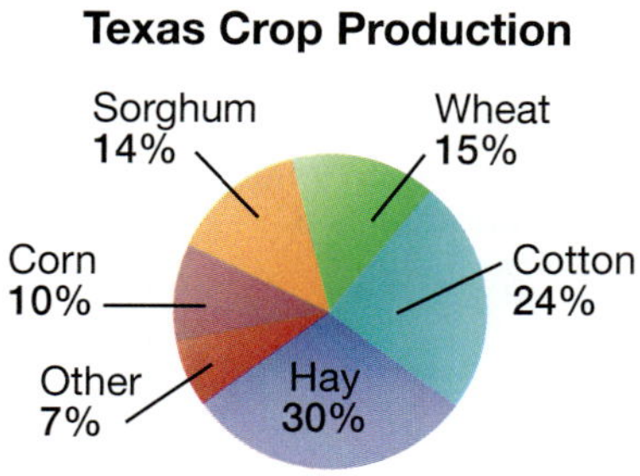

Source: *Texas Almanac*

1. Use the percent proportion to find the number of acres of hay.
2. Express the percent of hay as a decimal. Then multiply the decimal by 18.5 million, the number of acres. Compare the answers to Exercises 1 and 2.

In Lesson 8-2, you used a percent proportion to find the missing part, percent, or whole. You can also use an equation.

$$\frac{\text{part}}{\text{whole}} = \text{percent}$$ The percent is written as a decimal.

$$\frac{\text{part}}{\text{whole}} \cdot \text{whole} = \text{percent} \cdot \text{whole}$$ Multiply each side by the base.

$$\text{part} = \text{percent} \cdot \text{whole}$$ This form is called the **percent equation**.

EXAMPLE Find the Part

1 **What number is 12% of 150?** **Estimate** 12% of 150 ≈ 0.1 · 150 or 15

The percent is 12. The whole is 150. You need to find the part. Let p represent the part.

part = percent · whole

$p = 0.12 \cdot 150$ Write the percent equation.

$p = 18$ Multiply. The part is 18.

So, 18 is 12% of 150.

Check for Reasonableness 18 is close to 15. ✓

CHECK Your Progress

Write an equation for each problem. Then solve. Round to the nearest tenth if necessary.

a. What is 6% of 19?

b. Find 72% of 90.

EXAMPLE Find the Percent

2 **21 is what percent of 40?** Estimate $\frac{21}{40} \approx \frac{1}{2}$ or 50%

The part is 21. The whole is 40. You need to find the percent. Let n represent the percent.

part	=	percent	•	whole	
21	$=$	n	$\cdot$	40	Write the percent equation.
$\frac{21}{40}$	$=$	$\frac{40n}{40}$			Divide each side by 40.
$0.525 = n$					The percent is 52.5%.

So, 21 is 52.5% of 40.

Check for Reasonableness 52.5% ≈ 50% ✔

STUDY TIP

Percent Remember to write the decimal as a percent in your final answer.

CHECK Your Progress

Write an equation for each problem. Then solve. Round to the nearest tenth if necessary.

c. 35 is what percent of 70?

d. What percent of 125 is 75?

e. What percent of 40 is 9?

f. 27 is what percent of 150?

EXAMPLE Find the Whole

3 **13 is 26% of what number?** Estimate $\frac{1}{4}$ of 48 = 12

The part is 13. The percent is 26. You need to find the whole. Let w represent the whole.

part	=	percent	•	whole	
13	$=$	0.26	$\cdot$	w	Write the percent equation. 26% = 0.26
$\frac{13}{0.26}$	$=$	$\frac{0.26w}{0.26}$			Divide each side by 0.26.
50	$= w$				The number is 50.

So, 13 is 26% of 50.

Check for Reasonableness 50 is close to 48. ✔

CHECK Your Progress

Write an equation for each problem. Then solve. Round to the nearest tenth if necessary.

g. 39 is 84% of what number?

h. 26% of what number is 45?

i. 14% of what number is 7?

j. 24 is 32% of what number?

Real-World Link
In the U.S., Anchorage, Alaska, has the highest percent of cell phone users.
Source: Polk's Research

Real-World EXAMPLE

4 **CELL PHONES** **Luxembourg has the highest percent of people who have cell phones, 96.7%. If there are about 447,421 people in Luxembourg with cell phones, what is its population?**

Words	447,421 people is 96.7% of what number of people?
Variable	Let n represent the number of people.
Equation	$447{,}421 \quad = \quad 0.967 \quad \cdot \quad n$

$447{,}421 = 0.967 \cdot n$ — Write the percent equation. 96.7% = 0.967

$\frac{447{,}421}{0.967} = \frac{0.967n}{0.967}$ — Divide each side by 0.967. Use a calculator.

$462{,}690 \approx n$ — Simplify.

The population of Luxembourg is about 462,690.

CHECK Your Progress

k. **GEOGRAPHY** Of the U.S. Gulf Coast coastline, 22.5% is located in Texas. If Texas has 367 miles of coastline, how many miles of coastline are located in the Gulf Coast?

Online Personal Tutor at tx.msmath2.com

CONCEPT Summary — Types of Percent Problems

Type	Example	Proportion
Find the Part	What number is 50% of 6?	$p = 0.5 \cdot 6$
Find the Percent	3 is what percent of 6?	$3 = n \cdot 6$
Find the Whole	3 is 50% of what number?	$3 = 0.5 \cdot w$

CHECK Your Understanding

Examples 1–3 (pp. 405–406)

Write an equation for each problem. Then solve. Round to the nearest tenth if necessary.

1. What number is 88% of 300?
2. What number is 12% of 250?
3. 75 is what percent of 150?
4. 24 is what percent 120?
5. 3 is 12% of what number?
6. 84 is 60% of what number?

Example 4 (p. 407)

7. **BUSINESS** A local bakery sold 60 loaves of bread in one day. If 65% of these were sold in the afternoon, how many loaves were sold in the afternoon?

Exercises

HOMEWORK HELP

For Exercises	See Examples
8–11	1
12–15	2
16–19	3
20–23	4

Write an equation for each problem. Then solve. Round to the nearest tenth if necessary.

8. What number is 65% of 98?
9. Find 39% of 65.
10. Find 24% of 25.
11. What number is 53% of 470?
12. 9 is what percent of 45?
13. What percent of 96 is 26?
14. What percent of 392 is 98?
15. 30 is what percent of 64?
16. 33% of what number is 1.45?
17. 84 is 75% of what number?
18. 17 is 40% of what number?
19. 80% of what number is 64?

20. **BOOKS** Emma bought 6 new books for her collection. This increased her collection by 12%. How many books did she have before her purchases?

21. **VIDEO GAMES** A store sold 550 video games during the month of December. If this made up 12.5% of their yearly video game sales, about how many video games did the store sell all year?

22. **SALES** Ms. Allon received a $325 *commission* on her sales. If her sales totaled $8,125, what is the percent that she earns?

23. **LOBSTERS** Approximately 0.02% of North Atlantic lobsters are born bright blue in color. Out of 5,000 North Atlantic lobsters, how many would you expect to be blue in color?

Write an equation for each problem. Then solve. Round to the nearest tenth if necessary.

24. Find 135% of 64.
25. What number is 0.4% of 82.1?
26. 450 is 75.2% of what number?
27. What percent of 200 is 230?

28. **SALARY** A landscape architect who earns an annual salary of $57,680 receives a 2.5% raise. What will be her annual salary after the raise?

ANALYZE GRAPHS Almost 13.5 million acres are planted in cotton in the United States. For Exercises 29–31, use the graph at the right.

29. About what percent of U.S. cotton is planted in Texas?
30. About what percent of U.S. cotton is planted in Georgia?
31. About what percent of U.S. cotton is planted in states other than those listed?

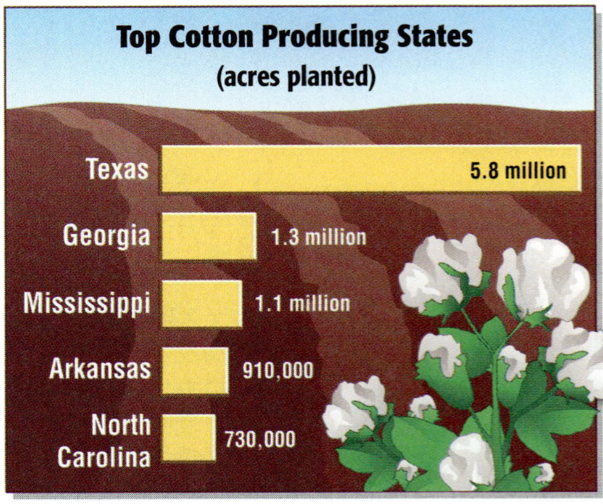

Source: National Cotton Council

EXTRA PRACTICE
See pages 737, 762.
Math Online
Self-Check Quiz at tx.msmath2.com

32. **SWIMMING POOLS** A pool that holds 320 cubic feet of water is 84% filled to capacity. Another pool that holds 400 cubic feet of water is 82.5% filled to capacity. Which pool contains more water? How much more?

H.O.T. Problems

33. **OPEN ENDED** Write a percent problem for which the percent is greater than 100% and the part is known. Use the percent equation to solve your problem to find the base.

34. **CHALLENGE** If you need to find the percent of a number, explain how you can predict whether the part will be less than, greater than, or equal to the number.

35. **WRITING IN MATH** Compare the percent equation and the percent proportion. Then explain when it might be easier to use the percent equation rather than the percent proportion.

TEST PRACTICE

36. In a survey, 150 students were asked to choose their favorite take-out food. The table shows the results.

Favorite Take-Out Food	
Type of Food	**Percent**
Pizza	40
Sandwiches	32
Fried chicken	28

Based on this data, predict how many out of 1,800 students would choose sandwiches.

A 504 C 680

B 576 D 720

37. How many programs were sold at the Troy High School football game if the athletic boosters sold 76% of the 125 programs they had available?

F 49 H 95

G 76 J 201

38. **GRIDDABLE** There are 1,400 students at West Elm Junior High. If approximately 11% of the student population is left-handed, predict the number of left-handed students at West Elm Junior High.

Spiral Review

39. **ROLLER COASTERS** A roller coaster travels its track length of 2,800 feet in about 2 minutes. What is a reasonable distance the coaster travels each second? Use the *reasonable answers* strategy. (Lesson 8-4)

Estimate by using fractions. (Lesson 8-3)

40. 11% of 79

41. 30.5% of 50

42. 48% of 311

GET READY for the Next Lesson

PREREQUISITE SKILL **Solve each proportion.** (Lesson 7-4)

43. $\frac{a}{125} = \frac{20}{100}$

44. $\frac{13}{x} = \frac{65}{100}$

45. $\frac{b}{575} = \frac{80}{100}$

CHAPTER 8 Mid-Chapter Quiz

Lessons 8-1 through 8-5

Find each number. Round to the nearest tenth if necessary. (Lesson 8-1)

1. Find 17% of 655.
2. What is 235% of 82?
3. Find 75% of 160.
4. What number is 162.2% of 55?
5. **TEST PRACTICE** Ayana has 220 coins in her piggy bank. Of those, 45% are pennies. How many coins are NOT pennies? (Lesson 8-1)

   A 121 **C** 109
   B 116 **D** 85

Find each number. Round to the nearest tenth if necessary. (Lesson 8-2)

6. What percent of 84 is 12?
7. 15 is 25% of what number?
8. 85% of 252 is what number?

ANALYZE GRAPHS **For Exercises 9 and 10, refer to the graph that shows the results of a survey of students' favorite TV programs.** (Lesson 8-2)

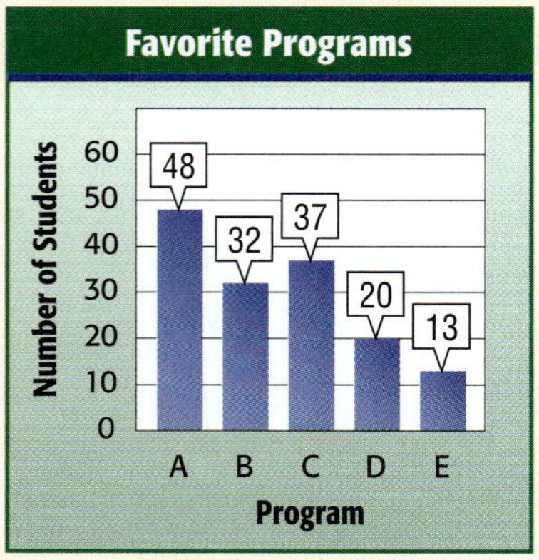

9. Of the 150 students surveyed, what percent of the students preferred Program A?
10. Of the five TV programs, which program did about 25% of the students report as their favorite?

Estimate. (Lesson 8-3)

11. 20% of 392
12. 78% of 112
13. 52% of 295
14. 30% of 42
15. 79% of 88
16. 41.5% of 212
17. **TEST PRACTICE** Miyoki has read 82% of a book that has 214 pages. About how many pages does she have left to read? (Lesson 8-3)

   F 16 pages **H** 65 pages
   G 40 pages **J** 80 pages

18. **SHOPPING** A desktop computer costs \$849.75 and the hard drive is 61.3% of the total cost. What is a reasonable estimate for the cost of the hard drive? (Lesson 8-4)

Write an equation for each problem. Then solve. Round to the nearest tenth if necessary. (Lesson 8-5)

19. What number is 35% of 72?
20. 16.1 is what percent of 70?
21. 27.2 is 68% of what number?
22. 16% of 32 is what number?
23. 55% of what number is 1.265?
24. 17 is 40% of what number?
25. **ANALYZE TABLES** The table shows the costs of owning a dog over an average 11-year lifespan. What percent of the total cost is veterinary bills? (Lesson 8-5)

Dog Ownership Costs

Item	Cost ($)
Food	4,020
Veterinary Bills	3,930
Grooming, Equipment	2,960
Training	1,220
Other	2,470

Source: American Kennel Club

8-6 Using Statistics to Predict

Main IDEA

Predict actions of a larger group by using a sample.

Targeted TEKS **7.3** The student solves problems involving direct proportional relationships. **(A)** estimate and **find solutions to application problems involving percent.** *Also addresses TEKS 7.13(A), 7.13(D).*

NEW Vocabulary

survey
population
random sample

GET READY for the Lesson

TELEPHONE The circle graph shows the results of a survey in which children ages 8 to 12 were asked whether they have a television in their bedroom.

1. Can you tell how many were surveyed? Explain.
2. Describe how you could use the graph to predict how many students in your school have television in their bedroom.

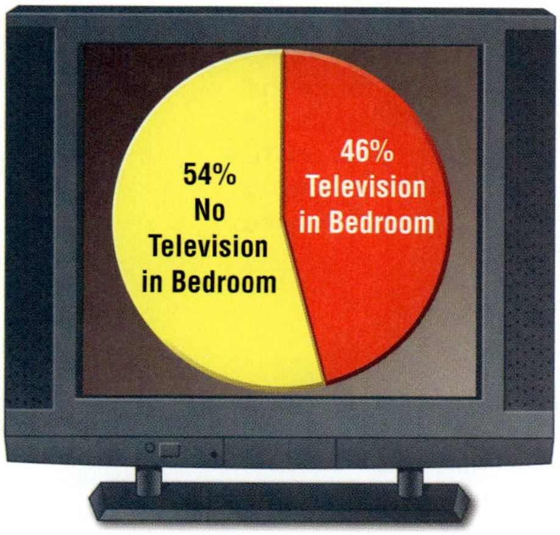

Source: www.mediafamily.org

A **survey** is designed to collect data about a specific group of people, called the **population**. If a survey uses a **random sample** of a population, or a sample chosen without preference, you can assume that the sample represents the population. Then you can use the results to make predictions about the population.

Real-World EXAMPLE

1 **TELEVISION Refer to the graphic above. Predict how many out of 1,250 students would not have a television in their bedroom.**

You can use the percent proportion and the survey results to predict what part p of the population of students have no TV in their bedroom.

part of the population → p; whole population → 1,250

$\frac{p}{1,250} = \frac{54}{100}$ } Survey results: 54%

$p \cdot 100 = 1,250 \cdot 54$ Find the cross products.

$100p = 67,500$ Simplify.

$\frac{100p}{100} = \frac{67,500}{100}$ Divide each side by 100.

$p = 675$ Simplify.

About 675 students do not have a television in their bedroom.

CHECK Your Progress

a. **TELEVISION** Refer to the same graphic. Predict how many out of 1,370 students have a television in their bedrooms.

READING in the Content Area

For strategies in reading this lesson, visit tx.msmath2.com.

Real-World EXAMPLE

Real-World Link A survey found that 85% of people use buddy icons on their instant messengers.
Source: AOL Research

2 **INSTANT MESSAGING** **Use the information at the left to predict how many of the 2,450 students at Washington Middle School use buddy icons on their instant messengers.**

You need to predict how many of the 2,450 students use buddy icons.

Words	What number of students is 85% of 2,450 students?
Variable	Let n represent the number of students.
Equation	$n \quad = \quad 0.85 \quad \cdot \quad 2{,}450$

$n = 0.85 \cdot 2{,}450$ Write the percent equation.

$n = 2{,}082.5$ Multiply.

About 2,083 of the students use buddy icons.

CHECK Your Progress

b. **INSTANT MESSAGING** This same survey found that 59% of people use sound on their instant messengers. Predict how many of the 2,450 students use sound on their instant messengers.

Online Personal Tutor at tx.msmath2.com

CHECK Your Understanding

Example 1 (p. 411)

SPENDING **For Exercises 1 and 2, use the circle graph that shows the results of a poll to which 60,000 teens responded.**

Source: *USA WEEKEND*

1. How many of the teens surveyed said that they would save their money?
2. Predict how many of the approximately 28 million teens in the United States would buy a music CD if they were given $20.

Example 2 (p. 412)

TRANSPORTATION **For Exercises 3 and 4, use the bar graph that shows the results of a survey in which working adults in America were asked how they get to work.**

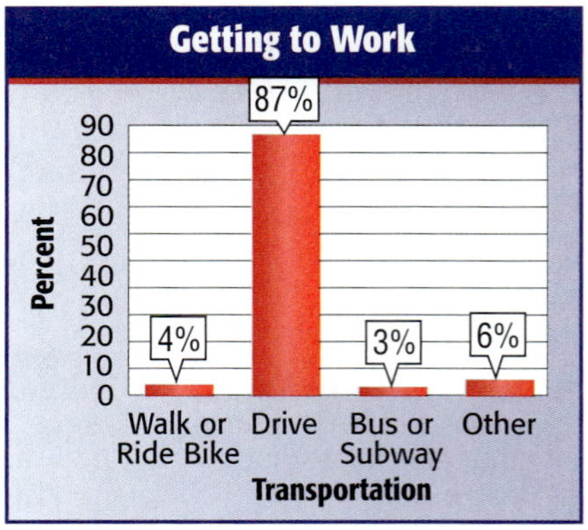

Source: Gallup Poll

3. Out of the 143 million working adults in America, predict how many ride a bicycle to work.
4. Predict how many working adults in America drive to work.

Exercises

HOMEWORK HELP	
For Exercises	See Examples
5–8	1, 2

COMPUTERS **For Exercises 5 and 6, use the table that shows the results of a survey in which students were asked how they use a personal computer at home.**

PC Use	Percent
Educational programs	93%
Homework	80%
Games	70%
Download music	95%

5. Predict how many of the 1,745 Allegheny Valley Middle School students use a PC for homework.

6. About how many of the students use a PC for games?

7. **CAMERAS** In a survey, 14% of teens said that they own a digital camera. Predict how many of the 420,000 teens in Arizona own digital cameras.

8. **VOLUNTEERING** A survey showed that 90% of teens donate money to a charity during the holidays. Based on that survey, how many teens in a class of 400 will donate money the next holiday season?

Match each situation with the appropriate equation or proportion.

9. 27% of MP3 owners download music weekly. Predict how many MP3 owners out of 238 owners download music weekly.

10. 27 MP3s is what percent of 238 MP3s?

11. 238% of 27 is what number?

a. $n = 27 \cdot 2.38$

b. $\frac{27}{100} = \frac{n}{238}$

c. $\frac{27}{238} = \frac{n}{100}$

CATS **For Exercises 12 and 13, use the graph that shows the percent of cat owners who train their cats in each category.**

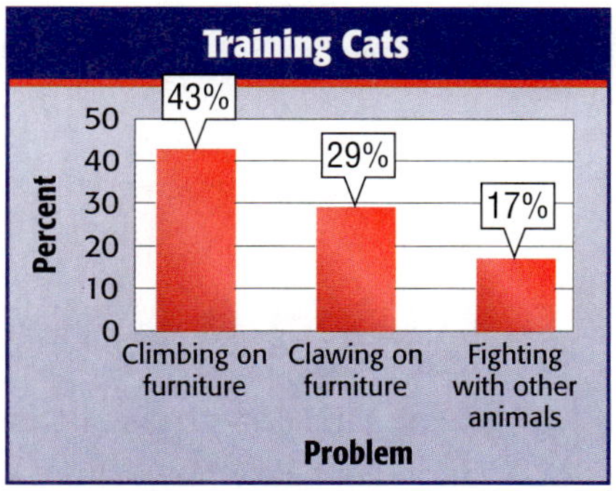

Source: Purina Cat Chow

12. Out of 255 cat owners, predict how many owners trained their cat not to climb on furniture.

13. Out of 316 cat owners, predict how many more cat owners have trained their cat not to claw on furniture than have trained their cat not to fight with other animals.

EXTRA PRACTICE

See pages 737, 762.

Math Online

Self-Check Quiz at tx.msmath2.com

14. **FIND THE DATA** Refer to the Texas Data File on pages 16–19. Choose some data and write a real-world problem in which you could use the percent proportion or percent equation to make a prediction.

H.O.T. Problems

15. **CHALLENGE** A survey found that 80% of teens enjoy going to the movies in their free time. Out of 5,200 teens, predict how many teens said that they do not enjoy going to the movies in their free time.

16. **OPEN ENDED** Select a newspaper or magazine article that contains a table or graph. Identify the population and explain how you think the results were found.

17. **SELECT A TOOL** A survey showed that 15% of the people in Tennessee over the age of 16 belong to a fitness center. Predict how many of the 5,900,962 people in Tennessee over the age of 16 belong to a fitness center. Select one or more of the following tools to solve the problem. Justify your selection(s).

make a model | calculator | paper/pencil | real objects

18. **WRITING IN MATH** Explain how to use a sample to predict what a group of people prefer. Then give an example of a situation in which it makes sense to use a sample.

TEST PRACTICE

19. A survey of 80 seventh graders at Lincoln Middle School was taken to find how they get to school each day. The results are shown in the table.

Getting to School	Percent
Take a Bus	33%
Walk	29%
Adult Drives	18%
Other	20%

Of the 423 seventh graders in the school, predict about how many walk to school.

A 23 **C** 123

B 64 **D** 394

20. Yesterday, a bakery baked 54 loaves of bread in 20 minutes. Today, the bakery needs to bake 375 loaves of bread. At this rate, predict how long it will take to bake the bread.

F 1.5 hours **H** 3.0 hours

G 2.3 hours **J** 3.75 hours

21. Of the 357 students in a freshman class, about 82% plan to go to college. How many students plan on going to college?

A 224 **C** 314

B 293 **D** 325

Spiral Review

Write an equation for each problem. Then solve. Round to the nearest tenth if necessary. (Lesson 8-5)

22. What number is 12% of 60?

23. 54 is 72% of what number?

24. **SHOPPING** Belinda wants to buy a coat that cost $149. On Friday, the coat will be 30% off. About how much money will Belinda save if she buys the coat on Friday? (Lesson 8-3)

Multiply. (Lesson 2-7)

25. -4×6

26. $5 \times (-8)$

27. $-6 \times (-9)$

28. 8×3

GET READY for the Next Lesson

PREREQUISITE SKILL **Simplify.** (Lesson 1-4)

29. $\frac{10 - 7}{10}$

30. $\frac{50 - 18}{50}$

31. $\frac{22 - 4}{4}$

32. $\frac{39 - 15}{15}$

8-7 Percent of Change

Main IDEA

Find the percent of increase or decrease.

Targeted TEKS **7.3** The student solves problems involving direct proportional relationships. **(A)** estimate and **find solutions to application problems involving percent.**

NEW Vocabulary

percent of change
percent of increase
percent of decrease

MINI Lab

Concepts in Motion
Interactive Lab tx.msmath2.com

You can use paper strips of equal length to model a 50% increase.

- Begin with two paper strips. On each strip, label 0% on the left side and 100% on the right side.

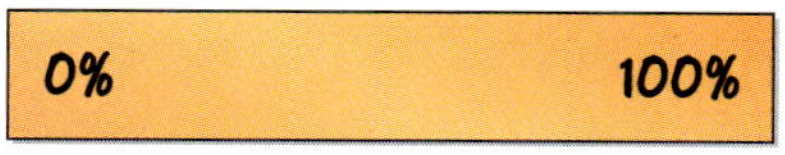

- Fold one of the paper strips in half. Mark 50% in the center.

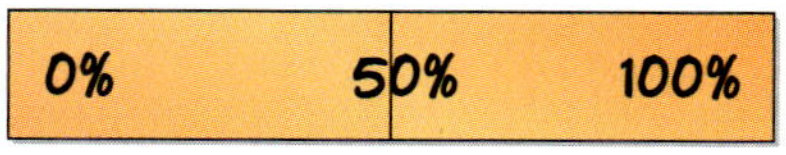

- Cut the second strip at the 50% mark and tape the piece onto the end of the first strip. The new longer strip represents a 50% increase or 150% of the original strip.

Model each percent of change.

1. 25% increase
2. 75% increase
3. 30% increase
4. Describe a model that represents a 100% increase, a 200% increase, and a 300% increase.
5. Describe how this process would change to show percent of decrease.

One way to describe a change in quantities is to use percent of change.

KEY CONCEPT — Percent of Change

Words A **percent of change** is a ratio that compares the change in quantity to the original amount.

Equation $\text{percent of change} = \dfrac{\text{amount of change}}{\text{original amount}}$

If the original quantity is increased, then it is called a **percent of increase**. If the original quantity is decreased, then it is called a **percent of decrease**.

$$\text{percent of increase} = \frac{\text{amount of increase}}{\text{original amount}} \leftarrow \text{new} - \text{original}$$

$$\text{percent of decrease} = \frac{\text{amount of decrease}}{\text{original amount}} \leftarrow \text{original} - \text{new}$$

EXAMPLE Find Percent of Increase

STUDY TIP

Percents
In the percent of change formula, the decimal must be written as a percent.

1 **TREES** **Find the percent of change in tree height from year 1 to year 10. Round to the nearest whole percent if necessary.**

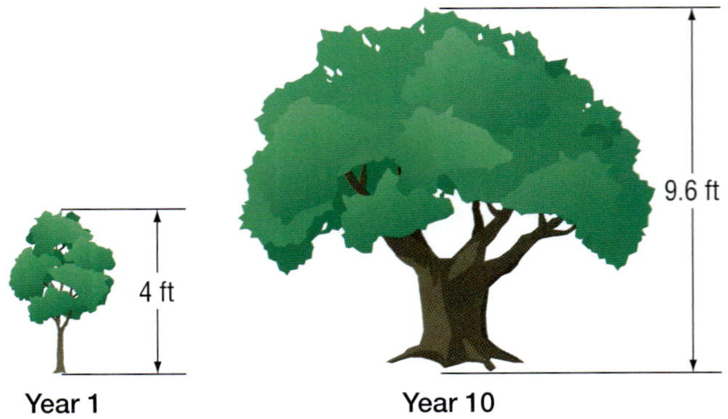

Since the new height is greater than the original height, this is a percent of increase. The amount of increase is 9.6 − 4 or 5.6 feet.

$$\text{percent of increase} = \frac{\text{amount of increase}}{\text{original amount}}$$

$= \frac{5.6}{4}$ Substitution

$= 1.4$ Simplify.

$= 140\%$ Write 1.4 as a percent.

CHECK Your Progress

a. **MEASUREMENT** Find the percent of change from 10 yards to 13 yards.

EXAMPLE Find Percent of Decrease

Real-World Career
How Does a Stockbroker Use Math?
A stockbroker must be able to compare percents of change of different stock prices.

Math Online For more information, go to tx.msmath2.com.

2 **STOCKS** **The table shows the original price of a stock and its new price after one month on the stock exchange. Find the percent of change in the price. Round to the nearest whole percent if necessary.**

Stock	Price
original	$75
new	$60

Since the new price is less than the original price, this is a percent of decrease. The amount of decrease is 75 − 60 or $15.

$$\text{percent of decrease} = \frac{\text{amount of decrease}}{\text{original amount}}$$

$= \frac{15}{75}$ Substitution

$= 0.2$ Simplify.

$= 20\%$ Write 0.2 as a percent.

CHECK Your Progress

b. **MONEY** Find the percent of change from $20 to $15.

TEST EXAMPLE

3 **The table shows about how many people attended the home games of a high school football team for five consecutive years. Which statement is supported by the information in the table?**

Attendance of Home Games	
Year	**Total Attendance (thousands)**
2000	16.6
2001	16.4
2002	15.9
2003	17.4
2004	17.6

A The attendance in 2003 was 15% greater than the attendance in 2002.

B The greatest decrease in attendance occurred from 2000 to 2001.

C The attendance in 2002 was 3% less than the attendance in 2001.

D The greatest increase in attendance occurred from 2003 to 2004.

Read the Test Item

You need to determine which statement is best supported by the information given in the table.

Solve the Test Item

- Check **A**. The percent of change from 2002 to 2003 was $\frac{17.4 - 15.9}{15.9}$ or about 10%, not 15%.
- Check **B**.
  From 2000 to 2001, the decrease was 16.6 − 16.4 or 0.2.
  From 2001 to 2002, the decrease was 16.4 − 15.9 or 0.5.
  This statement is not supported by the information.
- Check **C**. The percent of change from 2001 to 2002 was $\frac{16.4 - 15.9}{16.4}$ or about 3%. This statement is supported by the information.
- Check **D**.
  From 2002 to 2003, the increase was 17.4 − 15.9 or 1.5.
  From 2003 to 2004, the increase was 17.6 − 17.4 or 0.2.
  This statement is not supported by the information.

The solution is **C**.

Test-Taking Tip

Check the Results If you have time, check all of the choices given. By doing so, you will verify that your choice is correct.

CHECK Your Progress

c. Which of the following represents the greatest percent of change?

F A savings account that had $500 now has $470.

G An MP3 player that stored 15 GB now stores 30 GB.

H A plant grew from 3 inches to 8 inches in one month.

J An airplane ticket that was originally priced at $345 is now $247.

Online Personal Tutor at tx.msmath2.com

CHECK Your Understanding

Find each percent of change. Round to the nearest whole percent if necessary. State whether the percent of change is an *increase* or a *decrease*.

Examples 1, 2 (p. 416)

1. 30 inches to 24 inches
2. 20.5 meters to 35.5 meters
3. \$126 to \$150
4. \$75.80 to \$94.75

Example 3 (p. 417)

5. **TEST PRACTICE** The table shows the number of youth 7 years and older that played soccer from 1996 to 2004. Which statement is supported by the information in the table?

Playing Soccer

Year	Number (millions)
1996	13.9
1998	13.2
2000	12.9
2002	13.7
2004	13.3

Source: nsga.org

A The greatest decrease in the number of players occurred from 1998 to 2000.

B There were 7% fewer youth playing soccer in 2004 than in 2002.

C The number of players in 2002 was 6% greater than the number of players in 2000.

D There were 10% more youth playing soccer in 1998 than in 1996.

Exercises

HOMEWORK HELP

For Exercises	See Examples
6–7, 14–15 18–19	1
8–13 16–17	2
39, 40	3

For Exercises 6–19, find each percent of change. Round to the nearest whole percent if necessary. State whether the percent of change is an *increase* or a *decrease*.

6. 15 yards to 18 yards
7. 100 acres to 140 acres
8. \$12 to \$6
9. 48 notebooks to 14 notebooks
10. 125 centimeters to 87.5 centimeters
11. \$15.60 to \$11.70
12. 1.6 hours to 0.95 hour
13. 132 days to 125.4 days
14. \$240 to \$320
15. 624 feet to 702 feet

16. **BOOKS** On Monday, Kenya spent 60 minutes reading her favorite book. Today, she spent 45 minutes reading this book.

17. **EXERCISE** Three months ago, Ernesto could walk 2 miles in 40 minutes. Today he can walk 2 miles in 25 minutes.

18. **SCHOOL** Last school year the enrollment of Gilboa Middle School was 465 students. This year the enrollment is 525.

19. **MONEY** Jake had \$782 in his checking account. He now has \$798.

Find each percent of change. Round to the nearest whole percent if necessary. State whether the percent of change is an *increase* or a *decrease*.

20. $\frac{1}{2}$ to $\frac{1}{4}$
21. $\frac{4}{6}$ to $\frac{1}{6}$
22. $\frac{1}{5}$ to $\frac{4}{5}$
23. $\frac{2}{3}$ to $\frac{5}{3}$

GEOMETRY **For Exercises 24 and 25, refer to the rectangle at the right. Suppose the side lengths are doubled.**

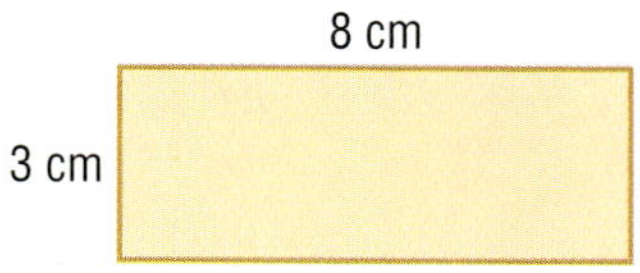

24. Find the percent of change in the perimeter.

25. Find the percent of change in the area.

26. **EDUCATION** In a recent year, a person with a high school diploma earned an average of $18,711 per year. A person who attended college earned an average of $21,982 per year. What was the percent of change?

27. **FIND THE DATA** Refer to the Texas Data File on pages 16–19. Choose some data and write a real-world problem in which you would find the percent of change.

28. **ANALYZE GRAPHS** Use the graphic shown to find the percent of change in hot dog consumption from 2003 to 2004 at American baseball parks.

Source: National Hotdog and Sausage Council

29. **ART** In 2001, the sales of fine art were $40.8 billion. Art sales increased by about 25% from 2001 to 2005. Find the projected amount of art sales in 2005.

30. **BABY-SITTING** The table shows how many hours Catalina spent baby-sitting during the months of April and May. If Catalina charges $6.50 per hour, what is the percent of change in the amount of money earned from April to May?

Month	Hours Worked
April	40
May	32

ANALYZE TABLES **For Exercises 31–33, refer to the table at the right.**

Age	Average Weekly Allowance
12	$9.58
13	$9.52
14	$13.47
15	$15.57
16	$17.84
17	$30.66

Source: kidsmoney.org

31. Find the percent of increase of allowance from age 13 to 14. Round to the nearest whole percent.

32. State two consecutive ages where the change in allowance is a percent of decrease. Then find the percent of decrease. Round to the nearest tenth.

33. Between which two consecutive years is the percent of increase the greatest? What is the percent of increase? Round to the nearest whole percent.

EXTRA PRACTICE
See pages 737, 762.
Math Online
Self-Check Quiz at tx.msmath2.com

H.O.T. Problems

34. **OPEN ENDED** Write a percent of change problem using the quantities 14 and 25, and state whether there is a percent of increase or decrease. Find the percent of change.

35. **NUMBER SENSE** The costs of two different sound systems were decreased by $10. The original costs of the systems were $90 and $60, respectively. Without calculating, which had greater percent of decrease? Explain.

36. **FIND THE ERROR** Jada and Monica are finding the percent of change from \$46 to \$130. Who is correct? Explain.

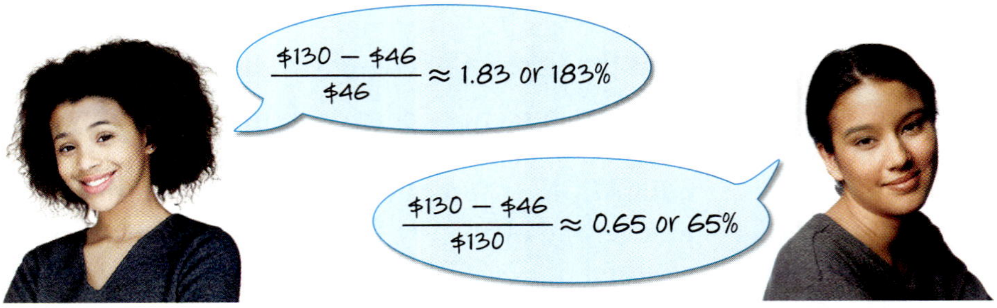

Jada Monica

37. **CHALLENGE** If a quantity increases by 10% and then decreases by 10%, will the result be the original quantity? Explain.

38. **WRITING IN MATH** Explain how you know whether a percent of change is a percent of increase or a percent of decrease.

TEST PRACTICE

39. Which of the following represents the least percent of change?

    A A coat that was originally priced at \$90 is now \$72.

    B A puppy who weighed 6 ounces at birth now weighs 96 ounces.

    C A child grew from 54 inches to 60 inches in 1 year.

    D A savings account increased from \$500 to \$550 in 6 months.

40. If each dimension of the rectangle is doubled, what is the percent of increase in the area?

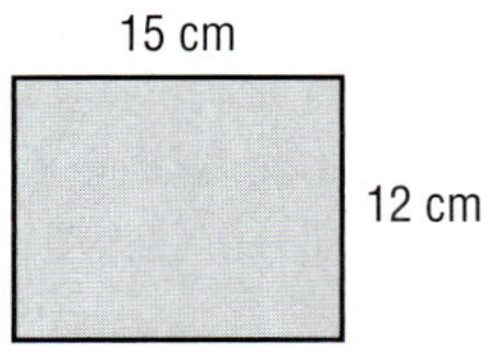

    F 100% H 300%

    G 200% J 400%

Spiral Review

41. **COLORS** In a survey of 150 students at Kennedy Middle School, 48% said that their favorite color is blue. Predict how many of the 1,375 students in the school like the color blue. (Lesson 8-6)

Write an equation for each problem. Then solve. Round to the nearest tenth if necessary. (Lesson 8-5)

42. 30% of what number is 17?

43. What is 21% of 62?

44. **SHOPPING** Four pounds of pecans costs \$12.75. How much is this per pound? (Lesson 7-2)

GET READY for the Next Lesson

PREREQUISITE SKILL **Write each percent as a decimal.** (Lesson 7-7)

45. 6.5%

46. $5\frac{1}{2}\%$

47. $8\frac{1}{4}\%$

48. $6\frac{3}{4}\%$

8-8 Sales Tax and Discount

Main IDEA

Solve problems involving sales tax and discount.

Targeted TEKS 7.3 The student solves problems involving direct proportional relationships. (A) estimate and **find solutions to application problems involving percent**.

NEW Vocabulary

sales tax
discount

STUDY TIP

Sales Tax and Discount
Sales tax is a percent of increase. Discount is a percent of decrease.

GET READY for the Lesson

COMPUTERS Julie Ann plans to buy a new flat screen monitor that costs $1,299. She lives in Florida where there is a 6% sales tax.

1. Calculate the sales tax by finding 6% of $1,299.
2. What will be the total costs including the sales tax?
3. Use a calculator to multiply 1.06 and 1,299. How does the result compare to your answer in Exercise 2?

Sales tax is an additional amount of money charged on items that people buy. The total cost of an item is the regular price plus the sales tax.

EXAMPLE Find the Total Cost

1 CALCULATORS A graphing calculator costs $90, and the sales tax is 4.25%. What is the total cost of the calculator?

METHOD 1 Add sales tax to the regular price.

First, find the sales tax.

4.25% of $90 = 0.0425 • 90	Write 4.5% as a decimal.
≈ 3.83	The sales tax is $3.83.

Next, add the sales tax to the regular price.
3.83 + 90 = 93.83

METHOD 2 Add the percent of tax to 100%.

100% + 4.25% = 104.25%	Add the percent of tax to 100%.

The total cost is 104.25% of the regular price.

104.25% of $90 = 1.0425 • 90	Write 104.25% as a decimal.
≈ 93.83	Use a calculator.

So, the total cost of the calculator is $93.83.

CHOOSE Your Method

a. **CLOTHES** What is the total cost of a sweatshirt if the regular price is $42 and the sales tax is $5\frac{1}{2}$%?

Discount is the amount by which the regular price of an item is reduced. The sale price is the regular price minus the discount.

EXAMPLE Find the Sale Price

2 **BOOGIE BOARDS** **A boogie board that has a regular price of $69 is on sale at a 35% discount. What is the sale price of the boogie board?**

METHOD 1 **Subtract the discount from the regular price.**

First, find the amount of the discount.

35% of \$69 = 0.35 • \$69	Write 35% as a decimal.
= \$24.15	The discount is \$24.15.

Next, subtract the discount from the regular price.
\$69 − \$24.15 = \$44.85

STUDY TIP

Subtracting Decimals
When subtracting decimals, remember to first align the decimal points. Then subtract.

METHOD 2 **Subtract the percent of discount from the 100%.**

100% − 35% = 65%	Subtract the discount from 100%.

The sale price is 65% of the regular price.

65% of \$69 = 0.65 • \$69	Write 65% as a decimal.
= 44.85	Use a calculator.

So, the sale price of the boogie board is \$44.85.

CHOOSE Your Method

b. **MUSIC** A CD that has a regular price of \$15.50 is on sale at a 25% discount. What is the sale price of the CD?

EXAMPLE Find the Percent of Discount

3 **MUSIC** **An electric guitar is on sale as shown at the right. What is the percent of discount?**

Original Price: ~~\$299.95~~
Now: \$179.99

First, find the *amount* of discount.

\$299.95 − \$179.99 = \$119.96

Next, use the percent equation to find the percent discount.

Words	\$119.96 is what percent of \$299.95?				
Variable	Let n represent the percent.				
Equation	119.96	=	n	•	299.95

$119.96 = n \cdot 299.95$	Write the equation.
$0.40 \approx n$	Divide each side by 299.95.

The percent of discount is about 40%.

CHECK Your Progress

c. Find the percent of discount if the sale price of the guitar is \$224.96.

Online **Personal Tutor at** tx.msmath2.com

CHECK Your Understanding

Find the total cost or sale price to the nearest cent.

Example 1 (p. 421)

1. $2.95 notebook; 5% tax
2. $46 shoes; 2.9% tax

Example 2 (p. 422)

3. $1,575 computer; 15% discount
4. $119.50 skateboard; 20% off

Example 3 (p. 422)

5. **IN-LINE SKATES** A pair of in-line skates that normally cost $99 is on sale for $90. To the nearest percent, what is the percent of discount?

Exercises

HOMEWORK HELP

For Exercises	See Examples
6–13	1–2
14–17	3

Find the total cost or sale price to the nearest cent.

6. $58 ski lift ticket; 20% discount
7. $1,500 computer; 7% tax
8. $99 CD player; 5% tax
9. $12.25 pen set; 60% discount
10. $4.30 makeup; 40% discount
11. $7.50 meal; 6.5% tax
12. $39.60 sweater; 33% discount
13. $89.75 scooter; $7\frac{1}{4}$% tax

14. **COSMETICS** A bottle of hand lotion that normally sells for $4.50 is on sale for $2.25. What is the percent of discount?

15. **TICKETS** At a movie theater, the cost of admission to a matinee is $5.25. The cost of admission to a regular evening movie is $7.50. Find the percent of discount to the nearest percent.

Find the percent of discount to the nearest percent.

16. calendar: regular price, $9
sale price, $2.25
17. telescope: regular price, $180
sale price, $126

18. **VIDEO GAMES** What is the sales tax of a $178.90 video game system if the tax rate is 5.75%?

19. **RESTAURANTS** A restaurant bill comes to $28.35. Find the total cost if the tax is 6.25% and a 20% tip is left on the amount before tax.

BIKES For Exercises 20–22, use the information below and the table shown.

Jason lives in California and is buying a bike that normally costs $575.

State	2005 Sales Tax Rate
California	6.25%
Mississippi	7%
North Carolina	4.5%
Texas	6.25%

Source: www.taxadmin.org

20. What is the total cost of the bike including tax?
21. If the bike is on sale with a 25% discount, how much will Jason save on the bike?
22. If Jason arrives at the store between 7 and 8 A.M. on the day of the sale, the bike will be discounted an additional 15% off the already discounted price. What will be the sale price if tax is calculated after both discounts?

EXTRA PRACTICE

See pages 738, 762.

Math Online
Self-Check Quiz at tx.msmath2.com

H.O.T. Problems

23. **CHALLENGE** A gift store is having a sale in which all items are discounted 20%. Including tax, Colin paid $21 for a picture frame. If the sales tax rate is 5%, what was the original price of the picture frame?

24. **OPEN ENDED** Give an example of the regular price of an item and the total cost including sales tax if the tax rate is 5.75%.

25. **Which One Doesn't Belong?** In each pair, the first value is the regular price of an item and the second value is the sale price. Identify the pair that does not have the same percent of discount as the other three. Explain.

$20, $15	$60, $35	$8, $6	$130, $97.50

26. **WRITING IN MATH** Describe two methods for finding the sale price of an item that is discounted 30%. Which method do you prefer? Explain.

TEST PRACTICE

27. A computer software store is having a sale. The table shows the regular price, *r*, and the sales price, *s*, of various items.

Item	Regular Price (*r*)	Sale Price (*s*)
A	$5.00	$4.00
B	$8.00	$6.40
C	$10.00	$8.00
D	$15.00	$12.00

Which formula can be used to calculate the sale price?

A $s = r \times 0.2$

B $s = r - 0.2$

C $s = r \times 0.8$

D $s = r - 0.8$

28. A chair that costs $210 was reduced by 40% for a one day sale. After the sale, the sale price was increased by 40%. What is the price of the chair?

F $176.40

G $185.30

H $205.50

J $210.00

29. A T-shirt at the mall costs $14.95. It is on sale for 30% off. What is the sale price to the nearest cent?

A $4.49 **C** $10.50

B $10.47 **D** $10.65

Spiral Review

Find each percent of change. Round to the nearest whole percent if necessary. State whether the percent of change is an *increase* or *decrease*. (Lesson 8-7)

30. 4 hours to 6 hours

31. $500 to $456

32. 20.5 meters to 35.5 meters

33. **BOOKS** In a survey, 34% of teens said that they prefer reading mystery books. Predict how many teens out of 1,500 prefer reading mysteries. (Lesson 8-6)

GET READY for the Next Lesson

PREREQUISITE SKILL Multiply. (Lessons 3-2 and 6-5)

34. $790 \cdot 0.185 \cdot 2$

35. $45 \cdot 0.04 \cdot 9$

36. $600 \cdot 0.03 \cdot 5\frac{1}{2}$

8-9 Simple Interest

Main IDEA

Solve problems involving simple interest.

Targeted TEKS **7.3** The student solves problems involving direct proportional relationships. **(A)** estimate and **find solutions to application problems involving percent.**

GET READY for the Lesson

INVESTING Jin plans to invest \$1,000 in a certificate of deposit (CD). The graph shows CD rates for one year at various banks.

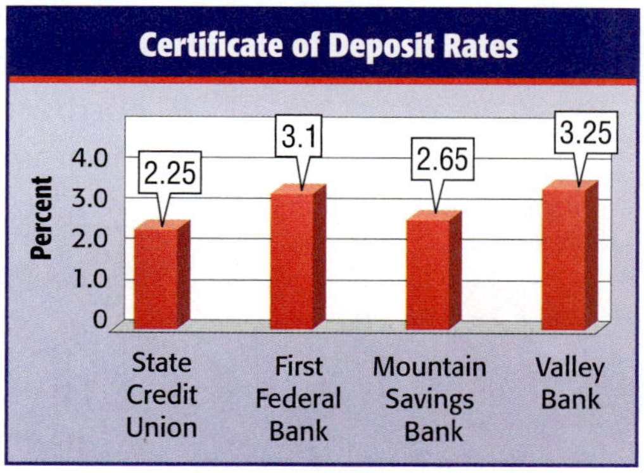

1. Calculate 2.25% of \$1,000 to find the amount of money that Jin can earn in one year for a CD at State Credit Union.
2. Find the amount of money that she can earn in one year at the other three banks.

NEW Vocabulary

simple interest
principal

Simple interest is the amount paid or earned for the use of money. To find simple interest I, use the following formula.

Principal is the amount of money deposited or borrowed.

$$I = prt$$

annual interest rate written as a decimal

amount of time, expressed in years that money is deposited or borrowed

EXAMPLES Find Interest Earned

SAVINGS Raini has \$750 in a savings account that pays 3% simple interest. How much interest will he earn in each amount of time?

1 **4 years**

$I = prt$	Formula for simple interest
$I = 750 \cdot 0.03 \cdot 4$	Replace p with \$750, r with 0.03, and t with 4.
$I = 90$	Simplify.

Raini will earn \$90 in interest in 4 years.

2 **9 months**

9 months $= \frac{9}{12}$ or 0.75 year	Write the time as years.
$I = prt$	Formula for simple interest
$I = 750 \cdot 0.03 \cdot 0.75$	$p = \$750, r = 0.03, t = 0.75$
$I \approx 16.88$	Simplify.

Raini will earn \$16.88 in interest in 9 months.

CHECK Your Progress

SAVINGS **Jenny has $1,560 in a savings account that pays 2.5% simple interest. How much interest will she earn in each amount of time?**

a. 3 years

b. 6 months

Online **Personal Tutor at** tx.msmath2.com

READING Math

Formulas Read $I = prt$ as *Interest is equal to principal times rate times time.*

The formula $I = prt$ can also be used to find the interest owed when you borrow money. In this case, p is the amount of money borrowed, and t is the amount of time the money is borrowed.

EXAMPLE Find Interest Paid on a Loan

3 **LOANS** **Rondell's parents borrow $1,200 from the bank for a new car. The interest rate is 8% per year. How much simple interest will they pay if they take 2 years to repay the loan?**

$I = prt$ — Formula for simple interest

$I = 1{,}200 \cdot 0.08 \cdot 2$ — Replace p with $1,200, r with 0.08, and t with 2.

$I = 192$ — Simplify.

Rondell's parents will pay $192 in interest in 2 years.

Real-World Link

A car loan on a $22,000 car over 60 months at 4.79 percent annual interest and no down payment will cost an additional $2,783 in interest payments alone.

Source: carloanclues.com

CHECK Your Progress

c. **LOANS** Mrs. Hanover borrows $1,400 at a rate of 5.5% per year. How much simple interest will she pay if it takes 8 months to repay the loan?

EXAMPLE Find Total Paid on a Credit Card

4 **CREDIT CARDS** **Cory charged a $600 TV on his credit card with an interest rate of 21%. If he has no other charges on the card, and does not pay off the balance at the end of the month how much money will he owe after one month?**

$I = prt$ — Formula for simple interest

$I = 600 \cdot 0.21 \cdot \frac{1}{12}$ — Replace p with $600, r with 0.21, and t with $\frac{1}{12}$.

$I = 10.5$ — Simplify.

The interest owed after one month is $10.50. So, the total amount owed would be $600 + $10.50 or $610.50.

CHECK Your Progress

d. **CREDIT CARDS** An office manager charged $425 worth of office supplies on a charge card with an interest rate of 9.9%. How much money will he owe if he makes no other charges on the card and does not pay off the balance at the end of the month?

CHECK Your Understanding

Examples 1, 2 (pp. 425-426)

Find the simple interest earned to the nearest cent for each principal, interest rate, and time.

1. $640, 3%, 2 years
2. $1,500, 4.25%, 4 years
3. $580, 2%, 6 months
4. $1,200, 3.9%, 8 months

Example 3 (p. 426)

Find the simple interest paid to the nearest cent for each loan, interest rate, and time.

5. $4,500, 9%, 3.5 years
6. $290, 12.5%, 6 months

Example 4 (p. 426)

7. **FINANCES** The Masters family financed a computer that costs $1,200. If the interest rate is 19%, how much will the family owe after one month if no payments are made?

Exercises

HOMEWORK HELP

For Exercises	See Examples
8–9	1
10–11	2
12–15	3
16–17	4

Find the simple interest earned to the nearest cent for each principal, interest rate, and time.

8. $1,050, 4.6%, 2 years
9. $250, 2.85%, 3 years
10. $500, 3.75%, 4 months
11. $3,000, 5.5%, 9 months

Find the simple interest paid to the nearest cent for each loan, interest rate, and time.

12. $1,000, 7%, 2 years
13. $725, 6.25%, 1 year
14. $2,700, 8.2%, 3 months
15. $175.80, 12%, 8 months

16. **CREDIT CARDS** Leon charged $75 at an interest rate of 12.5%. How much will Leon have to pay after one month if he makes no payments?

17. **TRAVEL** A family charged $1,345 in travel expenses. If no payments are made, how much will they owe after one month if the interest rate is 7.25%?

BANKING For Exercises 18 and 19, use the table.

18. What is the simple interest earned on $900 for 9 months?

19. Find the simple interest earned on $2,500 for 18 months.

Home Savings and Loan	
Time	**Rate**
6 months	2.4%
9 months	2.9%
12 months	3.0%
18 months	3.1%

INVESTING For Exercises 20 and 21, use the following information.

Manuel has $1,800 from his summer job to invest.

20. Suppose he invests the $1,800 for 2 years and earns $144. What was the rate of interest?

21. Manuel would like to have $2,340 altogether. If he invests his money at 5% interest, in how many years will he have $2,340?

EXTRA PRACTICE

See pages 738, 762.

Math Online

Self-Check Quiz at tx.msmath2.com

H.O.T. Problems

22. **OPEN ENDED** Suppose you earn 3% on a $1,200 deposit for 5 years. Explain how the simple interest is affected if the rate is increased by 1%. What happens if the time is increased by 1 year?

23. **CHALLENGE** Mrs. Williams deposits $600 in an account that pays 4.5% annually. At the end of the year, the interest earned is added to the principal. Find the total amount in her account each year for 3 years, if she does not withdraw any money in the 3 years.

24. **WRITING IN MATH** List the steps you would use to find the simple interest on a $500 loan at 6% interest rate for 18 months. Then find the simple interest.

TEST PRACTICE

25. Antonia opened a savings account that pays 6.5% simple interest. How much money will be in Antonia's account after 3 years if she deposited $250 at the beginning and never made any withdrawals or more deposits?

 A $48.75

 B $248.75

 C $298.75

 D $300.00

26. Mr. McMahon bought a $562 freezer using a credit card that charges 18% annual interest. If he does not make any payments or any additional charges, how much will he owe after 1 month?

 F $553.57

 G $570.43

 H $578.86

 J $663.16

Spiral Review

27. Find the total cost of a $19.99 DVD if the tax rate is 7%. (Lesson 8-8)

Find each percent of change. Round to the nearest whole percent if necessary. State whether the percent of change is an increase or decrease. (Lesson 8-7)

28. 35 birds to 45 birds

29. 60 inches to 38 inches

30. $2.75 to $1.80

Multiply. (Lesson 3-2)

31. 0.9×1.2

32. 1.5×3.67

33. $\$15.63 \times 5$

34. **PATTERNS** What is the next number in the sequence 23, 28, 33, …? (Lesson 1-8)

Cross-Curricular Project

Math and Science

Lions, Tigers, and Bears, Oh My! It's time to complete your project. Use the information and data you have gathered about the animals you selected to prepare a video or poster. Be sure to include a spreadsheet and all the necessary graphs with your project.

Math Online **Cross-Curricular Project at** tx.msmath2.com

Extend 8-9

Spreadsheet Lab
Simple Interest

Main IDEA

Use a spreadsheet to calculate simple interest.

Targeted TEKS **7.3** The student solves problems involving direct proportional relationships. **(A)** estimate and **find solutions to application problems involving percent.** *Also addresses TEKS 7.14(A).*

A computer spreadsheet is a useful tool for quickly calculating simple interest for different values of principal, rate, and time.

ACTIVITY

Max plans on opening a "Young Savers" account at his bank. The current rate on the account is 4%. He wants to see how different starting balances, rates, and times will affect his account balance. To find the balance at the end of 2 years for different principal amounts, he enters the values B2 = 4 and C2 = 2 into the spreadsheet below.

Simple Interest.xls

	A	B	C	D	E
1	Principal (*p*)	Rate (*r*)	Time (*t*)	Interest (*I*)	New Balance
2					
3	500	=B2/100	=C2	=A3*B3*C3	=A3+D3
4	1000	=B2/100	=C2	=A4*B4*C4	=A4+D4
5	1500	=B2/100	=C2	=A5*B5*C5	=A5+D5
6	2000	=B2/100	=C2	=A6*B6*C6	=A6+D6
7	2500	=B2/100	=C2	=A7*B7*C7	=A7+D7

Sheet 1 | Sheet 2 | Sheet 3

For each principal given in column A, simple interest is calculated for any values of rate and time entered in B2 and C2, respectively.

The spreadsheet adds simple interest to the principal.

ANALYZE THE RESULTS

1. Why is the rate in column B divided by 100?
2. What is the balance in Max's account after 2 years if the principal is \$1,500 and the simple interest rate is 4%?
3. How much interest does Max earn in 2 years if his account has a principal of \$2,000 and a simple interest rate of 4%?
4. Is the amount of principal proportional to the interest Max earns if his account earns 4% simple interest over 2 years? Explain.
5. Is the amount of principal proportional to the balance in Max's account if it earns 4% simple interest over 2 years? Explain.
6. What entries for cells B2 and C2 would you use to calculate the simple interest on a principal of \$1,500 at a rate of 7% for a 9-month period?
7. What is the balance of this account at the end of the 9 months?

CHAPTER 8 Study Guide and Review

STUDY TO GO Download Vocabulary Review from tx.msmath2.com

FOLDABLES™ Study Organizer

GET READY to Study

Be sure the following Key Concepts are noted in your Foldable.

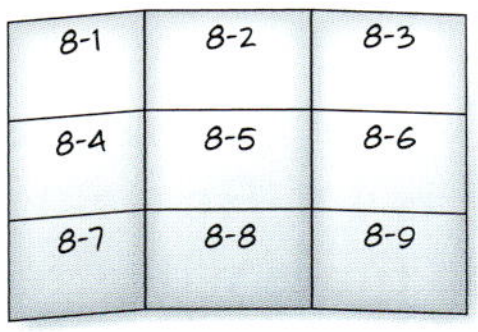

Key Concepts

Percent of a Number (Lesson 8-1)

- To find the percent of a number, first write the percent as either a fraction or decimal and then multiply.

Percent Proportion (Lesson 8-2)

$$\frac{\text{part}}{\text{whole}} = \left.\frac{n}{100}\right\} \text{percent}$$

Percent and Estimation (Lesson 8-3)

- One way to estimate the percent of a number is to use a fraction. The other way is to first find 10% of the number and then multiply.

Percent Equation (Lesson 8-5)

$$\text{part} = \text{percent} \cdot \text{whole}$$

Percent of Change (Lesson 8-7)

- A percent of change is ratio that compares the change in quantity to the original amount.

$$\text{percent of change} = \frac{\text{amount of change}}{\text{original amount}}$$

Sales and Discount (Lesson 8-8)

- Sales tax is an additional amount of money charged on items. The total cost of an item is the regular price plus the sales tax.
- Discount is the amount by which the regular price of an item is reduced. The sale price is the regular price minus the discount.

Simple Interest (Lesson 8-9)

- Simple interest is the amount paid or earned for the use of money.

$$I = prt$$

Key Vocabulary

discount (p. 421)
percent equation (p. 405)
percent of change (p. 415)
percent of decrease (p. 415)
percent of increase (p. 415)
percent proportion (p. 392)
population (p. 411)
principal (p. 425)
random sample (p. 411)
sales tax (p. 421)
simple interest (p. 425)
survey (p. 411)

Vocabulary Check

State whether each sentence is *true* or *false*. If *false*, replace the underlined word or number to make a true sentence.

1. The sale price of a discounted item is the regular price minus the discount.
2. When taking a survey, the total group of people that the survey is interested in is called the sample.
3. A percent proportion compares part of a quantity to the whole quantity using a percent.
4. The formula for simple interest is $I = prt$.
5. A method for estimating the percent of a number is to find 21% of the number and then multiply.
6. A sample is representative of the population if it is random.
7. The principal is the amount of money deposited or borrowed.
8. A tax is the amount by which the regular price of an item is reduced.
9. To find a percent of increase, compare the amount of the increase to the new amount.
10. A sample is a question or a set of questions designed to collect data about a specific group of people.

Math Online Vocabulary Review at tx.msmath2.com

Lesson-by-Lesson Review

8-1 Percent of a Number (pp. 386–390)

Find each number. Round to the nearest tenth if necessary.

11. Find 78% of 50.
12. 45.5% of 75 is what number?
13. What is 225% of 60?
14. 0.75% of 80 is what number?

Example 1 Find 24% of 200.

24% of 200

$= 24\% \times 200$ Write the expression.

$= 0.24 \times 200$ Write 24% as a decimal.

$= 48$ Multiply.

So, 24% of 200 is 48.

8-2 The Percent Proportion (pp. 392–396)

Find each number. Round to the nearest tenth if necessary.

15. **SOCCER** A soccer team lost 30% of their games. If they played 20 games, how many did they win?
16. 6 is what percent of 120?
17. Find 0.8% of 35.
18. What percent of 375 is 40?
19. **PHONE SERVICE** A family pays $21.99 each month for their long distance phone service. This is 80% of the original price of the phone service. What is the original price of the phone service? Round to the nearest tenth if necessary.

Example 2 What percent of 90 is 18?

$\frac{18}{90} = \frac{n}{100}$ Write the proportion.

$18 \cdot 100 = 90 \cdot n$ Find the cross products.

$1{,}800 = 90n$ Simplify.

$\frac{1{,}800}{90} = \frac{90n}{90}$ Divide each side by 90.

$20 = n$ So, 18 is 20% of 90.

Example 3 52 is 65% of what number?

$\frac{52}{w} = \frac{65}{100}$ Write the proportion.

$52 \cdot 100 = w \cdot 65$ Find the cross products.

$5{,}200 = 65w$ Simplify.

$\frac{5{,}200}{65} = \frac{65w}{65}$ Divide each side by 65.

$80 = w$ So, 52 is 65% of 80.

8-3 Percent and Estimation (pp. 397–402)

Estimate.

20. 25% of 81
21. 33% of 122
22. 77% of 38
23. 19.5% of 96

Estimate by using 10%.

24. 12% of 77
25. 88% of 400
26. **PETS** About 12% of 291 households in a neighborhood have fish. Estimate how many households have fish.

Example 4 Estimate 52% of 495.

$52\% \approx 50\%$ or $\frac{1}{2}$, and $495 \approx 500$.

52% of 495 $\approx \frac{1}{2} \cdot 500$ or 250

So, 52% of 495 is about 250.

Example 5 Estimate 68% of 80.

10% of 80 = $0.1 \cdot 80$ or 8 Find 10% of 80.

68% is about 70%.

$7 \cdot 8 = 56$ 70% of 80 $\approx 7 \cdot$ (10% of 80)

So, 68% of 80 is about 56.

8-4 PSI: Determine Reasonable Answers (pp. 403–404)

Determine a reasonable answer for each problem.

27. **CABLE TV** In a survey of 1,813 consumers, 18% said that they would be willing to pay more for cable if they got more channels. Is 3.3, 33, or 333 a reasonable estimate for the number of consumers willing to pay more for cable?

28. **SCHOOL** There are 880 students at Medina Middle School. If 68% of the students are involved in sports, would the number of students involved in sports be about 510, 630, or 720?

29. **VACATION** Suppose you are going on vacation for $689 and the airfare accounts for 43.5% of the total cost. What is a reasonable cost of the airfare?

Example 6 **Mr. Swanson harvested 1,860 pounds of apples from one orchard, 1,149 pounds from another, and 905 pounds from a third. The apples will be placed in crates that hold 42 pounds of oranges. Will Mr. Swanson need 100, 200, or 400 crates?**

Since an exact answer is not needed, we can estimate the total of pounds.

1,860	→	1,900
1,149	→	1,100
+ 905	→	+ 900
		3,900

Since 3,900 ÷ 40 is about 100, it is reasonable that 100 crates need to be ordered.

8-5 Algebra: The Percent Equation (pp. 405–409)

Write an equation for each problem. Then solve. Round to the nearest tenth if necessary.

30. 32 is what percent of 50?
31. 65% of what number is 39?
32. Find 42% of 300.
33. 7% of 92 is what number?
34. 12% of what number is 108?
35. **SALONS** A local hair salon increased their sales of hair products by about 12.5% this week. If they sold 48 hair products, how many hair products did they sell last week?

Example 7 **27 is what percent of 90?**

27 is the part and 90 is the base.
Let n represent the percent.

part = percent • base

$27 = n \cdot 90$ Write an equation.

$\frac{27}{90} = \frac{90n}{90}$ Divide each side by 90.

$0.3 = n$ The percent is 30%.

So, 27 is 30% of 90.

Mixed Problem Solving
For mixed problem-solving practice, see page 762.

8-6 Using Statistics to Predict (pp. 411–414)

CAREERS For Exercises 36 and 37, use the table that shows the results of a university survey of incoming freshman.

Career Goal	Percent
Elementary teacher	5.5%
Engineer	6.4%

36. Predict how many of the 3,775 freshmen would choose a career as an elementary teacher.
37. How many of the 3,775 freshmen would you expect to choose a career as an engineer?
38. **SHOES** A survey showed that 72% of teens bought new athletic shoes for the new school year. Based on that survey, how many teens in group of 225 bought new athletic shoes for the new school year?

Example 8 The circle graph shows the results of a survey to which 150 students at McAuliffe Middle School responded. Predict how many of the 644 students at the school have after-school jobs.

Do You Have an After-School Job?

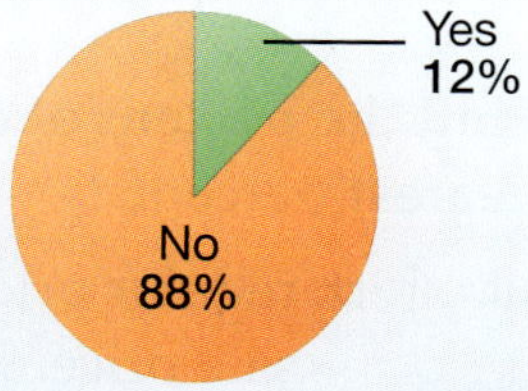

Find 12% of 644.

$n = 0.12 \cdot 644$ Write an equation.

$= 77.28$ Multiply.

So, you could predict that about 77 students at McAuliffe Middle School have after-school jobs.

8-7 Percent of Change (pp. 415–420)

Find each percent of change. Round to the nearest whole percent if necessary. State whether the percent of change is an *increase* or *decrease*.

39. original: 172
new: 254
40. original: $200
new: $386
41. original: 75
new: 60
42. original: $49.95
new: $54.95
43. **GAMES** A computer game that sold for $24.95 last year is now priced at $27.95. Find the percent of change.

Example 9 A magazine that originally cost $2.75 is now $3.55. Find the percent of change. Round to the nearest whole percent.

The new price is greater than the original price, so this is a percent of increase.

amount of increase = 3.55 − 2.75 or 0.80

$$\text{percent of increase} = \frac{\text{amount of increase}}{\text{original amount}}$$

$$= \frac{0.80}{2.75} \quad \text{Substitution}$$

$$\approx 0.29 \quad \text{Simplify.}$$

The percent of increase is about 29%.

8-8 Sales Tax and Discount (pp. 421–424)

Find the total cost or sale price to the nearest cent.

44. \$25 backpack; 7% tax
45. \$210 bicycle; 15% discount
46. \$8,000 car; $5\frac{1}{2}$% tax
47. \$40 sweater; 33% discount

Find the percent of discount to the nearest percent.

48. shirt: regular price: \$42
    sale price: \$36
49. boots: regular price, \$78
    sale price: \$70
50. **MONEY** A DVD that normally costs \$21.99 is on sale for 25% off. Tara buys the DVD and pays using a \$20 bill. Not including tax, how much change will she receive to the nearest cent?

Example 10 **A new computer system is priced at \$2,499. Find the total cost if the sales tax is 6.5%.**

First, find the sales tax.

$$6.5\% \text{ of } \$2{,}499 = 0.065 \cdot 2{,}499$$
$$\approx 162.44$$

Next, add the sales tax. The total cost is 162.44 + 2,499 or \$2,661.44.

Example 11 **A pass at a water park is \$58. At the end of the season, the same pass costs \$46.40. What is the percent of discount?**

$58 - 46.40 = 11.60$ Find the amount of discount.

Next, find what percent of 58 is 11.60.

$11.60 = n \cdot 58$ Write an equation.

$0.2 = n$ Divide each side by 58.

The percent of discount is 20%.

8-9 Simple Interest (pp. 425–428)

Find the interest earned to the nearest cent for each principal, interest rate, and time.

51. \$475, 5%, 2 years
52. \$5,000, 10%, 3 years
53. \$2,500, 11%, $1\frac{1}{2}$ years

Find the interest paid to the nearest cent for each loan balance, interest rate, and time.

54. \$3,200, 8%, 4 years
55. \$1,980, 21%, 9 months
56. **LOANS** Brian has a loan balance of \$1,000. If he pays off the balance in 2 years at an annual simple interest rate of 18%, how much total will he pay?

Example 12 **Find the interest earned on \$400 at 9% for 3 years.**

$I = prt$ Simple interest formula

$I = 400 \cdot 0.09 \cdot 3$ $p = \$400, r = 0.09, t = 3$

$I = 108$ Simplify.

The interest earned is \$108.

Example 13 **Elisa has a loan for \$1,300. The interest rate is 7%. If she pays it off in 6 months, how much interest will she pay?**

$I = prt$ Simple interest formula

$I = 1{,}300 \cdot 0.07 \cdot 0.5$ $p = \$1{,}300, r = 0.07, t = 0.5$

$I = 45.5$ Simplify.

The interest she will pay after 6 months is \$45.50.

CHAPTER 8

Practice Test

Find each number. Round to the nearest tenth if necessary.

1. Find 55% of 164.
2. What is 355% of 15?
3. Find 25% of 80.

4. **TEST PRACTICE** Of 365 students, 210 bought a hot lunch. About what percent of the students did NOT buy a hot lunch?
   A 35%
   B 42%
   C 56%
   D 78%

Estimate.

5. 18% of 246
6. 145% of 81
7. 71% of 324
8. 56% of 65.4

9. **COMMUNICATION** Theresa makes a long distance phone call and talks for 50 minutes. Of these minutes, 25% were spent talking to her brother. Would the time spent talking with her brother be about 8, 12, or 15 minutes? Explain your reasoning.

Write an equation for each problem. Then solve. Round to the nearest tenth if necessary.

10. Find 14% of 65.
11. What number is 36% of 294?
12. 82% of what number is 73.8?
13. 75 is what percent of 50?

Find each percent of change. Round to the nearest whole percent if necessary. State whether the percent of change is an *increase* or a *decrease*.

14. $60 to $75
15. 145 meters to 216 meters
16. 48 minutes to 40 minutes

BOOKS For Exercises 17 and 18, use the table below. It shows the results of a survey in which students at Haskell Middle School were asked to name their favorite types of fiction.

Type of Fiction	Percent
Historical Fiction	8%
Mystery	24%
Science Fiction	38%
Sports	30%

17. Predict how many of the 845 students at Haskell Middle School would choose science fiction as their favorite type.

18. How many of the 845 students would you expect to select mystery as their favorite type of fiction?

Find the total cost or sale price to the nearest cent.

19. $2,200 computer, $6\frac{1}{2}$% sales tax
20. $16 hat, 55% discount
21. $35.49 jeans, 33% discount

Find the simple interest earned to the nearest cent for each principal, interest rate, and time.

22. $750, 3%, 4 years
23. $1,050, 4.6%, 2 years
24. $2,600, 4%, 3 months

25. **TEST PRACTICE** Leah borrows $2,200 to buy new furniture. Her loan has an annual simple interest rate of 16%. If she does not make any payments or additional charges, about how much will she owe after one month?
   F $2,229
   G $2,552
   H $2,750
   J $3,520

CHAPTER 8

Texas Test Practice

Cumulative, Chapters 1–8

Read each question. Then fill in the correct answer on the answer document provided by your teacher or on a sheet of paper.

1. Sarah wants to buy pillows for her living room. Which store offers the best buy on pillows?

Store	Sale Price
A	3 pillows for $40
B	4 pillows for $50
C	2 pillows for $19
D	1 pillow for $11

A Store A

B Store B

C Store C

D Store D

2. The graph below shows the attendance at a summer art festival from 2000 to 2005. If the trend in attendance continues, which is the best prediction of the attendance at the art festival in 2008?

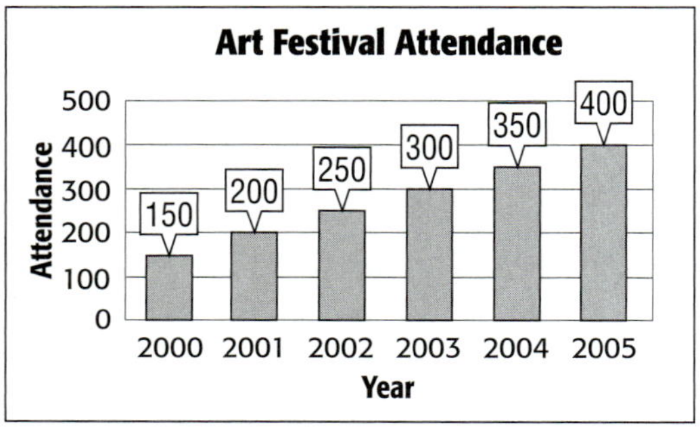

F Fewer than 200

G Between 500 and 600

H Between 700 and 800

J More than 800

3. **GRIDDABLE** At their annual car wash, the science club washes 30 cars in 45 minutes. At this rate, how many cars will they wash in 1 hour?

4. The cost of Ken's haircut was $23.95. If he wants to give his hair stylist a 15% tip, about how much of a tip should he leave?

A $2.40

B $3.60

C $4.60

D $4.80

5. At a pet store, 38% of the animals are dogs. If there are a total of 88 animals at the pet store, which equation can be used to find x, the number of dogs at the pet store?

F $\frac{x}{88} = \frac{100}{38}$

G $\frac{38}{88} = \frac{100}{x}$

H $\frac{x}{88} = \frac{38}{100}$

J $\frac{100}{88} = \frac{x}{38}$

6. An architect made a model of an office building using a scale of 1 inch equals 3 meters. If the height of the model is 12.5 inches, which of the following represents the actual height of the building?

A 40.0 m

B 37.5 m

C 36.0 m

D 28.4 m

7. Which of the following represents the greatest percent of change?

F A person who was earning $8.00 per hour is now earning $12.00 per hour.

G A baby who weighed 6 pounds at birth now weighs 20 pounds.

H A plant grew from 3 inches to 12 inches in one month.

J A pair of shoes that was originally priced at $50 is now $30.

Math Online Texas Test Practice at tx.msmath2.com

Get Ready for the Texas Test
For test-taking strategies and more practice, see pages TX1–TX23.

8. **GRIDDABLE** At a grocery store, half-gallons of milk are on sale 5 for \$4. Find the cost of 7 half-gallons of milk in dollars to the nearest cent.

9. If point *B* is translated 3 units to the left and 2 units up, what will be point *B*'s new coordinates?

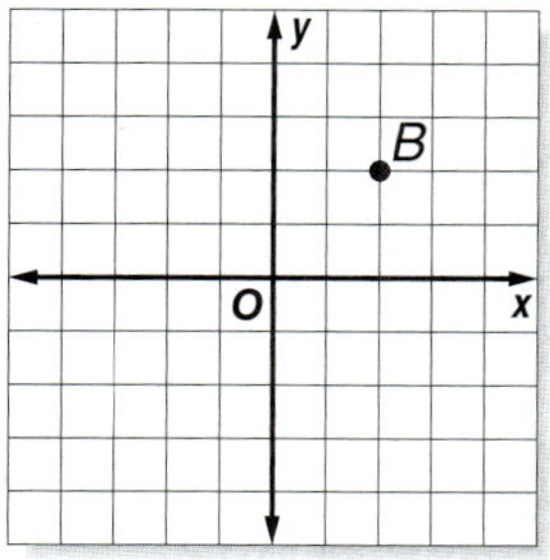

A (−3, 2) C (4, −1)
B (5, 0) D (−1, 4)

10. In Nadia's DVD collection, she has 8 action DVDs, 12 comedy DVDs, 7 romance DVDs, and 3 science fiction DVDs. What percent of Nadia's DVD collection are comedies?

F 25% H 35%
G 30% J 40%

11. Cassandra bought 2 dozen juice boxes priced at 6 juice boxes for \$2.29 and 24 snack packages priced at 8 snack packages for \$6.32. What is the total amount, not including tax, she spent on juice boxes and snack packages?

A \$34.44
B \$32.15
C \$28.12
D \$25.83

12. Which problem situation matches the equation below?

$$x - 6 = 13$$

F Jordan spent \$6 on a book. He now has \$13. What is *x*, the original amount of money Jordan had?

G Harley's portion of a lunch bill is \$6 more than Chris. If Chris paid \$6, find the amount *x*, that Harley pays.

H Suzanne read 6 pages in her book on Tuesday. She has read a total of 13 pages. What is *x*, the number of pages she read on Monday?

J The sum of two numbers is 13. One of the numbers is 6. What is *x*, the other number?

TEST-TAKING TIP

Question 13 Remember to show all of your work. You may be able to get partial credit for your answers, even if they are not entirely correct.

Pre-AP

Record your answers on a sheet of paper. Show your work.

13. The Sybil family is working on its budget.
   a. Their rent increased from \$750 to \$907.50 a month. What is the percent of increase?
   b. Their landlord said that she would decrease the \$907.50 monthly rent payment by 6% if the family paid their rent by the 10th day of the month. If the Sybil family takes the landlord's offer, describe two ways to find how much rent they would pay.

NEED EXTRA HELP?

If You Missed Question...	1	2	3	4	5	6	7	8	9	10	11	12	13
Go to Lesson...	7-2	8-6	7-2	8-1	8-1	7-6	8-7	7-4	2-3	8-5	7-1	4-2	8-8
For Help with Test Objective...	6	5	1	2	2	2	4	1	3	2	2	2	2

Unit 4
Statistics and Probability

Focal Point
Use statistical measures and probability to describe data.

CHAPTER 9
Statistics: Analyzing Data

BIG Idea Understand that the way a set of data is displayed influences its interpretation.

BIG Idea Use measures of central tendency and range to describe a set of data.

CHAPTER 10
Probability

BIG Idea Recognize that a physical or mathematical model can be used to describe the experimental and theoretical probability of real-life events.

Cross-Curricular Project

Math and Recreation

Step Right Up and Win A Prize What are my chances of winning? You may ask yourself that any time you play a game. You're about to embark on a gaming adventure. You'll investigate the mathematical probabilities of winning various carnival games. You'll also research and design a game of your own. So, come on and take a chance! Sharpen up that hand-eye coordination and grab your probability tool kit. This adventure is a win-win situation!

Math Online Log on to tx.msmath2.com to begin.

CHAPTER 9

Statistics: Analyzing Data

Knowledge and Skills

- Understand that the way a set of data is displayed influences its interpretation. **TEKS 7.11**
- Use measures of central tendency and range to describe a set of data. **TEKS 7.12**

Key Vocabulary

histogram (p. 462)

measures of central tendency (p. 448)

range (p. 443)

scatter plot (p. 477)

Real-World Link

Amusement Parks Six Flags Over Texas in Arlington, Texas, is home to some of the fastest roller coasters. You can use a bar graph to display and then compare the speeds of these coasters.

FOLDABLES™ Study Organizer

Statistics: Analyzing Data Make this Foldable to help you organize your notes. Begin with nine sheets of notebook paper.

1. **Fold** 9 sheets of paper in half along the width.

2. **Cut** a 1″ tab along the left edge through one thickness.

3. **Glue** the 1″ tab down. Write the lesson number and title on the front tab.

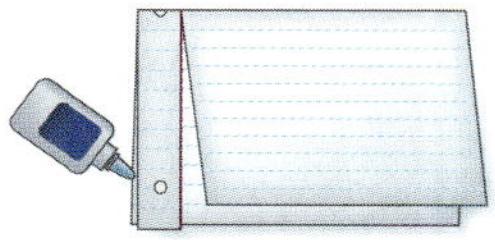

4. **Repeat** Steps 2 and 3 for the remaining sheets. Staple them together on the glued tabs to form a booklet.

GET READY for Chapter 9

Diagnose Readiness You have two options for checking Prerequisite Skills.

Option 2

Math Online Take the Online Readiness Quiz at tx.msmath2.com.

Option 1

Take the Quick Quiz below. Refer to the Quick Review for help.

QUICK Quiz

Order from least to greatest.
(Used in Lessons 9-2 and 9-3)

1. 96.2, 96.02, 95.89
2. 5.61, 5.062, 5.16
3. 22.02, 22, 22.012
4. **JEANS** A store sells bootcut jeans for $49.97, classic for $49.79, and flared for $47.99. Write these prices in order from least to greatest.

Order from greatest to least.
(Used in Lessons 9-2 and 9-3)

5. 74.65, 74.67, 74.7
6. 1.26, 1.026, 10.26
7. 3.304, 3.04, 3.340

Evaluate each expression.
(Used in Lesson 9-2)

8. $\dfrac{23 + 44 + 37 + 45}{4}$
9. $\dfrac{1.7 + 2.6 + 2.4 + 3.1 + 1.8}{5}$
10. **PIZZA** Four friends ordered a large pizza for $14.95, a salad for $3.75, and two bottles of soda for $2.25 each. If they split the cost evenly, how much does each person owe?

QUICK Review

Example 1

Order 47.7, 47.07, and 40.07 from least to greatest.

47.7
47.07
40.07

Line up the decimal points and compare place value.

The numbers in order from least to greatest are 40.07, 47.07, and 47.7.

Example 2

Order 2.08, 20.8, 0.28 from greatest to least.

2.08
20.8
0.28

Line up the decimal points and compare place value.

The numbers in order from greatest to least are 20.8, 2.08, and 0.28.

Example 3

Evaluate $\dfrac{3.4 + 4.5 + 3.8}{3}$.

$\dfrac{3.4 + 4.5 + 3.8}{3} = \dfrac{11.7}{3}$ Add 3.4, 4.5, and 3.8.

$= 3.9$ Divide 11.7 by 3.

9-1 Line Plots

Main IDEA

Display and analyze data using a line plot.

Targeted TEKS 7.11 The student understands that the way a set of data is displayed influences its interpretation. **(A) select and use an appropriate representation for presenting and displaying relationships among collected data, including line plot,** line graph, bar graph, stem and leaf plot, circle graph, and Venn diagrams, **and justify the selection.** *Also addresses TEKS 7.11(B), 7.12(A).*

NEW Vocabulary

statistics
data
line plot
cluster
outlier
range
analyze

READING in the Content Area

For strategies in reading this lesson, visit tx.msmath2.com.

GET READY for the Lesson

BUILDINGS The table shows the number of stories in Fort Worth's tallest buildings.

1. Do any of the values seem much greater or much less than the other data values?
2. Do some of the buildings have the same number of stories? Is this easy to see? Explain.

Fort Worth's Tallest Buildings Number of Stories

40	38	40	37	33
23	19	20	19	16
30	20	24	21	17
20	19	14	10	13

Source: fortwortharchitecture.com

Statistics deals with collecting, organizing, and interpreting data. **Data** are pieces of information, which are often numerical. One way to show how data are spread out is to use a line plot. A **line plot** is a diagram that shows the frequency of the data on a number line.

EXAMPLE Display Data Using a Line Plot

1 BUILDINGS **Make a line plot of the data shown above.**

Step 1 Draw a number line. The shortest building in the table has 10 stories, and the tallest has 40. You can use a scale of 5 to 40 and an interval of 5. Other scales and intervals could also be used.

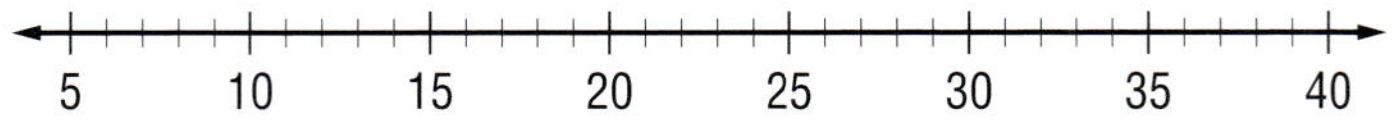

Step 2 Put an × above the number that represents the number of stories in each building. Include a title.

Fort Worth's Tallest Buildings Number of Stories

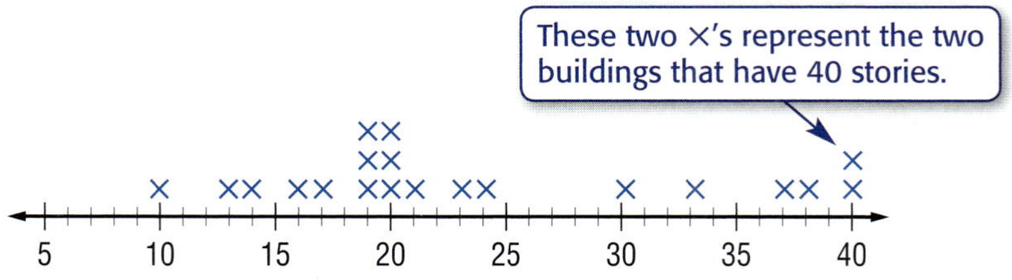

CHECK Your Progress

a. **BUILDINGS** The number of stories in the 15 tallest buildings in the world are listed at the right. Display the data in a line plot.

World's Tallest Buildings Number of Stories

101	88	88	110	88
88	80	69	102	78
72	54	73	85	80

Source: *The World Almanac*

Online Personal Tutor at tx.msmath2.com

Concepts in Motion
Interactive Lab tx.msmath2.com

You can make some observations about the *distribution* of data, or how data are grouped together or spread out. Consider the line plot below.

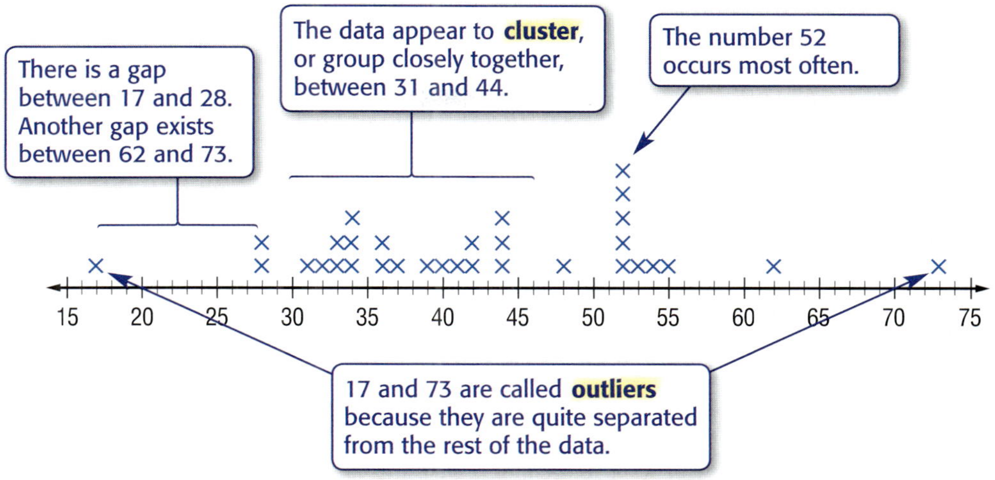

Vocabulary Link
Range
Everyday Meaning in music, all the notes between the high and low notes, as in a singer with a wide range.
Math Use the difference between the greatest number and least number in a set of data.

In a line plot, you can easily find the **range**, or spread, of the data, which is the difference between the greatest and least numbers. When you **analyze** data, you use these observations to describe, summarize, and compare data.

EXAMPLES Use a Plot to Analyze Data

2 **SHOES The line plot below shows the prices for different basketball shoes. Identify any clusters, gaps, and outliers and find the range.**

Prices ($) of Basketball Shoes

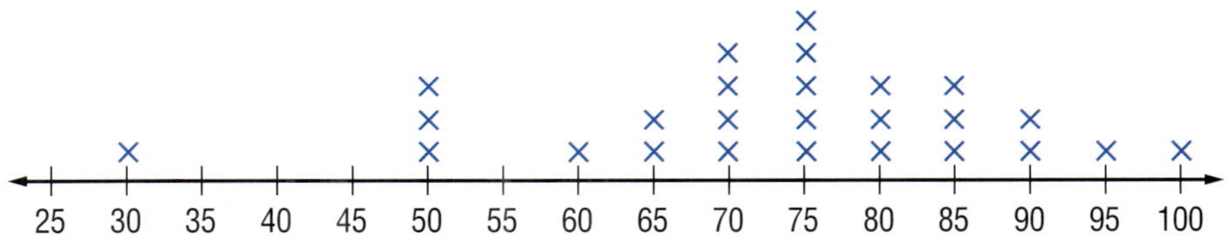

Many of the data cluster between \$70 and \$85.

There is a gap between \$30 and \$50.

Since \$30 is apart from the rest of the data, it could be an outlier.

The greatest price is \$100 and the least price is \$30. So the range of the prices is \$100 – \$30 or \$70.

STUDY TIP

Clusters
You can describe a cluster by stating a range of values or by giving a single value around which the data appear to be grouped.

3 **Write a few sentences that summarize the data based on your findings in Example 2.**

Most of the shoes cost from \$70 to \$85 and no shoes cost between \$30 and \$50. A price of \$30 is low and not representative of the data set.

CHECK Your Progress **Refer to Example 1.**

b. Identify any clusters, gaps, and outliers and find the range.

c. Write a few sentences that summarize the data based on your findings.

CHECK Your Understanding

Example 1 (p. 442) Display each set of data in a line plot.

1.

Costs of Video Games ($)			
20	29	40	50
45	20	50	50
20	25	50	40

2.

Sizes of Tennis Shoes					
8	10	9	8	7	6
9	10	9	6	5	7
7	8	11	6	8	7

MUSIC For Exercises 3 and 4, analyze the line plot below.

Number of Music CDs Owned

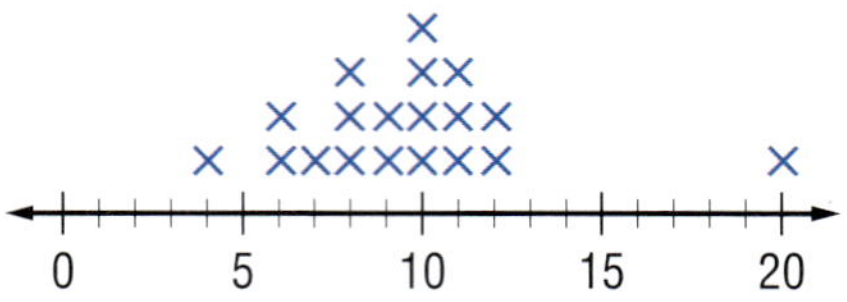

Example 2 (p. 443)

3. Identify any clusters, gaps, and outliers and find the range of the data.

Example 3 (p. 443)

4. Write a few sentences that summarize the data based on your findings.

SURVEYS For Exercises 5–8, analyze the line plot at the right and use the information below.

Jamie asked her classmates how many glasses of water they drink on a typical day. The results are shown.

Glasses of Water Consumed

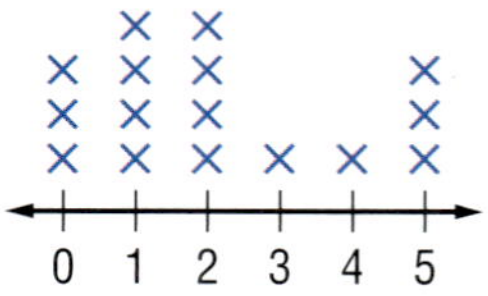

Example 2 (p. 443)

5. What was the most frequent response?
6. What was the least frequent response?
7. What is the range?

Example 3 (p. 443)

8. Summarize the data in a sentence or two.

Exercises

HOMEWORK HELP

For Exercises	See Examples
9–12	1
13–20	2–3

Display each set of data in a line plot.

9.

Heights of Desert Cacti (ft)				
30	10	1	15	10
10	10	10	2	10
20	3	2	15	5

10.

Test Scores (%)					
98	90	97	85	86	92
92	93	95	79	91	92
91	94	88	90	93	92

11.

Basketball Scores (pts)				
101	105	99	130	120
100	108	126	135	98
120	122	115	129	97

12.

Ages of Students (y)					
12	13	13	13	12	14
13	12	13	13	12	12
13	14	12	13	12	12

Real-World Link Monahans, Texas, holds the highest temperature ever recorded in Texas, 120°F.

Source: *The World Almanac*

WEATHER **For Exercises 13–16, analyze the line plot that shows the record high temperatures recorded by weather stations in each of the fifty states.**

Record High Temperatures (°F)

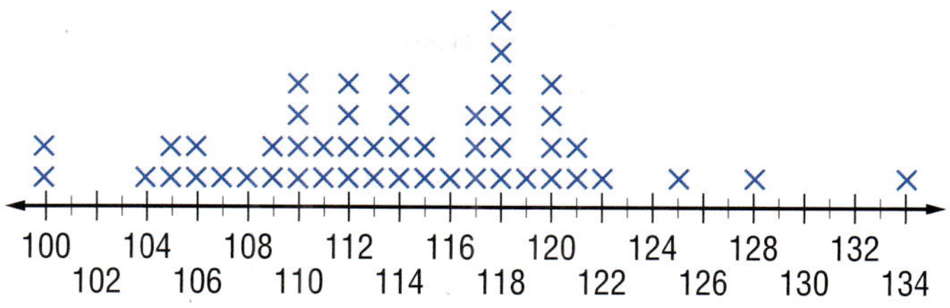

Source: *The World Almanac*

13. What is the range of the data?
14. What temperature occurred most often?
15. Identify any clusters, gaps, or outliers. Summarize the data by using these values.
16. Describe how the range of the data would change if 134°F were not part of the data set.

MOVIES **For Exercises 17–20, analyze the line plot below that shows the number of digital video discs various students have in their DVD collection.**

Digital Video Disc (DVD) Collection

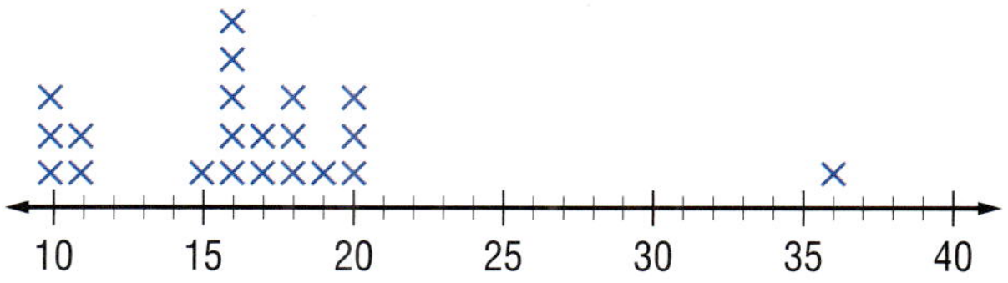

17. Find the range of the data.
18. What number of DVDs occurred most often?
19. How many students have more than 15 DVDs in their collection?
20. Are there any clusters, gaps, or outliers? If so, identify them and then summarize the data using these values.

Determine whether each statement is *sometimes*, *always*, or *never* true. Explain your reasoning.

21. You can determine the number of items in a data set from a line plot.
22. If there is a cluster, it will appear in the center of the line plot.

BOOKS **For Exercises 23–25, analyze the line plot at the right.**

Number of Books Read

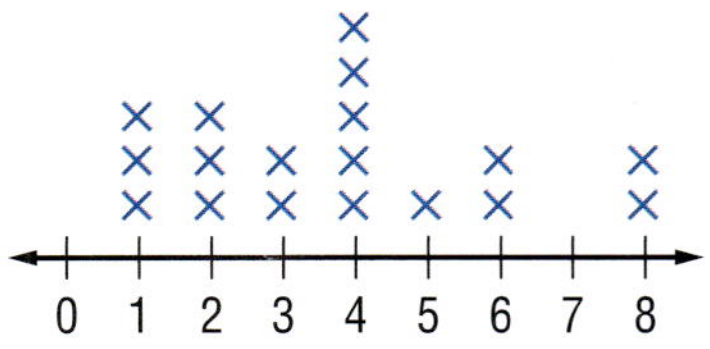

23. How many students read 4 or more books?
24. How many more students read 1–2 books than 5–6 books?
25. About what percent of the students read less than 5 books?

ANIMALS For Exercises 26–28, refer to the table.

Average Life Spans					
Animal	**Span (yr)**	**Animal**	**Span (yr)**	**Animal**	**Span (yr)**
black bear	18	giraffe	10	lion	15
camel	12	gorilla	20	pig	10
cat	12	grizzly bear	25	polar bear	20
chipmunk	6	horse	20	rhesus monkey	15
dog	12	kangaroo	7	squirrel	10
elephant	40	leopard	12	white rhinoceros	20

Source: *The World Almanac for Kids*

26. Display the data in a line plot.
27. Find the range and determine any clusters or outliers.
28. Use the line plot to summarize the data in a sentence or two.
29. The *maximum* life spans, in order, of the animals in the table above are 36, 50, 28, 10, 20, 77, 36, 54, 50, 50, 24, 23, 30, 27, 45, 37, 24, and 50 respectively. Display this data in a line plot. Compare this line plot to the line plot you made in Exercise 26. Include a discussion about clusters, outliers, range, and gaps in data.

EXTRA PRACTICE

See pages 738, 763.

Math Online

Self-Check Quiz at tx.msmath2.com

30. **COLLECT THE DATA** Conduct a survey of your classmates to determine how many hours of television they watch on a typical school night. Then display and analyze the data in a line plot. Use your analysis of the data to write a convincing argument about television viewing on a school night.

H.O.T. Problems

31. **OPEN ENDED** Create a set of data that are clustered between 20 and 30 with a range of 15.
32. **FIND THE ERROR** Ryan and Darnell are analyzing the data shown in the line plot at the right. Who is correct? Explain.

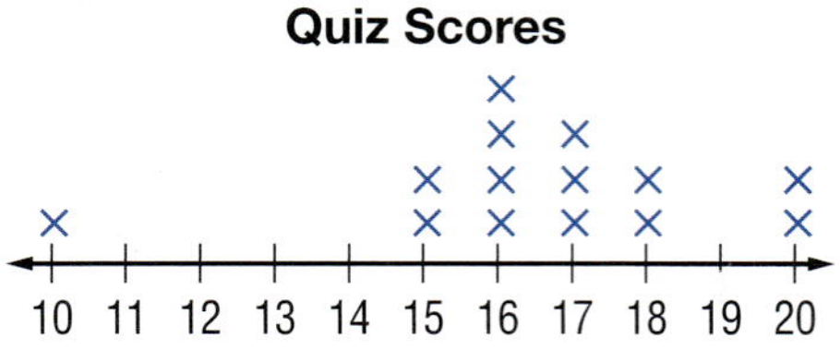

Ryan Darnell

33. **CHALLENGE** Compare and contrast line plots and frequency tables. Include a discussion about what they show and when it is better to use each one.

34. **WRITING IN MATH** The last 14 bowling scores of two people are shown. Describe which person is more consistent and explain how you know.

Bowling Scores

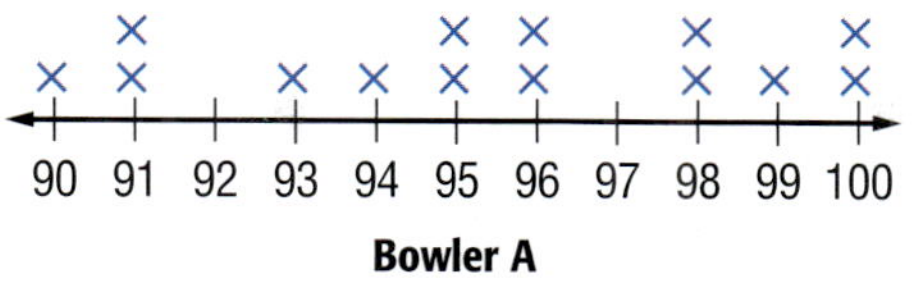

Bowling Scores

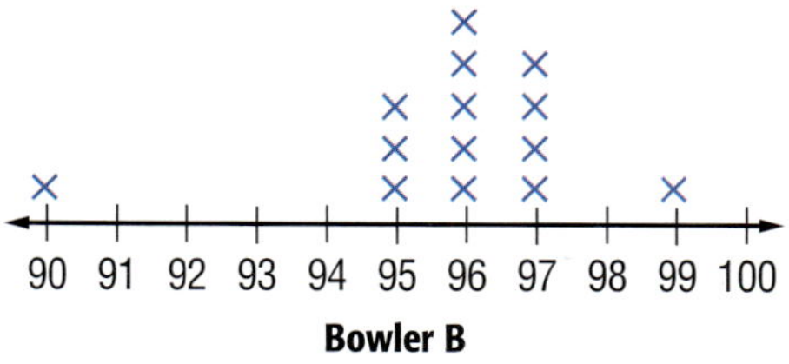

TEST PRACTICE

35. The graph shows the weight of the emperor penguins at a zoo.

Emperor Penguins Weight (kg)

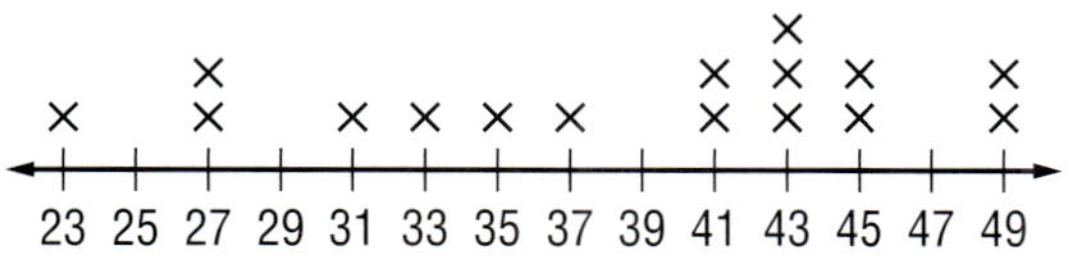

Which statement is NOT supported by the data?

A More than half of these penguins weigh at least 41 kilograms.

B There are 16 emperor penguins at the zoo.

C Of these penguins, 30% weigh between 30 and 38 kilograms.

D The range of the emperor penguins' weight is 49 − 23 or 26 kilograms.

36. The table shows the math scores for 24 students in Mr. Baker's class.

Math Test Scores					
90	86	96	89	85	91
100	65	73	85	85	93
71	70	75	80	82	99
93	82	77	84	89	75

What is the range of the test scores?

F 35

G 80

H 85

J 100

Spiral Review

Find the interest earned to the nearest cent for each principal, interest rate, and time. (Lesson 8-9)

37. \$300, 10%, 2 years

38. \$900, 5.5%, 4.5 years

39. **BASEBALL CARDS** What is the total cost of a package of baseball cards if the regular price is \$4.19 and the sales tax is 6.5%? (Lesson 8-8)

40. Solve $m + 18 = 33$ mentally. (Lesson 1-7)

GET READY for the Next Lesson

PREREQUISITE SKILL **Add or divide. Round to the nearest tenth if necessary.**

41. $16 + 14 + 17$

42. $4.6 + 2.5 + 9$

43. $\frac{202}{16}$

44. $\frac{255}{7}$

9-2 Measures of Central Tendency and Range

Main IDEA

Describe a set of data using mean, median, mode, and range.

Targeted TEKS **7.12** The student uses measures of central tendency and range to describe a set of data. **(B)** **choose among mean, median, mode, or range to describe a set of data and justify the choice for a particular situation.** *Also addresses TEKS 7.12(A).*

NEW Vocabulary

measures of central tendency
mean
median
mode

MINI Lab

The table shows scores for five quizzes.

- Place pennies in each cup to represent each score.

Quiz	Score
1	8
2	7
3	9
4	6
5	10

- Move the pennies among the cups so that each cup has the same number of pennies.

1. What was the average score for the five quizzes?
2. If the quiz score of 14 points is added to the data, how many pennies would be in each cup?

A number used to describe the *center* of a set of data is a **measure of central tendency**. The most common of these measures is the mean.

KEY CONCEPT — Mean

Words The **mean** of a set of data is the sum of the data divided by the number of items in the data set. The mean is also referred to as *average*.

Examples data set: 1 cm, 1 cm, 5 cm, 2 cm, 2 cm, 4 cm, 2 cm, 5 cm

mean: $\frac{1 + 1 + 5 + 2 + 2 + 4 + 2 + 5}{8}$ or 2.75 cm

EXAMPLE Find the Mean

1 **NUTRITION** **The table shows the grams of sugar in 20 different breakfast bars. Find the mean.**

Grams of Sugar in Breakfast Bars				
14	11	7	14	15
22	18	18	21	10
10	10	11	9	11
11	9	12	8	12

Source: www.cspinnet.org

$$\text{mean} = \frac{14 + 11 + \ldots + 12}{20} \begin{array}{l}\leftarrow \text{sum of data} \\ \leftarrow \text{number of data items}\end{array}$$

$$= \frac{253}{20} \text{ or } 12.65 \text{ grams}$$

CHECK Your Progress

a. **MONEY** Adam earned \$14, \$10, \$12, \$15, and \$13 by doing chores around the house. What is the mean amount Adam earned doing these chores?

Two other common measures of central tendency are median and mode.

Vocabulary Link
Median
Everyday Use the middle paved or planted section of a highway, as in median strip.
Math Use the middle number of the ordered data.

KEY CONCEPT

Median

Words The **median** of a set of data is the middle number of the ordered data, or the mean of the middle two numbers.

Example data set: 7 yd, 11 yd, 15 yd, 17 yd, 20 yd, 20 yd

median: $\frac{15 + 17}{2}$ or 16 yd — The median divides the data in half.

Mode

Words The **mode** or modes of a set of data is the number or numbers that occur most often.

Example data set: 50 mi, 45 mi, 45 mi, 52 mi, 49 mi, 56 mi, 56 mi

modes: 45 mi and 56 mi

EXAMPLE Find the Mean, Median, and Mode

2 **MOVIE RENTALS** **The number of DVDs rented during one week at Star Struck Movie Rental is shown in the table. What are the mean, median, and mode of the data?**

Star Struck Movie Rental Daily DVD Rentals						
S	M	T	W	TH	F	S
55	34	35	34	57	78	106

mean: $\frac{55 + 34 + 35 + 34 + 57 + 78 + 106}{7} = \frac{399}{7}$ or 57

median: 34, 34, 35, 55, 57, 78, 106 (55 = median)

mode: 34 — It is the only value that occurs more than once.

The mean is 57 DVDs, the median is 55 DVDs, and the mode is 34 DVDs.

CHECK Your Progress

b. **BICYCLES** The sizes of the bicycles owned by the students in Ms. Garcia's class are listed in the table. What are the mean, median, and mode of the data?

Students' Bicycle Sizes (in.)			
20	24	20	26
24	24	24	26
24	29	26	24

c. **FOOTBALL** The total number of points scored in each game by Darby Middle School's football team for 9 games are 21, 35, 14, 17, 28, 14, 7, 21, and 14. Find the mean, median, and mode.

TEST EXAMPLE

3 Twenty-nine students were asked how many times they used the Internet while doing a science project. The responses are shown.

Internet Use	
Number of Times Used	**Number of Students**
10	11
11	5
12	4
13	8
14	1

Which measure of data represents the most common number of times the students used the Internet?

A Mean
B Median
C Mode
D Range

Test-Taking Tip

Reading the Question
Read the question carefully. It may not be necessary to do any calculations in order to answer the question.

Read the Test Item

You are asked to identify the measure that represents the *most common number* of times the students used the Internet.

Solve the Test Item

The most common number is the one that occurs most often, which is the definition of a mode. So, the answer is C.

CHECK Your Progress

d. In which data set are the mean, median, mode, and range all the same number?

F {2, 4, 6, 6, 4, 2, 4}
G {2, 4, 6, 2, 4, 6, 2}
H {2, 6, 6, 6, 4, 6, 2}
J {4, 4, 2, 4, 6, 4, 6}

Online **Personal Tutor at** tx.msmath2.com

In addition to the mean, median, and mode, you can also use the range to describe a set of data. Below are some guidelines for using these measures.

CONCEPT Summary — Mean, Median, Mode, and Range

Measure	Most Useful When...
Mean	• data set has no outliers
Median	• data set has outliers • there are no big gaps in the middle of the data
Mode	• data set has many identical numbers
Range	• describing the spread of the data

STUDY TIP

Median
When there is an odd number of data, the median is the middle number of the ordered set. When there is an even number of data, the median is the mean of the two middle numbers.

EXAMPLE Choose Mean, Median, Mode, or Range

4 **TESTS** **The line plot shows the test scores of the students in Mrs. Hiroshi's math class. Would the mean, median, mode, or range best represent the test scores?**

Test Scores

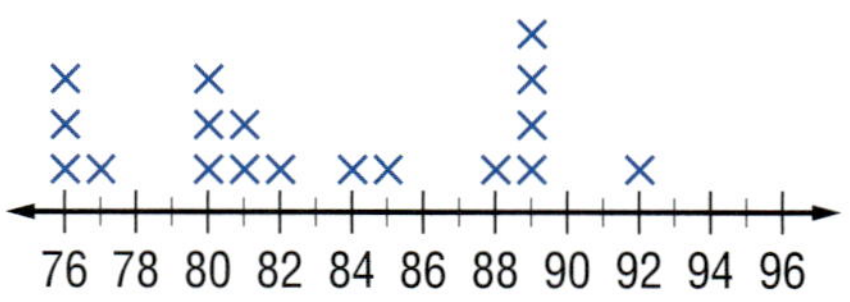

mean: $\frac{76 + 76 + 76 + ... + 92}{18}$ or 83

median: $\frac{\text{9th term} + \text{10th term}}{2} = \frac{81 + 82}{2}$ or 81.5

mode: 89

range: 92 – 76 or 16

The mode of 89 misrepresents the scores. Either the mean of 83 or the median of 81.5 best represents the scores.

CHECK Your Progress

e. **GAMES** The table shows the cost of various board games. Would the mean, median, mode, or range best represent the costs? Explain.

Board Game Costs ($)

12	15	40	22
14	40	15	17
20	18	40	19
16	21	19	16

CHECK Your Understanding

Examples 1, 2 (pp. 448–449)

Find the mean, median, and mode for each set of data. Round to the nearest tenth if necessary.

1. Miles traveled on the weekend: 29, 14, 80, 59, 78, 30, 59, 69, 55, 50

2.

Team	Number of Wins
Eagles	10
Hawks	8
Zipps	9
Falcons	11

3. **Quiz Scores**

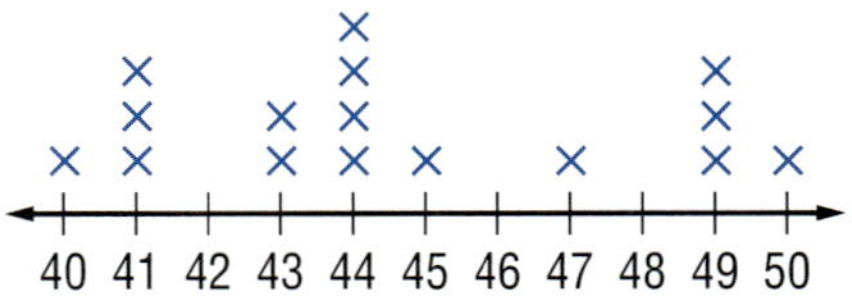

Example 3 (p. 450)

4. **TEST PRACTICE** During a week, the daily low temperatures were 52°F, 45°F, 50°F, 51°F, and 48°F. Which expression can be used to find the average daily low temperature during that week?

A 52 + 45 + (–50) + 51 + 48 ÷ 5

B (52 + 45 + 50 + 51 + 48) ÷ 5

C 52 + 45 + 50 + 51 + 48 ÷ 5

D [52 + 45 + 50 + 51 + 48] × 5

Example 4 (p. 451)

5. **SCHOOL** The line plot shows the number of times per day that students drink from the water fountain at school. Which measure best describes the data: mean, median, mode, or range? Explain.

Daily Drinks From the Water Fountain

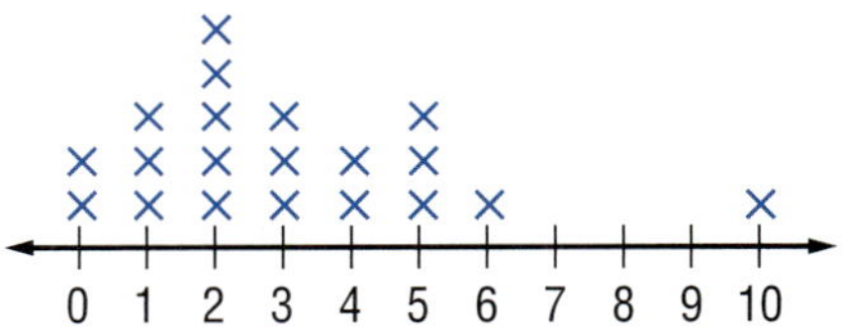

Exercises

HOMEWORK HELP

For Exercises	See Examples
6–11	1,2
30–32	3
12–13	4

Find the mean, median, and mode for each set of data. Round to the nearest tenth if necessary.

6. Number of dogs groomed each week: 65, 56, 57, 75, 76, 66, 64
7. Daily number of boats in a harbor: 93, 84, 80, 91, 94, 90, 78, 93, 80
8. Scores earned on a math test: 95, 90, 92, 94, 91, 90, 98, 88, 89, 100
9. Prices of books: $10, $18, $11, $6, $6, $5, $10, $11, $46, $7, $6, $8

10.

Cost	Number of Coats
$75	8
$80	3
$85	6

11. **Minutes Spent Exercising**

12. **MUSIC** The line plot shows the number of weeks that songs have been on the Top 20 Country Songs list. Would the mean, median, mode, or range best represent the data? Explain.

Country Songs
Number of Weeks in Top 20

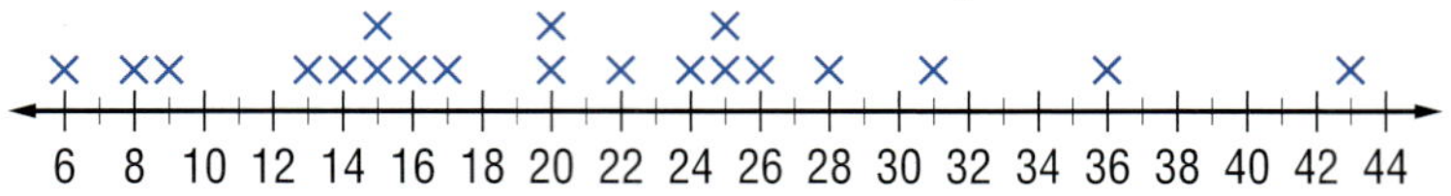

13. **SPACE** Twenty-seven countries have sent people into space. The table shows the number of individuals from each country. Which measure best describes the data: mean, median, mode, or range? Explain.

People in Space								
267	1	9	8	1	1	1	1	1
97	1	1	1	3	1	1	2	1
11	2	1	1	5	1	1	1	1

Source: *The World Almanac*

Real-World Link
The International Space Station measures 356 feet by 290 feet, and contains almost an acre of solar panels.
Source: *The World Almanac*

Find the mean, median, and mode for each set of data. Round to the nearest tenth if necessary.

14. Weight in ounces of various insects: 6.1, 5.2, 7.2, 7.2, 3.6, 9.0, 6.5, 7.4, 5.4
15. Miles traveled on a bicycle: 6.4, 6.5, 7.1, 6.4, 6.6, 6.4, 8.0, 6.6
16. Prices of magazines: $3.50, $3.75, $3.50, $4.00, $3.00, $3.50, $3.25
17. Daily low temperatures: −2°F, −8°F, −2°F, 0°F, −1°F, 1°F, −2°F, −1°F

SURVEY For Exercises 18 and 19, use the following information.

Conduct a survey of your classmates to determine how many minutes it takes them to travel from their home to the school.

18. Which measure best describes the data: mean, median, mode, or range?
19. Which measure might students use to convince the school board that the tardy bell should ring at a later time? Explain your reasoning.

DINOSAURS For Exercises 20–22, use the lengths of the dinosaurs shown below.

Tyrannosaurus Rex
Length: 480 inches

Corythosaurus
Length: 396 inches

Parasaurolophus
Length: 480 inches

20. What is the mean length of the dinosaurs?

21. One of the largest dinosaurs ever is the Brachiosaurus. Its length was 960 inches. If this data value is added to the lengths of the dinosaurs above, how will it affect the mean? Explain your reasoning.

22. Which measure best describes the data if the length of the Brachiosaurus is included: mean, median, mode, or range? If the length of the Brachiosaurus is *not* included? Explain any similarities or differences.

23. **SPORTS** The table shows the points scored by a lacrosse team so far this season. The team will play 14 games this season. How many points need to be scored during the last game so that the average number of points scored this season is 12? Explain.

Hawks Lacrosse Team Points Scored

11	15	12	10	10	10	13
14	13	13	10	15	12	■

EXTRA PRACTICE
See pages 739, 763.
Math Online
Self-Check Quiz at
tx.msmath2.com

24. **FIND THE DATA** Refer to the Texas Data File on pages 16–19. Choose some data and then describe it using the mean, median, mode and range.

H.O.T. Problems

25. **OPEN ENDED** Give an example of a set of data in which the mean is not the best representation of the data set. Explain why not.

26. **Which One Doesn't Belong?** Identify the term that does not have the same characteristic as the other three. Explain your reasoning.

mean	median	range	mode

27. **REASONING** Determine whether the median is *sometimes*, *always*, or *never* part of the data set. Explain your reasoning.

28. **CHALLENGE** Without calculating, would the mean, median, or mode be most affected by eliminating 1,000 from the data shown? Which would be the least affected? Explain your reasoning.

50, 100, 75, 60, 75, 1,000, 90, 100

29. **WRITING IN MATH** According to the U.S. Census Bureau, the typical number of family members per household in Texas is 3.28. State whether this measure is a mean or mode. Explain how you know.

TEST PRACTICE

30. The table below shows the number of soup labels collected in one week by each homeroom in grade 7.

Classroom	Number of Soup Labels
Mr. Martin	138
Ms. Davis	125
Mr. Cardona	89
Mrs. Turner	110
Mr. Wilhelm	130
Mrs. LaBash	?

Which number could be added to the set of data in order for the mode and median of the set to be equal?

A 89 **C** 125

B 110 **D** 130

31. The table shows the hourly wages for the employees at a pizza shop.

Hourly Wages				
$5.00	$6.25	$8.00	$5.25	$8.00
$6.50	$5.00	$6.75	$6.00	$5.00
$5.00	$6.00	$5.25	$6.25	$6.50
$5.25	$8.00	$6.00	$5.00	$6.25

Which measure of data is represented by $6.00?

F Mean **H** Range

G Mode **J** Median

32. **GRIDDABLE** An antique dealer purchased 5 antiques for a total of $850.00. He later bought another antique for $758.00. What was the mean cost of all the antiques?

Spiral Review

33. **NUTRITION** The table shows the grams of fiber in one serving of 15 different cereals. Make a line plot of the data. (Lesson 9-1)

Fiber in Cereal (g)				
5	5	4	3	3
3	1	1	1	2
1	1	1	1	0

Find the interest earned to the nearest cent for each principal, interest rate, and time. (Lesson 8-9)

34. $1,250, 3.5%, 2 years

35. $569, 5.5%, 4 months

36. **FOOD** The United States produced almost 11 billion pounds of apples in a recent year. Use the information in the graph to find how many pounds of apples were used to make juice and cider. (Lesson 8-1)

Uses of Apples in the United States

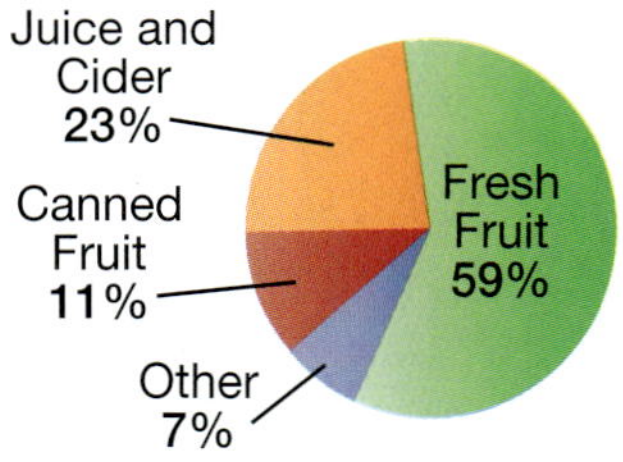

Source: usapple.org

Name the property shown by each statement. (Lesson 1-8)

37. $4 \times 6 = 6 \times 4$

38. $2(3 + 9) = 2 \cdot 3 + 2 \cdot 9$

GET READY for the Next Lesson

PREREQUISITE SKILL **Name the place value of the underlined digit.** (p. 709)

39. <u>5</u>81 **40.** 6,29<u>5</u> **41.** <u>4</u>,369 **42.** 2.<u>8</u>4

Extend 9-2

Graphing Calculator Lab
Mean and Median

Main IDEA

Use technology to calculate the mean and median of a set of data.

Targeted TEKS **7.12** The student uses measures of central tendency and range to describe a set of data. **(A)** **describe a set of data using mean, median, mode, and range.**

You can more efficiently calculate the mean and median of a large set data using a TI-83/84 Plus graphing calculator.

ACTIVITY

COMPUTERS **Kendrick surveys thirty seventh-graders and asks them how many times they had to wait longer than 5 minutes during the previous week to use a computer in the school library. The results are shown below.**

Number of Times a Student Had to Wait to Use the Library Computer									
5	2	9	1	1	2	1	2	5	2
3	4	2	1	4	0	4	2	2	5
4	2	2	3	2	1	3	9	5	2

Find the mean and median of the data.

STEP 1 Clear list L1 by pressing STAT ENTER ▲ CLEAR ENTER

STEP 2 Enter the number of times students had to wait in L1. Press 5 ENTER 2 ENTER . . . 2 ENTER.

STEP 3 Display a list of statistics for the data by pressing STAT ▶ ENTER 2nd 1 ENTER.

The first value, $\bar{x}$, is the mean.

Use the down arrow key to locate **Med**. The mean number of times a student waited was 3 and the median number of times was 2.

STUDY TIP

Median The median, 2 times, means that half of the students waited more than 2 times to use a computer and half waited fewer than 2 times.

ANALYZE THE RESULTS

1. **WRITING IN MATH** Kendrick claims that, on average, students had to wait more than 5 minutes about 3 times last week. Based on your own analysis of the data, write a convincing argument to dispute his claim. (*Hint*: Create and use a line plot of the data to support your argument.)

2. **COLLECT THE DATA** Collect some numerical data from your classmates. Then use a graphing calculator to calculate the mean and median of the data. After analyzing the data, write a convincing argument to support a claim you can make about your data.

9-3 Stem-and-Leaf Plots

Main IDEA

Display and analyze data in a stem-and-leaf plot.

Targeted TEKS 7.11 The student understands that the way a set of data is displayed influences its interpretation. **(A) select and use an appropriate representation for presenting and displaying relationships among collected data, including** line plot, line graph, bar graph, **stem and leaf plot,** circle graph, and Venn diagrams, **and justify the selection.** *Also addresses TEKS 7.11(B).*

NEW Vocabulary

stem-and-leaf plot
leaf
stem
inferences

GET READY for the Lesson

BIRDS The table shows the average chick weight in grams of sixteen different species of birds.

1. Which chick weight is the lightest?
2. How many of the weights are less than 10 grams?

Chick Weight (g)

19	6	7	10
11	13	18	25
21	12	5	12
20	21	11	12

Source: upatsix.com

In a **stem-and-leaf plot**, the data are organized from least to greatest. The digits of the least place value usually form the **leaves**, and the next place value digits form the **stems**.

EXAMPLE Display Data in a Stem-and-Leaf Plot

1 **BIRDS Display the data in the table above in a stem-and-leaf plot.**

Step 1 Choose the stems using digits in the tens place, 0, 1, and 2. The least value, 5, has 0 in the tens place. The greatest value, 25, has 2 in the tens place.

Step 2 List the stems from least to greatest in the *Stem* column. Write the leaves, the ones digits to the right of the corresponding stems.

Stem	Leaf
0	6 7 5
1	9 0 1 3 8 2 2 1 2
2	5 1 0 1

Step 3 Order the leaves and write a *key* that explains how to read the stems and leaves. Include a title.

Chick Weight (g)

Stem	Leaf
0	5 6 7
1	0 1 1 2 2 2 3 8 9
2	0 1 1 5

$1|2 = 12$ g

The tens digits of the data form the stems.
Always write each leaf even if it repeats.
The ones digits of the data form the leaves.
Include a key.

CHECK Your Progress

a. **HOMEWORK** The number of minutes the students in Mr. Blackwell's class spent doing their homework one night is shown. Display the data in a stem-and-leaf plot.

Homework Time (min)

42	5	75	30	45
47	0	24	45	51
56	23	39	30	49
58	55	75	45	35

Online Personal Tutor at tx.msmath2.com

Stem-and-leaf plots are useful in analyzing data because you can see all the data values, including the greatest, least, mode, and median value.

EXAMPLE Describe Data

2 CHESS The stem-and-leaf plot shows the number of chess matches won by members of the Avery Middle School Chess Team. Find the range, median, and mode of the data.

Chess Matches Won

Stem	Leaf
0	8 8 9
1	9
2	0 0 2 4 4 8 9
3	1 1 2 4 5 5 6 6 7 7 8
4	0 0 0 3 8 9
5	2 4
6	1

3|2 = 32 wins

range: greatest wins − least wins
$= 61 - 8$ or 53

median: middle value, or 35 wins

mode: most frequent value, 40

CHECK Your Progress

b. **BIRDS** Find the range, median, and mode of the data in Example 1.

When you analyze a set of data, you can make **inferences**. That is, you can draw conclusions based on the data.

Real-World Career
How Does a Nutritionist Use Math?
Nutritionists use statistical graphs to summarize and compare the nutritional values of various foods.

Math Online For more information, go to tx.msmath2.com.

EXAMPLE Analyze Data to Make Inferences

3 NUTRITION The average amount of pasta that people in different countries consume each year is shown in the stem-and-leaf plot. Based on the data, what inferences can be made about pasta consumption?

Amount of Pasta Consumed (lb)

Stem	Leaf
0	3 4 5 8 8 9 9
1	0 1 4 5 5 5 5 9
2	0 0 8
3	
4	
5	9

2|8 = 28 lb

Based on the data, you can make the following inferences about pasta consumption.

- Most of the countries consume less than 20 pounds of pasta per year.
- Of the amounts, 15 pounds of pasta per year is consumed most often.
- One country consumes much more pasta than any of the other countries.

CHECK Your Progress

c. **BIRDS** Based on the data in Example 1, write two inferences that can be made about the average chick weight of the sixteen different species of birds.

CHECK Your Understanding

Example 1 (p. 456)

Display each set of data in a stem-and-leaf plot.

1.

Height of Trees (ft)				
15	25	8	12	20
10	16	15	8	18

2.

Cost of Shoes ($)				
42	47	19	16	21
23	25	25	29	31
33	34	35	39	48

Examples 2, 3 (p. 457)

SCHOOL The stem-and-leaf plot at the right shows the ages of the students in a pottery class at Lake Champion Summer Camp.

Ages of Students

Stem	Leaf
0	9 9 9
1	0 1 1 1 1 2 2 3 3 4

1|0 = 10 yr

3. What is the range of the ages of the students?
4. Find the median and mode of the data.
5. Write two inferences that can be made about the students' ages.

Exercises

HOMEWORK HELP

For Exercises	See Examples
6–9	1
10, 11, 13, 14, 16–18	2
12, 15, 19	3

Display each set of data in a stem-and-leaf plot.

6.

Quiz Scores (%)			
70	96	72	91
80	80	79	93
76	95	73	93
90	93	77	91

7.

Low Temperatures (°F)				
15	13	28	32	38
30	31	13	36	35
38	32	38	24	20

8.

Floats at Annual Parade			
151	158	139	103
111	134	133	154
157	142	149	159

9.

School Play Attendance			
225	227	230	229
246	243	269	269
267	278	278	278

CYCLING The number of Tour de France titles won by eleven countries as of 2005 is shown.

Tour de France Titles Won by Eleven Countries

Stem	Leaf
0	1 1 1 2 2 4 8 9
1	0 8
2	
3	6

0|4 = 4 titles

10. Find the range of titles won.
11. Find the median and mode of the data.
12. Based on the data, write one inference that can be made about the data.

ELECTRONICS For Exercises 13–15, use the stem-and-leaf plot that shows the costs of various DVD players at an electronics store.

Costs of DVD Players

Stem	Leaf
8	2 5 5
9	9 9
10	0 0 2 5 6 8
11	0 0 5 5 5 9 9
12	5 7 7

11|5 = $115

13. What is the range of the prices?
14. Find the median and mode of the data.
15. Write three inferences that can be made based on the data.

HISTORY For Exercises 16–19, refer to the stem-and-leaf plot below.

Ages of Signers of Declaration of Independence

Stem	Leaf
2	6 6 9
3	0 1 3 3 3 4 4 5 5 5 5 7 7 8 8 9 9
4	0 1 1 1 2 2 2 4 5 5 5 5 6 6 6 6 7 8 9
5	0 0 0 0 2 2 3 3 5 7
6	0 0 2 3 5 6
7	0

3|1 = 31 years

16. How many people signed the Declaration of Independence?
17. What was the age of the youngest signer?
18. What is the range of the ages of the signers?
19. Based on the data, can you infer that the majority of the signers were 30–49 years old? Explain your reasoning.

Real-World Link
The saltwater crocodile is the largest living reptile. Some measuring 27–30 feet in length have been recorded in the wild.
Source: pbs.org

20. **GYMNASTICS** The scores for 10 girls in a gymnastics event are 9.3, 10.0, 9.9, 8.9, 8.7, 9.0, 8.7, 8.5, 8.8, 9.3. Analyze a stem-and-leaf plot of the data to make two inferences about the scores.

21. **REPTILES** The average lengths of certain species of crocodiles are given in the table. Analyze a stem-and-leaf plot of this data to write a convincing argument about a reasonable length for a crocodile.

Crocodile Average Lengths (ft)			
8.1	16.3	16.3	9.8
16.3	16.3	11.4	6.3
13.6	9.8	19.5	16.0

Source: Crocodilian Species List

EXTRA PRACTICE
See pages 739, 763.
Math Online
Self-Check Quiz at tx.msmath2.com

22. **FIND THE DATA** Refer to the Texas Data File on pages 16–19. Choose some data that can be presented in a stem-and-leaf plot. Then analyze the stem-and-leaf plot to make two inferences about the data.

H.O.T. Problems

23. **FIND THE ERROR** Selena and Diana are analyzing the data in the stem-and-leaf plot at the right. Diana says half of the pieces of ribbon are between 20 and 30 inches in length. Selena says there are no pieces of ribbon more than 50 inches in length. Who is correct? Explain.

Cut Ribbon Length

Stem	Leaf
2	6 6 9
3	
4	6
5	3 6

2|6 = 26 in.

24. **CHALLENGE** Create a stem-and-leaf plot in which the median of the data is 25.

25. **WRITING IN MATH** Present the data shown at the right in a frequency table, a line plot, and a stem-and-leaf plot. Describe the similarities and differences among the representations. Which representation do you prefer to use? Explain your reasoning.

Price of Jeans ($)			
40	45	38	30
35	32	33	24
26	36	56	36
26	38	49	34
28	40	40	35

26. **COLLECT THE DATA** Collect a set of data that represents the heights in inches of the people in your math class. Then write a question that can be solved by analyzing a stem-and-leaf plot of the data. Be sure to explain how the stem-and-leaf plot would be used to solve your problem.

TEST PRACTICE

27. Denzell's science quiz scores are 11, 12, 13, 21, and 35. Which stem-and-leaf plot best represents this data?

A

Stem	Leaf
1	1
2	1
3	5

$3|5 = 35$

B

Stem	Leaf
1	3
2	1
3	5

$3|5 = 35$

C

Stem	Leaf
1	1 2 3
2	1
3	5

$3|5 = 35$

D

Stem	Leaf
1	1
2	1 1
3	5

$3|5 = 35$

28. The stem-and-leaf plot shows the points scored by the Harding Middle School basketball team.

Points Scored

Stem	Leaf
7	0 0 2 3
8	1 7 7
9	0 2 9

$9|0 = 90$

Based on the information in the stem-and-leaf plot, which of the following is a reasonable inference?

F The team scored an average of 80 points per game.

G The scores ranged from 37 points to 99 points.

H Sixty percent of the games had a score more than 80 points.

J Half of the scores were less than 80 points.

Spiral Review

Find the mean, median, and mode for each set of data. Round to the nearest tenth if necessary. (Lesson 9-2)

29. 80, 23, 55, 58, 45, 32, 40, 55, 50

30. 3.6, 2.4, 3.0, 7.9, 7.8, 2.4, 3.6, 3.9

31. Make a line plot of the test scores shown. (Lesson 9-1)

Test Scores

83	94	78	78	85
86	88	83	82	92
90	77	83	81	89
90	88	87	88	85
84	81	83	85	91

32. **SCHOOL** The ratio of boys to girls in a school is 7 to 8. How many girls are in the school if there are 56 boys? (Lesson 7-1)

33. Write $\frac{9}{24}$ in simplest form. (Lesson 5-4)

GET READY for the Next Lesson

PREREQUISITE SKILL **Choose an appropriate interval and scale for each set of data.** (page 715)

34. 9, 0, 18, 19, 2, 9, 8, 13, 4

35. 30, 20, 60, 80, 90, 120, 40

9-4 Bar Graphs and Histograms

Main IDEA

Display and analyze data using bar graphs and histograms.

Targeted TEKS 7.11 The student understands that the way a set of data is displayed influences its interpretation. **(A) select and use an appropriate representation for presenting and displaying relationships among collected data, including** line plot, line graph, **bar graph,** stem and leaf plot, circle graph, and Venn diagrams, **and justify the selection.** *Also addresses TEKS 7.11(B), 7.14(A).*

NEW Vocabulary

bar graph
histogram

GET READY for the Lesson

ANIMALS The cheetah is the fastest known land animal. The table shows its fastest speed and the top speeds of four other land animals.

Animal	Speed (mph)
cheetah	70
wildebeest	50
lion	50
elk	45
zebra	40

Source: *The World Almanac*

1. What are the fastest and slowest speeds in the table?
2. How can you create a visual representation to summarize the data?
3. Do any of these representations show both the animal name and its speed?

A **bar graph** is one method of comparing data by using solid bars to represent quantities.

EXAMPLE Display Data Using a Bar Graph

1 **Display the data in the table above in a bar graph.**

Step 1 Draw a horizontal axis and a vertical axis. Label the axes as shown. In this case, the scale on the vertical axis is chosen so that it includes all the speeds. Add a title.

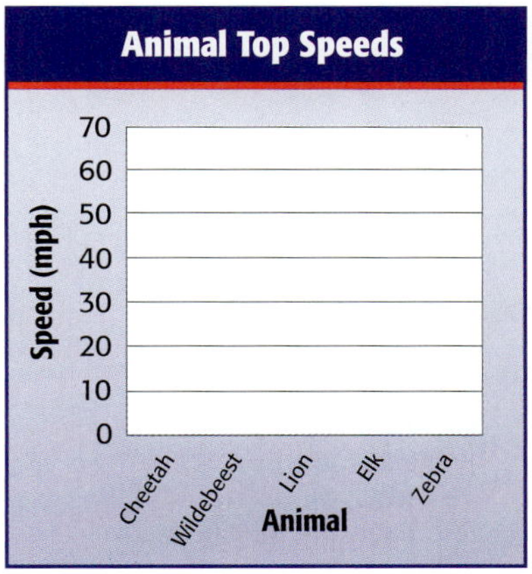

Step 2 Draw a bar to represent each category. In this case, a bar is used to represent the speed of each animal.

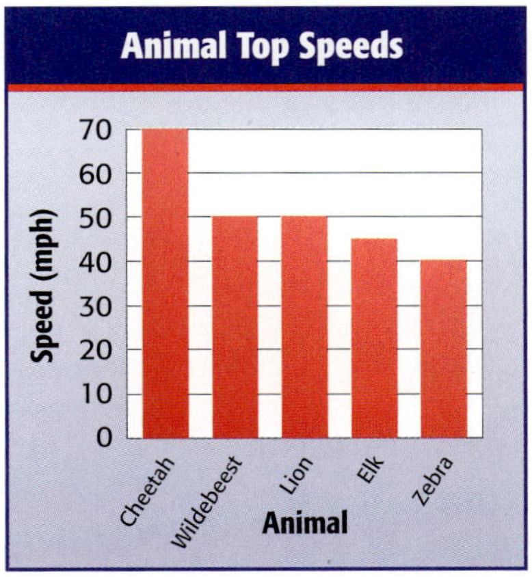

STUDY TIP

Bar Graphs The bars should be of equal width with equal spacing between them.

✓ CHECK Your Progress

a. **FLOWERS** The table shows the diameters of the world's largest flowers. Display the data in a bar graph.

Flower	Maximum Size (in.)
Rafflesia	36
Sunflower	19
Giant Water Lily	18
Brazilian Dutchman	14
Magnolia	10

Source: *Book of World Records*

A special kind of bar graph, called a **histogram**, uses bars to represent the frequency of numerical data that have been organized in intervals.

EXAMPLE Display Data Using a Histogram

2 **ANIMALS** **The top speeds of thirty different land animals have been organized into a frequency table. Display the data in a histogram.**

Maximum Speed (mph)	Number of Animals
11–20	5
21–30	5
31–40	10
41–50	8
51–60	0
61–70	2

Source: *The World Almanac*

Step 1 Draw and label horizontal and vertical axes. Add a title.

Step 2 Draw a bar to represent the frequency of each interval.

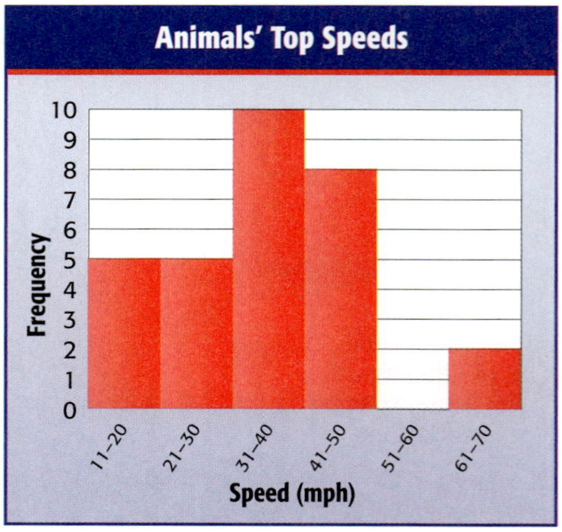

The two highest bars represent a majority of the data. From the graph, you can easily see that most of the animals have a top speed of 31–50 miles per hour.

STUDY TIP

Histograms
Because the intervals are equal, all of the bars have the same width, with no space between them. The space at 51–60 indicates that there are no data values on that interval.

CHECK Your Progress

b. **EARTHQUAKES** The magnitudes of the largest U.S. earthquakes are organized into the frequency table shown. Display the data in a histogram.

Magnitude	Frequency
7.0–7.4	4
7.5–7.9	14
8.0–8.4	5
8.5–8.9	2
9.0–9.4	1

Source: National Earthquake Information Center

Online Personal Tutor at tx.msmath2.com

STUDY TIP

Inferences
An inference is a conclusion that can be supported by data.

EXAMPLES Analyze Data to Make Inferences

WEATHER The bar graph shows the monthly number of tornadoes that occurred in the U.S. in 2004.

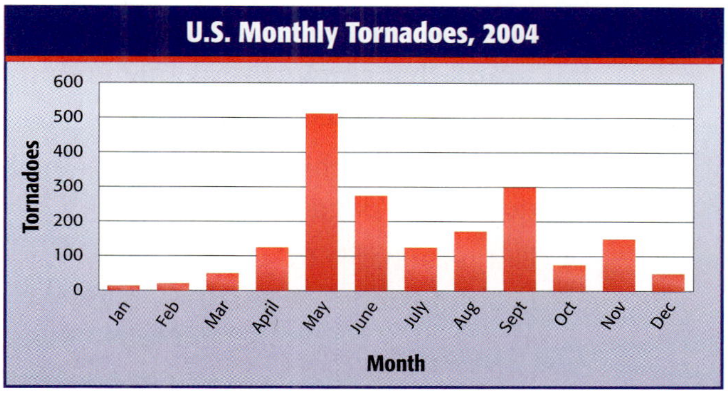

Source: NOAA National Weather Service

3 **Which season had the least number of tornadoes? Justify your answer.**

Look for the months with the least number of tornadoes. The graph shows that close to 0 tornadoes occurred in January and February. So, the least number of tornadoes occurred in winter.

4 **Compare the number of tornadoes that occurred in May and June.**

About 500 tornadoes occurred in May. About 275 tornadoes occurred in June. So, there were almost twice as many tornadoes in May than in June.

CHECK Your Progress

MALLS The histogram shows the number of stores in the largest malls in the U.S.

c. How many malls are represented in the histogram? Explain your reasoning.

d. Compare the number of malls with 275–349 stores to the malls with 425–499 stores.

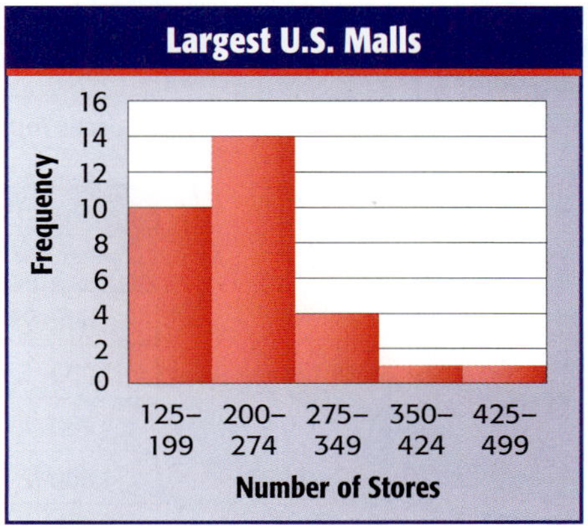

Source: Directory of Major Malls

CHECK Your Understanding

Examples 1, 2 (pp. 461–463)

Select the appropriate graph to display each set of data: bar graph or histogram. Then display the data in the appropriate graph.

1.

State Sales Tax Rates	
Percent	**States**
2.0–2.9	1
3.0–3.9	0
4.0–4.9	12
5.0–5.9	12
6.0–6.9	16
7.0–7.9	4

Source: www.taxadmin.org

2.

Men's Grand Slam Titles	
Player	**Titles**
Pete Sampras	14
Roy Emerson	12
Bjorn Borg	11
Rod Laver	11
Andre Agassi	8

Source: *Book of World Records*

Examples 3, 4 (p. 463)

TEXTBOOKS **For Exercises 3 and 4,use the bar graph that shows the average number of pages in various textbooks.**

3. On average, which textbook has the least number of pages?

4. Is it reasonable to say that on average, a health textbook has half as many pages as a science textbook? Explain.

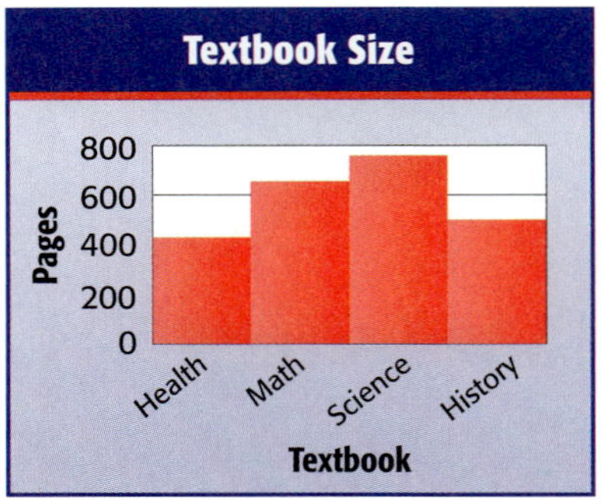

Exercises

HOMEWORK HELP	
For Exercises	**See Examples**
5–8	1, 2
9–15	3

Select the appropriate graph to display each set of data: bar graph or histogram. Then display the data in the appropriate graph.

5.

Most Threatened Reptiles	
Country	**Number of Species**
Australia	38
China	31
Indonesia	28
U.S.	27
India	25

Source: *Top 10 of Everything, 2005*

6.

Home Run Leaders, 1985–2004	
Home Runs	**Frequency**
31–36	1
37–42	4
43–48	7
49–54	5
55–60	3

Source: *The World Almanac*

7.

Major U.S. Rivers	
Length (mi)	**Frequency**
600–999	15
1,000–1,399	5
1,400–1,799	3
1,800–2,199	3
2,200–2,599	2

Source: *The World Almanac*

8.

City Skyscrapers	
City	**Skyscrapers**
New York	176
Hong Kong	163
Chicago	81
Shanghai	49
Tokyo	44

Source: *Book of World Records*

Real-World Link Giraffes live for 10–15 years in the wild, but average 25 years at zoos.
Source: zoo.org

GEOGRAPHY **For Exercises 9–12, use the graph that shows the number of bordering states for each of the fifty states.**

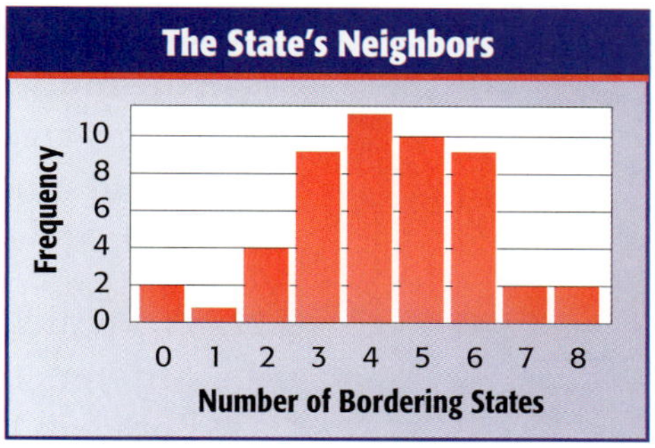

9. What is the most frequent number of states that borders another state?
10. How many states are bordered by 6 states?
11. How many states do not have any bordering states? Justify your answer.
12. **RESEARCH** Use the Internet or another source to find which states do not have any bordering states. Why do these states not have bordering states?

ZOOS **For Exercises 13–15, use the histogram that shows the attendance at the major U.S. zoos in a recent year.**

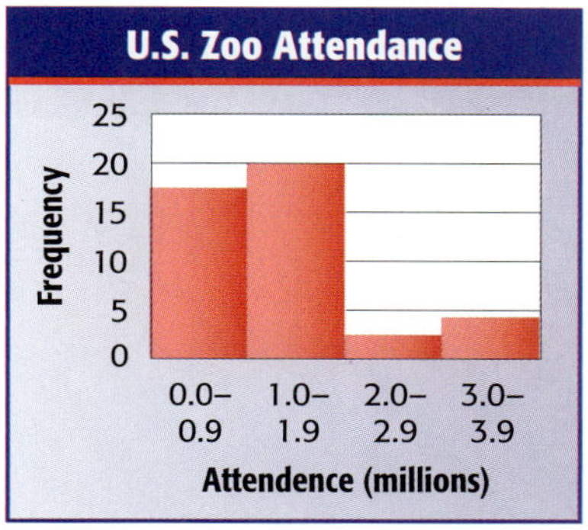

Source: The World Almanac

13. About how many zoos does the graph represent?
14. What is the range of attendance for most of the zoos?
15. Compare the number of zoos with 0.0–0.9 million visitors to the number of zoos with 3.0–3.9 million visitors.

Match each characteristic to the appropriate graph(s).

16. data display based upon place value
17. shows the frequency of data on a number line
18. compares data using solid bars
19. data is organized using intervals

a. line plot
b. histogram
c. stem-and-leaf plot
d. bar graph

CELL PHONES **For Exercises 20 and 21, use the bar graph shown below.**

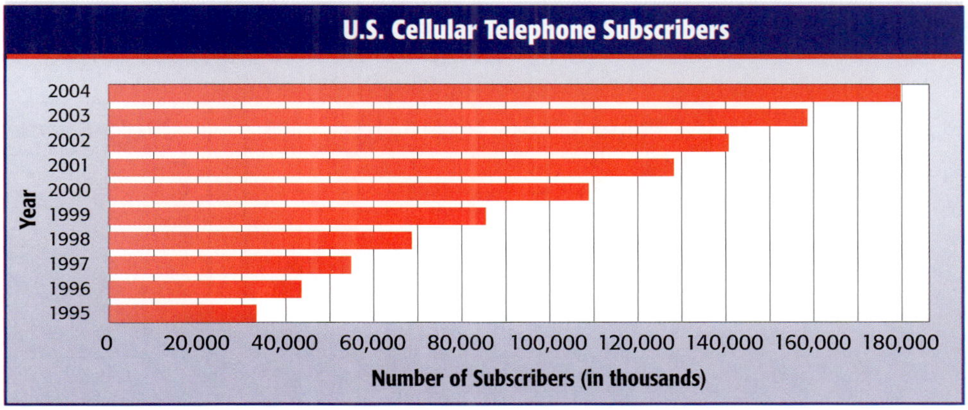

Source: *The World Almanac*

20. Describe how the number of cell phone subscribers has grown over the 10-year period.
21. Use the graph to predict the number of cell phone subscribers in 2010.

ELECTRICITY For Exercises 22 and 23, use the multiple bar graph that compares the annual costs of using old model appliances and using equivalent new model appliances.

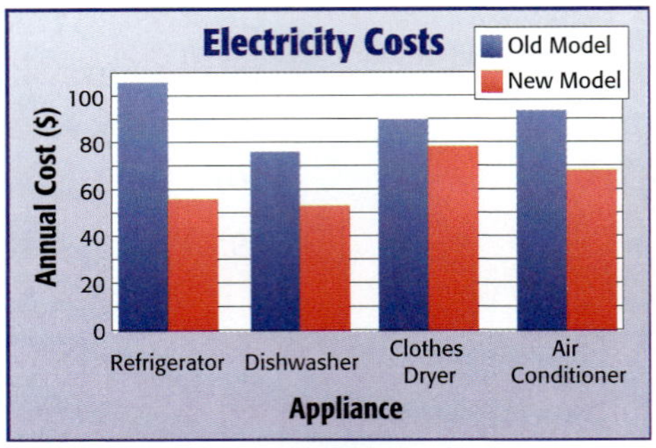

Source: *Association of Home Appliance Manufacturers*

22. For which appliance is the difference in electricity costs between the old and new model the greatest? Explain.

23. Describe an advantage of using a multiple-bar graph rather than two separate graphs to compare data.

EXERCISE For Exercises 24–27, refer to the graph below.

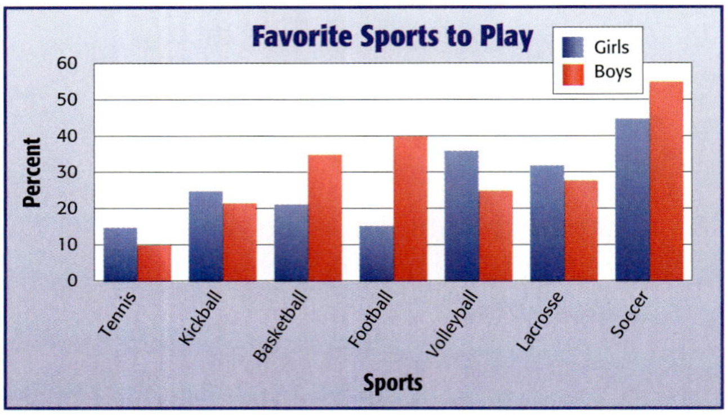

EXTRA PRACTICE
See pages 739, 763.
Math Online
Self-Check Quiz at tx.msmath2.com

24. Which sport did the girls surveyed prefer the most?
25. Which sport is the least favorite for the boys?
26. Based on this survey, boys prefer football 4 times more than what sport?
27. Write a convincing argument telling why you think that approximately the same number of boys and girls like to play kickball.

H.O.T. Problems

28. **CHALLENGE** The histograms show players' salaries for two major league baseball teams. Compare the salary distributions of the two teams.

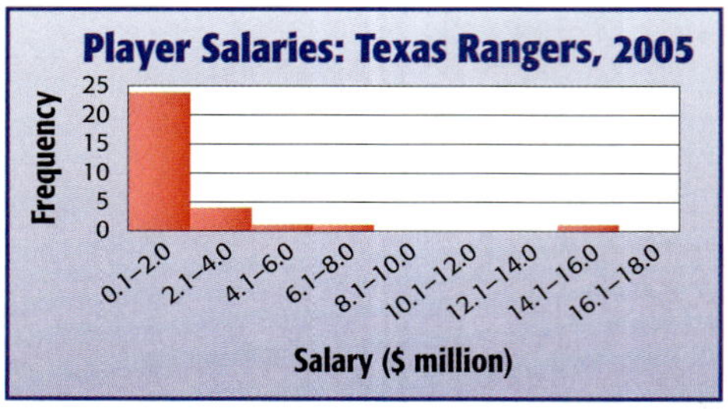

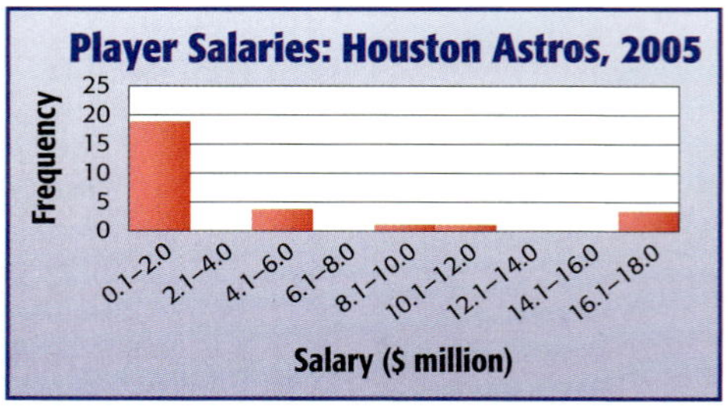

29. **DATA SENSE** Describe how to determine the number of values in a data set that is represented by a histogram.

30. **WRITING IN MATH** Can any data set be displayed using a histogram? If yes, explain why. If no, give a counterexample and explain why not.

TEST PRACTICE

31. The results of a survey are displayed in the graph.

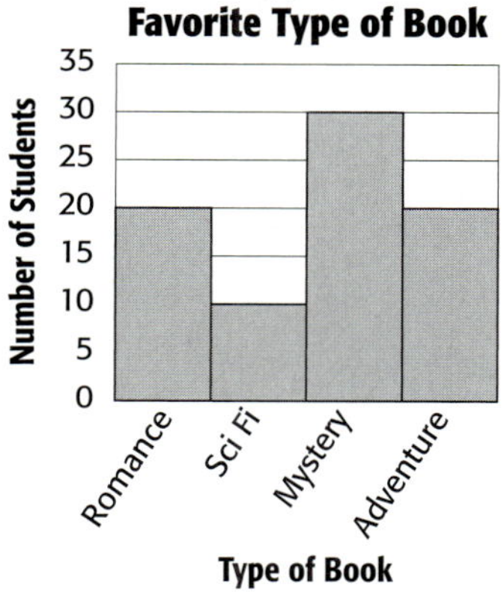

Which statement is best supported by the data?

A Twice as many students enjoy reading mysteries than romance.

B Most students enjoy reading adventure books.

C Twice as many students enjoy reading romance books than science fiction.

D Half as many students enjoy reading mysteries than romance.

32. The graph shows the average car sales per month at a car dealership.

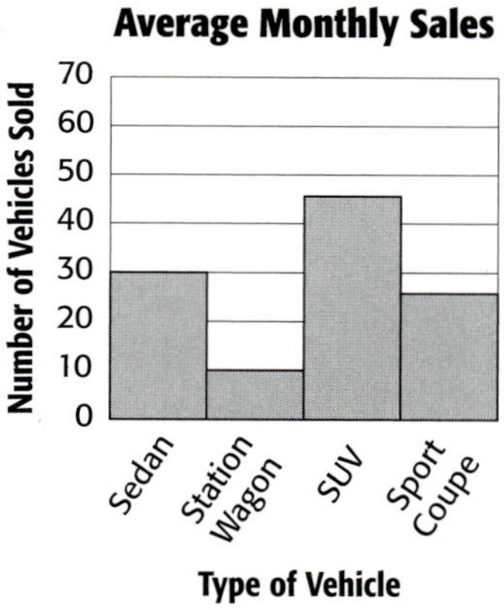

What is the best prediction for the number of station wagons the dealer sells in a year?

F 10

G 60

H 120

J 500

Spiral Review

SPORTS For Exercises 33 and 34, refer to the data that lists the number of games won by each team in a baseball league.

Number of Wins					
25	36	46	15	30	53
40	32	17	45	41	31
56	50	52	47	26	40
43	56	51	50	55	50
44	47	53	23	19	

33. Make a stem-and-leaf plot of the data. (Lesson 9-3)

34. What is the mean, median, and mode of the data? (Lesson 9-2)

35. SELECT A TECHNIQUE The video game that Neil wants to buy costs \$50. He has saved $\frac{1}{5}$ of the amount he needs. Which of the following techniques might Neil use to find how much more money he will need to buy the game? Justify your selection(s). Then use the technique(s) to solve the problem. (Lesson 6-5)

mental math | number sense | estimation

GET READY for the Next Lesson

36. WEATHER At 5:00 P.M., the outside temperature was 81°F. At 6:00 P.M., it was 80°F. At 7:00 P.M., it was 79°F. Use the *look for a pattern* strategy to predict the outside temperature at 8:00 P.M. (Lesson 2-6)

Extend 9-4

Spreadsheet Lab
Circle Graphs

Main IDEA

Use technology to create circle graphs.

Targeted TEKS 7.11 The student understands that the way a set of data is displayed influences its interpretation. (A) **select and use an appropriate representation for presenting and displaying relationships among collected data, including** line plot, line graph, bar graph, stem and leaf plot, **circle graph,** and Venn diagrams, **and justify the selection.**

Another type of display used to compare categories of data is a *circle graph*. Circle graphs are useful when comparing parts of a whole.

ACTIVITY

MAGAZINES The table shows the results of a survey in which students were asked to indicate their favorite type of magazine. Use a spreadsheet to make a circle graph of these data.

Magazine Preferences	
Type	**Frequency**
Comics	2
Fashion	7
Entertainment	5
News	3
Sports	6
Other	1

STEP 1 Enter the data in a spreadsheet as shown.

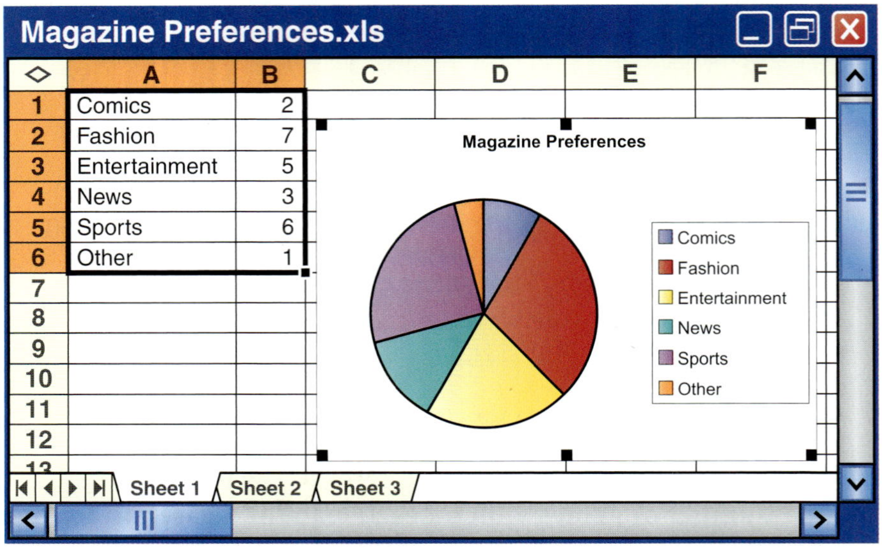

STEP 2 Select the information in cells A1 to B6. Click on the Chart Wizard icon. Choose the Pie chart type. Click Next twice. Enter the title Magazine Preferences. Then click Next and Finish.

STUDY TIP

Bar Graphs
To create a bar graph using a spreadsheet, follow the same steps used to create a circle graph, except choose Bar for the chart type.

ANALYZE THE RESULTS

1. **MAKE A CONJECTURE** Use the graph to determine which types of magazines were preferred by about $\frac{1}{3}$ and 25% of the students surveyed. Explain your reasoning. Then check your answers.

2. **COLLECT THE DATA** Collect some data that can be displayed in either a circle or bar graph. Record the data in a spreadsheet. Then use the spreadsheet to make both types of displays. Which display is more appropriate? Justify your selection.

9-5 Venn Diagrams

Main IDEA

Analyze data in Venn diagrams.

Targeted TEKS 7.11 The student understands that the way a set of data is displayed influences its interpretation. **(A) select and use an appropriate representation for presenting and displaying relationships among collected data, including** line plot, line graph, bar graph, stem and leaf plot, circle graph, and **Venn diagrams, and justify the selection.** *Also addresses TEKS 7.11(B).*

NEW Vocabulary

Venn diagram

GET READY for the Lesson

SURVEYS Nicholas asked 20 of his classmates what they use when taking notes: a pencil or a pen. The results are shown.

Taking Notes	
Writing Tool	**Number of Students**
Pencil	18
Pen	15
Neither	2

1. Display the information in a bar graph.
2. If Nicholas surveyed 20 classmates, why do the numbers in the second column have a sum of $18 + 15 + 2$ or 35?
3. Does the graph tell you how many people use both pencil and pen?

A **Venn diagram** is an arrangement of overlapping circles used to show how two or more sets of data are related.

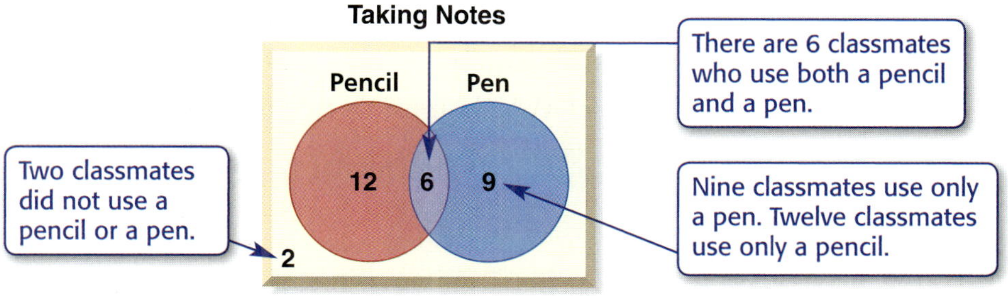

EXAMPLE Display Data in a Venn Diagram

1 **BAND** **Display the survey results shown at the right in a Venn diagram.**

Survey Results	
Jazz Band	Trina, Jerome, Logan, Kylie, Miguel
Orchestra	Natalie, Kylie, Jerome, Malina, Tyree

First, draw two overlapping circles to represent jazz band and orchestra. Label each circle.

Since Kylie and Jerome are in both jazz band and orchestra, write their names in the overlapping region.

Write each of the other names in the appropriate region.

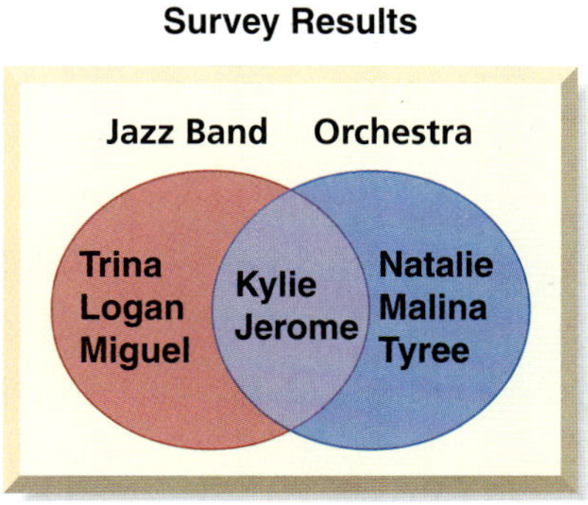

STUDY TIP

Shapes A Venn diagram is often two or more overlapping circles. However, other shapes can also be used.

CHECK Your Progress

a. **NUMBERS** Use a Venn diagram to show how the factors of 24 and 56 are related.

EXAMPLES Analyze a Venn Diagram

Real-World Link An adult squirrel needs to eat about a pound of food a week.
Source: squirrels.org

ANIMALS Refer to the Venn diagram at the right.

Animal Characteristics

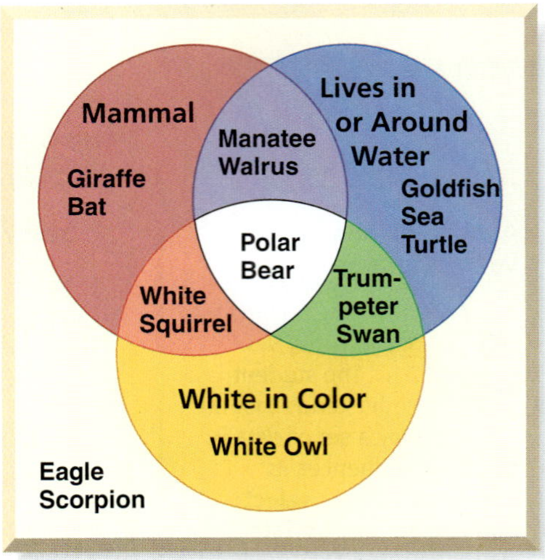

2 **Which animals are mammals that live in or around water?**

The area where the circle labeled *Mammal* and the circle labeled *Lives In or Around Water* overlap contains 3 animals, manatee, walrus, and polar bear.

3 **Which animals are mammals that do not live in or around water and are not white in color?**

The giraffe and bat are mammals that do not live in or around water and are not white in color.

CHECK Your Progress

b. Name the animals that are mammals that are white in color.
c. Which animals live in or around water and are not white in color?

Online Personal Tutor at tx.msmath2.com

CHECK Your Understanding

Example 1 (p. 469)

Draw a Venn diagram to show how the sets of data are related.

1.

Odd Numbers	Prime Numbers
1, 3, 5, 7, 9, 11, 13, 15, 17, 19	2, 3, 5, 7, 11, 13, 17, 19

2.

Pet Ownership	
Dog	Morgan, Enrique, Louis, Tia
Cat	Keith, Louis, Nikki, Morgan, Enrique

Examples 2, 3 (p. 470)

BOOKS For Exercises 3–6, use the Venn diagram that shows students' book preferences.

Book Preference

3. Which student(s) prefer to read mystery and romance books?
4. Which student(s) prefer to read historical but *not* mystery books?
5. Which student(s) prefer *not* to read romance or historical books?
6. What type of book(s) does Thom prefer to read?

Exercises

HOMEWORK HELP

For Exercises	See Examples
7–10	1
11–18	2, 3

For Exercises 7–12, draw a Venn diagram to show how the sets of data are related.

7.

Dessert Eaten at a Birthday Party	
Cake	Adelina, Jin, Rashid, Aisha, Santiago
Ice Cream	Rashid, Aisha, Todd, Reiko, Suzie

8.

Multiples of 4	Multiples of 6
0, 4, 8, 12, 16, 20, 24, 28, 32, 36	0, 6, 12, 18, 24, 30, 36

9.

Vegetable	Green in Color
Broccoli	Tree
Carrot	Grass
Corn	Frog
Peas	Broccoli
Onion	Peas

10.

Transportation to School	
Walk	Alejandro, Malcolm, Paige, Martin, Shandra, Mateo
Car/Bus	Jacob, Lisa, Ariel, Ellie, Malcolm, Diego, Kimberly

11. **TRAVEL** Of 50 people, 20 want to travel to Italy only, 16 want to travel to Germany only, and 14 want to travel to both Italy and Germany.

12. **FOOD** Of 60 people, 25 prefer pepperoni only on a pizza, 13 prefer sausage only, and 12 prefer both pepperoni and sausage.

SCHOOL For Exercises 13–15, refer to the Venn diagram.

Students' Favorite Subject

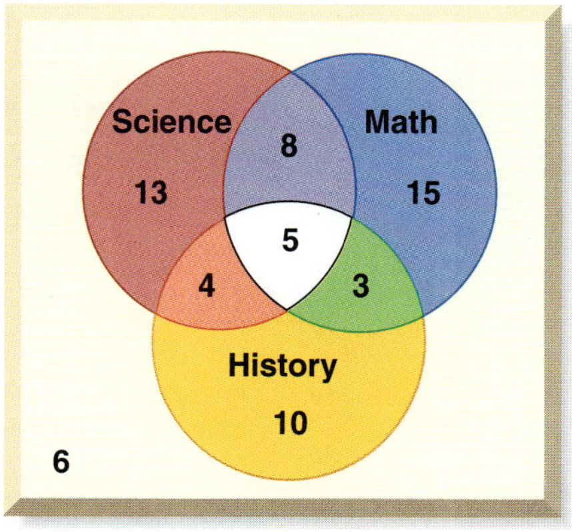

13. How many prefer only math?
14. How many said they prefer science and history?
15. How many prefer history but not math?

TIME For Exercises 16–18, refer to the Venn diagram.

Bedtime on a School Night

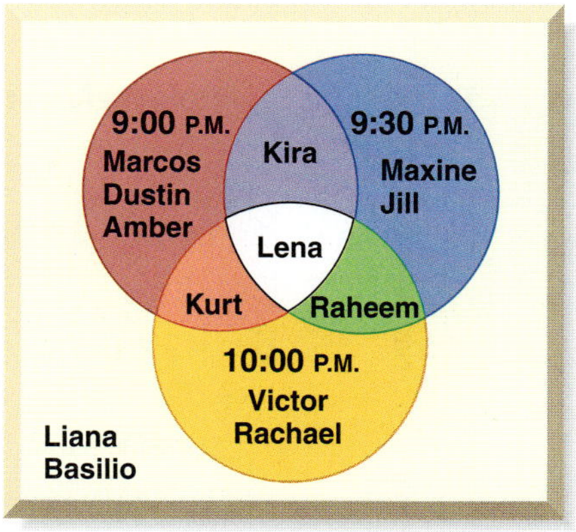

16. Who goes to bed at exactly 10:00 P.M.?
17. How many do not go to bed at any of these times?
18. How many were surveyed?

EXTRA PRACTICE
See pages 740, 763.
Math Online
Self-Check Quiz at tx.msmath2.com

19. **MUSIC** Kristy asked 43 people which format they like to listen to music, MP3 or CD. Of those surveyed, 20 said CD and 38 said MP3. However, 15 people said both CD and MP3. Use a Venn diagram to find how many classmates prefer MP3 format only.

H.O.T. Problems

20. **OPEN ENDED** Write two sets of data with a relationship that can be shown using a Venn diagram. Be sure to draw the Venn diagram.

21. **WRITING IN MATH** In your own words, explain what the area marked with an X in the Venn diagram at the right represents.

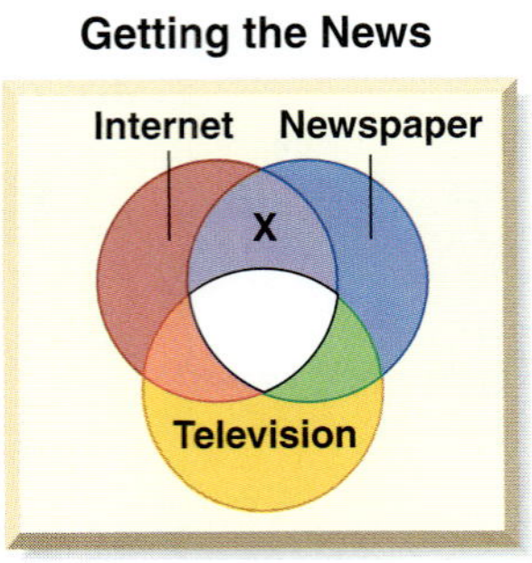

22. **CHALLENGE** Draw a Venn diagram to show the relationship between the characteristics of cats and dogs.

TEST PRACTICE

23. Sharon polled 15 friends to find out their music preferences. Which of the following gives the most detailed information about her friends' music preferences?

A

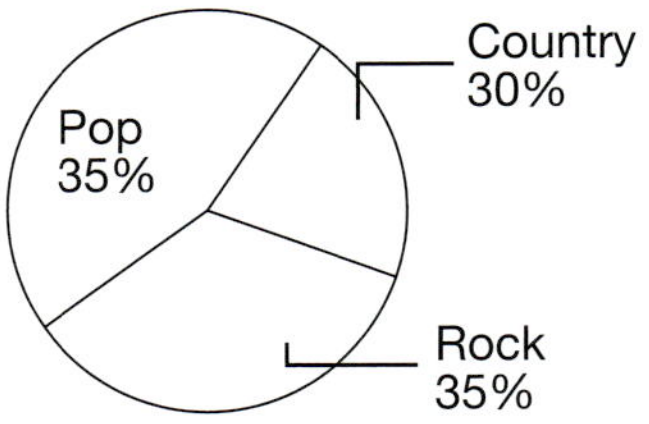

B

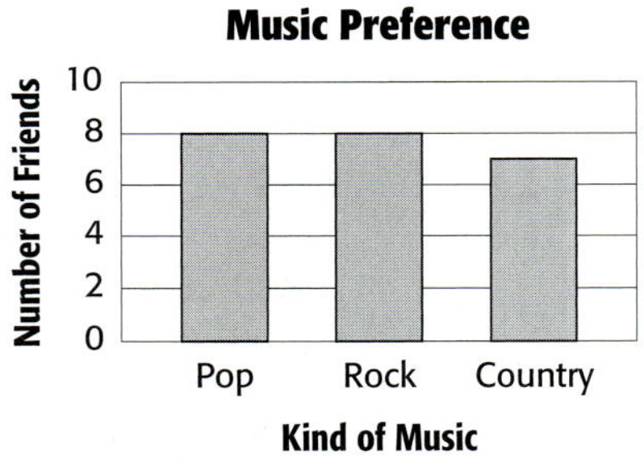

C

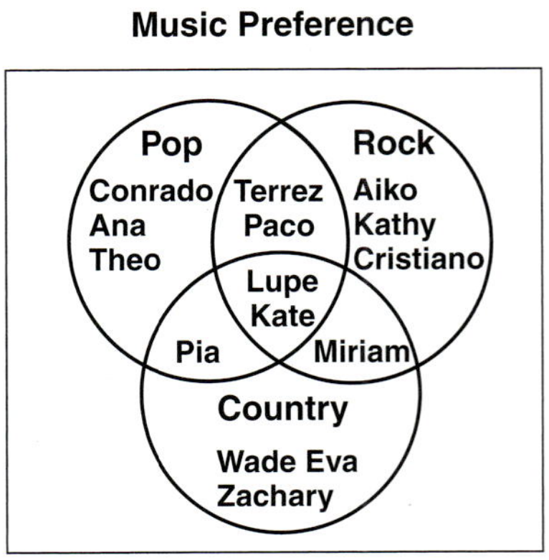

D

Music Preference	
Kind of Music	**Number of Friends**
Pop	8
Rock	8
Country	7

Spiral Review

24. **COLORS** Display the data at the right in a bar graph. (Lesson 9-4)

Favorite Color	
Color	**Students**
Red	13
Blue	16
Green	20
Yellow	8

Graph and label each point on a coordinate plane. (Lesson 2-3)

25. $A(-3, 2)$ 26. $N(-4, -5)$ 27. $J(1, 0)$

GET READY for the Next Lesson

28. **PREREQUISITE SKILL** Desireé bakes a pan of lasagna. She makes 3 cuts along the length of the rectangular pan and 4 cuts along the width. How many pieces of lasagna will be end pieces? Use the *make a diagram* strategy. (Lesson 7-5)

Chapter 9 Mid-Chapter Quiz

Lessons 9-1 through 9-5

1. **TEST PRACTICE** The table shows quiz scores of a math class. What is the range of test scores? (Lesson 9-1)

Math Scores						
89	92	67	75	95	89	82
92	88	89	80	91	79	90

A 89 **C** 67
B 82 **D** 28

For Exercises 2–4, use the data below. (Lesson 9-1)

Age Upon Receiving Driver's License									
16	17	16	16	18	21	16	16	18	18
17	25	16	17	17	17	17	16	20	16

2. Make a line plot of the data.
3. Identify any clusters, gaps, or outliers.
4. Describe how the range of data would change if 25 was not part of the data set.

5. **TEST PRACTICE** The table shows the average monthly rainfall for Amarillo. Which measure of data is represented by 1.2 inches? (Lesson 9-2)

Average Rain (in.)					
0.5	0.6	1.0	1.0	2.5	3.7
2.6	3.3	2.0	1.4	0.7	0.4

Source: countrystudies.us

F Mean **H** Range
G Median **J** Mode

Find the mean, median, and mode for each set of data. Round to the nearest tenth if necessary. (Lesson 9-2)

6. Jersey prices ($): 27, 32, 18, 24, 32, 39, 41
7. Tree heights (m): 7.6, 6.8, 6.5, 7.0, 7.9, 6.8, 7.0, 7.0, 6.8, 8.1

8. **SPEED** Display the data shown in a stem-and-leaf plot and write one inference based on the data. (Lesson 9-3)

Car Highway Speeds				
65	72	76	68	65
59	70	69	71	74
68	65	71	74	69

ATTENDANCE For Exercises 9 and 10, refer to the graph. (Lesson 9-4)

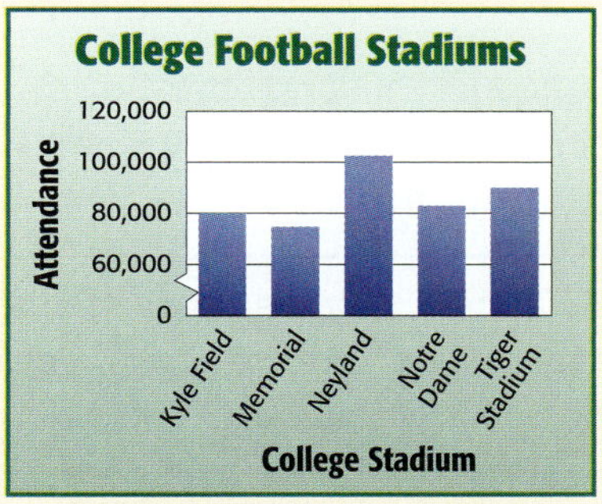

Source: msnbc.com

9. About how many people does the graph represent?
10. Which two stadiums house about the same number of people?

COMMUNICATION For Exercises 11 and 12, refer to the Venn diagram. (Lesson 9-5)

Communication Preferences

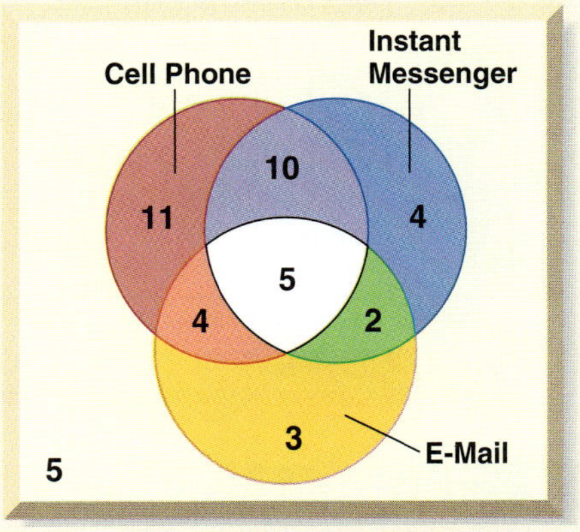

11. How many students prefer only instant messenger?
12. How many students prefer cell phones, but not e-mail?

9-6 Problem-Solving Investigation

MAIN IDEA: Solve problems by using a graph.

Targeted TEKS 7.11 The student understands that the way a set of data is displayed influences its interpretation. **(B)** **make inferences** and convincing arguments **based on an analysis of given** or collected **data**.

P.S.I. TEAM +

e-Mail: USE A GRAPH

YOUR MISSION: Use a graph to solve the problem.

THE PROBLEM: The table shows the study times and test scores of 13 students in Mrs. Collins' English class?

Yolanda: Based on this data, what would be the test score of a student who studied for 75 minutes?

Study Time and Test Scores

Study Time (min)	120	30	60	95	70	55	90	45	75	60	10
Test Score (%)	98	77	91	93	77	78	95	74	87	83	65

EXPLORE	You know the number of minutes studied. You need to predict the test score.	
PLAN	Organize the data in a graph so you can easily see any trends.	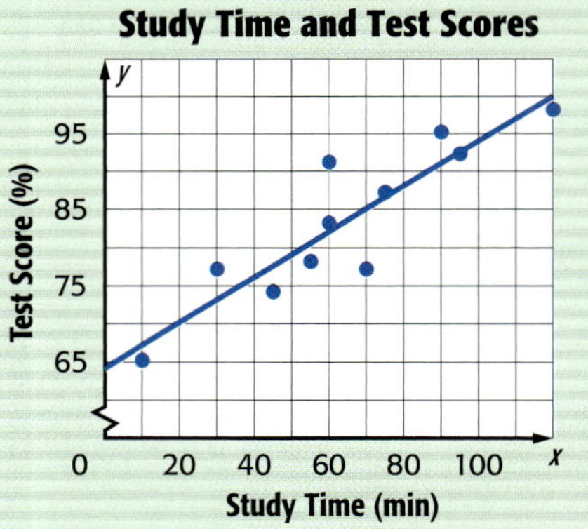
SOLVE	The graph shows that as the study times progress, the test scores increase. You can predict that the test score of a student who studied for 75 minutes is about 87%.	
CHECK	Draw a line that is close to as many of the points as possible, as shown. The estimate is close to the line so the prediction is reasonable.	

Analyze The Strategy

1. Explain why analyzing a graph is a useful way to quickly make conclusions about a set of data.
2. **WRITING IN MATH** Write a problem in which using a graph would be a useful way to check a solution.

Mixed Problem Solving

For Exercises 3 and 4, solve by using a graph.

3. **SCIENCE** Refer to the graph. Suppose the trends continue. Predict the average high temperature for the month of July.

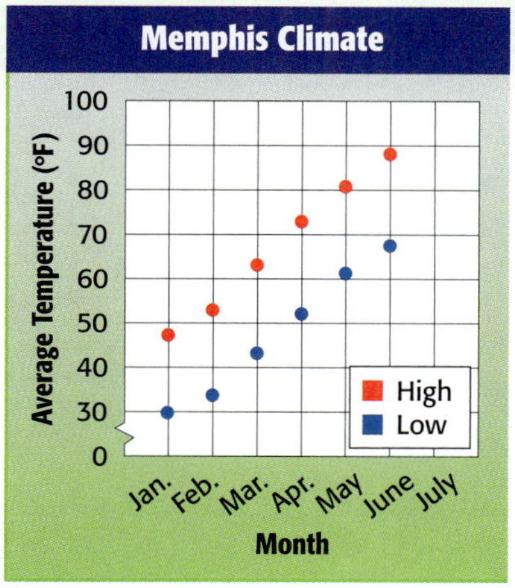

Source: weather.com

4. **SCHOOL** The graph shows the number of energy bars sold in the cafeteria. On which day did the cafeteria sell about half as many bars as it did on Friday?

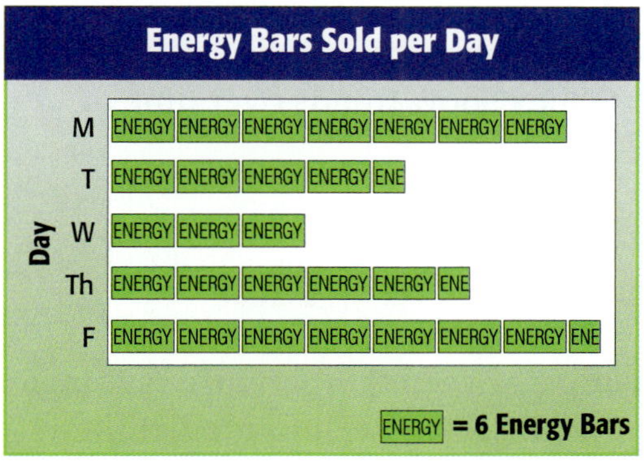

Use any strategy to solve Exercises 5–8. Some strategies are shown below.

PROBLEM-SOLVING STRATEGIES
- Guess and check.
- Look for a pattern.
- Use a graph.

5. **PATTERN** What are the next two numbers in the pattern 8, 18, 38, 78, ...?

6. **READING** Maya read 10 pages of a 150-page book on Monday and plans to read twice as many pages each day than she did the previous day. On what day will she finish the book?

7. **EXERCISE** The graph shows the number of minutes Jacob exercised during one week. According to the graph, which two days did he exercise about the same amount of time?

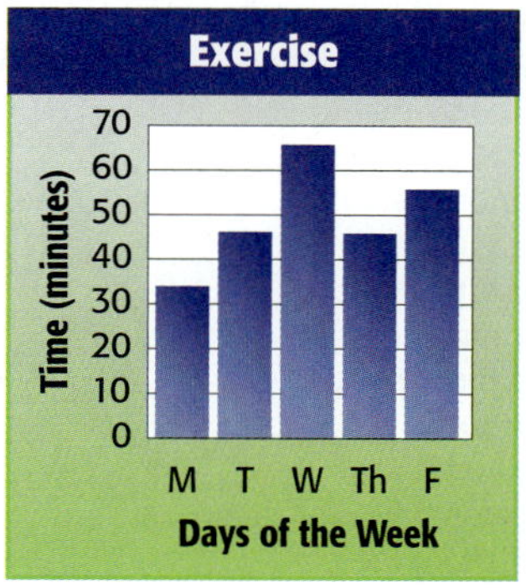

8. **NUMBER THEORY** Find two numbers with a sum of 56 and with a product of 783.

Select the Operation

For Exercises 9 and 10, select the appropriate operation(s) to solve the problem. Justify your selection(s) and solve the problem.

9. **SAFETY** An elevator sign reads *Do not exceed 2,500 pounds*. How many people, each weighing about 150 pounds, can be in the elevator at the same time?

10. **BOWLING** Tariq and three of his friends are going bowling, and they have a total of $70 to spend. Suppose they buy a large pizza, four beverages, and each rent bowling shoes. How many games can they bowl if they all bowl the same number of games?

Bowling Costs

Item	Price
large pizza	$15.75
beverage	$1.50
shoe rental	$3.50
game	$4.00

9-7 Line Graphs and Scatter Plots

Main IDEA

Analyze line graphs and scatter plots to make predictions and inferences.

Targeted TEKS 7.11 The student understands that the way a set of data is displayed influences its interpretation. **(A) select and use an appropriate representation for presenting and displaying relationships among collected data, including** line plot, **line graph,** bar graph, stem and leaf plot, circle graph, and Venn diagrams, **and justify the selection.** *Also addresses TEKS 7.11(B).*

MINI Lab

- Pour 1 cup of water into the drinking glass.
- Measure the height of the water, and record it in a table like the one shown.
- Place 5 marbles in the glass. Measure the height of the water. Record.
- Continue adding marbles, 5 at a time, until there are 20 marbles in the glass. After each time, measure and record the height of the water.

Number of Marbles	Height of Water (cm)
0	
5	
10	
15	
20	

1. By how much did the water's height change after each addition of marbles?
2. Predict the height of the water when 30 marbles are in the drinking glass. Explain how you made your prediction.
3. Test your prediction by placing 10 more marbles in the glass.
4. Draw a graph of the data that you recorded in the table.

NEW Vocabulary

line graph
scatter plot

You created a line graph in the Mini Lab. **Line graphs** can be useful in predicting future events because they show trends over time or relationships.

EXAMPLES Use a Line Graph to Predict

1 TEMPERATURE **The relationship between temperature readings in °C and °F is shown below. Use the line graph to predict the temperature reading 35°C in °F.**

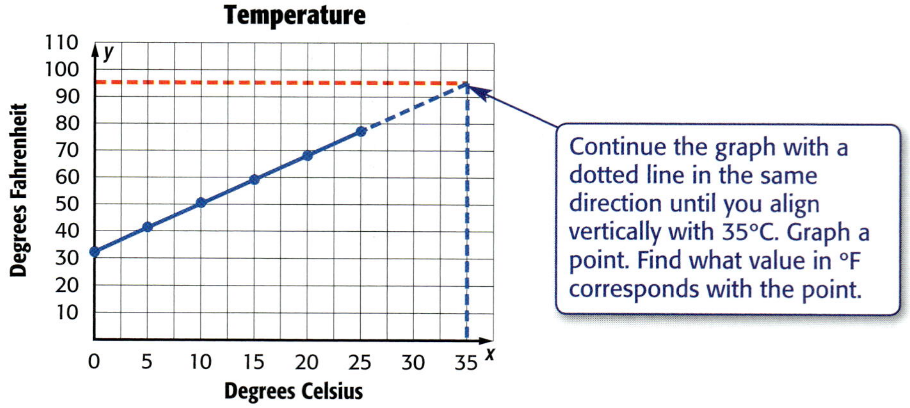

The temperature reading 35°C is equivalent to 95°F.

2 **SCHOOL** The graph shows the student enrollment at McDaniel Middle School for the past several years. If the trend continues, what will be the enrollment in 2010?

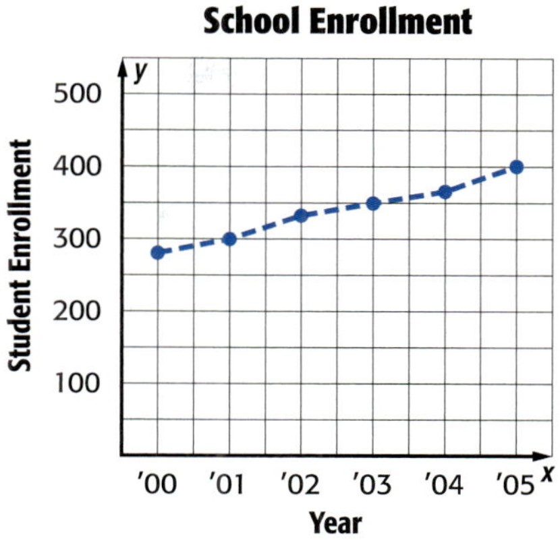

If the trend continues, the enrollment in 2010 will be about 525 students.

STUDY TIP

Broken Lines In Example 2, there are no data points between the points that represent enrollment. So, a broken line was used to help you easily see trends in the data.

CHECK Your Progress

a. **READING** Kerry is reading *The Game of Sunken Places* over summer break. The graph shows the time it has taken her to read the book so far. Predict the time it will take her to read 150 pages.

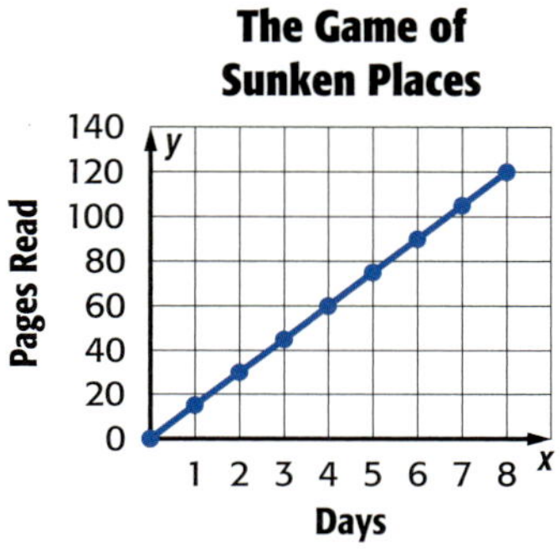

b. **JUICE BOXES** The table shows the number of juice boxes a cafeteria sold in a five-week period. Display the data in a line graph. If the trend continues, how many juice boxes will be sold in week 8?

Juice Box Sales

Week	Number Sold
1	50
2	52
3	56
4	60
5	62

A **scatter plot** displays two sets of data on the same graph. Like line graphs, scatter plots are useful for making predictions because they show trends in data. If the points on a scatter plot come close to lying on a straight line, the two sets of data are related.

STUDY TIP

Scatter Plots
In a positive relationship, as the value of x increases, so does the value of y. In a negative relationship, as the value of x increases, the value of y decreases.

CONCEPT Summary — Types of Relationships

Positive Relationship	Negative Relationship	No Relationship
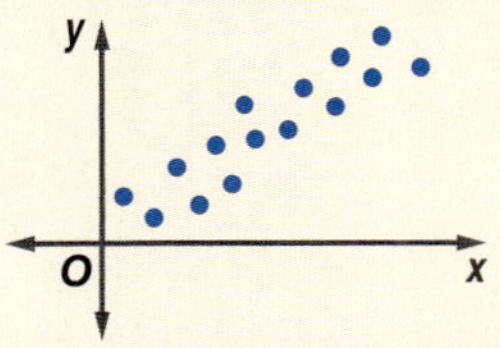	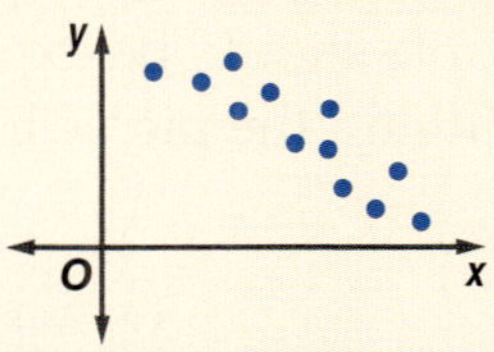	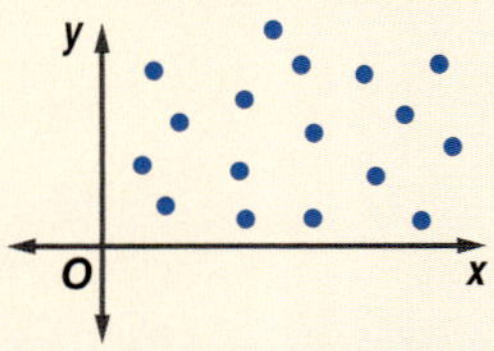

READING Math

Scatter Plots Another name for scatter plot is *scattergram.*

EXAMPLE Use a Scatter Plot to Predict

3 **SWIMMING** **The scatter plot shows the winning times for the women's 100-meter butterfly event at the Summer Olympics from 1968 to 2004. Predict a winning time for this event at the 2012 Olympics.**

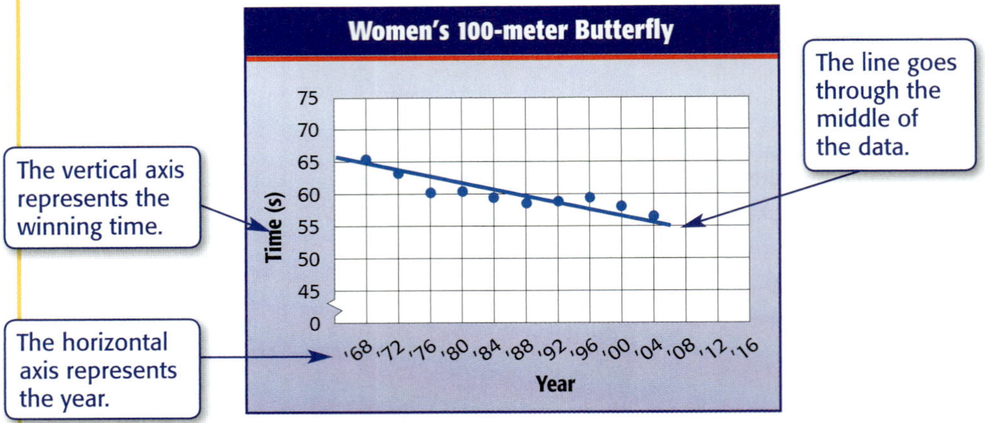

Source: *The World Almanac*

By looking at the pattern, we can predict that the winning time at the 2012 Olympics will be about 54 seconds.

CHECK Your Progress

c. **SWIMMING** Use the scatter plot above to predict a winning time for the Women's 100-meter Butterfly event at the 2016 Olympics.

Online Personal Tutor at tx.msmath2.com

CHECK Your Understanding

Examples 1, 2 (pp. 476–477)

TRACK **Sierra is training for cross-country try-outs. To make the team, she needs to be able to run 1 mile in under 8 minutes. The graph charts her progress.**

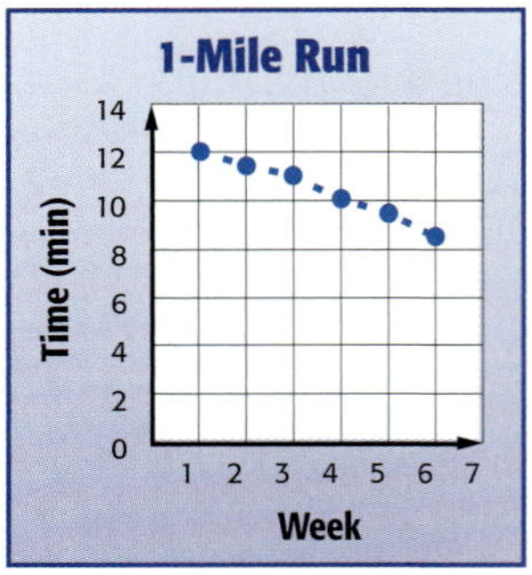

1. Describe the relationship between the two sets of data.
2. If the trend continues, will Sierra make the team? Explain.

Example 3 (p. 478)

3. **PICNICS** The scatter plot shows the number of people who attended a neighborhood picnic each year. How many people should be expected to attend the picnic in 2007?

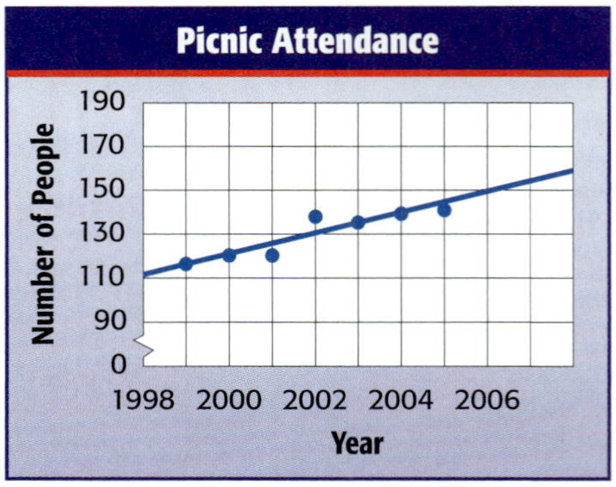

Exercises

HOMEWORK HELP	
For Exercises	See Examples
4–5	1, 2
6–7	3

MONUMENTS For Exercises 4 and 5, use the graph that shows the time it takes Ciro to climb the Statue of Liberty.

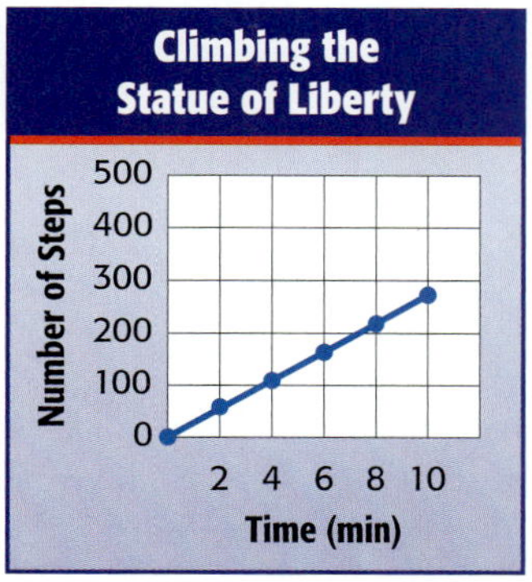

4. Predict the time it will take Ciro to climb 354 steps to reach the top.
5. How many steps will he have climbed after 14 minutes?

SCHOOL For Exercises 6 and 7, use the graph that shows the time students spent studying for a test and their test score.

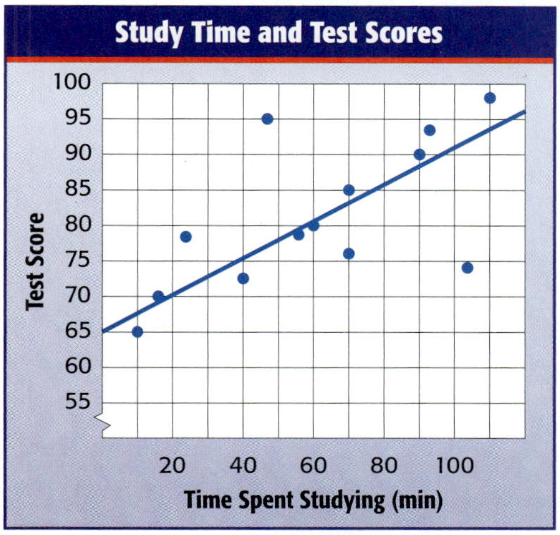

6. What score should a student who studies for 1 hour be expected to earn?
7. If a student scored 90 on the test, about how much time can you assume the student spent studying?

SAFETY For Exercises 8–10, use the table that shows the relationship between the speed of a vehicle and the distance required to stop.

Speed (mph)	Stopping Distance (ft)
55	273
60	312
65	355
70	400
75	447

8. Make a scatter plot of the data. Use the speed on the horizontal axis and the stopping distance on the vertical axis.
9. Describe the relationship, if any, between the two sets of data.
10. Predict the stopping distance for a car traveling 45 miles per hour.

OLYMPICS For Exercises 11–13, use the table that shows the number of nations that participated in the Summer Olympics from 1936 to 2004.

Year	Number of Nations	Year	Number of Nations
1936	49	1976	92
1948	59	1980	80
1952	69	1984	140
1956	72	1988	159
1960	83	1992	169
1964	93	1996	197
1968	112	2000	199
1972	121	2004	201

11. Display the data in a scatter plot.
12. Predict the number of nations that will participate in the 2012 Summer Olympics.
13. Describe the trend in the data.

SCHOOLS For Exercises 14 and 15, use the graphic that shows public school teachers' average salaries for the past few years.

Source: nea.org

14. Describe the relationship, if any, between the two sets of data.
15. If the trend continues, what will be the average annual salary in 2009?
16. **RESEARCH** Use the Internet or another source to find a real-world example of a scatter plot. Write a description of what the graph displays and extend the graph to show where the data will be in the future.
17. **POPULATION** The *multiple line graph* at the right shows the population of Miami-Dade and Broward Counties in Florida from 1950 to 2000. Do you think that the population of Broward County will catch up to the population of Miami-Dade County in the next census in 2010? Write a convincing argument as to why or why not.

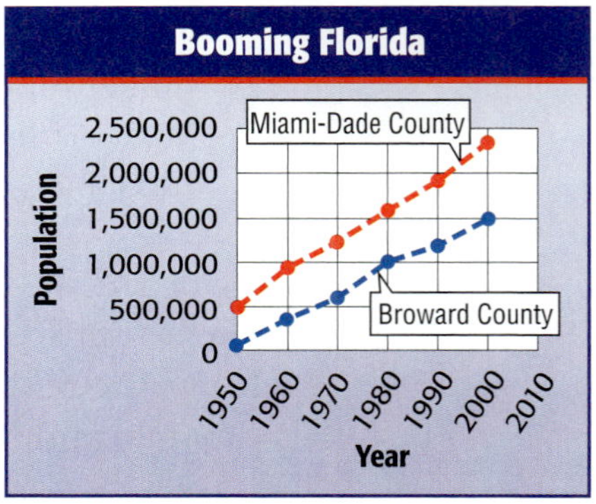

Source: U.S. Census Bureau

EXTRA PRACTICE

See pages 740, 763.

Math Online

Self-Check Quiz at tx.msmath2.com

H.O.T. Problems

18. **OPEN ENDED** Name two sets of data that can be graphed on a scatter plot.
19. **Which One Doesn't Belong?** Identify the term that does not have the same characteristic as the other three. Explain your reasoning.

line plot	mode	bar graph	scatter plot

20. **CHALLENGE** What can you conclude about the relationship between birth month and height shown in the scatter plot at the right?

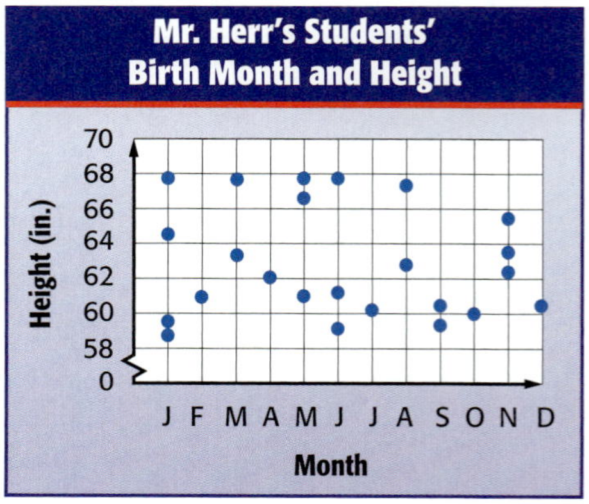

21. **WRITING IN MATH** Explain how a graph can be used to make predictions.

TEST PRACTICE

22. The number of laps Gaspar has been swimming each day is shown.

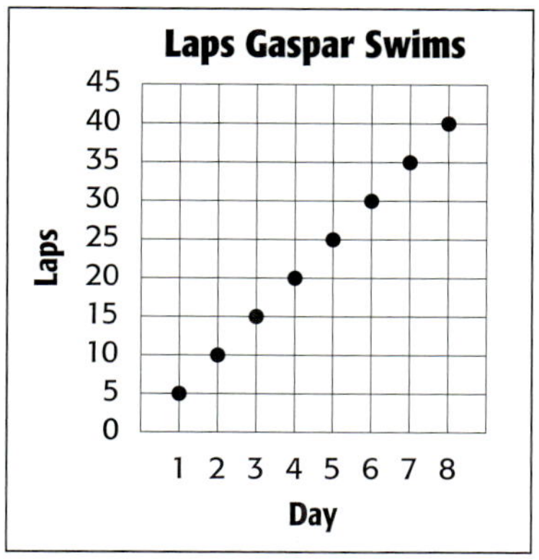

If the trend shown in the graph continues, what is the best prediction for the number of laps he will swim on day 10?

A 50

B 65

C 75

D 100

23. The number of customers at Clothes Palace at different times during the day is shown.

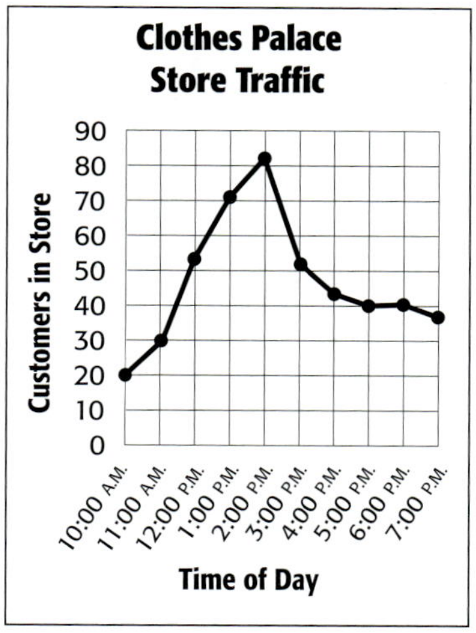

If extra workers are needed when the number of customers exceeds 50, between which hours is extra help needed?

F 12:00 P.M.–3:00 P.M.

G 11:00 A.M.–4:00 P.M.

H 1:00 P.M.–4:00 P.M.

J 1:00 P.M.–3:00 P.M.

Spiral Review

24. **SKATING** Use the *use a graph* strategy to compare the number of people who skate in California to the number of people who skate in Texas. (Lesson 9-6)

25. **FOOD** Of 77 students, 40 like pasta only, 15 like chicken only, and 22 like both pasta and chicken. Draw a Venn diagram to show how the sets of data are related. (Lesson 9-5)

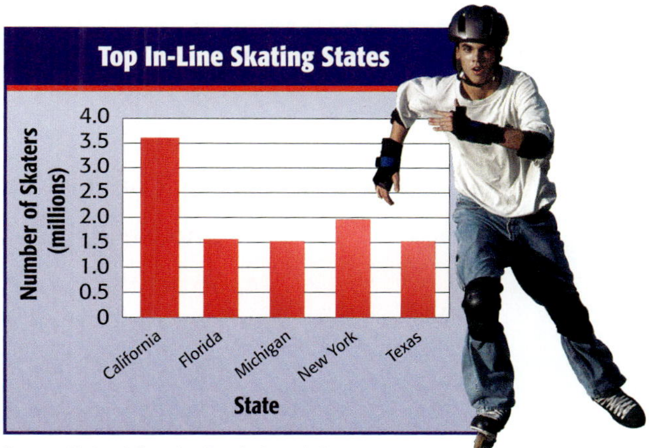

Source: National Sporting Goods Association

GET READY for the Next Lesson

PREREQUISITE SKILL Find the mean and median for each set of data. (Lesson 9-2)

26. 89 ft, 90 ft, 74 ft, 81 ft, 68 ft

27. 76°, 90°, 88°, 84°, 82°, 78°

Extend 9-7

Spreadsheet Lab
Multiple-Line and -Bar Graphs

Main IDEA

Use a spreadsheet to make a multiple-line graph and a multiple-bar graph.

Targeted TEKS 7.11 The student understands that the way a set of data is displayed influences its interpretation. **(A) select and use an appropriate representation for presenting and displaying relationships among collected data, including** line plot, **line graph, bar graph,** stem and leaf plot, circle graph, and Venn diagrams, **and justify the selection.**

In Lessons 9-4 and 9-7, you interpreted data in a multiple-bar graph and in a multiple-line graph, respectively. You can use a Microsoft® Excel® spreadsheet to make these two types of graphs.

ACTIVITY

1 The stopping distances for a car on dry pavement and on wet pavement are shown in the table at the right.

Speed (mph)	Stopping Distance (ft)	
	Dry Pavement	Wet Pavement
50	200	250
60	271	333
70	342	430
80	422	532

Source: *Continental Teves*

Set up a spreadsheet like the one shown below.

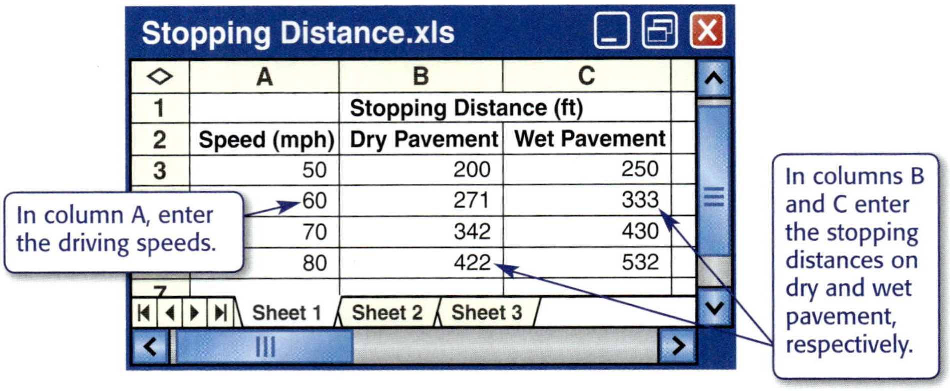

The next step is to "tell" the spreadsheet to make a double-line graph for the data.

1. Highlight the data in columns B and C, from B2 through C6.
2. Click on the Chart Wizard icon.
3. Choose the line graph and click Next.
4. To set the x-axis, choose the Series tab and press the icon next to the Category (X) axis labels.
5. On the spreadsheet, highlight the data in column A, from A3 through A6.
6. Press the icon on the bottom of the Chart Wizard box to automatically paste the information.
7. Click Next and enter the chart title and labels for the x- and y-axes.
8. Click Next and then Finish.

This tells the spreadsheet to read the data in columns B and C.

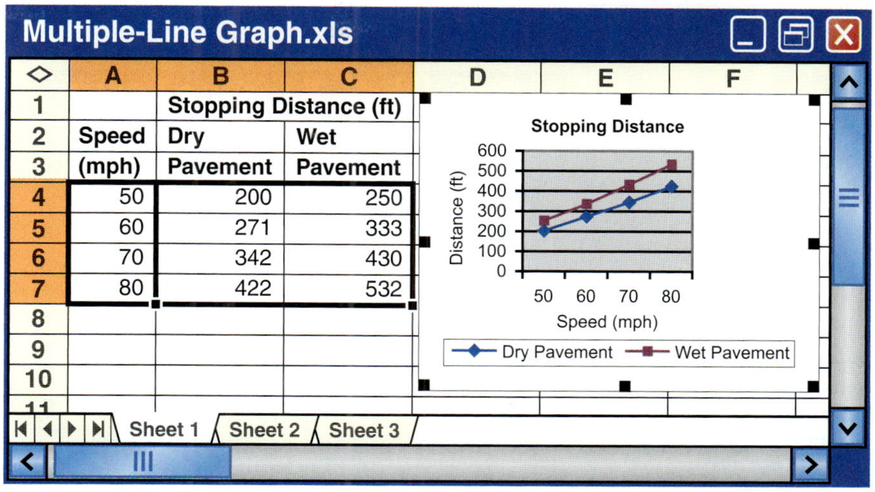

ACTIVITY

2 Use the same data to make a multiple-bar graph.

- Highlight the data in columns B and C, from B2 through C6.
- Click on the Chart Wizard icon.
- Click on Column and Next to choose the vertical bar graph.
- Complete steps 4–8 from Activity 1.

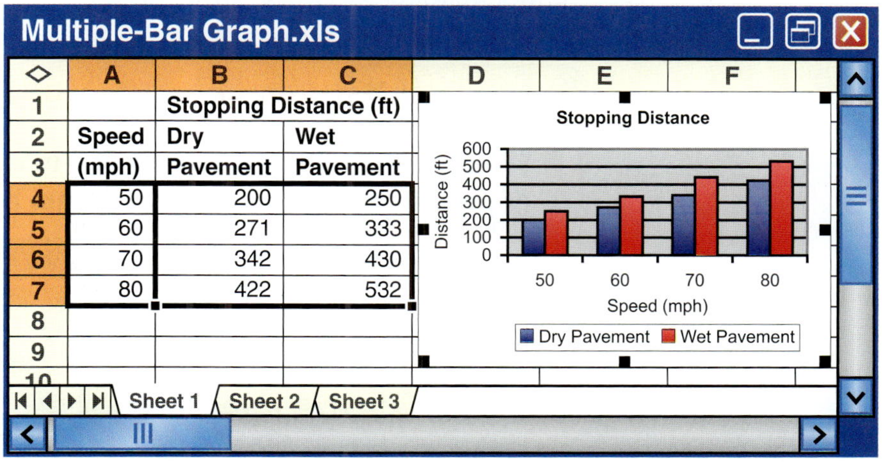

ANALYZE THE RESULTS

1. Explain the steps you would take to make a multiple-line graph of the stopping distances that include the speeds 55, 65, and 75.
2. **COLLECT THE DATA** Collect two sets of data that represent the number of boys and the number of girls in your class born in the Spring, Summer, Fall, and Winter. Use a spreadsheet to make a multiple-line or -bar graph of the data. Justify your selection.

9-8 Select an Appropriate Display

Main IDEA

Select an appropriate display for a set of data.

Targeted TEKS 7.11 The student understands that the way a set of data is displayed influences its interpretation. **(A) select and use an appropriate representation for presenting and displaying relationships among collected data, including line plot, line graph, bar graph, stem and leaf plot, circle graph, and Venn diagrams, and justify the selection.**

GET READY for the Lesson

CELL PHONES The displays at the right show the results of a survey in which teenagers were asked how many minutes they use their cell phone in one week.

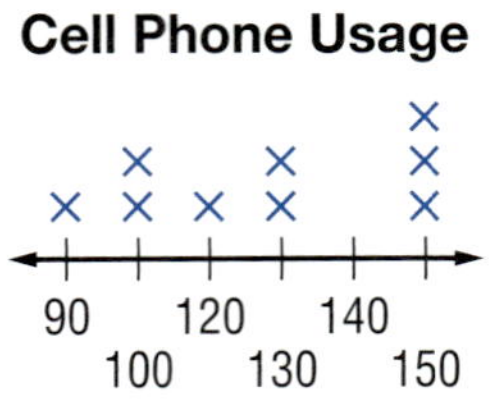

1. Which display shows who uses 150 minutes weekly?
2. Which display allows you to easily find the range?
3. Does either display show the percent of those surveyed who use 130 minutes? If not, which display could you use to display this data?

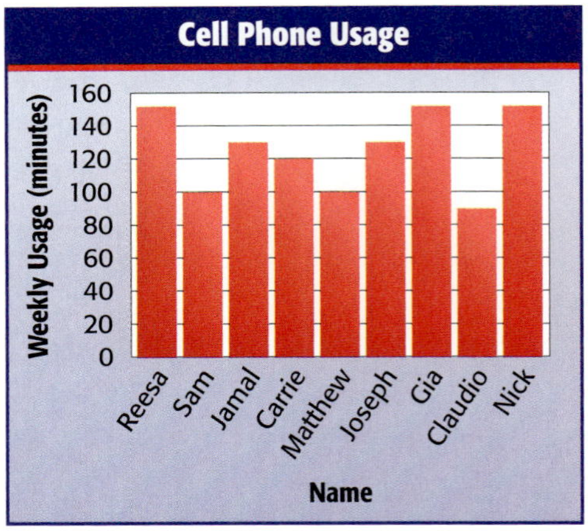

Some displays are more appropriate than others.

EXAMPLE Select an Appropriate Display

1 **SPORTS Which display allows you to easily see that the number of points scored by a volleyball team has been increasing?**

Points Scored

Stem	Leaf
1	7 8 9
2	0 2 2 3 5

1 | 7 = 17 points

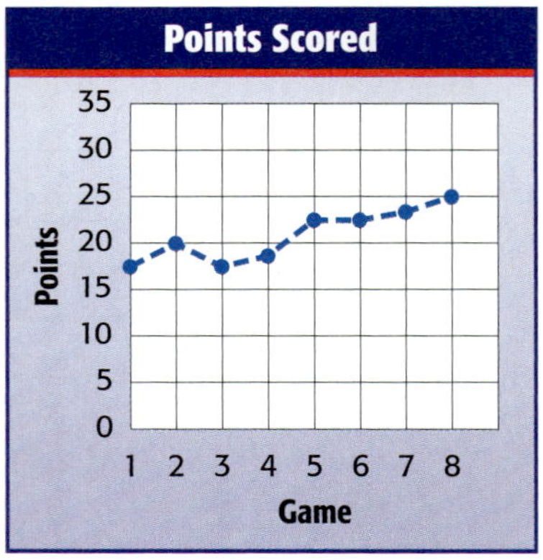

The line graph clearly shows that the number of points scored from game to game has been increasing.

CHECK Your Progress

a. **SPORTS** Which display allows you to easily see the greatest number of points scored?

Online Personal Tutor at tx.msmath2.com

Some ways of displaying data are more appropriate than others. When deciding on what type of display to use, ask the following questions.

- What type of data do you want to display?
- What should the graph or display show?

CONCEPT Summary — **Statistical Displays**

Display	Use
Bar Graph	shows the number of items in specific categories
Circle Graph	compares parts of the data to the whole
Histogram	shows frequency of data divided into equal intervals
Line Graph	shows change over a period of time
Line Plot	shows how many times each number occurs in the data
Stem-and-Leaf Plot	lists all individual numerical data in a condensed form
Venn Diagram	shows how two or more sets of data are related

Real-World Link The U.S. soap, bath and shower market totaled some $1.6 billion in 2004.

Source: *Mintel International Group*

EXAMPLE Select an Appropriate Display

2 **MARKETING** **A marketing company conducted a survey to determine what percent of those surveyed prefer bar soap to other types of hand soap. The table shows the results. Select an appropriate display for the data. Then make the display.**

Favorite Type of Hand Soap

Type of Soap	Responses
Bar	12
Liquid	29
Foam	9

If the company wants to show the specific numbers, a bar graph would be appropriate. However, the company wants to show how each part is related to the whole. So, a circle graph is best.

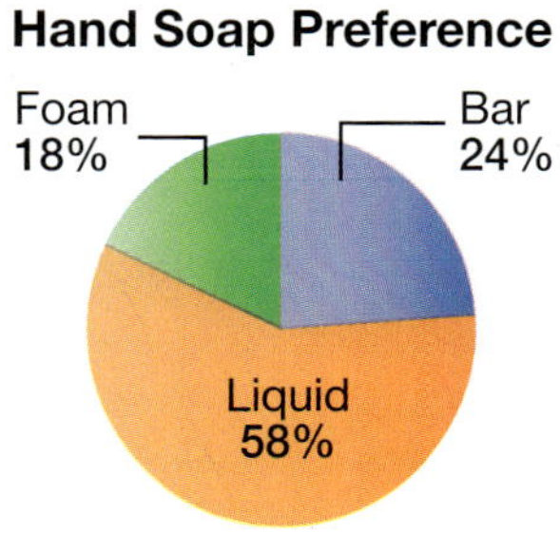

CHECK Your Progress

Select an appropriate display for each set of data. Then make the display.

b. **Hair Stylist's Daily Clients**

Clients per hour	Frequency
1–2	12
3–4	8
5–6	1

c. **Science Report Scores**

80	89	95	91
79	92	95	80
89	90	87	85

CHECK Your Understanding

Example 1 (p. 484)

1. Select an appropriate display for the number of siblings for each student in a classroom.

Examples 2 (p. 485)

Select an appropriate display for each set of data. Then make the display.

2.

Monthly Car Sales	
Month	**Number Sold**
January	10
February	8
March	12
April	25
May	31

3.

Decorating a Parade Float	
Number of Volunteers	**Completion Time (h)**
75	2
68	3
60	4
53	5

Exercises

HOMEWORK HELP	
For Exercises	See Examples
4–5	1
6–9	1, 2

Select an appropriate display for each situation.

4. the favorite dinner food of the seventh grade students
5. the portions of a piece of farm land used for planting various types of crops

Select an appropriate display for each situation. Then make the display.

6.

Ice Cream Cone Sales					
25	35	30	45	29	36
20	40	22	44	20	40
23	50	26	42	31	42
27	28	29	40	34	38
26	29	30	30	35	33

7.

Student Characteristics	
Name Begins with B	**Birthday in April**
Bret	Ashanti
Breanne	Blake
Bianca	Bret
Blake	Judie

8.

Daily Low Temperatures	
Day	**Temp. (°F)**
Monday	55
Tuesday	58
Wednesday	60
Thursday	58
Friday	65

9.

Favorite Color	
Color	**Number of Students**
Blue	18
Red	22
Green	14
Yellow	20

EXTRA PRACTICE
See pages 741, 763.
Math Online
Self-Check Quiz at tx.msmath2.com

10. **LAKES** The circle graph shows the approximate percent of the total volume each of the Great Lakes holds. Display the data using another type of display. Then write a convincing argument telling which display is most appropriate.

The Great Lakes

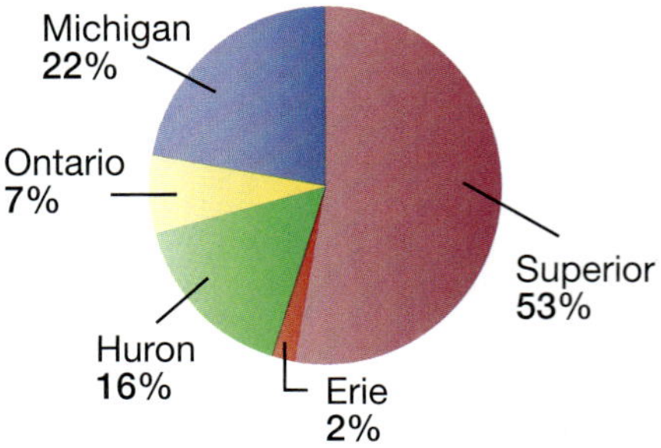

H.O.T. Problems

11. **OPEN ENDED** Give an example of a data set that would be best represented in a line graph.

12. **CHALLENGE** Which display(s) allows you to easily determine the range of the data set? Explain your reasoning.

13. **WRITING IN MATH** Explain when you would use a bar graph to display a set of data and when you would use a line graph.

TEST PRACTICE

14. Which type of display would allow you to easily see the relationship between the data in the table?

Fiction	Missy, Fran, Dwayne, Robin, Julie, Alma, Lakita
Mystery	Dwayne, Andrea, Alonso, Robin, Lakita, Fran, Takara

A line graph

B Venn diagram

C bar graph

D scatter plot

15. Which of the following situations involve data that are best displayed in a bar graph?

F A store's profit over the past month

G The test scores of 30 students in Mr. Thomas' math class.

H The size in square miles of each of the world's oceans.

J How much time students study for a test and their respective test scores.

Spiral Review

16. **HEALTH** Use the scatter plot at the right to predict the height of a 16-year-old. (Lesson 9-7)

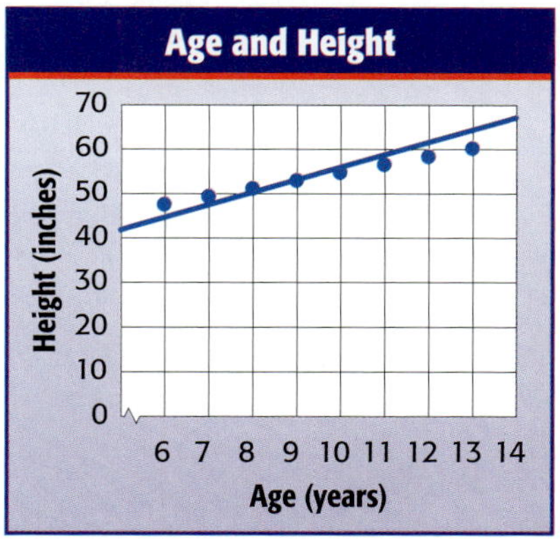

Draw a Venn diagram that represents each situation. (Lesson 9-5)

17. The factors of 20 are 1, 2, 4, 5, 10, and 20. The factors of 36 are 1, 2, 3, 4, 6, 9, 12, 18, and 36.

18. Of 16 flowers, 8 are yellow only, 5 are red only, and 3 are both yellow and red.

Find the percent of each number. (Lesson 8-1)

19. 30% of 80

20. 17% of 100

21. 75% of 120

GET READY for the Next Lesson

PREREQUISITE SKILL **Determine whether each statement is *true* or *false*.** (Lesson 9-7)

22. The vertical scale on a line graph must have equal intervals.

23. You do not need to label the axes of a line graph.

9-9 Misleading Statistics

Main IDEA

Recognize when statistics and graphs are misleading.

Targeted TEKS 7.11 The student understands that the way a set of data is displayed influences its interpretation. **(B) make inferences and convincing arguments based on an analysis of given or collected data.** *Also addresses TEKS 7.12(B), 7.13(A).*

GET READY for the Lesson

TRANSPORTATION A graph like the one at the right appeared in a brochure describing various modes of transportation.

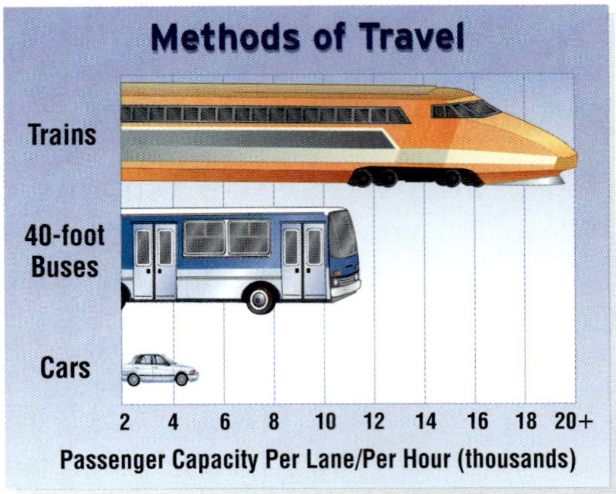

1. About how many more passengers per lane can a 40-foot bus transport in an hour than a car can transport?
2. Is the bus on the graph twice as large as the car? Explain.
3. Do you think the graph appeared in a brochure for a train/bus transit company or for a car company? What makes you think so?

Graphs let readers analyze and interpret data easily, but are sometimes drawn to influence conclusions by misrepresenting the data.

EXAMPLE Drawing Conclusions from Graphs

1 PETS Which graph below suggests that, in 2004, people spent more than twice the amount they spent in 1998? Is this a valid conclusion? Explain.

Graph A

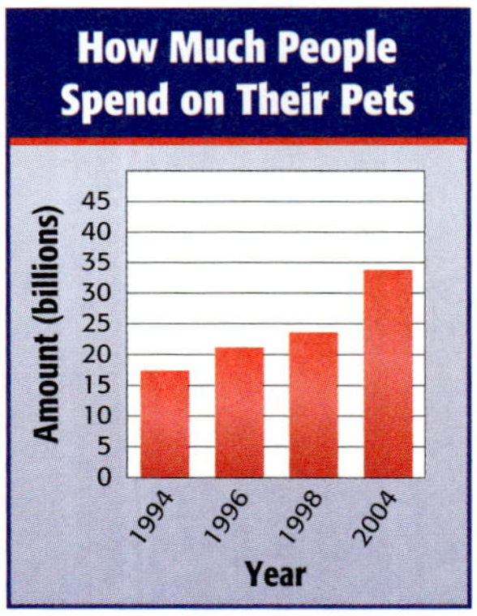

Graph B

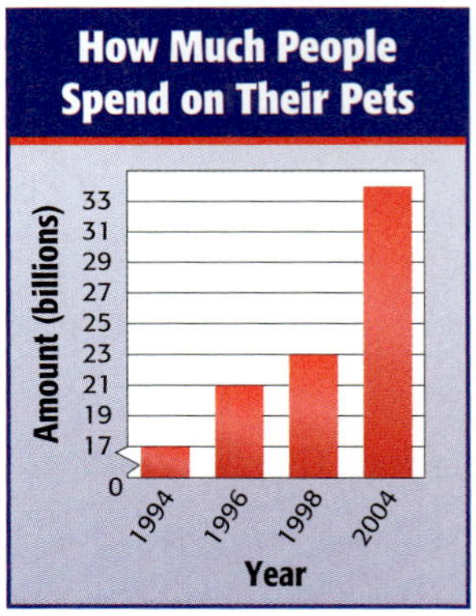

In Graph B, the lengths of the bars indicate that, in 2004, people spent more than twice the amount they spent in 1998. However, the amount spent in 2004, $34 billion, is not more than twice the amount spent in 1998, $23 billion.

A break in the scale in Graph B is a reminder that the scale had been compressed.

CHECK Your Progress

a. **TELEVISION** Both bar graphs show the percent of viewers that watch network television. Which graph makes it appear that the number of viewers is decreasing rapidly? Is this a valid conclusion? Explain.

Graph A

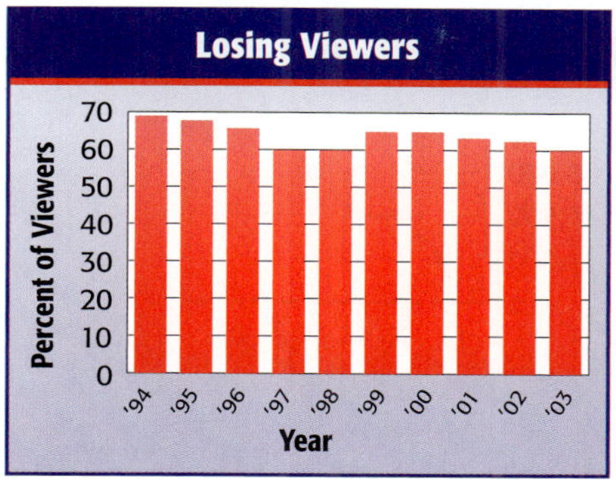

Graph B

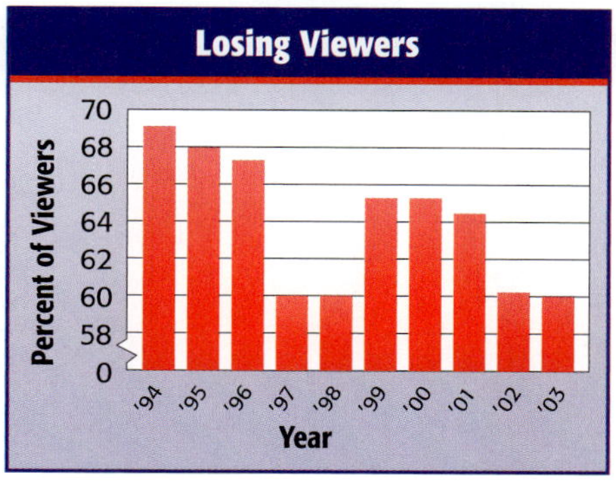

Online Personal Tutor at tx.msmath2.com

The use of different scales can influence conclusions drawn from graphs.

EXAMPLE Changing the Interval of Graphs

2 **SCHOOL DANCES** **The graphs show how the price of spring dance tickets increased.**

Graph A

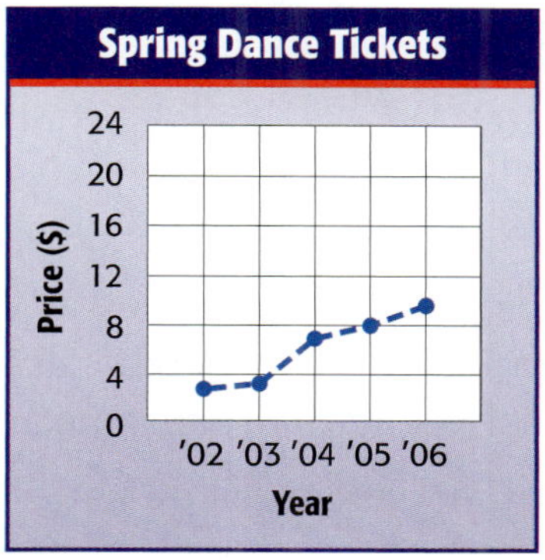

Graph B

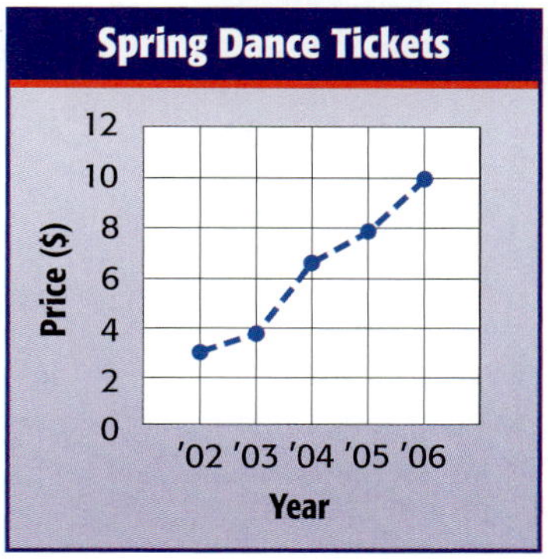

Do the graphs show the same data? If so, explain how they differ. The graphs show the same data. However, the graphs differ in that, on the vertical axis, Graph A uses an interval of 4, and Graph B uses an interval of 2.

Which graph makes it appear that the prices increased more rapidly? Graph B makes it appear that the prices increased more rapidly even though the price increase is the same.

Which graph might the student council use to show that while ticket prices have risen, the increase is not significant? Explain. They might use Graph A. The scale used on the vertical axis of this graph makes the increase appear less significant.

STUDY TIP

Changing Scales To emphasize a change over time, reduce the scale interval on the vertical axis.

CHECK Your Progress

b. **BUSINESS** The line graphs show monthly profits of a company from October to March. Which graph suggests that the business is extremely profitable? Is this a valid conclusion? Explain.

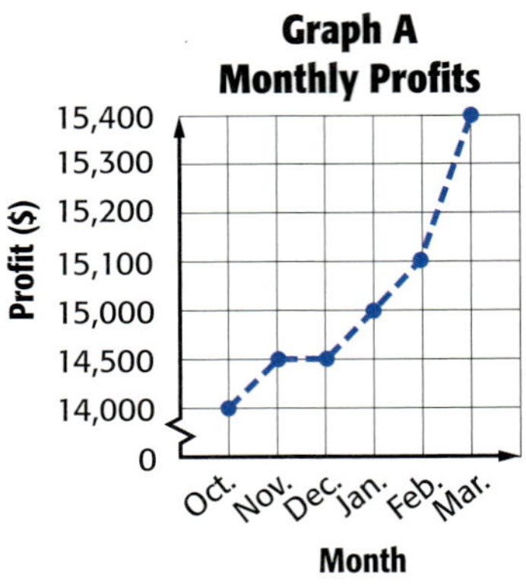

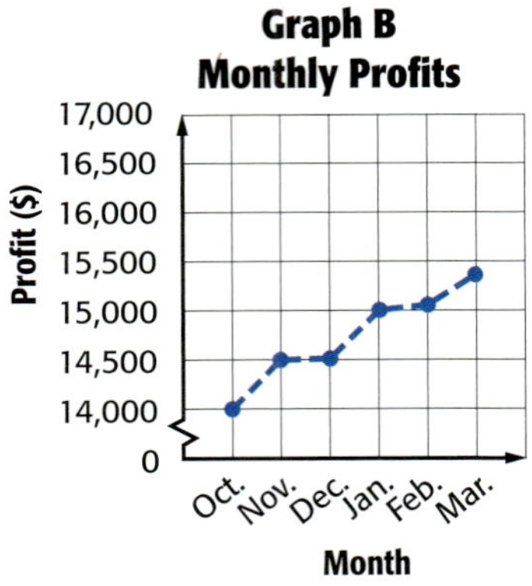

Statistics can also be used to influence conclusions.

EXAMPLE Misleading Statistics

3 MARKETING An amusement park boasts that the average height of their roller coasters is 170 feet. Explain how this is misleading.

Park Rollercoaster Heights	
Coaster	**Height (ft)**
Viper	109
Monster	135
Red Zip	115
Tornado	365
Riptide	126

mean: $\frac{109 + 135 + 115 + 365 + 126}{5} = \frac{850}{5}$

$= 170$

median: 109, 115, 126, 135, 365

mode: none

The average used by the park was the mean. This measure is much greater than most of the heights listed because of the outlier, 365 feet. So, it is misleading to use this measure to attract visitors.

A more appropriate measure to describe the data would be the median, 126 feet, which is closer to the height of most of the coasters.

Real-World Link
The tallest roller coaster in the world is the Kingda Ka in Jackson, New Jersey, with a height of 456 feet.
Source: ultimaterollercoaster.com

CHECK Your Progress

c. **SALARY** ABC Corporation claims the average salary for its employees is more than \$60,000, while the average salary at XYZ Incorporated is only \$25,000. Use the table to explain their reasoning and determine where you would prefer to work.

Position	Salary ($)	
	ABC Corp.	XYZ Inc.
President	500,000	120,000
1st Vice President	400,000	85,000
2nd Vice President	240,000	75,000
Sales Staff (5)	20,000	40,000
Supporting Staff (2)	15,000	25,000
Catalog Staff (7)	9,000	22,500

CHECK Your Understanding

Examples 1, 2
(pp. 488–490)

1. **BASEBALL** Refer to the graphs below. Which graph suggests that Hank Aaron hit four times as many home runs as Willie Mayes? Is this a valid conclusion? Explain.

Graph A

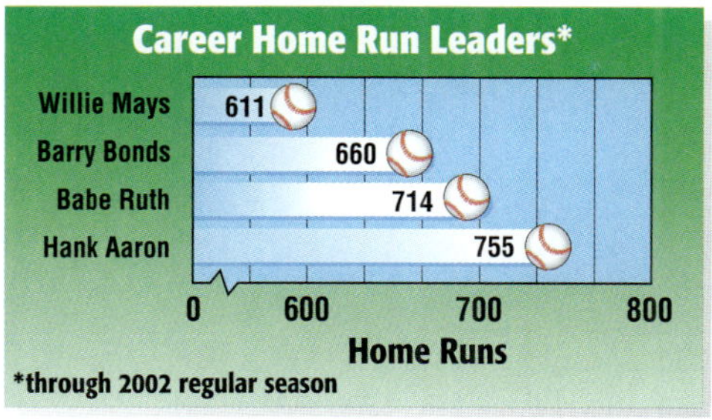

Graph B

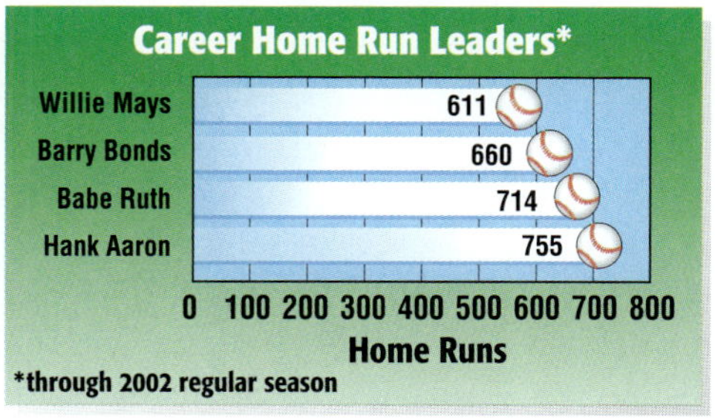

Example 3
(p. 490)

2. **TUNNELS** The table lists the five largest land vehicle tunnels in the U.S. Write a convincing argument for which measure of central tendency you would use to emphasize the average length of the tunnels.

U.S. Vehicle Tunnels on Land

Name	Length (ft)
Anton Anderson Memorial	13,300
E. Johnson Memorial	8,959
Eisenhower Memorial	8,941
Allegheny	6,072
Liberty Tubes	5,920

Source: Federal Highway Association

Exercises

HOMEWORK HELP

For Exercises	See Examples
3, 6–9	1, 2
4–5	3

3. **UTILITIES** The line graph shows the monthly electric bill for the condominium that Toshiko is interested in renting. Why is the graph misleading?

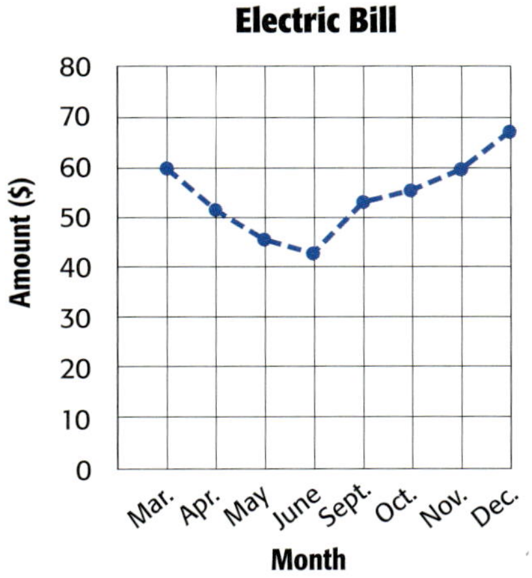

TRAVEL For Exercises 4 and 5, use the table.

4. Find the mean, median, and mode of the data. Which measure might be misleading in describing the average annual number of visitors that visit these sights? Explain.

5. Which measure would be best if you wanted a value close to the most number of visitors? Explain.

Annual Sight-Seeing Visitors

Sight	Visitors*
Cape Cod	4,600,000
Grand Canyon	4,500,000
Lincoln Memorial	4,000,000
Castle Clinton	4,600,000
Smoky Mountains	10,200,000

Source: *The World Almamac*
*Approximation

6. **STOCK** The graphs below show the increases and decreases in the monthly closing prices of Skateboard Depot's stock.

Graph A

Graph B

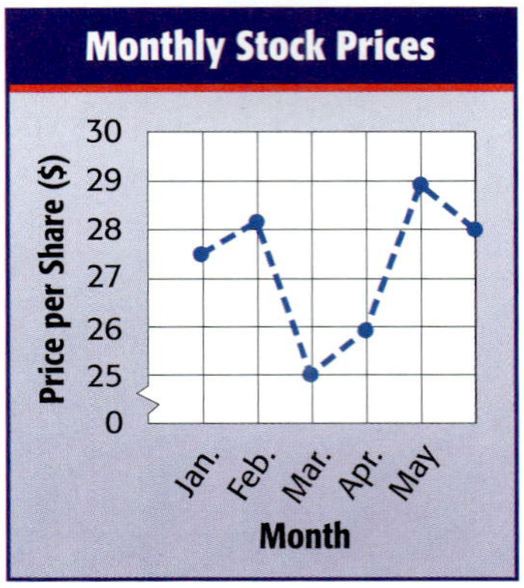

Suppose you are a stockbroker and want to show a customer that the price of the stock has been fairly stable since January. Write a convincing argument as to which graph you should show the customer.

MONEY For Exercises 7–9, use the graph that shows the cost of two cameras.

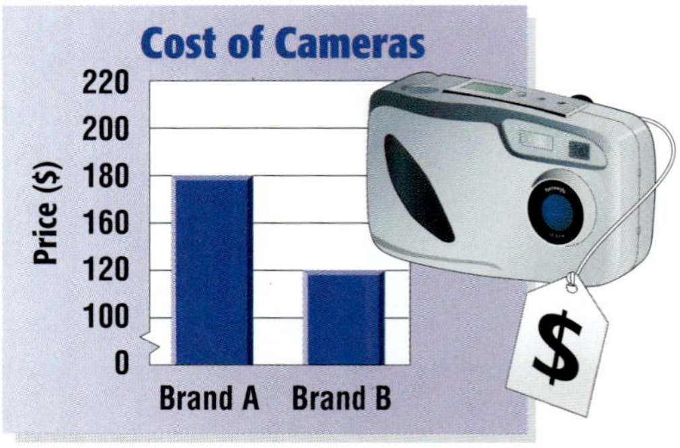

7. Based on the size of the bars, compare the costs of Brand A and Brand B.
8. Explain how this graph may be misleading.
9. Redraw the graph to show that Brand A and Brand B cost about the same.

GEOGRAPHY For Exercises 10–13, use the table that shows the sizes of the Caribbean Islands.

Caribbean Islands

Island	Area (sq mi)	Island	Area (sq mi)
Antigua	108	Martinique	425
Aruba	75	Puerto Rico	3,339
Barbados	166	Tobago	116
Curacao	171	Virgin Islands, UK	59
Dominica	290	Virgin Islands, U.S.	134

Source: U.S. Census Bureau

10. Find the mean, mode, and median of the data.
11. Which average would be misleading in describing the size of the islands? Explain your reasoning.
12. Which average would most accurately describe the data?
13. A travel agent tells you that most of the Caribbean islands are about 490 square miles in size. Which average is the agent using and is this average misleading? Explain your reasoning.

EXTRA PRACTICE
See pages 741, 763.
Math Online
Self-Check Quiz at tx.msmath2.com

H.O.T. Problems

14. **CHALLENGE** Does adding values that are much greater or much less than the other values in a set of data affect the median of the set? Give an example to support your answer.

15. **OPEN ENDED** Create a misleading graph given the following bowling scores. game 1: 134, game 2: 125, game 3: 150, and game 4: 160.

16. **WRITING IN MATH** Describe at least two ways in which the presentation of data can be misleading.

TEST PRACTICE

17. The bar graph shows the average number of hours each week that a group of students attend an extracurricular activity after school.

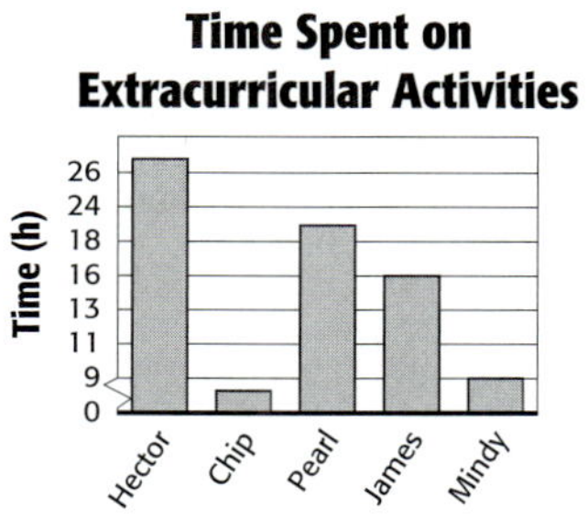

Which statement best tells why the graph may be misleading if you want to use the graph to compare the number of hours the students attend an extracurricular activity?

A The vertical scale should show days instead of hours.

B The graph does not show which activity each person attended.

C The intervals on the vertical scale are inconsistent.

D The graph's title is misleading.

18. A department store surveyed 100 teenagers about their preferred style of jeans. The table shows the results.

Survey Results	
Style of Jeans	**Number of Teenagers**
Boot Cut	22
Low Rise	45
Slouch	28
Relaxed	5

The store uses these survey results to order jeans. Which conclusion best reflects the data collected?

F Less than half of the order should be low rise jeans.

G About one fifth of the order should be relaxed fit jeans.

H Forty percent of the jeans ordered should be slouch jeans.

J About half of the jeans ordered should be boot cut jeans.

Spiral Review

19. Which graph would you use to display data that show change over a period of time? (Lesson 9-8)

20. **SNACKS** Refer to the graph that shows a grocery store's sales of salty snacks like potato chips and pretzels. If the trend continues, about what will be the sales in September? (Lesson 9-7)

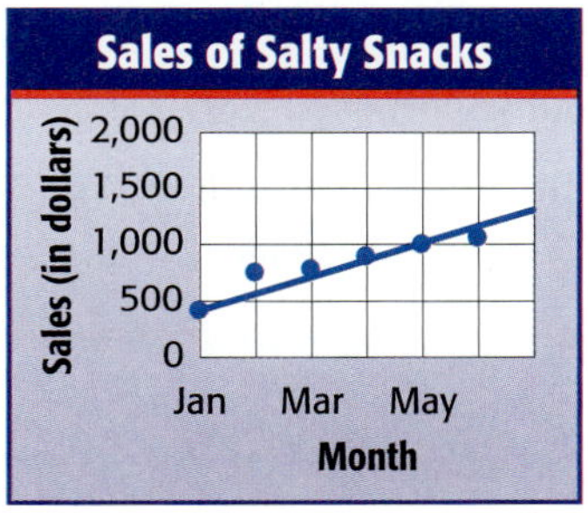

CHAPTER 9

Study Guide and Review

STUDY TO GO Download Vocabulary Review from tx.msmath2.com

FOLDABLES™ Study Organizer

GET READY to Study

Be sure the following Key Concepts are noted in your Foldable.

Key Concepts

Mean (Lesson 9-2)

- The mean of a set of data is the sum of the data divided by the number of items in a data set.

Median (Lesson 9-2)

- The median of a set of data is the middle number of the ordered data, or the mean of the middle two numbers.

Mode (Lesson 9-2)

- The mode or modes of a set of data is the number or numbers that occur most often.

Statistical Displays (Lessons 9-1, 9-3 through 9-9)

- Line plots show how many times each number occurs in a data set.
- Stem-and-leaf plots list all individual numerical data in a condensed form.
- Bar graphs show the number of items in specific categories.
- Histograms show the frequency of data divided into smaller intervals.
- Venn diagrams show how two or more sets of data are related.
- Circle graphs compare parts of the data to the whole.
- Line graphs show change over a period of time.
- Scatter plots determine if there is a relationship between two sets of data.

Key Vocabulary

analyze (p. 443)
bar graph (p. 461)
cluster (p. 443)
data (p. 442)
histogram (p. 462)
inferences (p. 457)
leaf (p. 456)
line graph (p. 476)
line plot (p. 442)
mean (p. 448)
measures of central tendency (p. 448)
median (p. 449)
mode (p. 449)
outlier (p. 443)
range (p. 443)
scatter plot (p. 477)
statistics (p. 442)
stem (p. 456)
stem-and-leaf plot (p. 456)
Venn diagram (p. 469)

Vocabulary Check

State whether each sentence is *true* or *false*. If *false*, replace the underlined word or number to make a true sentence.

1. The range is the difference between the greatest and the least values in a set of data.
2. The mode divides a set of data in half.
3. A graph that uses bars to make comparisons is a bar graph.
4. A scatter plot shows two sets of related data.
5. The median is a data value that is quite separated from the rest of the data.
6. The mean is the arithmetic average of a set of data.
7. The number or item that appears most often in a set of data is the mode.
8. The range is the middle number in a set of ordered data, or the mean of the middle two numbers.

Lesson-by-Lesson Review

9-1 Line Plots (pp. 442–447)

Display each set of data in a line plot. Identify any clusters, gaps, or outliers.

9. 10°, 12°, 10°, 8°, 13°, 10°, 8°, 12°.
10. 7 ft, 8 ft, 8 ft , 9 ft, 14 ft, 9 ft, 8 ft, 7 ft
11. Number of Calories: 43, 41, 42, 45, 43, 42, 43, 46, 44, 44

Example 1 **Display the test scores 72, 75, 72, 74, 73, 68, 73, 74, 74, 75, and 73 in a line plot. Identify any clusters, gaps, or outliers.**

Test Scores

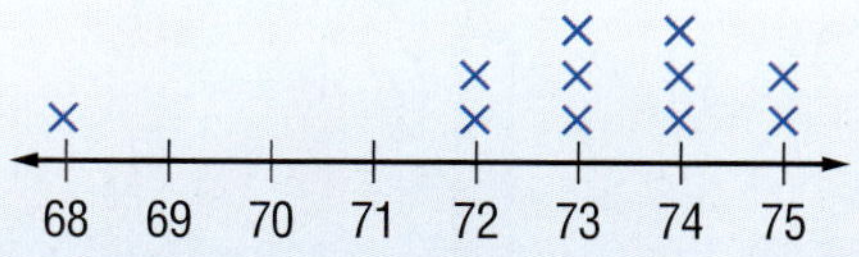

There is a cluster from 72 to 75, a gap between 68 and 72, and an outlier at 68.

9-2 Measures of Central Tendency and Range (pp. 448–454)

Find the mean, median, and mode. Round to the nearest tenth if necessary.

12. Number of siblings: 2, 3, 4, 3, 4, 3, 8, 7, 2
13. 89°, 76°, 93°, 100°, 72°, 86°, 74°
14. **MONEY** Which measure, mean, median, mode, or range best represents the amount of money students spent on clothing?

Money Spent ($)			
125	108	172	136
121	112	218	172

Example 2 **Find the mean, median, and mode for the following college students' ages: 23, 22, 19, 19, and 20.**

mean: $\frac{23 + 22 + 19 + 19 + 20}{5}$ or 20.6 years

median: 20, the middle value of the ordered set

mode: 19, the data value that occurs most often

9-3 Stem-and-Leaf Plots (pp. 456–460)

Display each set of data using a stem-and-leaf plot.

15. Hours worked: 29, 54, 31, 26, 38, 46, 23, 21, 32, 37
16. Number of points: 75, 83, 78, 85, 87, 92, 78, 53, 87, 89, 91
17. Birthdates: 9, 5, 12, 21, 18, 7, 16, 24, 11, 10, 3, 14

Example 3 **Display the number of pages read 12, 15, 17, 20, 22, 22, 23, 25, 27, and 35 in a stem-and-leaf plot.**

The tens digits form the stems, and the ones digits form the leaves.

Pages Read

Stem	Leaf
1	2 5 7
2	0 2 2 3 5 7
3	5

2|3 = 23 pages

9-4 Bar Graphs and Histograms (pp. 461–467)

ATTENDANCE For Exercises 18–20, refer to the graph.

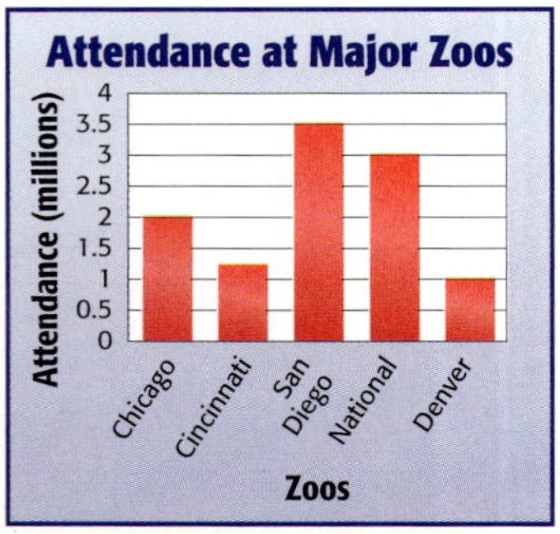

18. Which zoo did the most people attend?
19. About what was the total attendance for all five zoos?
20. Write a statement comparing the attendance at the National Zoo to the attendance at the Denver Zoo.

Example 4 The histogram below shows the heights of students in a classroom.

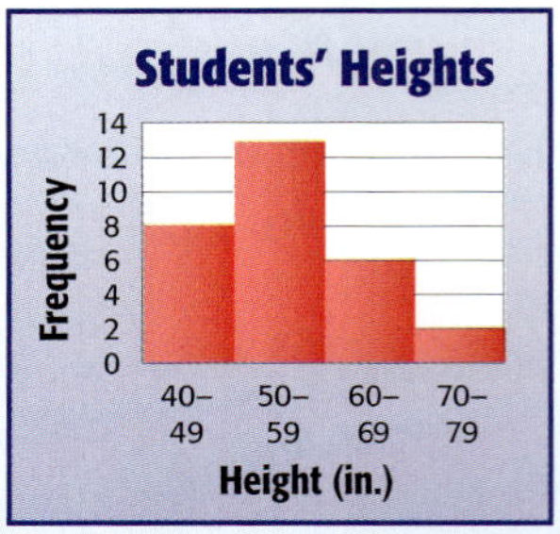

How many students are 50–59 inches tall?

13 students

Write a statement comparing the 70–79 interval to the 60–69 interval.

The 60–69 interval is three times larger than the 70–70 interval.

9-5 Venn Diagrams (pp. 469–472)

For Exercises 21 and 22, use the Venn diagram that shows students' favorite type of cookies.

Cookie Survey Results

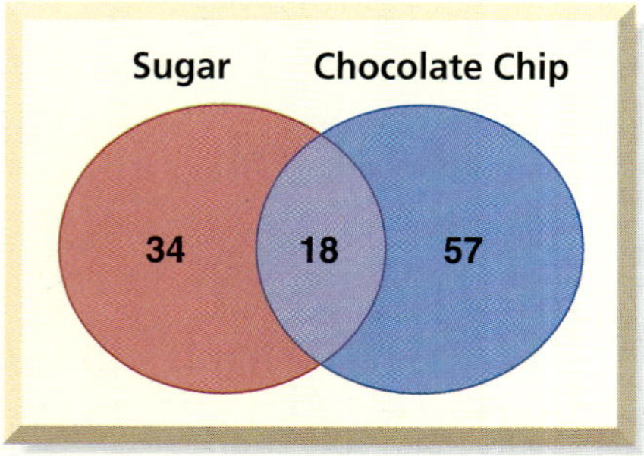

21. How many students only prefer chocolate chip cookies?
22. How many students were surveyed?

Example 5 Logan's Pet Store surveyed 120 residents. The results showed that 38 residents were cat owners, 66 residents were dog owners, and 18 residents owned both types of pets. How many residents owned neither a cat nor a dog?

Pet Ownership

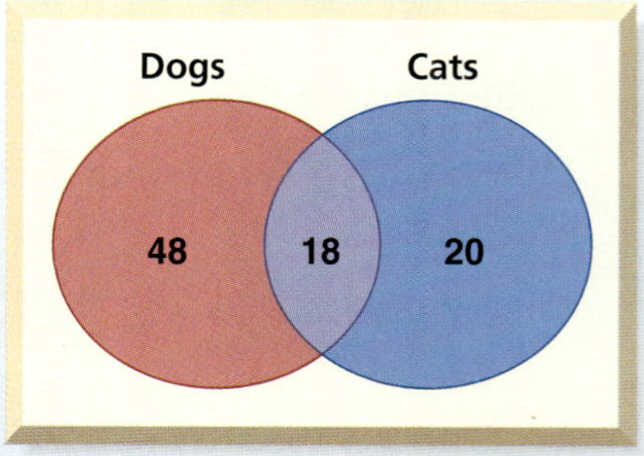

only dogs: $66 - 18 = 48$

only cats: $38 - 18 = 20$

neither dog nor cat: $120 - 48 - 20 - 18 = 34$

So, 34 residents owned neither type of pet.

Mixed Problem Solving
For mixed problem-solving practice, see page 763.

9-6 PSI: Use a Graph (pp. 474–475)

STATUES **For Exercises 23 and 24, use the graph that shows the heights of free-standing statues in the world.**

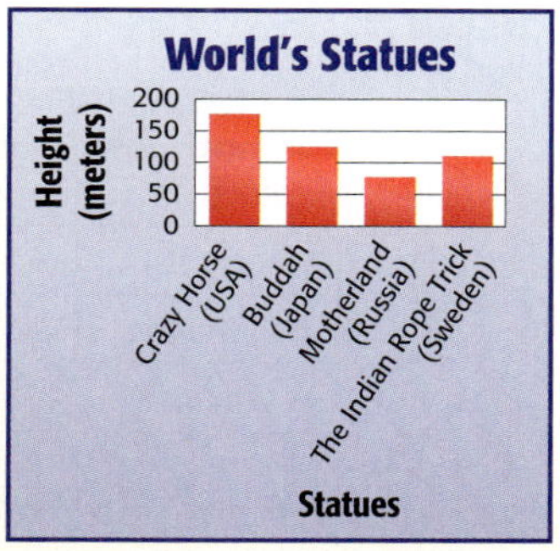

23. Which statue is the tallest?
24. Compare the height of the *Motherland* statue to the height of the *Crazy Horse* statue.

Example 6 **The graph shows the results of a survey about favorite vacation places.**

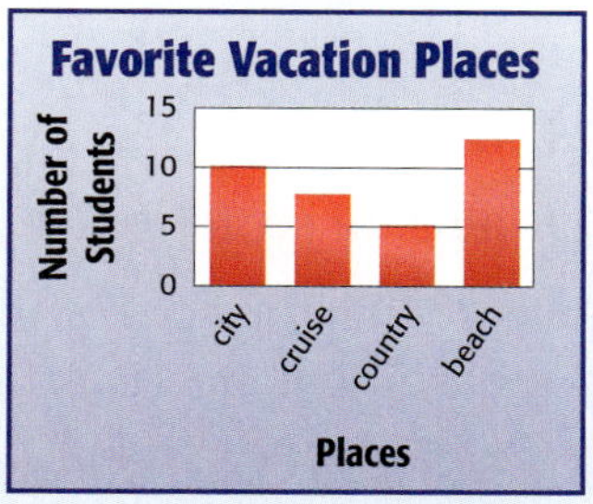

Which place was favored by most students?

The beach was favored by 12 students, which was the greatest number.

9-7 Line Graphs and Scatter Plots (pp. 476–481)

PHONE CALLS **For Exercises 25 and 26, use the graph showing the number of people in a family and the number of weekly calls.**

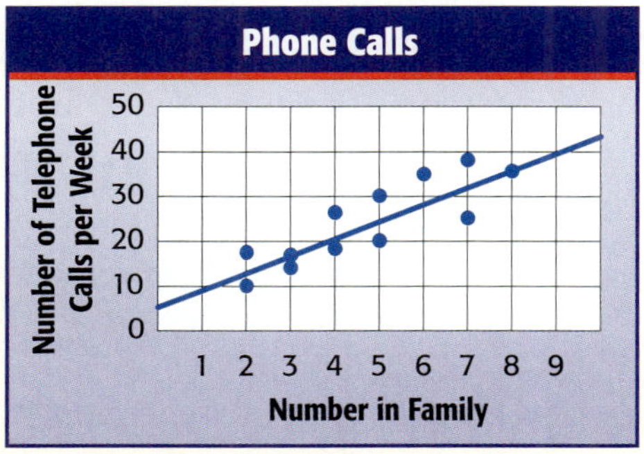

25. Describe the relationship between the two sets of data.
26. Predict the number of weekly phone calls for a family of 10.

Example 7 **The scatter plot below shows the keyboarding speeds in words per minute of 12 students.**

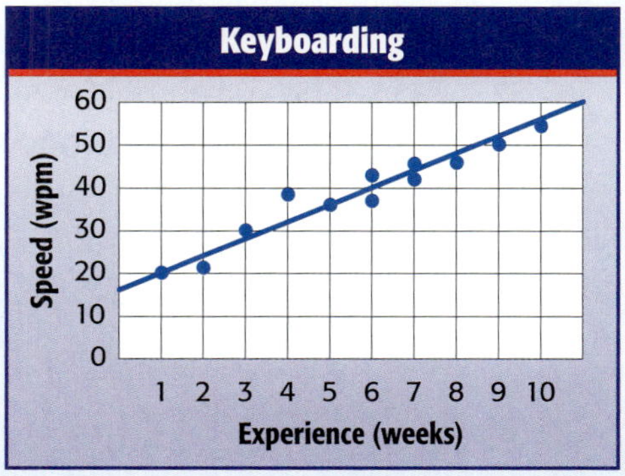

Describe the relationship between the two sets of data.

The graph shows a positive relationship. That is, as the weeks pass, speed increases.

9-8 Select an Appropriate Display (pp. 484–487)

Select an appropriate display for each situation.

27. the attendance at a theme park over 20 years
28. the parts of a family budget
29. a list of scores on an English test
30. the ticket prices of the top 20 money earning concerts arranged by intervals
31. **FRIENDS** Michelle surveyed her friends to find out their interests. Select and make an appropriate display.

Friends' Interests			
Favorite Color is Blue		Favorite Sport is Hockey	
J.T.	Colleen	Roger	Jessie
Miko	Gustavo	John	Shawnel
Julie	John	J.T.	Pam
Pam	Mara	Julie	Jean

Example 8 **Use the table to show the parts of the entire student body in each class. Select and make an appropriate display.**

Students in Each Class	
Seniors	185
Juniors	105
Sophomores	115
Freshman	95

You need to compare one class of students to the entire student body. So, use a circle graph.

Students in Each Class

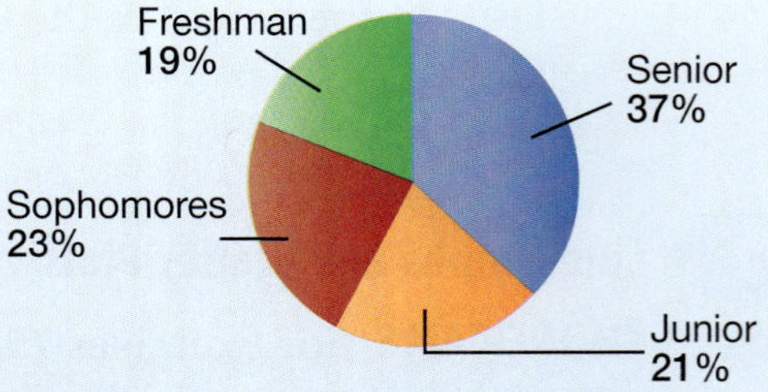

9-9 Misleading Statistics (pp. 488–493)

32. **SALES** The graph below shows the monthly CD sales for one year at the Music Madness Warehouse. Why might the graph be misleading?

Example 9 **The graph shows the pounds of cans recycled in eight weeks. Why might this graph be misleading?**

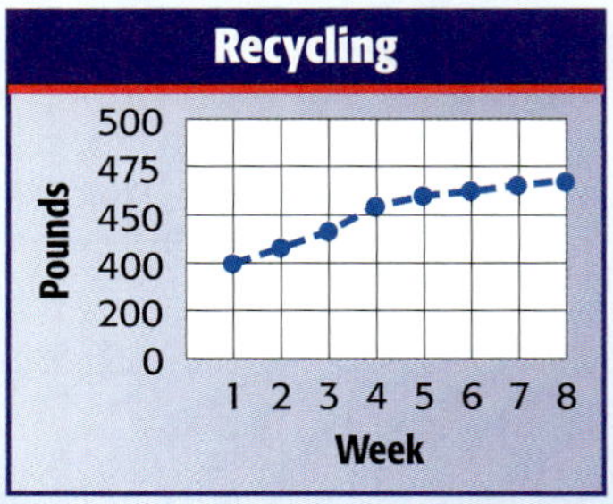

The scale is not divided into equal intervals. It has intervals of 200, 50, and 25.

Chapter 9 Practice Test

For Exercises 1 and 2, use the line plot that shows the number of hours students spend listening to the radio per week.

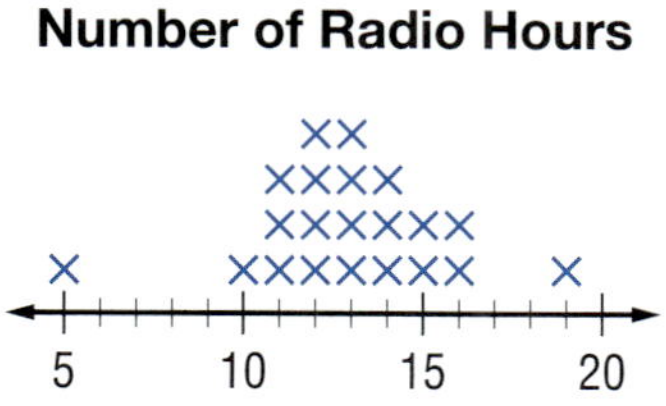

1. Identify any clusters, gaps or outliers.
2. Describe how the range of data would change if 5 was not part of the data set.

Find the mean, median, and mode for each set of data. Round to the nearest tenth if necessary.

3. 12.4 in., 17.9 in., 16.5 in., 10.2 in.
4. \$10, \$12, \$18, \$14, \$12

Display each data set in a stem-and-leaf plot.

5. 37°, 59°, 26°, 42°, 57°, 53°, 31°, 58°
6. \$461, \$422, \$430, \$425, \$425, \$467, \$429
7. **TEST PRACTICE** The graph below shows the type of amusement park rides students enjoy. Which statement is best supported by the data?

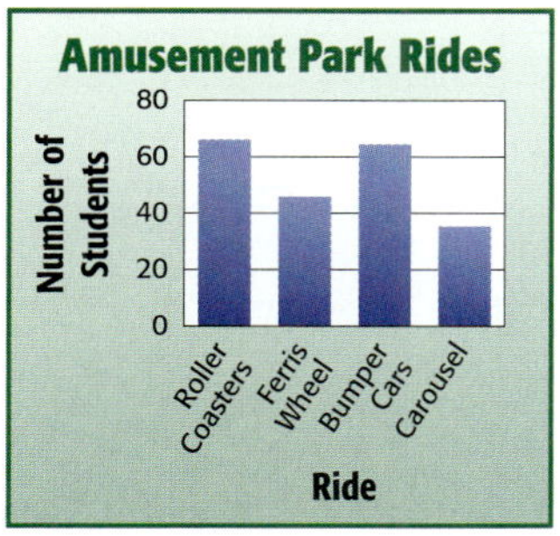

A Twice as many students enjoy riding roller coasters than the carousel.
B The Ferris wheel is liked least.
C Most students enjoy the bumper cars.
D About 50 students like the carousel.

8. **GRADES** Make a histogram for the following French test grades: 95, 76, 82, 90, 83, 76, 79, 82, 95, 85, 93, 81, and 63.

For Exercises 9 and 10, use the table.

Factors of 12	Factors of 18
1, 2, 3, 4, 6, 12	1, 2, 3, 6, 9, 18

9. Draw a Venn diagram of the factors. What are the total number of factors?
10. List the factors that are shared.
11. **EMPLOYMENT** The line graph show the percent of women who had jobs outside the home from 1975 to 2000. Use the graph to predict the number of women who will have jobs outside the home in 2010.

12. **TEST PRACTICE** The line graph shows ship sales at Marvin's Marina in thousands of dollars. Which statement best tells why the graph is misleading?

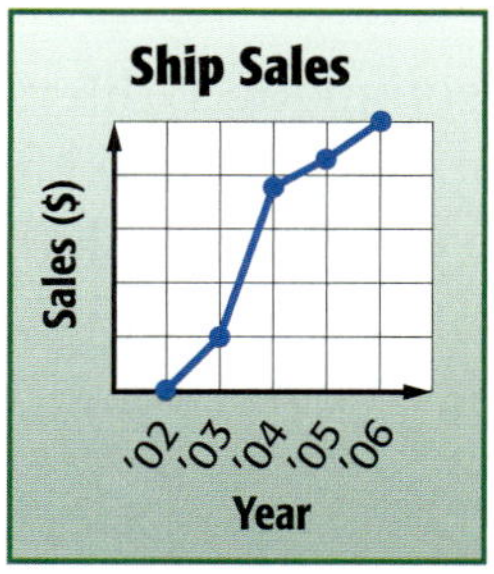

F The graph's title is misleading.
G The intervals on the horizontal scale are inconsistent.
H The graph does not show any data.
J The vertical axis is not labeled.

CHAPTER 9

Texas Test Practice

Cumulative, Chapters 1–9

Read each question. Then fill in the correct answer on the answer document provided by your teacher or on a sheet of paper.

1. Mr. Ed's Used Car Lot bought 5 used cars for $32,000. The business later bought another used car for $4,600. What was the mean cost of all of the used cars?

   A $3,200.00

   B $4,600.00

   C $6,100.00

   D $8,500.00

2. A fitness club charges a membership fee of $50 plus $25 each month you belong to the club. Which expression could be used to find the total cost of belonging to the club for 10 months?

   F $50(10) + 25$

   G $50 - 25(10)$

   H $50 + 25(10)$

   J $50(10) + 25(10)$

3. **GRIDDABLE** Sierra had 11.5 yards of fabric. She wants to use 20% of the fabric to make a flag. Determine the amount of fabric in yards she wants to use.

4. Ms. Thompson made 17 liters of punch for a party. The punch contained 5 liters of orange juice. Which equation could be used to find y, the percent of orange juice in the punch?

   A $\frac{17}{5} = \frac{y}{100}$

   B $\frac{5}{17} = \frac{y}{100}$

   C $\frac{5}{17} = \frac{100}{y}$

   D $\frac{17}{y} = \frac{100}{5}$

5. The table shows the relationship between the outside temperature, x, and a monthly heating bill, y.

Temperature, x (°F)	Heating Bill, y (dollars)
40	65
32	92
20	121
8	145

Which graph best represents the data?

F
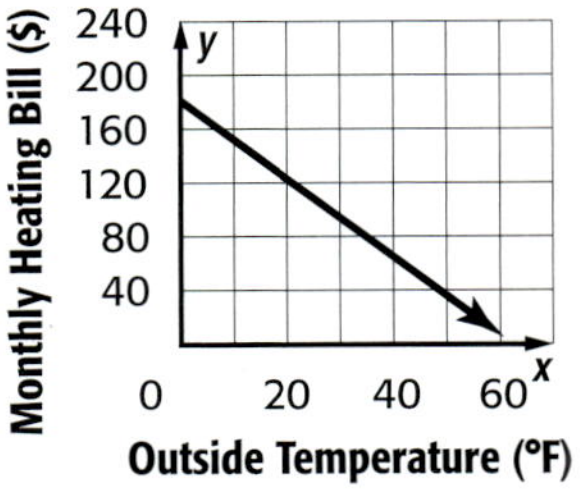

G
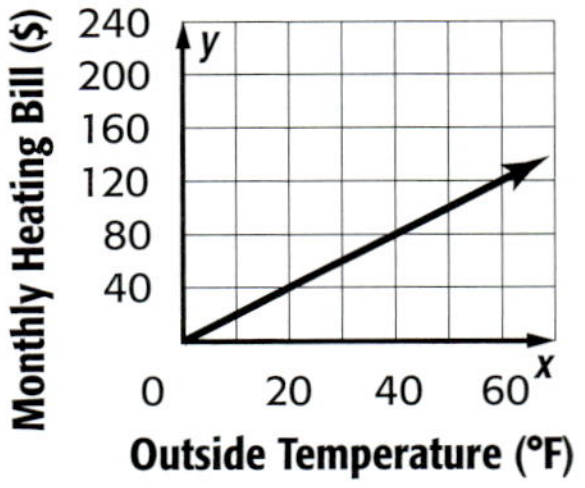

H
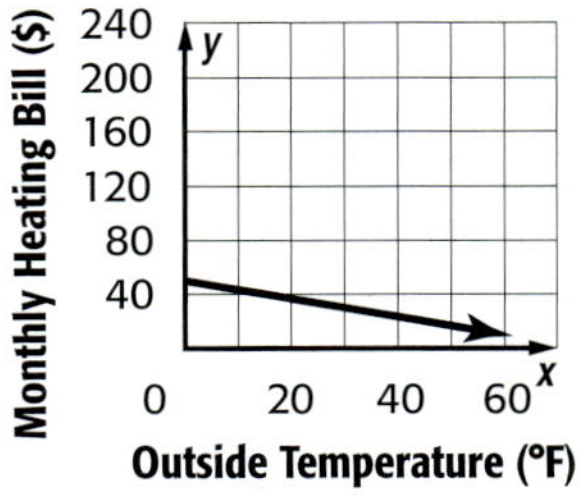

J
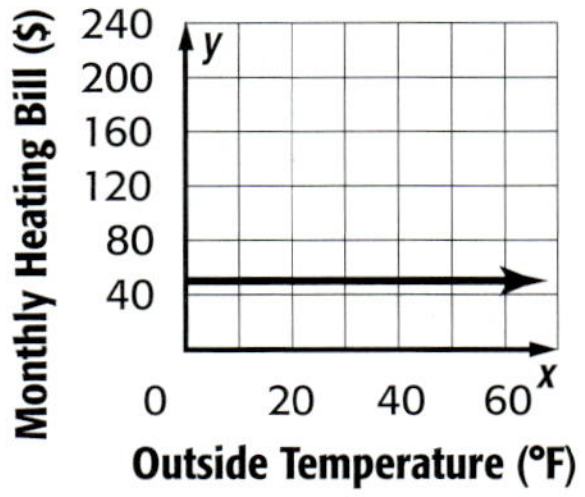

6. A football team scored 20, 32, 28, 21, and 24 points in their first five games. How many points should they score in the next game so that the median and mode scores are equal?

A 32 **C** 21
B 24 **D** 20

7. Which of the following displays gives the most detailed information about each of Kevin's friends and their music preferences?

F

Music Preferences	
Music	**Number of Students**
Rock	7
Rap	7
Hip Hop	7

G **Music Preferences**

H **Music Preferences**

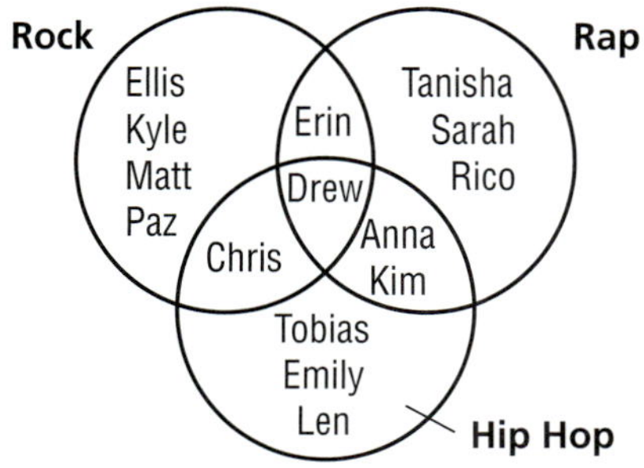

J **Music Preferences**

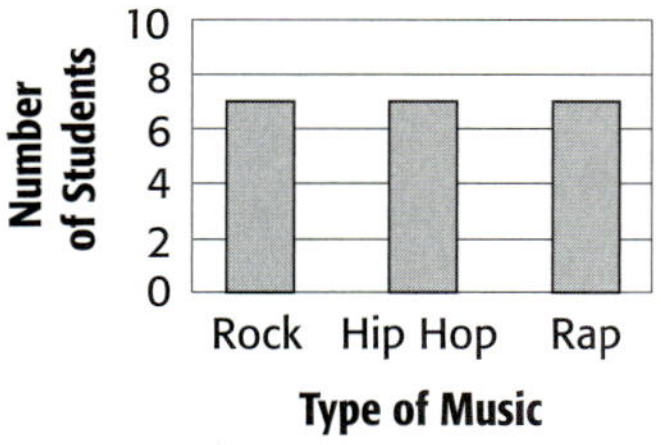

8. Taylor spends between $125 and $200 per month on food. Which is the best estimate of how much she spends on food in 6 months?

A From $1,500 to $2,400
B From $750 to $1,200
C From $250 to $400
D From $125 to $200

9. A store has 2,545 CDs. On Saturday, the store sold $12\frac{1}{2}\%$ of the CDs. What fraction of the CDs were sold on Saturday?

F $\frac{1}{8}$ **H** $\frac{2}{9}$
G $\frac{3}{25}$ **J** $\frac{2}{17}$

TEST-TAKING TIP

Question 10 If you find that you cannot answer every part of an open-ended question, do as much as you can. You may earn partial credit.

Pre-AP

Record your answers on a sheet of paper. Show your work.

10. The table shows how values of a painting increased over ten years.

Year	Value	Year	Value
1997	$350	2002	$1,851
1998	$650	2003	$2,151
1999	$950	2004	$2,451
2000	$1,200	2005	$2,752
2001	$1,551	2006	$3,052

a. Make a line graph of the data.
b. Use the graph to predict what the value of the painting will be in 2010.

NEED EXTRA HELP?										
If You Missed Question...	1	2	3	4	5	6	7	8	9	10
Go to Lesson...	9-2	1-6	8-1	8-2	9-7	9-2	9-8	1-1	5-6	9-7
For Help with Test Objective...	5	6	2	6	6	5	5	1	1	5

CHAPTER 10

Probability

Knowledge and Skills

- Recognize that a physical or mathematical model can be used to describe the experimental and theoretical probability of real-life events. **TEKS 7.10**

Key Vocabulary

composite event (p. 536)
independent event (p. 536)
probability (p. 504)
sample space (p. 509)

Real-World Link

GAMES Rolling number cubes allows you to advance forward or backward in many board games. Probability tells you that rolling doubles on a pair of number cubes happens only about 17% of the time.

FOLDABLES™ Study Organizer

Probability Make this Foldable to help you organize your notes. Begin with five sheets of $8\frac{1}{2}$" by 11" paper.

1. **Stack** five sheets of paper $\frac{3}{4}$ inch apart.

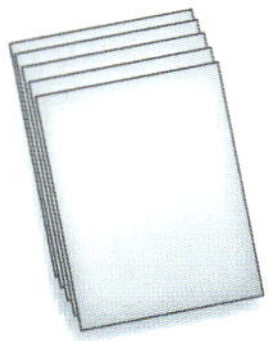

2. **Roll** up bottom edges so that all tabs are the same size.

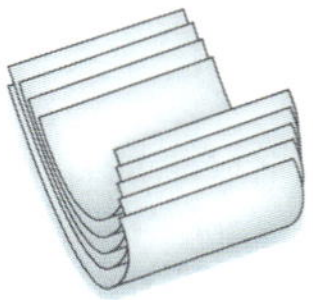

3. **Crease** and staple along the fold.

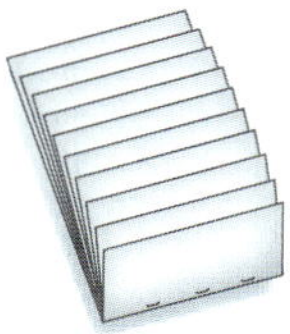

4. **Write** the chapter title on the front. Label each tab with a lesson number and title. Label the last tab *Vocabulary.*

GET READY for Chapter 10

Diagnose Readiness You have two options for checking Prerequisite Skills.

Option 2

Math Online Take the Online Readiness Quiz at tx.msmath2.com.

Option 1

Take the Quick Quiz below. Refer to the Quick Review for help.

QUICK Quiz

Multiply. (Used in Lessons 10-3 and 10-4)

1. 7×15
2. 24×6
3. 13×4
4. 8×21
5. 5×32
6. 30×8
7. $7 \times 6 \times 5$
8. $8 \times 7 \times 6$
9. $6 \times 5 \times 4 \times 3$
10. $4 \times 3 \times 2 \times 1$
11. $10 \times 9 \times 8 \times 7$
12. $11 \times 10 \times 9$
13. **JOBS** If you earn $9 an hour and work 5 hours each day for 7 days, how much have you earned?

Write each fraction in simplest form. Write *simplified* if the fraction is already in simplest form. (Used in Lessons 10-1, 10-7, and 10-8)

14. $\frac{8}{12}$
15. $\frac{3}{18}$
16. $\frac{4}{9}$
17. $\frac{5}{15}$
18. **SLEEP** If the average adult gets 8 hours of sleep, what fraction of the day, in simplest form, is spent asleep?

Find each value. (Used in Lesson 10-5)

19. $\frac{6 \times 5}{3 \times 2}$
20. $\frac{9 \times 8 \times 7}{5 \times 4 \times 3}$
21. $\frac{4 \times 3 \times 2}{3 \times 2 \times 1}$
22. $\frac{7 \times 6 \times 5 \times 4}{4 \times 3 \times 2 \times 1}$

QUICK Review

Example 1 Multiply $7 \times 6 \times 5 \times 4$.

$$7 \times 6 \times 5 \times 4 = 42 \times 5 \times 4$$
$$= 210 \times 4$$
$$= 840$$

Multiply from left to right.

Example 2 Write $\frac{21}{28}$ in simplest form.

$$\frac{21}{28} = \frac{3}{4} \quad (\div 7 \text{ numerator and denominator})$$

Divide the numerator and denominator by the GCF, 7.

Example 3 Find the value of $\frac{6 \times 5 \times 4}{3 \times 2 \times 1}$.

$$\frac{6 \times 5 \times 4}{3 \times 2 \times 1} = \frac{120}{6}$$ ← Multiply the numerator. ← Multiply the denominator.

$$= 20$$ Simplify.

10-1 Simple Events

Main IDEA

Find the probability of a simple event.

Targeted TEKS 7.10 The student recognizes that a physical or mathematical model can be used to describe the experimental and theoretical probability of real-life events. **(A) construct sample spaces for simple** or composite **experiments.**

NEW Vocabulary

outcome
simple event
probability
random
complementary event

READING Math

Probability
P(even number) is read *the probability of rolling an even number.*

GET READY for the Lesson

TAFFY A box of saltwater taffy contains six pieces of each flavor shown at the right.

Saltwater Taffy Flavors	
peppermint	chocolate
grape	raspberry
root beer	orange creme
cherry	vanilla

1. What fraction of the taffy is vanilla? Write in simplest form.
2. Suppose you take one piece of taffy from the box without looking. Are your chances of picking vanilla the same as picking root beer? Explain.

An **outcome** is any one of the possible results of an action. For the action of picking a piece of taffy out of the box described above, there are 48 total outcomes.

A **simple event** is one outcome or a collection of outcomes. For example, picking a piece of vanilla taffy is a simple event. The chance of that event happening is called its **probability**.

KEY CONCEPT — Probability

Words If all outcomes are equally likely, the probability of a simple event is a ratio that compares the number of favorable outcomes to the number of possible outcomes.

Symbols $P(\text{event}) = \dfrac{\text{number of favorable outcomes}}{\text{number of possible outcomes}}$

EXAMPLE Find Probability

1 What is the probability of rolling an even number on a number cube marked with 1, 2, 3, 4, 5, and 6 on its faces?

$$P(\text{even number}) = \frac{\text{even numbers possible}}{\text{total numbers possible}}$$
$$= \frac{3}{6} \text{ or } \frac{1}{2}$$

The probability of rolling an even number is $\frac{1}{2}$ or 50%.

CHECK Your Progress

Use the number cube above to find each probability. Write as a fraction in simplest form.

a. $P(\text{odd number})$ b. $P(5 \text{ or } 6)$ c. $P(\text{prime number})$

Outcomes occur at **random** if each outcome occurs by chance. For example, rolling a number on a number cube occurs at random.

Real-World Link
Parcheesi is derived from the Indian word *pacis*, which means 25.
Source: www.yesterdayland.com

Real-World EXAMPLE

2 PARCHEESI Jewel and her three friends are playing Parcheesi. To decide which player goes first, each player rolls a number cube. The player who rolls the lowest number goes first. If her friends rolled a 4, 3, and 5, what is the probability that Jewel will get to go first?

The possible outcomes of rolling a number cube are 1, 2, 3, 4, 5, and 6. In order for Jewel to go first, she will need to roll a 1 or 2.

Let $P(A)$ be the probability that Jewel will go first.

$$P(A) = \frac{\text{number of favorable outcomes}}{\text{number of possible outcomes}}$$

$$= \frac{2}{6}$$ There are 6 possible outcomes and 2 of them are favorable.

$$= \frac{1}{3}$$ Simplify.

The probability that Jewel will go first is $\frac{1}{3}$, or about 33%.

CHECK Your Progress

MUSIC The table at the right shows the numbers of brass instruments in the Dallas Wind Symphony. Suppose one brass instrument musician is randomly selected to be a featured performer. Find the probability of each event. Write as a fraction in simplest form.

Dallas Wind Symphony Brass Instruments	
Horn	5
Trombone	3
Trumpet	6
Tuba	2

d. P(trumpet)

e. P(brass)

f. P(flute)

g. P(horn or tuba)

Concepts in Motion
BrainPOP® tx.msmath2.com

The probability that an event will happen can be any number from 0 to 1, including 0 and 1, as shown on the number line below.

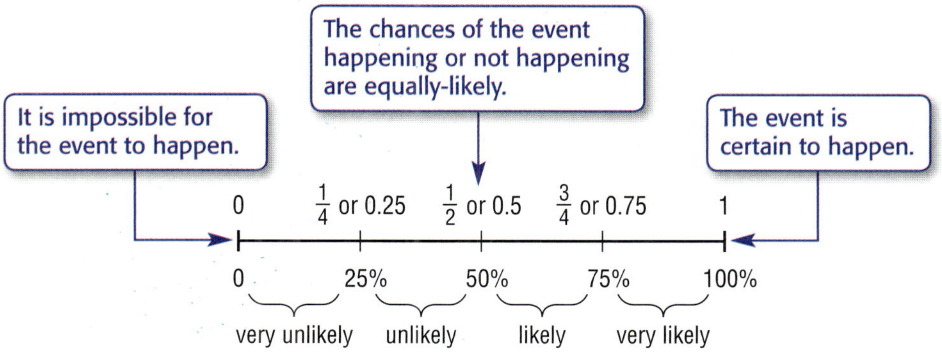

READING Math

Probability
P(not A) is read the probability of the complement of A.

Either Jewel will go first or she will *not* go first. These two events are **complementary events**. The sum of the probabilities of an event and its complement is 1 or 100%. In other words, $P(A) + P(not\ A) = 1$.

EXAMPLE Complementary Events

3 PARCHEESI Refer to Example 2. Find the probability that Jewel will *not* go first.

The probability that Jewel will *not* go first is the complement of the probability that Jewel will go first.

$P(A) + P(not\ A) = 1$ Definition of complementary events

$\frac{1}{3} + P(not\ A) = 1$ Substitute $\frac{1}{3}$ for $P(A)$.

$-\frac{1}{3} \qquad -\frac{1}{3}$ Subtract $\frac{1}{3}$ from each side.

$P(not\ A) = \frac{2}{3}$ $1 - \frac{1}{3}$ is $\frac{3}{3} - \frac{1}{3}$ or $\frac{2}{3}$

The probability that Jewel will *not* go first is $\frac{2}{3}$, or about 67%.

CHECK Your Progress

SCHOOL Ramón's teacher uses a spinner similar to the one shown at the right to determine the order in which each group will make their presentation. Use the spinner to find each probability. Write as a fraction in simplest form.

h. $P(not$ group 4)

i. $P(not$ group 1 or group 3)

Online Personal Tutor at tx.msmath2.com

CHECK Your Understanding

Example 1 (p. 504)

Use the spinner to find each probability. Write as a fraction in simplest form.

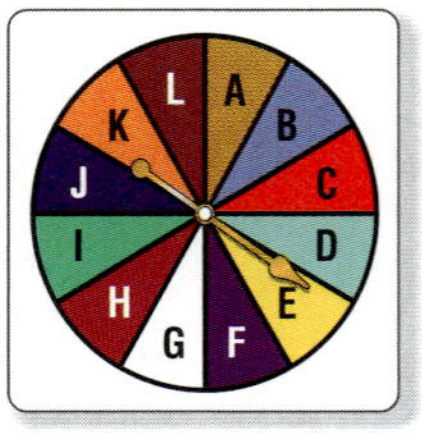

1. P(J)
2. P(E or H)
3. P(vowel)

Examples 2, 3 (pp. 505–506)

MARBLES Robert has a bag that contains 7 blue, 5 purple, 12 red, and 6 orange marbles. Find each probability if he draws one marble at random from the bag. Write as a fraction in simplest form.

4. P(purple)
5. P(red or orange)
6. P(green)
7. P(*not* blue)
8. P(*not* red or orange)
9. P(*not* yellow)

Example 3 (p. 506)

10. **SURVEYS** Shanté asked her classmates how many pets they own. The responses are in the table. If a student in her class is selected at random, what is the probability that the student does *not* own 3 or more pets?

Number of Pets	Response
None	6
1–2	15
3 or more	4

Exercises

HOMEWORK HELP

For Exercises	See Examples
11–14	1
17–22	2
15–16, 23–26	3

A set of 20 cards is numbered 1, 2, 3, . . ., 20. Suppose you pick a card at random without looking. Find the probability of each event. Write as a fraction in simplest form.

11. $P(1)$
12. $P(3 \text{ or } 13)$
13. $P(\text{multiple of } 3)$
14. $P(\text{even number})$
15. $P(\textit{not } 20)$
16. $P(\textit{not} \text{ a factor of } 10)$

STUDENT COUNCIL **The table shows the membership of the Student Council at Lincoln Middle School. Suppose one student is randomly selected as the president. Find the probability of each event. Write as a fraction in simplest form.**

Student Council	
girls	30
boys	20
8th graders	25
7th graders	15
6th graders	10

17. $P(\text{girl})$
18. $P(\text{boy})$
19. $P(\text{5th grader})$
20. $P(\text{8th grader})$
21. $P(\text{boy or girl})$
22. $P(\text{6th or 8th grader})$
23. $P(\textit{not} \text{ 6th grader})$
24. $P(\textit{not} \text{ 7th grader})$

25. **SOUP** A cupboard contains 20 soup cans. Seven are tomato, 4 are cream of mushroom, 5 are chicken, and 4 are vegetable. If one can is chosen at random from the cupboard, what is the probability that it is *neither* cream of mushroom *nor* vegetable soup? Write as a percent.

26. **VIDEOS** In a drawing, one name is randomly chosen from a jar of 75 names to receive free video rentals for a month. If Enola entered her name 8 times, what is the probability that she is *not* chosen to receive the free rentals? Write as a fraction in simplest form.

27. **TECHNOLOGY** The graph shows the cost of 22 digital cameras. If one of the 22 cameras is chosen at random, what is the probability that the cost ranges from \$111 up to \$160? Write as a fraction in simplest form.

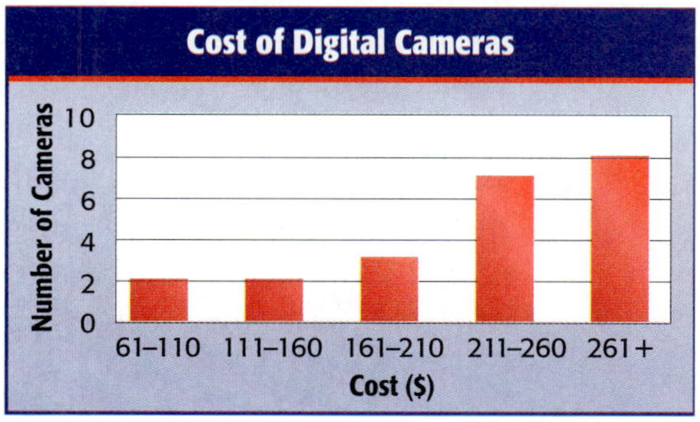

28. **MOVIES** The probability of buying a defective DVD is 0.002. What is the probability of buying a DVD that is *not* defective?

29. **WEATHER** The forecast for tomorrow says that there is a 37% chance of rain. Describe the complementary event and find its probability.

30. **FUND-RAISER** The Jefferson Middle School Band is selling raffle tickets for a new computer system. They sold 1,000 tickets at \$2 each. Ted's parents spent \$200 on tickets. What is the probability they will *not* win?

EXTRA PRACTICE

See pages 741, 764.

Math Online
Self-Check Quiz at tx.msmath2.com

H.O.T. Problems

31. **OPEN ENDED** Describe an event that has a probability of $\frac{1}{5}$.

32. **CHALLENGE** A bag contains 6 red marbles, 4 blue marbles, and 8 green marbles. How many marbles of each color should be added so that the total number of marbles is 27, but the probability of randomly selecting one marble of each color remains unchanged? Explain your reasoning.

33. **Which One Doesn't Belong?** Identify the pair of probabilities that does not represent probabilities of complementary events. Explain your reasoning.

$\frac{5}{8}, \frac{3}{8}$	0.65, 0.55	$\frac{4}{6}, \frac{1}{3}$	0.875, $\frac{1}{8}$

34. **WRITING IN MATH** Harmony and Hakan are playing a game by rolling two number cubes. Hakan gets a point each time the sum of the number cubes is 2, 3, 4, 9, 10, 11, or 12. Otherwise, Harmony gets a point. Determine whether this game is fair. Explain your reasoning.

TEST PRACTICE

35. In a school raffle, one ticket will be drawn out of 500 tickets. If the Hawkins family has 12 tickets, what is the probability that they will win?

A 0.002 C $\frac{3}{125}$

B 2% D $0.08\overline{3}$

36. What is the probability of the spinner landing on a number less than 3?

F 25% H 50%

G 37.5% J 75%

Spiral Review

37. **RAIN** The scatter plot shows the height of grass on several lawns and the amount of rain that has fallen on each lawn. Write a conclusion based on the graph. (Lesson 9-7)

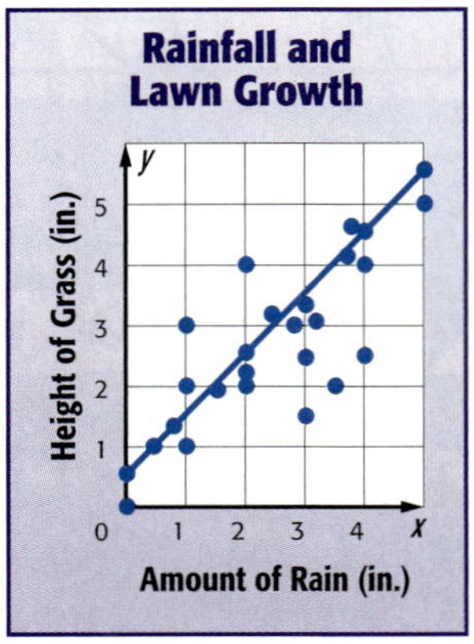

38. **TESTS** Rosa's test scores are shown in the line plot. Which measure of central tendency would give the highest test score? Would this number be misleading? Explain. (Lesson 9-6)

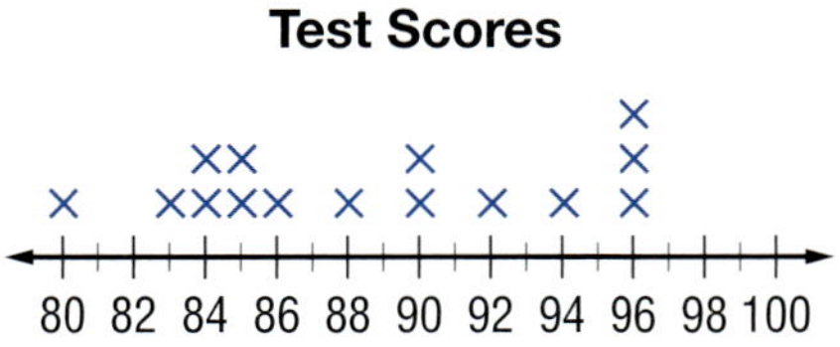

GET READY for the Next Lesson

PREREQUISITE SKILL Write each fraction in simplest form. Write *simplified* if the fraction is already in simplest form. (Lesson 5-4)

39. $\frac{2}{6}$ 40. $\frac{3}{8}$ 41. $\frac{15}{30}$ 42. $\frac{6}{16}$ 43. $\frac{18}{32}$

10-2 Sample Spaces

Main IDEA

Find sample spaces and probabilities.

Targeted TEKS 7.10 The student recognizes that a physical or mathematical model can be used to describe the experimental and theoretical probability of real-life events. **(A) construct sample spaces for simple or composite experiments.** *Also addresses TEKS 7.13(D).*

NEW Vocabulary

sample space
tree diagram
fair game

MINI Lab

Here is a probability game that you can play with two counters.

- Mark one side of the first counter A. Mark the other side B. Mark both sides of the second counter A.
- Player 1 tosses the counters. If both sides shown are the same, Player 1 wins a point. If the sides are different, Player 2 wins a point. Record your results.
- Player 2 then tosses the counters and the results are recorded. Continue alternating the tosses until each player has tossed the counters ten times. The player with the most points wins.

1. Before you play, make a conjecture. Do you think that each player has an equal chance of winning? Explain.
2. Now, play the game. Who won? What was the final score?

A list of all of the possible outcomes in a probability experiment is called the **sample space**. A table can be used to list the sample space.

EXAMPLE Find the Sample Space

1 ICE CREAM An ice cream vendor sells vanilla and chocolate ice cream. Customers can choose from a waffle or sugar cone and either hot fudge or caramel topping. Find the sample space for all possible orders of one scoop of ice cream in a cone with one topping.

Make a table that shows all of the possible outcomes.

Outcomes		
Vanilla	Waffle	Hot Fudge
Vanilla	Waffle	Caramel
Vanilla	Sugar	Hot Fudge
Vanilla	Sugar	Caramel
Chocolate	Waffle	Hot Fudge
Chocolate	Waffle	Caramel
Chocolate	Sugar	Hot Fudge
Chocolate	Sugar	Caramel

STUDY TIP

Making a Table Begin with one choice and list *all* of the outcomes that correspond with that choice before listing the outcomes that correspond with another choice.

CHECK Your Progress

a. **PETS** The animal shelter has both male and female Labradors in yellow, brown, or black. Find the sample space for all possible Labradors available at the shelter.

Online Personal Tutor at tx.msmath2.com

A **tree diagram** can also be used to construct a sample space.

TEST EXAMPLE

2 A scooter comes in silver, red, or purple with 125 or 180-millimeter wheel sizes. Which list shows all possible color-wheel size outcomes?

A

Outcomes	
silver	125 mm
silver	180 mm
red	125 mm
red	180 mm
purple	125 mm
purple	180 mm

B

Outcomes	
silver	125 mm
red	180 mm
purple	125 mm

C

Outcomes	
silver	125 mm
red	180 mm
purple	125 mm
silver	180 mm

D

Outcomes	
silver	125 mm
red	180 mm
purple	125 mm
silver	180 mm
purple	180 mm

Read the Test Item The scooter comes in 3 colors, silver, red, or purple, and 2 wheel sizes, 125 or 180 millimeters. Find all of the color-wheel size combinations.

Solve the Test Item

Make a tree diagram to show the sample space.

There are 6 different color-wheel size combinations. The answer is A.

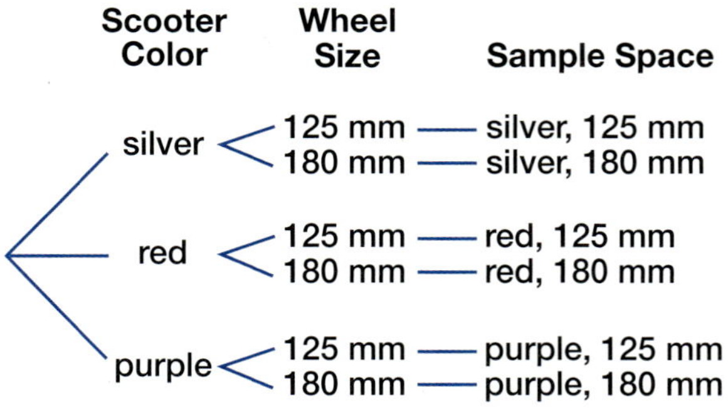

Test-Taking Tip

Educated Guess Find out if there is a penalty for incorrect answers. If there is no penalty, making an educated guess can only increase your score, or at worst, leave your score the same.

CHECK Your Progress

b. For dessert, you can have apple or cherry pie with or without ice cream. Which list shows all the possible outcomes of choosing pie and ice cream?

F

Outcomes	
apple	with ice cream
cherry	without ice cream

G

Outcomes	
apple	with ice cream
apple	without ice cream
cherry	with ice cream
cherry	without ice cream

H

Outcomes	
apple	without ice cream
cherry	with ice cream

J

Outcomes	
apple	with ice cream
cherry	with ice cream
apple	without ice cream

A **fair game** is one in which players have an equal chance of winning. To determine whether a game is fair, analyze its sample space.

EXAMPLE Determine Fairness of a Game

3 GAMES Refer to the Mini Lab at the start of this lesson. Find the sample space. Then determine whether the game is fair.

Since there are 4 equally-likely outcomes with 2 favoring each player, the probability that each player can win is $\frac{1}{2}$. So, the game is fair.

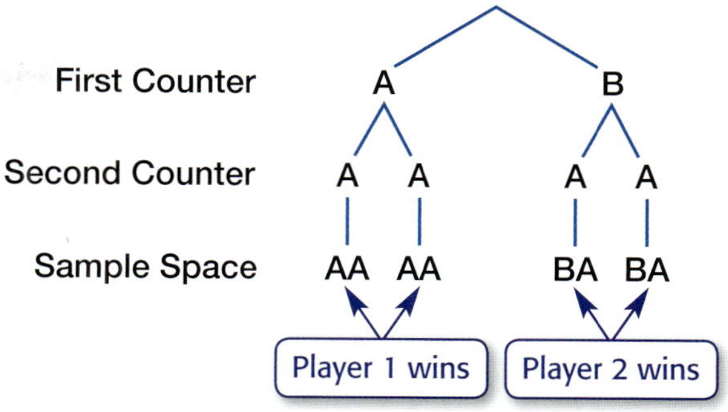

CHECK Your Progress

c. **GAMES** Pablo tosses three coins. If all three coins show up heads, Pablo wins. Otherwise, Kara wins. Find the sample space. Is this a fair game?

CHECK Your Understanding

Examples 1, 2 (pp. 509–510)

For each situation, find the sample space using a table or tree diagram.

1. A number cube is rolled twice.

2. A pair of brown or black sandals are available in sizes 7, 8, or 9.

Example 2 (p. 510)

3. **TEST PRACTICE** Sandwiches can be made with ham or turkey on rye, white, or sourdough breads. Which list shows all the possible outcomes?

A

Outcomes	
ham	rye
turkey	white
ham	sourdough
ham	rye
turkey	white
turkey	sourdough

B

Outcomes	
ham	rye
turkey	white
turkey	sourdough

C

Outcomes	
ham	rye
turkey	rye
ham	white
turkey	white
ham	sourdough
turkey	sourdough

D

Outcomes	
ham	rye
turkey	white
ham	sourdough

Example 3 (p. 511)

4. **GAMES** Brianna spins a spinner with four sections of equal size twice, labeled A, B, C, and D. If letter A is spun at least once, Brianna wins. Otherwise, Odell wins. Is this a fair game? Explain.

Exercises

HOMEWORK HELP	
For Exercises	See Examples
5–12	1, 2
28	2
13–14	3

For each situation, find the sample space using a table or tree diagram.

5. choosing a card with a shape and spinning the spinner from the choices at the right
6. choosing a card with a shape and either boots, gym shoes, or dress shoes
7. tossing a coin and rolling a number cube
8. picking a number from 1 to 5 and choosing the color red, white, or blue
9. choosing a purple, green, black, or silver mountain bike having 10, 18, 21, or 24 speeds
10. choosing a letter from the word SPACE and choosing a consonant from the word MATH

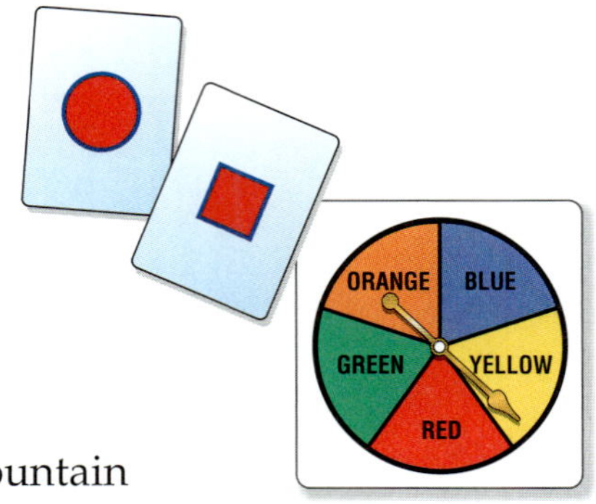

11. **CLOTHES** Jerry can buy a school T-shirt with either short sleeves or long sleeves in either gray or white and in small, medium, or large. Find the sample space for all possible T-shirts he can buy.

12. **FOOD** Three-course dinners can be made from the menu shown. Find the sample space for a dinner consisting of an appetizer, entrée, and dessert.

Appetizers	Entrees	Desserts
Soup Salad	Steak Chicken Fish	Carrot Cake Cheesecake

Real-World Link The average family size in the United States is 2.59 people.
Source: U.S. Census Bureau

For each game, find the sample space. Then determine whether the game is fair.

13. Elba tosses a quarter, a dime, and a nickel. If tails comes up at least twice, Steve wins. Otherwise Elba wins.
14. Ming rolls a number cube, tosses a coin, and chooses a card from two cards marked A and B. If an even number and heads appears, Ming wins, no matter which card is chosen. Otherwise Lashonda wins.

FAMILIES Mr. and Mrs. Romero are expecting triplets. Suppose the chance of each child being a boy is 50% and of being a girl is 50%. Find each probability.

15. P(all three children will be boys)
16. P(at least one boy and one girl)
17. P(two boys and one girl)
18. P(at least two girls)
19. P(the first two born are boys and the last born is a girl)

20. **GAMES** Determine whether the following game for two players is fair. Explain your reasoning.
    - Three counters are labeled according to the table at the right.
    - Toss the three counters.
    - If exactly 2 counters match, Player 1 scores a point. Otherwise, Player 2 scores a point.

	Side 1	Side 2
Counter 1	A	B
Counter 2	A	C
Counter 3	B	C

UNIFORMS For Exercises 21 and 22, use the information below and at the right.

Linus is a big fan of the Houston Astros baseball team and wears a different jersey and cap every time he goes to a game. The table shows the number of different jerseys and caps Linus owns.

	Home Jersey	Road Jersey	Practice Jersey	Cap
White	2	0	2	0
Black	1	0	0	1
Gray	0	1	0	0
Orange	1	1	0	2

21. How many jersey/cap combinations can Linus wear when he goes to the baseball game to cheer on the Astros?

22. If Linus picks a jersey/cap combination at random, what is the probability that he will pick a home jersey with a black cap?

EXTRA PRACTICE
See pages 742, 764.
Math Online
Self-Check Quiz at tx.msmath2.com

23. **RESEARCH** Use the Internet or another resource to find the number of jerseys and caps your favorite professional sports team has as part of its uniform. How many jersey/cap combinations are there for the team you picked?

H.O.T. Problems

24. **CHALLENGE** Refer to Exercise 20. Adjust the scoring of the game so that it is fair.

25. **SELECT A TOOL** Mei wants to determine the probability of guessing correctly on two true-false questions on her history test. Which of the following tools might Mei use to determine the probability of answering both questions correctly by guessing? Justify your selection(s). Then use the tool(s) to solve the problem.

draw a model | calculator | real objects

26. **FIND THE ERROR** Rhonda and Elise are finding all the possible unique outcomes of rolling an even number on a number cube and landing on A or B on the spinner shown. Who is correct? Explain your reasoning.

Rhonda

Outcomes	
Number Cube	Spinner
2	A
2	B
4	C
4	A
6	B
6	C

Elise

Outcomes	
Number Cube	Spinner
2	A
2	B
4	A
4	B
6	A
6	B

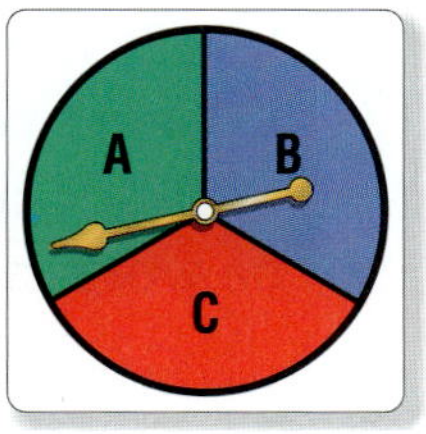

27. **WRITING IN MATH** Describe a fair game between two players using one coin. Then explain why your game is fair.

TEST PRACTICE

28. Theo played a game where he tossed a quarter and a nickel. Which list shows all of the possible unique outcomes of tossing a quarter and then tossing a nickel?

A

Quarter	Nickel
tails	heads
tails	tails
heads	heads
heads	tails

B

Quarter	Nickel
tails	heads
tails	tails

C

Quarter	Nickel
tails	heads

D

Quarter	Nickel
tails	tails
tails	heads
heads	tails

Spiral Review

PROBABILITY A spinner is equally likely to stop on each of its regions numbered 1 to 20. Find each probability as a fraction in simplest form. (Lesson 10-1)

29. a prime number
30. GCF(12, 18)
31. multiple of 2 or 3
32. *not* a multiple of 4
33. factor of 10 or 6
34. *not* an even number

UTILITIES For Exercises 35 and 36, use the graph that shows the prices for natural gas charged by an Illinois natural gas supplier. (Lesson 9-7)

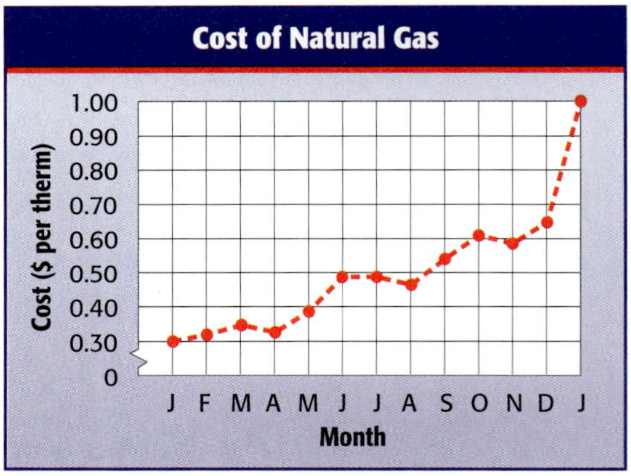

35. What trend seems to be revealed in the line graph?
36. What problems might there be in using this information to predict future prices of natural gas?

37. **INTEREST** If Carlota invests $2,100 in a CD for 5 years at a simple interest rate of 4.75%, how much will the CD be worth after 5 years? (Lesson 8-9)

Find each number. Round to the nearest tenth if necessary. (Lesson 8-1)

38. 43% of 266
39. 17% of 92
40. 2.5% of 44

GET READY for the Next Lesson

PREREQUISITE SKILL Multiply.

41. 7 • 22
42. 11 • 16
43. 23 • 20
44. 131 • 4

10-3 The Fundamental Counting Principle

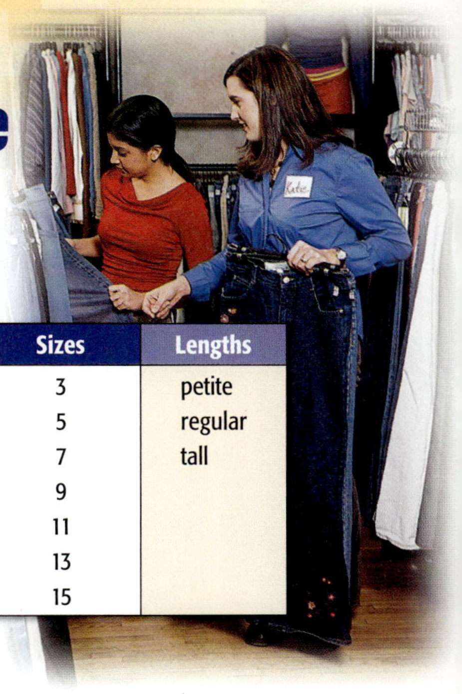

Main IDEA

Use multiplication to count outcomes.

Targeted TEKS 7.10 The student recognizes that a physical or mathematical model can be used to describe the experimental and theoretical probability of real-life events. **(A) construct sample spaces for simple or composite experiments.**

NEW Vocabulary

Fundamental Counting Principle

READING in the Content Area

For strategies in reading this lesson, visit tx.msmath2.com.

GET READY for the Lesson

RETAIL SALES The Jean Factory sells juniors' jeans in different sizes and lengths. The table shows what they have available.

Sizes	Lengths
3	petite
5	regular
7	tall
9	
11	
13	
15	

1. According to the table, how many sizes of juniors' jeans are there?
2. How many lengths are there?
3. Find the product of the two numbers you found in Exercises 1 and 2.
4. Draw a tree diagram to help you find the number of different size and length combinations. How does the number of outcomes compare to the product you found above?

In the activity above, you discovered that multiplication, instead of a tree diagram, can be used to find the number of possible outcomes in a sample space. This is called the **Fundamental Counting Principle**.

KEY CONCEPT — Fundamental Counting Principle

Words If event M has m possible outcomes and event N has n possible outcomes, then event M followed by event N has $m \times n$ possible outcomes.

EXAMPLE Find the Number of Outcomes

1 Find the total number of outcomes when a coin is tossed and a number cube is rolled.

number of outcomes on one coin		number of outcomes on one number cube		total number of outcomes	
2	·	6	=	12	Fundamental Counting Principle

There are 12 different outcomes.

Check Draw a tree diagram to show the sample space.

CHECK Your Progress

a. Find the total number of outcomes when choosing from bike helmets that come in three colors and two styles.

The Fundamental Counting Principle can be applied to find the number of possible outcomes when there are more than two events.

Real-World EXAMPLE

2 **FOOD** **A famous steak house allows customers to create their own steak dinners. The choices are shown at the right. Find the number of steak dinners possible. Then find the probability that a customer randomly selects a well-done ribeye steak and a baked potato.**

451 Steakhouse

Steak	How Steaks Are Cooked	Potatoes
New York Strip	rare	mashed
Ribeye	medium	baked
Filet	well	twice baked
Porterhouse		au gratin
T-Bone		

number of types of steaks		number of ways steaks can be cooked		number of types of potatoes		total number of steak dinners	
5	·	3	·	4	=	60	Fundamental Counting Principle

There are 60 different ways of choosing a steak dinner. Out of the 60 possible outcomes, only one is favorable. So, the probability of randomly selecting a well-done ribeye steak and a baked potato is $\frac{1}{60}$.

CHECK Your Progress

b. **FOOD** If the chef adds sirloin steak and scalloped potatoes to the menu, find the number of possible steak dinners. Then find the probability of randomly selecting a medium-done sirloin steak and mashed potatoes.

Online Personal Tutor at tx.msmath2.com

CHECK Your Understanding

Example 1 (p. 515)

Use the Fundamental Counting Principle to find the total number of outcomes in each situation.

1. tossing a quarter, a dime, and a nickel
2. choosing scrambled, sunny-side up, or poached eggs with bacon or sausage and milk, orange juice, or apple juice
3. choosing a card from 20 different cards and spinning the spinner at the right

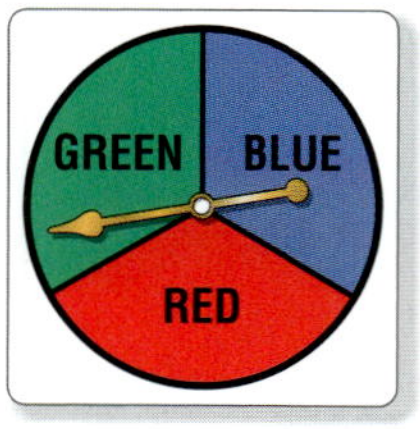

Example 2 (p. 516)

4. **CLOTHES** Beth has 3 sweaters, 4 blouses, and 6 skirts that coordinate. Find the number of different outcomes consisting of a sweater, blouse, and skirt that are possible. Then find the probability of randomly selecting a particular sweater-blouse-skirt outfit.

Exercises

HOMEWORK HELP

For Exercises	See Examples
5–10	1
11–12	2

Use the Fundamental Counting Principle to find the total number of outcomes in each situation.

5. choosing a bagel with one type of cream cheese from the list shown in the table

Bagels	Cream Cheese
plain	plain
blueberry	chive
cinnamon raisin	sun-dried tomato
garlic	

6. choosing a number from 1 to 20 and a color from 7 colors
7. picking a month of the year and a day of the week
8. choosing from a comedy, horror, or action movie each shown in four theaters
9. rolling a number cube and tossing two coins
10. choosing iced tea in regular, raspberry, lemon, or peach flavors; sweetened or unsweetened; and in a glass or a plastic container

11. **ROADS** Two roads, Broadway and State, connect the towns of Eastland and Harping. Three roads, Park, Fairview, and Main, connect the towns of Harping and Johnstown. Find the number of possible routes from Eastland to Johnstown that pass through Harping. Then find the probability that State and Fairview will be used if a route is selected at random.

Real-World Link A popular orchard in Medina, Texas, the Apple Capital of Texas, grows 11 varieties of apples including Granny Smith and Fuji.
Source: *The Handbook of Texas Online*

12. **APPLES** An orchard makes apple nut bread, apple pumpkin nut bread, and apple buttermilk bread using 6 different varieties of apples, including Fuji. Find the number of possible bread choices. Then find the probability of selecting a Fuji apple buttermilk bread if a customer buys a loaf of bread at random.

13. **GAMES** Find the number of possible outcomes if five number cubes are rolled at one time during a board game.

14. **PASSWORDS** Find the number of possible choices for a 2-digit password that is greater than 19. Then find the number of possible choices for a 4-digit Personal Identification Number (PIN) if the digits *cannot* be repeated.

15. **ADVERTISING** The Wake-Up Restaurant advertises that you can have a different pancake breakfast every day of the year. It offers 25 different kinds of pancakes and 14 flavored syrups. If the restaurant is open every day of the year, is its claim valid? Justify your answer.

EXTRA PRACTICE
See pages 742, 764.
Math Online
Self-Check Quiz at tx.msmath2.com

16. **ANALYZE TABLES** The table shows cell phone options offered by a wireless phone company. If a phone with one payment plan and one accessory is given away at random, find the probability that it will be Brand B and have a headset. Explain your reasoning.

Phone Brands	Payment Plans	Accessories
Brand A	Individual	Leather Case
Brand B	Family	Car Mount
Brand C	Business	Headset
	Government	Travel Charger

H.O.T. Problems

17. **CHALLENGE** Determine the number of possible outcomes for tossing one coin, two coins, and three coins. Then determine the number of possible outcomes for tossing *n* coins. Describe the strategy you used.

18. **Which One Doesn't Belong?** Identify the choices for event *M* and *N* that do *not* result in the same number of outcomes as the other two. Explain your reasoning.

12 meats, 8 breads	18 hats, 8 sizes	24 teams, 4 sports

19. **WRITING IN MATH** Explain when you might choose to use the Fundamental Counting Principle to find the number of possible outcomes and when you might choose to use a tree diagram.

TEST PRACTICE

20. A bakery offers white, chocolate, or yellow cakes with white or chocolate icing. There are also 24 designs that can be applied to a cake. If all orders are equally likely, what is the probability that a customer will order a white cake with white icing in one of these designs?

A $\frac{1}{30}$ **C** $\frac{1}{120}$

B $\frac{1}{64}$ **D** $\frac{1}{144}$

21. WritePen makes 8 different styles of pens in several colors with 2 types of grips. If the company makes 112 kinds of pens, how many different colors do they make?

F 7 **H** 16

G 8 **J** 1,792

Spiral Review

22. **SCHOOL** Horacio can choose from 2 geography, 3 history, and 2 statistics classes. Find the sample space for all possible schedules. (Lesson 10-2)

PROBABILITY Find the probability that the spinner shown at the right will stop on each of the following. Write as a fraction in simplest form. (Lesson 10-1)

23. an even number

24. a multiple of 4

Order each set of numbers from least to greatest. (Lesson 7-7)

25. $27\%, \frac{1}{5}, 0.22, 20.1$

26. $\frac{19}{20}, 88\%, 0.85, \frac{3}{4}$

GET READY for the Next Lesson

PREREQUISITE SKILL Multiply.

27. $3 \cdot 2 \cdot 1$

28. $9 \cdot 8 \cdot 7$

29. $5 \cdot 4 \cdot 3 \cdot 2$

30. $7 \cdot 6 \cdot 5 \cdot 4$

10-4 Permutations

Main IDEA

Find the number of permutations of a set of objects.

Targeted TEKS 7.13 The student applies Grade 7 mathematics to solve problems connected to everyday experiences, investigations in other disciplines, and activities in and outside of school. **(A) identify and apply mathematics to everyday experiences, to activities in and outside of school, with other disciplines, and other mathematical topics.** *Also addresses TEKS 7.13(D).*

NEW Vocabulary

permutation

MINI Lab

How many different ways are there to arrange your first 3 classes if they are math, science, and language arts?

STEP 1 Write math, science, and language arts on the index cards.

MATH	SCIENCE	LANGUAGE ARTS

STEP 2 Find and record all arrangements of classes by changing the order of the index cards.

1. When you first started to make your list, how many choices did you have for your first class?
2. Once your first class was selected, how many choices did you have for the second class? Then, the third class?

A **permutation** is an arrangement, or listing, of objects in which order is important. In the example above, the arrangement Science, Math, Language Arts is a permutation of Math, Science, Language Arts because the order of the classes is different. You can use the Fundamental Counting Principle to find the number of possible permutations.

EXAMPLE Find a Permutation

1 SCHEDULES Find the number of possible arrangements of classes in the Mini-Lab above using the Fundamental Counting Principle.

There are **3** choices for the first class.
There are **2** choices that remain for the second class.
There is **1** choice that remains for the third class.

$3 \cdot 2 \cdot 1 = 6$ ← The number of permutations of 3 classes

There are 6 possible arrangements, or permutations, of the 3 classes.

CHECK Your Progress

a. **VOLLEYBALL** In how many ways can the starting six players of a volleyball team stand in a row for a picture?

You can use a permutation to find the probability of an event.

Real-World EXAMPLE Find Probability

2 **SWIMMING** **The finals of the Northwest Swimming League features 8 swimmers. If each swimmer has an equally likely chance of finishing in the top two, what is the probability that Yumii will be in first place and Paquita in second place?**

Northwest League Finalists	
Octavia	Eden
Natasha	Paquita
Calista	Samantha
Yumii	Lorena

There are **8** choices for first place.

There are **7** choices that remain for second place.

$8 \cdot 7 = 56$ ← The number of permutations of the 2 places

There are 56 possible arrangements, or permutations, of the 2 places.

Since there is only one way of having Yumii come in first and Paquita second, the probability of this event is $\frac{1}{56}$.

CHECK Your Progress

b. **LETTERS** Two different letters are randomly selected from the letters in the word *math*. What is the probability that the first letter selected is *m* and the second letter is *h*?

Online Personal Tutor at tx.msmath2.com

CHECK Your Understanding

Example 1 (p. 519)

1. **TRANSPORTATION** In how many ways can the 7 students shown waiting at the bus stop board the bus when it arrives?

2. **COMMITTEES** In how many ways can a president, vice-president, and secretary be randomly selected from a class of 25 students?

Example 2 (p. 520)

3. **DVD** You have five seasons of your favorite TV show on DVD. If you randomly select two of them from a shelf, what is the probability that you will select season one first and season two second?

4. **PASSWORDS** A password consists of four letters, of which none are repeated. What is the probability that a person could guess the entire password by randomly selecting the four letters?

Exercises

HOMEWORK HELP

For Exercises	See Examples
5–8	1
9–12	2

5. **CONTESTS** In the Battle of the Bands contest, in how many ways can the four participating bands be ordered?

6. **ZIP CODES** How many different 5-digit zip codes are there if no digit is repeated?

7. **LETTERS** How many permutations are possible of the letters in the word *friend*?

8. **NUMBERS** How many different 3-digit numbers can be formed using the digits 9, 3, 4, 7, and 6? Assume no number can be used more than once.

9. **CAPTAINS** The members of the Evergreen Junior High Quiz Bowl team are listed at the right. What is the probability that Walter is selected as captain and Mi-Ling as co-captain?

Evergreen Junior High Quiz Bowl Team	
Jamil	Luanda
Savannah	Mi-Ling
Tucker	Booker
Ferdinand	Nina
Walter	Meghan

10. **BASEBALL** Adriano, Julián and three of their friends will sit in a row of five seats at a baseball game. If each friend is equally-likely to sit in any seat, what is the probability that Adriano will sit in the first seat and Julián will sit in the second seat?

11. **GAMES** Alex, Aiden, Dexter, and Dion are playing a video game. If they each have an equally-likely chance of getting the highest score, what is the probability that Dion will get the highest score and Alex the second highest?

12. **BLOCKS** A child has wooden blocks with the letters *G*, *R*, *T*, *I*, and *E*. Find the probability that the child randomly arranges the letters in the order *TIGER*.

Real-World Link At the 2005 Westminster Kennel Club Dog Show, *Carlee, a German Shorthaired Pointer* from the Sporting Group, won the Best in Show Trophy.
Source: *Westminster Kennel Club*

13. **SELECT A TOOL** Refer to the information in the table. The best dog in each breed competes to win one of four top ribbons in the group. Which of the following tools might you use to find the number of ways a ribbon can be awarded to a dog in the Working group? Justify your selection(s). Then use your tool(s) to solve the problem.

calculator | mental math | estimation

Westminster Kennel Club Dog Show Attendance 2005

Group	Number of Breeds
Herding	19
Hounds	25
Non-Sporting	18
Sporting	28
Terriers	28
Toy	23
Working	24

EXTRA PRACTICE
See pages 742, 764.
Math Online
Self-Check Quiz at tx.msmath2.com

14. **PHOTOGRAPHY** A family discovered they can stand in a row for their portrait in 720 different ways. How many members are in the family?

15. **STUDENT ID** Hamilton Middle School assigns a four-digit identification number to each student. The number is made from the digits 1, 2, 3, and 4, and no digit is repeated. If assigned randomly, what is the probability that an ID number will end with a 3?

H.O.T. Problems

16. **CHALLENGE** There are 1,320 ways for three students to win first, second, and third place during a debate match. How many students are there on the debate team? Explain your reasoning.

17. **WRITING IN MATH** Describe a real-world situation that has 6 permutations. Justify your answer.

TEST PRACTICE

18. The five finalists in a random drawing are shown. Find the probability that Sean is awarded first prize and Teresa is awarded second prize.

A $\frac{1}{5}$

B $\frac{1}{10}$

C $\frac{2}{5}$

D $\frac{1}{20}$

Finalists
Cesar
Teresa
Sean
Nikita
Alfonso

19. A baseball coach is setting a batting order for his nine starting players with the pitcher batting last. How many batting orders are possible?

F 8

G 72

H 40,320

J 362,880

Spiral Review

20. **BREAKFAST** Find the total number of outcomes if you can choose from 8 kinds of bagels, 3 toppings, and 4 beverages. (Lesson 10-3)

21. **LUNCH** Make a tree diagram showing different ways to make a sandwich with turkey, ham, or salami and either cheddar or Swiss cheese. (Lesson 10-2)

22. **PROBABILITY** What is the probability of rolling a number greater than four on a number cube? (Lesson 10-1)

Find each product. Write in simplest form. (Lesson 6-5)

23. $\frac{4}{5} \times 2\frac{1}{3}$

24. $11\frac{1}{8} \times \frac{1}{2}$

25. $4\frac{5}{6} \times \frac{7}{8}$

GET READY for the Next Lesson

PREREQUISITE SKILL Find each value. (Lesson 1-4)

26. $\frac{5 \cdot 4}{2 \cdot 1}$

27. $\frac{8 \cdot 7 \cdot 6}{3 \cdot 2 \cdot 1}$

28. $\frac{5 \cdot 4 \cdot 3}{4 \cdot 3 \cdot 2}$

29. $\frac{10 \cdot 9 \cdot 8 \cdot 7}{8 \cdot 7 \cdot 6 \cdot 5}$

CHAPTER 10

Mid-Chapter Quiz

Lessons 10-1 through 10-4

A number cube is rolled. Find each probability. Write as a fraction in simplest form. (Lesson 10-1)

1. P(an odd number)
2. P(a number not greater than 4)
3. P(a number less than 6)
4. P(a multiple of 2)

5. **DVDS** Andrés is starting a collection of DVDs. He has 2 action, 3 comedy, and 5 drama DVDs. If he randomly picks a DVD to watch, what is the probability that he will *not* pick a comedy? Write as a percent. (Lesson 10-1)

For each situation, find the sample space using a table or tree diagram. (Lesson 10-2)

6. A penny and a dime are tossed.
7. The spinner shown is spun, and a digit is randomly selected from the number 803.

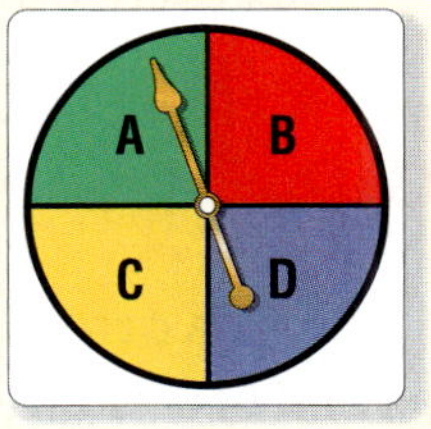

8. **TEST PRACTICE** At a diner, a customer can choose from eggs or pancakes as an entrée and from juice, coffee, or water as a beverage. Which expression gives the number of possible unique outcomes if a customer chooses an entrée and beverage? (Lesson 10-2)

   A $2 \times 2 \times 2$
   B 2×3
   C 3×3
   D $2 + 3$

9. **GAMES** Abbey rolls a number cube and chooses a card from among cards marked *A*, *B*, and *C*. If an odd number and a vowel turn up, Abbey wins. Otherwise Benny wins. Find the sample space. Then determine if this is a fair game. (Lesson 10-2)

For Exercises 10 and 11, use the Fundamental Counting Principle to find the total number of possible outcomes in each situation. (Lesson 10-3)

10. A customer chooses a paper color, size, and binding style for some copies.

Color	Size	Binding
white	8.5″ x 11″	paper clip
yellow	8.5″ x 14″	binder clip
green	8.5″ x 17″	staple

11. A number cube is rolled and three coins are tossed.

12. **CARS** A certain car model comes in the colors in the table and either automatic or manual transmission. Find the probability that a randomly selected car will have a black exterior, tan interior, and manual transmission if all combinations are equally likely. (Lesson 10-3)

Exterior	Interior
Black	Gray
White	Tan
Red	
Silver	

13. **STUDENT COUNCIL** In how many ways can a president, treasurer, and a secretary be chosen from among 8 candidates? (Lesson 10-4)

14. **TEST PRACTICE** Noriko packed five different sweaters for her weekend vacation. If she randomly selects one sweater to wear each day, what is the probability that she will select the brown sweater on Friday, the orange sweater on Saturday, and the pink sweater on Sunday? She will not wear each sweater more than once. (Lesson 10-4)

    F $\frac{1}{60}$
    G $\frac{1}{120}$
    H $\frac{3}{5}$
    J $\frac{1}{5}$

10-5 Combinations

Main IDEA

Find the number of combinations of a set of objects.

Targeted TEKS 7.13 The student applies Grade 7 mathematics to solve problems connected to everyday experiences, investigations in other disciplines, and activities in and outside of school. **(A) identify and apply mathematics to everyday experiences, to activities in and outside of school, with other disciplines, and with other mathematical topics.**

NEW Vocabulary

combination

Vocabulary Link
Combination
Everyday Use the result of putting objects together, as in a combination of ingredients
Math Use an arrangement of objects in which order is not important

GET READY for the Lesson

BASKETBALL Coach Chávez wants to select co-captains for her basketball team. She will select two girls from the four oldest members on the team: Jenna, Bailey, Oleta, and Danielle.

1. Use the first letter of each name to list all of the permutations of co-captains. How many are there?
2. Cross out any arrangement that contains the same letters as another one in the list. How many are there now?
3. Explain the difference between the two lists.

An arrangement, or listing, of objects in which order is not important is called a **combination**. In the activity above, choosing Jenna and Bailey is the same as choosing Bailey and Jenna.

Permutations and combinations are related. You can find the number of combinations of objects by dividing the number of permutations of the entire set by the number of ways each smaller set can be arranged.

EXAMPLE Find the Number of Combinations

1 **FOOD Terrence's Pizza Parlor is offering the special shown in the table. How many different two-topping pizzas are possible?**

Today's Special:
Large two-topping pizza for $14.99

Toppings
Pepperoni
Sausage
Green Peppers
Onions
Mushrooms

This is a combination problem because the order of the toppings on the pizza is not important.

METHOD 1 **Make a list.**

Use the first letter of each topping to list all of the permutations of the toppings taken two at a time. Then cross out the pizzas that are the same as another one.

p, s	~~s, p~~	~~g, p~~	~~o, p~~	~~m, p~~
p, o	s, o	~~g, s~~	~~o, s~~	~~m, s~~
p, m	s, m	~~g, o~~	o, m	~~m, o~~
p, g	s, g	~~g, m~~	o, g	m, g

So, there are 10 different two-topping pizzas.

METHOD 2 **Use a permutation.**

Step 1 Find the number of permutations of the entire set.

$5 \cdot 4 = 20$ A permutation of 5 toppings, taken 2 at time

Step 2 Find the number of permutations of the smaller set.

$2 \cdot 1 = 2$ Number of ways to arrange 2 toppings

Step 3 Find the number of combinations.

$\frac{20}{2}$ or 10 Divide the number of permutations of the entire set by the number of permutations of each smaller set.

So, there are 10 different two-topping pizzas.

CHOOSE Your Method

a. **FOOD** How many different three-topping pizzas are possible if Terrence adds ham and anchovies to the topping choices?

Online **Personal Tutor at** tx.msmath2.com

Real-World EXAMPLES

Real-World Link Checkers is played on an 8-by-8 board in the U.S., England, Australia, and Ireland. People in eastern Europe play on a 10-by-10 board.
Source: about.com

2 **CHECKERS** **A checkers tournament features each of the top 8 regional players playing every opponent one time. The 2 players with the best records will then play in a final championship round. How many matches will be played if there are no ties?**

Find the number of ways 2 players can be chosen from a group of 8.

There are $8 \cdot 7$ ways to choose 2 people. →
There are $2 \cdot 1$ ways to arrange 2 people. →
$\frac{8 \cdot 7}{2 \cdot 1} = \frac{56}{2}$ or 28

There are 28 matches plus 1 final match to determine the champion. So, there will be 29 matches played.

Check Make a diagram in which each person is represented by a point. Draw line segments between two points to represent the games. There are 28 line segments. Then add the final-round match to make a total of 29 matches.

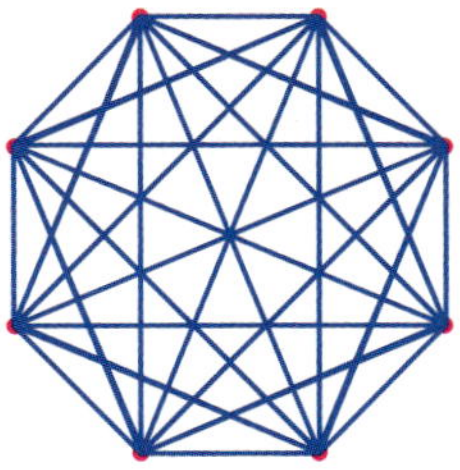

3 **If the players for the first match are selected at random, what is the probability that player 2 will play player 7 in the first match?**

Since there are 28 possible first matches and only one favorable outcome, the probability that player 2 will play player 7 in the first match is $\frac{1}{28}$.

CHECK Your Progress

b. **CHECKERS** What is the probability that player 2 will play player 16 in the first match if the top 16 regional players are invited to play in the tournament?

CHECK Your Understanding

Example 1 (pp. 524–525)

1. **PUPPIES** In how many ways can you pick 2 puppies from a litter of 7?
2. **SCIENCE FAIR** In how many ways can 3 out of 10 students be chosen to present their projects at a science fair?

Examples 2, 3 (p. 525)

PAINTING For Exercises 3 and 4, use the information below.

Jade is going to paint her room two different colors from among white, gray, sage, or yellow.

3. How many combinations of two paint colors are there?
4. Find the probability that two colors chosen randomly will be white and sage.

Exercises

HOMEWORK HELP

For Exercises	See Examples
5–8	1, 2
9–10	3

5. **ESSAYS** In how many ways can you select 4 essay questions out of 10?
6. **ART** In how many ways can 4 paintings out of 15 be chosen for display?
7. **INTERNET** Of 12 Web sites, in how many ways can you choose to visit 6?
8. **SPORTS** On an 8-member volleyball team, how many different 6-player starting teams are possible?
9. **STUDENT COUNCIL** The students listed are members of Student Council. Three will be chosen at random to form a committee. Find the probability that the three students chosen will be Placido, Maddie, and Akira.

Roster
Leon
Placido
Maddie
Adrahan
Matt
Akira

10. **FOOD** At a hot dog stand, customers can select three toppings from among chili, onions, cheese, mustard, or relish. What is the probability that three toppings selected at random will include onions, mustard, and relish?
11. **MUSIC** Marissa practiced the five pieces listed at the right for a recital. Find the number of different ways that three pieces will be randomly chosen for her to play. Then find the probability that all three were composed by Beethoven.

Recital Piece	Composer
Fur Elise	Ludwig van Beethoven
First Piano Sonata	Sergei Rachmaninoff
The Four Seasons	Antonio Vivaldi
Cappricio	Ludwig van Beethoven
Moonlight Sonata	Ludwig van Beethoven

Tell whether each problem represents a *permutation* or a *combination*. Then solve the problem.

12. Six children remain in a game of musical chairs. If two chairs are removed, how many different groups of four children can remain?
13. How many ways can first and second chair positions be awarded in a band that has 10 flute players?
14. How many ways can 12 books be stacked in a single pile?

EXTRA PRACTICE
See page 743, 764.

Math Online
Self-Check Quiz at tx.msmath2.com

H.O.T. Problems

15. **CHALLENGE** How many people were at a party if each person shook hands exactly once with every other person and there were 105 handshakes?

16. **FIND THE ERROR** Allison and Francisca are calculating the number of ways that a 3-member committee can be chosen from a 7-member club. Who is correct? Explain your reasoning.

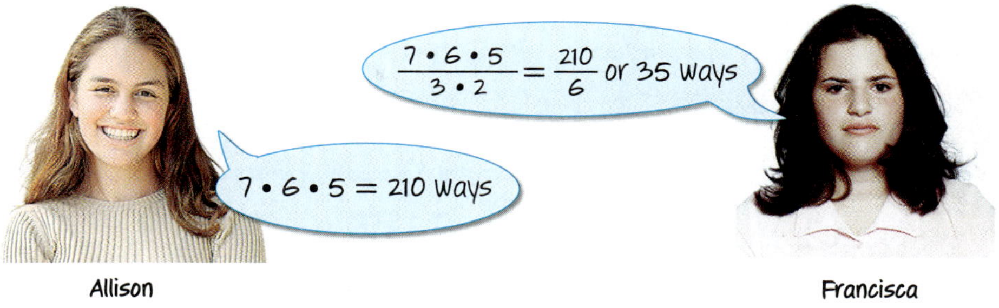

17. **WRITING IN MATH** Write about a real-world situation that can be solved using a combination. Then solve the problem.

TEST PRACTICE

18. **GRIDDABLE** If all 24 cheerleaders at a school give each other a high-five when their team wins, how many high-fives will there be between different cheerleaders?

19. Three students are to be chosen from a roster of 12 students to attend a science camp. In how many ways can these 3 students be chosen?

A 3 **C** 220

B 4 **D** 9,240

Spiral Review

20. **SAILING** Six sailboats are entered in a race. In how many different ways can the race be completed? Assume there are no ties. (Lesson 10-4)

21. **CARS** A certain brand of car has the choices listed in the table. How many different cars are possible? (Lesson 10-3)

Engine	Extras	Seats	Color
2.5 L	DVD-player	Cloth	Silver
3.1 L	CD-player	Leather	Green
4.0 L	CD-changer		Red
			White

Estimate. (Lesson 6-2)

22. $\frac{1}{10} + \frac{7}{8}$

23. $\frac{5}{12} - \frac{1}{9}$

GET READY for the Next Lesson

PREREQUISITE SKILL For Exercises 24 and 25, use the graph. (Lesson 9-6)

24. How many students were surveyed?

25. Find the probability that a student's favorite picnic game is sack racing.

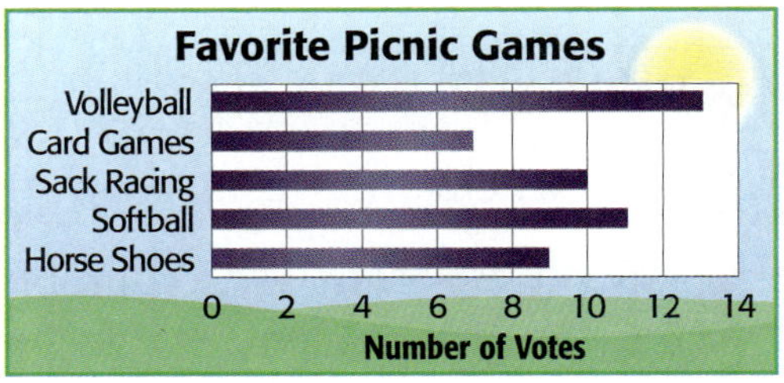

10-6 Problem-Solving Investigation

MAIN IDEA: Solve problems by acting it out.

Targeted TEKS 7.13 The student applies Grade 7 mathematics to solve problems connected to everyday experiences, investigations in other disciplines, and activities in and outside of school. **(C) select or develop an appropriate problem-solving strategy from a variety of different types, including… acting it out… to solve a problem**. *Also addresses TEKS 7.13(B).*

P.S.I. TEAM +

e-Mail: ACT IT OUT

YOUR MISSION: Solve the problem by acting it out.

THE PROBLEM: Determine the probability that Eddie makes two free-throws in a row.

Eddie: I make an average of 3 out of every 4 free-throws I try.

EXPLORE	You know that Eddie makes an average of 3 out of every 4 free throws. You could have Eddie actually make free throws, but that requires a basketball hoop. You could also act it out with a spinner.
PLAN	Spin a spinner, numbered 1 to 4, two times. If the spinner lands on 1, 2, or 3, he makes the free-throw. If the spinner lands on 4, he doesn't make it. Repeat the experiment of 10 times.
SOLVE	Spin the spinner and make a table of the results.
CHECK	Repeat the experiment several times to see whether the results agree.

Trials	1	2	3	4	5	6	7	8	9	10
First Spin	4	1	4	3	1	2	2	1	3	2
Second Spin	2	3	3	2	1	4	1	4	3	3

The highlighted columns show that six out of the 10 trials resulted in two free-throws in a row. So the probability is 60%.

Analyze The Strategy

1. Explain whether the results of the experiment would be the same if it were repeated.
2. **WRITING IN MATH** Write a problem that can be solved by acting it out. Then solve the problem by acting it out.

Mixed Problem Solving

For Exercises 3–6, use the *act it out* strategy.

3. **POP QUIZ** Determine whether using a spinner with four equal sections is a good way to answer a 5-question multiple-choice quiz if each question has choices A, B, C, and D. Justify your answer.

4. **PHOTOGRAPHS** Samuel is taking a photo of the Spanish Club's five officers. The president will always stand on the left, and the vice-president will always stand on the right. How many different ways can he arrange the officers for the photo?

5. **RUNNING** Six runners are entered in a race. Assuming no ties, in how many different ways can first and second places be awarded?

6. **MOVIES** In how many different ways can four friends sit in a row of four seats at the movies if two of the friends insist on sitting next to each other?

Use any strategy to solve Exercises 7–11. Some strategies are shown below.

PROBLEM-SOLVING STRATEGIES
- Use the four-step plan.
- Draw a diagram.
- Use reasonable answers.
- Act it out.

7. **SEASONS** Refer to the graph. In a middle school of 800 students, would about 150, 250, or 350 be a reasonable answer for the number of students that prefer autumn? Justify your solution.

Seasons of Change

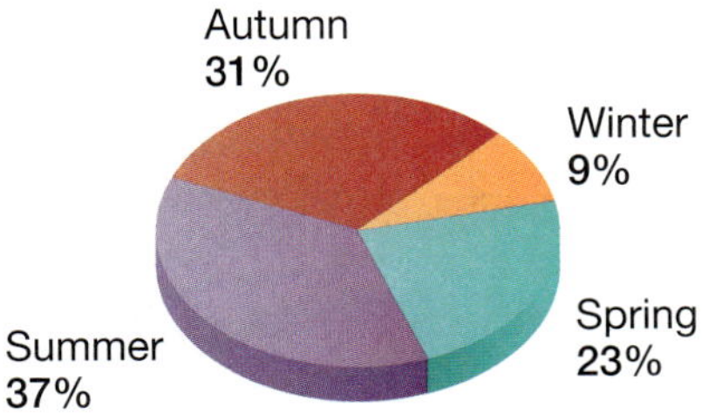

8. **SPACE SCIENCE** A 21-kilogram sample of rocks from the Moon is composed of 40% oxygen and 19.2% silicon. How many kilograms more is the oxygen than the silicon mass?

9. **PATTERNS** The pattern below is known as Pascal's Triangle. Would 1, 6, 10, 10, 6, 1 be a reasonable conjecture for the numbers in the 6th row? Justify your answer.

1st Row					1				
2nd Row				1		1			
3rd Row			1		2		1		
4th Row		1		3		3		1	
5th Row	1		4		6		4		1

10. **SOCCER** Sixteen teams are playing in a soccer tournament. If a team loses one game, it is eliminated. How many total games will be played in the tournament?

11. **SCHOOL** Suppose rolling an even number on a number cube corresponds to an answer of *true* and rolling an odd number corresponds to an answer of *false*. Determine whether rolling this number cube is a good way to answer a 5-question true-false quiz. Justify your answer.

Select the Operation

For Exercises 12–14, select the appropriate operation(s) to solve the problem. Justify your selection(s) and solve the problem.

12. **TRANSPORTATION** A taxi charges $3.25 for the first 0.4 mile and $0.75 for each additional 0.4 mile. Find the cost of a 4-mile taxi ride.

13. **MOUNTAINS** The mountain Mauna Kea in Hawaii, is about 1.38×10^4 feet tall while Mt. Everest is about 29,000 feet tall. About how many feet taller is Mt. Everest?

14. **MONEY** Lola purchased a $35 book bag at a sale price of $27.50. What was the approximate percent of decrease from the original price to the sale price?

10-7 Theoretical and Experimental Probability

Main IDEA

Find and compare experimental and theoretical probabilities.

Targeted TEKS 7.10 The student recognizes that a physical or mathematical model can be used to describe the experimental and theoretical probability of real-life events. **(A) construct sample spaces for simple or composite experiments.** *Also addresses TEKS 7.13(D).*

NEW Vocabulary

theoretical probability
experimental probability

REVIEW Vocabulary

sample space a list of all possible outcomes
(Lesson 10-2)

GET READY for the Lesson

Follow the steps to determine how many times a sum of 7 is expected to turn up when two number cubes are rolled.

Step 1 Use an addition table from 1 to 6 to help you find the expected number of times the sum of 7 should come up after rolling two number cubes 36 times. The top row represents one number cube, and the left column represents the other number cube.

+	1	2	3	4	5	6
1	2	3	4	5	6	7
2	3	4	5	6	7	8

Step 2 Roll two number cubes 36 times. Record the number of times the sum of the number cubes is 7.

1. Compare the number of times you *expected* to roll a sum of 7 with the number of times you *actually* rolled a sum of 7. Then compare your result to the results of other groups.
2. Write the probability of rolling a sum of 7 out of 36 rolls using the number of times you *expected* to roll a 7 from Step 1. Then write the probability of rolling a sum of 7 out of 36 rolls using the number of times you *actually* rolled a sum of 7 from Step 2.

In the Mini-Lab above, you found both the theoretical probability and the experimental probability of rolling a sum of 7 using two number cubes. **Theoretical probability** is a probability based on what *should* happen when conducting a probability experiment. This is the probability you have been using since Lesson 10-1. **Experimental probability** is based on what *actually* occurred during such an experiment.

Theoretical Probability

$\frac{6}{36}$ ← 6 rolls *should* occur
← total number of rolls

Experimental Probability

$\frac{n}{36}$ ← *n* rolls *actually* occured
← total number of rolls

The theoretical probability and the experimental probability of an event may or may not be the same. As the number of times an experiment is conducted increases, the theoretical probability and the experimental probability should become closer in value.

EXAMPLE Experimental Probability

1 **Two number cubes are rolled 75 times, and a sum of 9 is rolled 10 times. What is the experimental probability of rolling a sum of 9?**

$$P(9) = \frac{\text{number of these times a sum of 9 occurs}}{\text{total number of rolls}}$$

$$= \frac{10}{75} \text{ or } \frac{2}{15}$$

The experimental probability of rolling a sum of 9 is $\frac{2}{15}$.

CHECK Your Progress

a. In the above experiment, what is the experimental probability of rolling a sum that is *not* 9?

b. In the above experiment, what is the experimental probability of rolling a sum that is *not* six if a sum of six was rolled 18 times?

STUDY TIP

Trials A *trial* is one experiment in a series of successive experiments.

EXAMPLES Experimental and Theoretical Probability

2 **The graph shows the results of an experiment in which a coin was tossed thirty times. Find the experimental probability of tossing tails for this experiment.**

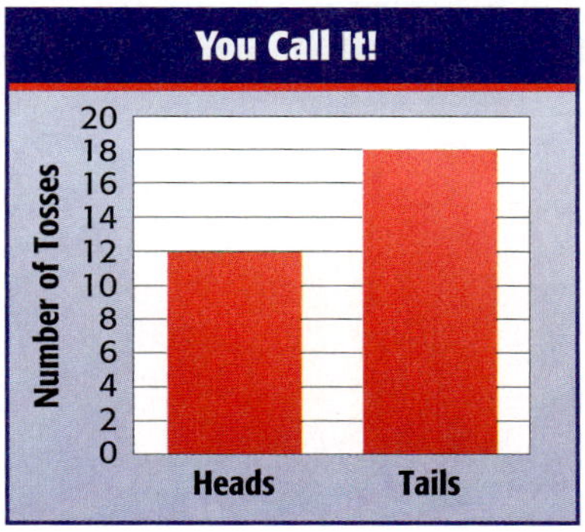

The frequency graph indicates that the coin landed on heads 12 times and tails 18 times.

$$P(\text{tails}) = \frac{\text{number of times tails occurs}}{\text{total number of tosses}}$$

$$= \frac{18}{30} \text{ or } \frac{3}{5}$$

The experimental probability of tossing tails was $\frac{3}{5}$.

3 **Compare the experimental probability you found in Example 2 to its theoretical probability.**

The coin has two possible outcomes, heads or tails. So, the theoretical probability of tossing tails on a coin is $\frac{1}{2}$. Since $\frac{3}{5} \approx \frac{1}{2}$, the experimental probability is close to the theoretical probability.

CHECK Your Progress

c. Refer to Example 2. If the coin was tossed 2 more times and landed on tails each time, find the experimental probability of tossing heads for this experiment.

d. Compare the experimental probability you found in Exercise c to its theoretical probability.

Online **Personal Tutor at** tx.msmath2.com

Real-World Career . . .
How Does a Chef Use Math? In addition to cooking, chefs order enough food and supplies based on customers' preferences and recent sales.

Math Online
For more information, go to tx.msmath2.com.

Experimental probability can be used to make predictions about future events.

Real-World EXAMPLES Predict Future Events

4 **FOOD** **In a survey, 100 people in a city were asked to name their favorite Independence Day side dishes. What is the experimental probability of macaroni salad being someone's favorite dish?**

Side Dish	Number of People
potato salad	55
green salad or vegetables	25
macaroni salad	12
coleslaw	8

There were 100 people surveyed and 12 chose macaroni salad. So, the experimental probability is $\frac{12}{100}$, or $\frac{3}{25}$.

5 **Suppose 2,500 people attend the city's Independence Day barbecue. Based on the survey results how many can be expected to choose macaroni salad as their favorite side dish?**

$\frac{3}{25} = \frac{x}{2{,}500}$ Write a proportion.

$3 \cdot 2{,}500 = 25 \cdot x$ Find the cross products.

$7{,}500 = 25x$ Multiply.

$300 = x$ Divide each side by 25.

About 300 will choose macaroni salad.

CHECK Your Progress

e. What is the experimental probability of potato salad being someone's favorite dish?

f. About how many people can be expected to choose potato salad as their favorite dish if 400 attend the barbecue?

CHECK Your Understanding

Examples 1–3 (p. 531)

For Exercises 1–3, a coin is tossed 50 times, and it lands on heads 28 times.

1. Find the experimental probability of the coin landing heads.
2. Find the theoretical probability of the coin landing heads.
3. Compare the probabilities in Exercises 1 and 2.

TRAFFIC **For Exercises 4 and 5, use the table of the types of vehicles that drove through an intersection between 3:00 and 4:00 P.M. one Saturday.**

Vehicle	Number of Vehicles
sedan	11
truck	15
sports car	6

Example 4 (p. 532)

4. Based on this information, what is the probability that a vehicle that drives through the intersection is a sports car?

Example 5 (p. 532)

5. If 128 vehicles drove through the intersection, about how many would you expect to be sports cars?

Exercises

HOMEWORK HELP

For Exercises	See Examples
6–7	1–3
8–9	4
10–11	5

For Exercises 6 and 7, a number cube is rolled 20 times and lands on 1 two times and on 5 four times.

6. Find the experimental probability of landing on 5. Compare the experimental probability to the theoretical probability.
7. Find the experimental probability of *not* landing on 1. Compare the experimental probability to the theoretical probability.

X GAMES For Exercises 8–11, use the graph of a survey of 50 students asked to name their favorite X Game sport.

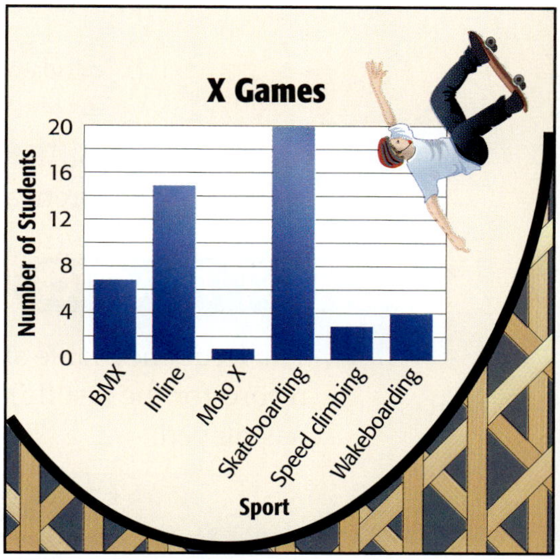

8. What is the probability of Moto X being someone's favorite sport?
9. What is the probability of skateboarding being someone's favorite sport?
10. Suppose 500 students attend the X Games. Predict how many will choose inline as their favorite sport.
11. Suppose 850 students attend. Predict how many will choose speed climbing as their favorite sport.

For Exercises 12–14, a spinner with three equal-sized sections marked A, B, and C was spun 100 times. The results are shown in the table.

Section	Frequency
A	24
B	50
C	26

12. What is the experimental probability of landing on A? Of landing on C?
13. If this spinner is spun 20 more times, predict how many of these times the pointer will land on B.
14. Make a drawing of what the spinner might look like based on its experimental probabilities. Explain your reasoning.

GIFTS For Exercises 15–17, use the graph at the right.

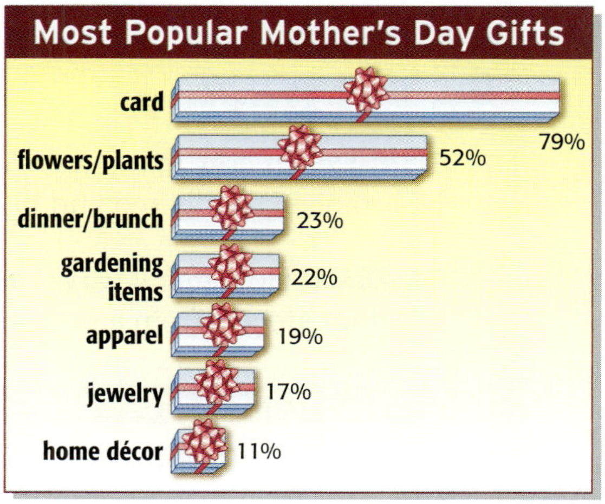

Source: Carlton Cards

15. What is the probability that a mother will receive a gift of flowers or plants? Write the probability as a fraction.
16. Out of 400 mothers that receive gifts, predict how many will receive flowers or plants.
17. Out of 750 mothers that receive gifts, is it reasonable to expect 250 mothers to receive jewelry? Why or why not?

EXTRA PRACTICE

See page 743, 764.

Math Online
Self-Check Quiz at tx.msmath2.com

H.O.T. Problems

18. **CHALLENGE** The experimental probability of a coin landing on heads is $\frac{7}{12}$. If the coin landed on tails 30 times, find the number of tosses.

19. **SELECT A TOOL** The results of rolling a number cube are shown. Which of the following tools could you use to determine the *minimum* number of additional rolls needed and their frequency of landing on each number so that the experimental probabilities will be equal to the theoretical probabilities? Justify your selection(s). Then use your tool(s) to solve the problem.

Number	Frequency
1	8
2	12
3	4
4	8
5	6
6	10

calculator   real object   paper/pencil

20. **WRITING IN MATH** Compare and contrast experimental probability and theoretical probability.

TEST PRACTICE

21. The frequency table shows Mitch's record for the last thirty par-3 holes he has played.

Mitch's Golf Results	
Score	**Number of Holes**
2	4
3	14
4	9
5	3

Based on this record, what is the probability that Mitch will score a 2 or 3 on the next par-3 hole?

A $\frac{7}{9}$ C $\frac{3}{10}$

B $\frac{3}{5}$ D $\frac{9}{50}$

22. J.R. tossed a coin 100 times and graphed the results.

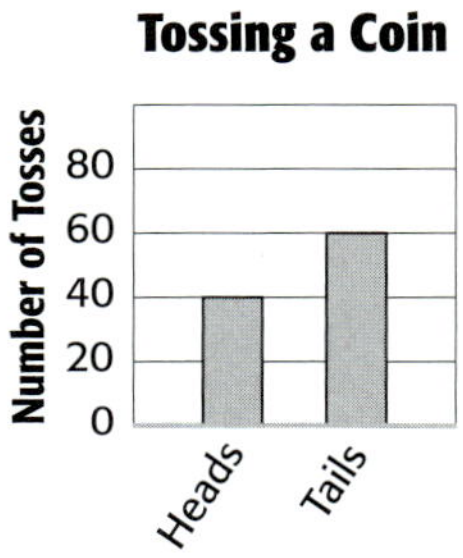

Based on this information, what is the experimental probability of tossing tails on the next toss?

F $\frac{1}{5}$ H $\frac{3}{5}$

G $\frac{2}{3}$ J $\frac{4}{5}$

Spiral Review

23. **SPINNERS** In how many ways could the colors in the spinner shown be arranged so that red and blue remain in the same places? (Lesson 10-6)

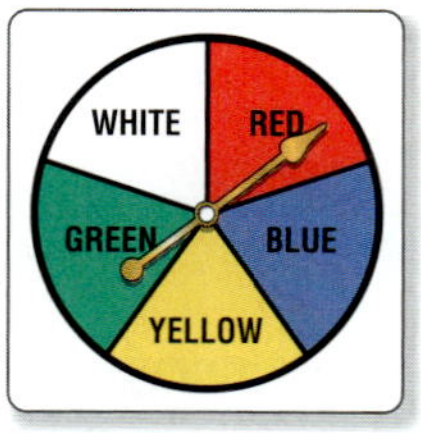

24. **BASEBALL** How many ways can a baseball coach select four starting pitchers from a pitching staff of eight? (Lesson 10-5)

GET READY for the Next Lesson

PREREQUISITE SKILL **Write each fraction as a percent.** (Lesson 7-7)

25. $\frac{4}{5}$ 26. $\frac{11}{20}$ 27. $\frac{7}{8}$ 28. $\frac{39}{50}$

Extend 10-7

Probability Lab
Simulations

Main IDEA

Investigate experimental probability by conducting a simulation.

Targeted TEKS **7.10** The student recognizes that a physical or mathematical model can be used to describe the experimental and theoretical probability of real-life events. **(A) construct sample spaces for simple or composite experiments.**

STUDY TIP

Assumption This simulation assumes that each prize is equally likely to appear in each box of cereal.

A *simulation* is a way of acting out a problem situation. Simulations often use models to act out events that would be difficult or impractical to perform. In this lab, you will simulate purchasing a box of cereal and getting one of four possible prizes inside.

ACTIVITY

STEP 1 Place four different colored cubes into a paper bag.

STEP 2 Without looking, draw a cube from the bag, record its color, and then place the cube back in the bag.

STEP 3 Repeat steps 1 and 2 until you have drawn a cube from the bag a total of four times.

ANALYZE THE RESULTS

1. Based on your results, find the experimental probability of getting each prize.
2. What is the theoretical probability of getting each prize?
3. How do your probabilities in Exercises 1 and 2 compare?
4. **MAKE A PREDICTION** Predict the probability of selecting all four prizes in four boxes of cereal.
5. Repeat the simulation above 20 times. Use this data to find the experimental probability of selecting all four prizes in four boxes of cereal.
6. Calculate the experimental probability describe in Exercise 5 using the combined data of five different groups. How does this probability compare with your prediction?
7. Describe a simulation that could be used to determine the experimental probability of taking a five question true/false test and getting all five questions correct by guessing. Choose from among two-sided counters, number cubes, coins, or spinners as your model.
8. **COLLECT THE DATA** Conduct 50 trials of the experiment you described in Exercise 7. Then calculate the experimental probability of getting all five questions correct by guessing.

10-8 Independent Events

Main IDEA

Find the probability of independent events.

Targeted TEKS 7.10 The student recognizes that a physical or mathematical model can be used to describe the experimental and theoretical probability of real-life events. **(B) find the probability of independent events.**

NEW Vocabulary

composite event
independent events

READING Math

Probability Notation
P(A, B) is read the probability of A followed by B.

GET READY for the Lesson

TRACK AND FIELD The 100-meter dash features 20 runners competing in a preliminary round of 4 heats. The winner of each heat advances to the final race. Before the race, each runner chooses a number from jar 1 to determine the heat in which he runs and a number from jar 2 to determine one of five lanes he occupies. Omar is the first runner to choose from the jars.

1. What is the probability of Omar being in the second heat? in lane 3?
2. Multiply your answers in Exercise 1. What does this number represent?

In the example above, choosing the heat and the lane is a compound, or *composite*, event. A **composite event** consists of two or more simple events. Since choosing the heat number does not affect choosing the lane number, the two events are called **independent events**. The outcome of one event does not affect the outcome of the other event.

EXAMPLE Independent Events

1 **A coin is tossed, and the spinner shown is spun. Find the probability of tossing heads and spinning a consonant.**

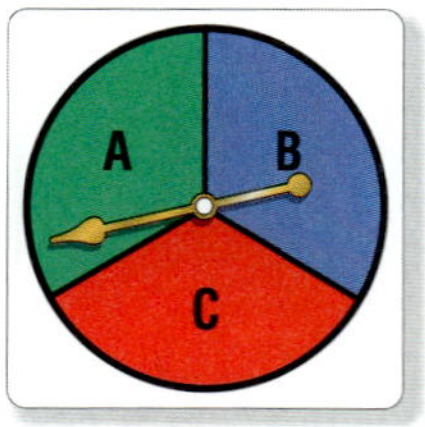

List the sample space. Use H for heads and T for tails.

H, A	H, B	H, C
T, A	T, B	T, C

$$P(\text{H and a consonant}) = \frac{\text{number of times heads and a consonant occurs}}{\text{number of possible coutcomes}}$$

$$P(\text{H and a consonant}) = \frac{2}{6} \text{ or } \frac{1}{3}$$

So, the probability is $\frac{1}{3}$ or about 33%.

CHECK Your Progress

A number cube is rolled, and the spinner in Example 1 is spun. Find each probability.

a. $P(4 \text{ and a consonant})$

b. $P(\text{odd and a B })$

The probability in Example 1 can also be found by multiplying the probabilities of each event. $P(\text{H}) = \frac{1}{2}$ and $P(\text{C}) = \frac{1}{3}$ and so $P(\text{H and C}) = \frac{1}{2} \cdot \frac{1}{3}$ or $\frac{1}{6}$. This leads to the following.

KEY CONCEPT — Probability of Independent Events

Words The probability of two independent events can be found by multiplying the probability of the first event by the probability of the second event.

Symbols $P(A \text{ and } B) = P(A) \cdot P(B)$

Real-World EXAMPLE

2 SNACKS Kayla chooses from a box containing 2 oatmeal, 3 strawberry, and 6 cinnamon snack bars. For a drink, she chooses from milk or water. If Kayla chooses a snack and a drink at random, find the probability that she chooses a cinnamon bar and milk.

$P(\text{cinnamon and milk}) = P(\text{cinnamon}) \cdot P(\text{milk})$

$= \frac{6}{11} \cdot \frac{1}{2}$ — 6 out of 11 bars are cinnamon. 1 out of 2 drink choices is milk.

$= \frac{\overset{3}{\cancel{6}}}{11} \cdot \frac{1}{\underset{1}{\cancel{2}}}$ or $\frac{3}{11}$ — Simplify.

So, the probability is $\frac{3}{11}$ or about 27%.

STUDY TIP

Reasonable Answer You can check your answer in Example 2 by listing the sample space or by making a tree diagram.

CHECK Your Progress

c. **SNACKS** If soda and juice are added to Kayla's drink choices, find the probability that she chooses an oatmeal bar and water.

Online Personal Tutor at tx.msmath2.com

CHECK Your Understanding

Example 1 (p. 536)

A number cube is rolled, and the spinner is spun. Find each probability.

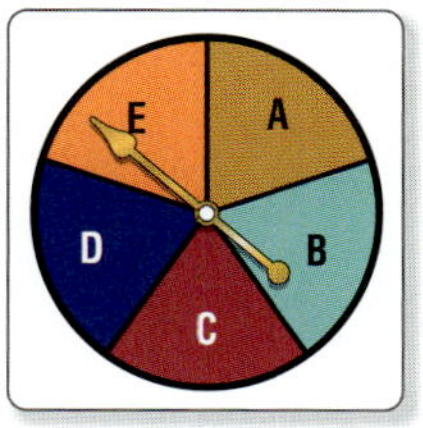

1. $P(\text{5 and E})$
2. $P(\text{2 and vowel})$
3. $P(\text{3 and a consonant})$
4. $P(\text{factor of 6 and D})$

Example 2 (p. 537)

5. **CLOTHES** Loretta has 2 pairs of black jeans, 3 pairs of blue jeans, and 1 pair of tan jeans. She also has 4 white and 2 red T-shirts. If Loretta chooses a pair of jeans and a T-shirt at random, what is the probability that she will choose a pair of black jeans and a white T-shirt?

6. **MARBLES** A jar contains 12 marbles. Four are red, 3 are white, and 5 are blue. A marble is randomly selected, its color recorded, and then the marble is returned to the jar. A second marble is randomly selected. Find the probability that both marbles selected are blue.

Math Online Extra Examples at tx.msmath2.com

Exercises

For Exercises	See Examples
7–12	1
13–14	2

HOMEWORK HELP

A coin is tossed, and a number cube is rolled. Find each probability.

7. P(heads and 1)
8. P(tails and multiple of 3)

A set of five cards is labeled 1–5. A second set of ten cards contains the following colors: 2 red, 3 purple, and 5 green. One card from each set is selected. Find each probability.

9. P(5 and green)
10. P(odd and red)
11. P(prime and purple)
12. P(even and yellow)

13. **MUSIC** Denzel is listening to a CD that contains 12 songs. If he presses the random button on his CD player, what is the probability that the first two songs played will be the first two songs listed on the album?

14. **JUICE POPS** Lakita has two boxes of juice pops with an equal number of pops in each flavor. Find the probability of randomly selecting a grape juice pop from the first box and randomly selecting a juice pop from the second box that is *not* grape.

A coin is tossed twice, and a letter is picked from the word *event*. Find each probability.

15. P(two heads and T)
16. P(tails, not tails, consonant)
17. P(heads, tails, not V)
18. P(two tails and vowel)

FAMILY For Exercises 19–21, use the fact that the probability for a boy or a girl is each $\frac{1}{2}$.

19. Copy and complete the table that gives the probability that all the children in a family are boys given the number of children in the family.
20. Find the probability that, in a family of ten children, all ten are boys.
21. Find the probability that, in a family of n children, all n are boys.

Number of Children	P(all boys)
1	$\frac{1}{2}$
2	$\frac{1}{2} \cdot \frac{1}{2}$ or $\frac{1}{4}$
3	■
4	■
5	■

22. **TRAFFIC** Two consecutive traffic signals on a street operate independently of each other. The first signal is green 45% of the time, and the second signal is yellow 10% of the time and red 40% of the time. What is the probability of a person driving down the street making both green lights? Write as a percent.

23. **CIVICS** In the 109th Congress, California had 33 Democrats and 20 Republicans serving in the House of Representatives while Texas had 11 Democrats and 21 Republicans. If a subcommittee of 2 representatives, one from each state, is randomly formed, what is the probability that both would be Republicans? Write as a percent to the nearest tenth.

EXTRA PRACTICE

See pages 744, 764.

Math Online

Self-Check Quiz at tx.msmath2.com

H.O.T. Problems

CHALLENGE For Exercises 24 and 25, use the spinner.

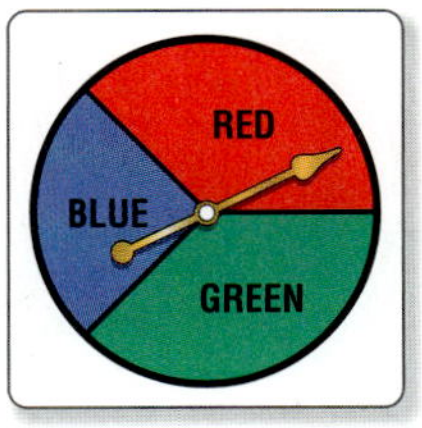

24. Use a tree diagram to construct the sample space of all the possible outcomes of three successive spins.

25. Suppose the spinner is designed so that for each spin there is a 40% probability of spinning red and a 20% chance of spinning blue. What is the probability of spinning two reds and then one blue?

26. **WRITING IN MATH** A shelf has books A, B, and C on it. You pick a book at random, place it on a table, and then pick a second book. Explain why the probability that you picked books A and B is *not* $\frac{1}{9}$.

TEST PRACTICE

27. You take a 4-question quiz made up of multiple-choice questions having 4 choices each. If you guess on all 4 questions, what is the probability you will get 100%?

A $\frac{1}{256}$ C $\frac{1}{16}$

B $\frac{1}{64}$ D $\frac{1}{4}$

28. What is the probability of spinning a red, the number 1, and the letter A on the three spinners below?

F $\frac{1}{3}$ G $\frac{1}{32}$ H $\frac{1}{12}$ J $\frac{1}{64}$

Spiral Review

29. **PROBABILITY** Paz performed a probability experiment by spinning a spinner 20 times. The results are shown in the table. If the spinner is divided into four equal sections, how many sections would you expect to be blue? (Lesson 10-7)

Color	Frequency
red	𝍸
green	𝍸 𝍸
blue	𝍸

30. **CHORES** This weekend, Brennen needs to do laundry, mow the lawn, and clean his room. How many different ways can he do these three chores? (Lesson 10-6)

Evaluate each expression if $a = 6$, $b = -4$, and $c = -3$. (Lesson 2-7)

31. $9c$ 32. $-8a$ 33. $2bc$ 34. $5b^2$

Cross-Curricular Project

Math and Recreation

Step Right Up and Win a Prize It's time to complete your project. Use the information and data you have gathered about carnival games to prepare a Web page or poster. Be sure to include a scale drawing of the game you design with your project.

Math Online **Cross-Curricular Project at** tx.msmath2.com

Study Guide and Review

STUDY TO GO Download Vocabulary Review from tx.msmath2.com

FOLDABLES™ Study Organizer

GET READY to Study

Be sure the following Key Concepts are noted in your Foldable.

Key Concepts

Probability (Lesson 10-1)

- The probability of a simple event is a ratio that compares the number of favorable outcomes to the number of possible outcomes.

Fundamental Counting Principle (Lesson 10-3)

- If event *M* has *m* possible outcomes and is followed by event *N* that has *n* possible outcomes, then the event *M* followed by *N* has $m \times n$ possible outcomes.

Permutations and Combinations (Lessons 10-4, 10-5)

- A permutation is an arrangement, or listing, of objects in which order is important.
- A combination is an arrangement, or listing, of objects in which order is *not* important.

Theoretical and Experimental Probability (Lesson 10-7)

- Theoretical probability is based on what *should* happen when conducting a probability experiment.
- Experimental probability is based on what *actually occurred* during a probability experiment.

Independent Events (Lesson 10-8)

- The probability of two independent events can be found by multiplying the probability of the first event by the probability of the second event.

Key Vocabulary

combination (p. 524)
complementary events (p. 506)
composite event (p. 536)
experimental probability (p. 530)
fair game (p. 511)
Fundamental Counting Principle (p. 515)
independent events (p. 536)
outcome (p. 504)
permutation (p. 519)
probability (p. 504)
random (p. 505)
sample space (p. 509)
simple event (p. 504)
theoretical probability (p. 530)
tree diagram (p. 510)

Vocabulary Check

State whether each sentence is *true* or *false*. If *false*, replace the underlined word or number to make a true sentence.

1. <u>Composite events</u> consists of two or more simple events.
2. A <u>random</u> outcome is an outcome that occurs by chance.
3. P(not A) is read the <u>permutation</u> of the complement of A.
4. The Fundamental Counting Principle counts the number of possible outcomes using the operation of <u>addition</u>.
5. Events in which the outcome of the first event does not affect the outcome of the other event(s) are <u>simple events</u>.
6. The <u>sample space</u> of an event is the set of outcomes not included in the event.
7. A game in which players of equal skill have an equal chance of winning is a <u>complementary event</u>.

Lesson-by-Lesson Exercises and Examples

10-1 Simple Events (pp. 504–508)

A bag contains 6 red, 3 pink, and 3 white bows. Suppose you draw a bow at random. Find the probability of each event. Write as a fraction in simplest form.

8. $P(\text{red})$
9. $P(\text{white})$
10. $P(\text{red or pink})$
11. $P(\textit{not}\text{ pink})$
12. $P(\text{red, white, or pink})$

13. **ARRIVALS** The probability that a plane will arrive at the airport on time is $\frac{23}{25}$. Find the probability that the plane will *not* arrive on time. Write as a percent.

Example 1 **What is the probability of rolling an odd number on a number cube?**

$$P(\text{odd}) = \frac{\text{number of odd outcomes}}{\text{total number of possible outcomes}}$$

$= \frac{3}{6}$ Three numbers are odd: 1, 3, and 5.

$= \frac{1}{2}$ Simplify.

Therefore, $P(\text{odd}) = \frac{1}{2}$.

10-2 Sample Spaces (pp. 509–514)

For each situation, find the sample space using a table or tree diagram.

14. rolling a number cube and tossing a coin
15. choosing from white, wheat, or rye bread and turkey, ham, or salami to make a sandwich.
16. **GAMES** Eliza and Zeke are playing a game in which Zeke spins the spinner shown and rolls a number cube. If the sum of the numbers is less than six, Eliza wins. Otherwise Zeke wins. Find the sample space. Then determine if this is a fair game.

Example 2 **Ginger and Micah are playing a game in which a coin is tossed twice. If heads comes up exactly once, Ginger wins. Otherwise Micah wins. Find the sample space. Then determine if this is a fair game.**

Make a tree diagram.

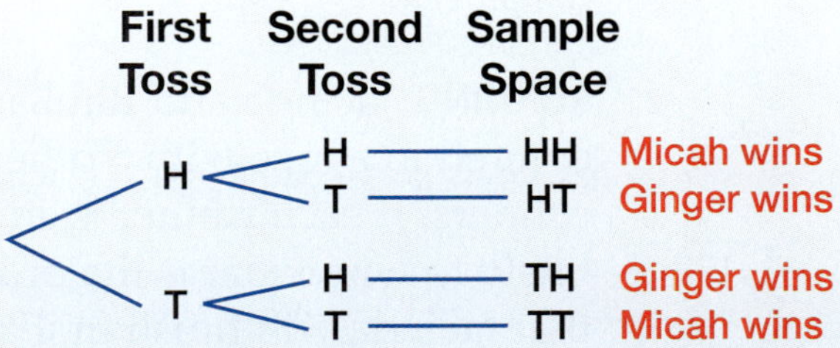

There are four equally-likely outcomes with 2 favoring each player. The probability that each player wins is $\frac{2}{4}$ or $\frac{1}{2}$. So, the game is fair.

10-3 The Fundamental Counting Principle (pp. 515–518)

Use the Fundamental Counting Principle to find the total number of outcomes in each situation.

17. rolling two number cubes
18. making an ice cream sundae selecting from 5 flavors of ice cream and 4 different toppings
19. **SHOPPING** A catalog offers a jogging suit in three colors, gray, pink, and black. It comes in sizes S, M, L, XL, and XXL and is available with a hood or without a hood. If a jogging suit is selected at random, what is the probability that it will be a pink hooded suit in size medium?

Example 3 **Use the Fundamental Counting Principle to find the total number of outcomes for a family that has four children.**

There are 2 possible outcomes, a boy or a girl, each time a child is born. For a family with four children, there are $2 \cdot 2 \cdot 2 \cdot 2$, or 16 outcomes.

Example 4 **Find the probability that, in a family of four children, all four children are girls.**

There are 16 outcomes. There is one possible outcome resulting in four girls. So, the probability that all four children are girls is $\frac{1}{16}$.

10-4 Permutations (pp. 519–522)

20. **BASKETBALL** In how many ways can five basketball players be placed in three positions: center, forward, and guard?
21. **LETTERS** How many permutations are there of the letters in the word *computer*?
22. **RUNNING** Jacinda and Raul are entered in a race with 5 other runners. If each runner is equally likely to win, what is the probability that Jacinda will finish first and Raul will finish second?

Example 5 **Nathaniel needs to choose two of the chores shown to do after school. If he is equally likely to choose the chores, what is the probability that he will walk the dog first and rake the leaves second?**

Chores
Walk the Dog
Do Homework
Clean the Kitchen
Rake the Leaves

There are $4 \cdot 3$, or 12, arrangements in which Nathaniel can complete the chores. There is one way in which he will walk the dog first and rake the leaves second. So, the probability that he will walk the dog first and rake the leaves second is $\frac{1}{12}$.

Mixed Problem Solving
For mixed problem-solving practice, see page 764.

10-5 Combinations (pp. 524–527)

23. **PIZZA** How many three-topping pizzas are possible given eight different toppings?

24. **KITTENS** How many groups of three kittens are possible from a litter of six?

25. **GAMES** In how many ways can Rondell select two board games from the ten games that his family owns?

26. **QUIZ** Frances must answer 3 of the 5 questions on a quiz, numbered 1–5. What is the probability that Frances will answer questions 2, 3, and 4?

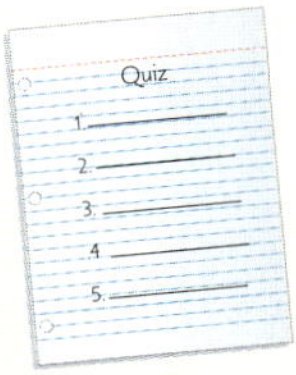

Example 6 **Caitlin and Román are playing a game in which Román chooses four different numbers from 1–15. What is the probability that Caitlin will guess all four numbers correctly?**

There are $15 \cdot 14 \cdot 13 \cdot 12$ permutations of four numbers chosen from 15 numbers.

There are $4 \cdot 3 \cdot 2 \cdot 1$ ways to arrange the 4 numbers.

$$\frac{15 \cdot 14 \cdot 13 \cdot 12}{4 \cdot 3 \cdot 2 \cdot 1} = \frac{32{,}760}{24} \text{ or } 1{,}365$$

There are 1,365 ways to choose four numbers from 15 numbers. There is one way to guess all four numbers correctly, so the probability that Caitlin will guess all four numbers correctly is $\frac{1}{1{,}365}$.

10-6 PSI: Act it Out (pp. 528–529)

Solve each problem. Use the *act it out* strategy.

27. **QUIZ** Determine whether tossing a coin is a good way to answer a 6-question true-false quiz. Justify your answer.

28. **FAMILY PORTRAIT** In how many ways can the Maxwell family pose for a portrait if Mr. and Mrs. Maxwell are sitting in the middle and their three children are standing behind them?

29. **AMUSEMENT PARK** In how many ways can 4 friends be seated in 2 rows of 2 seats each on a roller coaster if Judy and Harold must ride together?

Example 7 **In how many ways can three females and two males sit in a row of six seats at a concert if the females must sit in the first three seats?**

Place five desks or chairs in a row. Have three females and two males sit in any of the seats as long as the females sit in the first three seats. Continue rearranging until you find all the possibilities. Record the results.

$F_1\ F_2\ F_3\ M_1\ M_2$ $F_2\ F_3\ F_1\ M_1\ M_2$
$F_1\ F_2\ F_3\ M_2\ M_1$ $F_2\ F_3\ F_1\ M_2\ M_1$
$F_1\ F_3\ F_2\ M_1\ M_2$ $F_3\ F_2\ F_1\ M_1\ M_2$
$F_1\ F_3\ F_2\ M_2\ M_1$ $F_3\ F_2\ F_1\ M_2\ M_1$
$F_2\ F_1\ F_3\ M_1\ M_2$ $F_3\ F_1\ F_2\ M_1\ M_2$
$F_2\ F_1\ F_3\ M_2\ M_1$ $F_3\ F_1\ F_2\ M_2\ M_1$

There are 12 possible arrangements.

10-7 Theoretical and Experimental Probability (pp. 530–534)

The results of spinning a spinner labeled A–E fifty times are given. Find the experimental probability of each event.

Letter	Frequency
A	8
B	17
C	9
D	6
E	10

30. $P(\text{A})$
31. $P(\text{D})$
32. $P(\text{E})$
33. $P(\text{A or B})$
34. $P(\textit{not}\ \text{C})$
35. $P(\text{B or D})$
36. If the spinner is equally likely to land on each section, what is the theoretical probability of landing on B?

Example 8 **A coin is tossed 75 times, and it lands on tails 55 times. What is the experimental probability of the coin landing on heads?**

The coin landed on heads 20 times.

$$P(\text{heads}) = \frac{\text{number of times heads occurs}}{\text{total number of possible outcomes}}$$

$$= \frac{20}{75} \text{ or } \frac{4}{15}$$

So, the experimental probability of the coin landing on heads is $\frac{4}{15}$ or about 27%.

10-8 Independent Events (pp. 536–539)

A bag contains 6 green, 8 white, and 2 blue counters. Two counters are randomly drawn. Find each probability if the first counter is replaced before the second counter is drawn.

37. $P(\text{green, blue})$
38. $P(\text{2 white})$
39. $P(\text{blue, not green})$
40. $P(\text{not white, white})$
41. **PROBABILITY** A coin is tossed and a number cube is rolled. Find the probability that tails and a number less than 5 comes up.
42. **SHOPPING** The table gives the choices for cheese and milk at a grocery store. If Kaleb selects a package of cheese and a gallon of milk at random, what is the probability that she selects chocolate milk and Swiss cheese?

Cheese	Milk
Cheddar	Chocolate
Mozzarella	Vitamin D
Swiss	Skim
Colby	

Example 9 **A box contains 12 solid, 14 striped, and 10 spotted marbles. You reach in and grab two marbles. Find the probability of choosing a striped marble, replacing it, and then choosing a spotted marble.**

$P(\text{striped}) = \frac{14}{36}$

$P(\text{spotted, after replacing the striped}) = \frac{10}{36}$

$$\frac{14}{36} \cdot \frac{10}{36} = \frac{140}{1{,}296} \text{ or } \frac{35}{324}$$

So, the probability of choosing a striped marble, replacing it, and then choosing a spotted marble is $\frac{35}{324}$, or about 11%.

Chapter 10 Practice Test

The spinner shown has an equal chance of landing on each number. Find each probability.

1. P(odd number)
2. P(1 or 7)
3. P(*not* a prime number)
4. P(number greater than 1)

For each situation, use a table or a tree diagram to find the sample space.

5. A coin is tossed three times.
6. A letter is chosen from the word *MATH* and then a digit from the number 123.
7. **GAMES** Randall and Lucy are playing a game in which Lucy rolls a number cube and selects a card from the cards *A* and *B*. If a number less than 4 and a consonant comes up, Lucy wins. Otherwise Randall wins. Find the sample space. Then determine if this is a fair game.

Use the Fundamental Counting Principle to find the total number of outcomes in each situation.

8. A 3-digit security code is chosen.
9. A number cube is rolled four times.
10. **TEST PRACTICE** A certain store sells picture frames in sizes 5 inches by 7 inches and 8 inches by 10 inches. The frames can be either black, silver, wood, or white. Which expression correctly uses the Fundamental Counting Principle to find the number of possible outcomes of frames with these choices?

A 2×2
B 4×4
C 2×4
D $2 + 4$

11. **PARADES** If there are 50 floats in a parade, how many ways can a first place and a second place trophy be awarded?
12. **TEST PRACTICE** A brand of yogurt has 15 different flavors. Which of the following gives the number of ways in which you can choose three flavors?

F 2,730
G 455
H 45
J 5

13. **CAMPING** Four campers are chosen from nine to pitch the tents. If Sandy, Jarrod, Dyami, and Clara are among the nine campers, find the probability that they are chosen.
14. **SCHOOL** Determine whether spinning a spinner with five equal sections would be a good way to answer a 5-question multiple-choice quiz if each question has answer choices *A*, *B*, *C*, *D*, and *E*. Justify your answer.
15. **SURVEY** Two hundred fifty teenagers were asked what type of pet they owned. The results of the survey are in the table. What is the experimental probability that a teenager owns a pet? Write as a percent.

Pet	Number of Teenage Pet Owners
fish	26
cat	65
dog	86
bird	20
other	38
no pet	15

16. **POPCORN** Two variety bags of popcorn each contain 100 pieces of regular popcorn, 60 pieces of cheese popcorn, and 40 pieces of caramel popcorn. Peter picks one piece of popcorn from each bag. What is the probability that he picks caramel from the first bag and regular from the second bag?

Chapter 10 Texas Test Practice
Cumulative, Chapters 1–10

Read each question. Then fill in the correct answer on the answer document provided by your teacher or on a sheet of paper.

1. Jessica played a game where she spun each of the spinners shown below once. If she spins an even number on Spinner 1, red or yellow on Spinner 2, and a B on Spinner 3, how many possible unique combinations are there?

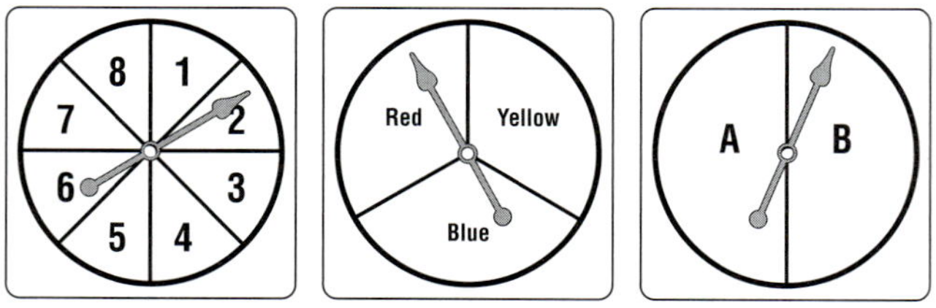

Spinner 1 Spinner 2 Spinner 3

A 4

B 8

C 10

D 16

2. Mr. Campos bought 40 pencils priced at 8 for \$0.99 and 3 dozen notebooks priced at 4 for \$2.49. Find the total amount, not including tax, Mr. Campos spent on pencils and notebooks.

F \$28.86

G \$27.36

H \$17.88

J \$15.96

3. In a movie theatre there are 168 seats. If 75% of the theatre is filled, how many people are sitting in the movie theatre?

A 156

B 148

C 134

D 126

4. **GRIDDABLE** Mr. Blackwell gave his math students a pop quiz. The students' scores are listed below. What is the median quiz score?

23	19	18	12	21	24	25

5. The results of an election for student body president showed that Trey received 250 votes, Marta 100 votes, and Ed 50 votes. Which of the following is NOT an appropriate way to display the election results?

F **Election Results**

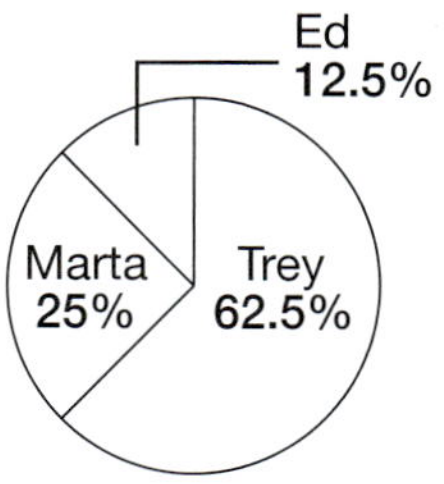

G

Election Results	
Candidates	**Votes**
Trey	250
Marta	100
Ed	50

H **Election Results**

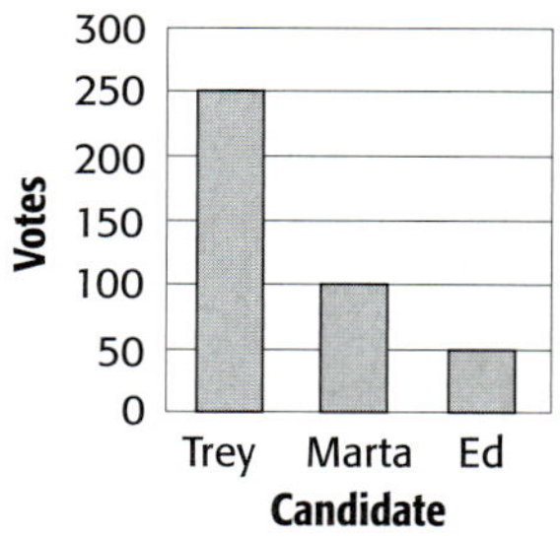

J **Election Results**

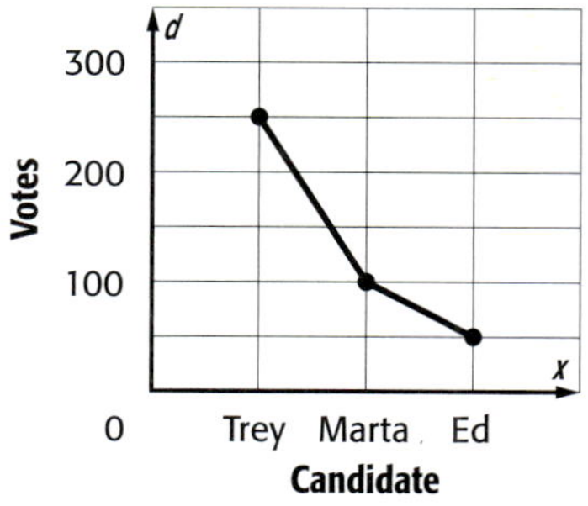

Get Ready for the Texas Test
For test-taking strategies and more practice, see pages TX1–TX23.

6. Hanako spins each spinner shown below once. Find the total possible letter/number combinations that could have resulted from Hanako's spins.

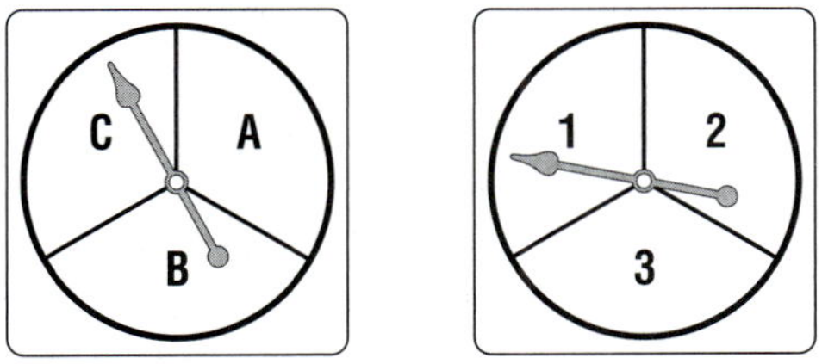

First Spinner   Second Spinner

A 3
B 6
C 9
D 12

7. Max has 3 pizzas to serve to his friends. If he gives each friend $\frac{1}{4}$ of a whole pizza, how many friends can Max serve?

F 4   **H** 12
G 8   **J** 16

8. The model below represents the equation $3x + 2 = 6y + 2$. What is the value of x?

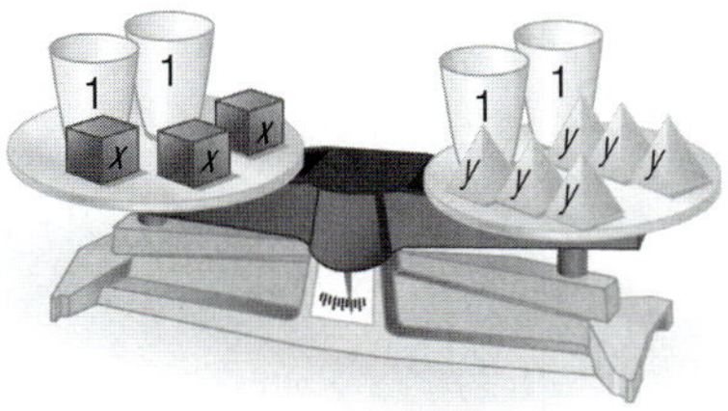

A $x = 2y$
B $x = 2y - 2$
C $x = 4y + 2$
D $x = 6y + 4$

9. **GRIDDABLE** Elizabeth spent $\frac{1}{2}$ of her baby-sitting money on a sweater and $\frac{1}{2}$ of the remaining amount on a pair of earrings. After she spent \$4.65 on a snack, she had \$7.35 left. How much baby-sitting money did Elizabeth have?

10. Wilson has 7 different pieces of fruit in his refrigerator. If he randomly selects 3 pieces of fruit, how many possible unique combinations are there?

F 7   **H** 21
G 14   **J** 35

TEST-TAKING TIP

Question 10 You may want to find your own answer before looking at the answer choices. Doing so keeps you from being tempted by wrong answer choices that look correct, but are still wrong.

Pre-AP

Record your answers on a sheet of paper. Show your work.

11. Paula has a 5-disc CD player. She has jazz, country, rap, pop, and R&B CDs in the player. She listens to the CDs on random mode on both Friday and Saturday night.
    a. Make a tree diagram that shows all of the possible outcomes.
    b. What is the probability that Paula will hear a country song first on Friday night?
    c. What is the probability that Paula will hear a rap song first on Friday night and a jazz song first on Saturday night?

NEED EXTRA HELP?											
If You Missed Question...	1	2	3	4	5	6	7	8	9	10	11
Go to Lesson...	10-2	3-2	8-1	9-2	9-8	10-2	6-7	4-5	4-4	10-5	10-8
For Help with Test Objective...	5	5	1	2	5	5	1	2	1	5	5

Unit 5

Geometry and Measurement

Focal Point

Use geometric properties, relationships, and formulas to model and analyze situations and solve problems.

CHAPTER 11
Geometry: Polygons

BIG Idea Use geometry to model and describe the physical world.

BIG Idea Use coordinate geometry to describe location on a plane.

CHAPTER 12
Measurement: Two- and Three-Dimensional Figures

BIG Idea Compare and classify two- and three-dimensional figures using geometric vocabulary and properties.

BIG Idea Solve application problems involving estimation and measurement.

CHAPTER 13
Extending Geometry and Algebra

BIG Idea Use indirect measurement to solve problems.

BIG Idea Use procedures to determine the measures of three-dimensional figures.

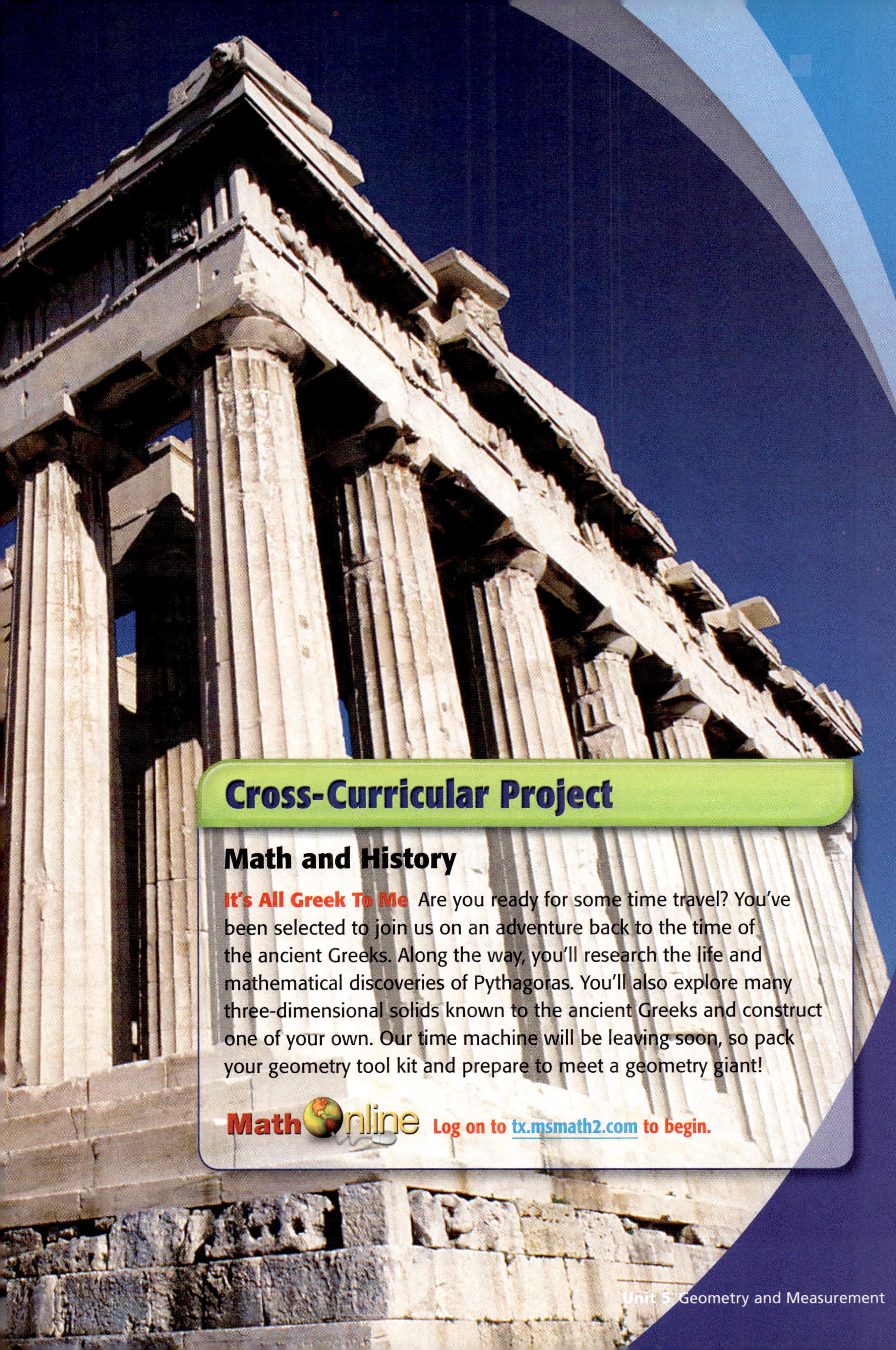

Cross-Curricular Project

Math and History

It's All Greek To Me Are you ready for some time travel? You've been selected to join us on an adventure back to the time of the ancient Greeks. Along the way, you'll research the life and mathematical discoveries of Pythagoras. You'll also explore many three-dimensional solids known to the ancient Greeks and construct one of your own. Our time machine will be leaving soon, so pack your geometry tool kit and prepare to meet a geometry giant!

Math Online **Log on to tx.msmath2.com to begin.**

CHAPTER 11

Geometry: Polygons

Knowledge and Skills

- Use coordinate geometry to describe location on a plane. **TEKS 7.7**
- Use geometry to model and describe the physical world. **TEKS 7.8**

Key Vocabulary

complementary angles (p. 553)
line of symmetry (p. 596)
similar figures (p. 578)
supplementary angles (p. 553)

Real-World Link

Tigers Geometry is used to explain how the face of a tiger shows a line of vertical reflection symmetry.

FOLDABLES™ Study Organizer

Geometry: Polygons Make this Foldable to help you organize your notes. Begin with a piece of 11″ by 17″ paper.

1. **Fold** a 2″ tab along the long side of the paper.

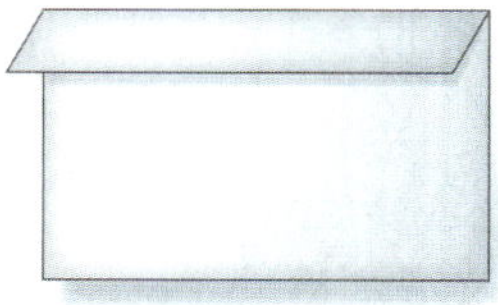

2. **Unfold** the paper and fold in thirds widthwise.

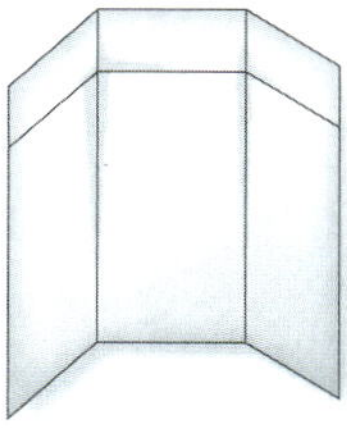

3. **Open** and draw lines along the folds. Label the head of each column as shown. Label the front of the folded table with the chapter title.

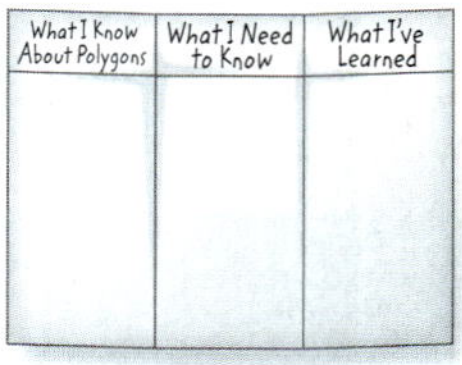

GET READY for Chapter 11

Diagnose Readiness You have two options for checking Prerequisite Skills.

Option 2

Math Online Take the Online Readiness Quiz at tx.msmath2.com.

Option 1

Take the Quick Quiz below. Refer to the Quick Review for help.

QUICK Quiz

Multiply or divide. Round to the nearest hundredth if necessary.

(Used in Lesson 11-2)

1. 360×0.85
2. $48 \div 191$
3. $24 \div 156$
4. 0.37×360
5. $33 \div 307$
6. 0.69×360

Solve each equation.

(Used in Lessons 11-3 and 11-4)

7. $122 + x + 14 = 180$
8. $45 + 139 + k + 17 = 360$
9. **SCHOOL** There are 180 school days at Lee Middle School. If school has been in session for 62 days and there are 13 days until winter break, how many school days are after the break?

Evaluate each expression.

(Used in Lesson 11-6)

10. $\frac{4}{a} = \frac{3}{9}$
11. $\frac{7}{16} = \frac{h}{32}$
12. $\frac{5}{8} = \frac{15}{y}$
13. $\frac{t}{42} = \frac{6}{7}$
14. **READING** Sandra can read 28 pages of a novel in 45 minutes. At this rate, how many pages can she read in 135 minutes?

QUICK Review

Example 1

Find 0.92×360.

$$\begin{array}{r} 360 \\ \times\ 0.92 \\ \hline 720 \\ +\ 32400 \\ \hline 331.20 \end{array}$$

$\times\ 0.92$ ← Two decimal places

331.20 ← Two decimal places

So, $0.92 \times 360 = 331.2$.

Example 2

Solve the equation.

$46 + 90 + p = 180$.

$46 + 90 + p = 180$	Write the equation.
$136 + p = 180$	Add 46 and 90.
$-136 \quad -136$	Subtract 136 from each side.
$p = 44$	

The solution to the equation $46 + 90 + p = 180$ is $p = 44$.

Example 3

Solve the proportion $\frac{3}{8} = \frac{g}{48}$.

$\frac{3}{8} = \frac{g}{48}$ Write a proportion.

$\frac{3}{8} = \frac{18}{48}$ (× 6 across the top and bottom) Since $8 \times 6 = 48$, multiply 3 by 6 to find g.

So, $g = 18$.

11-1 Angle Relationships

Main IDEA

Classify angles.

Targeted TEKS 7.6 The student compares and classifies two- and three-dimensional figures using geometric vocabulary and properties. **(A) use angle measurements to classify pairs of angles as complementary or supplementary.**

NEW Vocabulary

angle
degrees
vertex
congruent angles
right angle
acute angle
obtuse angle
straight angle
complementary angles
supplementary angles
perpendicular lines

READING Math

Geometry symbols

∠ *angle*
° *degree*

READING in the Content Area

For strategies in reading this lesson, visit tx.msmath2.com.

GET READY for the Lesson

CLOCKS The hands of a clock form angles of different sizes.

3:10 less than 90° | 3:00 90° | 3:40 greater than 90°

1. Name other times in which the hands of a clock form angles less than 90°, equal to 90°, and greater than 90°.
2. How many degrees is the angle that is formed by clock hands at 6:00?

An **angle** has two sides that share a common endpoint and is measured in units called **degrees**. If a circle were divided into 360 equal-sized parts, each part would have an angle measure of 1 degree (1°).

An angle can be named in several ways. The symbol for angle is ∠.

EXAMPLE Naming Angles

1 **Name the angle at the right.**

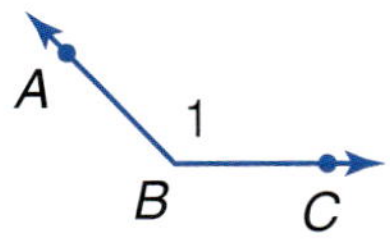

- Use the vertex as the middle letter and a point from each side.
  ∠*ABC* or ∠*CBA*
- Use the vertex only.
  ∠*B*
- Use a number.
  ∠1

The angle can be named in four ways: ∠*ABC*, ∠*CBA*, ∠*B*, or ∠1.

CHECK Your Progress

a. Name the angle shown in four ways.

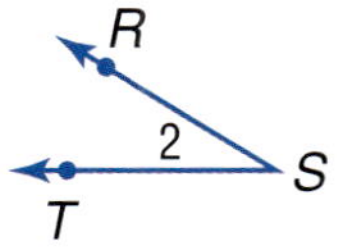

Angles are classified according to their measure. Two angles that have the same measure are said to be **congruent**.

KEY CONCEPT — Types of Angles

right angle

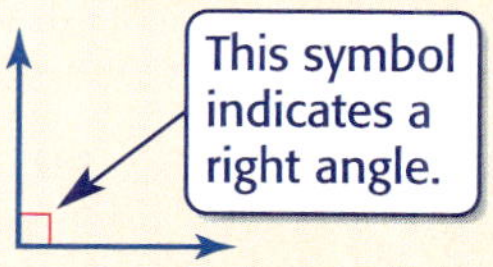

exactly 90°

acute angle

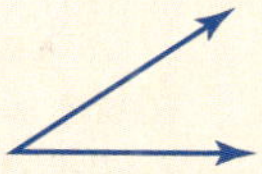

less than 90°

obtuse angle

between 90° and 180°

straight angle

exactly 180°

EXAMPLES Classify Angles

Classify each angle as *acute*, *obtuse*, *right*, or *straight*.

2

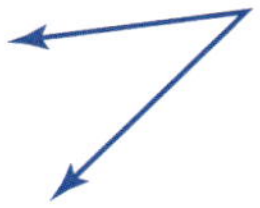

The angle is less than 90°, so it is an acute angle.

3

The angle is greater than 90°, so it is an obtuse angle.

CHECK Your Progress

Classify each angle as *acute*, *obtuse*, *right*, or *straight*.

b.

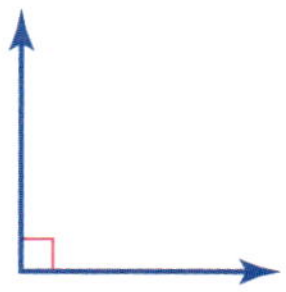

c.

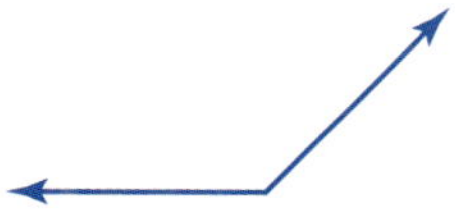

d.

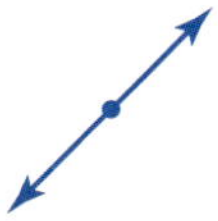

Some angle pairs share a special relationship.

KEY CONCEPT — Complementary Angles

Words Two angles are **complementary** if the sum of their measures is 90°.

Examples

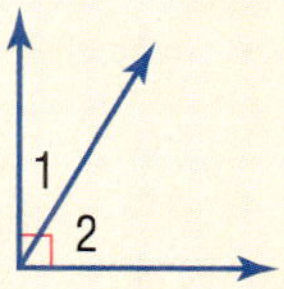

$m\angle 1 + m\angle 2 = 90°$

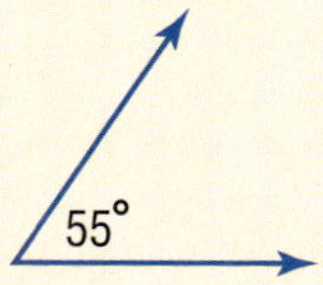

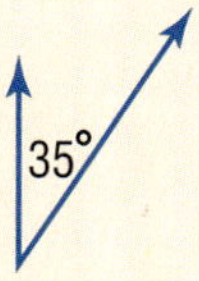

$55° + 35° = 90°$

Supplementary Angles

Words Two angles are **supplementary** if the sum of their measures is 180°.

Examples

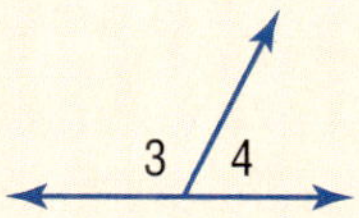

$m\angle 3 + m\angle 4 = 180°$

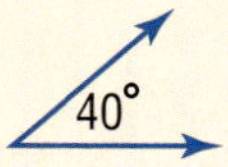

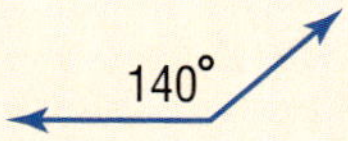

$40° + 140° = 180°$

READING Math

Angle Measure The notation $m\angle 1$ is read *the measure of angle 1*.

EXAMPLES Classify Angles

Classify each pair of angles as *complementary*, *supplementary*, or *neither*.

4

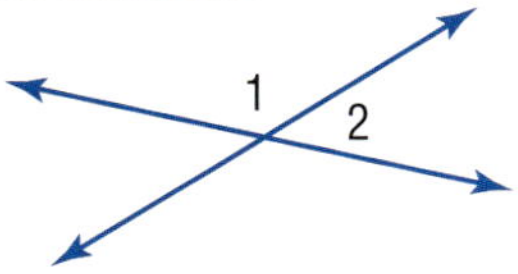

$\angle 1$ and $\angle 2$ form a straight angle. So, the angles are supplementary.

5

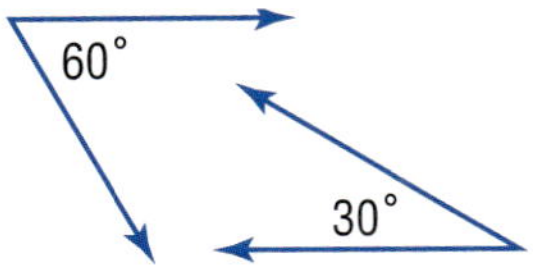

$60° + 30° = 90°$
The angles are complementary.

CHECK Your Progress

Classify each pair of angles as *complementary*, *supplementary*, or *neither*.

e.

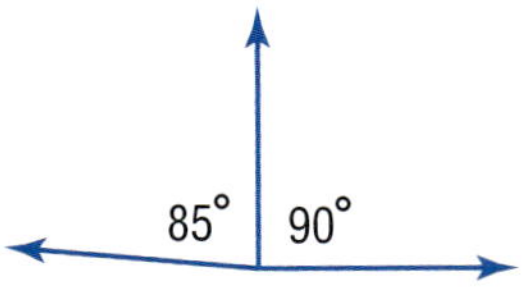

f.

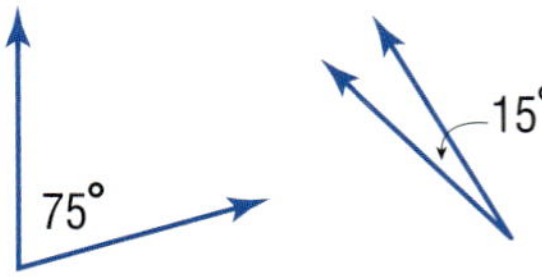

You can use angle relationships to find missing measures.

EXAMPLE Find a Missing Angle Measure

READING Math

Perpendicular Lines or sides that meet to form right angles are perpendicular.

6 **ALGEBRA** **Find the value of *x*.**

Since the two angles form a right angle, they are complementary.

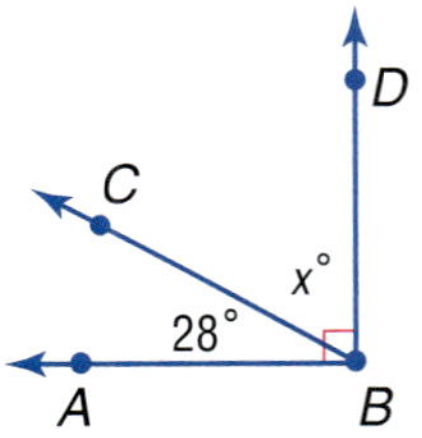

Words	The sum of the measures of $\angle ABC$ and $\angle CBD$	is	90°.
Variable	Let x represent the measure of $\angle CBD$.		
Equation	$28 + x$	=	90

$$\begin{aligned} 28 + x &= 90 & \text{Write the equation.} \\ -28 \quad &\quad -28 & \text{Subtract 28 from each side.} \\ x &= 62 & \end{aligned}$$

So, value of x is 62.

CHECK Your Progress

g. **ALGEBRA** Find the value of x.

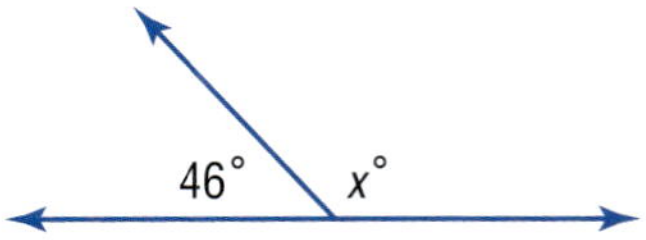

h. **ALGEBRA** If $\angle J$ and $\angle K$ are complementary and the measure of $\angle K$ is 65°, what is the measure of $\angle J$?

Online Personal Tutor at tx.msmath2.com

CHECK Your Understanding

Examples 1–3 (pp. 552–553)

Name each angle in four ways. Then classify the angle as *acute, right, obtuse,* or *straight*.

1. 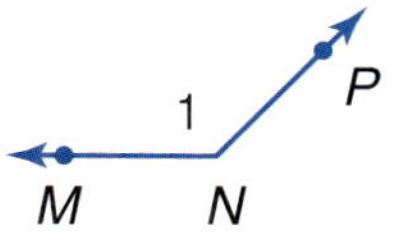

2. 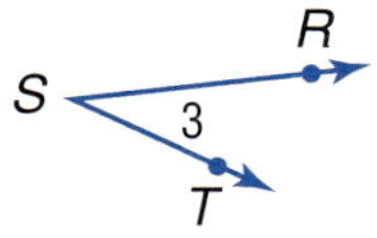

Examples 4, 5 (p. 554)

Classify each pair of angles as *complementary, supplementary,* or *neither*.

3. 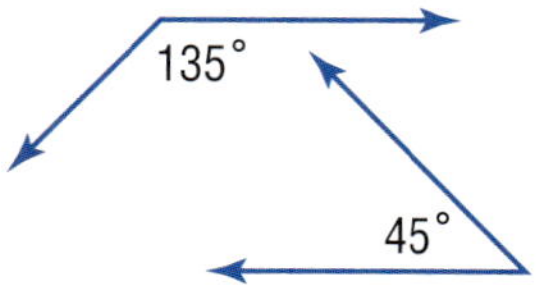

4. 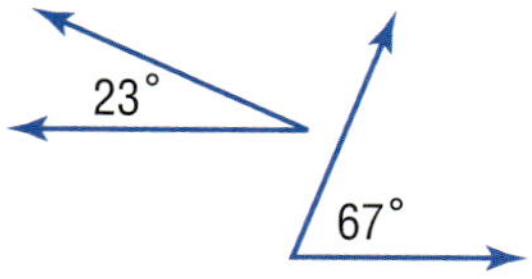

Example 6 (p. 554)

5. **ALGEBRA** Find the value of x.

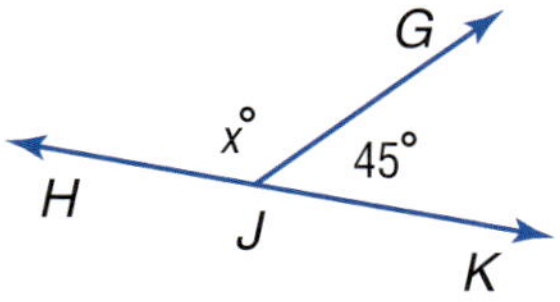

Exercises

HOMEWORK HELP

For Exercises	See Examples
6–11	1,3
12–17	4,5
18–21	6

Name each angle in four ways. Then classify the angle as *acute, right, obtuse,* or *straight*.

6. 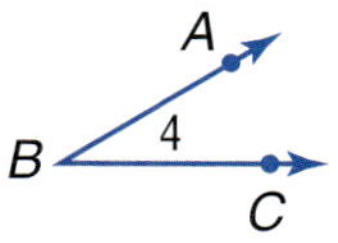

7. 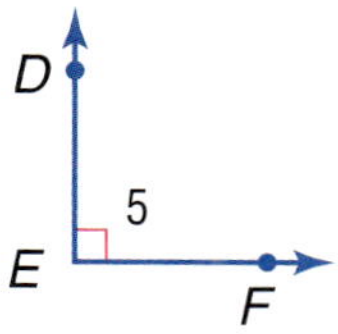

8. 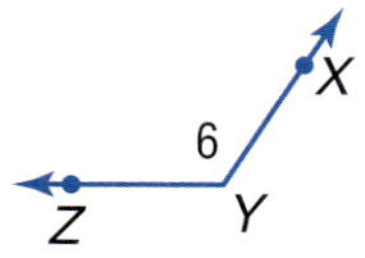

9. 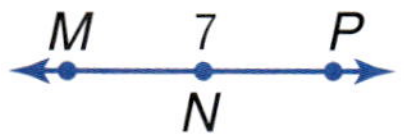

10. 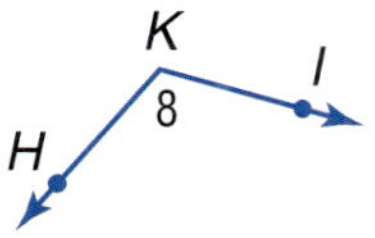

11. 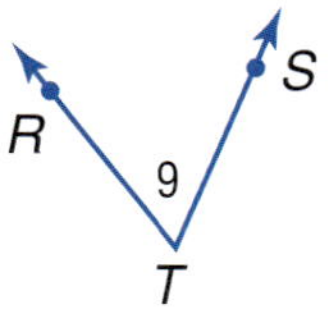

Classify each pair of angles as *complementary, supplementary,* or *neither*.

12. 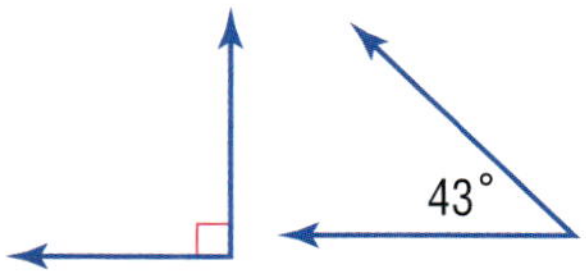

13. 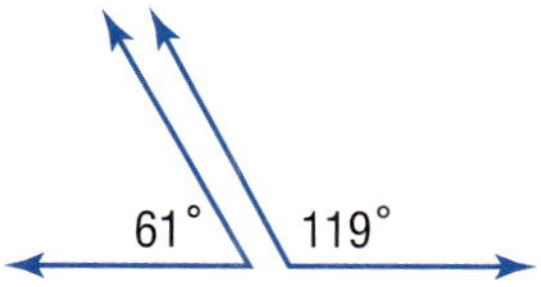

14. 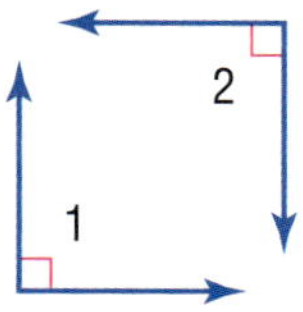

15. 

16. 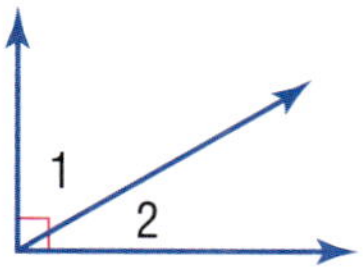

17. 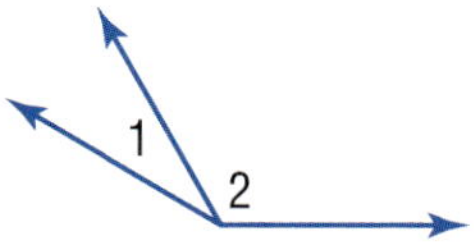

18. **ALGEBRA** If $\angle A$ and $\angle B$ are complementary and the measure of $\angle B$ is 67°, what is the measure of $\angle A$?

19. **ALGEBRA** What is the measure of $\angle J$ if $\angle J$ and $\angle K$ are supplementary and the measure of $\angle K$ is 115°?

20. **SCHOOL SUPPLIES** What is the measure of the angle given by the opening of the scissors, x?

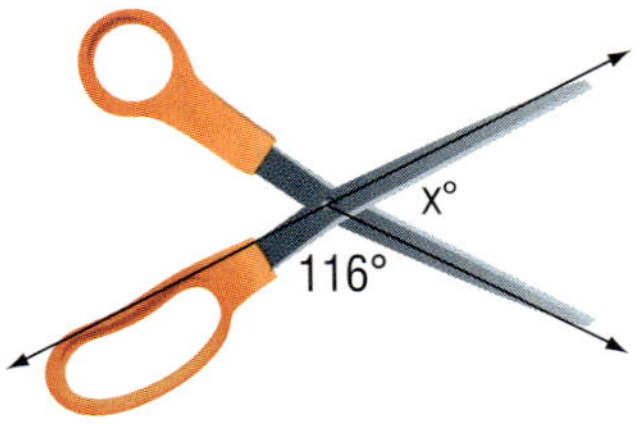

21. **CONSTRUCTION** Roof trusses like the one shown are used to support a roof. Find the value of x so that the indicated web and chord form a right angle.

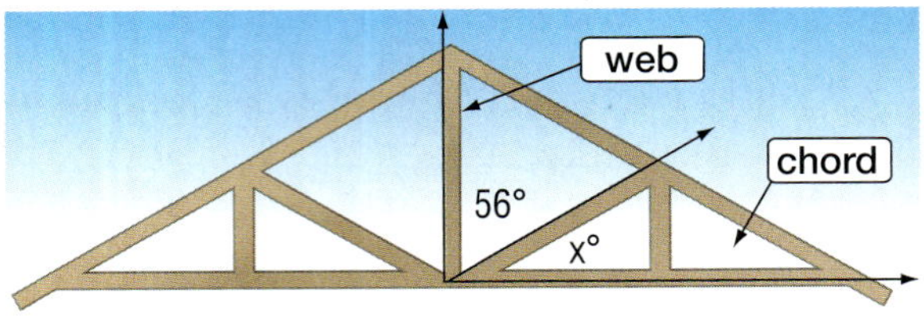

ALGEBRA Find the value of x in each figure.

22. 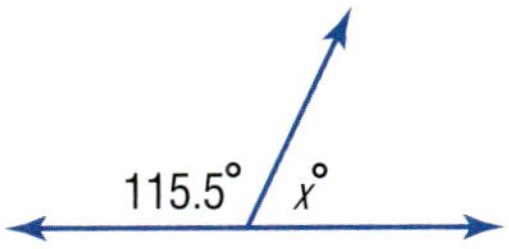

23. 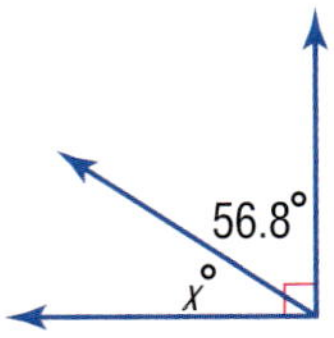

24. 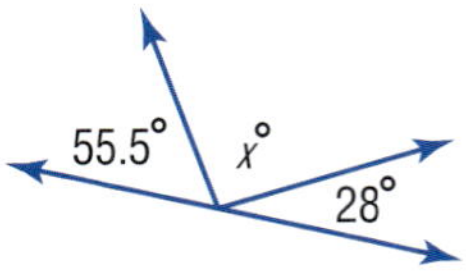

25. **BASKETBALL** Beatriz makes a bounce pass to Tyrone. Find the value of x so that Beatriz's pass hits Tyrone's hands.

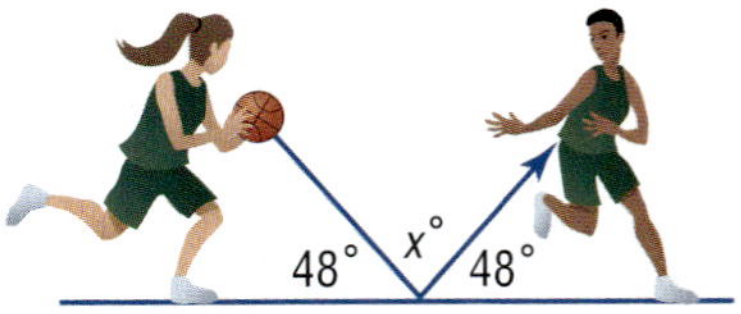

Use the figure at the right to name the following.

26. two obtuse angles
27. a pair of supplementary angles
28. two straight angles
29. a pair of complementary angles
30. four right angles

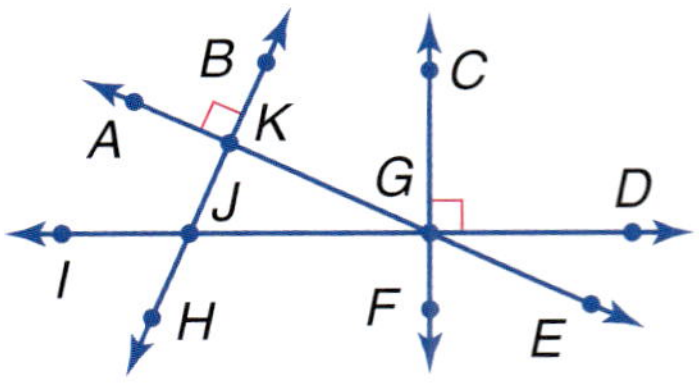

DRAFTING For Exercises 31 and 32, use the diagram that shows how drafting tools can be used to draw a 75° angle.

31. How many different obtuse angles can be drawn using the tools? List the measures of the obtuse angles.

32. Can the tools be arranged to show a pair of complementary angles? Explain your reasoning.

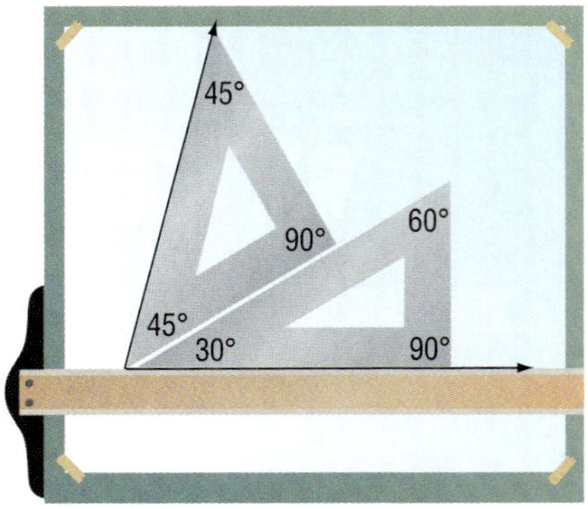

EXTRA PRACTICE
See pages 744, 765.
Math Online
Self-Check Quiz at
tx.msmath2.com

H.O.T. Problems

33. **CHALLENGE** Angles E and F are complementary. If $m\angle E = x - 10$ and $m\angle F = x + 2$, find the measure of each angle.

34. **REASONING** Determine whether the following statement is *sometimes*, *always*, or *never* true. Explain your reasoning.

All angles have both a supplement and a complement.

35. **REASONING** When two lines intersect, they form two pairs of opposite congruent angles called *vertical angles*. In the diagram, ∠1 and ∠2 are vertical angles. Describe whether a pair of angles can be both vertical and supplementary. Give an example or counterexample with angle measurements to support your answer.

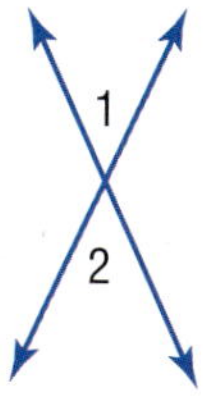

36. **WRITING IN MATH** Describe a strategy for determining whether two angles are *complementary*, *supplementary*, or *neither* without knowing or measuring each angle using a protractor.

TEST PRACTICE

37. Which two angles are NOT complementary?

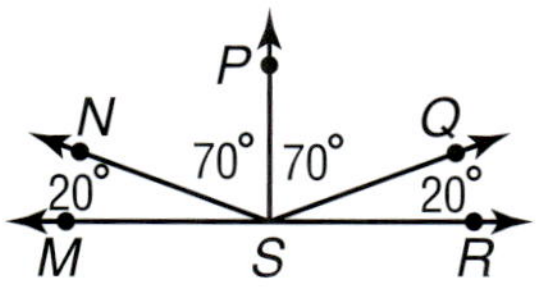

A ∠*NSP* and ∠*QSR*

B ∠*MSN* and ∠*QSR*

C ∠*MSN* and ∠*NSP*

D ∠*PSQ* and ∠*QSR*

38. If ∠*H* and ∠*J* are supplementary and the measure of ∠*H* is 65°, what is the measure of ∠*J*?

F 25° **H** 115°

G 105° **J** 120°

39. Which word best describes the angle marked in the figure?

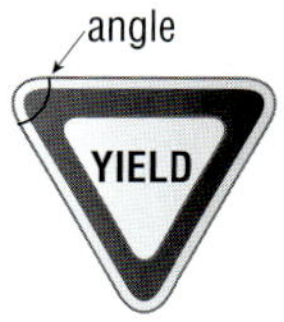

A acute

B complementary

C obtuse

D right

Spiral Review

PROBABILITY A number cube is rolled, and a coin is tossed. Find each probability. (Lesson 10-8)

40. *P*(5 and heads) 41. *P*(odd and tails) 42. *P*(even and heads or tails)

43. **PROBABILITY** Anica spins a spinner fifty times, and it lands on 3 fifteen times. What is the experimental probability of *not* landing on 3? (Lesson 10-8)

44. **REAL ESTATE** A house for sale has a rectangular lot with a length of 250 feet and a width of 120 feet. What is the area of the lot? (Lesson 4-6)

GET READY for the Next Lesson

PREREQUISITE SKILL Multiply or divide. Round to the nearest hundredth if necessary. (Lessons 3-2 and 3-4)

45. 0.62 • 360 46. 360 • 0.25 47. 17 ÷ 146 48. 63 ÷ 199

11-2 Statistics: Display Data in a Circle Graph

Main IDEA

Construct and interpret circle graphs.

Targeted TEKS 7.11 The student understands that the way a set of data is displayed influences its interpretation. **(A) select and use an appropriate representation for presenting and displaying relationships among collected data, including** line plot, line graph, bar graph, stem and leaf plot, **circle graph**, and Venn diagrams, **and justify the selection.** *Also addresses TEKS 7.11(B).*

NEW Vocabulary

circle graph

GET READY for the Lesson

COLORS In a recent survey, people ages 13–20 were asked to choose their favorite shade of blue. The results are shown in the table.

Favorite Shade of Blue for People Ages 13–20

Shade	Percent
Navy	35%
Sky/Light Blue	30%
Aquamarine	17%
Other	18%

Source: *American Demographics*

1. Explain how you know that each person surveyed chose only one shade of blue.
2. If 500 people took part in the survey, how many preferred aquamarine?

A graph that shows data as parts of a whole is called a **circle graph**. In a circle graph, the percents add up to 100.

EXAMPLE Display Data in a Circle Graph

1 **COLORS** **Display the data above in a circle graph.**

- There are 360° in a circle. Find the degrees for each part.

35% of 360° = 0.35 • 360° or 126° Round to the nearest whole degree.

30% of 360° = 0.30 • 360° or 108°

17% of 360° = 0.17 • 360° or about 61°

18% of 360° = 0.18 • 360° or about 65°

- Draw a circle with a radius as shown. Then use a protractor to draw the first angle, in this case 126°. Repeat this step for each section or *sector*.

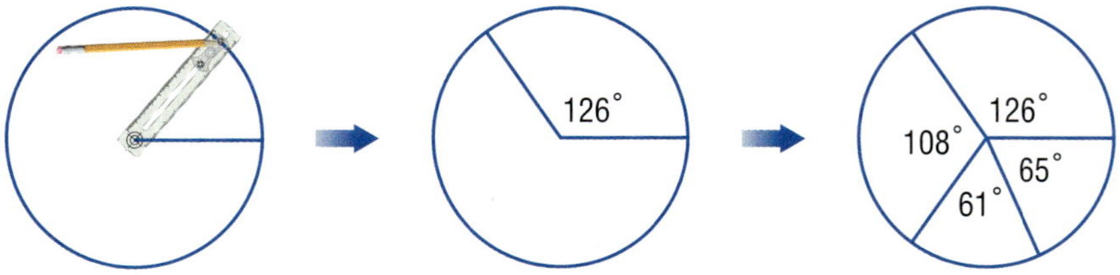

- Label each section of the graph with the category and percent it represents. Give the graph a title.

Check To draw an accurate circle graph, make sure the sum of the angle measures is equal to, or is approximately equal to, 360°.

Favorite Shade of Blue for People Ages 13–20

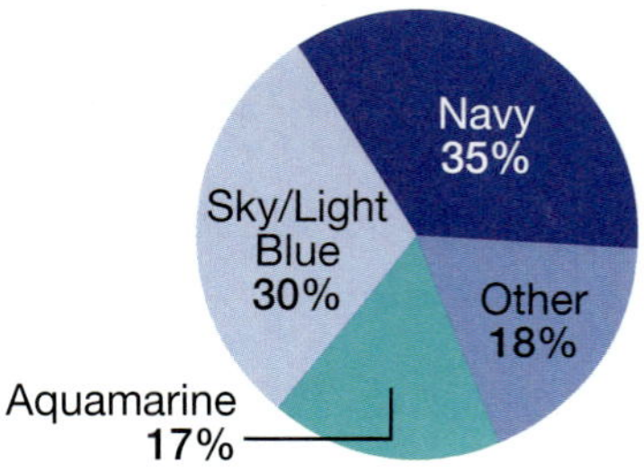

CHECK Your Progress

a. **SCIENCE** The table shows the present composition of Earth's atmosphere. Display the data in a circle graph.

Composition of Earth's Atmosphere

Element	Percent
Nitrogen	78%
Oxygen	21%
Other gases	1%

Source: www.nasa.gov

When constructing a circle graph, you may need to first convert the data to ratios and decimals and then to degrees and percents.

EXAMPLE Construct a Circle Graph

Real-World Link The United States has won 2,219 Summer Olympic medals through 2004, the most for any country.
Source: infoplease.com

2 **OLYMPICS** **The table shows the number of each type of medal won by the United States during the Summer Olympics from 1896 to 2004. Make a circle graph of the data.**

U.S. Summer Olympic Medals

Type	Number
Gold	907
Silver	697
Bronze	615

Source: infoplease.com

- Find the total number of medals: 907 + 697 + 615 or 2,219.
- Find the ratio that compares each number with the total. Write the ratio as a decimal rounded to the nearest hundredth.

gold: $\frac{907}{2{,}219} \approx 0.41$ silver: $\frac{697}{2{,}219} \approx 0.31$ bronze: $\frac{615}{2{,}219} \approx 0.28$

- Find the number of degrees for each section of the graph.

gold: $0.41 \cdot 360° \approx 148°$

silver: $0.31 \cdot 360° \approx 112°$

bronze: $0.28 \cdot 360° \approx 101°$

Because of rounding, the sum of the degrees is 361°.

- Draw the circle graph.

0.41 = 41%, 0.31 = 31%, 0.28 = 28%

U.S. Summer Olympic Medals

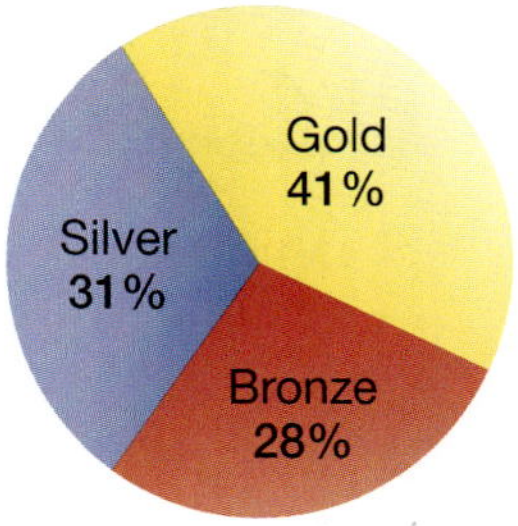

Check After drawing the first two sections, you can measure the last section of a circle graph to verify that the angles have the correct measures.

CHECK Your Progress

b. **OLYMPICS** The number of Winter Olympic medals won by the U.S. from 1924 to 2002 is shown in the table. Display the data in a circle graph.

U.S. Winter Olympic Medals

Type	Number
Gold	69
Silver	72
Bronze	52

Source: answers.com

EXAMPLES Analyze a Circle Graph

AUTOMOBILES The graph shows the percent of automobiles registered in the southwestern United States in a recent year.

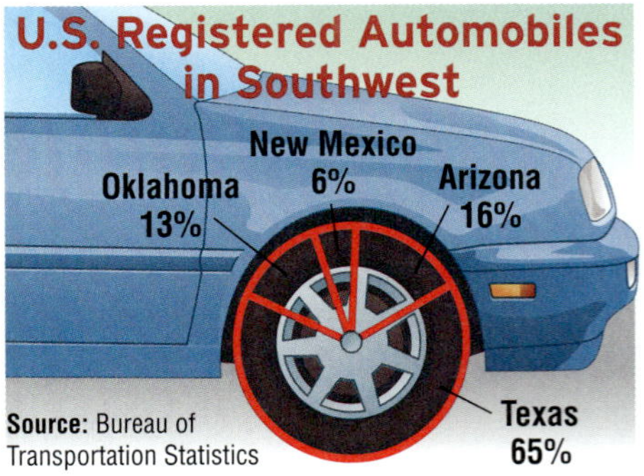

3 **Which state had the most registered automobiles?**

The largest section of the circle is the one representing Texas. So, Texas has the most registered automobiles.

4 **If 12.0 million automobiles were registered in these states, how many more automobiles were registered in Texas than in Arizona?**

Texas: 65% of 12.0 million → 0.65 × 12.0 or 7.8 million

Arizona: 16% of 12.0 million → 0.16 × 12.0 or 1.92 million

There were 7.8 million − 1.92 million or 5.88 million more registered automobiles in Texas than in Arizona.

> **STUDY TIP**
>
> **Check for Reasonableness** To check Example 4, you can estimate and solve the problem another way.
>
> 65% − 16% ≈ 50%
> 50% of 12.0 is 6
>
> Since 5.88 is about 6, the answer is reasonable.

CHECK Your Progress

c. Which state had the least number of registered automobiles? Explain.

d. What was the total number of registered automobiles in New Mexico and Oklahoma?

Online Personal Tutor at tx.msmath2.com

CHECK Your Understanding

Examples 1, 2 (pp. 558–559)

Display each set of data in a circle graph.

1.

Blood Types in the U.S.	
Blood Type	**Percent**
O	44%
A	42%
B	10%
AB	4%

Source: Stanford School of Medicine

2.

Population of U.S. by Region	
Region	**Population (millions)**
Northeast	54
Midwest	65
South	104
West	66

Source: U.S. Census Bureau, 2004

Examples 3, 4 (p. 560)

COLORS For Exercises 3 and 4, use the graph that shows the results of a survey.

3. What color is most favored?

4. If 400 people were surveyed, how many more people favored purple than red?

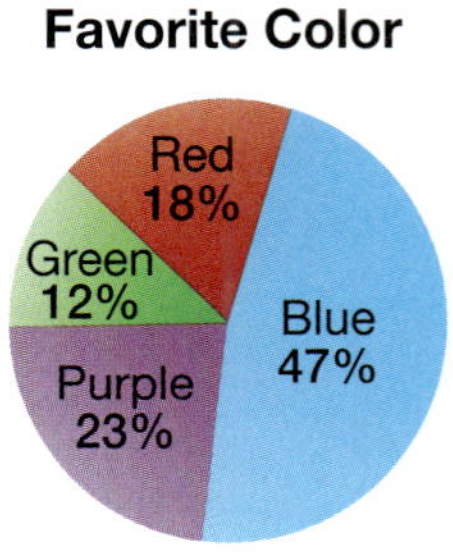

Exercises

HOMEWORK HELP	
For Exercises	See Examples
5–6	1
7–8	2
9–14	3,4

Display each set of data in a circle graph.

5.

U.S. Steel Roller Coasters	
Type	Percent
Sit down	86%
Inverted	8%
Other	6%

Source: rcdb.com

6.

New York City Commuters	
Transportation	Percent
Driving Alone	24%
Carpool/Other	23%
Public Transit	53%

Source: *Time Almanac*

7.

Endangered Species in U.S.	
Species	Number of Species
Mammals	68
Birds	77
Reptiles	14
Amphibians	11

Source: U.S. Fish and Wildlife Service

8.

Speed Limits in U.S.	
Speed Limit (mph)	Number of States
60	1
65	20
70	16
75	13

Source: *The World Almanac*

EDUCATION **For Exercises 9–11, use the circle graph that shows the percent of students by grade level in U.S. schools.**

Grade Level of U.S. Students

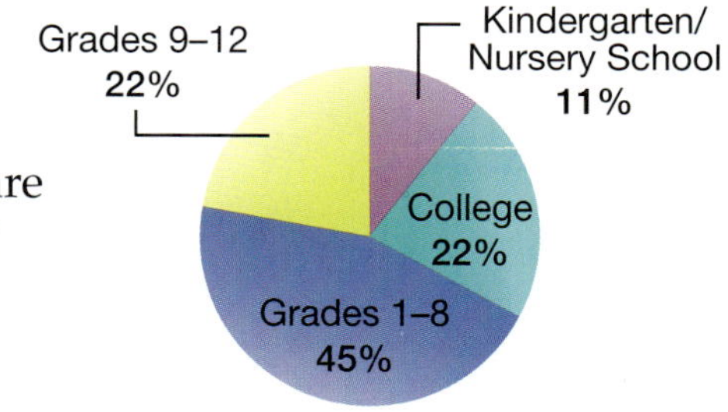

Source: U.S. Census Bureau

9. In which grades are most students?

10. About how many times more students are there in grades 1–8 than in grades 9–12?

11. There are about 75 million students in U.S. schools. How many students are in grades 9–12?

MONEY **For Exercises 12–14, use the graph that shows the results of a survey about a common currency for North America.**

Do Americans Favor Common North American Currency?

Source: Coinstar

12. What percent of Americans favor a common North American currency?

13. Based on these results, about how many of the approximately 298 million Americans would say "Don't Know" in response to this survey?

14. About how many more Americans oppose a common currency than favor it?

DATA SENSE For each graph, find the missing values.

15. **Dog Expenses**

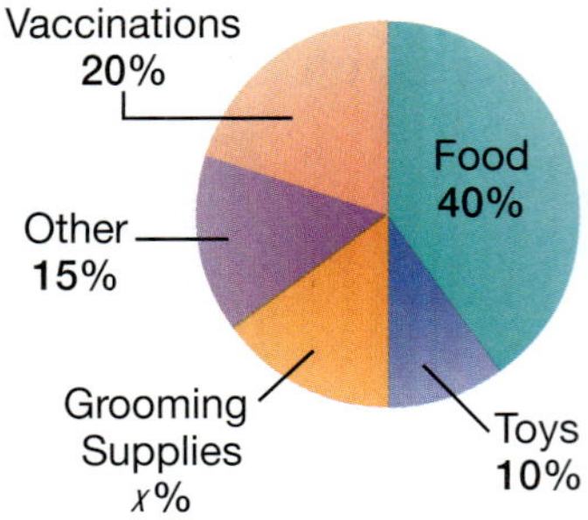

16. **Family Budget**

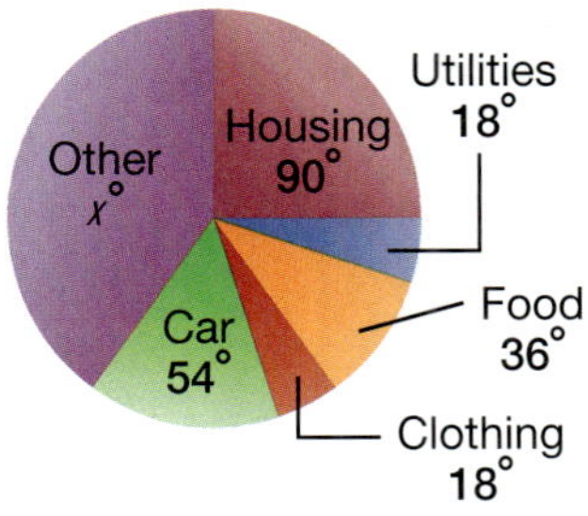

Select an appropriate type of graph to display each set of data: line graph, bar graph, or circle graph. Then display the data using the graph.

17.

Top 5 Presidential Birth States	
Place	**Presidents**
Virginia	8
Ohio	7
Massachusetts	4
New York	4
Texas	3

Source: *The World Book of Facts*

18.

Tanya's Day	
Activity	**Percent**
School	25%
Sleep	33%
Homework	12%
Sports	8%
Other	22%

GEOGRAPHY For Exercises 19–21, use the table.

19. Display the data in a circle graph.

20. Use your graph to find which two lakes equal the size of Lake Superior.

21. Compare the size of Lake Ontario to the size of Lake Michigan.

Sizes of U.S. Great Lakes	
Lake	**Size (sq mi)**
Erie	9,930
Huron	23,010
Michigan	22,400
Ontario	7,520
Superior	31,820

POLITICS For Exercises 22 and 23, use the graph and information below.

A group of students were asked whether people their age could make a difference in the political decisions of elected officials.

22. How many students participated in the survey?

23. Write a convincing argument explaining whether or not it is reasonable to say that 50% more students said they could make a difference than those who said they could not make a difference.

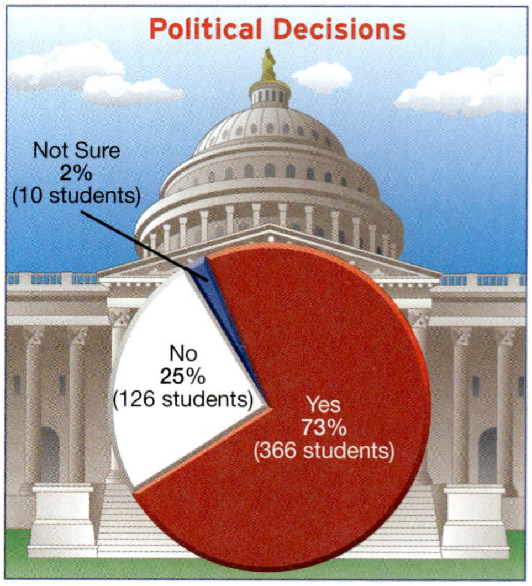

Source: momslife.com and *Mothering Magazine*

EXTRA PRACTICE
See pages 744, 765.
Math Online
Self-Check Quiz at
tx.msmath2.com

24. **FIND THE DATA** Refer to the Texas Data File on pages 16–19. Choose some data that can be displayed in a circle graph. Then display the data in a circle graph and write one statement analyzing the data.

H.O.T. Problems

25. **CHALLENGE** The graph shows the results of a survey about students' favorite school subject. About what percent of those surveyed said that math was their favorite subject? Explain your reasoning.

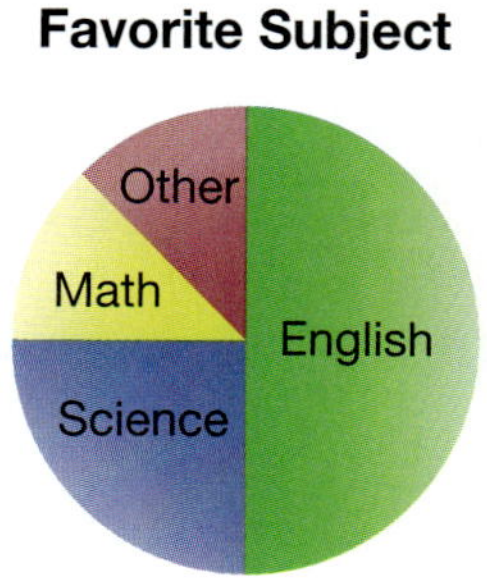

26. **COLLECT THE DATA** Collect some data from your classmates that can be represented in a circle graph. Then create the circle graph and write one statement analyzing the data.

27. **WRITING IN MATH** The table shows the percent of people that like each type of fruit juice. Can the data be represented in a circle graph? Justify your answer.

Fruit Juice	Percent
Apple	54%
Grape	48%
Orange	37%
Cranberry	15%

TEST PRACTICE

28. The results of a survey are shown in the table below.

Favorite Fast Foods of 100 People	
Food	**Number of People**
Pizza	25
Hamburger	15
Hotdog	10
Tacos	50

How many degrees make up the section of a circle graph representing those who preferred hamburgers?

A 25° **C** 54°

B 45° **D** 72°

29. The graph shows the types of vehicles registered in one state.

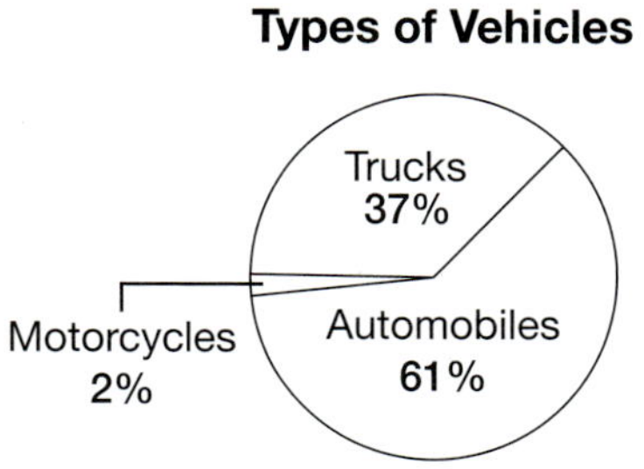

If there are about 30 million vehicles registered in the state, predict how many of the vehicles are motorcycles.

F 0.6 million **H** 16 million

G 11 million **J** 18 million

Spiral Review

30. Find the value of x in the figure. (Lesson 11-1)

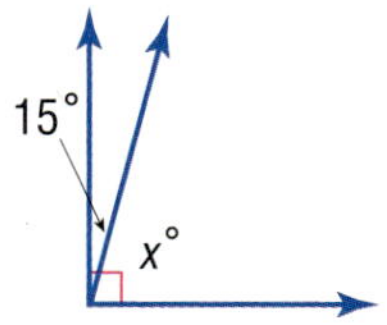

31. **PROBABILITY** Fernando has an after-school activity 15% of the time. Li-Cheng has an after-school activity 20% of the time. Find the probability that they will both have an after-school activity on the same day. (Lesson 10-8)

GET READY for the Next Lesson

PREREQUISITE SKILL **Solve each equation.** (Lesson 4-2)

32. $x + 112 = 180$ 33. $50 + t = 180$ 34. $180 = 79 + y$ 35. $180 = h + 125$

11-3 Triangles

Main IDEA

Identify and classify triangles.

Targeted TEKS **7.6** The student compares and classifies two- and three-dimensional figures using geometric vocabulary and properties. **(B) use properties to classify triangles** and quadrilaterals. *Also addresses TEKS 7.8(C).*

NEW Vocabulary

triangle
congruent segments
acute triangle
right triangle
obtuse triangle
scalene triangle
isosceles triangle
equilateral triangle

READING Math

△ triangle

MINI Lab

STEP 1 Use a straightedge to draw a triangle with three acute angles. Label the angles *A*, *B*, and *C*. Cut out the triangle.

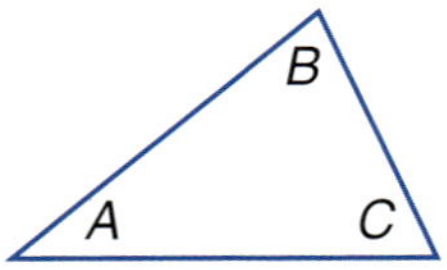

STEP 2 Fold ∠*A*, ∠*B*, and ∠*C* so the vertices meet on the line between angles *A* and *C*.

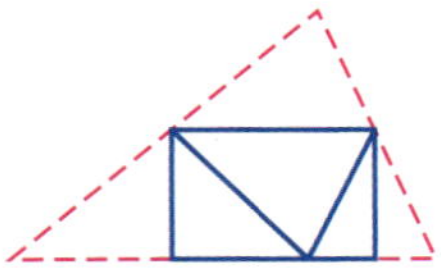

1. What kind of angle is formed where the three vertices meet?
2. Repeat the activity with another triangle. Make a conjecture about the sum of the measures of the angles of any triangle.

A **triangle** is a figure with three sides and three angles. The symbol for triangle is △. There is a relationship among the three angles in a triangle.

KEY CONCEPT — Angles of a Triangle

Words The sum of the measures of the angles of a triangle is 180°.

Algebra $x + y + z = 180$

Model

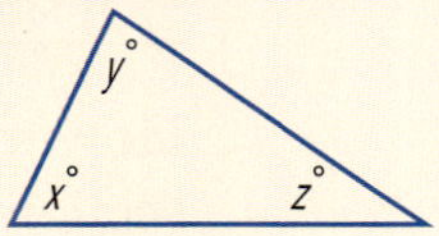

EXAMPLE Find a Missing Measure

1 ALGEBRA Find $m\angle Z$ in the triangle.

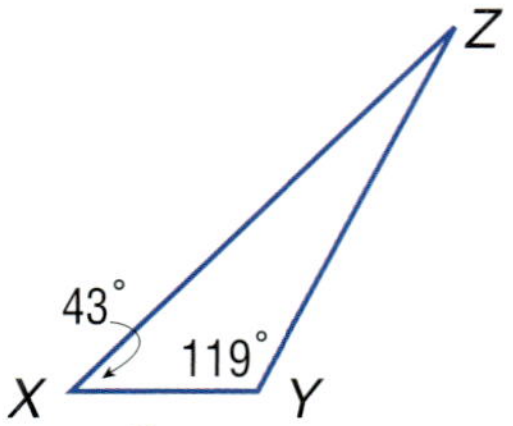

Since the sum of the angle measures in a triangle is 180°, $m\angle Z + 43° + 119° = 180°$.

$m\angle Z + 43° + 119° = 180°$		Write the equation.
$m\angle Z + 162° = 180°$		Simplify.
$-162° = -162°$		Subtract 162° from each side.
$m\angle Z = 18°$		

So, $m\angle Z$ is 18°.

CHECK Your Progress

a. **ALGEBRA** In △*ABC*, if $m\angle A = 25°$ and $m\angle B = 108°$, what is $m\angle C$?

TEST EXAMPLE

2 **A kite is constructed with two triangles as shown. What is the missing measure of the kite?**

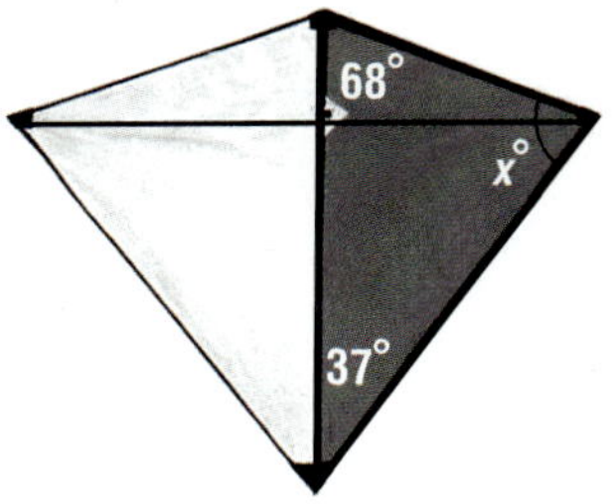

A 45° **C** 75°

B 52° **D** 80°

Read the Test Item

To find the missing measure, write and solve an equation.

Solve the Test Item

$x + 68 + 37 = 180$	The sum of the measures is 180.
$x + 105 = 180$	Simplify.
$-105 = -105$	Subtract 105 from each side.
$x = 75$	

The answer is C.

Test-Taking Tip

Check the Results To check the results, add the three angle measures to see if they equal 180.

$75 + 68 + 37 = 180$ ✔

The answer is correct.

CHECK Your Progress

b. The frame of a bicycle shows a triangle. What is the missing measure?

F 31° **H** 45°

G 40° **J** 50°

Online Personal Tutor at tx.msmath2.com

Every triangle has at least two acute angles. One way you can classify a triangle is by using the third angle. Another way to classify triangles is by their sides. Sides with the same length are **congruent segments**.

STUDY TIP

Congruent Segments The marks on the sides of the triangle indicate that those sides are congruent.

KEY CONCEPT

Classify Triangles Using Angles

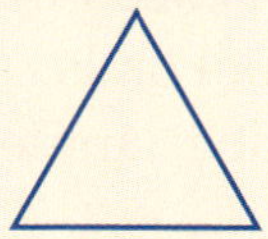

all acute angles

acute triangle

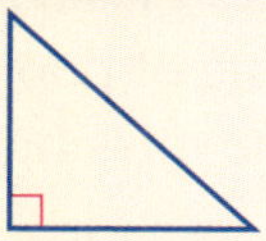

1 right angle

right triangle

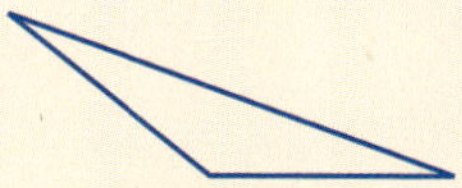

1 obtuse angle

obtuse triangle

Classify Triangles Using Sides

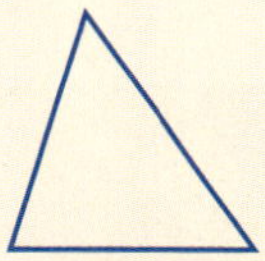

no congruent sides

scalene triangle

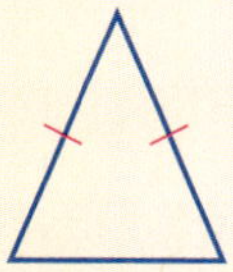

at least 2 congruent sides

isosceles triangle

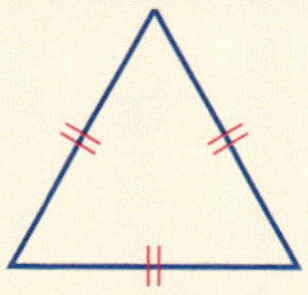

3 congruent sides

equilateral triangle

Real-World EXAMPLES

Classify the marked triangle on each object by its angles and by its sides.

3

The triangle on the side of a house has one obtuse angle and two congruent sides. So, it is an obtuse, isosceles triangle.

4

The triangle marked on the toy sailboat has three acute angles and no sides congruent. So, it is a scalene triangle.

CHECK Your Progress

c. 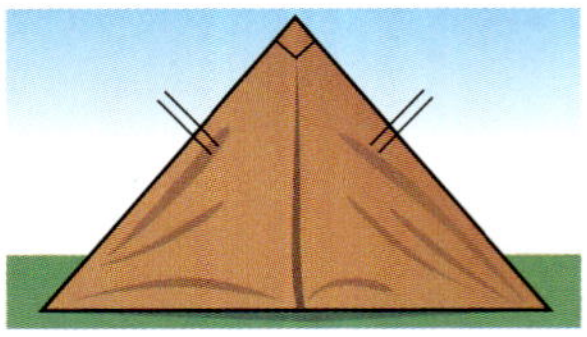

d. 

CHECK Your Understanding

Example 1 (p. 564)

Find the value of x.

1. 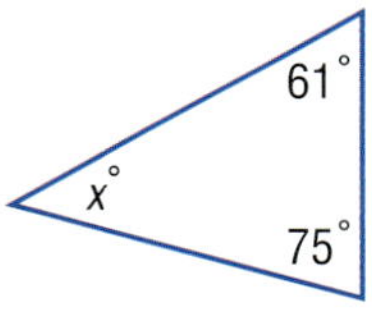

2. 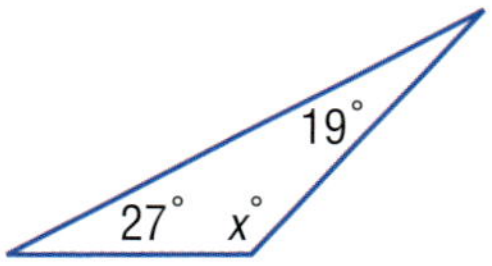

3. 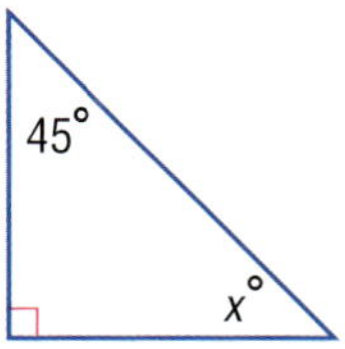

4. **ALGEBRA** Find $m\angle T$ in $\triangle RST$ if $m\angle R = 37°$ and $m\angle S = 55°$.

Example 2 (p. 565)

5. **TEST PRACTICE** A triangle is used in the game of pool to rack the pool balls. Find the missing measure of the triangle.

A 30° C 60°

B 40° D 75°

Examples 3, 4 (p. 566)

FLAGS **Classify the marked triangle in each flag by its angles and by its sides.**

6. 

Puerto Rico

7. 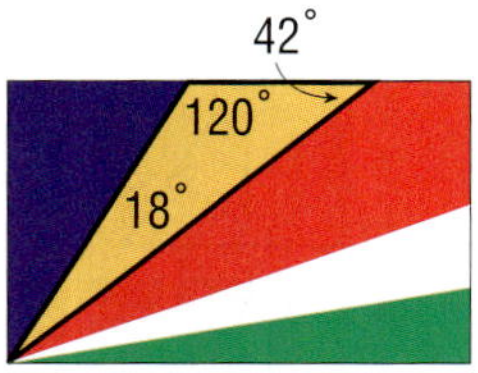

Seychelles Islands

8. 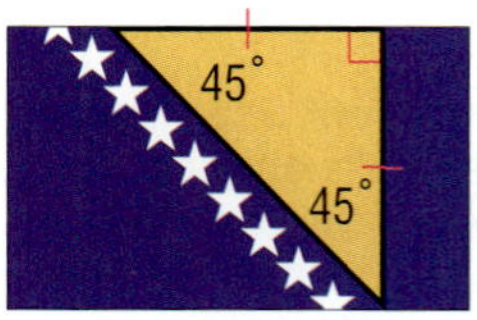

Bosnia-Herzegovina

Exercises

HOMEWORK HELP	
For Exercises	See Examples
9–16, 39–40	1–2
17–24	3–4

Find the value of x.

9. 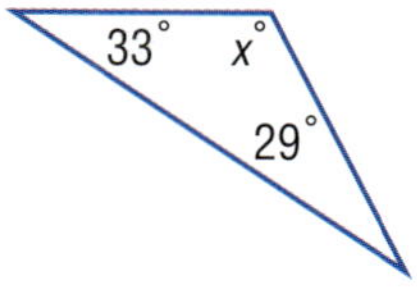

10. 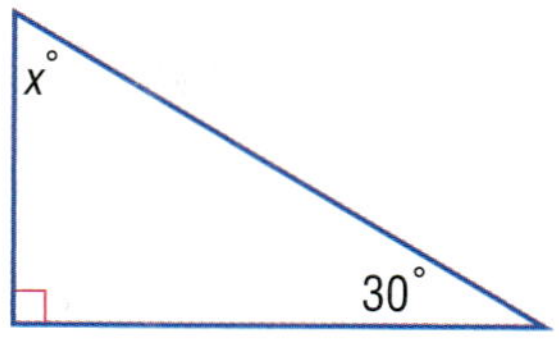

11. 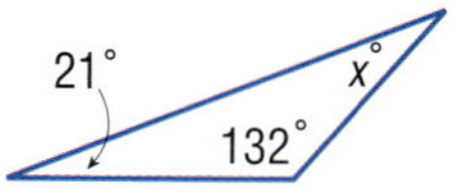

12. 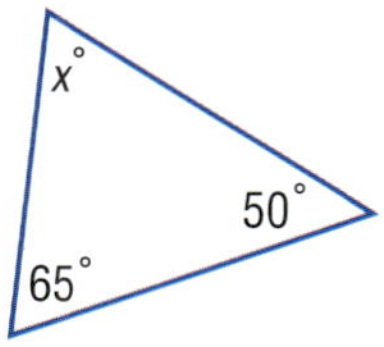

13. 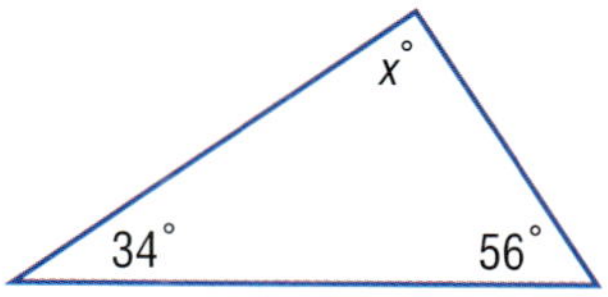

14. 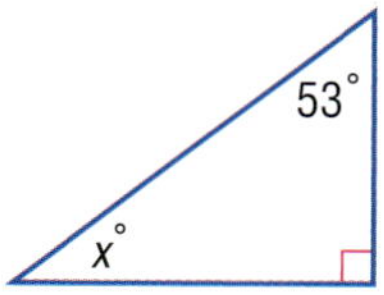

15. **ALGEBRA** Find $m\angle Q$ in $\triangle QRS$ if $m\angle R = 25°$ and $m\angle S = 102°$.

16. **ALGEBRA** In $\triangle EFG$, $m\angle F = 46°$ and $m\angle G = 34°$. What is $m\angle E$?

Classify the marked triangle in each object by its angles and by its sides.

17. 

18. 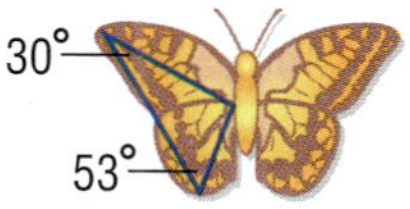

19. 

20. 

21. 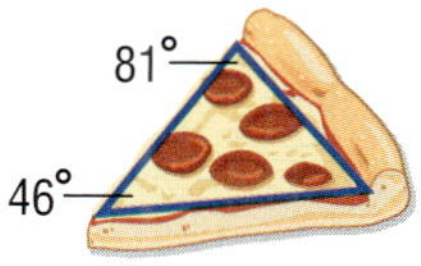

22. 

23. **ART** The sculpture at the right is entitled *Texas Triangles*. It is located in Lincoln, Massachusetts. What type of triangle is shown: *acute*, *right*, or *obtuse*?

Source: DeCordova Museum and Sculpture Park

24. **ARCHITECTURE** Use the photo at the left to classify the side view of the Transamerica building by its angles and by its sides.

Real-World Link
The Transamerica building in San Francisco is 853 feet tall.
Source: transamerica.com

Find the missing measure in each triangle with the given angle measures.

25. 80°, 20.5°, x°
26. 75°, x°, 50.2°
27. x°, 10.8°, 90°
28. 45.5°, x°, 105.6°
29. x°, 140.1°, 18.6°
30. 110.2°, x°, 35.6°
31. Find the third angle measure of a right triangle if one of the angles measures 10°.
32. What is the third angle measure of a right triangle if one of the angle measures is 45.8°?

EXTRA PRACTICE
See pages 745, 765.
Math Online
Self-Check Quiz at
tx.msmath2.com

ALGEBRA **Find the value of x in each triangle.**

33.
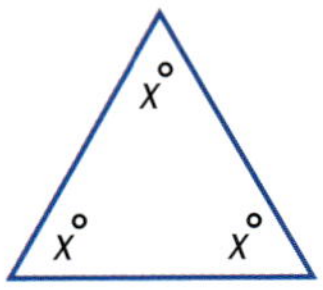

34.
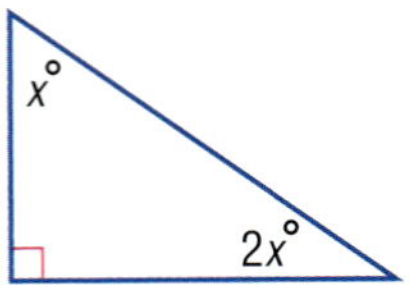

35.
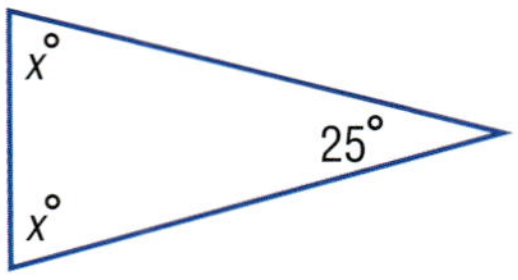

H.O.T. Problems

36. CHALLENGE Apply what you know about triangles to find the missing angle measures in the figure.

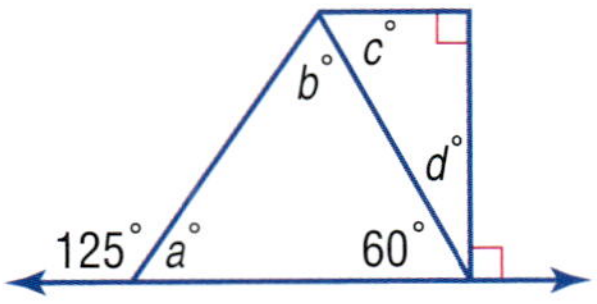

37. OPEN ENDED Draw an acute scalene triangle. Describe the angles and sides of the triangle.

38. WRITING IN MATH An isosceles triangle has two sides measuring 5 meters and 3 meters. What is the measure of the third side? Justify your answer.

TEST PRACTICE

39. How would you find $m\angle R$?

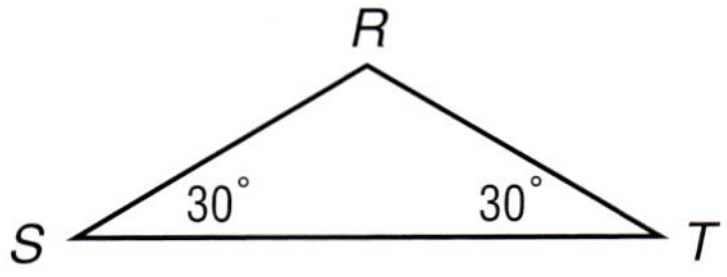

A Add 30° to 180°.

B Subtract 60° from 180°.

C Subtract 30° from 90°.

D Subtract 180° from 60°.

40. Mrs. Knouse installed triangular pieces of tile in her bathroom.

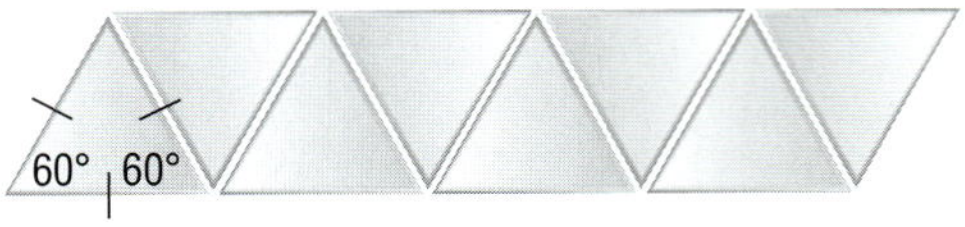

Which of the following best describes the triangle with the given measures?

F Acute isosceles triangle

G Obtuse isosceles triangle

H Acute equilateral triangle

J Right scalene triangle

Spiral Review

41. BIRDS A circle graph shows that 41% of birdwatchers live in the Northeast region of the U.S. What is the measure of the angle of the Northeast section of the graph? (Lesson 11-2)

Classify each pair of angles as *complementary*, *supplementary*, or *neither*. (Lesson 11-1)

42.
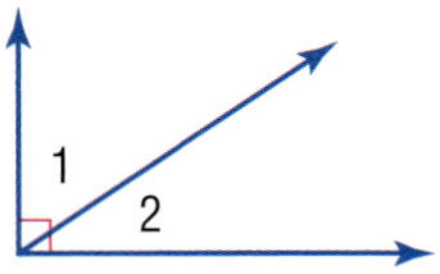

43.
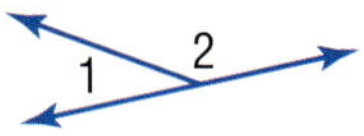

44.
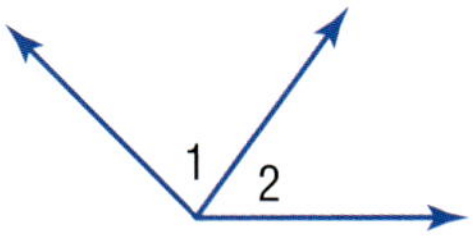

GET READY for the Next Lesson

45. PREREQUISITE SKILL If Jade buys 5 notebooks at $1.75 each, what will be the total cost of the notebooks; about $6, $7, or $9? (Lesson 8-4)

11-4 Problem-Solving Investigation

MAIN IDEA: Solve problems by using logical reasoning.

Targeted TEKS 7.13 The student applies Grade 7 mathematics to solve problems connected to everyday experiences, investigations in other disciplines, and activities in and outside of school. **(B) use a problem-solving model that incorporates understanding the problem, making a plan, carrying out the plan, and evaluating the solution for reasonableness.**

P.S.I. TEAM +

e-Mail: USE LOGICAL REASONING

YOUR MISSION: Use logical reasoning to solve the problem.

THE PROBLEM: Do the angles in an equilateral triangle have a special relationship?

> Dion: It looks like the angles in an equilateral triangle are congruent. Is that true?

EXPLORE	Equilateral triangles have sides that are congruent. You need to find whether the angles are congruent.
PLAN	Draw several equilateral triangles and measure the angles.
SOLVE	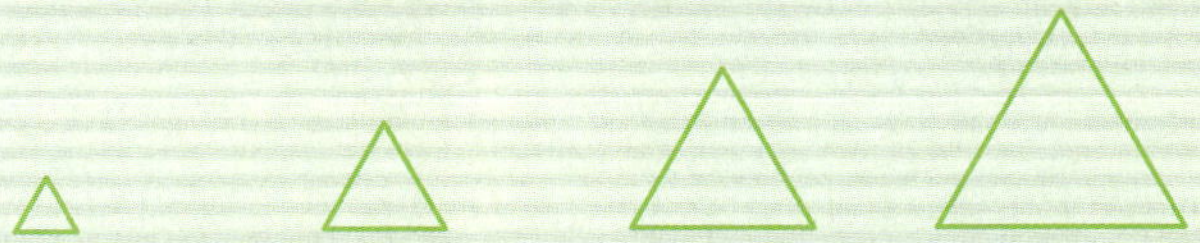 sides = 1 cm sides = 2 cm sides = 3 cm sides = 4 cm Each angle of the triangles is 60°. So, it seems like the angles in an equilateral triangle are congruent.
CHECK	Any triangle with angles measuring 60° is equilateral. If we try to draw a triangle with angle measures of 60° and different side lengths, the drawing would not be in the shape of a triangle. 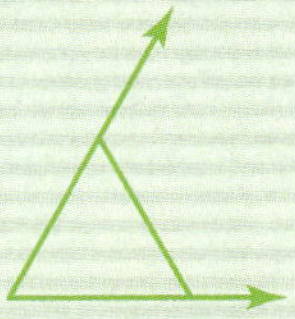

Analyze The Strategy

1. When you use *inductive reasoning*, you make a rule after seeing several examples. When you use *deductive reasoning*, you use a rule to make a decision. What type of reasoning did Dion use to solve the problem? Explain your reasoning.
2. Explain how the *look for a pattern* strategy is similar to inductive reasoning.

Mixed Problem Solving

For Exercises 3–5, use logical reasoning to solve the problem.

3. **GEOMETRY** Draw several isosceles triangles and measure their angles. What do you notice about the measures of the angles of an isosceles triangle?

4. **BASKETBALL** Placido, Dexter, and Scott play guard, forward, and center on a team, but not necessarily in that order. Placido and the center drove Scott to practice on Saturday. Placido does not play guard. Who is the guard?

5. **TOYS** Hannah was finding the relationship between the time it took a yo-yo to swing back and forth and its length. Predict the length of a yo-yo if it takes 5 seconds to swing back and forth.

Time (seconds)	Length (units)
1	1
2	4
3	9
4	16

Use any strategy to solve Exercises 6–10. Some strategies are shown below.

PROBLEM-SOLVING STRATEGIES
- Use the four-step plan.
- Look for a pattern.
- Use a graph.
- Use logical reasoning.

6. **RECTANGLES** Draw several rectangles and measure their diagonals. Find a relationship between the diagonals of a rectangle.

7. **TRAVEL** Mrs. Petricca drove at an average speed of 55 miles per hour for three hours. After stopping for lunch, she drove at an average speed of 40 miles for 2.5 hours. How far did she drive?

8. **PATTERNS** Find the next three numbers in the pattern below.

71, 64, 57, 50, ■, ■, ■

9. **GEOMETRY** The large square has been divided into 9 squares. The lengths of the squares are given. Find the area of the entire square.

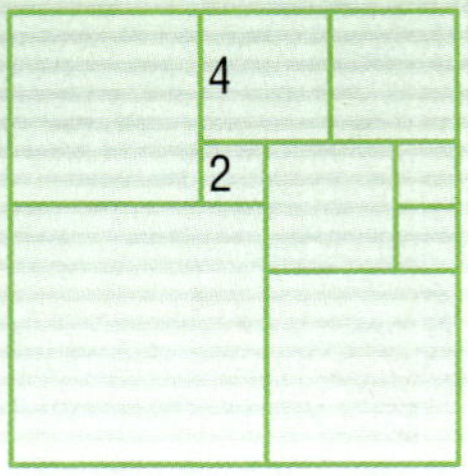

10. **SHOES** What can you conclude about the number of boys who favor brand C and the number of boys who prefer brand D?

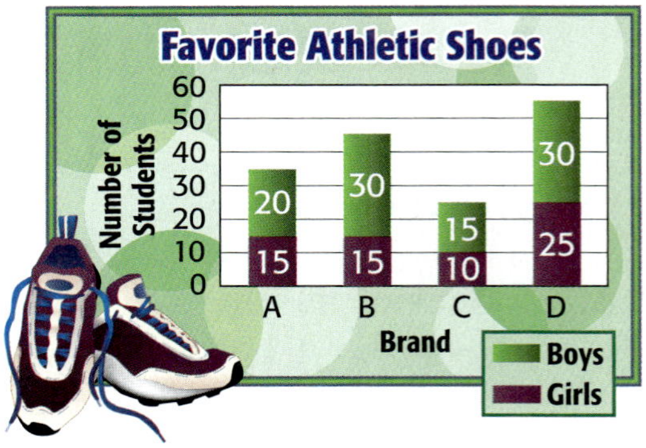

Select the Operation

For Exercises 11–13, select the appropriate operation(s) to solve the problem. Justify your selection(s) and solve the problem.

11. **GARDENING** Shelby wants to build a fence around her garden with the dimensions shown. How much fencing will she need?

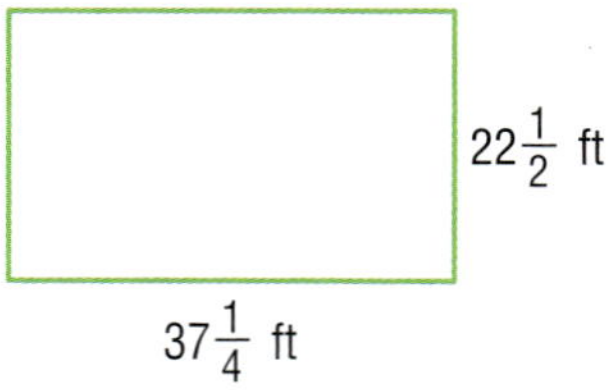

12. **PHOTOCOPYING** Suppose you enlarge a drawing to 120% of its original size on the copy machine. If the drawing is 2 inches long and 3 inches wide, what are the dimensions of the copy?

13. **GRADES** David has earned scores of 73, 85, 91 and 82 on the first four out of five math tests for the grading period. He would like to finish the grading period with a test average of at least 82. What is the minimum score David needs to earn on the fifth test in order to achieve his goal?

Explore 11-5

Geometry Lab
Investigating Quadrilaterals

Main IDEA

Investigate the properties of special quadrilaterals.

Targeted TEKS **7.6** The student compares and classifies two- and three-dimensional figures using geometric vocabulary and properties. **(B) use properties to classify** triangles and **quadrilaterals.** *Also addresses TEKS 7.15(A), 7.15(B).*

Four-sided figures are called *quadrilaterals*. In this lab, you will explore the properties of different types of quadrilaterals.

ACTIVITY

STEP 1 Draw the quadrilaterals shown on grid paper.

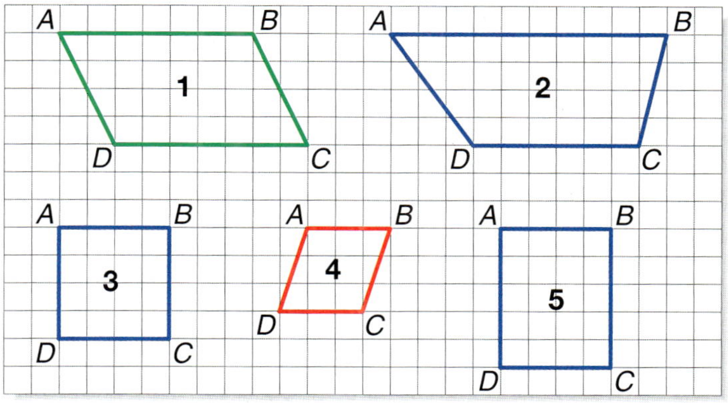

STEP 2 Use a ruler and a protractor to measure the sides and angles of each quadrilateral. Record your results in a table.

Quadrilateral	$m\angle A$	$m\angle B$	$m\angle C$	$m\angle D$	AB	BC	CD	DA
1								
2								

Analyze the Results

1. Describe any similarities or patterns in the angle measurements.

2. Describe any similarities or patterns in the side measurements.

3. **MAKE A VENN DIAGRAM** Cut out the quadrilaterals you drew in the activity. Then sort them into categories according to their similarities and differences. Arrange and record your categories in a two-circled Venn diagram. Be sure to label each circle with its category.

4. Create two other Venn diagrams illustrating two different ways of categorizing these quadrilaterals.

5. **WRITING IN MATH** Did you find shapes that did not fit a category? Where did you place these shapes? Did any shapes have properties allowing them to belong to more than one category? Could you arrange these quadrilaterals into a three-circled Venn diagram? If so, how?

11-5 Quadrilaterals

Main IDEA

Identify and classify quadrilaterals.

Targeted TEKS 7.6 The student compares and classifies two- and three-dimensional figures using geometric vocabulary and properties. **(B) use properties to classify** triangles and **quadrilaterals.** *Also addresses TEKS 7.8(C).*

NEW Vocabulary

quadrilateral
parallelogram
trapezoid
rhombus

GET READY for the Lesson

VIDEO GAMES The general shape of a video game controller is shown.

1. Describe the angles inside the four-sided figure.
2. Which sides of the figure appear to be parallel?
3. Which sides appear to be congruent?

A **quadrilateral** is a closed figure with four sides and four angles. Quadrilaterals are named based on their sides and angles. The diagram shows how quadrilaterals are related. Notice how it goes from the most general to the most specific.

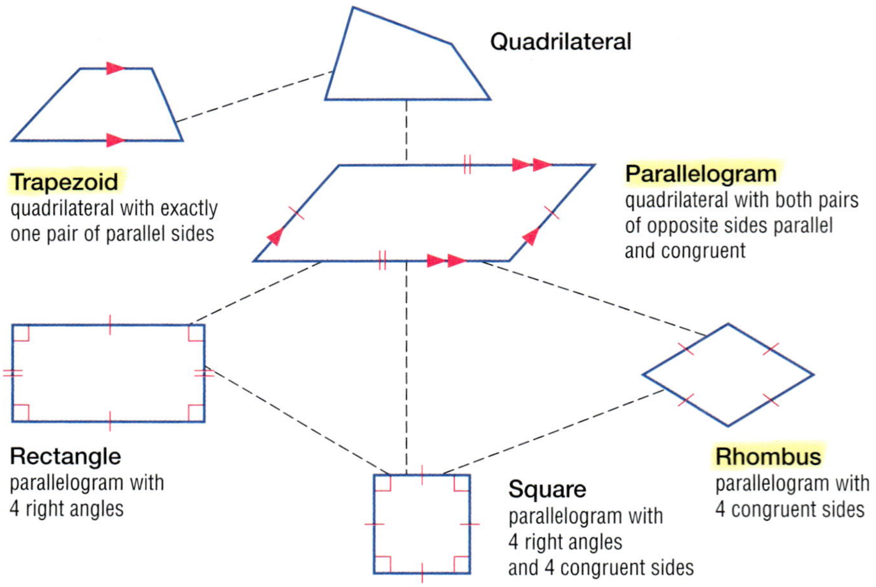

STUDY TIP

Parallel Lines The sides with matching arrows are parallel.

The name that *best* describes a quadrilateral is the one that is most specific.

- If a quadrilateral has all the properties of a parallelogram and a rhombus, then the *best* description of the quadrilateral is a rhombus.
- If a quadrilateral has all the properties of a parallelogram, rhombus, rectangle, and square, then the *best* description of the quadrilateral is a square.

EXAMPLES Classify Quadrilaterals

Classify the quadrilateral using the name that *best* describes it.

1 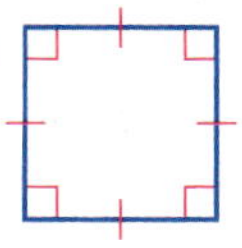 The quadrilateral has 4 right angles and 4 congruent sides. It is a square.

2 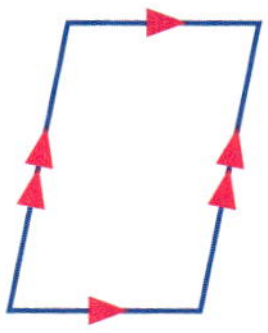 The quadrilateral has opposite sides parallel. It is a parallelogram.

CHECK Your Progress

Classify the quadrilateral using the name that best describes it.

a. 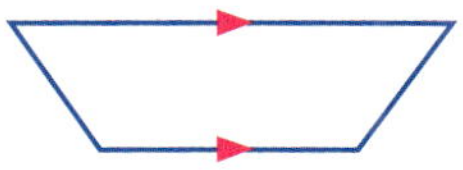

b. 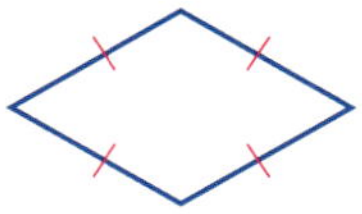

A quadrilateral can be separated into two triangles, *A* and *B*. Since the sum of the angle measures of each triangle is 180°, the sum of the angle measures of the quadrilateral is 2 • 180, or 360°.

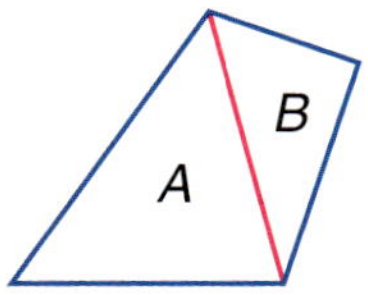

KEY CONCEPT — Angles of a Quadrilateral

Words The sum of the measures of the angles of a quadrilateral is 360°.

Algebra $w + x + y + z = 360$

Model 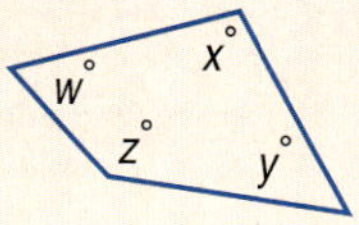

EXAMPLE Find a Missing Measure

3 **ALGEBRA Find the value of *x* in the quadrilateral shown.**

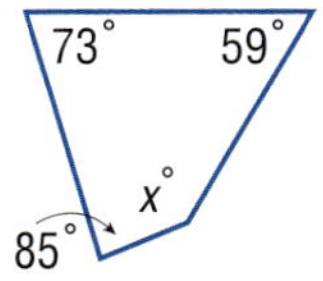

Write and solve an equation.

Words	The sum of the measures is 360°.
Variable	Let x represent the missing measure.
Equation	$85 + 73 + 59 + x = 360$

$$\begin{aligned} 85 + 73 + 59 + x &= 360 && \text{Write the equation.} \\ 217 + x &= 360 && \text{Simplify.} \\ -217 \quad &= -217 && \text{Subtract 217 from each side.} \\ x &= 143 \end{aligned}$$

So, the missing angle measure is 143°.

STUDY TIP

Check for Reasonableness
Since $\angle x$ is an obtuse angle, $m\angle x$ should be between 90° and 180°. Since $90° < 143° < 180°$, the answer is reasonable.

CHECK Your Progress

c. **ALGEBRA** Find the value of *x* in the quadrilateral shown.

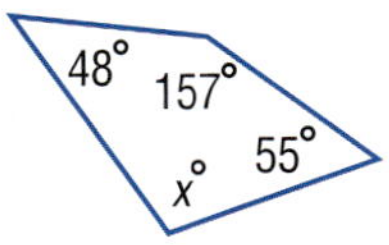

Online Personal Tutor at tx.msmath2.com

CHECK Your Understanding

Examples 1, 2 (p. 573)

Classify each quadrilateral using the name that *best* describes it.

1. 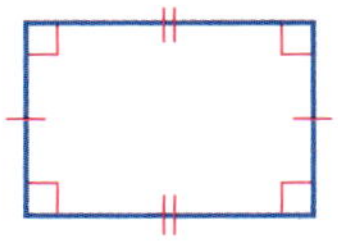

2. 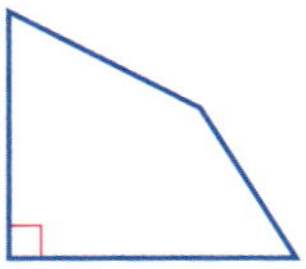

3. 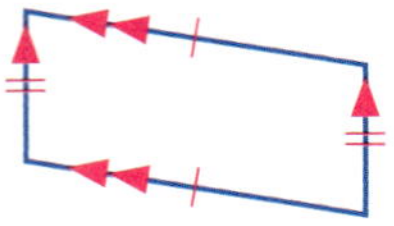

4. **BOATS** The photo shows a sailboat called a schooner. What type of quadrilateral does the indicated sail best represent?

Example 3 (p. 573)

5. **ALGEBRA** In quadrilateral *DEFG*, $m\angle D = 57°$, $m\angle E = 78°$, $m\angle G = 105°$. What is $m\angle F$?

ALGEBRA Find the missing angle measure in each quadrilateral.

6. 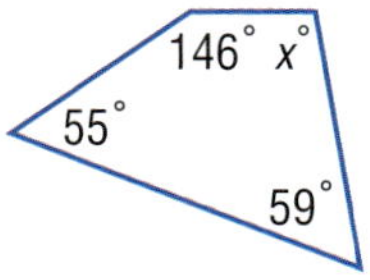

7. 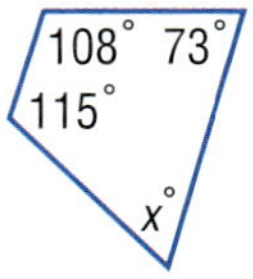

8. 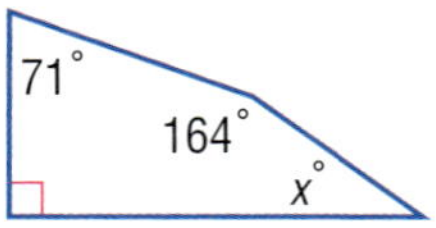

Exercises

HOMEWORK HELP

For Exercises	See Examples
9–14, 23–24	1, 2
15–22	3

Classify each quadrilateral using the name that *best* describes it.

9. 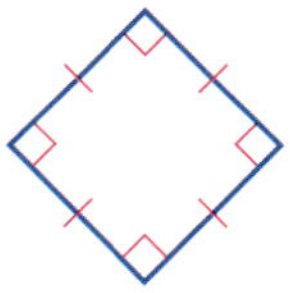

10. 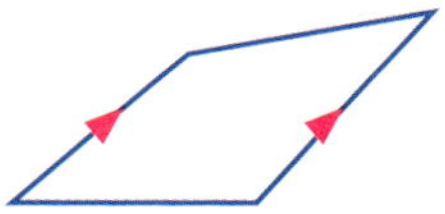

11. 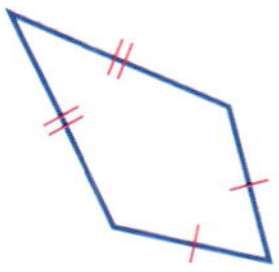

12. 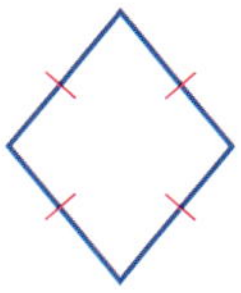

13. 

14. 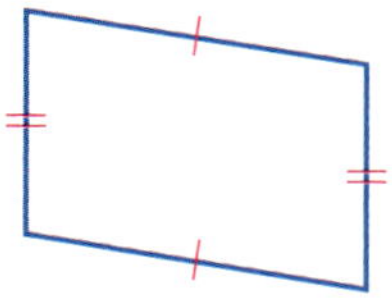

ALGEBRA Find the missing angle measure in each quadrilateral.

15. 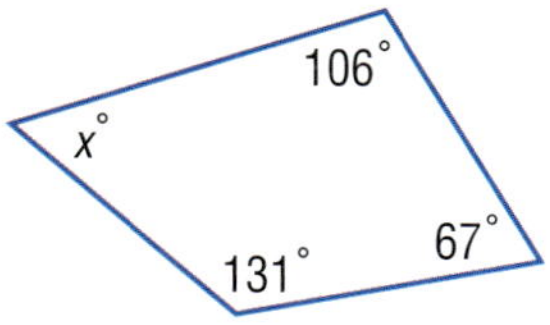

16. 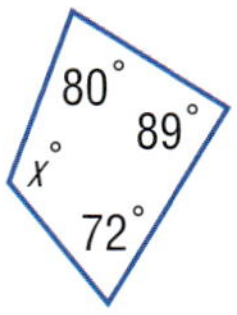

17. 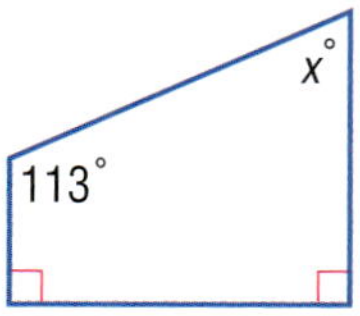

18. 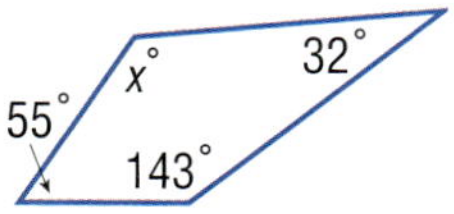

19. 

20. 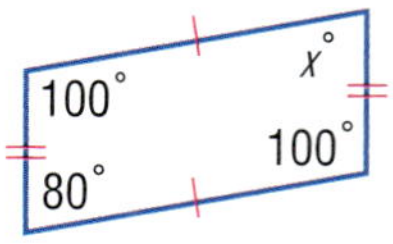

21. **ALGEBRA** Find $m\angle B$ in quadrilateral *ABCD* if $m\angle A = 87°$, $m\angle C = 135°$, and $m\angle D = 22°$.

22. **ALGEBRA** What is $m\angle X$ in quadrilateral *WXYZ* if $m\angle W = 45°$, $m\angle Y = 128°$, and $\angle Z$ is a right angle?

Math Online Extra Examples at tx.msmath2.com

23. **LANDSCAPE** Identify the shapes of the bricks used in the design at the right. Use the names that *best* describe the bricks.

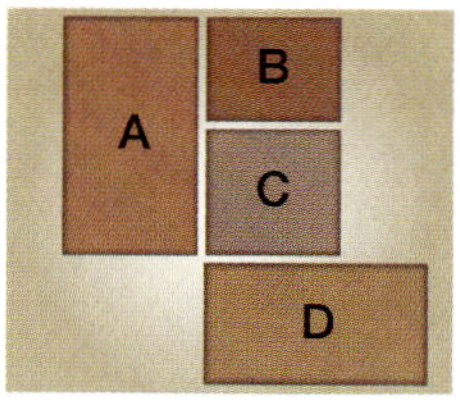

24. **ART** Sculptor George W. Hart is known for his sculptures that incorporate geometric patterns and relationships. The work shown is entitled *Yin and Yang*. What types of quadrilaterals did he use in the sculpture?

Source: georgehart.com

Find the missing measure in each quadrilateral with the given angle measures.

25. 37.5°, 78°, 115.4°, x°

26. x°, 108.3°, 49.8°, 100°

27. 25.5°, x°, 165.9°, 36.8°

28. 79.1°, 120.8°, x°, 65.7°

ART For Exercises 29–31, identify the types of triangles and quadrilaterals used in each quilt block pattern. Use the names that *best* describe the figures.

29. 

30. 

31. 

EXTRA PRACTICE
See page 745, 765.

Math Online
Self-Check Quiz at tx.msmath2.com

ALGEBRA Find the value of x in each quadrilateral.

32. 

33. 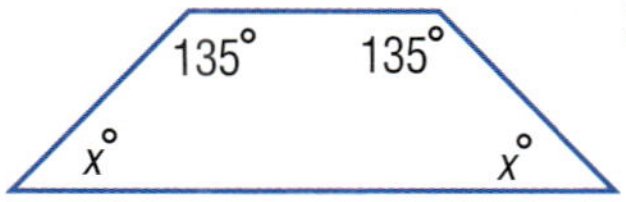

34. 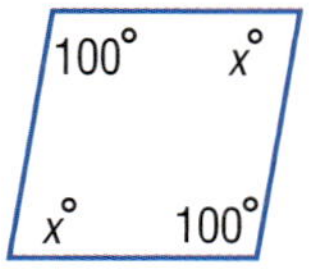

H.O.T. Problems

CHALLENGE Determine whether each figure described below can be drawn. If the figure can be drawn, draw it. If not, explain why not.

35. a quadrilateral that is both a rhombus and a rectangle

36. a trapezoid with three right angles

37. a trapezoid with two congruent sides

REASONING Determine whether each statement is *sometimes*, *always*, or *never* true. Explain your reasoning.

38. A quadrilateral is a trapezoid.

39. A trapezoid is a parallelogram.

40. A square is a rectangle.

41. A rhombus is a square.

H.O.T. Problems

42. **FIND THE ERROR** Isabelle and Justin are describing a square. Who is more accurate? Explain.

43. **WRITING IN MATH** Write a real-world word problem in which you would need to find a missing measure in a quadrilateral.

TEST PRACTICE

44. Identify the name that does NOT describe the quadrilateral shown.

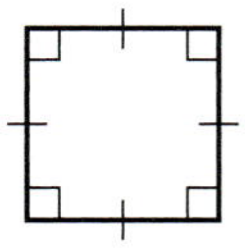

A square

B rectangle

C rhombus

D trapezoid

45. Which statement is always true about a rhombus?

F It has 4 right angles.

G The sum of the measures of the angles is 180°.

H It has exactly one pair of parallel sides.

J It has 4 congruent sides.

Spiral Review

46. **SCHOOL** Neva, Sophie, and Seth have a turtle, a dog, and a hamster for a pet, but not in that order. Sophie's pet lives in a glass aquarium and does not have fur. Neva never has to give her pet a bath. Who has what pet? Use the *logical reasoning* strategy. (Lesson 11-4)

Classify each triangle by its angles and by its sides. (Lesson 11-3)

47. 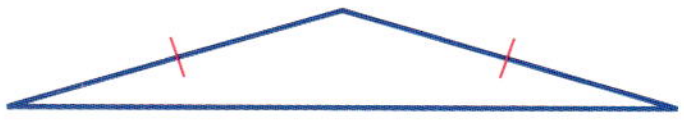

48. 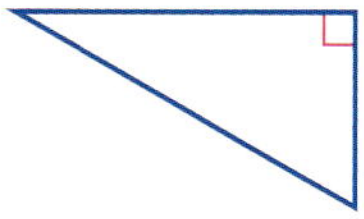

49. 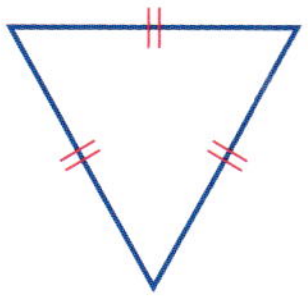

50. Angle RST and $\angle TSU$ are supplementary. Find $m\angle TSU$ if $m\angle RST$ is 76°. (Lesson 11-1)

Find the sales tax or discount to the nearest cent. (Lesson 8-8)

51. \$54 jacket; 7% sales tax

52. \$23 hat; 15% discount

GET READY for the Next Lesson

PREREQUISITE SKILL **Solve each proportion.** (Lesson 7-4)

53. $\frac{3}{5} = \frac{x}{75}$

54. $\frac{a}{7} = \frac{18}{42}$

55. $\frac{7}{9} = \frac{28}{m}$

56. $\frac{3.5}{t} = \frac{16}{32}$

57. $\frac{3}{6} = \frac{c}{5}$

CHAPTER 11 Mid-Chapter Quiz

Lessons 11-1 through 11-5

Name each angle in four ways. Then classify each angle as *acute, obtuse, right,* or *straight.* (Lesson 11-1)

1. 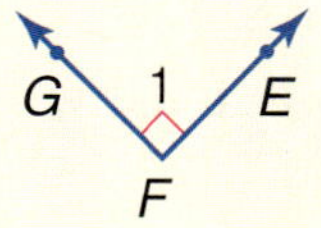

2. 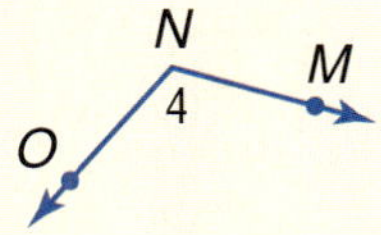

3. **TEST PRACTICE** Which angle is complementary to ∠*CBD*? (Lesson 11-1)

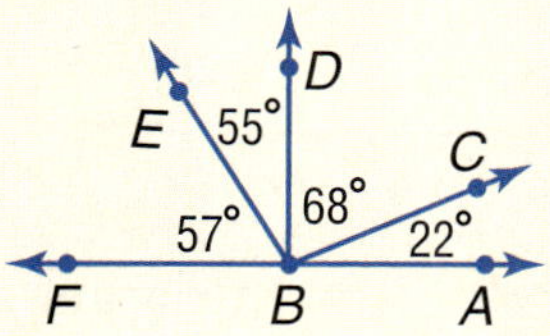

A ∠*ABC* C ∠*DBE*
B ∠*FBC* D ∠*EBF*

4. **SOCCER** Display the data in a circle graph. (Lesson 11-2)

Injuries of High School Girls' Soccer Players	
Position	**Percent**
Halfbacks	37%
Fullbacks	23%
Forward Line	28%
Goalkeepers	12%

Source: National Athletic Trainers' Association

BEVERAGES **For Exercises 5 and 6, use the graph that shows the results of a survey.** (Lesson 11-2)

Favorite Dinner Beverage

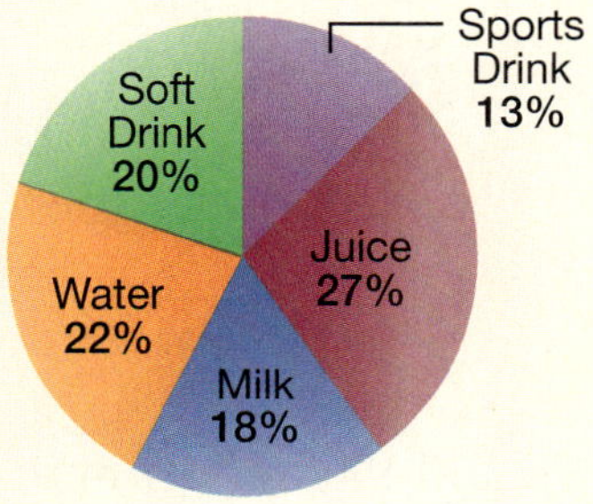

5. What beverage is liked most by students?
6. About how many more students drink juice than sport drinks with dinner?

ALGEBRA **Find the value of *x*.** (Lesson 11-3)

7. 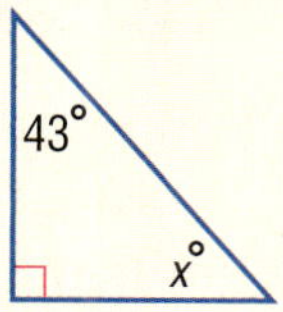

8. 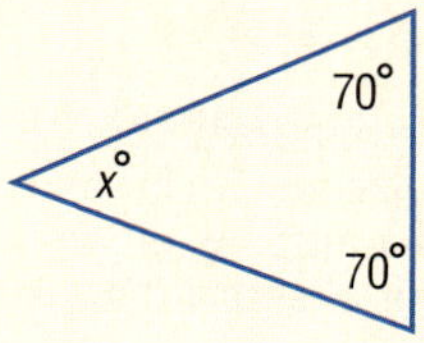

9. **TEST PRACTICE** In triangle *ABC*, $m\angle A = 62°$ and $m\angle C = 44°$. What is $m\angle B$? (Lesson 11-3)

F 90° H 64°
G 74° J 42°

10. **RACES** Norberto, Isabel, Fiona, Brock, and Elizabeth were the first five finishers of a race. From the given clues, find the order in which they finished. Use the *logical reasoning* strategy. (Lesson 11-4)
- Norberto passed Fiona just before the finish line.
- Elizabeth finished 5 seconds ahead of Norberto.
- Isabel crossed the finish line after Fiona.
- Brock was fifth at the finish line.

Classify the quadrilateral using the name that *best* describes it. (Lesson 11-5)

11. 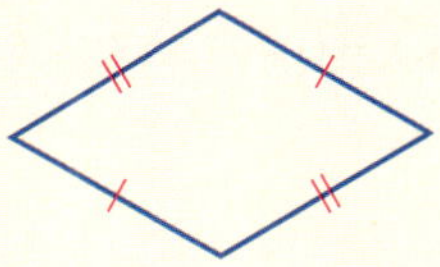

12. 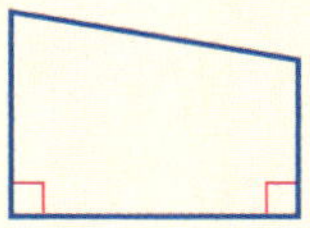

ALGEBRA **Find the value of *x* in each quadrilateral.** (Lesson 11-5)

13. 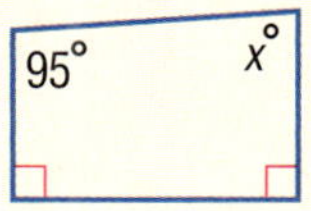

14. 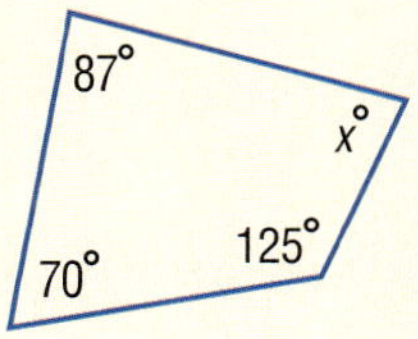

15. **ALGEBRA** What is $m\angle A$ in quadrilateral *ABCD* if $m\angle B = 36°$, $m\angle C = 74°$, and ∠*D* is a right angle? (Lesson 11-5)

11-6 Similar Figures

Main IDEA

Determine whether figures are similar and find a missing length in a pair of similar figures.

Targeted TEKS 7.6 The student compares and classifies two- and three-dimensional figures using geometric vocabulary and properties. **(D) use critical attributes to define similarity**. *Also addresses TEKS 7.3(B).*

NEW Vocabulary

similar figures
corresponding sides
corresponding angles
indirect measurement

MINI Lab

The figures in each pair below have the same shape but different sizes. Copy each pair onto dot paper. Then find the measure of each angle using a protractor and the measure of each side using a centimeter ruler.

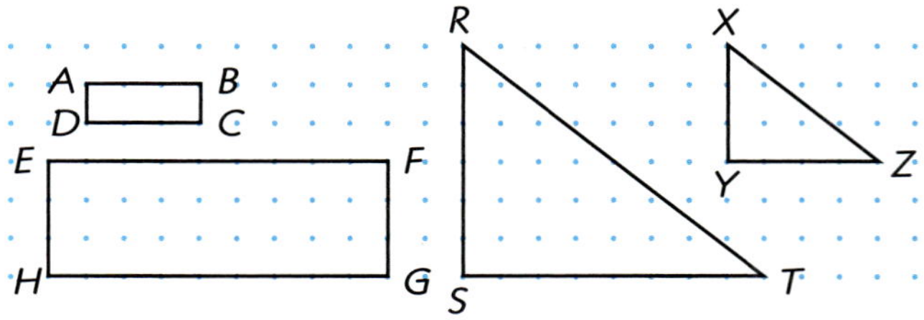

1. $\overline{AB}$ on the smaller rectangle matches $\overline{EF}$ on the larger rectangle. Name all pairs of matching sides in each pair of figures.
   The notation $\overline{AB}$ means the segment with endpoints at *A* and *B*.
2. Write each ratio in simplest form.
   The notation *AB* means the *measure* of segment *AB*.
   a. $\frac{AB}{EF}, \frac{BC}{FG}, \frac{DC}{HG}, \frac{AD}{EH}$ b. $\frac{RS}{XY}, \frac{ST}{YZ}, \frac{RT}{XZ}$
3. What do you notice about the ratios of matching sides?
4. Name all pairs of matching angles in the figures above. What do you notice about the measure of these angles?
5. **MAKE A CONJECTURE** about figures that have the same shape but not necessarily the same size.

Figures that have the same shape but not necessarily the same size are **similar figures**. In the figures below, triangle *RST* is similar to triangle *XYZ*. That is, $\triangle RST \sim \triangle XYZ$.

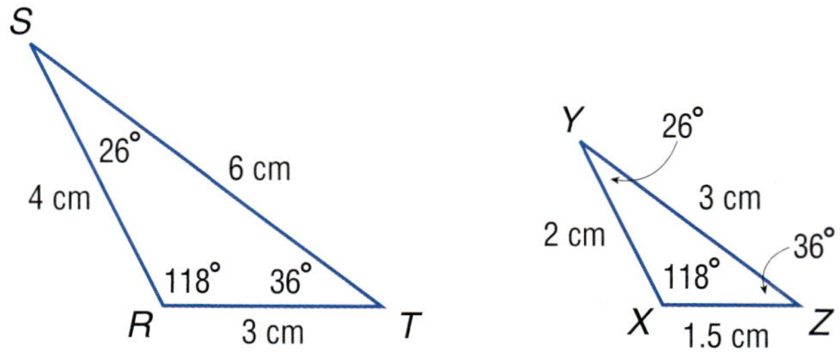

The matching sides are $\overline{ST}$ and $\overline{YZ}$, $\overline{SR}$ and $\overline{YX}$, and $\overline{RT}$ and $\overline{XZ}$.

The sides of similar figures that "match" are **corresponding sides**.

The matching angles are $\angle S$ and $\angle Y$, $\angle R$ and $\angle X$, and $\angle T$ and $\angle Z$.

The angles of similar figures that "match" are **corresponding angles**.

The Mini Lab illustrates the following definition.

KEY CONCEPT — Similar Figures

Words If two figures are similar, then
- the corresponding sides are proportional, and
- the corresponding angles are congruent.

Models

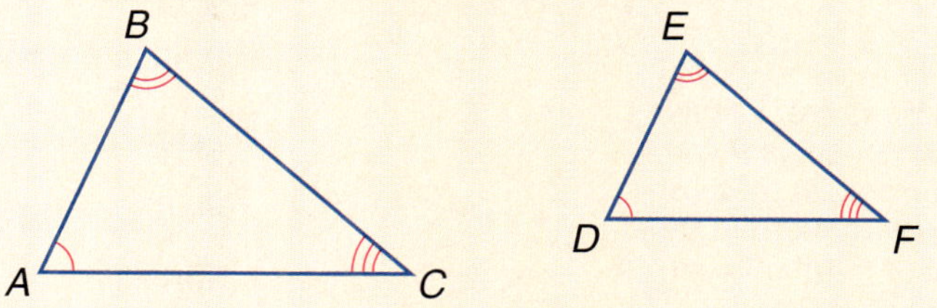

Symbols $\triangle ABC \sim \triangle DEF$ The symbol $\sim$, means *is similar to.*

corresponding sides: $\frac{AB}{DE} = \frac{BC}{EF} = \frac{AC}{DF}$

corresponding angles: $\angle A \cong \angle D$; $\angle B \cong \angle E$; $\angle C \cong \angle F$

READING Math

Geometry Symbols

$\sim$ is similar to

$\cong$ is congruent to

EXAMPLE Identify Similar Figures

1 **Which trapezoid below is similar to trapezoid *DEFG*?**

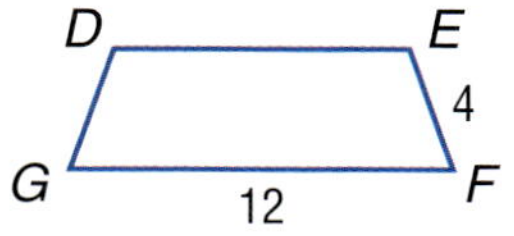

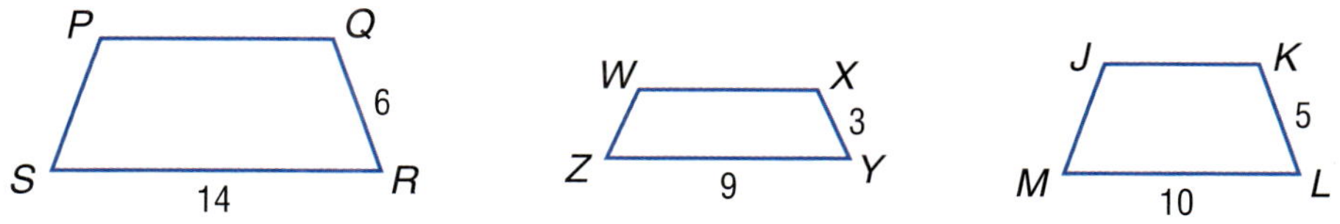

Find the ratios of the corresponding sides to see if they form a constant ratio.

Trapezoid *PQRS*	**Trapezoid *WXYZ***	**Trapezoid *JKLM***
$\frac{EF}{QR} = \frac{4}{6}$ or $\frac{2}{3}$	$\frac{EF}{XY} = \frac{4}{3}$	$\frac{EF}{KL} = \frac{4}{5}$
$\frac{FG}{RS} = \frac{12}{14}$ or $\frac{6}{7}$	$\frac{FG}{YZ} = \frac{12}{9}$ or $\frac{4}{3}$	$\frac{FG}{LM} = \frac{12}{10}$ or $\frac{6}{5}$
Not similar	Similar	Not similar

So, trapezoid *WXYZ* is similar to trapezoid *DEFG*.

CHECK Your Progress

a. Which triangle below is similar to triangle *DEF*?

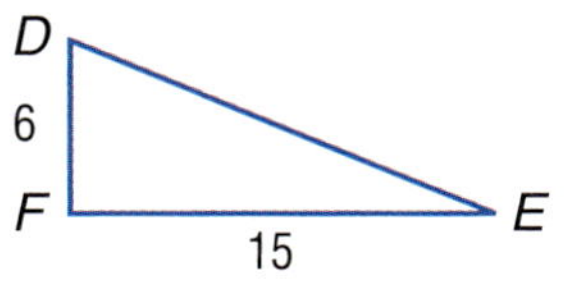

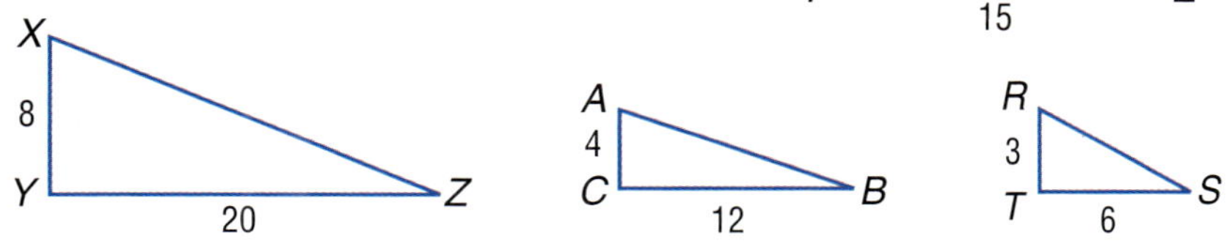

EXAMPLE Find Side Measures of Similar Triangles

2 **If $\triangle RST \sim \triangle XYZ$, find the length of $\overline{XY}$.**

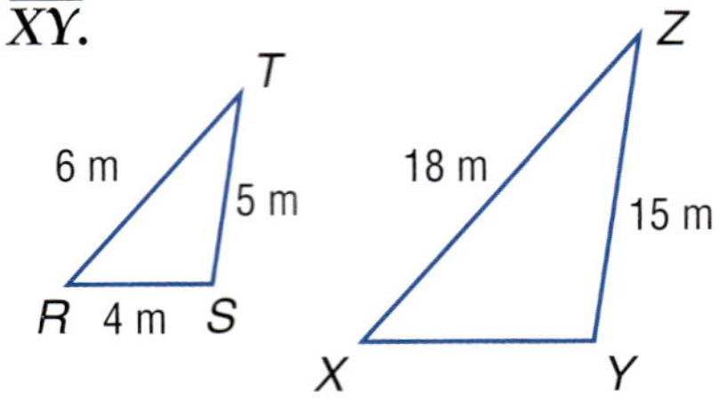

Since the two triangles are similar, the ratios of their corresponding sides are equal. Write and solve a proportion to find XY.

$\frac{RT}{XZ} = \frac{RS}{XY}$ Write a proportion.

$\frac{6}{18} = \frac{4}{n}$ Let n represent the length of $\overline{XY}$. Then substitute.

$6n = 18(4)$ Find the cross products.

$6n = 72$ Simplify.

$n = 12$ Divide each side by 6. The length of $\overline{XY}$ is 12 meters.

READING Math

Segment Measure Just as the measure of angle *A* can be written as $m\angle A$, there is a special way to indicate the measure of a segment. The measure of $\overline{AB}$ is written as *AB*, without the bar over it.

CHECK Your Progress

b. If $\triangle ABC \sim \triangle EFD$, find the length of $\overline{AC}$.

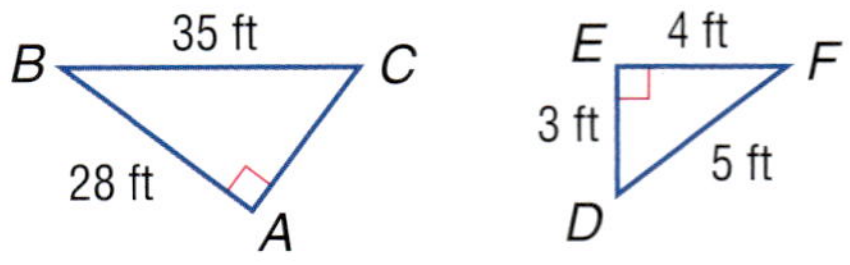

Indirect measurement uses similar figures to find the length, width, or height of objects that are too difficult to measure directly.

Real-World EXAMPLE

3 **GEYSERS Old Faithful in Yellowstone National Park shoots water 60 feet into the air that casts a shadow of 42 feet. What is the height of a nearby tree that casts a shadow 63 feet long? Assume the triangles are similar.**

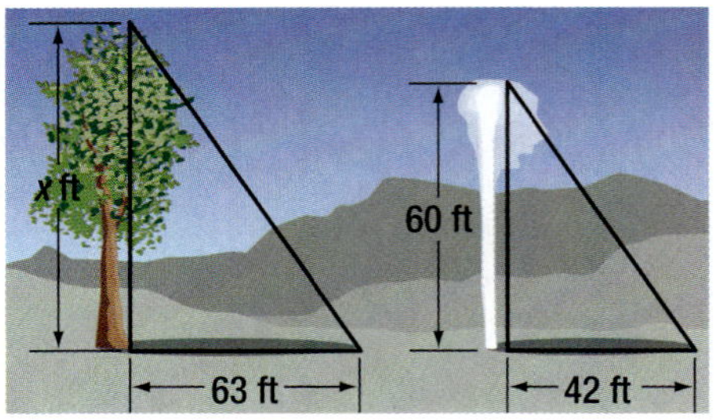

Tree **Old Faithful**

$\frac{x}{63} = \frac{60}{42}$ ← height ← shadow

$x \cdot 42 = 63(60)$ Find the cross products.

$42x = 3{,}780$ Simplify.

$x = 90$ Divide each side by 42.

The tree is 90 feet tall.

CHECK Your Progress

c. **PHOTOGRAPHY** Destiny wants to resize a 4-inch wide by 5-inch long photograph for the school newspaper. It is to fit in a space that is 2 inches wide. What is the length of the resized photograph?

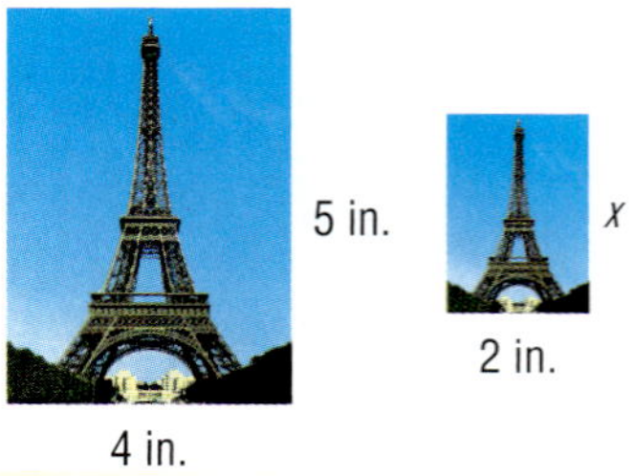

Online Personal Tutor at tx.msmath2.com

CHECK Your Understanding

Example 1 (p. 579)

1. Which rectangle below is similar to rectangle *ABCD*?

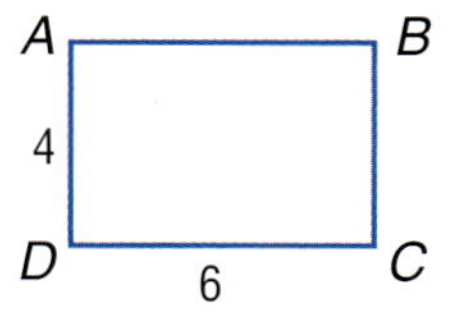

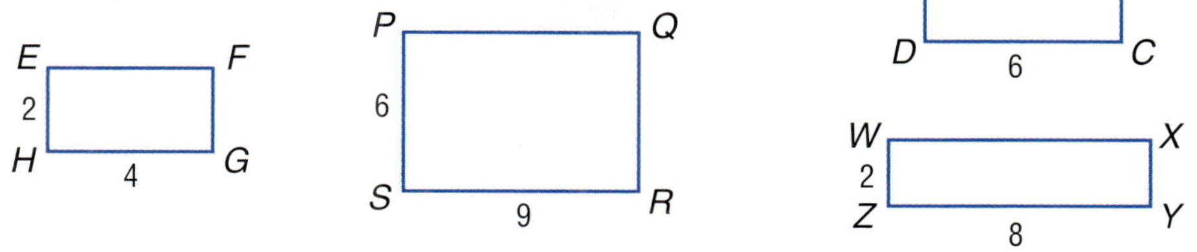

Example 2 (p. 580)

Find the value of *x* in each pair of similar figures.

2. 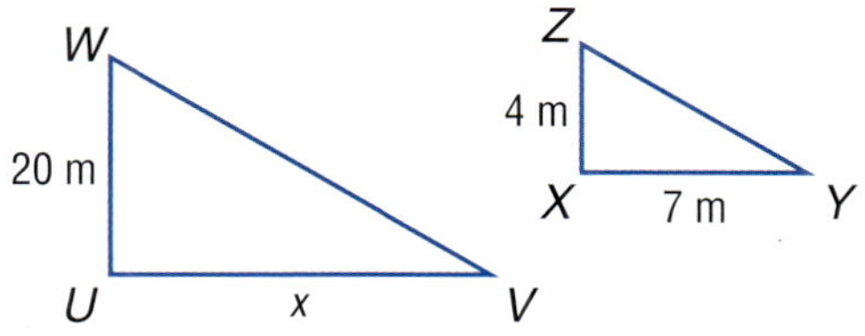

3. 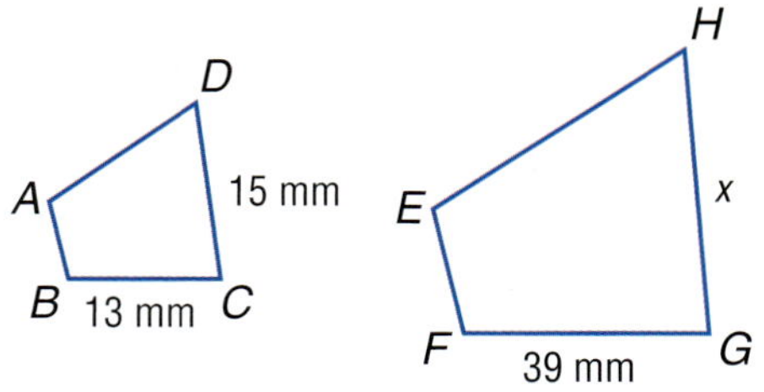

Example 3 (p. 580)

4. **TREES** A certain tree casts a 40-foot shadow. At the same time, Roberto who is 6 feet tall, casts a 5-foot shadow. What is the height of the tree? Assume the triangles are similar.

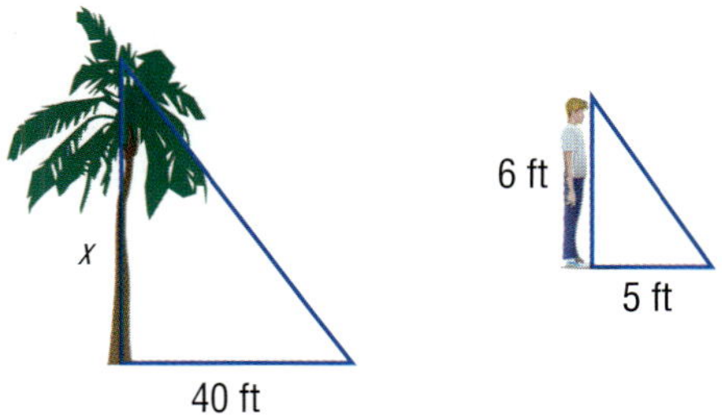

Exercises

HOMEWORK HELP

For Exercises	See Examples
5–6	1
7–10	2
11–12	3

5. Which triangle below is similar to triangle *FGH*?

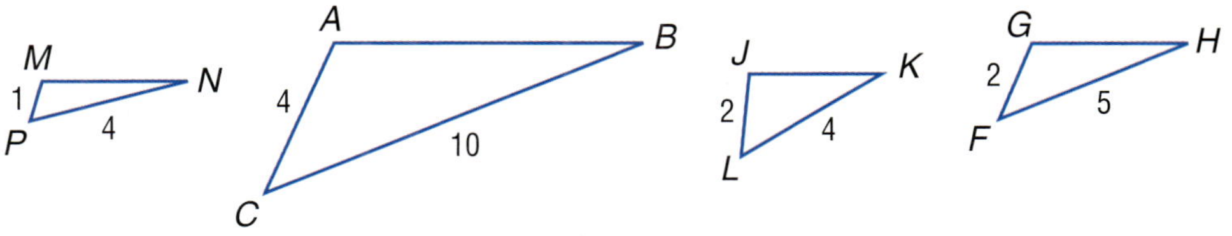

6. Which parallelogram below is similar to parallelogram *HJKM*?

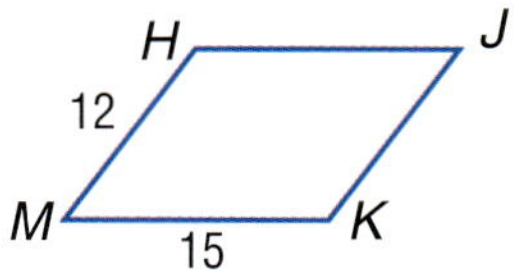

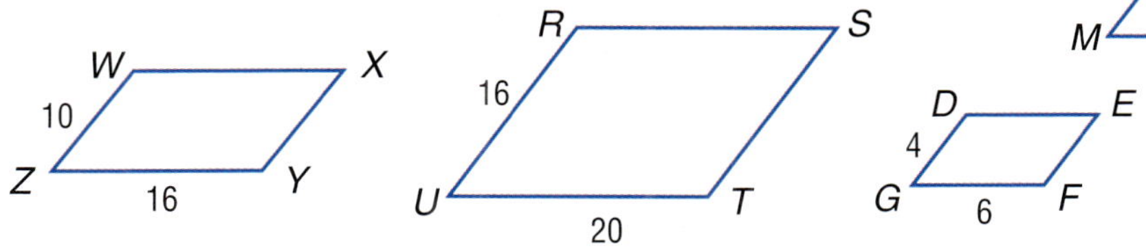

Find the value of *x* in each pair of similar figures.

7. 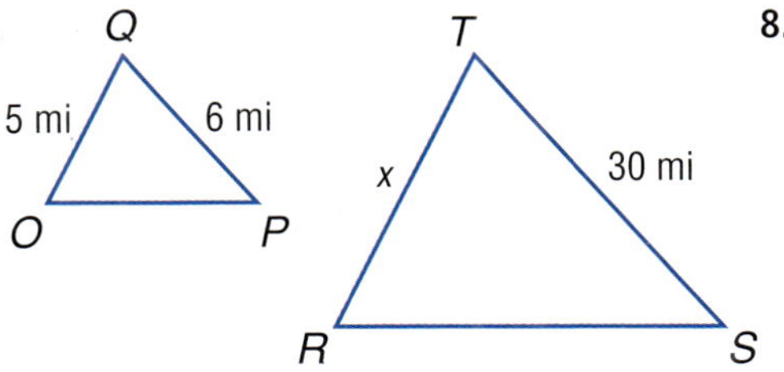

8. 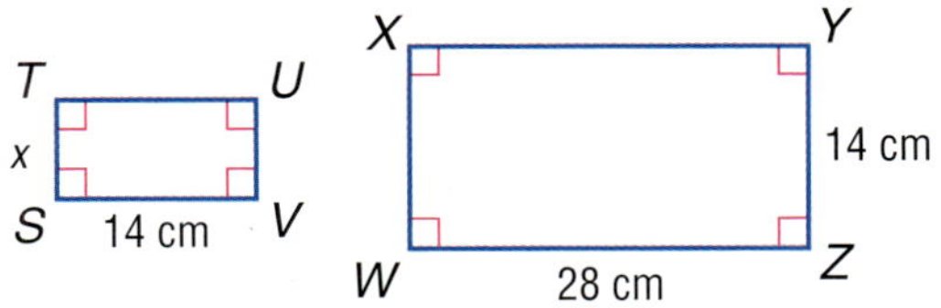

Find the value of x in each pair of similar figures.

9. 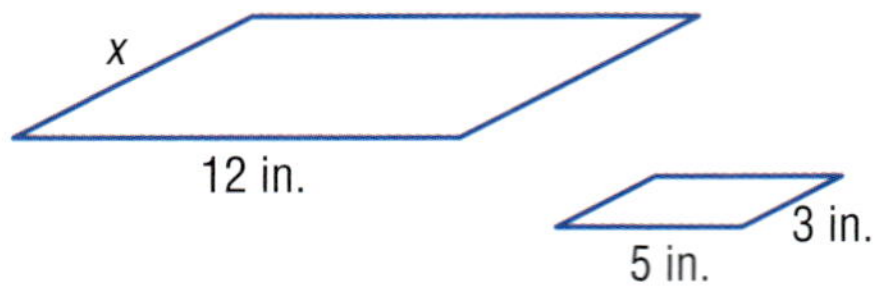

10. 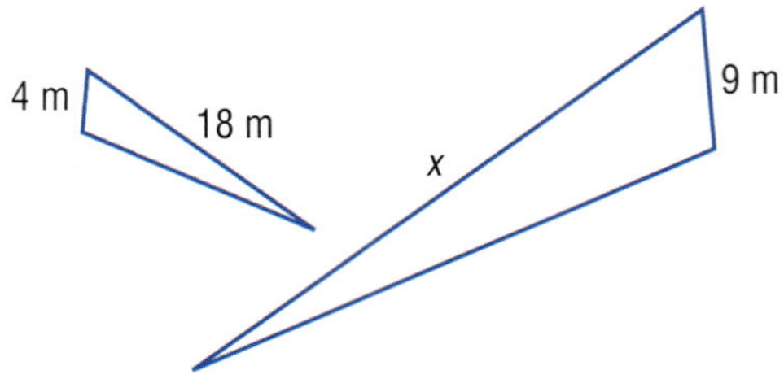

11. **PARKS** Ruth is at the park standing next to a slide. Ruth is 5 feet tall, and her shadow is 4 feet long. If the shadow of the slide is 4.8 feet long, what is the height of the slide? Assume the triangles are similar.

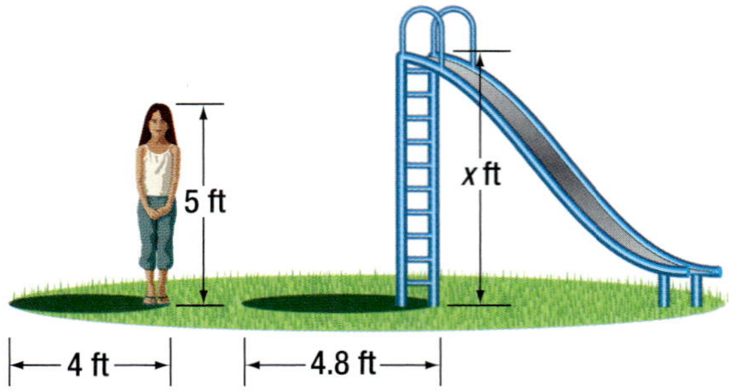

12. **FURNITURE** A child's desk is made so that it is a replica of a full-sized adult desk. Suppose the top of the full-size desk measures 54 inches long by 36 inches wide. If the top of a child's desk is 24 inches wide and is similar to the full-size desk, what is the length?

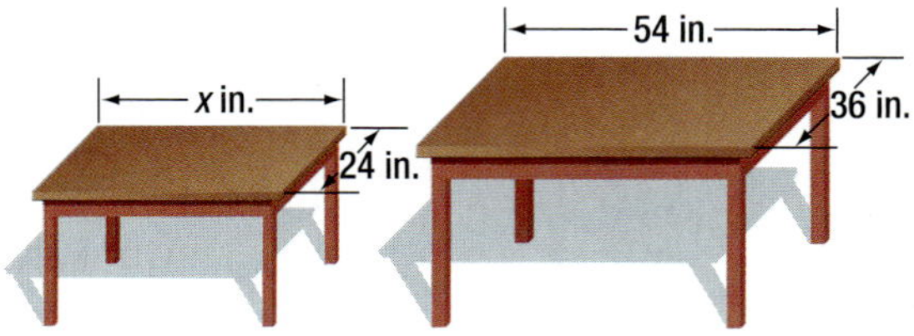

Real-World Link The Statue of Liberty stands 305 feet tall from the foundation of the pedestal to the top of the torch.
Source: Staten Island Information and Services

Find the value of x in each pair of similar figures.

13. 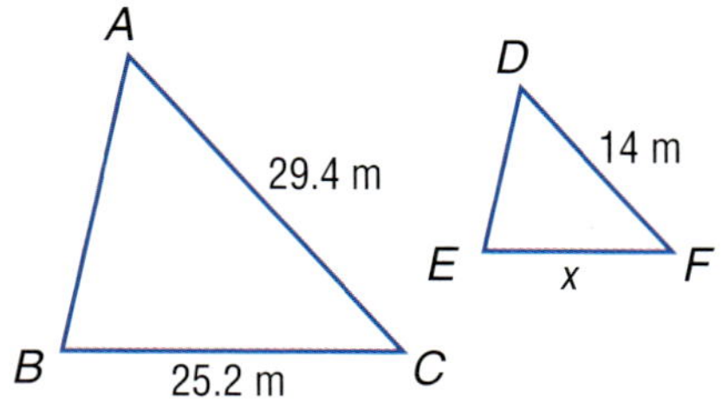

14. 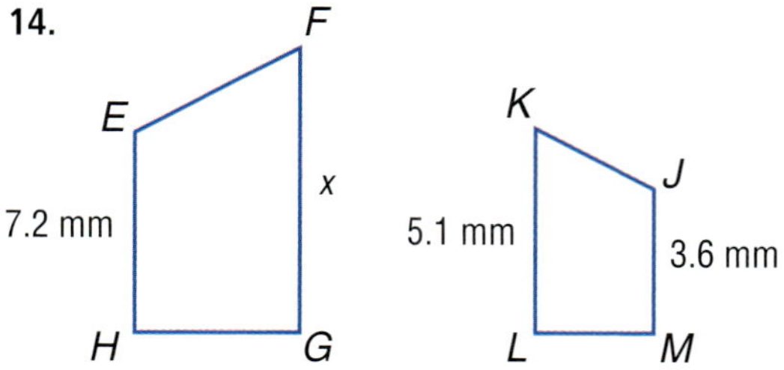

STATUES For Exercises 15 and 16 use the information below and at the left.

Alyssa has a miniature replica of the Statue of Liberty. The replica is 9 inches tall, and the length of the statue's right arm holding the torch is $1\frac{1}{4}$ inches.

15. About how long is the actual Statue of Liberty's right arm?
16. Alyssa's friend has a smaller replica in which the length of the statue's right arm is $\frac{3}{4}$ inch. How tall is the smaller statue?
17. **GEOMETRY** The ratio of the length of square A to the length of square B is 3:5. If the length of square A is 18 meters, what is the perimeter of square B?

EXTRA PRACTICE
See pages 746, 765.
Math Online
Self-Check Quiz at tx.msmath2.com

H.O.T. Problems

CHALLENGE **For Exercises 18 and 19, use the following information.**

Two rectangles are similar. The ratio of their corresponding sides is 1:4.

18. Find the ratio of their perimeters.

19. What is the ratio of their areas?

20. **WRITING IN MATH** Write a problem about a real-world situation that could be solved using proportions and the concept of similarity. Then use what you have learned in this lesson to solve the problem.

TEST PRACTICE

21. Which rectangle is similar to the rectangle shown?

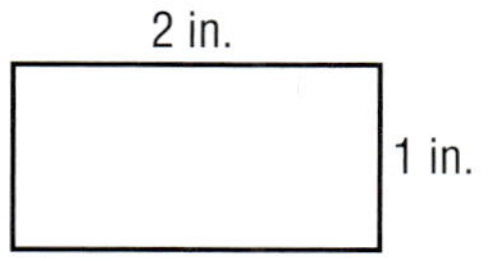

A
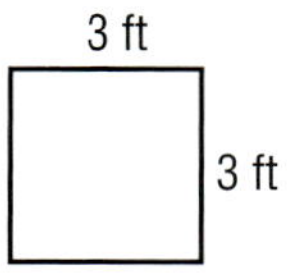

B
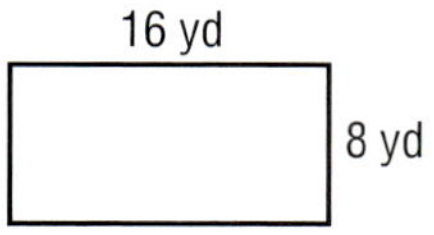

C
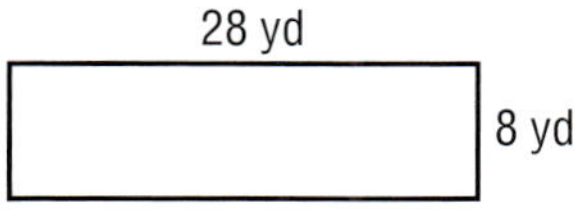

D
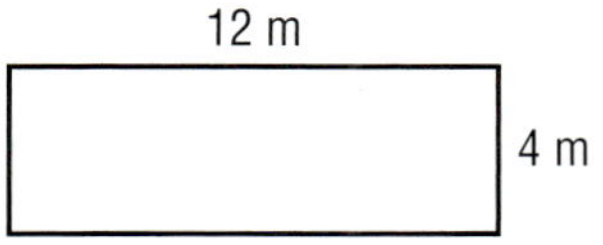

22. Which of the following statements is NOT true?

    F All squares are similar.

    G All rhombi are similar.

    H Some trapezoids are similar.

    J All equilateral triangles are similar.

23. Horatio is 6 feet tall and casts a shadow of 3 feet long. What is the approximate height of a nearby cellular telephone tower if it casts a shadow 25 feet long at the same time?

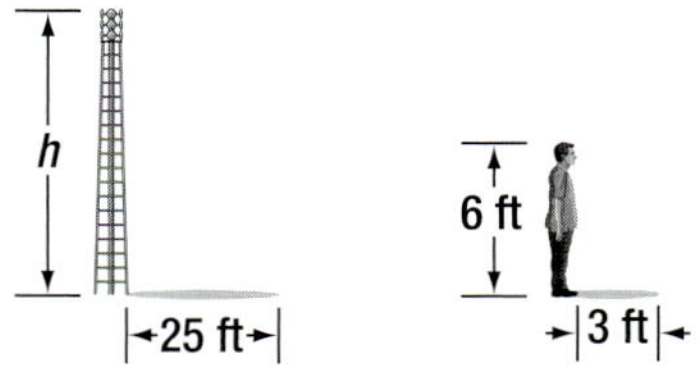

A 25 feet **C** 50 feet

B 45 feet **D** 75 feet

Spiral Review

Classify the quadrilateral using the name that *best* describes it. (Lesson 11-5)

24. 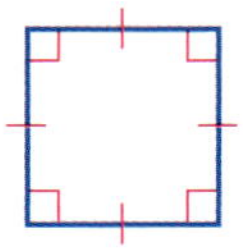

25. 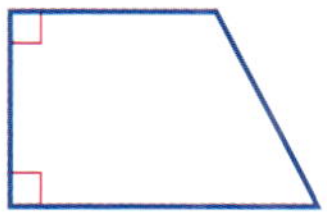

26. 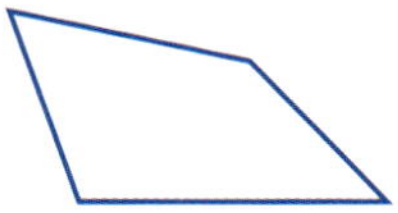

27. **SAILING** A triangular-shaped sail has angle measures of 44° and 67°. Find the measure of the third angle. (Lesson 11-3)

GET READY for the Next Lesson

PREREQUISITE SKILL **Solve each equation.** (Lesson 4-3)

28. $5a = 120$ 29. $360 = 4x$ 30. $940 = 8n$ 31. $6t = 720$

11-7 Polygons and Tessellations

Main IDEA

Classify polygons and determine which polygons can form a tessellation.

Targeted TEKS **7.8** The student uses geometry to model and describe the physical world. **(C) use geometric concepts and properties to solve problems in fields such as art** and architecture. *Also addresses TEKS 7.13(A), 7.15(A).*

NEW Vocabulary

polygon
pentagon
hexagon
heptagon
octagon
nonagon
decagon
regular polygon
tessellation

GET READY for the Lesson

GEOGRAPHY The size and shape of each state in the United States is different. Analyze the shapes of the states in both groups at the right.

Group 1	Group 2
Utah	Kentucky
Wyoming	Michigan
New Mexico	Mississippi
Colorado	Texas

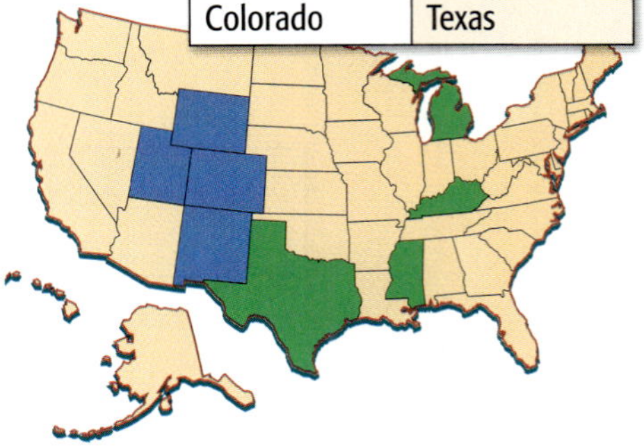

1. Find the difference between the shapes of the states in Group 1 (blue states) and the shapes of the states in Group 2 (green states).
2. Why do most states have boundaries that are not straight line segments?

A **polygon** is a simple, closed figure formed by three or more straight lines. A *simple figure* does not have lines that cross each other. You have drawn a *closed figure* when your pencil ends up where it started.

Polygons	Not Polygons

• Line segments are called sides. • Sides meet only at their endpoints. • Points of intersection are called vertices.	• Figures with sides that overlap. • Figures that are open. • Figures that have curved sides.

READING Math

Polygons The polygons shown at the right have special names. Other polygons are named using a number. For example, a polygon with 11 sides is an 11-gon.

A polygon can be classified by the number of sides it has.

Words	pentagon	hexagon	heptagon	octagon	nonagon	decagon
Number of Sides	5	6	7	8	9	10
Models	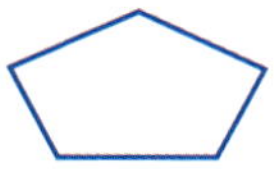		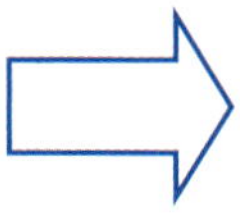			

A polygon that has all sides congruent and all angles congruent is called a **regular polygon**. Equilateral triangles and squares are regular polygons.

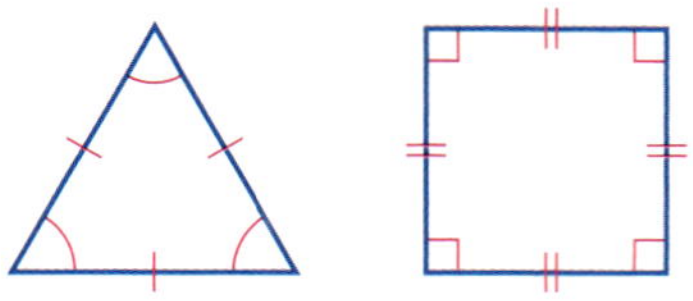

EXAMPLES Classify Polygons

READING Math

Regular Polygons Since regular polygons have *equal–sized angles*, they are also called *equiangular*.

Determine whether each figure is a polygon. If it is, classify the polygon and state whether it is regular. If it is not a polygon, explain why.

1

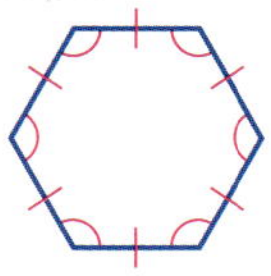

The figure has 6 congruent sides and 6 congruent angles. It is a regular hexagon.

2

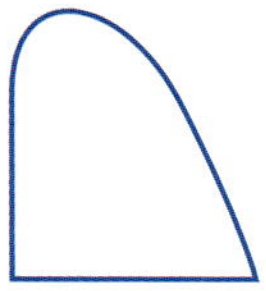

The figure is not a polygon since it has a curved side.

CHECK Your Progress

Determine whether each figure is a polygon. If it is, classify the polygon and state whether it is regular. If it is *not* a polygon, explain why.

a.

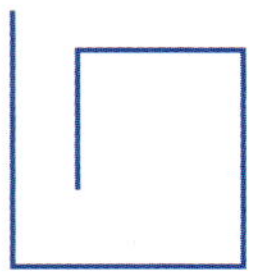

b.

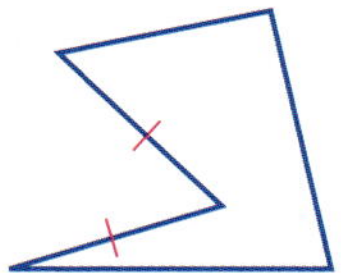

The sum of the measures of the angles of a triangle is 180°. You can use this relationship to find the measures of the angles of regular polygons.

EXAMPLE Angle Measures of a Polygon

STUDY TIP

Diagonal
A diagonal of a polygon is a line segment that connects two vertices that are not next to each other.

3 **ALGEBRA Find the measure of each angle of a regular pentagon.**

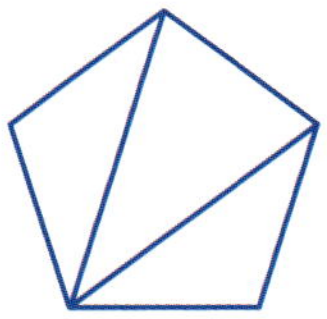

- Draw all of the diagonals from one vertex as shown and count the number of triangles formed.
- Find the sum of the angle measures in the polygon.

number of triangles formed × 180° = sum of angle measures in polygon

$$3 \times 180° = 540°$$

- Find the measure of each angle of the polygon. Let n represent the measure of one angle in the pentagon.

$5n = 540$ There are five congruent angles.

$n = 108$ Divide each side by 5.

The measure of each angle in a regular pentagon is 108°.

CHECK Your Progress

Find the measure of an angle in each polygon.

c. regular octagon

d. equilateral triangle

Concepts in Motion
Interactive Lab tx.msmath2.com

A repetitive pattern of polygons that fit together with no overlaps or holes is called a **tessellation**. The surface of a chessboard is an example of a tessellations of squares.

The sum of the measures of the angles where the vertices meet in a tessellation is 360°.

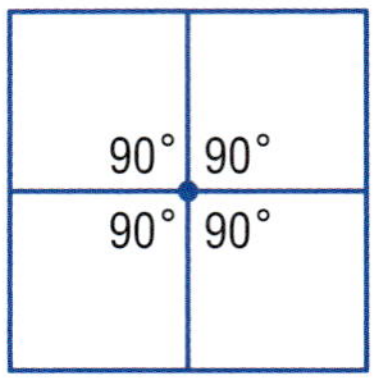

$4 \times 90° = 360°$

Real-World Career.
How Does a Landscape Architect Use Math?
A landscape architect uses math when arranging bricks to create a patio.

Math Online
For more information, go to tx.msmath2.com.

Real-World EXAMPLE

4 **LANDSCAPING** **Mr. Brooks bought pentagonal-shaped bricks to create a patio. Can Mr. Brooks make a tessellation using the bricks?**

The measure of each angle in a regular pentagon is 108°.

The sum of the measures of the angles where the vertices meet must be 360°. So, solve $108n = 360$.

$108n = 360$	Write the equation.
$\frac{108n}{108} = \frac{360}{108}$	Divide each side by 108.
$n = 3.\overline{3}$	Use a calculator.

Since 108° does not divide evenly into 360°, the sum of the measures of the angles where the vertices meet is not 360°. So, Mr. Brooks cannot tessellate the bricks.

Check

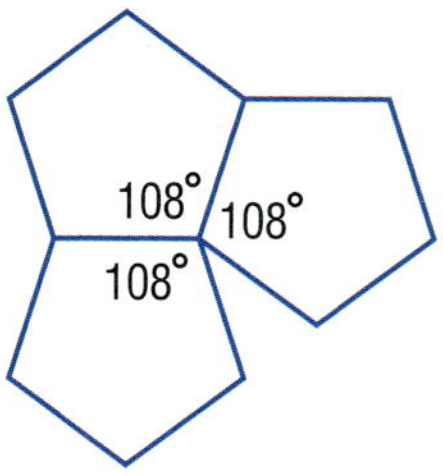

CHECK Your Progress

e. **LANDSCAPING** Can Mr. Brooks use stones that are equilateral triangles to pave the patio? Explain.

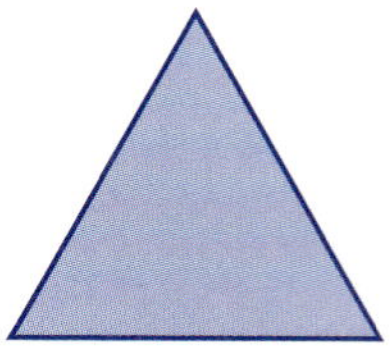

Online **Personal Tutor at** tx.msmath2.com

CHECK Your Understanding

Examples 1, 2 (p. 585)

Determine whether each figure is a polygon. If it is, classify the polygon and state whether it is regular. If it is *not* a polygon, explain why.

1. 

2. 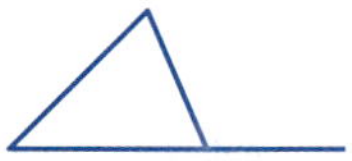

3. 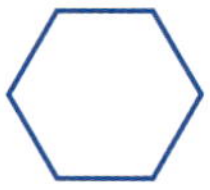

Example 3 (p. 585)

Find the measure of an angle in each polygon if the polygon is regular. Round to the nearest tenth of a degree if necessary.

4. hexagon
5. heptagon

Example 4 (p. 586)

6. **ART** In art class, Trisha traced and then cut several regular octagons out of tissue paper. Can she use the figures to create a tessellation? Explain.

Exercises

HOMEWORK HELP

For Exercises	See Examples
7–12	1,2
13–16	3
17–18	4

Determine whether each figure is a polygon. If it is, classify the polygon and state whether it is regular. If it is *not* a polygon, explain why.

7. 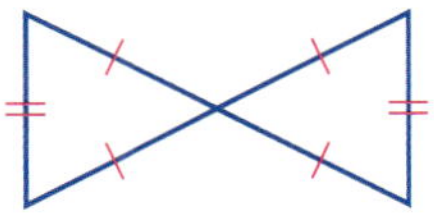

8. 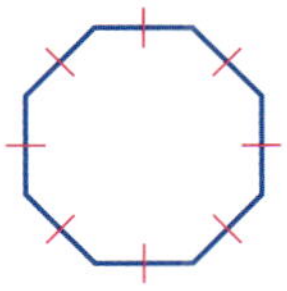

9. 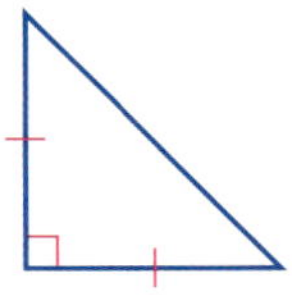

10. 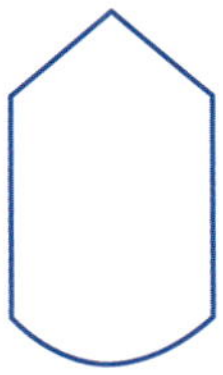

11. 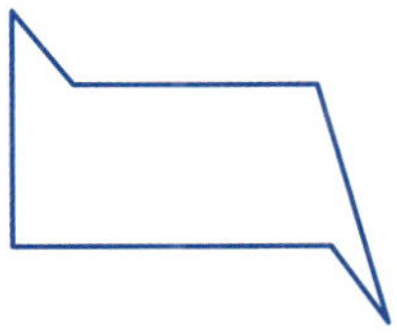

12. 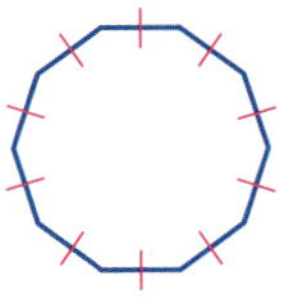

Find the measure of an angle in each polygon if the polygon is regular. Round to the nearest tenth of a degree if necessary.

13. decagon
14. nonagon
15. quadrilateral
16. 11-gon

17. **TOYS** Marty used his magnetic building set to build the regular decagon at the right. Assume he has enough building parts to create several of these shapes. Can the figures be arranged in a tessellation? Explain.

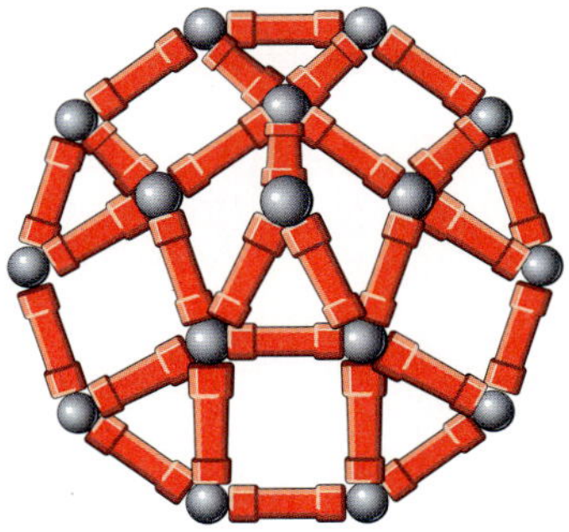

18. **COASTERS** Paper coasters are placed under a beverage glass to protect the table surface. The coasters are shaped like regular heptagons. Can the coasters be arranged in a tessellation? Explain your reasoning.

Classify the polygons that are used to create each tessellation.

19.

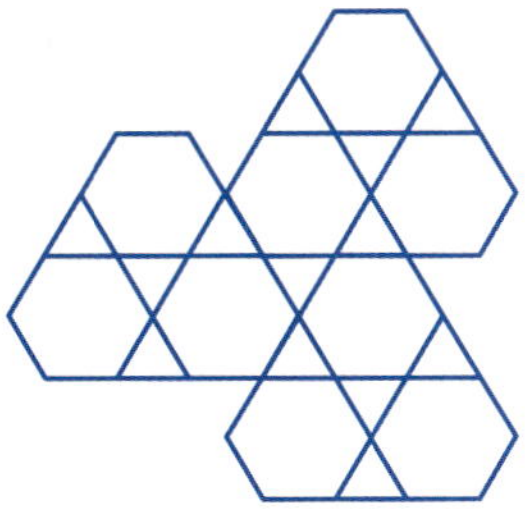

20.

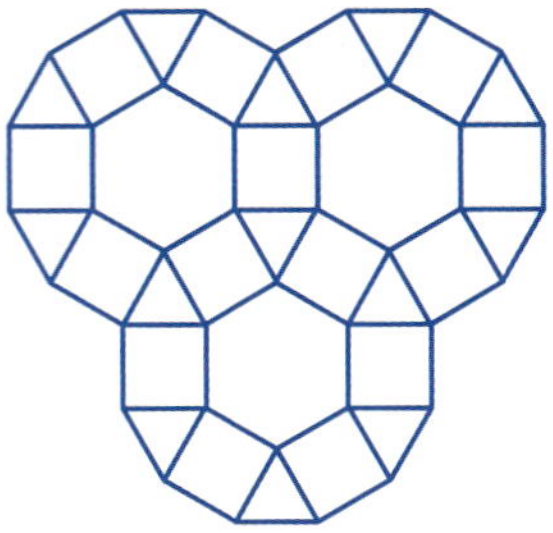

21.

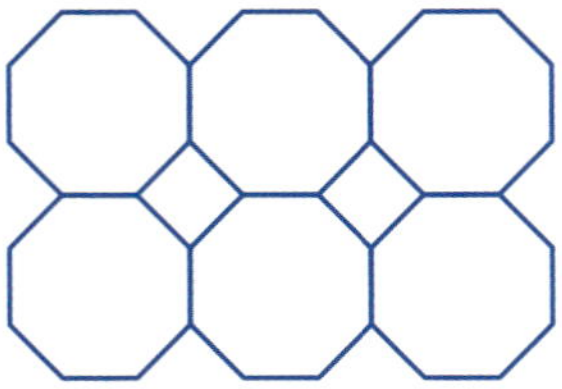

22. What is the perimeter of a regular nonagon with sides 4.8 centimeters?

23. Find the perimeter of a regular pentagon having sides $7\frac{1}{4}$ yards long.

24. **ART** The mosaic shown is decorated with handmade tiles from Pakistan. Name the polygons used in the tessellation.

25. **SIGNS** Refer to the photo at the left. Stop signs are made from large sheets of steel. Suppose one sheet of steel is large enough to cut nine signs. Can all nine signs be arranged on the sheet so that none of the steel goes to waste? Explain.

Real-World Link All stop signs have the same shape and meaning. In Spanish-speaking countries, the signs read "ALTO" (halt) or "PARE" (stop).

26. **RESEARCH** Use the Internet or another source to find the shape of other road signs. Name the type of sign, its shape, and state whether or not it is regular.

SCHOOL For Exercises 27–29, use the information below and the graphic of the cafeteria tray shown.

A company designs cafeteria trays so that four students can place their trays around a square table without bumping corners. The top and bottom sides of the tray are parallel.

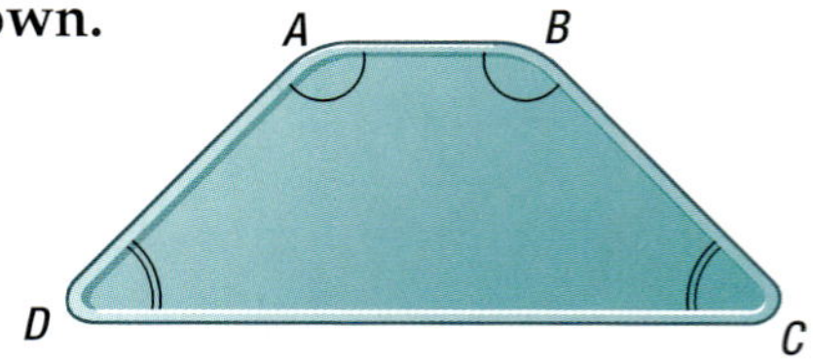

27. Classify the shape of the tray.

28. If $\angle A \cong \angle B$, $\angle C \cong \angle D$, and $m\angle A = 135°$, find $m\angle B$, $m\angle C$, and $m\angle D$.

29. Name the polygon formed by the outside of four trays when they are placed around the table with their sides touching. Justify your answer.

EXTRA PRACTICE See pages 746, 765.

Math Online Self-Check Quiz at tx.msmath2.com

H.O.T. Problems

30. **REASONING** *True* or *False*? Only a regular polygon can tessellate a plane.

31. **OPEN ENDED** Draw examples of a pentagon and a hexagon that represent real-world objects.

32. **CHALLENGE** You can make a tessellation with equilateral triangles. Can you make a tessellation with any isosceles or scalene triangles? If so, explain your reasoning and make a drawing.

33. **WRITING IN MATH** Analyze the parallelogram at the right and then explain how you know the parallelogram can be used by itself to make a tessellation.

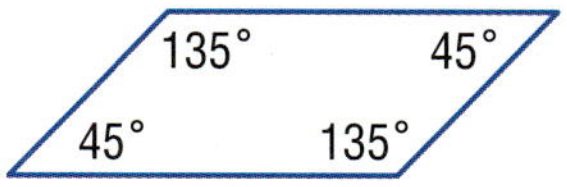

TEST PRACTICE

34. Which term identifies the shape of the solitaire game board?

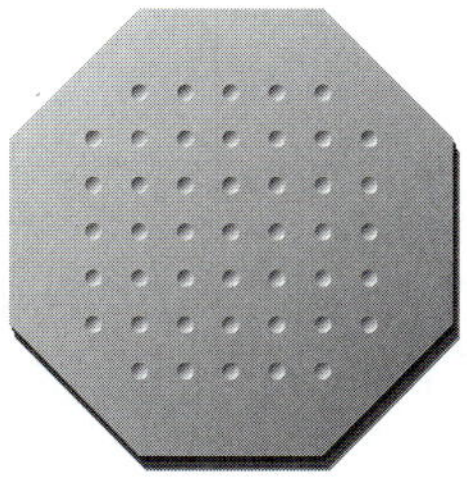

A pentagon

B hexagon

C octagon

D nonagon

35. Which statement is NOT true about polygons?

F A polygon is classified by the number of sides it has.

G The sides of a polygon overlap.

H A polygons is formed by 3 or more line segments.

J The sides of a polygon meet only at its endpoints.

36. **GRIDDABLE** What is the measure in degrees of ∠1?

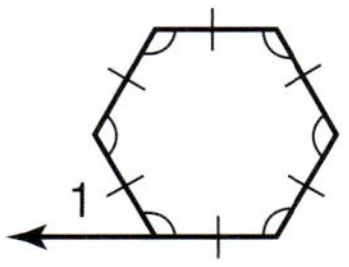

Spiral Review

For Exercises 37 and 38, use the figures at the right.

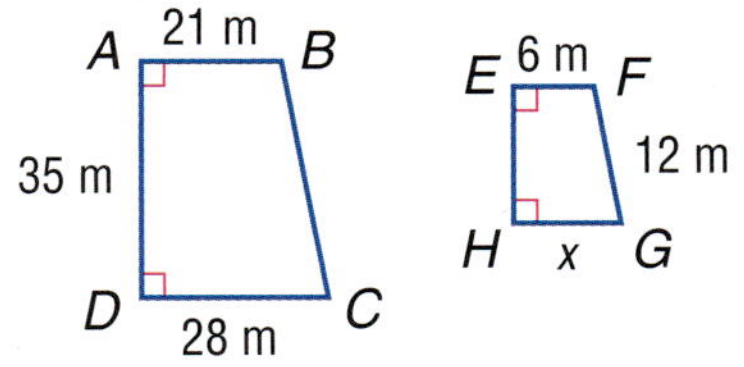

37. The quadrilaterals are similar. Find the value of x. (Lesson 11-6)

38. Classify figure $ABCD$. (Lesson 11-5)

39. **SCHOOL** Two students will be randomly selected from a group of seven to present their reports. If Carla and Pedro are in the group of 7, what is the probability that Carla will be selected first and Pedro selected second? (Lesson 10-4)

40. **MEASUREMENT** How many $\frac{1}{2}$-cup servings of ice cream are there in a gallon of chocolate ice cream? (Lesson 7-3)

Add or subtract. Write each sum or difference in simplest form. (Lesson 6-3)

41. $3\frac{2}{9} + 5\frac{4}{9}$ 42. $5\frac{1}{3} - 2\frac{1}{6}$ 43. $1\frac{3}{7} + 6\frac{1}{4}$ 44. $9\frac{4}{5} - 4\frac{7}{8}$

GET READY for the Next Lesson

PREREQUISITE SKILL **Graph and label each point on the same coordinate plane.** (Lesson 2-3)

45. $A(-2, 3)$ 46. $B(4, 3)$ 47. $C(2, -1)$ 48. $D(-4, -1)$

Extend 11-7

Geometry Lab
Tessellations

Main IDEA

Create tessellations.

Targeted TEKS 7.8 The student uses geometry to model and describe the physical world. **(C) use geometric concepts and properties to solve problems in fields such as art** and architecture. *Also addresses TEKS 7.13(A).*

In this lab, you will create tessellations.

ACTIVITY

STEP 1 Draw a square on the back of an index card. Then draw a triangle on the inside of the square and a trapezoid on the bottom of the square as shown.

STEP 2 Cut out the square. Then cut out the triangle and slide it from the right side of the square to the left side of the square. Cut out the trapezoid and slide it from the bottom to the top of the square.

STEP 3 Tape the figures together to form a pattern.

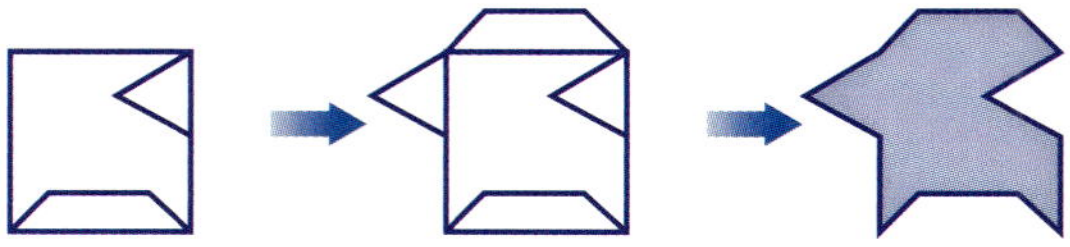

STEP 4 Trace this pattern onto a sheet of paper as shown to create a tessellation.

CHECK Your Progress **Create a tessellation using each pattern.**

a. 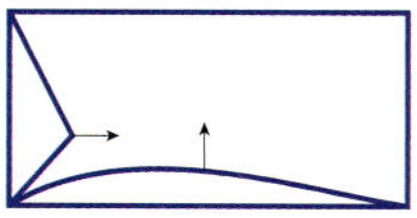

b. 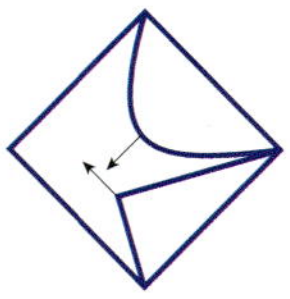

c. 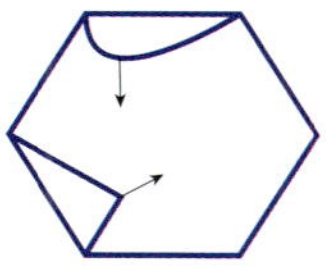

Analyze the Results

1. Design and describe your own tessellation pattern.
2. **MAKE A CONJECTURE** Could a tessellation be made from sliding an equilateral triangle? Explain your reasoning.

11-8 Translations

Main IDEA

Graph translations of polygons on a coordinate plane.

Targeted TEKS 7.7 The student uses coordinate geometry to describe location on a plane. **(B)** graph reflections across the horizontal or vertical axis and **graph translations on a coordinate plane**.

NEW Vocabulary

transformation
translation
congruent figures

MINI Lab

Concepts in Motion
Interactive Lab tx.msmath2.com

STEP 1 Trace a parallelogram-shaped pattern block onto a coordinate grid. Label the vertices *ABCD*.

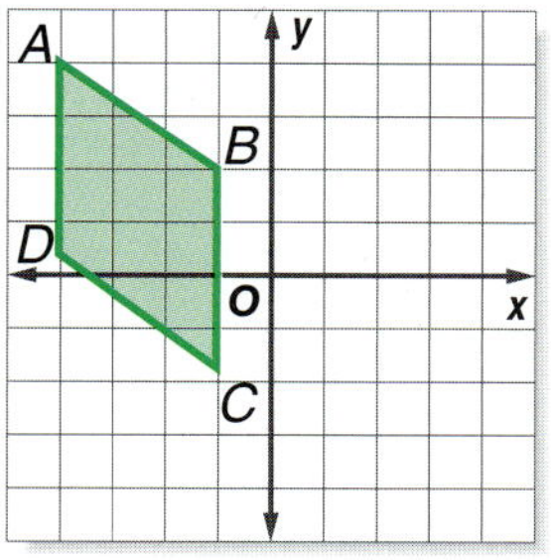

STEP 2 Slide the pattern block over 5 units to the right and 2 units down.

STEP 3 Trace the figure in its new position. Label the vertices *A*′, *B*′, *C*′, and *D*′.

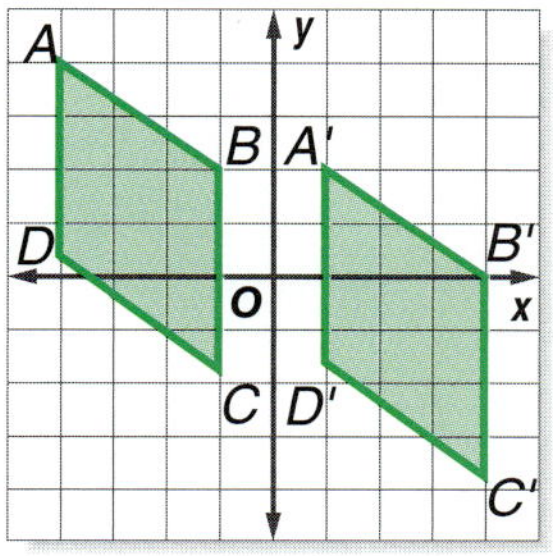

1. Trace the horizontal and vertical path between corresponding vertices. What do you notice?
2. Add 5 to each *x*-coordinate of the vertices of the original figure. Then subtract 2 from each *y*-coordinate of the vertices of the original figure. What do you notice?

A **transformation** maps one figure onto another. When you move the figure without turning it, the motion is a **translation**.

When translating a figure, every point of the original figure is moved the same distance and in the same direction.

READING Math

Prime Symbols Use prime symbols for vertices in transformed image.

A → *A*′
B → *B*′
C → *C*′

A′ is read *A prime*.

EXAMPLE Graph a Translation

1 Translate quadrilateral *HIJK* 2 units left and 5 units up. Graph quadrilateral *H*′ *I*′ *J*′ *K*′.

- Move each vertex of the figure 2 units left and 5 units up. Label the new vertices *H*′, *I*′, *J*′, and *K*′.
- Connect the vertices to draw the trapezoid. The coordinates of the vertices of the new figure are *H*′(−4, 1), *I*′(−3, 4), *J*′(1, 3), and *K*′(−1, 1).

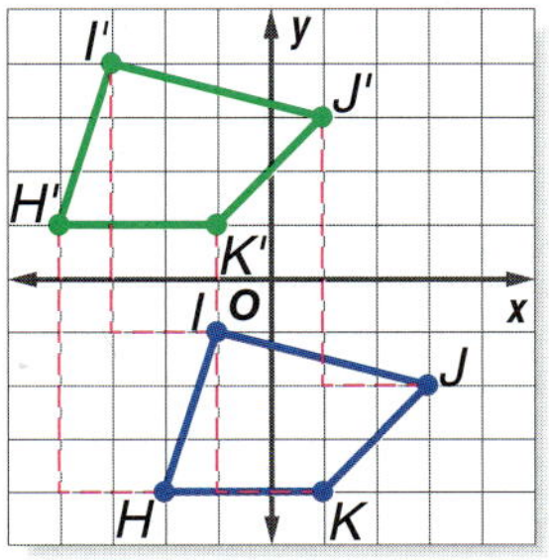

CHECK Your Progress

a. Translate quadrilateral *HIJK* 4 units up and 2 units right. Graph quadrilateral *H*′ *I*′ *J*′ *K*′.

When a figure has been translated, the original figure and the translated figure, or *image*, are congruent. **Congruent figures** have the same size and same shape, and the corresponding sides and angles have equal measure.

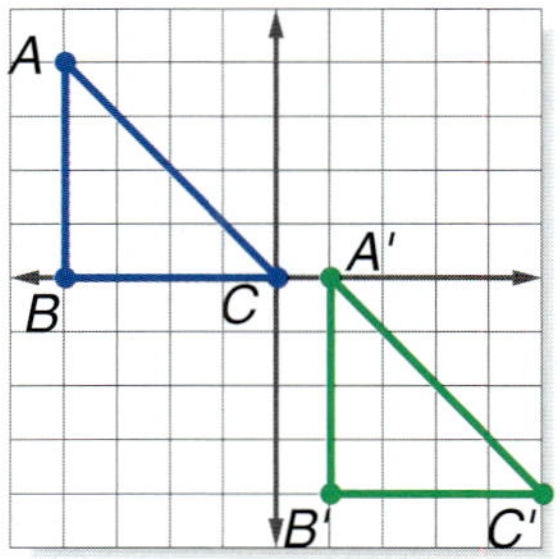

$\triangle ABC \cong \triangle A'B'C'$

You can also add to or subtract from the coordinates of the vertices of a figure to find the vertices of the translated image.

STUDY TIP

Integers
Recall that to subtract an integer, add its opposite.

A *positive* integer describes a translation right or up on a coordinate plane. A *negative* integer describes a translation left or down.

EXAMPLE Find Coordinates of a Translation

2 **Triangle LMN has vertices $L(-1, -2)$, $M(6, -3)$, and $N(2, -5)$. Find the vertices of $\triangle L'M'N'$ after a translation of 6 units left and 4 units up. Then graph the figure and its translated image.**

The vertices can be found by adding -6 to the x-coordinates and 4 to the y-coordinates.

Add -6 to each x-coordinate.

Add 4 to each y-coordinate.

Vertices of $\triangle LMN$	$(x + (-6), y + 4)$	Vertices of $\triangle L'M'N'$
$L(-1, -2)$	$(-1 + (-6), -2 + 4)$	$L'(-7, 2)$
$M(6, -3)$	$(6 + (-6), -3 + 4)$	$M'(0, 1)$
$N(2, -5)$	$(2 + (-6), -5 + 4)$	$N'(-4, -1)$

Use the vertices of $\triangle LMN$ and of $\triangle L'M'N'$ to graph each triangle.

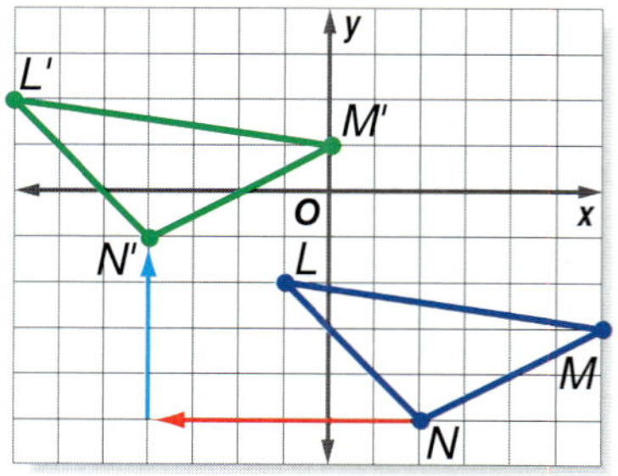

STUDY TIP

Check for Reasonableness
After graphing the original figure and its image on the same coordinate plane, check to see that the figures are congruent.

CHECK Your Progress

b. Triangle TUV has vertices $T(6, -3)$, $U(-2, 0)$, and $V(-1, 2)$. Find the vertices of $\triangle T'U'V'$ after a translation of 3 units right and 4 units down. Then graph the figure and its translated image.

Online **Personal Tutor at** tx.msmath2.com

In Example 2, $\triangle LMN$ was translated 6 units left and 4 units up. This translation can be described using the ordered pair $(-6, 4)$. In Check Your Progress b., $\triangle TUV$ was translated 3 units right and 4 units down. This translation can be described using the ordered pair $(3, -4)$.

CHECK Your Understanding

Example 1 (p. 591)

1. Translate $\triangle ABC$ 3 units left and 3 units down. Graph $\triangle A'B'C'$.

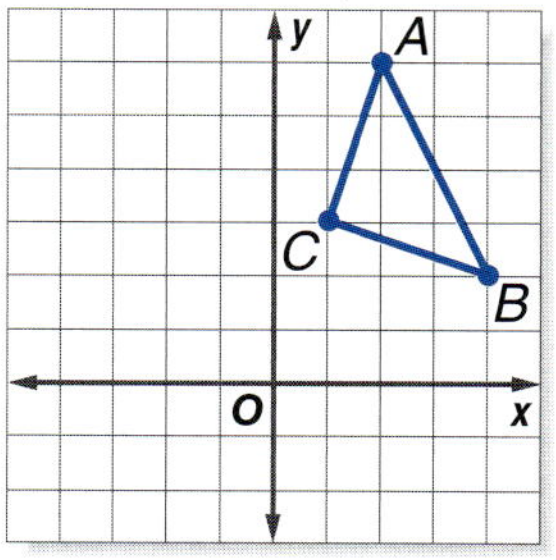

Example 2 (p. 592)

Quadrilateral $DEFG$ has vertices $D(1, 0)$, $E(-2, -2)$, $F(2, 4)$, and $G(6, -3)$. Find the vertices of $D'E'F'G'$ after each translation. Then graph the figure and its translated image.

2. 4 units right, 5 units down
3. 6 units right

4. **GAMES** When playing chess, the rook can only move vertically or horizontally across a chessboard. The chessboard at the right shows the movement of a rook after two turns. Describe this translation in words and as an ordered pair.

Exercises

HOMEWORK HELP	
For Exercises	See Examples
5–6	1
7–12	2

5. Translate $\triangle HIJ$ 2 units right and 6 units down. Graph $\triangle H'I'J'$.

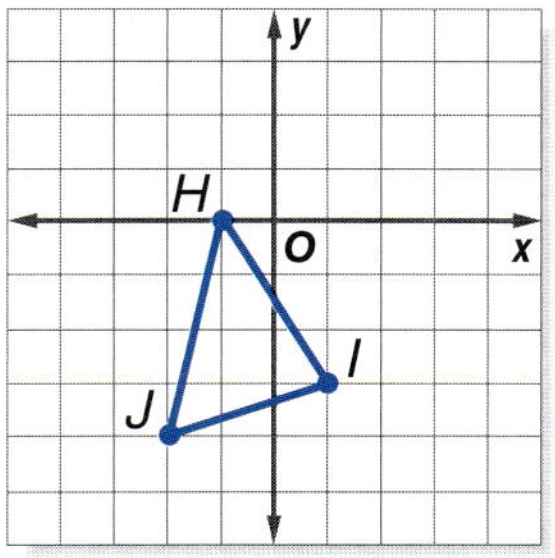

6. Translate rectangle $KLMN$ 1 unit left and 3 units up. Graph rectangle $K'L'M'N'$.

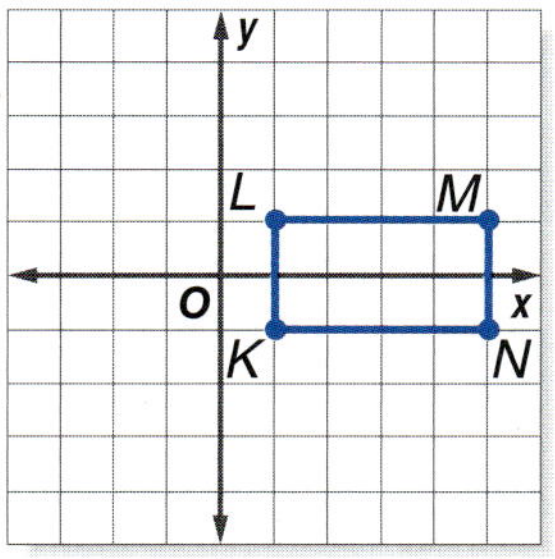

Triangle PQR has vertices $P(0, 0)$, $Q(5, -2)$, and $R(-3, 6)$. Find the vertices of $P'Q'R'$ after each translation. Then graph the figure and its translated image.

7. 6 units right, 5 units up
8. 8 units left, 1 unit down
9. 3 units left
10. 9 units down

MAPS Payat lives at the corner of Wabash and Ohio. His school is located at Huron and Dearborn. Describe each of the following as a translation and as an ordered pair of the number of blocks.

11. Payat's walk from school to home
12. Payat's walk from home to school

13. Triangle ABC is translated 2 units left and 3 units down. Then the translated figure is translated 3 units right. Graph the resulting triangle.

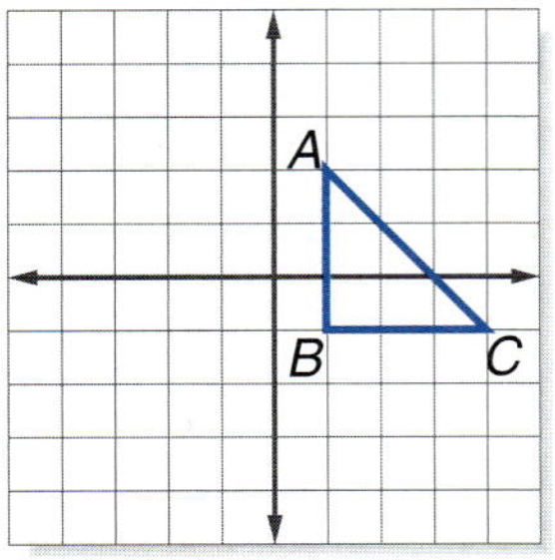

14. Parallelogram $RSTU$ is translated 3 units right and 5 units up. Then the translated figure is translated 2 units left. Graph the resulting parallelogram.

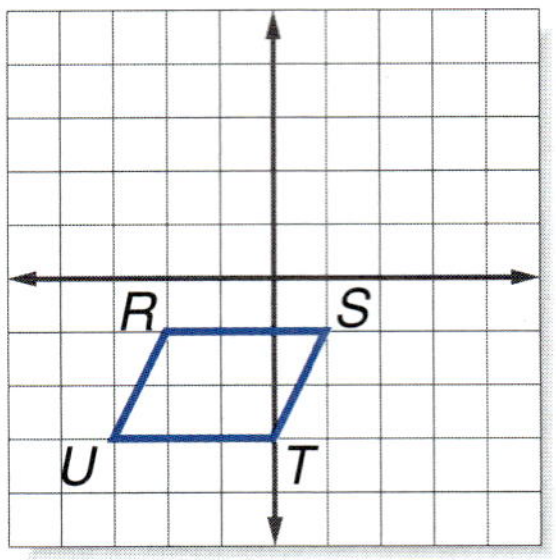

15. **ART** Explain how translations and tessellations were used in *Horsemen*, created by M.C. Escher at the right.

16. **RESEARCH** Use the Internet or another source to find other pieces of art that contain tessellations of translations. Describe how the artists incorporated both ideas into their work.

17. Triangle FGH has vertices $F(7, 6)$, $G(3, 4)$, $H(1, 5)$. Find the coordinates of $\triangle F'G'H'$ after a translation $1\frac{1}{2}$ units right and $3\frac{1}{2}$ units down. Then graph the figure and its translated image.

Horsemen by M.C. Escher. © Cordon Art-Baarn-Holland. All rights reserved.

EXTRA PRACTICE
See pages 747, 765.
Math Online
Self-Check Quiz at tx.msmath2.com

REASONING The coordinates of a point and its image after a translation are given. Describe the translation in words and as an ordered pair.

18. $N(0, -3) \rightarrow N'(2, 2)$
19. $M(2, 4) \rightarrow M'(-3, 1)$
20. $P(-2, -1) \rightarrow P'(3, -2)$
21. $Q(-4, 0) \rightarrow Q'(1, 4)$

H.O.T. Problems

22. **CHALLENGE** Is it possible to make a tessellation with translations of equilateral triangles? Explain your reasoning.

23. **Which One Doesn't Belong?** Identify the transformation that is not the same as the other three. Explain your reasoning.

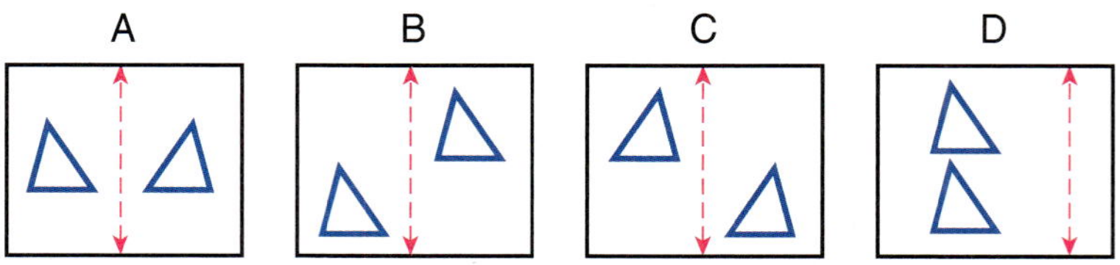

24. **WRITING IN MATH** Triangle ABC is translated 4 units right and 2 units down. Then the translated image is translated again 7 units left and 5 units up. Describe the final translated image in words.

TEST PRACTICE

25. Which graph shows a translation of the letter Z?

A
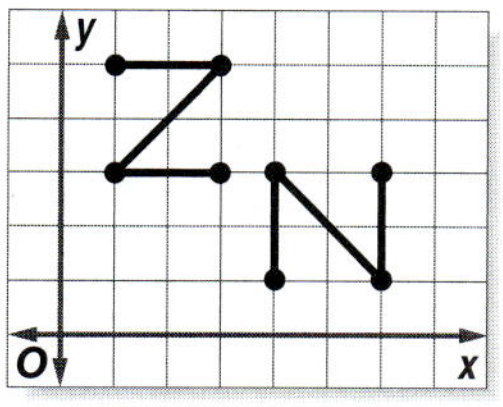

C
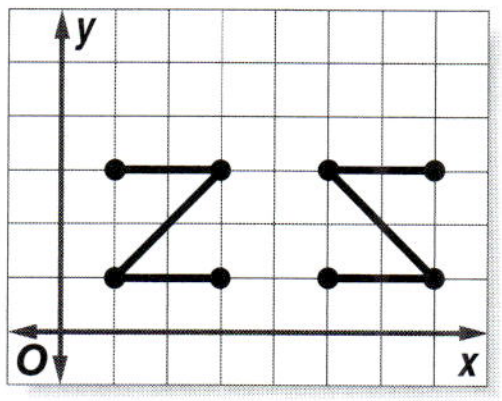

B
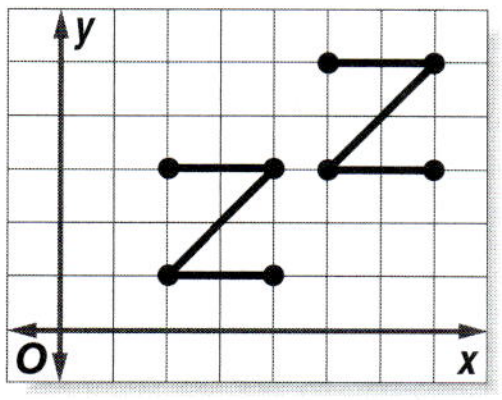

D
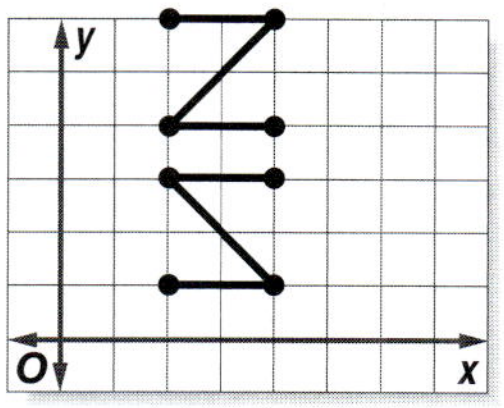

26. If point A is translated 4 units left and 3 units up, what will be the coordinates of point A in its new position?

F (4, 4)

G (−5, 5)

H (−5, −1)

J (−4, 3)

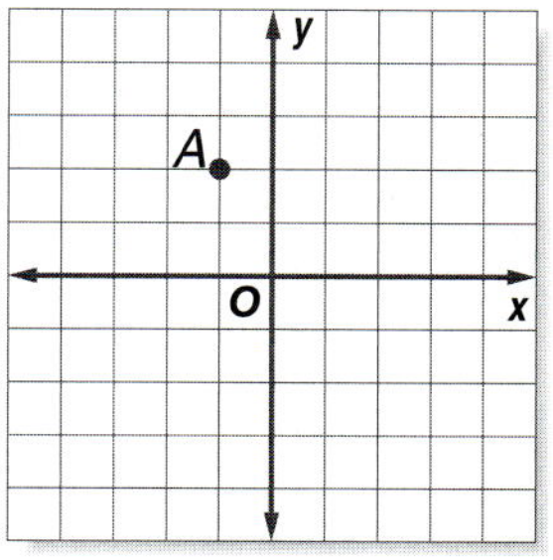

Spiral Review

27. **GEOMETRY** What is the name of a polygon with eight sides? (Lesson 11-7)

28. **GEOMETRY** The triangles at the right are similar. What is the measure of $\angle F$? (Lesson 11-6)

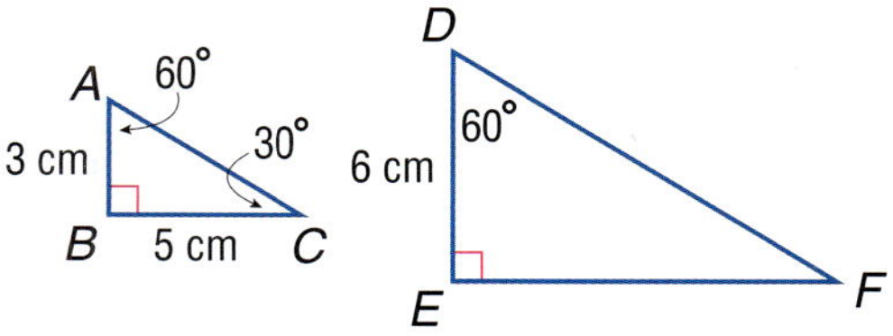

29. **FOOD** For dinner, you can choose one of two appetizers, one of four entrées, and one of three desserts. How many possible unique dinners can you choose? (Lesson 10-3)

Write each percent as a decimal. (Lesson 5-7)

30. 83.8%
31. 56.7%
32. 3.8%
33. 102.6%

Estimate. (Lesson 3-1)

34. $3.8 + 6.1$
35. $8.9 - 4.8$
36. 5.6×3.2
37. $10.3 \div 1.8$

GET READY for the Next Lesson

PREREQUISITE SKILL **Determine whether each figure can be folded in half so that one side matches the other. Write *yes* or *no*.**

38. 

39. 

40. 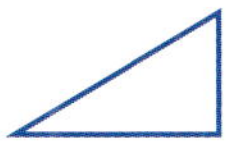

41. 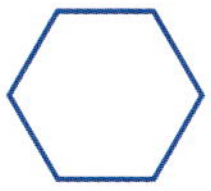

11-9 Reflections

Main IDEA

Identify figures with line symmetry and graph reflections on a coordinate plane.

Targeted TEKS **7.7** The student uses coordinate geometry to describe location on a plane. **(B)** **graph reflections across the horizontal or vertical axis** and graph translations **on a coordinate plane**.

NEW Vocabulary

line symmetry
line of symmetry
reflection
line of reflection

MINI Lab

- Write your first name in capital letters on a sheet of paper.
- Use the geomirror to trace the reflection of the letters in your name.
- Write a classmate's name. Draw the reflection of the letters without using the geomirror.

1. Describe how you drew the reflection of your classmate's name.
2. Explain why the line where the geomirror and paper meet is called the *line of symmetry*.

Figures that match exactly when folded in half have **line symmetry**. The figures at the right have line symmetry.

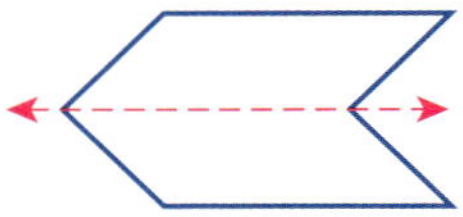

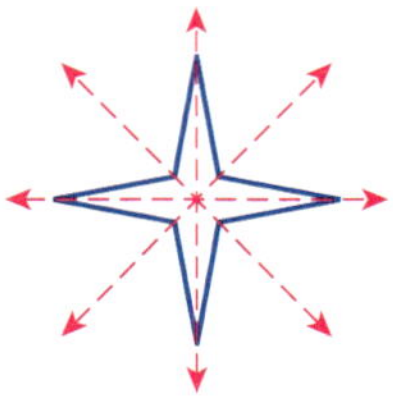

Each fold line is called a **line of symmetry**.

Real-World EXAMPLES

GRAPHIC DESIGN **Determine whether each figure has line symmetry. If so, copy the figure and draw all lines of symmetry.**

1

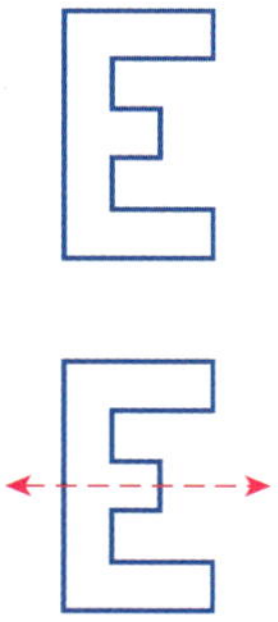

2

no symmetry

3

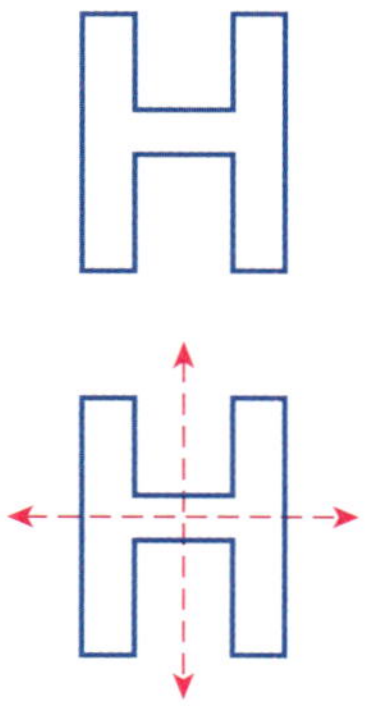

CHECK Your Progress

a.

b.

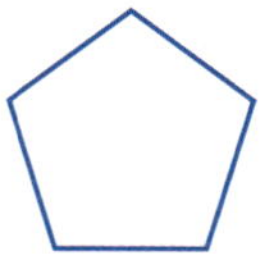

c.

A **reflection** is a transformation of a figure over a line called a **line of reflection**.

STUDY TIP

Congruent Figures As with translations, the original figure and the reflected image are congruent.

EXAMPLE Reflect a Figure Over the *x*-axis

4 **Triangle ABC has vertices $A(5, 2)$, $B(1, 3)$, and $C(-1, 1)$. Graph the figure and its reflected image over the x-axis. Then find the coordinates of the reflected image.**

The x-axis is the line of reflection. So, plot each vertex of $A'B'C'$ the same distance from the x-axis as its corresponding vertex on ABC.

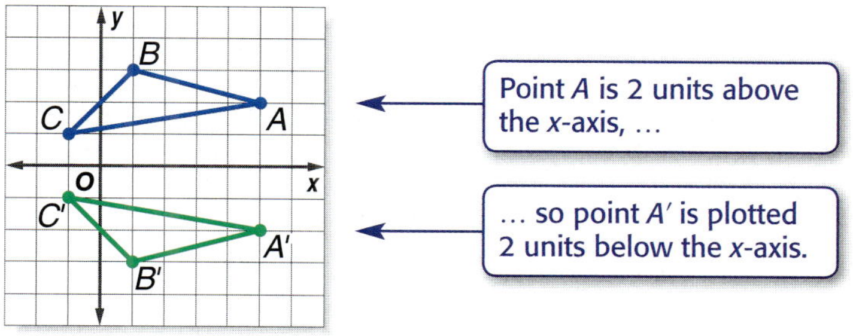

The image coordinates are $A'(5, -2)$, $B'(1, -3)$, and $C'(-1, -1)$.

CHECK Your Progress

d. Rectangle $GHIJ$ has vertices $G(3, -4)$, $H(3, -1)$, $I(-2, -1)$, and $J(-2, -4)$. Graph the figure and its image after a reflection over the x-axis. Then find the coordinates of the reflected image.

Online Personal Tutor at tx.msmath2.com

EXAMPLE Reflect a Figure Over the *y*-axis

5 **Quadrilateral $KLMN$ has vertices $K(2, 3)$, $L(5, 1)$, $M(4, -2)$, and $N(1, -1)$. Graph the figure and its reflected image over the y-axis. Then find the coordinates of the reflected image.**

STUDY TIP

Reflections An image and reflection are mirror images of each other with respect to either the *x*-axis or the *y*-axis.

The y-axis is the line of reflection. So, plot each vertex of $K'L'M'N'$ the same distance from the y-axis and its corresponding vertex on $KLMN$.

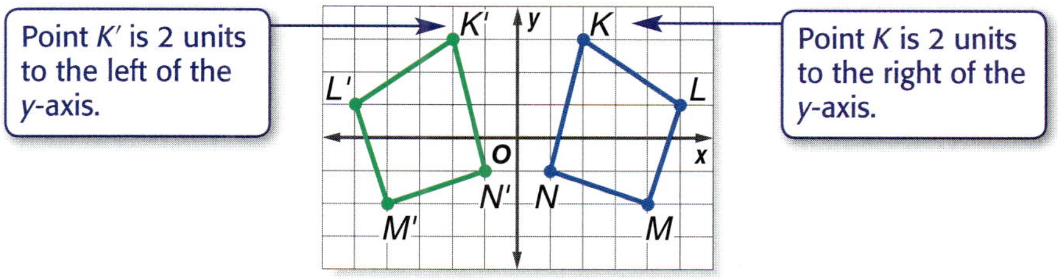

The image coordinates are $K'(-2, 3)$, $L'(-5, 1)$, $M'(-4, -2)$, and $N'(-1, -1)$.

CHECK Your Progress

e. Triangle PQR has vertices $P(1, 5)$, $Q(3, 7)$, and $R(5, -1)$. Graph the figure and its reflection over the y-axis. Then find the coordinates of the reflected image.

CHECK Your Understanding

Examples 1–3 (p. 596)

Determine whether each figure has line symmetry. If so, copy the figure and draw all lines of symmetry.

1. 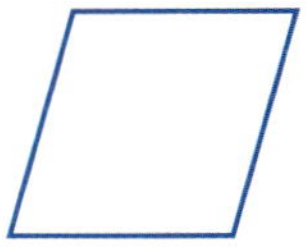

2. 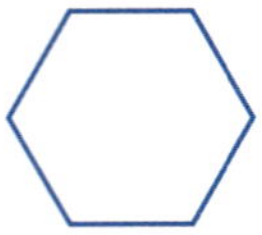

3. 

4. **INSECTS** Identify the number of lines of symmetry in the photo of the butterfly at the right.

Example 4 (p. 597)

Graph each figure and its reflection over the x-axis. Then find the coordinates of the reflected image.

5. $\triangle ABC$ with vertices $A(5, 8)$, $B(1, 2)$, and $C(6, 4)$
6. quadrilateral $DEFG$ with vertices $D(-3, 6)$, $E(-2, -3)$, $F(2, 2)$, and $G(4, 9)$

Example 5 (p. 597)

Graph each figure and its reflection over the y-axis. Then find the coordinates of the reflected image.

7. $\triangle QRS$ with vertices $Q(2, -5)$, $R(4, -5)$, and $S(2, 3)$
8. parallelogram $WXYZ$ with vertices $W(-4, -2)$, $X(-4, 3)$, $Y(-2, 4)$, and $Z(-2, -1)$

Exercises

HOMEWORK HELP

For Exercises	See Examples
9–14 23–24	1,3
15–18	4
19–22	5

Determine whether each figure has line symmetry. If so, copy the figure and draw all lines of symmetry.

9. 

10. 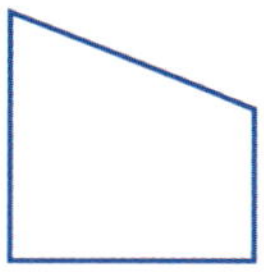

11. 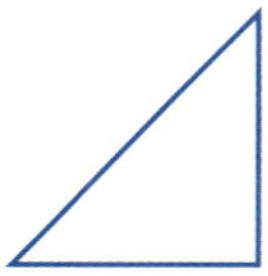

12. 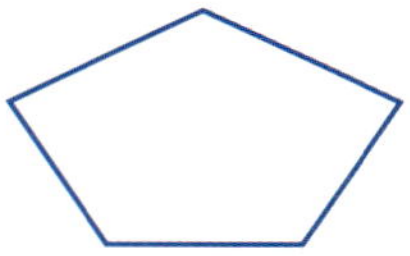

13. 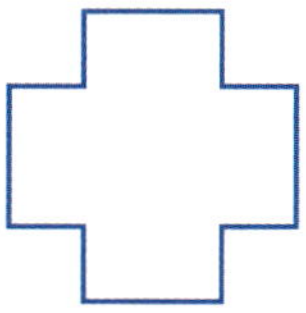

14. 

Graph each figure and its reflection over the x-axis. Then find the coordinates of the reflected image.

15. $\triangle TUV$ with vertices $T(-6, -1)$, $U(-2, -3)$, and $V(5, -4)$
16. $\triangle MNP$ with vertices $M(2, 1)$, $N(-3, 1)$, and $P(-1, 4)$
17. square $ABCD$ with vertices $A(2, 4)$, $B(-2, 4)$, $C(-2, 8)$, and $D(2, 8)$
18. trapezoid $WXYZ$ with vertices $W(-1, -1)$, $X(4, 1)$, $Y(4, 5)$, and $Z(1, 7)$

Graph each figure and its reflection over the y-axis. Then find the coordinates of the reflected image.

19. $\triangle RST$ with vertices $R(-5, 3)$, $S(-4, -2)$, and $T(-2, 3)$

20. $\triangle GHJ$ with vertices $G(4, 2)$, $H(3, -4)$, and $J(1, 1)$

21. parallelogram $HIJK$ with vertices $H(-1, 3)$, $I(-1, -1)$, $J(2, -2)$, and $K(2, 2)$

22. quadrilateral $DEFG$ with vertices $D(1, 0)$, $E(1, -5)$, $F(4, -1)$, and $G(3, 2)$

23. **BUILDINGS** Describe the location of the line(s) of symmetry in the photograph of the Taj Mahal, which is in India.

24. **SIGNAL FLAGS** International Marine Signal Flags are used by sailors to send messages at sea. The signal flags shown spell out the word *MATH*. Which flags have line symmetry? Draw all lines of symmetry.

Real-World Link
A violin is usually around 14 inches long.

25. **MUSIC** Use the photo at the left to determine how many lines of symmetry the body of a violin has.

For Exercises 26–29, use the graph shown at the right.

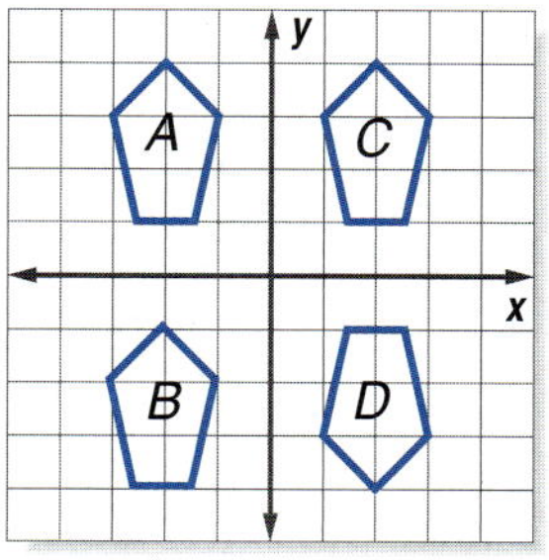

26. Identify the pair(s) of figures for which the x-axis is the line of reflection.

27. For which pair(s) of figures is the line of reflection the y-axis?

28. What type of transformation do figures B and C represent?

29. Describe the possible transformation(s) required to move figure A onto figure D.

30. $\triangle RST$ is reflected over the x-axis and then translated 3 units to the left and 2 units down. Graph the resulting triangle.

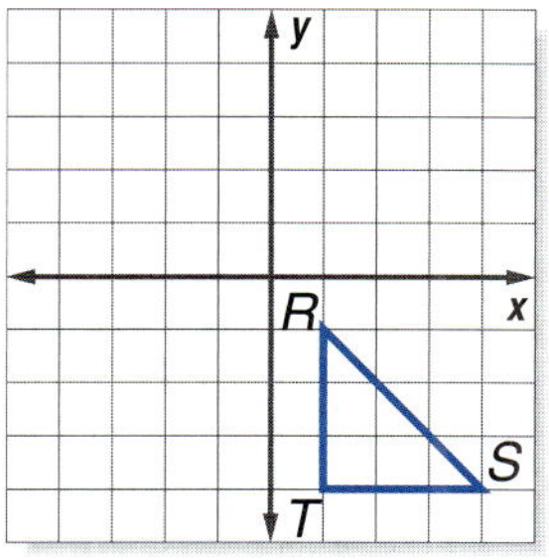

31. $\triangle MNP$ is translated 2 units right and 3 units up. Then the translated figure is reflected over the y-axis. Graph the resulting triangle.

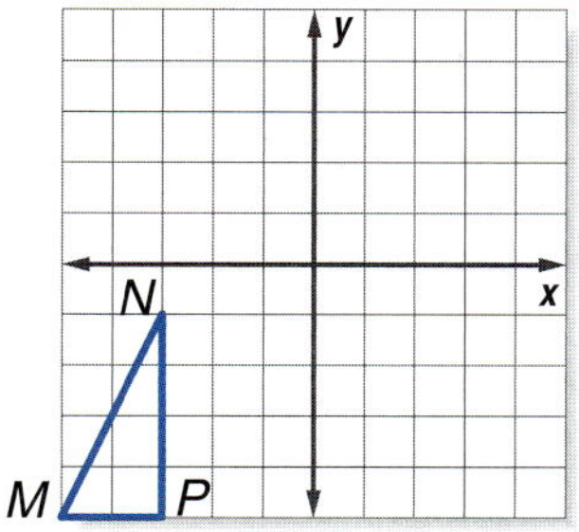

EXTRA PRACTICE
See pages 747, 765.
Math Online
Self-Check Quiz at
tx.msmath2.com

The coordinates of a point and its image after a reflection are given. Describe the reflection as over the *x*-axis or *y*-axis.

32. $A(-3, 5) \rightarrow A'(3, 5)$

33. $M(3, 3) \rightarrow M'(3, -3)$

34. $X(-1, -4) \rightarrow X'(-1, 4)$

35. $W(-4, 0) \rightarrow W'(4, 0)$

H.O.T. Problems

36. **OPEN ENDED** Make a tessellation using a combination of translations and reflections of polygons. Explain your method.

37. **CHALLENGE** Triangle *JKL* has vertices $J(-7, 4)$, $K(7, 1)$, and $L(2, -2)$. Without graphing, find the new coordinates of the vertices of the triangle after a reflection first over the *x*-axis and then over the *y*-axis.

38. **WRITING IN MATH** Draw a figure on a coordinate plane and its reflection over the *y*-axis. Explain how the *x*- and *y*-coordinates of the reflected figure relate to the *x*- and *y*-coordinates of the original figure. Then repeat, this time reflecting the figure over the *x*-axis.

TEST PRACTICE

39. The figure shown was transformed from quadrant II to quadrant III.

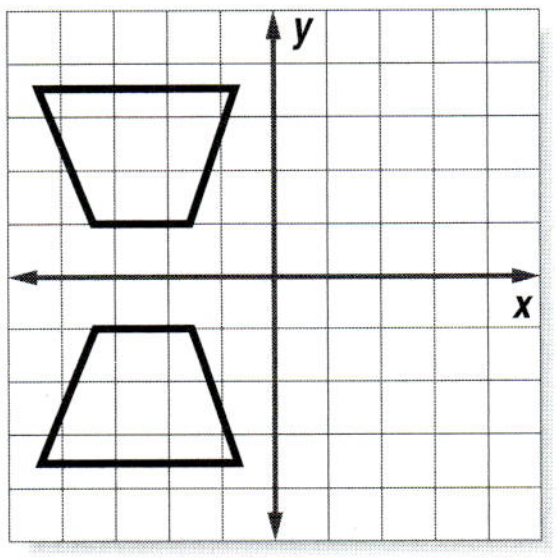

This transformation best represents which of the following?

A translation
B tessellation
C reflection
D rotation

40. If *ABCD* is reflected over the *x*-axis and translated 5 units to the right, which is the resulting image of point *B*?

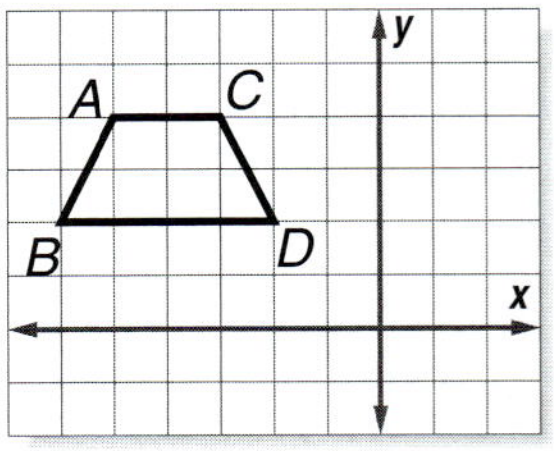

F $(-1, -2)$
G $(-11, 2)$
H $(-1, 2)$
J $(11, 2)$

Spiral Review

41. **GEOMETRY** Triangle *FGH* has vertices $F(-3, 7)$, $G(-1, 5)$, and $H(-2, 2)$. Graph the figure and its image after a translation 4 units right and 1 unit down. Write the ordered pairs for the vertices of the image. (Lesson 11-8)

42. **ART** Melissa wishes to construct a tessellation for a wall hanging made only from regular decagons. Is this possible? Explain. (Lesson 11-7)

Estimate. (Lesson 6-1)

43. $\frac{4}{9} + 8\frac{1}{9}$

44. $\frac{1}{9} \times \frac{2}{5}$

45. $12\frac{1}{4} \div 5\frac{6}{7}$

CHAPTER 11

Study Guide and Review

STUDY TO GO Download Vocabulary Review from tx.msmath2.com

FOLDABLES™ Study Organizer — GET READY to Study

Be sure the following Key Concepts are noted in your Foldable.

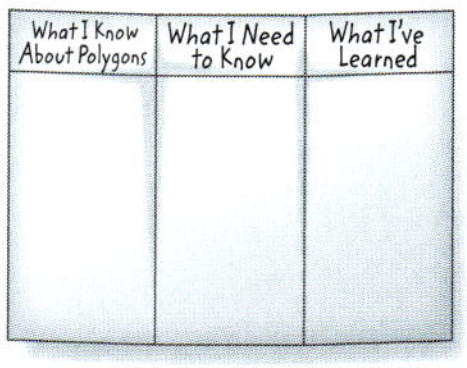

Key Concepts

Angles (Lesson 11-1)

- Two angles are complementary if the sum of their measures is 90°.
- Two angles are supplementary if the sum of their measures is 180°.

Triangles (Lesson 11-3)

- An acute triangle has all acute angles.
- A right triangle has one right angle.
- An obtuse triangle has one obtuse angle.
- A scalene triangle has no congruent sides.
- An isosceles triangle has at least 2 congruent sides.
- An equilateral triangle has 3 acute congruent sides.

Quadrilaterals (Lesson 11-5)

- The sum of the measures of the angles of a quadrilateral is 360°.

Similar Figures (Lesson 11-6)

- If two figures are similar then the corresponding sides are proportional and the corresponding angles are congruent.

Transformations (Lessons 11-8 and 11-9)

- When translating a figure, every point in the original figure is moved the same distance in the same direction.
- When reflecting a figure, every point in the original figure is the same distance from the line of reflection as its corresponding point on the original figure.

Key Vocabulary

acute angle (p. 553)
angle (p. 552)
circle graph (p. 558)
complementary angles (p. 553)
congruent angles (p. 553)
congruent figures (p. 592)
degrees (p. 552)
hexagon (p. 584)
indirect measurement (p. 580)
line of symmetry (p. 596)
line symmetry (p. 596)
obtuse angle (p. 553)
octagon (p. 584)
parallelogram (p. 572)
pentagon (p. 584)
polygon (p. 584)
quadrilateral (p. 572)
reflection (p. 597)
regular polygon (p. 584)
rhombus (p. 572)
right angle (p. 553)
similar figures (p. 578)
straight angle (p. 553)
supplementary angles (p. 553)
tessellation (p. 586)
transformation (p. 591)
translation (p. 591)
trapezoid (p. 572)
triangle (p. 564)
vertex (p. 552)

Vocabulary Check

State whether each sentence is *true* or *false*. If *false*, replace the underlined word or number to make a true sentence.

1. Two angles whose measures add to 180° are called complementary angles.
2. A hexagon is a polygon with 6 sides.
3. An angle whose measure is less than 90° is called a right angle.
4. The vertex is where the sides of angle meet.
5. The point (3, −2) when translated up 3 units and to the left 5 units becomes (6, −7).
6. A trapezoid has both pairs of opposite sides parallel.

Lesson-by-Lesson Review

11-1 Angle Relationships (pp. 552–557)

7. Name the angle shown in four ways. Then classify the angle as *acute*, *right*, *obtuse*, or *straight*.

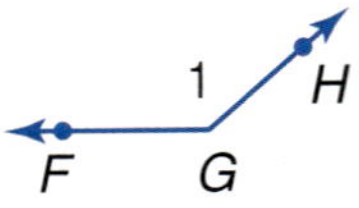

Classify each pair of angles as *complementary*, *supplementary*, or *neither*.

8. 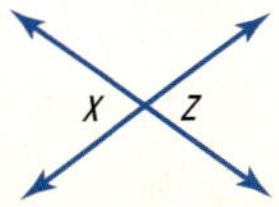

9. 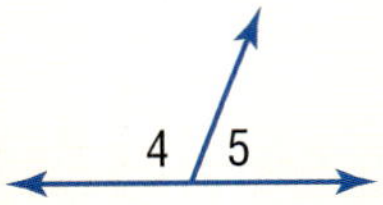

10. **ALGEBRA** If $\angle Y$ and $\angle Z$ are supplementary and $m\angle Z = 35°$, what is the measure of $\angle Y$?

Example 1 **Name the angle in four ways.**

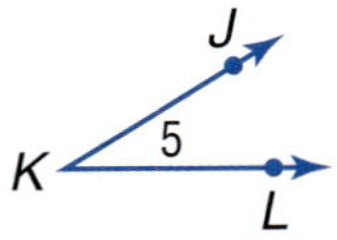

The angle can be named as $\angle JKL$, $\angle LKJ$, $\angle K$, or $\angle 5$.

Example 2 **Find the value of x.**

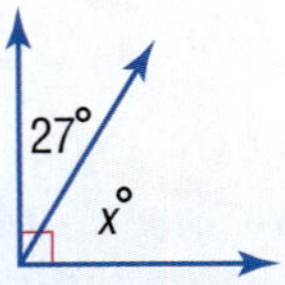

Since the two angles form a right angle, they are complementary. The sum of their measures is 90°.

$$x + 27 = 90 \quad \text{Write the equation.}$$
$$-27 = -27 \quad \text{Subtract 27 from each side.}$$
$$x = 63$$

11-2 Statistics: Display Data in a Circle Graph (pp. 558–563)

11. **SOFT DRINKS** The table shows favorite soft dinks. Display the set of data in a circle graph.

Favorite Soft Drink	
Soft Drink	**Percent**
Cola	36%
Diet Cola	28%
Root Beer	15%
Lemon Lime	7%
Other	14%

Example 3 **Refer to the graph. Which season was chosen by about twice as many who chose fall?**

Spring, since 40% is about twice as much as 22%.

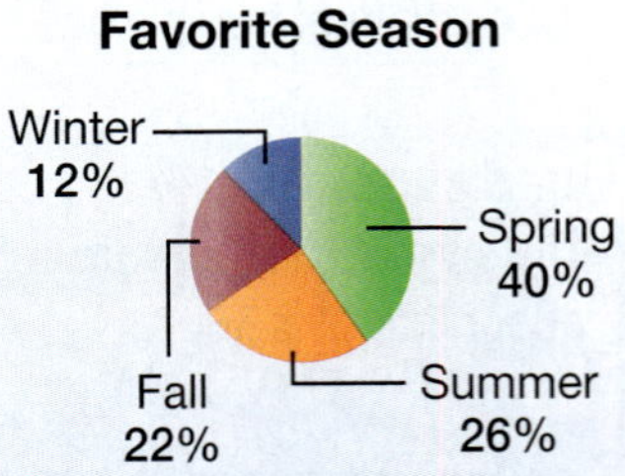

11-3 Triangles (pp. 564–568)

ALGEBRA **Find the value of x.**

12. 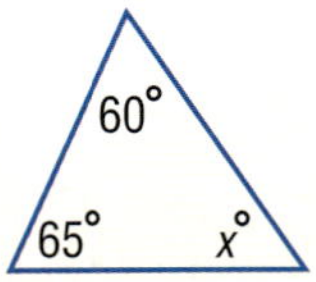

13. 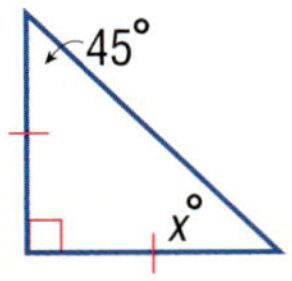

14. **ALGEBRA** Find $m\angle S$ in $\triangle RST$ if $m\angle R = 28°$ and $m\angle T = 13°$.

Example 4 **Find the value of x.**

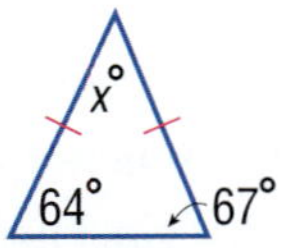

The sum of the angle measures in a triangle is 180°.

$$x + 64 + 67 = 180 \quad \text{Write the equation.}$$
$$x + 131 = 180$$
$$-131 = -131 \quad \text{Subtract 131 from each side.}$$
$$x = 49$$

Mixed Problem Solving
For mixed problem-solving practice, see page 765.

11-4 PSI: Logical Reasoning (pp. 569–570)

15. **SPORTS** Donnie, Jenna, Milo, and Barbara play volleyball, field hockey, golf, and soccer but not in that order. Use the clues given below to find the sport each person plays.
    - Donnie does not like golf, volleyball, or soccer.
    - Neither Milo nor Jenna likes golf.
    - Milo does not like soccer.

16. **FOOD** Angelo's Pizza Parlor makes square pizzas. After baking, the pizzas are cut along one diagonal into two triangles. Classify the triangles made.

Example 5 **Todd, Virginia, Elaine, and Peter are siblings. Todd was born after Peter, but before Virginia. Elaine is the oldest. Who is the youngest in the family?**

Use logical reasoning to determine the youngest of the family.

You know that Elaine is the oldest, so she is first on the list. Todd was born after Peter, but before Virginia. So, Peter was second and then Todd was born. Virginia is the youngest of the family.

11-5 Quadrilaterals (pp. 572–576)

Classify the quadrilateral using the name that *best* describes it.

17. 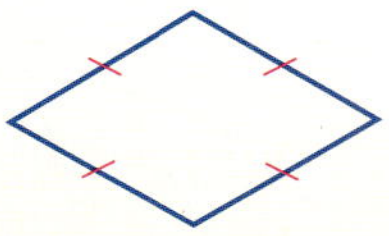

18. 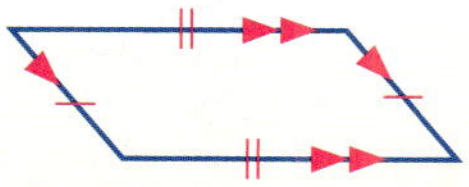

19. **SHAPES** What type of quadrilateral does not have opposite sides congruent?

Example 6 **Classify the quadrilateral using the name that *best* describes it.**

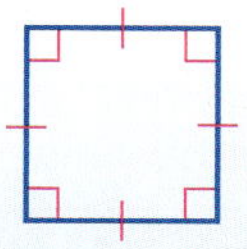

The quadrilateral is a parallelogram with 4 right angles and 4 congruent sides. It is a square.

11-6 Similar Figures (pp. 578–583)

Find the value of x in each pair of similar figures.

20. 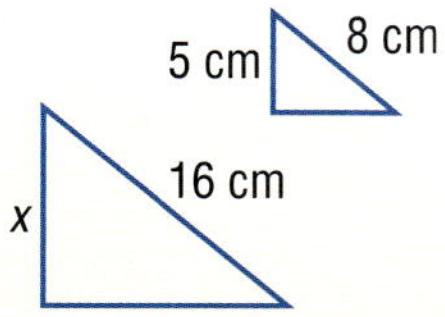

21. 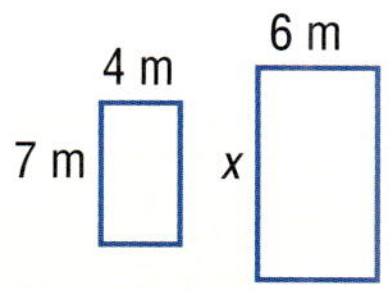

22. **FLAGPOLES** Hiroshi is 1.6 meters tall and casts a shadow 0.53 meter in length. How tall is a flagpole if it casts a shadow 2.65 meters in length?

Example 7

Find the value of x in the pair of similar figures.

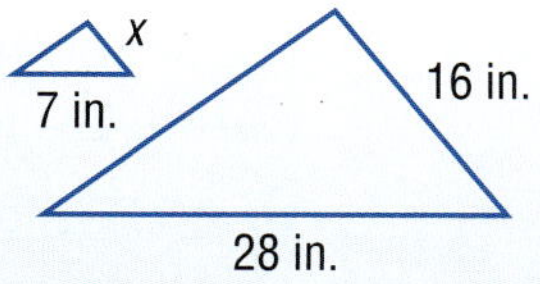

$\frac{7}{28} = \frac{x}{16}$ Write a proportion.

$28 \cdot x = 7 \cdot 16$ Find the cross products.

$28x = 112$ Simplify.

$\frac{28x}{28} = \frac{112}{28}$ Divide each side by 28.

$x = 4$ Simplify.

So, the value of x is 4.

11-7 Polygons and Tessellations (pp. 584–589)

Determine whether each figure is a polygon. If it is, classify the polygon and state whether it is regular. If it is *not* a polygon, explain why.

23. 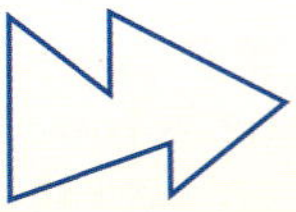

24. 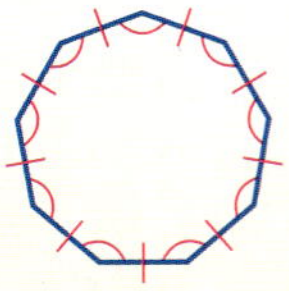

25. **ALGEBRA** Find the measure of each angle of a regular 12-gon.

Example 8 **Determine whether the figure is a polygon. If it is, classify the polygon and state whether it is regular. If it is *not* a polygon, explain why.**

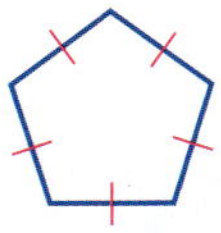

Since the polygon has 5 congruent sides and 5 congruent angles, it is a regular pentagon.

11-8 Translations (pp. 591–595)

Triangle PQR has coordinates $P(4, -2)$, $Q(-2, -3)$, and $R(-1, 6)$. Find the coordinates of $P'Q'R'$ after each translation. Then graph each translation.

26. 6 units left, 3 units up
27. 4 units right, 1 unit down
28. 3 units left
29. 7 units down

Example 9 **Find the coordinates of $\triangle G'H'I'$ after a translation of 2 units left and 4 units up.**

The vertices of $\triangle G'H'I'$ are $G'(-2, 7)$, $H'(2, 3)$, and $I'(-4, 1)$.

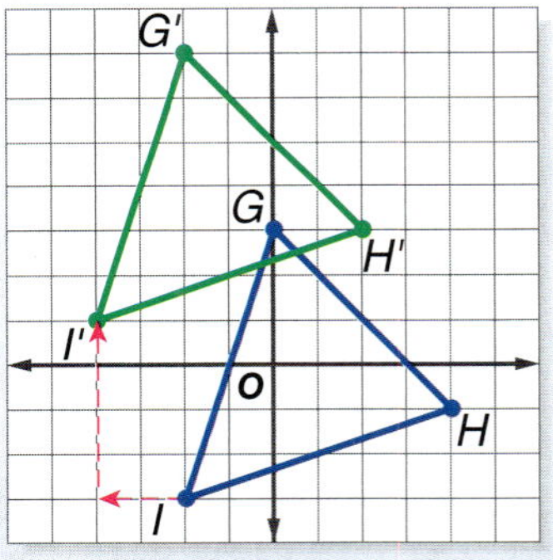

11-9 Reflections (pp. 596–600)

Find the coordinates of each figure after a reflection over the given axis. Then graph the figure and its reflected image.

30. $\triangle RST$ with coordinates $R(-1, 3)$, $S(2, 6)$, and $T(6, 1)$; x-axis
31. parallelogram $ABCD$ with coordinates $A(1, 3)$, $B(2, -1)$, $C(5, -1)$, and $D(4, 3)$; y-axis
32. rectangle $EFGH$ with coordinates $E(4, 2)$, $F(-2, 2)$, $G(-2, -5)$, and $H(4, -5)$; x-axis

Example 10 **Find the coordinates of $\triangle C'D'E'$ after a reflection over the y-axis. Then graph its reflected image.**

The vertices of $\triangle C'D'E'$ are $C'(-3, 4)$, $D'(-2, 1)$, and $E'(-5, 3)$.

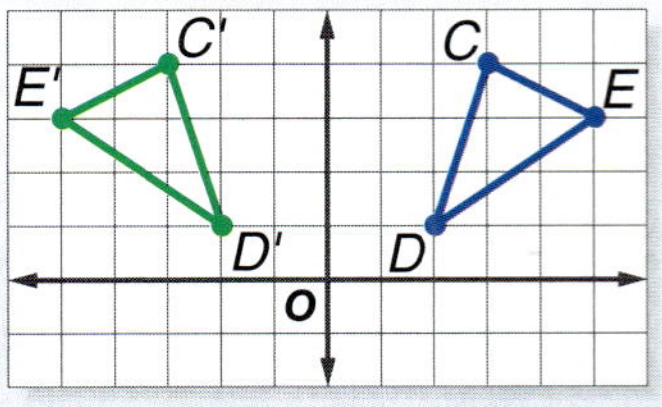

Chapter 11 Practice Test

Name each angle in four ways. Then classify each angle as *acute*, *obtuse*, *right*, or *straight*.

1. 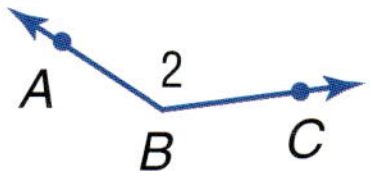

2. 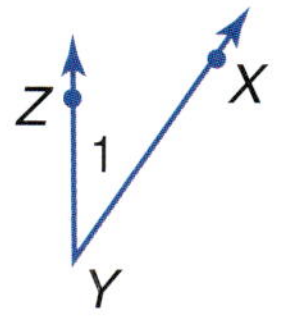

Classify each pair of angles as *complementary*, *supplementary*, or *neither*.

3. 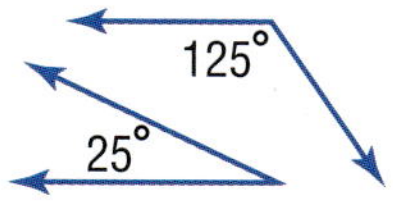

4. 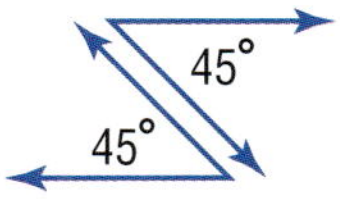

5. **TEST PRACTICE** The table shows the results of a survey. The results are to be displayed in a circle graph. Which statement about the graph is NOT true?

Favorite Type of Books	
Type	**Students**
mystery	24
science fiction	8
sports	26
romance	30

A The science fiction section on the graph will have an angle measure of about 33°.
B Romance books were preferred more than any other type of book.
C About 30% of students chose sports books as their favorite.
D The mystery and sports sections on the circle graph are supplementary angles.

Find the missing measure in each triangle with the given angle measures.

6. 75°, 25.5°, x°
7. x°, 58°, 64°
8. 23.5°, x°, 109.5°

9. **DIVISION** Numbers ending in zero or five are divisible by five. Are the numbers 25, 893, 690 divisible by 5? Use the *logical reasoning* strategy.

ALGEBRA Find the value of x in each quadrilateral.

10. 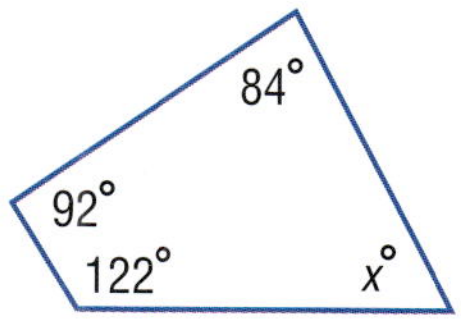

11. 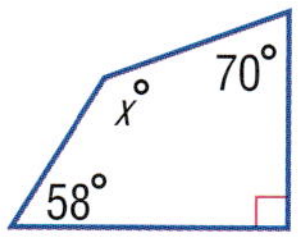

12. **GEOGRAPHY** A map is drawn so that it is similar to a map in an atlas. The map in the atlas is 7 inches long and 10 inches wide. If the hand-drawn map has a length of 17.5 inches, what is its width?

13. **GEOMETRY** Can a regular heptagon, with angle measures that total 900°, be used by itself to make a tessellation? Explain your reasoning.

14. **TEST PRACTICE** Which quadrilateral does NOT have opposite sides congruent?

F parallelogram
G square
H trapezoid
J rectangle

15. **SQUARES** Square $ABCD$ is shown. What are the vertices of $A'B'C'D'$ after a translation 2 units right and 2 units down? Graph the translated image.

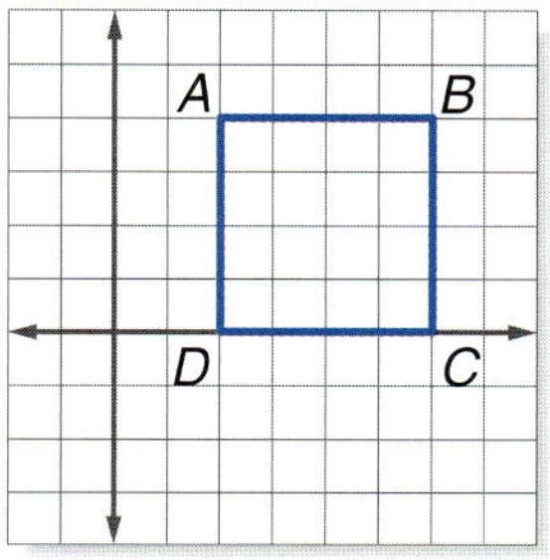

16. **FIGURES** Draw a figure with one line of symmetry. Then draw a figure with no lines of symmetry.

CHAPTER 11

Texas Test Practice

Cumulative, Chapters 1–11

Read each question. Then fill in the correct answer on the answer document provided by your teacher or on a sheet of paper.

1. Which of the following two angles are complementary?

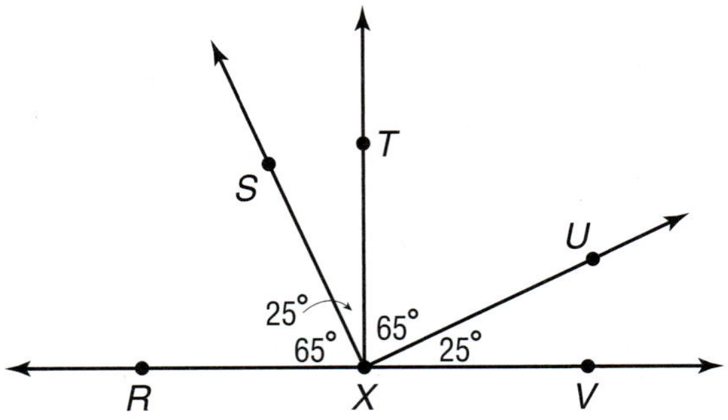

A $\angle RXS$ and $\angle TXU$

B $\angle SXT$ and $\angle TXU$

C $\angle RXS$ and $\angle SXV$

D $\angle SXR$ and $\angle SXV$

2. A square is divided into 9 congruent squares. Which of the following methods can be used to find the area of the larger square, given the area of one of the smaller squares?

F Multiply the area of the larger square by 9.

G Add 9 to the area of one of the smaller squares.

H Multiply the area of one of the smaller squares by 9.

J Add the area of the larger square to the sum of the areas of each of the 9 smaller squares.

3. **GRIDDABLE** Brian bought 5 paintings at an art gallery for a total of $3,500. Later he bought another painting for $970. What was the mean price in dollars of all the paintings Brian bought?

4. Which of the following groups does NOT contain equivalent fractions, decimals, and percents?

A $\frac{9}{20}$, 0.45, 45%

B $\frac{3}{10}$, 0.3, 30%

C $\frac{7}{8}$, 0.875, 87.5%

D $\frac{1}{100}$, 0.1, 1%

5. Jasmine recorded the number of Calories in various protein bars in the table below. Which measure of the data is represented by 375 Calories?

Protein Bar Calories	
Protein Bar	**Calories**
A	280
B	342
C	570
D	245
E	444
F	369

F Mean

G Median

H Mode

J Range

6. Seth has $858.60 in his savings account. He plans to spend 15% of his savings on a bicycle. Which of the following represents the amount Seth plans to spend on the bicycle?

A $128.79

B $171.72

C $182.79

D $122.79

Get Ready for the Texas Test
For test-taking strategies and more practice, see pages TX1–TX23.

7. The prices of 3 different bottles of laundry detergent are given in the table below. Which size bottle of laundry detergent has the lowest price per ounce?

Bottle Size (ounces)	Price
32	\$2.79
64	\$4.49
96	\$8.09

F The 32-oz bottle only
G The 32-oz bottle and the 64-oz bottle
H The 64-oz bottle only
J The 96-oz bottle only

8. Which of the following is true about similar figures?
A Similar figures never have the same shape.
B Similar figures always have the same size.
C Similar figures always have corresponding angles that are equal.
D Similar figures never have corresponding sides that are proportional.

9. **GRIDDABLE** Mrs. Stuart bought 2 dozen bottles of orange juice priced at 6 bottles for \$3.95 and 18 cookies priced at 6 cookies for \$1.95. What is the total amount in dollars she spent on orange juice and cookies?

TEST-TAKING TIP

Question 10 Most standardized tests allow you to write in the test booklet. Use it to work out the problems. For example, plot a figure and its translation in the booklet. Doing so will help keep you from making careless errors.

10. Point *D* has the coordinates (2, 3). If point *D* is translated 5 units to the left and 4 units down, what will be the new coordinates of point *D*?
F (−3, −1)
G (3, 1)
H (−3, 1)
J (3, −1)

Pre-AP

Record your answers on a sheet of paper. Show your work.

11. Edmundo plotted the polygon *JKLM* on the coordinate plane below.

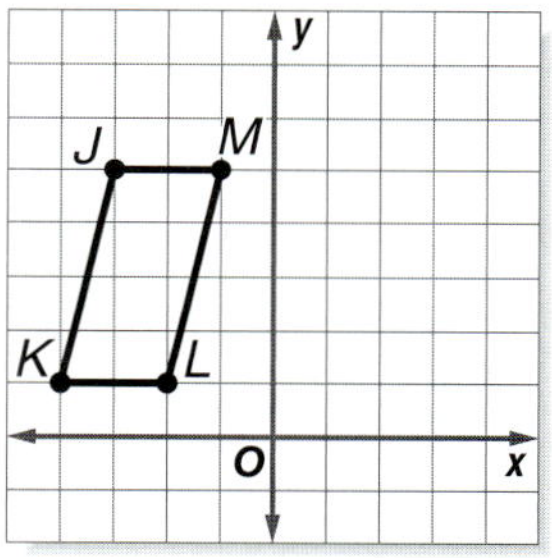

a. Classify ∠*J*.
b. Classify ∠*M*.
c. Classify the polygon *JKLM* using the name that *best* describes it.
d. Can polygon *JKLM* be used by itself to make a tessellation? Explain your reasoning.
e. If polygon *JKLM* is translated 2 units right and 5 units down, what are the coordinates of the new figure?
f. If polygon *JKLM* is reflected over the *x*-axis, what are the coordinates of the new figure?

NEED EXTRA HELP?											
If You Missed Question...	1	2	3	4	5	6	7	8	9	10	11
Go to Lesson...	11-1	11-5	9-2	5-6	9-2	8-1	7-2	11-6	3-5	11-8	11-9
For Help with Test Objective...	3	6	5	1	5	2	2	3	1	3	3

CHAPTER 12

Measurement: Two- and Three-Dimensional Figures

Knowledge and Skills

- Compare and classify two- and three-dimensional figures using geometric vocabulary and properties. **TEKS 7.6**
- Solve application problems involving estimation and measurement. **TEKS 7.9**

Key Vocabulary

circumference (p. 622)
cylinder (p. 642)
pyramid (p. 641)
volume (p. 651)

Real-World Link

Architecture If you visit the Aquarium Pyramid and the Rainforest Pyramid at the Moody Gardens in Galveston, Texas, you will see examples of three-dimensional figures used in architecture.

FOLDABLES™ Study Organizer

Measurement: Two- and Three-Dimensional Figures Make this Foldable to help you organize your notes. Begin with a sheet of $8\frac{1}{2}$" by 11" construction paper and two sheets of notebook paper.

1. **Fold** the construction paper in half lengthwise. Label the chapter title on the outside.

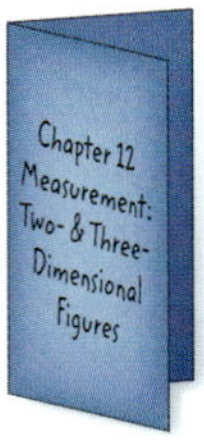

2. **Fold** the sheets of notebook paper in half lengthwise. Then fold top to bottom twice.

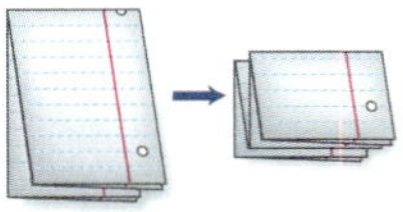

3. **Open** the notebook paper. Cut along the second folds to make four tabs.

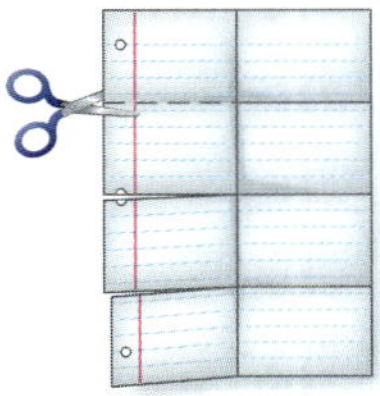

4. **Glue** the uncut notebook paper side by side onto the construction paper. Label each tab as shown.

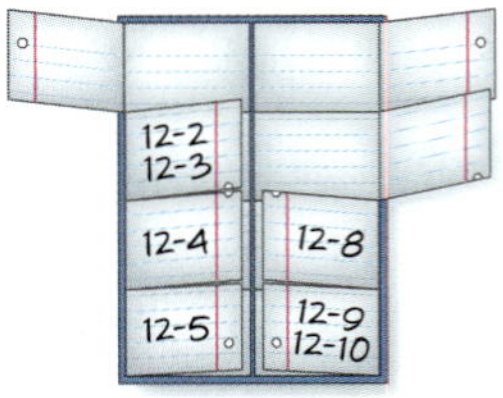

GET READY for Chapter 12

Diagnose Readiness You have two options for checking Prerequisite Skills.

Option 2

Math Online Take the Online Readiness Quiz at tx.msmath2.com.

Option 1

Take the Quick Quiz below. Refer to the Quick Review for help.

QUICK Quiz

Evaluate each expression.

(Used in Lessons 12-1, 12-2, and 12-9)

1. 8×17
2. 5.6×9.8
3. $12 \times 4 \times 26$
4. $4.5 \times 3.2 \times 1.7$
5. $\left(\frac{1}{2}\right)(11)(14)$
6. $\left(\frac{1}{2}\right)(8.8)(2.3)$
7. **SHOPPING** Margo bought 3 sweaters that originally cost \$27.78 each. If they were on sale for half the price, what was the total cost of the sweaters, not including tax?

Evaluate each expression.

(Used in Lessons 12-4, 12-9, and 12-10)

8. 3^2
9. 11 squared
10. 5 to the third power
11. 6 to the second power
12. **CHESS** If a chessboard has 8^2 squares, how many squares is this?

Use the π button on your calculator to evaluate each expression. Round to the nearest tenth.

(Used in Lessons 12-3 and 12-4)

13. $\pi \times 4$
14. $\pi \times 13.8$
15. $(2)(\pi)(5)$
16. $(2)(\pi)(1.7)$
17. $\pi \times 9^2$
18. $\pi \times 6^2$

QUICK Review

Example 1 Find $1.2 \cdot 3.4$.

$$\begin{array}{rl} 1.2 & \leftarrow \text{1 decimal place} \\ \times\ 3.4 & \leftarrow \text{+1 decimal place} \\ \hline 48 & \\ 36\ & \\ \hline 4.08 & \leftarrow \text{2 decimal places} \end{array}$$

Example 2 Find $\left(\frac{1}{2}\right)(26)(19)$.

$\left(\frac{1}{2}\right)(26)(19) = (13)(19)$ Multiply $\frac{1}{2}$ by 26.

$= 247$ Multiply 13 by 19.

Example 3 Evaluate 7^3.

$7^3 = 7 \cdot 7 \cdot 7$ or 343

Example 4 Evaluate 2 to the fourth power.

2 to the fourth power is written 2^4.

$2^4 = 2 \cdot 2 \cdot 2 \cdot 2$ or 16

Example 5 Use the π button on your calculator to evaluate $\pi \times 5^2$. Round to the nearest tenth.

$\pi \cdot 5^2 = \pi \cdot 25$ $\quad 5^2 = 25$

$= 78.5$ Multiply π by 25.

12-1 Area of Parallelograms

Main IDEA

Find the areas of parallelograms.

Targeted TEKS 7.4 The student represents a relationship in numerical, geometric, verbal, and symbolic form. **(A) generate formulas involving** unit conversions, perimeter, **area**, circumference, volume, and scaling. *Also addresses TEKS 7.8(C), 7.9(A).*

MINI Lab

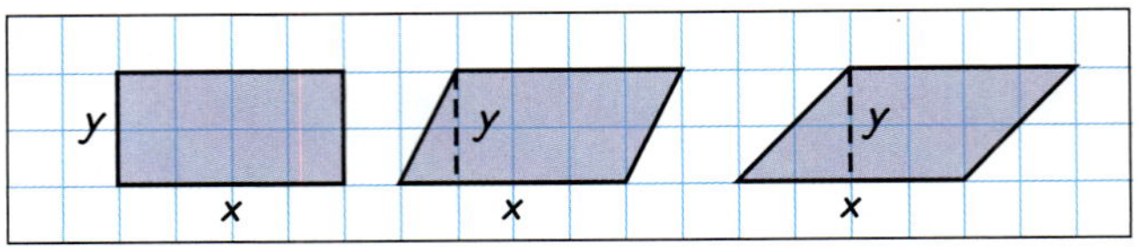

1. What is the value of x and y for each parallelogram?
2. Count the grid squares to find the area of each parallelogram.
3. On grid paper, draw three different parallelograms in which $x = 5$ units and $y = 4$ units. Find the area of each.
4. **MAKE A CONJECTURE** Explain how to find the area of a parallelogram if you know the values of x and y.

You can find the area of a parallelogram by using the values for the base and height, as described below.

The **base** is any side of a parallelogram.

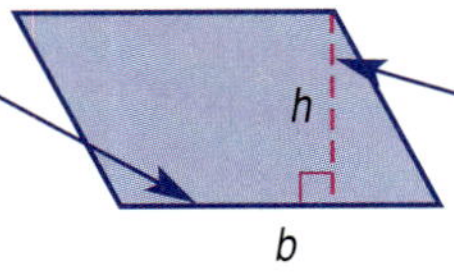

The **height** is the length of the segment perpendicular to the base with endpoints on opposite sides.

NEW Vocabulary

base
height

KEY CONCEPT — Area of a Parallelogram

Words The area A of a parallelogram equals the product of its base b and height h.

Symbols $A = bh$

Model

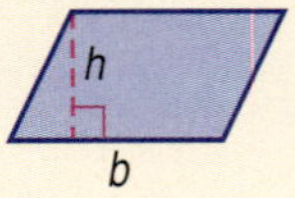

REVIEW Vocabulary

parallelogram quadrilateral with both pairs of opposite sides parallel and congruent (Lesson 11-5)

EXAMPLES Find the Area of a Parallelogram

Find the area of a parallelogram.

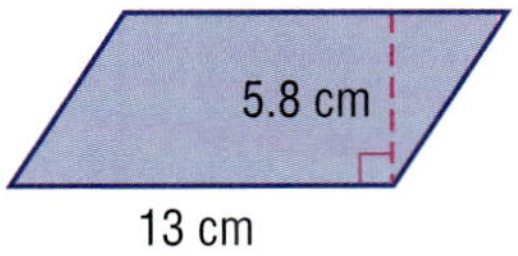

1 **Estimate** $A = 13 \cdot 6$ or $78\ \text{cm}^2$

$A = bh$	Area of a parallelogram
$A = 13 \cdot 5.8$	Replace b with 13 and h with 5.8.
$A = 75.4$	Multiply.

The area is 75.4 square centimeters.

Check for Reasonableness $75.4 \approx 78$ ✔

STUDY TIP

Common Error When finding the area of a parallelogram, be sure to use the base and the height, not the base and a side.

2 **Find the area of the parallelogram.**

The base is 11 inches, and the height is 9 inches.

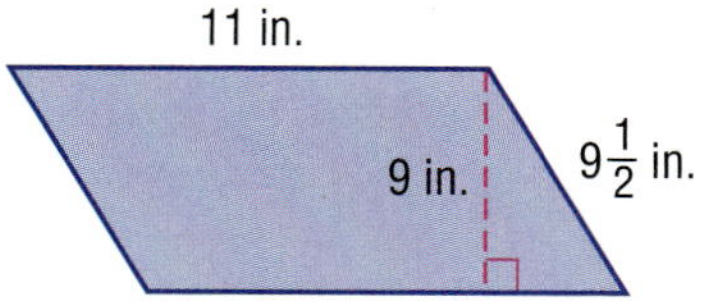

Estimate $A = 10 \cdot 10$ or 100 in^2

$A = bh$	Area of a parallelogram
$A = 11 \cdot 9$	Replace b with 11 and h with 9.
$A = 99$	Multiply.

The area of the parallelogram is 99 square inches.

Check for Reasonableness $99 \approx 100$ ✔

CHECK Your Progress

Find the area of each parallelogram.

a.

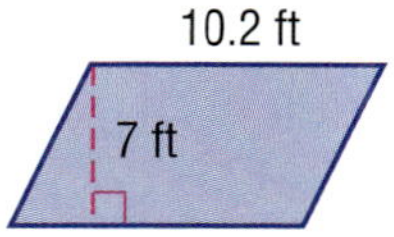

b.

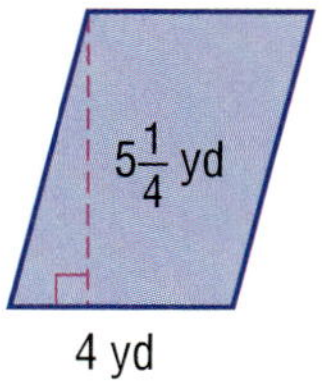

Online Personal Tutor at tx.msmath2.com

Real-World Link In 2004, there were 1,819 tornadoes in the U.S. with 509 of these ocurring in May.
Source: NOAA

Real-World EXAMPLE

3 **WEATHER The map shows the region of a state that is under a tornado warning. What is the area of this region?**

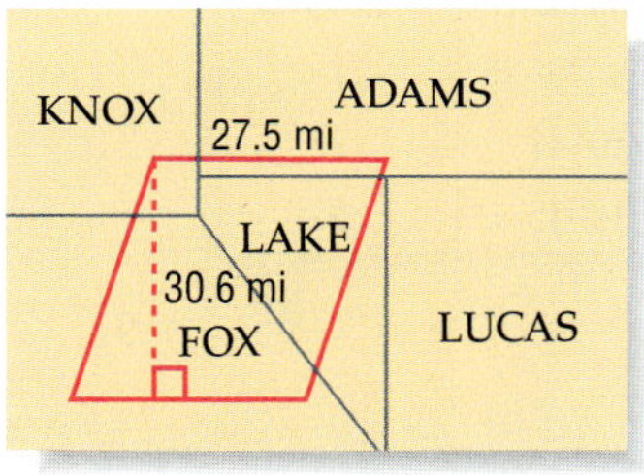

Estimate $A = 30 \cdot 30$ or 900 mi^2

$A = bh$	Area of a parallelogram
$A = 27.5 \cdot 30.6$	Replace b with 27.5 and h with 30.6.
$A = 841.5$	Multiply.

The area of the region is 841.5 square miles.

Check for Reasonableness $841.5 \approx 900$ ✔

CHECK Your Progress

c. **SAFETY** A street department painted the pavement markings shown at the right on the surface of a highway to reduce traffic speeds and crashes. What is the area inside one of the markings?

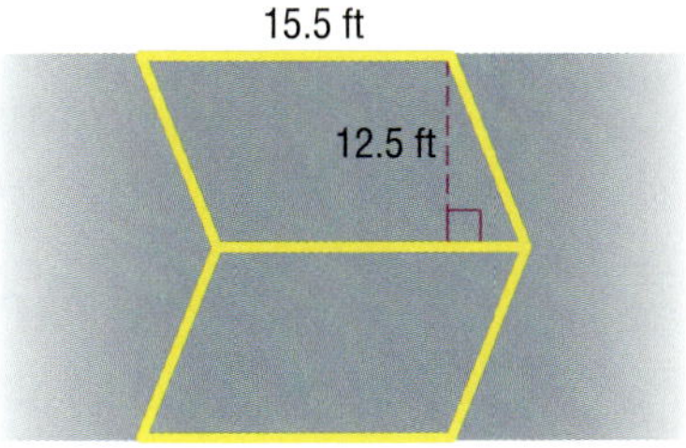

CHECK Your Understanding

Example 1 (p. 610)

Find the area of each parallelogram. Round to the nearest tenth if necessary.

1. 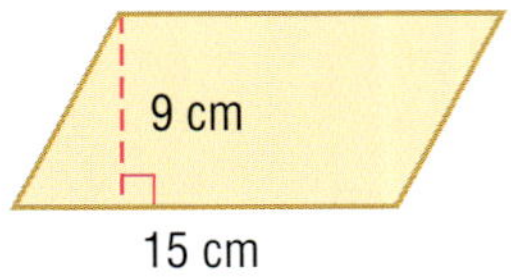

2. 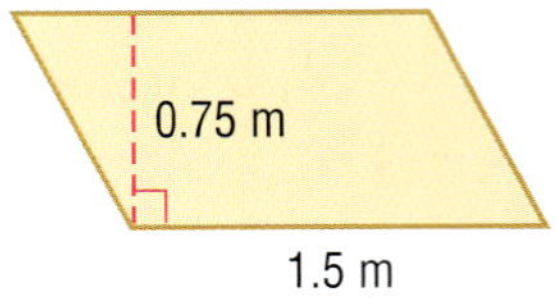

Example 2 (p. 611)

3. 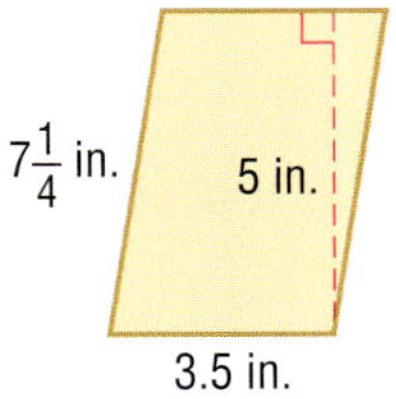

4. 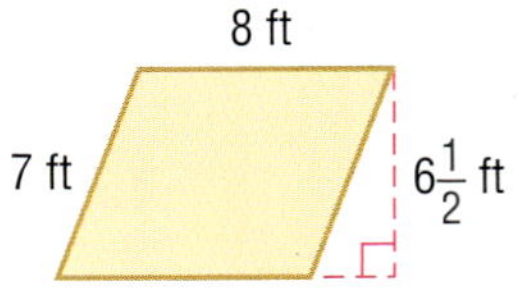

Example 3 (p. 611)

5. **ART** Martina designs uniquely-shaped ceramic wall tiles. What is the area of the tile shown?

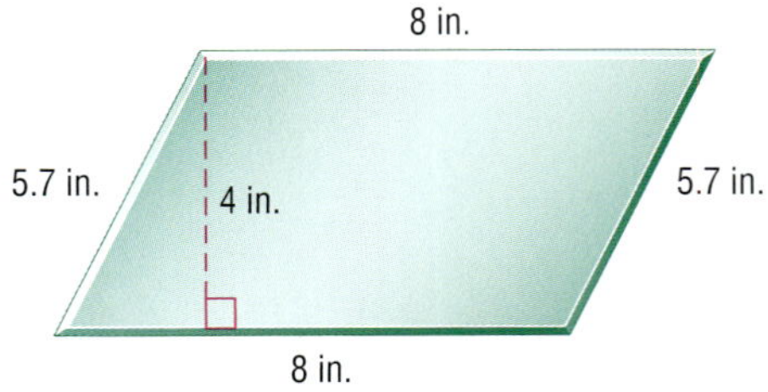

Exercises

HOMEWORK HELP

For Exercises	See Examples
6–9, 12–13	1
10–11	2
14–15	3

Find the area of each parallelogram. Round to the nearest tenth if necessary.

6. 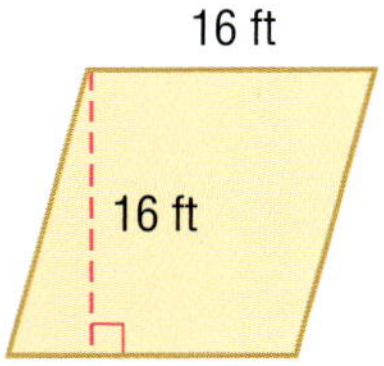

7. 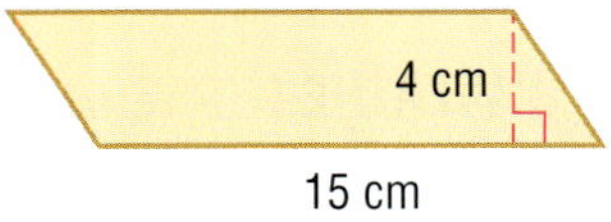

8. 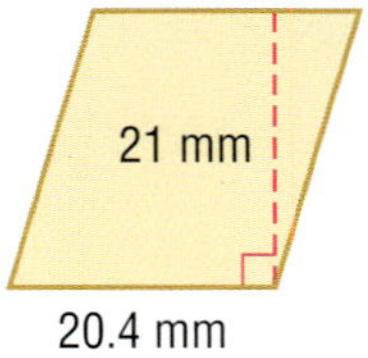

9. 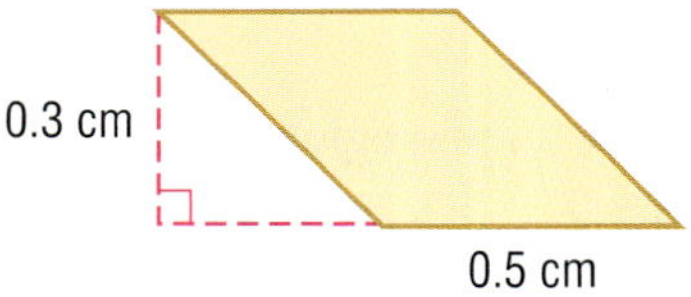

10. 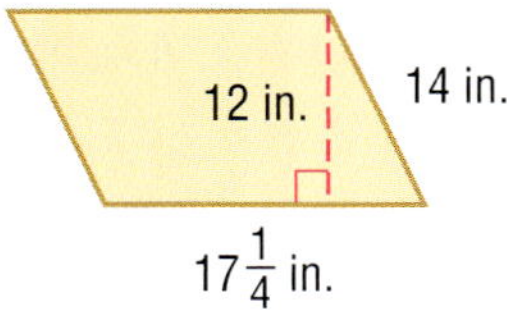

11. 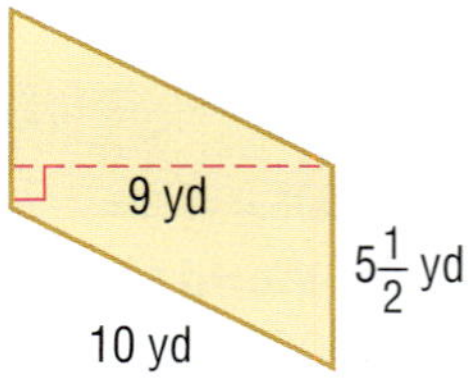

12. What is the area of a parallelogram with base $10\frac{3}{4}$ yards and height 7 yards?

13. Find the area of a parallelogram with base 12.5 meters and height 15.25 meters.

14. **WALLPAPER** The design of the wallpaper border at the right contains parallelograms. How much space on the border is covered by the parallelograms?

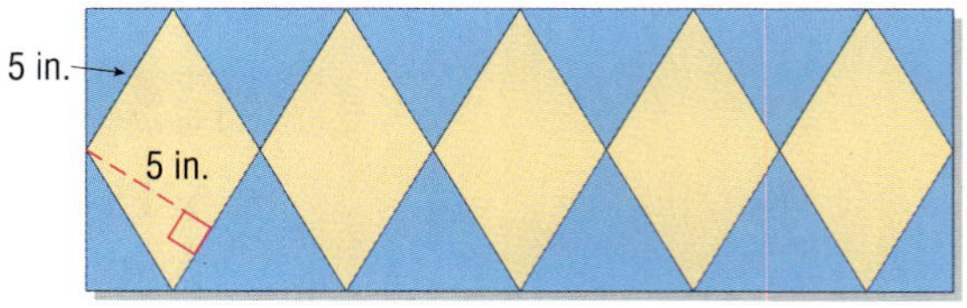

15. **PATTERN BLOCKS** What is the area of the parallelogram-shaped pattern block shown at the right?

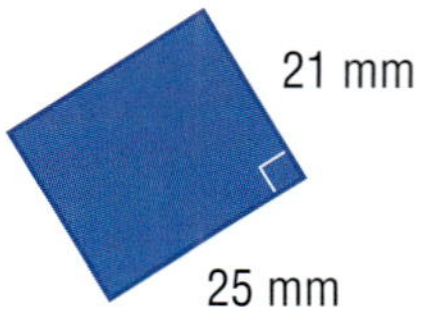

Real-World Link The first parking meter was installed in Oklahoma City, Oklahoma in 1935.
Source: 50states.com

16. **PARKING SPACES** A city ordinance requires that all parking spaces have a minimum area of 162 square feet. Do the measurements of the parking spaces shown below meet the requirements? Explain.

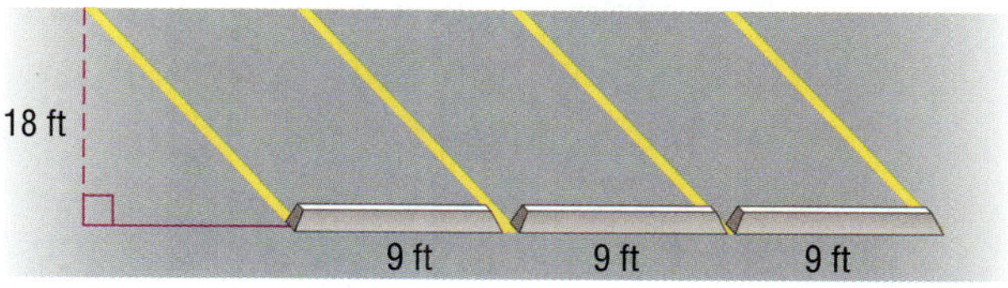

Find the area of each parallelogram. Round to the nearest tenth if necessary.

17.
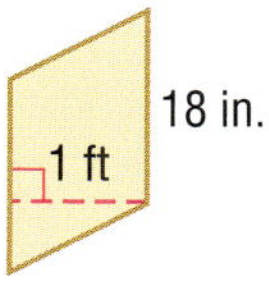

18.
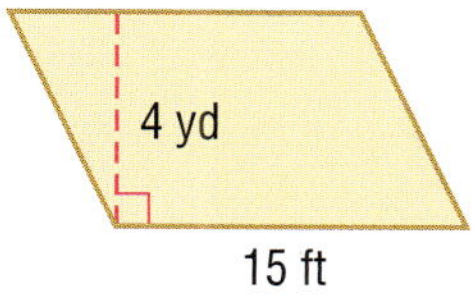

19.
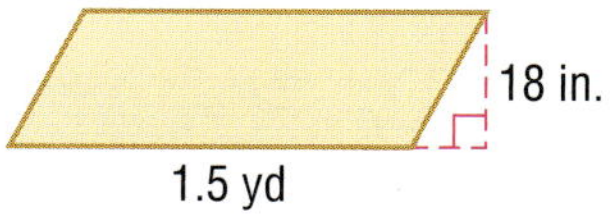

GEOGRAPHY **Estimate the area of each state.**

20.

21.

22. **ALGEBRA** A parallelogram has an area of 75 square feet. Find the base of the parallelogram if the height is 3 feet.

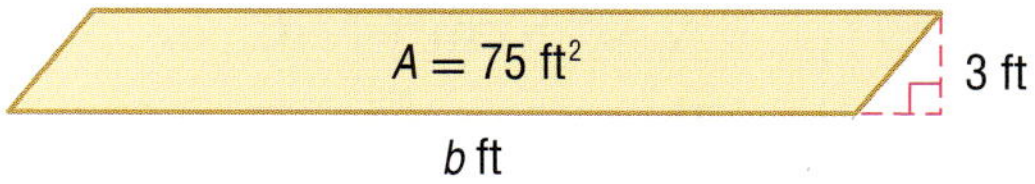

23. **ALGEBRA** What is the height of a parallelogram if the base is 24 inches and the area is 360 square inches?

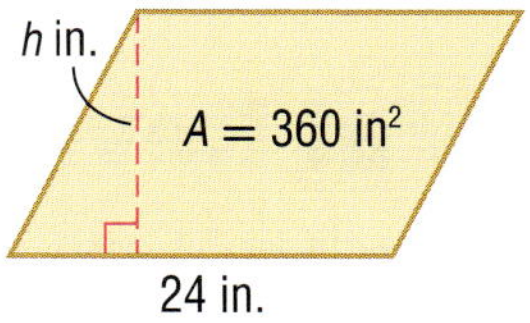

QUILTING **For Exercises 24 and 25, use the four quilt blocks shown and following information.**

Each quilt block uses eight parallelogram-shaped pieces of fabric that have a height of $3\frac{1}{3}$ inches and a base of $3\frac{3}{4}$ inches.

24. Find the amount of fabric in square inches needed to make the parallelogram-shaped pieces for one quilt block.

25. How much fabric is needed to make the parallelogram pieces for a quilt that is made using 24 blocks? Write in square feet. (*Hint*: 144 $\text{in}^2 = 1\ \text{ft}^2$)

EXTRA PRACTICE
See pages 748, 766.
Math Online
Self-Check Quiz at tx.msmath2.com

H.O.T. Problems

26. **OPEN ENDED** Draw three different parallelograms, each with an area of 24 square units.

27. **CHALLENGE** *True* or *False*? The area of a parallelogram doubles if you double the base and the height. Explain or give a counterexample to support your answer.

28. **WRITING IN MATH** Compare and contrast the formula for the area of a rectangle and a parallelogram.

TEST PRACTICE

29. A scale drawing of a piece of land is shown below.

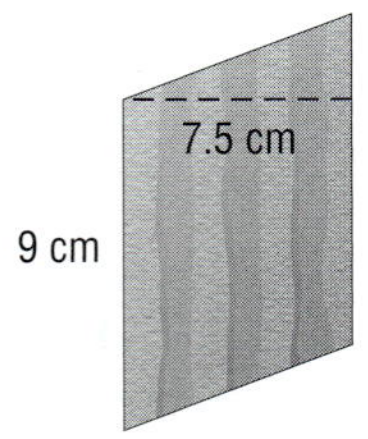

What is the actual area of the land if the scale on the drawing is 10 km = 1 cm?

A 67.5 cm^2 **C** 675 km^2

B 67.5 km^2 **D** 6,750 km^2

30. Ms. Cruz painted one wall in her living room. She did not paint the window.

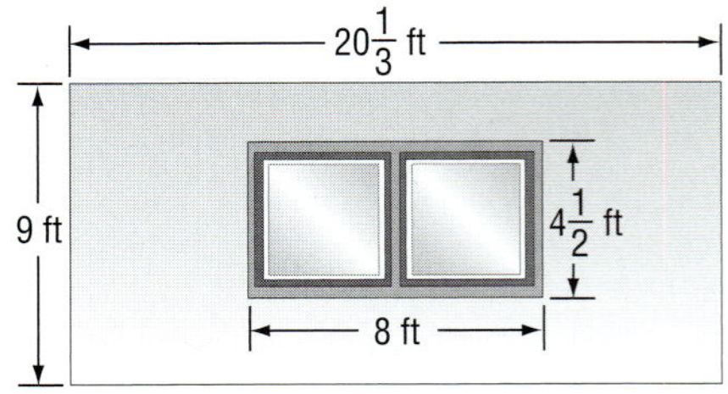

Which of the following is closest to the painted area of the wall in square feet?

F 180 ft^2 **H** 120 ft^2

G 150 ft^2 **J** 34 ft^2

Spiral Review

For Exercises 31 and 32, refer to $\triangle ABC$ at the right. Find the vertices of $\triangle A'B'C'$ after each transformation. Then graph the triangle and its reflected or translated image.

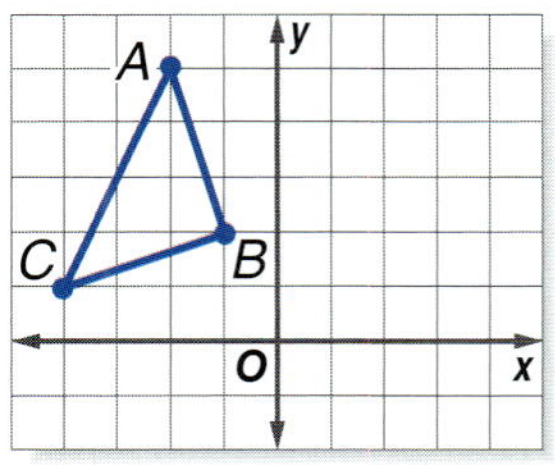

31. $\triangle ABC$ reflected over the y-axis (Lesson 11-9)

32. $\triangle ABC$ translated 5 units right and 1 unit up (Lesson 11-8)

33. **TESSELLATIONS** Explain how to determine whether an octagon tessellates the plane. (Lesson 11-7)

34. **FRUIT** If 2 out of every 3 pieces of fruit in a fruit basket are oranges, how many oranges are there if the fruit basket has 18 pieces of fruit? (Lesson 7-4)

GET READY for the Next Lesson

PREREQUISITE SKILL Find each value. (Lesson 1-4)

35. $6(4 + 10)$ 36. $\frac{1}{2}(8)(8)$ 37. $\frac{1}{2}(24 + 15)$ 38. $\frac{1}{2}(5)(13 + 22)$

Explore 12-2

Geometry Lab
Triangles and Trapezoids

Main IDEA

Find the areas of triangles and trapezoids using models.

Targeted TEKS **7.4** The student represents a relationship in numerical, geometric, verbal, and symbolic form. The student is expected to: **(A) generate formulas involving** unit conversions, perimeter, **area**, circumference, volume, and scaling. *Also addresses TEKS 7.15(B).*

ACTIVITY

STEP 1 On grid paper, draw a triangle with a base of 6 units and a height of 3 units. Label the base b and the height h as shown.

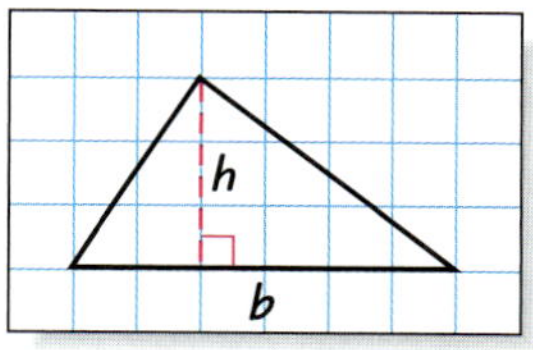

STEP 2 Fold the grid paper in half and cut out the triangle through both sheets so that you have two congruent triangles.

STEP 3 Turn the second triangle upside down and tape it to the first triangle.

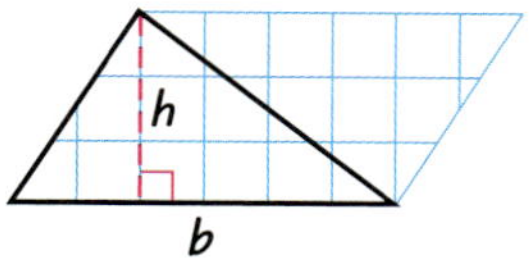

Analyze the Results

1. What figure is formed by the two triangles?
2. Write the formula for the area of the figure. Then find the area.
3. What is the area of each of the triangles? How do you know?
4. Repeat the activity above, drawing a different triangle in Step 1. Then find the area of each triangle.
5. Compare the area of a triangle to the area of a parallelogram with the same base and height.
6. **MAKE A CONJECTURE** Write a formula for the area of a triangle with base b and height h.

For Exercises 7–10, refer to the information below.

On grid paper, cut out two identical trapezoids. Label the bases b_1 and b_2, respectively, and label the heights h. Then turn one trapezoid upside down and tape it to the other trapezoid as shown.

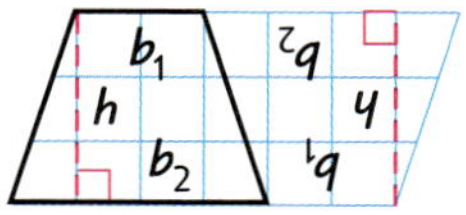

7. Write an expression to represent the base of the parallelogram.
8. Write a formula for the area A of the parallelogram using b_1, b_2, and h.
9. How does the area of each trapezoid compare to the area of the parallelogram?
10. **MAKE A CONJECTURE** Write a formula for the area A of a trapezoid with bases b_1 and b_2, and height h.

12-2 Area of Triangles and Trapezoids

Main IDEA

Find the areas of triangles and trapezoids.

Targeted TEKS 7.4 The student represents a relationship in numerical, geometric, verbal, and symbolic form. The student is expected to: **(A) generate formulas involving** unit conversions, perimeter, **area**, circumference, volume, and scaling. *Also addresses TEKS 7.8(C), 7.9(A).*

MINI Lab

- Draw a parallelogram with a base of 6 units and a height of 4 units.
- Draw a diagonal as shown.
- Cut out the parallelogram.

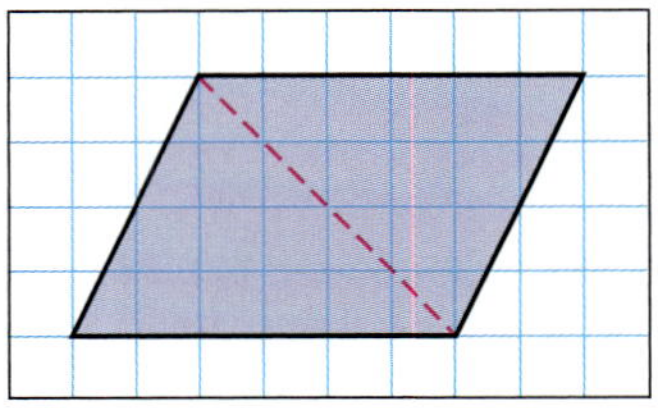

1. What is the area of the parallelogram?
2. Cut along the diagonal. What is true about the triangles formed?
3. What is the area of each triangle?
4. If the area of a parallelogram is bh, then write an expression for the area A of each of the two congruent triangles that form the parallelogram.

You can find the area of a triangle by using the base and height.

The *base* of a triangle can be any of its sides.

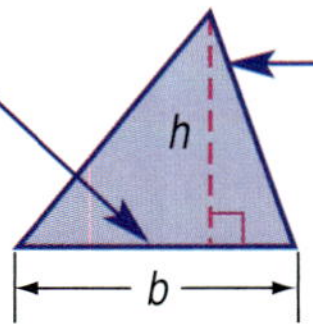

The *height* is the perpendicular distance from the vertex opposite the base to the line containing the base.

REVIEW Vocabulary

perpendicular lines lines that meet to form right angles (Lesson 11-1)

KEY CONCEPT — Area of a Triangle

Words The area A of a triangle equals half the product of its base b and height h.

Symbols $A = \frac{1}{2}bh$

Model

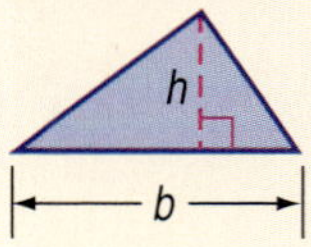

EXAMPLE Find the Area of a Triangle

1 **Find the area of the triangle below.**

Estimate $A = \frac{1}{2}(10)(7)$ or 35

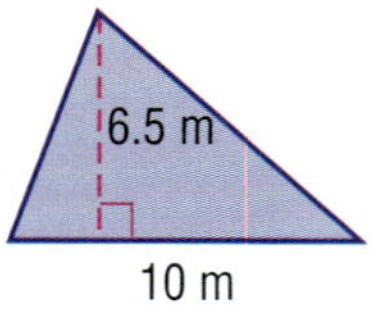

$A = \frac{1}{2}bh$	Area of a triangle
$A = \frac{1}{2}(10)(6.5)$	Replace b with 10 and h with 6.5.
$A = 32.5$	Multiply.

The area of the triangle is 32.5 square meters.

Check for Reasonableness $32.5 \approx 35$ ✔

CHECK Your Progress

Find the area of each triangle. Round to the nearest tenth if necessary.

a. 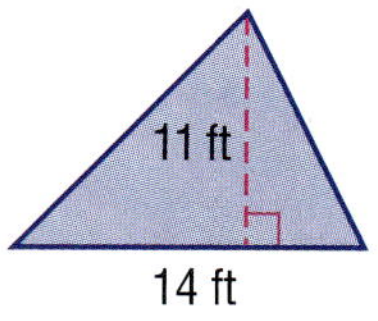

b. 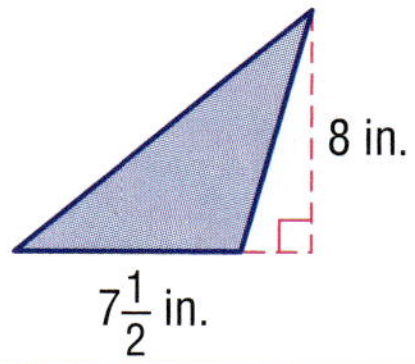

A trapezoid has two bases, b_1 and b_2. The bases are always the two sides that are parallel. The height of a trapezoid is the perpendicular distance between the bases.

Concepts in Motion
Interactive Lab tx.msmath2.com

KEY CONCEPT — Area of a Trapezoid

Words The area A of a trapezoid equals half the product of the height h and the sum of the bases $b_1 + b_2$.

Symbols $A = \frac{1}{2}h(b_1 + b_2)$

Model 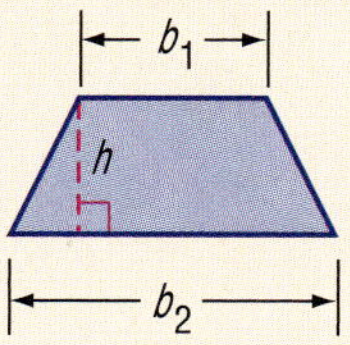

EXAMPLE Find the Area of a Trapezoid

READING Math

Subscripts Read b_1 as *b sub 1*. Read b_2 as *b sub 2*.The subscripts mean that b_1 and b_2 represent different variables.

2 Find the area of the trapezoid.

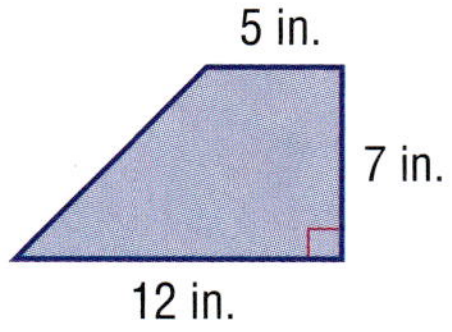

The bases are 5 inches and 12 inches. The height is 7 inches.

$A = \frac{1}{2}h(b_1 + b_2)$ Area of a trapezoid

$A = \frac{1}{2}(7)(5 + 12)$ Replace h with 7, b_1 with 5, and b_2 with 12.

$A = \frac{1}{2}(7)(17)$ Add 5 and 12.

$A = 59.5$ Multiply.

The area of the trapezoid is 59.5 square inches.

CHECK Your Progress

Find the area of each trapezoid. Round to the nearest tenth if necessary.

c. 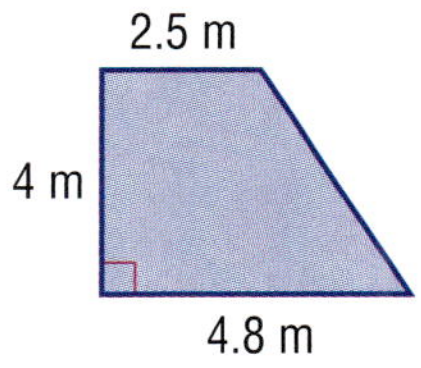

d. 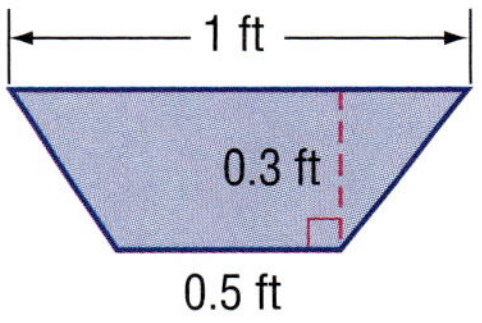

Math Online Personal Tutor at tx.msmath2.com

Real-World Link In southwestern Val Verde County, the Pecos River flows into the Rio Grande.

Source: The Handbook of Texas Online

Real-World EXAMPLE

3 **GEOGRAPHY** **The shape of Val Verde County resembles a trapezoid. Find the approximate area of this county.**

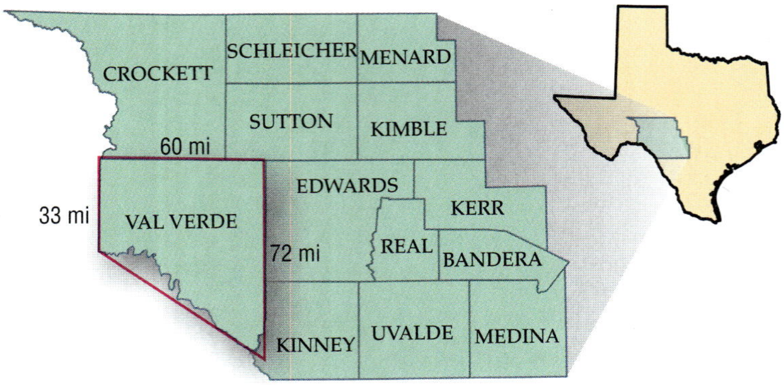

$A = \frac{1}{2}h(b_1 + b_2)$ — Area of a trapezoid

$A = \frac{1}{2}(60)(33 + 72)$ — Replace h with 60, b_1 with 33, and b_2 with 72.

$A = \frac{1}{2}(60)(105)$ — Add 33 and 72.

$A = 3{,}150$ — Multiply.

The area of Val Verde County is approximately 3,150 square miles.

CHECK Your Progress

e. **GEOGRAPHY** The shape of the state of Arkansas resembles a trapezoid. Find the approximate area of Arkansas.

CHECK Your Understanding

Examples 1, 2 (pp. 616–617)

Find the area of each figure. Round to the nearest tenth if necessary.

1. 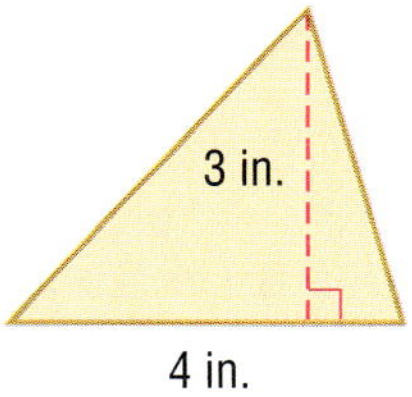

2. 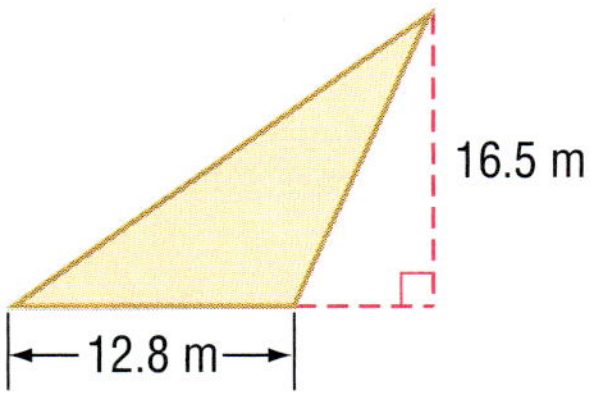

3. 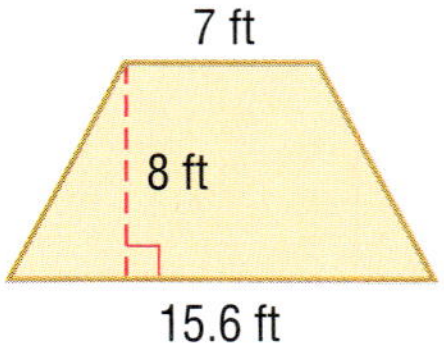

Example 3 (p. 618)

4. **GEOGRAPHY** Nevada has a shape that looks like a trapezoid, as shown at the right. Find the approximate area of Nevada.

Exercises

HOMEWORK HELP	
For Exercises	See Examples
5, 6, 9	1
7, 8, 10	2
11, 12	3

Find the area of each figure. Round to the nearest tenth if necessary.

5. 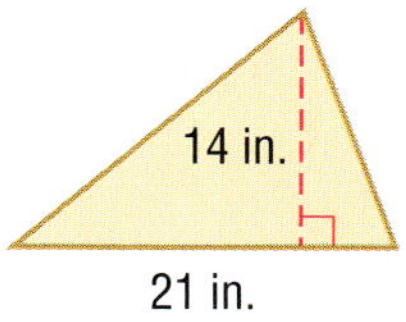

6. 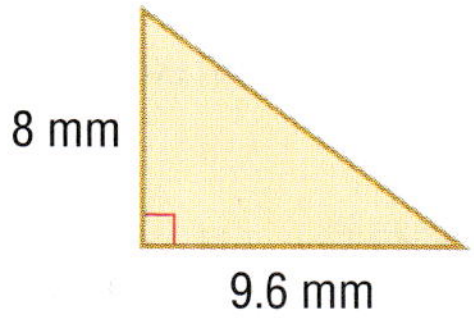

7. 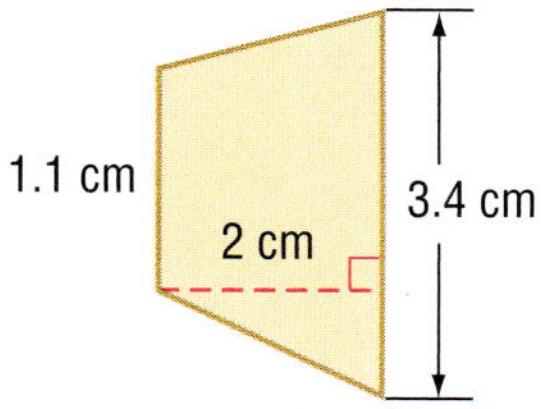

8. 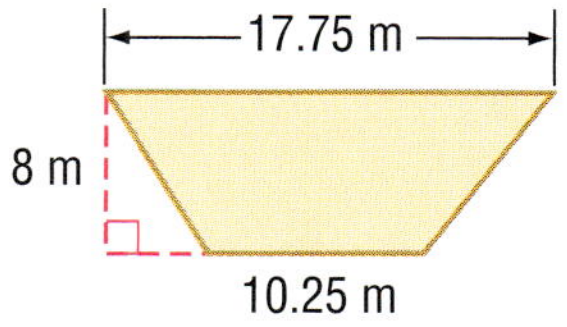

9. 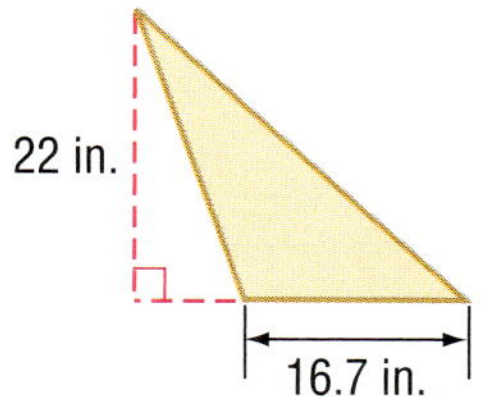

10. 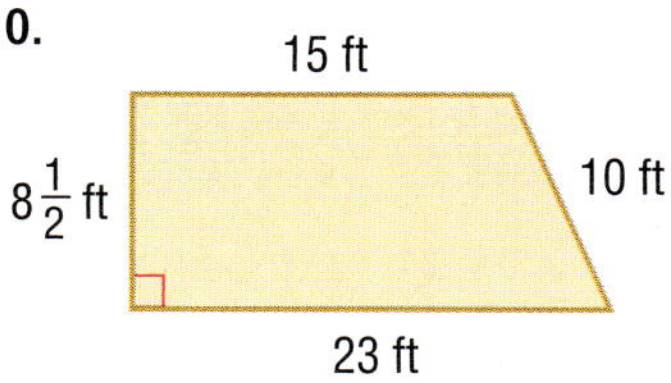

11. **GEOGRAPHY** The shape of Idaho is roughly triangular with a base of 380 miles and a height of 500 miles. Find the approximate area of Idaho.

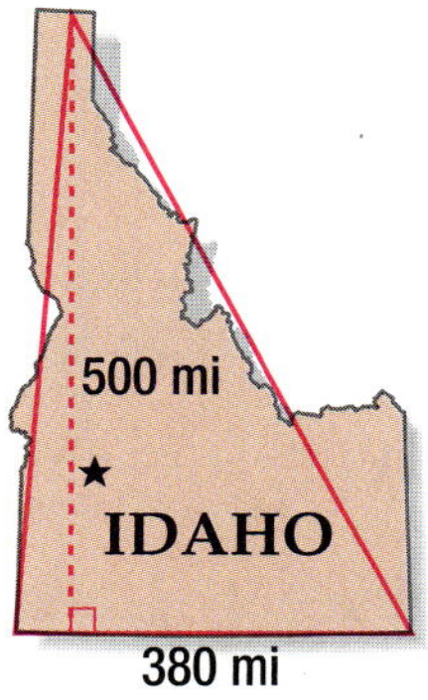

12. **ALGEBRA** Find the area of a trapezoid with bases 13 inches and 15 inches and a height of 7 inches.

ALGEBRA Find the height of each figure.

13. 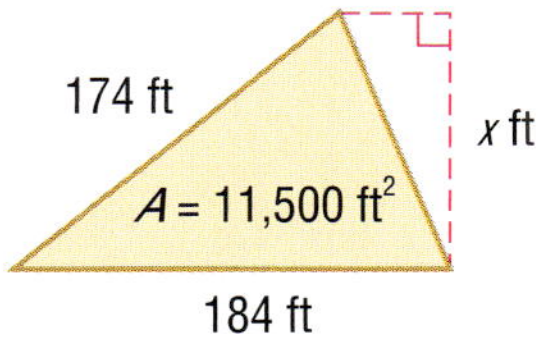

14. 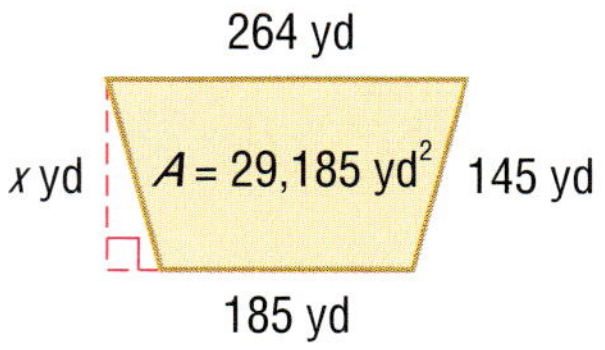

Draw and label each figure. Then find the area.

15. a triangle with no right angles and an area less than 12 square centimeters
16. a trapezoid with a right angle and an area greater than 40 square meters
17. a trapezoid with no right angles and an area less than 25 square feet

18. **ARCHITECTURE** The blueprints for a patio are shown at the right. If the cost of the patio is $4.50 per square foot,what will be the total cost of the patio?

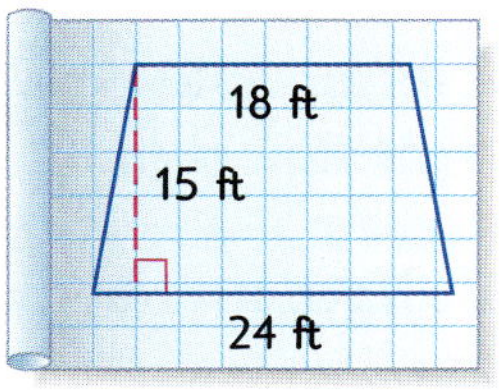

LANDSCAPING For Exercises 19 and 20, use the diagram that shows the lawn that surrounds an office building.

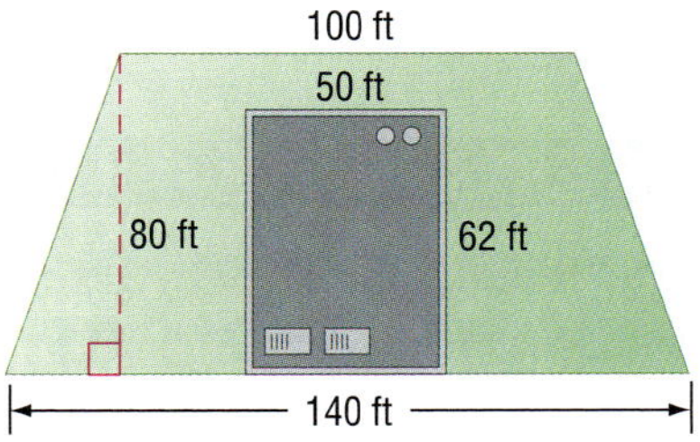

19. What is the area of the lawn?
20. If one bag of grass seed covers 2,000 square feet, how many bags are needed to seed the lawn?

EXTRA PRACTICE

See pages 748, 766.

Math Online
Self-Check Quiz at tx.msmath2.com

H.O.T. Problems

21. **CHALLENGE** A triangle has height h. Its base is 4. Create an algebraic equation for the area of the triangle in terms of h.

22. **REASONING** Apply what you know about rounding to explain how to estimate the height h of the trapezoid shown if the area is 235.5 in^2.

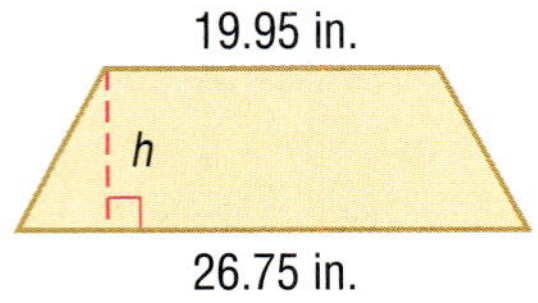

23. **WRITING IN MATH** Describe the relationship between the area of a parallelogram and the area of a triangle with the same height and base.

TEST PRACTICE

24. $\triangle FGH$ and $\triangle JKM$ are similar.

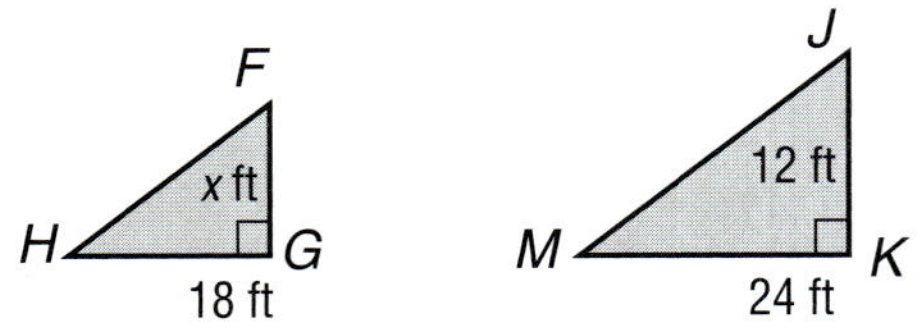

Which choice shows the equations that can be used to find the area of $\triangle FGH$?

A $\frac{18}{24} = \frac{12}{x}$ and then $\frac{1}{2}(18x)$

B $\frac{18}{24} = \frac{x}{12}$ and then $18x$

C $\frac{18}{24} = \frac{x}{12}$ and then $\frac{1}{2}(18x)$

D $\frac{18}{24} = \frac{12}{x}$ and then $18x$

25. Randy was hired to put in sod on a piece of land shaped like a trapezoid as shown. How many square feet of sod are needed?

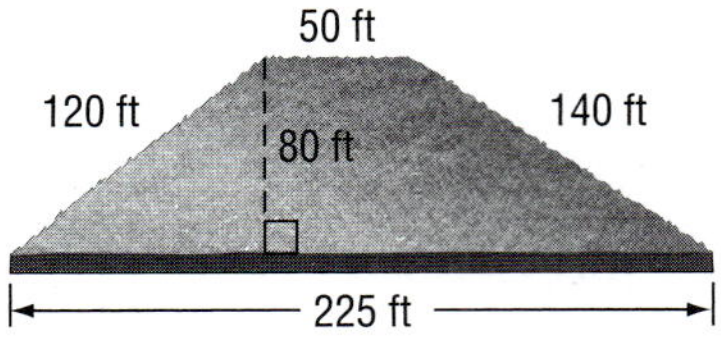

F 4000 ft^2

G 11,000 ft^2

H 20,400 ft^2

J 32,000 ft^2

Spiral Review

26. **GEOMETRY** Find the area of a parallelogram having a base of 2.3 inches and a height of 1.6 inches. Round to the nearest tenth. (Lesson 12-1)

27. **GEOMETRY** Graph $\triangle JLK$ with vertices $J(-1, -4)$, $K(1, 1)$, and $L(3, -2)$ and its reflection over the x-axis. Write the ordered pairs for the vertices of the new figure. (Lesson 11-9)

Find each number. Round to the nearest tenth if necessary. (Lesson 8-5)

28. What number is 56% of 600?

29. 24.5 is what percent of 98?

30. 72 is 45% of what number?

31. 62.5% of 250 is what number?

GET READY for the Next Lesson

PREREQUISITE SKILL **Use a calculator to find each product to the nearest tenth.** (Lesson 1-4)

32. $\pi \cdot 13$

33. $\pi \cdot 29$

34. $\pi \cdot 16^2$

35. $\pi \cdot 4.8^2$

Explore 12-3

Geometry Lab
Circumference of Circles

Main IDEA

Find a relationship between circumference and diameter.

Targeted TEKS **7.4** The student represents a relationship in numerical, geometric, verbal, and symbolic form. **(A)** **generate formulas involving** unit conversions, perimeter, area, **circumference**, volume, and scaling.

In this lab, you will investigate how the *circumference*, or the distance around a circle, is related to its *diameter*, or the distance across a circle through its center.

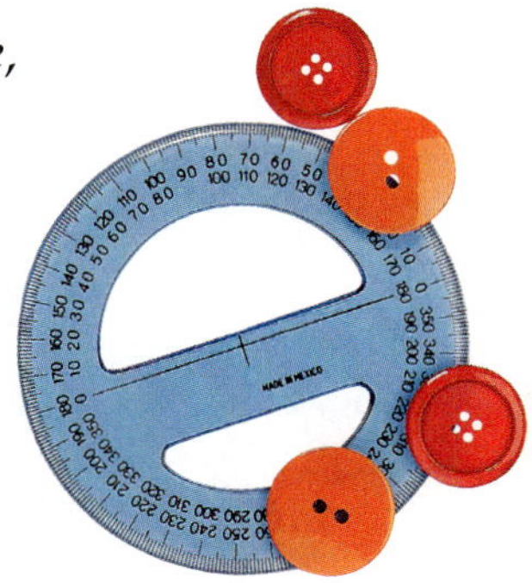

ACTIVITY

STEP 1 Use a ruler to measure the diameter of a circular object. Record the measure in a table like the one shown below.

Object	Diameter (cm)	Circumference (cm)

STEP 2 Make a small mark at the edge of the circular object. Place a measuring tape on a flat surface. Place the mark you made on the circular object at the beginning of the measuring tape. Roll the object along the tape for one revolution, until you reach the mark again.

STEP 3 Record the length in the table. This is the circumference.

STEP 4 Repeat this activity with circular objects of various sizes.

Analyze the Results

1. For each object, divide the circumference by the diameter. Add another column to your table and record the results. Round to the nearest tenth if necessary.
2. What do you notice about the ratio of each circumference to each diameter?
3. Graph the ordered pair (diameter, circumference) on a coordinate plane for each object. What do you notice?
4. Use the graph to predict the circumference of a circular object that has a diameter of 18 centimeters.
5. **MAKE A CONJECTURE** Write a rule describing how you would find the circumference C of a circle if you know the diameter d.
6. Use your rule to approximate the circumference of a circular object that has a diameter of 45 centimeters.

12-3 Circles and Circumference

Main IDEA

Find the circumference of circles.

Targeted TEKS **7.9** The student solves application problems involving estimation and measurement. **(A) estimate measurements and solve application problems involving length (including** perimeter and **circumference)** and area **of** polygons and **other shapes**.

NEW Vocabulary

circle
center
diameter
circumference
radius
π (pi)

GET READY for the Lesson

FERRIS WHEELS The London Eye Ferris wheel, in London, England, measures 450 feet across.

1. Which point appears to be the center of the Ferris wheel?
2. Is the distance from G to F greater than, less than, or equal to the distance from G to J?
3. How does the distance from G to H compare to the distance from F to J?
4. Find the distance from G to F.

A **circle** is the set of all points in a plane that are the same distance from a given point, called the **center**.

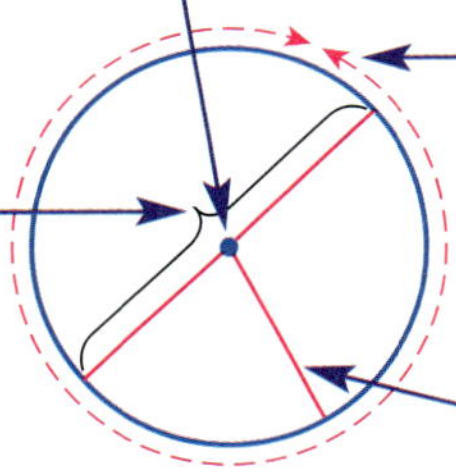

The diameter of a circle is 2 times the radius, or $d = 2r$. Another relationship that is true of all circles is $\frac{C}{d} = 3.1415926\ldots$.
This nonterminating and nonrepeating number is represented by the Greek letter **π (pi)**. An approximation often used for π is 3.14.

KEY CONCEPT — Circumference of a Circle

Words The circumference C of a circle is equal to its diameter d times π, or 2 times its radius r times π.

Symbols $C = \pi d$ or $C = 2\pi r$

You can use the approximation for π of 3.14 to find the circumference of a circle.

STUDY TIP

Estimation
To estimate the circumference of a circle, you can use 3 for π since $\pi \approx 3$.

Real-World EXAMPLE Find Circumference

1 **FERRIS WHEELS** **Refer to the lesson opener. Find the circumference of the London Eye Ferris wheel.**

Estimate $C = 3 \cdot 450$ or 1,350 ft

$C = \pi d$ Circumference of a circle

$C \approx 3.14(450)$ Replace π with 3.14 and d with 450.

$C \approx 1{,}413$ Multiply.

So, the distance around the Ferris wheel is about 1,413 feet.

Check for Reasonableness $1{,}413 \approx 1{,}350$ ✔

CHECK Your Progress

Find the circumference of each circle. Use 3.14 for π. Round to the nearest tenth if necessary.

a.
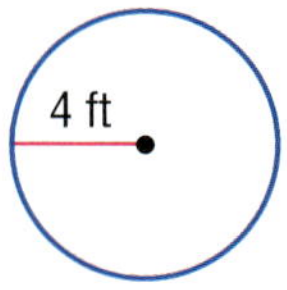

b.
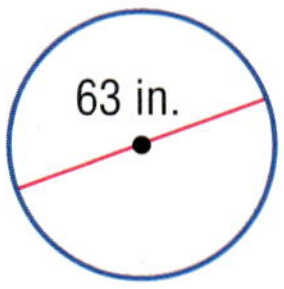

Online Personal Tutor at tx.msmath2.com

Another approximation for π is $\frac{22}{7}$. Use this value when the radius or diameter is a multiple of 7 or has a multiple of 7 in its numerator if the radius is a fraction.

EXAMPLE Find Circumference

2 **Find the circumference of a circle with a radius of 21 inches.**

Since 21 is a multiple of 7, use $\frac{22}{7}$ for π.

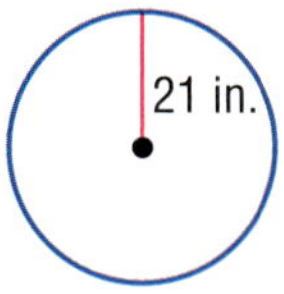

$C = 2\pi r$ Circumference of a circle

$C \approx 2 \cdot \frac{22}{7} \cdot 21$ Replace π with $\frac{22}{7}$ and r with 21.

$C \approx 2 \cdot \frac{22}{\cancel{7}_1} \cdot \frac{\cancel{21}^3}{1}$ Divide by the GCF, 7.

$C \approx 132$ Simplify.

The circumference of the circle is about 132 inches.

STUDY TIP

Technology
You can use a calculator to find the circumference. To find $2\pi(21)$, press 2 [π] [×] 21 [ENTER]. The circumference is about 131.9468915.

CHECK Your Progress

Find the circumference of each circle. Use $\frac{22}{7}$ for π. Round to the nearest tenth if necessary.

c.
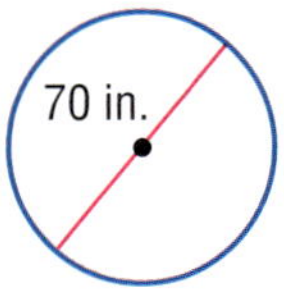

d.
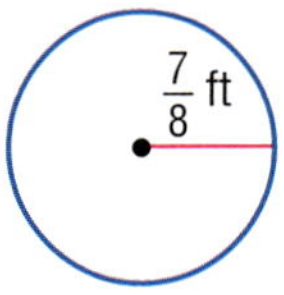

CHECK Your Understanding

Examples 1, 2
(p. 623)

Find the circumference of each circle. Use 3.14 or $\frac{22}{7}$ for π. Round to the nearest tenth if necessary.

1.
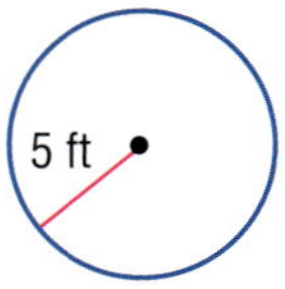

2.
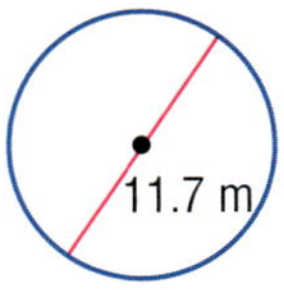

3.
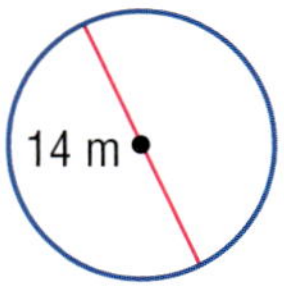

4.
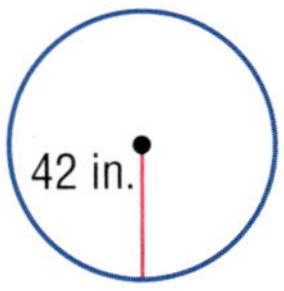

5. **CLOCKS** To the nearest tenth, how many centimeters does the tip of the minute hand of the clock shown travel each hour?

Exercises

HOMEWORK HELP	
For Exercises	See Examples
6–9, 14–15 20–21	1
10–13, 16–19	2

Find the circumference of each circle. Use 3.14 or $\frac{22}{7}$ for π. Round to the nearest tenth if necessary.

6.
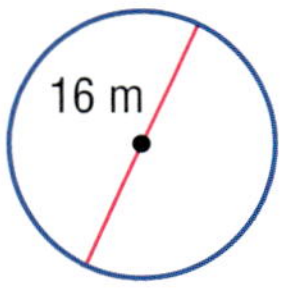

7.
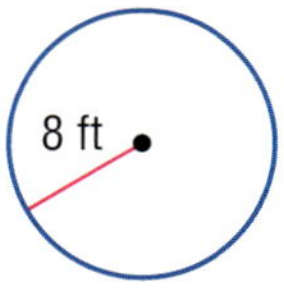

8.
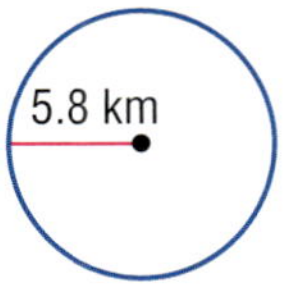

9.
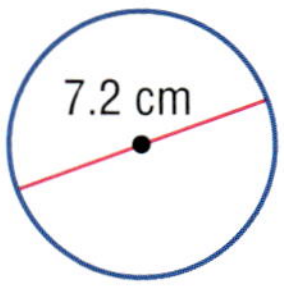

10.
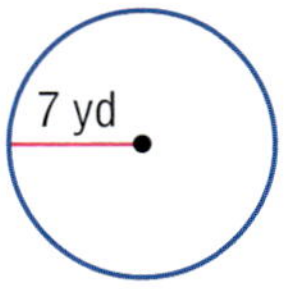

11.
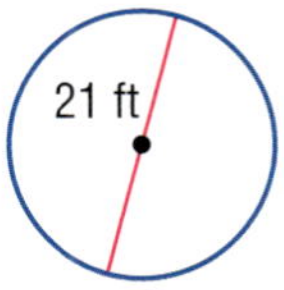

12. radius $= 1\frac{3}{4}$ in.

13. diameter $= 10\frac{1}{2}$ in.

14. diameter $= 15.1$ m

15. diameter $= 10.8$ km

16. radius $= 2\frac{5}{8}$ in.

17. diameter $= 12\frac{1}{4}$ mi

18. **SPORTS** A flying disc has a diameter of $9\frac{5}{8}$ inches. Find its circumference.

19. **PETS** A hamster wheel has a radius of $4\frac{1}{2}$ inches. How far will the wheel turn in one revolution?

20. **PATCHES** The Texas National Guard military patch has a diameter of 2.5 inches. What is its circumference to the nearest tenth?

21. **POOLS** The Cole family owns an above-ground circular swimming pool that has walls made of aluminum. Find the length ℓ of aluminum surrounding the pool as shown if the radius is 15 feet. Round to the nearest tenth.

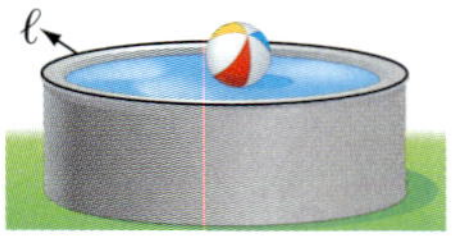

LABELS Determine the length of each can's label.

22. 

23. 

24. 

Estimate to find the approximate circumference of each circle. State which approximation of π you used.

25. 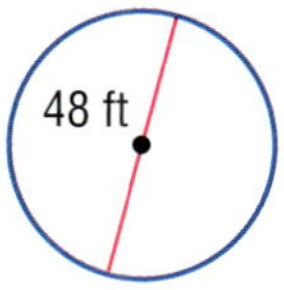

26. 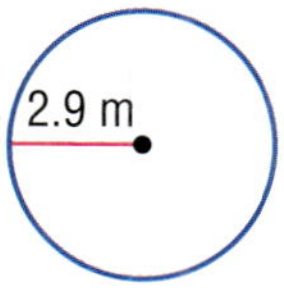

27. 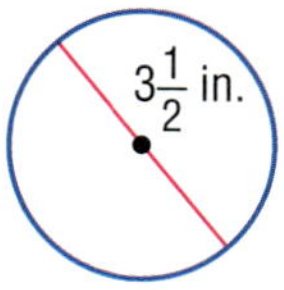

ALGEBRA **Find the diameter or radius of each circle. Use 3.14 for π. Round to the nearest tenth if necessary.**

28. $C = 25$ ft, diameter = ■ ft

29. $C = 54$ cm, diameter = ■ cm

30. $C = 30$ yd, radius = ■ yd

31. $C = 48$ km, radius = ■ km

32. **GARDENING** A circular garden with a radius of 10 feet is to be outlined with bricks measuring 10 inches long. About how many bricks are needed if the bricks are laid end to end?

Real-World Link The record for the longest unicycle ride is 9,126 miles.
Source: Guinness World Records

33. **UNICYCLES** A unicycle wheel has a radius of 10 inches. How many feet will the unicycle travel in 5 revolutions? Explain how you solved this problem.

34. **CROPS** The crop circle shown was created in England in a single night by an unknown source. About how many strides would it take for a person to walk around the circle if each stride is 3 feet?

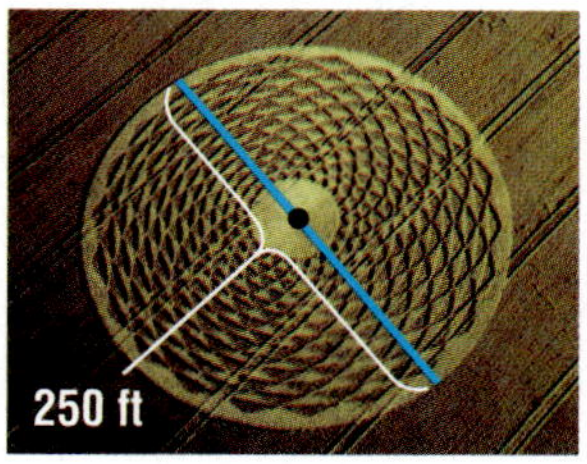

EXTRA PRACTICE
See pages 748, 766.
Math Online
Self-Check Quiz at tx.msmath2.com

35. **FIND THE DATA** Refer to the Texas Data File on pages 16–19. Choose some data and write a real-world problem in which you would find the circumference of a circle.

H.O.T. Problems

36. **OPEN ENDED** Select a real-world situation in which finding the circumference of a circle would be useful.

37. **FIND THE ERROR** Aidan and Mya are finding the circumference of a circle with a radius of 5 inches. Who is correct? Explain.

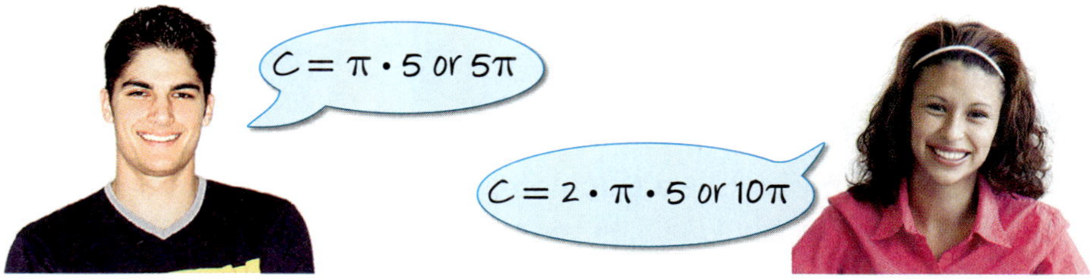

Aidan　　　Mya

CHALLENGE **For Exercises 38 and 39, use the circle at the right.**

38. How many lengths x will fit on the circumference of the circle?

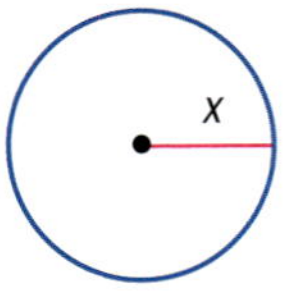

39. If the value of x is doubled, what effect will this have on the diameter? on the circumference? Explain your reasoning.

40. **WRITING IN MATH** *True* or *False*? All circles are similar. Justify your answer.

TEST PRACTICE

41. Malik's bike tire has a radius of 8 inches. Which equation could be used to find the circumference of the tire in inches?

A $C = \pi \cdot 4$

B $C = \pi \cdot 16 \times 2$

C $C = \pi \cdot 16$

D $C = \pi \cdot 8$

42. The distance around a tree trunk is the girth of the tree. Which measure is closest to the girth of the cross-section of the tree shown below?

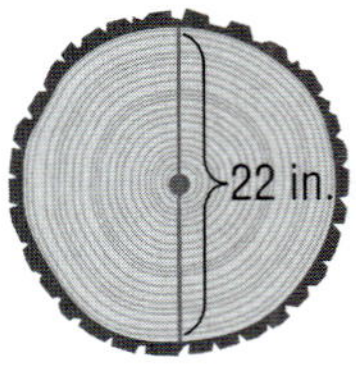

F 34.5 in.

G 69.1 in.

H 138.2 in.

J 380.0 in.

Spiral Review

GEOMETRY **Find the area of each figure. Round to the nearest tenth if necessary.** (Lesson 12-2)

43.

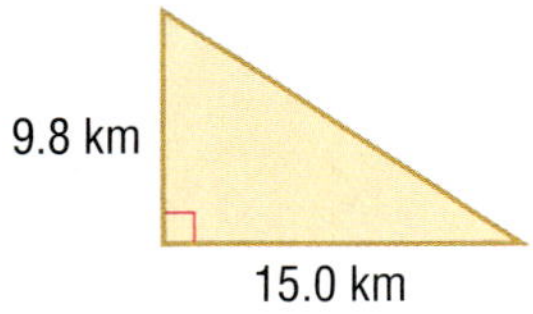

44.

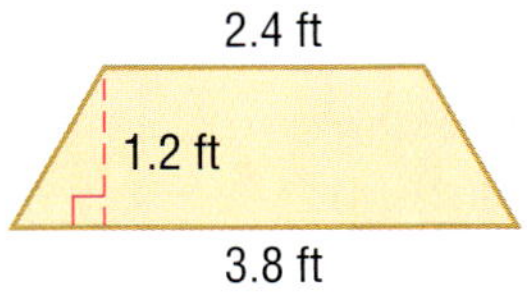

45. **GEOMETRY** Find the area of a parallelogram with base 6.5 meters and height 7.0 meters. (Lesson 12-1)

46. **ALGEBRA** What is $m\angle Y$ in quadrilateral $WXYZ$ if $m\angle W = 35°$, $m\angle X = 115°$, and $\angle Z$ is a right angle? (Lesson 11-5)

47. **PROBABILITY** Jorge rolled a number cube several times and recorded the results in the table shown. Find the experimental probability that an odd number turned up. (Lesson 10-7)

Outcome	Frequency
1	𝍸 I
2	III
3	𝍸 II
4	𝍸
5	II
6	IIII

GET READY for the Next Lesson

PREREQUISITE SKILL **Use a calculator to find each product to the nearest tenth. Use 3.14 for π.** (Lesson 1-4)

48. $\pi \cdot 5^2$

49. $\pi \cdot 7^2$

50. $\pi \cdot (2.4)^2$

51. $\pi \cdot (4.5)^2$

12-4 Area of Circles

Main IDEA

Find the areas of circles.

Targeted TEKS **7.9** The student solves application problems involving estimation and measurement. **(A) estimate measurements and solve application problems involving** length (including perimeter and circumference) and **area of** polygons and **other shapes**. *Also addresses TEKS 7.4(A), 7.8(C).*

MINI Lab

- Fold a paper plate in half four times to divide it into 16 equal-sized sections.
- Label the radius r as shown. Let C represent the circumference of the circle.
- Cut out each section; reassemble to form a parallelogram-shaped figure.

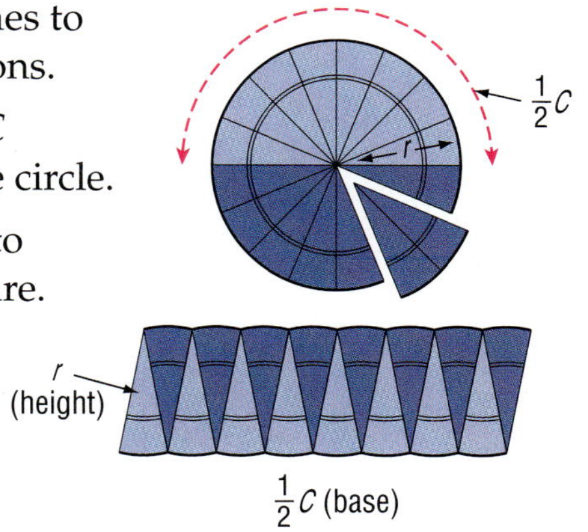

1. What is the measurement of the base and the height?
2. Substitute these values into the formula for the area of a parallelogram.
3. Replace C with the expression for the circumference of a circle, $2\pi r$. Simplify the equation and describe what it represents.

In the Mini Lab, the formula for the area of a parallelogram was used to develop a formula for the area of a circle.

KEY CONCEPT — Area of a Circle

Words The area A of a circle equals the product of π and the square of its radius r.

Symbols $A = \pi r^2$

Model

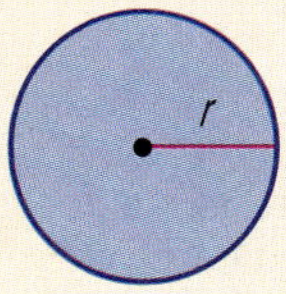

EXAMPLE Find the Area of a Circle

1 **Find the area of the circle.**

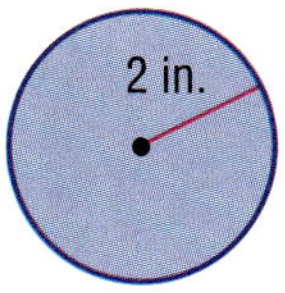

$A = \pi r^2$ Area of a circle

$A = \pi \cdot 2^2$ Replace r with 2.

[π] [×] 2 [x^2] [ENTER] 12.56637061

The area of the circle is approximately 12.6 square inches.

CHECK Your Progress

a. Find the area of a circle with a radius of 3.2 centimeters. Round to the nearest tenth.

Real-World EXAMPLE

2 **COINS** **Find the area of the face of the Texas quarter shown.**

The diameter of the quarter is 24 millimeters, so the radius is $\frac{1}{2}(24)$ or 12 millimeters.

$A = \pi r^2$ — Area of a circle

$A = \pi \cdot 12^2$ — Replace r with 12.

$A \approx 452.4$ — Use a calculator.

The area is approximately 452.4 square millimeters.

CHECK Your Progress

b. **POOLS** The bottom of a circular swimming pool with diameter 30 feet is painted blue. How many square feet are blue?

TEST EXAMPLE

3 Ellis draws a circle with a diameter of 16 inches similar to the one shown. He then shades one region of the circle. Find the approximate area of the shaded region.

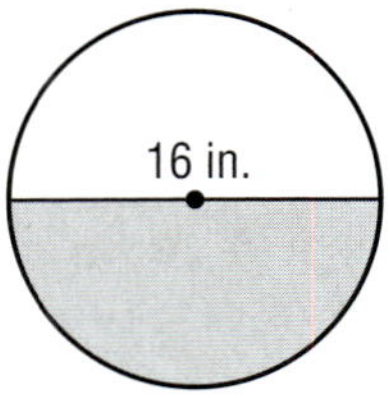

A 100 in^2 **C** 402 in^2

B 201 in^2 **D** 804 in^2

Test-Taking Tip

Identifying What is Given Before finding area, be sure to read the question carefully and identify if the radius or diameter is given.

Read the Test Item

Since the segment in the figure is a diameter, you know that the shaded region represents half of the area of the circle. To find the area of the shaded region, you can find the total area of the circle and then divide by 2.

Solve the Test Item

$A = \pi r^2$ — Area of a circle

$A = \pi \cdot 8^2$ — Replace r with 16 ÷ 2 or 8.

$A \approx 200$ — Multiply. Use 3.14 for π.

Half of the total area is approximately $\frac{1}{2}(200)$ or 100 square inches. The answer is A.

CHECK Your Progress

c. Ray drew one circle with a radius of 7 centimeters and another circle with a radius of 10 centimeters. Find the approximate difference between the areas of the circles.

F 28 cm^2 **G** 40 cm^2 **H** 160 cm^2 **J** 254 cm^2

Online Personal Tutor at tx.msmath2.com

CHECK Your Understanding

Examples 1, 2 (pp. 627–628)

Find the area of each circle. Round to the nearest tenth.

1. 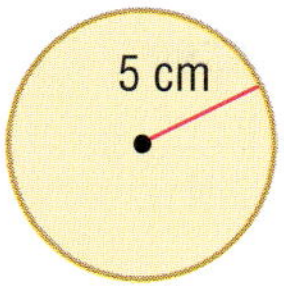

2. 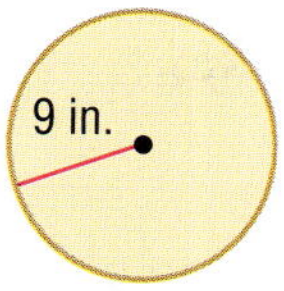

3. diameter = 16 m

4. diameter = 13 ft

Example 3 (p. 628)

5. **TEST PRACTICE** Kenneth draws the circle shown at the right. He shades one region of the circle. What is the approximate area of the shaded region?

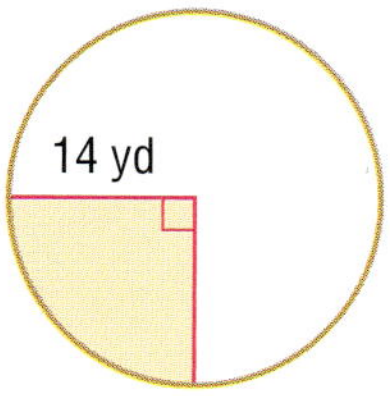

A 88 yd^2 **C** 310 yd^2

B 154 yd^2 **D** 615 yd^2

Exercises

HOMEWORK HELP

For Exercises	See Examples
6–7, 10–11, 14–15, 19	1
8–9, 12–13, 16–18	2
36–37	3

Find the area of each circle. Round to the nearest tenth.

6. 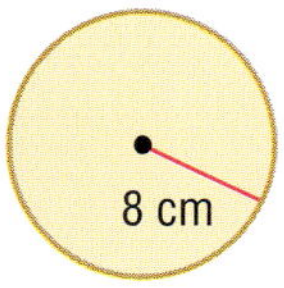

7. 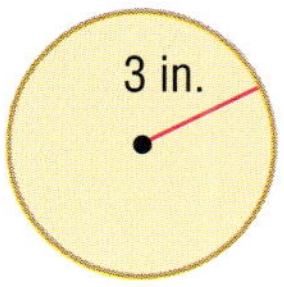

8. 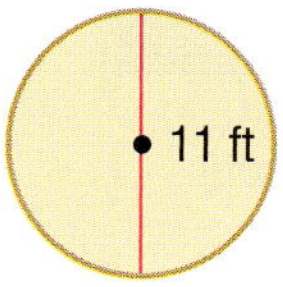

9. 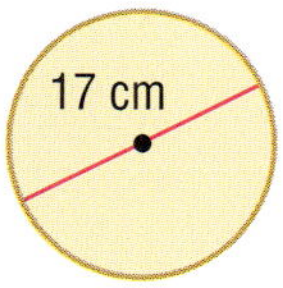

10. 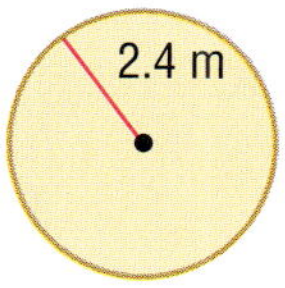

11. 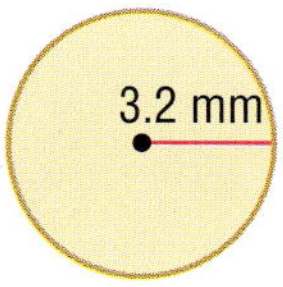

12. diameter = 8.4 m

13. diameter = 12.6 cm

14. radius = $4\frac{1}{2}$ in.

15. radius = $3\frac{3}{4}$ ft

16. diameter = $9\frac{1}{4}$ mi

17. diameter = $20\frac{3}{4}$ yd

18. **PATCHES** Find the area of the Girl Scout patch shown if the diameter is 1.25 inches. Round to the nearest tenth.

19. **TOOLS** A sprinkler that sprays water in a circular area can be adjusted to spray up to 30 feet. To the nearest tenth, what is the maximum area of lawn that can be watered by the sprinkler?

ESTIMATION **Estimate to find the approximate area of each circle.**

20. 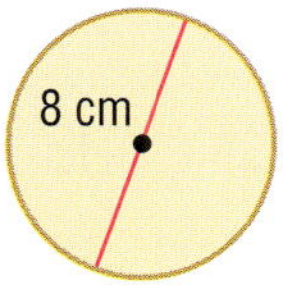

21. 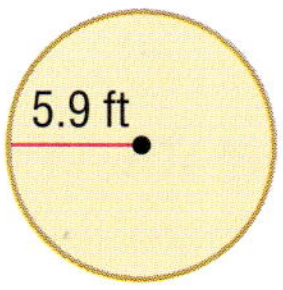

22. 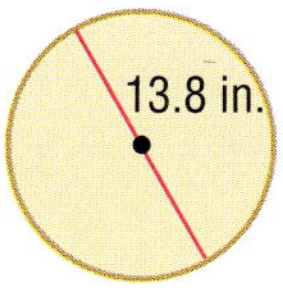

For Exercises 23–26, match each figure with its approximate area.

23. parallelogram: base = 3.2 m, height = 8 m
24. trapezoid: bases = 5.5 m and 8 m, height = 4 m
25. circle: diameter = 10 m
26. triangle: base = 8.2 m, height = 14 m

a. $78.5\ m^2$
b. $57.4\ m^2$
c. $25.6\ m^2$
d. $27.0\ m^2$

Real-World Math The Roman Pantheon has a diameter of 142 feet.
Source: Great Building Online

27. A *semicircle* is half a circle. Find the area of the semicircle to the nearest tenth.

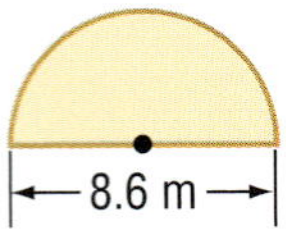

28. Which has a greater area, a triangle with a base of 100 feet and a height of 100 feet or a circle with diameter of 100 feet? Justify your selection.

29. **ARCHITECTURE** The Roman Pantheon is a circular structure that was completed about 126 A.D. Use the information at the left to find the approximate area of the floor in square yards. (*Hint*: 1 sq ft ≈ 0.1 sq yd)

30. **LANDSCAPE DESIGN** A circular stone path is to be installed around a birdbath with radius 1.5 feet, as shown at the right. What is the area of the path? (*Hint*: Find the area of the large circle minus the area of the small circle.)

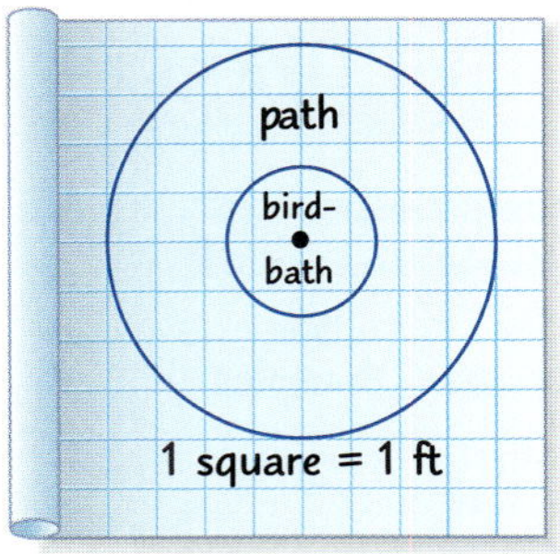

EXTRA PRACTICE
See pages 749, 766.
Math Online
Self-Check Quiz at tx.msmath2.com

H.O.T. Problems

CHALLENGE **Find the area of the shaded region in each figure. Round to the nearest tenth.**

31.
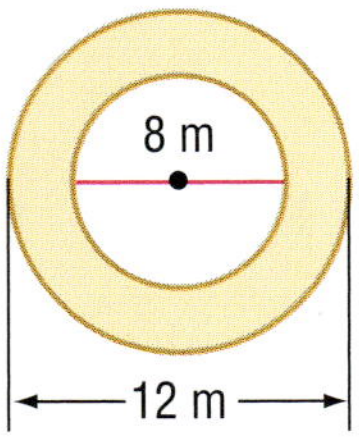

32.
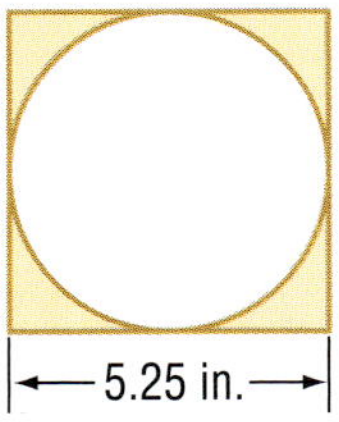

33.
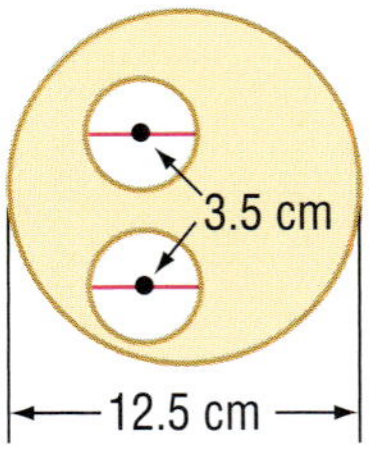

34. **FIND THE ERROR** Domingo and Bradley are finding the area of a circle that has a diameter of 12 centimeters. Who is correct? Explain.

Domingo

Bradley

35. **WRITING IN MATH** Write and solve a real-world problem in which you would solve the problem by finding the area of a circle.

TEST PRACTICE

36. Use a ruler to measure the radius of the half dollar in centimeters.

Which of the following is closest to the area of the face of the half dollar?

A 12 cm^2

B 15 cm^2

C 28 cm^2

D 735 cm^2

37. Which two figures have the same area?

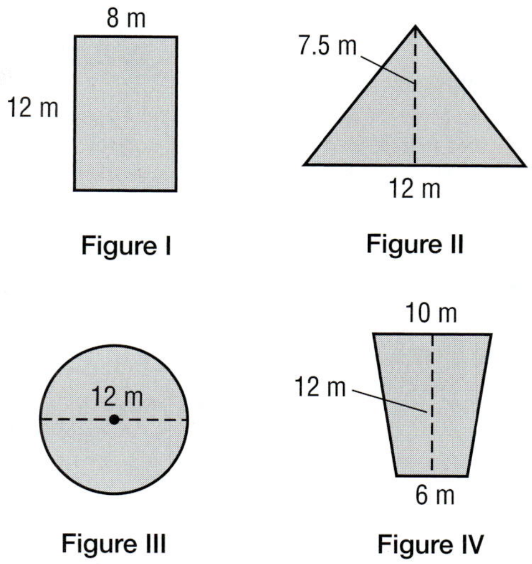

F Figure I and Figure IV

G Figure I and Figure II

H Figure II and Figure IV

J Figure II and Figure III

Spiral Review

38. **GEOMETRY** What is the circumference of a circle that has a radius of 8 yards? Use 3.14 for π and round to the nearest tenth if necessary. (Lesson 12-3)

39. **GEOMETRY** Find the area of a triangle with a base of 21 meters and a height of 27 meters. (Lesson 12-2)

Find the area of each parallelogram. Round to the nearest tenth if necessary. (Lesson 12-1)

40.
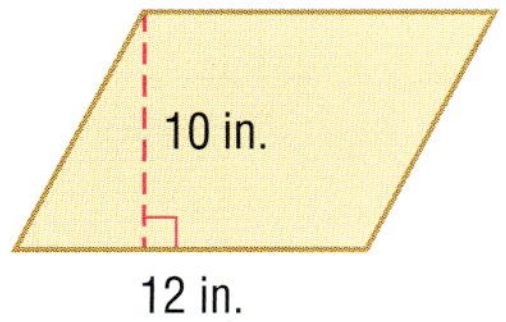

41.
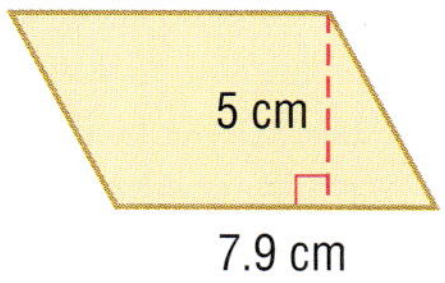

42.
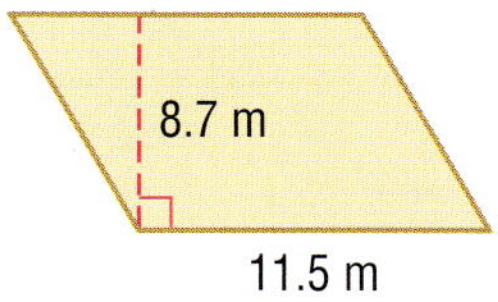

43. **MONEY** Toya buys a coat for $189, not including tax. If the tax rate is 8.5%, what is a reasonable total cost of the coat; $190, $205, $245? (Lesson 8-4)

GET READY for the Next Lesson

PREREQUISITE SKILL **Simplify each expression.** (Lessons 1-2, 1-3, and 1-4)

44. 8.5^2

45. $3.14 \cdot 6^2$

46. $\frac{1}{2} \cdot 5.4^2 + 11$

47. $\frac{1}{2} \cdot 7^2 + (9)(14)$

12-5 Problem-Solving Investigation

MAIN IDEA: Solve problems by solving a simpler problem.

Targeted TEKS 7.13 The student applies Grade 7 mathematics to solve problems connected to everyday experiences… and activities in and outside of school. **(C) select or develop an appropriate problem-solving strategy from a variety of different types, including… working a simpler problem, … to solve a problem.** *Also addresses TEKS 7.13(B).*

P.S.I. TEAM +

e-Mail: SOLVE A SIMPLER PROBLEM

YOUR MISSION: Solve the problem by solving a simpler problem.

THE PROBLEM: How much wallpaper is needed to cover the entire front of the backdrop?

Liam: The diagram shows the backdrop for our fall play. We need to find the total area of the backdrop.

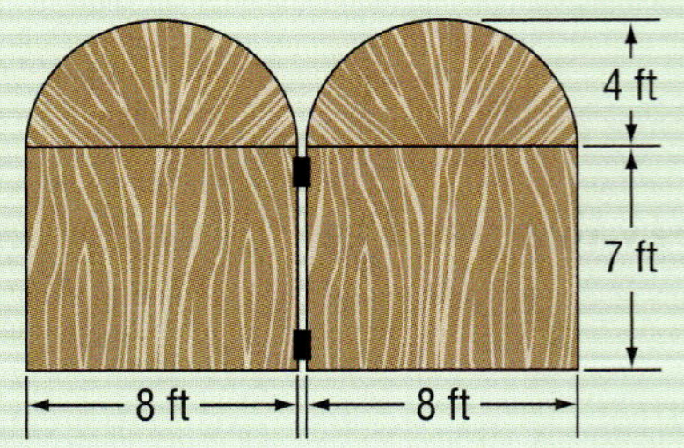

EXPLORE	You know that the backdrop is made of one large rectangle and two semicircles, which equal an entire circle.
PLAN	Find the areas of the rectangle and the circle, and then add.
SOLVE	area of rectangle: $A = \ell w$ $A = (8 + 8)7$ or 112 area of circle: $A = \pi r^2$ $A = \pi \cdot 4^2$ or about 50.3 The total area is 112 + 50.3 or 162.3 square feet. So, at least 162.3 square feet of wallpaper is needed.
CHECK	Use estimation to check. The backdrop is 16 feet long and 11 feet high. However, it is less than a complete rectangle, so the area should be less than 16 • 11 or 176 feet. Since 162.3 is less than 176, the answer is reasonable.

Analyze The Strategy

1. Explain why simplifying this problem is a good strategy to solve this problem.
2. Describe another way that the problem could have been solved.
3. **WRITING IN MATH** Write a problem that can be solved by breaking it down into simpler problems. Solve the problem and explain your answer.

Mixed Problem Solving

Solve Exercises 4–5. Use the *solve a simpler problem* strategy.

4. **LANDSCAPING** Mr. James is installing a circular sidewalk around a flower bed, as shown. What is the area, in square feet, of the sidewalk? Use 3.14 for π.

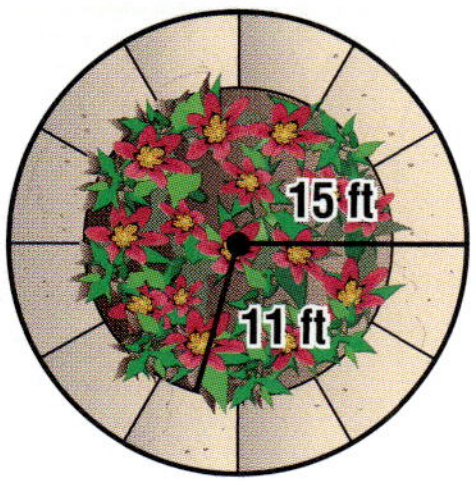

5. **COMMUNICATION** According to a recent report, one city has 2,945,000 phone lines assigned to three different area codes. Approximately how many of the phone lines are assigned to each area code?

Area Code	Percent
888	44.3%
777	23.7%
555	31.5%

Use any strategy to solve Exercises 6–9. Some strategies are shown below.

PROBLEM-SOLVING STRATEGIES
- Use the four-step plan.
- Eliminate possibilities.
- Draw a diagram.
- Solve a simpler problem.

6. **SALES** Dee needs to sell \$3,000 in ads for the school newspaper. The prices of the ads and the number of ads that she has sold are shown in the table. Which is the smallest single ad she could sell in order to meet her quota?

Ad Size	Cost per Ad	Number Sold
quarter-page	\$75	15
half-page	\$125	8
full-page	\$175	4

7. **AREA** Morgan is painting one wall in her room, as shown by the shaded region below. What is the area that she is painting?

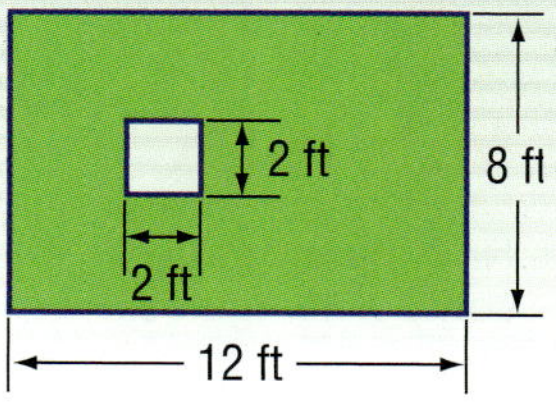

A 92 ft^2

B 94 ft^2

C 96 ft^2

D 100 ft^2

8. **MUSIC** On Mondays, you practice piano for 45 minutes. For each successive day of the week, you practice $\frac{1}{3}$ hour more than the day before. How many hours and minutes do you practice the piano on Saturdays?

9. **TELEVISION** The graph shows the results of a survey in which 365,750 people were asked to name their favorite television programs. About how many people chose sitcoms as their favorite?

Favorite TV Shows

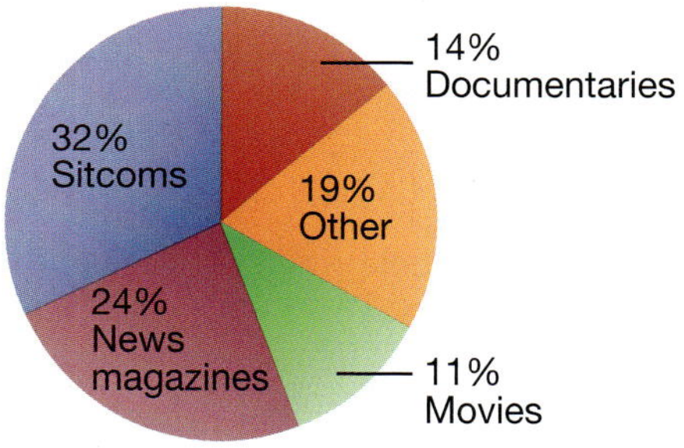

Select the Operation

For Exercises 10 and 11, select the appropriate operation(s) to solve the problem. Justify your selection(s) and solve the problem.

10. **THEATER** Mr. Marquez is purchasing new fabric for curtains for a theatrical company. The front of the stage is 15 yards wide and 5 yards high. The fabric is sold on bolts that are 60 inches wide and 20 yards long. How many bolts are needed to make the curtains?

11. **WORK** For every 150 hours Clark works, he receives 10 hours of vacation time. How many hours has he worked if he has 108 vacation hours?

12-6 Area of Composite Figures

Main IDEA

Find the areas of composite figures.

Targeted TEKS **7.9** The student solves application problems involving estimation and measurement. **(A) estimate measurements and solve application problems involving** length (including perimeter and circumference) and **area of polygons and other shapes.**

NEW Vocabulary

composite figure
semicircle

Vocabulary Link
Composite
Everyday Use a whole made up of distinct parts
Math Use a figure made of triangles, quadrilaterals, semicircles, and other two-dimensional figures

GET READY for the Lesson

ARCHITECTURE Rooms in a house are not always square or rectangular, as shown in the diagram.

1. Describe the shape of the kitchen.
2. How could you determine the area of the kitchen?
3. How could you determine the total square footage of a house with rooms shaped like these?

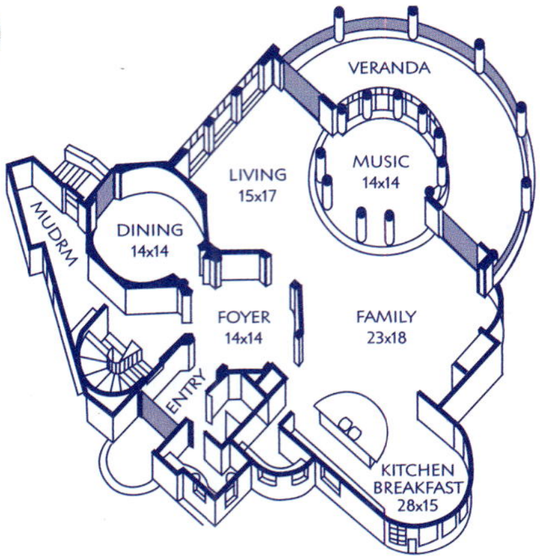

A **composite figure** is made of triangles, quadrilaterals, semicircles, and other two-dimensional figures. A **semicircle** is half of a circle.

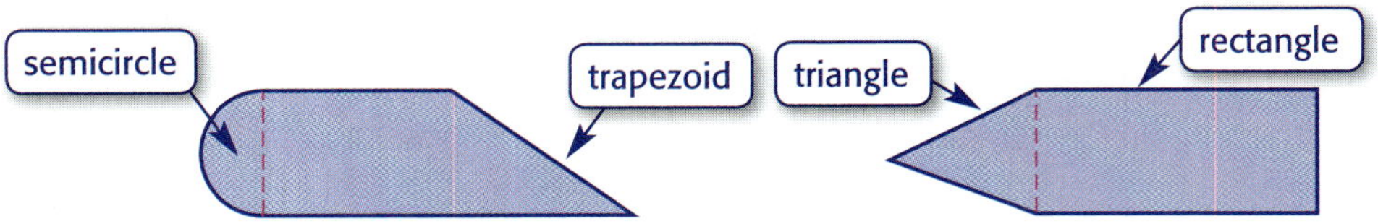

To find the area of a composite figure, separate it into figures with areas you know how to find, and then add those areas.

EXAMPLE Find the Area of a Composite Figure

1 **Find the area of the figure at the right.**

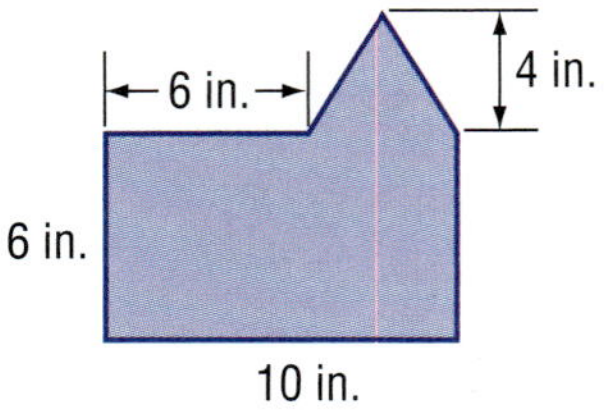

The figure can be separated into a rectangle and a triangle. Find the area of each.

Area of Rectangle

$A = \ell w$

$A = 10 \cdot 6$ or 60

Area of Triangle

$A = \frac{1}{2}bh$

$A = \frac{1}{2}(4)(4)$ or 8

The base of the triangle is 10 − 6 or 4 inches.

The area is 60 + 8 or 68 square inches.

CHECK Your Progress **Find the area of each figure.**

a.

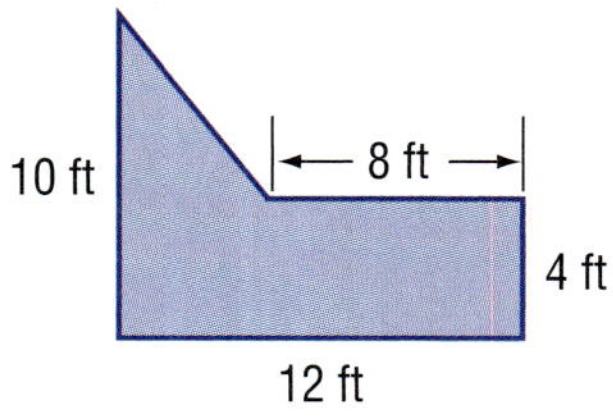

b.

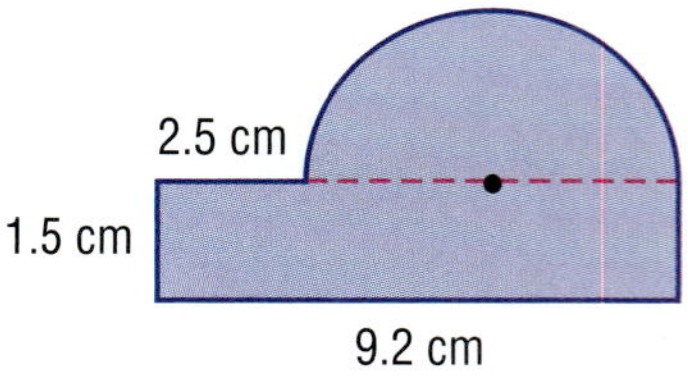

Real-World EXAMPLE

2 **ARCHITECTURE** **Refer to the diagram of the house at the beginning of the lesson. The kitchen is 28 feet by 15 feet, as shown at the right. Find the area of the kitchen. Round to the nearest tenth.**

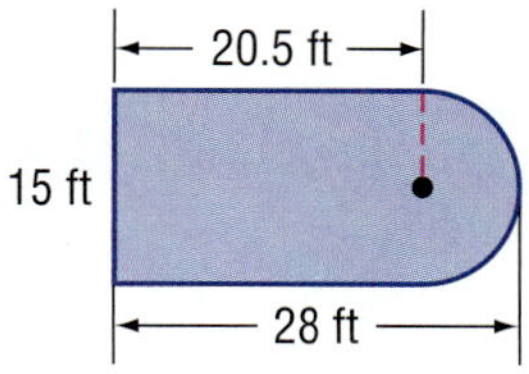

The figure can be separated into a rectangle and a semicircle.

Area of Rectangle

$A = \ell w$

$A = 20.5 \cdot 15$

$A = 307.5$

Area of Semicircle

$A = \frac{1}{2}\pi r^2$

$A = \frac{1}{2}\pi(7.5)^2$

$A \approx 88.4$

The area is approximately 307.5 + 88.4 or 395.9 square feet.

CHECK Your Progress

c. **DECKS** Find the area of the deck shown.

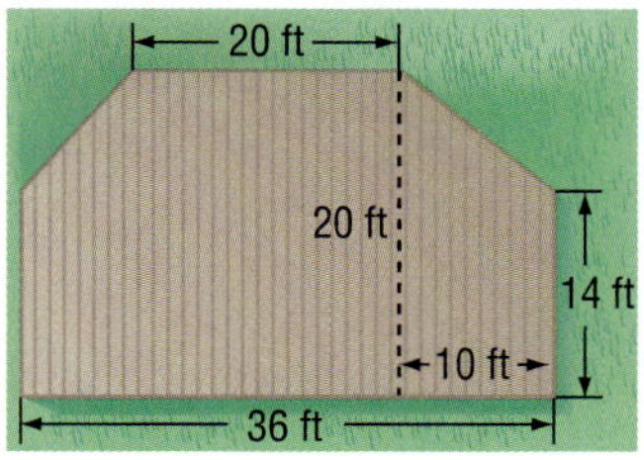

Online Personal Tutor at tx.msmath2.com

CHECK Your Understanding

Example 1 (p. 634)

Find the area of each figure. Round to the nearest tenth if necessary.

1.

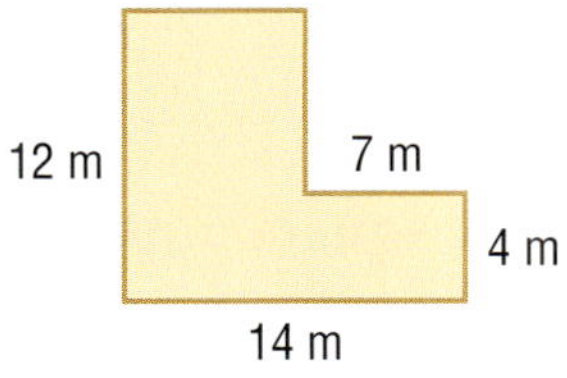

2.

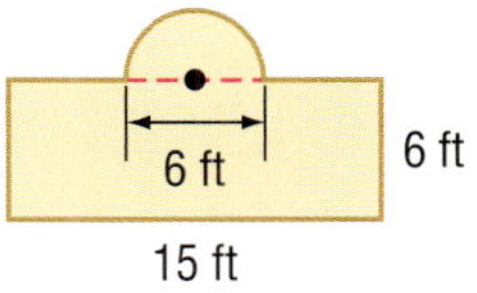

3.

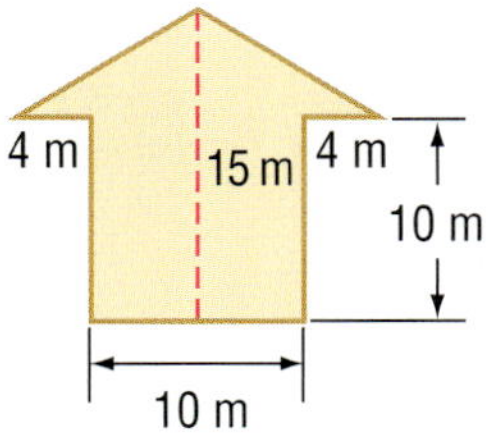

Example 2 (p. 635)

4. **APARTMENTS** The manager of an apartment complex will install new carpeting in a studio apartment. The floor plan is shown at the right. What is the total area that needs to be carpeted?

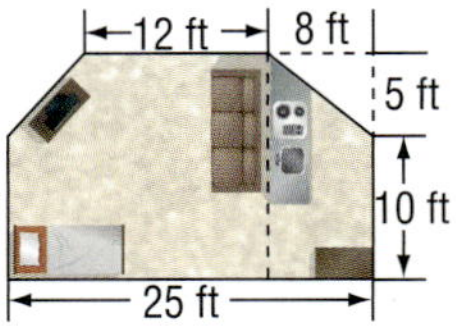

5. **TILING** A kitchen, shown at the right, has a bay window. If the entire kitchen floor is to be tiled, including the section by the bay window, how many square feet of tile are needed?

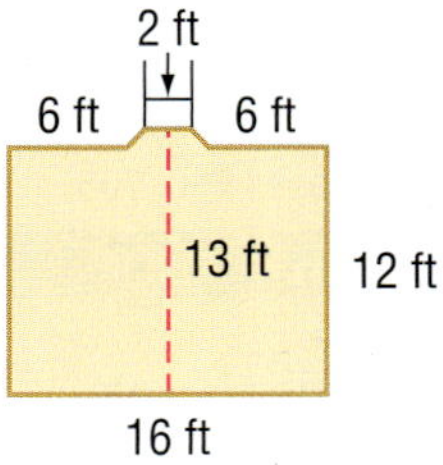

Exercises

HOMEWORK HELP

For Exercises	See Examples
6–11	1
12–13	2

Find the area of each figure. Round to the nearest tenth if necessary.

6. 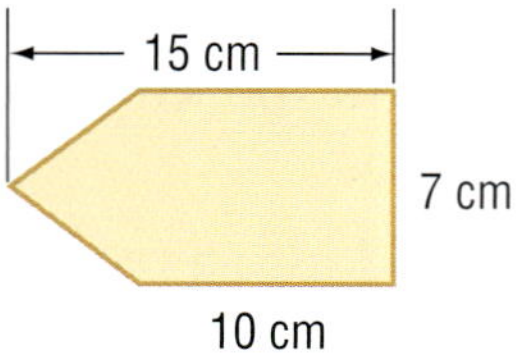

7. 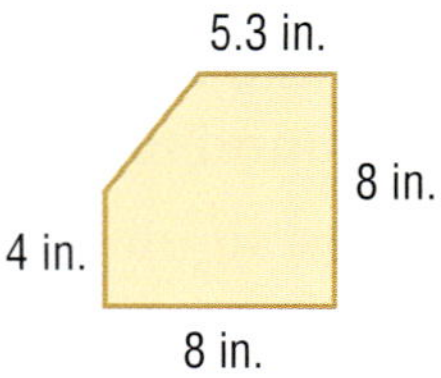

8. 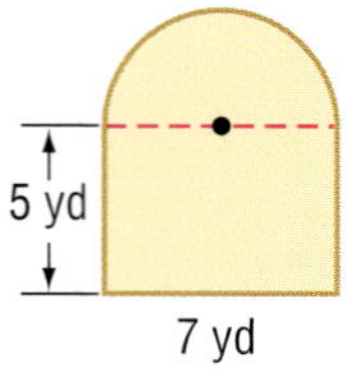

9. 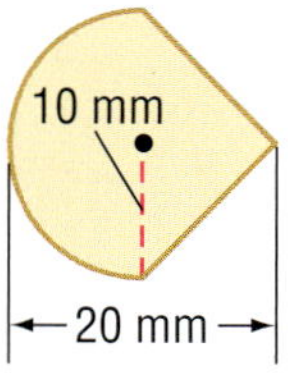

10. 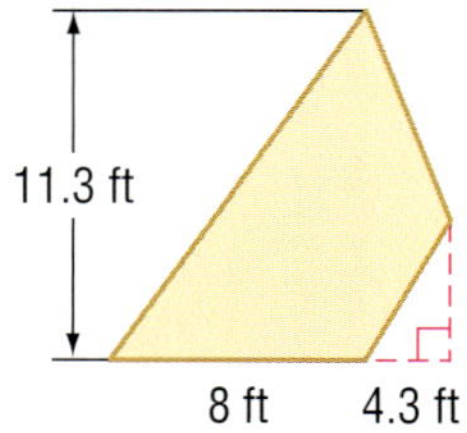

11. 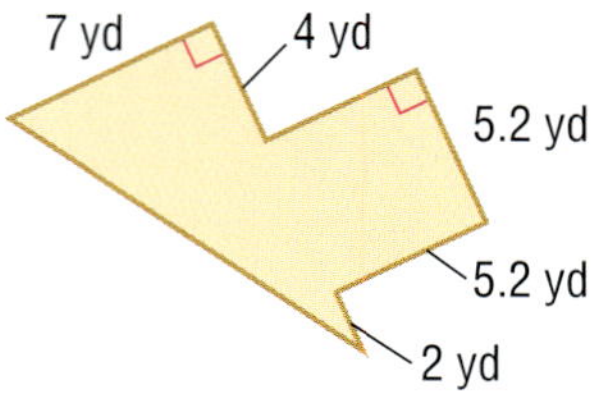

12. **BLUEPRINTS** On a blueprint, a rectangular room 14 feet by 12 feet has a semicircular sitting area attached with a diameter of 12 feet. What is the total area of the room and the sitting area?

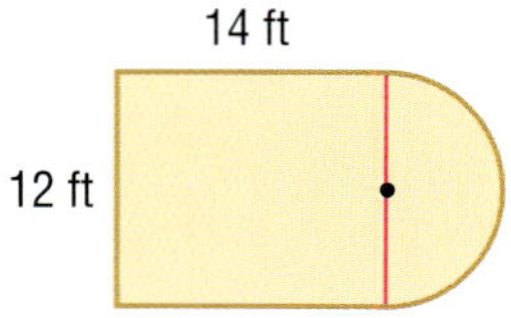

13. **POOLS** The diagram at the right gives the dimensions of a swimming pool. If a cover is needed for the pool, what will be the approximate area of the cover?

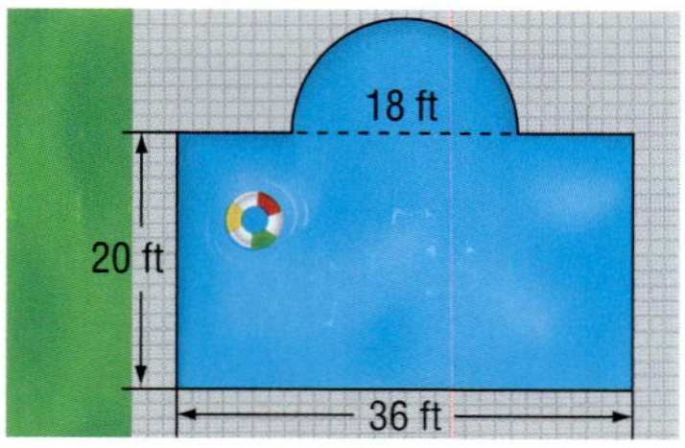

Find the area of each figure. Round to the nearest tenth if necessary.

14. 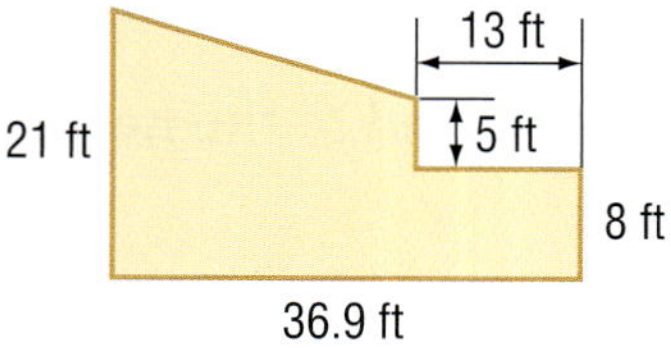

15. 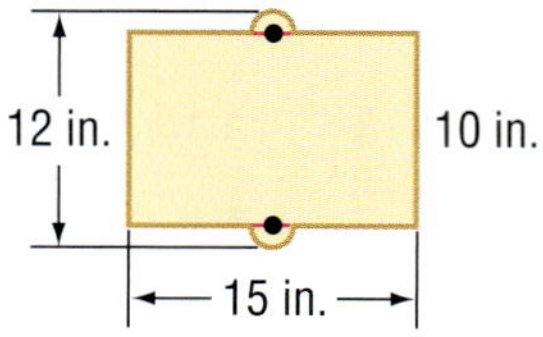

Find the area of each figure. One square unit represents 5 square feet.

16. 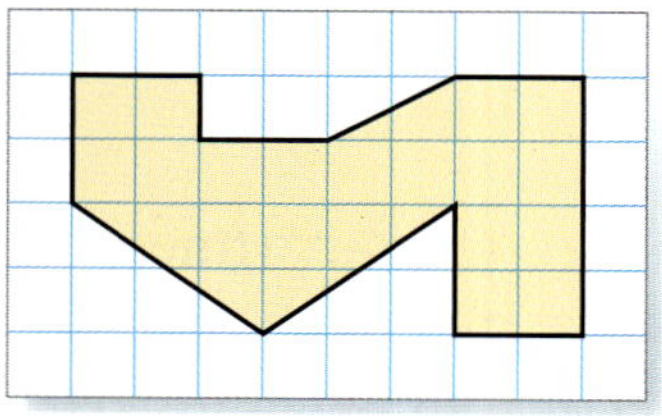

17. 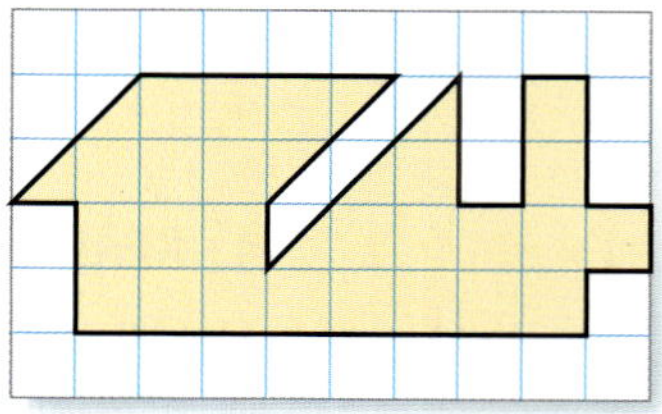

PAINTING **For Exercises 18 and 19, use the diagram that shows one side of a storage barn.**

18. This side of the storage barn needs to be painted. Find the total area to be painted.

19. Each gallon of paint costs $20 and covers 350 square feet. Find the total cost to paint this side once. Justify your answer.

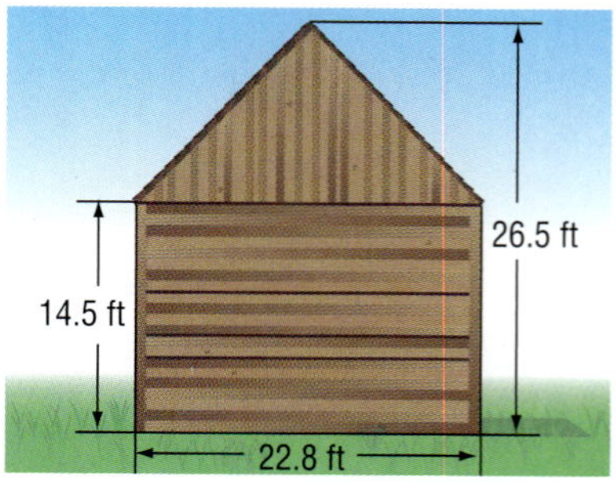

EXTRA PRACTICE

See pages 750, 766.

Math Online

Self-Check Quiz at tx.msmath2.com

H.O.T. Problems

CHALLENGE **Describe the figures each state can be separated into. Then use these figures to estimate the area of each state if one square unit equals 1,900 square miles. Justify your answer.**

20. 

21. 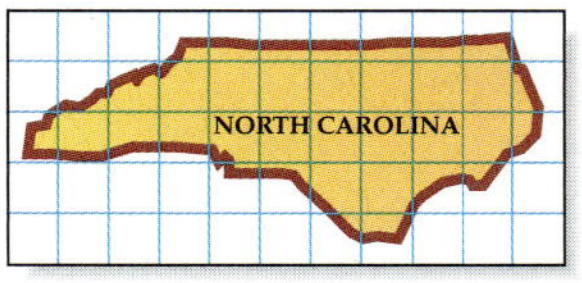

22. **WRITING IN MATH** Describe how you would find the area of the figure shown at the right.

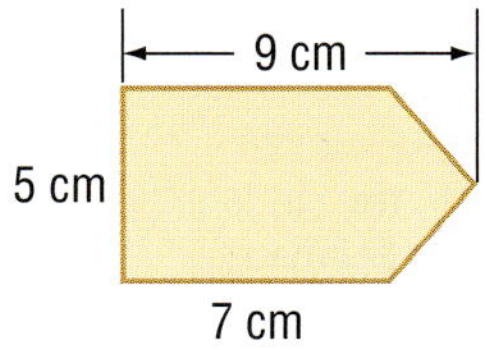

TEST PRACTICE

23. **GRIDDABLE** The Diaz family plans to separate their basement into a laundry room and a recreation room. They want to install carpeting in the recreation room and tile in the square laundry room.

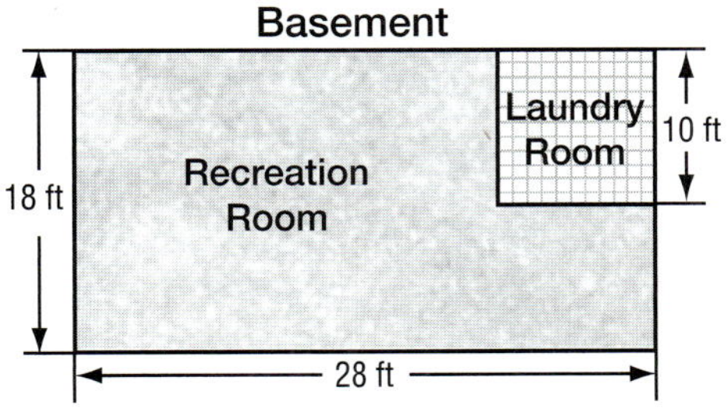

Find the area, in square feet, of the room they plan to carpet.

24. The shaded part of the grid represents the plans for a fish pond.

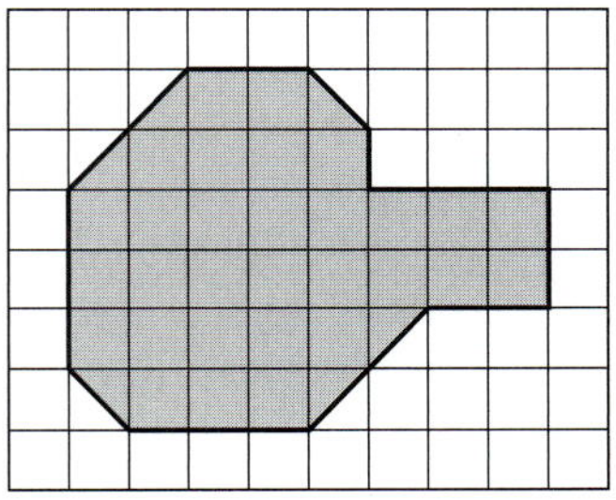

If each square on the grid represents 5 square feet, what is the approximate area of the fish pond?

A 175 ft^2
B 165 ft^2
C 150 ft^2
D 33 ft^2

Spiral Review

25. **MONEY** Over the weekend, Mrs. Lobo spent \$534. Of that, about 68% was spent on groceries. About how much money was *not* spent on groceries? Use the *solve a simpler problem* strategy. (Lesson 12-5)

Find the area of each circle. Round to the nearest tenth. (Lesson 12-4)

26. radius = 4.7 cm
27. radius = 12 in.
28. diameter = 15 in.

GET READY for the Next Lesson

PREREQUISITE SKILL **Sketch each object.**

29. ice cream cone
30. shoe box
31. drinking straw

Extend 12-6

Geometry Lab
Nets and Surface Area

Main IDEA

Use nets to find the surface area of rectangular prisms.

Targeted TEKS 7.8 The student uses geometry to model and describe the physical world. (B) **make a net (two-dimensional model) of the surface area of a three-dimensional figure.**

Suppose you cut a cardboard box along its edges, open it up, and lay it flat.

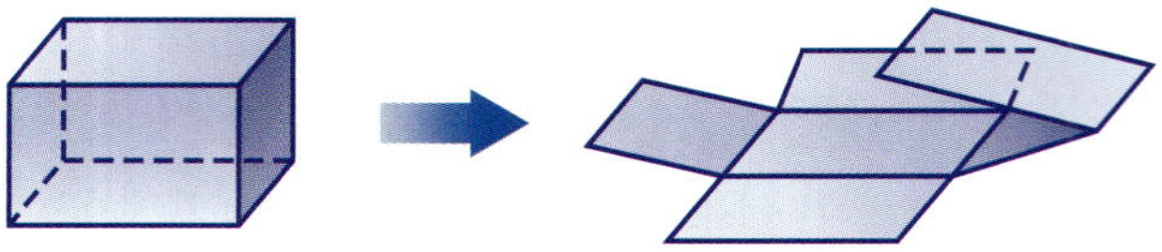

The result is a complex figure called a **net**. A net can help you see the regions or faces that make up the surface of a figure.

ACTIVITY

STEP 1 Place the box in the middle of a large sheet of paper as shown. Trace the outline of the bottom of the box.

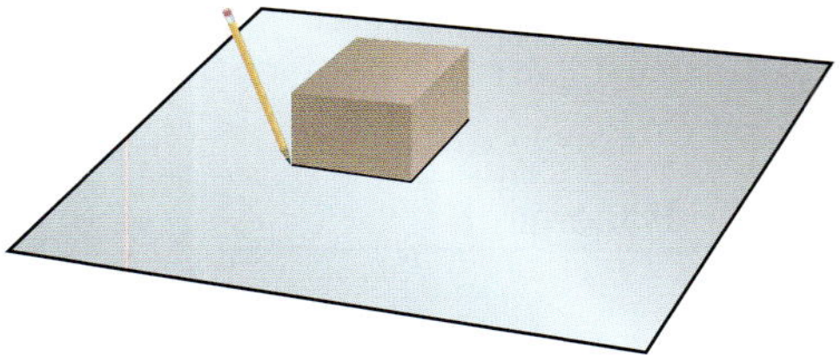

STEP 2 Roll the box onto its right side and label the outline you traced "Bottom". Trace and label each of the sides and top in this same way as shown below.

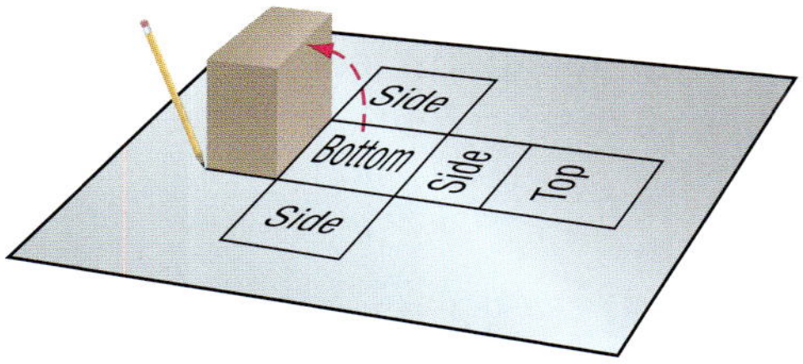

STEP 3 Cut out the resulting complex figure.

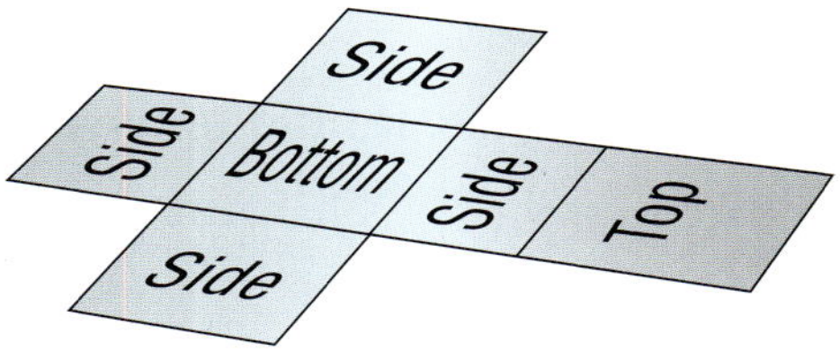

CHECK Your Progress

a–b. Make nets for two other rectangular boxes.

Check Your Net
To check that you have created a correct net for a figure, cut out the net, fold it, and tape it together to form the figure.

Analyze the Results

1. The net shown in the Activity is made of rectangles. How many rectangles are in the net?
2. Explain how you can find the total area of the rectangles.

Draw a net for each figure. Find the area of the net.

3. 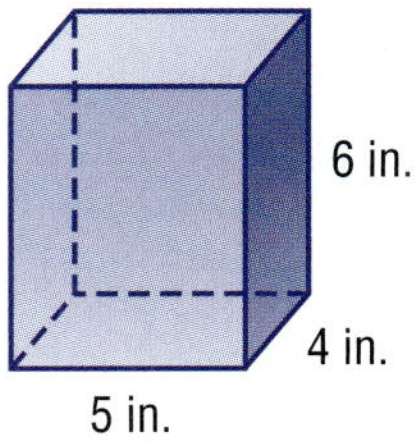

4. 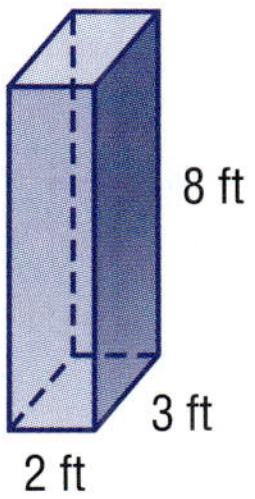

5. 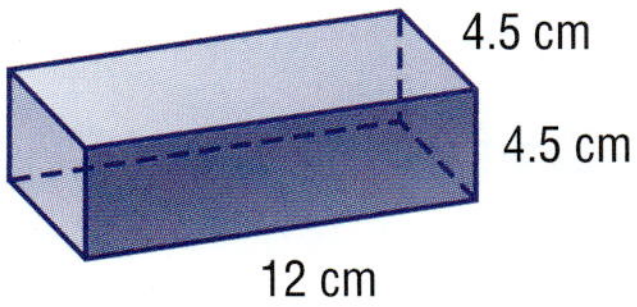

6. The *surface area* of a prism is the total area of its net. Write an equation that shows how to find the surface area of the prism below using the length ℓ, width w, and height h.

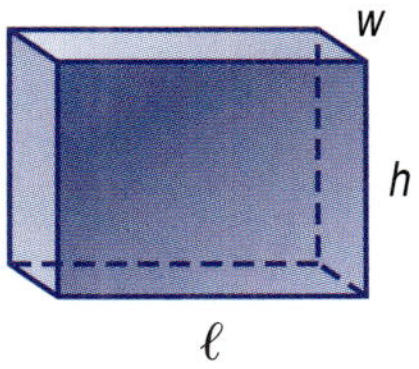

7. Find the surface areas of cubes whose edges are 1 unit, 2 units, and 3 units and graph the ordered pairs (side length, surface area) on a coordinate plane. Describe the graph.
8. **MAKE A CONJECTURE** Describe what happens to the surface area of a cube as its dimensions are doubled? tripled?

Draw a net for each figure.

9. 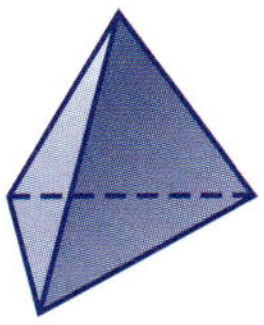
tetrahedron

10. 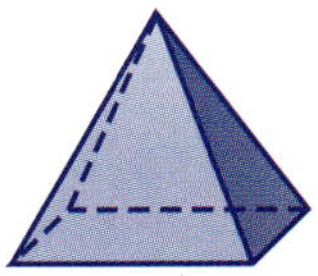
square-based pyramid

11. Explain how the net of a tetrahedron differs from the net of a square-based pyramid.
12. Describe how you could find the surface area of a tetrahedron.
13. Describe how you could find the surface area of a square-based pyramid.
14. Find the surface area of a square-based pyramid if the square base has a side length of 8 centimeters and the height of each triangular side of the pyramid has a height of 5 centimeters.

CHAPTER 12 Mid-Chapter Quiz

Lessons 12-1 through 12-6

Find the area of each parallelogram. Round to the nearest tenth if necessary. (Lesson 12-1)

1. base = 7 cm height = 4 cm
2. base = 4.3 in. height = 9 in.
3. base = $11\frac{3}{4}$ ft height = $8\frac{1}{3}$ ft

4. **TEST PRACTICE** A scale drawing of a deck is shown. What is the actual area of deck if the scale drawing is 10 m = 1 mm? (Lesson 12-1)

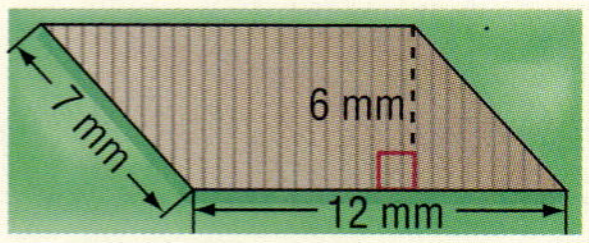

A $7{,}200 \text{ m}^2$
B 720 m^2
C 720 mm^2
D 24 m^2

Find the area of each figure. Round to the nearest tenth if necessary. (Lesson 12-2)

5.

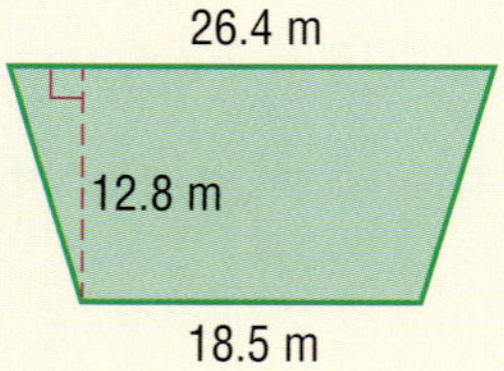

6.

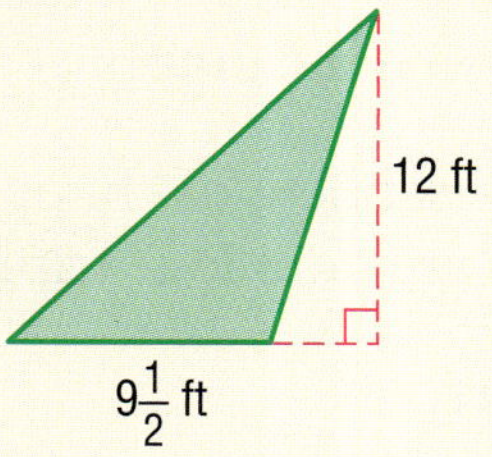

7. **ALGEBRA** Find the area of a triangle with a base of 23 centimeters and a height of 18 centimeters. (Lesson 12-2)

Find the circumference of each circle. Use 3.14 or $\frac{22}{7}$ for π. Round to the nearest tenth if necessary. (Lesson 12-3)

8. radius = $10\frac{7}{8}$ in.
9. diameter = 21 ft

10.

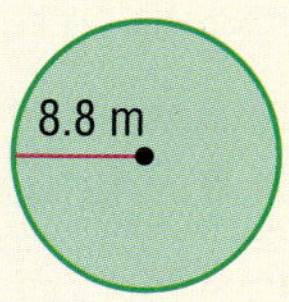

11.

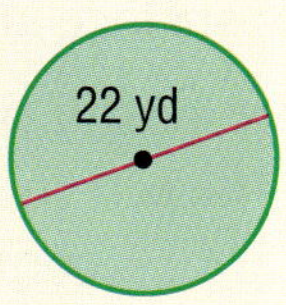

12. **TEST PRACTICE** What is the approximate circumference of a circular patio table with a diameter of 8.9 feet? (Lesson 12-3)

F 14.0 ft
G 27.9 ft
H 32.3 ft
J 55.9 ft

Find the area of each circle. Round to the nearest tenth. (Lesson 12-4)

13. radius = $4\frac{1}{4}$ cm
14. diameter = $6\frac{4}{5}$ ft
15. diameter = 14.6 m
16. radius = $7\frac{3}{4}$ yd

17. **SALES** A manager at the local cell phone store reported to his employees that sales had increased 19.5% over last month's total of \$25,688. About how much did the store sell this month? Use the *solve a simpler problem* strategy. (Lesson 12-5)

Find the area of each figure. (Lesson 12-6)

18.

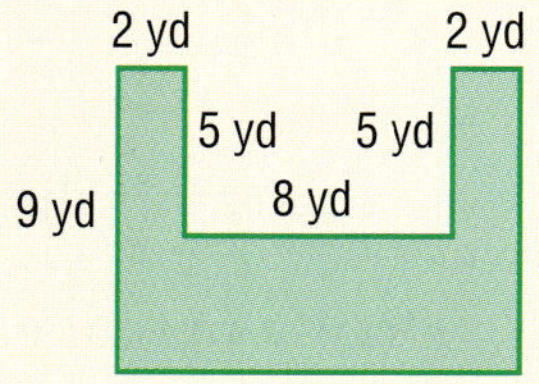

19.

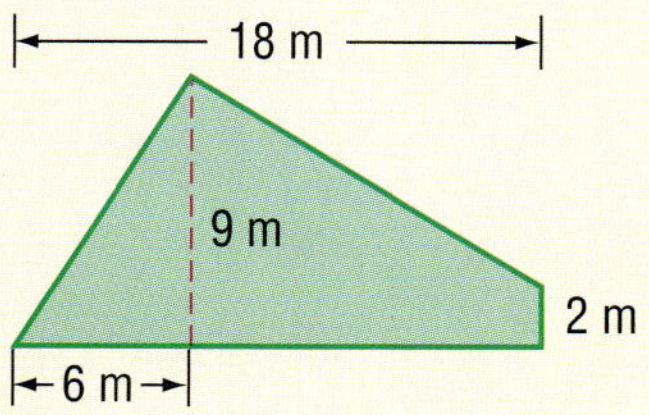

20. **WINDOWS** How many square feet of glass is needed to make the window shown? Round to the nearest tenth. (Lesson 12-6)

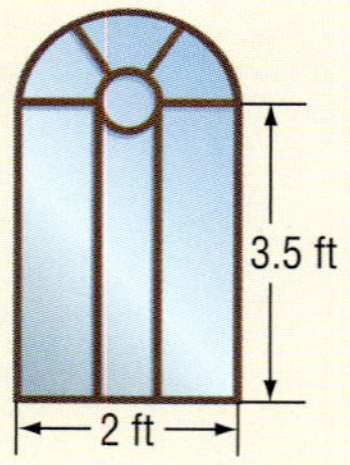

12-7 Three-Dimensional Figures

Main IDEA

Classify three-dimensional figures.

Targeted TEKS 7.6 The student compares and classifies two- and three-dimensional figures using geometric vocabulary and properties. **(C) use properties to classify three-dimensional figures, including pyramids, cones, prisms, and cylinders.** *Also addresses TEKS 7.15(A).*

NEW Vocabulary

three-dimensional figure
face
edge
lateral face
vertex (vertices)
prism
base
pyramid
cone
cylinder
sphere
center

GET READY for the Lesson

Study the shape of each common object below.
Then compare and contrast the properties of each object.

Many common shapes are **three-dimensional figures**. That is, they have length, width, and depth (or height). Some terms associated with three-dimensional figures are shown below.

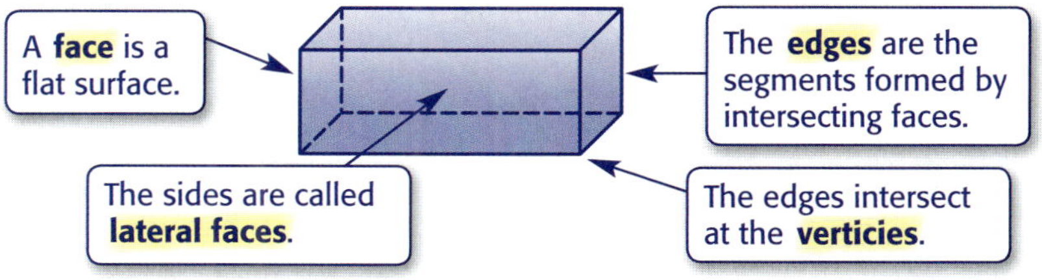

Two types of three-dimensional figures are prisms and pyramids.

KEY CONCEPT — Prisms and Pyramids

Figure	Properties
Prism	• Has at least three lateral faces that are parallelograms. • The top and bottom faces, called the **bases**, are congruent parallel polygons. • The shape of the base tells the name of the prism. Rectangular prism 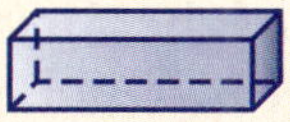 Triangular prism 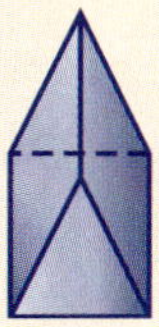 Square prism or cube 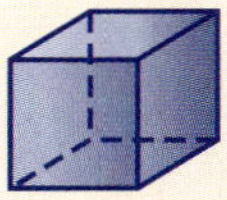
Pyramid	• Has at least three lateral faces that are triangles. • Has only one base, which is a polygon. • The shape of the base tells the name of the pyramid. Triangular pyramid  Square pyramid 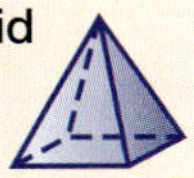

STUDY TIP

Three-Dimensional Figures In three-dimensional figures, dashed lines are used to indicate edges that are hidden from view.

Some three dimensional figures have curved surfaces.

KEY CONCEPT — Cones, Cylinders, and Spheres

Figure	Properties	
Cone	• Has only one base. • The base is a circle. • Has one vertex.	
Cylinder	• Has only two bases. • The bases are congruent circles. • Has no vertices and no edges.	
Sphere	• All of the points on a sphere are the same distance from the **center**. • No faces, bases, edges, or vertices.	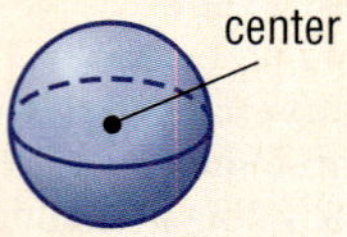

> **STUDY TIP**
>
> **Prisms and Pyramids** Prisms and pyramids are examples of *polyhedra*, or solids with flat surfaces that are polygonal regions. Cones, cylinders, and spheres are not examples of polyhedra.

EXAMPLES Classify Three-Dimensional Figures

For each figure, identify the shape of the base(s). Then classify the figure.

1 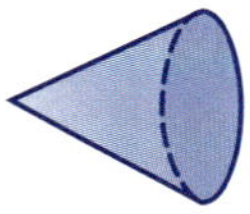

The figure has one circular base, one edge, and one vertex.

The figure is a cone.

2 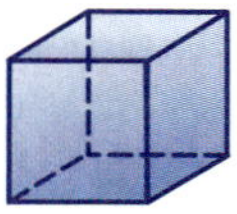

The base and all other faces are squares.

The figure is a square prism or cube.

CHECK Your Progress

a. 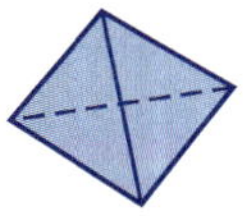

b. 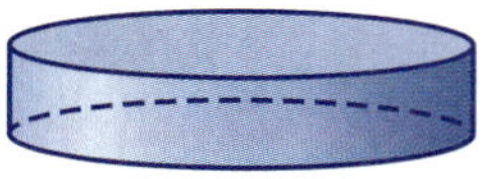

Real-World EXAMPLE

3 **CAMERAS Classify the shape of the body of the digital camera, not including the lens, as a three-dimensional figure.**

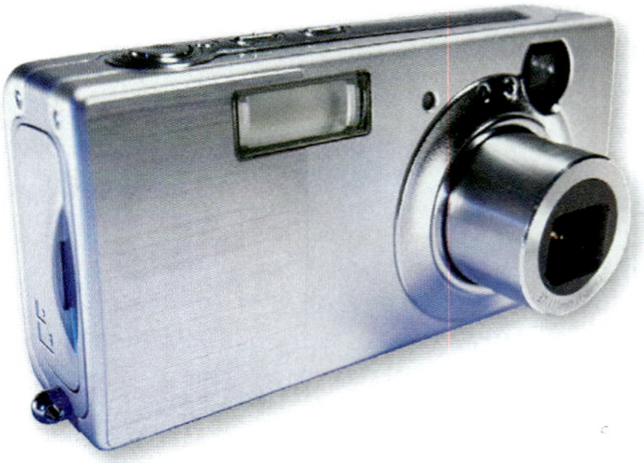

The body of the camera is a rectangular prism.

CHECK Your Progress

c. Classify the shape of the zoom lens as a three-dimensional figure.

Online **Personal Tutor at** tx.msmath2.com

CHECK Your Understanding

Examples 1, 2 (p. 642)

For each figure, identify the shape of the base(s). Then classify the figure.

1. 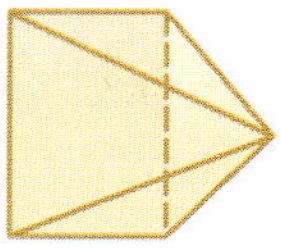

2. 

3. 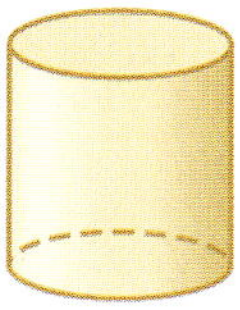

Example 3 (p. 642)

4. **SPORTS** An official major league baseball has 108 stitches. Classify the shape of a baseball as a three-dimensional figure.

Exercises

HOMEWORK HELP

For Exercises	See Examples
5–8	1–2
9–10	3

For each figure, identify the shape of the base(s). Then classify the figure.

5. 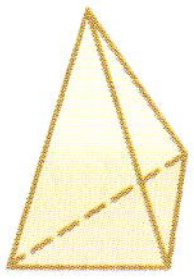

6. 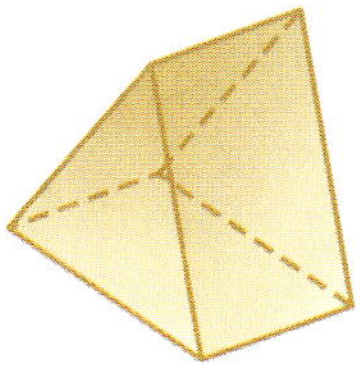

7. 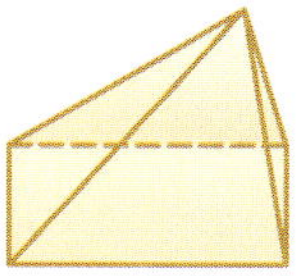

8. 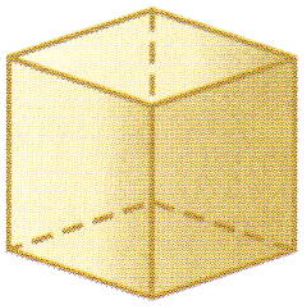

9. **FOOD** What three-dimensional figure describes the item shown?

10. **SCHOOL SUPPLIES** Classify the shape of your math textbook as a three-dimensional figure.

For each figure, identify the shape of the base(s). Then classify the figure.

11. 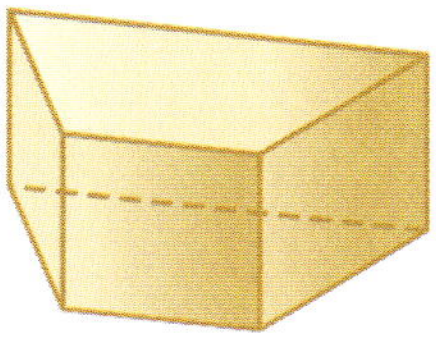

12. 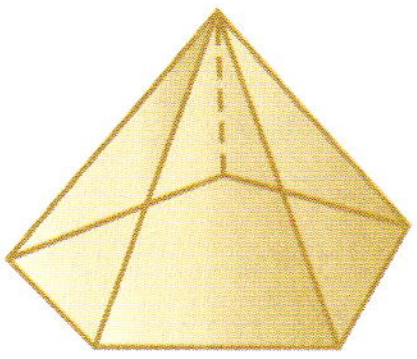

13. 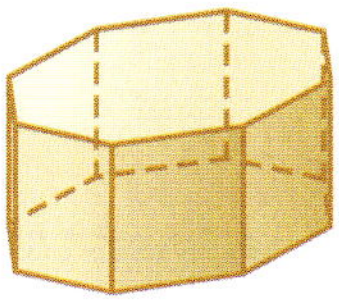

14. **SCHOOL SUPPLIES** The model of the pencil shown is made of two geometric figures. Classify these figures.

EXTRA PRACTICE

See pages 750, 766.

Math Online

Self-Check Quiz at tx.msmath2.com

15. **HOUSES** The model of the house shown is made of two geometric figures. Classify these figures.

H.O.T. Problems

16. **REASONING** Two sets of figures were sorted according to a certain rule. The figures in Set A follow the rule and the figures in Set B do not follow the rule. Describe the rule.

Set A	Prism	Pyramid	Cube
Set B	Cylinder	Cone	Sphere

17. **CHALLENGE** What figure is formed if only the height of a cube is increased? Draw a figure to justify your answer.

18. **OPEN ENDED** Select one three-dimensional figure in which you could use the term *congruent* to describe the bases of the figure. Then write a sentence using *congruent* to describe the figure.

19. **WRITING IN MATH** Apply what you know about the properties of geometric figures to compare and contrast cones and pyramids.

TEST PRACTICE

20. Which statement is true about all triangular prisms?
    - **A** All of the edges are congruent line segments.
    - **B** There are exactly 6 faces.
    - **C** The bases are congruent triangles.
    - **D** All of the faces are triangles.

21. Which figure is shown?

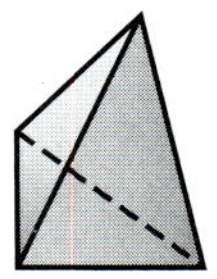

   - **F** triangular pyramid
   - **G** square pyramid
   - **H** rectangular pyramid
   - **J** triangular prism

Spiral Review

22. **GEOMETRY** Find the area of the figure shown at the right if each triangle has a height of 3.5 inches and the square has side lengths of 4 inches. (Lesson 12-6)

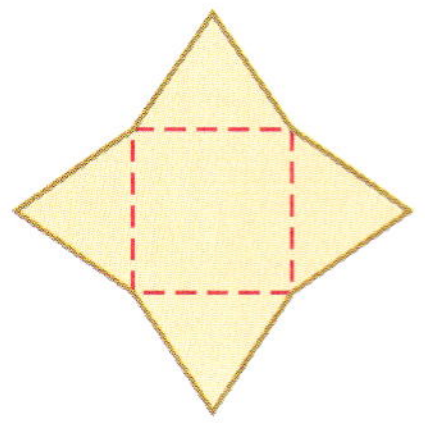

23. **GEOMETRY** Find the area of a circle with a radius of 5.7 meters. Round to the nearest tenth. (Lesson 12-4)

ALGEBRA Find the missing angle measure in each quadrilateral. (Lesson 11-5)

24.

25.

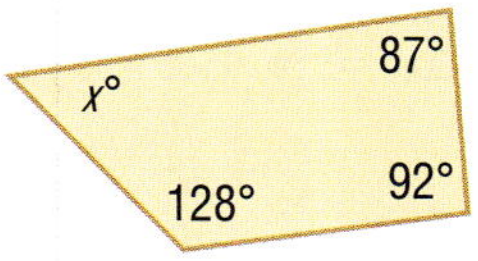

26.

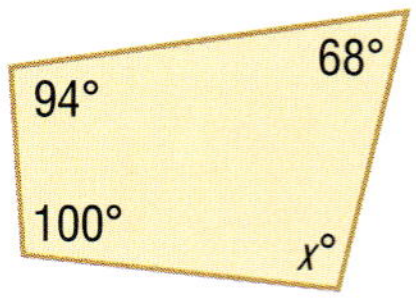

GET READY for the Next Lesson

PREREQUISITE SKILL **Describe the shape seen when each object is viewed from the top.**

27. number cube
28. cereal box
29. soup can

Explore 12-8

Geometry Lab
Three-Dimensional Figures

Main IDEA

Build three-dimensional figures given the top, side, and front views.

Targeted TEKS **7.8** The student uses geometry to model and describe the physical world. **(A)** **sketch a three-dimensional figure when given the top, side, and front views.**

Cubes are examples of three-dimensional figures because they have length, width, and depth. In this lab, you will use centimeter cubes to build other three-dimensional figures.

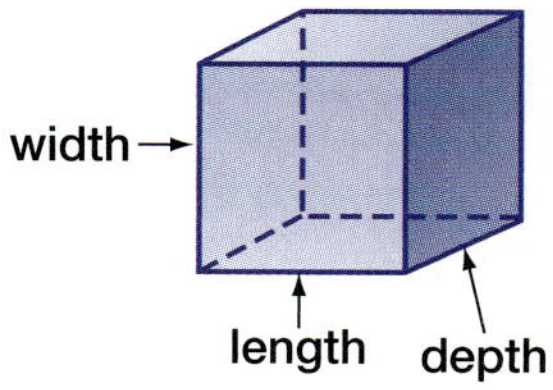

ACTIVITY

The top view, side view, and front view of a three-dimensional figure are shown below. Use centimeter cubes to build the figure. Then make a sketch of the figure.

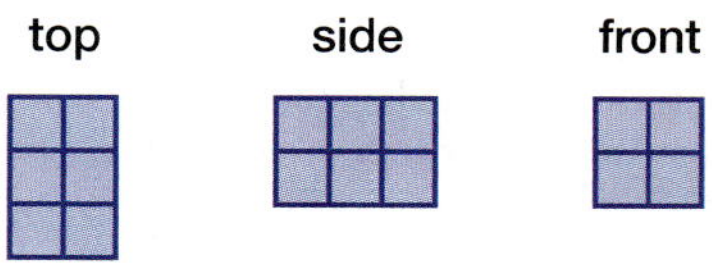

STEP 1 Use the top view to build the figure's base.

STEP 2 Use the side view to complete the figure.

STEP 3 Use the front view to check the figure.

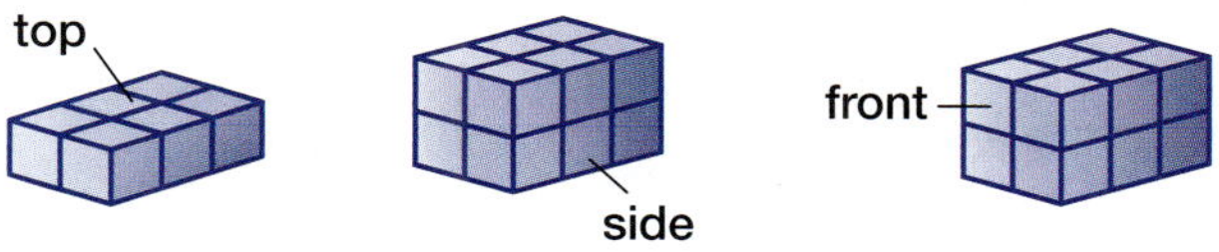

CHECK Your Progress

a. 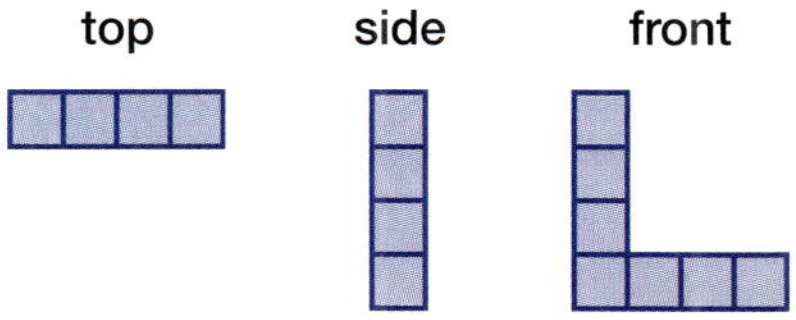

b. 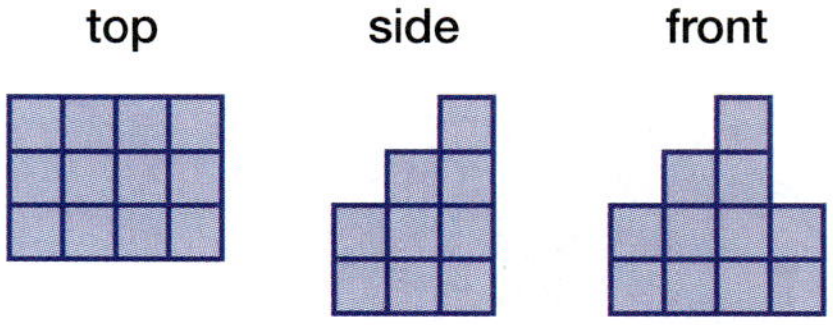

Analyze the Results

1. Explain how you began building the figures in Exercises a and b.
2. Determine whether there is more than one way to build each model. Explain your reasoning.
3. Build two different models that would look the same from two views, but not the third view. Draw a top view, side view, and front view of each model.
4. Describe a real-world situation where it might be necessary to draw a top, side, and front view of a three-dimensional figure.

12-8 Drawing Three-Dimensional Figures

Main IDEA

Draw a three-dimensional figure given the top, side, and front views.

Targeted TEKS 7.8 The student uses geometry to model and describe the physical world. **(A) sketch three-dimensional figures when given the top, side, and front views.** *Also addresses TEKS 7.8(C), 7.13(A).*

GET READY for the Lesson

Concepts in MOtion Interactive Lab tx.msmath2.com

COMICS **For Exercises 1 and 2, refer to the comic below.**

SHOE

1. Which view of the Washington Monument is shown in the comic?
2. Find a photograph of the Washington Monument and draw a side view.

You can draw different views of three-dimensional figures. The most common views drawn are the top, side, and front views.

EXAMPLE Draw a Three-Dimensional Figure

STUDY TIP

Plane Figures In geometry, three-dimensional figures are *solids* and two-dimensional figures such as triangles, circles, and squares are *plane* figures.

1 **Draw a top, a side, and a front view of the figure at the right.**

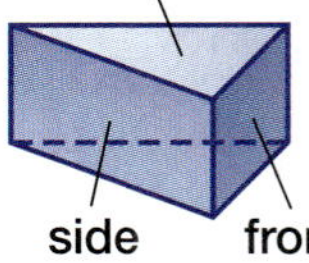

The top view is a triangle.

The side and front view are rectangles.

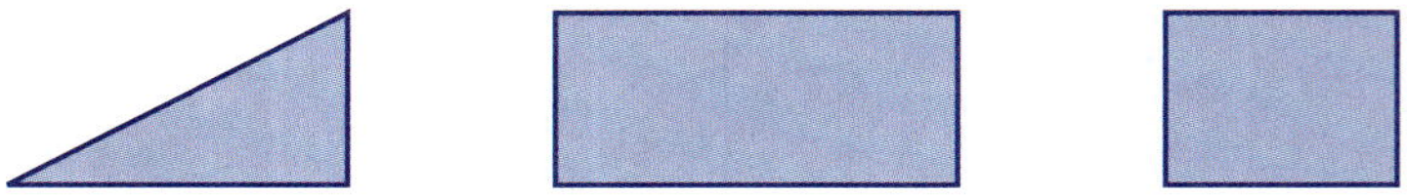

CHECK Your Progress

Draw a top, a side, and a front view of each solid.

a.

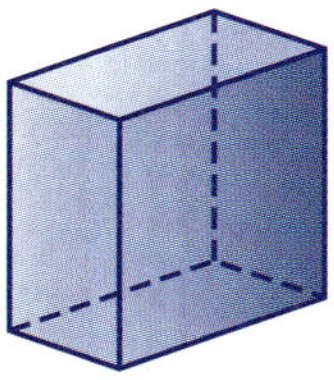

b.

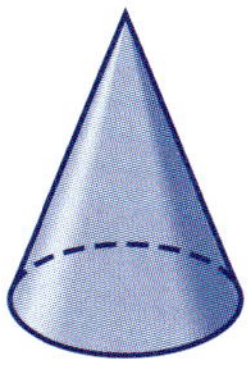

Real-World EXAMPLE

2 **VIDEO GAMES** **Draw a top, a side, and a front view of the video console shown.**

The top view is a rectangle.

The side and front views are two rectangles.

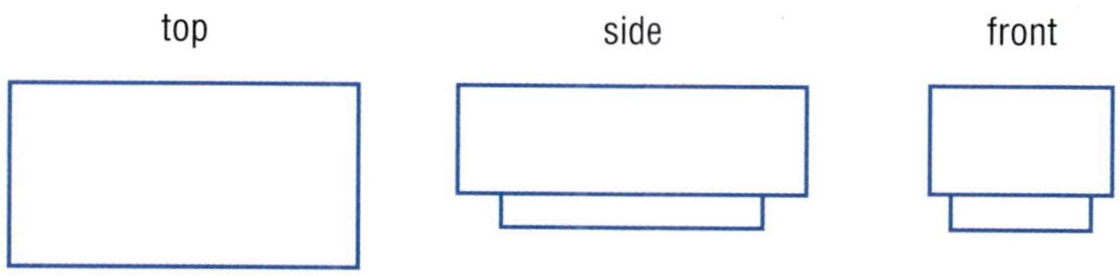

CHECK Your Progress

c. **TENTS** Draw a top, a side, and a front view of the tent shown.

Online Personal Tutor at tx.msmath2.com

The top, side, and front views of a three-dimensional figure can be used to draw the figure.

EXAMPLE Draw a Three-Dimensional Figure

3 **Draw the three-dimensional figure whose top, side, and front views are shown.**

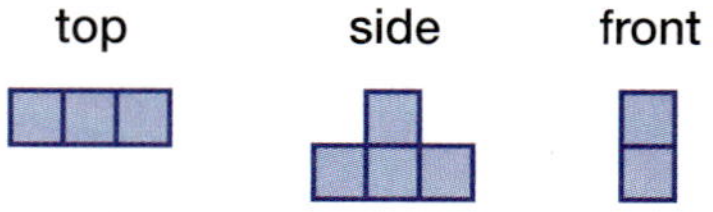

Step 1 Use the top view to draw the base of the figure, a 1-by-3 rectangle.

Step 2 Add edges to make the base a solid figure.

Step 3 Use the side and front views to complete the figure.

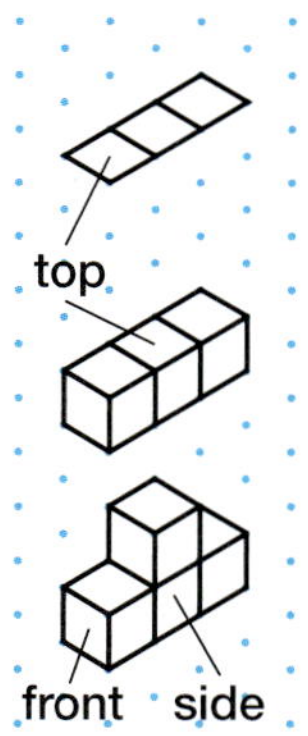

STUDY TIP

Paper Use isometric dot paper for the drawings in this lesson, as shown at the right.

CHECK Your Progress

d. Draw the three-dimensional figure whose top, side, and front views are shown. Use isometric dot paper.

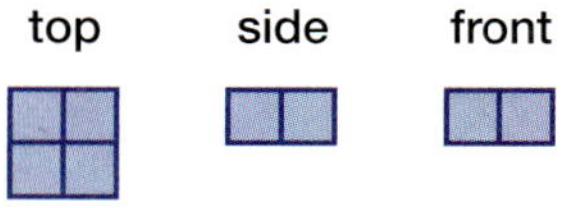

CHECK Your Understanding

Example 1
(p. 646)

Draw a top, a side, and a front view of each solid.

1.

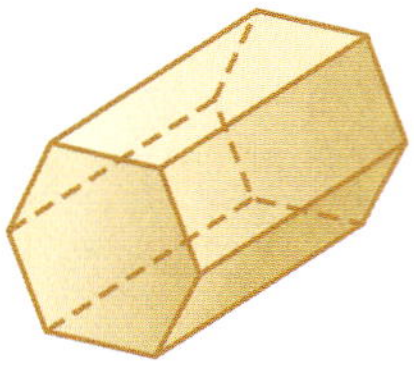

2.

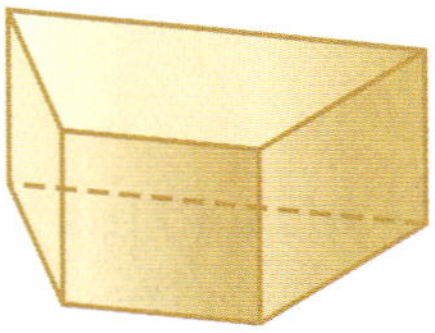

Example 2
(p. 647)

3. **SCIENCE** A transparent prism can be used to refract or disperse a beam of light. Draw a top, a side, and a front view of the prism shown at the right.

Example 3
(p. 647)

4. **Draw the solid whose top, side, and front views are shown. Use isometric dot paper.**

top side front

Exercises

HOMEWORK HELP	
For Exercises	See Examples
5–10	1
15–16	2
11–14	3

Draw a top, a side, and a front view of each solid.

5.

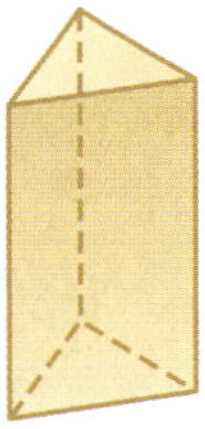

6.

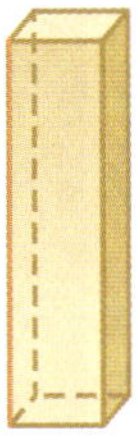

7.

8.

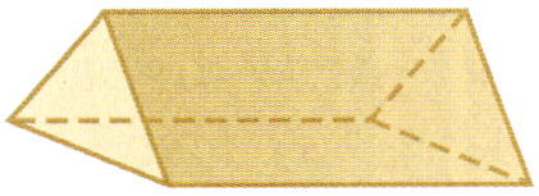

9.

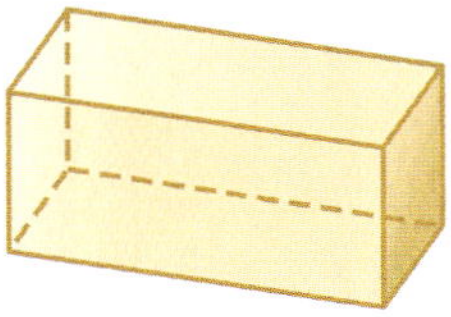

10.

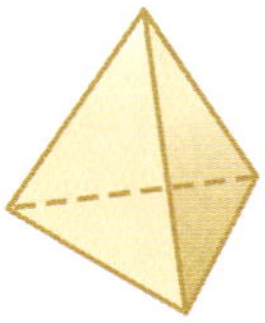

Draw each solid whose top, side, and front views are shown. Use isometric dot paper.

11. top side front

12. top side front

13. top side front

14. top side front

15. **SCHOOL** Draw a top, a side, and a front view of the eraser shown.

16. **TABLES** Draw a top, a side, and a front view of a square table.

Draw each solid whose top, side, and front views are shown. Use isometric dot paper.

17. 

18. 

19. **ARCHITECTURE** The Quetzalcoatl pyramid in Mexico is the largest pyramid in the world. Use the photo at the left to sketch views from the top, side, and front of the pyramid.

Real-World Link
The Quetzalcoatl pyramid is about 30 meters tall. It was constructed by the Mayans 1000–1200 A.D.
Source: Guinness World Records

20. **RESEARCH** Use the Internet or another source to find a photograph of the only Wonder of the Ancient World existing today, the Great Pyramid of Giza. Draw a top view, a side view, and a front view of the pyramid.

Draw a top, a side, and a front view of each solid.

21. 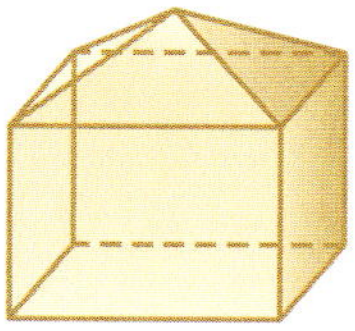

22. 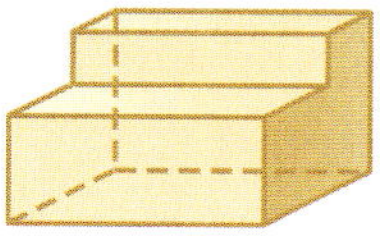

23. 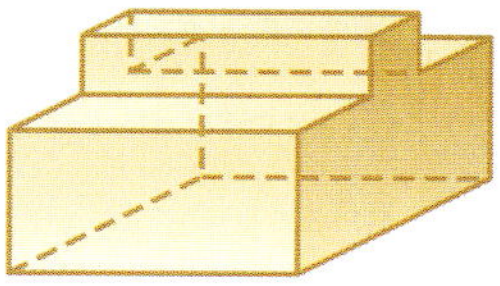

EXTRA PRACTICE
See pages 751, 766.
Math Online
Self-Check Quiz at tx.msmath2.com

24. **TRANSPORTATION** Sketch views of the top, side, and front of the school bus shown at the right.

H.O.T. Problems

25. **CHALLENGE** Draw a three-dimensional figure in which the front and top views each have a line of symmetry but the side view does not. (*Hint*: Refer to Lesson 11-9 to review line symmetry).

26. **Which One Doesn't Belong?** Identify the figure that does not have the same characteristic as the other three. Explain your reasoning.

27. **OPEN ENDED** Choose an object in your classroom or in your home. Sketch any view of the object. Choose among a top, a side, or a front view.

28. **WRITING IN MATH** Apply what you have learned about views of three-dimensional figures to write a problem about the bridge shown.

TEST PRACTICE

29. The top, side, and front view of a solid figure made of cubes are shown.

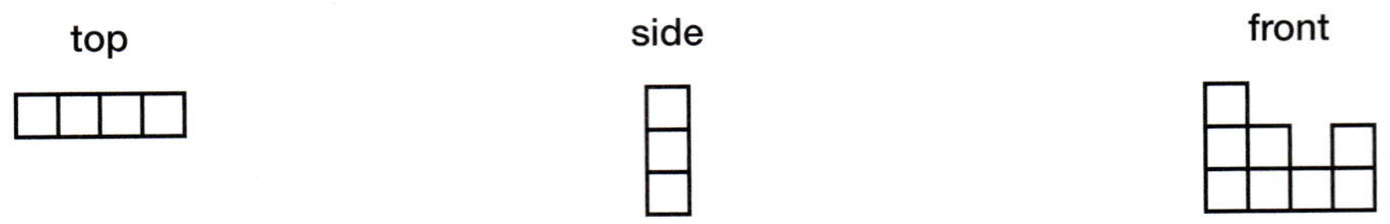

Which solid figure is best represented by these views?

A 

B 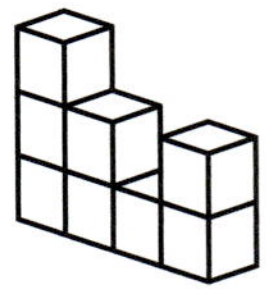

C 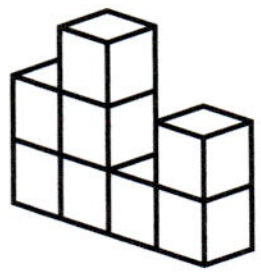

D 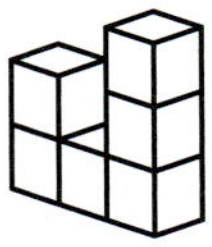

Spiral Review

Classify each figure. (Lesson 12-7)

30. 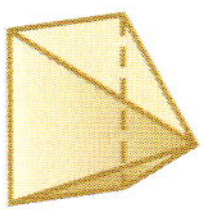

31. 

32. 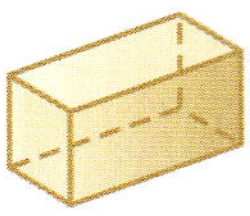

GEOMETRY **Find the area of each figure. Round to the nearest tenth if necessary.** (Lesson 12-6)

33. 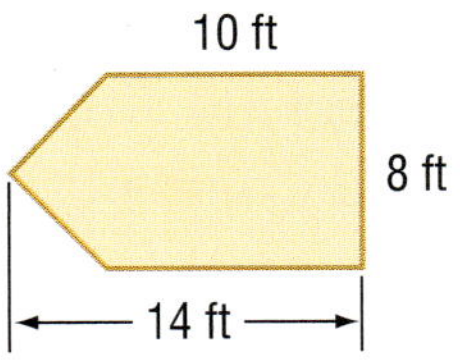

34. 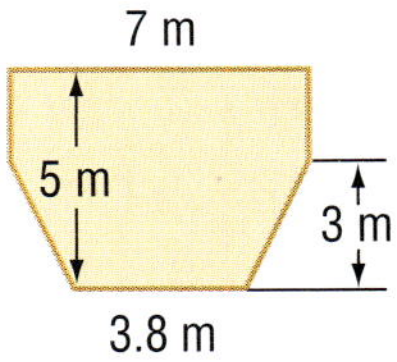

35. 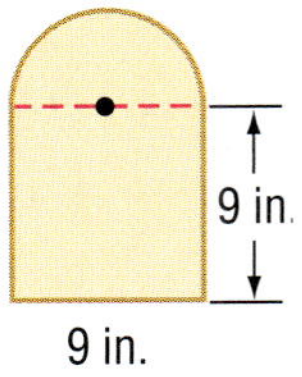

36. **STATISTICS** Jordan buys a soccer ball for \$15, a baseball for \$8, a basketball for \$18, and a football for \$19. Find the mean amount spent. (Lesson 9-2)

37. **SAVINGS** Ernesto deposited \$75 into a savings account earning 4.25% annual interest. What is his balance 9 months later if he makes no withdrawals or no more deposits? Round to the nearest cent. (Lesson 8-9)

GET READY for the Next Lesson

PREREQUISITE SKILL **Multiply.** (Lesson 6-5)

38. $7\frac{1}{2} \cdot 6$

39. $8 \cdot 2\frac{3}{4}$

40. $\frac{5}{6} \cdot 1\frac{4}{5}$

41. $10\frac{1}{5} \cdot 6\frac{2}{3}$

12-9 Volume of Prisms

Main IDEA

Find the volumes of rectangular and triangular prisms.

Targeted TEKS 7.9 The student solves application problems involving estimation and measurement. **(B) connect models for volume of prisms (triangular and rectangular)** and cylinders **to formulas of prisms (triangular and rectangular)** and cylinders. *Also addresses TEKS 7.4(A), 7.8(C), 7.9(C), 7.14(A).*

NEW Vocabulary

volume
rectangular prism
triangular prism

Vocabulary Link

Volume

Everyday Use bulk or mass, as in shipping a large volume of merchandise

Math Use measure of space occupied by a three-dimenional figure

MINI Lab

- On a piece of grid paper, cut out a square that is 10 centimeters on each side.
- Cut a 1-centimeter square from each corner. Fold the paper and tape the corners together to make a box.

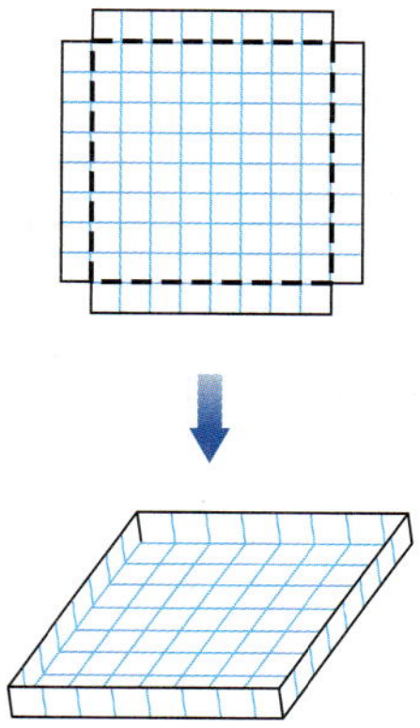

1. What is the area of the base, or bottom, of the box? What is the height of the box?
2. How many centimeter cubes fit in the box?
3. What do you notice about the product of the base area and the height of the box?

The **volume** of a three-dimensional figure is the measure of space occupied by it. It is measured in cubic units such as cubic centimeters (cm^3) or cubic inches (in^3). The volume of the figure at the right can be shown using cubes.

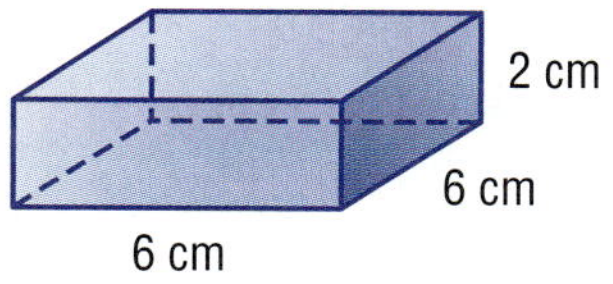

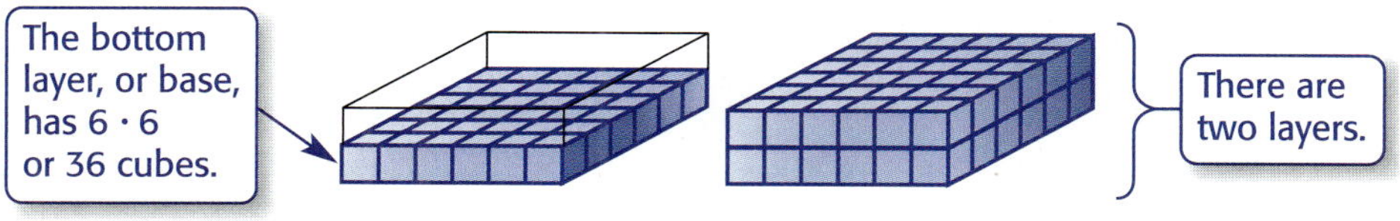

It takes 36 • 2 or 72 cubes to fill the box. So, the volume of the box is 72 cubic centimeters.

The figure above is a rectangular prism. A **rectangular prism** is a prism that has rectangular bases.

KEY CONCEPT — Volume of a Rectangular Prism

Words The volume V a rectangular prism is the area of the base B times the height h. It is also the product of the length ℓ, the width w, and the height h.

Model

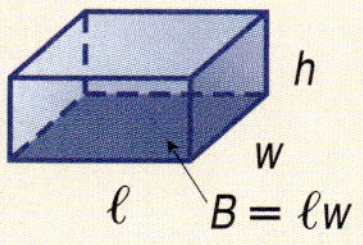

Symbols $V = Bh$ or $V = \ell wh$

You can use the formula $V=Bh$ or $V = lwh$ to find the volume of a rectangular prism.

EXAMPLE Volume of a Rectangular Prism

1 **Find the volume of the rectangular prism.**

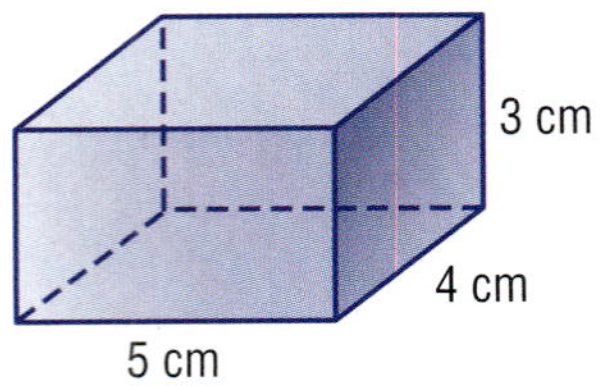

$V = \ell wh$ — Volume of a prism

$V = 5 \cdot 4 \cdot 3$ — $\ell = 5$, $w = 4$, and $h = 3$

$V = 60$ — Multiply.

The volume is 60 cubic centimeters or 60 cm^3.

CHECK Your Progress

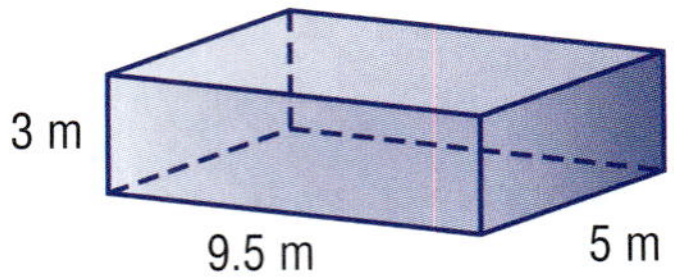

a. Find the volume of the rectangular prism at the right.

Real-World Career . . . .
Market researchers use tools such as statistics, surveys, focus groups, and product tests to determine what drives people to buy a product.

Math Online
For more information, go to tx.msmath2.com.

Real-World EXAMPLE

2 **MARKETING** **A company needs to decide which size box to use to package its new cereal. Which box shown will hold more cereal?**

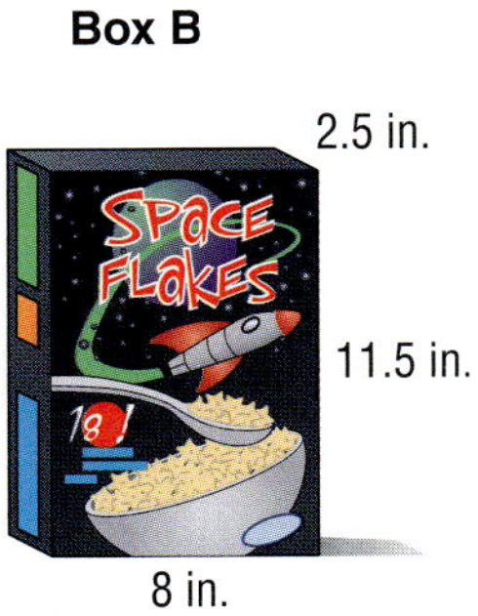

Find the volume of each box. Then compare.

Box A

$V = \ell wh$ — Volume of a rectangular prism

$V = 7.5 \cdot 2.5 \cdot 12$ — $\ell = 7.5$, $w = 2.5$, and $h = 12$

$V = 225 \text{ in}^3$ — Multiply.

Box B

$V = \ell wh$ — Volume of a rectangular prism

$V = 8 \cdot 2.5 \cdot 11.5$ — $\ell = 8$, $w = 2.5$, and $h = 11.5$

$V = 230 \text{ in}^3$ — Multiply.

Since $230 \text{ in}^3 > 225 \text{ in}^3$, Box B will hold more cereal.

CHECK Your Progress

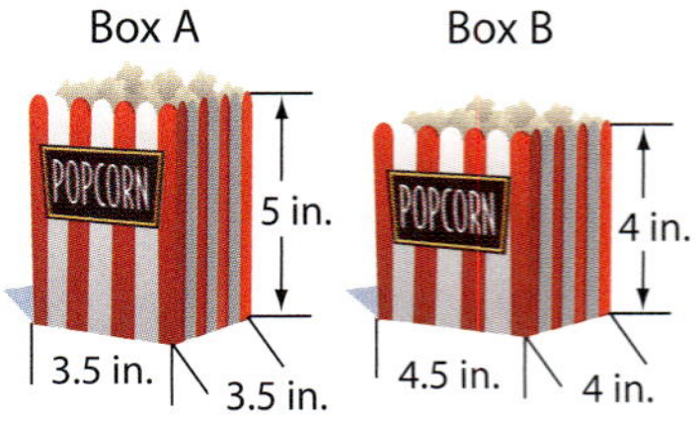

b. **PACKAGING** A movie theater serves popcorn in two different container sizes. Which container holds more popcorn? Justify your answer.

READING in the Content Area

For strategies in reading this lesson, visit tx.msmath2.com.

A **triangular prism** is a prism that has triangular bases. The diagram below shows that the volume of a triangular prism is also the product of the area of the base B and the height of the prism h.

STUDY TIP

Height Be sure not to confuse the height of the triangular base with the height of the prism.

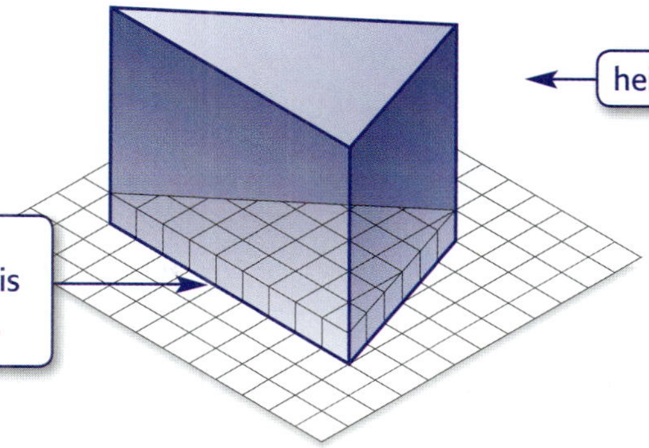

KEY CONCEPT — Volume of a Triangular Prism

Words The volume V of a triangular prism is the area of the base B times the height.

Symbols $V = Bh$

Model

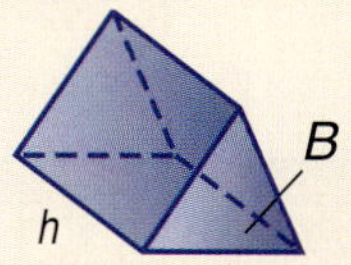

EXAMPLE Volume of a Triangular Prism

STUDY TIP

Base Before finding the volume of a prism, identify the base. In Example 3, the base is a triangle so you replace B with $\frac{1}{2}bh$.

3 **Find the volume of the triangular prism shown.**

The area of the triangle is $\frac{1}{2} \cdot 6 \cdot 8$ so replace B with $\frac{1}{2} \cdot 6 \cdot 8$.

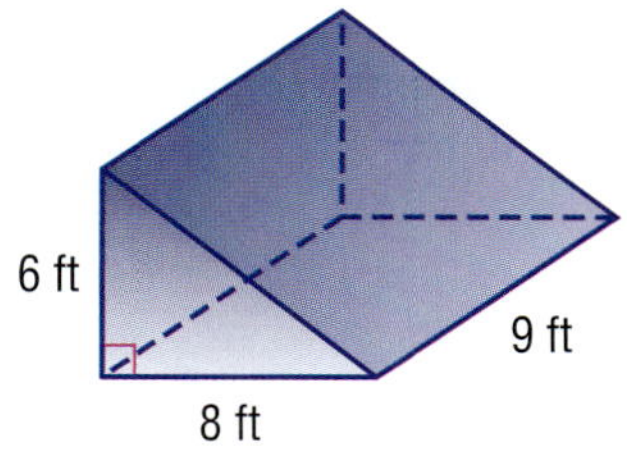

$V = Bh$	Volume of a prism
$V = \left(\frac{1}{2} \cdot 6 \cdot 8\right)h$	Replace B with $\frac{1}{2} \cdot 6 \cdot 8$.
$V = \left(\frac{1}{2} \cdot 6 \cdot 8\right)9$	The height of the prism is 9.
$V = 216$	Multiply.

The volume is 216 cubic feet or 216 ft^3.

CHECK Your Progress

Find the volume of each triangular prism.

c.

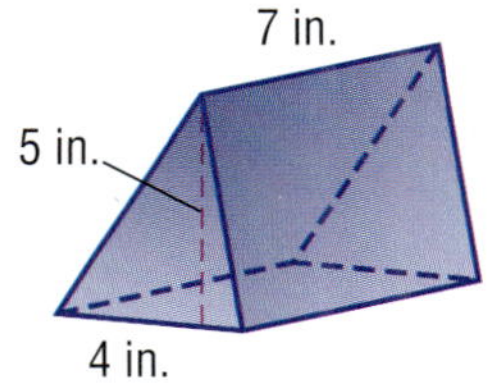

d.

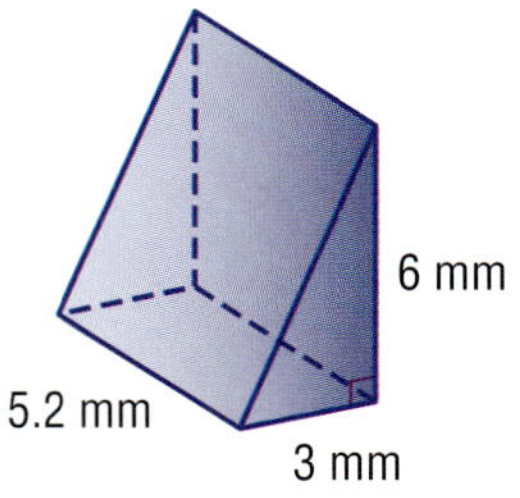

Math Online Personal Tutor at tx.msmath2.com

CHECK Your Understanding

Example 1 (p. 652)

Find the volume of each prism. Round to the nearest tenth if necessary.

1. 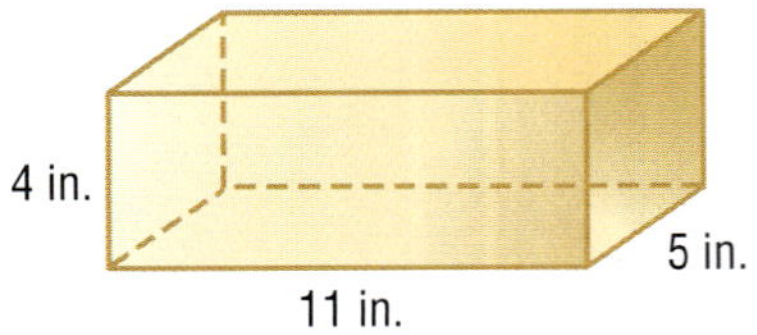

2. 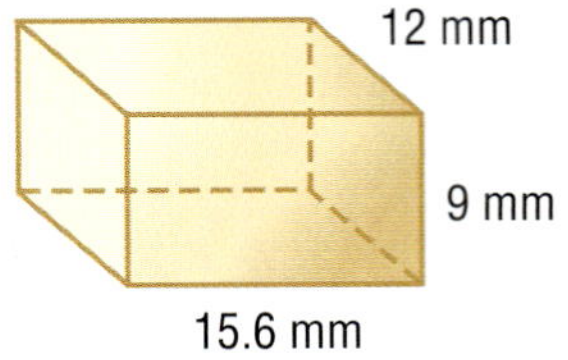

Example 3 (p. 653)

3. 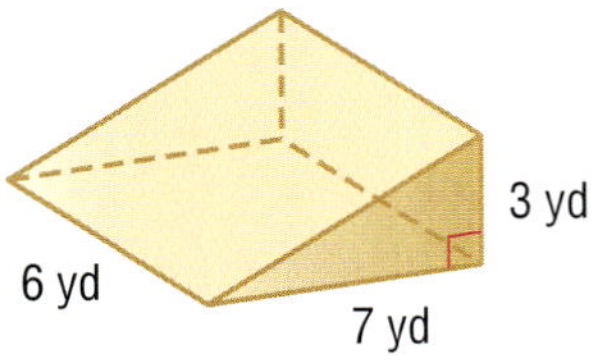

4. 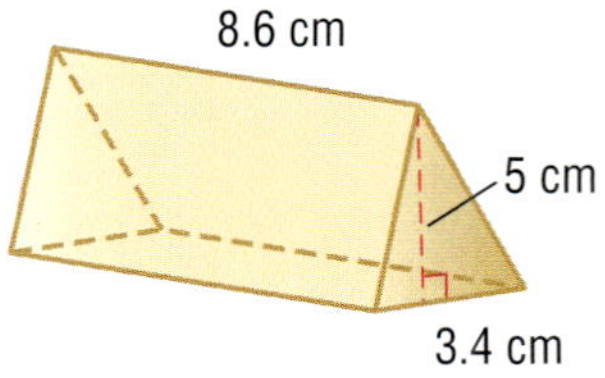

Example 2 (p. 652)

5. **STORAGE** One cabinet measures 3 feet by 2.5 feet by 5 feet. A second measures 4 feet by 3.5 feet by 4.5 feet. Which cabinet has the greater volume?

Exercises

HOMEWORK HELP

For Exercises	See Examples
6–9	1
14–15	2
10–13	3

Find the volume of each prism. Round to the nearest tenth if necessary.

6. 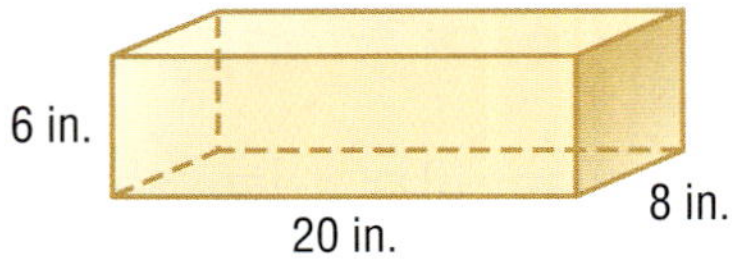

7. 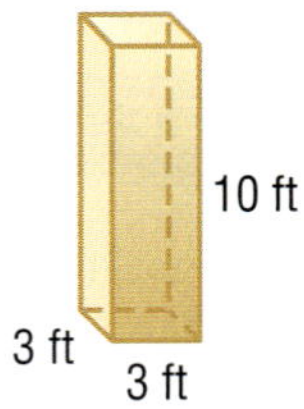

8. 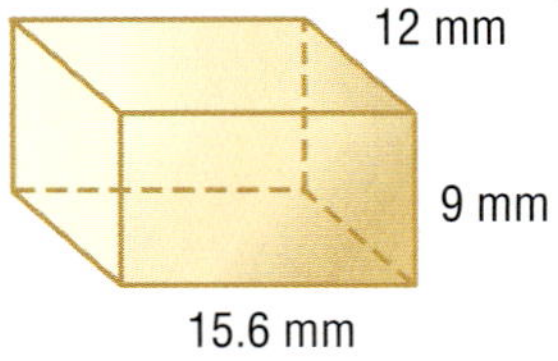

9. 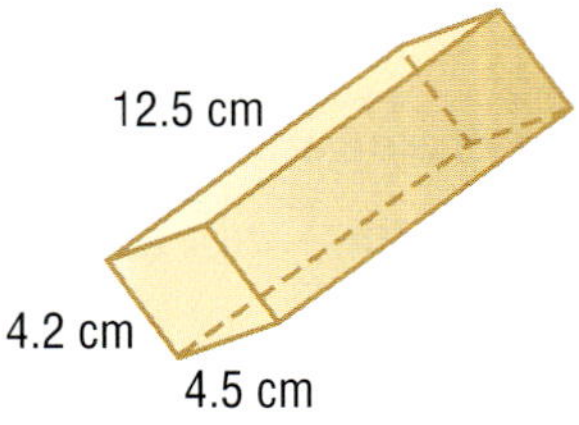

10. 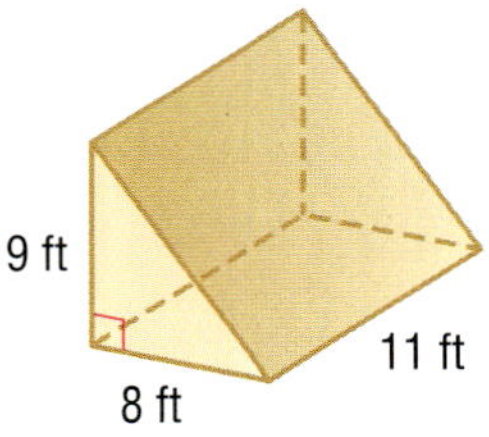

11. 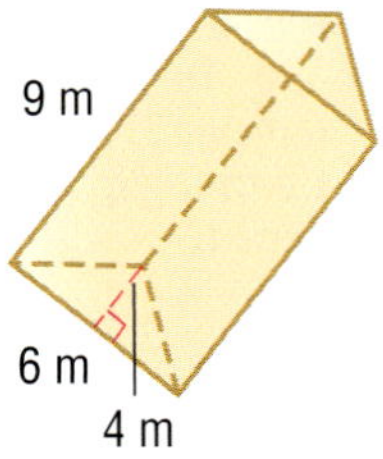

12. 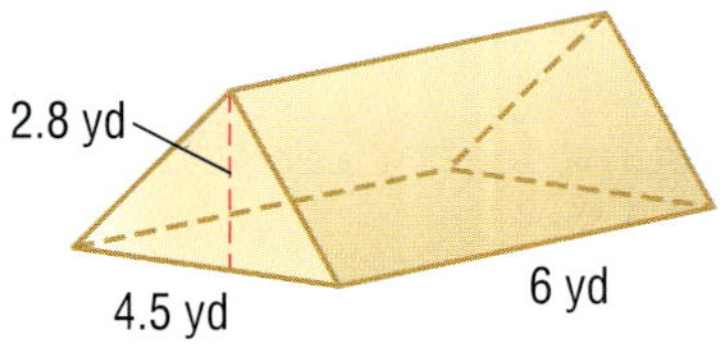

13. 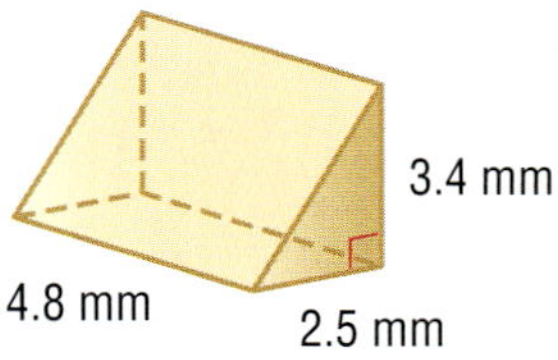

14. **PACKAGING** A soap company sells laundry detergent in two different containers. Which container holds more detergent? Justify your answer.

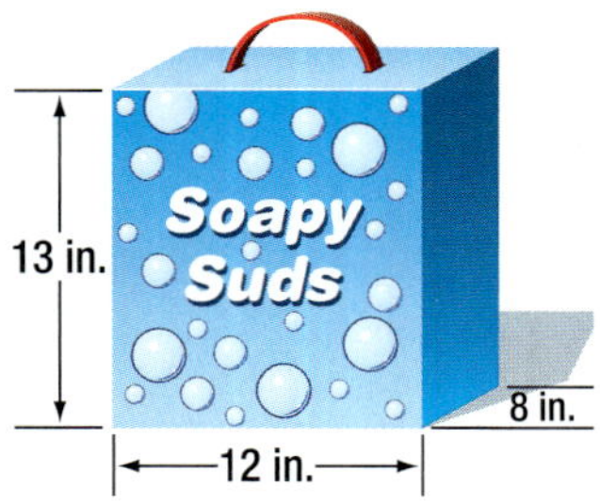

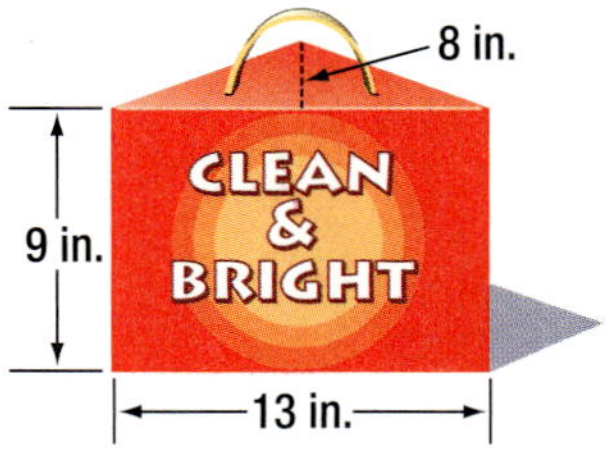

Real-World Math The Flatiron Building in New York City resembles a triangular prism.
Source: greatbuildings.com

15. **TOYS** A toy company makes rectangular sandboxes that measure 6 feet by 5 feet by 1.2 feet. A customer buys a sandbox and 40 cubic feet of sand. Did the customer buy too much or too little sand? Justify your answer.

Find the volume of each prism.

16.

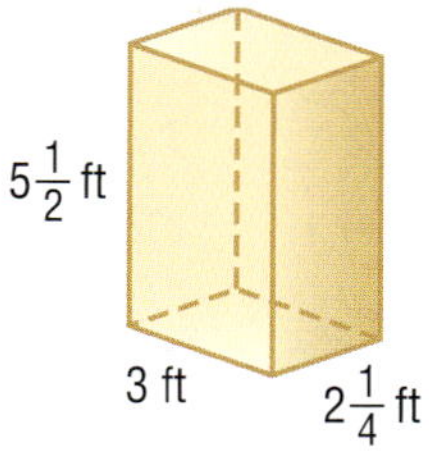

17.

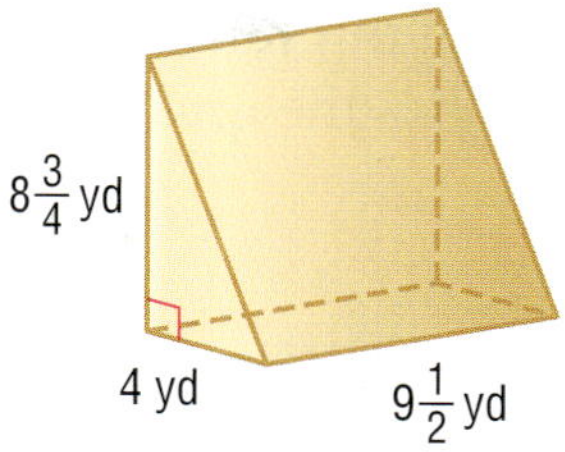

18.

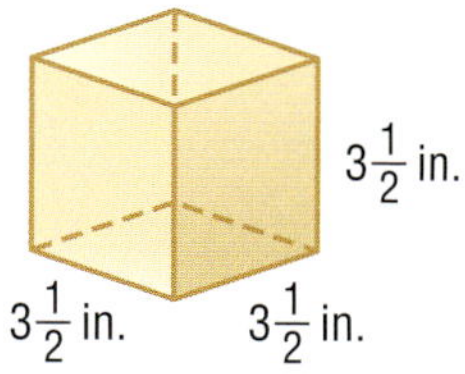

ARCHITECTURE For Exercises 19 and 20, use the diagram at the right that shows the approximate dimensions of the Flatiron Building in New York City.

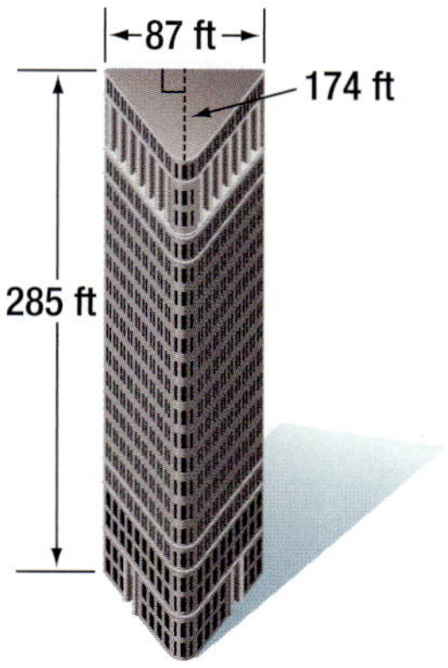

19. What is the approximate volume of the Flatiron Building?

20. The building is a 22-story building. Estimate the volume of each story.

21. **ALGEBRA** The base of a rectangular prism has an area of 19.4 square meters and a volume of 306.52 cubic meters. Write an equation that can be used to find the height h of the prism. Then find the height of the prism.

ESTIMATION Estimate to find the approximate volume of each prism.

22.

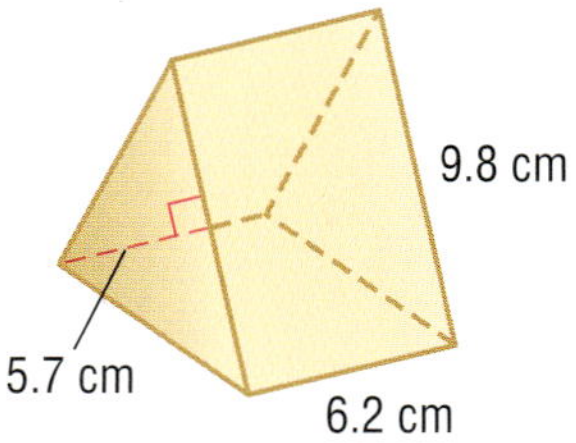

23.

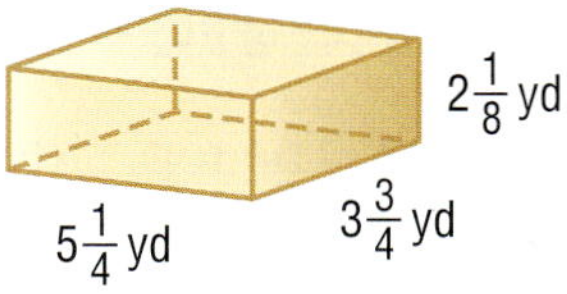

24. **MONEY** The diagram shows the dimensions of an office. It costs about 11¢ per year to air condition one cubic foot of space. On average, how much does it cost to air condition the office for one month?

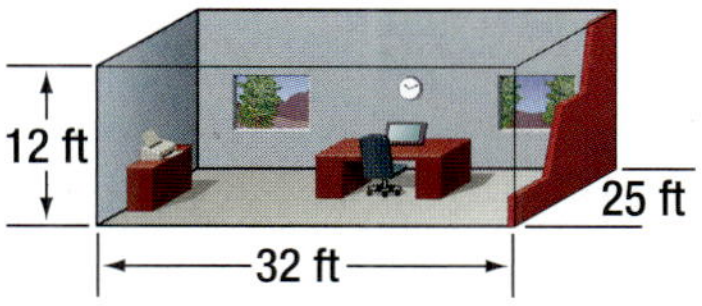

25. **POOLS** The Garrett family is building a pool in the shape of a rectangular prism in their backyard. The pool will cover an area 18 feet by 25 feet and will hold 2,700 cubic feet of water. If the pool is equal depth throughout, find that depth.

EXTRA PRACTICE
See pages 751, 766.
Math Online
Self-Check Quiz at tx.msmath2.com

H.O.T. Problems

26. **CHALLENGE** How many cubic inches are in a cubic foot?

27. **NUMBER SENSE** Without calculating, determine whether the volumes of the two prisms are equal. If so, explain your reasoning. If not, tell which has the greater volume.

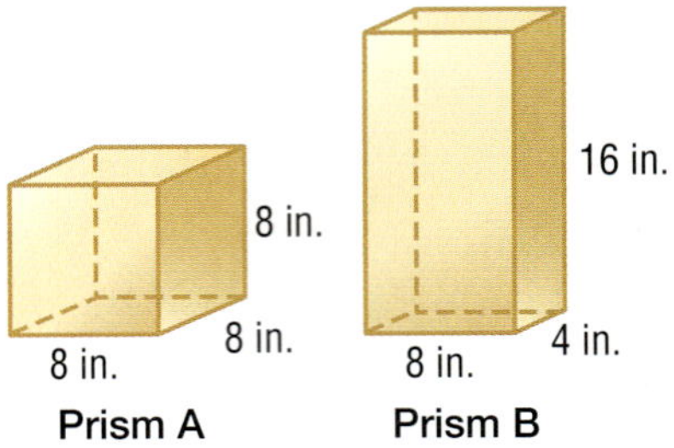

28. **WRITING IN MATH** Explain the similarities and differences in finding the volume of a rectangular prism and a triangular prism.

TEST PRACTICE

29. **GRIDDABLE** A fish aquarium is shown.

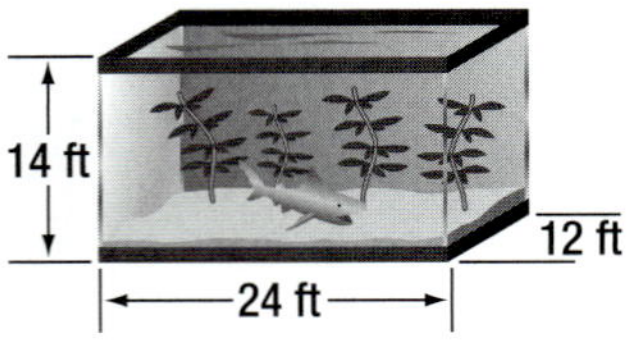

What is the volume of the aquarium in cubic feet?

30. Use a ruler to measure the dimensions of the paper clip box in centimeters.

Which is closest to the volume of the box?

A 1.5 cm^3 **C** 4.5 cm^3
B 2.5 cm^3 **D** 5.5 cm^3

Spiral Review

31. **GEOMETRY** The top, side, and front view of a geometric figure are shown at the right. Make a sketch of the geometric figure. (Lesson 12-8)

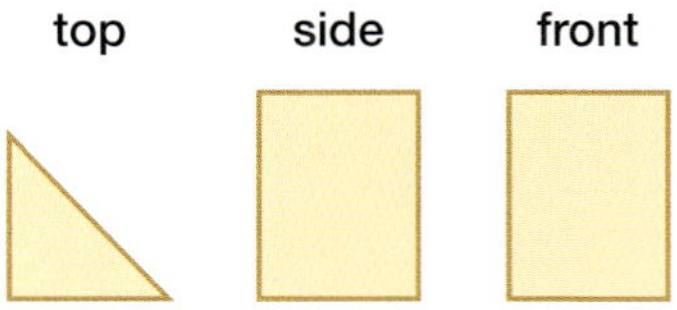

For each figure, identify the shape of the base(s). Then classify the figure. (Lesson 12-7)

32. 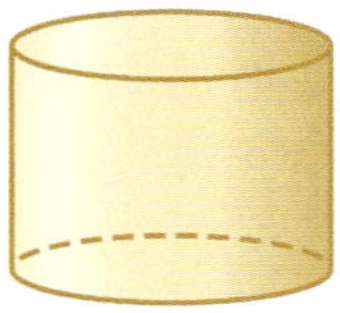

33. 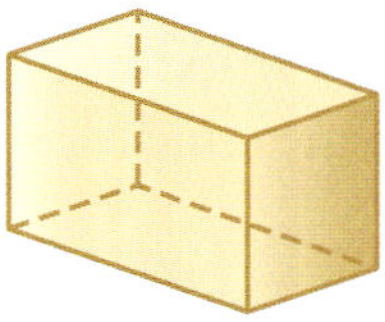

34. 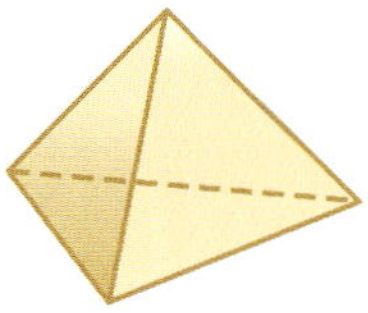

35. **RATES** A car travels 180 miles in 3.6 hours. What is the average rate of speed in miles per hour? (Lesson 7-2)

GET READY for the Next Lesson

PREREQUISITE SKILL **Estimate.** (page 712)

36. $3.14 \cdot 6$
37. $5 \cdot 2.7^2$
38. $9.1 \cdot 8.3$
39. $3.1 \cdot 1.75^2 \cdot 2$

12-10 Volume of Cylinders

Main IDEA

Find the volumes of cylinders.

Targeted TEKS 7.9 The student solves application problems involving estimation and measurement. **(B) connect models for volume of** prisms (triangular and rectangular) and **cylinders to formulas of** prisms (triangular and rectangular) and **cylinders**. *Also addresses TEKS 7.4(A), 7.9(C).*

MINI Lab

Set a soup can on a piece of grid paper and trace around the base, as shown at the right.

1. Estimate the number of centimeter cubes that would fit at the bottom of the can. Include parts of cubes.
2. If each layer is 1 centimeter high, how many layers would it take to fill the cylinder.
3. **MAKE A CONJECTURE** How can you find the volume of the soup can?

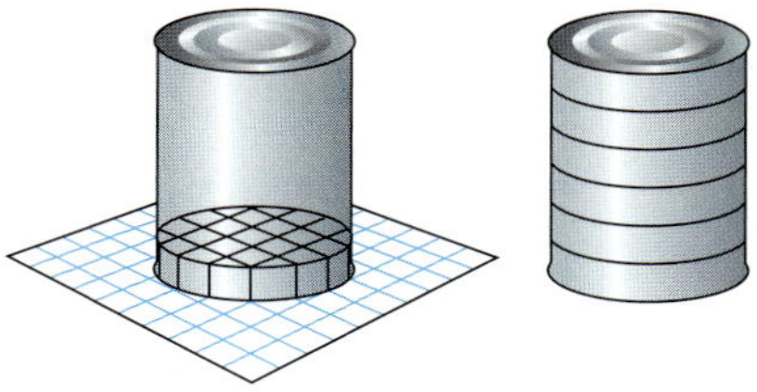

As with prisms, the area of the base of a cylinder tells the number of cubic units in one layer. The height tells how many layers there are in the cylinder.

KEY CONCEPT — Volume of a Cylinder

Words The volume V of a cylinder with radius r is the area of the base B times the height h.

Symbols $V = Bh$ where $B = \pi r^2$ or $V = \pi r^2 h$

Model

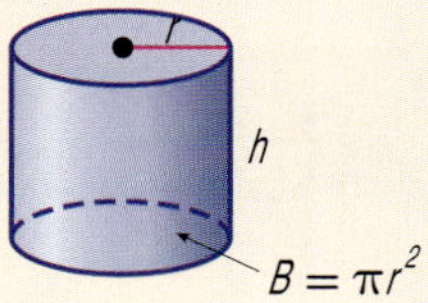

STUDY TIP

Check for Reasonableness Use estimation to check for reasonableness.

$\pi(5)^2(8.3) \approx 3(5)^2(8)$

≈ 600

Since $600 \approx 651.9$, the answer is reasonable.

EXAMPLE Find the Volume of a Cylinder

1 **Find the volume of the cylinder. Round to the nearest tenth.**

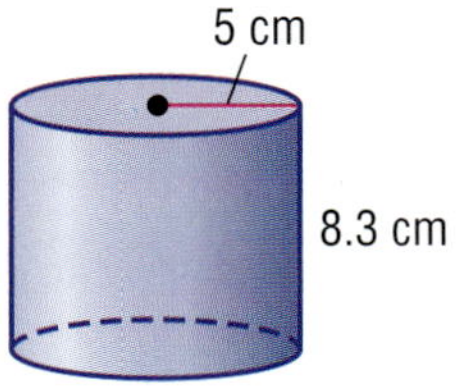

$V = \pi r^2 h$ — Volume of a cylinder

$V = \pi(5)^2(8.3)$ — Replace r with 5 and h with 8.3.

Use a calculator.

[π] [×] 5 [x²] [×] 8.3 [ENTER] 651.8804756

The volume is about 651.9 cubic centimeters.

CHECK Your Progress

Find the volume of each cylinder. Round to the nearest tenth.

a. 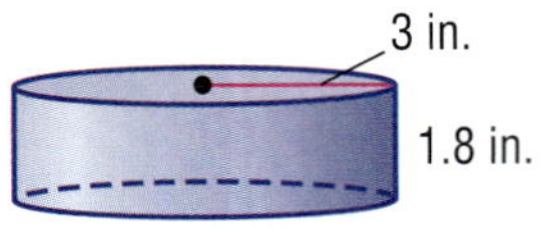

b. 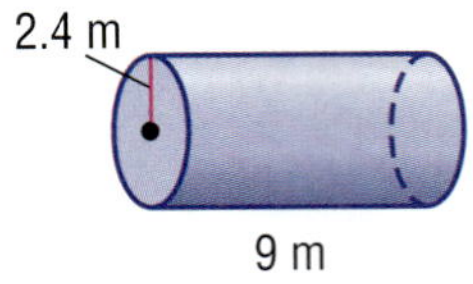

Real-World EXAMPLE

STUDY TIP

Circles Recall that the radius is half the diameter.

2 **WEATHER** **The decorative rain gauge shown has a height of 13 centimeters and a diameter of 3 centimeters. How much water can the rain gauge hold?**

$V = \pi r^2 h$ Volume of a cylinder

$V = \pi(1.5)^2 13$ Replace r with 1.5 and h with 13.

$V \approx 91.9$ Simplify.

The rain gauge can hold about 91.9 cubic centimeters.

CHECK Your Progress

c. **PAINT** Find the volume of a cylinder-shaped paint can that has a diameter of 4 inches and a height of 5 inches.

Online **Personal Tutor at** tx.msmath2.com

CHECK Your Understanding

Find the volume of each cylinder. Round to the nearest tenth.

Example 1 (p. 657)

1. 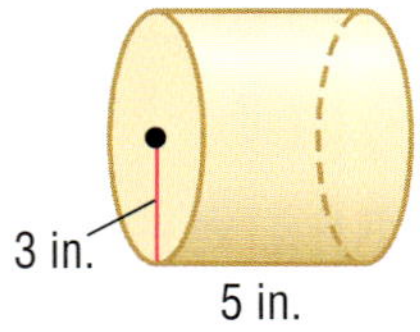

2. 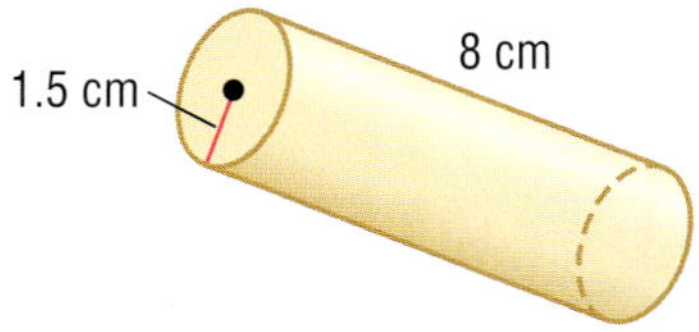

3. 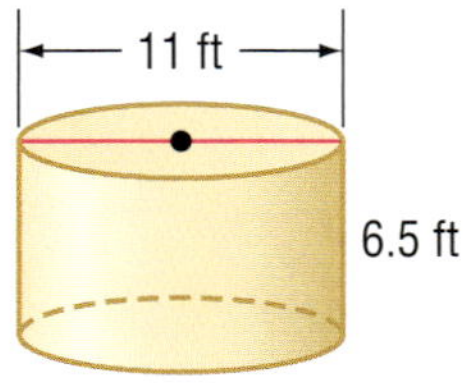

Example 2 (p. 658)

4. **HOCKEY** An official hockey puck has a diameter of 3 inches and a height of 1 inch. What is the volume of the hockey puck?

5. **CANDLES** A scented candle is in the shape of a cylinder. The radius is 4 centimeters and the height is 12 centimeters. Find the volume of the candle.

Exercises

HOMEWORK HELP	
For Exercises	See Examples
6–15	1
16, 17	2

Find the volume of each cylinder. Round to the nearest tenth.

6. 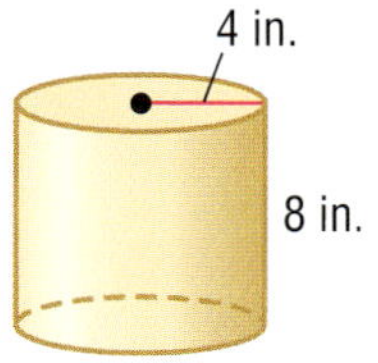

7. 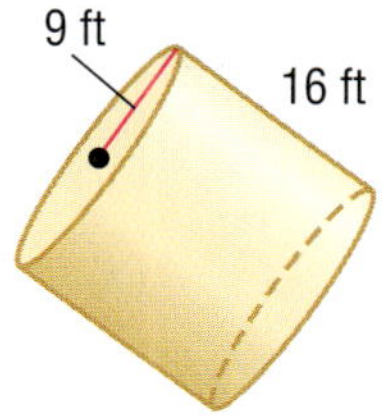

8. 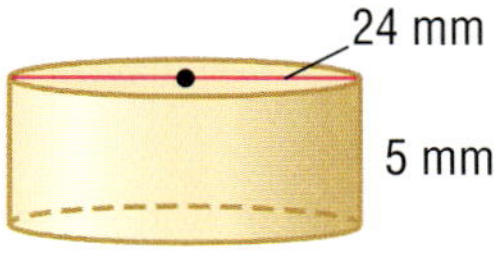

9. 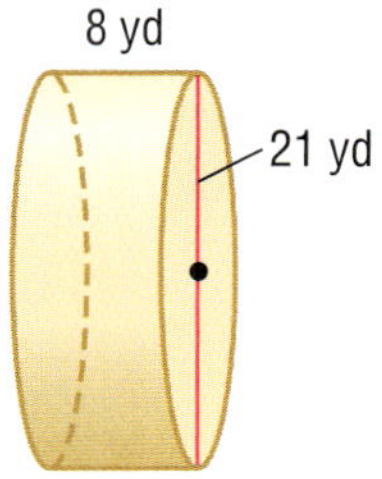

10. 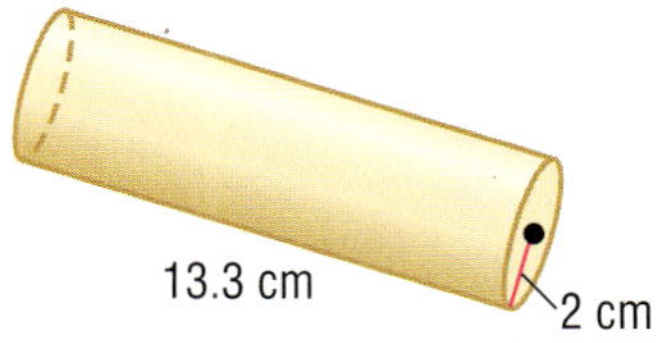

11. 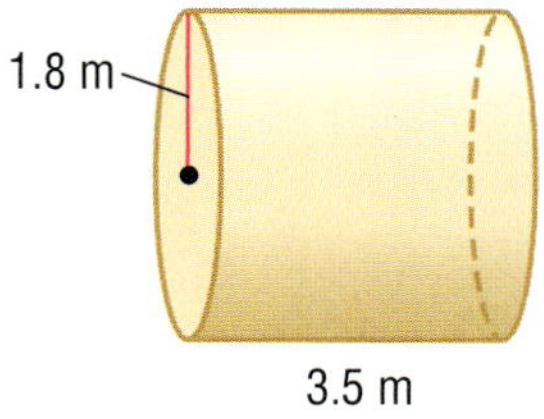

12. diameter = 15 mm
height = 4.8 mm

13. diameter = 4.5 m
height = 6.5 m

14. radius = 6 ft
height = $5\frac{1}{3}$ ft

15. radius = $3\frac{1}{2}$ in.
height = $7\frac{1}{2}$ in.

16. **FOOD** What is the volume of a can of potato chips that has a radius of $1\frac{1}{2}$ inches and a height of 8 inches?

17. **SCIENCE** The Hubble Space Telescope is cylinder-shaped. Use the information at the left to find its volume to the nearest tenth.

Real-World Link
The Hubble Space Telescope has a diameter of 4 meters and a height of 13 meters.

Find the volume of each cylinder. Round to the nearest tenth.

18. 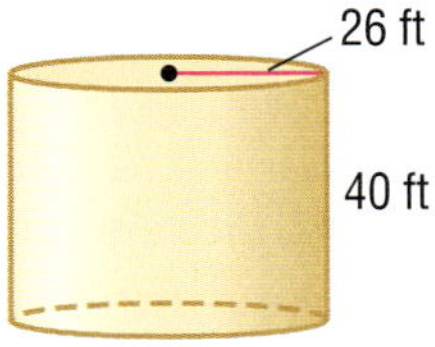

19. 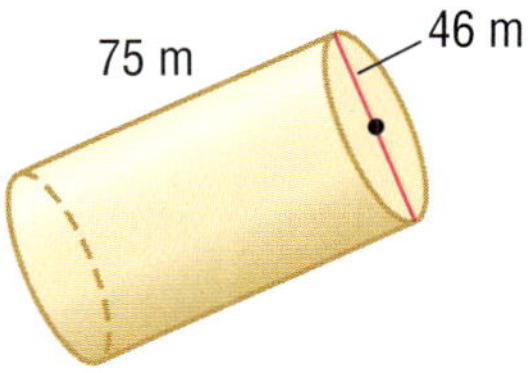

20. 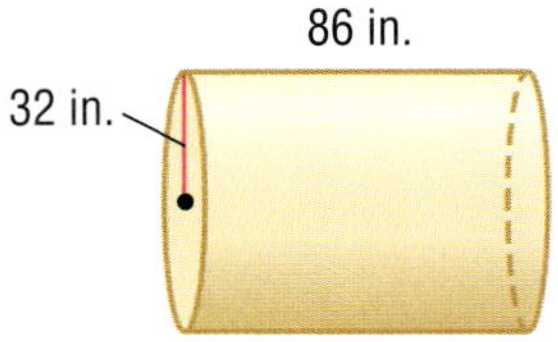

ESTIMATION **Match each cylinder with its approximate volume.**

21. radius = 4.1 ft, height = 5 ft
22. diameter = 8 ft; height = 2.2 ft
23. diameter = 6.2 ft, height = 3 ft
24. radius = 2 ft, height = 3.8 ft

a. 91 ft^3
b. 48 ft^3
c. 111 ft^3
d. 264 ft^3

25. **PACKAGING** A cylinder-shaped popcorn tin has a height of 1.5 feet and a diameter of 10 inches. Find the volume to the nearest cubic inch. Use 3.14 for π.

26. **BAKING** Which will hold more cake batter, the rectangular pan, or the two round pans? Explain.

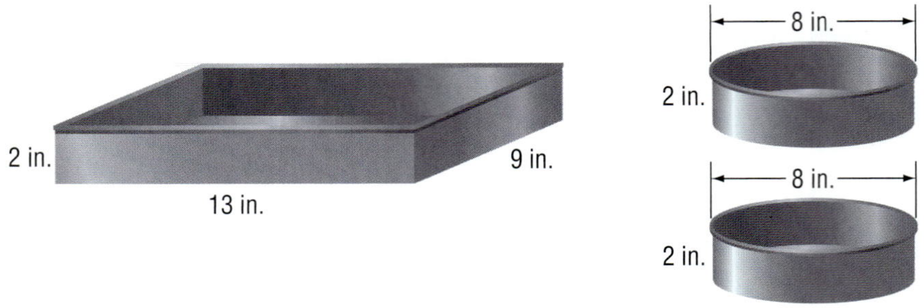

27. **PACKAGING** The two cans at the right have the same volume. What is the value of *h*?

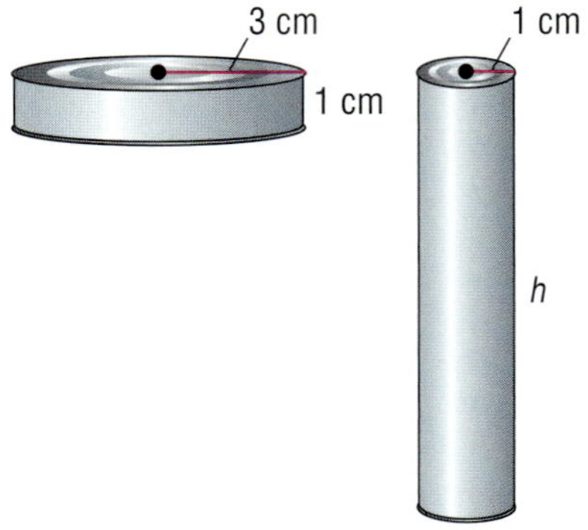

MEASUREMENT For Exercises 28 and 29, use the following information.

Firewood is usually sold by a unit of measure called a *cord*. A cord is a stack of wood that is 8 feet long, 4 feet wide, and 4 feet high.

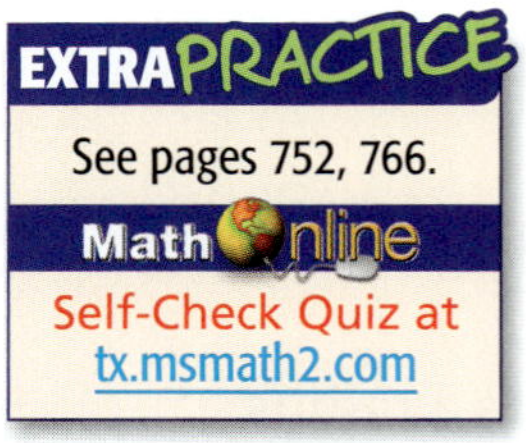

28. What is the volume of a cord of wood?

29. Suppose a tree has a diameter of 2 feet. Find the height of the tree trunk that would produce about 1 cord of firewood.

H.O.T. Problems

30. **CHALLENGE** Two equal-size sheets of paper are rolled along the length and along the width, as shown. Which cylinder do you think has the greater volume? Explain.

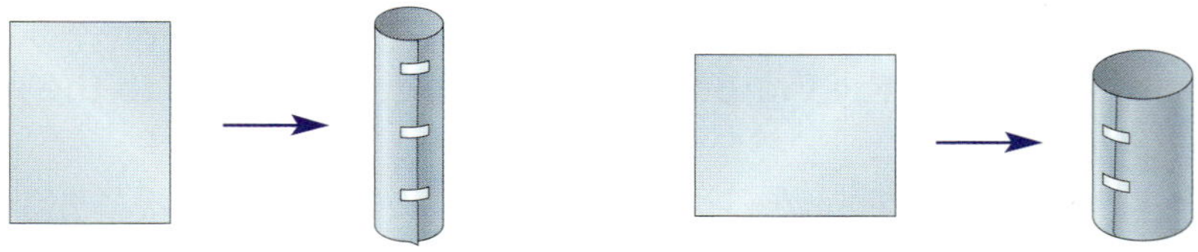

31. **OPEN ENDED** Draw and label a cylinder that has a larger radius, but less volume than the cylinder shown at the right.

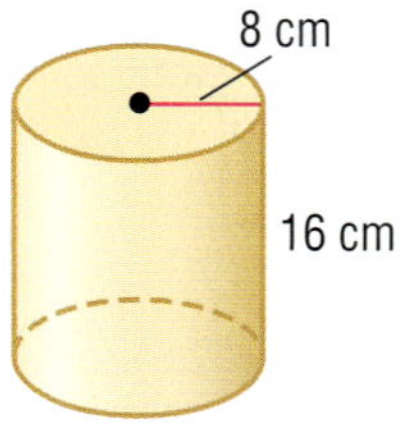

32. **NUMBER SENSE** What is the ratio of the volume of a cylinder to the volume of a cylinder having twice the height but the same radius?

33. **NUMBER SENSE** Suppose cylinder A has the same height but twice the radius of cylinder B. What is the ratio of the volume of cylinder B to cylinder A?

34. 

MATH Explain how the formula for the volume of a cylinder is similar to the formula for the volume of a rectangular prism.

TEST PRACTICE

35. The oatmeal container shown has a diameter of $3\frac{1}{2}$ inches and a height of 9 inches.

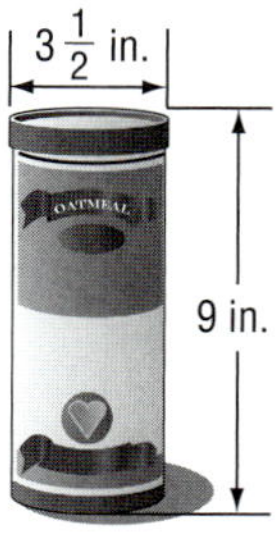

Which is closest to the number of cubic inches it will hold when filled?

A 32

B 42.78

C 75.92

D 85.56

36. Which statement is true about the volumes of the cylinders shown?

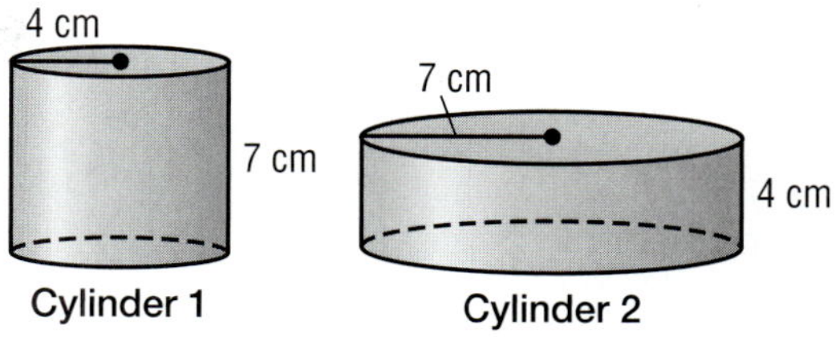

F The volume of cylinder 1 is greater than the volume of cylinder 2.

G The volume of cylinder 2 is greater than the volume of cylinder 1.

H The volumes are equal.

J The volume of cylinder 1 is twice the volume of cylinder 2.

Spiral Review

37. **GEOMETRY** Find the volume of a rectangular prism with a length of 6 meters, a width of 4.9 meters, and a height of 5.2 meters. (Lesson 12-9)

Make a sketch of each geometric figure using the top, side, and front views shown. (Lesson 12-8)

38.

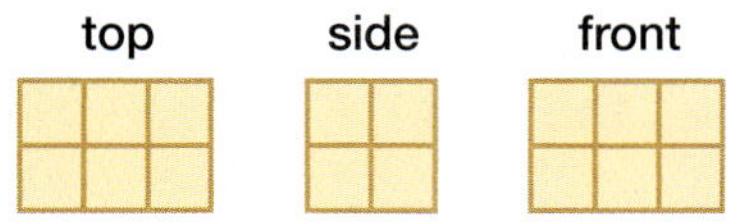

39.

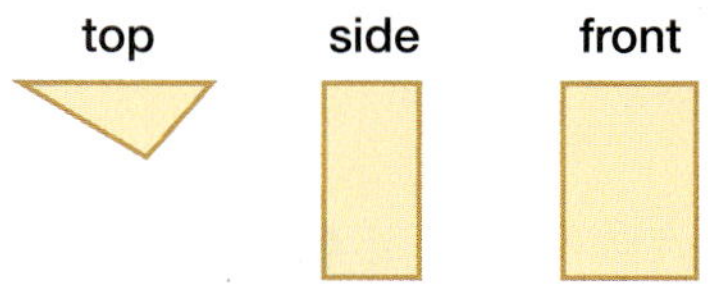

PROBABILITY A coin is tossed and a number cube is rolled. Find the probability of each of the following. (Lesson 10-8)

40. P(heads and 4)

41. P(tails and an odd number)

42. P(heads and *not* 5)

43. P(*not* tails and not 2)

44. **TEST SCORES** The list gives the scores on a recent history test. Find each measure of central tendency and range. Round to the nearest tenth if necessary. Then state which measure best represents the data. Explain your reasoning. (Lesson 9-2)

History Test Scores									
78,	92,	83,	88,	89,	91,	96,	72,	74,	99
81,	88,	86,	95,	73,	97,	78,	78,	60	
84,	85,	90,	92,	98,	74,	76,	80,	83	

Extend **12-10**

Graphing Calculator Lab

Graphing Geometric Relationships

Main IDEA

Use technology to graph data in order to demonstrate geometric relationships.

Targeted TEKS 7.4 The student represents a relationship in numerical, geometric, verbal, and symbolic form. **(B) graph data to demonstrate relationships in familiar concepts such as conversions, perimeter, area, circumference, volume, and scaling.** *Also addresses TEKS 7.14(A).*

In this lab, you will use a TI-83/84 Plus graphing calculator to analyze geometric relationships among the base, height, and area of several parallelograms.

ACTIVITY

1

STEP 1 Draw five parallelograms that each have a height of 4 centimeters on centimeter grid paper.

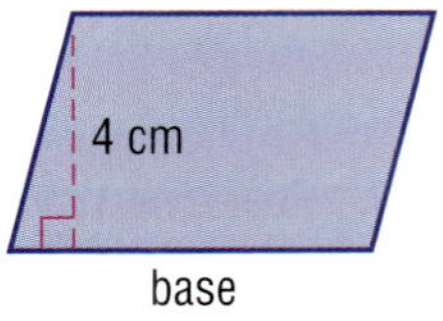

STEP 2 Copy and complete the table shown for each parallelogram.

Base (cm)	Height (cm)	Area (cm^2)
	4	
	4	
	4	
	4	
	4	

STEP 3 Next enter the data into your graphing calculator. Press [STAT] 1 and enter the length of each base in L1. Then enter the area of each parallelogram in L2.

STEP 4 Turn on the statistical plot by pressing [2nd] [STAT PLOT] [ENTER] [ENTER]. Select the scatter plot and enter or confirm L1 as the Xlist and L2 as the Ylist.

STEP 5 Graph the data by pressing [ZOOM] 9. Use the Trace feature and the left and right arrow keys to move from one point to another.

Analyze the Results

1. What does an ordered pair on your graph represent?
2. Sketch and describe the shape of the graph.
3. **MAKE A CONJECTURE** Write an equation for your graph. Check your equation by pressing [Y=], entering your equation into Y1, and then pressing [GRAPH]. What does this equation mean?
4. As the length of the base of the parallelogram increases, what happens to its area? Does this happen at a constant rate? How can you tell this from the table? from the graph?

Math Online Other Calculator Keystrokes at tx.msmath2.com

ACTIVITY

2

STEP 1 Draw five rectangles that each have an area of 36 square centimeters on centimeter grid paper. The length should be greater than or equal to its width.

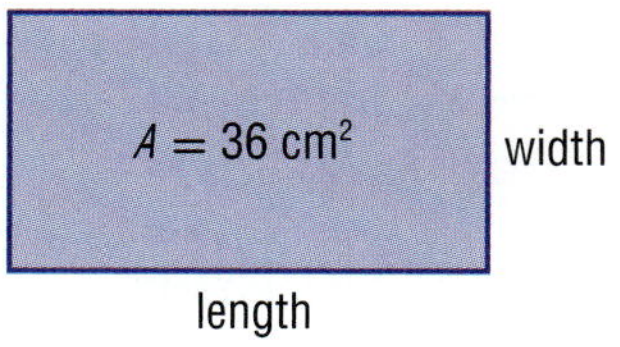

STEP 2 Copy and complete the table shown for each rectangle.

Length (cm)	Width (cm)	Area (cm^2)
		36
		36
		36
		36
		36

STEP 3 Clear list L1 and L2 by pressing [STAT] 4 [2nd] [L1] , [2nd] [L2] [ENTER]. Then press [STAT] 1 and enter the length of each rectangle in L1 and the width of each rectangle in L2.

STEP 4 Follow Steps 4 and 5 of Activity 1 to graph the data.

Analyze the Results

5. What does an ordered pair on your graph represent?
6. Sketch and describe the shape of the graph.
7. **MAKE A CONJECTURE** Write an equation for your graph. Use the calculator to graph and check your equation. What does this equation mean?
8. As the length of the rectangle increases, what happens to its width? Does this happen at a constant rate? How can you tell this from the table? from the graph?
9. **MAKE A PREDICTION** Draw five cubes with different edge lengths. Predict the shape of the graph of the relationship between the edge length and volume of the cube.
10. Create a table to record the edge length and volume of each cube. Then graph the data to show the relationship between the edge length and volume of the cube. Sketch and describe the shape of the graph.
11. **MAKE A CONJECTURE** Write an equation for your graph. Use the calculator to graph and check your equation. What does this equation mean?
12. As the length of the cube's edge increases, what happens to the volume?

CHAPTER 12

Study Guide and Review

STUDY TO GO Download Vocabulary Review from tx.msmath2.com

FOLDABLES Study Organizer — GET READY to Study

Be sure the following Key Concepts are noted in your Foldable.

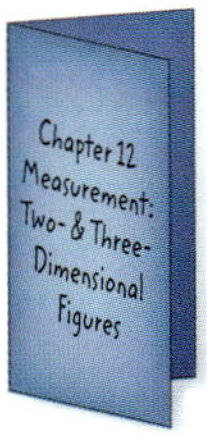

Key Concepts

Area (Lessons 12-1, 12-2, and 12-6)

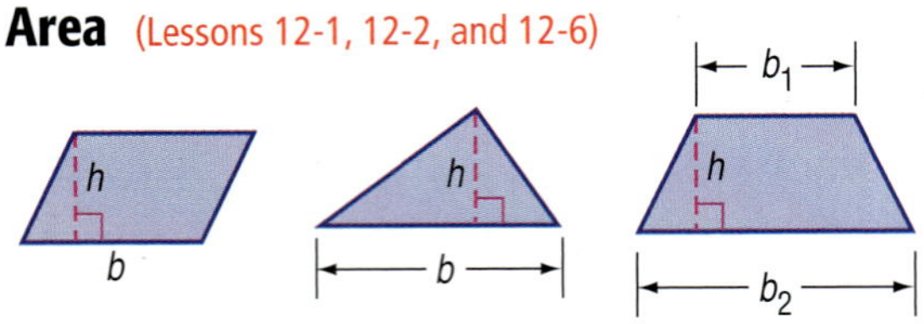

parallelogram $A = bh$

triangle $A = \frac{1}{2}bh$

trapezoid $A = \frac{1}{2}h(b_1 + b_2)$

Circles (Lessons 12-3 and 12-4)

- circumference
  $C = \pi d$ or $C = 2\pi r$
- area
  $A = \pi r^2$

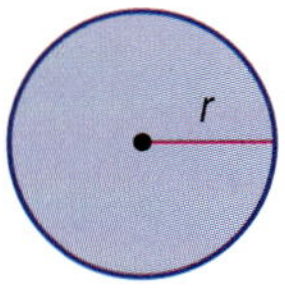

Volume (Lessons 12-9 and 12-10)

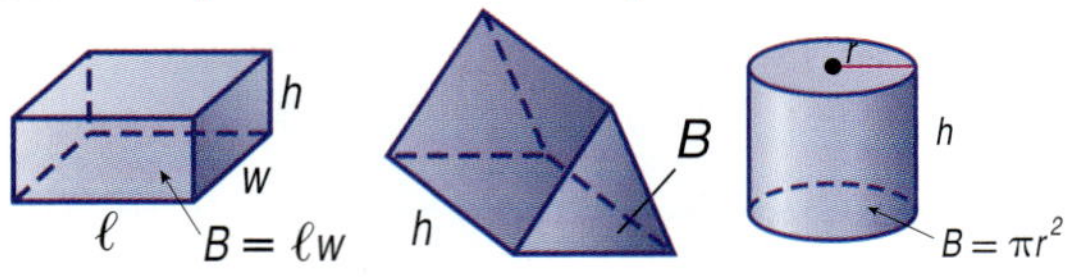

rectangular prism, triangular prism: $V = Bh$

cylinder: $V = Bh$ or $\pi r^2 h$

Key Vocabulary

base (p. 610)
center (p. 622)
circle (p. 622)
circumference (p. 622)
composite figure (p. 634)
cone (p. 642)
cylinder (p. 642)
diameter (p. 622)
edge (p. 641)
face (p. 641)
height (p. 610)
lateral face (p. 641)
π (pi) (p. 622)
prism (p. 641)
pyramid (p. 641)
radius (p. 622)
rectangular prism (p. 651)
semicircle (p. 646)
sphere (p. 642)
three-dimensional figure (p. 641)
triangular prism (p. 653)
vertex (p. 641)
volume (p. 651)

Vocabulary Check

Choose the correct term or number to complete each sentence.

1. A (rectangular prism, rectangle) is a three-dimensional figure that has three sets of parallel congruent sides.
2. The (volume, surface area) of a three-dimensional figure is the measure of the space occupied by it.
3. $A = \frac{1}{2}h(b_1 + b_2)$ is the formula for the area of a (triangle, trapezoid).
4. Volume is measured in (square, cubic) units.
5. A (cylinder, prism) is a three-dimensional figure that has two congruent, parallel circles as its bases.
6. The volume of a rectangular prism is found by (adding, multiplying) the length, the width, and the height.
7. The formula for the area of a (square, circle) is $A = \pi r^2$.

Math Online Vocabulary Review at tx.msmath2.com

Lesson-by-Lesson Review

12-1 Area of Parallelograms (pp. 610–614)

Find the area of each parallelogram. Round to the nearest tenth if necessary.

8.

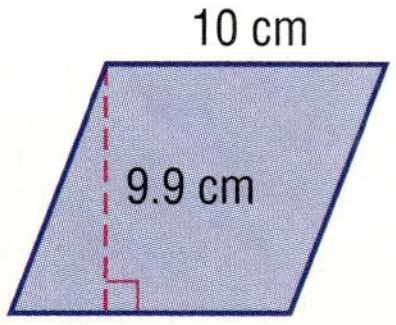

9.

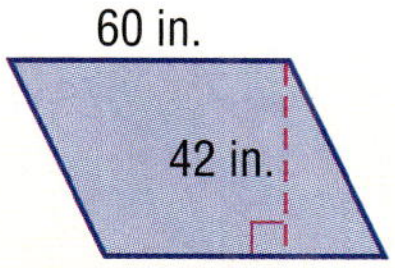

10. ALGEBRA A parallelogram has an area of 57 square inches. Find the base of the parallelogram if the height is 6 inches.

Example 1 **Find the area of a parallelogram if the base is 15 inches and the height is 8 inches.**

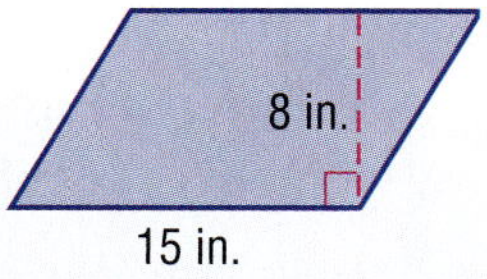

$A = bh$ — Area of a parallelogram

$A = 15 \cdot 8$ — Replace b with 15 and h with 8.

$A = 120$ in. — Multiply.

12-2 Area of Triangles and Trapezoids (pp. 616–620)

Find the area of each figure. Round to the nearest tenth if necessary.

11.

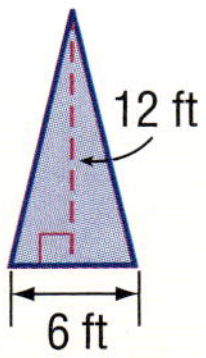

12.

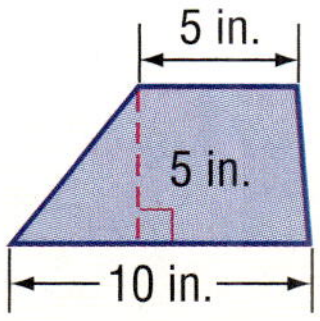

13. trapezoid: bases 22 yd and 35 yd
height 18.5 yd

14. ALGEBRA The area of a triangle is 26.9 square inches. If the base is 9.6 inches, what is the height of the triangle?

Example 2 **Find the area of a triangle with a base of 8 meters and a height of 11.2 meters.**

$A = \frac{1}{2}bh$ — Area of a triangle

$A = \frac{1}{2}(8)(11.2)$ or 44.8 m^2 — $b = 8, h = 11.2$

Example 3 **Find the area of the trapezoid.**

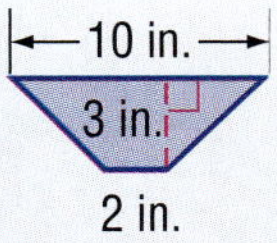

$A = \frac{1}{2}h(b_1 + b_2)$

$A = \frac{1}{2}(3)(2 + 10)$ — $h = 3, b_1 = 2, b_2 = 10$

$A = \frac{1}{2}(3)(12)$ or 18 in^2 — Simplify.

12-3 Circles and Circumference (pp. 622–626)

Find the circumference of each circle. Use 3.14 or $\frac{22}{7}$ for π. Round to the nearest tenth if necessary.

15. radius = 12 in.

16. diameter = 28 m

17. diameter = $8\frac{2}{5}$ ft

18. radius = 4.4 cm

19. LIFE SCIENCE A circular nest built by bald eagles has a diameter of $9\frac{1}{2}$ feet. Find the nest's circumference.

Example 4 **Find the circumference of a circle with a diameter of 12.2 meters.**

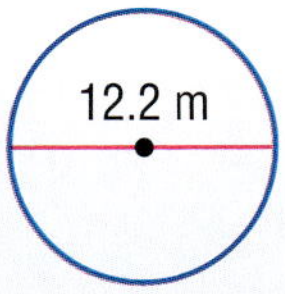

$C = \pi d$ — Circumference of a circle

$C \approx 3.14(12.2)$ — $\pi \approx 3.14$ and $d = 12.2$

$C \approx 38.3$ — Multiply.

The circumference is about 38.3 meters.

CHAPTER 12

Study Guide and Review

12-4 Area of Circles (pp. 627–631)

Find the area of each circle. Round to the nearest tenth.

20. radius = 11.4 in.

21. diameter = 44 cm

22. **GARDENING** A lawn sprinkler can water a circular area with a radius of 20 feet. Find the area that can be watered. Round to the nearest tenth.

Example 5 **Find the area of a circle with a radius of 5 inches.**

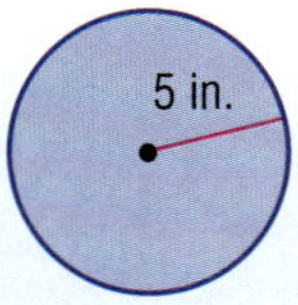

$A = \pi r^2$ Area of a circle

$A = \pi(5)^2$ Replace *r* with 5.

$A \approx 78.5$ Multiply.

The area of the circle is about 78.5 square inches.

12-5 PSI: Solve a Simpler Problem (pp. 632–633)

23. **BAKING** The local baker can make 10 cakes in 2 days. How many cakes can 8 bakers make working at the same rate in 20 days?

24. **TRAVEL** Mrs. Whitmore left Chicago at 6:45 A.M. and arrived in St. Louis at 11:15 A.M., driving a distance of approximately 292 miles. Find her approximate average speed.

25. **SHOPPING** Mercedes spent \$175.89 over the weekend. Of the money she spent, 40% was spent on shoes. About how much money was *not* spent on shoes?

Example 6 **A total of 950 residents voted on whether to build a neighborhood playground. Of those that voted, 70% voted for the playground. How many residents voted for the playground?**

Find 10% of 950 and then use the result to find
70% of 950.

10% of 950 = 95

Since there are seven 10%s in 70%, multiply 95 by 7.

So, 95 × 7 or 665 residents voted for the playground.

12-6 Area of Composite Figures (pp. 634–637)

Find the area of each figure. Round to the nearest tenth if necessary.

26.

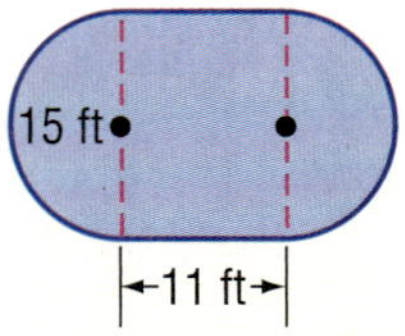

27.

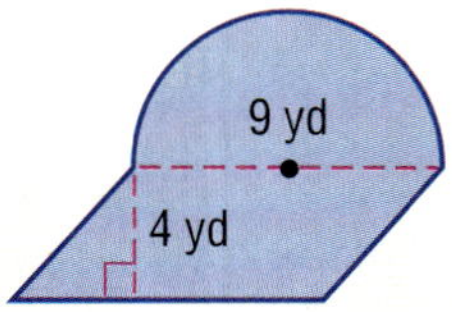

28. **PATIOS** The McAllister family is installing a brick patio like the one shown. What is the total area of the patio?

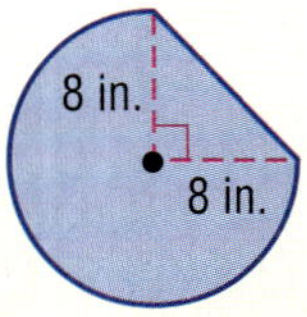

Example 7 **Find the area of the figure. Round to the nearest tenth.**

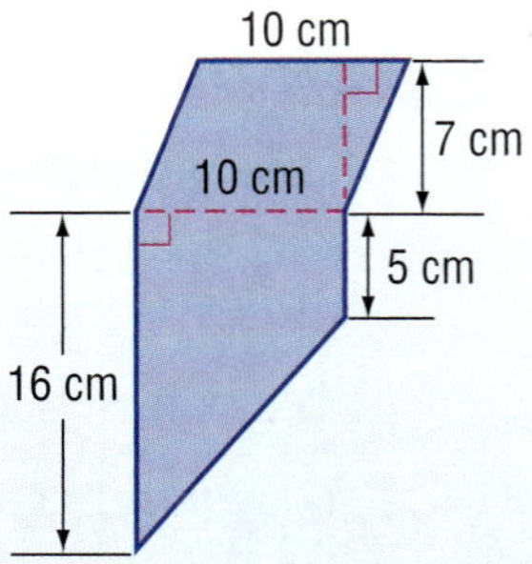

The figure can be separated into a parallelogram and a trapezoid.

parallelogram: $A = 10 \cdot 7$ or 70

trapezoid: $A = \frac{1}{2}(10)(16 + 5)$ or 105

The area is 70 + 105 or 175 cm^2.

Mixed Problem Solving
For mixed problem-solving practice, see page 766.

12-7 Three-Dimensional Figures (pp. 641–644)

For each figure, identify the shape of the base(s). Then classify the figure.

29. 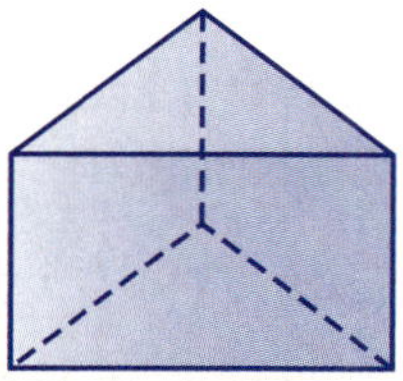

30. 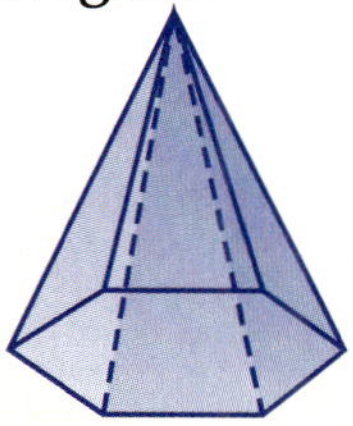

31. **VEGETABLES** Classify the shape of a can of green beans.

DOGHOUSE For Exercises 32 and 33, use the figure of the doghouse shown.

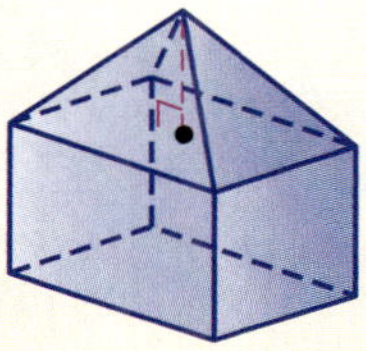

32. What geometric figure is represented by the main part of the doghouse?
33. Identify the top figure of the doghouse.

Example 8 **For the figure, identify the shape of the base(s). Then classify the figure.**

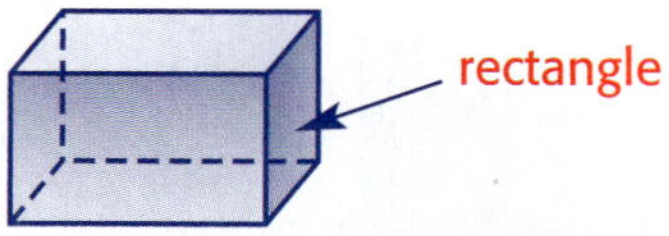

Since the figure has 6 rectangular faces, parallel bases, and a rectangular base, the figure is a rectangular prism.

Example 9 **Classify the shape of a basketball.**

The figure has no faces, bases, edges, or vertices. The figure is a sphere.

12-8 Drawing Three-Dimensional Figures (pp. 646–650)

Draw a top, a side, and a front view of each solid.

34. 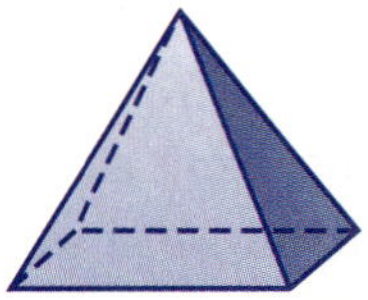

35. 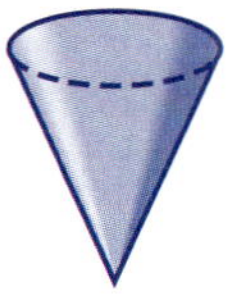

36. Draw a solid using the top, side, and front views shown. Use isometric dot paper.

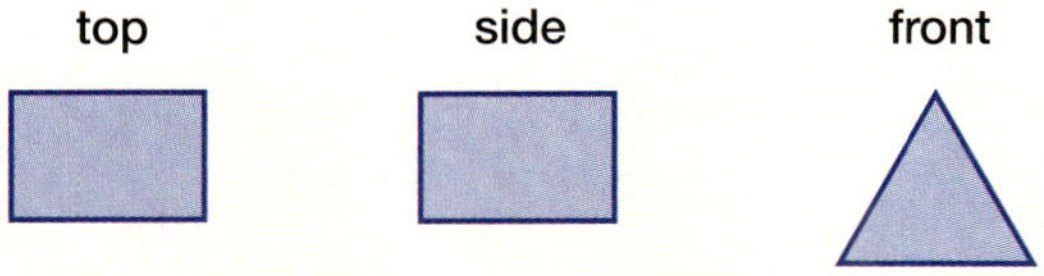

37. **CRAFTS** Alejandra put all of her craft supplies in the box shown. Draw a top, a side, and a front view of the box.

Example 10 **Draw the solid by using the top, side, and front views shown.**

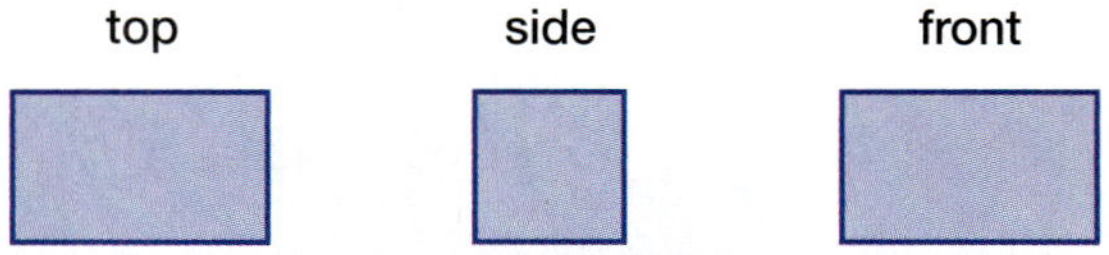

The side view is a square. The top and front views are rectangles.

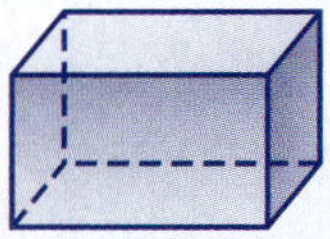

The figure drawn is a rectangular prism.

12-9 Volume of Prisms (pp. 651–656)

Find the volume of each prism. Round to the nearest tenth if necessary.

38.

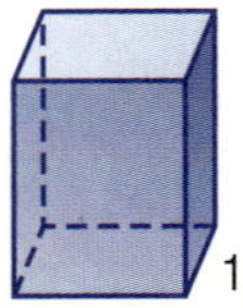

39.

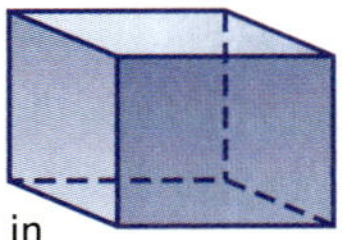

40. **POOLS** A competition swimming pool is 25 yards long and has 8 lanes that are each 3 yards wide. The pool is filled to a depth of 6 feet. Find the number of cubic feet of water in the pool.

41. **TRUCKS** The dimensions of the bed of a dump truck are length 20 feet, width 7 feet, and height $9\frac{1}{2}$ feet. What is the volume of the bed of the dump truck?

Example 11 **A local city provides residents with a rectangular container for recycling products. Find the volume of the rectangular container.**

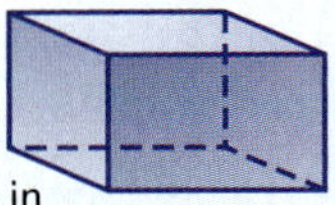

$V = \ell wh$	Volume of a rectangular prism
$V = (24)(14)(15)$	Replace ℓ with 24, w with 14 and h with 15.
$V = 5{,}040$	Multiply.

The volume of the rectangular container is 5,040 cubic inches.

12-10 Volume of Cylinders (pp. 657–661)

Find the volume of each cylinder. Round to the nearest tenth.

42.

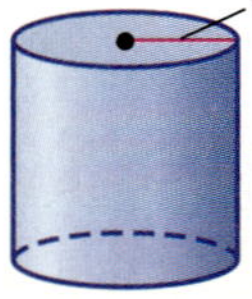

43.

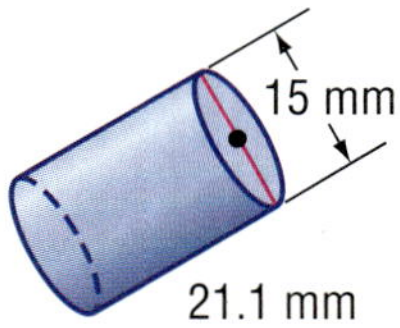

44. **POTTERY** In his art class, Benjamin made a vase in the shape of a cylinder. The diameter is 5 inches, and the height is 10 inches. Find the maximum volume of water the vase can hold.

45. **COOKIES** Mrs. Delagado stores cookies in a cylinder-shaped jar that has a height of 12 inches and a diameter of 10 inches. Find the volume to the nearest cubic inch. Use 3.14 for π.

Example 12 **Marquez stores his toys in a cylinder-shaped can like the one shown below. Find the volume of the cylinder-shaped can. Round to the nearest tenth.**

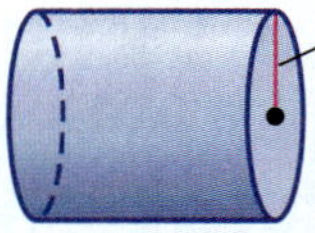

$V = \pi r^2 h$	Volume of a cylinder
$= \pi 3^2(7)$	Replace r with 3 and h with 7.
≈ 197.9	Multiply.

The volume of the cylinder-shaped can is 197.9 cubic feet.

CHAPTER 12 Practice Test

Find the area of each figure. Round to the nearest tenth if necessary.

1. 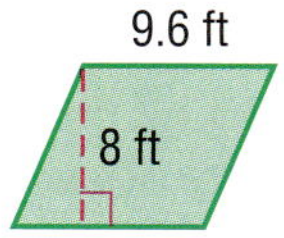

2. 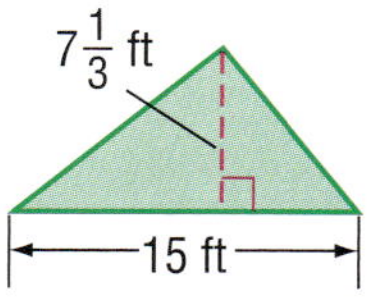

3. 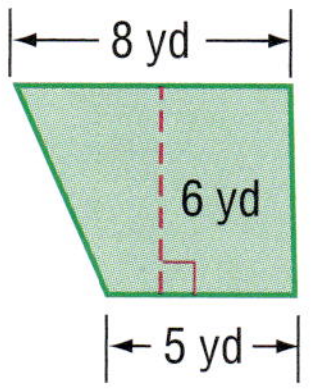

4. 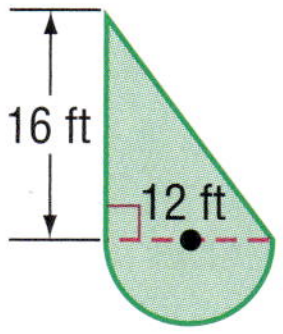

5. **RUGS** Mrs.Torres has a circular rug underneath her dining room table. What is the approximate circumference of the rug if it has a radius of $3\frac{1}{2}$ yards?

Find the area of each circle. Round to the nearest tenth.

6. radius = 9 ft
7. diameter = 5.2 m

8. **TEST PRACTICE** A fountain is in the shape of a semicircle. If the fountain has a diameter of 8.8 meters, what is the area of the base of the fountain?

   A 60.8 m^2
   B 30.4 m^2
   C 27.6 m^2
   D 13.8 m^2

9. **SWIMMING POOL** The Gruseser family wants to build a swimming pool like the one shown below. If they have 85 square feet of land available for the pool, do they have enough space for the swimming pool? Justify your response.

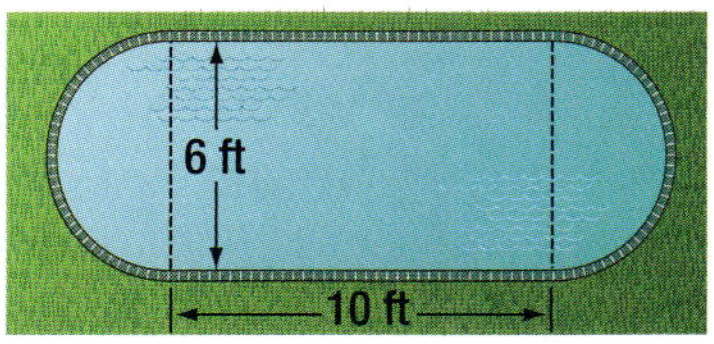

For each figure, identify the shape of the base(s). Then classify the figure.

10. 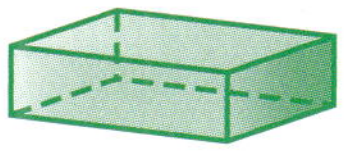

11. 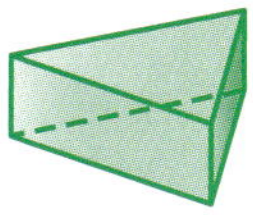

12. **PAPER TOWELS** Classify the shape of a roll of paper towels.

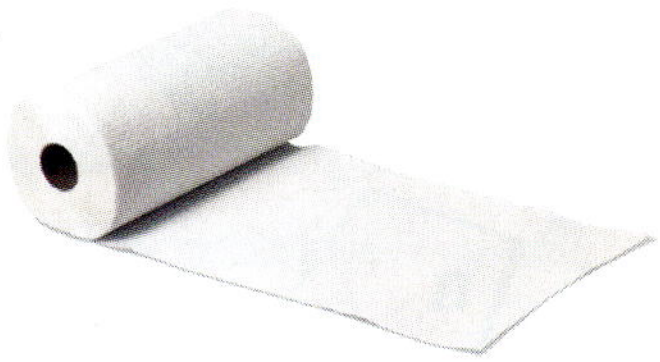

13. **SHAPES** Which geometric shape has at least three lateral faces that are triangles and only one base?

Draw a top, a side, and a front view of each solid.

14. 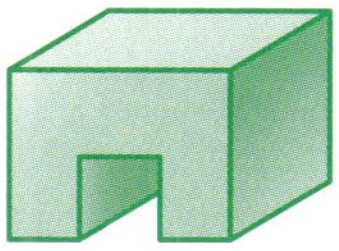

15. 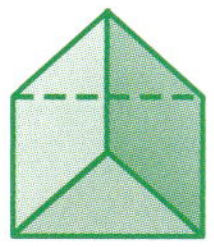

Find the volume of each prism and cylinder. Round to the nearest tenth.

16. 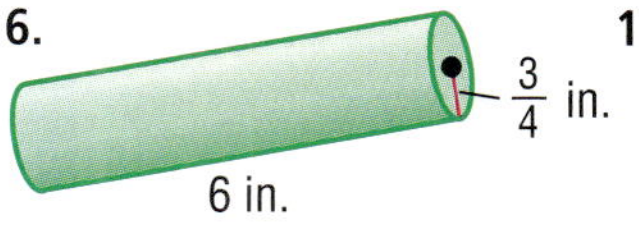

17. 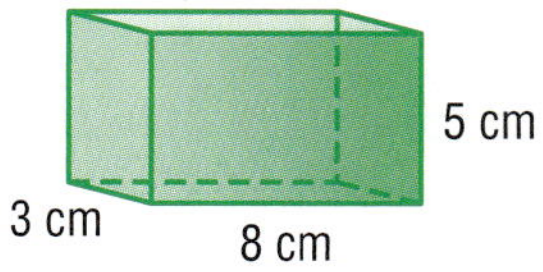

18. 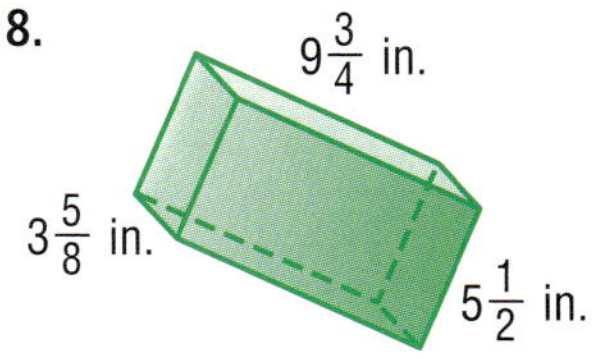

19. 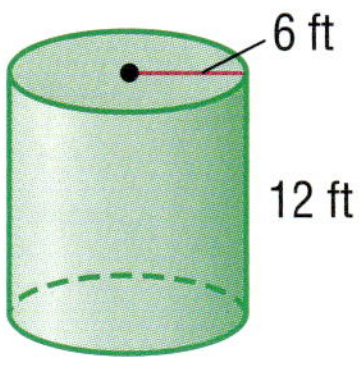

20. **TEST PRACTICE** The standard-size drinking straw has a radius of $\frac{1}{8}$ inch and a height of $7\frac{3}{4}$ inches. How much liquid is contained in the straw if it is only half full?

   F 0.2 in^3
   G 1.5 in^3
   H 3.4 in^3
   J 3.8 in^3

CHAPTER 12

Texas Test Practice

Cumulative, Chapters 1–12

Read each question. Then fill in the correct answer on the answer document provided by your teacher or on a sheet of paper.

1. Stephanie shaded part of a circle like the one shown below. What is the approximate area of the shaded region?

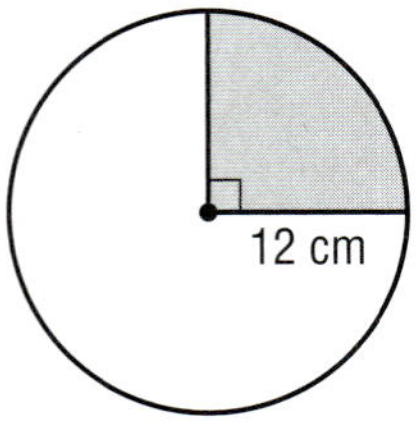

A 113 cm^2

B 364 cm^2

C 452 cm^2

D 728 cm^2

TEST-TAKING TIP

Question 1 The Texas Test includes a Mathematics Chart in the test booklet. Refer to the chart for area and volume formulas.

2. Shandra designed a new flower bed, as shown in the shaded part of the grid below. Each square on the grid represents 4 square feet. What will be the approximate area of the flower bed?

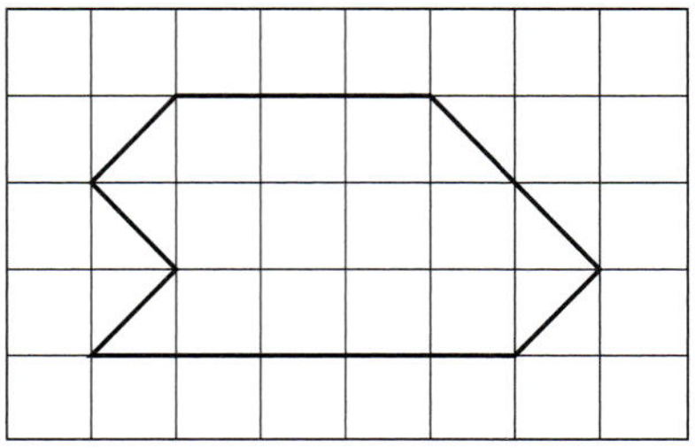

F 14 ft^2

G 16 ft^2

H 56 ft^2

J 72 ft^2

3. **GRIDDABLE** Angle D and angle E are complementary angles. If $\angle D$ is 35°, what is the measure of $\angle E$?

4. If the corresponding angles of 2 trapezoids are congruent and the lengths of the corresponding sides of the trapezoids are proportional, the trapezoids are —

A regular

B congruent

C symmetric

D similar

5. Which description shows the relationship between a term and n, its position in the sequence?

Position	1	2	3	4	5	n
Value of Term	2	5	8	11	14	

F Add 1 to n

G Multiply n by 2 and add 3

H Multiply n by 3 and subtract 1

J Add 9 to n

6. A metal toolbox has a length of 11 inches, a width of 5 inches, and a height of 6 inches. What is the volume of the toolbox?

A 22 in^3

B 121 in^3

C 210 in^3

D 330 in^3

7. **GRIDDABLE** Miguel deposited $1,528 in an account earning 6% annual interest. What is the balance in dollars and cents in the account 2 years later if he makes no additional deposits or withdrawals?

Get Ready for the Texas Test
For test-taking strategies and more practice, see pages TX1–TX23.

8. Mr. Jenkins is using the triangular piece of wood shown below for a project. Which of the following best describes the triangle?

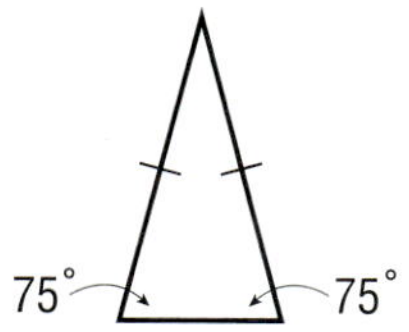

F Obtuse equilateral triangle

G Acute isosceles triangle

H Right scalene triangle

J Right isosceles triangle

9. Ms. Williams recorded the time it took six of her top students to complete a math quiz. The results are shown in the table below. What is the median time for these six students?

Math Quiz Times	
Student	**Time (minutes)**
1	12.8
2	23.1
3	19.6
4	15.7
5	27.3
6	20.5

A 12.8 minutes

B 16 minutes

C 20.05 minutes

D 27.3 minutes

10. **GRIDDABLE** Katie has 3 apples to serve to her friends. If Katie serves each friend $\frac{1}{3}$ of a whole apple, how many friends can she serve?

11. If point B is translated 2 units to the left and 4 units down, what will be point B's new coordinates?

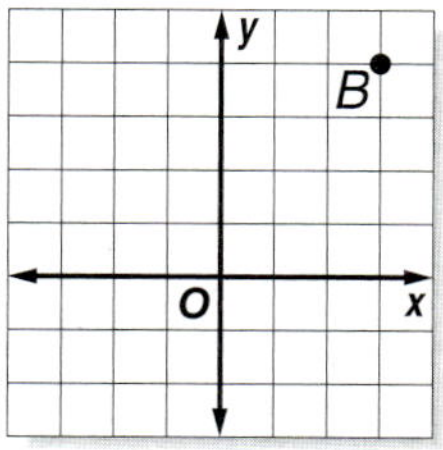

F $(-2, -4)$

G $(3, 4)$

H $(5, 8)$

J $(1, 0)$

Pre-AP

Record your answers on a sheet of paper. Show your work.

12. Suppose you bought a new tent with the dimensions shown below.

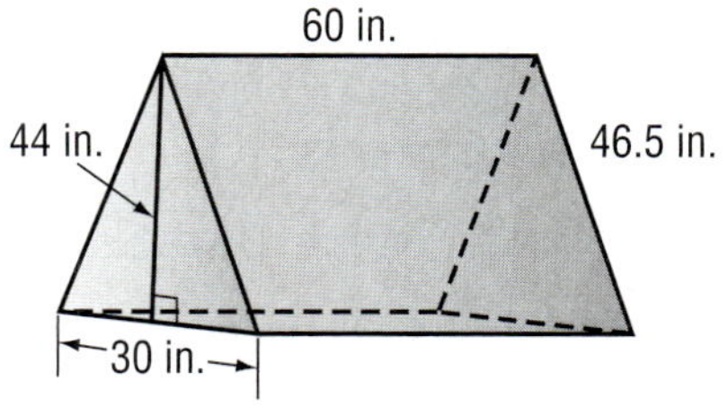

a. Is the area of the parallelogram-shaped side of the tent greater than or less than the area of the floor? Explain.

b. The front and back triangular regions are covered with screens. What is the total area of the screens?

NEED EXTRA HELP?												
If You Missed Question...	1	2	3	4	5	6	7	8	9	10	11	12
Go to Lesson...	12-4	12-6	11-1	11-6	1-9	12-9	8-9	11-3	9-2	6-7	11-8	12-2
For Help with Test Objective...	4	4	3	3	2	4	3	3	5	1	3	4

Get Ready for the Texas Test

It's almost time for the Texas Test. And you may have many questions about it. Here are some answers to frequently-asked questions.

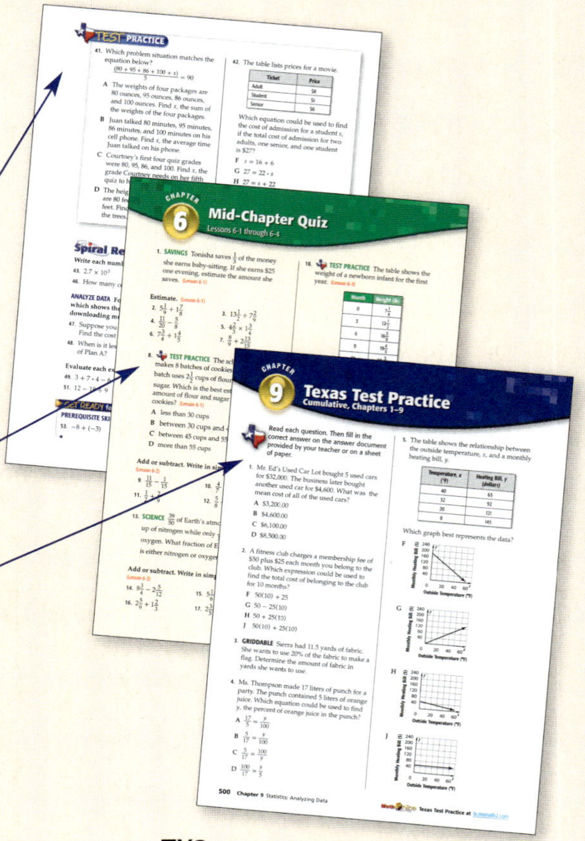

Should I Study for the Test?

The good news is that you've been studying all along for the test—a little bit every day. Here are some of the ways your textbook has been preparing you for the test.

- **Every Day** Each lesson had practice questions that are similar to the questions on the test.
- **Every Week** The Mid-Chapter Quiz and Practice Test had several practice questions.
- **Every Month** The Texas Test Practice pages at the end of each chapter had even more questions similar to those on the Texas Test.

Can I Still Review Before the Test?

Absolutely! The following pages contain even more practice for each test objective.

Math Online **Additional Texas Test Practice at** tx.msmath2.com

What Kinds of Questions are on the Test?

There are two kinds of questions on the test.

- **Multiple-Choice Questions:** Most of the questions are multiple-choice questions that have four answer choices. These are labeled A, B, C, D, or F, G, H, J.
- **Griddable Questions:** Some questions are short-answer questions in which you mark the answer on a grid printed on your answer sheet. The answers to griddable questions cannot be negative numbers or fractions.

What Does the Grid Look Like?

The answer grid contains seven columns. One of those columns is for the decimal point. Notice on the sample below that there are four columns to the left of the decimal point and two columns to the right of the decimal point.

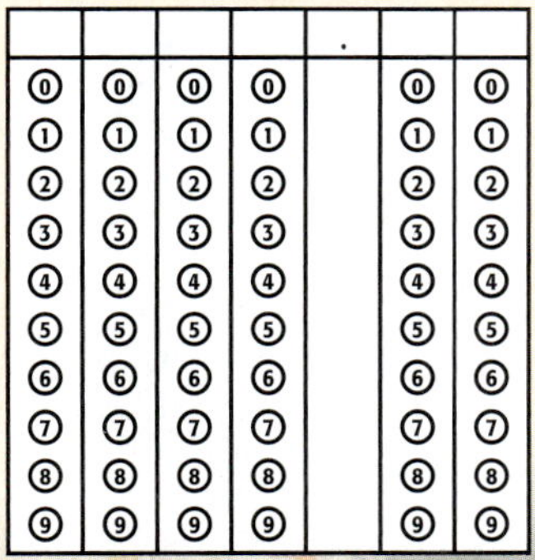

How Many Questions Are on the Test?

There are about 50 different questions on the test.

What Happens if I Forget a Formula?

Don't worry! A Mathematics Chart that contains measurement conversions (for example, 1 quart = 2 pints) and formulas for perimeter, circumference, area, and volume—as well as the value of π—is included with the test.

There is a Mathematics Chart similar to the one provided with the test on the inside back cover of your textbook.

Should I Bring a Ruler?

No. Metric and customary rulers are found on the Mathematics Chart.

Can I Use a Calculator?

Your teacher will tell you whether you are permitted to use a calculator on the test.

Tips for SUCCESS

Before the Test

- Go to bed early the night before the test. You will think more clearly after a good night's rest.
- Become familiar with common formulas and when they should be used.
- Think positively.

During the Test

- Read each problem carefully. Underline key words and think about different ways to solve the problem.
- Watch for key words like NOT. Also look for order words like *least, greatest, first,* and *last*.
- Answer questions you are sure about first. If you do not know the answer to a question, skip it and go back to that question later.
- Check your answer to make sure it is reasonable.
- Make sure that the number of the question on the answer sheet matches the number of the question on which you are working in your test booklet.

Whatever you do...

- Don't try to do it all in your head. If no figure is provided, draw one.
- Don't rush. Try to work at a steady pace.
- Don't give up. Some problems may seem hard to you, but you may be able to figure out what to do if you read each question carefully or try another strategy.

Multiple-Choice Questions

Incomplete shading
(A) (B) (C) (D)
Too light shading
(A) (B) (C) (D)
Correct shading
(A) (B) (C) (D)

Multiple-choice questions are the most common type of question on the Texas Test. You are asked to choose the best answer from four possible answers.

To record a multiple-choice answer, you will be asked to shade in a bubble that is a circle. Always make sure that your shading is dark enough and completely covers the bubble.

TEST EXAMPLE

1 Mrs. Hon's seventh grade students are purchasing stuffed animals to donate to a charity. They bought 3 boxes containing eight animals each and 5 boxes containing twelve animals each. Which expression *cannot* be used to find the total number of animals they bought to give to the charity?

Notice that the problem asks for the expression that *cannot* represent the situation.

A $8 + 8 + 8 + 12 + 12 + 12 + 12 + 12$

B $3 \times 8 + 5 \times 12$

C $3(8) + 5(12)$

D $8 \times (8 + 12)$

Read the problem carefully and locate the important information. There are 3 boxes that have eight animals, so that is 3×8, or 24 animals. There are 5 boxes of twelve animals, so that is 5×12, or 60 animals. The total number of animals is $24 + 60$, or 84.

You know from reading the problem that you are looking for the expression that *does not* simplify to 84. Simplify each expression to find the answer.

A $8 + 8 + 8 + 12 + 12 + 12 + 12 + 12$
$= (8 + 8 + 8) + (12 + 12 + 12 + 12 + 12)$
$= 24 + 60$
$= 84$

B $3 \times 8 + 5 \times 12 = 24 + 60$
$= 84$

C $3(8) + 5(12) = 24 + 60$
$= 84$

D $8 \times (8 + 12) = 8 \times 20$
$= 160$

The only expression that *does not* simplify to 84 is D.
The correct choice is D.

TEST EXAMPLE

2 **On a hiking trip, Grace and Alicia traveled 10 miles south and 4 miles west as part of a rectangular hiking path. If they complete the path back to their starting point, how far will they have hiked?**

F 14 mi **G** 20 mi **H** 28 mi **J** 32 mi

STRATEGY

Diagrams Draw a diagram for the situation. If you cannot write in the test booklet, draw a diagram on scratch paper.

To solve this problem, you need to draw a diagram of the situation. Label the directions and the important information from the problem.

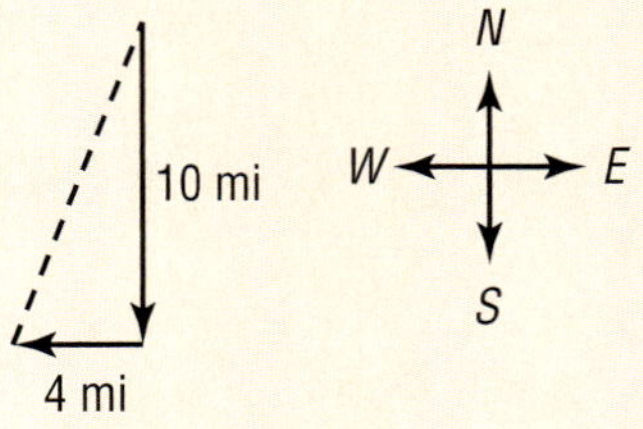

To find the distance hiked, find the perimeter of the rectangle.

$P = 2\ell + 2w$	Perimeter of a rectangle
$P = 2(10) + 2(4)$	Replace ℓ with 10 and w with 4.
$P = 20 + 8$	Multiply.
$P = 28$	Add.

The total distance hiked will be 28 miles. The correct choice is H.

Some problems give more information than needed to solve the problem. Read the question carefully to determine the information you need.

TEST EXAMPLE

3 **One of the biggest pieces of cheese ever produced was made in 1866 in Ingersoll, Canada. It weighed 7,300 pounds. It was shaped as a cylinder with a diameter of 7 feet and a height of 3 feet. To the nearest cubic foot, what was the volume of the cheese? Use 3.14 for π.**

A 462 ft^3 **B** 143 ft^3 **C** 115 ft^3 **D** 63 ft^3

You need to use the formula for the volume of a cylinder. The diameter is 7 feet, so the radius is $\frac{7}{2}$ or 3.5 feet. The height is 3 feet.

STRATEGY

Formulas Use the Mathematics Chart to find the correct formula.

$V = \pi r^2 h$	Volume of a cylinder
$V \approx (3.14)(3.5)^2(3)$	Replace π with 3.14, r with 3.5, and h with 3.
$V \approx 115.395$	Simplify.

The volume of the cheese is about 115 cubic feet. The correct choice is C.

Griddable Questions

Griddable questions are another type of question on the Texas Test. For griddable questions, you mark your answer on a grid printed on your answer sheet.

The grid contains a row of seven boxes at the top—six for numbers and one for the decimal point. Below the boxes are six columns of bubbles separated by a blank column. An example of a grid showing the number 960 is shown below.

TEST EXAMPLE

1 Mr. Byrd builds and sells storage buildings. The dimensions of his most popular model are shown in the diagram. What is the volume of the building in cubic feet? Record your answer and fill in the bubbles on your answer document. Be sure to use the correct place value.

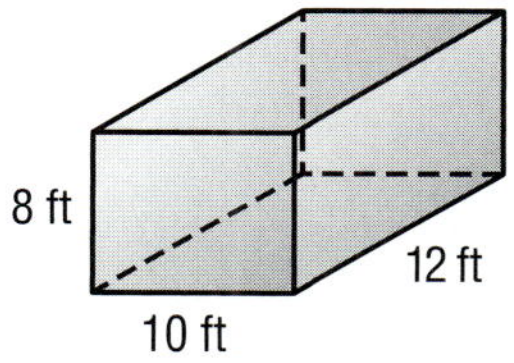

You need to find the volume of a rectangular prism. Use the formula and the dimensions given in the diagram.

$V = \ell wh$	Volume of a rectangular prism
$V = 12 \cdot 10 \cdot 8$	Replace ℓ with 12, w with 10, and h with 8.
$V = 960$	Multiply.

The volume is 960 cubic feet.

STRATEGY

Formulas Use the Mathematics Chart to find the formula you need.

Fill in the Grid

- Write your answer in the answer boxes so that 9 is in the hundreds place.
- Write only one digit or symbol in each answer box.
- Do not write any digits or symbols outside the answer boxes.
- You may leave blank any boxes you do not need.
- Fill in only one bubble for every answer box that you have written in. Be sure not to fill in a bubble under a blank answer box.

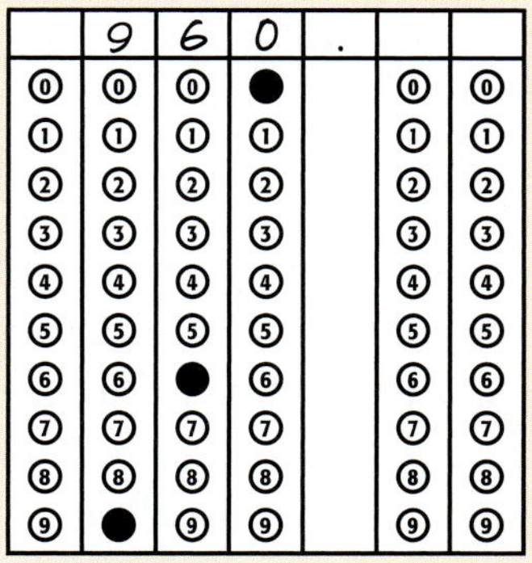

Practice by Objective

Objective 1: The student will demonstrate an understanding of numbers, operations, and quantitative reasoning.

DIRECTIONS

Read each question. Then fill in the correct answer on your answer document. If a correct answer is <u>not here</u>, mark the letter for "Not here."

QUICK Practice

1. Mrs. Adams paints seashells. She paints 30 shells in 80 minutes. How long will it take her to paint 90 shells if she continues painting at the same rate?

   A 18 min **C** 150 min

   B 27 min **D** 240 min

2. Anya planted $\frac{3}{8}$ of the area of her garden with rose bushes as shown.

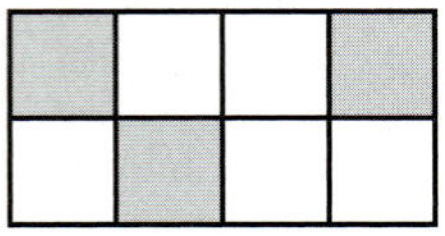

   What percent of her garden did Anya plant with rose bushes?

   F 11% **H** $37\frac{1}{2}\%$

   G 24% **J** $66\frac{2}{3}\%$

3. The mayor of Blue Hills estimates that 31.4% of the residents of Blue Hills regularly use public transportation. Which number is NOT equivalent to 31.4%?

   A $\frac{314}{1{,}000}$ **C** 3.14

   B $\frac{31.4}{100}$ **D** 0.314

QUICK Review

STRATEGY Which answers can you eliminate because they are not reasonable?

This question can be answered using a proportion.

$$\frac{30 \text{ shells}}{80 \text{ minutes}} = \frac{90 \text{ shells}}{x \text{ minutes}}$$

For more help with proportions, see page 348.

READING HINT Percent means *per hundred.* Ask yourself: How much is $\frac{3}{8}$ of 100?

You can answer this question by solving a proportion.

$$\frac{3}{8} = \frac{x}{100}$$

You can also write $\frac{3}{8}$ as a decimal and then write the decimal as a percent.

For more help with percents, see page 250.

STRATEGY As you examine each choice, put a check beside the ones that ARE equivalent. The one without a check is the correct answer.

To change a percent to the decimal, move the decimal point two places to the left and remove the percent sign.

For more help with decimals and percents, see page 254.

QUICK Practice

4. Simplify the expression below.

$9 + 8(11 - 6) \div 2^2$

F 12

G 19

H 125

J 409

QUICK Review

STRATEGY Recall that the rules of order of operations detail the steps to follow to simplify this type of expression.

To simplify, do all operations within grouping symbols first. Next, evaluate the power and then multiply and divide in order from left to right. Finally, complete the addition.

For more help with order of operations, see page 38.

5. The model represents which of the following expressions?

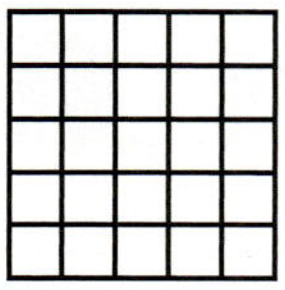

A $\sqrt{25}$ **C** 5^2

B $5 + 5$ **D** $2 \cdot 5$

STRATEGY What operation is best described by using a square model?

Count the number of rows, columns, and total blocks. Note that $5 \cdot 5$, or 5^2, equals 25.

For more help with exponents, see page 30.

6. **GRIDDABLE** During a visit to his favorite bookstore, Kevin bought 3 hardback books priced at \$14.99 each, and 4 paperbacks priced at \$7.99 each. Find the total of Kevin's purchase in dollars before tax is included.

STRATEGY Record your answer carefully in the grid being careful to put the decimal point in the proper place. Place one digit in each block.

Using order of operations, multiply to find the cost of the hardback books and the cost of the paperbacks. Then add to find the total.

For more help with multiplying decimals, see page 134.

7. Order the set of numbers from least to greatest.

$$18.5\%, 0.85, \frac{5}{8}, 1.85$$

F $18.5\%, \frac{5}{8}, 0.85, 1.85$

G $\frac{5}{8}, 0.85, 1.85, 18.5\%$

H $0.85, \frac{5}{8}, 1.85, 18.5\%$

J $18.5\%, 0.85, 1.85, \frac{5}{8}$

STRATEGY Recall that, in order to compare and order numbers, they must be written in the same form.

Write all numbers as decimals. Compare each number, using place value. Then write the numbers in order from least to greatest.

For more help with comparing and ordering numbers, see page 263.

Practice on Your Own

Objective 1

8. Mr. Connor discovers that $\frac{3}{5}$ of the tiles on his bathroom floor are cracked and in need of replacement. What percent of the tiles need to be replaced?

A 15%

B 35%

C 60%

D 167%

9. Which expression can be used to solve the problem below?

To rent a car while on a business trip, John must pay $39.50 per day plus $0.35 per mile driven. Which expression represents the total cost for a 4-day rental driven 72 miles?

F $4 \times 39.50 + 0.35 + 72$

G $4 \times 39.50 + 0.35 \times 72$

H $4 \times 72 + 0.35 \times 39.50$

J $4 \times 0.35 + 72 \times 39.50$

10. A local waterpark offers several different package deals. The prices are given in the table.

Package	Price
3-Day Pass	$24.50
5-Day Pass	$40.95
10-Day Pass	$74.95

Which package deal(s) offer(s) the lowest price per day?

A The 3-day pass alone

B The 3-day pass and the 5-day pass

C The 5-day pass alone

D The 10-day pass alone

11. **GRIDDABLE** Aurelio and his friends ate $\frac{7}{8}$ of a pizza. What percent of the pizza did they eat?

12. What is the value of the expression below?

$(9 - 5)^2 \div 8 - 3 \times 2$

F -12

G -4

H 2

J 6

13. Kelley is making a quilt using two different colors of fabric for the square pieces. In the pattern, $\frac{2}{5}$ of the squares are black, as shown.

What percent of the squares did Kelley make black?

A 25%

B 40%

C 52%

D 65%

14. Ben drives from his home to a vacation spot at a rate of 62 miles per hour. He travels for 3.5 hours. About how far was Ben's vacation spot from his home?

F Less than 200 miles

G Between 200 and 250 miles

H Between 250 and 300 miles

J More than 300 miles

15. Apples are on sale for $0.88 a pound. Lawrence purchased 4.85 pounds of apples. About how much did he pay for the apples?

A Less than $4.00

B Between $4.00 and $4.50

C Between $4.50 and $5.00

D More than $5.00

Practice by Objective

Objective 2: The student will demonstrate an understanding of patterns, relationships, and algebraic thinking.

DIRECTIONS

Read each question. Then fill in the correct answer on your answer document. If a correct answer is not here, mark the letter for "Not here."

QUICK Practice

1. The gym teacher at Middlebrook Elementary school uses a circular mat with a circumference of 38 feet. Which expression could be used to find the radius of the mat?

   A $38 - 2\pi$ **C** $\frac{38}{\pi}$

   B $\frac{38}{2\pi}$ **D** $38 + 2\pi$

QUICK Review

READING HINT Circumference means *distance around the circle,* and radius means *distance from the center of the circle to any point on the circle.*

This question can be answered by solving the formula for the circumference of a circle, $C = 2\pi r$ for r.

For more help with circumference, see page 622.

2. In his marble collection of 40 marbles, Nick has 7 red marbles. Which equation can be used to find x, the percent of red marbles in Nick's marble collection?

   F $\frac{x}{40} = \frac{7}{100}$ **H** $\frac{40}{7} = \frac{x}{100}$

   G $\frac{100}{40} = \frac{7}{x}$ **J** $\frac{7}{40} = \frac{x}{100}$

READING HINT Percent means *per hundred.* Ask yourself: How much is $\frac{7}{40}$ of 100?

You can answer this question by solving a proportion.

$$\frac{7}{40} = \frac{x}{100}$$

For more help with percents, see page 392.

3. The model represents the equation $x - 3 = 7$.

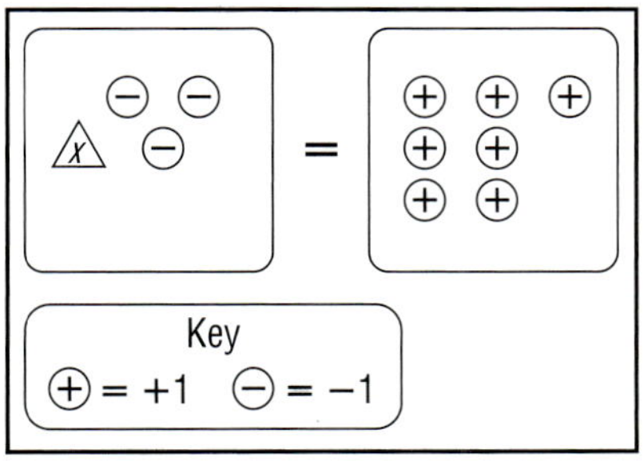

   What is the value of x?

   A $x = -10$ **C** $x = 4$

   B $x = -4$ **D** $x = 10$

STRATEGY Which answers can you eliminate because they are not reasonable?

To solve a subtraction equation, recall the Addition Property of Equality. If you add the same number to each side of an equation, the two sides remain equal.

For more help with solving addition and subtraction equations, see page 184.

QUICK Practice

4. Which of the following sequences follows the rule $4n - 3$, where n represents the position of a term in the sequence?

   F 3, 9, 14, 22, 31, …

   G 18, 15, 12, 9, 6, …

   H 1, 5, 9, 13, 17, …

   J 24, 20, 16, 12, 8, …

QUICK Review

STRATEGY Look at the rule and determine whether the terms of the sequence should increase or decrease. This will narrow the possibilities.

To find the terms of a sequence, evaluate the rule for values of n beginning with $n = 1$.

For more help with sequences, see page 57.

5. The length of a rectangular plot of land is five less than twice its width w.

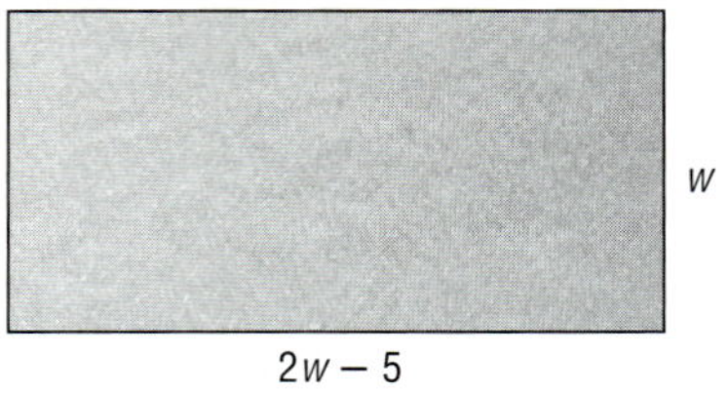

   Which equation below represents the perimeter P of the plot of land?

   A $P = 4w - 10$

   B $P = 6w - 10$

   C $P = 3w - 5$

   D $P = 2w^2 - 5w$

READING HINT Perimeter means *distance around a figure.*

The formula for the perimeter of a rectangle is $P = 2\ell + 2w$. Substitute $2w - 5$ for ℓ and simplify the expression.

For more help with perimeter, see page 204.

6. Which description shows the relationship between a term and n, its position in the sequence?

Position	1	2	3	4	5	n
Value of Term	5	7	9	11	13	

   F Add 4 to n.

   G Multiply n by 3 and then add 2.

   H Multiply n by 3 and then subtract 2.

   J Multiply n by 2 and then add 3.

STRATEGY Look for a pattern among the value of the terms.

The same rule must apply to every term in the sequence. Test each term to determine if it follows the rule.

For more help with sequences, see page 57.

Practice on Your Own

7. Mrs. Eakin has 24 students in her seventh grade geography class. Eight of the students are boys. What percent of the students are boys?

A 8%

B $33\frac{1}{3}\%$

C $37\frac{1}{2}\%$

D $66\frac{2}{3}\%$

8. The Delicious Deli is advertising a special on corned beef sandwiches. The advertised price is 3 sandwiches for $12.99. What is the sale price of one sandwich?

F $3.00

G $3.99

H $4.33

J $6.49

9. A triangular piece of plywood has an area of 50 square meters. Which of the following expresses the height h of the triangle in terms of its area and base b?

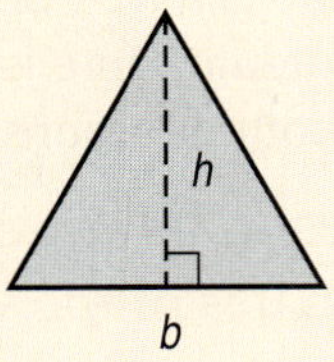

A $h = \frac{100}{b}$

B $h = 50b$

C $h = \frac{2b}{50}$

D $h = \frac{b}{200}$

10. Which of the following relationships is best represented by the data in the graph?

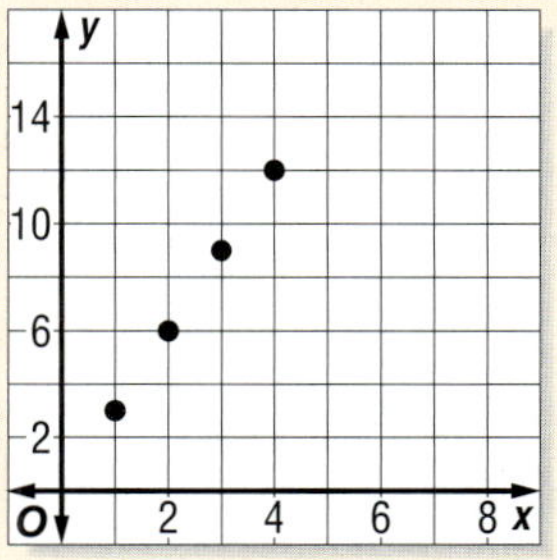

F Conversion of feet to inches

G Conversion of inches to yards

H Conversion of miles to feet

J Conversion of yards to feet

11. Which sequence follows the rule $7n - 5$, where n represents the position of a term in the sequence?

A 37, 30, 23, 16, 9, …

B 14, 19, 24, 29, 34, …

C 2, 9, 16, 23, 30, …

D 1, 2, 3, 4, 5, …

12. Mary is mixing 50 pounds of nuts to package for sale in her candy store. She uses 12 pounds of cashews in the 50-pound mix. Which equation can be used to find x, the percent of cashews in the nut mix?

F $\frac{x}{50} = \frac{12}{100}$

G $\frac{100}{x} = \frac{12}{50}$

H $\frac{50}{12} = \frac{x}{100}$

J $\frac{12}{50} = \frac{x}{100}$

Practice by Objective

Objective 3: The student will demonstrate an understanding of geometry and spatial reasoning.

DIRECTIONS

Read each question. Then fill in the correct answer on your answer document. If a correct answer is not here, mark the letter for "Not here."

QUICK Practice

1. Use the protractor to measure each angle.

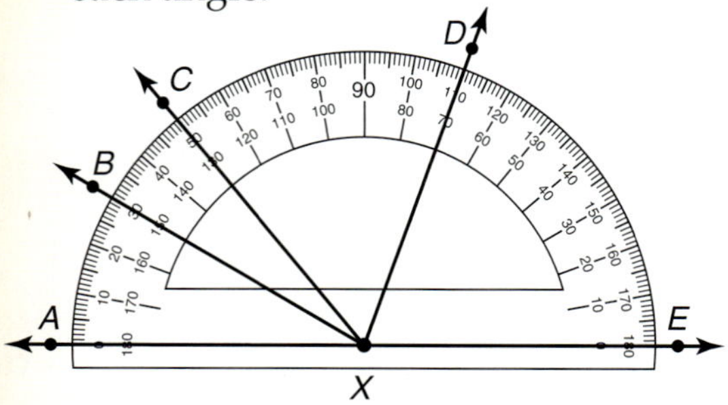

Name one pair of complementary angles.

A $\angle AXB$ and $\angle BXE$

B $\angle CXD$ and $\angle DXE$

C $\angle AXB$ and $\angle CXD$

D $\angle DXE$ and $\angle AXC$

QUICK Review

READING HINT Two angles are complementary if the sum of their measures is 90°.

Use a protractor to find the measure of each angle. Then determine which two angles have measures with a sum of 90°.

For more help with complementary angles, see page 552.

2. Katie sketched a trapezoid on graph paper. She wants to translate the trapezoid so that a vertex originally having coordinates $(-4, -2)$ moves to coordinates $(1, -3)$. Which steps will complete the translation?

F Move each vertex 3 units to the left and 1 unit down.

G Move each vertex 5 units to the right and 1 unit down.

H Move each vertex 4 units to the right and 5 units up.

J Move each vertex 5 units to the left and 3 units up.

READING HINT A translation is a type of transformation where a geometric figure is slid horizontally, vertically, or in both directions.

You can answer this question by graphing both the original coordinates of the vertex and the new coordinates of the vertex on the same set of axes. Then, determine the horizontal and vertical change.

For more help with translations, see page 591.

QUICK Practice

3. Mrs. Adams is planting a flower garden on a triangular plot of land as shown below.

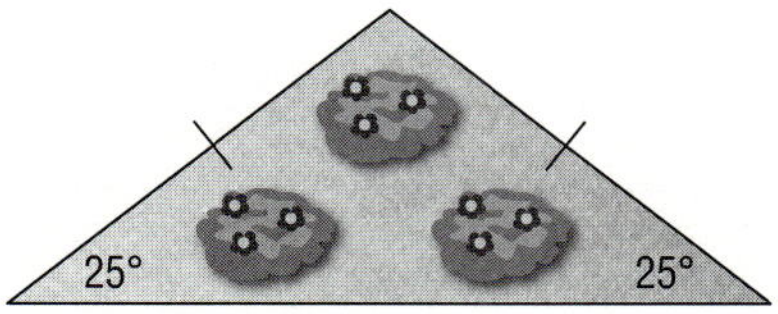

Which of the following best describes the triangle with the given measures?

A Acute equilateral triangle

B Obtuse isosceles triangle

C Right scalene triangle

D Right isosceles triangle

4. The figure was transformed from quadrant I to quadrant II.

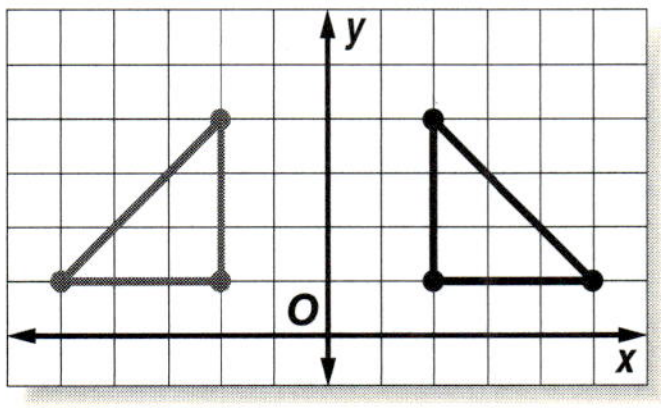

This transformation best represents which of the following?

F translation **H** rotation

G tessellation **J** reflection

5. If $\angle M$ and $\angle N$ are supplementary and the measure of $\angle M$ is 80°, what is the measure of $\angle N$?

A 10° **C** 100°

B 80° **D** 180°

QUICK Review

STRATEGY As you examine each choice, eliminate the answers that have terms that do not describe the triangle shown.

The triangle shown has two congruent sides and an obtuse angle.

For more help with triangles, see page 564.

READING HINT A translation is a slide vertically, horizontally, or both. A tessellation is a repetitive pattern of polygons. A rotation occurs when a figure is turned. A reflection is the flip of a figure over a line of symmetry.

The figure shows the triangle being flipped over the horizontal axis.

For more help with transformations, see page 596.

READING HINT Two angles are supplementary if the sum of their measures is 180°.

Solve the equation $x + 80 = 180$, where x is the measure of angle N.

For more help with supplementary angles, see page 552.

Practice on Your Own

Objective 3

6. If the corresponding angles of two polygons are congruent and the lengths of the corresponding sides of the polygons are proportional, which of the following describes the polygons?

F Regular
G Congruent
H Symmetric
J Similar

7. Which of the following has two parallel bases that are not polygons?

A Cone
B Sphere
C Cylinder
D Prism

8. If point H is translated 3 units to the right and 2 units down, what will the new coordinates of point H be?

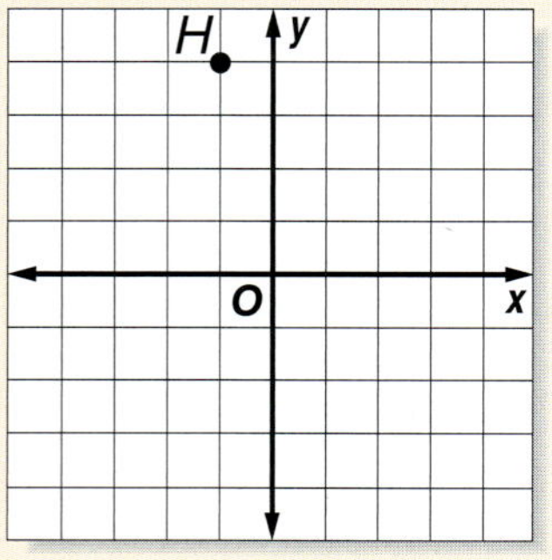

F (2, 2)
G (−3, 2)
H (2, 6)
J (−4, −2)

9. Which statement is always true about an equilateral triangle?

A It has three congruent angles.
B It has one right angle.
C It has exactly two congruent sides.
D The sum of any two angles is 180°.

10. Use the protractor to read the measure of each angle.

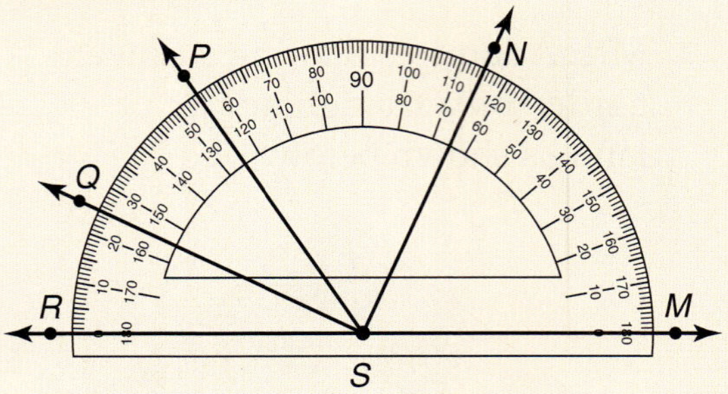

Name one pair of complementary angles.

F $\angle RSQ$ and $\angle NSM$
G $\angle QSM$ and $\angle RSN$
H $\angle QSN$ and $\angle RSN$
J $\angle PSN$ and $\angle RSN$

11. Identify the three-dimensional figure that can be formed from this net.

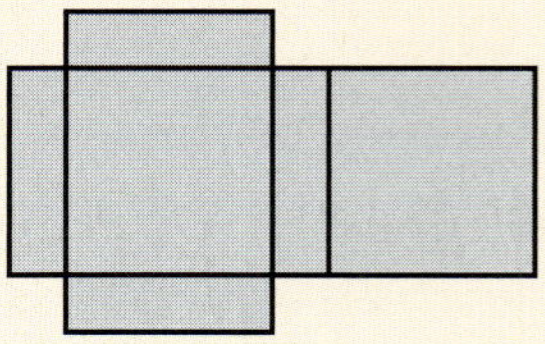

A Cube
B Rectangular pyramid
C Triangular prism
D Rectangular prism

12. Which of the following coordinates lie within the circle graphed below?

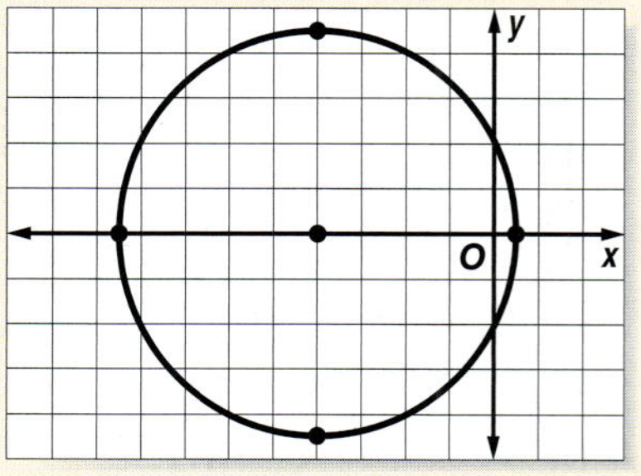

F (1, 4)
G (−2, 7)
H (−1, −4)
J (−5, −2)

Practice by Objective

Objective 4: The student will demonstrate an understanding of the concepts and uses of measurement.

DIRECTIONS

Read each question. Then fill in the correct answer on your answer document. If a correct answer is <u>not here</u>, mark the letter for "Not here."

QUICK Practice

1. Find the exact number of cubes measuring 4 centimeters on an edge that will fill a box shaped like a rectangular prism that measures 32 centimeters by 24 centimeters by 12 centimeters.

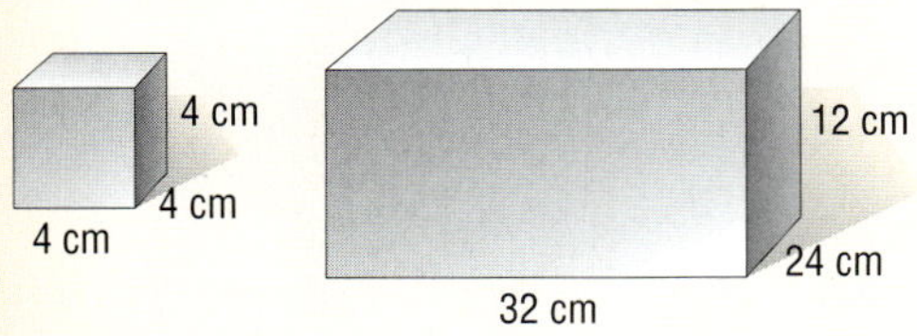

A 17 cubes C 144 cubes

B 48 cubes D 212 cubes

2. **GRIDDABLE** Mrs. Cantor plans to paint one wall of her bedroom. The wall measures 18 feet long and 9 feet high. There is one window on the wall that has dimensions 4.2 feet by 3.5 feet. Find the area, in square feet, of the wall surface Mrs. Cantor is planning to paint.

3. Ellie is using the circular dish shown to make a cookie tray. Which of the following is closest to the area of the dish?

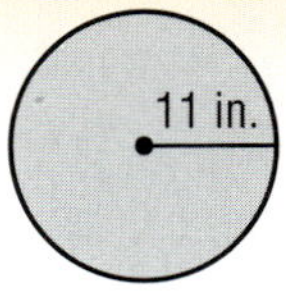

F 34 in^2 H 254 in^2

G 121 in^2 J 380 in^2

QUICK Review

READING HINT The volume of a rectangular prism is found by multiplying the length, the width, and the height.

Determine how many cubes with edges of 4 centimeters it will take to make up the length, width, and height. Then multiply those values.

For more help with finding the volume of a rectangular prism, see page 651.

STRATEGY Record your answer carefully in the grid being careful to put the decimal point in the proper place. Place one digit in each block.

Find both the area of the entire wall and the area of the window. Then subtract the area of the window from the area of the entire wall.

For more help with finding the area of a rectangle, see page 204.

STRATEGY Which answers can you eliminate because they are not reasonable?

To answer the question, use the formula for the area of a circle, $A = \pi r^2$.

For more help with finding the area of a circle, see page 627.

QUICK Practice

4. Dave is designing a plastic box to be used to store a garden hose when it is not in use. The storage box is to be 20 inches long, 24 inches wide, and 18 inches high.

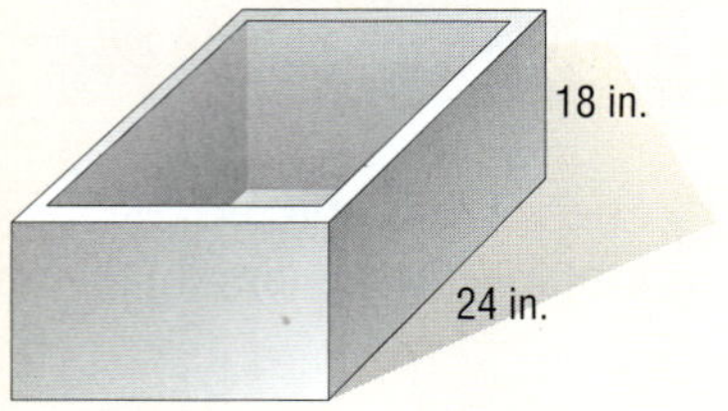

What is the volume of the storage box in cubic inches?

A 62 in.^3

B 480 in.^3

C $2{,}650 \text{ in.}^3$

D $8{,}640 \text{ in.}^3$

5. Daniel is building a picture frame. The outside dimensions of the frame are 18 inches by 12 inches. The inside dimensions of the frame are 14 inches by 8 inches. Find the area of the picture frame.

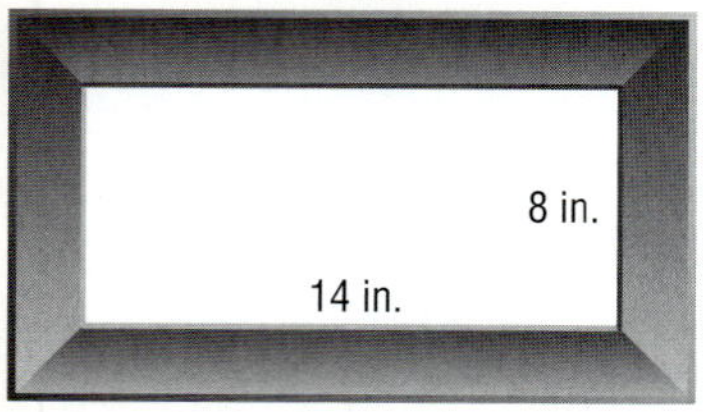

F 8 in.^2

G 104 in.^2

H 112 in.^2

J 216 in.^2

QUICK Review

READING HINT Recall that the volume of a rectangular prism can be found by multiplying the length, width, and height.

The volume of this box can be found by finding $20 \cdot 24 \cdot 18$.

For more help with finding the volume of a rectangular prism, see page 651.

STRATEGY Which answers can you eliminate because they are not reasonable?

First find the areas of both the outer and inner rectangles. Then, subtract the smaller area from the larger area to find the area of the frame.

For more help with finding the area of a rectangle, see page 204.

Practice on Your Own

6. A box of cereal has a length of 8 inches, a width of 3 inches, and a height of 14 inches. What is the volume of the cereal box?

   A 25 in.^{3}

   B 38 in.^{3}

   C 154 in.^{3}

   D 336 in.^{3}

7. While working on a project for art class, Sarah drew a circle with a radius of 12 centimeters and another circle with a radius of 9 centimeters. What is the approximate difference to the nearest whole number between the areas of the two circles?

   F 64 cm^2 H 198 cm^2

   G 144 cm^2 J 215 cm^2

8. Samantha is planning to wallpaper the largest wall in her living room. The wall has dimensions 21 feet by 10 feet. There are two windows on the wall, each measuring 4 feet by 5 feet. Find the area that needs covering with wallpaper.

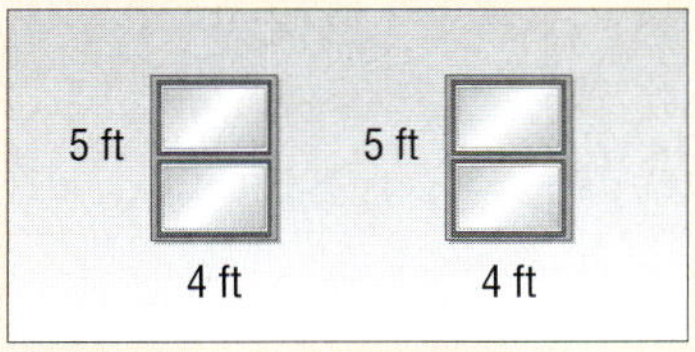

   A 20 ft^2

   B 40 ft^2

   C 170 ft^2

   D 210 ft^2

9. Andrew is painting a geometric design on the bottom of a circular swimming pool. The pool has a radius of 10 feet. If Andrew paints 25% of the pool's bottom green, what is the approximate area of the green portion of the bottom of the pool?

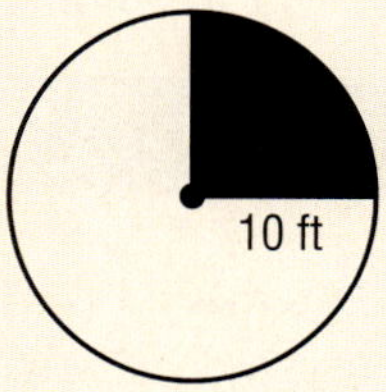

   F 78.5 ft^2 H 214.8 ft^2

   G 124 ft^2 J 314 ft^2

10. Nicole wants to fence her rectangular backyard for her new puppy. The back wall of her house will serve as one side of the fence. The length of the fenced area will be 40 feet, and the width will be 25 feet. How much fencing does Nicole need to purchase to complete the project?

   A 65 ft C 130 ft

   B 90 ft D 1,000 ft

11. **GRIDDABLE** A cylindrical can of soup measures 10.4 centimeters high and has a diameter of 9.8 centimeters. Find the volume of the can of soup in cubic centimeters. Round to the nearest tenth. Use 3.14 for π.

Practice by Objective

Objective 5: The student will demonstrate an understanding of probability and statistics.

DIRECTIONS

Read each question. Then fill in the correct answer on your answer document. If a correct answer is not here, mark the letter for "Not here."

QUICK Practice

1. A probability experiment consists of first tossing a coin and then rolling a number cube. How many outcomes are possible?

   A 8

   B 12

   C 16

   D 64

2. A police officer monitoring a certain stretch of highway recorded the speeds of five cars. The results are shown below.

Car	Speed (mph)
1	62
2	81
3	74
4	68
5	65

   What is the range of the speeds and the median speed for these five cars?

   F Range = 19 mph
   Median = 68 mph

   G Range = 81 mph
   Median = 68 mph

   H Range = 24 mph
   Median = 62 mph

   J Range = 19 mph
   Median = 74 mph

QUICK Review

READING HINT An outcome is one possible result of a probability event. For example, when a coin is tossed, heads is an outcome.

Create a tree diagram to determine all possible outcomes in the sample space.

For more help with sample spaces, see page 509.

READING HINT Range measures the difference between the greatest and least piece of data. The median is the data value that falls in the middle when the data is ranked in numeric order.

You can find the range of this data by subtracting the lowest speed from the highest speed. The median of the five data values will be the third value when the data is ranked.

For more help with range, see page 442.
For more help with median, see page 448.

QUICK Practice

3. Kyle spun each spinner once.

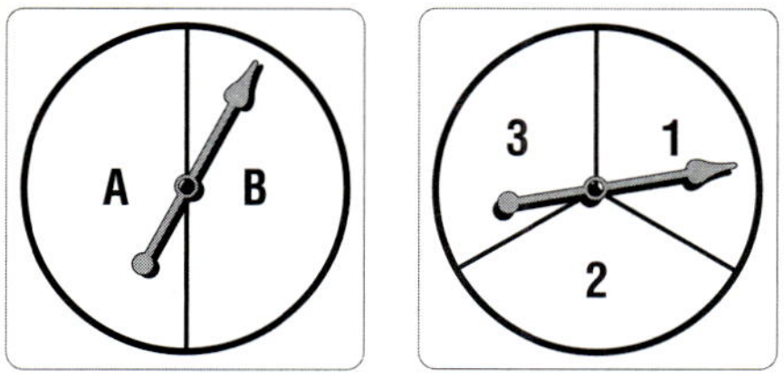

First Spinner   Second Spinner

Which shows all the possible unique combinations of letters and numbers that could have resulted from Kyle's spins?

A {A, B, 1, 2, 3}

B {A1, B2, A3}

C {A1, A2, A3, B1, B2, B3}

D {AB, 12, 13, 23}

QUICK Review

READING HINT Recall that a sample space is the set of all possible outcomes of a probability experiment.

A tree diagram can be used to accurately list all of the possible outcomes to this experiment.

For more help with finding the outcomes of a sample space, see page 509.

---

4. The graph shows the favorite flavors of ice cream for a group of 100 middle school students.

Which flavor is the most popular?

F vanilla

G chocolate

H cookie dough

J strawberry

STRATEGY Which answers can you eliminate because they are not reasonable?

To solve the problem, look at the graph to determine which bar is the tallest. This represents the most frequently given answer.

For more help with interpreting bar graphs, see page 461.

Practice on Your Own

5. Mrs. Hastings gave an algebra quiz to her seventh grade class. The scores are shown.

   8, 7, 10, 5, 7, 6, 9, 9, 10

   What is the range of the quiz scores?

   A 5 **C** 7

   B 6 **D** 8

6. Matt is working on a probability experiment that involves tossing a coin 3 times. How many unique outcomes are possible for this experiment?

   F 3 **H** 8

   G 6 **J** 9

7. The table gives the ages of students enrolled in a college statistics course.

Age of Students			
23	18	33	27
21	37	23	22
20	22	21	19
18	25	24	31

   What is the mean age of a student in the course?

   A 18 **C** 27

   B 24 **D** 37

8. Andrea is creating a circle graph to display data she has collected in a survey of her friends' favorite movies. The most popular movie was chosen by 40% of Andrea's friends. How large a section of the circle graph should be reserved for this movie choice?

   F 40° **H** 144°

   G 60° **J** 175°

9. During a survey of customers at a car dealership, 250 customers were asked about their favorite color of car. 105 customers selected silver, 85 selected blue, and 60 selected white. Which representation of the data is NOT an appropriate way to display the survey results?

   A **Favorite Car Color**

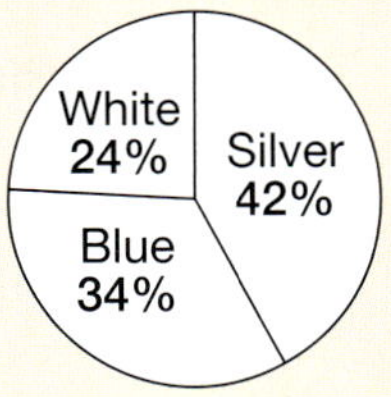

   B **Favorite Car Color**

Color	Customers
Silver	105
Blue	85
White	60

   C **Favorite Car Color**

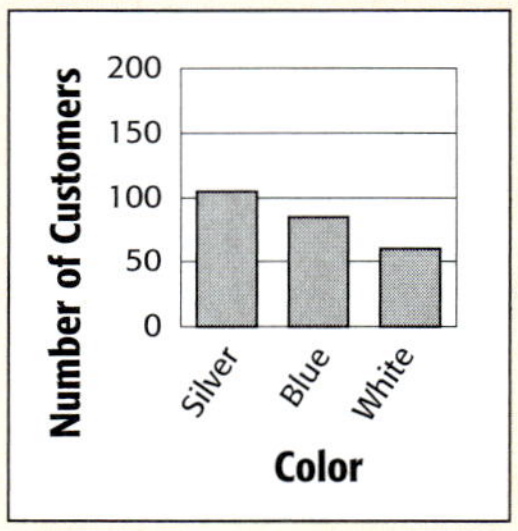

   D **Favorite Car Color**

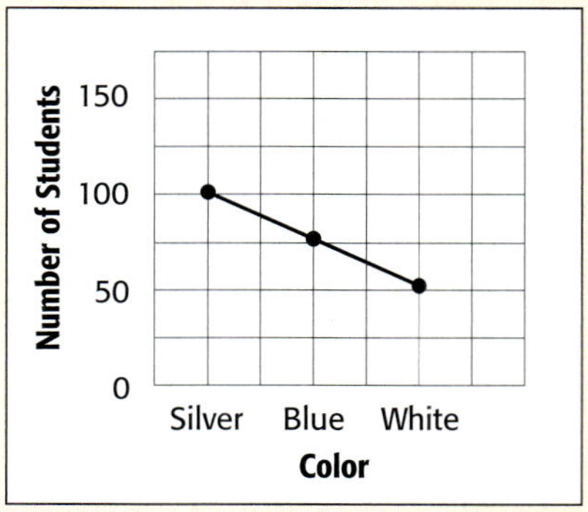

Practice by Objective

Objective 6: The student will demonstrate an understanding of the mathematical processes and tools used in problem solving.

DIRECTIONS

Read each question. Then fill in the correct answer on your answer document. If a correct answer is not here, mark the letter for "Not here."

QUICK Practice

1. Identify the equation below that models $(ab)^c = a^cb^c$.

   A $4^3 = 4 \cdot 4 \cdot 4$

   B $4^34^2 = 16^5$

   C $(3x)^4 = 3^4x^4$

   D $(3 + 2)^4 = 3^42^4$

2. The table shows the heights of nine students in Mr. Adams' physical education class.

Student	1	2	3	4	5	6	7	8	9
Height (in.)	58	61	54	65	60	49	55	66	59

   What should Mr. Adams do to organize the data to identify which students have heights less than the median height?

   F He should add the heights.

   G He should list the student numbers in order from greatest to least.

   H He should list the heights in order from least to greatest with their corresponding student numbers.

   J He should list the student numbers in order from least to greatest with their corresponding heights.

QUICK Review

STRATEGY Use the operations included in the model to help eliminate answers that are not similar in form.

The model suggests that a product raised to a power is equal to the product of the individual factors each raised to that same power.

For more help with exponents, see page 30.

READING HINT The median of a set of data is the value in the middle when the data are ranked in order.

To find the median, list the heights in increasing order. The median will be the data value in the 5th position.

For more help with finding the median of a set of data, see page 448.

QUICK Practice

3. Samantha bought 3 pairs of jeans for \$19.50 each, 2 sweatshirts for \$24.95 each, and 4 pairs of socks for \$3.25 each. She paid 7.5% tax on the entire purchase. What other information is necessary to find Samantha's correct change?

   A The total cost of the purchase

   B Amount she paid in tax

   C Amount she gave the cashier

   D Reason for buying the clothes

4. Peter is constructing a circular stage for a school performance. The diameter of the structure is 11.5 feet.

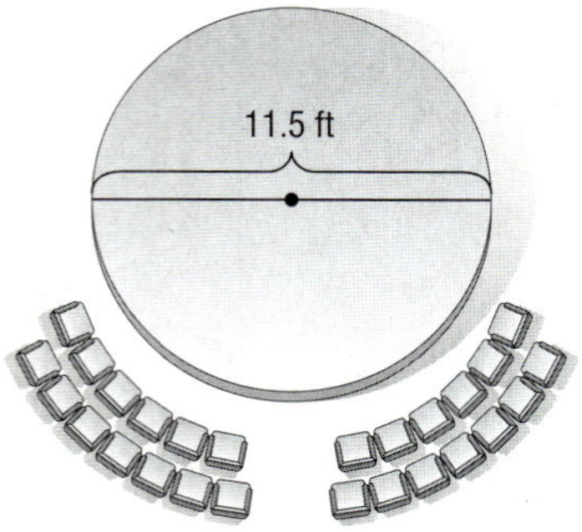

   Which of the following gives the area, in square feet, of the stage? Use $\pi = 3.14$ and round your answer to the nearest hundredth.

   F 415.27 ft^2

   G 103.82 ft^2

   H 72.22 ft^2

   J 36.11 ft^2

QUICK Review

STRATEGY Which answers can you eliminate because they are not reasonable?

The total cost of the purchase can be determined by finding the sum of the costs for each type of item and the adding the tax for the total amount.

For more help with problem solving, see page 25.

STRATEGY Use estimation to eliminate answers that are not reasonable.

The formula for finding the area of a circle is $A = \pi r^2$. Remember that the radius is equal to one half of the diameter.

For more help with finding the area of a circle, see page 627.

Practice on Your Own

5. Which expression can be used to find the maximum number of 0.4-foot lengths of wood that can be cut from a 8.5-foot length of wood?

   A $0.4 \div 8.5$ C $8.5 \div 0.4$
   B $8.5 - 0.4$ D $0.4 - 8.5$

6. Mr. Brauen is building a toy box for his grandchildren that has dimensions 3 feet by 2 feet by 2.5 feet.

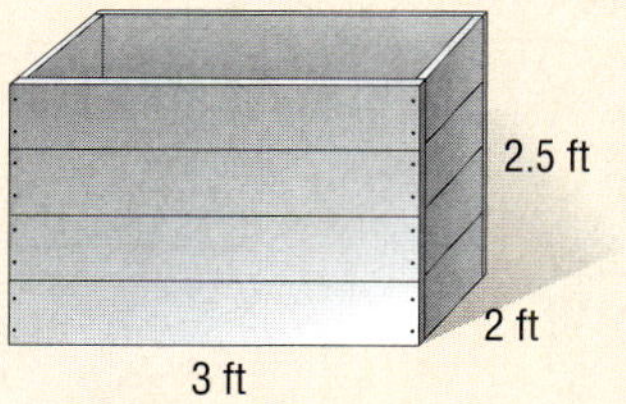

   What is the volume of the toy box?

   F 6 ft^3
   G 7.5 ft^3
   H 15 ft^3
   J 24.5 ft^3

7. The table below gives the distance in miles that students in Miss Marks' class live from school.

Distance (mi)		
2.4	1.2	3.0
4.1	0.8	2.6
1.5	2.3	4.3
2.5	2.8	2.5

   What is the mean distance?

   A 1.3 mi
   B 2.5 mi
   C 2.8 mi
   D 4.3 mi

8. Howard spent one half of his Saturday earnings on a video game and half of the remaining amount on a CD. After he spent $5.85 on lunch, he had $8.15 left. How much did Howard earn on Saturday?

   F $31.50
   G $47
   H $56
   J $72

9. The prices of three different bottles of laundry detergent are given in the table.

Bottle Size (ounces)	Price ($)
36	3.99
48	4.59
64	6.09

   Which size bottle of laundry detergent has the lowest price per ounce?

   A The 36-oz bottle only
   B The 48-oz bottle only
   C The 64-oz bottle only
   D All three botttle sizes have the same price per ounce.

10. A movie company distributed 120 children's videos last year and 30 of them became best-sellers. Which best represents the percent of videos the company distributed that did NOT become best-sellers?

   F 25%
   G 30%
   H 75%
   J 83%

Chapter 13

Extending Algebra and Geometry

Knowledge and Skills

- Use indirect measurement to solve problems. **Preparation for TEKS 8.9**
- Use procedures to determine measures of three-dimensional figures. **Preparation for TEKS 8.8**

Key Vocabulary

hypotenuse (p. 678)

irrational number (p. 675)

Pythagorean Theorem (p. 678)

surface area (p. 688)

Real-World Link

SPAGHETTI The shape of many spaghetti boxes are rectangular prisms, and the shape of many cans are cylinders. You can use the formula $S = 2\ell w + 2\ell h + 2wh$ to find the surface area of a box of spaghetti given the length ℓ, the width w, and the height h of the box.

FOLDABLES™ Study Organizer

Extending Algebra and Geometry Make this Foldable to help you organize your notes. Begin with a piece of 11″ by 17″ paper.

1. **Fold** the paper in fourths lengthwise.

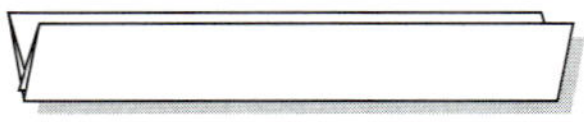

2. **Open** and fold a 2″ tab along the short side. Then fold the rest in half.

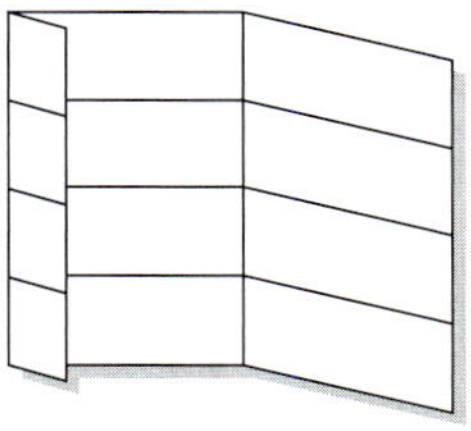

3. **Draw** lines along the folds and label as shown.

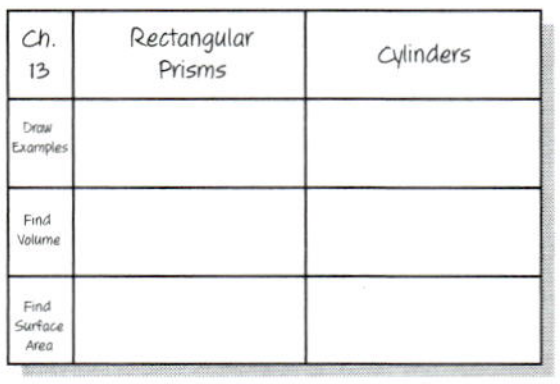

GET READY for Chapter 13

Diagnose Readiness You have two options for checking Prerequisite Skills.

Option 2

Math Online Take the Online Readiness Quiz at tx.msmath2.com.

Option 1

Take the Quick Quiz below. Refer to the Quick Review for help.

QUICK Quiz

Evaluate each expression.
(Used in Lessons 13-1 and 13-2)

1. 4^2
2. 7^2
3. 13^2
4. 24^2
5. $5^2 + 8^2$
6. $10^2 + 6^2$
7. $9^2 + 12^2$
8. $15^2 + 17^2$
9. **AGES** Samuel's mother is 7^2 years old, and his grandmother is 9^2 years old. Find the sum of their ages.

Evaluate the expression $2ab + 2bc + 2ac$ for each value of the variables indicated. (Used in Lesson 13-4)

10. $a = 4, b = 5, c = 8$
11. $a = 2, b = 7, c = 11$
12. $a = 3.1, b = 2.4, c = 9.9$
13. $a = 2.1, b = 1.7, c = 4.6$

Use the π button on your calculator to evaluate each expression below. Round to the nearest tenth.
(Used in Lesson 13-5)

14. $(2)(\pi)(3^2) + (2)(\pi)(3)(8)$
15. $(2)(\pi)(7^2) + (2)(\pi)(7)(5)$

QUICK Review

Example 1
Evaluate $3^2 + 5^2$.

$3^2 + 5^2 = 9 + 25$ — Evaluate 3^2 and 5^2.
$= 34$ — Add 9 and 25.

Example 2
Evaluate the expression $2ab + 2bc + 2ac$ for $a = 3$, $b = 5$, and $c = 6$.

$2ab + 2bc + 2ac$
$= 2(3)(5) + 2(5)(6) + 2(3)(6)$ — Replace *a* with 3, *b* with 5, and *c* with 6.
$= 30 + 60 + 36$ — Multiply.
$= 126$ — Add.

Example 3
Use the π button on your calculator to evaluate $(2)(\pi)(4^2) + (2)(\pi)(4)(6)$. Round to the nearest tenth.

$(2)(\pi)(4^2) + (2)(\pi)(4)(6)$
$= (2)(\pi)(16) + (2)(\pi)(4)(6)$ — Evaluate 4^2.
$= (32)(\pi) + (48)(\pi)$ — Multiply.
≈ 251.3 — Multiply and add.

13-1 Estimating Square Roots

Main IDEA

Estimate square roots.

Preparing for TEKS 8.1 The student understands that different forms of numbers are appropriate for different situations. **(C) approximate (mentally and with calculators) the value of irrational numbers as they arise from problem situations (such as π, $\sqrt{2}$).**

NEW Vocabulary

irrational number

READING in the Content Area

For strategies in reading this lesson, visit tx.msmath2.com.

MINI Lab

Estimate the square root of 27.

- Arrange 27 tiles into the largest square possible. You will use 25 tiles and 2 will remain.
- Add tiles to make the next larger square. So, add 9 tiles to make a square with 36 tiles.
- The square root of 27 is between 5 and 6. Since 27 is much closer to 25 than 36, we can expect that the square root of 27 is closer to 5 than 6.

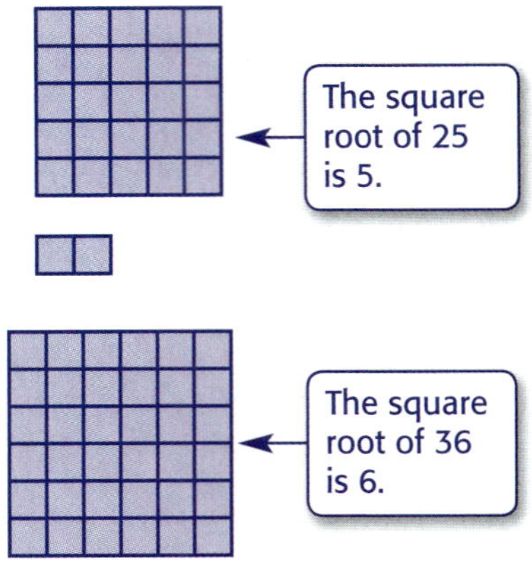

Use algebra tiles to estimate the square root of each number to the nearest whole number.

1. 40 **2.** 28 **3.** 85 **4.** 62

5. Describe another method that you could use to estimate the square root of a number.

The square root of a perfect square is an integer. You can estimate the square root of a number that is *not* a perfect square.

EXAMPLE Estimate a Square Root

1 Estimate $\sqrt{78}$ to the nearest whole number.

List some perfect squares.

1, 4, 9, 16, 25, 36, 49, 64, 81, ...

78 (between 64 and 81)

$64 < 78 < 81$ — 78 is between the perfect squares 64 and 81.

$\sqrt{64} < \sqrt{78} < \sqrt{81}$ — Find the square root of each number.

$8 < \sqrt{78} < 9$ — $\sqrt{64} = 8$ and $\sqrt{81} = 9$

So, $\sqrt{78}$ is between 8 and 9. Since 78 is much closer to 81 than to 64, the best whole number estimate is 9. Verify with a calculator.

CHECK Your Progress

a. Estimate $\sqrt{50}$ to the nearest whole number.

Online **Personal Tutor at** tx.msmath2.com

A number that cannot be written as a fraction is an **irrational number**.

Irrational Numbers $\sqrt{2}$, π, 0.636336333...

Vocabulary Link
Irrational
Everyday Use lacking usual or normal clarity, as in irrational thinking
Math Use a number that cannot be written as a fraction

The square root of any number that is not a perfect square is an irrational number. You can use a calculator to estimate square roots that are irrational numbers.

EXAMPLE Use a Calculator to Estimate

2 **Use a calculator to find the value of $\sqrt{42}$ to the nearest tenth.**

2nd [√] 42 ENTER 6.480740698

$\sqrt{42} \approx 6.5$

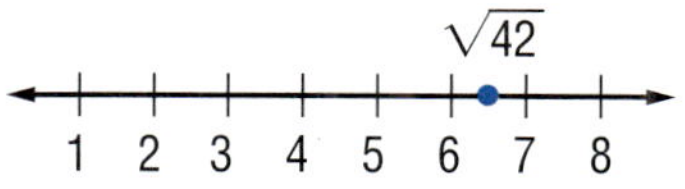

Check for Reasonableness
$6^2 = 36$ and $7^2 = 49$. Since 42 is between 36 and 49, the answer, 6.5, is reasonable.

CHECK Your Progress

Use a calculator to find each square root to the nearest tenth.

b. $\sqrt{6}$ c. $\sqrt{23}$ d. $\sqrt{309}$

The Venn diagram shows the relationship among sets of numbers.

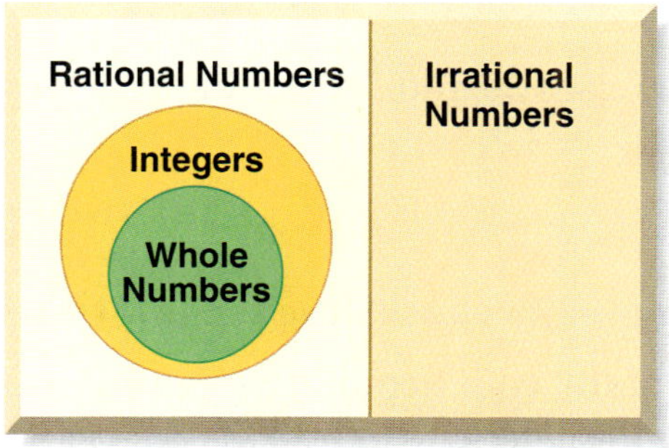

Whole Numbers: 0, 1, 2, 3, ...
Integers: ..., −2, −1, 0, 1, 2, ...
Rational Numbers: $\frac{1}{2}$, 0.25, −0.2, 0.333...
Irrational Numbers: π, $\sqrt{2}$, 0.124543...

CHECK Your Understanding

Example 1 (p. 674)

Estimate each square root to the nearest whole number.

1. $\sqrt{39}$ 2. $\sqrt{106}$ 3. $\sqrt{90}$ 4. $\sqrt{140}$

Example 2 (p. 675)

Use a calculator to find each square root to the nearest tenth.

5. $\sqrt{7}$ 6. $\sqrt{51}$ 7. $\sqrt{135}$ 8. $\sqrt{462}$

9. **FLOOR PLANS** The diagram at the right shows the floor plan of a square kitchen. Use a calculator to find the length of one side of the kitchen floor to the nearest tenth.

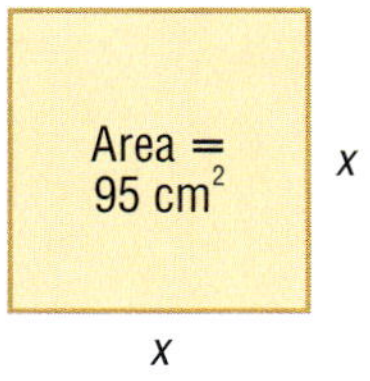

Exercises

HOMEWORK HELP	
For Exercises	See Examples
10–17, 27	1
18–26	2

Estimate each square root to the nearest whole number.

10. $\sqrt{11}$
11. $\sqrt{20}$
12. $\sqrt{35}$
13. $\sqrt{65}$
14. $\sqrt{89}$
15. $\sqrt{116}$
16. $\sqrt{137}$
17. $\sqrt{409}$

Use a calculator to find each square root to the nearest tenth.

18. $\sqrt{15}$
19. $\sqrt{8}$
20. $\sqrt{44}$
21. $\sqrt{89}$
22. $\sqrt{160}$
23. $\sqrt{573}$
24. $\sqrt{645}$
25. $\sqrt{2{,}798}$

26. **BAKING** The bottom of the square baking pan has an area of 67 square inches. What is the approximate length of one side of the pan?

27. **ALGEBRA** What whole number is closest to $\sqrt{m - n}$ if $m = 45$ and $n = 8$?

Estimate each square root to the nearest whole number.

28. $\sqrt{925}$
29. $\sqrt{2{,}480}$
30. $\sqrt{1{,}610}$
31. $\sqrt{6{,}500}$

Estimate each square root to the nearest tenth.

32. $\sqrt{0.25}$
33. $\sqrt{0.49}$
34. $\sqrt{1.96}$
35. $\sqrt{2.89}$

ALGEBRA For Exercises 36 and 37, evaluate each expression to the nearest tenth if $a = 8$ and $b = 3.7$.

36. $\sqrt{a + b}$
37. $\sqrt{6b - a}$

STAMPS For Exercises 38 and 39, use the information below.

The Special Olympics' commemorative stamp is square in shape with an area of 1,008 square millimeters.

38. Find the length of one side of the postage stamp to the nearest tenth.
39. What is the length of one side in centimeters?

40. **DISTANCE** The formula $D = 1.22 \times \sqrt{h}$ can be used to estimate the distance D in miles you can see from a point h feet above Earth's surface. Use the formula to find the distance D in miles you can see from the top of a 120-foot hill. Round to the nearest tenth.

EXTRA PRACTICE
See pages 752, 767.
Math Online
Self-Check Quiz at tx.msmath2.com

41. **FIND THE DATA** Refer to the Texas Data File on pages 16–19. Choose some data and write a real-world problem in which you would estimate a square root.

H.O.T. Problems

42. **Which One Doesn't Belong?** Identify the number that does not have the same characteristic as the other three. Explain your reasoning.

$\sqrt{5}$	π	$\sqrt{81}$	0.535335333...

43. **OPEN ENDED** Select three numbers with square roots between 4 and 5.

44. **NUMBER SENSE** Explain why 7 is the best whole number estimate for $\sqrt{51}$.

CHALLENGE A cube root of a number is one of its three equal factors. Estimate the cube root of each of the following to the nearest whole number.

45. $\sqrt[3]{9}$ 46. $\sqrt[3]{26}$ 47. $\sqrt[3]{120}$ 48. $\sqrt[3]{500}$

49. **WRITING IN MATH** Apply what you know about numbers to explain why $\sqrt{30}$ is an irrational number.

TEST PRACTICE

50. Reina wrote four numbers on a piece of paper. She then asked her friend Tyron to select the number closest to 5. Which number should he select?

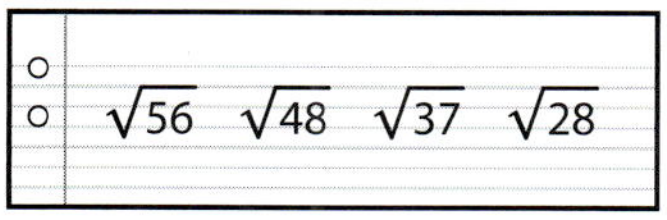

A $\sqrt{56}$
B $\sqrt{48}$
C $\sqrt{37}$
D $\sqrt{28}$

51. The following expression can be used to find the speed of a car in miles per hour if it left skid marks *d* feet long.

$$\sqrt{39d}$$

About how fast was a car traveling if it left skid marks 67.5 feet long?

F 39 mph
G 51 mph
H 62 mph
J 71 mph

Spiral Review

52. **FOOD** Find the volume of a can of vegetables with a diameter of 3 inches and a height of 4 inches. (Lesson 12-10)

53. **GEOMETRY** A rectangular prism is 14 inches long, 4.5 inches wide, and 1 inch high. What is the volume of the prism? (Lesson 12-9)

GEOMETRY For Exercises 54–57, use the graph at the right. Classify the angle that represents each category as *acute*, *obtuse*, *right*, or *straight*. (Lesson 11-1)

54. 30–39 hours 55. 1–29 hours
56. 40 hours 57. 41–50 hours

Hours Worked in a Typical Week

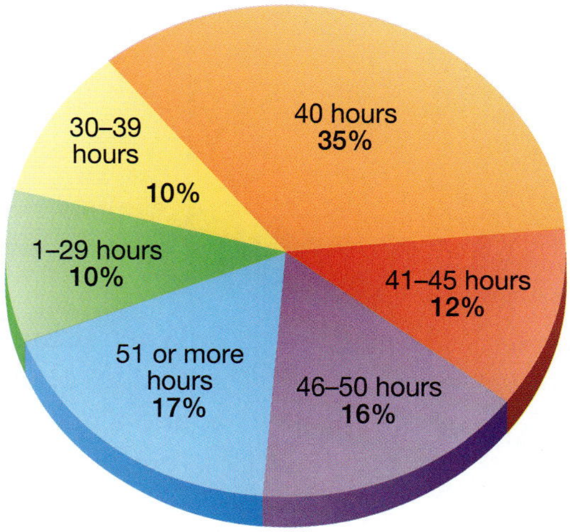

Source: Heldrich Work Trends Survey

GET READY for the Next Lesson

PREREQUISITE SKILL Solve each equation. (Lesson 1-7)

58. $7^2 + 5^2 = c$ 59. $4^2 + b = 36$
60. $3^2 + a = 25$ 61. $9^2 + 2^2 = c$

13-2 The Pythagorean Theorem

Main IDEA

Find length using the Pythagorean Theorem.

Preparing for TEKS 8.9 The student uses indirect measurement to solve problems. **(A) use the Pythagorean Theorem to solve real-life problems.** *Also addresses TEKS 8.7(C).*

MINI Lab

Concepts in Motion BrainPOP® tx.msmath2.com

Three squares with sides 3, 4, and 5 units are used to form the right triangle shown.

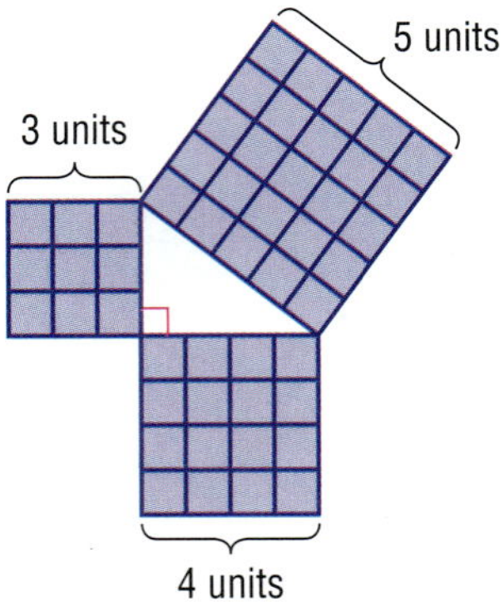

1. Find the area of each square.
2. How are the squares of the sides related to the areas of the squares?
3. Find the sum of the areas of the two smaller squares. How does the sum compare to the area of the larger square?
4. Use grid paper to cut out three squares with sides 5, 12, and 13 units. Form a right triangle with these squares. Compare the sum of the areas of the two smaller squares with the area of the larger square.

NEW Vocabulary

leg
hypotenuse
Pythagorean Theorem

In a right triangle, the sides have special names.

The two sides adjacent to the right angle are the **legs**.

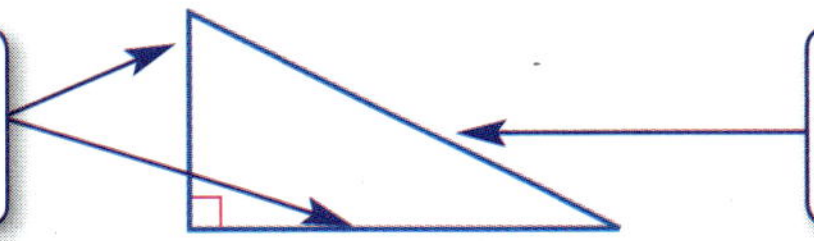

The side opposite the right angle is the **hypotenuse**.

The **Pythagorean Theorem** describes the relationship between the length of the hypotenuse and the lengths of the legs.

KEY CONCEPT — Pythagorean Theorem

Words In a right triangle, the square of the length of the hypotenuse equals the sum of the squares of the lengths of the legs.

Model

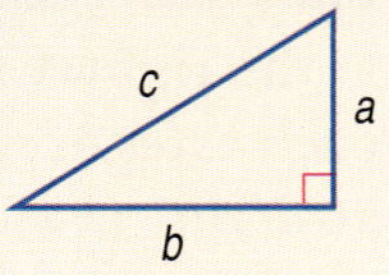

Symbols $c^2 = a^2 + b^2$

READING Math

Square Roots Read $\pm\sqrt{5}$ as *plus or minus the square root of* 5.

When using the Pythagorean Theorem, you will encounter equations that involve square roots. Every positive number has both a positive and a negative square root. By the definition of square roots, if $n^2 = a$, then $n = \pm\sqrt{a}$. The notation $\pm\sqrt{}$ indicates both the positive and negative square root of a number. You can use this relationship to solve equations that involve squares.

EXAMPLE Find the Length of the Hypotenuse

STUDY TIP

Check for Reasonableness You can eliminate −8.9 as a solution because the length of a side of a triangle cannot be a negative number.

1 **Find the length of the hypotenuse of the triangle.**

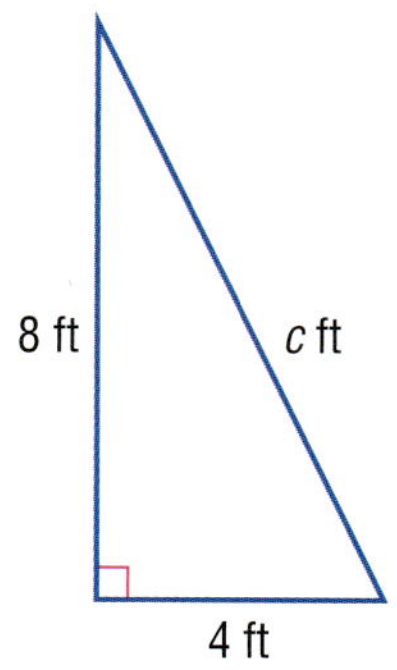

$c^2 = a^2 + b^2$	Pythagorean Theorem
$c^2 = 8^2 + 4^2$	Replace *a* with 8 and *b* with 4.
$c^2 = 64 + 16$	Evaluate 8^2 and 4^2.
$c^2 = 80$	Add.
$c = \pm\sqrt{80}$	Definition of square root
$c \approx \pm 8.9$	Simplify.

The length of the hypotenuse is about 8.9 feet.

CHECK Your Progress

a. Find the length of the hypotenuse of a right triangle with legs 5 yards and 7 yards. Round to the nearest tenth.

Real-World Career . . .
How Does an Archeologist Use Math? Before digging, archaeologists use the Pythagorean Theorem to calculate the diagonal of an excavation site to be sure that the area is a rectangle.

Math Online For more information, go to tx.msmath2.com.

Real-World EXAMPLE

2 **ARCHAEOLOGY** **Archaeologists placed corner stakes to mark a rectangular excavation site as shown at the right. If their stakes are placed correctly, what is the measure of the diagonal of the excavation site?**

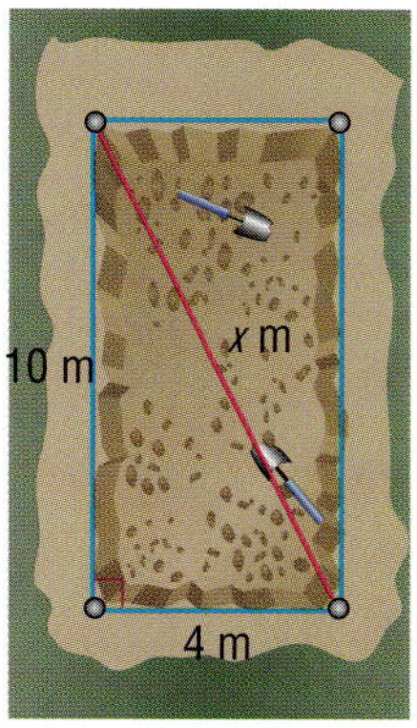

The diagonal of the rectangle is the hypotenuse of a right triangle. Write and solve an equation for x.

$c^2 = a^2 + b^2$	Pythagorean Theorem
$x^2 = 4^2 + 10^2$	Replace *c* with *x*, *a* with 4, and *b* with 10.
$x^2 = 16 + 100$	Evaluate 4^2 and 10^2.
$x^2 = 116$	Add.
$x = \pm\sqrt{116}$	Definition of square root
$x \approx \pm 10.8$	Simplify.

The length of the diagonal of the excavation site is about 10.8 meters.

CHECK Your Progress

b. **SOFTBALL** A softball diamond is a square measuring 60 feet on each side. How far does a player on second base throw when she throws from second base to home? Round to the nearest tenth.

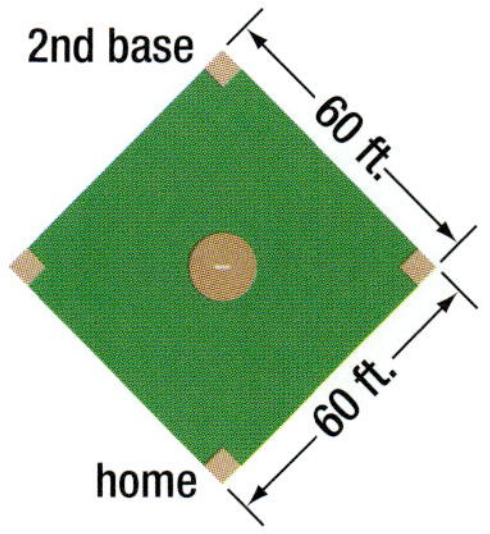

You can also use the Pythagorean Theorem to find the measure of a leg if the measure of the other leg and the hypotenuse are known.

EXAMPLE Find the Length of a Leg

3 **Find the missing measure of the triangle. Round to the nearest tenth if necessary.**

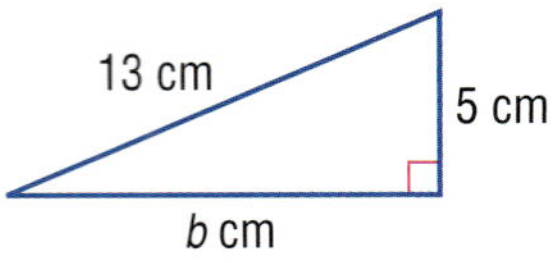

The missing measure is of a leg.

$c^2 = a^2 + b^2$	Pythagorean Theorem
$13^2 = 5^2 + b^2$	Replace a with 5 and c with 13.
$169 = 25 + b^2$	Evaluate 13^2 and 5^2.
$-25 = -25$	Subtract 25 from each side.
$144 = b^2$	Simplify.
$\pm\sqrt{144} = b$	Definition of square root
$12 = b$	Simplify.

The length of the leg is 12 centimeters.

CHECK Your Progress

c.

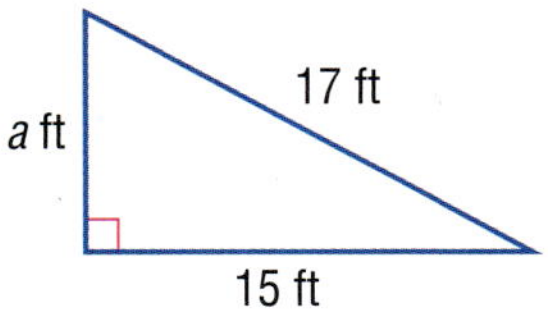

d.

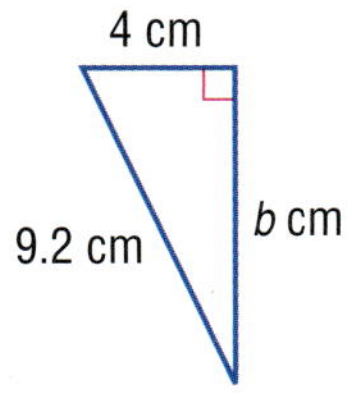

e. $b = 7$ in., $c = 25$ in.

TEST EXAMPLE

4 **Mr. Thomson created a mosaic tile in the shape of a square to place in his kitchen.**

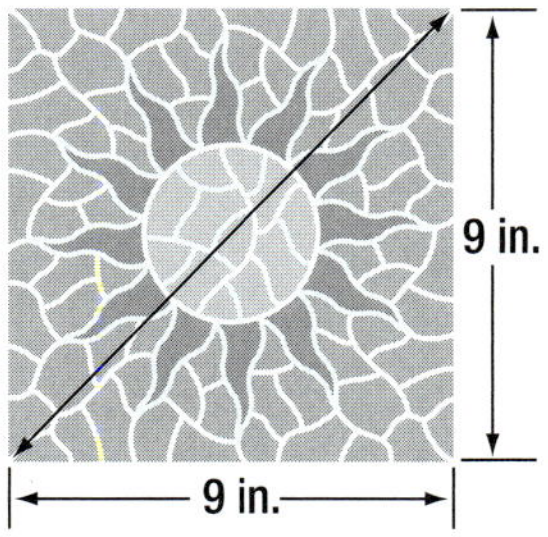

Which is closest to the length of the diagonal of the tile?

A 10 in.

B 13 in.

C 15 in.

D 17 in.

Test-Taking Tip

Formulas Some formulas will be given to you during the test. It is a good idea to familiarize yourself with the formulas before the test.

Read the Test Item

You need to use the Pythagorean Theorem to find the diagonal length.

Solve the Test Item

$c^2 = a^2 + b^2$	Pythagorean Theorem
$c^2 = 9^2 + 9^2$	Replace *a* with 9 and *b* with 9.
$c^2 = 81 + 81$	Evaluate 9^2 and 9^2.
$c^2 = 162$	Add.
$c = \pm\sqrt{162}$	Definition of square root
$c \approx \pm 12.7$	Simplify.

The length is about 12.7 inches. The answer choice closest to 12.7 inches is 13 inches. So, the answer is B.

CHECK Your Progress

f. A painter leans a ladder against the side of a building. How far from the bottom of the building is the top of the ladder?

F 38.2 ft H 21.8 ft
G 28.0 ft J 20.0 ft

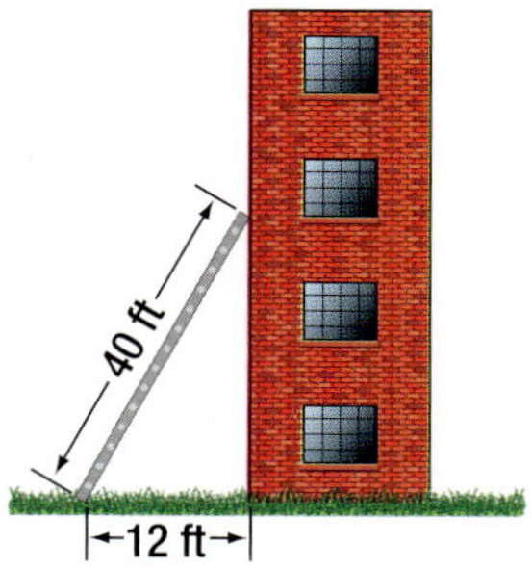

Online Personal Tutor at tx.msmath2.com

CHECK Your Understanding

Examples 1, 3 (pp. 679–680)

Find the missing measure of each triangle. Round to the nearest tenth if necessary.

1.
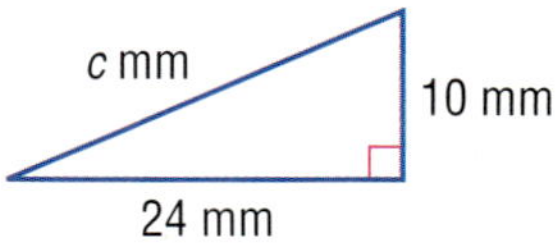

2.
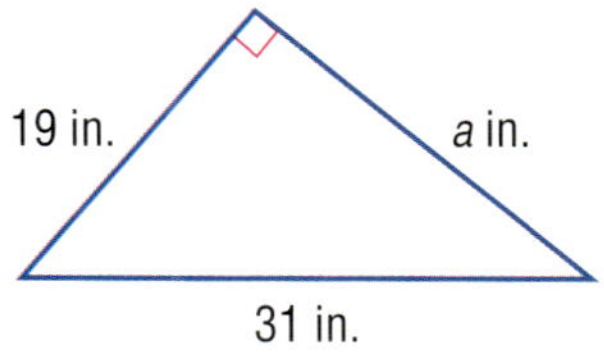

3. $b = 21$ cm, $c = 28$

4. $a = 11$ yd, $b = 12$ yd

Example 2 (p. 679)

5. **ARCHITECTURE** What is the width of the the fence gate shown at the right? Round to the nearest tenth.

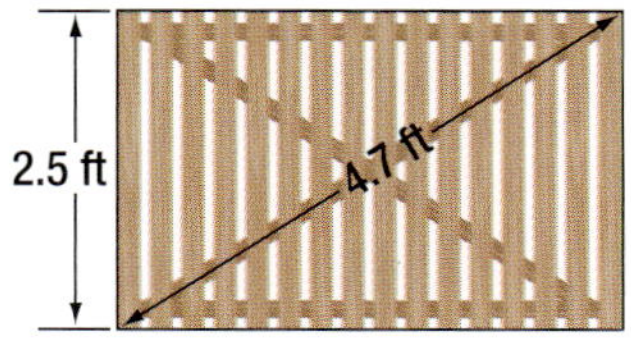

Example 4 (pp. 680–681)

6. **TEST PRACTICE** A company designed a public play area in the shape of a square. The play area will include a pathway, as shown. Which is closest to the length of the pathway?

A 100 ft C 140 ft
B 125 ft D 175 ft

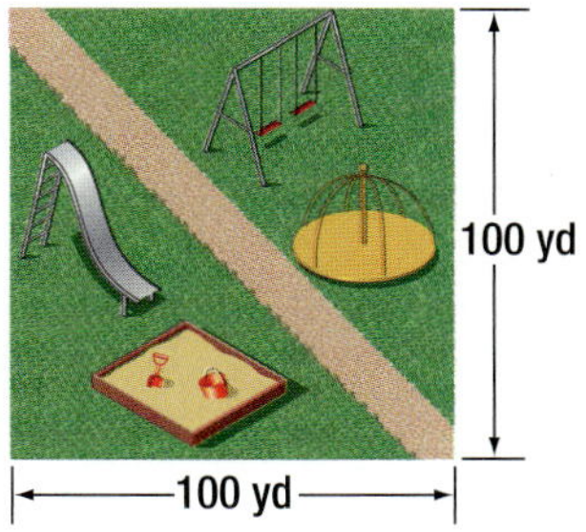

Exercises

For Exercises	See Examples
7–8, 11–12, 15–16	1
17–20	2
9–10, 13–14	3
37–39	4

HOMEWORK HELP

Find the missing measure of each triangle. Round to the nearest tenth if necessary.

7.
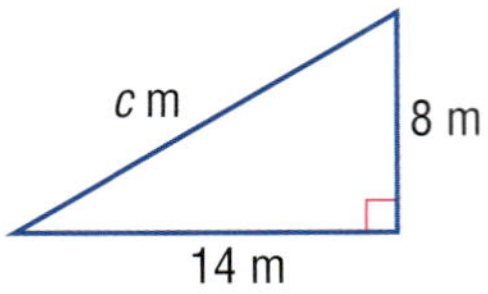

8.
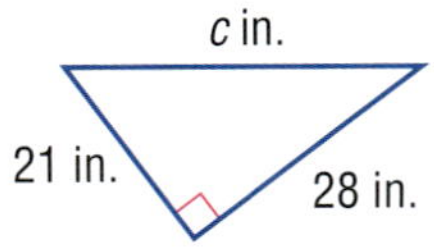

9.
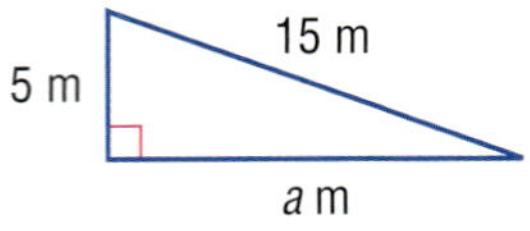

10.
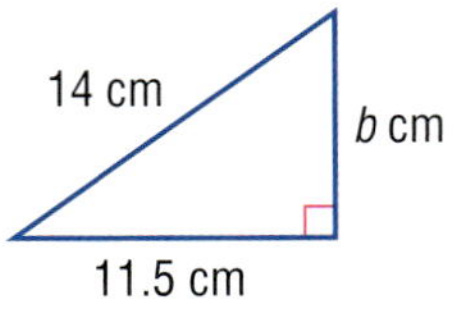

11.
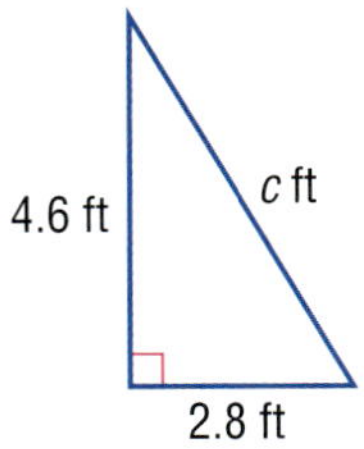

12.
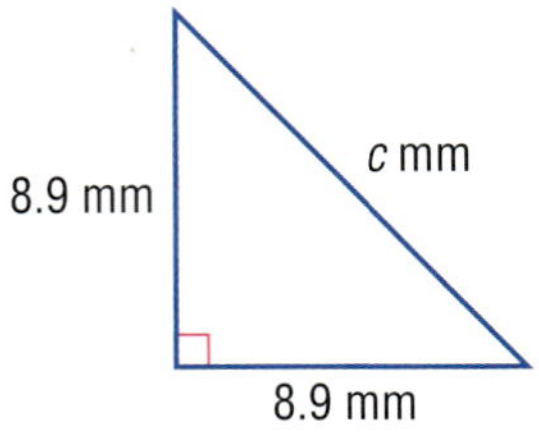

13. $a = 2.4$ yd, $c = 3.7$ yd

14. $b = 8.5$ m, $c = 10.4$ m

15. $a = 7$ in., $b = 24$ in.

16. $a = 13.5$ mm, $b = 18$ mm

DISTANCE **For Exercises 17 and 18, find each distance to the nearest tenth.**

17.
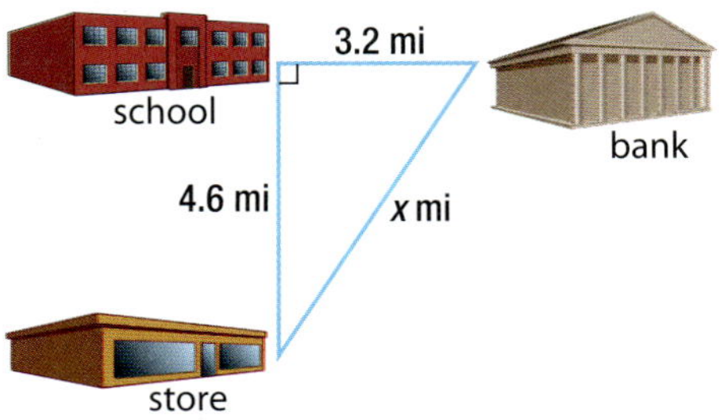

18.
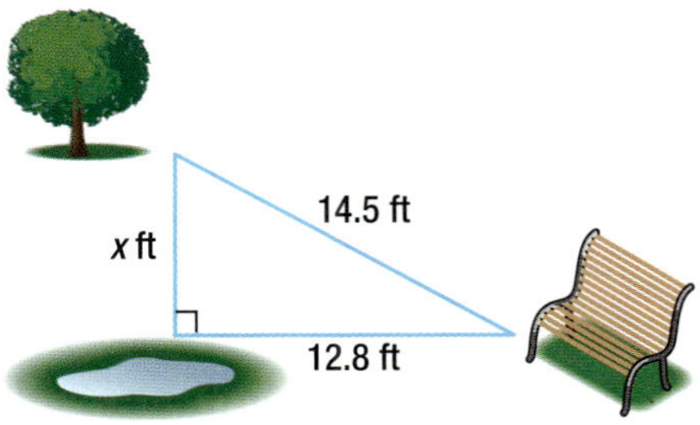

SPORTS **For Exercises 19 and 20, find the length or width of each piece of sports equipment. Round to the nearest tenth.**

19.
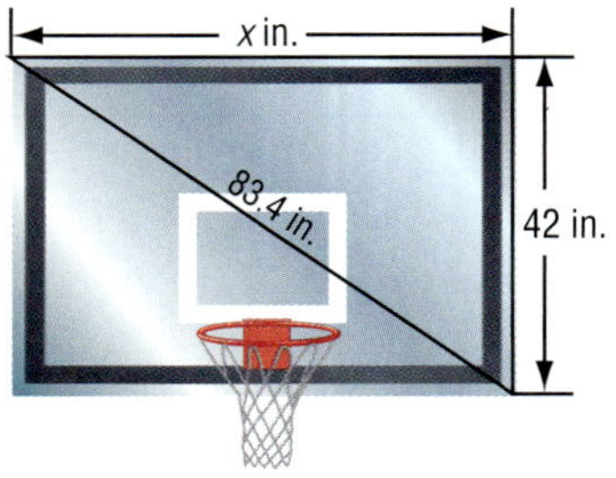

20.
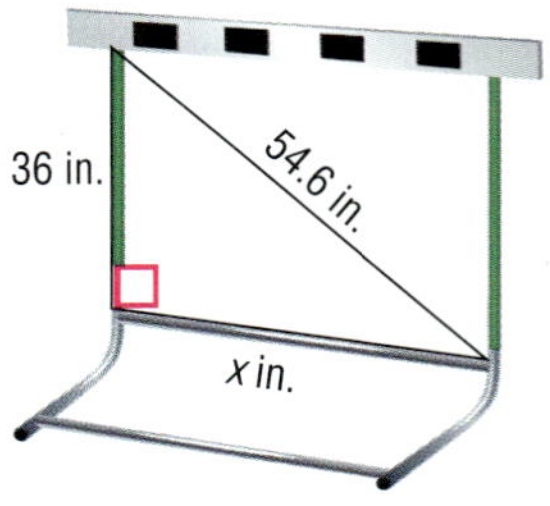

Find the missing measure of each triangle. Round to the nearest tenth if necessary.

21. $a = 3\frac{1}{2}$ in., $b = 4$ in.

22. $a = 5\frac{1}{4}$ m, $b = 6\frac{3}{4}$ m

23. $a = 5\frac{1}{2}$ cm, $c = 9\frac{1}{2}$ cm

24. $b = 4\frac{1}{2}$ yd, $c = 15\frac{1}{5}$ yd

If a triangle has sides a, b, and c so that $a^2 + b^2 = c^2$, then the triangle is a right triangle. Determine whether a triangle with the given side lengths is a right triangle. Write *yes* or *no*.

25. 12 cm, 16 cm, 20 cm

26. 11 ft, 14 ft, 17 ft

27. 18 in., 18 in., 36 in.

Real-World Link According to a survey, the best water park in the U.S. is Schlitterbahn Waterparks in New Braunfels, Texas.
Source: The Travel Channel

EXTRA PRACTICE
See pages 753, 767.
Math Online
Self-Check Quiz at tx.msmath2.com

H.O.T. Problems

Find the missing measure in each figure. Round to the nearest tenth if necessary.

28. 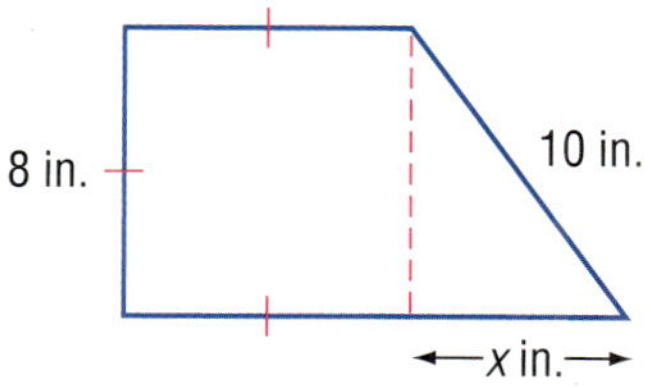

29. 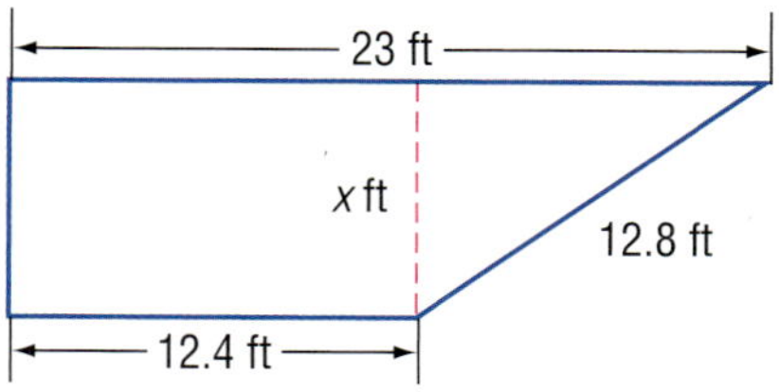

30. **WATER PARKS** The diagram shows the dimensions of a water slide. Jonathan goes down the slide at a rate of 5 feet per second. How long will it take him to reach the bottom of the slide?

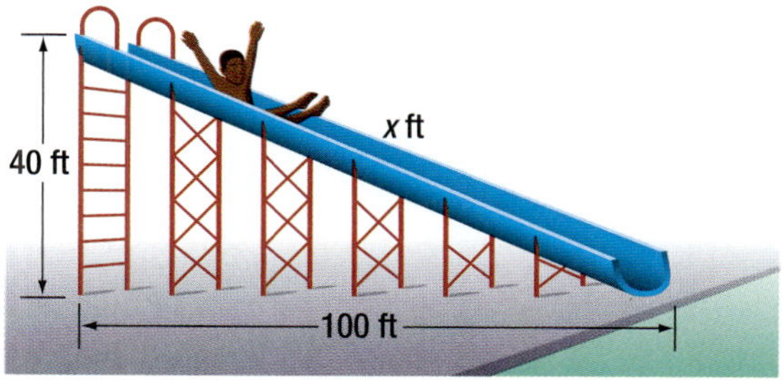

31. **MOVING** The doorway of a house is 3 feet wide and 6.5 feet tall. A square mirror 7 feet on each side must be delivered through the doorway. Can the mirror fit through the doorway? Justify your answer.

32. **TRAVEL** You drive 80 miles east, then 50 miles north, then 140 miles west, and finally 95 miles south. How far are you from your starting point? Justify your answer with a drawing.

33. **CHALLENGE** What is the length of the diagonal shown in the cube at the right?

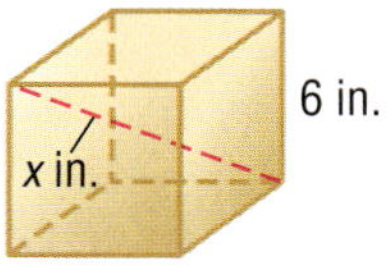

34. **OPEN ENDED** Draw and label a right triangle that has one side measuring 14 units. Write the length of another side. Then find the length of the third side to the nearest tenth.

35. **FIND THE ERROR** Devin and Jamie are writing an equation to find the missing measure of the triangle at the right. Who is correct? Explain.

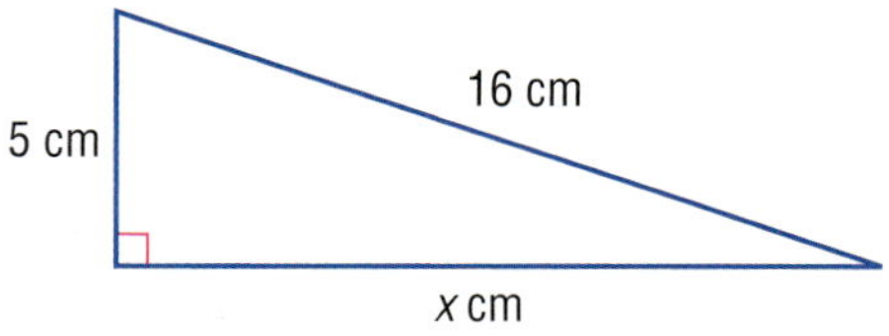

36. **WRITING IN MATH** Write a problem about a real-world situation in which you would use the Pythagorean Theorem.

TEST PRACTICE

37. Which triangle has sides a, b, and c so that the relationship $a^2 + b^2 = c^2$ is true?

A

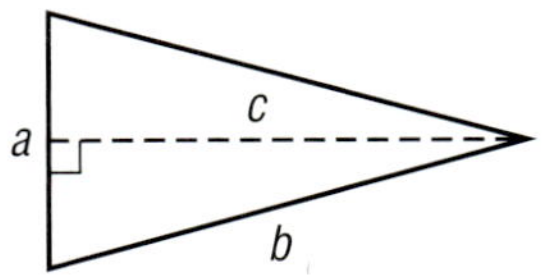

B

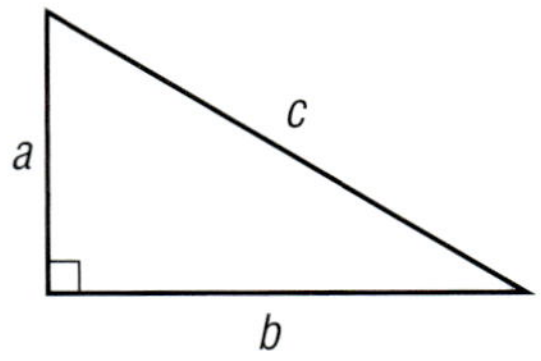

C

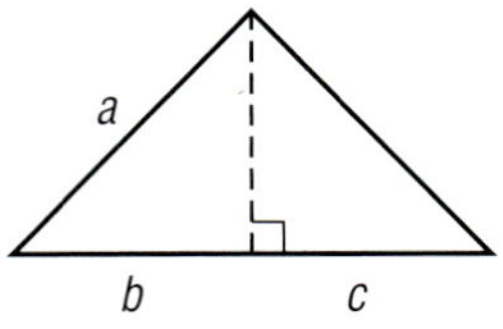

D

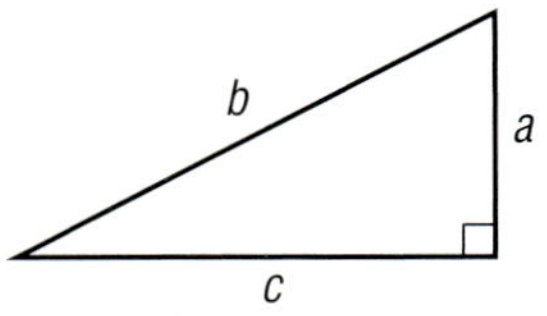

38. Each day, Aurelio walks home from school by cutting straight through the park.

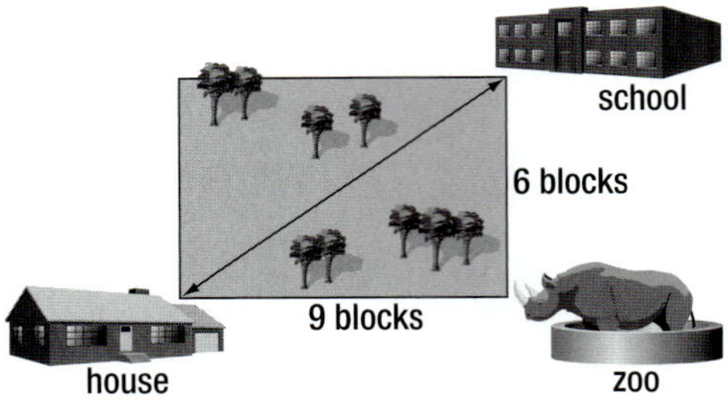

Which is closest to the distance Tyler walks from school to his home?

F 10 blocks

G 11 blocks

H 12 blocks

J 13 blocks

39. **GRIDDABLE** An isosceles right triangle has legs that are 8 inches long. What is the length of the hypotenuse in inches to the nearest tenth?

Spiral Review

40. **ESTIMATION** Which is closer to $\sqrt{55}$: 7 or 8? (Lesson 13-1)

41. **POPCORN** A cylinder-shaped popcorn tin has a height of 1.5 feet and a diameter of 10 inches. Find the volume to the nearest cubic inch. Use 3.14 for π. (Lesson 12-10)

42. **BRIDGES** There are 48,457 bridges in Texas. Of these, 66% are owned by the state. What is a reasonable estimate for the number of bridges in Texas that are owned by the state? (Lesson 8-3)

Write each percent as a decimal. (Lesson 5-7)

43. 45%

44. 8%

45. 124%

46. 265%

GET READY for the Next Lesson

47. **PREREQUISITE SKILL** The average person takes about 15 breaths per minute. At this rate, how many breaths does the average person take in one week? Use the *solve a simpler problem* strategy. (Lesson 12-5)

13-3 Problem-Solving Investigation

MAIN IDEA: Solve problems by making a model.

Targeted TEKS 7.13 The student applies Grade 7 mathematics to solve problems connected to everyday experiences, investigations in other disciplines, and activities in and outside of school. **(B) use a problem-solving model that incorporates understanding the problem, making a plan, carrying out the plan, and evaluating the solution for reasonableness.**

P.S.I. TEAM +

e-Mail: MAKE A MODEL

YOUR MISSION: Make a model to solve the problem.

THE PROBLEM: How much fabric is needed to make one cube if there is a $\frac{1}{2}$-inch seam on each side?

Libby: I'm going to help my mom make 3-inch soft alphabet blocks for the children at her daycare center. A model can be used to find out how much fabric is needed.

EXPLORE	You know that each cube is 3 inches long with $\frac{1}{2}$-inch seams.
PLAN	Make a cardboard model of a cube with sides 3 inches long. Then cut the model into six squares and add $\frac{1}{2}$-inch paper extensions to each side as seams.
SOLVE	Make the cardboard model and unfold the cube. 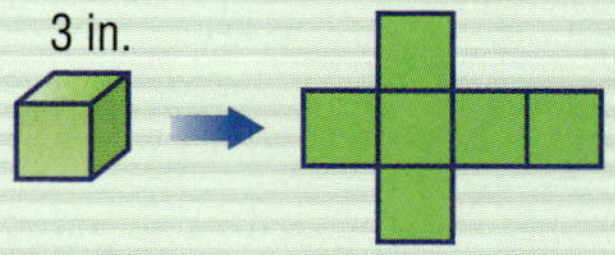 Then cut the cube into six squares. Take one of the squares and tape $\frac{1}{2}$-inch seams on each side. One side of the cube is 4 in. $\times$ 4 in. or *about* 16 in^2. 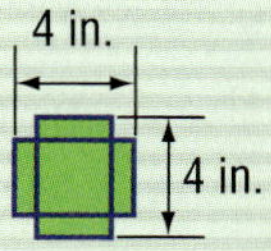 Since one cube has six sides, you will need 6 $\times$ 16 in^2 or 96 in^2 of fabric.
CHECK	If the 4-inch by 4-inch pattern pieces were laid as two columns and three rows, it would be 8 inches wide and 12 inches long or 96 square inches.

Analyze The Strategy

1. Explain why you think Libby started with the three-dimensional model to make her pattern.
2. **WRITING IN MATH** Write a problem that can be solved by making a model. Then solve the problem.

Mixed Problem Solving

For Exercises 3–5, make a model to solve the problem.

3. **ART** Rodrigo is creating a layout of his bedroom for art class. The room measures 15 feet by 12 feet. If he uses a scale of 1 ft = $\frac{3}{4}$ inch, what are the dimensions of his bedroom on the model?

4. **BICYCLES** Eight customers stood outside The Bike Shop with either a bicycle or a tricycle that needed repair. If there was a total of 21 wheels, how many tricycles and bicycles were there?

5. **PHOTOS** Francis has a photo that measures 10 inches by $8\frac{1}{2}$ inches. If the frame he uses is $1\frac{1}{4}$ inches wide, what is the perimeter of the framed picture?

Use any strategy to solve Exercises 6–9. Some strategies are shown below.

PROBLEM-SOLVING STRATEGIES
- Use the four-step plan.
- Draw a diagram.
- Use logical reasoning.
- Make a model.

6. **COMMUNITY SERVICE** There are four drop-off centers for the community food drive. The table shows the total collections for each center. Suppose a newsletter reports that over 13,000 cans of food were collected. Is this estimate reasonable? Explain.

Center	Number of Cans
A	3,298
B	2,629
C	4,429
D	2,892

7. **SPORTS** Len can swim one 20-meter lap in 1.25 minutes. How long will it take her to swim 100 meters at the same rate?

8. **TRAFFIC** At the four-way intersection shown below, the traffic lights change every 90 seconds. About 8 cars in one lane travel through each light change. Determine the approximate number of cars in all lanes that travel through the intersection in 3 minutes.

9. **REMODELING** How many square feet of wallpaper are needed to cover a wall that measures 9 feet by 16 feet?

Select the Operation

For Exercises 10–12, select the appropriate operation(s) to solve the problem. Justify your selection(s) and solve the problem.

10. **MONEY** Duante deposited $450 in a new savings account in January, withdrew $175 in February, and then began monthly deposits of $75 from March through December. How much money does he have in his savings account?

11. **BASEBALL** A regulation baseball diamond is a square with an area of 8,100 square feet. If it is laid out on a field that is 172 feet wide and 301 feet long, how much greater is the distance around the whole field than the distance around the diamond?

12. **DVDS** Marc currently has 68 DVDs in his collection. By the end of the next four months, he wants to have 92 DVDs in his collection. How many DVDs must he buy each month to obtain his goal?

CHAPTER 13 Mid-Chapter Quiz

Lessons 13-1 through 13-3

Estimate each square root to the nearest whole number. (Lesson 13-1)

1. $\sqrt{32}$
2. $\sqrt{80}$
3. $\sqrt{105}$
4. $\sqrt{230}$

GEOMETRY **Estimate the side length of each square to the nearest whole number.** (Lesson 13-1)

5. 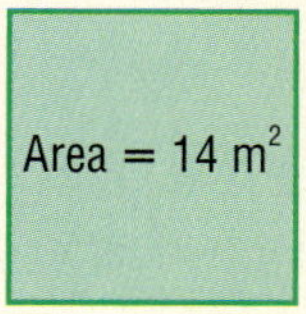

6. 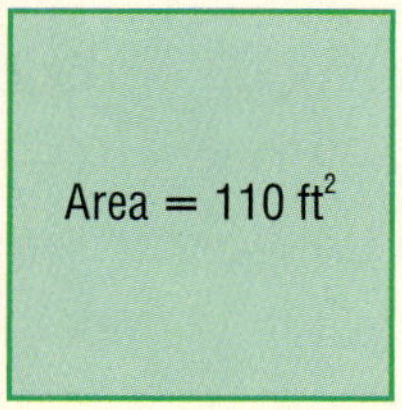

ALGEBRA **Evaluate each expression to the nearest tenth if $a = 20$ and $b = 7$.** (Lesson 13-1)

7. $\sqrt{a + b}$
8. $\sqrt{a - b}$

9. **TEST PRACTICE** Imani is playing a review game in math class. She needs to pick the card that is labeled with a number closest to 8. Which should she pick? (Lesson 13-1)

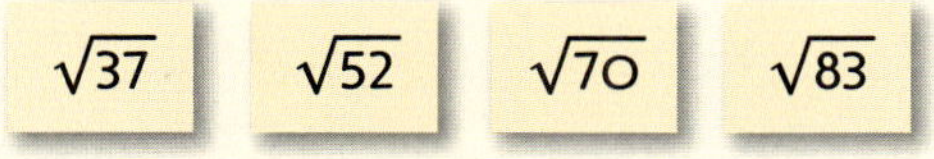

A $\sqrt{37}$
B $\sqrt{52}$
C $\sqrt{70}$
D $\sqrt{83}$

Find the length of the hypotenuse of each triangle. Round to the nearest tenth if necessary. (Lesson 13-2)

10. 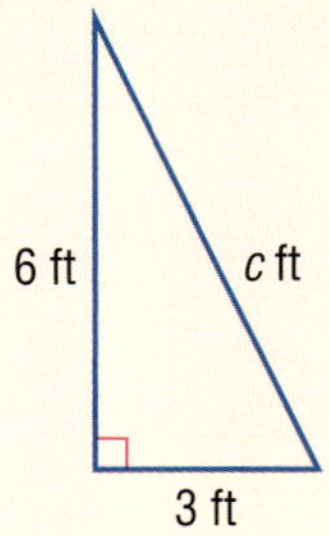

11. 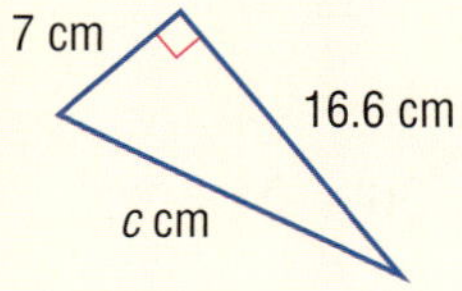

Find the missing measure of each triangle. Round to the nearest tenth if necessary. (Lesson 13-2)

12. 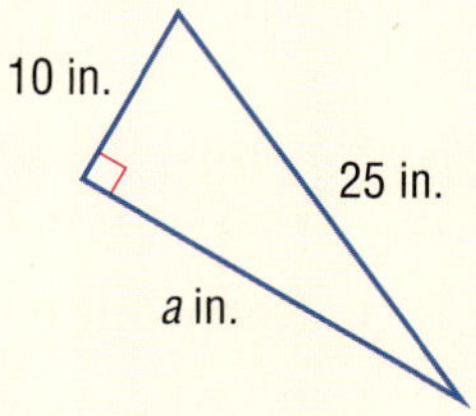

13. 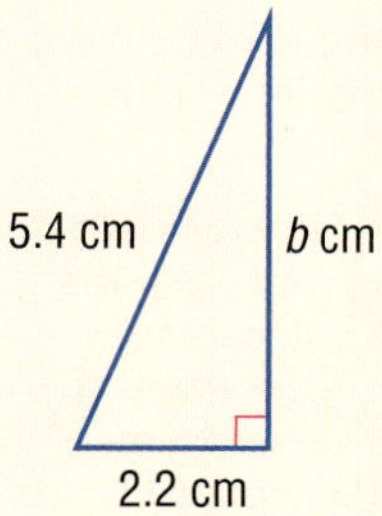

14. **TECHNOLOGY** On a computer monitor, the diagonal measure of the screen is 17 inches.

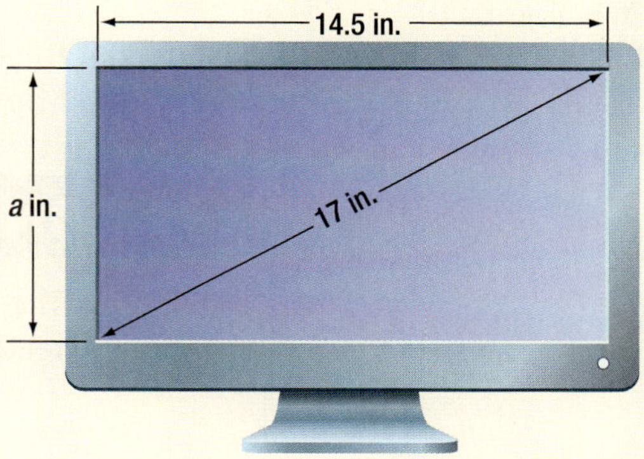

If the screen length is 14.5 inches, what is the height of the screen to the nearest tenth? (Lesson 13-2)

15. **TEST PRACTICE** Eduardo jogs 5 kilometers north and 5 kilometers west. To the nearest kilometer, how far is he from his starting point? (Lesson 13-2)

F 25 km
G 10 km
H 7 km
J 5 km

16. **SCIENCE** A certain type of bacteria doubles every hour. If there are two bacteria initially in a sample, how many will be present after five hours? Use the *make a model* strategy. (Lesson 13-3)

17. **MODELS** A scale model is made of an office building measuring 120 feet long, 75 feet wide, and 45 feet high. If the scale is 1 inch = 15 feet, what are the dimensions of the model? Use the *make a model* strategy. (Lesson 13-3)

13-4 Surface Area of Rectangular Prisms

Main IDEA

Find the surface areas of rectangular prisms.

Preparing for TEKS 8.8 The student uses procedures to determine measures of three-dimensional figures [solids]. **(A) find** lateral and **total surface area of prisms, pyramids, and cylinders using concrete models and nets (two dimensional models).** *Also addresses TEKS 8.8(C), 7.13(D).*

NEW Vocabulary

surface area

MINI Lab

- Use the cubes to build a rectangular prism with a length of 8 centimeters.

- Count the number of squares on each side. The sum is the *surface area.*

1. Record the dimensions, volume, and surface area in a table.
2. Build two more prisms using all of the cubes. For each, record the dimensions, volume, and surface area.
3. Describe the prisms with the greatest and least surface areas.

The sum of the areas of all of the surfaces, or faces, of a three-dimensional figure is the **surface area**.

KEY CONCEPT — Surface Area of a Rectangular Prism

Words The surface area S of a rectangular prism with length ℓ, width w, and height h is the sum of the areas of the faces.

Model

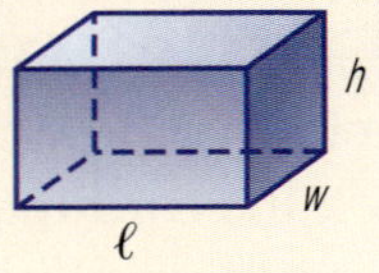

Symbols $S = 2\ell w + 2\ell h + 2wh$

EXAMPLES Find Surface Area

1 Find the surface area of the rectangular prism.

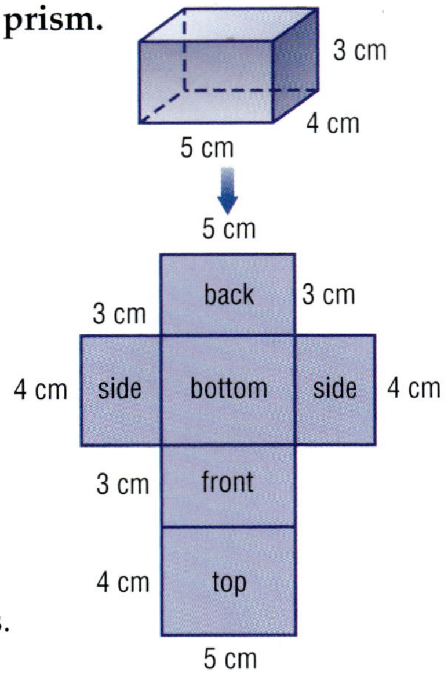

There are three pairs of congruent faces.

- top and bottom
- front and back
- two sides

Faces	**Area**
top and bottom	$2(5 \cdot 4) = 40$
front and back	$2(5 \cdot 3) = 30$
two sides	$2(3 \cdot 4) = 24$
sum of the areas	$40 + 30 + 24 = 94$

The surface area is 94 square centimeters.

STUDY TIP

Surface Area When you find the surface area of a three-dimensional figure, the units are square units, not cubic units.

2 **Find the surface area of the rectangular prism.**

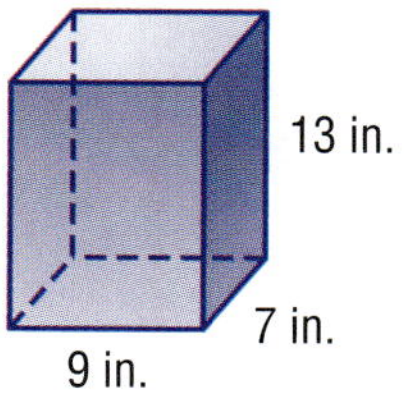

Replace ℓ, with 9, w with 7, and h with 13.

$$\begin{aligned} \text{surface area} &= 2\ell w + 2\ell h + 2wh \\ &= 2 \cdot 9 \cdot 7 + 2 \cdot 9 \cdot 13 + 2 \cdot 7 \cdot 13 \\ &= 126 + 234 + 182 \quad \text{Multiply first. Then add.} \\ &= 542 \end{aligned}$$

The surface area of the prism is 542 square inches.

CHECK Your Progress

Find the surface area of each rectangular prism.

a. 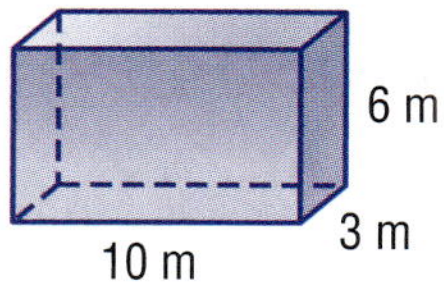

b. 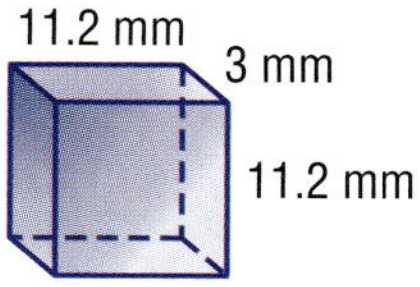

Real-World EXAMPLE

3 **GIFTS** **Rafael is wrapping a gift. He places it in a box 8 inches long, 2 inches wide, and 11 inches high. If Rafael bought a roll of wrapping paper that is 1 foot wide and 2 feet long, did he buy enough paper to wrap the gift? Justify your answer.**

STEP 1 Find the surface area of the package.
Replace ℓ with 8, w with 2, and h with 11.

$$\begin{aligned} \text{surface area} &= 2\ell w + 2\ell h + 2wh \\ &= 2 \cdot 8 \cdot 2 + 2 \cdot 8 \cdot 11 + 2 \cdot 2 \cdot 11 \\ &= 252 \text{ in}^2 \end{aligned}$$

STEP 2 Find the area of the wrapping paper.

area = 12 in. $\cdot$ 24 in. or 288 in^2

Since 288 > 252, Rafael bought enough wrapping paper.

CHECK Your Progress

c. **BOXES** The largest corrugated cardboard box ever constructed measured about 23 feet long, 9 feet high, and 8 feet wide. Would 950 square feet of paper be enough to cover the box? Justify your answer.

d. **BOXES** If 1 foot was added to each dimension of the largest corrugated cardboard box, ever constructed, would 950 square feet of paper still be enough to cover the box? Justify your answer.

Online Personal Tutor at tx.msmath2.com

EXAMPLE Use the Pythagorean Theorem

4 Find the surface area of the rectangular prism.

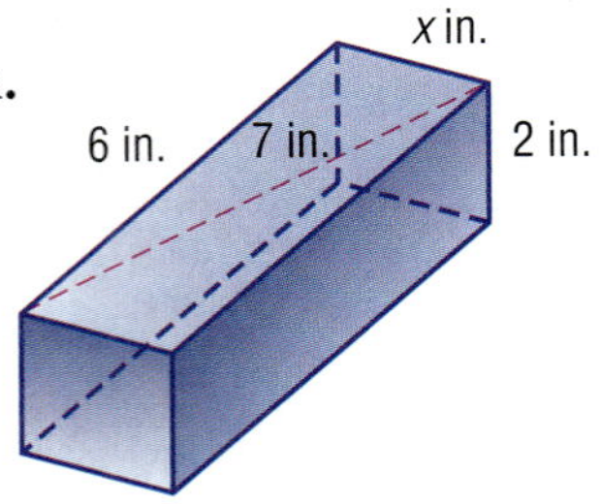

The width and height of the prism are given. To find the surface area, you need to find the length of the prism. Notice that the diagonal, length, and width of the top face of the prism form a right triangle.

$c^2 = a^2 + b^2$	Pythagorean Theorem
$7^2 = 6^2 + x^2$	Replace *c* with 7, *a* with 6, and *b* with *x*.
$49 = 36 + x^2$	Evaluate 7^2 and 6^2.
$49 - 36 = 36 + x^2 - 36$	Subtract 36 from each side.
$13 = x^2$	Simplify.
$\pm\sqrt{13} = x$	Definition of square root
$\pm 3.6 \approx x$	Simplify.

The length of the prism is about 3.6 inches. Find the surface area.

surface area $= 2\ell w + 2\ell h + 2wh$

$= 2(3.6)(6) + 2(3.6)(2) + 2(6)(2)$ or 81.6

The surface area of the prism is about 81.6 square inches.

STUDY TIP

Square Roots The equation $13 = x^2$ has two solutions, 3.6 and −3.6. However, the length of the prism must be positive, so choose the positive solution.

CHECK Your Progress

e. Find the surface area of the rectangular prism to the nearest tenth.

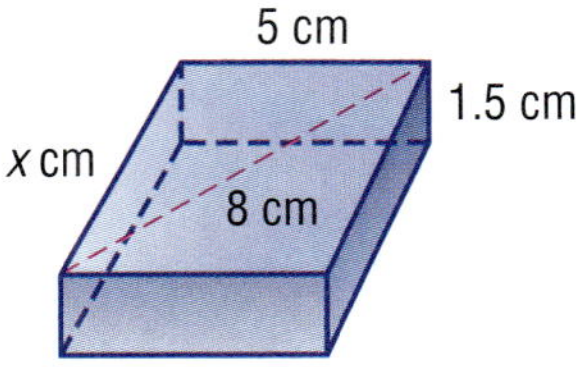

CHECK Your Understanding

Examples 1, 2 (pp. 688–689)

Find the surface area of each rectangular prism. Round to the nearest tenth if necessary.

1.

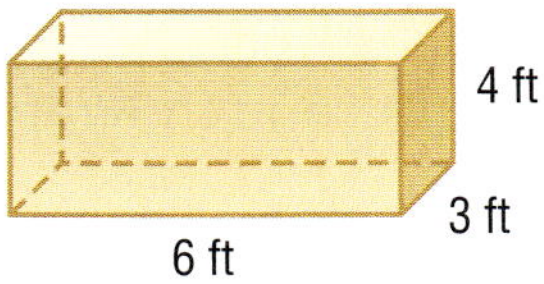

2.

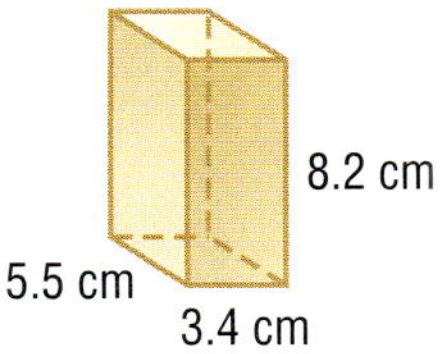

Example 3 (p. 689)

3. **PAINTING** Lars built a toy box 5 feet long, 2 feet wide, and 2 feet high. If he has 1 quart of paint that covers about 87 square feet, does he have enough to paint the toy box twice? Justify your answer.

Example 4 (p. 690)

4. **GEOMETRY** Find the surface area of the rectangular prism at the right. Round to the nearest tenth if necessary.

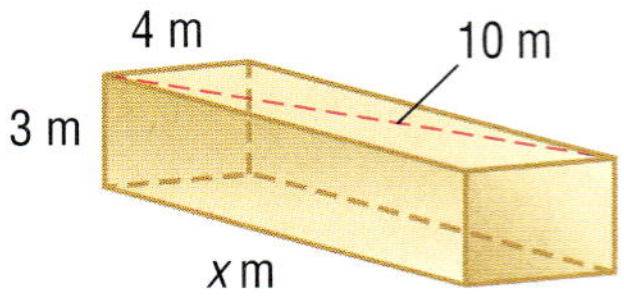

Math Online Extra Examples at tx.msmath2.com

Exercises

HOMEWORK HELP

For Exercises	See Examples
5–10	1, 2
11–12	3
13–14	4

Find the surface area of each rectangular prism. Round to the nearest tenth if necessary.

5.
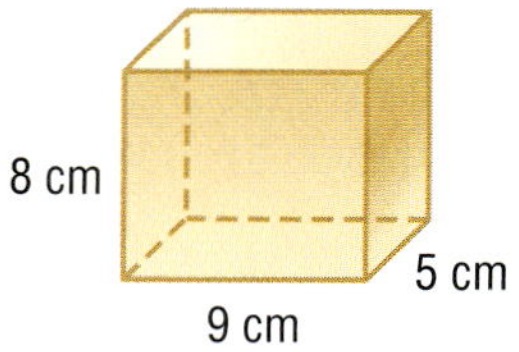

6.
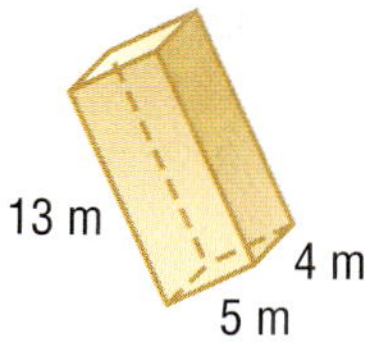

7.
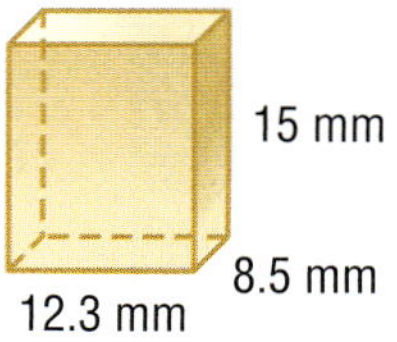

8.
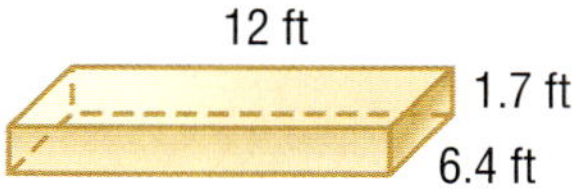

9.
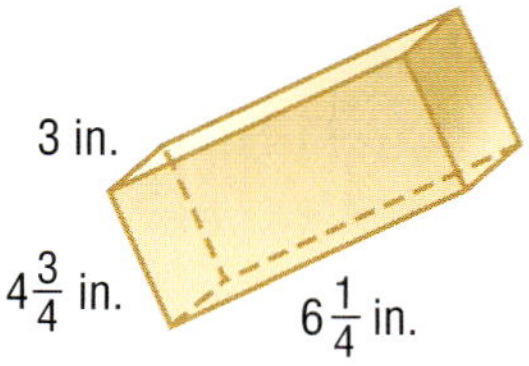

10.
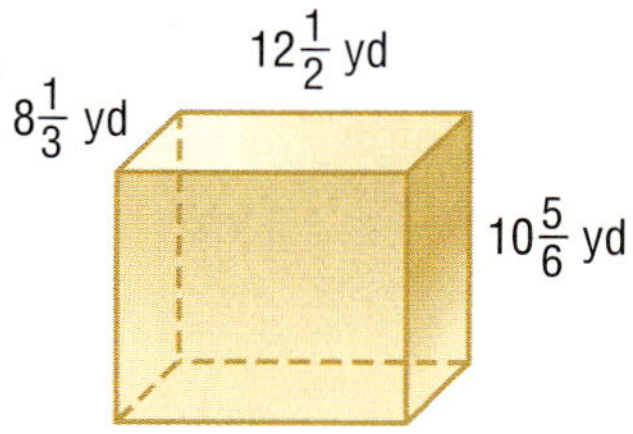

11. **BOOKS** When making a book cover, Anwar adds an additional 20 square inches to the surface area to allow for overlap. How many square inches of paper will Anwar use to make a book cover for a book 11 inches long, 8 inches wide, and 1 inch high?

12. **FENCES** If one gallon of paint covers 350 square feet, will 8 gallons of paint be enough to paint the inside and outside of the fence shown once? Explain.

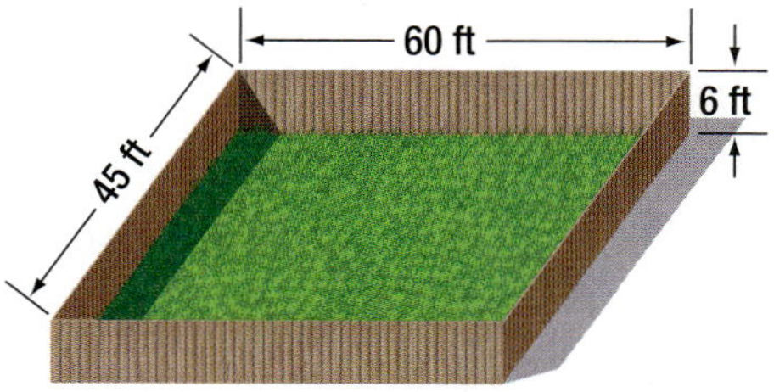

Find the surface area of each rectangular prism. Round to the nearest tenth if necessary.

13.
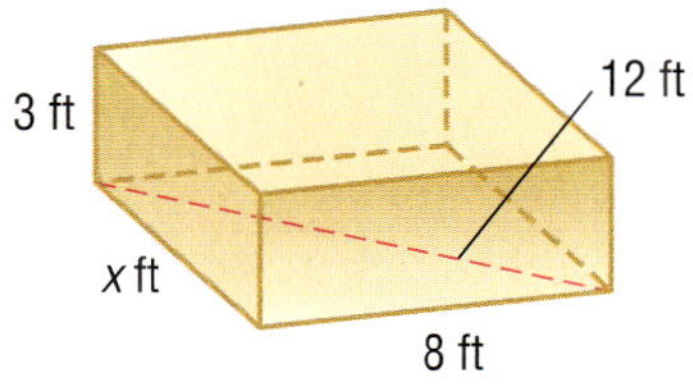

14.
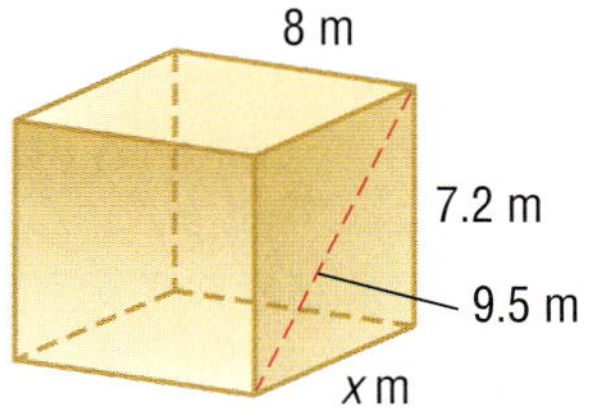

Find the surface area of each rectangular prism. Round to the nearest tenth if necessary.

15. length = 50 yd
width = 45 yd
height = 35 yd

16. length = 28.9 cm
width = 14.8 cm
height = 37.5 cm

17. length = 75.2 m
width = 80.5 m
height = 60.0 m

18. **MUSIC** To the nearest tenth, find the approximate amount of plastic covering the outside of the CD case.

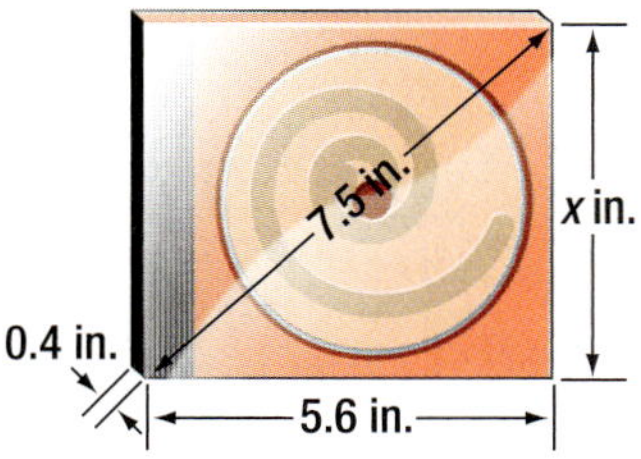

19. **GEOMETRY** What is the surface area of a rectangular prism that has a length of 6.5 centimeters, a width of 2.8 centimeters, and a height of 9.7 centimeters?

ESTIMATION **Estimate the surface area of each prism.**

20. 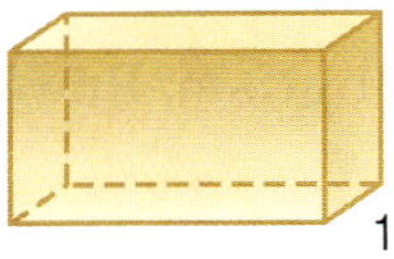

21. 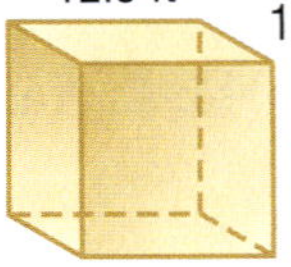

22. **ALGEBRA** Write a formula for the surface area of a cube in which each side measures x units.

Real-World Link Sugar cane is a tropical grass that grows 10–20 feet high. Four U.S. states produce sugar cane: Florida, Hawaii, Louisiana, and Texas.
Source: sugar.org

INDUSTRY **For Exercises 23–25, use the following information.**

Granulated sugar dissolves faster in water than sugar cubes.

granulated sugar

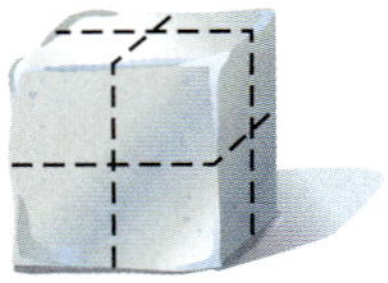
sugar cube

23. Suppose the length of each edge of a sugar cube is 1 centimeter. Find the surface area of the cube.
24. Imagine cutting the cube once in half horizontally and vertically. Find the total surface area of the eight cubes.
25. Make a conjecture as to why granulated sugar dissolves faster than a sugar cube.

CEREAL **For Exercises 26 and 27, use the following information.**

A company needs to make a trial size cereal box that holds 100 cubic centimeters of cereal.

26. Find the whole number dimensions of the box that would use the least amount of cardboard.
27. If cardboard costs $0.05 per 100 square centimeters, how much would it cost to make 100 boxes?

EXTRA PRACTICE
See pages 754, 767.
Math Online
Self-Check Quiz at tx.msmath2.com

H.O.T. Problems

28. **SELECT A TOOL** A storage cabinet measures 2 feet by 3 feet by 7 feet. Suppose you want to find the surface area of the cabinet in square inches. You know that 1 square foot = 144 square inches. Which of the following tools might you use to find the surface area on square inches? Justify your selection(s). Then use the tool(s) to solve the problem.

paper/pencil	real objects	technology	manipulatives

29. **CHALLENGE** The figure at the right is made by placing a cube with 12-centimeter sides on top of another cube with 15-centimeter sides. Find the surface area.

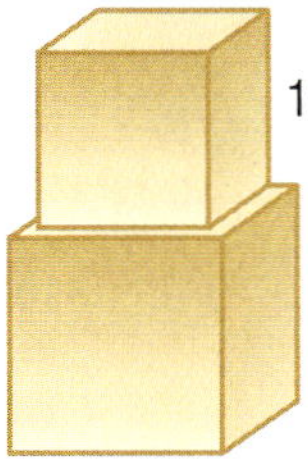

30. **WRITING IN MATH** Explain why surface area of a three-dimensional figure is measured in square units rather than in cubic units.

TEST PRACTICE

31. The surface area of the cube shown is 384 square centimeters.

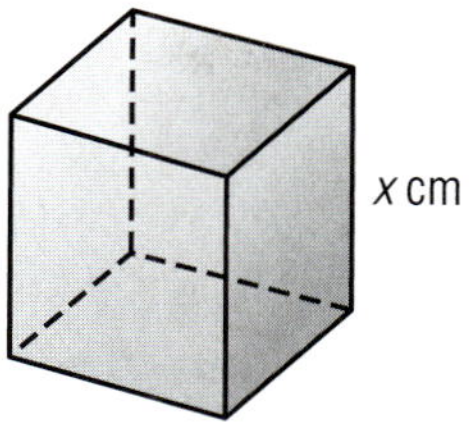

What is the length of one edge of the cube?

A 6 centimeters

B 8 centimeters

C 9 centimeters

D 12 centimeters

32. Annabelle's pet fish live in an aquarium that has the dimensions shown below. The top of the aquarium is open.

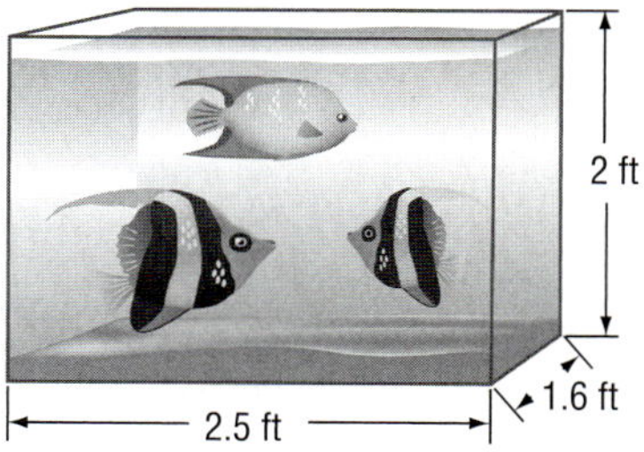

Which is closet to the surface area of the aquarium?

F 15.2 ft^2

G 17 ft^2

H 19.8 ft^2

J 20.4 ft^2

Spiral Review

33. **LANDSCAPE** A rectangular-shaped yard that measures 50 feet by 70 feet is bordered by a flowerbed that is 2 feet wide. What is the perimeter of the entire yard? Use the *make a model* strategy. (Lesson 13-3)

34. **GEOMETRY** What is the missing measure of a right triangle in which $a = 13$ feet and $c = 18$ feet? Round to the nearest tenth. (Lesson 13-2)

ESTIMATION Estimate each square root to the nearest whole number. (Lesson 13-1)

35. $\sqrt{61}$ 36. $\sqrt{147}$ 37. $\sqrt{40}$ 38. $\sqrt{277}$

39. **GEOMETRY** What is the volume of the cylinder shown at the right? Round to the nearest tenth. (Lesson 12-10)

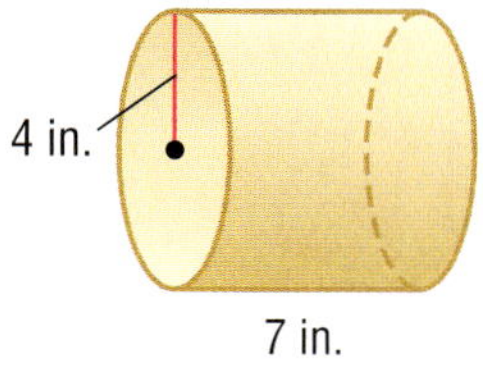

GET READY for the Next Lesson

PREREQUISITE SKILL Find the area of each circle. Round to the nearest tenth. (Lesson 12-4)

40. 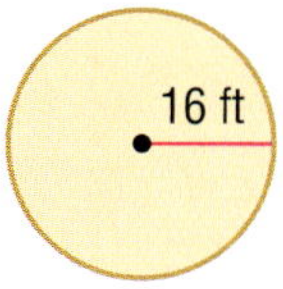

41. 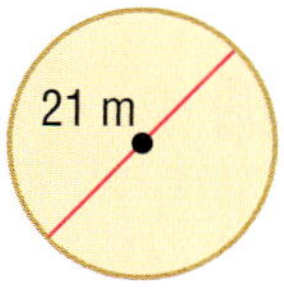

42. diameter = 13.6 yd

43. radius = 23 km

Extend 13-4

Geometry Lab
Changes in Volume and Surface Area

Main IDEA

Investigate changes in volume and surface area.

Preparing for TEKS 8.10 The student describes how changes in dimensions affect linear, area, and volume measures. **(B) describe the resulting effect on volume when dimensions of a solid are changed proportionally.** *Also addresses TEKS 7.4(A).*

Suppose you have a model of a rectangular prism and you are asked to create a similar model whose dimensions are twice as large. In this lab, you will investigate how changing the dimensions of a three-dimensional figure affects the surface area and volume.

ACTIVITY

1

STEP 1 Draw a cube on dot paper that measures 1 unit on each side. Calculate the volume and the surface area of the cube. Then record the data in a table like the one shown below.

STEP 2 Double the side lengths of the cube. Calculate the volume and the surface area of this cube. Record the data in your table.

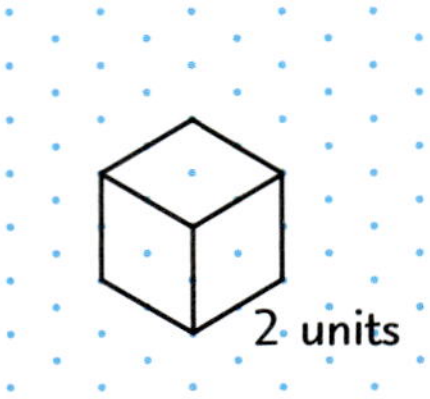

STEP 3 Triple the side lengths of the original cube. Now each side measures 3 units long. Calculate the volume and the surface area of the cube and record the data.

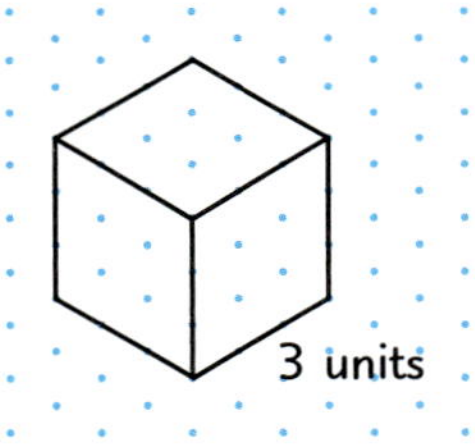

STEP 4 For each cube, write a ratio comparing the side length and the volume. Then write a ratio comparing the side length and the surface area. The first one is done for you.

Side Length (units)	Volume (units^3)	Surface Area (units^2)	Ratio of Side Length to Volume	Ratio of Side Length to Surface Area
1	$1^3 = 1$	$6(1^2) = 6$	1:1	1:6
2				
3				
4				
5				
s				

CHECK Your Progress

a. Complete the table above.

ACTIVITY

2 **STEP 1** Draw a cube on dot paper that measures 8 units on each side. Calculate the volume and the surface area of the cube. Record the data in a table like the one shown below.

STEP 2 Halve the side lengths of the cube in Step 1. Calculate the volume and the surface area of this cube and record the data.

STEP 3 Halve the side lengths of the cube in Step 2. Calculate the volume and the surface area of the cube and record the data.

STEP 4 For each cube, write a ratio comparing the side length and the volume and a ratio comparing the side length and the surface area. The first one is done for you.

STUDY TIP

Ratios If you're looking for a pattern among ratios, it is sometimes helpful to reduce each ratio first.

Side Length (units)	Volume ($units^3$)	Surface Area ($units^2$)	Ratio of Side Length to Volume	Ratio of Side Length to Surface Area
8	$8^3 = 512$	$6(8^2) = 384$	8:512 or 1:64	8:384 or 1:48
4				
2				
s				

CHECK Your Progress

b. Complete the table above.

ANALYZE THE RESULTS

1. Write a formula for the volume V of a cube with side length s.
2. Write a formula for the surface area A of a cube with side length s.

MAKE A CONJECTURE **Complete each sentence.**

3. If the side length of a cube is doubled, the volume is ■ times greater.
4. If the side length of a cube is doubled, the surface area is ■ times greater.
5. If the side length of a cube is tripled, the volume increases by ■ times and the surface area increases by ■ times.
6. If the side length of a cube decreases by $\frac{1}{2}$, the surface area decreases by ■.

13-5 Surface Area of Cylinders

Main IDEA

Find the surface area of a cylinder.

Preparing for TEKS 8.8 The student uses procedures to determine measures of three-dimensional figures. **(A) find** lateral and **total surface area of** prisms, pyramids, and **cylinders using concrete models and nets (two dimensional models).** *Also addresses TEKS 8.8(C).*

MINI Lab

STEP 1 Trace the top and bottom of the can on grid paper. Then cut out the shapes.

STEP 2 Cut a long rectangle from the grid paper. The width of the rectangle should be the same as the height of the can. Wrap the rectangle around the side of the can. Cut off the excess paper so that the edges just meet.

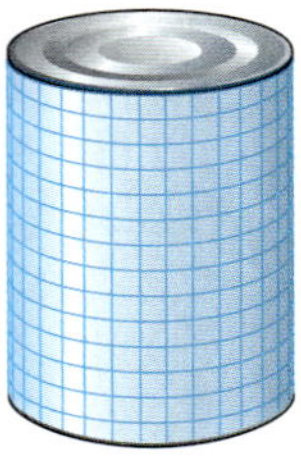

1. Make a net of the cylinder.
2. Name the shapes in the net.
3. How is the length of the rectangle related to the circles?
4. Explain how to find the surface area of the cylinder.

You can put two circles and a rectangle together to make a cylinder.

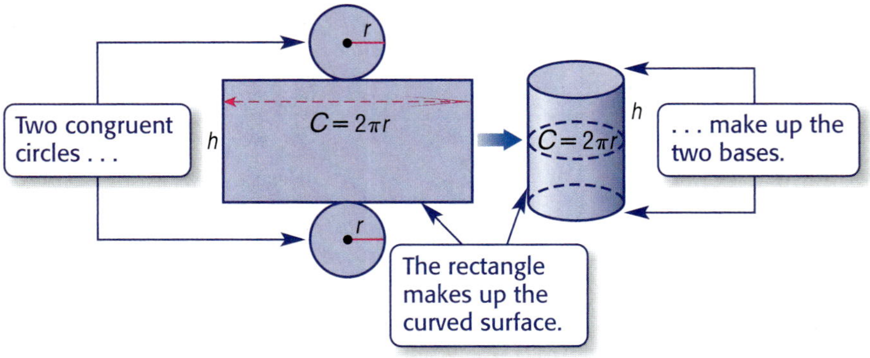

REVIEW Vocabulary

circumference the distance around a circle (Lesson 12-3)

In the diagram above, the length of the rectangle is the same as the circumference of the circle. Also, the width of the rectangle is the same as the height of the cylinder.

The surface area of a cylinder	equals	the area of two bases	plus	the area of the curved surface.
S	$=$	$2(\pi r^2)$	$+$	$(2\pi r)h$

KEY CONCEPT — Surface Area of a Cylinder

Words The surface area S of a cylinder with height h and radius r is the sum of the areas of the circular bases and the area of the curved surface.

Model

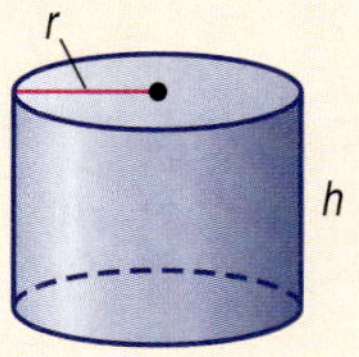

Symbols $S = 2\pi r^2 + 2\pi rh$

EXAMPLE Find the Surface Area of a Cylinder

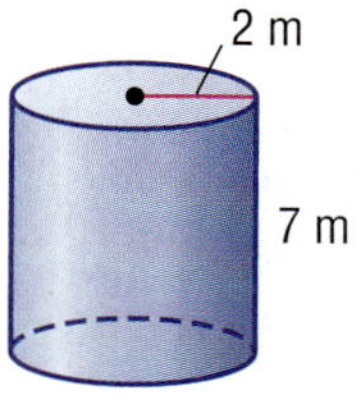

1 **Find the surface area of the cylinder. Round to the nearest tenth.**

$S = 2\pi r^2 + 2\pi rh$ — Surface area of a cylinder

$= 2\pi(2)^2 + 2\pi(2)(7)$ — Replace r with 2 and h with 7.

≈ 113.1 — Simplify.

The surface area is about 113.1 square meters.

CHECK Your Progress

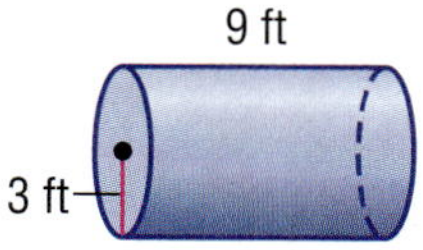

a. Find the surface area of the cylinder. Round to the nearest tenth.

Real-World EXAMPLE

2 **DESIGN A can of soup is 5 inches high, and its base has a diameter of 4 inches. How much paper is needed to make the label on the can?**

Only the curved side of the can has a label. So, you do not need to include the areas of the top and bottom of the can.

$S = 2\pi rh$ — Curved surface of a cylinder

$= 2\pi(2)(5)$ — Replace r with 2 and h with 5.

≈ 62.8 — Simplify.

So, about 62.8 square inches of paper is needed to make the label.

CHECK Your Progress

b. **DESIGN** Find the area of the label of a can of tuna with a radius of 5.1 centimeters and a height of 2.9 centimeters.

Online Personal Tutor at tx.msmath2.com

CHECK Your Understanding

Example 1 (p. 697)

Find the surface area of each cylinder. Round to the nearest tenth.

1. 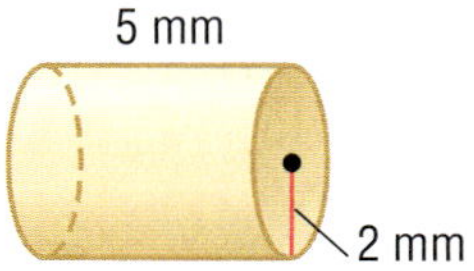

2. 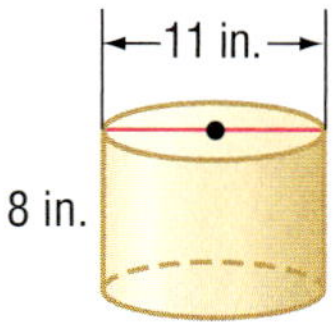

Example 2 (p. 697)

3. **STORAGE** The height of a water tank is 10 meters, and it has a diameter of 10 meters. What is the surface area of the tank?

Exercises

HOMEWORK HELP

For Exercises	See Examples
4–9	1
10–11	2

Find the surface area of each cylinder. Round to the nearest tenth.

4. 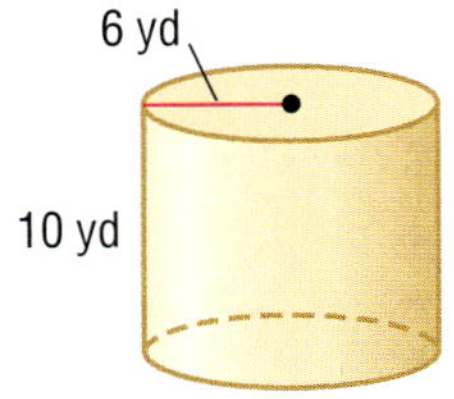

5. 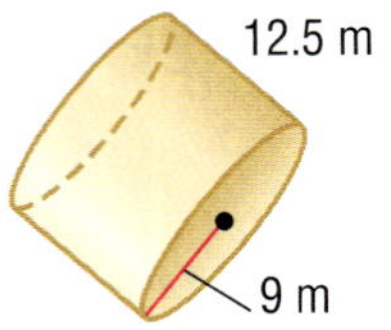

6. 

7. 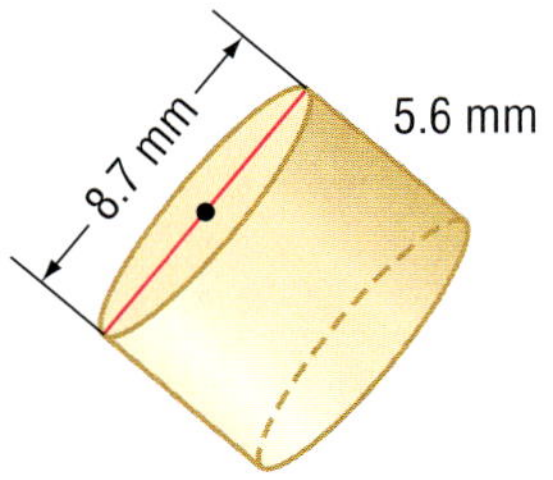

8. 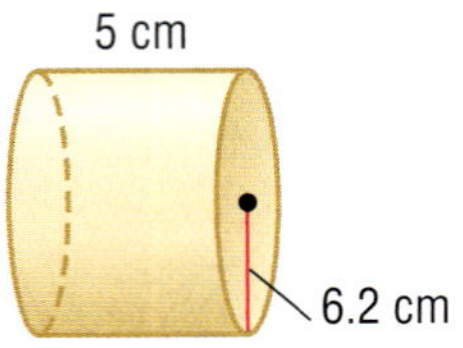

9. 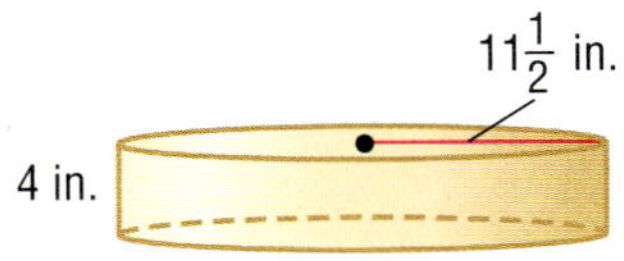

10. **CANDLES** A cylindrical candle has a diameter of 4 inches and a height of 7 inches. What is the surface area of the candle?

11. **PENCILS** Find the surface area of an unsharpened cylindrical pencil that has a radius of 0.5 centimeter and a height of 19 centimeters.

ESTIMATION Estimate the surface area of each cylinder

12. 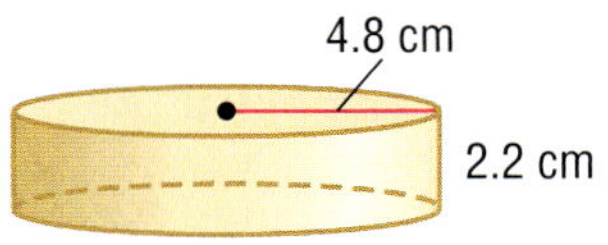

13. 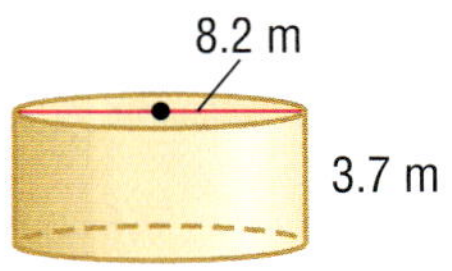

14. 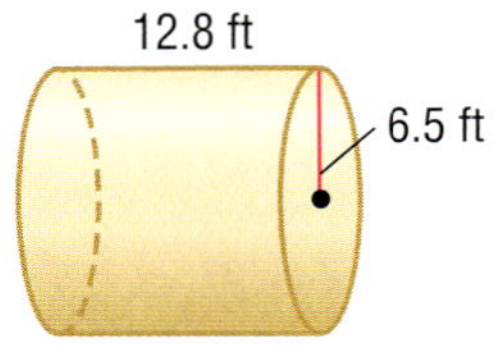

15. **BAKING** Mrs. Jones baked a cake 5 inches high and 9 inches in diameter. If Mrs. Jones covers the top and sides of the cake with frosting, find the area that the frosting covers to the nearest tenth.

EXTRA PRACTICE
See pages 754, 767.
Math Online
Self-Check Quiz at tx.msmath2.com

16. **PACKAGING** The mail tube shown is made of cardboard and has plastic end caps. Approximately what percent of the surface area of the mail tube is cardboard?

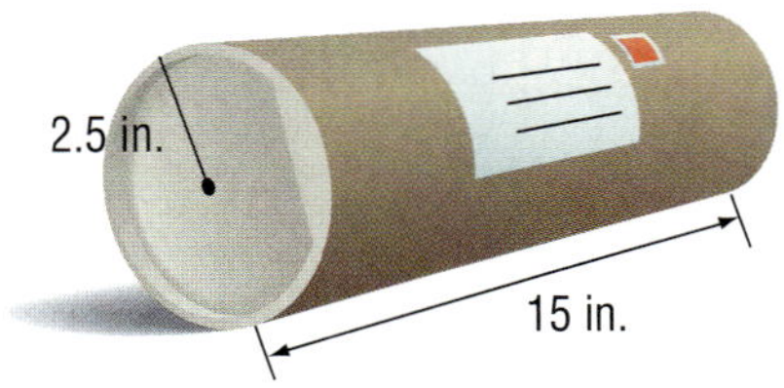

H.O.T. Problems

17. **CHALLENGE** If the height of a cylinder is doubled, will its surface area also double? Explain your reasoning.

18. **WRITING IN MATH** Write a problem about a real-world situation in which you would find the surface area of a cylinder. Be sure to include the answer to your problem.

19. **REASONING** Which has more surface area, a cylinder with radius 6 centimeters and height 3 centimeters or a cylinder with radius 3 centimeters and height 6 centimeters? Explain your reasoning.

TEST PRACTICE

20. Stacey has a cylindrical paper clip holder with the net shown. Use a centimeter ruler to measure the dimensions of the net in centimeters.

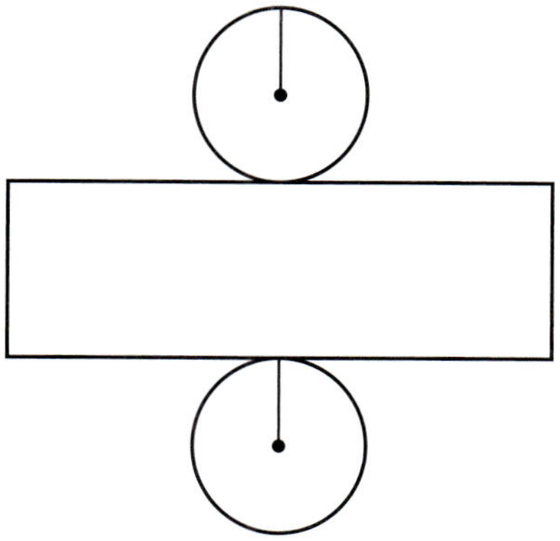

Which is closest to the surface area of the cylindrical paper clip holder?

A 6.0 cm^2

B 6.5 cm^2

C 10.0 cm^2

D 15.5 cm^2

21. The three containers below each hold about 1 liter of liquid. Which container has the greatest surface area?

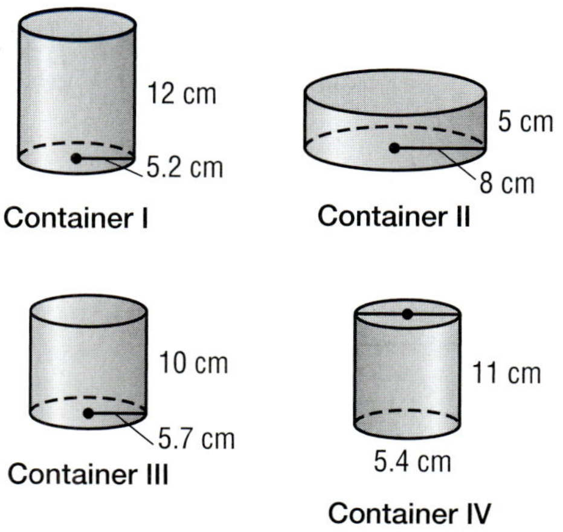

F Container I

G Container II

H Container III

J Container IV

Spiral Review

GEOMETRY **Find the surface area of each rectangular prism.** (Lesson 13-4)

22.

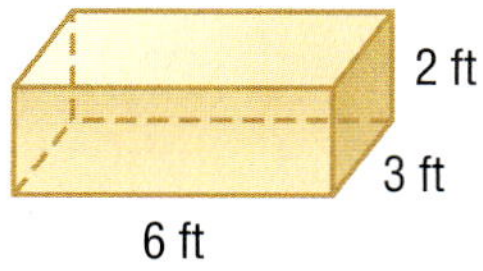

23.

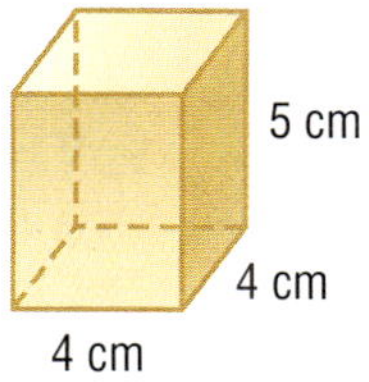

24.

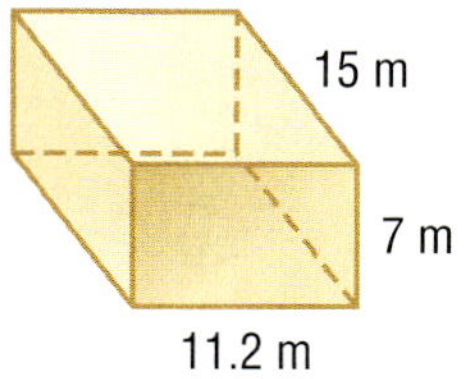

GEOMETRY **Find the missing measure of each right triangle. Round to the nearest tenth if necessary.** (Lesson 13-2)

25. $a = 8$ in., $b = 10$ in.

26. $a = 12$ ft, $c = 20$ ft

27. $b = 12$ cm, $c = 14$ cm

Cross-Curricular Project

Math and History

It's All Greek to Me It's time to complete your project. Use the information and data you have gathered about Pythagoras to prepare a Web page or poster. Be sure to include the three-dimensional solid you created with your project.

Math Online **Cross-Curricular Project at** tx.msmath2.com

CHAPTER 13

Study Guide and Review

STUDY TO GO Download Vocabulary Review from tx.msmath2.com

FOLDABLES™ Study Organizer

GET READY to Study

Be sure the following Key Concepts are noted in your Foldable.

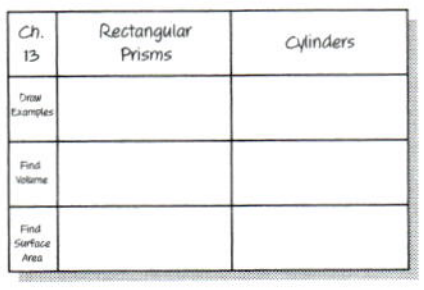

Key Concepts

Irrational Numbers (Lesson 13-1)

- An irrational number is a number that *cannot* be written as a fraction.

Pythagorean Theorem (Lesson 13-2)

- In a right triangle, the square of the length of the hypotenuse equals the sum of the squares of the lengths of the legs.

Surface Area (Lessons 13-4, 13-5)

- The surface area S of a rectangular prism with length ℓ, width w, and height h is the sum of the areas of the faces. $S = 2\ell w + 2\ell h + 2wh$

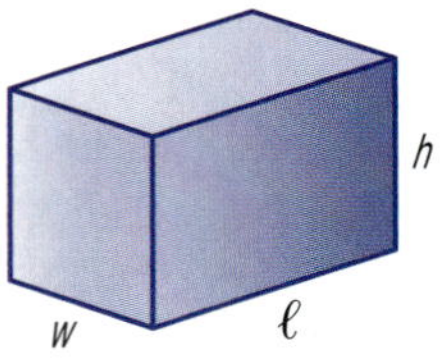

- The surface area of S of a cylinder with height h and a radius r is the sum of the area of the circular bases and the area of the curved surface. $S = 2\pi r^2 + 2\pi rh$

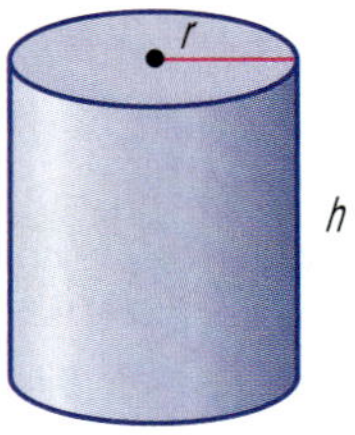

Key Vocabulary

hypotenuse (p. 678)
irrational number (p. 675)
leg (p. 678)
Pythagorean Theorem (p. 678)
surface area (p. 688)

Vocabulary Check

State whether each sentence is *true* or *false*. If *false*, replace the underlined word or number to make a true sentence.

1. The side opposite the right angle in a scalene triangle is called a hypotenuse.
2. Either of the two sides that form the right angle of a right triangle is called a hypotenuse.
3. An irrational number is a number that cannot be written as a fraction.
4. The Pythagorean Theorem states that in a right triangle, the square of the length of the hypotenuse equals the difference of the squares of the lengths of the legs.
5. The sum of the areas of all the surfaces of a three-dimensional figure is called the surface area.
6. The formula for finding the surface area of a cylinder is $S = 2\ell w + 2\ell h + 2wh$.
7. Rational numbers include only positive numbers.
8. The Pythagorean Theorem can be used to find length of the hypotenuse of a right triangle if the measures of both legs are known.
9. To find the surface area of a rectangular prism, you must know the measurements of the height and the radius.
10. The square root of a perfect square is a rational number.

Math Online Vocabulary Review at tx.msmath2.com

Mixed Problem Solving
For mixed problem-solving practice, see page 767.

Lesson-by-Lesson Review

13-1 Estimating Square Roots (pp. 674–677)

Estimate each square root to the nearest whole number.

11. $\sqrt{6}$
12. $\sqrt{99}$
13. $\sqrt{48}$
14. $\sqrt{76}$
15. $\sqrt{19}$
16. $\sqrt{52}$

Use a calculator to find each square root to the nearest tenth.

17. $\sqrt{61}$
18. $\sqrt{132}$
19. $\sqrt{444}$
20. $\sqrt{12}$

21. **SWIMMING POOL** The bottom of Marcia's square swimming pool has an area of 118 square feet. What is the approximate length of one of the sides?

Example 1 Estimate $\sqrt{29}$ to the nearest whole number.

$25 < 29 < 36$	29 is between the perfect squares 25 and 36.
$\sqrt{25} < \sqrt{29} < \sqrt{36}$	Find the square root of each number.
$5 < \sqrt{29} < 6$	$\sqrt{25} = 5$ and $\sqrt{36} = 6$

So, $\sqrt{29}$ is between 5 and 6. Since 29 is closer to 25 than to 36, the best whole number estimate is 5.

13-2 The Pythagorean Theorem (pp. 678–684)

Find the missing measure of each triangle. Round to the nearest tenth if necessary.

22.
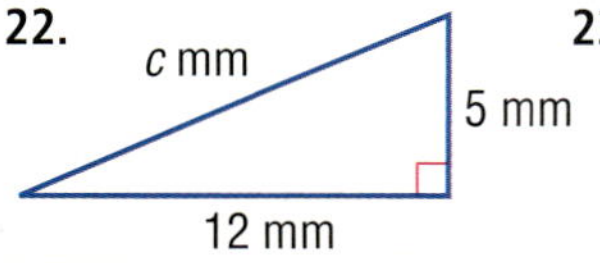

23.
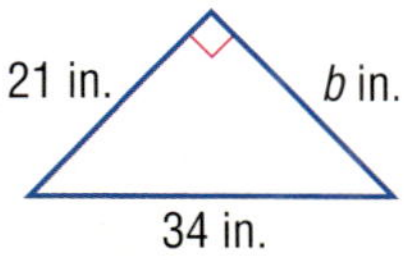

24. $a = 5$ ft, $b = 6$ ft
25. $b = 10$ yd, $c = 12$ yd
26. $a = 7$ m, $c = 15$ m

27. **COMMUNICATION** Find the length of the wire x that is attached to the telephone pole. Round to the nearest tenth.

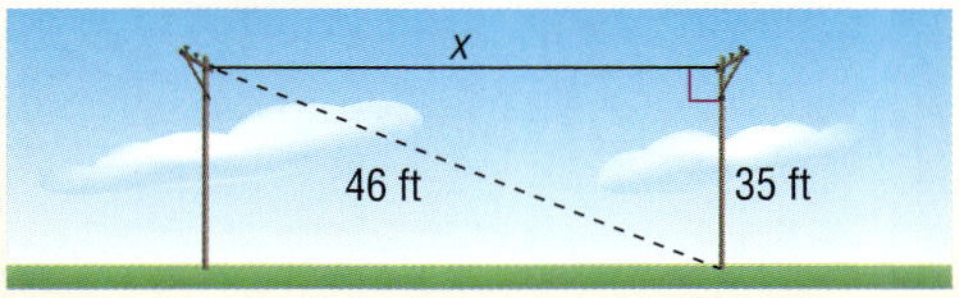

28. **LADDERS** Bartolo has a 26-foot ladder. He places it 10-feet away from the base of a building. What is the height of the building where the top of ladder rests?

Example 2 Find the missing measure of the triangle shown at the right. Round to the nearest tenth if necessary.

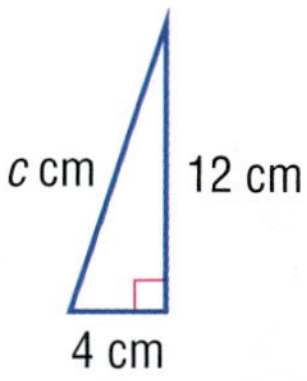

Use the Pythagorean Theorem to solve for c.

$c^2 = a^2 + b^2$	Pythagorean Theorem
$c^2 = 4^2 + 12^2$	$a = 4$ and $b = 12$
$c^2 = 16 + 144$	Evaluate.
$c^2 = 160$	Add.
$\sqrt{c^2} = \sqrt{160}$	Take the square root of each side.
$c \approx \pm 12.6$	Simplify.

Since length cannot be negative, the length of the hypotenuse is about 12.6 centimeters.

CHAPTER 13 Study Guide and Review

13-3 PSI: Make a Model (pp. 685–686)

Solve the problem by using the *make a model* strategy.

29. **FRAMING** A painting 15 inches by 25 inches is bordered by a mat that is 3 inches wide. The frame around the mat is 2 inches wide. Find the area of the picture with the frame and mat.

30. **DVDS** A video store arranges its best-selling DVDs in their front window. In how many different ways can five best-seller DVDs be arranged in a row?

Example 3 **The bottom layer of a display of soup cans has 6 cans in it. If there is one less can in each layer above it and there are 4 layers in the display, how many cans are there in the display?**

So, based on the model there are 18 cans.

13-4 Surface Area of Rectangular Prisms (pp. 688–693)

Find the surface area of each rectangular prism. Round to the nearest tenth if necessary.

31.

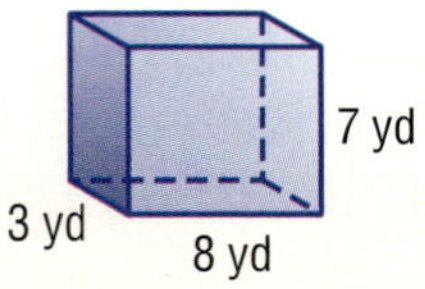

32.

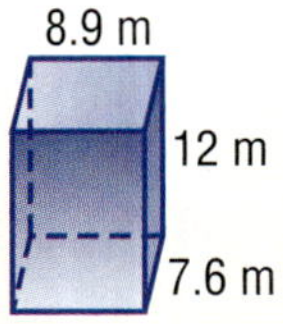

33. **MOVING** A large wardrobe box is 2.25 feet long, 2 feet wide, and 4 feet tall. How much cardboard is needed to make the box?

Example 4 **Find the surface area of a rectangular prism.**

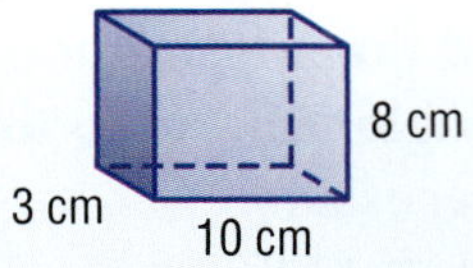

$$\text{surface area} = 2\ell w + 2\ell h + 2wh$$
$$= 2(10)(3) + 2(10)(8) + 2(3)(8)$$
$$= 268$$

The surface area is 268 square centimeters.

13-5 Surface Area of Cylinders (pp. 696–699)

Find the surface area of each cylinder. Round to the nearest tenth.

34.

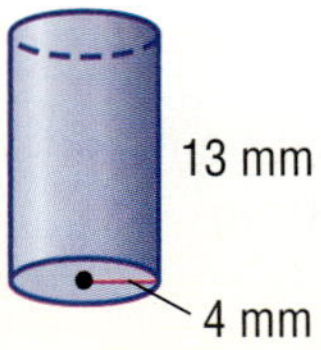

35.

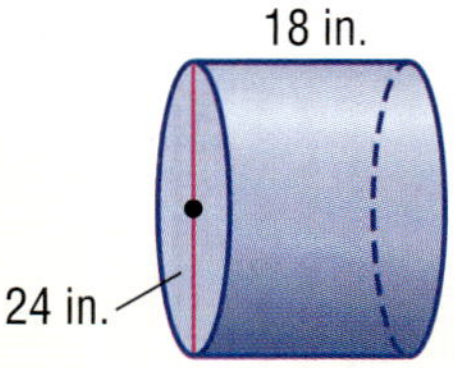

36. **DESIGN** A can of black beans is $5\frac{1}{2}$ inches high, and its base has a radius of 2 inches. How much paper is needed to make the label on the can?

Example 5 **Find the surface area of the cylinder. Round to the nearest tenth.**

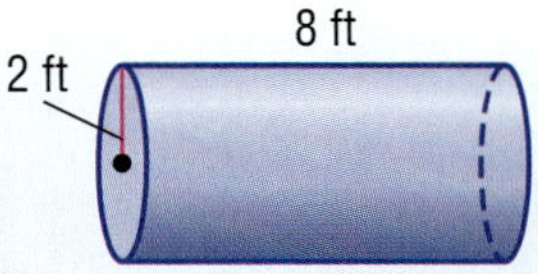

$$\text{surface area} = 2\pi r^2 + 2\pi rh$$
$$= 2(\pi)(2^2) + 2(\pi)(2)8$$
$$\approx 125.7 \text{ ft}^2$$

The surface area is 125.7 square feet.

CHAPTER 13

Practice Test

Estimate each square root to the nearest whole number.

1. $\sqrt{500}$
2. $\sqrt{95}$
3. $\sqrt{265}$

Use a calculator to find each square root to the nearest tenth.

4. $\sqrt{570}$
5. $\sqrt{7}$
6. $\sqrt{84}$

7. **TEST PRACTICE** The length of one side of a square sandbox is 7 feet. Which number is closest to the length of the diagonal of the sandbox?

   A $\sqrt{100}$
   B $\sqrt{50}$
   C $\sqrt{14}$
   D $\sqrt{7}$

Find the missing measure of each right triangle. Round to the nearest tenth if necessary.

8. $a = 5$ m, $b = 4$ m
9. $b = 12$ in., $c = 14$ in.
10. $a = 7$ in., $c = 13$ in.

11. **DISTANCE** Use the diagram below to find the distance from the library to the post office. Round to the nearest tenth.

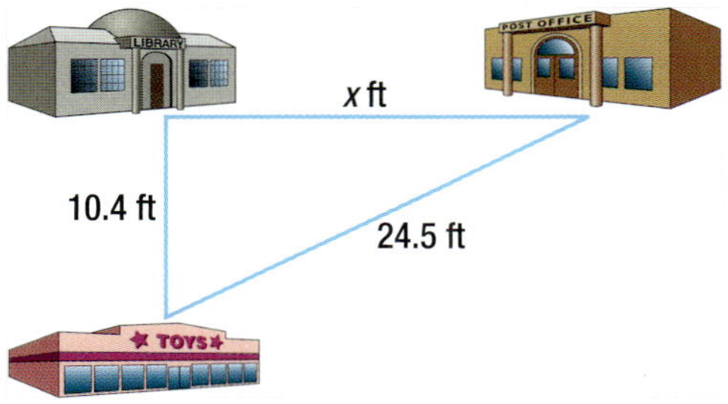

12. **CHAIRS** Chris is responsible for arranging the chairs at the meeting. There are 72 chairs, and he wants to have twice as many chairs in each row as he has in each column. How many chairs should he put in each row? How many rows does he need?

Find the surface area of each rectangular prism and cylinder. Round to the nearest tenth if necessary.

13.
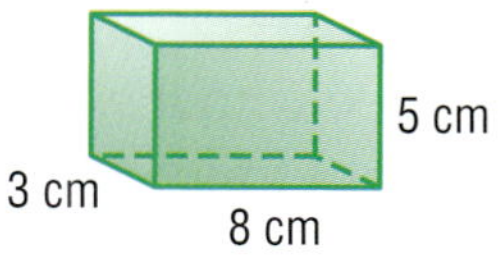

14.
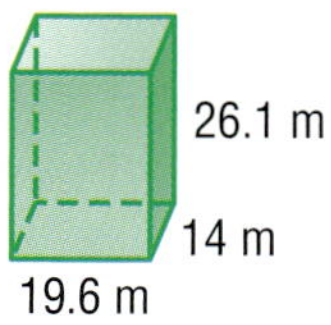

15.
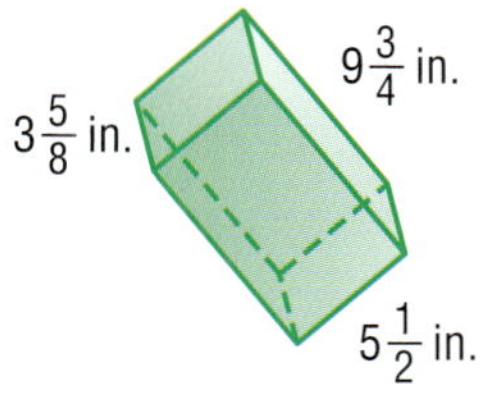

16.
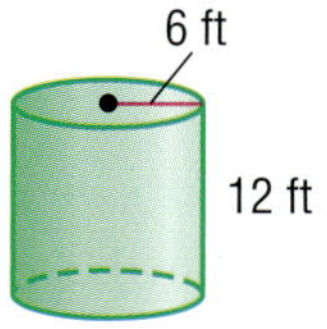

17.
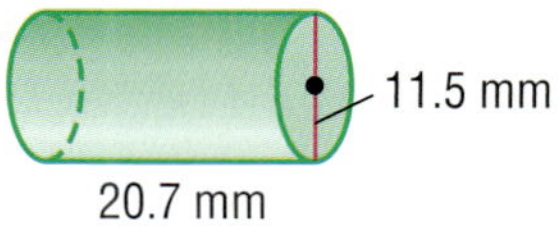

18.
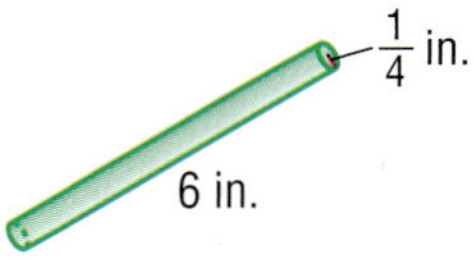

19. **PACKAGING** Mrs. Rodriguez is wrapping a gift. What is the least amount of wrapping paper she will need to wrap the box below?

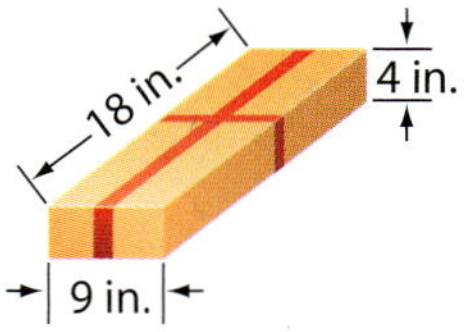

20. **TEST PRACTICE** The dimensions of four containers are given below. Which container has the greatest surface area?

F
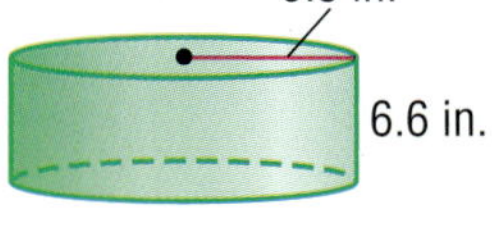

H
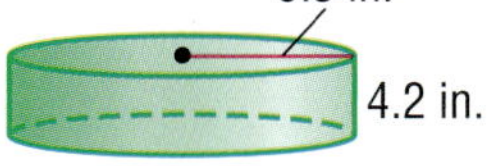

G
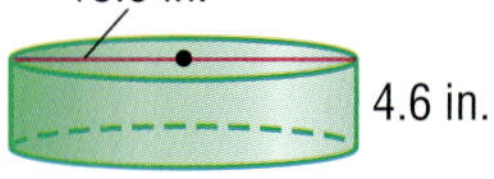

J
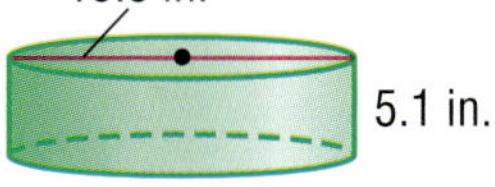

CHAPTER 13 Texas Test Practice

Cumulative, Chapters 1–13

Read each question. Then fill in the correct answer on the answer document provided by your teacher or on a sheet of paper.

1. Which of the following three-dimensional figures could be formed from this net?

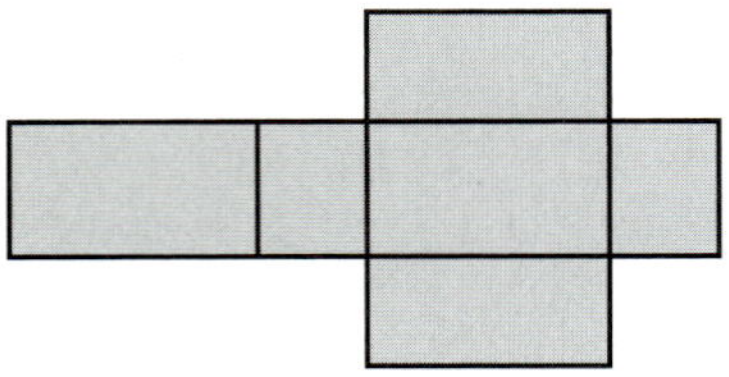

A Cube

B Rectangular pyramid

C Triangular prism

D Rectangular prism

2. Which of the following nets could be used to make a cylinder?

F

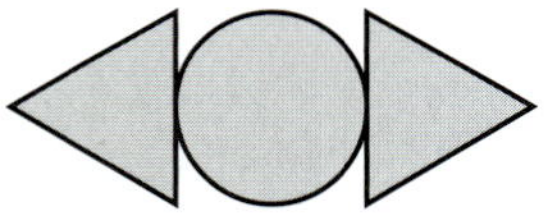

G

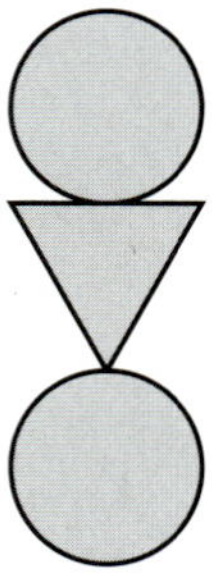

H

J

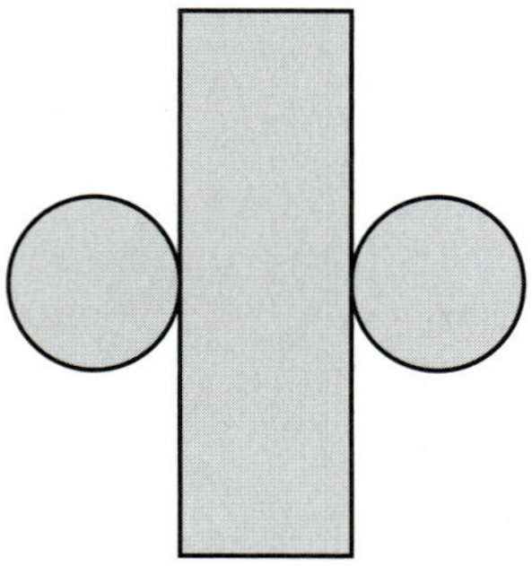

3. Carla has an above-ground swimming pool with a circumference of 20 feet. Which of the following equations could be used to find r, the radius of the pool?

A $r = \frac{10}{\pi}$

B $r = \frac{40}{\pi}$

C $r = \frac{10}{2\pi}$

D $r = \frac{\pi}{20}$

4. Of the following figures that Ryan drew, which 2 figures have the same area?

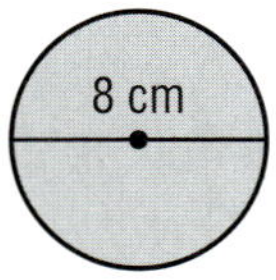

Figure I

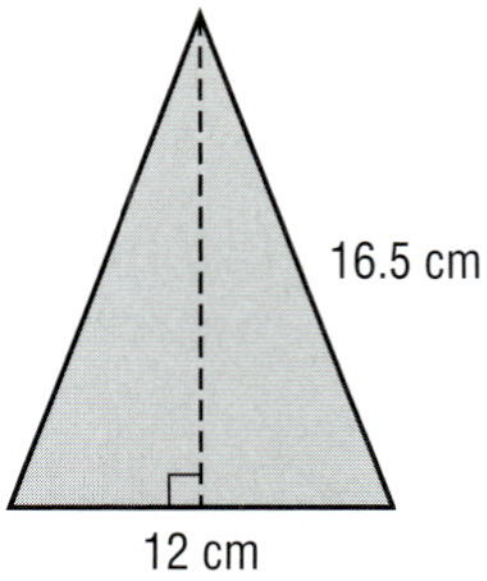

Figure II

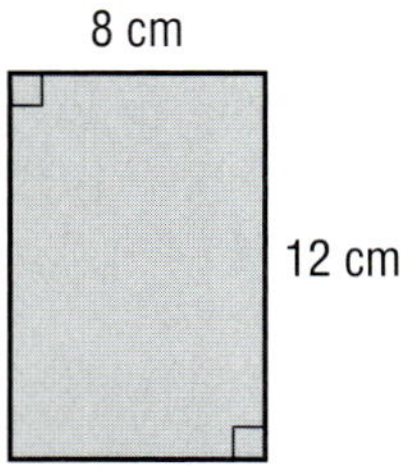

Figure III

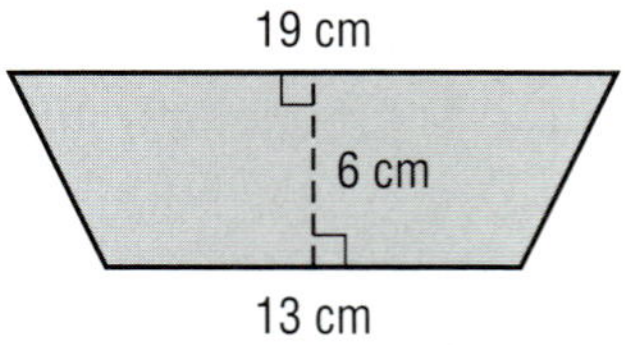

Figure IV

F Figure I and II

G Figure II and III

H Figure II and IV

J Figure III and IV

5. **GRIDDABLE** Cassandra drew a circle with a radius of 12 inches and another circle with a radius of 8 inches. What is the approximate difference in square inches between the areas of the 2 circles? Use $\pi = 3.14$.

Get Ready for the Texas Test
For test-taking strategies and more practice, see pages TX1–TX23.

6. Sarah's parents asked her to save $\frac{1}{4}$ of her allowance each week to help pay for her music lessons. What percent of her allowance did Sarah's parents ask her to save?

   A 25% **C** 50%
   B 40% **D** 75%

7. Dave can run 30 yards in 8.2 seconds. During a race, he ran 120 yards. If Dave's rate of speed remained the same, how long did it take him to run the race?

   F 43 seconds **H** 24.6 seconds
   G 32.8 seconds **J** 18.4 seconds

8. **GRIDDABLE** Find the perimeter in yards of the rectangle shown below.

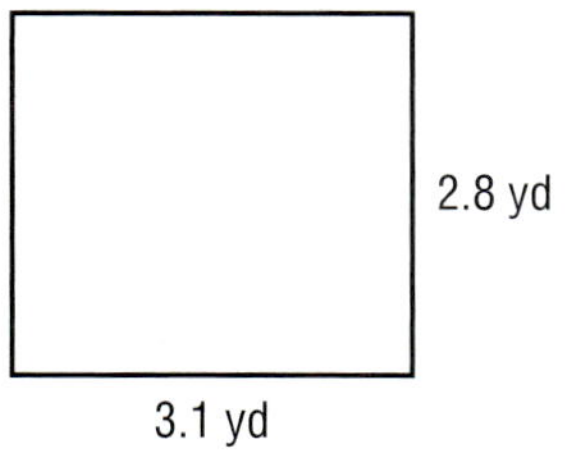

TEST-TAKING TIP

Question 8 When answering GRIDDABLE questions, first fill in the answer on the top row. Then pencil in exactly one bubble under each number or symbol

9. Which statement is NOT true about an equilateral triangle?

   A The sum of the 3 angles is 180°.
   B It has 3 congruent angles.
   C It has 1 right angle.
   D It has exactly 3 congruent sides.

10. Bill's Electronics bought 5 computers for a total of \$3,000. The business later bought another computer for \$600. What was the mean price of all the computers?

   F \$600.00 **H** \$3,600.00
   G \$3,200.00 **J** \$6,100.00

11. The net of a cylinder is shown below. Find the total surface area of this cylinder to the nearest square centimeter.

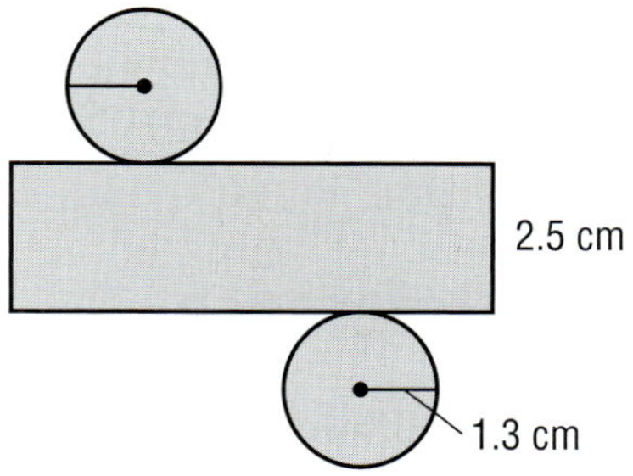

   A 22 cm^2 **C** 28 cm^2
   B 24 cm^2 **D** 31 cm^2

Pre-AP

Record your answers on a sheet of paper. Show your work.

12. The cylindrical gasoline storage tank on Mrs. Simon's farm needs to be painted. The dimensions are shown below.

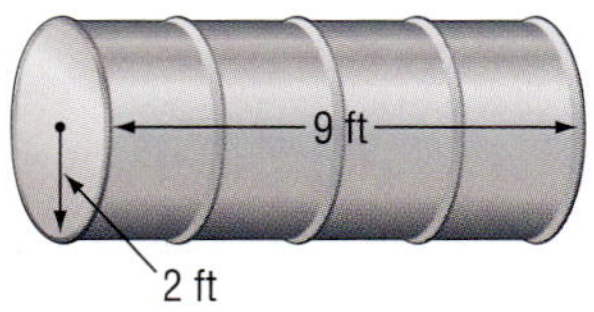

   a. What is the surface area of the tank?
   b. If one quart of paint covers 85 square feet, how many quarts does Mrs. Simon need for this job?

NEED EXTRA HELP?												
If You Missed Question...	1	2	3	4	5	6	7	8	9	10	11	12
Go to Lesson...	13-4	13-5	12-3	12-2	12-4	5-6	7-4	4-6	11-3	9-2	13-5	13-5
For Help with Test Objective...	3	3	6	4	4	1	2	4	3	5	4	4

Student Handbook

Built-In Workbooks

Reference

How to Use the Student Handbook

A Student Handbook is the additional skill and reference material found at the end of books. The Student Handbook can help answer these questions.

What If I Forget What I Learned Last Year?

Use the Prerequisite Skills section to refresh your memory about things you have learned in other math classes. Here's a list of the topics covered in your book.

1. Divisibility Patterns
2. Place Value and Decimals
3. Comparing and Ordering Decimals
4. Rounding Decimals
5. Estimating with Decimals
6. Adding and Subtracting Decimals
7. Mixed Numbers and Improper Fractions
8. Frequency Tables
9. Measuring and Drawing Angles

What If I Need More Practice?

You, or your teacher, may decide that working through some additional problems would be helpful. The **Extra Practice** section provides these problems for each lesson so you have ample opportunity to practice new skills.

What If I Have Trouble with Word Problems?

The **Mixed Problem Solving** portion of the book provides additional word problems that use the skills presented in each chapter. These problems give you real-world situations where the math can be applied.

What If I Forget a Vocabulary Word?

The **English-Spanish Glossary** provides a list of important, or difficult, words used throughout the textbook. It provides a definition in English and Spanish as well as the page number(s) where the word can be found.

What If I Need to Check a Homework Answer?

The answers to the odd-numbered problems are included in **Selected Answers**. Check your answers to make sure you understand how to solve all of the assigned problems.

What If I Need to Find Something Quickly?

The **Index** alphabetically lists the subjects covered throughout the entire textbook and the pages on which each subject can be found.

What If I Forget a Formula?

Inside the back cover of your math book is a **Mathematics Chart** that lists formulas and symbols that are used in the book.

Prerequisite Skills

1 Divisibility Patterns

In $54 \div 6 = 9$, the quotient, 9, is a whole number. So, we say that 54 is **divisible** by 6. You can use the following rules to determine whether a number is by 2, 3, 4, 5, 6, 9, and 10.

A number is divisible by:

- 2 if the ones digit is divisible by 2.
- 3 if the sum of the digits is divisible by 3.
- 4 if the number formed by the last two digits is divisible by 4.
- 5 if the ones digit is 0 or 5.
- 6 if the number is divisible by both 2 and 3.
- 9 if the sum of the digits is divisible by 9.
- 10 if the ones digit is 0.

EXAMPLE Use Divisibility Rules

Determine whether 972 is divisible by 2, 3, 4, 5, 6, 9, or 10.

2: Yes; the ones digit, 2, is divisible by 2.
3: Yes; the sum of the digits, $9 + 7 + 2 = 18$, is divisible by 3.
4: Yes; the number formed by the last two digits, 72, is divisible by 4.
5: No; the ones digit is not 0 or 5.
6: Yes; the number is divisible by 2 and 3.
9: Yes; the sum of the digits, 18, is divisible by 9.
10: No; the ones digit is not 0.

Exercises

Use divisibility rules to determine whether the first number is divisible by the second number.

1. 447; 3
2. 135; 6
3. 240; 4
4. 419; 3
5. 831; 3
6. 4,408; 4
7. 7,110; 5
8. 1,287; 9
9. 2,984; 9
10. 7,026; 6
11. 1,260; 10
12. 8,903; 6

Determine whether each number is divisible by 2, 3, 4, 5, 6, 9, or 10.

13. 712
14. 1,035
15. 8,901
16. 462
17. 270
18. 1,005
19. 32,221
20. 8,340
21. 920
22. 50,319
23. 64,042
24. 3,498

25. **MEASUREMENT** Jordan has 5,280 feet of rope. Can he cut the rope into 9-foot pieces and use all of the rope? Explain.

2 Place Value and Decimals

Our number system is based on units of ten. Numbers like 1.35, 0.8, and 25.09 are called decimals.

You can use a place-value chart like the one at the right to help you read decimals and write them in words. Use the word *and* to represent the decimal point.

10,000	1,000	100	10	1		0.1	0.01	0.001	0.0001	0.00001
ten thousands	thousands	hundreds	tens	ones	decimal point	tenths	hundredths	thousandths	ten-thousandths	hundred-thousandths
			2	5	•	0	9			

EXAMPLES Write Decimal in Words

Write each decimal in words

1 **20.09**

tens	ones	decimal point	tenths	hundredths
2	0	•	0	9

twenty and nine hundredths

2 **6.738**

ones	decimal point	tenths	hundredths	thousandths
6	•	7	3	8

six and seven hundred thirty-eight thousandths

You can also write decimals in **expanded notation** using place value and decimals or their fraction equivalents as shown at the right.

Decimal	0.1	0.01	0.001	0.0001
Fraction	$\frac{1}{10}$	$\frac{1}{10^2}$	$\frac{1}{10^3}$	$\frac{1}{10^4}$

EXAMPLE Write a Decimal in Expanded Notation

3 **Write 2.814 in expanded notation using decimals and using fractions.**

Write the product of each digit and its place value.

$$2.814 = (2 \times 1) + (8 \times 0.1) + (1 \times 0.01) + (4 \times 0.001)$$

$$2.814 = (2 \times 1) + \left(8 \times \frac{1}{10}\right) + \left(1 \times \frac{1}{10^2}\right) + \left(4 \times \frac{1}{10^3}\right)$$

Replace the decimals with their fraction equivalents.

Exercises

Write each decimal in words.

1. 6.37 **2.** 13.7 **3.** 145.66 **4.** 92.03 **5.** 4,280.899

6. 0.6 **7.** 0.69 **8.** 0.00012 **9.** 7.005 **10.** 2000.0002

Write each decimal in expanded notation using decimals and using fractions.

11. 0.8 **12.** 5.3 **13.** 6.79 **14.** 9.132 **15.** 65.002

16. 0.625 **17.** 0.0072 **18.** 100.001 **19.** 548.845 **20.** 4,260.705

21. **BATS** The northern blossom bat is one of the world's smallest bats. It weighs just 0.53 ounce. Write its weight in expanded notation using fractions.

3 Comparing and Ordering Decimals

To determine which of two decimals is greater, you can compare the digits in each place-value position, or you can use a number line.

EXAMPLES Order Decimals

1 Which is greater, 7.4 or 7.63?

METHOD 1 Use place value.

7.4 Line up the decimal points.

7.63 Starting at the left, compare the digits in each place-value position.

↑

The digits in the tenths place are not the same.

Since 6 tenths $>$ 4 tenths, $7.63 > 7.4$.

METHOD 2 Use a number line.

Graph each decimal on a number line and compare.

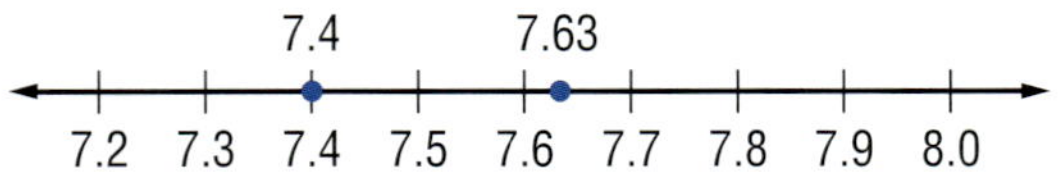

On a number line, numbers to the right are greater than numbers to the left.

7.63 is to the right of 7.4, so $7.63 > 7.4$.

2 Order 12.15, 12.08, and 12.103 from least to greatest.

12.15 Line up the decimal points.

12.08 12.08 is less than 12.15 and 12.103 since $0 < 1$ in the tenths place.

12.103 12.103 is less than 12.15 since $0 < 5$ in the hundredths place.

So, the numbers from least to greatest are 12.08, 12.103, and 12.15.

Exercises

Replace each ● with $<$, $>$, or $=$ to make a true sentence.

1. 1.22 ● 1.02
2. 0.97 ● 1.06
3. 7.90 ● 7.9
4. 1.3 ● 1.31
5. 4.03 ● 4.01
6. 0.77 ● 0.69
7. 0.8 ● 0.08
8. 0.68 ● 0.680
9. 3.28 ● 3.279
10. 25.23 ● 25.32
11. 77.55 ● 77.65
12. 1.29 ● 1.43
13. 310.36 ● 310.3600
14. 0.0034 ● 0.034
15. 9.09 ● 9

Order each group of decimals from least to greatest.

16. 5.13, 5.07, 5.009
17. 7.9, 7.088, 8.02, 7.98
18. 0.087, 0.901, 2, 1.001
19. 12.3, 12.008, 12.54, 12
20. 60.5, 60.05, 60.55, 60.505
21. 505.9, 505.09, 505.91, 505.99
22. 0.02, 0.2, 0.022, 0.002
23. 0.99, 0.90, 0.09, 0.999, 0.099

4 Rounding Decimals

When a number has more decimal places than you want or need, you can **round** it. Use the rules below to round a number to any place value.

Rounding Decimals	Look at the digit to the right of the place being rounded. • If the digit is 4 or less, the digit being rounded remains the same. • If the digit is 5 or greater, the digit being rounded is rounded up.

EXAMPLES Round Decimals

1 Round 3.92 to the nearest tenth.

tenths place ↓

3.92 Look at the digit to the right of the tenths place.
Since 2 is less than 5, the digit in the tenths place stays the same.

3.92 rounded to the nearest tenth is 3.9.

2 Round 46.297 to the nearest hundredth.

hundredths place ↓

46.297 Look at the digit to the right of the hundredths place.
Since 7 is greater than 5, round 9 up.

46.297 rounded to the nearest hundredth is 46.30.

Exercises

Round each number to the given place value.

1. 0.315; tenth
2. 0.2456; hundredth
3. 17.499; tenth
4. 43.219; hundredth
5. 15.522; tenth
6. 9.6; ones
7. 7.0375; thousandth
8. 16.399; tenth
9. 6.95; tenth
10. 99.1283; thousandth
11. 1,000.37; tenth
12. 750.523; ones
13. 0.445; hundredth
14. 490.299; ones
15. 999.99; tenth
16. 476.835; hundredth
17. 682.596; tenth
18. 1,000.562; ones

Round each number to the underlined place-value position.

19. $0.7\underline{8}9$
20. $0.\underline{9}6$
21. $1.5\underline{7}246$
22. $2\underline{3}.48$
23. $1.7\underline{0}4$
24. $0.\underline{1}63$
25. $15.\underline{4}51$
26. $4.52\underline{9}88$
27. $0.\underline{7}87$
28. $3\underline{8}.56$
29. $5\underline{9}.61$
30. $\underline{0}.555$
31. $0.\underline{5}55$
32. $0.5\underline{5}5$
33. $10.\underline{9}29$
34. $10.9\underline{2}9$
35. $42\underline{5}.599$
36. $0.929\underline{2}9$
37. **HORSES** A trainer recorded a racehorse running at 47.54 miles per hour. Round this speed to the nearest mile per hour.
38. **POPULATION** In 2000, the population of Texas was 20.85 million. Round to the nearest million.

Prerequisite Skills

Prerequisite Skills

5 Estimating with Decimals

Estimation can be used to provide quick answers when an exact answer is not necessary. It is also an excellent way to check whether your answer is reasonable. One method of estimating is to use rounding. Round numbers to any place value that makes estimation easier.

EXAMPLES Estimate by Rounding

Estimate by rounding.

1 **23.485 − 9.757**

$$\begin{array}{rcr} 23.485 & \rightarrow & 23 \\ -\ 9.757 & \rightarrow & -\ 10 \\ \hline & & 13 \end{array}$$

Round to the nearest whole numbers.

The difference is about 13.

2 **6.43 + 2.17 + 9.1 + 4.87**

$$\begin{array}{rcr} 6.43 & \rightarrow & 6 \\ 2.17 & \rightarrow & 2 \\ 9.1 & \rightarrow & 9 \\ +\ 4.87 & \rightarrow & +\ 5 \\ \hline & & 22 \end{array}$$

Round to the nearest whole numbers.

The sum is about 22.

Another way to estimate sums is to use **clustering**. This strategy is used when all the numbers are close to a common value.

EXAMPLE Estimate by Clustering

3 **Estimate 9.775 + 9.862 + 9.475 + 9.724 by clustering.**

All of the numbers are clustered around 10. There are four numbers.

So, the sum is about 4 × 10 or 40.

Exercises

Estimate by rounding.

1. 8.56 + 5.34
2. 34.84 − 17.69
3. 6.8 + 2.4
4. 40.79 − 6.8
5. 6.9 + 5.2
6. 23.84 + 12.13
7. 34.3 − 18.9
8. 7.5 + 8.4
9. 65.48 − 9.3
10. 26.3 + 9.7
11. 33.21 − 8.23
12. 67.86 − 24.35
13. 8.99 − 2.6
14. 121.5 + 487.8
15. 32.5 + 81.4

Estimate by clustering.

16. 18.4 + 22.5 + 20.7
17. 56.9 + 63.2 + 59.3 + 61.1
18. 42.3 + 41.5 + 39.8 + 40.4
19. 77.8 + 75.6 + 81.2 + 79.9
20. 239.8 + 242.43 + 236.20 + 240.77
21. 9.9 + 10.0 + 10.3 + 11.1 + 9.8 + 11.2
22. 50.4 + 51.1 + 48.9 + 49.5 + 50.8
23. 100.5 + 97.8 + 101.6 + 100.2 + 99.3

6 Adding and Subtracting Decimals

To add or subtract decimals, write the numbers in a column and line up the decimal points. In some cases, you may want to *annex*, or place zeros at the end of the decimals, to help align the columns. Then add or subtract as with whole numbers and bring down the decimal point. Always estimate first to see whether your answer is reasonable.

EXAMPLES Add and Subtract Decimals

Find each sum or difference.

1 **12.6 + 4.5** Estimate 13 + 5 = 18

12.6	Line up the decimal points.
+ 4.5	Add.
17.1	The sum is close to the estimate.

2 **42.17 − 15.85** Estimate 42 − 16 = 26

42.17	Line up the decimal points.
− 15.85	Subtract.
26.32	The difference is close to the estimate.

3 **57.125 + 7.63** Estimate 57 + 8 = 65

57.125	
+ 7.630	Annex a zero to align the columns.
64.755	Compare to the estimate.

4 **25 − 15.25** Estimate 25 − 15 = 10

25.00	Annex a zero to align the columns.
+ 15.25	
9.75	Compare to the estimate.

Exercises

Find each sum or difference.

1. $\begin{array}{r} 0.132 \\ \underline{-\ 0.021} \end{array}$ **2.** $\begin{array}{r} 3.78 \\ \underline{+\ 0.21} \end{array}$ **3.** $\begin{array}{r} 13.2 \\ \underline{+\ 12.8} \end{array}$ **4.** $\begin{array}{r} 5.86 \\ \underline{-\ 1.51} \end{array}$ **5.** $\begin{array}{r} 42.07 \\ \underline{-\ 38.78} \end{array}$

6. $\begin{array}{r} 14.7 \\ \underline{+\ 351.82} \end{array}$ **7.** $\begin{array}{r} 42.3 \\ \underline{+\ 0.81} \end{array}$ **8.** $\begin{array}{r} 12.3 \\ \underline{-\ 0.847} \end{array}$ **9.** $\begin{array}{r} 342.9 \\ \underline{-\ 0.18} \end{array}$ **10.** $\begin{array}{r} 282.45 \\ \underline{-\ 111.3} \end{array}$

11. $\begin{array}{r} 100 \\ \underline{-\ 0.48} \end{array}$ **12.** $\begin{array}{r} 82.23 \\ \underline{+\ 0.88} \end{array}$ **13.** $\begin{array}{r} 128.01 \\ \underline{-\ 39.117} \end{array}$ **14.** $\begin{array}{r} 80.05 \\ \underline{-\ 79.06} \end{array}$ **15.** $\begin{array}{r} 104.98 \\ \underline{-\ 0.12} \end{array}$

16. 0.42 + 0.68
17. 0.48 + 2.901
18. 5.8 + 3.92
19. 38.63 + 38.63
20. 8 − 2.54
21. 16.354 − 0.2
22. 0.125 + 0.78
23. 8.2 − 6.9
24. 1.245 + 3.842
25. 3.2 + 1.23
26. 0.889 − 0.3
27. 22.22 + 1.475
28. 10 − 0.25
29. 33.16 − 0.08
30. 1.254 + 0.5
31. 44.698 − 14.903
32. 10 − 0.005
33. 722.86 + 0.024
34. 100.211 + 8.004
35. 86.124 + 32.822
36. 6.9 + 1.1
37. 75 − 0.24
38. 13 − 0.324
39. 0.8 + 1.2

40. What is the sum of 35.009 and 3.6?

41. Find 9.1 minus 5.625.

42. **AIR TRAVEL** The numbers of passengers, in millions, passing through four airports in a recent year were 80.2, 72.1, 68.5, and 60.7. Find the total number of passengers for the four airports.

Prerequisite Skills

7 Mixed Numbers and Improper Fractions

A **mixed number** is the sum of a whole number and a fraction. An **improper fraction** is a fraction with a numerator that is greater than or equal to the denominator.

mixed number: $8\frac{1}{2}$ improper fraction: $\frac{17}{2}$

To write a mixed number as an improper fraction, use the following steps.

- Multiply the whole number by the denominator.
- Add the numerator.
- Write the sum as the numerator of the improper fraction.

EXAMPLES Write Mixed Numbers as Improper Fractions

Write each mixed number as an improper fraction.

1 $6\frac{1}{2}$

$6\frac{1}{2} = \frac{(6 \cdot 2) + 1}{2}$ ← Multiply 6 by 2. Add 1. ← The denominator is 2.

$= \frac{12 + 1}{2}$ or $\frac{13}{2}$ Simplify.

2 $3\frac{4}{5}$

$3\frac{4}{5} = \frac{(3 \cdot 5) + 4}{5}$ ← Multiply 3 by 5. Add 4. ← The denominator is 5.

$= \frac{15 + 4}{5}$ or $\frac{19}{5}$ Simplify.

To write an improper fraction as a mixed number, divide the numerator by the denominator. Write the remainder as the numerator of the fraction.

EXAMPLE Write Improper Fractions as Mixed Numbers

3 **Write $\frac{7}{4}$ as a mixed number.**

$7 \div 4 = 1\text{ R }3$ Divide the numerator by the denominator.

$= 1\frac{3}{4}$ Write the remainder as the numerator of the function.

So, $\frac{7}{4} = 1\frac{3}{4}$.

Exercises

Write each mixed number as an improper fraction.

1. $2\frac{1}{3}$ **2.** $1\frac{5}{8}$ **3.** $4\frac{5}{7}$ **4.** $3\frac{3}{4}$ **5.** $9\frac{1}{3}$

6. $1\frac{1}{10}$ **7.** $10\frac{2}{3}$ **8.** $12\frac{1}{4}$ **9.** $6\frac{3}{8}$ **10.** $11\frac{1}{2}$

11. $2\frac{3}{8}$ **12.** $20\frac{3}{5}$ **13.** $5\frac{7}{8}$ **14.** $27\frac{1}{3}$ **15.** $5\frac{2}{3}$

Write each improper fraction as a mixed number.

16. $\frac{15}{2}$ **17.** $\frac{9}{7}$ **18.** $\frac{15}{8}$ **19.** $\frac{100}{3}$ **20.** $\frac{28}{5}$

21. $\frac{3}{3}$ **22.** $\frac{19}{8}$ **23.** $\frac{17}{10}$ **24.** $\frac{51}{3}$ **25.** $\frac{17}{6}$

26. $\frac{5}{3}$ **27.** $\frac{99}{3}$ **28.** $\frac{25}{7}$ **29.** $\frac{46}{9}$ **30.** $\frac{27}{4}$

8 Frequency Tables

A **frequency table** organizes data by grouping repeating values together and counting their frequency using tally marks. Intervals are sometimes used when the values in the data set can easily be grouped into equal ranges of numbers. The scale of a set of numerical data must include the lowest and highest numbers in the data set.

EXAMPLE Construct a Frequency Table of a Set Data

1 The list gives the daily high temperatures of a certain city, in degrees Fahrenheit, for thirty days.

75, 76, 74, 73, 80, 66, 65, 60, 72, 74, 78, 59, 60, 60, 61,
62, 70, 75, 76, 77, 71, 68, 67, 65, 60, 55, 53, 60, 70, 69

To organize the data into a frequency table, intervals are appropriate since the range of values is a large number, 80−53, or 27. Since there are three temperatures in the interval 50−59, place three tally marks in the tally column and write a frequency of 3 in the frequency column. Repeat this process until all temperatures have been accounted for.

Daily High Temperatures

Interval (°F)	Tally	Frequency
50–59	|||	3
60–69	𝍸 𝍸 |||	13
70–79	𝍸 𝍸 |||	13
80–89			1

Exercises

Construct a frequency table for the each data set.

1. The results of a coin toss where Paul recorded each head as an "H" and each tail as a "T" are given.
   H, T, H, H, T, H, T, T, T, H, H, T, T, T, H, H, H, H, H, T
2. The number of foul (1), two-point (2), and three-point basketball shots (3) Aaron made are given.
   1, 2, 1, 2, 2, 3, 2, 3, 2, 2, 1, 1, 3, 3, 2, 3, 2, 3, 2, 2
3. The results of a poll where students gave their favorite color are given.
   yellow, white, green, blue, red, blue, purple, red, red, blue, green, purple, black, blue, blue, yellow, red, orange, green, black, black, white, white, red, blue
4. The results of rolling a number cube are given.
   1, 4, 4, 6, 5, 3, 2, 1, 2, 3, 5, 6, 6, 6, 2, 3, 4, 4
5. The results of the student council presidential election are given.
   Simona, Jeffrey, Malik, Malik, Jeffrey, Simona, Lawanda, Malik, Simona, Jeffrey, Lawanda, Malik, Simona, Jeffrey, Malik, Lawanda, Simona, Simona, Malik, Jeffrey, Simona, Malik, Lawanda, Lawanda, Malik, Malik, Jeffrey

9 Measuring and Drawing Angles

An angle is formed by two rays, with a common endpoint, called a **vertex**. The measure of the tilt of one side of the angle compared to the other can be given in degrees measured with a **protractor**. Angles can be classified by their measure.

- Angles with measures less than 90° are called **acute** angles.
- Angles with measures of exactly 90° are called **right** angles.
- Angles with measures between 90° and 180° are called **obtuse** angles.
- Angles with measures of exactly 180° are called **straight** angles.

EXAMPLE Measure an Angle

1 Use a protractor to measure $\angle ABC$. State whether the angle is acute, right, obtuse, or straight.

Step 1 Place the center point of the protractor's base on vertex B. Align the straight side with side $\overrightarrow{BC}$ so that the marker for 0° is on side $\overrightarrow{BC}$.

Step 2 Use the scale that begins with 0° at $\overrightarrow{BC}$. Read where the other side of the angle, $\overrightarrow{BA}$, crosses this scale.

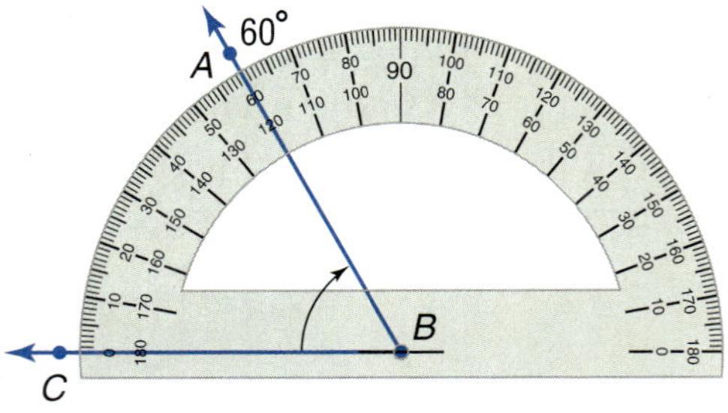

The measure of angle ABC is 60°. Using symbols, $m\angle ABC = 60°$.
Since $m\angle ABC < 90°$, the angle is acute.

EXAMPLE Draw an Angle

2 Draw $\angle F$ having a measure of 135°.

Step 1 Draw a ray. Label the endpoint F.

Step 2 Place the center point of the protractor's base on point F. Align the mark labeled 0 with the ray.

Step 3 Use the scale that begins with 0. Locate the mark labeled 135. Then draw the other side of the angle.

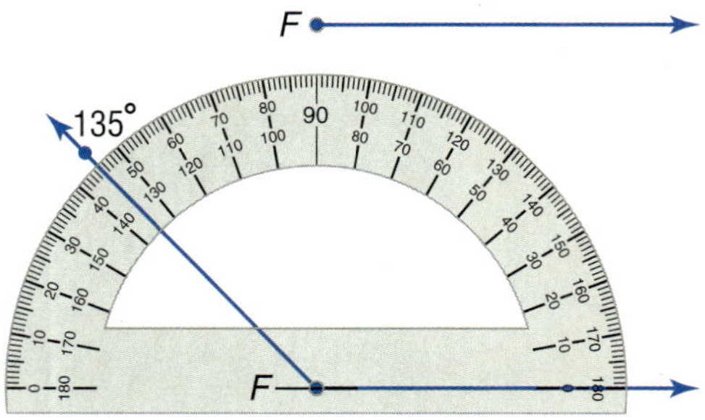

Exercises

Measure the following angles and state whether they are acute or obtuse.

1.

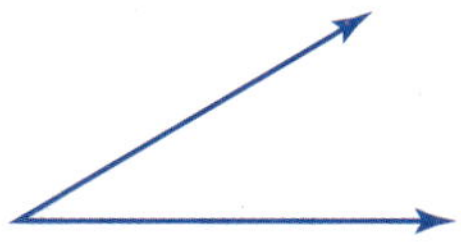

2.

3.

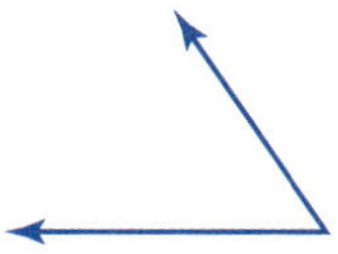

4.

Draw the following angles using a protractor.

5. 45° **6.** 120° **7.** 76° **8.** 153°

Extra Practice

Lesson 1-1

Pages 25–29

Use the four-step plan to solve each problem.

1. The Reyes family rode their bicycles for 9 miles to the park. The ride back was along a different route for 14 miles. How many miles did they ride in all?
2. A farmer planted 389 acres of land with 78,967 corn plants. How many plants were planted per acre?
3. A group of 251 people is eating dinner at a school fund-raiser. If each person pays $8.00 for their meal, how much money is raised?
4. When Tamika calls home from college, she talks ten minutes per call for 3 calls per week. How many minutes does she call in a 15-week semester?
5. Darren runs at 6 feet per second and Kim runs at 7 feet per second. If they both start a race at the same time, how far apart are they after one minute?

Lesson 1-2

Pages 30–33

Write each power as a product of the same factor.

1. 13^4 2. 9^6 3. 1^7
4. 12^2 5. 5^8 6. 15^4

Evaluate each expression.

7. 5^6 8. 17^3 9. 2^{12} 10. 3^5
11. 1^4 12. 5^3 13. 10^2 14. 2^8
15. 8^2 16. 7^4 17. 20^3 18. 42^3

Write each product in exponential form.

19. $2 \cdot 2 \cdot 2 \cdot 2 \cdot 2$ 20. $3 \cdot 3$ 21. $1 \cdot 1 \cdot 1 \cdot 1 \cdot 1 \cdot 1$
22. $18 \cdot 18 \cdot 18 \cdot 18$ 23. $9 \cdot 9 \cdot 9 \cdot 9 \cdot 9 \cdot 9 \cdot 9 \cdot 9$ 24. $10 \cdot 10 \cdot 10 \cdot 10 \cdot 10 \cdot 10$

Lesson 1-3

Pages 34–37

Find the square of each number.

1. 4 2. 19 3. 13 4. 25
5. 9 6. 2 7. 14 8. 24
9. 40 10. 50 11. 100 12. 250

Find each square root.

13. $\sqrt{324}$ 14. $\sqrt{900}$ 15. $\sqrt{2{,}500}$ 16. $\sqrt{576}$
17. $\sqrt{8{,}100}$ 18. $\sqrt{676}$ 19. $\sqrt{100}$ 20. $\sqrt{784}$
21. $\sqrt{1{,}024}$ 22. $\sqrt{841}$ 23. $\sqrt{2{,}304}$ 24. $\sqrt{3{,}025}$

Lesson 1-4

Pages 38–41

Evaluate each expression.

1. $14 - (5 + 7)$
2. $(32 + 10) - 5 \times 6$
3. $(50 - 6) + (12 + 4)$
4. $12 - 2 \cdot 3$
5. $16 + 4 \times 5$
6. $(5 + 3) \times 4 - 7$
7. $2 \times 3 + 9 \times 2$
8. $6 \cdot (8 + 4) \div 2$
9. $7 \times 6 - 14$
10. $8 + (12 \times 4) \div 8$
11. $13 - 6 \cdot 2 + 1$
12. $(80 \div 10) \times 8$
13. $14 - 2 \cdot 7 + 0$
14. $156 - 6 \times 0$
15. $30 - 14 \cdot 2 + 8$
16. $3 \times 4 - 3^2$
17. $10^2 - 5$
18. $3 + (10 - 5 + 1)^2$
19. $(4 + 3)^2 \div 7$
20. 8×10^3
21. $10^4 \times 6$
22. 4.5×10^3
23. 1.8×10^2
24. $3 + 5(1.7 + 2.3)$
25. $4(3.6 + 5.4) - 9$
26. $10 + 3(6.1 + 3.7)$
27. $6(7.5 + 2.1) - 2.3$

Lesson 1-5

Pages 42–43

Use the *guess and check* strategy to solve each problem.

1. **NUMBERS** A number is divided by 3. Then 8 is added to the quotient. The result is 15. What is the number?
2. **NUMBERS** Benny is thinking of two numbers. Their product is 32 and their difference is 4. Find the numbers.
3. **MONEY** A theater is charging \$5 for children under 12 and \$8 for everyone else. If the total for a group of people was \$36, how many people under the age of 12 were in the group?
4. **PLACE VALUE** Mindy wrote down a decimal number. The digit in the tenth's place is half the digit in the hundredth's place. If the product of the two digits is 18, what is the number?
5. **MONEY** Penny has 14 coins totaling \$1.55. She has one more nickel than she has dimes, and three less quarters than nickels. How many quarters, dimes, and nickels does she have if these are the only coin types she has?
6. **FRUIT** Mason places 4 apples and 3 oranges into each fruit basket he makes. If he has used 24 apples and 18 oranges, how many fruit baskets has he made?

Lesson 1-6

Pages 44–47

Evaluate each expression if $a = 3$, $b = 4$, $c = 12$, and $d = 1$.

1. $a + b$
2. $c - d$
3. $a + b + c$
4. $b - a$
5. $c - ab$
6. $a + 2d$
7. $b + 2c$
8. ab
9. $a + 3b$
10. $6a + c$
11. $\frac{c}{d}$
12. abc
13. $2(a + b)$
14. $\frac{2c}{b}$
15. $144 - abc$
16. $2ab$
17. $\frac{b}{2}$
18. a^2
19. $c^2 - 100$
20. $a^3 + 3$
21. $2b^2$
22. $b^3 + c$
23. $\frac{a^2}{d}$
24. $5a^2 + 2d^2$
25. $\frac{4d^2}{b}$
26. $\frac{15}{a}$
27. $3a^2$
28. $10d^3$
29. $\frac{ab}{c}$
30. $\frac{(a + b)}{d}$
31. $2.5b + c$
32. $\frac{10}{d}$
33. $\frac{(2c + b)}{b}$
34. $\frac{(b^2 + 2d)}{a}$
35. $\frac{(2c + ab)}{c}$
36. $\frac{(3.5c + 2)}{11}$

Lesson 1-7

Pages 49–52

Solve each equation mentally.

1. $b + 7 = 12$	2. $a + 3 = 15$	3. $s + 10 = 23$	4. $9 + n = 13$
5. $20 = 24 - n$	6. $4x = 36$	7. $2y = 10$	8. $15 = 5h$
9. $j \div 3 = 2$	10. $14 = w - 4$	11. $24 \div k = 6$	12. $b - 3 = 12$
13. $c \div 10 = 8$	14. $6 = t \div 5$	15. $14 + m = 24$	16. $3y = 39$
17. $\frac{f}{2} = 12$	18. $16 = 4v$	19. $81 = 80 + a$	20. $9 = \frac{72}{x}$
21. $66 = 22m$	22. $77 - 12 = a$	23. $9k = 81$	24. $95 + d = 100$
25. $b = \frac{72}{6}$	26. $z = 15 + 22$	27. $15b = 225$	28. $43 + s = 57$
29. $4w = 52$	30. $e - 10 = 0$	31. $62 - d = 12$	32. $14f = 14$
33. $48 \div n = 8$	34. $a - 82 = 95$	35. $\frac{x}{2} = 36$	36. $99 = c \div 2$

Lesson 1-8

Pages 53–56

Use the Distributive Property to evaluate each expression.

1. $3(4 + 5)$	2. $(2 + 8)6$	3. $4(9 - 6)$
4. $8(6 - 3)$	5. $5(200 - 50)$	6. $20(3 + 6)$
7. $(20 - 5)8$	8. $50(8 + 2)$	9. $15(1{,}000 - 200)$
10. $3(2{,}000 + 400)$	11. $12(1{,}000 + 10)$	12. $7(1{,}000 - 50)$

Name the property shown by each statement.

13. $7(2 + 3) = 7(2) + 7(3)$	14. $7 \times 8 = 8 \times 7$	15. $(4 + 2) + 8 = 4 + (2 + 8)$
16. $92 + 3 = 3 + 92$	17. $4(2) + 4(3) = 4(2 + 3)$	18. $z \cdot 1 = z$
19. $(1 \times 5) \times 2 = 1 \times (5 \times 2)$	20. $7 + (8 + 1) = (7 + 8) + 1$	21. $4 \cdot (x \cdot y) = (4 \cdot x) \cdot y$
22. $a + 0 = a$	23. $a \times b = b \times a$	24. $43 + z = z + 43$

Lesson 1-9

Pages 57–61

Describe the relationship between the terms in each arithmetic sequence. Then write the next three terms in each sequence.

1. 5, 9, 13, 17, …	2. 3, 5, 7, 9, …	3. 10, 15, 20, 25, …
4. 90, 93, 96, 99, …	5. 8, 14, 20, 26, …	6. 4.5, 5.4, 6.3, 7.2, …
7. 0.3, 0.4, 0.5, …	8. 2.3, 3.4, 4.5, 5.6, …	9. 8.9, 9.1, 9.3, 9.5, …
10. 3, 11, 19, 27, …	11. 350, 375, 400, 425, …	12. 620, 635, 650, 665, …
13. 2, 7, 12, 17, …	14. 10, 17, 24, 31, …	15. 0, 7, 14, 21, …
16. 1, 7, 13, 19, …	17. 95, 101, 107, 113, …	18. 9, 90, 171, 252, …
19. 2.6, 2.8, 3.0, 3.2, …	20. 4.1, 4.6, 5.1, 5.6, …	21. 6.6, 7.7, 8.8, 9.9, …
22. 19.5, 21, 22.5, 24, …	23. 14.5, 14.8, 15.1, 15.4, …	24. 0.1, 0.4, 0.7, 1.0, …

Lesson 1-10

Pages 63–67

Copy and complete each function table. Then identify the domain and range.

1.

x	$2x$	y
0		
1		
2		
3		

2.

x	$3x + 1$	y
1		
2		
3		
4		

3.

x	$x - 2$	y
3		
4		
5		
6		

4.

x	$x + 0.1$	y
2		
3		
4		
5		

Lesson 2-1

Pages 80–83

Write an integer for each situation.

1. seven degrees below zero
2. a loss of 3 pounds
3. a loss of 20 yards
4. a profit of $25
5. 112°F above 0
6. 2,830 feet above sea level

Graph each set of integers on a number line.

7. $\{-2, 0, 2\}$
8. $\{1, 3, 5\}$
9. $\{-2, -5, 3\}$
10. $\{7, -1, 4\}$

Evaluate each expression.

11. $|1|$
12. $|-8|$
13. $|0|$
14. $|-82|$
15. $|64|$
16. $|-128|$
17. $|-22| + 5$
18. $|-40| - 8$
19. $|-18| + |10|$
20. $|-7| + |-1|$
21. $|98| - |-5|$
22. $|-49| - |-10|$

Lesson 2-2

Pages 84–87

Replace each ● with < or > to make a true sentence.

1. 7 ● −7
2. −8 ● 4
3. −4 ● −9
4. −3 ● 0
5. 8 ● 10
6. −5 ● −4
7. 6 ● −7
8. −12 ● −13
9. 3 ● 1
10. −2 ● 2
11. 7 ● −1
12. −15 ● −20
13. −40 ● 30
14. 0 ● −3
15. −5 ● 0
16. 85 ● −17

Order the integers from least to greatest.

17. −2, −8, 4, 10, −6, −12
18. 19, −19, −21, 32, −14, 18
19. 18, 23, 95, −95, −18, −23, 2
20. 46, −48, −47, −52, −18, 12
21. 0, −10, −6, −8, 12
22. −15, 18, −1, 0, 14, −20

Lesson 2-3

Pages 88–92

Write the ordered pair for each point graphed at the right. Then name the quadrant or axis on which each point is located.

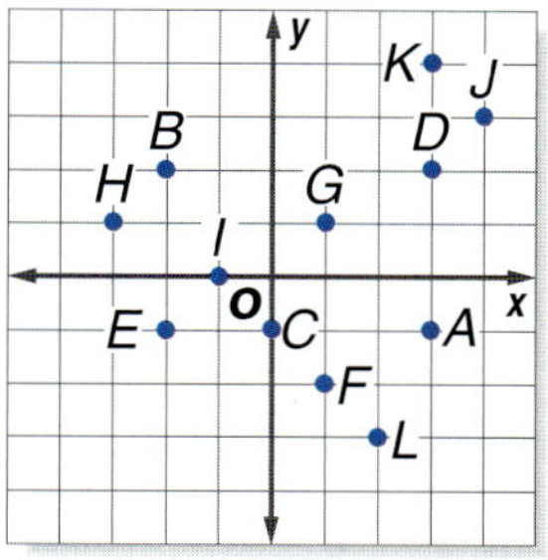

1. A
2. B
3. C
4. D
5. E
6. F
7. G
8. H
9. I
10. J
11. K
12. L

On graph paper, draw a coordinate plane. Then graph and label each point.

13. $N(-4, 3)$
14. $K(2, 5)$
15. $W(-6, -2)$
16. $X(5, 0)$
17. $Y(4, -4)$
18. $M(0, -3)$
19. $Z(-2, 0.5)$
20. $S(-1, -3)$
21. $A(0, 2)$
22. $C(-2, -2)$
23. $E(0, 1)$
24. $G(1, -1)$

Lesson 2-4

Pages 95–99

Add.

1. $-4 + 8$
2. $14 + 16$
3. $-7 + (-7)$
4. $-9 + (-6)$
5. $-18 + 11$
6. $-36 + 40$
7. $42 + (-18)$
8. $-42 + 29$
9. $18 + (-32)$
10. $12 + (-9)$
11. $-24 + 9$
12. $-7 + (-1)$

Evaluate each expression if $a = 6$, $b = -2$, $c = -6$, and $d = 3$.

13. $-96 + a$
14. $b + (-5)$
15. $c + (-32)$
16. $d + 98$
17. $-120 + b$
18. $-120 + c$
19. $5 + b$
20. $a + d$
21. $c + a$
22. $d + (-9)$
23. $b + c$
24. $d + c$

Lesson 2-5

Pages 103–106

Subtract.

1. $3 - 7$
2. $-5 - 4$
3. $-6 - 2$
4. $8 - 13$
5. $6 - (-4)$
6. $12 - 9$
7. $-2 - 23$
8. $63 - 78$
9. $0 - (-14)$
10. $15 - 6$
11. $18 - 20$
12. $-5 - 8$
13. $21 - (-37)$
14. $-60 - 32$
15. $57 - 63$

Evaluate each expression if $k = -3$, $p = 6$, $n = 1$, and $d = -8$.

16. $55 - k$
17. $p - 7$
18. $d - 15$
19. $n - 12$
20. $-51 - d$
21. $k - 21$
22. $n - k$
23. $-99 - k$
24. $p - k$
25. $d - (-1)$
26. $k - d$
27. $n - d$

Extra Practice

Lesson 2-6

Pages 107–108

Solve using the *look for a pattern* strategy.

1. **NUMBERS** Determine the next three numbers in the pattern below.

   15, 21, 27, 33, 39, ...

2. **TIME** Determine the next two times in the pattern below.

   2:30 A.M., 2:50 A.M., 3:10 A.M., 3:30 A.M., ...

3. **MONEY** The table shows Abigail's savings. If the pattern continues, what will be the total amount in week 6?

Week	Total ($)
1	$400
2	$800
3	$1,200
4	$1,600
5	$2,000
6	■

4. **SCIENCE** A single rotation of Earth takes about 24 hours. Copy and complete the table to determine the number of hours in a week.

Number of Days	Number of Hours
1	24
2	48
3	72
4	■
5	■
6	■
7	■

Lesson 2-7

Pages 109–113

Multiply.

1. $5(-2)$
2. $6(-4)$
3. $4(21)$
4. $-11(-5)$
5. $-6(5)$
6. $-50(0)$
7. $-5(-5)$
8. $-4(8)$
9. $3(-13)$
10. $12(-5)$
11. $-9(-12)$
12. $15(-8)$
13. $(-6)^2$
14. $(-2)^2$
15. $(-4)^3$
16. $(-5)^3$

Evaluate each expression if $a = -5$, $b = 2$, $c = -3$, and $d = 4$.

17. $-2d$
18. $6a$
19. $3ab$
20. $-12d$
21. $-4b^2$
22. $-5cd$
23. a^2
24. $13ab$

Lesson 2-8

Pages 114–118

Divide.

1. $4 \div (-2)$
2. $16 \div (-8)$
3. $-14 \div (-2)$
4. $\frac{32}{8}$
5. $18 \div (-3)$
6. $-18 \div 3$
7. $8 \div (-8)$
8. $0 \div (-1)$
9. $-25 \div 5$
10. $\frac{-14}{-7}$
11. $-32 \div 8$
12. $-56 \div (-8)$
13. $-81 \div 9$
14. $-42 \div (-7)$
15. $121 \div (-11)$
16. $-81 \div (-9)$
17. $18 \div (-2)$
18. $\frac{-55}{11}$
19. $\frac{25}{-5}$
20. $-21 \div 3$

Evaluate each expression if $a = -2$, $b = -7$, $x = 8$, and $y = -4$.

21. $-64 \div x$
22. $\frac{16}{y}$
23. $x \div 2$
24. $\frac{a}{2}$
25. $ax \div y$
26. $\frac{bx}{y}$
27. $2y \div 1$
28. $\frac{x}{ay}$
29. $-y \div a$
30. $x^2 \div y$
31. $\frac{ab}{1}$
32. $\frac{xy}{a}$

Lesson 3-1

Pages 128–131

Estimate each product.

1. 4.6×5.5
2. 8.4×4.6
3. 3.9×7.1
4. 12.3×10.1
5. 9.6×7.8
6. 10.4×2.8
7. 25.2×4.3
8. 3.89×11.7
9. 3.25×47.6

Estimate each quotient.

10. $11.8 \div 2.7$
11. $19.4 \div 3.7$
12. $14.8 \div 2.6$
13. $52.1 \div 9.8$
14. $37.8 \div 4.7$
15. $34.9 \div 7.3$
16. $62.1 \div 6.3$
17. $12.3 \div 1.8$
18. $48.2 \div 9.4$

Use estimation to determine whether each answer is reasonable. If the answer is reasonable, write *yes*. If not, write *no* and provide a reasonable estimate.

19. $24.76 \times 8.22 = 312.98$
20. $99.8 \times 9.34 = 932.13$
21. $17.6 \times 41.98 = 1{,}000$
22. $75.9 \div 2.8 = 34.2$

Lesson 3-2

Pages 134–139

Multiply.

1. 0.2×7
2. 0.1×8
3. 0.3×6
4. 0.5×4
5. 0.8×9
6. 0.7×5
7. 2.6×7
8. 3.4×8
9. 1.45×2
10. 2.76×4
11. 1.45×6
12. 8.62×5
13. 0.09×6
14. 0.17×8
15. 0.78×4
16. 0.067×7
17. 0.082×9
18. 0.6×0.9
19. 1.8×1.6
20. 3.4×7.8
21. 1.18×0.3
22. 2.49×0.53
23. 3.97×1.23
24. 8.76×2.75
25. 0.008×4.3
26. 0.017×5.6
27. 0.034×8.7

Lesson 3-3

Pages 140–144

Find each product.

1. 0.89×10
2. 11.8×10
3. 17.45×10
4. 6.9×100
5. 2.24×100
6. 22.8×100
7. $0.87 \times 1{,}000$
8. $2.57 \times 1{,}000$
9. $1.56 \times 1{,}000$
10. $5.2 \times 10{,}000$
11. $4.55 \times 10{,}000$
12. $9.997 \times 10{,}000$
13. 0.4×0.1
14. 2.85×0.1
15. 2.87×0.1
16. 12.14×0.01
17. 36.14×0.01
18. 0.4×0.01
19. 9.23×0.1
20. 23.54×0.01
21. 0.63×0.001
22. 1.56×0.001
23. 14.76×0.001
24. 421.25×0.001

Write each of the following in standard form.

25. 56.7 thousand
26. 12.8 million
27. 77.56 million

Lesson 3-4

Pages 147–152

Divide.

1. $4.2 \div 2$
2. $5.7 \div 3$
3. $21.7 \div 7$
4. $6.6 \div 5$
5. $8.1 \div 3$
6. $1.08 \div 6$
7. $2.16 \div 4$
8. $8.19 \div 9$
9. $1.24 \div 4$
10. $7.48 \div 5$
11. $12.22 \div 2$
12. $0.012 \div 3$
13. $0.014 \div 5$
14. $7.968 \div 6$
15. $0.84 \div 0.2$
16. $32.8 \div 0.4$
17. $14.4 \div 1.2$
18. $44.2 \div 8.5$
19. $278.4 \div 4.8$
20. $138.6 \div 1.4$
21. $150.4 \div 3.2$
22. $1.43 \div 1.3$
23. $12.54 \div 6.6$
24. $62.4 \div 2.6$
25. $6.25 \div 0.5$
26. $3.25 \div 2.5$
27. $5.76 \div 4.8$
28. $35.8 \div 0.04$
29. $24.2 \div 0.55$
30. $77.5 \div 0.31$

Lesson 3-5

Pages 154–155

Choose the best method of computation. Then use the method to solve the problem.

POPULATION **For Exercises 1–2, use the table shown below.**

Country	2005 Population (million)
China	1,306.3
India	1,080.2
United States	295.7
Indonesia	242.0
Brazil	186.1

Source: www.factmonster.com

1. About how many people lived in the world's five most populous countries in 2005?
2. About how many times greater was the population of India than Brazil in 2005?
3. **GEOGRAPHY** The Missouri River is 2,540 miles long. The Brazos River is 1,280 miles long. How much longer is the Missouri River than the Brazos River?
4. **APPLES** Maxine's family owns an apple orchard. Her father pays her $2 for each pound of apples she picks. If she picks 1,000 pounds of apples, how much will she earn?
5. **MILEAGE** Stan's car uses a gallon of gasoline for every 24.5 miles he travels. How far can Stan's car travel on 11.25 gallons of gas?

Lesson 3-6

Pages 157–161

Complete.

1. 400 mm = ■ cm
2. 4 km = ■ m
3. 660 cm = ■ m
4. 0.3 km = ■ m
5. 30 mm = ■ cm
6. 84.5 m = ■ km
7. ■ m = 54 cm
8. 18 km = ■ cm
9. ■ mm = 45 cm
10. 4 kg = ■ g
11. 632 mg = ■ g
12. 4,497 g = ■ kg
13. ■ mg = 21 g
14. 61.2 mg = ■ g
15. 61 g = ■ mg
16. ■ mg = 0.51 kg
17. 0.63 kg = ■ g
18. ■ kg = 563 g
19. 662 m = ■ km
20. 5,283 mL = ■ L
21. 0.24 cm = ■ mm
22. 380 kL = ■ L
23. 10.8 g = ■ mg
24. 83,000 mL = ■ L
25. 17.8 m = ■ cm
26. 2 km = ■ m
27. 0.75 m = ■ mm

Lesson 3-7

Pages 162–166

Write each number in scientific notation.

1. 1,400
2. 91,200
3. 51,000
4. 145,000
5. 90,100
6. 123,000,000,000
7. 4,500
8. 1,700,000
9. 10,000,000
10. 820,000,000
11. 680,000
12. 5 million
13. 6.6 million
14. 39 billion
15. 5.7 billion

Write each number in standard form.

16. 7.6×10^2
17. 2.6×10^3
18. 4.7×10^5
19. 1.0×10^2
20. 6.4×10^6
21. 8.3×10^4
22. 2.76×10^3
23. 6.17×10^5
24. 8.70×10^5
25. 1.28×10^7

16. 4.32×10^9

27. 5.01×10^2
28. 1.89×10^6
29. 7.43×10^4
30. 3.03×10^9

Lesson 4-1

Pages 176–181

Write each phrase as an algebraic expression.

1. six less than p
2. twenty more than c
3. the quotient of a and b
4. Juana's age plus 6
5. x increased by twelve
6. $1,000 divided by z
7. 3 divided into y
8. the product of 7 and m
9. the difference of f and 9
10. twenty-six less q
11. 19 decreased by z
12. two less than x

Write each sentence as an algebraic equation.

13. Three times a number less four is 17.
14. The sum of a number and 6 is 5.
15. Twenty more than twice a number is −30.
16. The quotient of a number and −2 is −42.
17. Four plus three times a number is 18.
18. Five times a number minus 15 is 92.
19. Eight times a number plus twelve is 36.
20. The difference of a number and 24 is −30.

Lesson 4-2

Pages 184–189

Solve each equation. Check your solution.

1. $r - 3 = 14$
2. $t + 3 = 21$
3. $s + 10 = 23$
4. $7 + a = -10$
5. $14 + m = 24$
6. $-9 + n = 13$
7. $s - 2 = -6$
8. $6 + f = 71$
9. $x + 27 = 30$
10. $a - 7 = 23$
11. $-4 + b = -5$
12. $w + 18 = -4$
13. $k - 9 = -3$
14. $j + 12 = 11$
15. $-42 + v = -42$
16. $s + 1.3 = 18$
17. $x + 7.4 = 23.5$
18. $p + 3.1 = 18$
19. $w - 3.7 = 4.63$
20. $m - 4.8 = 7.4$
21. $x - 1.3 = 12$
22. $y + 3.4 = 18$
23. $7.2 + g = 9.1$
24. $z - 12.1 = 14$
25. $v - 18 = 13.7$
26. $w - 0.1 = 0.32$
27. $r + 6.7 = 1.2$

Lesson 4-3

Pages 190–194

Solve each equation. Check your solution.

1. $2m = 18$
2. $-42 = 6n$
3. $72 = 8k$
4. $-20r = 20$
5. $420 = 5s$
6. $325 = 25t$
7. $-14 = -2p$
8. $18q = 36$
9. $40 = 10a$
10. $100 = 20b$
11. $416 = 4c$
12. $45 = 9d$
13. $0.5m = 3.5$
14. $1.8 = 0.6x$
15. $0.4y = 2$
16. $1.86 = 6.2z$
17. $-8x = 24$
18. $8.34 = 2r$
19. $1.67t = 10.02$
20. $243 = 27a$
21. $0.9x = 4.5$
22. $4.08 = 1.2y$
23. $8d = 112$
24. $5f = 180.5$
25. $59.66 = 3.14m$
26. $98.4 = 8p$
27. $208 = 26k$

Lesson 4-4

Pages 196–197

Use the *work backward* strategy to solve each problem.

1. **NUMBERS** A number is divided by 2. Then 4 is added to the quotient. Next, the sum of these numbers is multiplied by 3. The result is 21. Find the number.
2. **MONEY** Holly spent $13.76 on a birthday present for her mom. She also spent $3.25 on a snack for herself. If she now has $7.74, how much money did she have initially?
3. **TIME** Timothy gets to school at 9:00 A.M. It takes him 45 minutes to get ready and 25 minutes for him to walk to the school. At what time did Timothy get up?
4. **LOGIC** A small container has 4 tennis balls inside of it. There are 6 of these small boxes inside a medium sized box. There are 8 medium sized boxes inside each large box, and there are 100 large boxes shipped in a large semi-truck. How many tennis balls are on the truck?
5. **FOOD** After four days, 0.5 pound of lunch meat was left in the refrigerator. If half this amount was eaten on each of the previous four days, how much lunch meat was initially in the refrigerator?

Lesson 4-5

Pages 199–203

Solve each equation. Check your solution.

1. $3x + 6 = 6$
2. $2r - 7 = -1$
3. $-10 + 2d = 8$
4. $2b + 4 = -8$
5. $5w - 12 = 3$
6. $5t - 4 = 6$
7. $2q - 6 = 4$
8. $2g - 3 = -9$
9. $15 = 6y + 3$
10. $3s - 4 = 8$
11. $18 - 7f = 4$
12. $13 + 3p = 7$
13. $7.5r + 2 = -28$
14. $4.2 + 7z = 2.8$
15. $-9m - 9 = 9$
16. $32 + 0.2c = 1$
17. $5t - 14 = -14$
18. $-0.25x + 0.5 = 4$
19. $5w - 4 = 8$
20. $4d - 3 = 9$
21. $2g - 16 = -9$
22. $4k + 13 = 20$
23. $7 = 5 - 2x$
24. $8z + 15 = -1$
25. $92 - 16b = 12$
26. $14e + 14 = 28$
27. $1.1j + 2 = 7.5$

Lesson 4-6

Pages 204–209

Find the perimeter and area of each rectangle.

1.
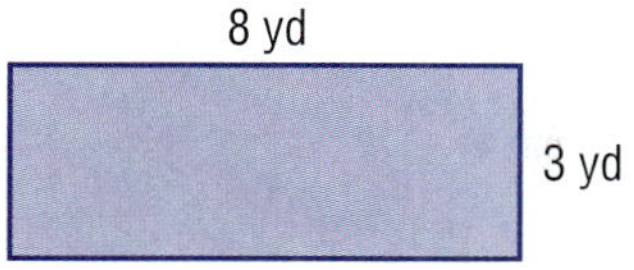

2.
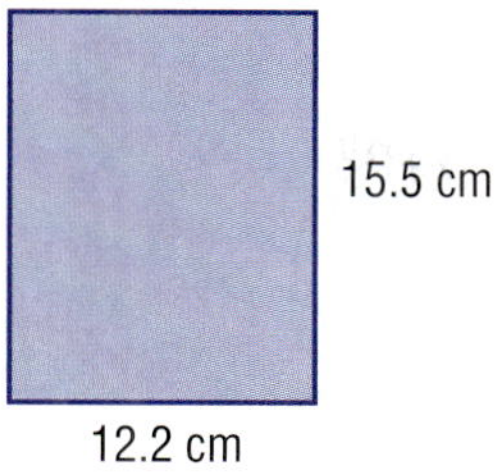

3.
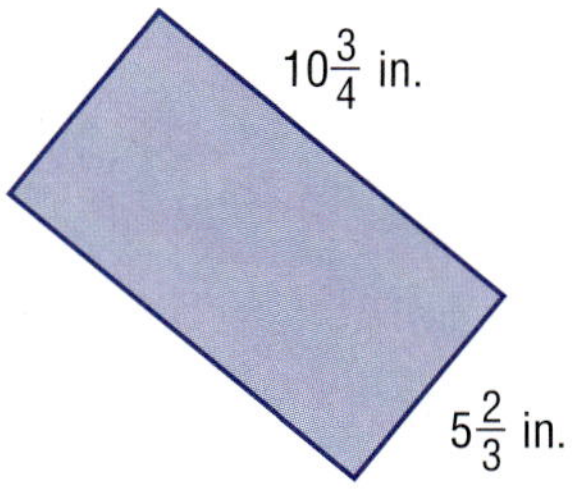

4. $\ell = 80$ yd, $w = 20$ yd
5. $\ell = 75$ cm, $w = 25$ cm
6. $\ell = 5.25$ km, $w = 1.5$ km
7. $\ell = 8.6$ cm, $w = 2.5$ cm
8. $\ell = 20.25$ m, $w = 4.75$ m
9. $\ell = 12$ ft, $w = 3$ ft
10. $\ell = 5\frac{1}{4}$ mi, $w = 2\frac{1}{2}$ mi
11. $\ell = 10\frac{2}{3}$ ft, $w = 5\frac{5}{6}$ ft

Lesson 4-7

Pages 211–215

Graph the function represented by the table.

1.

Total Cost of Tennis Balls	
Number of Tennis Balls	Total Cost ($)
3	6
4	8
5	10
6	12

2.

Convert Gallons to Quarts	
Gallon	Quarts
1	4
2	8
3	12
4	16

Graph each equation.

3. $y = 3x$
4. $y = 2x + 3$
5. $y = -x$
6. $y = 0.5x + 2$
7. $y = -x + 3$
8. $y = 0.25x + 6$
9. $y = -3x + 6$
10. $y = -x + 1$
11. $y = 5 - 0.5x$

Lesson 5-1

Pages 229–232

Determine whether each number is *prime* or *composite*.

1. 32
2. 41
3. 52
4. 21
5. 71
6. 102
7. 239
8. 93
9. 123

Find the prime factorization of each number.

10. 81
11. 72
12. 144
13. 245
14. 423
15. 525
16. 750
17. 914
18. 975

Factor each expression.

19. $35xy$
20. $14a^2$
21. $30n$
22. $27cd^2$
23. $4s^2t^2$
24. $60p^2qr$

Lesson 5-2

Pages 234–237

Find the GCF of each set of numbers.

1. 12, 16
2. 63, 81
3. 225, 500
4. 37, 100
5. 32, 240
6. 412, 640
7. 36, 81
8. 140, 350
9. 72, 170
10. 51, 255
11. 48, 72
12. 86, 200
13. 12, 18, 42
14. 24, 56, 120
15. 48, 60, 84
16. 32, 80, 96
17. 14, 49, 70
18. 8, 10, 20

Find the GCF of each set of expressions.

19. $18b$, $24b$
20. $2a$, $3a$
21. $5n$, $5mn$
22. $12cd$, $24c$
23. $30x$, $50x^2$
24. $15az$, $25az$
25. $2c$, $4ac$, $8a$
26. d, $6c^2d$, $12d$
27. $10ab$, $15bc$, $20b^2$

Lesson 5-3

Pages 238–239

Use the *make a list* strategy to solve each problem.

1. **FOOD** The table shows the choices for ordering a deli sandwich at The Sandwich Shop. How many different subs could be made using one choice from just bread and meat?

The Sandwich Shop	
Bread	White, Wheat, Whole Grain
Meat	Ham, Turkey, Roast Beef
Cheese	American, Swiss
Dressing	Italian, Ranch

2. **SHOPPING** Charmaine went to the store and bought a yellow shirt, a blue shirt, and a red shirt. She also bought a pair of jeans and a pair of khaki dress pants. How many different outfits can be made using one shirt and one pair of pants?

3. **WORK** The following four numbers are used for employee identification numbers at a small company: 0, 1, 2, and 3. How many different employee identification numbers can be made?

Lesson 5-4

Pages 240–243

Write each fraction in simplest form.

1. $\frac{14}{28}$
2. $\frac{15}{25}$
3. $\frac{100}{130}$
4. $\frac{14}{35}$
5. $\frac{9}{51}$
6. $\frac{54}{56}$
7. $\frac{75}{90}$
8. $\frac{24}{40}$
9. $\frac{180}{270}$
10. $\frac{312}{390}$
11. $\frac{240}{448}$
12. $\frac{71}{82}$
13. $\frac{333}{900}$
14. $\frac{85}{255}$
15. $\frac{84}{128}$
16. $\frac{64}{96}$
17. $\frac{99}{99}$
18. $\frac{3}{99}$
19. $\frac{44}{55}$
20. $\frac{57}{69}$
21. $\frac{15}{37}$
22. $\frac{204}{408}$
23. $\frac{5}{125}$
24. $\frac{144}{216}$
25. $\frac{15}{75}$

Lesson 5-5

Pages 244–248

Write each fraction or mixed number as a decimal. Use bar notation if the decimal is a repeating decimal.

1. $\frac{16}{20}$
2. $\frac{25}{120}$
3. $1\frac{7}{8}$
4. $\frac{1}{6}$
5. $\frac{11}{40}$
6. $5\frac{13}{50}$
7. $\frac{55}{300}$
8. $1\frac{1}{2}$
9. $\frac{5}{9}$
10. $2\frac{3}{4}$
11. $\frac{9}{11}$
12. $4\frac{1}{9}$

Write each decimal as a fraction or mixed number in simplest form.

13. 0.26
14. 0.75
15. 0.4
16. 0.1
17. 4.48
18. 9.8
19. 0.91
20. 11.15

Lesson 5-6

Pages 250–253

Write each ratio as a percent.

1. 39 out of 100
2. $\frac{23}{100}$
3. 17:100
4. 72 per 100
5. 4 to 100
6. 98 in 100

Write each fraction as a percent.

7. $\frac{1}{2}$
8. $\frac{2}{5}$
9. $\frac{60}{100}$
10. $\frac{17}{20}$
11. $\frac{7}{25}$
12. $\frac{1}{20}$
13. $\frac{8}{100}$
14. $\frac{7}{7}$
15. $\frac{9}{10}$
16. $\frac{1}{100}$
17. $\frac{50}{50}$
18. $\frac{49}{50}$

Write each percent as a fraction in simplest form.

19. 12%
20. 23%
21. 1%
22. 94%
23. 36%
24. 4%
25. 72%
26. 100%
27. 65%
28. 47%
29. 15%
30. 48%

Lesson 5-7

Pages 254–258

Write each percent as a decimal.

1. 42%
2. 100%
3. 8%
4. 20%
5. 35%
6. 3%
7. 62%
8. 50%
9. 28%
10. 87%
11. 7.5%
12. 87.5%
13. 1.8%
14. 99.9%
15. $85\frac{1}{4}\%$
16. $24\frac{1}{2}\%$
17. $64\frac{4}{5}\%$
18. $36\frac{3}{4}\%$
19. $1\frac{1}{5}\%$
20. $2\frac{1}{2}\%$

Write each decimal as a percent.

21. 0.16
22. 0.1
23. 0.5
24. 0.98
25. 0.31
26. 0.76
27. 0.07
28. 0.8
29. 0.02
30. 0.10
31. 0.90
32. 1.00
33. 0.666
34. 0.725
35. 0.138
36. 0.899
37. 0.256
38. 0.038
39. 0.0525
40. 0.017

Lesson 5-8

Pages 259–262

Find the LCM of each set of numbers.

1. 4, 9
2. 6, 16
3. 24, 36
4. 48, 84
5. 8, 9
6. 49, 56
7. 42, 66
8. 15, 39
9. 56, 64
10. 24, 42
11. 80, 250
12. 16, 24
13. 13, 14
14. 36, 48
15. 10, 100
16. 25, 200
17. 1, 2, 5
18. 2, 3, 7
19. 1, 9, 27
20. 2, 24, 36
21. 7, 21, 35
22. 12, 18, 28
23. 32, 80, 96
24. 5, 18, 45
25. 11, 22, 33
26. 35, 70, 140
27. 25, 200, 400
28. 100, 200, 300

Extra Practice

Lesson 5-9

Pages 263–268

Replace each ● with <, >, or = to make a true sentence.

1. $\frac{7}{9}$ ● $\frac{3}{5}$
2. $\frac{14}{25}$ ● $\frac{3}{4}$
3. $\frac{8}{24}$ ● $\frac{20}{60}$
4. $\frac{5}{12}$ ● $\frac{4}{9}$
5. $\frac{18}{24}$ ● $\frac{10}{18}$
6. $\frac{4}{6}$ ● $\frac{5}{9}$
7. $\frac{11}{49}$ ● $\frac{12}{42}$
8. $\frac{5}{14}$ ● $\frac{2}{6}$

Determine whether each number is rational. Write *yes* or *no*.

9. $4.\overline{28}$
10. $-\frac{5}{4}$
11. $\frac{0.5}{4}$
12. $\frac{1}{7}$
13. 0.414114111…
14. 10.987…
15. 7.22…
16. $3\frac{2}{5}$

Order each set of numbers from least to greatest.

17. 70%, 0.6, $\frac{2}{3}$
18. 0.8, $\frac{17}{20}$, 17%
19. $\frac{61}{100}$, 0.65, 61.5%
20. $0.\overline{42}$, $\frac{3}{7}$, 42%
21. 0.15, 10.5%, $\frac{7}{50}$
22. $\frac{1}{8}$, 0.81, 18%

Lesson 6-1

Pages 278–283

Estimate.

1. $\frac{3}{7} + \frac{6}{8}$
2. $\frac{3}{9} + \frac{7}{8}$
3. $\frac{1}{8} + \frac{8}{9}$
4. $3\frac{1}{8} + 7\frac{6}{7}$
5. $4\frac{2}{3} + 6\frac{7}{8}$
6. $3\frac{2}{3} \times 2\frac{1}{3}$
7. $\frac{4}{5} \cdot 3$
8. $9\frac{7}{8} - 6\frac{2}{3}$
9. $\frac{3}{7} - \frac{1}{15}$
10. $\frac{3}{4} \cdot \frac{7}{8}$
11. $7\frac{1}{4} \div \frac{2}{3}$
12. $\frac{5}{6} \div \frac{2}{3}$
13. $9\frac{3}{5} + 3\frac{1}{8}$
14. $5\frac{1}{3} - 2\frac{3}{4}$
15. $13\frac{7}{8} - 2\frac{1}{3}$
16. $\frac{13}{15} \cdot \frac{3}{8}$
17. $\frac{1}{9} \div 2$
18. $\frac{5}{8} - \frac{1}{16}$
19. $9\frac{2}{3} + 4\frac{7}{8}$
20. $\frac{1}{2} \cdot 25$
21. $35\frac{1}{3} \div 6\frac{3}{4}$
22. $100 \div 3\frac{3}{4}$
23. $\frac{1}{3} \cdot 38$
24. $\frac{15}{16} - \frac{3}{4}$
25. $\frac{1}{5} \cdot 16$
26. $47\frac{1}{2} \div 6\frac{5}{8}$
27. $\frac{1}{9} \cdot 79$

Lesson 6-2

Pages 284–289

Add or subtract. Write in simplest form.

1. $\frac{5}{11} + \frac{9}{11}$
2. $\frac{5}{8} - \frac{1}{8}$
3. $\frac{7}{10} + \frac{7}{10}$
4. $\frac{9}{12} - \frac{5}{12}$
5. $\frac{2}{9} + \frac{1}{3}$
6. $\frac{1}{2} + \frac{3}{4}$
7. $\frac{1}{4} - \frac{3}{12}$
8. $\frac{3}{7} + \frac{6}{14}$
9. $\frac{1}{4} + \frac{3}{5}$
10. $\frac{4}{9} + \frac{1}{2}$
11. $\frac{5}{7} - \frac{4}{6}$
12. $\frac{3}{4} - \frac{1}{6}$
13. $\frac{3}{5} + \frac{3}{4}$
14. $\frac{2}{3} - \frac{1}{8}$
15. $\frac{9}{10} + \frac{1}{3}$
16. $\frac{8}{15} + \frac{2}{9}$
17. $\frac{6}{7} + \frac{6}{9}$
18. $\frac{3}{4} - \frac{3}{7}$

Evaluate each expression if $a = \frac{2}{3}$ and $b = \frac{7}{12}$.

19. $\frac{1}{5} + a$
20. $a - \frac{1}{2}$
21. $b + \frac{7}{8}$
22. $\frac{7}{8} - a$
23. $a + b$
24. $a - b$

Lesson 6-3

Pages 290–294

Add or subtract. Write in simplest form.

1. $2\frac{1}{3} + 1\frac{1}{3}$
2. $5\frac{2}{7} - 2\frac{3}{7}$
3. $6\frac{3}{8} + 7\frac{1}{8}$
4. $2\frac{3}{4} - 1\frac{1}{4}$
5. $5\frac{1}{2} - 3\frac{1}{4}$
6. $2\frac{2}{3} + 4\frac{1}{9}$
7. $7\frac{4}{5} + 9\frac{3}{10}$
8. $3\frac{3}{4} + 5\frac{5}{8}$
9. $10\frac{2}{3} + 5\frac{6}{7}$
10. $17\frac{2}{9} - 12\frac{1}{3}$
11. $6\frac{5}{12} + 12\frac{5}{12}$
12. $7\frac{1}{4} + 15\frac{5}{6}$
13. $6\frac{1}{8} + 4\frac{2}{3}$
14. $7 - 6\frac{4}{9}$
15. $8\frac{1}{12} + 12\frac{6}{11}$
16. $7\frac{2}{3} + 8\frac{1}{4}$
17. $12\frac{3}{11} + 14\frac{3}{13}$
18. $21\frac{1}{3} + 15\frac{3}{8}$
19. $19\frac{1}{7} + 6\frac{1}{4}$
20. $9\frac{2}{5} - 8\frac{1}{3}$
21. $18\frac{1}{4} - 3\frac{3}{8}$
22. $1\frac{1}{8} + 2\frac{1}{12}$
23. $2\frac{1}{12} - 1\frac{1}{8}$
24. $10 - \frac{2}{3}$

Lesson 6-4

Pages 295–296

Eliminate possibilities to solve each problem.

1. **TRAINS** A train passes through an intersection at the rate of 3 cars per 30 seconds. Assume that it takes 5 minutes for the train to completely pass through the intersection. How many cars does the train have altogether?

   A 6 cars

   B 15 cars

   C 30 cars

   D 45 cars

2. **PIZZA** A pizza shop used 100 pounds of pizza dough to make 125 pizzas. If a large pizza requires 1 pound of dough and a medium pizza requires $\frac{1}{2}$ pound, how many large and medium-sized pizzas were made?

   F 40 large, 85 medium

   G 65 large, 60 medium

   H 55 large, 70 medium

   J 75 large, 50 medium

Extra Practice

Extra Practice

Lesson 6-5

Pages 300–305

Multiply. Write in simplest form.

1. $\frac{2}{3} \times \frac{3}{5}$
2. $\frac{1}{6} \times \frac{2}{5}$
3. $\frac{4}{9} \times \frac{3}{7}$
4. $\frac{5}{12} \times \frac{6}{11}$
5. $\frac{3}{8} \times \frac{8}{9}$
6. $\frac{2}{5} \times \frac{5}{8}$
7. $\frac{7}{15} \times \frac{3}{21}$
8. $\frac{5}{6} \times \frac{15}{16}$
9. $\frac{2}{3} \times \frac{3}{13}$
10. $\frac{4}{9} \times \frac{1}{6}$
11. $3 \times \frac{1}{9}$
12. $5 \times \frac{6}{7}$
13. $\frac{3}{5} \times 15$
14. $3\frac{1}{2} \times 4\frac{1}{3}$
15. $\frac{4}{5} \times 2\frac{3}{4}$
16. $6\frac{1}{8} \times 5\frac{1}{7}$
17. $2\frac{2}{3} \times 2\frac{1}{4}$
18. $\frac{7}{8} \times 16$
19. $5\frac{1}{5} \times 2\frac{1}{2}$
20. $7 \times \frac{1}{14}$
21. $22 \times \frac{3}{11}$
22. $8\frac{2}{3} \times 1\frac{1}{2}$
23. $4 \times 6\frac{1}{2}$
24. $\frac{1}{2} \times 10\frac{2}{3}$
25. $\frac{2}{3} \times 21\frac{1}{3}$
26. $\frac{7}{8} \times \frac{8}{7}$
27. $21 \times \frac{1}{2}$
28. $11 \times \frac{1}{4}$

Lesson 6-6

Pages 306–311

Find the multiplicative inverse of each number.

1. $\frac{2}{3}$
2. $\frac{5}{4}$
3. 1
4. 10
5. $\frac{1}{7}$
6. $\frac{9}{16}$
7. $1\frac{1}{3}$
8. $3\frac{3}{4}$
9. $7\frac{3}{8}$
10. $6\frac{2}{5}$
11. $33\frac{1}{3}$
12. $66\frac{2}{3}$

Solve each equation. Check your solution.

13. $\frac{a}{13} = 2$
14. $\frac{8}{9}x = 24$
15. $\frac{3}{8}r = 36$
16. $\frac{3}{4}t = \frac{1}{2}$
17. $16 = \frac{h}{4}$
18. $\frac{m}{8} = 12$
19. $\frac{5}{8}n = 45$
20. $10 = \frac{b}{10}$
21. $\frac{1}{7}x = 7$
22. $5 = \frac{1}{5}y$
23. $\frac{4}{3}m = 28$
24. $\frac{2}{3}z = 20$
25. $\frac{c}{9} = 81$
26. $\frac{m}{9} = 9$
27. $16 = \frac{4}{9}f$
28. $\frac{15}{8}x = 225$

Lesson 6-7

Pages 313–318

Divide. Write in simplest form.

1. $\frac{2}{3} \div \frac{3}{2}$
2. $\frac{3}{5} \div \frac{2}{5}$
3. $\frac{7}{10} \div \frac{3}{8}$
4. $\frac{5}{9} \div \frac{2}{5}$
5. $4 \div \frac{2}{3}$
6. $8 \div \frac{4}{5}$
7. $9 \div \frac{5}{9}$
8. $\frac{2}{7} \div 2$
9. $\frac{1}{14} \div 7$
10. $\frac{2}{13} \div \frac{5}{26}$
11. $\frac{4}{7} \div \frac{6}{7}$
12. $\frac{7}{8} \div \frac{1}{3}$
13. $15 \div \frac{3}{5}$
14. $\frac{9}{14} \div \frac{3}{4}$
15. $\frac{7}{8} \div 10$
16. $16 \div \frac{3}{4}$
17. $\frac{3}{8} \div 2\frac{1}{2}$
18. $5\frac{1}{2} \div 2\frac{1}{2}$
19. $3\frac{1}{4} \div 5\frac{1}{2}$
20. $12\frac{5}{6} \div 2\frac{1}{6}$
21. $7\frac{1}{2} \div 3\frac{1}{2}$

Lesson 7-1

Pages 330–334

LUNCH **Use the survey results to write each ratio as a fraction in simplest form.**

Favorite School Lunch	Votes
Pizza	64
Hamburger	15
Macaroni and Cheese	14
Fish Sticks	4
Other	3

1. fish sticks:macaroni and cheese
2. pizza:macaroni and cheese
3. all votes:macaroni and cheese
4. pizza:all votes
5. other:hamburger
6. pizza:hamburger and other

Determine whether the following ratios are equivalent. Explain.

7. 4 out of 6 balloons popped, 8 out of 12 balloons popped
8. 20 out of 25 students agree, 16 out of 30 students agree
9. 20 shoppers to 15 cashiers, 30 shoppers to 25 cashiers
10. 36 comedies to 63 thrillers, 28 comedies to 49 thrillers

Lesson 7-2

Pages 335–340

Find each unit rate. Round to the nearest hundredth if necessary.

1. $240 for 4 days
2. 250 people in 5 buses
3. 500 miles in 10 hours
4. 18 cups for 24 pounds
5. 32 people in 8 cars
6. $4.50 for 3 dozen
7. 245 tickets in 5 days
8. 12 classes in 4 semesters
9. 60 people in 4 rows
10. 48 ounces in 3 pounds
11. 20 people in 4 groups
12. 1.5 pounds for $3.00
13. 45 miles in 60 minutes
14. $5.50 for 10 disks
15. 360 miles for 12 gallons
16. $8.50 for 5 yards
17. 24 cups for $1.20
18. 160 words in 4 minutes
19. $60 for 5 books
20. $24 for 6 hours

Lesson 7-3

Pages 342–347

Complete.

1. 4,000 lb = ▒ T
2. 5 T = ▒ lb
3. 5 lb = ▒ oz
4. 12,000 lb = ▒ T
5. $\frac{1}{4}$ lb = ▒ oz
6. 12 pt = ▒ c
7. 3 gal = ▒ pt
8. 24 fl oz = ▒ c
9. 8 pt = ▒ c
10. 10 pt = ▒ qt
11. $2\frac{1}{4}$c = ▒ fl oz
12. 6 lb = ▒ oz
13. 10 gal = ▒ qt
14. 4 qt = ▒ fl oz
15. 4 pt = ▒ c
16. 13,200 ft = ▒ mi
17. 120 oz = ▒ lb
18. $9\frac{1}{4}$ gal = ▒ qt
19. 7,480 yd = ▒ mi
20. $12\frac{1}{2}$ lb = ▒ oz
21. $7\frac{1}{2}$ qt = ▒ pt
22. $3\frac{1}{8}$ c = ▒ fl oz
23. $2\frac{1}{4}$ mi = ▒ ft
24. $3\frac{2}{3}$ T = ▒ lb

Lesson 7-4

Pages 348–353

Determine if the quantities in each pair of ratios are proportional. Explain your reasoning.

1. **MONEY** 2 coins for every 3 bills and 6 coins for every 9 bills
2. **SCALE** 3 feet for every 1 in and 15 feet for every 6 in
3. **FAMILY** 2 children for every 1 adult and 8 children for every 3 adults
4. **TRAVEL** 1 hour for every 60 miles and 6 hours for every 360 miles
5. **SHOPPING** 4 for \$1.60 and 9 for \$3.40
6. **HOTEL** \$159.95 for 1 night stay and \$315.90 for two night stay

Solve each proportion.

7. $\frac{u}{72} = \frac{2}{4}$
8. $\frac{12}{m} = \frac{15}{10}$
9. $\frac{36}{90} = \frac{16}{t}$
10. $\frac{g}{32} = \frac{8}{64}$
11. $\frac{5}{14} = \frac{10}{a}$
12. $\frac{k}{18} = \frac{5}{3}$
13. $\frac{15}{w} = \frac{60}{4}$
14. $\frac{81}{90} = \frac{y}{20}$
15. $\frac{45}{8} = \frac{36}{d}$
16. $\frac{125}{v} = \frac{20}{5}$
17. $\frac{4}{5} = \frac{x}{3}$
18. $\frac{45}{75} = \frac{j}{3}$

Lesson 7-5

Pages 356–357

Use the *draw a diagram* strategy to solve the following problems.

1. **DISTANCE** Alejandro and Pedro are riding their bikes to school. After 2 miles, they are $\frac{4}{5}$ of the way there. How much farther do they have to go?
2. **CARPENTRY** Six inches were cut from a board that is now 12 inches long. The board this piece was cut from is one of 4 boards of equal length cut from the original piece. How long was the original piece?
3. **RACES** Four girls are in a race. Anna is just ahead of Pilar. Pilar is two places behind Isabela. Isabela is a few seconds behind the leader, Mary. Place the girls in order from first to last.
4. **FRACTIONS** Marta ate a quarter of a whole pie. Edwin ate $\frac{1}{4}$ of what was left. Cristina then ate $\frac{1}{3}$ of what was left. What fraction of the pie remains?

Lesson 7-6

Pages 358–364

On a map, the scale is 1 inch = 50 miles. For each map distance, find the actual distance.

1. 5 inches
2. 12 inches
3. $2\frac{3}{8}$ inches
4. $\frac{4}{5}$ inch
5. $2\frac{5}{6}$ inches
6. 3.25 inches
7. 4.75 inches
8. 5.25 inches

On a scale drawing, the scale is $\frac{1}{2}$ inch = 2 feet. Find the dimensions of each room in the scale drawing.

9. 14 feet by 18 feet
10. 32 feet by 6 feet
11. 3 feet by 5 feet
12. 20 feet by 30 feet

Lesson 7-7

Pages 366–370

Write each percent as a fraction in simplest form.

1. 32%	**2.** 89%	**3.** 72%	**4.** 11%
5. 1%	**6.** 28%	**7.** 55%	**8.** 18.5%
9. 22.75%	**10.** 25.2%	**11.** 75.5%	**12.** 48.25%
13. 6.5%	**14.** 1.25%	**15.** 88.9%	**16.** $52\frac{1}{4}\%$

Write each fraction as a percent. Round to the nearest hundredth if necessary.

17. $\frac{14}{25}$	**18.** $\frac{28}{50}$	**19.** $\frac{14}{20}$	**20.** $\frac{7}{10}$
21. $\frac{17}{17}$	**22.** $\frac{80}{125}$	**23.** $\frac{9}{12}$	**24.** $\frac{4}{6}$
25. $\frac{11}{12}$	**26.** $\frac{9}{16}$	**27.** $\frac{8}{9}$	**28.** $\frac{3}{16}$
29. $\frac{5}{32}$	**30.** $\frac{1}{16}$	**31.** $\frac{8}{15}$	**32.** $\frac{9}{11}$

Lesson 7-8

Pages 371–374

Write each percent as a decimal and as a mixed number or fraction in simplest form.

1. 895%	**2.** 555%	**3.** 480%	**4.** 920%
5. 122%	**6.** 825%	**7.** 0.3%	**8.** 0.42%
9. 0.78%	**10.** 765%	**11.** 0.99%	**12.** 1,000%

Write each decimal as a percent.

13. 3.5	**14.** 12	**15.** 0.002	**16.** 6.78
17. 0.0056	**18.** 1.95	**19.** 0.0077	**20.** 0.0102
21. 14.0	**22.** 0.0064	**23.** 16.2	**24.** 44.3

Write each mixed number or fraction as a percent.

25. $\frac{1}{250}$	**26.** $\frac{7}{400}$	**27.** $1\frac{1}{4}$	**28.** $7\frac{9}{10}$
29. $\frac{9}{10}$	**30.** $\frac{1}{500}$	**31.** $12\frac{1}{2}$	**32.** $\frac{1}{1,000}$
33. $4\frac{3}{4}$	**34.** 25	**35.** 900	**36.** $18\frac{2}{5}$

Lesson 8-1

Pages 386–390

Find each number. Round to the nearest tenth if necessary.

1. 5% of 40	**2.** 10% of 120	**3.** 12% of 150	**4.** 12.5% of 40
5. 75% of 200	**6.** 13% of 25.3	**7.** 250% of 44	**8.** 0.5% of 13.7
9. 600% of 7	**10.** 1.5% of $25	**11.** 81% of 134	**12.** 43% of 110
13. 61% of 524	**14.** 100% of 3.5	**15.** 20% of 58.5	**16.** 45% of 125.5
17. 23% of 500	**18.** 80% of 8	**19.** 90% of 72	**20.** 32% of 54

Lesson 8-2

Pages 392–396

Find each number. Round to the nearest tenth if necessary.

1. What number is 25% of 280?
2. 38 is what percent of 50?
3. 54 is 25% of what number?
4. 24.5% of what number is 15?
5. What number is 80% of 500?
6. 12% of 120 is what number?
7. Find 68% of 50.
8. What percent of 240 is 32?
9. 99 is what percent of 150?
10. Find 75% of 1.
11. What number is $33\frac{1}{3}\%$ of 66?
12. 50% of 350 is what number?
13. What percent of 450 is 50?
14. What number is $37\frac{1}{2}\%$ of 32?
15. 95% of 40 is what number?
16. Find 30% of 26.
17. 9 is what percent of 30?
18. 52% of what number is 109.2?
19. What number is 65% of 200?
20. What number is 15.5% of 45?

Lesson 8-3

Pages 397–402

Estimate by using fractions.

1. 28% of 48
2. 99% of 65
3. 445% of 20
4. 9% of 81
5. 73% of 240
6. 65.5% of 75
7. 48.2% of 93
8. 39.45% of 51
9. 287% of 122
10. 53% of 80
11. 414% of 72
12. 59% of 105

Estimate by using 10%.

13. 30% of 42
14. 70% of 104
15. 90% of 152
16. 67% of 70
17. 78% of 92
18. 12% of 183
19. 51% of 221
20. 23% of 504
21. 81% of 390
22. 41% of 60
23. 59% of 178
24. 22% of 450

Estimate.

25. 50% of 37
26. 18% of 90
27. 300% of 245
28. 1% of 48
29. 70% of 300
30. 35% of 35
31. 60.5% of 60
32. $5\frac{1}{2}\%$ of 100
33. 40.01% of 16
34. 80% of 62
35. 45% of 119
36. 14.81% of 986

Lesson 8-4

Pages 403–404

Solve each problem using the *reasonable answers* strategy.

1. **SKIING** Benito skied for 13.5 hours and estimated that he spent 30% of his time on the ski lift. Did he spend about 4, 6, or 8 hours on the ski lift?
2. **CLASS TRIP** The class trip at Wilson Middle School costs $145 per student. A fund-raiser earns 38% of this cost. Will each student have to pay about $70, $80, or $90?
3. **GAS MILEAGE** Miguel's car gets 38 miles per gallon and has 2.5 gallons of gasoline left in the tank. Can he drive for 85, 95, or 105 more miles before he runs out of gas?
4. **DINING** At a restaurant, the total cost of a meal is $87.50. Nadia wants to leave a 20% tip. Should she leave a total of $95, $105, or $115?

Lesson 8-5

Pages 405–409

Write an equation for each problem. Then solve. Round to the nearest tenth if necessary.

1. Find 45% of 50.
2. 75 is what percent of 300?
3. 16% of what number is 2?
4. 75% of 80 is what number?
5. 5% of what number is 12?
6. Find 60% of 45.
7. 90 is what percent of 95?
8. $28\frac{1}{2}$% of 64 is what number?
9. Find 46.5% of 75.
10. What number is 55.5% of 70?
11. 80.5% of what number is 80.5?
12. $66\frac{2}{3}$% of what number is 40?
13. Find 122.5% of 80.
14. 250% of what number is 75?

Lesson 8-6

Pages 411–414

1. The table shows the results of a survey of students' favorite cookies. Predict how many of the 424 students at Scobey High School prefer chocolate chip cookies.

Cookie	Number
chocolate chip	49
peanut butter	12
oatmeal	10
sugar	8
raisin	3

2. The circle graph shows the results of a survey of teens and where they would prefer to spend a family vacation. Predict how many of 4,000 teens would prefer to go to an amusement park.

Vacation Survey

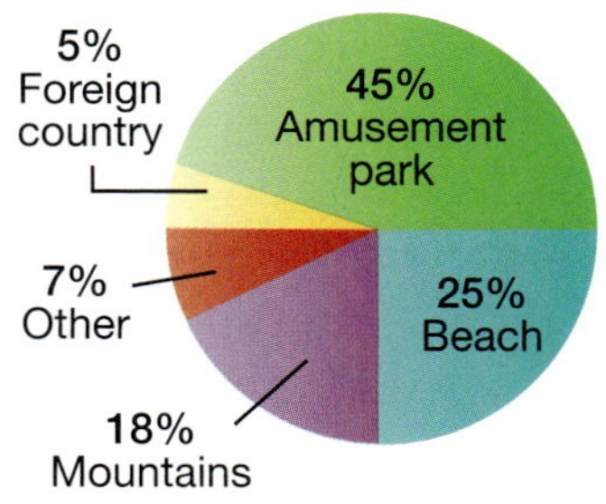

3. In 2000, about 29% of the foreign visitors to the U.S. were from Canada. If a particular hotel had 150,000 foreign guests in one year, how many would you predict were from Canada?

Lesson 8-7

Pages 415–420

Find each percent of change. Round to the nearest whole percent if necessary. State whether the percent of change is an *increase* or *decrease*.

1. 450 centimeters to 675 centimeters
2. 77 million to 200.2 million
3. 500 albums to 100 albums
4. 350 yards to 420 yards
5. 3.25 meters to 2.95 meters
6. $65 to $75
7. 180 dishes to 160 dishes
8. 450 pieces to 445.5 pieces
9. 700 grams 910 grams
10. 55 women to 11 women
11. 412 children to 1,339 children
12. 464 kilograms to 20 kilograms
13. 24 hours to 86 hours
14. 16 minutes to 24 minutes

Lesson 8-8

Pages 421–424

Find the total cost or sale price to the nearest cent.

1. \$45 sweater; 6% tax
2. \$18.99 CD; 15% discount
3. \$199 ring; 10% discount
4. \$29 shirt; 7% tax
5. \$19 purse; 25% discount
6. \$145 coat; 6.25% tax
7. \$12 meal; 4.5% tax
8. \$899 computer; 20% discount
9. \$105 skateboard; $7\frac{1}{2}$% tax
10. \$599 TV; 12% discount
11. \$12,500 car; $3\frac{3}{4}$% tax
12. \$49.95 gloves; $5\frac{1}{4}$% tax

Find the percent of discount to the nearest percent.

13. sneakers: regular price, \$72
    sale price, \$60
14. dress shirt: regular price, \$90
    sale price, \$22.50
15. portable game player: regular price, \$125
    sale price, \$100
16. car: regular price, \$25,000
    sale price, \$22,000

Lesson 8-9

Pages 425–428

Find the simple interest earned to the nearest cent for each principal, interest rate, and time.

1. \$2,000, 8%, 5 years
2. \$500, 10%, 8 months
3. \$750, 5%, 1 year
4. \$175.50, $6\frac{1}{2}$%, 18 months
5. \$236.20, 9%, 16 months
6. \$89, $7\frac{1}{2}$%, 6 months
7. \$800, 5.75%, 3 years
8. \$225, $1\frac{1}{2}$%, 2 years
9. \$12,000, $4\frac{1}{2}$%, 40 months

Find the simple interest paid to the nearest cent for each loan, interest rate, and time.

10. \$750, 18%, 2 years
11. \$1,500, 19%, 16 months
12. \$300, 9%, 1 year
13. \$4,750, 19.5%, 30 months
14. \$2,345, 17%, 9 months
15. \$689, 12%, 2 years
16. \$390, 18.75%, 15 months
17. \$1,250, 22%, 8 months
18. \$3,240, 18%, 14 months

Lesson 9-1

Pages 442–447

Display each set of data in a line plot. Identify any clusters, gaps, or outliers.

1.

Number of Pets in the Home				
0	1	3	4	0
2	1	0	1	1
10	0	1	5	2

2.

High Temperatures for 18 Days (°F)					
75	81	75	65	76	81
77	80	65	65	80	80
76	85	66	75	80	75

3.

Number of Stories for Buildings in Denver				
56	43	36	42	29
54	42	32	34	
52	40	32	32	

Source: *The World Almanac and Book of Facts*

4.

Ages of Children at Sunny Day Care (years)					
4	1	6	4	5	3
4	5	1	2	5	4
3	2	4	1	3	3

Lesson 9-2

Pages 448–454

Find the mean, median, and mode for each set of data.

1. 1, 5, 9, 1, 2, 6, 8, 2
2. 2, 5, 8, 9, 7, 6, 3, 5, 1, 4
3. 82, 79, 93, 91, 95, 95, 81
4. 117, 103, 108, 120
5. 256, 265, 247, 256
6. 47, 54, 66, 54, 46, 66
7. 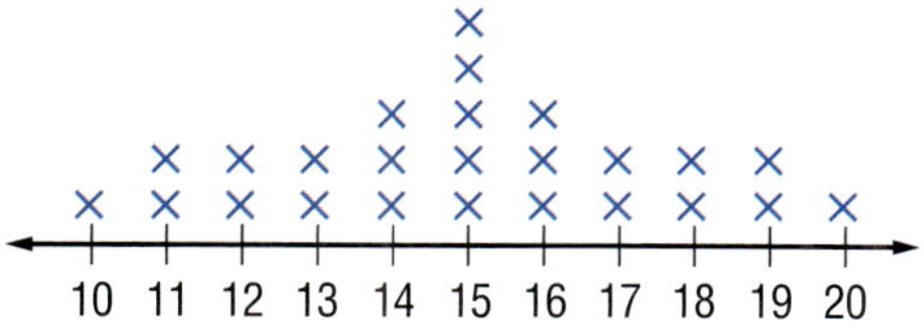

8.

Number of Absences	Tally	Frequency
0	IIII	4
1	卌 IIII	9
2	卌 I	6
3	卌	5

Lesson 9-3

Pages 456–460

Display each set of data in a stem-and-leaf plot.

1. 23, 15, 39, 68, 57, 42, 51, 52, 41, 18, 29
2. 189, 182, 196, 184, 197, 183, 196, 194, 184
3.

Average Monthly High Temperatures in Albany, NY (°F)			
21	46	72	50
24	58	70	40
34	67	61	27

Source: *The World Almanac and Book of Facts*

4.

Super Bowl Winning Scores 1987-2004					
39	55	52	27	34	20
42	20	30	35	23	48
20	37	49	31	34	32

Source: *The World Almanac and Book of Facts*

Lesson 9-4

Pages 461–467

Select the appropriate graph to display each set of data: bar graph or histogram. Then display the data in the appropriate graph.

1.

Longest Snakes	
Snake Name	**Length (ft)**
Royal python	35
Anaconda	28
Indian python	25
Diamond python	21
King cobra	19
Boa constrictor	16

Source: *The Top 10 of Everything*

2.

Least Densely Populated States	
State	**People Per Square Mile**
Alaska	1
Wyoming	5
Montana	6
North Dakota	9
South Dakota	10
New Mexico	15

Source: *The Top 10 of Everything*

3.

Cost of a Movie Ticket at Selected Theaters			
\$5.25	\$6.50	\$3.50	\$3.75
\$7.50	\$9.25	\$10.40	\$4.75
\$10.00	\$4.50	\$8.75	\$7.25
\$3.50	\$6.70	\$4.20	\$7.50

4.

Highest Recorded Wind Speeds For Selected U.S. Cities (mph)					
52	55	81	46	73	57
75	54	58	76	46	58
60	91	53	53	51	56
80	60	73	46	49	47

Source: *The World Almanac and Book of Facts*

Lesson 9-5

Pages 469–472

Use the Venn diagram that shows student hobby interests.

1. Which students prefer to be outside and active?
2. Which students prefer to be outside but not be active?
3. Which students would rather just read a book?
4. Explain Abby's preferences.

Draw a Venn diagram to show how the sets of data are related.

5.

Favorite Colors	
Blue	Amy, Sara, Alana, Nicholas
Green	Alana, Jorge, Zuza, Paulo
Red	Stephanie, Simon, Jorge, Alana

6.

Even Numbers	Multiples of 3
2, 4, 6, 8, 10, 12, 14, 16, 18, 20, 22, 24, 26, 28, 30	3, 6, 9, 12, 15, 18, 21, 24, 27, 30

Lesson 9-6

Pages 474–475

WEATHER **For Exercises 1–3, solve by using the graph.**

1. In which month is the average high temperature about twice as high as the average low temperature for January?
2. What is the approximate difference between the average high temperature and the average low temperature each month?
3. Predict the high and low temperatures for June based on the data given on the graph.

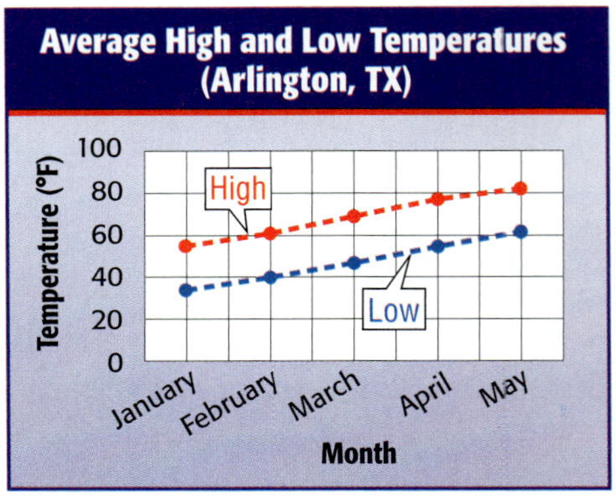

Lesson 9-7

Pages 476–481

1. Rachel's quiz scores in science have been steadily going up since her parents hired a tutor for her. If the trend continues, predict Rachel's score on the next quiz.

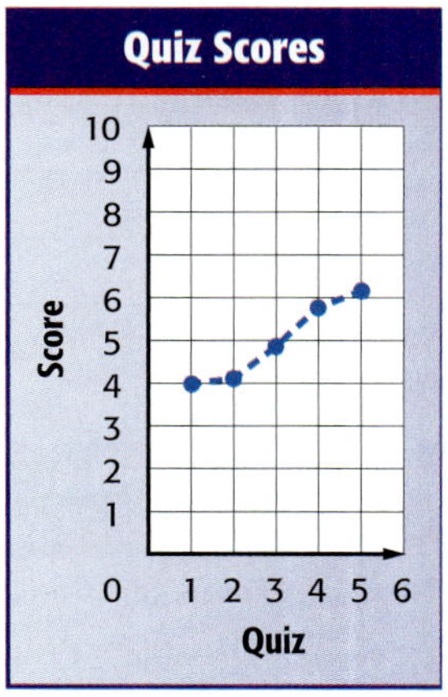

2. **The table shows the average price paid to farmers per 100 pounds of sheep they sold.**
   a. Make a scatter plot of the data.
   b. Describe the relationship, if any, between the two sets of data.
   c. Predict the price per 100 pounds for 2010. Explain.

Year	Price Per 100 Pounds ($)
1940	4
1950	12
1960	6
1970	8
1980	21
1990	23
2000	34

Source: *The World Almanac and Book of Facts*

Lesson 9-8

Pages 484–487

Select an appropriate display for each situation.

1. the average daily high temperatures for Wichita, KS recorded for two weeks
2. the favorite new release movies recorded in a survey of seventh grade students
3. the birth years of a population arranged by intervals
4. the population of a country by ethnicity
5. a comparison of students who like vanilla ice cream, chocolate ice cream, both, or neither.

Select an appropriate display for each situation. Then make the display.

6.

Should the Name of Deer Valley Middle School be Changed?	
Vote	**Number of Votes**
Yes	15
No	21
Don't Know	8

7.

Object Characteristics	
Red in Color	**Begins with R**
Ruby	Rose
Stop Sign	Raincoat
Rose	Rhinoceros
Tomato	Ruby

Lesson 9-9

Pages 488–493

Which graph could be misleading? Explain your reasoning.

1. Both graphs show pounds of grapes sold to Westview School in one week.

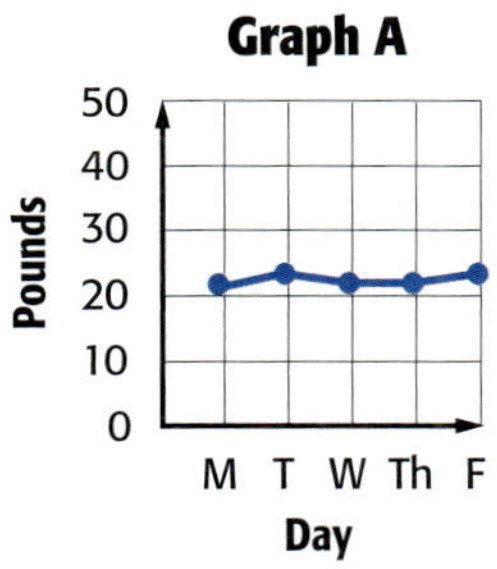

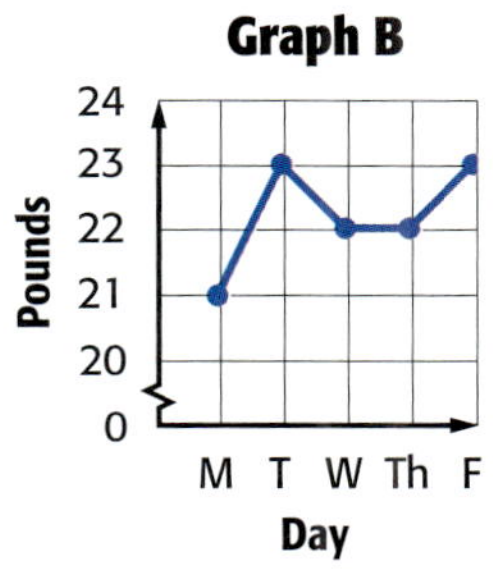

2. Both graphs show commissions made by Mr. Turner for a four-week pay period.

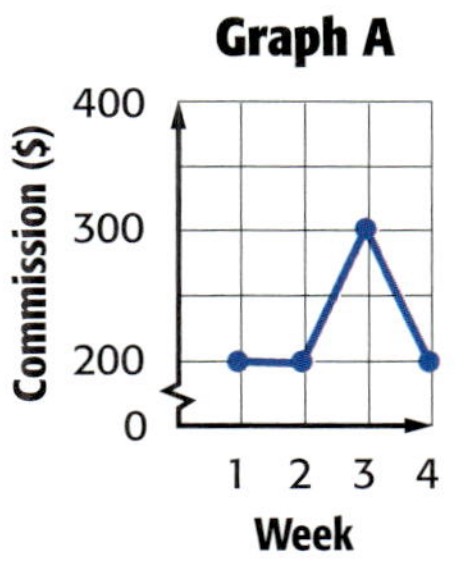

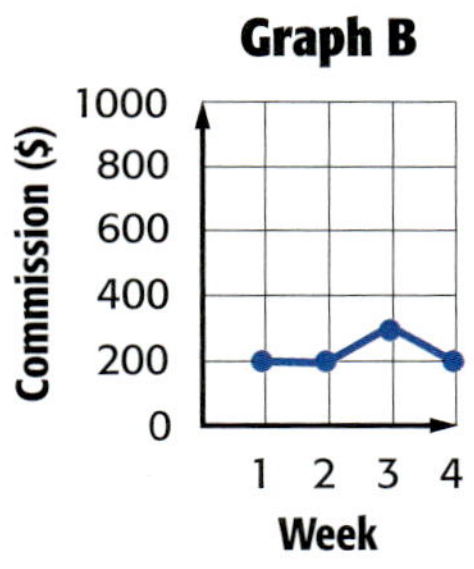

Lesson 10-1

Pages 504–508

Use the spinner at the right to find each probability. Write as a fraction in simplest form.

1. *P*(even number)
2. *P*(prime number)
3. *P*(factor of 12)
4. *P*(composite number)
5. *P*(greater than 10)
6. *P*(neither prime nor composite)

A package of balloons contains 5 green, 3 yellow, 4 red, and 8 pink balloons. Suppose you reach in the package and choose one balloon at random. Find the probability of each event. Write as a fraction in simplest form.

7. *P*(red balloon)
8. *P*(yellow balloon)
9. *P*(pink balloon)
10. *P*(orange balloon)
11. *P*(red or yellow balloon)
12. *P*(*not* green balloon)

Lesson 10-2

Pages 509–514

For each situation, find the sample space using a tree diagram.

1. rolling 2 number cubes
2. choosing an ice cream cone from waffle, plain, or sugar and a flavor of ice cream from chocolate, vanilla, or strawberry
3. making a sandwich from white, wheat, or rye bread, cheddar or Swiss cheese and ham, turkey, or roast beef
4. flipping a penny twice
5. choosing one math class from algebra and geometry and one foreign language class from French, Spanish, or Latin

Lesson 10-3

Pages 515–518

Use the Fundamental Counting Principle to find the total number of outcomes in each situation.

1. choosing a local phone number if the exchange is 398 and each of the four remaining digits is different
2. choosing a way to drive from Millville to Westwood if there are 5 roads that lead from Millville to Miamisburg, 3 roads that connect Miamisburg to Hathaway, and 4 highways that connect Hathaway to Westwood
3. tossing a quarter, rolling a number cube, and tossing a dime
4. spinning the spinners shown below

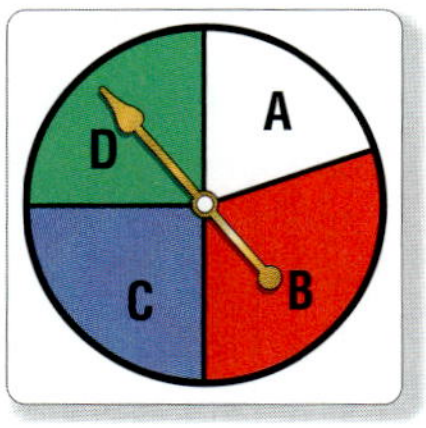

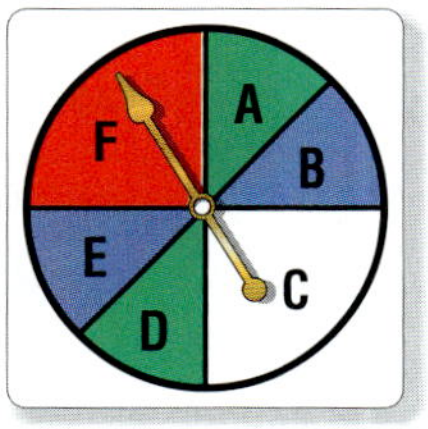

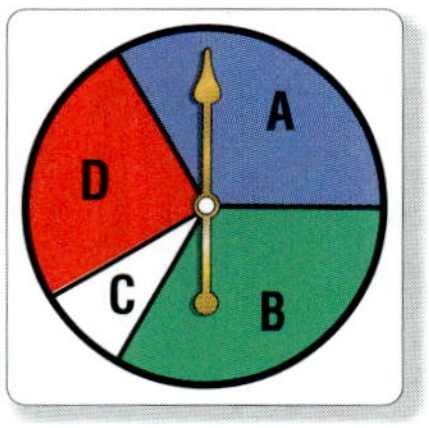

Lesson 10-4

Pages 519–522

1. **RACES** Eight runners are competing in a 100-meter sprint. In how many ways can the gold, silver, and bronze medals be awarded?
2. **LOCKERS** Five-digit locker combinations are assigned using the digits 1–9. In how many ways can the combinations be formed if no digit can be repeated?
3. **SCHEDULES** In how many ways can the classes math, language arts, science, and social studies be ordered on student schedules as the first four classes of their day?
4. **TOYS** At a teddy bear workshop, customers can select from black, brown, golden, white, blue, or pink for their bear's color. If a father randomly selects two bear colors, what is the probability that he will select a white bear for his son and a pink bear for his daughter? The father cannot pick the same color for both bears.
5. **WRITING** If you randomly select three of your last seven writing assignments to submit to an essay contest, what is the probability that you will select your first, fourth, and sixth essays in that order?

Lesson 10-5

Pages 524–527

1. **EXERCISE** How many ways can you choose to exercise three days of a week?
2. **BOOKS** In how many ways can six books be selected from a collection of 12?
3. **REPORTS** In how many ways can you select three report topics from a total of 8 topics?
4. **GROUPS** How many ways can four students be chosen from a class of 26?
5. **ROLLER COASTERS** In how many ways can you ride five out of nine roller coasters if you don't care in what order you ride them?

Lesson 10-6

Pages 528–529

Use the *act it out* strategy to solve each problem.

1. **STAIRS** Lynnette lives on a certain floor of her apartment building. She goes up two flights of stairs to put a load of laundry in a washing machine on that floor. Then she goes down five flights to borrow a book from a friend. Next, she goes up 8 flights to visit another friend who is ill. How many flights up or down does Lynette now have to go to take her laundry out of the washing machine?
2. **LOGIC PUZZLE** Suppose you are on the west side of a river with a fox, a duck, and a bag of corn. You want to take all three to the other side of the river, but...
   - your boat is only large enough to carry you and either the fox, duck, or bag of corn.
   - you cannot leave the fox alone with the duck.
   - you cannot leave the duck alone with the corn.
   - you cannot leave the corn alone on the east side of the river because some wild birds will eat it.
   - the wild birds are afraid of the fox.
   - you cannot leave the fox, duck, and the corn alone.
   - you can bring something across the river more than once.

   If there is no other way to cross the river, how do you get everything to the other side?

Lesson 10-7

Pages 530–534

The frequency table shows the results of a fair number cube rolled 40 times.

1. Find the experimental probability of rolling a 4.
2. Find the theoretical probability of *not* rolling a 4.
3. Find the theoretical probability of rolling a 2.
4. Find the experimental probability of *not* rolling a 6.
5. Suppose the number cube was rolled 500 times. About how many times would it land on 5?

Face	Frequency
1	5
2	9
3	2
4	8
5	12
6	4

Extra Practice

Lesson 10-8

Pages 536–539

1. Two evenly balanced nickels are flipped. Find the probability that one head and one tail result.
2. A wallet contains four \$5 bills, two \$10 bills, and eight \$1 bills. A bill is selected, replaced, and then a second bill is selected. Find P(\$5 and \$5).
3. Two chips are selected from a box containing 6 blue chips, 4 red chips, and 3 green chips. The first chip selected is replaced before the second is drawn. Find P(red, green).
4. A bag contains 7 blue, 4 orange, 8 red, and 5 purple marbles. Suppose one marble is chosen and then replaced. A second marble is then chosen. Find P(purple, red).

Lesson 11-1

Pages 552–557

Classify each pair of angles as *complementary*, *supplementary*, or *neither*.

1.

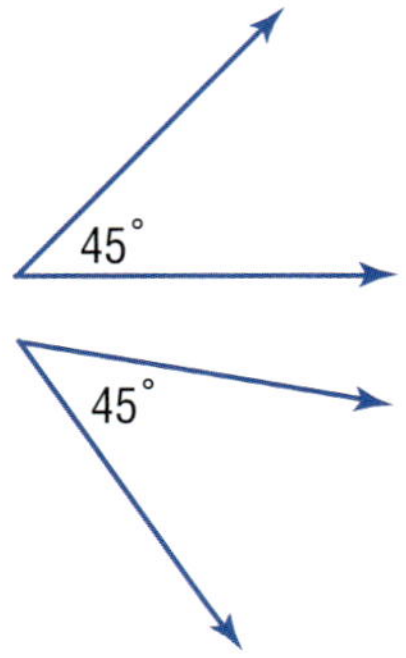

2.

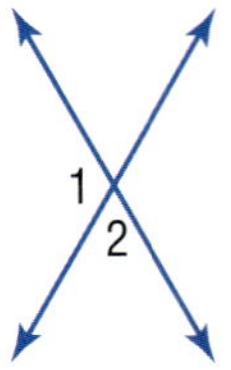

3.

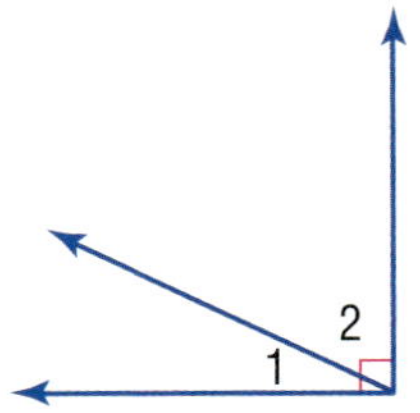

Find the value of x in each figure.

4.

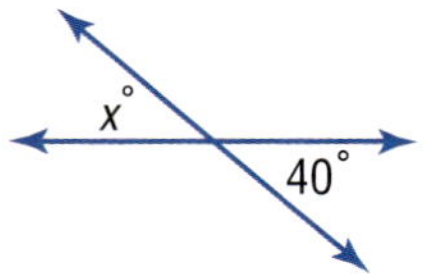

5.

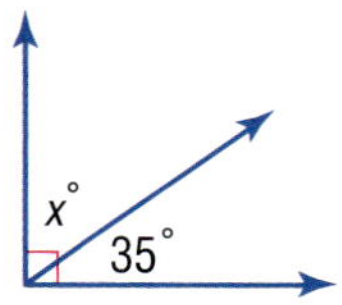

6.

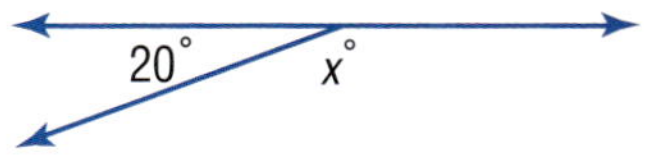

Lesson 11-2

Pages 558–563

Display each set of data in a circle graph.

1.

Car Sales	
Style	**Percent**
sedan	45%
SUV	22%
pickup truck	9%
sports car	13%
compact car	11%

2.

Favorite Flavor of Ice Cream	
Flavor	**Number**
vanilla	11
chocolate	15
strawberry	8
mint chip	5
cookie dough	3

Lesson 11-3

Pages 564–568

Find the value of x.

1. 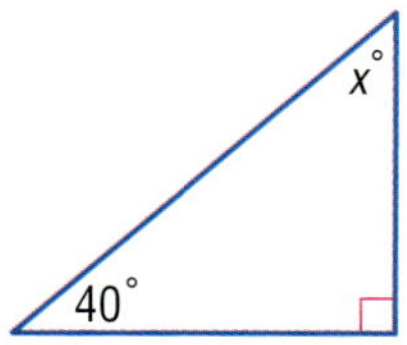

2. 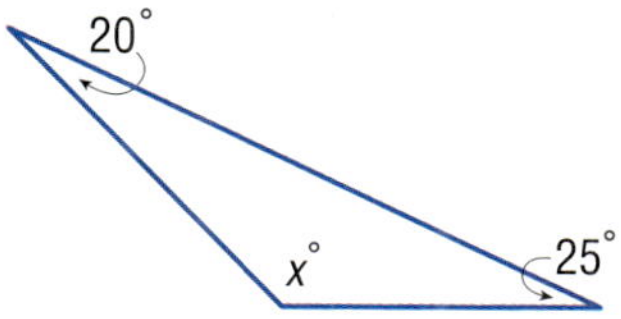

3. 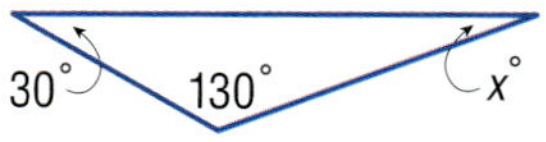

Classify each triangle by its angles and by its sides.

4. 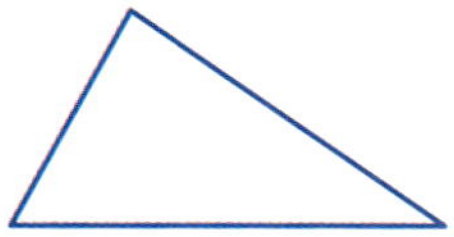

5. 

6. 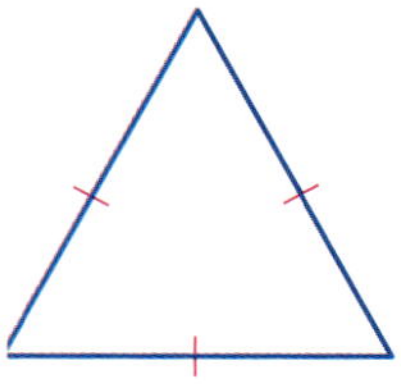

Lesson 11-4

Pages 569–570

Use the *logical reasoning* strategy to solve each problem.

1. **HOUSE NUMBERS** Rico's house number contains four digits. The digits are 5, 8, 3, and 2. If his house number is odd, divisible by 3, and the middle two numbers are a perfect square, what is his house number?
2. **FRUIT** Julio, Rashanda, and Perry each brought a fruit with their lunch. The fruits brought were a mango, a banana, and an orange. If Perry did not bring a banana and Julio brought a mango, what type of fruit did each student bring?
3. **MONEY** Corelia has twice as many quarters in her purse as dimes and half as many nickels as dimes. If she has 12 quarters in her purse, how much money total does she have?

Lesson 11-5

Pages 572–576

Classify each quadrilateral using the name that *best* describes it.

1. 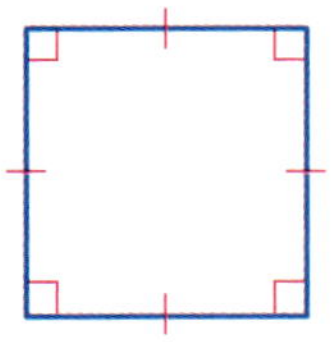

2. 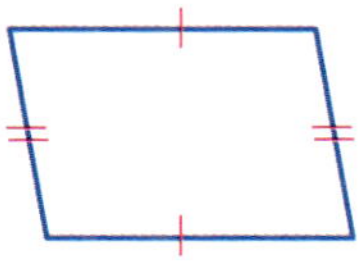

3. 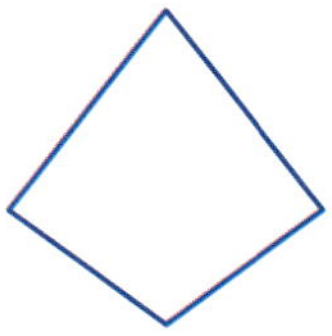

Find the missing angle measure in each quadrilateral.

4. 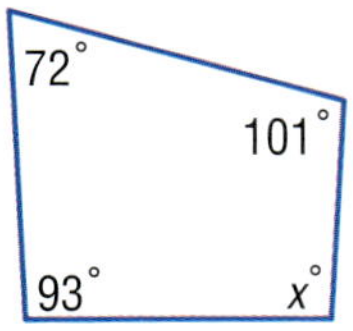

5. 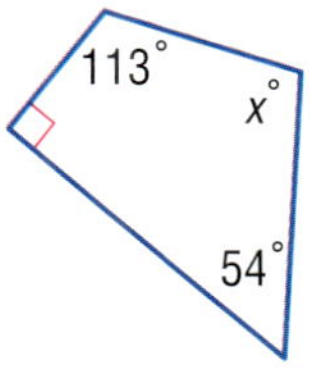

6. 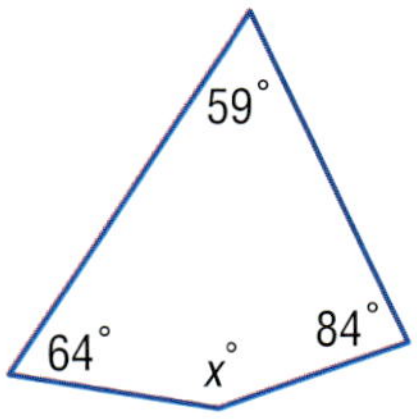

7. **GEOMETRY** In quadrilateral $RSTV$, $m\angle R = 47°$, $m\angle S = 108°$, and $\angle T$ is a right angle. Find the measure of $\angle V$.

Lesson 11-6

Pages 578–583

Find the value of *x* in each pair of similar figures.

1. 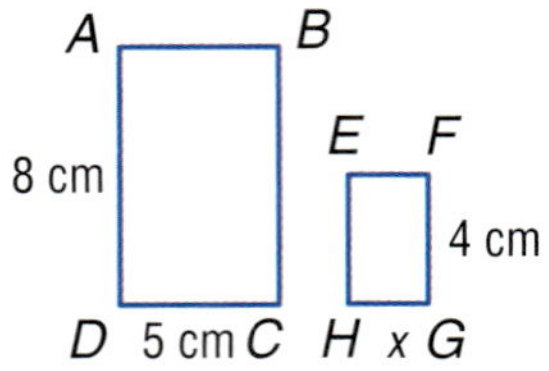

2. 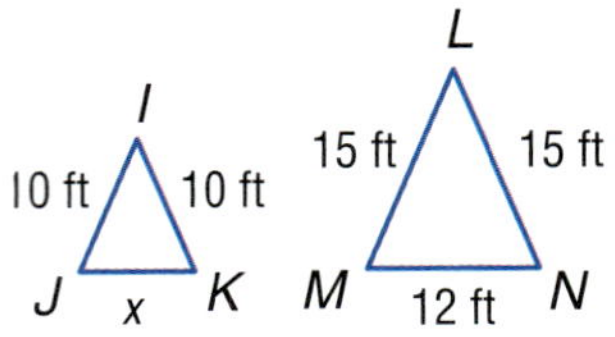

3. 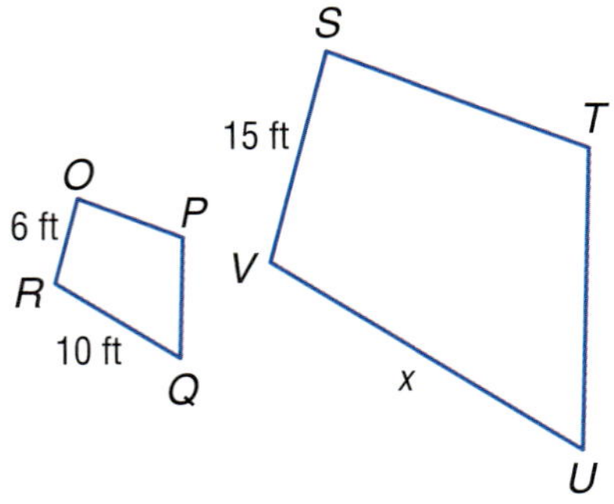

4. 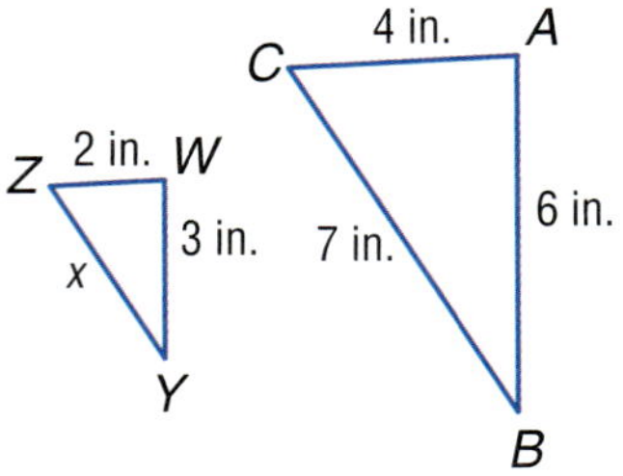

5. 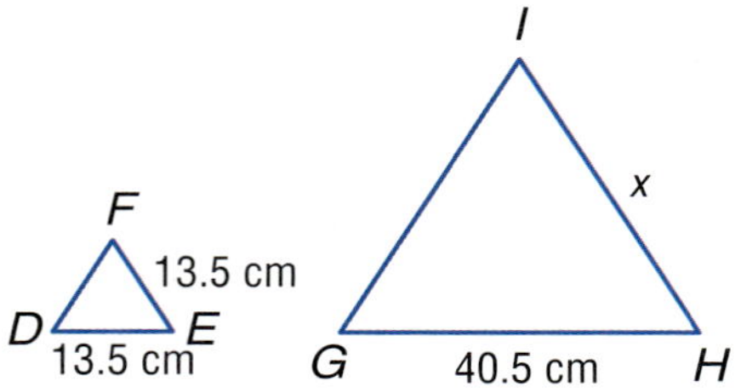

6. 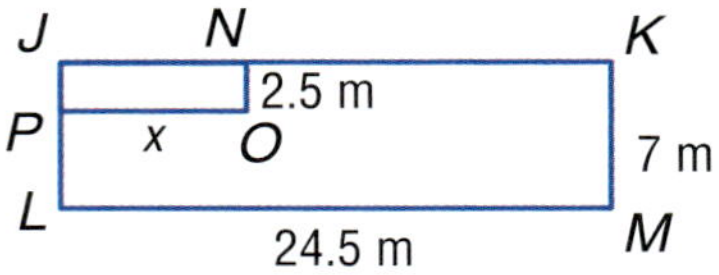

Lesson 11-7

Pages 584–589

Determine whether each figure is a polygon. If it is, classify the polygon and state whether it is regular. If it is *not* a polygon, explain why.

1. 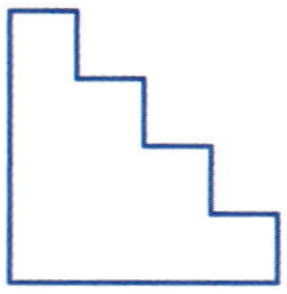

2. 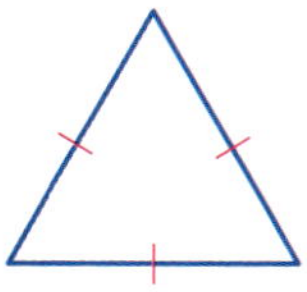

3. 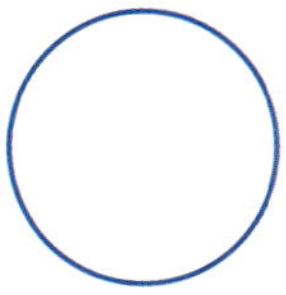

4. 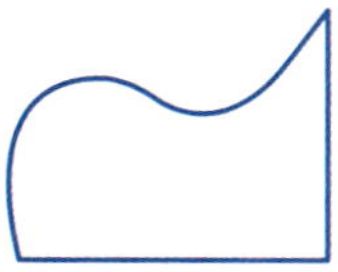

5. 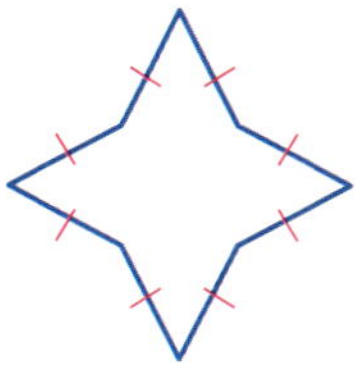

6. 

Find the measure of an angle in each polygon if polygon is regular. Round to the nearest tenth of a degree if necessary.

7. triangle
8. 30-gon
9. 18-gon
10. 14-gon
11. hexagon
12. nonagon
13. 27-gon
14. octagon

Lesson 11-8

Pages 591–595

1. Translate $\triangle ABC$ 2 units right and 1 unit down.

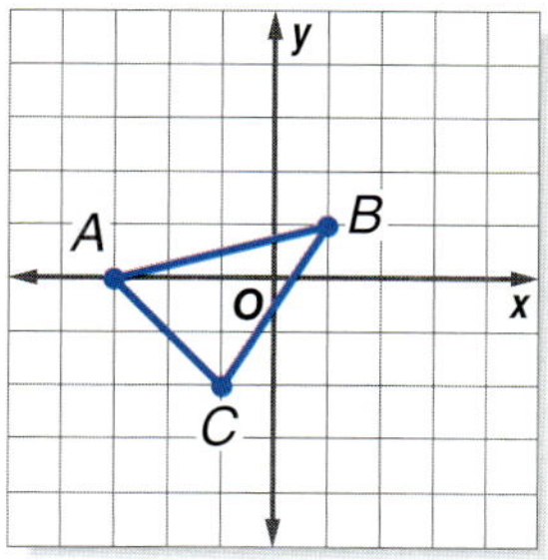

2. Translate quadrilateral $RSTU$ 4 units left and 3 units down.

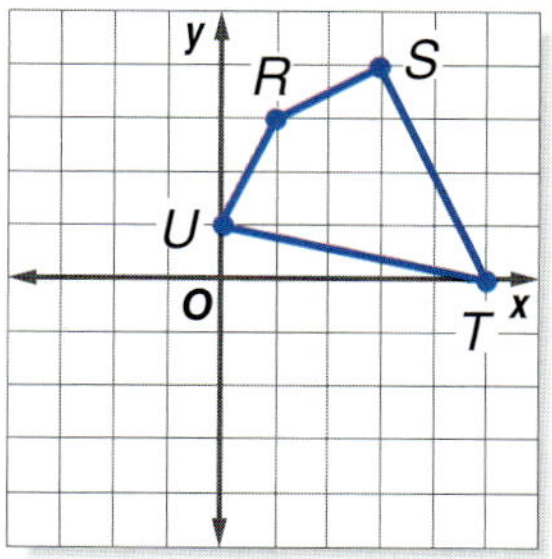

Triangle TRI has vertices $T(1, 1)$, $R(4, -2)$, and $I(-2, -1)$. Find the vertices of $T'R'I'$ after each translation. Then graph the figure and its translated image.

3. 2 units right, 1 unit down
4. 5 units left, 1 unit up
5. 3 units right
6. 2 units up

Lesson 11-9

Pages 596–600

Determine whether each figure has line symmetry. If so, copy the figure and draw all lines of symmetry.

1. 

2. 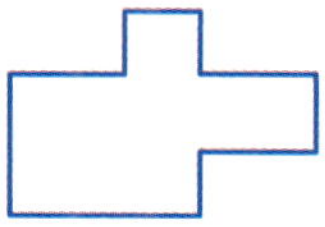

3. 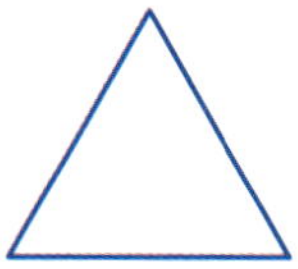

4. 

5. 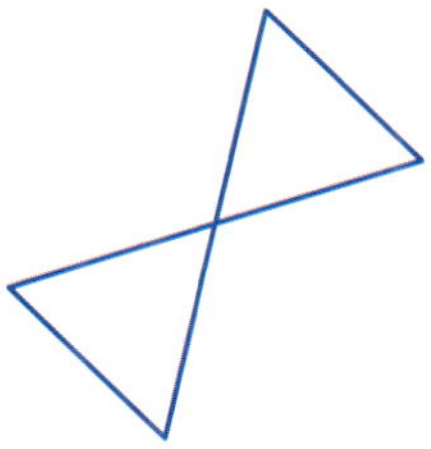

6. 

Graph each figure and its reflection over the x-axis. Then find the coordinates of the reflected image.

7. quadrilateral $QUAD$ with vertices $Q(-1, 4)$, $U(2, 2)$, $A(1, 1)$, and $D(-2, 2)$
8. triangle $\triangle ABC$ with vertices $A(0, -1)$, $B(4, -3)$, and $C(-4, -5)$

Graph each figure and its reflection over the y-axis. Then find the coordinates of the reflected image.

9. parallelogram $PARL$ with vertices $P(3, 5)$, $A(5, 4)$, $R(5, 1)$, and $L(3, 2)$
10. pentagon $PENTA$ with vertices $P(-1, 3)$, $E(1, 1)$, $N(0, -2)$, $T(-2, -2)$, and $A(-3, 1)$

Lesson 12-1

Pages 610–614

Find the area of each parallelogram. Round to the nearest tenth if necessary.

1. 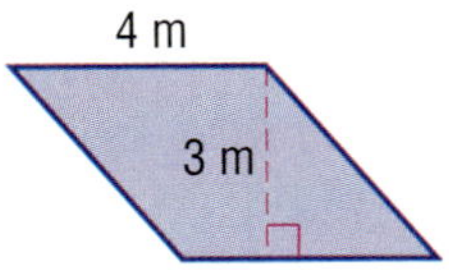

2. 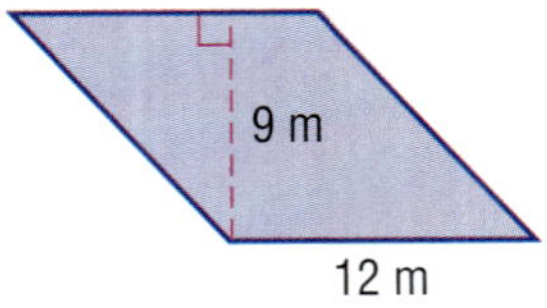

3. 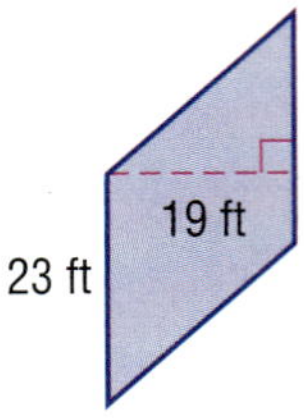

4. base = 19 m
   height = 6 m
5. base = 135 in.
   height = 15 in.
6. base = 8.2 cm
   height = 5.5 cm
7. base = 29.3 m
   height = 10.1 m

Lesson 12-2

Pages 616–620

Find the area of each figure. Round to the nearest tenth if necessary.

1. 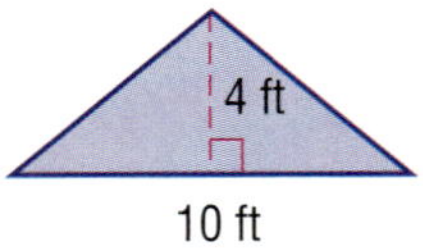

2. 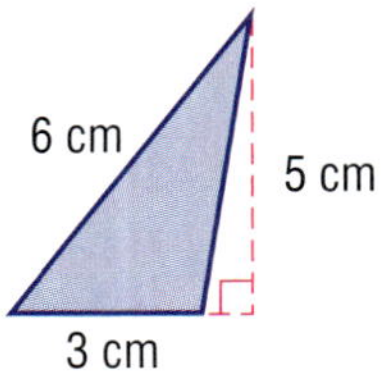

3. 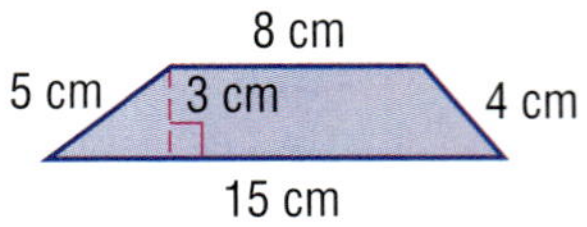

4. triangle: base = 5 in., height = 9 in.
5. trapezoid: bases = 3 cm and 8 cm, height = 12 cm
6. trapezoid: bases = 10 ft and 15 ft, height = 12 ft
7. triangle: base = 12 cm, height = 8 cm
8. trapezoid: bases = 82.6 cm and 72.2 cm, height = 44.5 cm
9. triangle: base = 500.5 ft, height = 254.5 ft

Lesson 12-3

Pages 622–626

Find the circumference of each circle. Use 3.14 or $\frac{22}{7}$ for π. Round to the nearest tenth if necessary.

1. 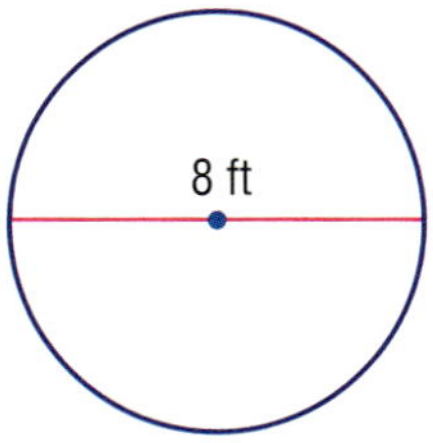

2. 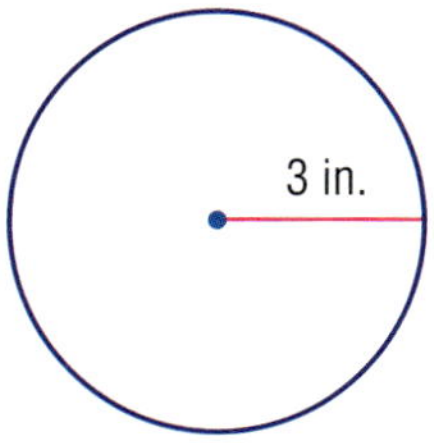

3. 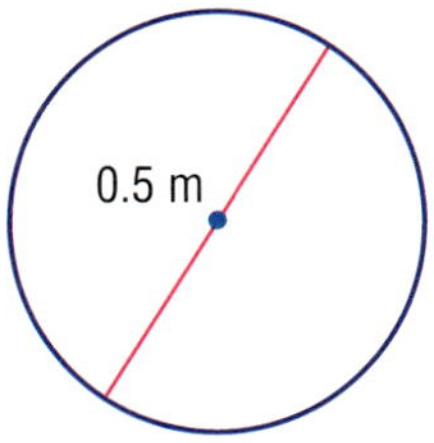

4. 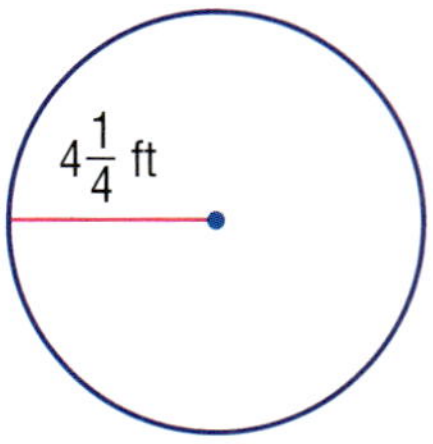

5. $r = 1$ m
6. $d = 2$ yd
7. $d = 5{,}280$ ft
8. $r = 0.5$ cm
9. $d = 6.4$ m
10. $r = 10.7$ km
11. $d = \frac{3}{16}$ in.
12. $r = 5\frac{1}{2}$ mi
13. $d = 42\frac{3}{4}$ ft

Lesson 12-4

Pages 627–631

Find the area of each circle. Round to the nearest tenth.

1. 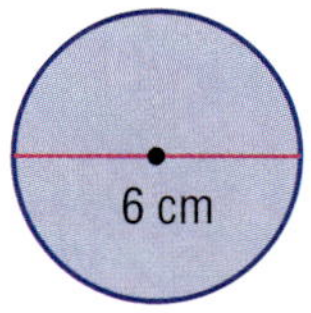

2. 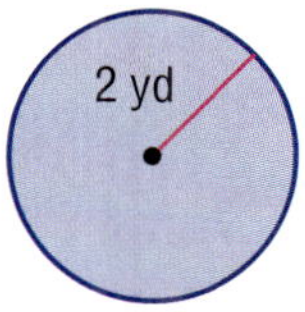

3. 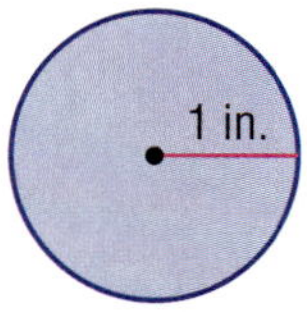

4. radius = 8 in.
5. diameter = 5 ft
6. radius = 24 cm
7. diameter = 2.3 m
8. diameter = 82 ft
9. radius = 68 cm
10. radius = 9.8 mi
11. diameter = 25.6 m
12. diameter = 6.75 in.
13. radius = $1\frac{1}{4}$ ft
14. diameter = $5\frac{2}{3}$ yd
15. diameter = $45\frac{1}{2}$ mi

Lesson 12-5

Pages 632–633

Use the *solve a simpler problem* strategy to solve each problem.

1. **EARNINGS** Cedric makes $51,876 each year. If he is paid once every two weeks and actually takes home about 67% of his wages after taxes, how much does he take home each paycheck? Round to the nearest cent if necessary.

2. **CARS** Jorge plans to decorate the rims on his tires by putting a strip of shiny metal around the outside edge on each rim. The diameter of each tire is 17 inches, and each rim is 2.75 inches from the outside edge of each tire. If he plans to cut the four individual pieces for each tire from the same strip of metal, how long of a strip should he buy? Round to the nearest tenth.

3. **SAVINGS** Erin's aunt invested a total of $1,500 into three different savings accounts. She invested $450 into a savings account with an annual interest rate of 3.25% and $600 into a savings account with an annual interest rate of 4.75%. The third savings account had an annual interest rate of 4.375%. After 3 years, how much money will Erin's aunt have in the three accounts altogether if she made no more additional deposits or withdrawals? Round to the nearest cent.

BIOLOGY For Exercises 4–6, use the following information.
About five quarts of blood are pumped through the average human heart in one minute.

4. At this rate, how many quarts of blood are pumped through the average human heart in one year? (Use 365 days = 1 year)

5. If the average heart beats 72 times per minute, how many quarts of blood are pumped with each beat? Round to the nearest tenth.

6. How many total gallons of blood are pumped through the average human heart in one week?

7. **LAND** A rectangular plot of land measures 1,450 feet by 850 feet. A contractor wishes to section off a portion of this land to build an apartment complex. If the complex is 425 feet by 550 feet, how many square feet of land will not be sectioned off to build it?

Lesson 12-6

Pages 634–637

Find the area of each figure. Round to the nearest tenth if necessary.

1.

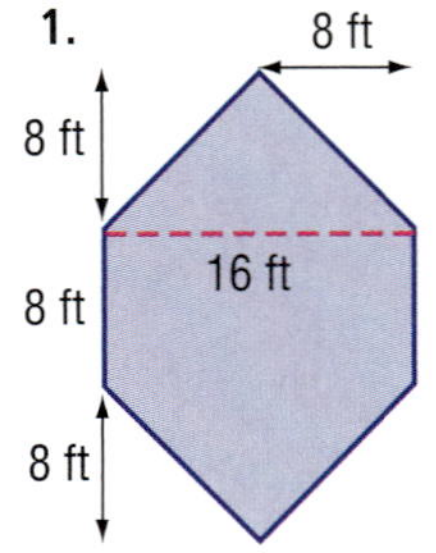

2.

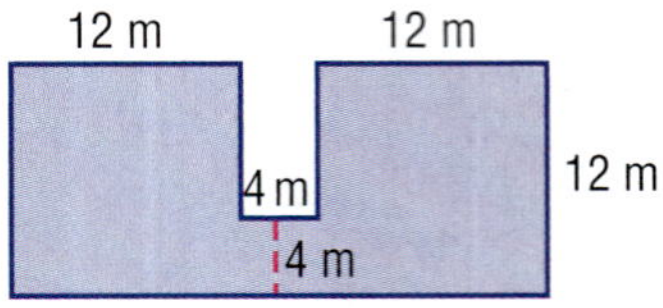

3.

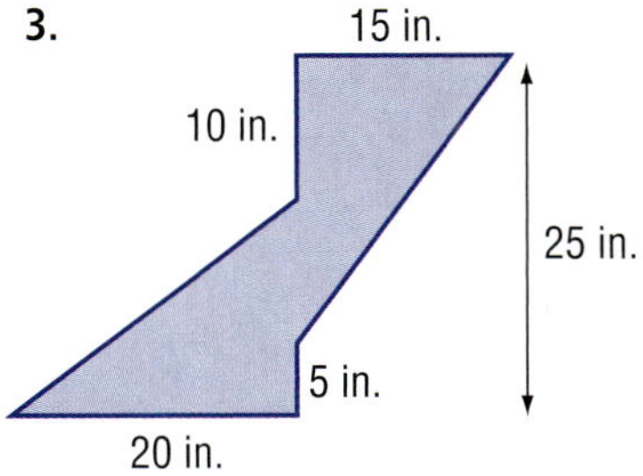

4.

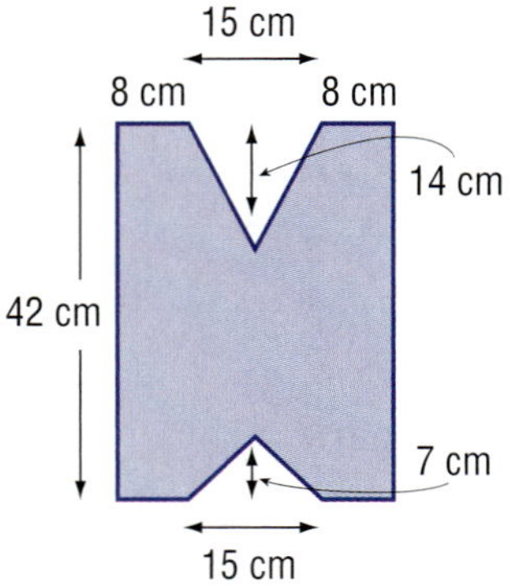

5.

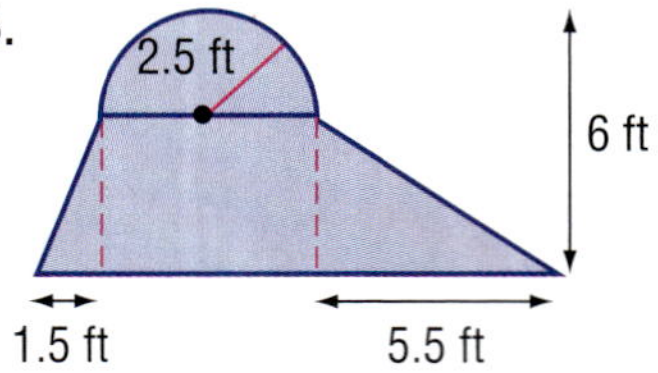

6.

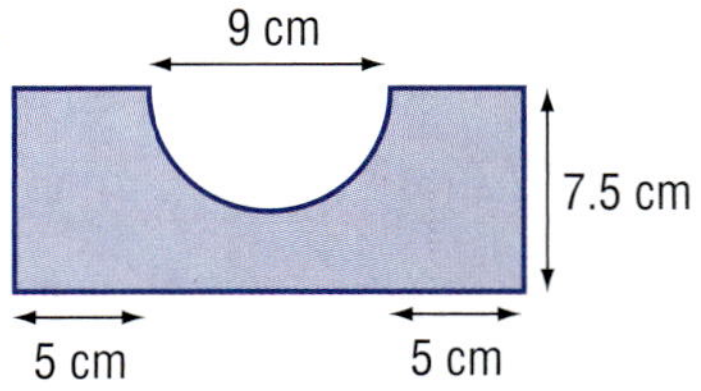

7.

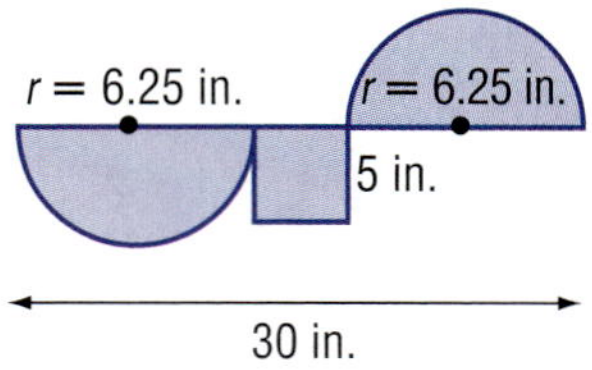

8.

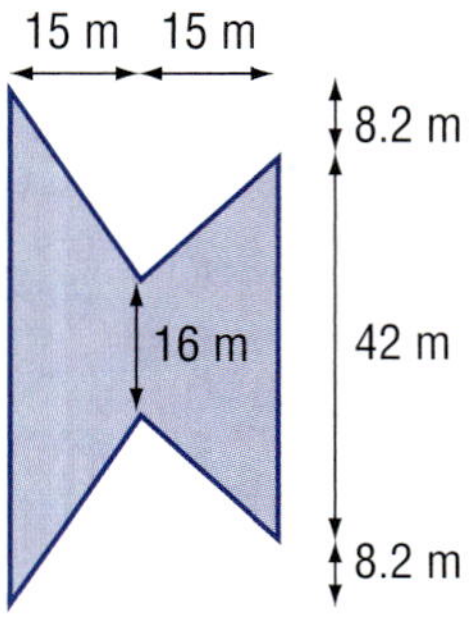

9.

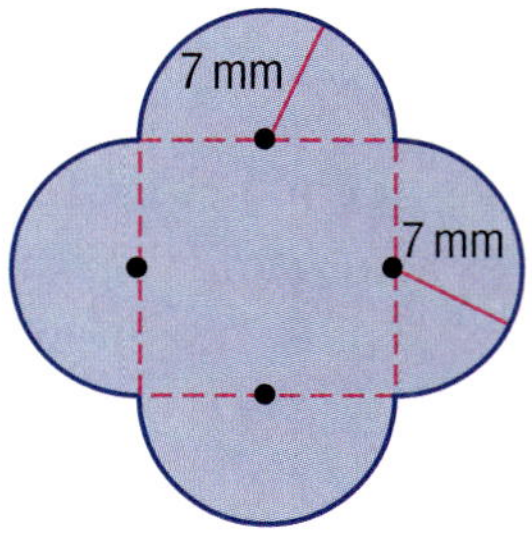

Lesson 12-7

Pages 641–644

For each figure, identify the shape of the base(s). Then classify the figure.

1.

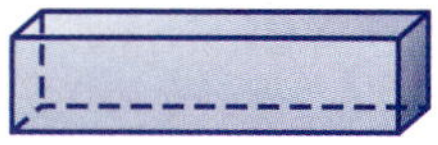

2.

3.

4.

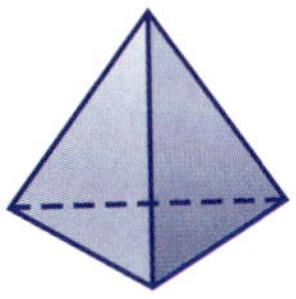

5.

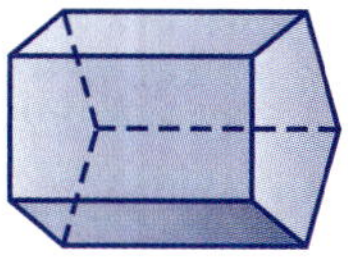

6.

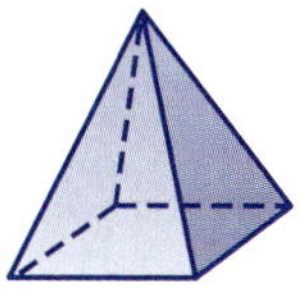

7. **SOUP** Classify the shape of a soup can as a three-dimensional figure.
8. **APPLIANCES** Classify the shape of a microwave oven as a three-dimensional figure.

Lesson 12-8

Pages 646–650

Draw a top, a side, and a front view of each solid.

1. 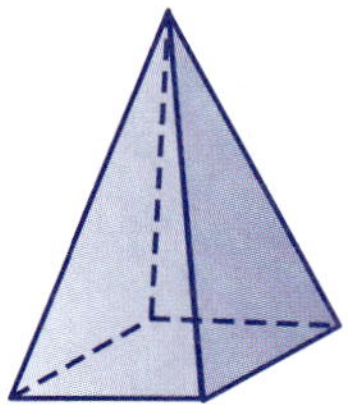

2. 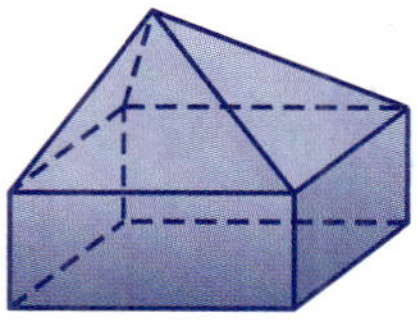

3. 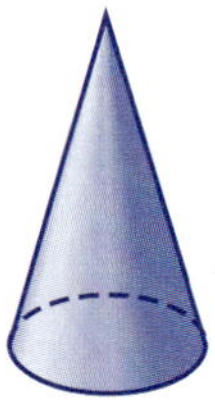

Draw each solid using the top, side, and front views shown. Use isometric dot paper.

4. 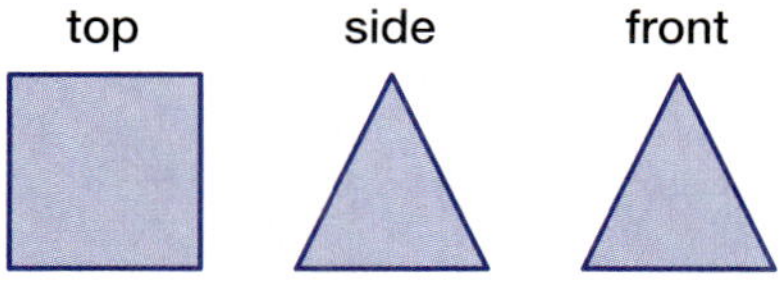

5. 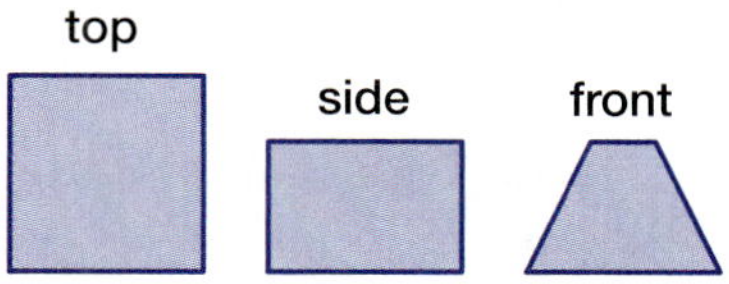

Lesson 12-9

Pages 651–656

Find the volume of each prism. Round to the nearest tenth if necessary.

1. 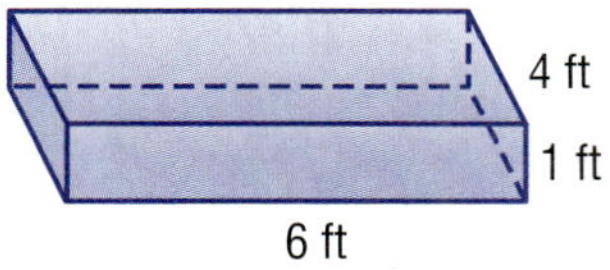

2. 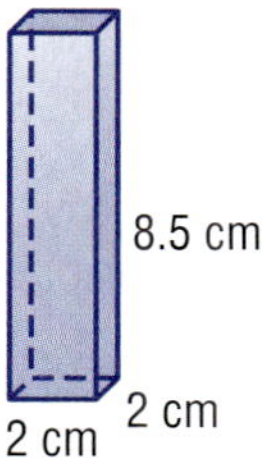

3. 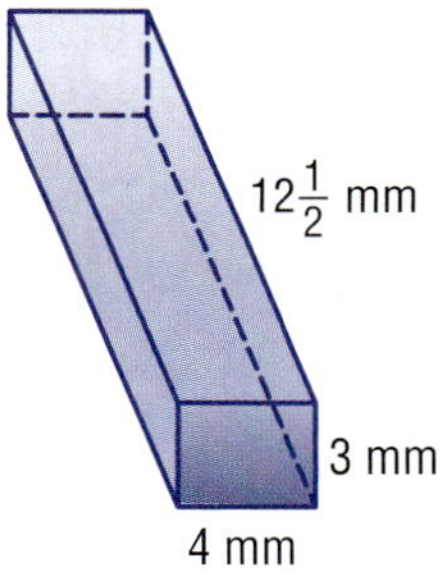

4. 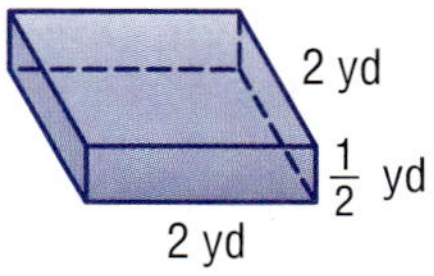

5. 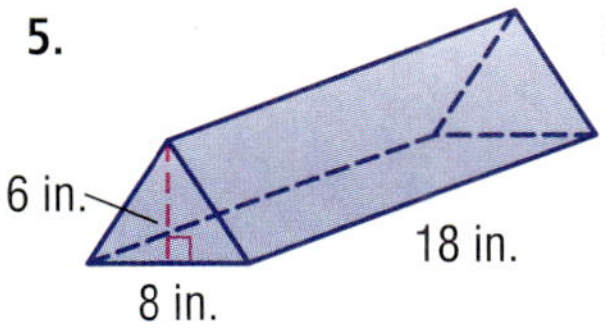

6. 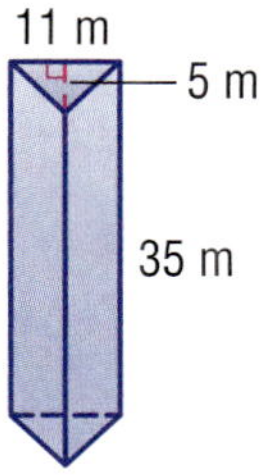

7. 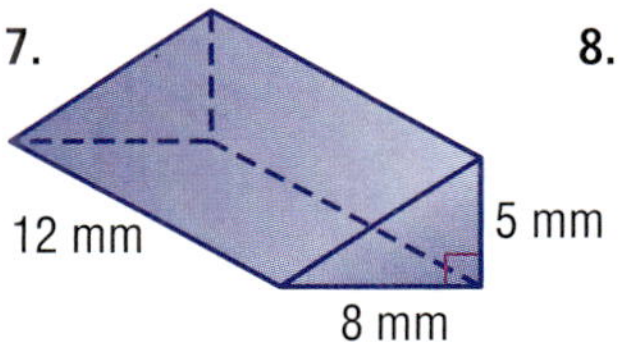

8. 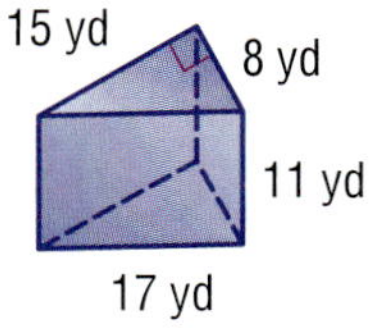

Find the volume of each rectangular prism. Round to the nearest tenth if necessary.

9. length = 3 ft
width = 10 ft
height = 2 ft

10. length = 18 cm
width = 23 cm
height = 15 cm

11. length = 25 mm
width = 32 mm
height = 10 mm

12. length = 1.5 in.
width = 3 in.
height = 6 in.

13. length = 4.5 cm
width = 6.75 cm
height = 2 cm

14. length = 16 mm
width = 0.7 mm
height = 12 mm

15. length = $3\frac{1}{2}$ ft
width = 10 ft
height = 6 ft

16. length = $5\frac{1}{2}$ in.
width = 12 in.
height = $3\frac{3}{8}$ in.

17. Find the volume of a rectangular prism with a length of 3 yards, a width of 5 feet, and a height of 12 feet.

18. Find the volume of a triangular prism whose base has an area of 416 square feet and whose height is 22 feet.

Lesson 12-10

Pages 657–661

Find the volume of each cylinder. Round to the nearest tenth.

1. 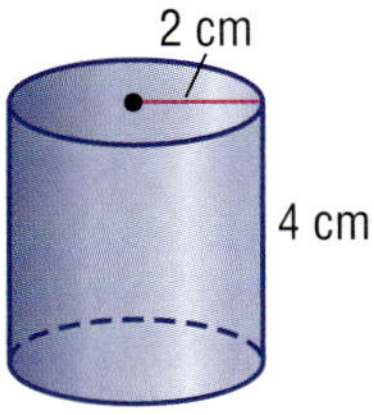

2. 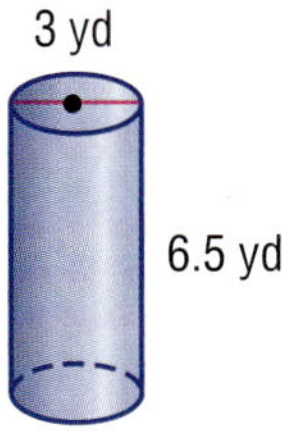

3. 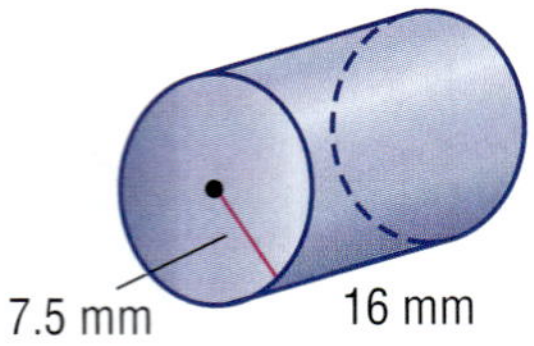

4. 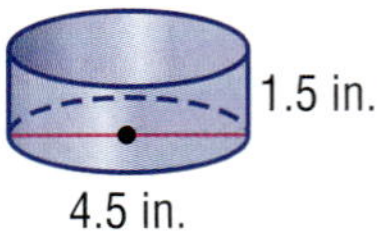

5. radius = 6 in.
height = 3 in.
6. radius = 8 ft
height = 10 ft
7. radius = 6 km
height = 12 km
8. radius = 8.5 cm
height = 3 cm
9. diameter = 16 yd
height = 4.5 yd
10. diameter = 3.5 mm
height = 2.5 mm
11. diameter = 12 m
height = 4.75 m
12. diameter = $\frac{5}{8}$ in.
height = 4 in.
13. diameter = 100 ft
height = 35 ft
14. radius = 40.5 m
height = 65.1 m
15. radius = 0.5 cm
height = 1.6 cm
16. diameter = $8\frac{3}{4}$ in.
height = $5\frac{1}{2}$ in.
17. Find the volume of a cylinder whose diameter is 6 inches and height is 2 feet. Round to the nearest tenth.
18. How tall is a cylinder that has a volume of 2,123 cubic meters and a radius of 13 meters? Round to the nearest tenth.
19. A cylinder has a volume of 310.2 cubic yards and a radius of 2.9 yards. What is the height of the cylinder? Round to the nearest tenth.
20. Find the height of a cylinder whose diameter is 25 centimeters and volume is 8,838 cubic centimeters. Round to the nearest tenth.

Lesson 13-1

Pages 674–677

Estimate each square root to the nearest whole number.

1. $\sqrt{27}$
2. $\sqrt{112}$
3. $\sqrt{249}$
4. $\sqrt{88}$
5. $\sqrt{1,500}$
6. $\sqrt{612}$
7. $\sqrt{340}$
8. $\sqrt{495}$
9. $\sqrt{264}$
10. $\sqrt{350}$
11. $\sqrt{834}$
12. $\sqrt{3,700}$
13. $\sqrt{298}$
14. $\sqrt{101}$
15. $\sqrt{800}$

Use a calculator to find each square root to the nearest tenth.

16. $\sqrt{58}$
17. $\sqrt{750}$
18. $\sqrt{1,200}$
19. $\sqrt{1,000}$
20. $\sqrt{5,900}$
21. $\sqrt{999}$
22. $\sqrt{374}$
23. $\sqrt{512}$
24. $\sqrt{3,750}$
25. $\sqrt{255}$
26. $\sqrt{83}$
27. $\sqrt{845}$
28. $\sqrt{200}$
29. $\sqrt{500}$
30. $\sqrt{10,001}$
31. **ALGEBRA** Evaluate $\sqrt{a - b}$ to the nearest tenth if $a = 16$ and $b = 4$.
32. **ALGEBRA** Estimate the value of $\sqrt{x + y}$ to the nearest whole number if $x = 64$ and $y = 25$.

Lesson 13-2

Pages 678–684

Find the missing measure of each triangle. Round to the nearest tenth if necessary.

1.
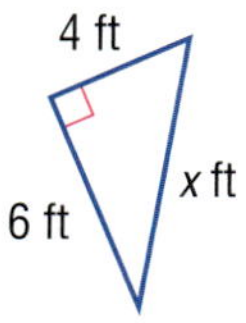

2.
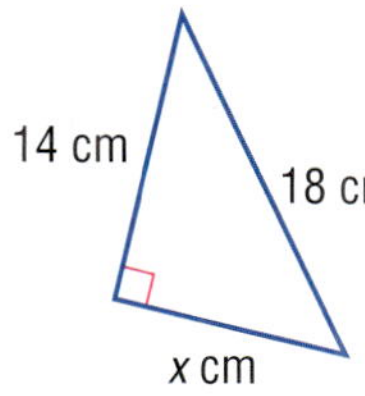

3.
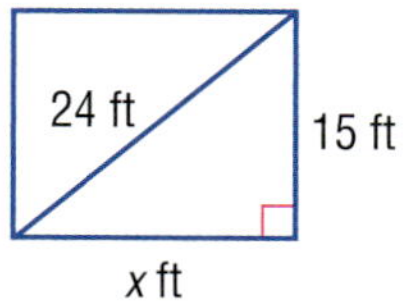

4. $a = 12$ cm, $b = 25$ cm
5. $a = 5$ yd, $c = 10$ yd
6. $b = 12$ mi, $c = 20$ mi
7. $a = 15$ yd, $b = 24$ yd
8. $a = 4$ m, $c = 12$ m
9. $a = 8$ mm, $b = 11$ mm
10. $a = 1$ mi, $c = 3$ mi
11. $a = 5$ yd, $b = 8$ yd
12. $b = 7$ in., $c = 19$ in.
13. $a = 50$ km, $c = 75$ km
14. $b = 82$ ft, $c = 100$ ft
15. $a = 100$ m, $b = 200$ m

Lesson 13-3

Pages 685–686

Use the *make a model* strategy to solve each problem.

1. **ARCHITECTURE** An architect is designing a large skyscraper for a local firm. The skyscraper is to be 1,200 feet tall, 500 feet long, and 400 feet wide. If his model has a scale of 80 feet = 1 inch, find the volume of the model.

2. **STACKING BOXES** Box A has twice the volume of Box B. Box B has a height of 10 centimeters and a length of 5 centimeters. Box A has a width of 20 centimeters, a length of 10 centimeters, and a height of 5 centimeters. What is the width of Box B?

3. **TRAVEL** On Monday, Mara drove 400 miles as part of her journey to see her sister. She drove 60% of this distance on Tuesday. If the distance she drove on Tuesday represents one third of her total journey, how many more miles does she still need to drive?

4. **PIZZA** On Monday, there was a whole pizza in the refrigerator. On Tuesday, Enrico ate $\frac{1}{3}$ of the pizza. On Wednesday, he ate $\frac{1}{3}$ of what was left. On Thursday, he ate $\frac{1}{2}$ of what remained. What fractional part of the pizza is left?

5. **GARDENS** Mr. Blackwell has a circular garden in his backyard. He wants to build a curved brick pathway around the entire garden. The garden has a radius of 18 feet. The distance from the center of the garden to the outside edge of the brick pathway will be 21.5 feet. Find the area of the brick pathway. Round to the nearest tenth.

Lesson 13-4

Pages 688–694

Find the surface area of each rectangular prism. Round to the nearest tenth if necessary.

1. 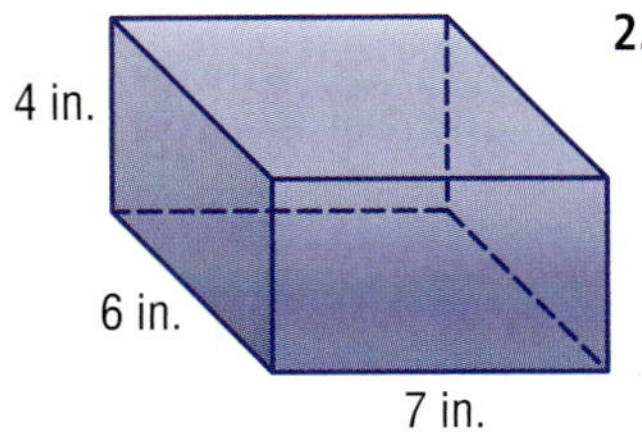

2. 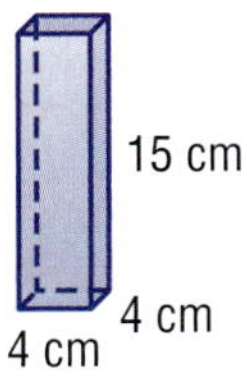

3. 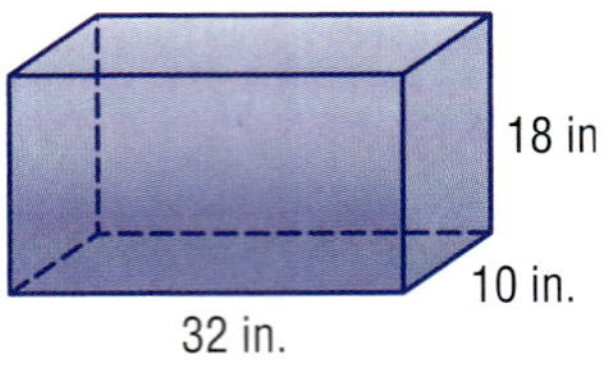

4. 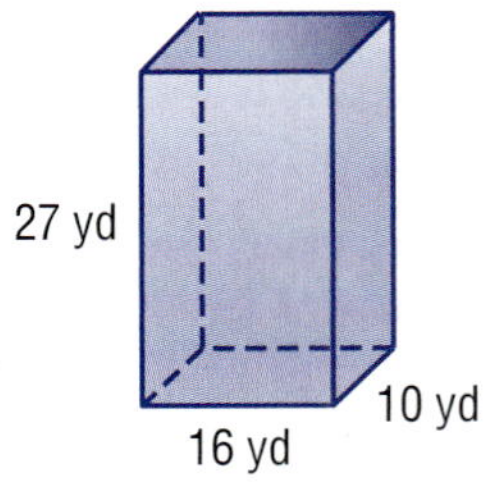

5. length = 10 m
width = 6 m
height = 7 m

6. length = 20 mm
width = 15 mm
height = 25 mm

7. length = 16 ft
width = 20 ft
height = 12 ft

8. length = 52 cm
width = 48 cm
height = 45 cm

9. length = 8 ft
width = 6.5 ft
height = 7 ft

10. length = 9.4 m
width = 2 m
height = 5.2 m

11. length = 20.4 cm
width = 15.5 cm
height = 8.8 cm

12. length = 8.5 mi
width = 3 mi
height = 5.8 mi

13. length = $7\frac{1}{4}$ ft
width = 5 ft
height = $6\frac{1}{2}$ ft

14. length = $15\frac{2}{3}$ yd
width = $7\frac{1}{3}$ yd
height = 9 yd

15. length = $4\frac{1}{2}$ in.
width = 10 in.
height = $8\frac{3}{4}$ in.

16. length = 12.2 mm
width = 7.4 mm
height = 7.4 mm

17. Find the surface area of an open-top box with a length of 18 yards, a width of 11 yards, and a height of 14 yards.

18. Find the surface area of a rectangular prism with a length of 1 yard, a width of 7 feet, and a height of 2 yards.

Lesson 13-5

Pages 696–699

Find the surface area of each cylinder. Round to the nearest tenth.

1. 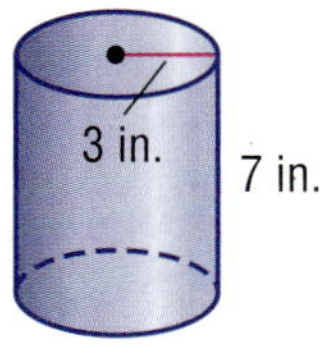

2. 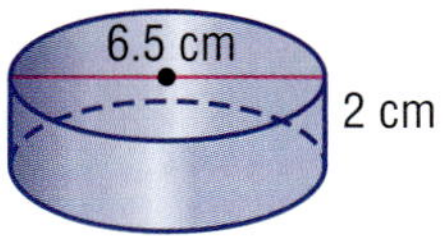

3. 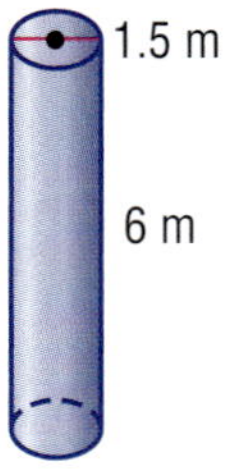

4. 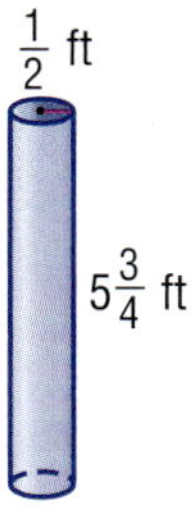

5. height = 6 cm
radius = 3.5 cm

6. height = 16.5 mm
diameter = 18 mm

7. height = 22 yd
radius = 10.5 yd

8. height = 6 ft
radius = 18.5 ft

9. height = 10.2 mi
diameter = 4 mi

10. height = 8.6 cm
diameter = 8.2 cm

11. height = 5.8 km
diameter = 3.6 km

12. height = 32.7 m
radius = 21.5 m

13. height = $2\frac{2}{3}$ yd
diameter = 6 yd

14. height = $12\frac{3}{4}$ ft
radius = $7\frac{1}{4}$ ft

15. height = $5\frac{1}{5}$ mi
radius = $18\frac{1}{3}$ mi

16. height = $5\frac{1}{2}$ in.
diameter = 3 in.

Mixed Problem Solving

Chapter 1 Introduction to Algebra and Functions

Pages 22–77

1. **HISTORY** In 1932, Amelia Earhart flew 2,026 miles in 14 hours 56 minutes. To the nearest mile, what was her speed in miles per minute? (Lesson 1-1)

2. **LIGHT** The speed of light is about 67^3 kilometers per second. How many kilometers per second is this? (Lesson 1-2)

3. **FARMING** Find the length of one side of a square field whose area is 180,625 square feet. (Lesson 1-3)

4. **SALES** A department store is having a back-to-school sale. The table shows the prices of three popular items.

Item	Price ($)
Jeans	37.99
Sweatshirt	19.88
Polo Shirt	22.50

Latonia wants to buy 2 pairs of jeans, 3 sweatshirts, and 1 polo shirt. Write and evaluate a numerical expression that represents the total cost of all three items. (Lesson 1-4)

5. **MONEY** Mateo has $2.58 in coins. If he has quarters, dimes, nickels, and pennies, how many of each coin does he have? Use the *guess and check* strategy. (Lesson 1-5)

6. **FITNESS** You can estimate how fast you walk in miles per hour by evaluating the expression $\frac{n}{30}$, where n is the number of steps you take in one minute. Find your speed in miles per hour if you take 96 steps in one minute. (Lesson 1-6)

7. **BASEBALL** Last year, Scott attended 13 Minnesota Twins baseball games. This year, he attended 24. Solve $13 + n = 24$ to find how many more games he attended this year than last. (Lesson 1-7)

8. **HOT AIR BALLOONS** Miyoki paid $140 for a four-hour hot air balloon ride over the Bridger Mountains. Solve $4h = 140$ to find the cost per hour of the ride. (Lesson 1-7)

ENTERTAINMENT For Exercises 9 and 10, use the following information.
The five members of the Wolff family went to an amusement park. They each purchased an all-day ride pass and a water park pass, as shown below. (Lesson 1-8)

Item	Price ($)
All-day Ride Pass	14.95
Water Park Pass	6.50

9. Use the Distributive Property to write two different expressions that represent the total cost for the family.

10. Find the total cost of the passes.

11. **NUMBER THEORY** Numbers that can be represented by a square arrangement of dots are called *square numbers*. The first four square numbers are shown below. (Lesson 1-9)

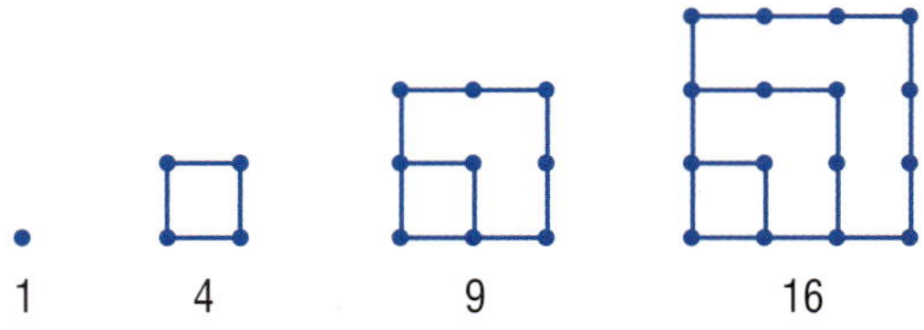

Write a sequence formed by the first eight square numbers.

12. **TIME** Copy and complete the function table showing how many days y there are in various number of weeks x. Then identify the domain and range. (Lesson 1-10)

x	$7x$	y
1		
2		
3		
4		

1. **AIR CONDITIONING** Jacob turned on the air conditioning and the temperature in his apartment decreased 8 degrees. Write an integer to represent the change in temperature. (Lesson 2-1)

EARTH SCIENCE For Exercises 2 and 3, use the table below. It describes the deepest land depressions in the world in feet below sea level.

Depth (ft)			
220	436	511	282
383	505	235	230

Source: *The Top 10 Everything*

2. Write an integer to represent each depth. (Lesson 2-1)
3. Order the integers from greatest depth to least depth. (Lesson 2-2)

ENTERTAINMENT For Exercises 4–8, use the diagram below. It shows the locations of several rides at the Outlook Amusement Park. (Lesson 2-3)

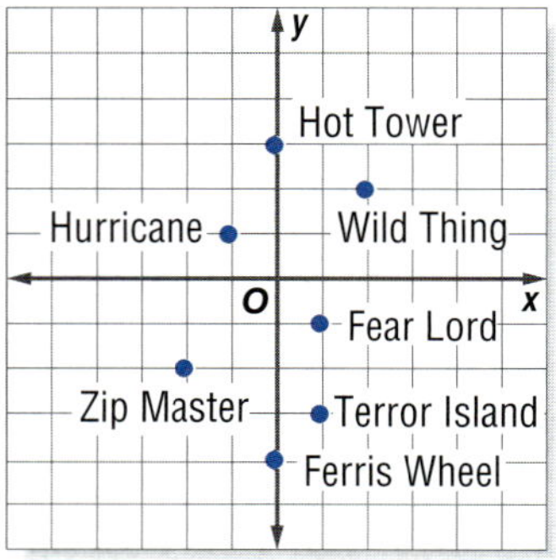

4. Which ride(s) is located in quadrant III?
5. Which ride(s) is located on the y-axis? Name the coordinates.
6. Which ride(s) has coordinates in which the x- coordinates and y-coordinates are equal?
7. In which quadrant is the Hurricane located?
8. A new ride is built with a location on the x-axis and 5 units left of the origin. Name the coordinates of this point.

9. **CAVERNS** Adriana is 52 feet underground touring the Lewis and Clark Caverns. She climbs a ladder up 15 feet. What is her new location? (Lesson 2-4)

10. **RECORDS** The lowest temperature recorded in Verkhoyansk, Russia, was about −90°F. The highest temperature was about 99°F. What is the difference between these temperatures? (Lesson 2-5)

11. **EARTH SCIENCE** The highest and lowest points in California are shown in the table. What is the difference in elevations? (Lesson 2-5)

Location	Elevation
Mount Whitney	14,494 ft above sea level
Death Valley	282 ft below sea level

Source: *The World Almanac of the U.S.A.*

12. **SPORTS** Every 12 times at bat, Simon hits the ball 3 times. About how many times will he hit the ball after 20 times at bat? 40? 84? Use the *look for a pattern* strategy. (Lesson 2-6)

Times at Bat	Number of Hits
12	3
20	■
40	■
84	■

13. **RIDES** A glider ride over the Crazy Mountains has a maximum altitude of 12,000 feet. It is descending at a rate of about 300 feet per minute. At what altitude will the glider be 20 minutes later? (Lesson 2-7)

14. **TEMPERATURE** A temperature of −89°C was recorded in Antarctica. Use the expression $\frac{9C}{5} + 32$, where C is the temperature in degrees Celsius, to find the temperature in degrees Fahrenheit. (Lesson 2-8)

Mixed Problem Solving

Chapter 3 Applying Decimals

Pages 126–173

1. **TIME** The average one-way commute time for workers in Amarillo, Texas was 18.4 minutes in 2000 and 17.3 minutes in 1990. About how many more hours would a worker spend commuting in 2000 than in 1990 if they worked 290 days a year? (Lesson 3-1)

2. **SPORTS** Refer to the table which gives the highest and lowest payrolls in the National League of Baseball in 2005.

Team	Total Payroll (millions of dollars)
New York Mets	101.3
Pittsburgh Pirates	38.1

About how many times greater is New York's payroll than Pittsburgh's? (Lesson 3-1)

3. **MONEY** Daphne owns 6 shares in a company whose stock is worth $41.85 a share. How much is her stock worth? (Lesson 3-2)

4. **CYCLING** Jimmy cycled for 5.5 hours at an average speed of 15.25 miles per hour. How many miles did he cycle? (Lesson 3-2)

5. **GEOGRAPHY** The Mississippi River is 2.348 thousand miles long. Write the distance in standard notation. (Lesson 3-3)

6. **SPACE** The Sun is 93 million miles from the earth. How far is this in standard notation? (Lesson 3-3)

7. **POPULATION** In 2004, the population of California was estimated to be about 35.89 million people. Write this number in standard notation. (Lesson 3-3)

8. **WEATHER** The United States record (from 1970–2000) for average rainfall per year is held by the town of Quillayute, Washington. The average rainfall is 101.72 inches per year. Find the average daily rainfall. (1 year = 365 days) Round to the nearest hundredth, if necessary. (Lesson 3-4)

9. **MONEY** Bob paid $20.79 for gas which cost $2.20 per gallon. How many gallons of gasoline did this buy? Round to the nearest hundredth if necessary. (Lesson 3-4)

10. **EARNINGS** Ernesto earned $21.25 on his first paycheck. He worked 4.25 hours. How much money does Ernesto make per hour? Use the *choose the method of computation* strategy. (Lesson 3-5)

11. **TRAVEL** Darren drove an average of 58 miles per hour on Monday and an average of 53 miles per hour on Tuesday. If he drove for 3.5 hours on Monday and 4.75 hours on Tuesday, how many more miles did he drive on Tuesday than on Monday? Choose the best method of computation. (Lesson 3-5)

12. **WATER** A bottle contains 1,065 milliliters of water. How many liters of water does the bottle hold? (Lesson 3-6)

13. **BUILDINGS** A skyscraper is 0.484 kilometers tall. What is the height of the skyscraper in meters? (Lesson 3-6)

14. **BIRDS** The world's smallest bird, the bee hummingbird, has a mass of only about 1.6 grams. How many milligrams is this? (Lesson 3-6)

15. **BRIDGES** The Akashi Kaikyo bridge in Japan is 2,003 meters long. What is the length of the bridge in kilometers? (Lesson 3-6)

16. **SPACE** The Andromeda Spiral is a galaxy 2,200,000 light years from Earth. Write this distance in scientific notation. (Lesson 3-7)

17. **SPACE** Pluto is approximately 3.6 billion miles from the Sun. Write this number in scientific notation. (Lesson 3-7)

18. **DEBT** The national debt of the United States in January 2006 was approximately $8,160,000,000,000. Write this amount in scientific notation. (Lesson 3-7)

1. **TOURISM** The Statue of Liberty in New York, New York, and the Eiffel Tower in Paris, France, were designed by the same person. The Statue of Liberty is 152 feet tall. It is 732 feet shorter than the Eiffel Tower, x. Write an equation that models this situation. (Lesson 4-1)

ELECTIONS For Exercises 2 and 3, use the table below and the following information. New York has one more electoral vote than Texas. Pennsylvania has 9 fewer electoral votes than Texas. (Lesson 4-2)

Number of Electoral Votes 2000	
California	54
New York	33
Texas	
Florida	25
Pennsylvania	23

2. Write two different equations to find the number of electoral votes in Texas, n.
3. Find the number of electoral votes

4. **ROLLER COASTERS** The track length of a popular roller coaster is 5,106 feet. The roller coaster has an average speed of about 2,000 feet per minute. At that speed, how long will it take to travel its length of 5,106 feet? Use the formula $d = rt$. (Lesson 4-3)

5. **NUMBERS** A number is halved. Then three is subtracted from the quotient, and 5 is multiplied by the difference. Finally, 1 is added to the product. If the ending number is 26, what was the beginning number? Use the *work backward* strategy. (Lesson 4-4)

6. **BUSINESS** Carla's Catering charges a \$25 fee to serve 15 or fewer people. In addition to that fee, they charge \$10 per appetizer. You are having a party for 12 people and can spend a total of \$85. How many appetizers can you order from Carla's Catering? (Lesson 4-5)

CHESS For Exercises 7–10, use the chess board below. (Lesson 4-6)

12 in.

12 in.

7. What is the perimeter of the chess board?
8. What is the area of the chess board?
9. What is the area of each small square?
10. A travel chess board has half the length and width of the board shown. What is the perimeter and area?

11. **FENCING** Mr. Hernandez will build a fence to enclose a rectangular yard for his horse. If the area of the yard to be enclosed is 1,944 square feet, and the length of the yard is 54 feet, how much fencing is needed? (Lesson 4-6)

12. **GEOMETRY** The formula for the perimeter of a square is $P = 4s$, where P is the perimeter and s is the length of a side. Graph the equation. (Lesson 4-7)

AGES For Exercises 13–16, use the table below. It shows how Jared's age and his sister Emily's age are related. (Lesson 4-7)

Jared's age (yr)	1	2	3	4	5
Emily's age (yr)	7	8	9	10	11

13. Write a verbal expression to describe how the ages are related.
14. Write an equation for the verbal expression. Let x represent Jared's age and y represent Emily's age.
15. Predict how old Emily will be when Jared is 10 years old.
16. Graph the equation.

LAND **For Exercises 1–3, use the information below.**
A section of land is one mile long and one mile wide. (Lesson 5-1)

1. Write the prime factorization of 5,280.
2. Find the area of the section of land in square feet. (*Hint*: 1 mile = 5,280 feet)
3. Write the prime factorization of the area that you found in Exercise 2.

DECORATIONS **For Exercises 4 and 5, use the information below.**
Benito is cutting streamers from crepe paper for a party. He has a red roll of crepe paper 144 inches long, a white roll 192 inches long, and a blue roll 360 inches long. (Lesson 5-2)

4. If he wants to have all colors of streamers the same length, what is the longest length that he can cut?
5. If he cuts the longest possible length, how many streamers can he cut?

6. **PRIZES** By reaching into a bag that has the letters A, B, and C, George will select three winners in order. How many possible combinations are there of the people who could win? Use the *make an organized list* strategy. (Lesson 5-3)

OLYMPICS **For Exercises 7 and 8, refer to the table below. It shows the medals won by the top three countries in the 2000 Summer Olympics.**

Country	Medals		
	Gold	Silver	Bronze
United States	40	24	33
Russia	32	28	28
China	28	16	15

Source: *The World Almanac*

7. Write the number of gold medals that Russia won as a fraction of the total number that Russia won in simplest form. (Lesson 5-4)
8. Write the fraction that you wrote in Exercise 7 as a decimal. (Lesson 5-5)

9. **SPORTS** At Belgrade Intermediate School, 75 out of every 100 students participate in sports. What percent of students do *not* participate in sports? (Lesson 5-6)

ADVERTISING **For Exercises 10–13, use the table below. It shows the results of a survey in which teens were asked which types of advertising they pay attention to.**

Type of Advertising	Percent of Teens
Television	80%
Magazine	62%
Product in a Movie	48%
Ad in an E-mail	24%

Source: *E-Poll*

Write each percent as a fraction in simplest form. (Lesson 5-6)

10. television
11. magazine
12. product in a movie
13. ad in an e-mail

GEOMETRY **For Exercises 14–16, refer to the grid at the right.** (Lesson 5-7)

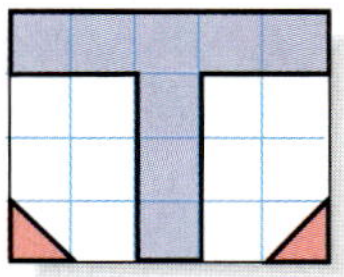

14. Write a decimal and a percent to represent the "T" shaded area.
15. Write a decimal and a percent to represent the area shaded pink.
16. What percent of the grid is *not* shaded?

17. **FLOWERS** Roses can be ordered in bunches of 6 and carnations in bunches of 15. If Ingrid wants to have the same number of roses as carnations for parent night, what is the least number of each flower that she must order? (Lesson 5-8)

18. **WATER** The table at the right shows the fraction of each state that is water. Order the states from least to greatest fraction of water. (Lesson 5-9)

What Part is Water?	
State	Fraction
Alaska	$\frac{3}{41}$
Michigan	$\frac{40}{97}$
Wisconsin	$\frac{1}{6}$

Source: *The World Almanac of the U.S.A*

1. **MEALS** A box of instant potatoes contains 20 cups of flakes. A family-sized bowl of potatoes uses $3\frac{2}{3}$ cups of the flakes. Estimate how many family-sized bowls can be made from one box. (Lesson 6-1)

2. **BAKING** A recipe calls for $2\frac{1}{3}$ cups of flour. Theo wants to make six batches of this recipe. About how much flour should he have available to use? (Lesson 6-1)

3. **CRAFTS** Kyle bought $\frac{5}{6}$ yard of fabric to make a craft item. He used $\frac{3}{4}$ yard in making the item. How much fabric was left over? (Lesson 6-2)

RAINFALL For Exercises 4 and 5, use the table. It shows the average annual precipitation for three of the driest locations on Earth. (Lesson 6-2)

Location	Precipitation (in.)
Arica, Chile	$\frac{3}{100}$
Iquique, Chile	$\frac{1}{5}$
Callao, Peru	$\frac{12}{25}$

Source: *The Top 10 Everything*

4. How much more rain does Iquique get per year than Arica?

5. How much more annual rain does Callao get than Iquique?

6. **INTERIOR DESIGN** A living room wall is $16\frac{1}{4}$ feet long. A window runs from the floor to the ceiling and has a length along the floor of $6\frac{3}{8}$ feet. How long is the wall without the window? (Lesson 6-3)

7. **HEALTH** The human body is about $\frac{7}{10}$ water. About how much would a person weigh if they had 70 pounds of water weight? Use the *eliminate possibilities* strategy. (Lesson 6-4)

   A 200 pounds
   B 100 pounds
   C 150 pounds
   D 70 pounds

8. **FOOD** The table below shows the carry-out menu for a Benito's Restaurant.

Take-out	Price ($)
Main Dish	5.00
Side Dishes	1.00
Dessert	2.00

A family of four spent $24.00 dollars for a take-home meal. What combination is possible for their meal? Use the *eliminate possibilities* strategy. (Lesson 6-4)

   F 3 main dishes and 2 side dishes
   G 4 main dishes and 3 side dishes
   H 3 main dishes, 3 side dishes, and 3 desserts
   J 4 main dishes and 4 desserts

9. **STARS** The star Sirius is about $8\frac{7}{10}$ light years from Earth. Alpha Centauri is half this distance from Earth. How far is Alpha Centauri from Earth? (Lesson 6-5)

10. **LIFE SCIENCE** Use the table below. It shows the average growth per month of hair and fingernails. Solve $3 = \frac{1}{2}t$ to find how long it takes hair to grow 3 inches. (Lesson 6-6)

Average Monthly Growth	
Hair	$\frac{1}{2}$ in.
Fingernails	$\frac{2}{25}$ in.

11. **SEWING** Jocelyn has nine yards of fabric to make table napkins for a senior citizens' center. She needs $\frac{3}{8}$ yard for each napkin. Use $\frac{3}{8}c = 9$ to find the number of napkins that she can make with this amount of fabric. (Lesson 6-6)

12. **WHALES** During the first year, a baby whale gains about $27\frac{3}{5}$ tons. What is the average weight gain per month? (Lesson 6-7)

1. **SCHOOLS** In a recent year, Oregon had 924 public elementary schools and 264 public high schools. Write a ratio in simplest form comparing the number of public high schools to elementary schools. (Lesson 7-1)

2. **MONTHS** Write a ratio in simplest form comparing the number of months that begin with the letter J to the total number of months in a year. (Lesson 7-1)

3. **EXERCISE** A person jumps rope 14 times in 10 seconds. What is the unit rate in jumps per second? (Lesson 7-2)

4. **FOOD** A 16-ounce box of cereal costs $3.95. Find the unit price to the nearest cent. (Lesson 7-2)

5. **LIFE SCIENCE** An adult has about 5 quarts of blood. If a person donates 1 pint of blood, how many pints are left? (Lesson 7-3)

6. **COFFEE** In Switzerland, the average amount of coffee consumed per year is 1,089 cups per person. How many pints is this? (Lesson 7-3)

7. **PHOTOGRAPHS** Mandy is enlarging a photograph that is 3 inches wide and 4.5 inches long. If she wants the width of the enlargement to be 10 inches, what will be the length? (Lesson 7-4)

8. **GEOMETRY** If the ratio of length to width of a rectangle is about 1.6 to 1, then the rectangle is said to be a *golden rectangle*. Determine whether either figure below is golden rectangle. (Lesson 7-4)

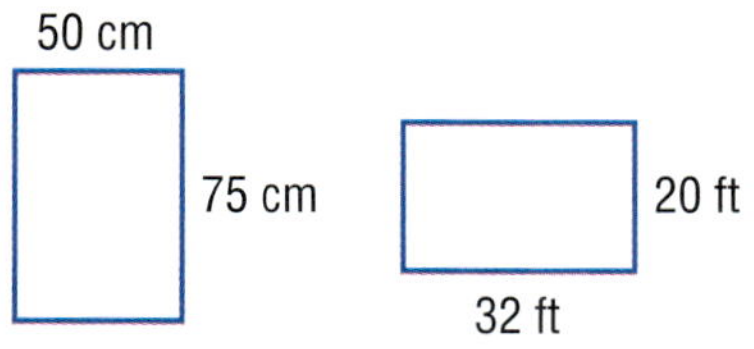

9. **TILES** A kitchen is 10 feet long and 8 feet wide. If kitchen floor tiles are $2\frac{1}{2}$ inches by 3 inches, how many tiles are needed for the kitchen? Use the *draw a diagram* strategy. (Lesson 7-5)

10. **MAPS** Washington, D.C., and Baltimore, Maryland, are $2\frac{7}{8}$ inches apart on a map. If the scale is $\frac{1}{2}$ inch : 6 miles, what is the actual distance between the cities? (Lesson 7-6)

11. **MODELS** Ian is making a miniature bed for his daughter's doll house. The actual bed is $6\frac{3}{4}$ feet long. If he uses the scale $\frac{1}{2}$ inch $= 1\frac{1}{2}$ feet, what will be the length of the miniature bed? (Lesson 7-6)

12. **POPULATION** According to the U.S. Census Bureau, 6.6% of all people living in Florida are 10–14 years old. What fraction is this? Write in simplest form. (Lesson 7-7)

13. **INTERNET** In 2001, 50.5% of U.S. households had access to the Internet. Write this percent as a fraction in simplest form. (Lesson 7-7)

COINS For Exercises 14 and 15, use the table below. It shows the fraction of a quarter that is made up of the metals nickel and copper. Write each fraction as a percent. Round to the nearest hundredth if necessary. (Lesson 7-7)

Metal	Fraction of Quarter
Nickel	$\frac{1}{12}$
Copper	$\frac{11}{12}$

14. nickel

15. copper

16. **FARMS** Approximately 0.0009 of the land in Montana is farmland. Write this as a percent. (Lesson 7-8)

17. **POPULATION** In 2003, 0.1% of the U.S. population was of Hawaiian descent. Write this percent as a fraction in simplest form. (Lesson 7-8)

18. **HEIGHT** Jackson is 1.4 times as tall as his sister. Write this decimal as a percent. (Lesson 7-8)

1. **SEEDS** A packet of beans guarantees that 95% of its 200 seeds will germinate. How many seeds are expected to germinate? (Lesson 8-1)

2. **SKIS** Toshiro spent $520 on new twin-tip skis. This was 40% of the money he earned at his summer job. How much did he earn at his summer job? (Lesson 8-2)

3. **GEOGRAPHY** In Washington, about 5.7% of the total area is water. If the total area of Washington is 70,637 square miles, estimate the number of square miles of water by using 10%. (Lesson 8-3)

4. **DVDs** A store has 1,504 DVDs in stock. The store sold 19.8% of the DVDs last month. About how many DVDs did they sell last month? Use the *reasonable answers* strategy. (Lesson 8-4)

5. **GOVERNMENT** Of the 435 members in the U.S. House of Representatives, 53 are from California and 13 are from North Carolina. To the nearest whole percent, what percent of the representatives are from California? from North Carolina? (Lesson 8-5)

FOOD For Exercises 6 and 7, use the graph below. It shows the results of a survey in which people were asked how they determine how long food has been in their freezer. (Lesson 8-6)

Frozen Foods

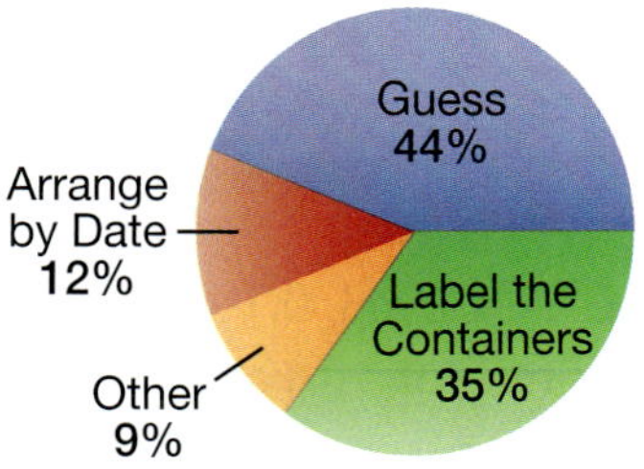

Source: Opinion Research Corporation

6. In a city of 56,000 people, predict how many of them guess to determine how long food has been in their freezer.

7. Suppose 420 people surveyed said they label their freezer containers. How many people took part in the survey?

SPORTS For Exercises 8 and 9, use the table below. It shows the number of participants ages 7 to 17 in the sports listed. (Lesson 8-7)

Sport	Number (millions)	
	1990	2000
In-line Skating	3.6	21.8
Snowboarding	1.5	4.3
Roller Hockey	1.5	2.2
Golf	23.0	26.4

Source: *National Sporting Goods Association*

8. What is the percent of change in in-line skaters 7 to 17 years old from 1990 to 2000? Round to the nearest percent and state whether the percent of change is an *increase* or *decrease*.

9. Find the percent of change from 1990 to 2000 in the number of children and teens who played roller hockey. Round to the nearest percent.

COMPUTERS For Exercises 10 and 11, use the following information.
The Wares want to buy a new computer with a regular price of $1,049. (Lesson 8-8)

10. If the store is offering a 20% discount, what will be the sale price of the computer?

11. If the sales tax on the computer is 5.25%, what will be the total cost with the discount?

BANKING For Exercises 12–15, complete the table below. The interest earned is simple interest. (Lesson 8-9)

	Principal	Rate	Time (yr)	Interest Earned
12.	$1,525.00	5%	$2\frac{1}{2}$	■
13.	$2,250.00	4%	■	$337.50
14.	■	3.5%	4	$498.40
15.	$5,080.00	■	3	$952.50

Chapter 9 Statistics: Analyzing Data

NUTRITION For Exercises 1–3, use the data below, that gives the grams of carbohydrates in fifteen different energy bars.

24, 16, 16, 16, 2, 20, 26, 14, 20, 20, 16, 16, 16, 15, 20

1. Make a line plot of the data. (Lesson 9-1)
2. What is the range of the data? (Lesson 9-1)
3. Identify any clusters, gaps, or outliers and explain what they represent. (Lesson 9-1)

BASKETBALL For Exercises 4–5, refer to the table below. It shows the number of games played by Michael Jordan each year from 1986–1987 to 2001–2002.

Number of Games Played							
82	82	81	82	82	80	78	0
17	82	82	82	0	0	0	60

Source: www.nba.com

4. Find the mean, median, and mode of the data. (Lesson 9-2)
5. Make a stem-and-leaf plot of the data. (Lesson 9-3)
6. **TOURISTS** The table shows the countries from which the most tourists in the United States came. Make a bar graph of the data. (Lesson 9-4)

Country	Visitors (millions)
Canada	14.6
Mexico	10.3
Japan	5.0
United Kingdom	4.7

Source: *Department of Commerce*

7. **NUMBERS** Where would 144 be placed on the Venn diagram shown below? (Lesson 9-5)

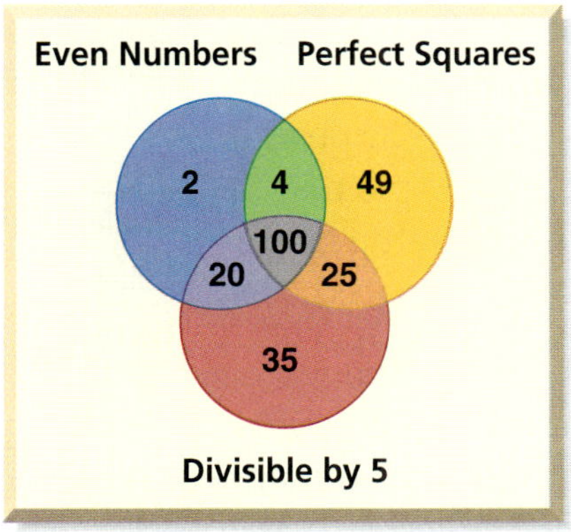

LUNCHES For Exercises 8 and 9, use the bar graph. (Lesson 9-6)

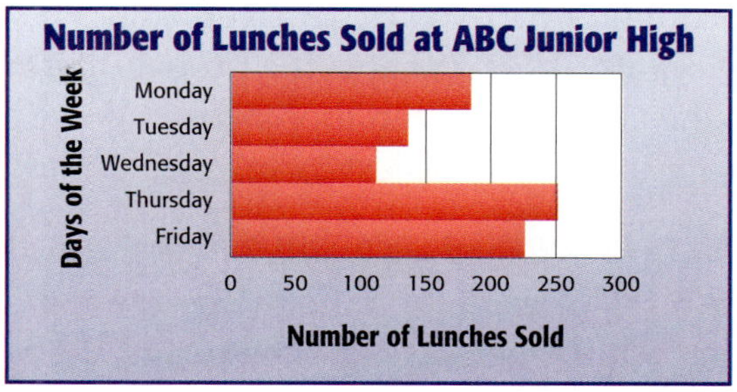

8. On what day were about twice as many lunches sold as on Wednesday?
9. The junior high sold about $\frac{3}{4}$ as many lunches Monday as on Thursday. Is this statement accurate? Explain.

SWIMMING For Exercises 10 and 11, refer to the table. It shows the winning Olympic times for the Women's 4 × 100-meter Freestyle Relay in swimming. (Lesson 9-7)

Year	Time (s)
1976	225
1980	223
1984	224
1988	221
1992	220
1996	219
2000	217

Source: *ESPN Sports Almanac*

10. Make a line graph of the data.
11. Predict the winning time in 2008.
12. Select the appropriate display for the following set of data. Then make the display. (Lesson 9-8)

Daily Rainfall	Inches
Monday	1
Tuesday	0.5
Wednesday	0.25
Thursday	1.1

13. **CELL PHONES** The table shows the number of monthly minutes Mallory used on her cell phone during the past year. She claims that the average number of minutes used is about 324. Explain how this is misleading. (Lesson 9-8)

284	322	286	359	318	294
602	278	292	267	299	285

1. **DENTISTS** A dental hygienist randomly chooses a toothbrush in a drawer containing 17 white, 12 green, and 5 blue toothbrushes. What is the probability that she chooses a green toothbrush? Write as a fraction in simplest form. (Lesson 10-1)

SURVEYS For Exercises 2 and 3, use the table below. It shows the results of a survey in which adults were asked how proud they were to be an American. (Lesson 10-1)

How Proud Are You?	
Response	**Number**
Extremely	650
Very	250
Moderately	60
Little/Not at All	30
No Opinion	10

Source: *Gallup Poll*

2. If one person participating in the survey is chosen at random, what is the probability that the person is extremely patriotic? Write as a fraction in simplest form.
3. If one person participating in the survey is chosen at random, what is the probability that he is *not* moderately patriotic? Write as a fraction in simplest form.

RANCHING For Exercises 4 and 5, use the following information.
For Roger to reach his cattle pasture, he must pass through three consecutive gates. Any of the three gates can be either *open* or *closed*. (Lesson 10-2)

4. Make a tree diagram to show all of the possible positions of the gates.
5. What is the probability that all three gates will be closed when Roger visits this pasture? Write as a fraction.
6. **SKATEBOARDS** World Sports makes skateboards with different deck patterns. You can choose one of four deck lengths and one of six types of wheels. If they have 120 different skateboards, how many deck patterns are there? (Lesson 10-3)
7. **READING** Mr. Steadman plans to read eight children's novels to his second graders during the school year. In how many ways can he arrange the books to be read? (Lesson 10-4)
8. **CRAFTS** Marina has print fabric in pink, blue, magenta, green, yellow, and tan. How many different stuffed bears can she make if each bear has only four different fabrics, and the order of the fabrics is not important? (Lesson 10-5)
9. **TRAVEL** There are four seats in Pedro's car: two in the front and two in the back. If Benny, Carlita, and Juanita are all in the car with Pedro, how many ways can they be seated in the car if Pedro is driving? Use the *act it out* strategy. (Lesson 10-6)
10. **FOOD** The graph shows the results of a survey in which 7th graders at Plentywood Middle School were asked to name their favorite fruit. If a 7th grader at the school is randomly selected, what is the probability that they chose bananas as their favorite? Write as a fraction in simplest form. (Lesson 10-7)

Favorite Fruits

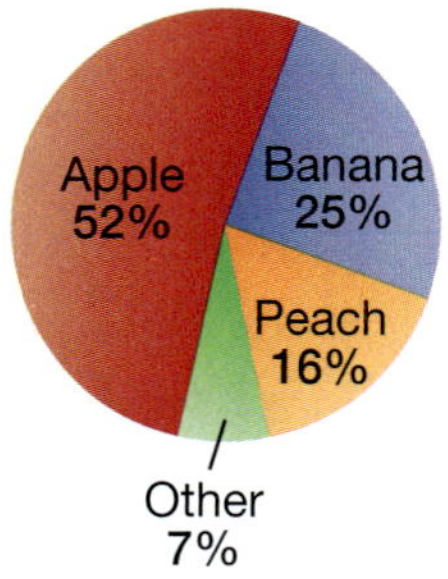

MARBLES For Exercises 11 and 12, refer to the table. (Lesson 10-8)

11. What is the probability of randomly selecting one yellow marble and then one purple marble? Assume that the first marble is replaced.

Color	Number
Red	10
Blue	6
Purple	10
Yellow	4
Green	2

12. What is the probability of randomly selecting two red marbles? Assume that the first marble is replaced.

Chapter 11 Geometry: Polygons

Pages 550–607

ART For Exercises 1 and 2, use the diagram of the Native American artifact. (Lesson 11-1)

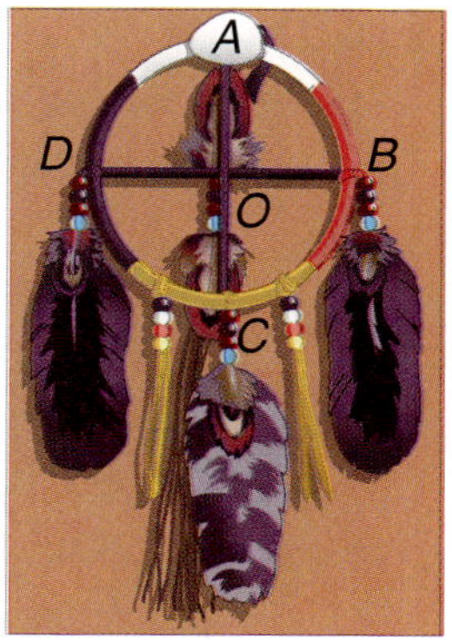

1. Name a right angle and a straight angle.
2. Suppose one side of an angle is $\overline{OA}$. Describe the location of point E so that $\angle AOE$ is acute.

TELEVISION For Exercises 3 and 4, use the survey results shown in the table below. (Lesson 11-2)

Channels Families Watch

Number	Percent
5 or fewer	30%
6–12	33%
13–25	19%
26 or more	14%

3. The fifth category in the survey is *no T.V. or no opinion*. What percent of the people surveyed were in this category?
4. Make a circle graph of the data.
5. **ART** Victor drew a right triangle so that one of the acute angles measures 55°. Without measuring, describe how Victor can determine the measure of the other acute angle in the triangle. Then find the angle measure. (Lesson 11-3)
6. **GARDENING** Mr. Sanchez has a flower bed with a length of 10 meters and a width of 5 meters. If he can only change the width of the flower bed, describe what he can do to increase the perimeter by 12 meters. Use the *logical reasoning* strategy. (Lesson 11-4)
7. **RUNNING** Four friends are entered in a race. Deirdre finishes directly ahead of Carlos. Mitchell finishes three places ahead of Tramaine and directly ahead of Deirdre. If Tramaine finishes fourth, place the runners in order from first to last. Use logical reasoning. (Lesson 11-4)

For Exercises 8 and 9, use the figure below.

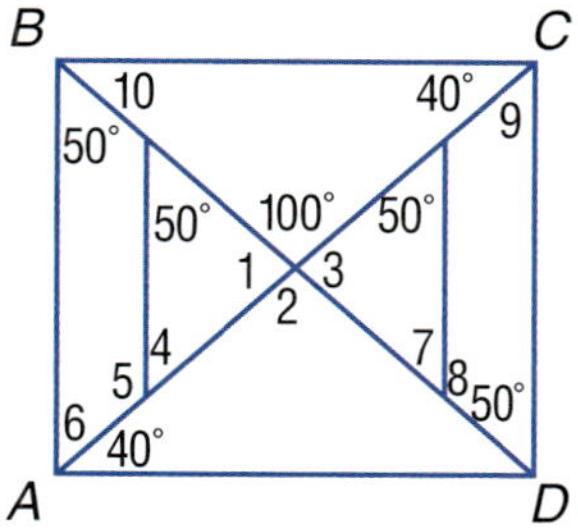

8. Find the measure of each angle numbered from 1–10. (Lesson 11-3)
9. Find the *best* name to classify quadrilateral $ABCD$. Explain your reasoning. (Lesson 11-5)
10. **CRAFTS** Priscilla makes porcelain dolls that are proportional to a real child. If Jody is $4\frac{2}{3}$ feet tall with a 23-inch waist, what should be the waist measure of a doll that is 13 inches tall? Round to the nearest inch. (Lesson 11-6)
11. **ART** Draw a tessellation using two of the polygons listed at the right. Identify the polygons and explain why the tessellation works. (Lesson 11-7)

regular triangles
quadrilaterals
pentagons
hexagons
octagons

For Exercises 12 and 13, use the quadrilateral *MOVE* shown below.

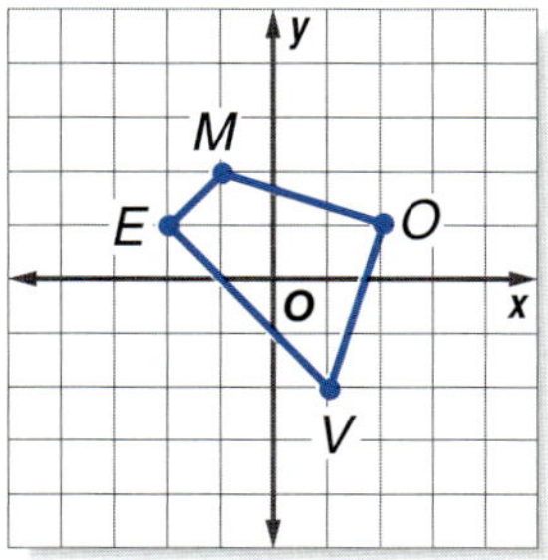

12. Describe the translation that will move M to the point at (2, −2). Then graph quadrilateral $M'O'V'E'$ using this translation. (Lesson 11-8)
13. Find the coordinates of the vertices of quadrilateral $MOVE$ after a reflection over the y-axis. Then graph the reflection. (Lesson 11-9)

1. **CRAFTS** A quilt pattern uses 25 parallelogram-shaped pieces of fabric, each with a base of 4 inches and a height of $2\frac{1}{2}$ inches. How much fabric is used to make the 25 pieces? (Lesson 12-1)

2. **FURNITURE** A corner table is in the shape of a right triangle. If the side lengths of the tabletop are 3.5 feet, 3.5 feet, and 4.9 feet, what is the area? Round to the nearest tenth if necessary. (Lesson 12-2)

3. **PUZZLES** Find the area of each small and large shaded triangle. Round to the nearest whole. (Lesson 12-2)

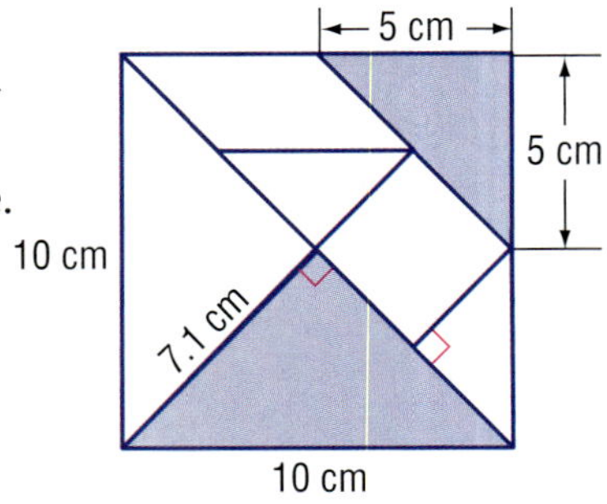

4. **EARTH SCIENCE** Earth has a diameter of 7,926 miles. Use the formula for the circumference of a circle to approximate the circumference of Earth at its equator. (Lesson 12-3)

5. **COOKIES** In New Zealand, a giant circular chocolate chip cookie was baked with a diameter of 81 feet 8 inches. To the nearest square foot, what was the area of the cookie? (Lesson 12-4)

6. **SPORTS PROFIT** A stadium seats 1,001,800 people. 22% of the tickets cost \$134.87 each. 45% of the tickets cost \$67.99 each. The remaining 33% cost only \$35.87 each. About how much revenue is made from one game which each seat is sold out? Use the *solve a simpler problem* strategy. (Lesson 12-5)

7. **LANDSCAPING** Find the area of the flower garden shown in the diagram at the right. Round to the nearest square foot. (Lesson 12-6)

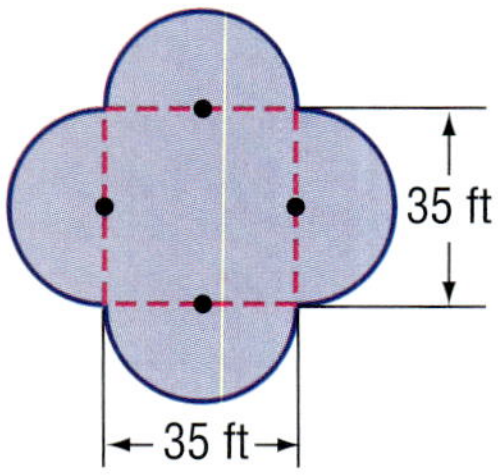

8. **GEOMETRY** A certain three-dimensional figure has four triangular faces and one square face. Classify this figure. (Lesson 12-7)

9. **RECORDS** According to the *Guinness Book of World Records*, the tallest hotel in the world is the 1,053-foot sail-shaped Burj Al Arab in Dubai, United Arab Emirates.

Draw possible sketches of the top, side, and front views of the hotel. (Lesson 12-8)

OCEANS For Exercises 10 and 11, use the following information.
The Atlantic Ocean has an area of about 33,420,000 square miles. Its average depth is 11,730 feet. (Lesson 12-9)

10. To the nearest hundredth, what is the average depth of the Atlantic Ocean in miles? (*Hint*: 1 mi = 5,280 ft)

11. What is the approximate volume of the Atlantic Ocean in cubic miles?

WATER For Exercises 12–13, use the cylinder-shaped water tank. (Lesson 12-10)

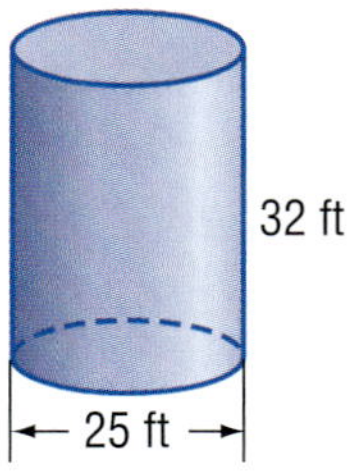

12. Find the volume of the tank. Round to the nearest cubic foot.

13. One cubic foot is approximately 7.48 gallons. Find the approximate volume of the water tank to the nearest gallon.

1. **OMELETS** In Japan, a gigantic omelet was made with an area of 1,383 square feet. If the omelet was a square, what would be its side lengths? Round to the nearest tenth. (Lesson 13-1)

2. **SOFTBALL** A softball diamond is a square measuring 60 feet on each side.

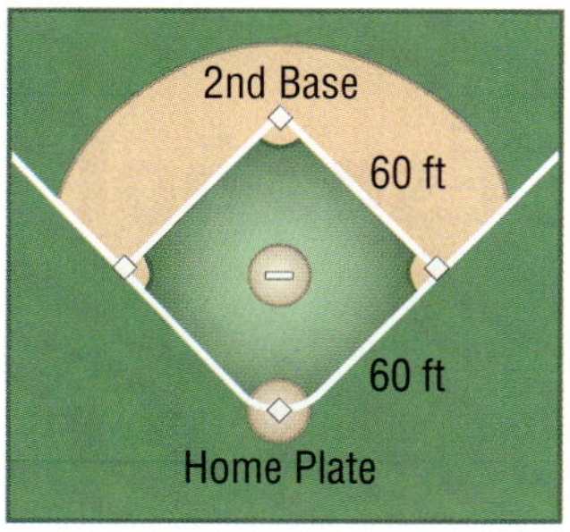

How far does a player on second base throw when she throws from second base to home? Round to the nearest tenth. (Lesson 13-2)

3. **BANDS** Mr. Garcia is planning a band formation at a football game. The diagram shows the dimensions of the field.

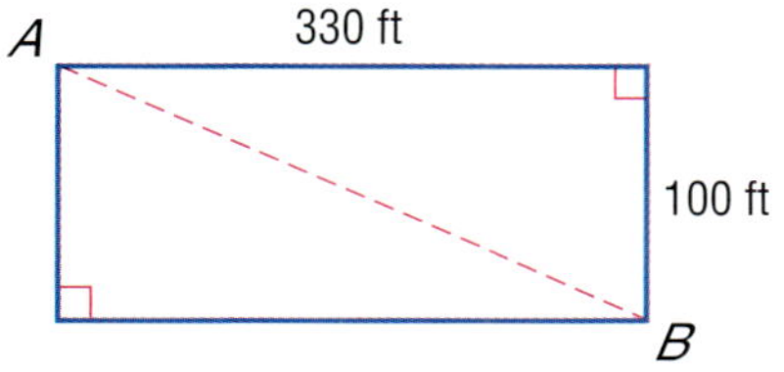

To the nearest foot, what is the distance from A to B? (Lesson 13-2)

4. **GEOMETRY** Two right triangles are side by side such that they form a larger isosceles triangle. If the two right triangles are congruent and each have angle measures of 90°, 45°, and 45°, what type of triangle will the new isosceles triangle be? Use the *make a model* strategy. (Lesson 13-3)

5. **CUBES** A rectangular prism is formed from 48 centimeter cubes such that the height of the prism is one-half of the width and one-third of the length of the prism. Find the dimensions of the rectangular prism. Use the *make a model* strategy. (Lesson 13-3)

For Exercises 6 and 7, use the following information.
Liz is designing some gift boxes. The small box is 6 inches long, 4 inches wide, and 2.5 inches high. The medium box has dimensions that are each 3 times the dimensions of the small box. (Lesson 13-4)

6. Find the surface area of the small box.
7. What are the dimensions of the medium box? Then find the surface area of the medium box.

STORAGE For Exercises 8–10, use the following information.
The two canisters shown below each have a volume of about 628.3 cubic inches. (Lesson 13-5)

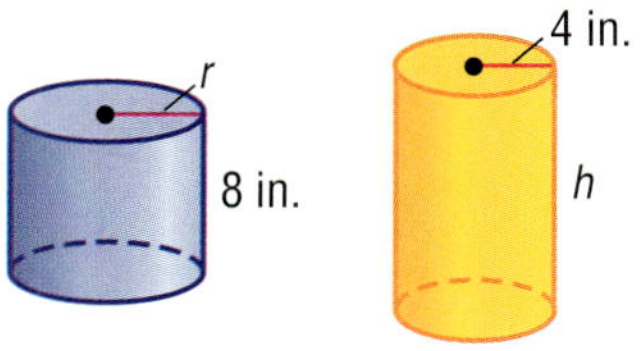

8. What is the radius of the blue canister? Round to the nearest tenth.
9. What is the height of the yellow canister? Round to the nearest tenth.
10. What is the difference between the surface areas of the two canisters?

HATS For Exercises 11–13, use the following information. (Lesson 13-5)
A certain cylinder-shaped hat box has a height of 9 inches and a radius of 5.5 inches. Its lid is also shaped as a cylinder, with a slightly larger diameter so that the lid fits over the box.

11. How many square inches of material are needed to make the hat box, not including the lid? Round to the nearest tenth.
12. If the lid has a height of 3.5 inches and a diameter of 11.8 inches, how many square inches of material are needed to make the lid? Round to the nearest tenth.
13. How many times more material is needed to make the hat box than the lid? Round to the nearest tenth.

Glossary/Glosario

Math Online A mathematics multilingual glossary is available at www.math.glencoe.com/multilingual_glossary. The glossary includes the following languages.

Arabic	Cantonese	Korean	Urdu
Bengali	English	Russian	Vietnamese
Brazilian Portuguese	Haitian Creole	Spanish	
	Hmong	Tagalog	

Cómo usar el glosario en español:

1. Busca el término en inglés que desees encontrar.
2. El término en español, junto con la definición, se encuentran en la columna de la derecha.

English

A

absolute value (p. 81) The distance the number is from zero on a number line.

acute angle (p. 553) An angle with a measure greater than 0° and less than 90°.

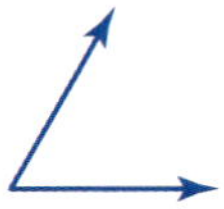

acute triangle (p. 565) A triangle having three acute angles.

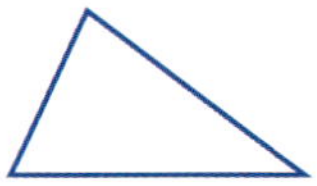

Addition Property of Equality (p. 186) If you add the same number to each side of an equation, the two sides remain equal.

additive inverse (p. 96) The opposite of an integer. The sum of an integer and its additive inverse is zero.

algebra (p. 44) The branch of mathematics that involves expressions with variables.

algebraic expression (p. 44) A combination of variables, numbers, and at least one operation.

analyze (p. 443) To describe, summarize, and compare data.

angle (p. 552) Two rays with a common endpoint form an angle. The rays and vertex are used to name the angle.

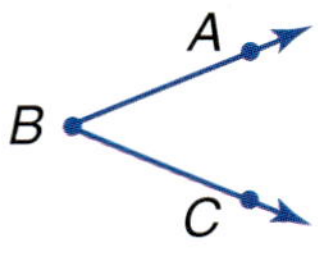

$\angle ABC$, $\angle CBA$, or $\angle B$

Español

valor absoluto Distancia a la que se encuentra un número de cero en la recta numérica.

ángulo agudo Ángulo que mide más de 0° y menos de 90°.

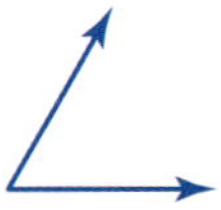

triángulo acutángulo Triángulo con tres ángulos agudos.

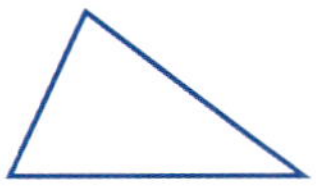

propiedad de adición de la igualdad Si sumas el mismo número a ambos lados de una ecuación, los dos lados permanecen iguales.

inverso aditivo El opuesto de un entero. La suma de un entero y su inverso aditivo es cero.

álgebra Rama de las matemáticas que involucra expresiones con variables.

expresión algebraica Combinación de variables, números y por lo menos una operación.

analizar Describir, resumir o comparar datos.

ángulo Dos rayos con un extremo común forman un ángulo. Los rayos y el vértice se usan para nombrar el ángulo.

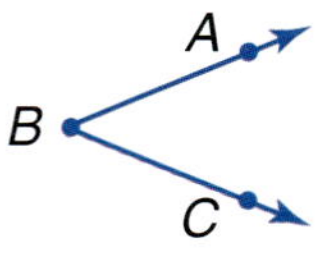

$\angle ABC$, $\angle CBA$, o $\angle B$

area (p. 605) The number of square units needed to cover a surface enclosed by a geometric figure.

área El número de unidades cuadradas necesarias para cubrir una superficie cerrada por una figura geométrica.

arithmetic sequence (p. 57) A sequence in which each term is found by adding the same number to the previous term.

sucesión aritmética Sucesión en que cada término se encuentra sumando el mismo número al término anterior.

Associative Property (p. 54) The way in which three numbers are grouped when they are added or multiplied does not change their sum or product.

propiedad asociativa La manera de agrupar tres números al sumarlos o multiplicarlos no cambia su suma o producto.

average (p. 448) The mean of a set of data.

promedio La media de un conjunto de datos.

B

bar graph (p. 461) A graphic form using bars to make comparisons of statistics.

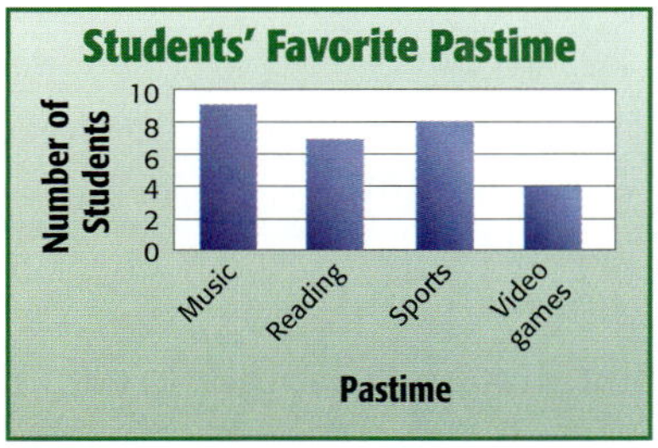

gráfica de barras Forma gráfica que usa barras para hacer comparaciones estadísticas.

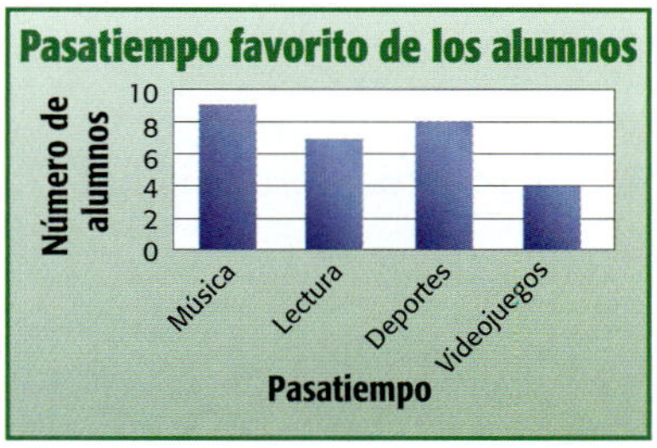

bar notation (p. 245) In repeating decimals, the line or bar placed over the digits that repeat. For example, $2.\overline{63}$ indicates that the digits 63 repeat.

notación de barra Línea o barra que se coloca sobre los dígitos que se repiten en decimales periódicos. Por ejemplo, $2.\overline{63}$ indica que los dígitos 63 se repiten.

base (p. 30) In a power, the number used as a factor. In 10^3, the base is 10. That is, $10^3 = 10 \times 10 \times 10$.

base En una potencia, el número usado como factor. En 10^3, la base es 10. Es decir, $10^3 = 10 \times 10 \times 10$.

base (p. 610) The base of a parallelogram or triangle is any side of the figure. The bases of a trapezoid are the parallel sides.

base La base de un paralelogramo o triángulo es el lado de la figura. Las bases de un trapecio son los lados paralelos.

base (p. 641) The top or bottom face of a three-dimensional figure.

base La cara inferior o superior de una figura tridimensional.

C

center (p. 622) The given point from which all points on a circle or sphere are the same distance.

centro Un punto dado del cual equidistan todos los puntos de un círculo o de una esfera.

circle (p. 622) The set of all points in a plane that are the same distance from a given point called the center.

círculo Conjunto de todos los puntos en un plano que equidistan de un punto dado llamado centro.

circle graph (p. 558) A type of statistical graph used to compare parts of a whole.

gráfica circular Tipo de gráfica estadística que se usa para comparar las partes de un todo.

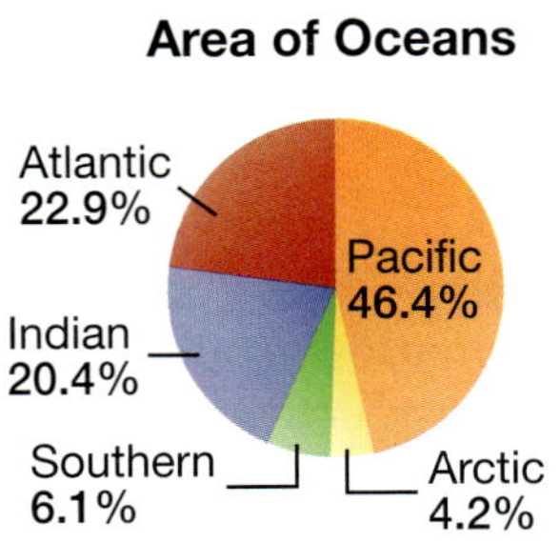

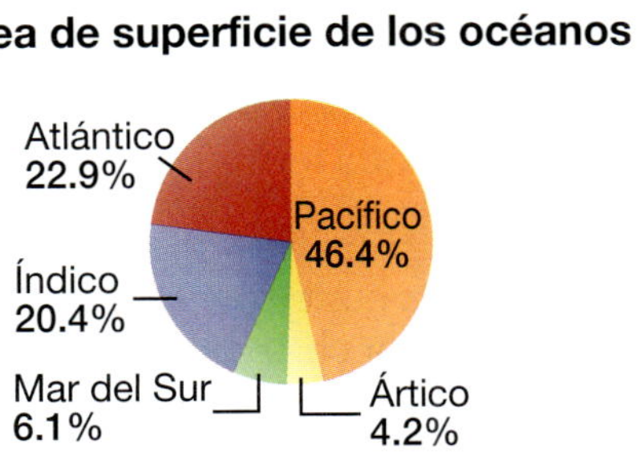

circumference (p. 622) The distance around a circle.

circunferencia La distancia alrededor de un círculo.

cluster (p. 443) Data that are grouped closely together.

agrupamiento Datos estrechamente agrupados.

coefficient (p. 45) The numerical factor of a term that contains a variable.

coeficiente El factor numérico de un término que contiene una variable.

combination (p. 524) An arrangement, or listing, of objects in which order is not important.

combinación Arreglo o lista de objetos donde el orden no es importante.

common denominator (p. 263) A common multiple of the denominators of two or more fractions. 24 is a common denominator for $\frac{1}{3}$, $\frac{5}{8}$, and $\frac{3}{4}$ because 24 is the LCM of 3, 8, and 4.

común denominador El múltiplo común de los denominadores de dos o más fracciones. 24 es un denominador común para $\frac{1}{3}$, $\frac{5}{8}$ y $\frac{3}{4}$ porque 24 es el mcm de 3, 8 y 4.

Commutative Property (p. 54) The order in which two numbers are added or multiplied does not change their sum or product.

propiedad conmutativa El orden en que se suman o multiplican dos números no afecta su suma o producto.

compatible numbers (p. 129) Numbers that are easy to compute mentally.

números compatibles Números que son fáciles de computar mentalmente.

complementary angles (p. 553) Two angles are complementary if the sum of their measures is 90°.

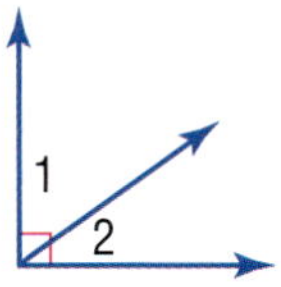

$\angle 1$ and $\angle 2$ are complementary angles.

ángulos complementarios Dos ángulos son complementarios si la suma de sus medidas es 90°.

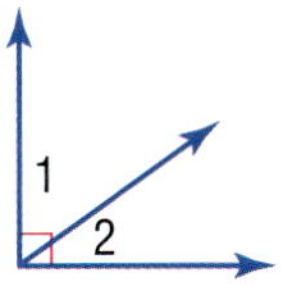

$\angle 1$ y $\angle 2$ son complementarios.

complementary events (p. 506) The events of one outcome happening and that outcome not happening are complementary events. The sum of the probabilities of complementary events is 1.

eventos complementarios Se dice de los eventos de un resultado que ocurren y el resultado que no ocurre. La suma de las probabilidades de eventos complementarios es 1.

composite event (p. 536) An event consisting of two or more simple events.

evento compuesto Un evento que consiste en dos o más eventos simples.

composite figure (p. 634) A figure made of circles, rectangles, squares, and other two-dimensional figures.

figura compuesto Una figura compuesta por círculos, rectángulos, cuadrados y otras dos figuras bidimencionales.

composite number (p. 229) A whole number greater than 1 that has more than two factors.

número compuesto Un número entero mayor que 1 que tiene más de dos factores.

cone (p. 642) A three-dimensional figure with a curved surface and a circular base.

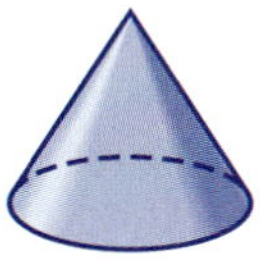

cono Figura tridimensional con una superficie curva y una base circular.

congruent angles (p. 553) Angles that have the same measure.

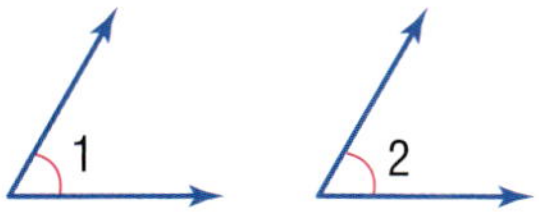

∠1 and ∠2 are congruent angles.

ángulos congruentes Ángulos que tienen la misma medida.

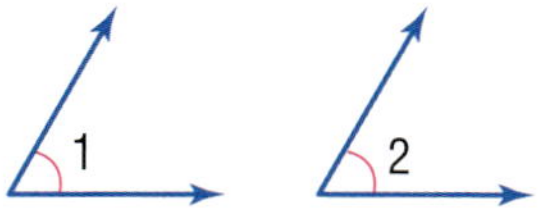

∠1 y ∠2 son congruentes.

congruent figures (p. 592) Figures with equal corresponding sides of equal length and corresponding angles of equal measure.

figuras congruentes Figuras cuyos lados y ángulos correspondientes son iguales.

congruent segments (p. 565) Segments having the same measure.

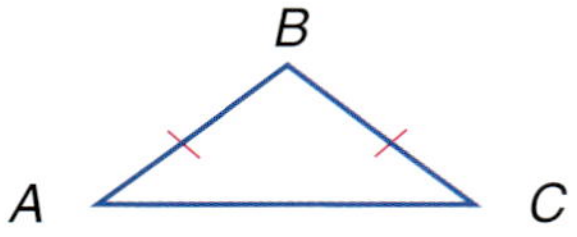

Side $\overline{AB}$ is congruent to side $\overline{BC}$.

segmentos congruentes Los segmentos que tienen la misma medida.

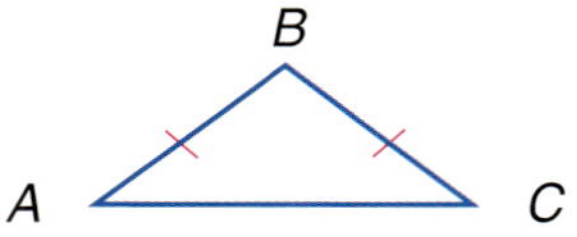

$\overline{AB}$ es congruente a $\overline{BC}$.

coordinate plane (p. 88) A plane in which a horizontal number line and a vertical number line intersect at their zero points. Also called a coordinate grid.

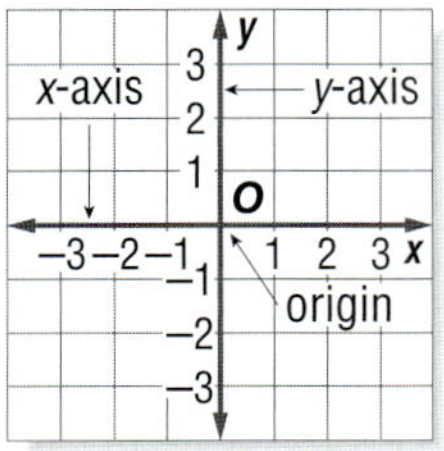

plano de coordenadas Plano en el cual se han trazado dos rectas numéricas, una horizontal y una vertical, que se intersecan en sus puntos cero. También conocido como sistema de coordenadas.

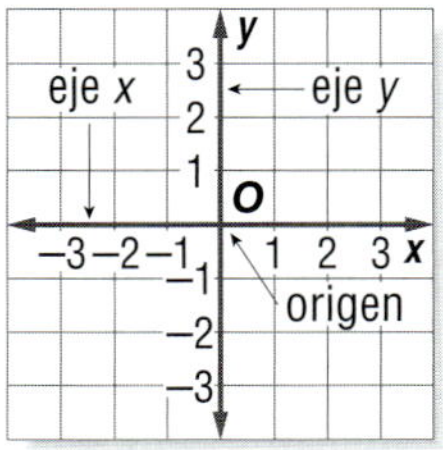

Glossary/Glosario

corresponding angles (p. 578) Congruent angles of similar figures.

corresponding sides (p. 578) Congruent or proportional sides of similar figures.

counterexample (p. 56) An example showing that a statement is not true.

cross product (p. 348) In a proportion, a cross product is the product of the numerator of one ratio and the denominator of the other ratio.

cubed (p. 30) The product in which a number is a factor three times. Two cubed is 8 because $2 \times 2 \times 2 = 8$.

cylinder (p. 642) A three-dimensional figure with two parallel congruent circular bases.

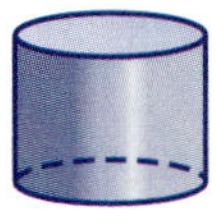

ángulos correspondientes Ángulos iguales de figuras semejantes.

lados correspondientes Lados iguales o proporcionales de figuras semejantes.

contraejemplo Ejemplo que demuestra que un enunciado no es verdadero.

productos cruzados En una proporción, un producto cruzado es el producto del numerador de una razón y el denominador de la otra razón.

al cubo El producto de un número por sí mismo, tres veces. Dos al cubo es 8 porque $2 \times 2 \times 2 = 8$.

cilindro Figura tridimensional que tiene dos bases circulares congruentes y paralelas.

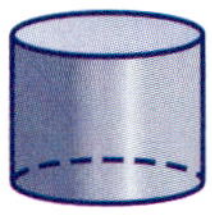

D

data (p. 422) Pieces of information, which are often numercical.

decagon (p. 584) A polygon having ten sides.

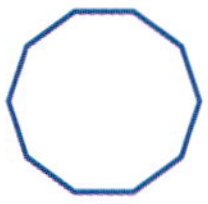

defining the variable (p. 50) Choosing a variable to represent an unknown value in a problem, and using it to write an expression or equation to solve the problem.

degrees (p. 552) The most common unit of measure for angles. If a circle were divided into 360 equal-sized parts, each part would have an angle measure of 1 degree.

diameter (p. 622) The distance across a circle through its center.

Distributive Property (p. 53) To multiply a sum by a number, multiply each addend of the sum by the number outside the parentheses.

Division Property of Equality (p. 190) If you divide each side of an equation by the same nonzero number, the two sides remain equal.

datos Información, la cual a menudo se presenta de manera numérica.

decágono Un polígono con diez lados.

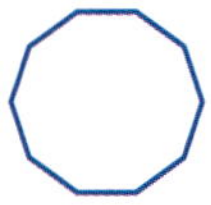

definir una variable El elegir una variable para representar un valor desconocido en un problema y usarla para escribir una expresión o ecuación para resolver el problema.

grados La unidad más común para medir ángulos. Si un círculo se divide en 360 partes iguales, cada parte tiene una medida angular de 1 grado.

diámetro La distancia a través de un círculo pasando por el centro.

propiedad distributiva Para multiplicar una suma por un número, multiplica cada sumando de la suma por el número fuera del paréntesis.

propiedad de igualdad de la división Si divides ambos lados de una ecuación entre el mismo número no nulo, los lados permanecen iguales.

domain (p. 63) The set of input values for a function.

dominio El conjunto de valores de entrada de una función.

E

edge (p. 641) The segment formed by intersecting faces of a three-dimensional figure.

arista Segmento de recta formado por la intersección de las caras en una figura tridimensional.

equation (p. 49) A mathematical sentence that contains an equals sign, =.

ecuación Enunciado matemático que contiene un signo de igualdad, =.

equilateral triangle (p. 565) A triangle having three congruent sides.

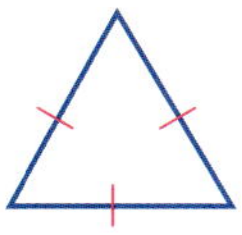

triángulo equilátero Triángulo con tres lados congruentes.

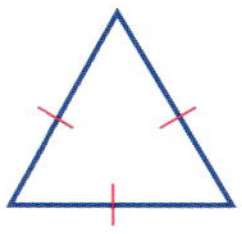

equivalent expressions (p. 53) Expressions that have the same value.

expresiones equivalentes Expresiones que tienen el mismo valor.

equivalent fractions (p. 240) Fractions that have the same value. $\frac{2}{3}$ and $\frac{4}{6}$ are equivalent fractions.

fracciones equivalentes Fracciones que tienen el mismo valor. $\frac{2}{3}$ y $\frac{4}{6}$ son fracciones equivalentes.

equivalent ratios (p. 330) Two ratios that have the same value.

razones equivalentes Dos razones que tienen el mismo valor.

evaluate (p. 31) To find the value of an expression.

evaluar Calcular el valor de una expresión. probabilidad experimental

experimental probability (p. 530) An estimated probability based on the relative frequency of positive outcomes occurring during an experiment.

probabilidad experimental Estimado de una probabilidad que se basa en la frecuencia relativa de los resultados positivos que ocurren durante un experimento.

exponent (p. 30) In a power, the number that tells how many times the base is used as a factor. In 5^3, the exponent is 3. That is, $5^3 = 5 \times 5 \times 5$.

exponente En una potencia, el número que indica las veces que la base se usa como factor. En 5^3, el exponente es 3. Es decir, $5^3 = 5 \times 5 \times 5$.

exponential form (p. 31) Numbers written with exponents.

forma exponencial Números escritos usando exponentes.

F

face (p. 641) The flat surface of a three-dimensional figure.

cara Superficies planas de una figura tridimensional.

factor tree (p. 230) A diagram showing the prime factorization of a number. The factors branch out from the previous factors until all of the factors are prime numbers.

diagrama de árbol Diagrama que muestra la factorización prima de un número. Los factores se ramifican a partir de los factores previos hasta que todos los factores son números primos.

factors (p. 30) Two or more numbers that are multiplied together to form a product.

factores Dos o más números que se multiplican entre sí para formar un producto.

fair game (p. 511) A game in which players of equal skill have an equal chance of winning.

juego justo Juego en que jugadores con la misma habilidad tienen igual oportunidad de ganar.

formula (p. 192) An equation that shows the relationship among certain quantities.

fórmula Ecuación que muestra la relación entre ciertas cantidades.

function (p. 63) A relation in which each element of the input is paired with exactly one element of the output according to a specified rule.

función Relación en que cada elemento de entrada es apareado con un único elemento de salida, según una regla específica.

function rule (p. 63) The operation performed on the input of a function.

regla de función Operación que se efectúa en el valor de entrada.

function table (p. 63) A table used to organize the input numbers, output numbers, and the function rule.

tabla de funciones Tabla que organiza las entradas, la regla y las salidas de una función.

Fundamental Counting Principle (p. 515) Uses multiplication of the number of ways each event in an experiment can occur to find the number of possible outcomes in a sample space.

Principio Fundamental de Contar Este principio usa la multiplicación del número de veces que puede ocurrir cada evento en un experimento para calcular el número de posibles resultados en un espacio muestral.

G

gram (p. 157) A unit of mass in the metric system equivalent to 0.001 kilogram.

gramo Unidad de masa del sistema métrico. Un gramo equivale a 0.001 de kilogramo.

graph (p. 80) The process of placing a point on a number line at its proper location.

graficar Proceso de dibujar o trazar un punto en una recta numérica en su ubicación correcta.

greatest common factor (GCF) (p. 234) The greatest of the common factors of two or more numbers. The GCF of 18 and 24 is 6.

máximo común divisor (MCD) El mayor factor común de dos o más números. El MCD de 18 y 24 es 6.

H

height (p. 610) The length of the segment perpendicular to the base with endpoints on opposite sides. In a triangle, the distance from a base to the opposite vertex.

altura Longitud del segmento perpendicular a la base y con extremos en lados opuestos. En un triángulo, es la distancia desde una base al vértice opuesto.

heptagon (p. 584) A polygon having seven sides.

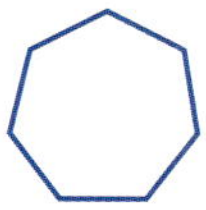

hexagon (p. 584) A polygon having six sides.

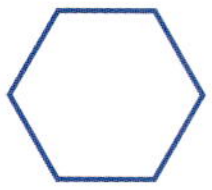

histogram (p. 462) A special kind of bar graph in which the bars are used to represent the frequency of numerical data that have been organized in intervals.

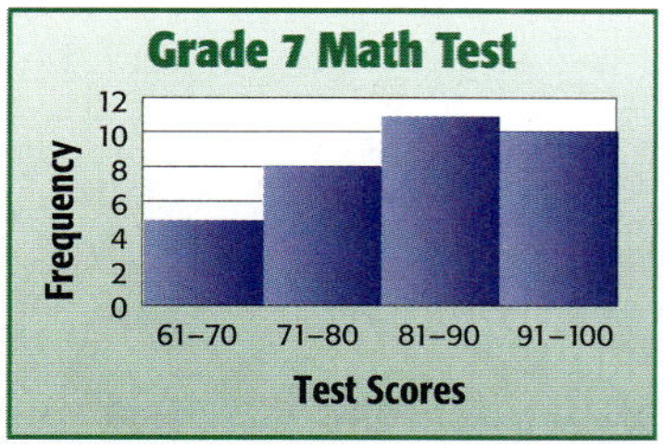

hypotenuse (p. 678) The side opposite the right angle in a right triangle.

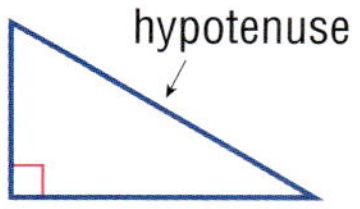

heptágono Polígono con siete lados.

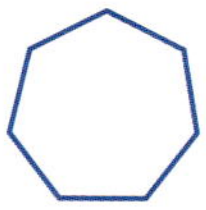

hexágono Polígono con seis lados.

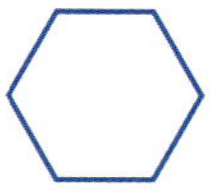

histograma Tipo especial de gráfica de barras que usa barras para representar la frecuencia de los datos numéricos, los cuales han sido organizados en intervalos iguales.

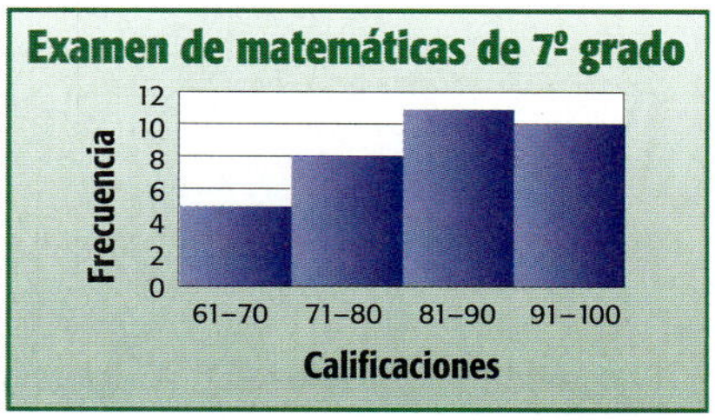

hipotenusa El lado opuesto al ángulo recto en un triángulo rectángulo.

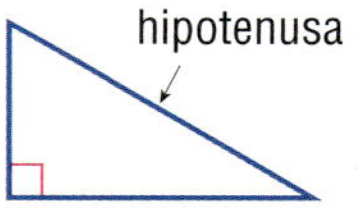

I

Identity Property (p. 54) The sum of an addend and 0 is the addend. The product of a factor and 1 is the factor.

independent events (p. 536) Two or more events in which the outcome of one event does not affect the outcome of the other event(s).

indirect measurement (p. 580) Finding a measurement by using similar triangles and writing a proportion.

inference (p. 457) A conclusion drawn based on data.

integer (p. 80) Any number from the set {... , −4, −3, −2, −1, 0, 1, 2, 3, 4, ...}

inverse operations (p. 184) Operations that "undo" each other. Addition and subtraction are inverse operations.

propiedad de identidad La suma de un sumando y 0 es el sumando mismo. El producto de un factor y 1 es el factor mismo.

eventos independientes Dos o más eventos en los cuales el resultado de uno de ellos no afecta el resultado de los otros eventos.

medida indirecta Técnica que se usa para calcular una medida a partir de triángulos semejantes y proporciones.

inferencia Conclusión que se saca en base a los datos.

entero Todo número del conjunto {... , −4, −3, −2, −1, 0, 1, 2, 3, 4, ...}

operaciones inversas Operaciones que se "anulan" mutuamente. La adición y la sustracción son operaciones inversas.

irrational number (p. 675) A number that cannot be written as a fraction.

número irracional Número que no se puede escribir como fracción.

isosceles triangle (p. 565) A triangle having at least two congruent sides.

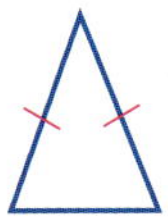

triángulo isósceles Triángulo que tiene por lo menos dos lados congruentes.

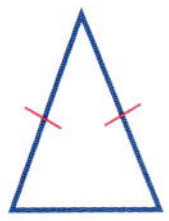

K

kilogram (p. 157) The base unit of mass in the metric system equivalent to 1,000 grams.

kilogramo Unidad fundamental de masa del sistema métrico. Un kilogramo equivale a mil gramos.

L

lateral face (p. 641) One side of a three-dimesional figure.

cara lateral Lado de una figura tridimensional.

leaf (p. 456) The second greatest place value of data in a stem-and-leaf plot.

hoja El segundo valor de posición mayor en un diagrama de tallo y hojas.

least common denominator (LCD) (p. 263) The least common multiple of the denominators of two or more fractions.

mínimo común denominador (mcd) El menor múltiplo común de los denominadores de dos o más fracciones.

least common multiple (LCM) (p. 259) The least of the common multiples of two or more numbers. The LCM of 2 and 3 is 6.

mínimo común múltiplo (mcm) El menor múltiplo común de dos o más números. El mcm de 2 y 3 es 6.

leg (p. 678) Either of the two sides that form the right angle of a right triangle.

cateto Cualquiera de los lados que forman el ángulo recto de un triángulo rectángulo.

like fractions (p. 284) Fractions that have the same denominator.

fracciones semejantes Fracciones con el mismo denominador.

line graph (p. 476) A type of statistical graph using lines to show how values change over a period of time.

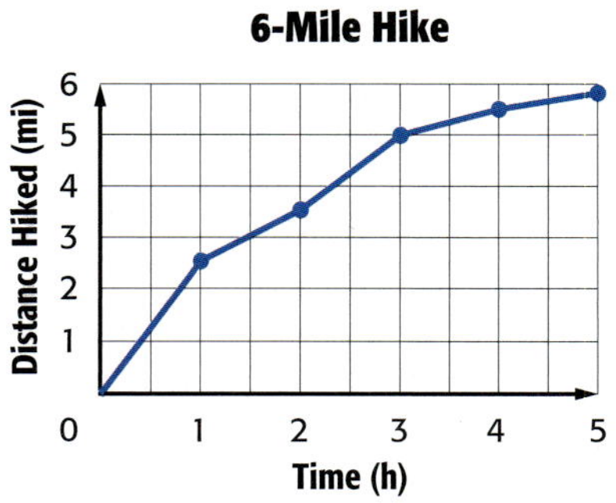

gráfica lineal Tipo de gráfica estadística que usa segmentos de recta para mostrar cómo cambian los valores durante un período de tiempo.

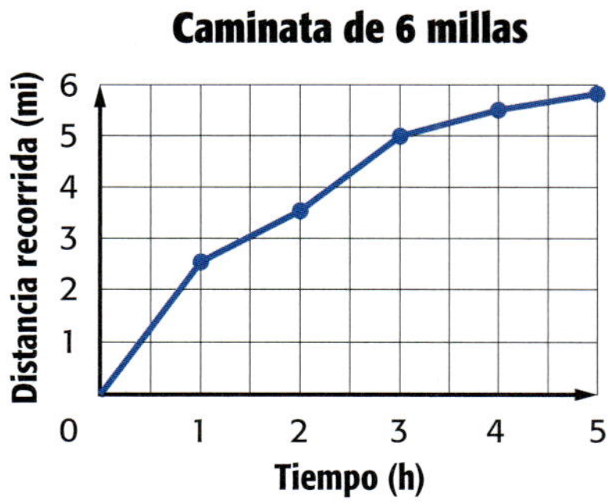

line of reflection (p. 597) The line over which a figure is reflected.

eje de reflexión La línea sobre la cual se refleja una figura.

line of symmetry (p. 596) A line that divides a figure into two halves that are reflections of each other.

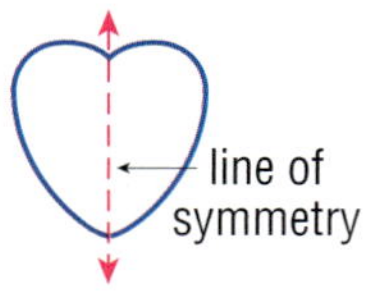

eje de simetría Recta que divide una figura en dos mitades que son reflexiones entre sí.

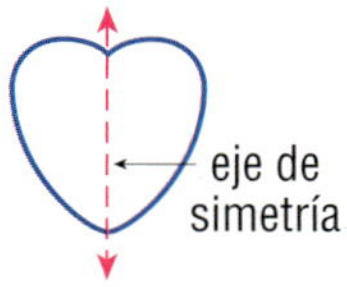

line plot (p. 442) A diagram that shows the frequency of data. An × is placed above a number on a number line each time that number occurs in a set of data.

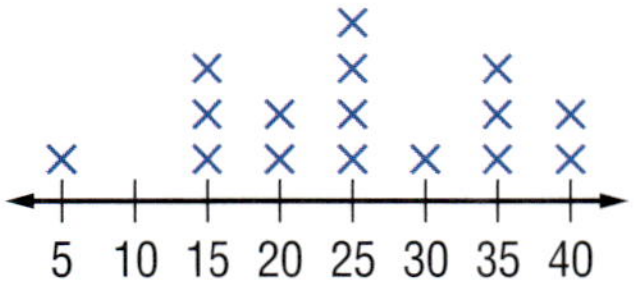

esquema lineal Grafica que muestra la frecuencia de datos. Se coloca una × sobre la recta numérica, cada vez que el número aparece en un conjunto de datos.

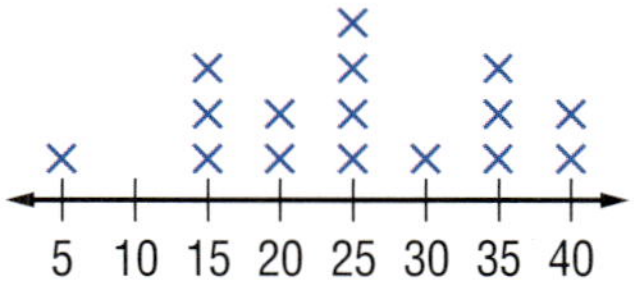

line symmetry (p. 596) Figures that match exactly when folded in half have line symmetry.

simetría lineal Exhiben simetría lineal las figuras que coinciden exactamente al doblarse una sobre otra.

linear equation (p. 212) An equation for which the graph is a straight line.

ecuación lineal Ecuación cuya gráfica es una recta.

liter (p. 157) The base unit of capacity in the metric system. A liter is a little more than a quart.

litro Unidad básica de capacidad del sistema métrico. Un litro es un poco más de un cuarto de galón.

M

mean (p. 448) The sum of the data divided by the number of items in the data set.

media La suma de los datos dividida entre el número total de artículos en el conjunto de datos.

measures of central tendency (p. 448) Numbers that are used to describe the center of a set of data. These measures include the mean, median, and mode.

medidas de tendencia central Números que se usan para describir el centro de un conjunto de datos. Estas medidas incluyen la media, la mediana y la moda.

median (p. 449) The middle number in a set of data when the data are arranged in numerical order. If the data has an even number, the median is the mean of the two middle numbers.

mediana Número central de un conjunto de datos, una vez que los datos han sido ordenados numéricamente. Si hay un número par de datos, la mediana es el promedio de los dos datos centrales.

meter (p. 157) The base unit of length in the metric system.

metro Unidad fundamental de longitud del sistema métrico.

metric system (p. 157) A base-ten system of measurement using the base units: meter for length, kilogram for mass, and liter for capacity.

sistema métrico Sistema de medidas de base diez que usa las unidades fundamentales: metro para longitud, kilogramo para masa y litro para capacidad.

mode (p. 449) The number or numbers that appear most often in a set of data.

moda Número o números que aparece(n) más frecuentemente en un conjunto de datos.

multiple (p. 259) The product of a number and any whole number.

múltiplo El producto de un número y cualquier número entero.

Multiplication Property of Equality (p. 307) If you multiply each side of an equation by the same nonzero number, the two sides remain equal.

propiedad de multiplicación de la igualdad Si multiplicas ambos lados de una ecuación por el mismo número no nulo, lo lados permanecen iguales.

multiplicative inverse (p. 306) The product of a number and its multiplicative inverse is 1. The multiplicative inverse of $\frac{2}{3}$ is $\frac{3}{2}$.

inverso multiplicativo El producto de un número y su inverso multiplicativo es 1. El inverso multiplicativo de $\frac{2}{3}$ es $\frac{3}{2}$.

N

negative integer (p. 80) An integer that is less than zero.

entero negativo Un entero menor que cero.

net (p. 638) A two-dimensional figure that can be used to build a three-dimensional figure.

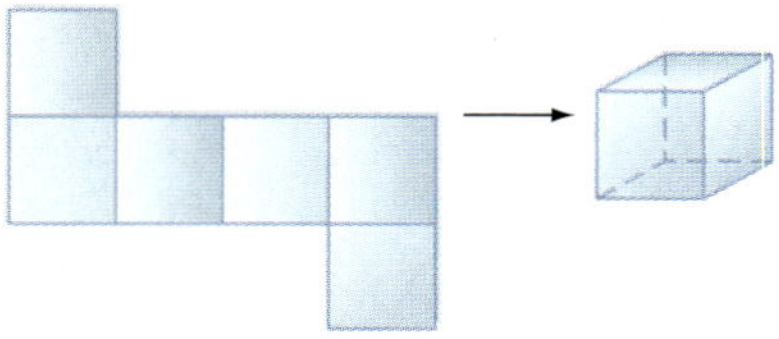

red Figura bidimensional que sirve para hacer una figura tridimensional.

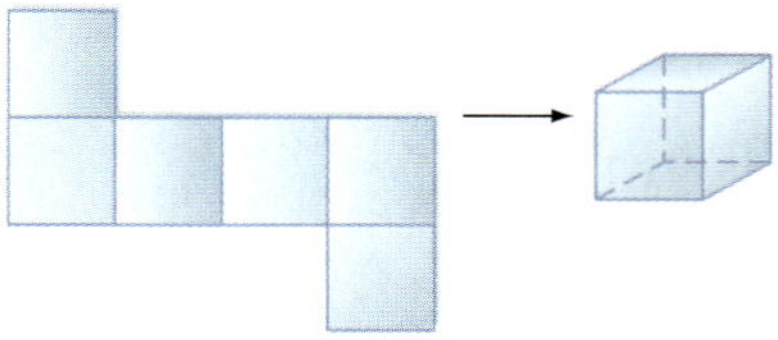

nonagon (p. 584) A polygon having nine sides.

enágono Polígono que tiene nueve lados.

numerical expression (p. 38) A combination of numbers and operations.

expresión numérica Combinación de números y operaciones.

O

obtuse angle (p. 553) Any angle that measures greater than 90° but less than 180°.

ángulo obtuso Cualquier ángulo que mide más de 90° pero menos de 180°.

obtuse triangle (p. 565) A triangle having one obtuse angle.

triángulo obtusángulo Triángulo que tiene un ángulo obtuso.

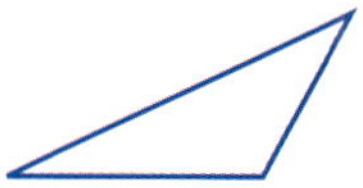

octagon (p. 584) A polygon having eight sides.

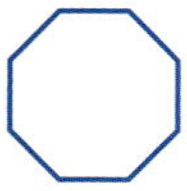

opposites (p. 96) Two integers are opposites if they are represented on the number line by points that are the same distance from zero, but on opposite sides of zero. The sum of two opposites is zero.

order of operations (p. 38) The rules to follow when more than one operation is used in a numerical expression.

1. Evaluate the expressions inside grouping symbols
2. Evaluate all powers
3. Multiply and divide in order from left to right.
4. Add and subtract in order from left to right.

ordered pair (p. 88) A pair of numbers used to locate a point in the coordinate plane. An ordered pair is written in the form (x-coordinate, y-coordinate).

origin (p. 88) The point at which the x-axis and the y-axis intersect in a coordinate plane.

outcome (p. 504) One possible result of a probability event. For example, 4 is an outcome when a number cube is rolled.

outlier (p. 443) A piece of data that is quite separated from the rest of the data.

P

parallel lines (p. 572) Lines in a plane that do not intersect.

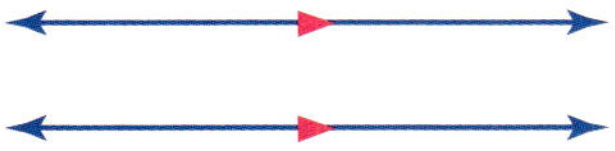

parallelogram (p. 572) A quadrilateral with opposite sides parallel and opposite sides congruent.

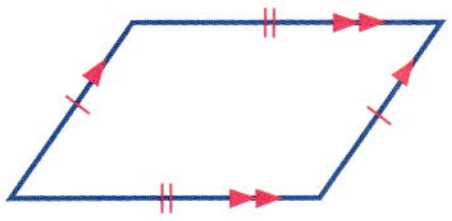

octágono Polígono que tiene ocho lados.

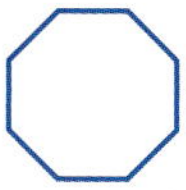

opuestos Dos enteros son opuestos si, en la recta numérica, están representados por puntos que equidistan de cero, pero en direcciones opuestas. La suma de dos opuestos es cero.

orden de operaciones Reglas a seguir cuando se usa más de una operación en una expresión numérica.

1. Primero ejecuta todas las operaciones dentro de los símbolos de agrupamiento
2. Evalúa todas las potencias antes que las otras operaciones.
3. Multiplica y divide en orden de izquierda a derecha.
4. Suma y resta en orden de izquierda a derecha.

par ordenado Par de números que se utiliza para ubicar un punto en un plano de coordenadas. Se escribe de la siguiente forma: (coordenada x, coordenada y).

origen Punto en que el eje x y el eje y se intersecan en un plano de coordenadas.

resultado Uno de los resultados posibles de un evento probabilístico. Por ejemplo, 4 es un resultado posible cuando se lanza un dado.

valor atípico Dato que se encuentra muy separado del resto de los datos.

líneas paralelas Rectas situadas en un mismo plano y que no se intersecan.

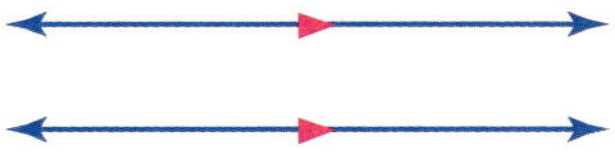

paralelogramo Cuadrilátero cuyos lados opuestos son paralelos y congruentes.

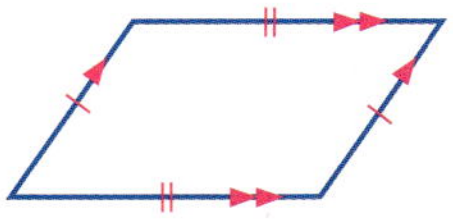

part (p. 392) In a percent proportion, the number that is compared to the whole quantity.

pentagon (p. 584) A polygon having five sides.

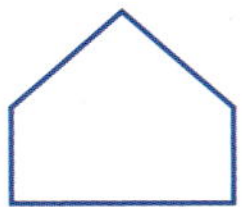

percent (p. 250) A ratio that compares a number to 100.

percent equation (p. 405) An equation that describes the relationship between the part, whole, and percent.
part = percent • whole

percent of change (p. 415) A ratio that compares the change in a quantity to the original amount.

percent of decrease (p. 415) A percent of change when the original quantity decreased.

percent of increase (p. 415) A percent of change when the original quantity increased.

percent proportion (p. 392) Compares part of a quantity to the whole quantity using a percent.

$$\frac{\text{part}}{\text{whole}} = \frac{\text{percent}}{100}$$

perfect squares (p. 35) Numbers whose square roots are whole numbers. 25 is a perfect square because the square root of 25 is 5.

perimeter (p. 204) The distance around a closed geometric figure.

permutation (p. 519) An arrangement, or listing, of objects in which order is important.

perpendicular lines (p. 554) Lines that meet to form right angles.

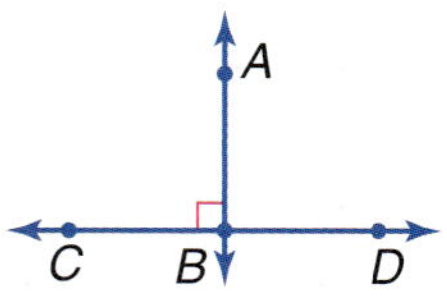

pi (π) (p. 622) The ratio of the circumference of a circle to its diameter. An approximation often used for π is 3.14.

polygon (p. 584) A simple closed figure in a plane formed by three or more line segments.

parte En una proporción porcentual, el número que se compara con la cantidad total.

pentágono Polígono que tiene cinco lados.

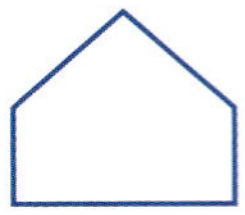

por ciento Razón que compara un número con 100.

ecuación porcentual Ecuación que describe la relación entre la parte, el todo y el por ciento.
parte = por ciento • todo.

porcentaje de cambio Razón que compara el cambio en una cantidad, con la cantidad original.

porcentaje de disminución Porcentaje de cambio cuando disminuye la cantidad original.

porcentaje de aumento Porcentaje de cambio cuando aumenta la cantidad original.

proporción porcentual Comparar partes de una cantidad, a la cantidad entera, usando un porcentaje.

$$\frac{\text{parte}}{\text{todo}} = \frac{\text{porcentaje}}{100}$$

cuadrados perfectos Números cuya raíz cuadrada es un número entero. 25 es un cuadrado perfecto porque la raíz cuadrada de 25 es 5.

perímetro La distancia alrededor de una figura geométrica cerrada.

permutación Arreglo o lista en que el orden es importante.

rectas perpendiculares Rectas que al encontrarse forman ángulos rectos.

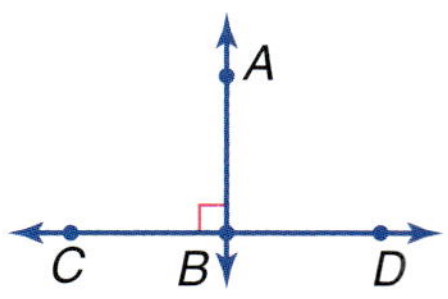

pi (π) Razón entre la circunferencia de un círculo y su diámetro. A menudo, se usa 3.14 como aproximación del valor de π.

polígono Figura simple cerrada en un plano, formada por tres o más segmentos de recta.

population (p. 411) The entire group of items or individuals from which the samples under consideration are taken.

positive integer (p. 80) An integer that is greater than zero.

powers (p. 30) Numbers expressed using exponents. The power 3^2 is read *three to the second power, or three squared.*

prime factorization (p. 230) Expressing a composite number as a product of prime numbers. For example, the prime factorization of 63 is $3 \times 3 \times 7$.

prime number (p. 229) A whole number greater than 1 that has exactly two factors, 1 and itself.

principal (p. 425) The amount of money deposited or invested.

prism (p. 641) A three-dimensional figure with at least three rectangular lateral faces and top and bottom faces parallel.

probability (p. 504) The chance that some event will happen. It is the ratio of the number of ways a certain event can occur to the number of possible outcomes.

properties (p. 54) Statements that are true for any number or variable.

proportional (p. 348) The relationship between two ratios with a constant rate or ratio.

protractor (p. 716) An instrument used to measure angles.

pyramid (p. 641) A three-dimensional figure with at least three lateral faces that are triangles and only one base.

Pythagorean Theorem (p. 678) In a right triangle, the square of the length of the hypotenuse is equal to the sum of the squares of the lengths of the legs. $c^2 = a^2 + b^2$

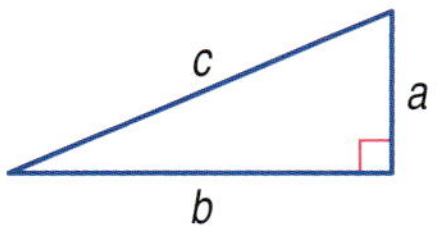

población El grupo total de individuos o de artículos del cual se toman las muestras bajo estudio.

entero positivo Un entero mayor que cero.

potencias Números que se expresan usando exponentes. La potencia 3^2 se lee *tres a la segunda potencia o tres al cuadrado.*

factorización prima Escritura de un número compuesto como el producto de números primos. La factorización prima de 63 es $3 \times 3 \times 7$.

número primo Número entero mayor que 1 que sólo tiene dos factores, 1 y sí mismo.

capital La cantidad de dinero depositada o invertida.

prisma Figura tridimensional que tiene por lo menos tres caras laterales rectangulares y caras paralelas superior e inferior.

probabilidad La posibilidad de que suceda un evento. Es la razón del número de maneras en que puede ocurrir un evento al número total de resultados posibles.

propiedades Enunciados que se cumplen para cualquier número o variable.

proporcional Relación entre dos razones con una tasa o razón constante.

transportador Instrumento que sirve para medir ángulos.

pirámide Figura tridimensional que tiene por lo menos tres caras laterales triangulares que son triángulos y una sola base.

Teorema de Pitágoras En un triángulo rectángulo, el cuadrado de la longitud de la hipotenusa es igual a la suma de los cuadrados de las longitudes de los catetos. $c^2 = a^2 + b^2$

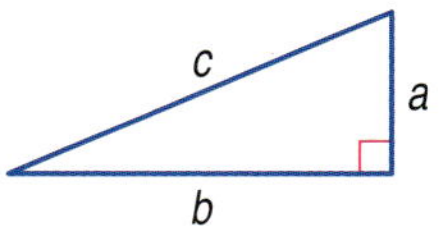

Q

quadrant (p. 88) One of the four regions into which the two perpendicular number lines of the coordinate plane separate the plane.

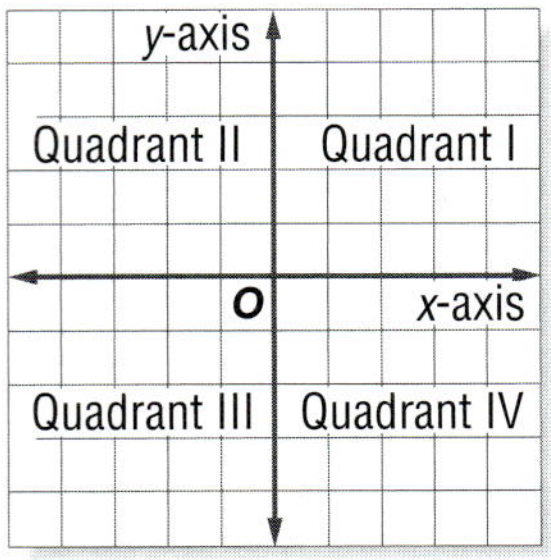

cuadrante Una de las cuatro regiones en que dos rectas numéricas perpendiculares dividen el plano de coordenadas.

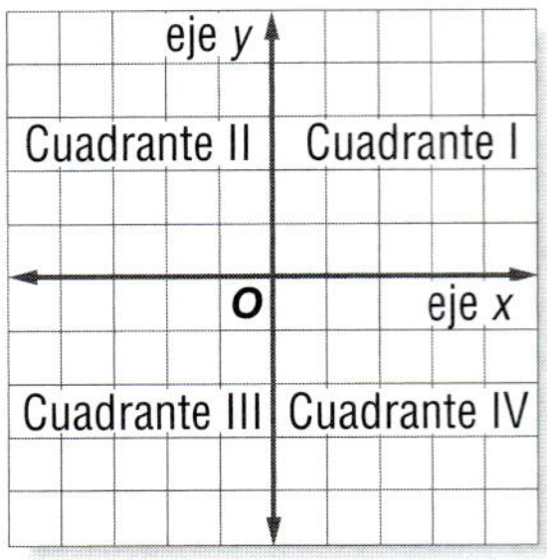

quadrilateral (p. 572) A closed figure having four sides and four angles.

cuadrilátero Figura cerrada que tiene cuatro lados y cuatro ángulos.

R

radical sign (p. 35) The symbol used to indicate a nonnegative square root, $\sqrt{\ }$.

signo radical Símbolo que se usa para indicar una raíz cuadrada no negativa, $\sqrt{\ }$.

radius (p. 622) The distance from the center of a circle to any point on the circle.

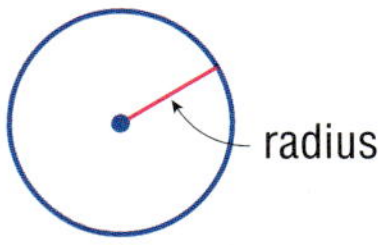

radio Distancia desde el centro de un círculo hasta cualquier punto del mismo.

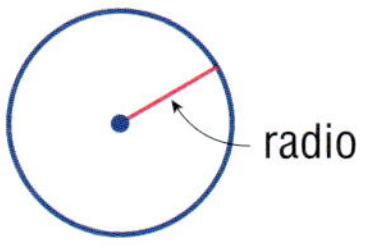

random (p. 505) Outcomes occur at random if each outcome is equally likely to occur.

aleatorio Un resultado ocurre al azar si la posibilidad de ocurrir de cada resultado es equiprobable.

random sample (p. 411) A sample in which the members are selected purely on the basis of chance.

muestra aleatoria Muestra en que todos sus miembros se eligen al azar.

range (p. 63) The set of output values for a function.

rango Conjunto de los valores de salida de una función.

range (p. 443) The difference between the greatest and least numbers in a data set.

rango La diferencia entre el número mayor y el menor en un conjunto de datos.

rate (p. 335) A ratio that compares two quantities with different kinds of units.

tasa Razón que compara dos cantidades que tienen distintas unidades de medida.

rate of change (p. 341) A ratio that shows a change in one quantity with respect to a change in another quantity.

tasa de cambio Razón que representa el cambio en una cantidad con respecto al cambio en otra cantidad.

ratio (p. 250) A comparison of two numbers by division. The ratio of 2 to 3 can be written as 2 out of 3, 2 to 3, 2 : 3, or $\frac{2}{3}$.

rational number (p. 264) A number that can be expressed as a fraction.

reciprocal (p. 306) The multiplicative inverse of a number.

rectangle (p. 572) A parallelogram having four right angles.

rectangular prism (p. 651) A solid figure that has two parallel and congruent bases that are rectangles.

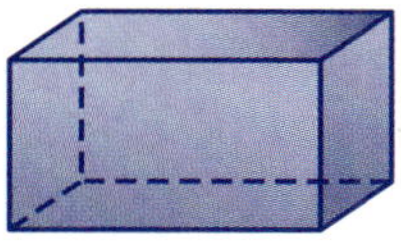

reflection (p. 597) A type of transformation in which a figure is flipped over a line of symmetry.

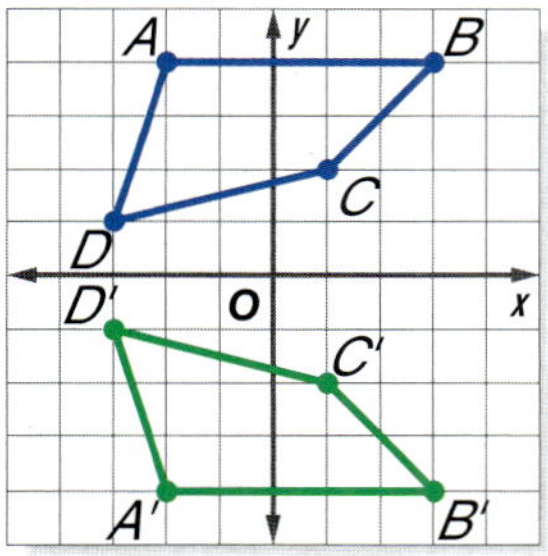

regular polygon (p. 584) A polygon that has all sides congruent and all angles congruent.

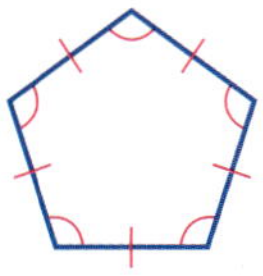

repeating decimals (p. 245) A decimal whose digits repeat in groups of one or more. Examples are 0.181818... and 0.83333... .

rhombus (p. 572) A parallelogram having four congruent sides.

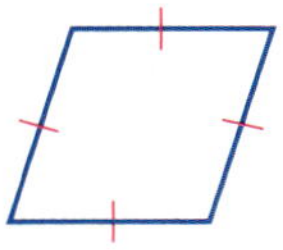

razón Comparación de dos números mediante división. La razón de 2 a 3 puede escribirse como 2 de cada 3, 2 a 3, 2:3 ó $\frac{2}{3}$.

número racional Número que puede expresarse como fracción.

recíproco El inverso multiplicativo de un número.

rectángulo Paralelogramo con cuatro ángulos rectos.

prisma rectangular Figura sólida con dos bases paralelas y congruentes que son rectángulos.

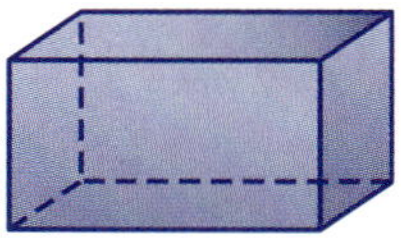

reflexión Tipo de transformación en el que se da vuelta a una figura sobre un eje de simetría.

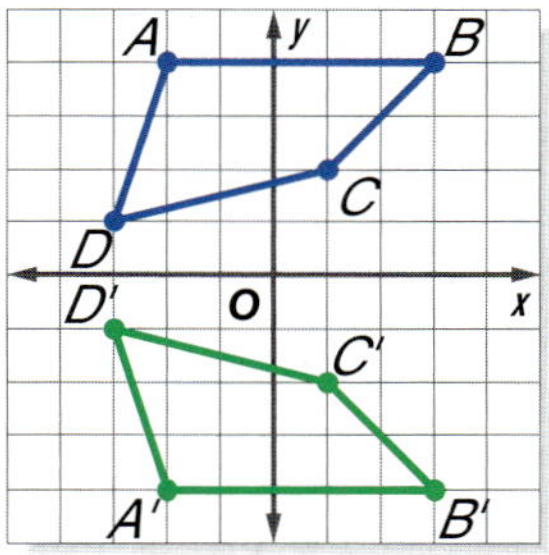

polígono regular Polígono con todos los lados y todos los ángulos congruentes.

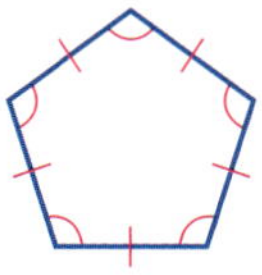

decimales periódicos Decimal cuyos dígitos se repiten en grupos de uno o más. Por ejemplo: 0.181818... y 0.83333... .

rombo Paralelogramo que tiene cuatro lados congruentes.

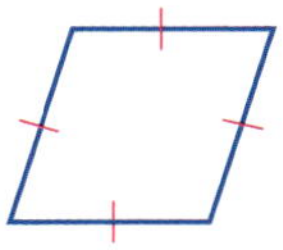

right angle (p. 553) An angle that measures 90°.

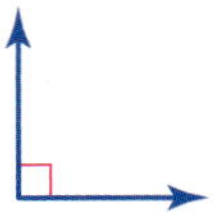

right triangle (p. 565) A triangle having one right angle.

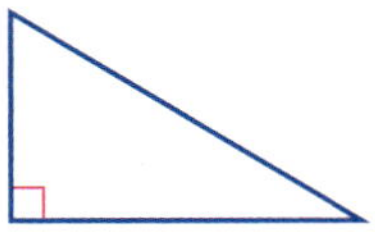

ángulo rect Ángulo que mide exactamente 90°.

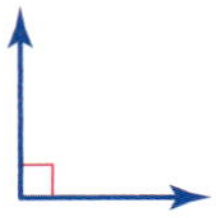

triángulo rectángulo Triángulo que tiene un ángulo recto.

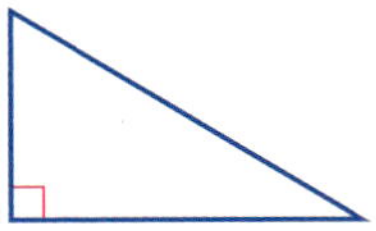

S

sample space (p. 509) The set of all possible outcomes of a probability experiment.

sampling (p. 354) A practical method used to survey a representative group.

scale (p. 358) On a map, intervals used representing the ratio of distance on the map to the actual distance.

scale drawing (p. 358) A drawing that is similar but either larger or smaller than the actual object.

scale factor (p. 360) A scale written as a ratio in simplest form.

scale model (p. 358) A model used to represent something that is too large or too small for an actual-size model.

scalene triangle (p. 565) A triangle having no congruent sides.

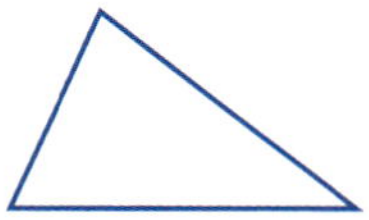

scatter plot (p. 477) In a scatter plot, two sets of related data are plotted as ordered pairs on the same graph.

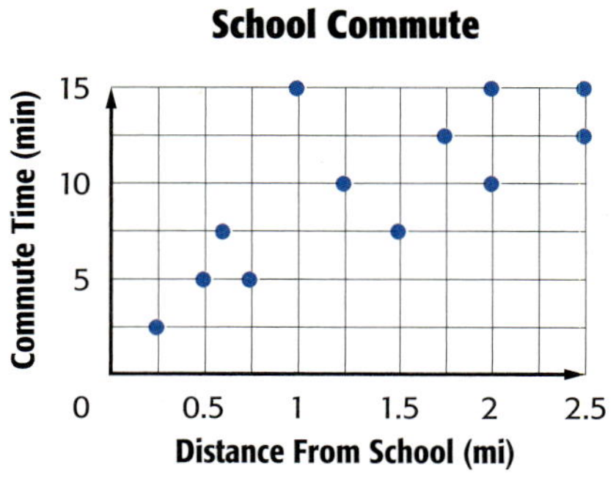

espacio muestral Conjunto de todos los resultados posibles de un experimento probabilístico.

muestreo Método conveniente que facilita la elección y el estudio de un grupo representativo.

escala En un mapa, los intervalos que se usan para representar la razón de las distancias en el mapa a las distancias verdaderas.

dibujo a escala Dibujo que es semejante, pero más grande o más pequeño que el objeto real.

factor de escala Escala escrita como una tasa en forma reducida.

modelo a escala Réplica de un objeto real, el cual es demasiado grande o demasiado pequeño como para construirlo de tamaño natural.

triángulo escaleno Triángulo sin lados congruentes.

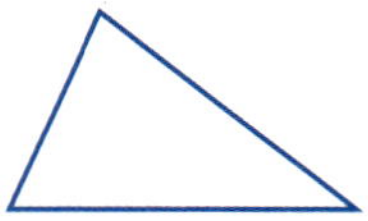

diagrama de dispersión Diagrama en que dos conjuntos de datos relacionados aparecen graficados como pares ordenados en la misma gráfica.

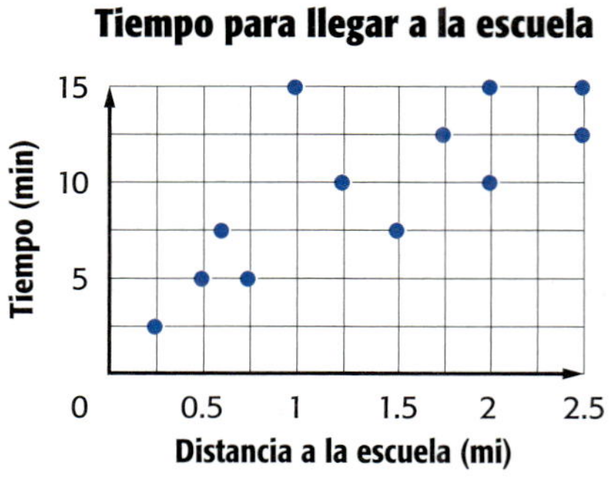

scientific notation (p. 162) A number written as a product of a number that is at least 1 but less than 10, and a power of ten. For example, $687{,}000 = 6.87 \times 10^5$.

semicircle (p. 634) Half of a circle.

sequence (p. 57) A list of numbers in a certain order, such as 0, 1, 2, 3, or 2, 4, 6, 8.

similar figures (p. 578) Figures that have the same shape but not necessarily the same size.

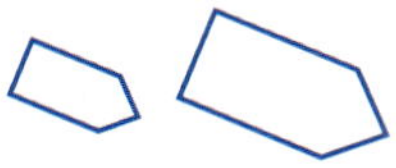

simple event (p. 504) One outcome or a collection of outcomes.

simple interest (p. 425) The amount paid or earned for the use of money. The formula for simple interest is $I = prt$.

simplest form (p. 240) A fraction is in simplest form when the GCF of the numerator and the denominator is 1.

simulate (p. 535) A way of acting out or modeling a problem situation.

solution (p. 49) A value for the variable that makes an equation true. The solution of $12 = x + 7$ is 5.

solving an equation (p. 49) The process of finding a solution to an equation.

sphere (p. 642) A three-dimensional figure in which all points are equal distance from the center.

square (p. 34) The product of a number and itself. 36 is the square of 6.

square (p. 572) A parallelogram having four right angles and four congruent sides.

square root (p. 35) One of the two equal factors of a number. The square root of 9 is 3.

standard form (p. 31) Numbers written without exponents.

statistics (p. 442) The branch of mathematics that deals with collecting, organizing, and interpreting data.

notación científica Números escritos como el producto de un número que es al menos igual a 1, pero menor que 10, por una potencia de diez. Por ejemplo, $687{,}000 = 6.87 \times 10^5$.

semicírculo Mitad de un círculo con el mismo diámetro.

sucesión Lista de números en cierto orden, tales como 0, 1, 2, 3 ó 2, 4, 6, 8.

figuras semejantes Figuras que tienen la misma forma, pero no necesariamente el mismo tamaño.

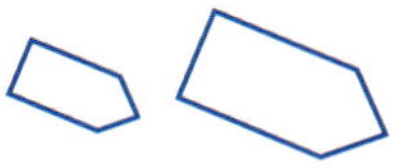

eventos simples Un resultado o una colección de resultados.

interés simple Cantidad que se paga o que se gana por el uso del dinero. La fórmula para calcular el interés simple es $I = prt$.

forma reducida Una fracción está escrita en forma reducida si el MCD de su numerador y denominador es 1.

simulación Manera de modelar o representar un problema.

solución Valor de la variable de una ecuación que hace verdadera la ecuación. La solución de $12 = x + 7$ es 5.

resolver una ecuación Proceso de encontrar el número o números que satisfagan una ecuación.

esfera Figura tridimensional en que todos los puntos están equidistantes del centro.

cuadrado El producto de un número por sí mismo. 36 es el cuadrado de 6.

cuadrado Paralelogramo con cuatro ángulos rectos y cuatro lados congruentes.

raíz cuadrada Uno de dos factores iguales de un número. La raíz cuadrada de 9 es 3.

forma estándar Números escritos sin exponentes.

estadística Rama de las matemáticas cuyo objetivo primordial es la recopilación, organización e interpretación de datos.

stem (p. 456) The greatest place value common to all the data values is used for the stem of a stem-and-leaf plot.

tallo El mayor valor de posición común a todos los datos es el que se usa como tallo en un diagrama de tallo y hojas.

stem-and-leaf plot (p. 456) A system used to condense a set of data where the greatest place value of the data forms the stem and the next greatest place value forms the leaves.

diagrama de tallo y hojas Sistema que se usa para condensar un conjunto de datos y en el cual el mayor valor de posición de los datos forma el tallo y el segundo mayor valor de posición de los datos forma las hojas.

straight angle (p. 553) An angle that measures exactly 180°.

ángulo llano Ángulo que mide exactamente 180°.

Subtraction Property of Equality (p. 184) If you subtract the same number from each side of an equation, the two sides remain equal.

propiedad de sustracción de la igualdad Si restas el mismo número de ambos lados de una ecuación, los dos lados permanecen iguales.

supplementary angles (p. 553) Two angles are supplementary if the sum of their measures is 180°.

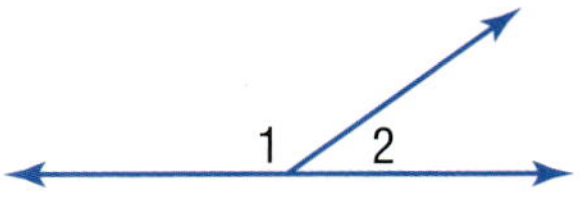

$\angle 1$ and $\angle 2$ are supplementary angles.

ángulos suplementarios Dos ángulos son suplementarios si la suma de sus medidas es 180°.

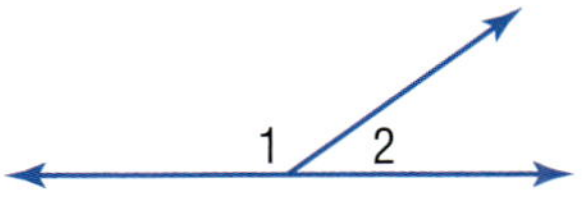

$\angle 1$ y $\angle 2$ son suplementarios.

surface area (p. 688) The sum of the areas of all the surfaces (faces) of a three-dimensional figure.

área de superficie La suma de las áreas de todas las superficies (caras) de una figura tridimensional.

survey (p. 411) A question or set of questions designed to collect data about a specific group of people.

encuesta Pregunta o conjunto de preguntas diseñadas para recoger datos sobre un grupo específico de personas.

T

term (p. 57) Each number in a sequence.

término Cada número en una sucesión.

terminating decimals (p. 245) A decimal whose digits end. Every terminating decimal can be written as a fraction with a denominator of 10, 100, 1,000, and so on.

decimales terminales Decimal cuyos dígitos terminan. Todo decimal terminal puede escribirse como una fracción con un denominador de 10, 100, 1,000, etc.

tessellation (p. 586) A repetitive pattern of polygons that fit together with no holes or gaps.

teselado Un patrón repetitivo de polígonos que coinciden perfectamente, sin dejar huecos o espacios.

theoretical probability (p. 530) The ratio of the number of ways an event can occur to the number of possible outcomes.

probabilidad teórica La razón del número de maneras en que puede ocurrir un evento al número total de resultados posibles.

three-dimensional figures (p. 641) A figure with length, width, and depth (or height).

figuras tridimensionales Figuras que poseen largo, ancho y profundidad (o altura).

transformation (p. 591) A movement of a geometric figure.

transformación Movimientos de figuras geométricas.

translation (p. 591) One type of transformation where a geometric figure is slid horizontally, vertically, or both.

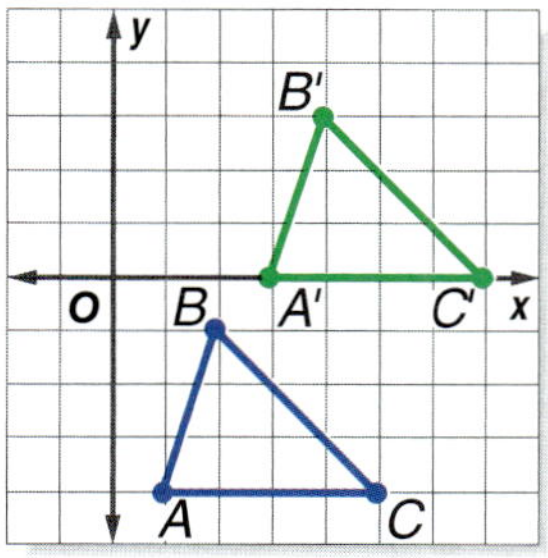

traslación Tipo de transformación en que una figura se desliza horizontal o verticalmente o de ambas maneras.

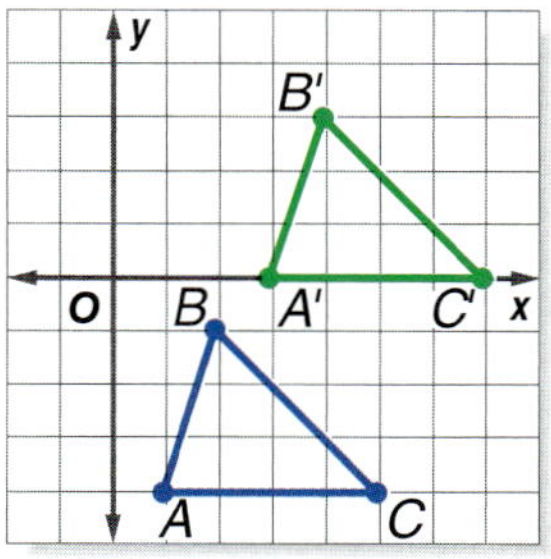

trapezoid (p. 572) A quadrilateral with one pair of parallel sides.

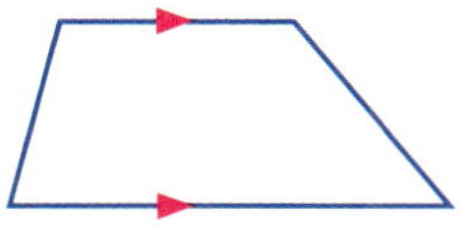

trapecio Cuadrilátero con un único par de lados paralelos.

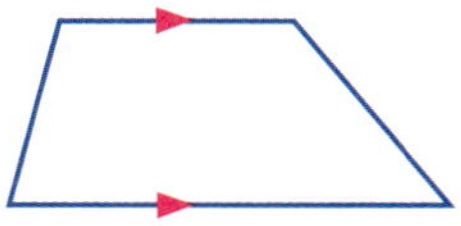

tree diagram (p. 510) A diagram used to show the total number of possible outcomes in a probability experiment.

diagrama de árbol Diagrama que se usa para mostrar el número total de resultados posibles en experimento probabilístico.

triangle (p. 564) A polygon that has three sides and three angles.

triángulo Polígono que posee tres lados y tres ángulos.

triangular prism (p. 653) A prism that has bases that are triangles.

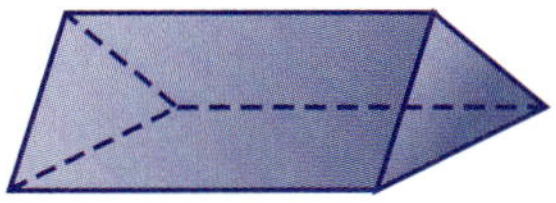

prisma triangular Prisma cuyas bases son triángulos.

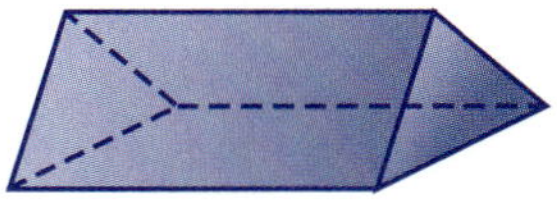

two-step equation (p. 199) An equation having two different operations.

ecuación de dos pasos Ecuación que contiene dos operaciones distintas.

U

unit rate (p. 335) A rate with denominator of 1.

tasa unitaria Una tasa con un denominador de 1.

unit ratio (p. 343) A unit rate where the denominator is one unit.

razón unitaria Tasa unitaria en que el denominador es la unidad.

unlike fractions (p. 285) Fractions with different denominators.

fracciones con distinto denominador Fracciones cuyos denominadores son diferentes.

V

variable (p. 44) A placeholder, usually a letter, used to represent an unspecified value in mathematical expressions or sentences. In $3 + a = 6$, a is a variable.

variable Marcador de posición, por lo general, una letra, que se usa para representar un valor desconocido en expresiones o enunciados matemáticos. En $3 + a = 6$, a es una variable.

Venn diagram (p. 234) A diagram that uses overlapping circles to show how elements among sets of numbers or objects are related.

diagrama de Venn Diagrama que usa círculos para mostrar la relación entre los elementos en un conjunto de números u objetos

vertex (p. 552) A vertex of an angle is the common endpoint of the rays forming the angle.

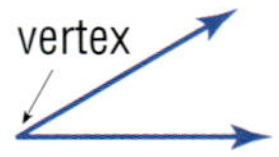

vértice El vértice de un ángulo es el extremo común de los rayos que lo forman.

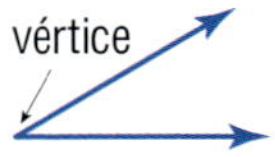

vertex (p. 641) The point where the edges of a three dimensional figure intersect.

vértice Punto donde se intersecan las aristas de una figura tridimensional.

vertical angles (p. 557) Opposite angles formed by the intersection of two lines.

$\angle 1$ and $\angle 2$ are vertical angles.

ángulos opuestos por el vértice Ángulos opuestos que se forman de la intersección de dos rectas.

$\angle 1$ y $\angle 2$ son ángulos opuestos por el vértice.

volume (p. 651) The number of cubic units needed to fill the space occupied by a solid.

volumen Número de unidades cúbicas que se requieren para llenar el espacio que ocupa un sólido.

W

whole (p. 392) In a percent proportion, the number to which the part is being compared.

todo En una proporción porcentual, el número con que se compara la parte.

X

x-axis (p. 88) The horizontal number line in a coordinate plane.

eje x La recta numérica horizontal en el plano de coordenadas.

x-coordinate (p. 88) The first number of an ordered pair. It corresponds to a number on the x-axis.

coordenada x El primer número de un par ordenado. Corresponde a un número en el eje x.

Y

***y*-axis** (p. 88) The vertical number line in a coordinate plane.

eje *y* La recta numérica vertical en el plano de coordenadas.

***y*-coordinate** (p. 88) The second number of an ordered pair. It corresponds to a number on the *y*-axis.

coordenada *y* El segundo número de un par ordenado. Corresponde a un número en el eje *y*.

Z

zero pair (p. 93) The result when one positive counter is paired with one negative counter.

par nulo Resultado que se obtiene cuando una ficha positiva se aparea con una ficha negativa.

Selected Answers

Chapter 1 Introduction to Algebra and Functions

Page 23 ***Chapter 1*** ***Getting Ready***

1. 105.8 **3.** 60.64 **5.** $72.94 **7.** 2.5 **9.** 6.2 **11.** 29.4 **13.** 10.2 **15.** 5.3 **17.** 4.46

Pages 27–29 ***Lesson 1-1***

1. three times **3.** 3,000 **5.** $4,169

7.

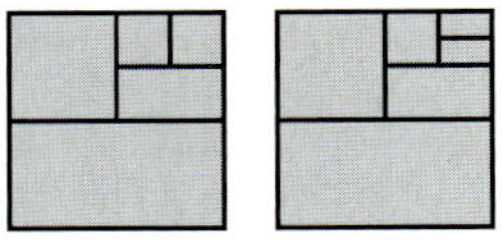

9. every 45 minutes **11.** 1:30 P.M. **15.** 21 wk **17.** Sample answer: For the school bake sale, Samantha bakes 79 cookies and 42 brownies. If two other students baked the same amount of cookies and brownies, how many items did they bake altogether? **19.** C **21.** 100 **23.** 625

Pages 31–33 ***Lesson 1-2***

1. $9 \cdot 9 \cdot 9$ **3.** $8 \cdot 8 \cdot 8 \cdot 8 \cdot 8$ **5.** 49 **7.** Sample answer: 282,000,000 people **9.** 1^4 **11.** $1 \cdot 1 \cdot 1 \cdot 1 \cdot 1$ **13.** $3 \cdot 3 \cdot 3 \cdot 3 \cdot 3 \cdot 3 \cdot 3 \cdot 3$ **15.** $9 \cdot 9 \cdot 9$ **17.** 64 **19.** 2,401 **21.** 1 **23.** 1,000,000 **25.** 3^2 **27.** 1^8 **29.** $4 \cdot 4 \cdot 4 \cdot 4 \cdot 4$ **31.** 1,296 **33.** $1^3, 2^3, 3^3, 4^3, 5^3$ **35.** $5^4 \cdot 4^3$ **37.** $1^{14}, 17^3, 6^5, 4^{10}$ **39.** $7^2, 5^3, 2^{11}, 4^6$ **41.** 50; 50 cannot be expressed as a power: $4 = 2^2, 9 = 3^2, 16 = 4^2$ **43.** Sample answer: The pattern is that each successive term is $\frac{1}{2}$ of the previous one, so $2^0 = 1$. Likewise, $2^{-1} = \frac{1}{2}$. **45.** about twice as many **47.** 4 **49.** 25

Pages 36–37 ***Lesson 1-3***

1. 36 **3.** 289 **5.** 3 **7.** 11 **9.** 24 in. by 24 in. **11.** 1 **13.** 121 **15.** 400 **17.** 1,156 **19.** 4 **21.** 10 **23.** 16 **25.** 25 **27.** 40 ft **29.** 361 **31.** 96,721 mi^2

33.

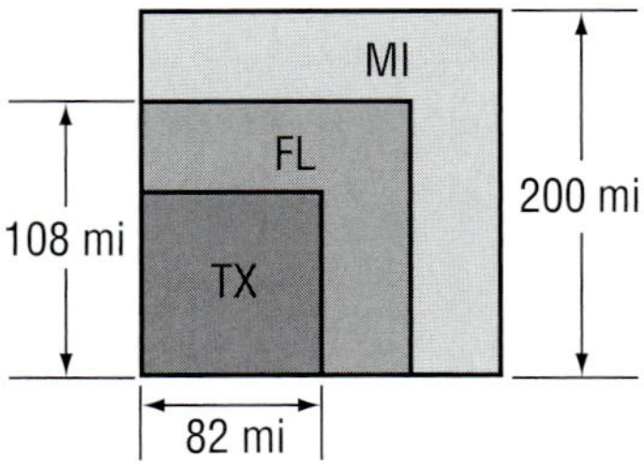

35. 55 m^2 greater; The area of an 8 by 8 square has an area of 64 m^2. **37.** Yes; for example, a garden that measures 30 feet by 30 feet has the same perimeter, but its area is 900 square feet, which is greater than 500 square feet. **39.** Sample answer: It is called squaring the number because the area of a square is found by multiplying the two side lengths together. **41.** J **43.** $8 \cdot 8 \cdot 8 \cdot 8 \cdot 8 \cdot 8$ **45.** $2 \cdot 2 \cdot 2 \cdot 2 \cdot 2 \cdot 2 \cdot 2$ **47.** 21 **49.** 30

Pages 40–41 ***Lesson 1-4***

1. 11 **3.** 11 **5.** 400 **7.** 11 **9.** $3(0.05) + 2(0.25) + 2(0.10) + 7(0.01)$; $0.92 **11.** 3 **13.** 1 **15.** 8 **17.** 5 **19.** 30,000 **21.** 386 **23.** 75 **25.** 22 **27.** 23 **29.** $3(2) + 2(3) + 4$; 16 h/wk **31.** 40 **33.** 64 **35.** $30 - (2 \times 8 + 2 \times 2 + 4)$; $6 **37.** Cynthia; the first step is to do the division, $24 \div 6$. Yutaka incorrectly multiplied 6 and 2 first. **41.** H **43.** 45 **45.** 32 million

Pages 42–43 ***Lesson 1-5***

1. Sample answer: You need to keep track of what numbers you have already guessed, so that you do not make the same guess twice. You also need to know what numbers produce answers that are too large or too small, so you can make better guesses. **3.** 9 cars and 7 SUVs **5.** Songs B, C, D, E, G, and H run for a total of 29.65 minutes, or 29 minutes and 39 seconds. **7.** The circumference of Earth is 24,900 miles long at the Equator. **9.** 512 and 1,024 **11.** addition; 324.8 in. of snow.

Pages 46–47 ***Lesson 1-6***

1. 10 **3.** 2 **5.** 32 **7.** 22 **9.** 7 **11.** 3 **13.** 4 **15.** 7 **17.** 5 **19.** 12 **21.** 48 **23.** 4 **25.** 18 **27.** 36 **29.** 5 **31.** 118 **33.** 5.1 **35.** 2, 2.5, 3 **37.** 64 ft **39.** Sample answer: $5x - 37$ if $x = 8$ **41.** sometimes; $x - 3$ and $y - 3$ represent the same value only when $x = y$ **43.** G **45.** 28 **47.** 56 **49.** 19 **51.** false

Pages 51–52 ***Lesson 1-7***

1. 3 **3.** 54 **5.** $2.25 **7.** 7 **9.** 28 **11.** 46 **13.** 33 **15.** 64 **17.** 7 **19.** 11 **21.** m = the number of miles Derrick walked on Monday; $m + 2.5 = 6.3$; 3.8 mi **23.** 5.4 **25.** 4.4 **27.** 1.2 **29.** $5{,}000 - 1{,}500 = n$ or $5{,}000 = 1{,}500 + n$; 3,500 mi **31.** Ivan; $75 - 25 = 50$ is a true statement. $25 - 25 \neq 50$ **33.** A **35.** 15 **37.** 29 **39.** 58 tables **41.** 72 **43.** 168

Pages 55–56 ***Lesson 1-8***

1. $7(4) + 7(3)$; 49 **3.** $(2)3 + (5)3$; 21 **5.** $4(12 + 5)$; $68 **7.** Commutative Property (+) **9.** $2(6) + 2(7)$; 26 **11.** $(3)4 + (8)4$; 44 **13.** Associative Property (×) **15.** Identity Property (×) **17.** Commutative Property (+) **19.** Associative Property (+) **21.** Distributive Property **23.** $5(20 + 7)$; 135 million **25.** $2(5) - 2(4)$; 2 **27.** $9(7) - 9(3)$; 36 **29.** $y + 5$ **31.** $32b$ **33.** $2x + 6$ **35.** $6c + 6$ **37.** $610 + 195 = 195 + 610$ **39.** Sample answer: $(5 + z) + 9 = 5 + (z + 9)$ **41.** Sample answer: Since $24 \div (12 \div 2) = 4$ and $(24 \div 12) \div 2 = 1$, $24 \div (12 \div 2) \neq (24 \div 12) \div 2$. **43.** B **45.** 11.3 **47.** 84 years **49.** 10 **51.** 4.6

Pages 59–61 ***Lesson 1-9***

1. 9 is added to each term; 36, 45, 54 **3.** 0.1 is added to each term; 1.4, 1.5, 1.6 **5.** $3n$; 36 in. **7.** 6 is added to each term; 25, 31, 37 **9.** 12 is added to each term; 67,

79, 91 **11.** 5 is added to each term; 53, 58, 63 **13.** 0.8 is added to each term; 5.6, 6.4, 7.2 **15.** 1.5 is added to each term; 10.5, 12.0, 13.5 **17.** 4 is added to each term; 20.6, 24.6, 28.6 **19.** $7n$; 42 laps **21.** 25 is added to each term; 120, 145, 170 **23.** 256, 1,024, 4,096 **25.** 324, 972, 2,916 **27.** 1,200 **29.** 4,950 **31.** The Fibonacci sequence is 1, 1, 2, 3, 5, 8, 13, …. In this sequence, each term after the second term is the sum of the two terms before it. Fibonacci numbers occur in many areas of nature, including pine cones, shell spirals, and branching plants. **33.** + 2, + 4, + 6, + 8, …; 30, 42, 56 **35.** Sample answer: paper/pencil; Write the equation that represents this situation, $15n$. Since 2 years = 24 months, evaluate the expression when n is 24. 15(24) = 360. So, after 2 years, $360 will be saved. **37.** D **39.** Comm. (+) **41.** 29 **43.** 20 **45.** 8 **47.** 3

Pages 65–67 ***Lesson 1-10***

1.

x	3x	y
1	3 • 1	3
2	3 • 2	6
3	3 • 3	9
4	3 • 4	12

; domain: {1, 2, 3, 4}; range: {3, 6, 9, 12}

3.

x	8x	y
1	8 • 1	8
2	8 • 2	16
3	8 • 3	24
4	8 • 4	32

; domain: {1, 2, 3, 4}; range: {8, 16, 24, 32}

5. 320 feet

7.

x	6x	y
1	6 • 1	6
2	6 • 2	12
3	6 • 3	18
4	6 • 4	24

; domain: {1, 2, 3, 4}; range: {6, 12, 18, 24}

9.

x	25x	y
1	25 • 1	25
2	25 • 2	50
3	25 • 3	75
4	25 • 4	100

; domain: {1, 2, 3, 4}; range: {25, 50, 75, 100}

11. $c = 20m$ **13.** $t = 35m$

15.

x	x − 1	y
1	1 − 1	0
2	2 − 1	1
3	3 − 1	2
4	4 − 1	3

; domain: {1, 2, 3, 4}; range: {0, 1, 2, 3}

17.

x	x + 0.25	y
0	0 + 0.25	0.25
1	1 + 0.25	1.25
2	2 + 0.25	2.25
3	3 + 0.25	3.25

; domain: {0, 1, 2, 3}; range: {0.25, 1.25, 2.25, 3.25}

19.

Width (units)	6w	Area (sq units)
2	6 • 2	12
3	6 • 3	18
4	6 • 4	24
5	6 • 5	30

21. $m = 8s$ **23.** 480 mi; 1,140 mi **25.** $y = 3x$ **27.** Sample answer: Sam charges $3 for each dog that he walks. In the equation $y = 3x$, x represents the number of dogs and y represents the total amount of money earned. **29.** C **31.** G **33.** 5(9) + 5(7); 80 **35.** 8(7) − 8(2); 40 **37.** 10 **39.** 8 **41.** Sample answer: $8 × 50 × 2 or $800

Pages 70–74 ***Chapter 1*** ***Study Guide and Review***

1. false, equivalent expressions **3.** false, domain **5.** true **7.** false, square **9.** $89.40 **11.** 3 • 3 • 3 • 3 **13.** 5 **15.** 5 • 5 • 5 • 5 **17.** 40, 353, 607 **19.** 324 **21.** 100 **23.** 8 **25.** 169 **27.** 18 **29.** 25 **31.** 33 **33.** 36 ÷ 4 + 12 ÷ 3; 13 **35.** 22 **37.** 5 **39.** 48 **41.** 8 **43.** 108 **45.** 9 + x = 15; 6 tickets **47.** Distributive **49.** Associative (×) **51.** Each term is found by adding 0.8 to the previous term; 6.6, 7.4, 8.2 **53.** 4.50n$

55.

x	4x	y
5	4(5)	20
6	4(6)	24
7	4(7)	28
8	4(8)	32

; The domain is {5, 6, 7, 8}. The range is {20, 24, 28, 32}.

Chapter 2 Integers

Page 79 ***Chapter 2*** ***Getting Ready***

1. < **3.** < **5.** Garrett **7.** 20 **9.** 9 **11.** 216 **13.** 29 **15.** 1,900 mi

Pages 82–83 ***Lesson 2-1***

1. −11 **3.** 16 **5.** −21

7.
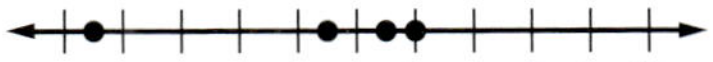

9. 8 **11.** 9 **13.** −53 **15.** −2 **17.** 12 **19.** −7

21.

23.

25. 10 **27.** 2 **29.** 14 **31.** 25 **33.** 5 **35.** 17 positive charges: 17; 25 negative charges: −25 **37.** false; 0 **39.** D

41.

x	x − 4	y
4	4 − 4	0
5	5 − 4	1
6	6 − 4	2
7	7 − 4	3

; domain: {4, 5, 6, 7}; range: {0, 1, 2, 3}

43.

x	$5x + 1$	y
1	$5 \cdot 1 + 1$	6
2	$5 \cdot 2 + 1$	11
3	$5 \cdot 3 + 1$	16
4	$5 \cdot 4 + 1$	21

; domain: {1, 2, 3, 4}; range: {6, 11, 16, 21}

45. > **47.** >

Pages 85–87 ***Lesson 2-2***

1. > **3.** >
5. {−18, −16, −10, 12, 19}
7. < **9.** > **11.** > **13.** <
15. {−8, −5, −3, 6, 11}
17. {−7, −6, −4, 1, 3, 5}
19. Sunlight, Twilight, Midnight, Abyssal, Hadal
21. < **23.** < **25.** Jan. 7, Jan. 5, Jan. 6, Jan. 8, Jan. 4, Jan. 9, Jan. 3
27. +15, −13, +10, −4, +13, −5
29. true **31.** true **33.** −1
35. C **37.** −9 **39.** $r = 6t$

41–44.

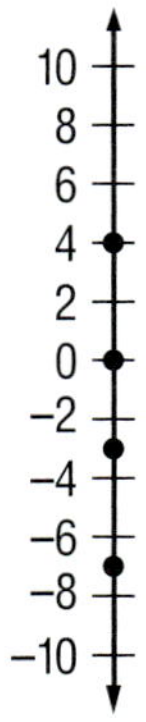

Pages 90–92 ***Lesson 2-3***

1. (−2, −4), III **3.** (0, 3), y-axis

5–8.

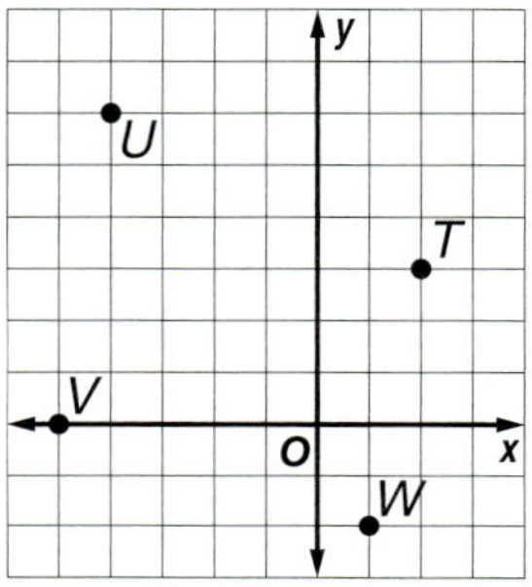

9. China
11. (−2, 2), II
13. (−5, 0), x-axis
15. (2, −2), IV
17. (−4, −1), III
19. (2, 2), I
21. (0, 4); y-axis

23–34.

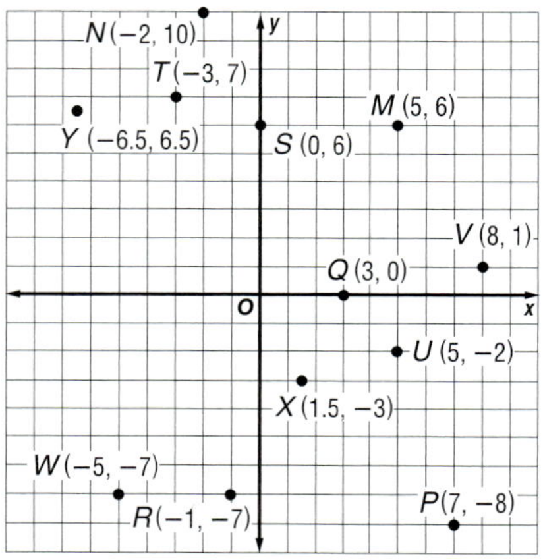

35. Children's Zoo **37.** (−3, −2)

39–41.

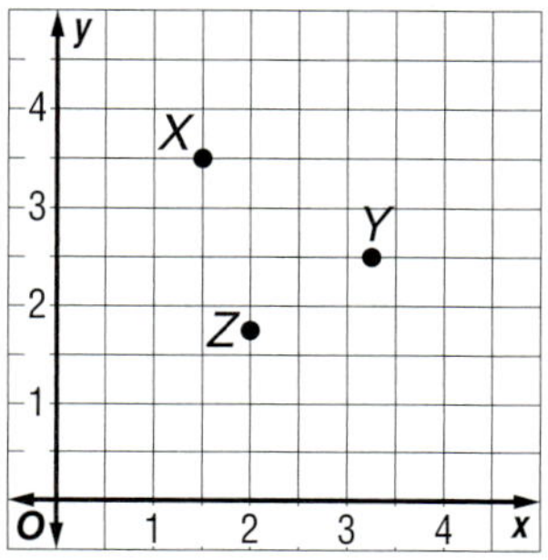

43. Sample answer: Rene Descarte is often credited with inventing the coordinate plane and so the coordinate plane is sometimes called the Cartesian plane, in his honor. The myth is that while a child, Descarte lay in bed one day watching a fly crawling around on the ceiling. In wondering how to tell someone else where the fly was, he realized that he could describe its position by its distance from the walls of the room. **45.** Sample answer: Sometimes; both (−2, 0) and (2, 0) lie on the x-axis.

47. Sample answer: Using the graphic, you can see that an ordered pair such as (−5, −4) is in Quadrant III.

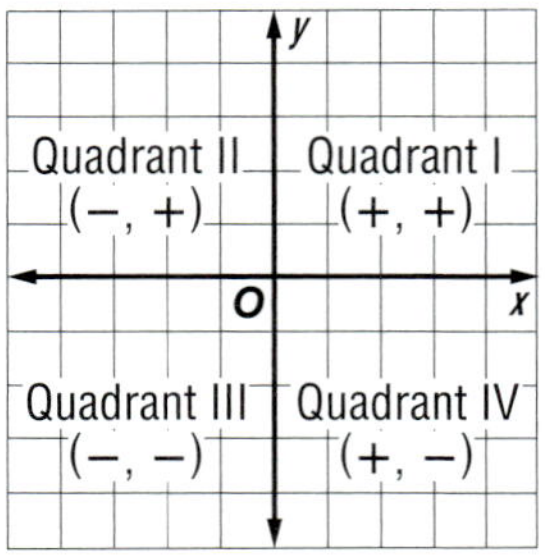

49. Sample answer: Point A is 1 unit to the right and 2 units down from the origin, in quadrant IV. Point B is 2 units to the left and 1 unit up from the origin, in quadrant II. **51.** G **53.** > **55.** < **57.** 48 mi **59.** 1,326 **61.** 11,737

Pages 98–99 ***Lesson 2-4***

1. −14 **3.** 7 **5.** −4 **7.** 0 **9.** −\$25 + \$18; −\$7; Camilia still owes her brother \$7. **11.** −25 **13.** 28 **15.** −6 **17.** −13 **19.** −2 **21.** 2 **23.** 0 **25.** 22 **27.** −19 **29.** 8 + (−14); −6; Hakeem is now 6 feet below street level. **31.** −5 + (−15); −20; The quarterback must now start at a point 20 yards behind the first line of scrimmage. **33.** −13 **35.** −18 **39.** a **41.** $m + (-15)$ **43.** Sample answer: Look at the signs. If the numbers being added are both positive, the sum is positive. If the numbers being added are both negative, the sum is negative. If the numbers being added have different signs, subtract their absolute values and give the sum the sign of the number with the greatest absolute value. If the numbers being added are opposites, the sum is zero. **45.** 1200 **47.** (0, −2); y-axis **49.** (1, 1); I **51.** 162 **53.** 3,265

Pages 105–106 ***Lesson 2-5***

1. −3 **3.** −12 **5.** 24 **7.** −2 **9.** −21 **11.** 22 **13.** −10 **15.** −14 **17.** 23 **19.** 31 **21.** −14 **23.** −30 **25.** 104 **27.** 6 **29.** 0 **31.** 0 **33.** 15 **35.** 11 **37.** 8,757 ft **39.** 5,066 ft **41.** −31 **43.** 23 **45.** Mitsu; Alicia did not add the additive inverse of −19. **47.** Sample answer: To subtract an integer, add its additive inverse. **49.** J **51.** −11 **53.** −14 **55.** 8

Pages 107–111 ***Lesson 2-6***

1. Sample answer: Use the look for a pattern strategy when there is a data table, a series of numbers, or a geometric pattern as part of the problem. **3.** Sample answer: Amanda has \$2 in change in her bank. If she adds \$0.50 each week for 7 weeks, how much money will be in her bank? $5.50 **5.** 9, 12, 18 **7.** Sample answer: 1 half-dollar, 3 quarters, 1 nickel, and 2 pennies **9.** 2 letters and 10 postcards **11.** multiplication; 8,524,425 **13.** division; 0.5 m

Pages 112–113 Lesson 2-7

1. −60 **3.** −28 **5.** 45 **7.** 64 **9.** −12 **11.** 100(−3) = −300; Monifa's investment is now worth $300 less than it was before the price of the stock dropped. **13.** 70 **15.** −220 **17.** −70 **19.** −50 **21.** 80 **23.** −125 **25.** 81 **27.** −45 **29.** 49 **31.** −24 **33.** 24 **35.** 64 **37.** −160 **39.** 5(−650) = −3,250; Ethan burns 3,250 Calories each week. **41.** −243 **43.** 88

47.

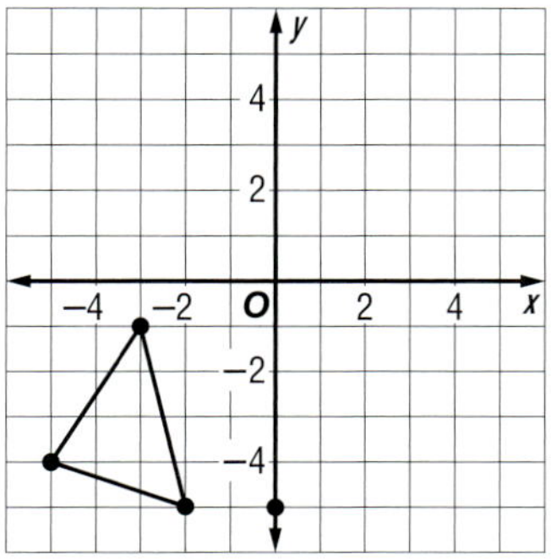

Sample answer: new triangle *P'Q'R'* is on the other side of the origin (in quadrant III) from original triangle *PQR* (which is in quadrant I). **49.** Sample answer: −6 × 3 = −18

51. Sample answer: 1; (−1)(−1) = 1. Since there are 50 ÷ 2 = 25 pairs of (−1) factors, $(-1)^{50} = 1^{25}$. One raised to any power is still 1. **53.** Sample answer: The product of three integers is positive when exactly two intergers are negative or all three integers are positive. **55.** J **57.** 8 **59.** −21 **61.** −6 **63.** −9 **65.** 52, 47, 36, 27, 13, 0, −2, −3, −6, −14 **67.** 20 **69.** 5

Pages 116–118 Lesson 2-8

1. −4 **3.** −6 **5.** 5 **7.** −3 **9.** −42.8°C **11.** −7 **13.** −9 **15.** 10 **17.** −7 **19.** −9 **21.** 9 **23.** 5 **25.** −12 **27.** −3 **29.** 2 **31.** −1 **33.** −10°F **35.** 8 **37.** 1 **39.** −$18 million **41.** −18 ÷ (−9) has a positive quotient; the others have negative quotients **43.** −20, −10, −5, −4, −2, −1, 1, 2, 4, 5, 10, 20 **45.** A **47.** −28 **49.** −35 **51.**

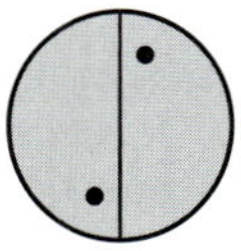

53. −12 **55.** 30

Pages 119–122 Chapter 2 Study Guide and Review

1. false, negative **3.** false, opposite **5.** false, *y*-coordinate **7.** true **9.** false, positive **11.** 350 ft **13.** −12° **15.** 32 **17.** −48 mL **19.** > **21.** < **23.** < **25.** {−32, −23, −21, 14, 19, 25} **27.** 3, 1, 0, −1, −2

28–31.

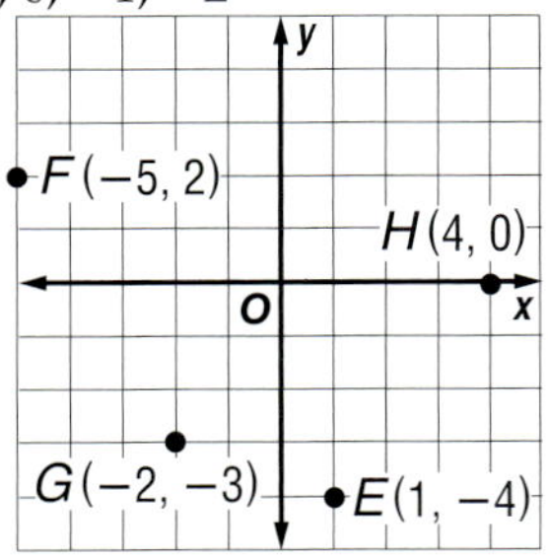

33. 2 **35.** −5 **37.** −5 **39.** −3 **41.** 4 **43.** 17,280 **45.** 576 ft **47.** – 48 **49.** −80 **51.** −15 **53.** 140 **55.** −3 **57.** 9

Chapter 3 Applying Decimals

Page 127 Chapter 3 Getting Ready

1. 46 **3.** 17 **5.** $379 **7.** 972 **9.** 1,015 **11.** 9 **13.** 14 **15.** $49 **17.** 10 • 10 • 10 • 10 • 10 = 100,000 **19.** 10 • 10 • 10 • 10 = 10,000

Pages 129–131 Lesson 3-1

1–37. Sample answers are given. **1.** 6 × 4 or 24 **3.** 60 × 30 or 1,800 **5.** 25 ÷ 5 or 5 **7.** 1,000 ÷ 40 or 2 **9.** 10 × 3 or 30 **11.** 20 × 8 or 160 **13.** 30 × 80 or 2,400 **15.** 40 × 2 or 80 million tons **17.** 30 ÷ 3 or 10 **19.** 80 ÷ 20 or 4 **21.** 36 ÷ 12 or 3 **23.** $49 ÷ 7 or $7 per yd **25.** yes **27.** no; 2 × 5 × 7 or 70 **29.** no; 75 ÷ 25 or 3 **31.** 80 × 40 or 3,200 **33.** 70 × 70 or 4,900 **35.** 300 ÷ 120 or 2.5 **37.** 60 × 10 or 600 ft **41.** Sample answer: 2.1 × 4.2 × 4.8 **43.** Sample answer: 17.5 ÷ 3.7; Use 20 and 4 since 20 and 4 are compatible numbers. 17.5 ÷ 3.7 → 20 ÷ 4 or 5. **45.** G **47.** −8 **49.** −11 **51.** 16 **53.** −54 **55.** 24 **57.** 72

Pages 136–139 Lesson 3-2

1. 2.7 **3.** 0.015 **5.** 0.415 tsp **7.** 4.05 **9.** 0.7904 **11.** 3.5 **13.** 14.4 **15.** 12.78 **17.** 12.04 **19.** 0.06 **21.** 0.066 **23.** 10.8 yd **25.** 0.42 **27.** 1.36 **29.** 1.83 **31.** 0.216 **33.** 12.288 **35.** 4.3125 **37.** 3.25 mi **39.** 0.0325 **41.** 0.3 × 1.4; 0.42 **43.** 3,474 **45.** 23 **47.** 6.5 **49.** 67.44 **51.** $791.44 **53.** 3 nickels, 3 quarters or nickels and a dime **55.** 35.8 **57.** Each term is 3 times the previous term.; 97.2 **59.** Sample answer: 2 × 2 × 3 or $12; $8.91; The estimate was low because both 1.5 and 1.98 were rounded up to the nearest whole number. **61.** 0.5 **63.** 1.2 **65.** never; 1.5 × 2.3 = 3.45 and 3.45 > 1.5 and 2.3 **67.** Sample answer: number sense; Since 0.9 is less than 1, she can determine that 125 × 0.9 would be less than 125 × 1 or 125. **69.** 474.5 **71.** Sample answer: 50 × 2 or 100 **73.** Sample answer: 75 ÷ 25 or 3 **75.** −7 **77.** 2 × 36 + 3 × 24 **79.** 1,000

Pages 142–144 Lesson 3-3

1. 6.7 **3.** 8,950 **5.** 0.045 **7.** 0.0032 **9.** 25 **11.** 9 **13.** 7,620 **15.** 6.7 **17.** 95,300 **19.** 17,201 **21.** 28,600,000 mi **23.** 0.003 **25.** 0.87 **27.** 0.00346 **29.** 0.002 **31.** 0.00045 **33.** 0.00003 **35.** $89 **37.** 78 **39.** 0.0075 **41.** 0.0341 **43.** 0.32 **45.** 0.12 **47.** $22.50 **49.** Sample answer: Find the product of 0.1 and the number and triple it; 7.5. **51.** Sample answer: Move the decimal point in $4.95 one place to the right. The cost of the 10 items would be $49.50 **53.** H **55.** 21.93 **57.** 0.01992 **59.** Sample answer: 30 × 8 or 240 **61.** Sample answer: 40 ÷ 5 or 8 **63.** 3.2 **65.** 27.5

Pages 150–152 Lesson 3-4

1. 2.9 **3.** 1.09 **5.** 32.7 **7.** 825 **9.** 0.06

11. 20.5 min **13.** 1.8 **15.** 3.6 **17.** 1.08 **19.** 0.88 **21.** 1.218 **23.** 0.0075 **25.** 24.8 g **27.** 41.2 **29.** 0.14 **31.** 10 **33.** 2.05 **35.** 20.3 **37.** 9.5 **39.** \$0.49 per lb **41.** 18.85 **43.** 7.2 **45.** 10 **47.** 8.0 m/s **49.** about 6.2 times **51.** One large-sized package cost \$4.89 and two regular-sized packages costs 2(\$2.59) or \$5.18. So, it makes sense to buy one large-sized package. **53.** Sample answer: $3.5 \div 0.5 = 7.0$ and $0.5 \div 3.5 = 0.1428571429$ **55.** $2.4 \div 6$ would be less than 1 since the divisor is greater than the dividend. **57.** Sample answer: Divide as you would if the decimals were whole numbers. Then estimate the quotient. Use the estimate to place the decimal point. **59.** 26 **61.** 8.5 **63.** 0.0572 **65.** Sample answer: 7 + 20 or about 27 **67.** Sample answer: 10×60 or about 600 **69.** 82°F, 84°F, 81°F **71.** −8, −5, −2, 7, 8 **73.** 1.75

Pages 154–155 ***Lesson 3-5***

1. Sample answer: When you need an exact answer and the calculations are not simple. **3.** Sample answer: A 10-package of pens costs \$7.90. What is the cost for each pen? Using mental math, ask yourself, what number times 10 is \$7.90. Since $0.79 \times 10 = 7.90$, the cost for each pen is \$0.79. **5.** Calculator; 1156.716 m **7.** Mental math; \$3.10 **9.** 587,322,000 mi **11.** Sample answer: 6,400,000 − 4,200,000 or 2,200,000 **13.** Subtraction followed by division; \$32.10 each month

Pages 159–161 ***Lesson 3-6***

1. 370 **3.** 45,000 **5.** 1.46 **7.** 1.6 km **9.** 0.983 **11.** 30 **13.** 7,500 **15.** 73,200 **17.** 0.0821 **19.** 9,100 **21.** 130,500 **23.** 57 **25.** 0.51 kg **27.** 156,500 g **29.** 0.022 **31.** 93,000 **33.** 0.04 **35.** 200 cm **37.** 100 g to 1,200 g **39.** 0.02 km, 3,000 cm, 50 m **41.** 35,100 mg, 0.32 kg, 345 g **43.** Since 1 km = 1,000 m, the bridges that are about 1 kilometer long are Mackinac, George Washington, and Tacoma Narrows II **45.** 5 cobblers **47.** Hunter; Arturo multiplied 45.7 by 1,000; he should have divided by 1,000. **49.** Sample answer: How many kilometers are in 500 meters? 0.5 km **51.** B **53.** 1724 **55.** mental math; 60 mi **57.** 0.35 **59.** 164,000 **61.** 9 **63.** −18 **65.** 100,000 **67.** 10,000

Pages 164–166 ***Lesson 3-7***

1. 4.1×10^5 **3.** 1.58×10^7 **5.** 2.6×10^6 **7.** 1.5×10^{11} **9.** 7,050,000 **11.** about 8.5 times more **13.** 3.6×10^4 **15.** 1.54×10^5 **17.** 8.406×10^6 **19.** 2.48×10^7 **21.** 4.0×10^6 **23.** 3.0×10^{10} **25.** 1.42×10^{10} people **27.** 4,900 **29.** 5,400,000 **31.** 248,000 **33.** 980,000,000 **35.** 151,200,000 **37.** = **39.** < **41.** 63,400, 6.03×10^5, 5,980,100, 6.98×10^6, **43.** 3.63×10^9 **45.** 0.18 **47.** 0.0072 **49.** Sample answer: Numbers written in standard form do not contain exponents, 8,100,000,000. A number written as the product of a number and a power of ten is written in scientific notation, 8.1×10^9. **51.** The number 36.42×10^5 is not written in scientific notation because 36.42 is not less than 10. **53.** G **55.** 0.036 **57.** 1,280,000 **59.** (−1, −3); III **61.** (2, −1); IV **63.** 0.7 is added to each term; 8.9, 9.6, 10.3

Pages 167–170 ***Chapter 3*** ***Study Guide and Review***

1. false; gram **3.** false; meter **5.** true **7.** false; 6 **9.** false; left **11.** Sample answer: 9×3 or 27 **13.** Sample answer: 18×20 or 360 **15.** Sample answer: $100 \div 5$ or 20 **17.** $14 \div 2$ or 7 bags of pretzels **19.** 0.021 **21.** 0.496 **23.** 8.5701 **25.** 81 **27.** 0.175 **29.** 186,000 mi/s **31.** 577 **33.** 5.472 **35.** mental math; $100 \times 14.5 = 1{,}450$ g **37.** 76,500 **39.** 0.118 **41.** 24,140 m **43.** 2.3149×10^6 **45.** 2.0×10^{10} **47.** 69,400 **49.** about 21.96 or 22 times greater

Chapter 4 Algebra: Linear Equations and Functions

Page 175 ***Chapter 4*** ***Getting Ready***

1. 4 **3.** −11

5.

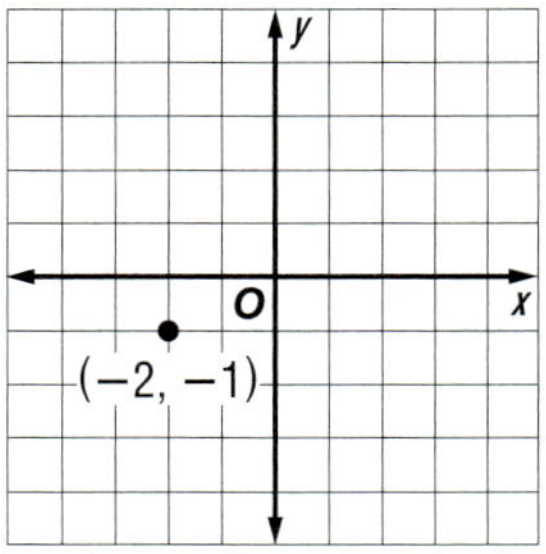

7. −8 **9.** 4 **11.** −11 **13.** 14 **15.** 2 **17.** −2

Pages 179–181 ***Lesson 4-1***

1. $n + 8$ **3.** $n - 9 = 24$ **5.** $2m = 18$ **7.** $x - 3 = 32.3$ **9.** $15 + t$ **11.** $n - 10$ **13.** $8r$ **15.** $\frac{a}{3}$ **17.** $n + 4 = -8$ **19.** $5d = -20$ **21.** $h - 10 = 26$ **23.** $c + 3.5 = 5.5$ **25.** the length is 4 times the width **27.** the width is 5 less than the length **29.** $j - 9$ **31.** $s + 2$ **33.** $c + 300$ **35.** \$20 bill **37.** Sample answer: 5 dollars more than my allowance is 8 dollars **39.** $x + 2$; $x - 2$ **41.** C **43.** 2,700 **45.** 9,360,000 **47.** about \$1.33 per song **49.** 25 **51.** 10 **53.** −11 **55.** −8

Pages 187–189 ***Lesson 4-2***

1. 2 **3.** −2 **5.** $d + 120 = 364$; 244 ft **7.** 5 **9.** 7 **11.** 7 **13.** −3 **15.** −9 **17.** 17 **19.** 7 **21.** $7 = w + 2$; 5 **23.** $15 = t - 3$; 18 years old **25.** 61 **27.** −5 **29.** −12 **31.** 18.4 **33.** 6.4 **35.** −0.68 **37.** $d - 5 = 18$; \$23 **39.** $35 + 45 + x = 180$; 100° **41.** $2 + 4 + s = 0$; −6 **43.** $h + 105 = 415$; 310 ft **45.** $s - 93 = 7$; 100 mph **47.** The value of y decreases by 3. **49.** C **51.** $p + 180$ **53.** 3.782 km **55.** 2.6 **57.** 1.52

Pages 192–194 ***Lesson 4-3***

1. 3 **3.** −3 **5.** 15 h **7.** 7 **9.** −3 **11.** 7 **13.** −9 **15.** 4 **17.** −8 **19.** $15w = 300$; 20 weeks **21.** $1{,}500 = 600h$; 2.5 hr **23.** 23 **25.** 18 **27.** 4.7

29. Sample answer: The *Magnum* has the greater speed. The track is almost twice as long, and yet the ride only takes 15 more seconds than the *Blue Streak*. **31.** $6k = 600$; $k = 100$ seconds **33.** Jesse; the variable is multiplied by -5. To solve for x, you need to divide each side of the equation by the entire coefficient, -5. **35.** Sample answer: Billie has twice as many cards as Tyree. If Billie has 16 cards, how many does Tyree have? **37.** Sample answer: If it takes a scuba diver 4 seconds to swim 8 meters below the surface of the water, what is the rate of descent? **39.** 2250 **41.** -10 **43.** -3 **45.** 11 days

Pages 196–197 Lesson 4-4

1. When you are given the final result and asked to find an earlier amount. **3.** Sample answer: In the first four games, Hannah scored a total of 83 points. In the fourth game she scored 19 points. In game three, she scored 27 points and in the second game she scored 22 points. How many points did she score in the first game? To solve, first subtract 19 from 83, which is 64. Then subtract 27 from 64 to get 37. Finally, subtract 22 from 37. So, Hannah scored 15 points in her first game. **5.** 4 **7.** Greg rented 9 videos, Paloma rented 5, Grace rented 1, and Jack rented 10. **9.** Maya is 15 years old.

11.

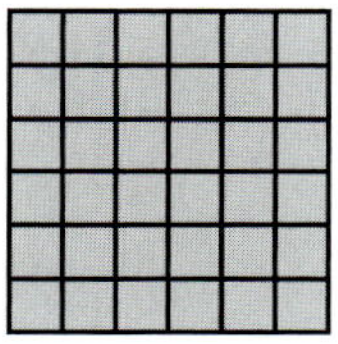

13. Multiplication followed by subtraction; Mikhail's car gets 17,74,074 more inches per gallon than an aircraft carrier.

Pages 201–203 Lesson 4-5

1. 2 **3.** 3 **5.** 3 **7.** $14c + 23 = 65$; 3 CDs **9.** 3 **11.** -4 **13.** 4 **15.** 9 **17.** 8 **19.** 11 **21.** $74 + 15w = 149$; 5 wk **23.** 2.25 **25.** 2.1 **27.** 28 **29.** $8 + 47.6d = 960$; 20 days **31.** Less than; -3°F is about -19.4°C. **33.** $\frac{1}{2}(20x) - 18 = 200$; $x = 21.8$; They must sell at least 22 subscriptions. **35.** Sample answer: A flower shop charges \$2 for each flower in a vase and \$5 for the vase. How many flowers can you place in a vase if you have \$15 to spend? **37.** 2.92 **39.** 7 **41.** 41 **43.** 14 ft **45.** 14 **47.** 16

Pages 206–209 Lesson 4-6

1. 18 yd **3.** 7 in. **5.** 26.25 ft^2 **7.** 36 ft **9.** 14.8 mm **11.** 11 ft **13.** 18 in. **15.** 78 ft^2 **17.** 183.6 m^2 **19.** 6.5 in^2 **21.** 5 squares **23.** $\ell = 33$ ft **25.** 17,010 ft^2 **27.** perimeter; 4 mi **29.** area; 13 ft **31.** 270 m^2 **35.** 9 yd;

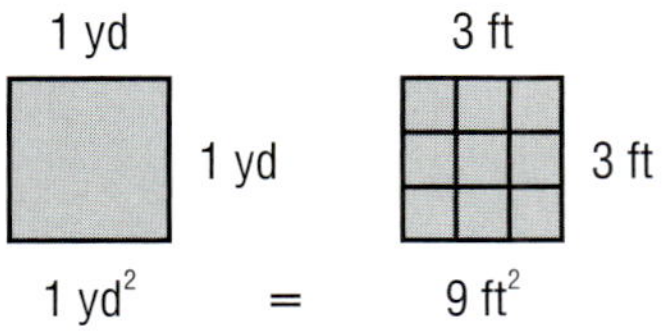

37. 144 yd;

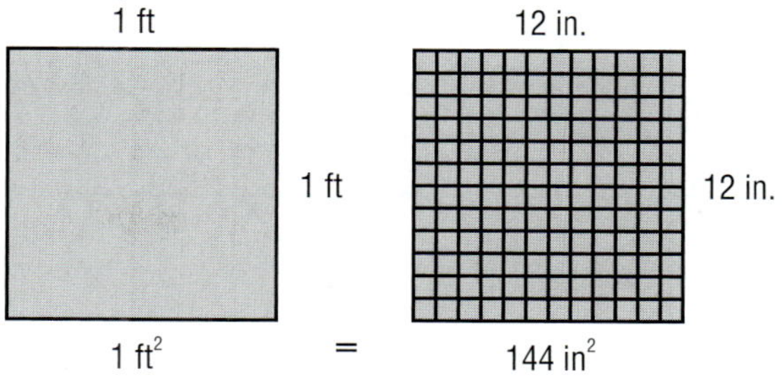

39. When the width of a rectangle is doubled, the perimeter becomes $2\ell + 4w$ and the area becomes $2\ell w$, or in other words, the area is doubled. **41.** $P = 2(3w + 1) + 2w$ or $P = 8w + 2$ **43.** A **45.** -2 **47.** 3.5 **49.** $5x = 11.25$; \$2.25 **51.** < **53.** 11 years old

55.

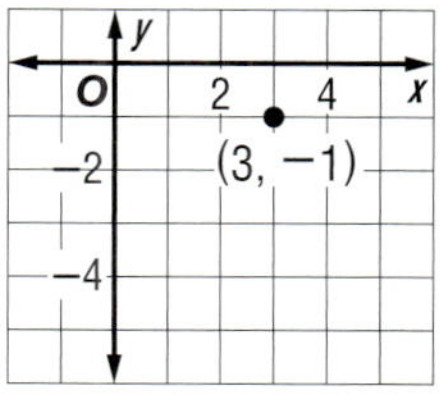

57.

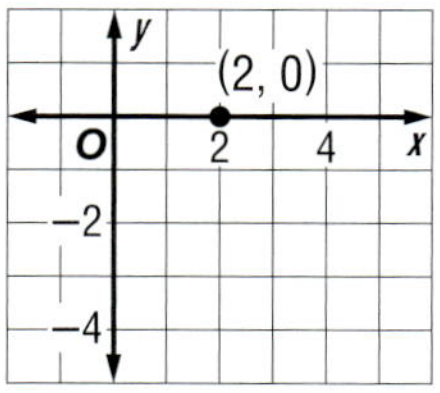

Pages 214–215 Lesson 4-7

1.

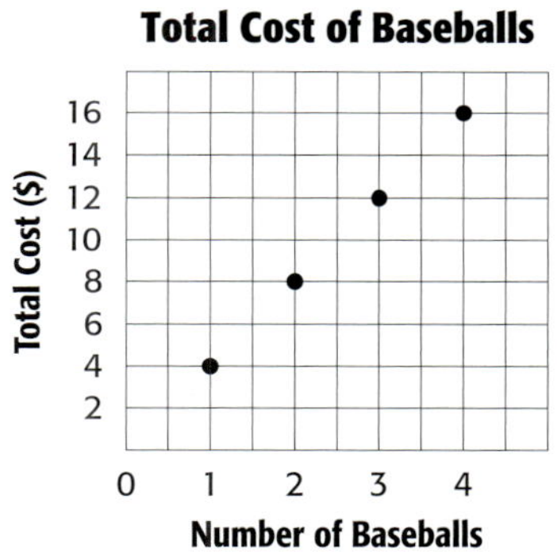

3.

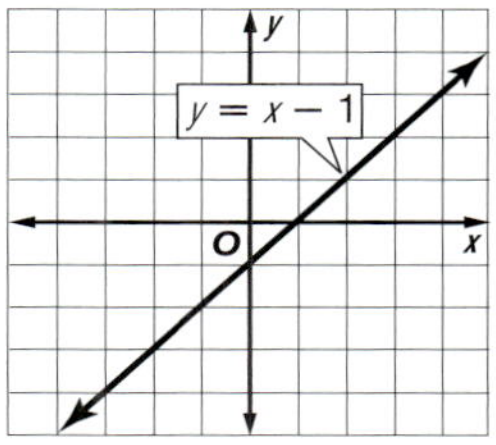

5.

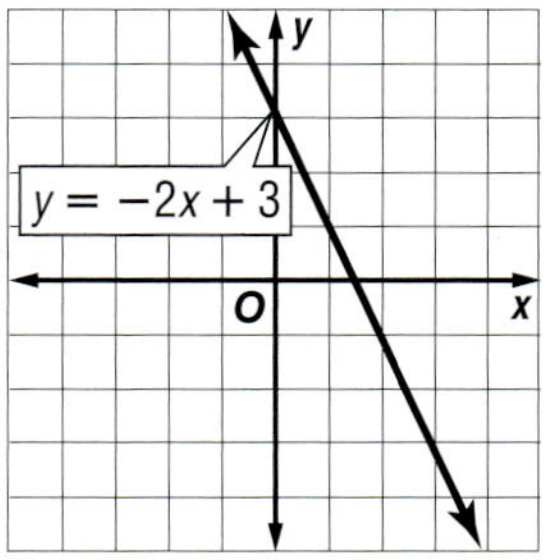

7.

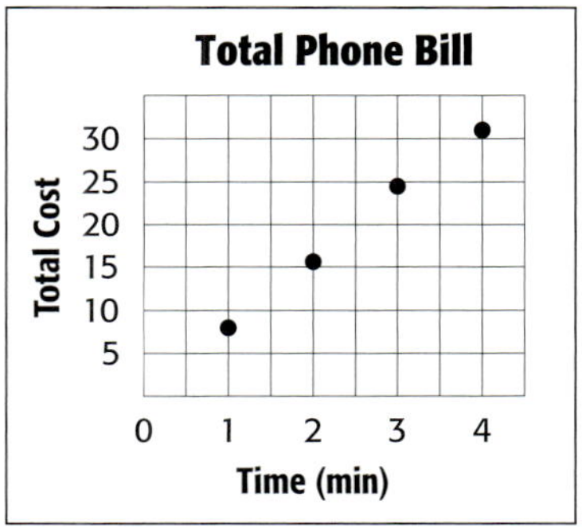

Selected Answers

9.

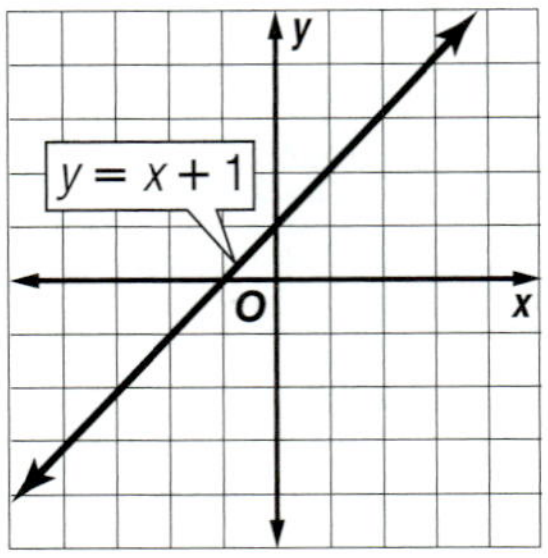

11.

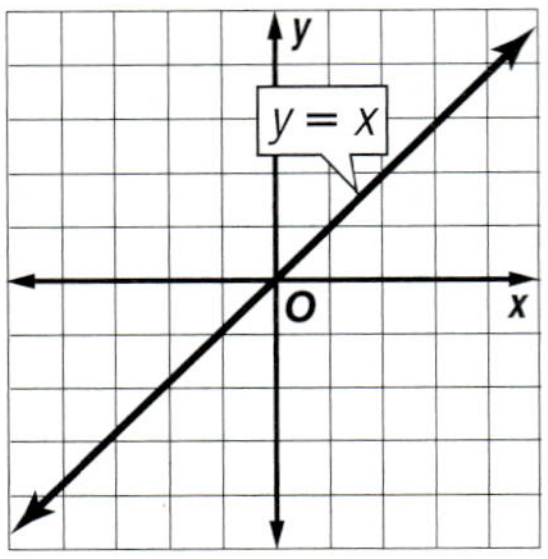

13.

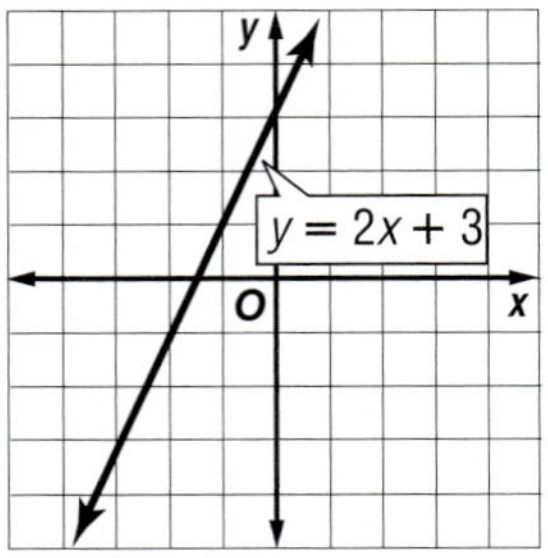

15.

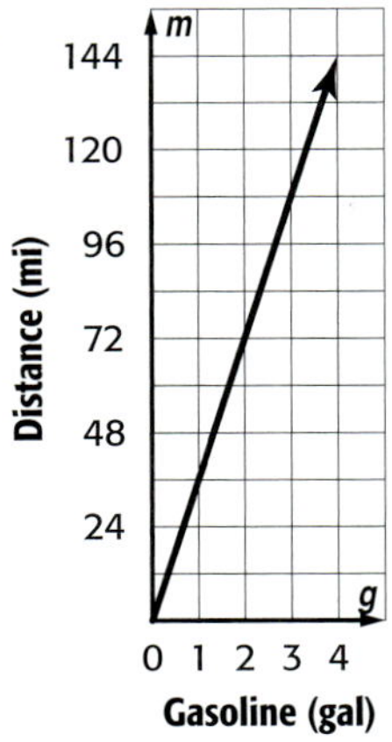

17.

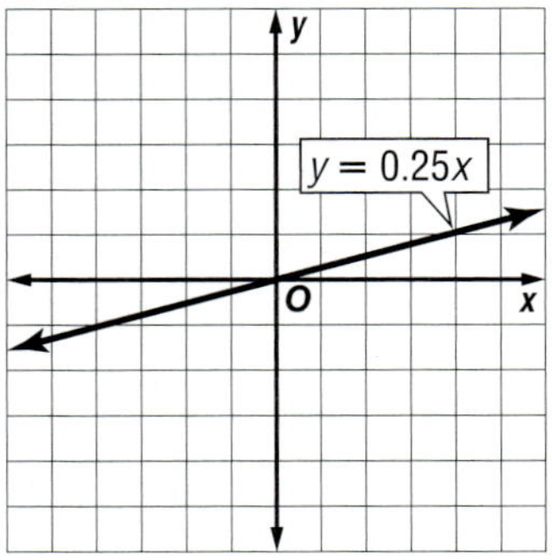

19.

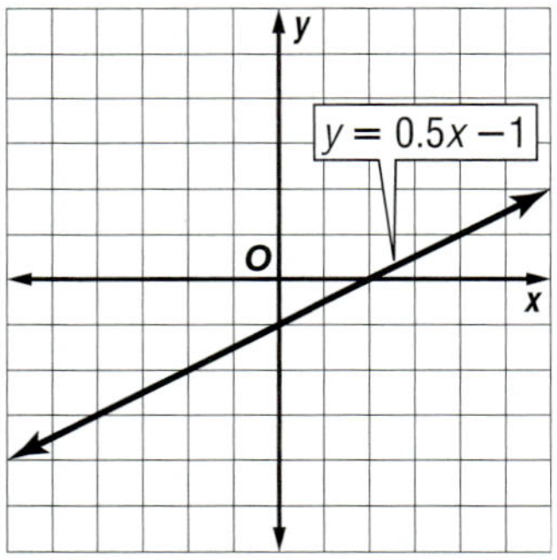

21. Sample answer: (2, 1), (3, 1.5), (4, 2) **23.**

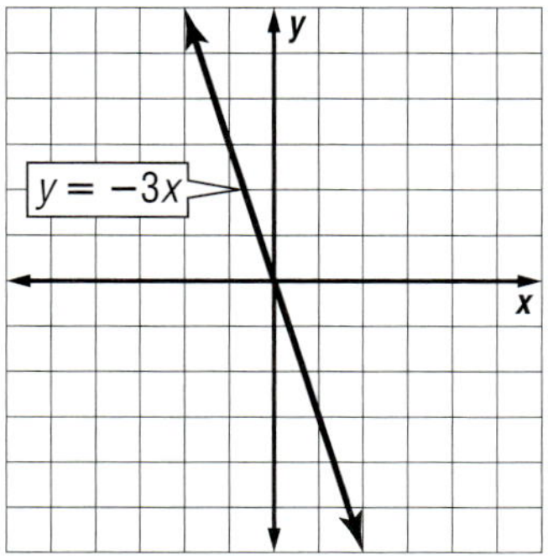

25. C **27.** −3 **29.** 4 **31.** 15

Pages 217–220 Chapter 4 Study Guide and Review

1. true **3.** true **5.** true **7.** false; subtract 3 from each side **9.** true **11.** false; perimeter **13.** $x + 5$ **15.** $2a$ **17.** $n - 4 = 19$ **19.** $t = f + \$8.75$ **21.** −6 **23.** 23 **25.** 37 **27.** 4 **29.** −9 **31.** $14w = 98$; 7 weeks **33.** $146.70 **35.** 4 **37.** −2 **39.** 5 **41.** 53.4 in.; 142.82 in^2 **43.** 7 mi

45. 16 yd **47.** 12 ft

49.

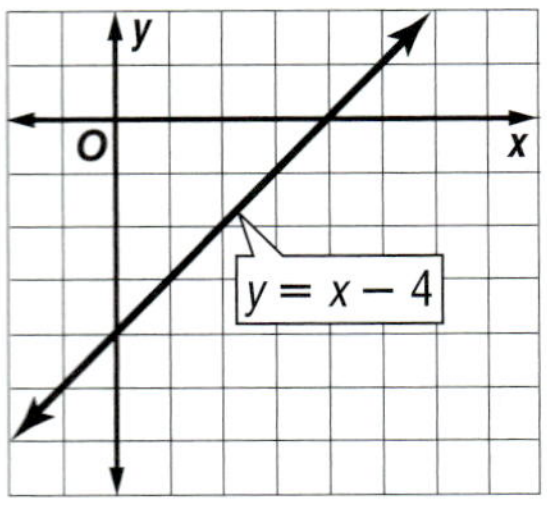

51.

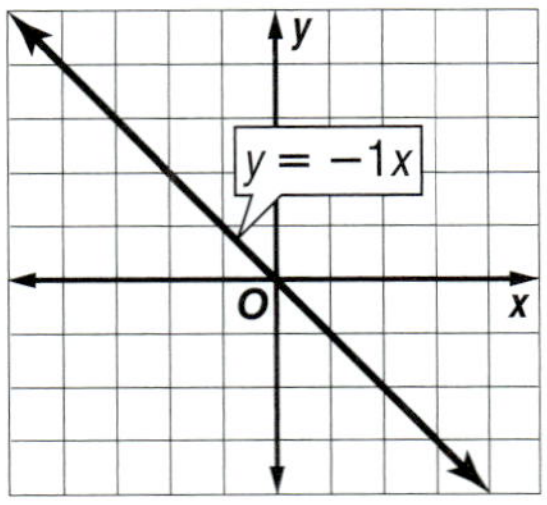

53.

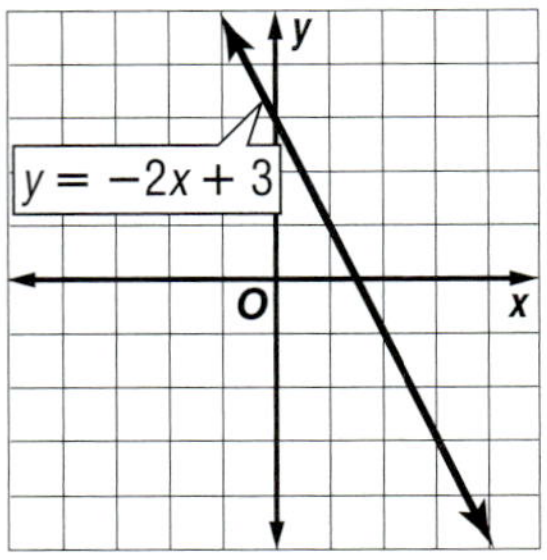

55. $y = 6x$

Chapter 5 Fractions, Decimals, and Percents

Page 227 Chapter 5 Getting Ready

1. 0.61 **3.** 0.33 **5.** Kirsten **7.** 2, 3, 6 **9.** Yes; the sum of the digits, 6, is divisible by 3. **11.** 6 **13.** 0.75 **15.** $5 \times 5 \times 5 \times 5 \times 5$ **17.** $9 \times 9 \times 9 \times 9$

Pages 231–232 Lesson 5-1

1. prime **3.** prime **5.** 2×17 **7.** $2^2 \times 3$ **9.** $2 \cdot 2 \cdot 2 \cdot 2 \cdot x \cdot x$ **11.** composite **13.** prime **15.** composite **17.** prime **19.** $2^5 \times 3$ **21.** $3^2 \times 11$ **23.** $2 \times 3 \times 5 \times 7$ **25.** $2 \times 3^2 \times 7$ **27.** $2 \cdot 5^2$ **29.** $3 \cdot 5 \cdot m \cdot n$ **31.** $2 \cdot 17 \cdot j \cdot k \cdot m$ **33.** $2 \cdot 2 \cdot 13 \cdot g \cdot h \cdot h$ **35.** 7 **37.** 5^2 **39.** $2^8 \times 5$ **41.** prime **43.** $2^3 \times 3 \times 5$ **45.** Sample answer: twenty 2 ft-by-3 ft tiles, or twelve 2 ft-by-5 ft tiles **47.** 36 **49.** If $n = 1$, $2n$ is a prime number. If $n > 1$, $2n$ is a composite number with at least three factors. **51.** H **53.** 36 ft; 65 ft^2 **55.** −4 **57.** 0 **59.** 2, 5, 10 **61.** 3, 9

Pages 236–237 Lesson 5-2

1. 6 **3.** 10 **5.** 4 **7.** 9 **9.** 10 **11.** 16 **13.** 15 **15.** 5 **17.** 12 **19.** 2 **21.** 4 in. **23.** 3 ft **25.** $10mn$ **27.** Sample answer: 18 and 81 **29.** Sample answer: 15 and 45 **31.** $14 **33.** never **35.** sometimes **37.** 2 **39.** $3 \times 5 \times 5$

41.

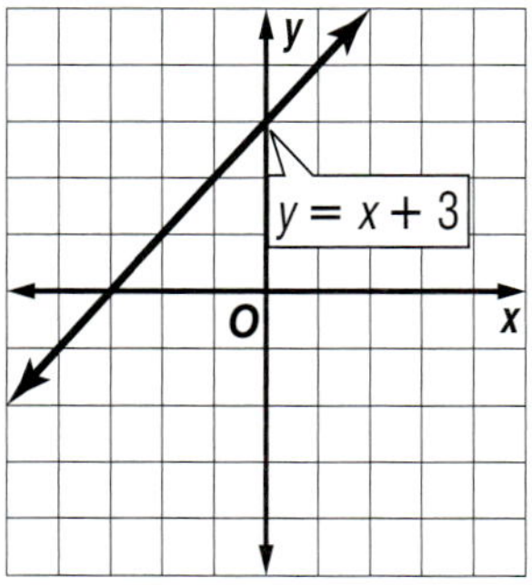

43. Sample answer: 80 + 70 + 70 + 60 or 280

Pages 238–239 ***Lesson 5-3***

1. Sample answer: By making an organized list, you can show all the possible ways to make a woodwind trio. Count the number of trios to determine the answer. **3.** 12 **5.** 6 **7.** 27, 29 **9.** 40 cookies **11.** 7 in. **13.** addition followed by division; \$1,200 + \$288 + \$360 = \$1,848; \$1,848 ÷ 24 = \$77

Pages 242–243 ***Lesson 5-4***

1. $\frac{1}{3}$ **3.** $\frac{2}{5}$ **5.** $\frac{2}{3}$ **7.** $\frac{5}{7}$ **9.** $\frac{7}{10}$ **11.** $\frac{4}{7}$ **13.** $\frac{6}{7}$ **15.** 1 **17.** $\frac{5}{6}$ **19.** $\frac{5}{7}$ **21.** $\frac{2}{5}$ **23.** $\frac{1}{5}$ **25.** $\frac{3}{4}$ **27.** $\frac{1}{3}$ **31.** No, because both the numerator and denominator can be divided by 2. **33.** Sample answer: A fraction is in simplest form if the GCF of the numerator and denominator is 1. **35.** F **37.** 9 **39.** 5 **41.** 0.5 **43.** 0.7

Pages 247–248 ***Lesson 5-5***

1. 0.4 **3.** 7.5 **5.** 0.125 **7.** $0.\overline{5}$ **9.** $\frac{11}{50}$ **11.** $4\frac{3}{5}$ **13.** 0.8 **15.** 4.16 **17.** 0.3125 **19.** 0.6 **21.** 5.875 **23.** $0.\overline{4}$ **25.** $0.\overline{16}$ **27.** $5.1\overline{3}$ **29.** $\frac{1}{5}$ **31.** $\frac{11}{20}$ **33.** $5\frac{24}{25}$ **35.** $30\frac{1}{2}$ cm **39.** $0.54\overline{6}$ **41.** $8.0\overline{3}$ **43.** Felisa; Sample answer: Felisa's batting average is about 0.286. Harmony's batting average is about 0.263. 0.286 > 0.263, so Felisa's average is better than Harmony's. **45.** Sample answer: $3\frac{1}{7} \approx 3.14286\ldots$ and $3\frac{10}{71} \approx 3.14085$; Since 3.1415927… is between $3\frac{1}{7}$ and $3\frac{10}{71}$, Archimedes was correct. **47.** B **49.** $\frac{5}{12}$ **51.** $\frac{2}{7}$ **53.** 9 pizzas **55.** $\frac{3}{9}$ or $\frac{1}{3}$ **57.** $\frac{4}{12}$ or $\frac{1}{3}$

Pages 252–253 ***Lesson 5-6***

1. 57% **3.** 25% **5.** 85% **7.** $\frac{9}{10}$ **9.** $\frac{11}{50}$ **11.** 42% **13.** 99.9% **15.** $66\frac{2}{3}\%$ **17.** 80% **19.** 26% **21.** 60% **23.** 100% **25.** 30% **27.** $\frac{3}{10}$ **29.** $\frac{22}{25}$ **31.** $\frac{13}{100}$ **33.** 3 **35.** < **37.** = **39.** > **41.** 64% **43.** 1%; the other ratios equal 10% **45.** C **47.** $\frac{3}{5}$ **49.** $2\frac{4}{5}$ **51.** 3 **53.** 4 **55.** 71 **57.** 0.791

Pages 256–258 ***Lesson 5-7***

1. 0.68 **3.** 0.276 **5.** 9% **7.** 73% **9.** 0.27 **11.** 0.06 **13.** 0.185 **15.** 0.022 **17.** 0.277 **19.** 0.3025 **21.** 0.686 **23.** 70% **25.** 580% **27.** 95% **29.** 17% **31.** 67.5% **33.** 1.2% **35.** 72.7% **37.** Memorial, Houston **39.** < **41.** > **43.** < **45.** 0.044; 0.02083; 0.0115; 0.00625; 0.0045 **47.** 5.625 in. **49.** Sample answer: 0.25, $\frac{1}{4}$, 25% **51.** 37.5% **53.** 3.125% **55.** D **57.** 72% **59.** 3.1% **61.** \$218.75 **63.** 2 × 5 × 5 **65.** 2 × 2 × 19

Pages 261–262 ***Lesson 5-8***

1. 28 **3.** 60 **5.** 60 **7.** 2016 **9.** 72 **11.** 72 **13.** 315 **15.** 72 **17.** 420 **19.** 144 **21.** 6:00 P.M. **23.** 50¢ **25.** Sample answer: 5, 7 **27.** Sample answer: 10, 35 **29.** 4 packages of juice boxes and 5 packages of oatmeal snack bars **31.** $2^2 \cdot 5^2$, or 100 **33.** Sample answer: 3, 10, 15 **35.** C **37.** 0.55 **39.** 0.0025 **41.** $\frac{17}{25}$ **43.** 4.8×10^8 mi **45.** <

Pages 266–268 ***Lesson 5-9***

1. > **3.** < **5.** Yes; it is written as a fraction. **7.** C **9.** < **11.** = **13.** < **15.** > **17.** > **19.** < **21.** > **23.** = **25.** Cecil; $\frac{11}{15} > \frac{5}{18}$ **27.** no; Sample answer: Since the number neither terminates nor repeats, it is not rational. **29.** no; Sample answer: Since the number neither terminates nor repeats, it is not rational. **31.** yes; Sample answer: Since the number repeats, it is rational. **33.** $\frac{8}{10}$, 0.805, 81% **35.** $1\frac{1}{25}$, 1.25, 1.4 **37.** 44%, 0.47, $\frac{4}{7}$ **39.** > **41.** Eastern Chipmunk **43.** Bustos: 0.346; Kretschman: 0.333; Nuveman: 0.313; Watley: 0.400; Watley **45.** 0.06; 0.06 equals 6% and the other ratios equal 60%.

47. Sample answer: Gwen needs $\frac{2}{5}$ yard of fabric and $\frac{3}{8}$ yard of ribbon to make a pillow. Which item does she need more, fabric or ribbon? Answer: fabric **49.** F **51.** 42 **53.** 48 **55.** 0.13 **57.** 18 **59.** 12

Pages 269–272 ***Chapter 5*** ***Study Guide and Review***

1. false; division **3.** true **5.** false; least common multiple **7.** true **9.** 2^7 **11.** 5 × 19 **13.** 65 = 5 × 13 **15.** 6 **17.** 21 **19.** \$12 **21.** 15 different plans **23.** $\frac{7}{12}$ **25.** $\frac{2}{9}$ **27.** $\frac{1}{2}$ **29.** 0.75 **31.** $0.\overline{5}$ **33.** 6.4 **35.** $\frac{7}{10}$ **37.** $\frac{1}{20}$ **39.** $\frac{27}{50}$ **41.** $5.\overline{13}$ min **43.** 44% **45.** 40% **47.** $\frac{19}{20}$ **49.** $\frac{4}{25}$ **51.** 0.48 **53.** 0.125 **55.** 61% **57.** 19% **59.** 0.23 **61.** 8 **63.** 24 **65.** 120 **67.** < **69.** > **71.** English

Chapter 6 Applying Fractions

Page 277 ***Chapter 6*** ***Getting Ready***

1. 35 **3.** 30 **5.** 21.6 **7.** 0.83 **9.** 4 **11.** $2\frac{6}{5}$ **13.** $5\frac{5}{4}$ **15.** $\frac{5}{3}$ or $1\frac{2}{3}$ c

Pages 281–283 ***Lesson 6-1***

1–41. Sample answers are given. **1.** 8 + 2 = 10 **3.** 6 × 3 = 18 **5.** $0 + \frac{1}{2} = \frac{1}{2}$ **7.** $\frac{1}{2} \times 1 = \frac{1}{2}$ **9.** $\frac{1}{4} \cdot 16 = 4$ **11.** 12 ÷ 4 or about 3 shelves **13.** 1 + 6 = 7 **15.** 4 − 2 = 2 **17.** 2 · 3 = 6 **19.** 9 ÷ 3 = 3 **21.** $\frac{1}{2} + \frac{1}{2} = 1$ **23.** $1 - \frac{1}{2} = \frac{1}{2}$ **25.** $\frac{1}{2} \cdot 1 = \frac{1}{2}$ **27.** 0 ÷ 1 = 0 **29.** 16 + 1 or 17 in. **31.** $\frac{1}{6} \times 36 = 6$ **33.** 25 ÷ 5 = 5 **35.** 24 ÷ 2 = 12 **37.** 39 **39.** 24 **41.** $\frac{1}{2} \times 200$ or 100 **43.** Sample answer: $\frac{1}{4} \times 60$ inches or 15 inches **45.** Sample answer: $\frac{11}{12}$ and $\frac{7}{15}$; $\frac{11}{12} - \frac{7}{15} \approx 1 - \frac{1}{2}$ or $\frac{1}{2}$ and $\frac{11}{12} \cdot \frac{7}{15} \approx 1 \cdot \frac{1}{2}$ or $\frac{1}{2}$ **47.** Estimation;

Dion doesn't need an exact answer. Sample answer: $3\frac{1}{4} + 1\frac{2}{3} + 1\frac{2}{3}$ is about halfway between 6 and 7 cups. Since this is more than 6 cups, Dion cannot use this bowl to mix the ingredients. **49.** C **51.** $>$ **53.** $<$ **55.** 5 pkg. of necklaces and 3 pkg. of bracelets **57.** 37.5% **59.** 1.9% **61.** 10 **63.** 15

Pages 286–289 ***Lesson 6-2***

1. $\frac{2}{3}$ **3.** $\frac{1}{4}$ **5.** $\frac{13}{24}$ **7.** $\frac{1}{4}$ **9.** $\frac{11}{16}$ in. **11.** $\frac{4}{7}$ **13.** $\frac{2}{3}$ **15.** $\frac{2}{3}$ **17.** $1\frac{13}{24}$ **19.** $\frac{4}{9}$ **21.** $\frac{14}{45}$ **23.** $1\frac{11}{20}$ ft **25.** $\frac{3}{8}$ **27.** $\frac{23}{28}$ **29.** $\frac{7}{12}$ **31.** $1\frac{1}{4}$ **33.** $2\frac{2}{3}$ **35.** Jon; $\frac{1}{18}$ of the race **37.** $\frac{2}{3} - \left(\frac{1}{6} + \frac{1}{4}\right) = \frac{1}{4}$ **39.** $\frac{2}{15}$ **41.** $1\frac{7}{12}$ **43.** $\frac{3}{4}$ **45.** Sample answer: The sum of two unit fractions $\frac{1}{a}$ and $\frac{1}{b}$, where a and b are not 0, is $\frac{a+b}{ab}$.

$\frac{1}{a} + \frac{1}{b} = \frac{1 \cdot b}{a \cdot b} + \frac{1 \cdot a}{b \cdot a}$	Rename each fraction using the LCD, ab.
$= \frac{b}{ab} + \frac{a}{ab}$	Simplify.
$= \frac{b+a}{ab}$	Add the numerators.
$= \frac{a+b}{ab}$	Commutative Property

So, $\frac{1}{99} + \frac{1}{100} = \frac{99 + 100}{99 \cdot 100}$ or $\frac{199}{9{,}900}$ **47.** Lourdes; Meagan did not rename the fractions using the LCD. **49.** A **51.** Sample answer: $1 - \frac{1}{2} = \frac{1}{2}$ **53.** Sample answer: $16 \div 8 = 2$ **55.** friend/family **57.** −1 **59.** 5 **61.** 9 **63.** $4\frac{3}{8}$

Pages 292–294 ***Lesson 6-3***

1. $9\frac{6}{7}$ **3.** $4\frac{2}{3}$ **5.** $1\frac{1}{2}$ **7.** $4\frac{5}{8}$ **9.** $8\frac{1}{6}$ gal **11.** $7\frac{5}{7}$ **13.** $2\frac{1}{7}$ **15.** $7\frac{5}{12}$ **17.** $18\frac{17}{24}$ **19.** $3\frac{1}{2}$ **21.** $2\frac{11}{20}$ **23.** $5\frac{7}{8}$ **25.** $7\frac{1}{6}$ **27.** 570 ft **29.** $3\frac{1}{4}$ in. **31.** $15\frac{1}{4}$ **33.** $1\frac{3}{4}$ **35.** $7\frac{1}{8}$ yd **37.** Sample answer: $4\frac{2}{3} - 1\frac{5}{6}$ **39.** 20 ft; If the initial string is 20 feet and cut in half, the two halves would each be 10 feet. Cutting one-fifth of one of these 10 foot halves would require splitting the 10 feet into five equal parts. Each part would be 2 feet. So, cutting one-fifth of 10 feet would be the same as cutting 2 feet. The remaining portion would be 8 feet long.

41. D **43.** $\frac{7}{15}$ **45.** Sample answer: $4 + 7 = 11$ **47.** Sample answer: $4 - 1 = 3$ **49.** 3:55 P.M.

Pages 295–296 ***Lesson 6-4***

1. Sample answer: Use estimation, look for a pattern, work backward. **3.** Sample answer: A fishbowl holds $1\frac{1}{2}$ gallons of water. If there is $\frac{1}{3}$ gallon of water in the bowl, how many more gallons are needed to fill the bowl; $\frac{2}{3}$ gallons, $1\frac{1}{6}$ gallons, or $2\frac{1}{6}$ gallons. Answer: $\frac{2}{3}$ gallon is not enough because that would make exactly 1 gallon of water in the tank. $2\frac{1}{6}$ gallons is too much, since the tank only holds $1\frac{1}{2}$ gallons. The answer is $1\frac{1}{6}$ gallons. **5.** J **7.** $\frac{5}{8}$ in.

9.

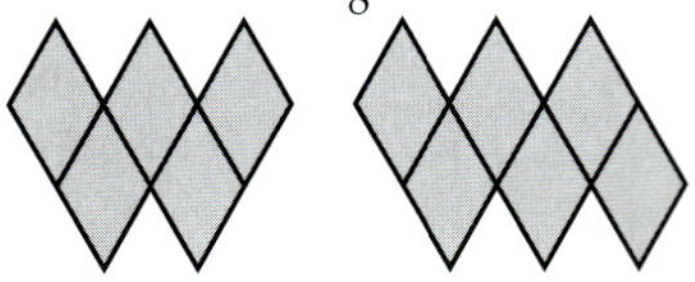

11. 1 in.

13. Addition followed by subtraction; $\frac{2}{5} + \frac{1}{3} = \frac{11}{15}$; $1 - \frac{11}{15} = \frac{4}{5}$

Pages 303–305 ***Lesson 6-5***

1. $\frac{2}{9}$ **3.** $\frac{2}{3}$ **5.** $1\frac{1}{2}$ **7.** $2\frac{1}{2}$ in. **9.** $\frac{4}{15}$ **11.** $4\frac{4}{5}$ **13.** $\frac{1}{9}$ **15.** $\frac{1}{20}$ **17.** $\frac{3}{8}$ **19.** $\frac{3}{4}$ **21.** $\frac{3}{16}$ **23.** 14 c **25.** $1\frac{9}{16}$ **27.** 30 **29.** $31\frac{1}{3}$ **31.** 20 **33.** $7\frac{1}{20}$ mi **35.** $\frac{8}{21}$ **37.** $\frac{11}{48}$ **39.** $16\frac{1}{3}$ yd; $10\frac{5}{6}$ yd^2 **41.** one pint **43.** one centimeter **45.** $15\frac{3}{4}$ **47.** $28\frac{3}{4}$ **49.** broccoli: $1\frac{7}{8}$ c, pasta: $5\frac{5}{8}$ c, salad dressing: 1 c, cheese: 2 c; Multiply each amount by $1\frac{1}{2}$. **51.** $\frac{2}{3} \times \frac{3}{5}$; $\frac{6}{25}$ **53.** Always; Sample answer: A model showing the product of two fractions will always be partially shaded, representing a part of a whole or less than 1. **55.** Sample answer: $3\frac{2}{5} \times 4\frac{5}{12} = \left(3 + \frac{2}{5}\right) \times \left(4 + \frac{5}{12}\right) \neq (3 \times 4) + \left(\frac{2}{5} \times \frac{5}{12}\right)$. We cannot perform multiple operations in any order. If the only operation was addition or if the only operation was multiplication, we could add in any order or multiply in any order, respectively. But when there is both addition and multiplication, we must follow the order of operations, which tells us that we need to perform the operations inside the parentheses, in this case addition of each whole number and fraction, before multiplying.

57. H **59.** $2\frac{1}{10}$ in. **61.** $>$ **63.** 6 **65.** 6 **67.** 5

Pages 309–311 ***Lesson 6-6***

1. $\frac{5}{8}$ **3.** $\frac{5}{29}$ **5.** 32 **7.** 20.5 **9.** 32 **11.** 32 **13.** $\frac{6}{5}$ or $1\frac{1}{5}$ **15.** $\frac{6}{1}$ or 6 **17.** $\frac{1}{3}$ **19.** $\frac{8}{41}$ **21.** 36 **23.** 14.4 **25.** 2.88 **27.** 30 **29.** $\frac{20}{21}$ **31.** $6\frac{2}{3}$ **33.** 137.5 mi **35.** −75 **37.** 41.4 **39.** $1\frac{1}{2}$ **41.** x = number of species; $\frac{3}{4}x = 540$; 720 species **43.** x = number of servings; $\frac{3}{4}x = 16\frac{1}{2}$; 22 servings **45.** x = the person's age; $\frac{1}{3}x = 26$; 78 years old **47.** Sample answer: By solving $8 = \frac{m}{4}$, you find that $m = 32$. So, replace m with 32 to find $32 - 12 = 20$. **49.** Sample answer: Use the Multiplicative Property to multiply each side by 2. Then use the Division Property to divide each side by h. So, $b = \frac{2A}{h}$. **51.** A **53.** $\frac{1}{6}$ **55.** $\frac{2}{5}$ **57.** $3\frac{5}{12}$ c **59.** 0.08 **61.** 1.23 **63.** 4,720 **65.** 11,700 **67.** Sample answer: $18 \div 3 = 6$ **69.** $0 \div 1 = 0$

Pages 315–318 ***Lesson 6-7***

1. $\frac{3}{8}$ **3.** $3\frac{1}{2}$ **5.** $\frac{1}{15}$ **7.** $1\frac{1}{5}$ **9.** 51 bookmarks **11.** $\frac{7}{16}$ **13.** $1\frac{1}{3}$ **15.** 12 **17.** $\frac{2}{3}$ **19.** 12 **21.** $\frac{4}{15}$ **23.** $\frac{2}{3}$ **25.** $2\frac{17}{20}$ **27.** $7\frac{4}{5}$ **29.** 36 **31.** 3 **33.** $\frac{2}{3}$ **35.** $\frac{3}{10}$ **37.** 25 **39.** $\frac{1}{22}$ **41.** $\frac{3}{11}$ **43.** 4 **45.** $7\frac{9}{10}$ times as many **47.** 6:30 P.M.; Sample answer: $105 \div 35 = 3$, The storm will travel 105 miles in 3 sets of $\frac{1}{2}$ hour, or $1\frac{1}{2}$ hours. Adding $1\frac{1}{2}$ hours to 5:00 P.M. will make it 6:30 P.M. **49.** Sample answer; You could use paper and pencil; $\frac{3}{4}$ of what number is $1\frac{1}{2}$? $1\frac{1}{2}$ feet $\div \frac{3}{4} = \frac{3}{2}$ feet $\cdot \frac{4}{3} = 2$ feet. **51.** Yes. If the first proper fraction is larger than the second proper fraction then the resulting quotient will be a whole number or mixed number. **53.** H **55.** $\frac{13}{4}$ or $3\frac{1}{4}$ **57.** $\frac{4}{21}$ **59.** 4.5 ft

Pages 319–322 ***Chapter 6*** ***Study Guide and Review***

1. numerators **3.** reciprocal **5.** unlike **7.** $1\frac{11}{7}$ **9.** 3 **11.** reciprocal **13.** Sample answer: $3 \div 1 = 3$ **15.** Sample answer: $1 \times 0 = 0$ **17.** Sample answer: $\frac{1}{2} \times 26 = 13$ **19.** Sample answer: 19×10 or about 190 ft^2 **21.** $\frac{1}{6}$ **23.** $\frac{2}{3}$ **25.** $\frac{5}{24}$ **27.** $\frac{5}{8}$ in. **29.** $9\frac{11}{15}$ **31.** $10\frac{1}{7}$ **33.** $2\frac{4}{15}$ **35.** $15\frac{1}{8}$ **37.** $7\frac{11}{12}$ h **39.** G **41.** $\frac{5}{27}$ **43.** $2\frac{3}{5}$ **45.** $9\frac{3}{8}$ **47.** $\frac{12}{7}$ or $1\frac{5}{7}$ **49.** $\frac{3}{10}$ **51.** 15 **53.** 0.75 **55.** $\frac{7}{10}$ **57.** $3\frac{3}{10}$ **59.** $1\frac{21}{22}$ **61.** 54

Chapter 7 Ratios and Proportions

Page 329 ***Chapter 7*** ***Getting Ready***

1. 48.1 **3.** 7.4 **5.** $\frac{1}{5}$ **7.** $\frac{19}{23}$ **9.** $\frac{39}{50}$ **11.** $\frac{3}{50}$ **13.** 450 **15.** 2,200

Pages 332–334 ***Lesson 7-1***

1. $\frac{2}{15}$ **3.** $\frac{1}{51}$ **5.** yes. $\frac{12}{20} = \frac{3}{5}$ and $\frac{6}{10} = \frac{3}{5}$ **7.** no; Sample answer: $\frac{2 \text{ boxes}}{\$5} \neq \frac{6 \text{ boxes}}{\$20}$, since $2 \cdot 3 = 6$, but $5 \cdot 3 \neq 20$ **9.** $\frac{3}{2}$ **11.** $\frac{1}{3}$ **13.** $\frac{2}{5}$ **15.** $\frac{21}{1,600}$ **17.** $\frac{21}{32}$ **19.** yes; $\frac{4}{16} = \frac{1}{4}$ and $\frac{10}{40} = \frac{1}{4}$, so $\frac{4}{16} = \frac{10}{40}$ **21.** no; $\frac{8}{6} = \frac{4}{3}$ and $\frac{12}{10} = \frac{6}{5}$, so $\frac{8}{6} \neq \frac{12}{10}$ **23.** no; Sample answer: $\frac{12 \text{ in.}}{3 \text{ in.}} = \frac{4}{1}$ and $\frac{6 \text{ in.}}{1 \text{ in.}} = \frac{6}{1}$, so $\frac{12 \text{ in.}}{3 \text{ in.}} \neq \frac{6 \text{ in.}}{1 \text{ in.}}$ **25.** yes; $1 : 1.5 = \frac{2}{3}$, $5 : 7.5 = \frac{2}{3}$. The picture will fit the frame. **27.** 9 lbs **29.** $\frac{80}{20} = \frac{4}{1}$; 4 times **31.** Areas A and C; both ratios simplify to a growth-to-removal ratio of $\frac{11}{30}$. **33.** 80; Sample answer: $440 + 80 = 520$; $\frac{520}{1,200} = \frac{13}{30}$ which is the same ratio as area B **35.** 4; The ratios of successive terms increase by 1; $\frac{480}{240} = 2$, $\frac{240}{80} = 3$, $\frac{80}{20} = 4$ **37.** B **39.** $\frac{6}{7}$ **41.** $1\frac{2}{3}$ **43.** $5\frac{2}{3}$ **45.** 4.9 **47.** \$0.31

Pages 337–340 ***Lesson 7-2***

1. 6 mi per gal **3.** \$0.50 per lb **5.** C **7.** 60 mi/h **9.** 30.4 people per class **11.** 3.5 m/s **13.** \$0.14/oz **15.** about \$0.50 per pair **17.** Susanna; 1.78 m/s > 1.66 m/s > 1.23 m/s **19.** Soft drink A and B have about 3 grams of sodium per ounce and Soft drink C has about 6 grams per ounce. **21.** 510 words **23.** Sample answer: about 60 **25.** 168.3 **27.** 38¢ per lb; $\$1.89 \div 5 \approx \$1.90 \div 5$ or \$0.38 **29.** 3 c **31.** about 1 h 36 min 24 s **33.** The bear's heart beats 120 times in 2 minutes when it is active. **35.** the bear's heart rate in beats per minute **37.** when it is active; Sample answer: The active line increases faster than the hibernating line when read from left to right. **41.** Always; every rate is a ratio, because it is a comparison of two quantities by division. **43.** Sample answer: a; $\frac{30 \text{ ft}}{2 \text{ min}} = 15$ ft/min, $\frac{40 \text{ ft}}{2 \text{ min}} = 20$ ft/min **45.** C **47.** $\frac{2}{9}$ **49.** $\frac{9}{14}$ **51.** 8 subs **53.** 14 **55.** 2.1

Pages 345–347 ***Lesson 7-3***

1. 48 **3.** 52 **5.** 3 **7.** $7\frac{1}{2}$ **9.** 1,280 times greater; 4 lb = 4 lb $\cdot \frac{16 \text{ oz}}{\text{lb}}$ or 64 lb; 64 oz ÷ 0.05 oz or 1,280 **11.** $4\frac{1}{2}$ **13.** 16 **15.** 24 **17.** 6,600 **19.** $6\frac{1}{2}$ **21.** 6,750 **23.** 3,520 ft **25.** $17\frac{1}{2}$ qt **27.** 50 bushels; 1 ton = 2,000 lb and 2,000 lb $\div \frac{40 \text{ lb}}{1 \text{ bushel}} = 50$ bushels **29.** No; 15 in. $+ 4\frac{1}{2}$ in. $+ 6\frac{3}{4}$ in. $= 26\frac{1}{4}$ in. and $26\frac{1}{4} \div 12 = 2\frac{3}{16}$. So, it snowed a total of $2\frac{3}{16}$ ft or about 2 ft, not $2\frac{1}{2}$ ft. **31.** $\frac{1}{2}$ **33.** $2\frac{1}{4}$ **35.** 112,000 **37.** The x-value represents the number of quarts and the y-value represents the equivalent number of gallons. **39.** Sample answer: The point on the line whose y-value is equal to 2.5 is (2.5, 10), so 2.5 qt = 10 gal. **41.** Sample answer: Annabelle is making brownies. The recipe calls for 2 cups of sour cream. She has 2 pints of sour cream. Does she have enough sour cream to make the brownies? **43.** >; Sample answer: $8\frac{3}{4}$ gal is equivalent to 35 qt, Since 35 qt > 32 qt, $8\frac{3}{4}$ gal > 32 qt. **45.** Yes; 2 qt = 8 c, so the ratio of cups vinegar to water in the recommended mixture is $\frac{\frac{3}{4} \text{ c}}{2 \text{ qt}} = \frac{\frac{3}{4} \text{ c}}{8 \text{ c}} = \frac{3}{4} \div 8 = \frac{3}{4} \cdot \frac{1}{8}$ or $\frac{3}{32}$. The ratio of the new mixture is $\frac{1.5 \text{ oz}}{16 \text{ oz}} = \frac{1.5 \cdot 2}{16 \cdot 2}$ or $\frac{3}{32}$. The mixtures have the same ratio of vinegar to water. **47.** D **49.** \$11.90 **51.** $\frac{18}{1}$ **53.** $\frac{17}{1}$ **55.** $\frac{381}{4}$ **57.** $40r = 300$; \$7.50/h **59.** $7.5t = 11.25$; 1.5 **61.** 8 **63.** 22

Pages 351–353 ***Lesson 7-4***

1. No; sample answer: $\frac{10 \text{ children}}{2 \text{ adults}} = \frac{5 \text{ children}}{1 \text{ adult}}$ and $\frac{12 \text{ children}}{3 \text{ adults}} = \frac{4 \text{ children}}{1 \text{ adult}}$. The unit rates are not equal. **3.** Yes; sample answer: The cross products of the ratios $\frac{8}{21}$ and $\frac{12}{31.5}$, 8 × 31.5 and 21 × 12, are both equal to 252. **5.** 15 **7.** 29.4 **9.** 20 **11.** $8.33 **13.** No; sample answer: The cross products of the ratios $\frac{20}{6}$ and $\frac{16}{5}$, 20 × 5 or 100 and 6 × 16 or 96, are not equal. **15.** Yes; sample answer: The cross products of the ratios $\frac{16}{200}$ and $\frac{28}{350}$, 16 × 350 and 200 × 28, are both equal to 5,600. **17.** No; sample answer: The cross products of the ratios $\frac{1.4 \text{ T}}{18 \text{ days}}$ and $\frac{10.5 \text{ T}}{60 \text{ days}}$, 1.4 × 60 or 84 and 18 × 10.5 or 189, are not equal. **19.** No; $\frac{45 \text{ min}}{25 \text{ pages}} = \frac{1.8 \text{ min}}{1 \text{ page}}$ and $\frac{60 \text{ min}}{30 \text{ pages}} = \frac{2 \text{ min}}{1 \text{ page}}$. These rates are not equivalent. **21.** 15 **23.** 3 **25.** 1.5 **27.** 63 **29.** 2.4 **31.** 13.5 **33.** 4.2 lb **35.** 7 stalks **37.** $10\frac{2}{3}$ oz **39.** 1.6 oz **41.** $19.50 **43.** $\frac{325}{13} = \frac{100}{x}$; 4 **45.** $5.70 for 6 lb; Sample answer: This ratio has a unit rate of 0.95/lb, while all of the other ratios have a unit rate of $0.90/lb. **47.** Sample answer: Mental math; $10 is 4 times more than $2.50, so the number of ears is 4 times more than a dozen, which is 4 dozen or 48 ears of corn. **49.** B **51.** 10 **53.** 7 **55.** $20\frac{9}{16}$ **57.** $17\frac{5}{32}$

Pages 356–357 ***Lesson 7-5***

1. 270 mi; Sample answer:

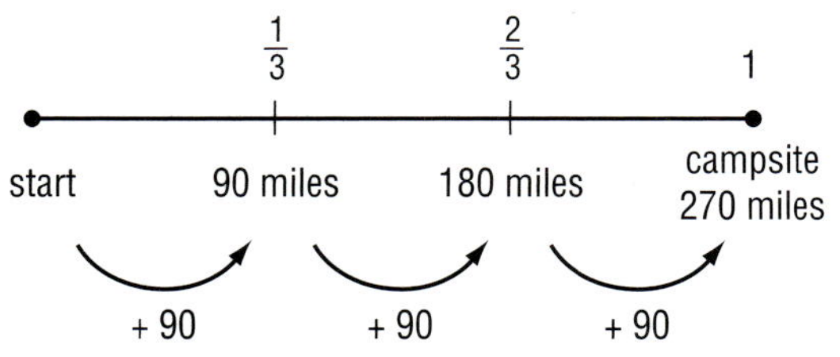

3. $\frac{5}{8}$ ft **5.** 125 minutes **7.** 15 games **9.** Subtraction; $2 × 10^9

Pages 361–364 ***Lesson 7-6***

1. 50 km **3.** 130 km **5.** 21 ft **7.** $16\frac{2}{3}$ in. **9.** $\frac{1}{48}$ **11.** $\frac{1}{63{,}360}$ **13.** 81 mi **15.** 40 mi **17.** 12 ft by 9 ft **19.** $11\frac{3}{5}$ in.; $\frac{1}{90}$ **21.** 6 in.; $\frac{1}{720}$ **23.** 26 mi **25.** $\frac{1}{12}$; 60 ft **29.** $\frac{5{,}000}{1}$ **31a.** A; 0.5 cm is larger than 1 mm. If 0.5 cm on the model is equal to 1 mm on the actual figure, then model A must be larger than the actual figure. **31b.** 1.5 mm is smaller than 4 cm. If 1.5 mm on the model is equal to 4 cm on the actual figure, then model B must be smaller than the actual figure. **31c.** C; 0.25 cm is equal to 2.5 mm. If 0.25 cm on the model is equal to 2.5 mm on the actual figure, then model C must be the same size as the actual figure. **33.** Sample answer: Using the scale given on the map, look at the distance between the two cities on the map and then estimate the actual distance based on the distance given in the scale. **35.** 72 **37.** 10.5 ft **39.** 3.3¢ per oz **41.** 45 mi **43.** 36.1 **45.** 8,000 **47.** 5,300 **49.** $\frac{13}{30}$ **51.** $\frac{7}{8}$

Pages 369–370 ***Lesson 7-7***

1. $\frac{27}{100}$ **3.** $\frac{3}{40}$ **5.** $\frac{5}{8}$ **7.** 16% **9.** 11.11% **11.** $\frac{5}{8}$ **13.** $\frac{23}{80}$ **15.** $\frac{1}{3}$ **17.** $\frac{15}{16}$ **19.** $\frac{33}{500}$ **21.** 55% **23.** 37.5% **25.** 96.67% **27.** 71.43% **29.** 1.25% **31.** 41.67% **33.** 2.5% **35.** $<$ **37.** $>$ **39.** $\frac{1}{2}$%, $\frac{2}{5}$, 0.48, 0.5 **43.** Less than; $\frac{26}{125}$ = 20.8% **45.** Sample answer: One method is to write a proportion using the given fraction and $\frac{n}{100}$. Then find the cross products, solve for n, and add a %. Another method is to write the fraction as a decimal. Then multiply by 100 and add a %. **47.** G **49.** 6 **51.** 2 **53.** $\frac{4}{5}$ **55.** $4\frac{1}{12}$ **57.** $1\frac{2}{3}$

Pages 372–374 ***Lesson 7-8***

1. 3.25; $3\frac{1}{4}$ **3.** 4.8; $4\frac{4}{5}$ **5.** 0.0015; $\frac{3}{2{,}000}$ **7.** 0.009; $\frac{9}{1{,}000}$ **9.** 0.15% **11.** 275% **13.** 325% **15.** 3.5; $3\frac{1}{2}$ **17.** 6 **19.** 0.006; $\frac{3}{500}$ **21.** 0.0055; $\frac{11}{2{,}000}$ **23.** 0.001; $\frac{1}{1{,}000}$ **25.** 850% **27.** 264% **29.** 0.9% **31.** 0.34% **33.** 140% **35.** 350% **37.** 0.4% **39.** 0.00125 **41.** 0.0012 **43.** 0.003; $\frac{3}{1{,}000}$; So, 0.003 of the population of the United States was Japanese. **45.** 0.0005 **47.** about 0.595% **49.** Julie; the first step is to divide 3 by 2,000. The next step is to convert to a percent by multiplying by 100. Mikasi multiplied by 10,000. **53.** G **55.** $\frac{3}{250}$ **57.** $\frac{37}{40}$ **59.** 0.85 **61.** 0.369

Pages 375–378 ***Chapter 7*** ***Study Guide and Review***

1. ratio **3.** rate **5.** scale drawing **7.** scale factor **9.** unit rate **11.** $\frac{4}{3}$ **13.** $\frac{2}{3}$ **15.** no; $\frac{18}{24} = \frac{3}{4}$, $\frac{5}{20} = \frac{1}{4}$, and $\frac{3}{4} \neq \frac{1}{4}$ **17.** Yes; sample answer: 2:28 = $\frac{1}{14}$ and 12:168 = $\frac{28}{168}$ or $\frac{1}{14}$, so the recommended ratio is met. **19.** 90 mi per day **21.** 64-oz bottle **23.** 24 **25.** $4\frac{1}{2}$ **27.** 6 **29.** 12.5 **31.** 9 **33.** 721.8 lb **35.** 45 **37.** 94 cm **39.** $\frac{27}{500}$ **41.** 12.5% **43.** 17.5% **45.** 1.25; $1\frac{1}{4}$ **47.** 0.005; $\frac{1}{200}$ **49.** 475% **51.** 1.35; $1\frac{7}{20}$

Chapter 8 Applying Percents

Page 383 ***Chapter 8*** ***Getting Ready***

1. 48 **3.** 1,512 **5.** $54.75 **7.** 0.34 **9.** 0.75 **11.** 75 **13.** 38.9 **15.** 0.17 **17.** 1.57 **19.** 0.075

Pages 388–390 ***Lesson 8-1***

1. 4 **3.** 110.5 **5.** 23 **7.** $3.25 **9.** $194.40 **11.** 45.9

13. 14.7 **15.** 17.5 **17.** 62.5 **19.** \$290 **21.** 3.5 **23.** 97.8 **25.** 92.5 **27.** \$19.95 **29.** 3.3 **31.** 990 **33.** 520 **35.** 0.24 **37.** \$9.75 **39.** \$297 **41.** about 1,432 **43.** Sample answer: 53% of 60 → 50% × 60 or $\frac{1}{2} \times 60 = 30$ **45.** Sample answer: 75% of 19 → 75% × 20 or $\frac{3}{4} \times 20 = 15$ **47.** 80 **49.** Sample answer: 24% × 250 or 60 people prefer cherries. So, 250 − 60 or 190 people did not prefer cherries. **51.** 15 **53.** Sample answer: Determine the number of questions answered correctly on a test and find how much to tip a restaurant server. **55.** Less than the original number; you are subtracting 10% of a greater number. **57.** B **59.** 7.5 **61.** 0.0004 **63.** 71% **65.** 3.45×10^5 **67.** 31, 38, 45 **69.** 70

Pages 395–396 ***Lesson 8-2***

1. 36% **3.** 0.7 **5.** 75 **7.** 3 c **9.** 7.5% **11.** 8.6 **13.** 375 **15.** \$12.50 **17.** 40% **19.** 4.1 **21.** 192 **23.** 0.2% **25.** \$8 **27.** about 3.4% **29.** about 6,378 km **31.** 20% of 500, 20% of 100, 5% of 100; If the percent is the same but the base is greater, then the part is greater. If the base is the same but the percent is greater, then the part is greater. **33.** B **35.** 30 **37.** 2.75 **39.** 3 **41.** 30 **43.** 18

Pages 399–402 ***Lesson 8-3***

1. 5; $\frac{1}{2} \cdot 10 = 5$; $0.1 \cdot 10 = 1$ and $5 \cdot 1 = 5$ **3.** 24; $\frac{2}{5} \cdot 60 = 24$; $0.1 \cdot 60 = 6$ and $4 \cdot 6 = 24$ **5.** $(1 \cdot 70) + \left(\frac{1}{2} \cdot 70\right) = 105$ **7.** about \$50; $\frac{1}{4} \cdot \$200 = \$50$; $0.1 \cdot 200 = 20$ and $2.5 \cdot 20 = \$50$ **9.** about 160,000 acres; $0.1 \cdot 20{,}000{,}000 = 200{,}000$ and $\frac{4}{5}$ of $200{,}000 = 160{,}000$ **11.** 18; $\frac{1}{5} \cdot 90 = 18$; $0.1 \cdot 90 = 9$ and $2 \cdot 9 = 18$ **13.** 135; $\frac{3}{4} \cdot 180 = 135$; $0.1 \cdot 180 = 18$ and $7.5 \cdot 18 = 135$ **15.** 90; $\frac{9}{100} \cdot 100 = 90$; $0.1 \cdot 100 = 10$ and $9 \cdot 10 = 90$ **17.** 36; $\frac{3}{10} \cdot 120 = 36$; $0.1 \cdot 120 = 12$ and $3 \cdot 12 = 36$ **19.** 90; $\frac{3}{5} \cdot 150 = 90$; $0.1 \cdot 150 = 15$ and $6 \cdot 15 = 90$ **21.** 168; $\frac{7}{10} \cdot 240 = 168$; $0.1 \cdot 240 = 24$ and $7 \cdot 24 = 168$ **23.** about 12 muscles; $\frac{3}{10} \cdot 40 = 12$ **25.** $(2 \cdot 300) + \left(\frac{1}{4} \cdot 300\right) = 675$ **27.** $0.01 \cdot 200 = 2$ and $\frac{3}{4} \cdot 2 = 1.5$ **29.** $0.01 \cdot 70 = 7$ **31.** about 2,700 birds; $0.01 \cdot 450{,}000 = 4{,}500$ and $\frac{3}{5} \cdot 4{,}500 = 2{,}700$ **33.** $\frac{1}{2} \cdot 80 = 40$ **35.** $\frac{1}{10} \cdot 240 = 24$ **37.** $1 \cdot 45 = 45$ **39.** about 3 hours; Method 1: $\frac{1}{3} \cdot 24 = 8$ and $\frac{1}{5} \cdot 24 \approx 5$; $8 - 5 = 3$ **41.** Sample answer: about 150; $\frac{1}{4} \cdot 1{,}000 = 250$; $\frac{1}{10} \cdot 1{,}000 = 100$; $250 - 100 = 150$ **43.** Sample answer: about 2,100,000 people; $0.1 \cdot 21{,}000{,}000 = 2{,}100{,}000$ **45.** Sample answer: about 0.15 lb; $0.01 \cdot 15 = 0.15$ **47.** Sample answer: Find 1% of \$800, then multiply by $\frac{3}{8}$. **49.** Sometimes; sample answer: one estimate for 37% of 60 is $\frac{2}{5} \times 60 = 24$. This is greater than the actual answer because $\frac{2}{5}$ is greater than 37%. Another estimate is $\frac{1}{3} \times 60 = 20$. This is less than the actual answer because $\frac{1}{3}$ is less than 37%. **51.** B **53.** 40% **55.** 72 **57.** 20 **59.** Sample answer: $1 + 0 = 1$ **61.** Sample answer: $1 - \frac{1}{2} = \frac{1}{2}$ **63.** 50 **65.** 357.1 **67.** 37 yr

Pages 403–404 ***Lesson 8-4***

1. Sample answer: Look for a rule or pattern in the data or number facts, estimation, guess and check, make an organized list, or work backwards. **3.** \$4 **5.** $0.7 \cdot 400$ or 280 teens **7.** 2 quarters, 1 dime, 4 nickels, and 3 pennies **9.** 10 times **11.** 8 **13.** multiplication followed by addition and finally division; $15 \cdot 18 + 18 \cdot 20 = 630\ \text{ft}^3$. Then convert $630\ \text{ft}^3$ to square yards; $630 \div (3 \cdot 3) = 70\ \text{yd}^2$

Pages 407–409 ***Lesson 8-5***

1. $p = 88 \cdot 300$; 264 **3.** $75 = n \cdot 150$; 50% **5.** $3 = 0.12 \cdot w$; 25 **7.** 39 loaves **9.** $p = 0.39 \cdot 65$; 25.4 **11.** $p = 0.53 \cdot 470$; 249.1 **13.** $26 = n \cdot 96$; 27.1% **15.** $30 = n \cdot 64$; 46.9% **17.** $84 = 0.75 \cdot w$; 112 **19.** $64 = 0.8 \cdot w$; 80 **21.** 4,400 games **23.** 1 **25.** $p = 0.4 \cdot 82.1$; 0.3 **27.** $230 = n \cdot 200$; 115% **29.** about 43% **31.** about 27% **33.** Sample answer: 30 is 125% of what number?; 24 **35.** Sample answer: It may be easier if the percent and the base are known because after writing the percent as a decimal or fraction, the only step is to multiply. When using the percent proportion, you must first find the cross products and then divide. **37.** H **39.** Sample answer: about 3,000 ÷ 100 or 30 ft/s **41.** 15; $\frac{3}{10} \cdot 50 = 15$ **43.** 25 **45.** 460

Pages 412–414 ***Lesson 8-6***

1. 19,800 **3.** 5.72 million **5.** 1,396 students **7.** 58,800 teens **9.** b. **11.** a. **13.** about 38 people **15.** about 1,040 **17.** Sample answer: Since large numbers are involved, use a calculator; $0.15 \cdot 5{,}900{,}962 = 885{,}144.3$ so about 885,000 people would belong to a fitness center **19.** C **21.** B **23.** $54 = 0.72 \cdot w$; 75 **25.** −24 **27.** 54 **29.** $\frac{3}{10}$ or 0.3 **31.** $\frac{9}{2}$ or 4.5

Pages 418–420 ***Lesson 8-7***

1. 20% decrease **3.** 19% increase **5.** C **7.** 40% increase **9.** 71% decrease **11.** 25% decrease **13.** 5% decrease **15.** 13% increase **17.** 38% decrease **19.** 2% increase **21.** 75% decrease **23.** 150% increase **25.** 300% **29.** \$51 billion **31.** 41% **33.** 16 to 17; 72% **35.** The \$60 sound system since 10 is a greater part of 60 than of 90. **37.** No; after a 10% increase, the quantity is greater then the original quantity. Decreasing a larger number by the same percent results in a greater change. **39.** D **41.** 660 **43.** $n = 0.21 \cdot 62$; 13.0 **45.** 0.065 **47.** 0.0825

Pages 423–424 ***Lesson 8-8***

1. \$3.10 **3.** \$1,338.75 **5.** about 9% **7.** \$1,605 **9.** \$4.90 **11.** \$7.99 **13.** \$96.26 **15.** 30% **17.** 30% **19.** \$35.79 **21.** \$143.75 **23.** \$25 **25.** \$60, \$35; The percent of discount is about 42%. All of the other pairs have a discount of 25%. **27.** C **29.** B **31.** 9% decrease **33.** 510 teens **35.** 16.2

Pages 427–428 Lesson 8-9

1. \$38.40 **3.** \$5.80 **5.** \$1,417.50 **7.** \$1,219.00 **9.** \$21.38 **11.** \$123.75 **13.** \$45.31 **15.** \$14.06 **17.** \$1,353.13 **19.** \$116.25 **21.** 6 yr **23.** \$627, \$655.22, \$684.70 **25.** C **27.** \$21.39 **29.** 37% decrease **31.** $1\frac{1}{5}$ **33.** $2\frac{2}{15}$

Pages 430–434 Chapter 8 Study Guide and Review

1. true **3.** true **5.** false; 10% **7.** true **9.** false; original **11.** 39 **13.** 135 **15.** 14 games **17.** 0.3 **19.** \$27.49 **21.** Sample answer: 40; $\frac{1}{3} \cdot 120 = 40$ **23.** Sample answer: 20; $\frac{1}{5} \cdot 100 = 20$ **25.** Sample answer: 360; $0.1 \cdot 400 = 40$; $9 \cdot 40 = 360$ **27.** 333 **29.** Sample answer: $\$700 \times 0.4 = \$280$ **31.** $39 = 0.65 \cdot w$; 60 **33.** $n = 0.07 \cdot 92$; 6.4 **35.** $\$700 \times 0.4 = \$280$ **37.** about 242 **39.** 48% increase **41.** 20% decrease **43.** about 12% increase **45.** \$178.50 **47.** \$26.80 **49.** 10% **51.** \$47.50 **53.** \$412.50 **55.** \$311.85

Chapter 9 Statistics: Analyzing Data

Page 441 Chapter 9 Getting Ready

1. 95.89, 96.02, 96.2 **3.** 22, 22.012, 22.02 **5.** 74.7, 74.67, 74.65 **7.** 3.340, 3.304, 3.04 **9.** 2.32

Pages 444–447 Lesson 9-1

1.

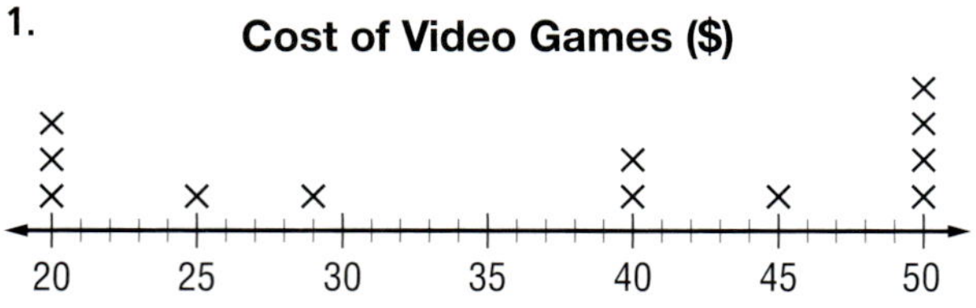

3. clusters: 6–12; gaps: 12–20; outlier: 20; range: 20 − 4, or 16 **5.** 1 or 2 glasses per day **7.** 5 glasses

9.

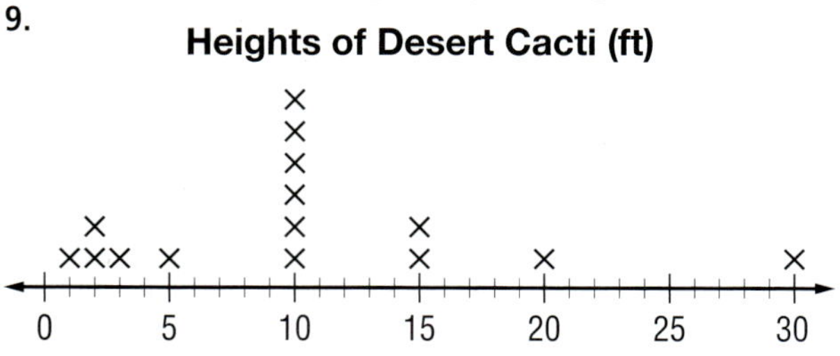

11.

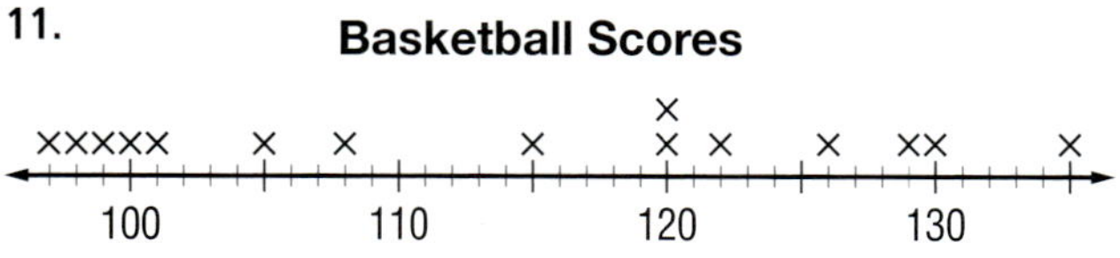

13. 34°F **15.** Sample answer: cluster 104°F–122°F, indicates that most of the temperatures are between 104°F and 122°F; gaps 100°F–104°F, 122°F–125°F, 125°F–128°F, and 128°F–134°F, indicate where no temperatures fall; outliers 100°F and 134°F, indicate temperatures that are significantly lower and significantly higher than the other temperatures. **17.** 36 − 10 or 26 **19.** 15 **21.** Always; each data item is plotted. **23.** 10 **25.** about 72% **27.** Sample answer: range 34 yr; cluster 10–12 yr; outlier 40 yr

29.

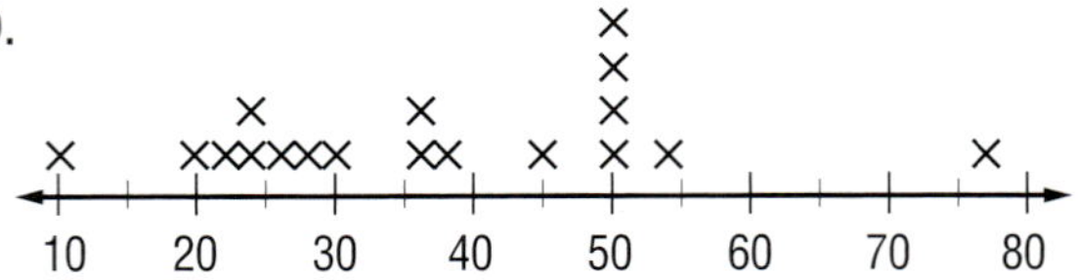

Sample answer: The data are more spread out, with a range of 67 compared with the previous range of 34. There is a cluster from 20 to 30 and a gap between 54 and 77. The piece of data that occurs most frequently is 50, which means that the maximum life span of more animals is 50 years than any other number of years. **31.** Sample answer: {21, 22, 24, 25, 25, 28, 21, 25, 26, 26, 36} **33.** Sample answer: A frequency table shows the number of times data occur by using tally marks. A line plot shows the number of times data occur by using ×s. A frequency table usually shows intervals of data and is useful when a summary is needed. A line plot shows individual data points and is useful when you need to see how all the data points are spread out. **35.** C **37.** \$60 **39.** \$4.46 **41.** 47 **43.** 12.6

Pages 451–454 Lesson 9-2

1. 52.3; 57; 59 **3.** 44.6; 44; 44 **5.** Sample answer: Either the mean, median, or mode could be used to represent the data. The mean is slightly greater than most of the data items, and therefore is a less accurate description of the data. **7.** 87; 90; 80 and 93 **9.** \$12; \$9; \$6 **11.** 26.5; 25.5; 23 and 25 **13.** Sample answer: The mean, 15.6, is higher than most of the data. The median, 1, or mode, 1, best represents the data. **15.** 6.75, 6.55, 6.4 **17.** −1.9°F, −1.5°F, −2°F **21.** Sample answer: A length of 960 inches is much greater than the other pieces of data. So, if this piece of data is added, the mean will increase. **23.** 10 points; Sample answer: The sum of the points for the first thirteen games is 158. In order for the average number of points to be 12, the total number of points for fourteen games would need to be 12 × 14 or 168. So, 168 – 158 or 10 points need to be scored during the last game. **25.** Sample answer: 4, 5, 2, 2, 3, 3, 1, 0, 1, 2, 4, 68, 5; the mean, 7.7, is not the best representation since it is greater than all the data items except one. **27.** Sometimes; if there is an odd number of items, the median is the middle number. If there is an even number of items, the median is the mean of the two middle numbers. **29.** Mean; a mode must be a member of the data set, and it is impossible to have 3.28 family members. **31.** J

33.

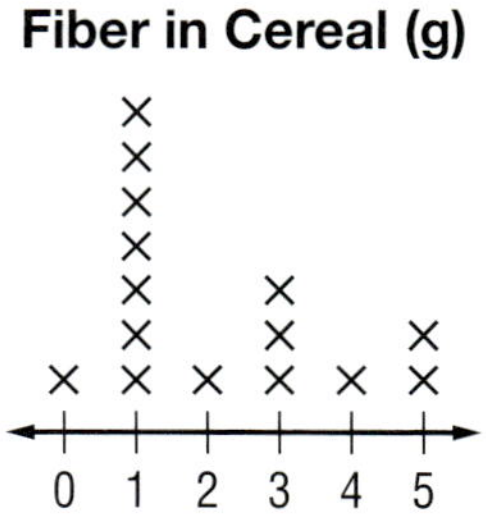

35. \$10.43 **37.** Commutative (×) **39.** hundreds **41.** thousands

Pages 458–460 ***Lesson 9-3***

1. Height of Trees(ft)

Stem	Leaf
0	8 8
1	0 2 5 5 6 8
2	0 5

2|0 = 20 ft

3. 5 **5.** Sample answer: Most of the students are between 10 and 14 years old. There are only a few students under the age of 10.

7.

Low Temperatures (°F)

Stem	Leaf
1	3 3 5
2	0 4 8
3	0 1 2 2 5 6 8 8 8

1|3 = 13°F

9.

School Play Attendance

Stem	Leaf
22	5 7 9
23	0
24	3 6
25	
26	7 9 9
27	8 8 8

26|7 = 267 people

11. 4; 1 **13.** $45 **15.** Sample answer: Most of the DVD players cost between $100 and $120. The most expensive players at the store sell for less than $130. If you want to buy a DVD player, you will spend at least $82. **17.** 26 **19.** Sample answer: Yes; Thirty-six of the 56 signers were 30–49 years. Since 36 out of 56 is greater than half, you can say that the majority of the signers were 30–49 years old.

21. Average Length (ft) of Crocodiles

Stem	Leaf
6	3
7	
8	1
9	8 8
10	
11	4
12	
13	6
14	
15	
16	0 3 3 3 3
17	
18	
19	5

13|6 = 13.6 ft

Sample answer: A reasonable length for an average crocodile is about 16 feet. **23.** Diana; three out of the six or 50% of the pieces of ribbon are 20–30 inches in length.

25.

Price ($)	Tally	Frequency
20–29	||||	4
30–39	卌 卌	10
40–49	卌	5
50–59	|	1

Price of Jeans ($)

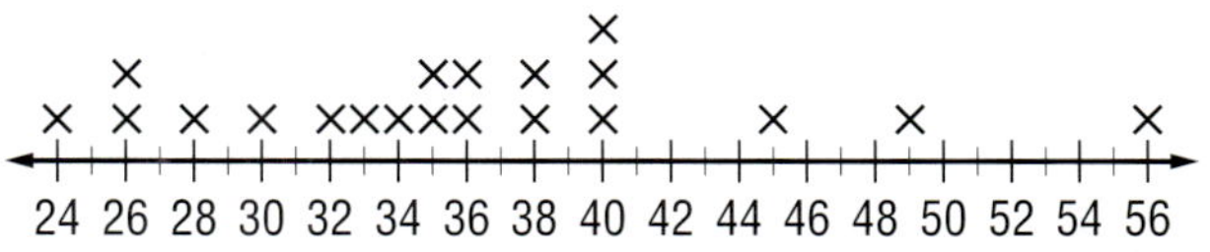

Price of Jeans ($)

Stem	Leaf
2	4 6 6 8
3	0 2 3 4 5 5 6 6 8 8
4	0 0 0 5 9
5	6

2|0 = $20

All three representations show the frequency of data occurring. The frequency table shows intervals of data and is useful in comparing price ranges. The line plot gives a good picture of the spread of the data. The stem-and-leaf plot shows individual prices as in the line plot, as well as intervals, such as $20s, $30s, and so on. See students' favorites and reasons. **27.** C **29.** 48.7; 50; 55

31. **Test Scores**

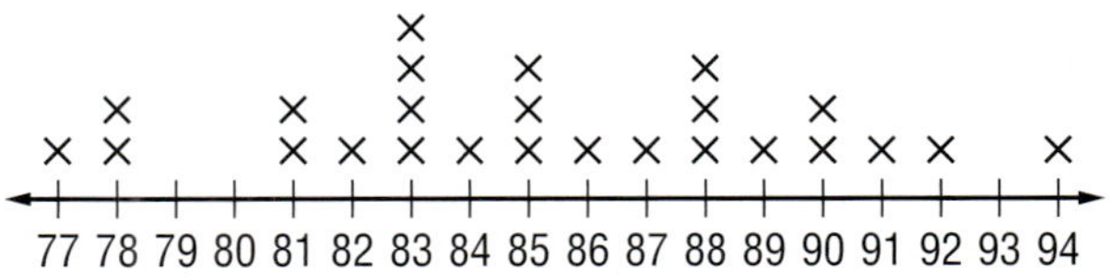

33. $\frac{3}{8}$ **35.** Sample answer: 20; 20–120

Pages 464–467 ***Lesson 9-4***

1. histogram

State Sales Tax Rate

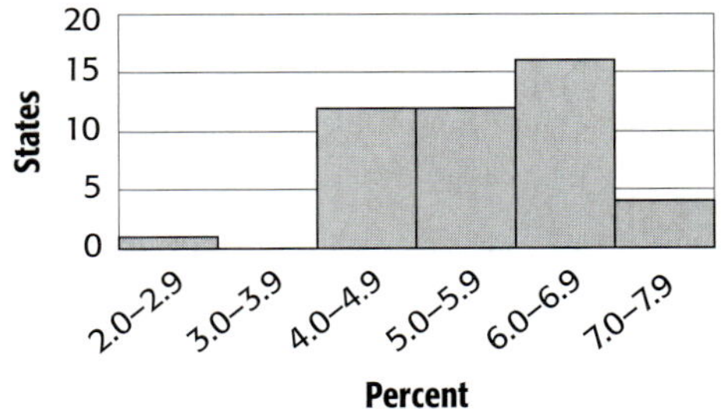

3. health

5. bar graph

Most Threatened Reptiles

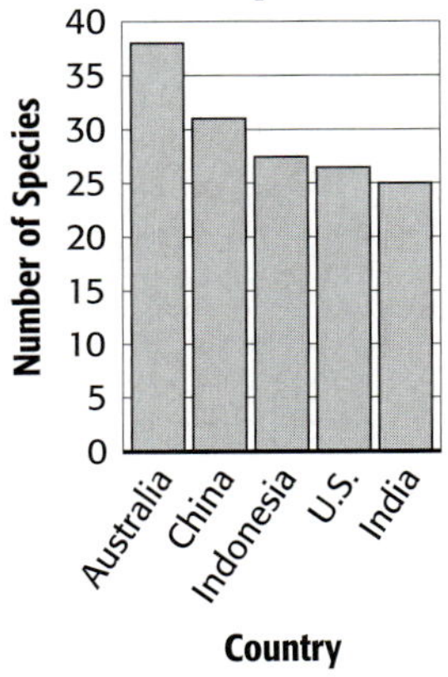

7. histogram

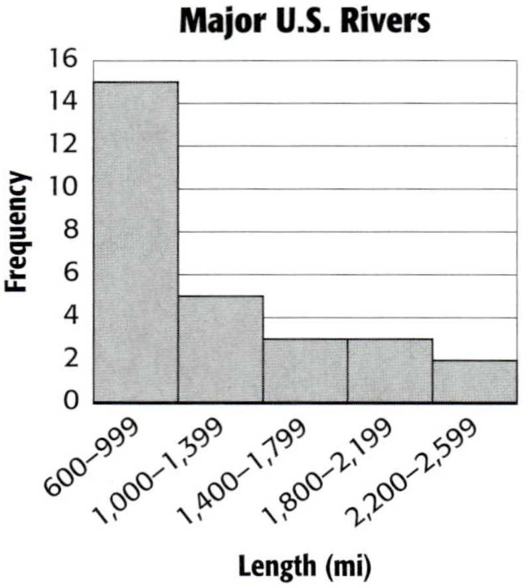

9. 4 **11.** 2; The bar for 0 is 2 high. **13.** 43 **15.** Sample answer: The number of zoos with 0.0–0.9 million visitors is about 4 times the number of zoos with 3.0–3.9 million visitors. **17.** a **19.** b

21. Sample answer: 210,000 thousand, or 210,000,000 **23.** Sample answer: It is easier to compare two sets of data. **25.** tennis **27.** Sample answer: The number of boys and girls is the same because kickball is a sport that mostly everyone can play and the only sports equipment needed is a kickball. **29.** Sample answer: Each interval represents a portion of the data set. The number of items in each interval is indicated by the frequency, typically shown along the vertical scale. By adding the frequencies for each interval, you can determine the number of values in the data set. **31.** C

33.

Number of Wins

Stem	Leaf
1	5 7 9
2	3 5 6
3	0 1 2 6
4	0 0 1 3 4 5 6 7 7
5	0 0 0 1 2 3 3 5 6 6
	5|3 = 53 wins

35. Mental math; the numbers are easy to computer mentally. Sample answer: $\frac{1}{5}$ of \$50 is \$10 and \$50 − \$10 = \$40. So, he will need an additional \$40.

Pages 470–472 ***Lesson 9-5***

1. **Odd Numbers and Prime Numbers**

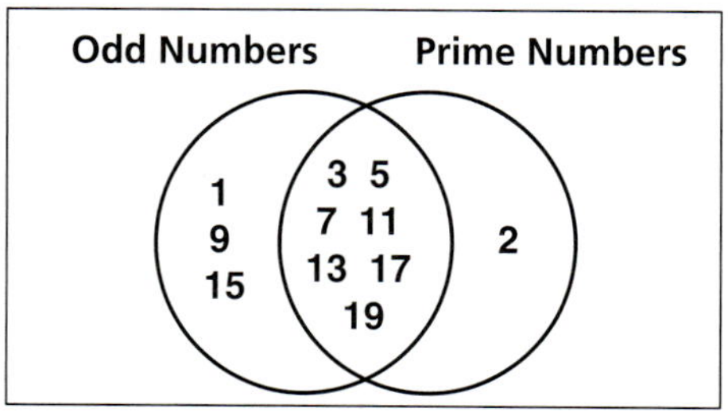

3. Pedro, Gracia, Lizzy **5.** Luke, Adam, Sara

7. **Dessert Eaten at a Birthday Party**

9. **Characteristics**

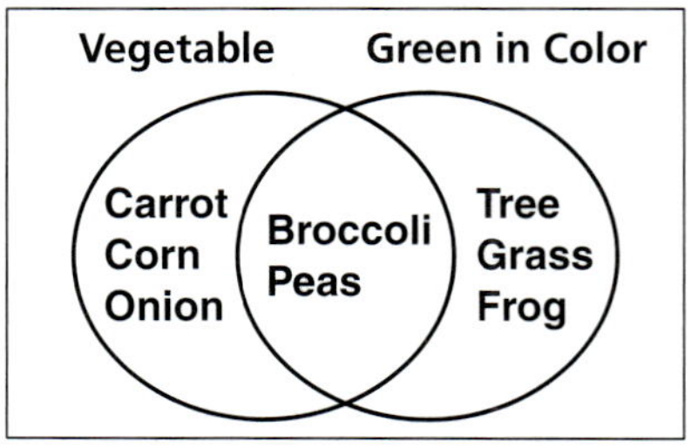

11. **Travel Destinations**

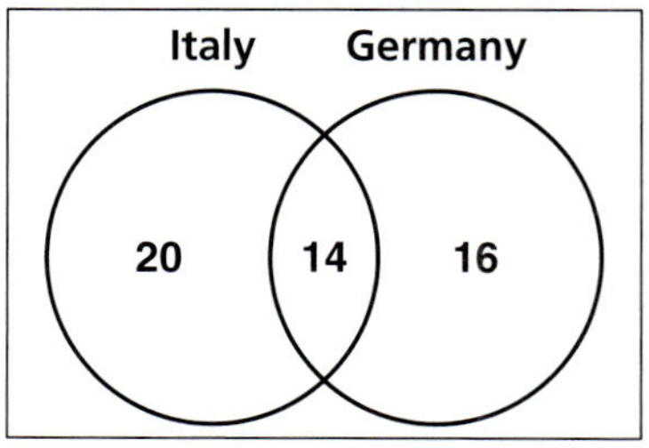

13. 15 **15.** 14 **17.** 2 **19.** 38 − 15 or 23; See students' diagram.

21. Sample answer:

Pet Characteristics

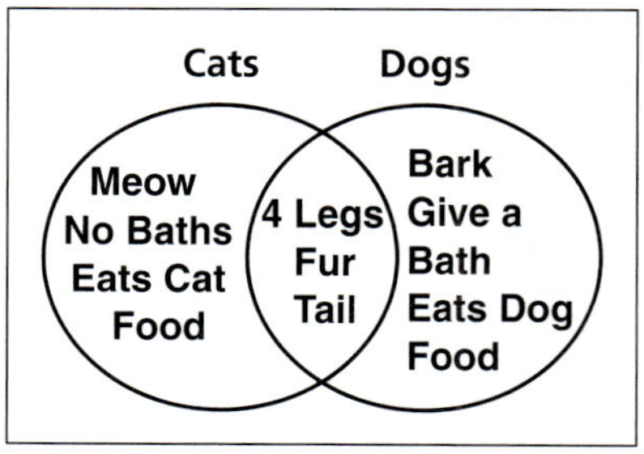

23. C

25–27.

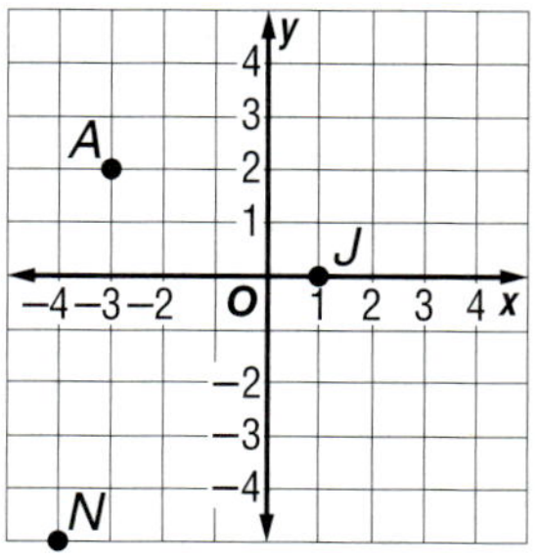

Pages 474–475 **Lesson 9-6**

1. Sample answer: Graphs provide a visual representation of a situation involving comparisons. A graphical model can sometimes show conclusively what is often difficult to interpret from looking at lists alone. **3.** Sample answer: 95°F **5.** 158, 318 **7.** Tuesday and Thursday **9.** division; 2,500 ÷ 150 is about 16 people

Pages 478–481 **Lesson 9-7**

1. Sample answer: The graph shows a negative relationship. That is, as the weeks pass, the time decreases. **3.** about 155–160 people **5.** about 400 **7.** about 95 min **9.** Sample answer: As the speed increases, the distance required to come to a complete stop increases.

11. **Olympic Participation**

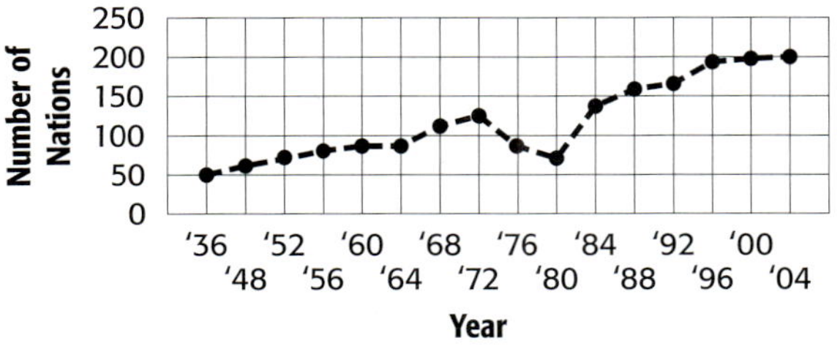

13. Sample answer: In most years, the number of participants increases. **15.** about $55,000 **17.** No; if the trend continues for both counties, then the population in Miami-Dade County will still be greater than the population in Broward County. The gap between the populations will actually widen. **19.** Mode; the other three are ways to display data. **21.** Graphs often show trends over time. If you continue the pattern, you can use it to make a prediction. **23.** F

25. **Food Preferences**

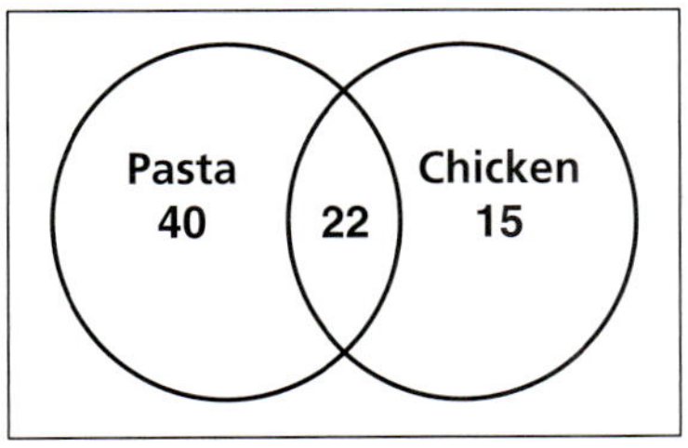

27. 83°; 83°

Pages 486–487 **Lesson 9-8**

1. Sample answer: line plot

3. Sample answer: scatter plot

Decorating a Parade Float

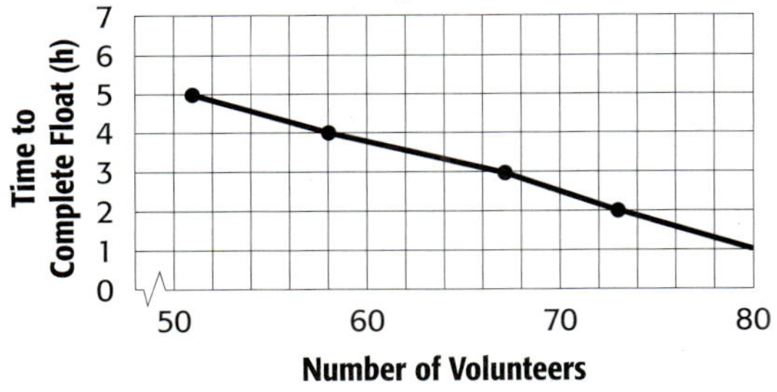

5. Sample answer: circle graph

7. Venn diagram.

Student Characteristics

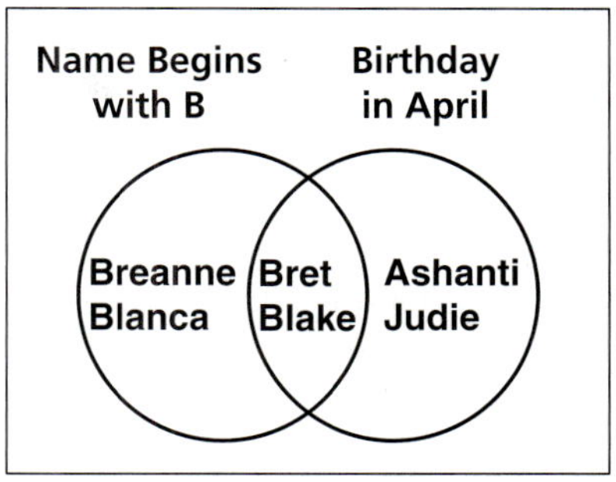

9. Sample answer: bar graph

Favorite Color

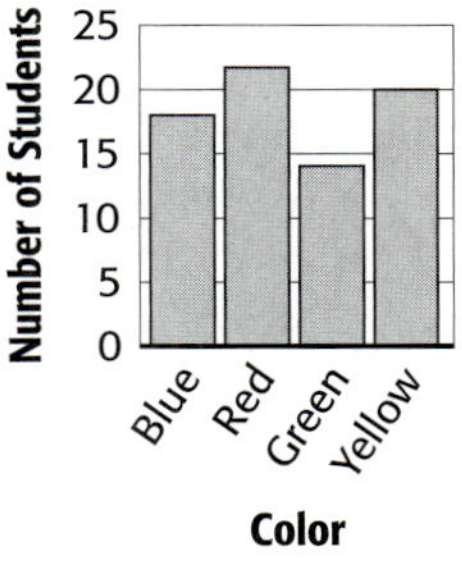

11. Sample answer: The number of surf boards a store sells over the past five years. **13.** Sample answer: A bar graph would be used to display the specific number of items in each category. A line graph would be used to show how the data changes over time. **15.** H

17.

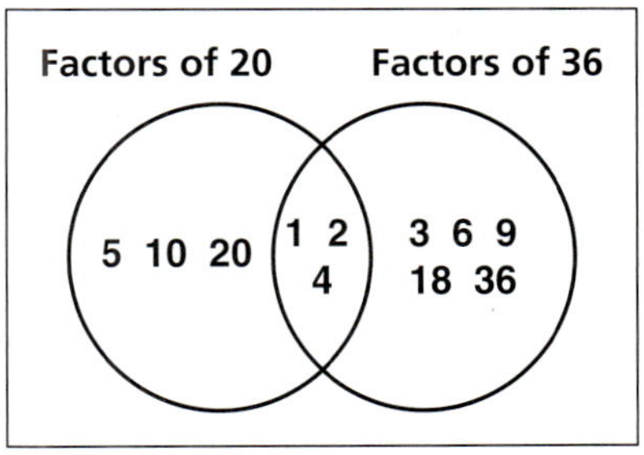

19. 24 **21.** 90 **23.** false

Pages 491–493 **Lesson 9-9**

1. Graph A; From the length of the bars, it appears that Hank Aaron hit about 4 times as many home runs as Willie Mayes. However, Willie Mayes hit about 600 home runs and Hank Aaron hit about 750 home runs. So, the conclusion is not valid. **3.** Sample answer: The graph does not include the very hot summer months or the very cold winter months, which would have higher electricity bills. **5.** The median or the mode because it is much closer in value to most of the pieces of data. **7.** Brand B appears to cost half as much as Brand A.

9.

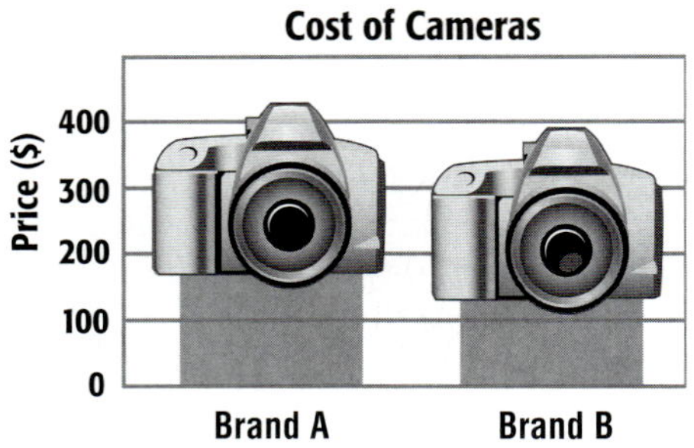

11. The mean could be misleading, since the areas of all but one of the islands are less than that value.
13. Mean; yes; Sample answer: Only one island has an area greater than the mean. The majority of the islands have areas that are much smaller than the mean.
17. C **19.** line graph

Pages 494–498 Chapter 9 Study Guide and Review

1. true **3.** true **5.** false; outlier **7.** true

9.

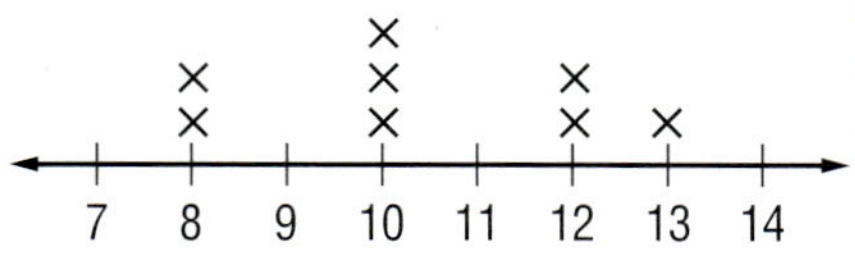

; Sample answer: no significant clusters, gaps or outliers.

11.

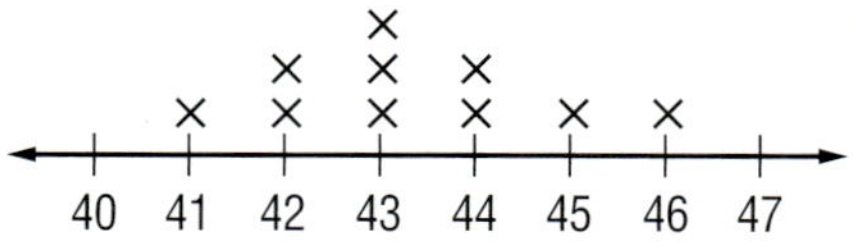

; Sample answer: cluster 42–44; no gaps or outliers.

13. 84.3°; 86°; none

15. **Hours Worked**

Stem	Leaf
2	1 3 6 9
3	1 2 7 8
4	6
5	4

3|2 = 32 hours

17. **Birthdates**

Stem	Leaf
0	3 5 7 9
1	0 1 2 4 6 8
2	1 4

1|2 = 12

19. 10.75 million **21.** 57 **23.** *Crazy Horse*
25. Sample answer: The graph shows a positive relationship. That is, as the number of people in a family increases, the number of telephone calls per week increases. **27.** line graph **29.** stem-and-leaf plot

31.

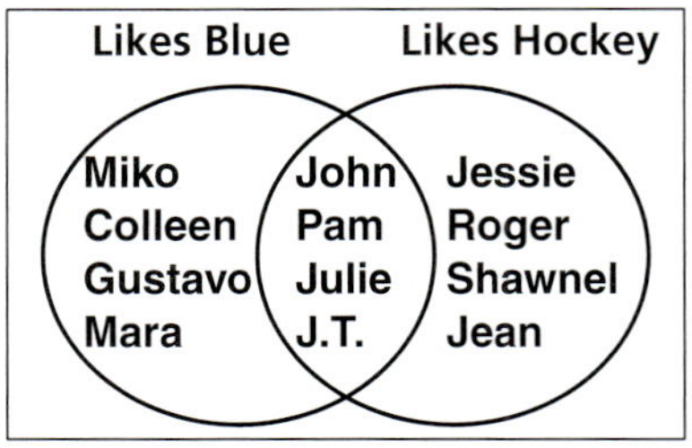

Chapter 10 Probability

Page 503 Chapter 10 Getting Ready

1. 105 **3.** 52 **5.** 160 **7.** 210 **9.** 360 **11.** 5,040
13. \$315 **15.** $\frac{1}{6}$ **17.** $\frac{1}{3}$ **19.** 5 **21.** 4

Pages 506–508 Lesson 10-1

1. $\frac{1}{12}$ **3.** $\frac{1}{4}$ **5.** $\frac{3}{5}$ **7.** $\frac{23}{30}$ **9.** 1 **11.** $\frac{1}{20}$ **13.** $\frac{3}{10}$ **15.** $\frac{19}{20}$
17. $\frac{3}{5}$ **19.** 0 **21.** 1 **23.** $\frac{4}{5}$ **25.** 60% **27.** $\frac{1}{11}$
29. Sample answer: The complementary event is the chance of no rain. Its probability is 63%. **31.** Sample answer: a spinner with 5 equal sections labeled A, B, C, D, and E. Spinning the letter B has a probability of $\frac{1}{5}$. **33.** 0.65, 0.55 are probabilities that are not complementary because $0.65 + 0.55 \neq 1$. The other sets of probability are complementary. **35.** C **37.** Sample answer: The more it rains, the taller the grass becomes.
39. $\frac{1}{3}$ **41.** $\frac{1}{2}$ **43.** $\frac{9}{16}$

Pages 511–514 Lesson 10-2

1. Sample answer:

	Outcomes					
	1	**2**	**3**	**4**	**5**	**6**
1	1, 1	1, 2	1, 3	1, 4	1, 5	1, 6
2	2, 1	2, 2	2, 3	2, 4	2, 5	2, 6
3	3, 1	3, 2	3, 3	3, 4	3, 5	3, 6
4	4, 1	4, 2	4, 3	4, 4	4, 5	4, 6
5	5, 1	5, 2	5, 3	5, 4	5, 5	5, 6
6	6, 1	6, 2	6, 3	6, 4	6, 5	6, 6

3. C
5. Sample answer:

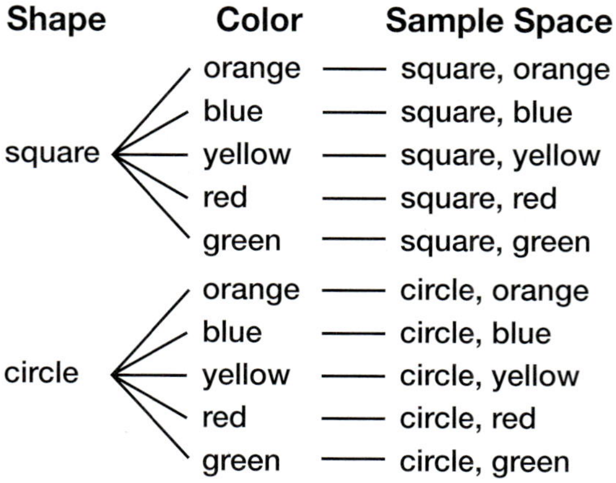

7. Sample answer:

Coin	Number Cube	Sample Space
H	1	H 1
	2	H 2
	3	H 3
	4	H 4
	5	H 5
	6	H 6
T	1	T 1
	2	T 2
	3	T 3
	4	T 4
	5	T 5
	6	T 6

9. Sample answer:

Color	Speeds	Sample Space
purple	10	purple, 10-speed
	18	purple, 18-speed
	21	purple, 21-speed
	24	purple, 24-speed
green	10	green, 10-speed
	18	green, 18-speed
	21	green, 21-speed
	24	green, 24-speed
black	10	black, 10-speed
	18	black, 18-speed
	21	black, 21-speed
	24	black, 24-speed
silver	10	silver, 10-speed
	18	silver, 18-speed
	21	silver, 21-speed
	24	silver, 24-speed

11. Sample answer:

Outcomes		
Short Sleeve	Gray	Small
Short Sleeve	Gray	Medium
Short Sleeve	Gray	Large
Short Sleeve	White	Small
Short Sleeve	White	Medium
Short Sleeve	White	Large
Long Sleeve	Gray	Small
Long Sleeve	Gray	Medium
Long Sleeve	Gray	Large
Long Sleeve	White	Small
Long Sleeve	White	Medium
Long Sleeve	White	Large

13. Sample answer:

Quarter	Dime	Nickel	Sample Space	
H	H	H	H, H, H	Elba wins
		T	H, H, T	Elba wins
	T	H	H, T, H	Elba wins
		T	H, T, T	Steve wins
T	H	H	T, H, H	Elba wins
		T	T, H, T	Steve wins
	T	H	T, T, H	Steve wins
		T	T, T, T	Steve wins

There are 8 equally-likely outcomes with 4 favoring Elba and 4 favoring Steve. So, the probability that each player wins is $\frac{1}{2}$. Thus, the game is fair.

15. $\frac{1}{8}$ **17.** $\frac{3}{8}$ **19.** $\frac{1}{8}$ **21.** 24 **25.** Sample answer: Mei can draw a model of the situation using a tree diagram to show the sample space. Then she can determine the probability. The probability of guessing correctly is $\frac{1}{4}$.

True/False	True/False	Sample Space
T	T	T, T
	F	T, F
F	T	F, T
	F	F, F

27. Sample game: Each player tosses a coin 10 times. If it comes up heads, player 1 receives 1 point. If it comes up tails, player 2 receives
1 point. The player with the most points at the end of 20 tosses wins. **29.** $\frac{2}{5}$ **31.** $\frac{13}{20}$ **33.** $\frac{3}{10}$ **35.** The cost is increasing over time. In about a year's time, the cost has more than tripled. **37.** \$2,598.75 **39.** 15.6 **41.** 154 **43.** 460

Pages 516–518 ***Lesson 10-3***

1. 8 **3.** 60 **5.** 12 **7.** 84 **9.** 24 **11.** 6 possible routes; $\frac{1}{6}$ **13.** 7,776 **15.** No; the number of selections is 25 • 14 or 350, which is less than 365. **17.** 2; 4; 8; 2^n; Sample answer: I used a pattern to determine the number of outcomes for n coins. One coin: 2^1 outcomes, two coins: 2 • 2 or 2^2 outcomes, three coins: 2 • 2 • 2 or 2^3 outcomes, n coins: 2^n outcomes.
19. Sample answer: When there are multiple events, the Fundamental Counting Principle is a much faster method of obtaining the total number of outcomes than drawing a tree diagram. The Fundamental Counting Principle also saves paper space and can often be done mentally. When you need to see what the specific outcomes are, make a tree diagram since the Fundamental Counting Principle only gives the number of outcomes. **21.** F **23.** $\frac{1}{2}$ **25.** $\frac{1}{5}$, 0.22, 27%, 20.1 **27.** 6 **29.** 120

Pages 520–522 *Lesson 10-4*

1. 5,040 **3.** $\frac{1}{20}$ **5.** 24 **7.** 720 **9.** $\frac{1}{90}$ **11.** $\frac{1}{12}$ **13.** Sample answer: Calculator; An exact answer is required. $24 \times 23 \times 22 \times 21 = 255{,}024$ **15.** $\frac{1}{4}$ **17.** Sample answer: The number of ways you can order 3 books on a shelf is $3 \cdot 2 \cdot 1$ or 6. **19.** H

21.

Meat	Cheese	Outcomes
turkey	cheddar	turkey, cheddar
	Swiss	turkey, Swiss
ham	cheddar	ham, cheddar
	Swiss	ham, Swiss
salami	cheddar	salami, cheddar
	Swiss	salami, Swiss

23. $1\frac{13}{15}$ **25.** $4\frac{11}{48}$ **27.** 56 **29.** 3

Pages 526–527 *Lesson 10-5*

1. 21 ways **3.** 6 **5.** 210 **7.** 924 **9.** $\frac{1}{20}$ **11.** 10; $\frac{1}{10}$ **13.** permutation; 90 **15.** 15 **17.** The number of ways you can choose three CDs from a collection of ten CDs is 120 ways. **19.** C **21.** 72 **23.** Sample answer: $\frac{1}{2} - 0 = \frac{1}{2}$ **25.** $\frac{1}{5}$

Pages 528–529 *Lesson 10-6*

1. Sample answer: Results would vary slightly. **3.** No; Sample answer: the experiment produces about 1–2 correct answers, so using a spinner with 4 sections is not a good way to answer a 5-question multiple-choice quiz. **5.** 30 **7.** 250 is a reasonable answer since 31% of 800 is 248. **9.** No, the 6th row should have the numbers 1, 5, 10, 10, 5, 1. **11.** No; Sample answer: the experiment produces about 2–3 correct answers, so using a number cube is not a good way to answer a 5-question true-false quiz. **13.** subtraction; $29{,}000 - 1.38 \times 10^4 = 15{,}200$ ft

Pages 532–534 *Lesson 10-7*

1. $\frac{14}{25}$ **3.** The experimental probability, $\frac{14}{25}$ or 56%, is close to its theoretical probability of $\frac{1}{2}$ or 50%. **5.** 24 **7.** $\frac{9}{10}$; the experimental probability, $\frac{9}{10}$ or 90%, is close to its theoretical probability of $\frac{5}{6}$, or about 83%. **9.** $\frac{2}{5}$ **11.** 51 **13.** 10 **15.** $\frac{13}{25}$ **17.** No; The experimental probability that a mother will receive jewelry is $\frac{17}{100}$. Out of 750 mothers that receive gifts, only about 128 can expect to receive jewelry not 250. **19.** Sample answer: Paper/Pencil; The number that has occurred the most is 2 with a frequency of 12. If this number remained unchanged then there would need to be a total of 12×6, or 72, rolls of the number cube to make the theoretical probability of $\frac{1}{6}$ equal the experimental probability. Thus, there needs to be an additional 24 rolls. Each number needs to have a frequency of 12. So, the number 1 needs to come up 4 more times, the number 3 needs to come up 8 more times, the number 4 needs to come up 4 more times, the number 5 needs to come up 6 more times, and the number 6 needs to come up 2 more times. **21.** B **23.** 6 **25.** 80% **27.** 87.5%

Pages 537–539 *Lesson 10-8*

1. $\frac{1}{30}$ **3.** $\frac{1}{10}$ **5.** $\frac{2}{9}$ **7.** $\frac{1}{12}$ **9.** $\frac{1}{10}$ **11.** $\frac{9}{50}$ **13.** $\frac{1}{144}$ **15.** $\frac{1}{20}$ **17.** $\frac{1}{5}$

19.

Number of Children	*P*(all boys)
1	$\frac{1}{2}$
2	$\frac{1}{2} \cdot \frac{1}{2}$ or $\frac{1}{4}$
3	$\frac{1}{2} \cdot \frac{1}{2} \cdot \frac{1}{2}$ or $\frac{1}{8}$
4	$\frac{1}{2} \cdot \frac{1}{2} \cdot \frac{1}{2} \cdot \frac{1}{2}$ or $\frac{1}{16}$
5	$\frac{1}{2} \cdot \frac{1}{2} \cdot \frac{1}{2} \cdot \frac{1}{2} \cdot \frac{1}{2}$ or $\frac{1}{32}$

21. $\frac{1}{2^n}$ **23.** 24.8% **25.** 0.032 **27.** A **29.** 1 **31.** −27 **33.** 24

Pages 540–544 *Chapter 10* *Study Guide and Review*

1. true **3.** false; probability **5.** false; independent events **7.** false; fair game **9.** $\frac{1}{4}$ **11.** $\frac{3}{4}$ **13.** 8%

15. Sample answer:

Outcomes	
White	Turkey
White	Ham
White	Salami
Wheat	Turkey
Wheat	Ham
Wheat	Salami
Rye	Turkey
Rye	Ham
Rye	Salami

17. 36 **19.** $\frac{1}{30}$ **21.** 40,320 **23.** 56 **25.** 45 **27.** No; Sample answer: the experiment produces about 3 correct answers, so tossing a coin is not a good way to answer a 6-question true-false quiz. **29.** 8

31. $\frac{3}{25}$ **33.** $\frac{1}{2}$ **35.** $\frac{23}{50}$ **37.** $\frac{3}{64}$ **39.** $\frac{5}{64}$ **41.** $\frac{1}{3}$

Chapter 11 Geometry: Polygons

Page 551 *Chapter 11* *Getting Ready*

1. 306 **3.** 0.15 **5.** 0.11 **7.** 44 **9.** 105 **11.** 14 **13.** 36

Pages 555–557 *Lesson 11-1*

1. ∠*MNP*, ∠*PNM*, ∠*N*, ∠1; obtuse **3.** supplementary **5.** 135 **7.** ∠*DEF*, ∠*FED*, ∠*E*, ∠5; right **9.** ∠*MNP*, ∠*PNM*, ∠*N*, ∠7; straight **11.** ∠*RTS*, ∠*STR*, ∠*T*, ∠9; acute **13.** supplementary

15. supplementary **17.** neither **19.** 65° **21.** 34 **23.** 33.2 **25.** 84 **27.** Sample answer: $\angle IJK$, $\angle KJG$ **29.** Sample answer: $\angle CGK$, $\angle KGJ$ **31.** 4; 30° + 90° = 120°, 60° + 45° = 105°, 60° + 90° = 150°, 90° + 45° = 135° **33.** $m\angle E = 39°$, $m\angle F = 51°$ **35.** Yes; $\angle 1$ and $\angle 2$ are vertical angles and $m\angle 1 = 90°$ and $m\angle 2 = 90°$. **37.** B **39.** A **41.** $\frac{1}{4}$ **43.** $\frac{7}{10}$ **45.** 223.2 **47.** 0.12

Pages 560–563 ***Lesson 11-2***

1.

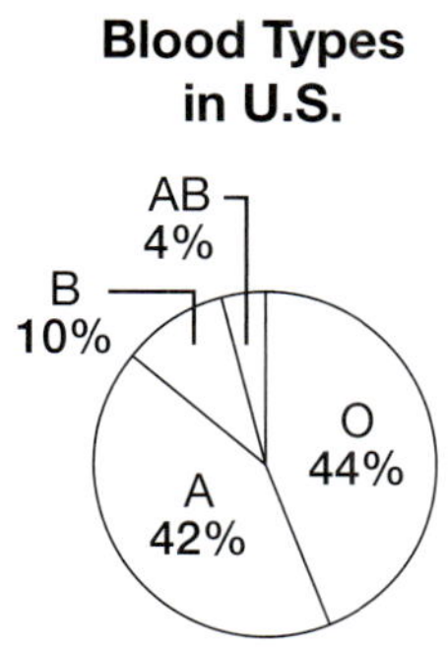

3. blue

5.

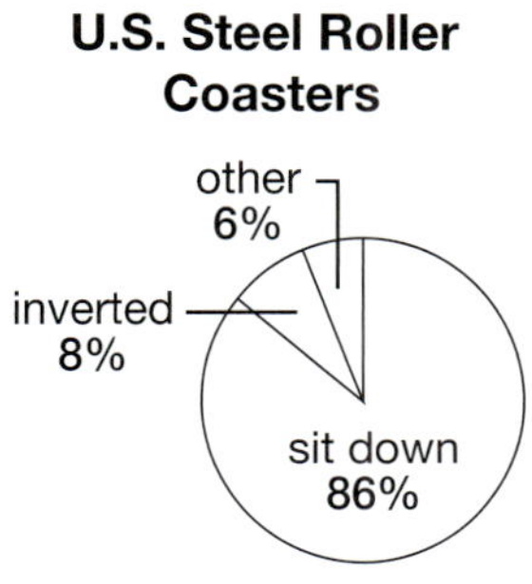

7.

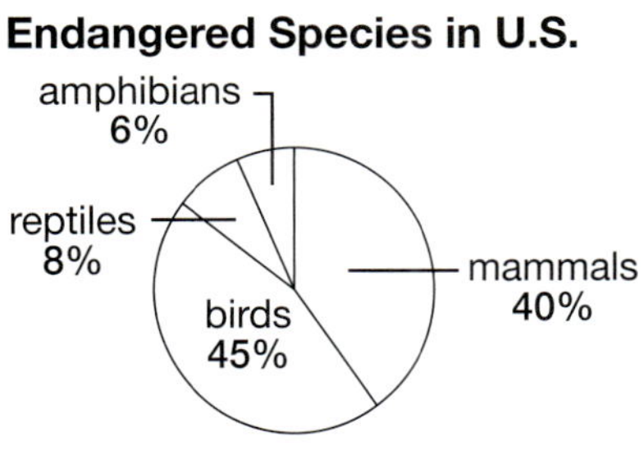

9. grades 1–8 **11.** about 16.5 million **13.** about 12 million **15.** 15

17. bar graph

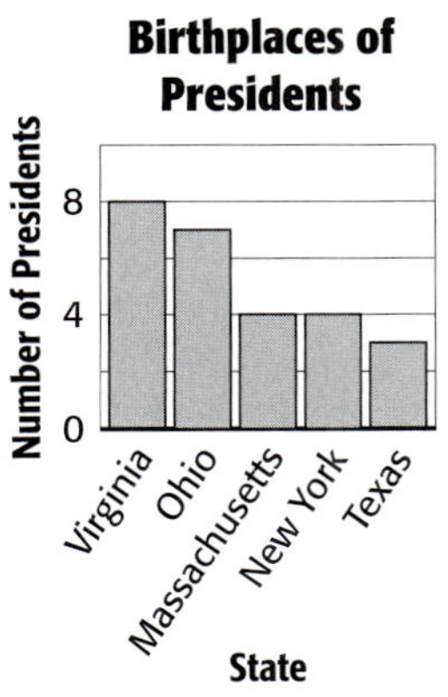

19.

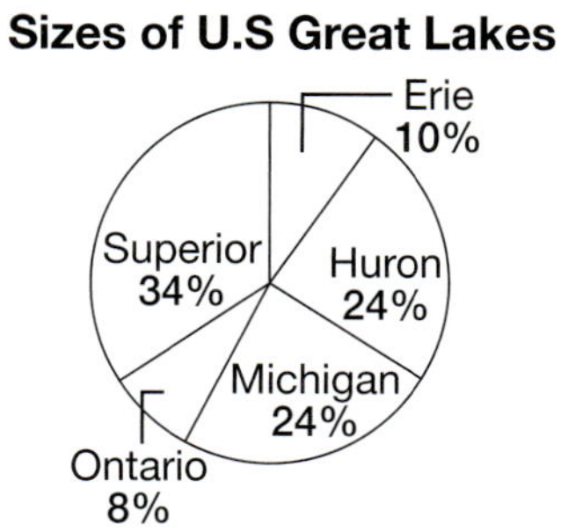

21. Lake Ontario is one-third the size of Lake Michigan. **23.** No; a 50% increase in 126 students is 189 and 189 is not equal to 366. So, it is not reasonable to say that 50% more students said they could make a difference. Since 300% of 126 is 378, it is reasonable to say that 300% more students said they could make a difference than those who said they cannot make a difference. **25.** 12.5%; English is half of the circle. Since Science is half of English, Science is half of 50% or 25%. Math is half of Science which is half of 25% or 12.5%. **27.** Sample answer: No; the sum of the percents is greater than 100. The people surveyed must have been able to choose more than one fruit juice. **29.** F **31.** 3% **33.** 130 **35.** 55

Pages 566–568 ***Lesson 11-3***

1. 44 **3.** 45 **5.** C **7.** obtuse, scalene **9.** 118 **11.** 27 **13.** 90 **15.** 53° **17.** acute, equilateral **19.** right, isosceles **21.** acute, scalene **23.** right **25.** 79.5 **27.** 79.2 **29.** 21.3 **31.** 80° **33.** 60 **35.** 77.5

37.

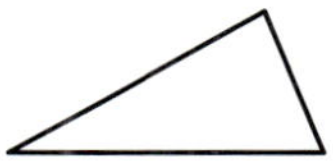

Sample answer: All of the angles are acute and there are no congruent sides. **39.** B **41.** 147.6° **43.** supplementary **45.** about \$9

Pages 569–570 ***Lesson 11-4***

1. Sample answer: They used inductive reasoning because they made a rule after seeing four examples. **3.** Two angles are congruent. **5.** 25 units **7.** 265 mi **9.** 196 sq units **11.** Sample answer: addition; $22\frac{1}{2} + 22\frac{1}{2} + 37\frac{1}{4} + 37\frac{1}{4} = 119\frac{1}{2}$ ft **13.** Sample answer: addition and division; Find the score that when added to the others, the total sum divided by the number of scores, 5, is equal to 82. The answer is 79.

Pages 574–576 ***Lesson 11-5***

1. rectangle **3.** parallelogram **5.** 120° **7.** 64° **9.** square **11.** quadrilateral **13.** trapezoid **15.** 56° **17.** 67° **19.** 90° **21.** 116° **23.** Bricks A, B, and D are rectangles and brick C is a square. **25.** 129.1° **27.** 131.8° **29.** trapezoids, squares, scalene triangles, equilateral triangles **31.** right isosceles triangles, squares, trapezoids **33.** 45

35. A square is a rhombus and a rectangle.

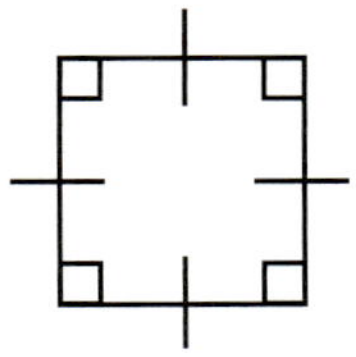

37. Yes; one pair of opposite sides are parallel, while the other pair of opposite sides are congruent. This figure is called an isosceles trapezoid.

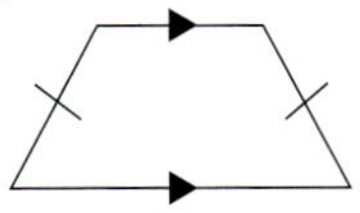

39. Never; Sample answer: A trapezoid has only one pair of parallel sides. A parallelogram has 2 pairs of parallel sides.
41. Sometimes; Sample answer; A rhombus is only a square if all 4 angles are right angles. **45.** J
47. obtuse, isosceles **49.** acute, equilateral **51.** \$3.78
53. 45 **55.** 36 **57.** 2.5

Pages 581–583 Lesson 11-6

1. rectangle *PQRS* **3.** 45 mm **5.** triangle *CAB* **7.** 25 mi **9.** 7.2 in. **11.** 6 ft **13.** 12 m **15.** about 42 ft **17.** 120 m **19.** 1:16 **21.** B **23.** C **25.** trapezoid **27.** 69° **29.** 90 **31.** 120

Pages 587–589 Lesson 11-7

1. decagon; not regular **3.** hexagon; regular **5.** 128.6° **7.** not a polygon; the figure is not simple **9.** isosceles triangle; not regular **11.** hexagon; not regular **13.** 144° **15.** 90° **17.** No; the figure is a decagon. Each angle of a decagon measures 144°, Since 144° does not divided evenly into 360°, a decagon cannot make a tessellation. **19.** hexagon and triangle **21.** octagon and square **23.** $36\frac{1}{4}$ yd **25.** No; the stop sign is an octagon in shape. An octagon cannot make a tessellation. So, there will be some steel that is wasted after the nine signs are cut from the sheet.
27. trapezoid
29. square **31.** pentagon hexagon

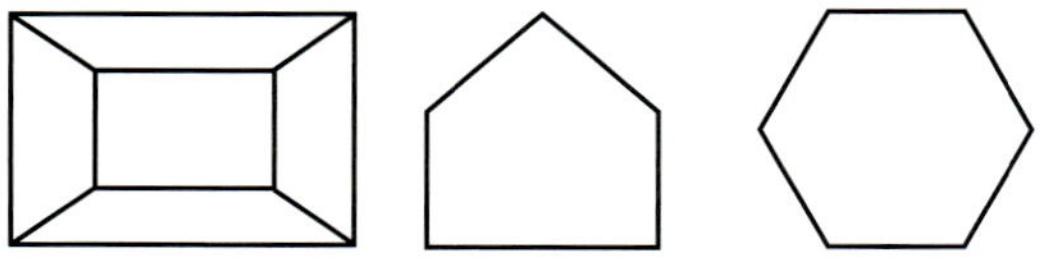

the Pentagon section of honeycomb

33. Sample answer; A copy of the parallelogram can fit next to it since 45° + 135° = 180° and above or below it since 135° + 45° = 180°. **35.** G **37.** 8 m **39.** $\frac{1}{42}$
41. $8\frac{2}{3}$ **43.** $7\frac{19}{28}$

45–48.

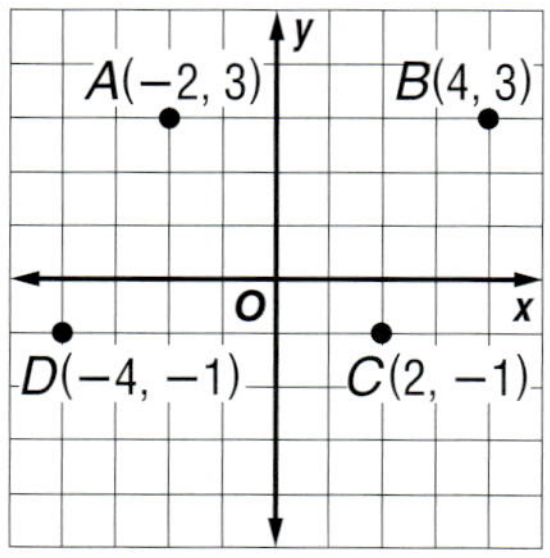

Pages 593–595 Lesson 11-8

1.

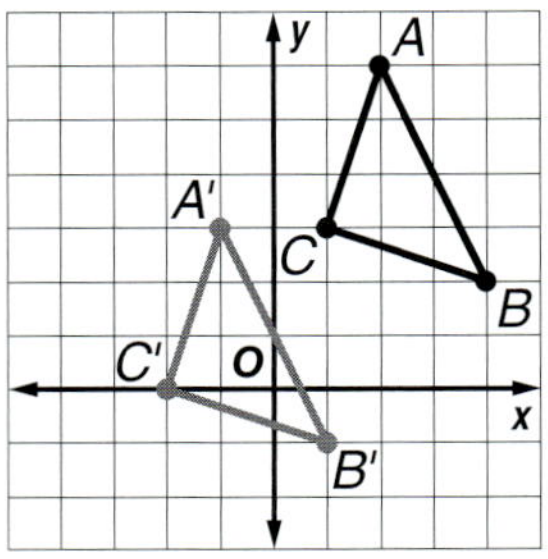

3. *D′* (7, 0), *E′* (4, −2), *F′* (8, 4), *G′* (12, −3)

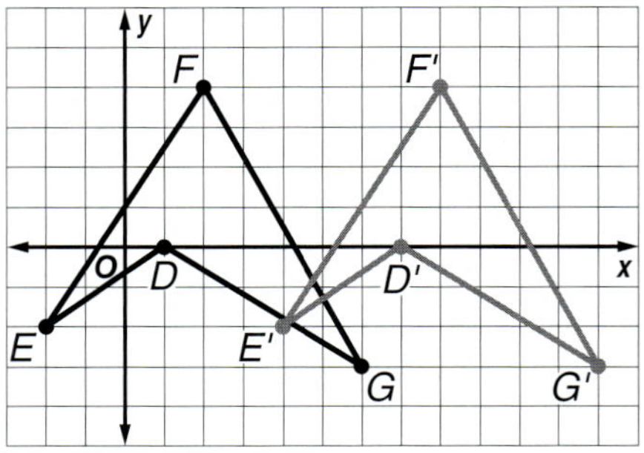

5.

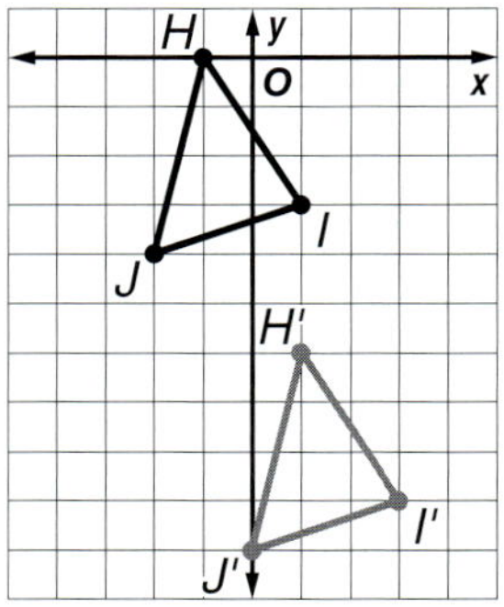

7. *P′* (6, 5), *Q′* (11, 3), *R′* (3, 11)

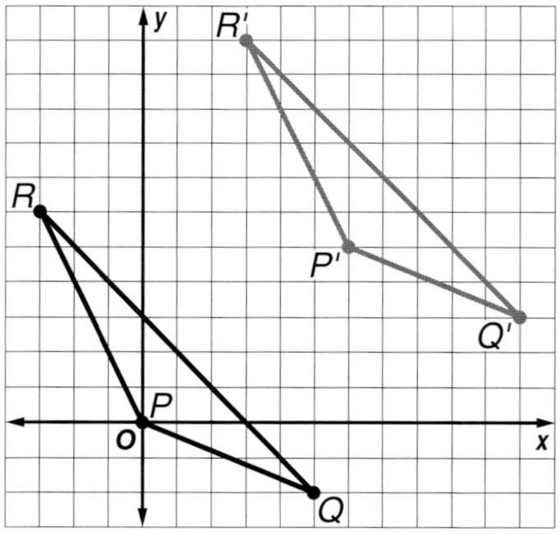

9. *P′* (−3, 0), *Q′* (2, −2), *R′* (−6, 6)

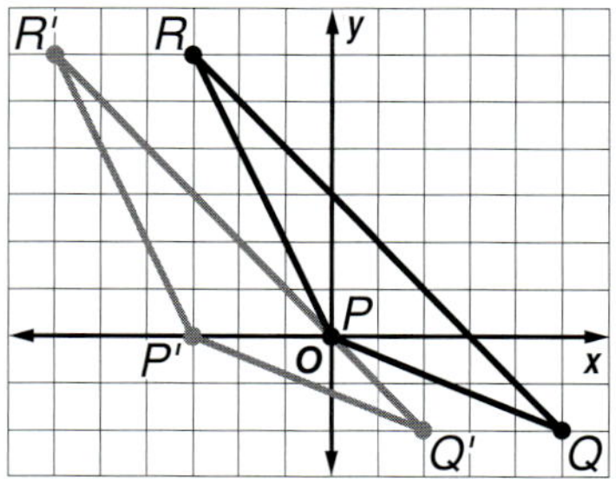

Selected Answers

11. right 2, down 3; (2, −3)

13.

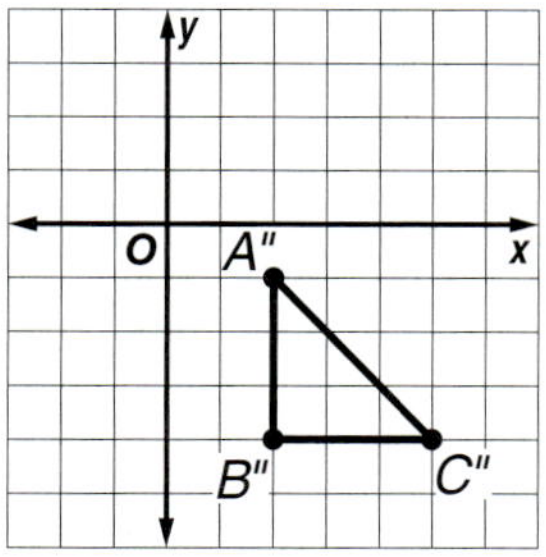

15. Sample answer: There are two main images, the brown horseman and the white horseman. Both main horsemen are translated to different parts of the picture. These translations allow for the tessellation of both horsemen.

17. $F'\left(8\frac{1}{2}, 2\frac{1}{2}\right)$, $G'\left(4\frac{1}{2}, \frac{1}{2}\right)$, $H'\left(2\frac{1}{2}, 1\frac{1}{2}\right)$

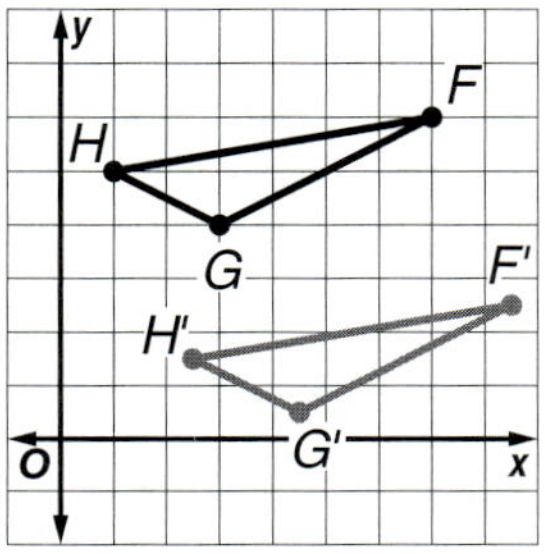

19. 5 units left and 3 units down; (−5, −3) **21.** 5 units right and 4 units up; (5, 4) **23.** Transformation A is a reflection; the others are translations. **25.** B **27.** octagon **29.** 2 × 4 × 3 or 24 dinners **31.** 0.567 **33.** 1.026 **35.** Sample answer: 9 − 5 or 4 **37.** Sample answer: 10 ÷ 2 or 5 **39.** no **41.** yes

Pages 598–600 ***Lesson 11-9***

1. no **3.** yes

5. $A'(5, -8)$, $B'(1, -2)$, and $C'(6, -4)$

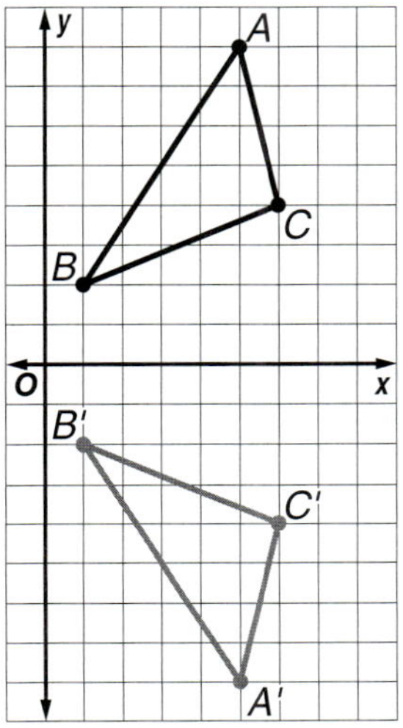

7. $Q'(-2, -5)$, $R'(-4, -5)$, and $S'(-2, 3)$

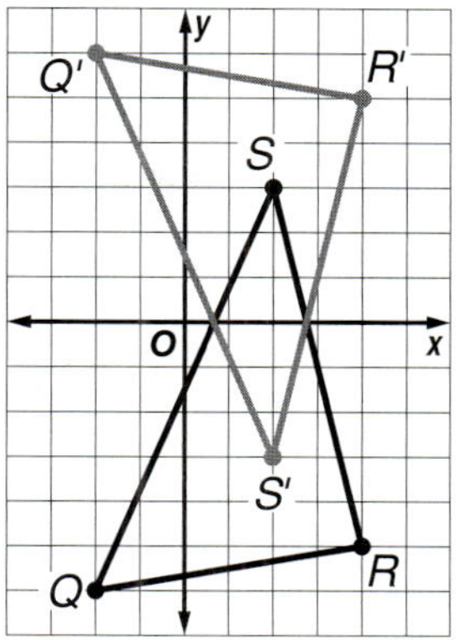

9. yes

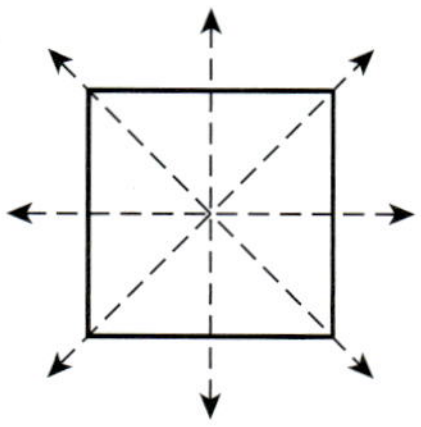

11. yes

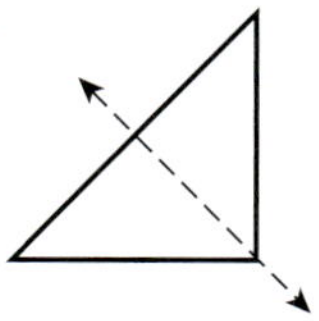

13. yes

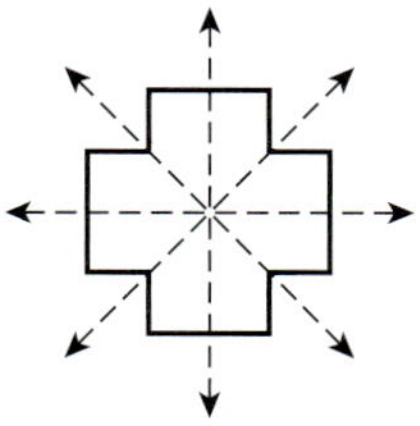

15. $T'(-6, 1)$, $U'(-2, 3)$, and $V'(5, 4)$

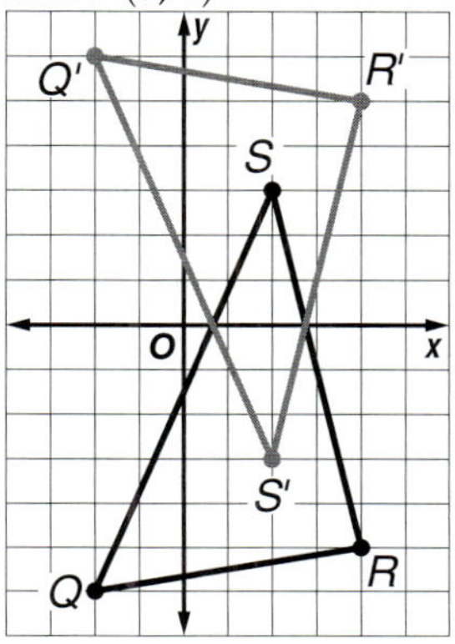

17. $A'(2, -4)$, $B'(-2, -4)$, $C'(2, -8)$, $D'(-2, -8)$

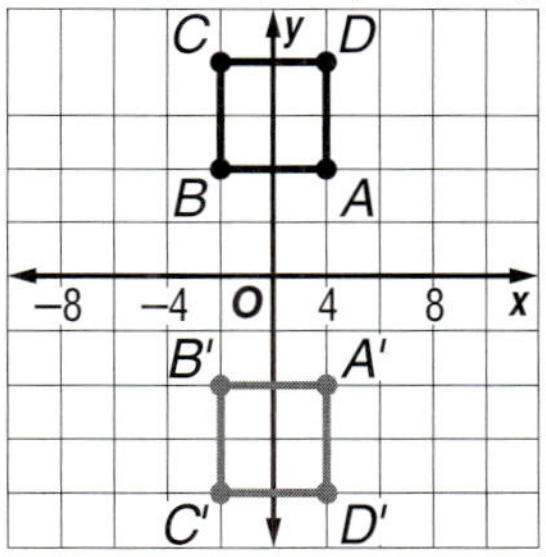

19. $R'(5, 3)$, $S'(4, -2)$, $T'(2, 3)$

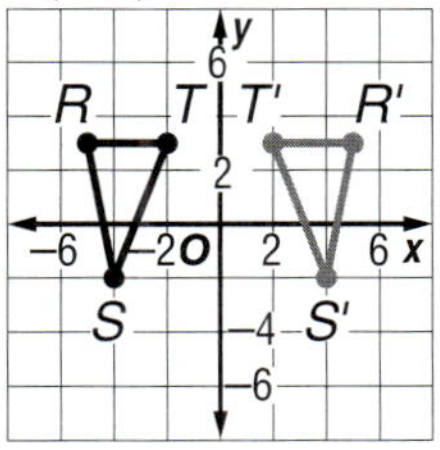

21. $H'(1, 3)$, $I'(1, -1)$, $J'(-2, -2)$, and $K'(-2, 2)$

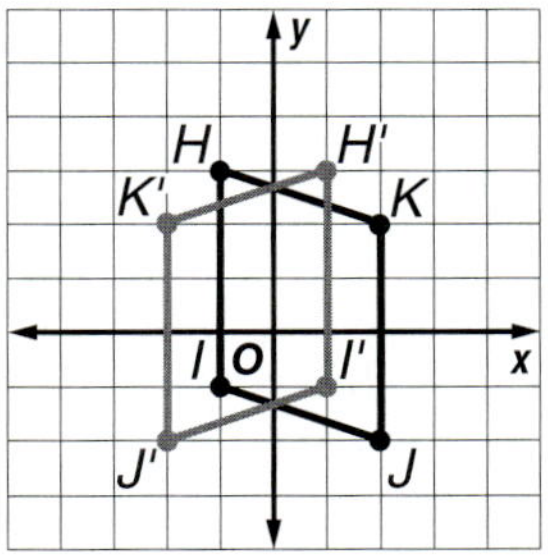

23. Sample answer: One is vertically down the center of the picture. The other is horizontally with the reflection of the water. **25.** 0 **27.** figures *A* and *C* **29.** Sample answer; A reflection over the *y*-axis followed by a reflection over the *x*-axis.

31. 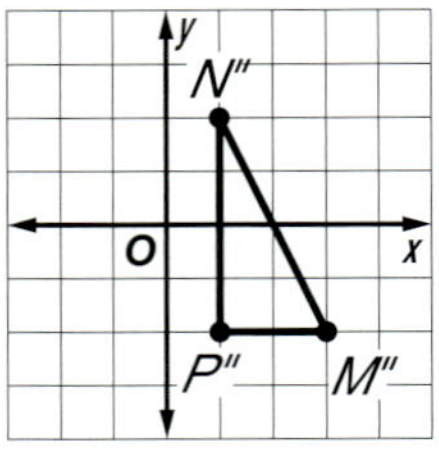

33. x-axis 35. y-axis 37. $J''(7, -4)$, $K''(-7, -1)$, and $L''(-2, 2)$ 39. C
41. $F'(1, 6)$, $G'(3, 4)$, $H'(2, 1)$

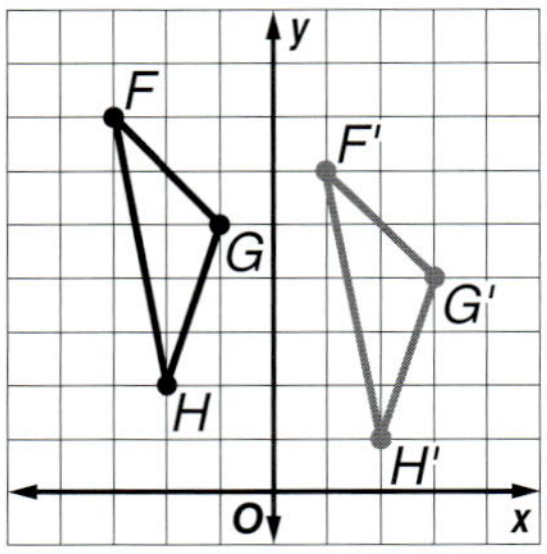

43. Sample answer: $\frac{1}{2} + 8 = 8\frac{1}{2}$
45. Sample answer: $12 \div 6 = 2$

Pages 601–604 Chapter 11 Study Guide and Review

1. false; supplementary angles 3. false; acute angle 5. true 7. $\angle FGH$, $\angle HGF$, $\angle G$, or $\angle 1$; obtuse 9. supplementary

11. **Favorite Soft Drinks**

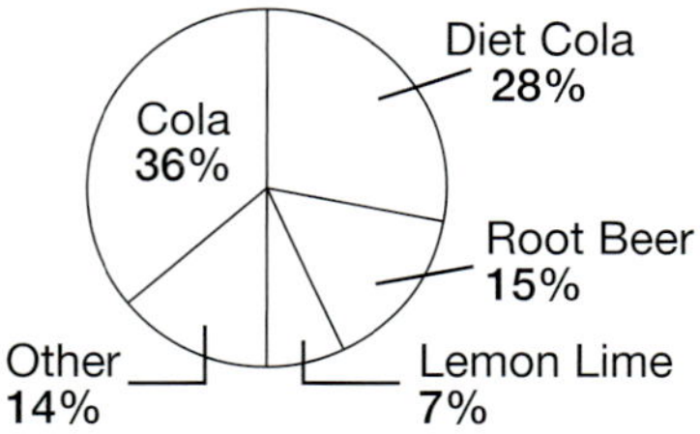

13. 47 15. Donnie, field hockey; Barbara, golf; Milo, volleyball; Jenna, soccer 17. rhombus
19. trapezoid 21. 10.5 m 23. heptagon; not regular 150° 25. 156° 27. $P'(8, -3)$, $Q'(2, -4)$, and $R'(3, 5)$

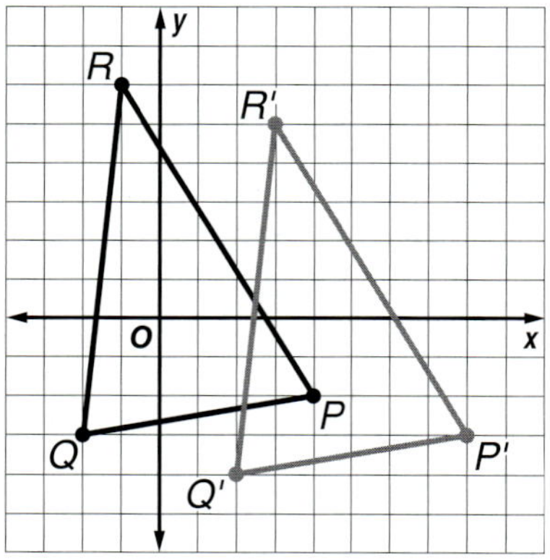

29. $P'(4, -9)$, $Q'(-2, -10)$, and $R'(-1, -1)$

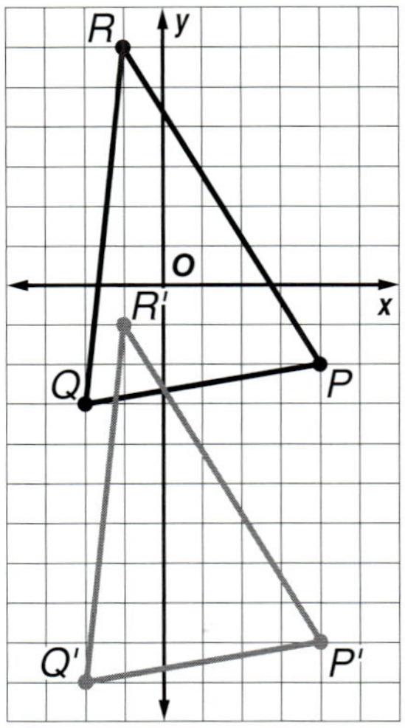

31. $A'(-1, 3)$, $B'(-2, -1)$, $C'(-5, -1)$, $D'(-4, 3)$

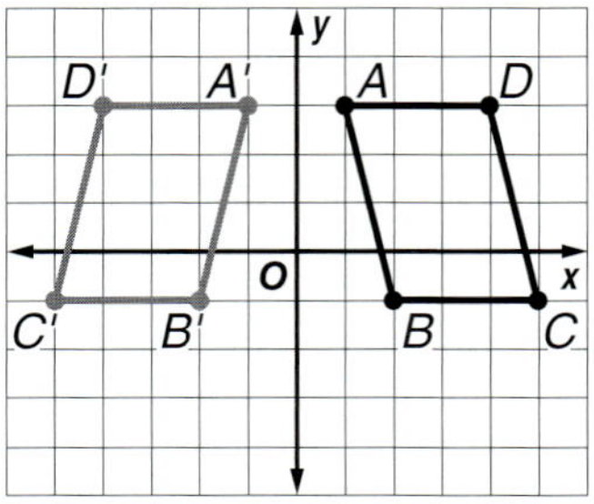

Chapter 12 Measurement: Two- and Three-Dimensional Figures

Page 609 Chapter 12 Getting Ready

1. 136 3. 1,248 5. 77 7. $41.67 9. 121 11. 36
13. 12.6 15. 31.4 17. 254.3

Pages 612–614 Lesson 12-1

1. 135 cm^2 3. 17.5 in^2 5. 32 in^2 7. 60 cm^2
9. 0.2 cm^2 11. 49.5 yd^2 13. 190.625 m^2
15. 525 mm^2 17. 216 in^2 or 1.5 ft^2 19. 972 in^2 or 0.8 yd^2 21. 42,000 mi^2 23. 15 in. 25. $16\frac{2}{3}$ ft^2 27. False; if the base and height are each doubled, then the area is $2b \cdot 2h = 4bh$, or 4 times greater. 29. D
31. $A'(2, 5)$, $B'(1, 2)$, $C'(4, 1)$

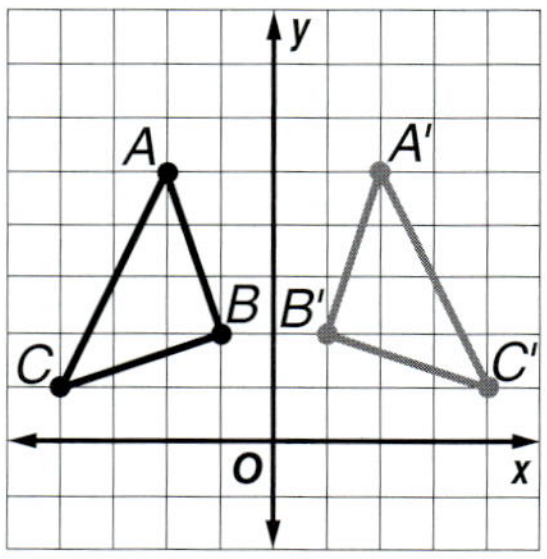

33. Sample answer: The sum of the measures of an octagon is 1,080°. Each angle measure is 1,080° ÷ 8 or 135°. Since 135 does not go into 360 evenly, an octagon does not tessellate the plane. 35. 84 37. 19.5

Pages 618–620 ***Lesson 12-2***

1. 6 in^2 **3.** 90.4 ft^2 **5.** 147 in^2 **7.** 4.5 cm^2 **9.** 183.7 in^2 **11.** about 95,000 mi^2 **13.** 125 ft **15.** Sample answer: 10 cm^2 **17.** Sample answer: 7 ft^2

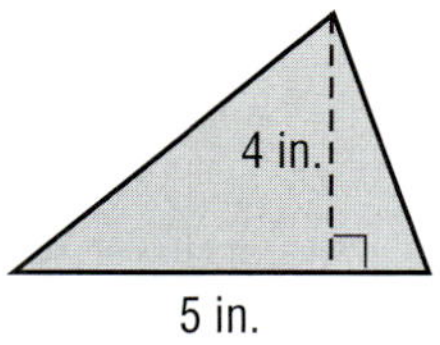

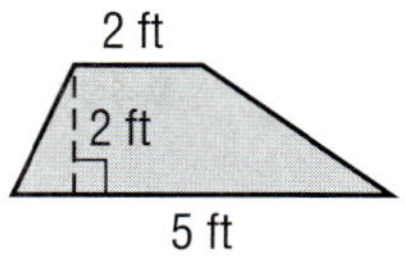

19. 6,500 ft^2 **21.** $A = 2h$ **23.** The area of a triangle is half the area of a parallelogram with the same base and height, because two of these triangles make up the parallelogram. **25.** G

27. $J'(-1, 4)$, $L'(1, -1)$, $K'(3, 2)$ **29.** 25% **31.** 156.3 **33.** 91.1 **35.** 72.4

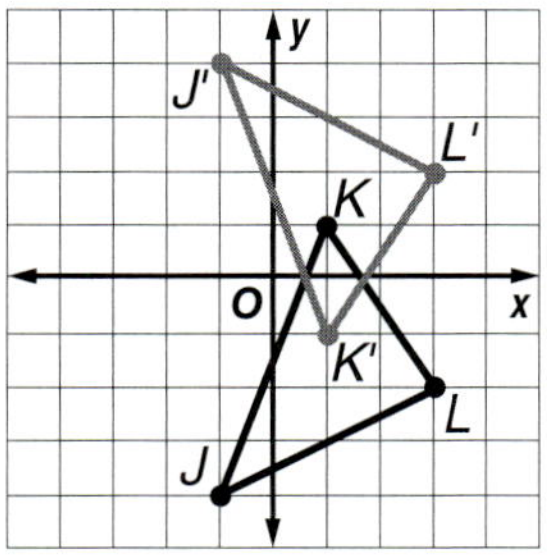

Pages 624–626 ***Lesson 12-3***

1. 31.4 ft **3.** 44 m **5.** 67.2 in. **7.** 50.2 ft **9.** 22.6 cm **11.** 66 ft **13.** 33 in. **15.** 33.9 km **17.** $38\frac{1}{2}$ mi **19.** $28\frac{2}{7}$ in. **21.** 94.2 ft **23.** 11.0 in. **25.** Sample answer: 48 is about 50 and 3.14 is about 3 so, 50 × 3 or 150 ft **27.** Sample answer: $3\frac{1}{2}$ is about 4 and $\frac{22}{7}$ is about $\frac{3}{1}$ so, $4 \times \frac{3}{1}$ or 12 in. **29.** 17.2 **31.** 7.6

33. Sample answer: Using the circumference formula, you find that the unicycle travels 3.14 • 10 • 2 or 62.8 inches on one revolution. So, in 5 revolutions, it will travel 62.8 • 5 or 314 inches. To change into feet, divide 314 by 12. So, the unicycle will travel $26\frac{1}{6}$ feet in 5 revolutions. **37.** Mya; Aidan incorrectly applied the formula that uses the diameter.

39. Both will be doubled. If the value of x is doubled, the diameter will be $2x$ instead of x. The circumference will increase from $2\pi x$ to $2\pi(2x)$ to $4\pi x$. **41.** C

43. 73.5 km^2 **45.** 45.5 m^2 **47.** $\frac{15}{27}$ or $\frac{5}{9}$ **49.** 153.9 **51.** 63.6

Pages 629–631 ***Lesson 12-4***

1. 78.5 cm^2 **3.** 201.1 m^2 **5.** B **7.** 28.3 in^2 **9.** 227.0 cm^2 **11.** 32.2 mm^2 **13.** 124.7 cm^2 **15.** 44.2 ft^2 **17.** 338.2 yd^2 **19.** 2,827.4 ft^2 **21.** Sample answer: $3 \cdot 6^2 = 108$ ft^2 **23.** c. **25.** a. **27.** 29.0 m^2 **29.** $\pi \cdot 71^2 \approx 15{,}836.8$ ft^2 and $15.836.8 \cdot 0.1 = 1{,}583.7$ yd^2 **31.** 62.8 m^2 **33.** 103.5 cm^2 **35.** Sample answer: If the radius of a circular garden is 6 feet, how much room is there for gardening? about 113.1 ft^2 **37.** F **39.** 283.5 m^2 **41.** 39.5 cm^2 **43.** $205 **45.** 113.04 **47.** 150.5

Pages 632–633 ***Lesson 12-5***

1. Sample answer: Finding the areas of the separate geometric figures and then adding is easier than trying to find the area of the irregular figure as a whole.
3. Sample answer: Find the area of the wall below to determine how much paint to buy. To solve, find the area of the triangle and the area of the rectangle, then add. The answer is 77 ft^2.

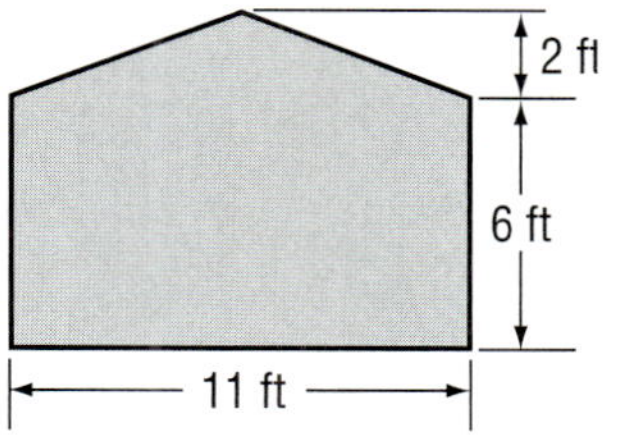

5. Sample answer: 0.44 × 3,000,000 or 1,320,000 phone lines have 888 area code; 0.24 × 3,000,000 or 720,000 phone lines have 777 area code; 0.32 × 3,000,000 or 960,000 phones lines have 555 area code. **7.** A

9. Sample answer: $\frac{1}{3} \times 360{,}000$ or 120,000 people

11. multiplication flowed by division; $150 \times 108 = 16{,}200$; $16{,}200 \div 10 = 1{,}620$; 1,620 h

Pages 635–637 ***Lesson 12-6***

1. 112 m^2 **3.** 145 m^2 **5.** 195 ft^2 **7.** 58.6 in^2 **9.** 257.1 mm^2 **11.** 66.2 yd^2 **13.** approximately 847.2 ft^2 **15.** 153.1 in^2 **17.** 142.5 ft^2 **19.** $467.4 \div 350 \approx 1.34$; Since only whole gallons of paint can be purchased, you will need 2 gallons of paint. At $20 each, the cost will be 2 • $20 or $40. **21.** Sample answer: Add the areas of a trapezoid and a triangle. Area of a trapezoid: $\left[\frac{1}{2} \times 2.5\,(7 + 10)\right] = 21.25$; Area of a triangle: $\frac{1}{2} \times 6 \times 2 = 6$; $21.25 + 6 = 27.25$. So, an approximate area is 27.25 × 1,900 or 51,775 mi^2.
23. 404 **25.** Sample answer: about 30% of $500 or $150 **27.** 452.4 in^2

29.

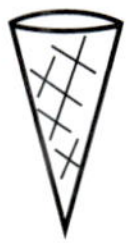

31.

Pages 643–644 ***Lesson 12-7***

1. square; square pyramid **3.** circle; cylinder **5.** triangle; triangular pyramid **7.** rectangle; rectangular pyramid **9.** cone **11.** trapezoid; trapezoidal prism **13.** octagon; octagonal prism
15. triangular prism and rectangular prism
17. rectangular prism

19. Sample answer: A cone has only one base that is a circle. A pyramid also has only one base but its base is a polygon. They both have only one vertex. A cone does not have any lateral faces and a pyramid has at least three lateral faces. **21.** F **23.** 102.1 m^2 **25.** 53° **27.** square **29.** circle

Pages 648–650 **Lesson 12-8**

1.

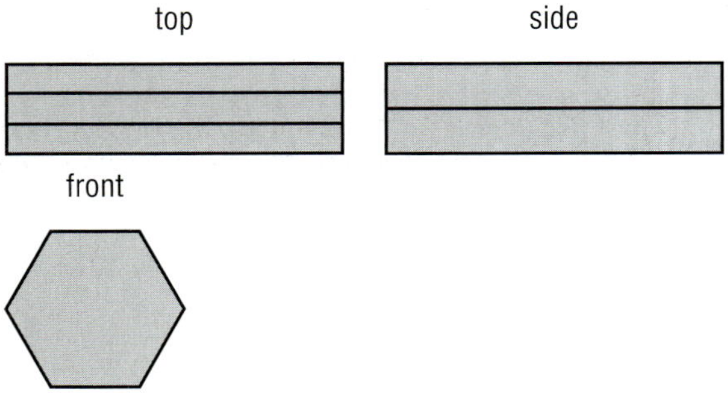

3.

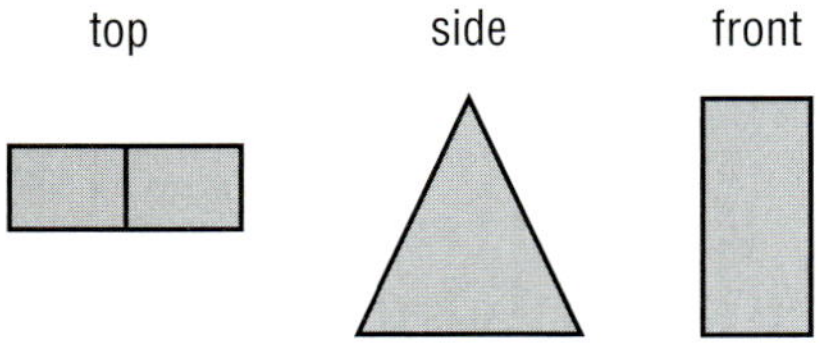

5.

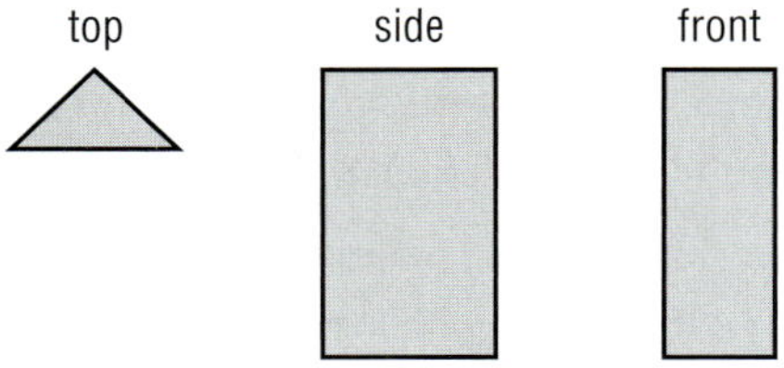

7.

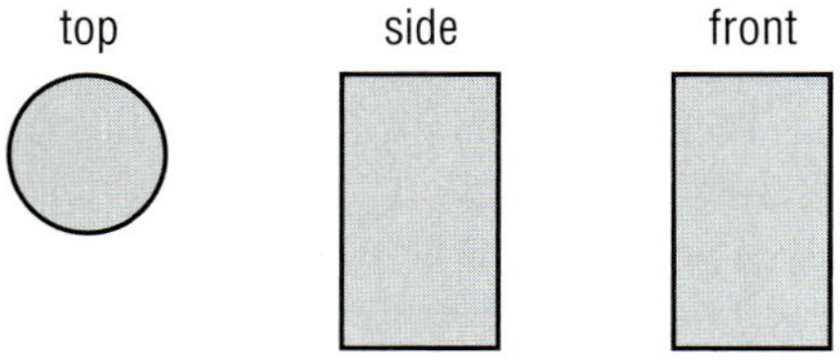

9.

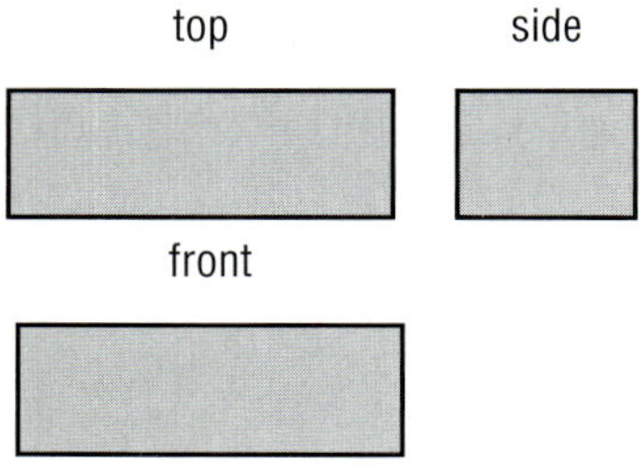

11.

13.

15.

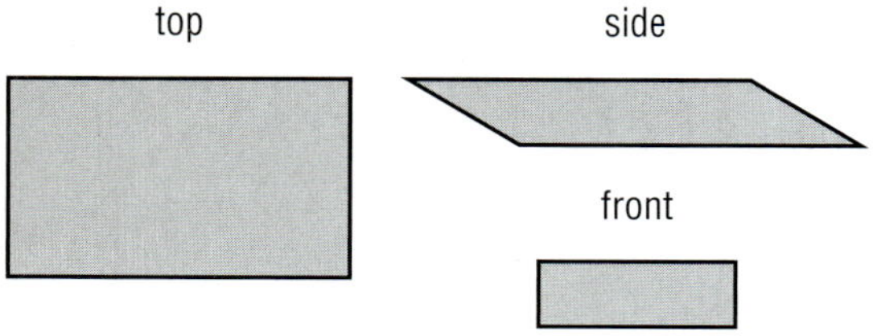

17.

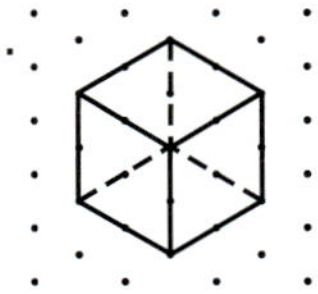

19. Sample answer:

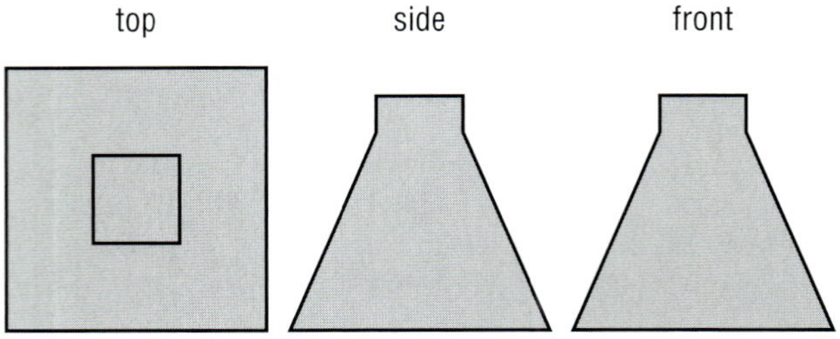

21.

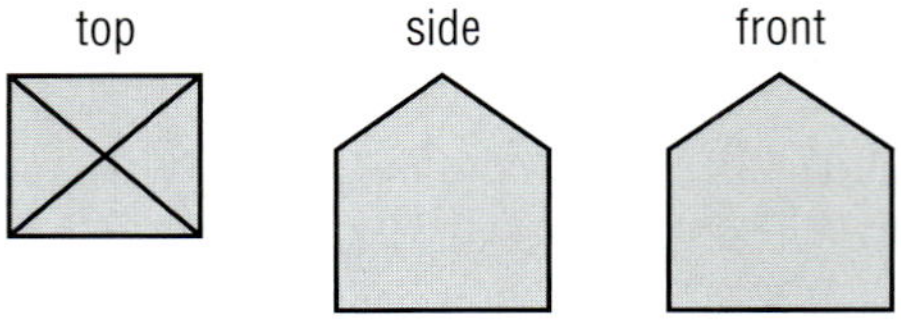

23.

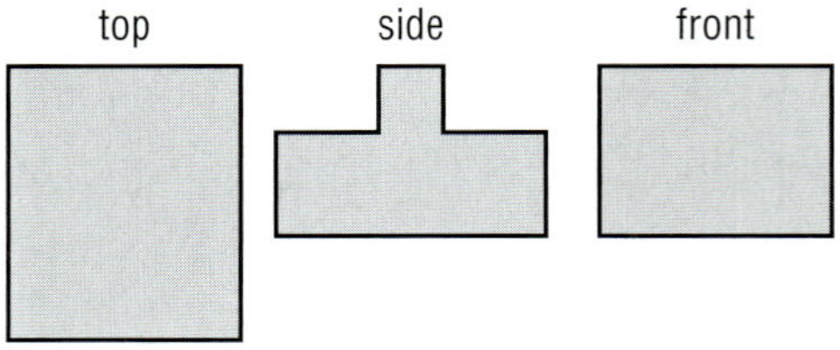

25. Sample answer:

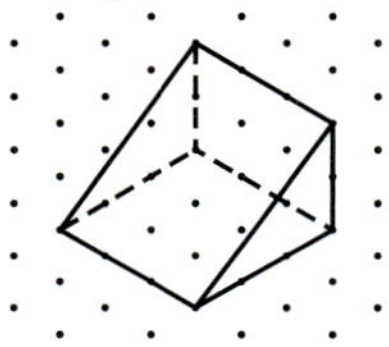

29. B **31.** sphere **33.** 96 ft^2 **35.** 112.8 in^2 **37.** \$77.39 **39.** 22 **41.** 68

Pages 654–656 **Lesson 12-9**

1. 220 in^3 **3.** 63 yd^3 **5.** 37.5 ft^3 < 63 ft^3; second cabinet **7.** 90 ft^3 **9.** 236.3 cm^3 **11.** 108 m^3 **13.** 20.4 mm^3 **15.** 40 ft^3 > 36 ft^3, so too much was bought **17.** $166\frac{1}{4}$ yd^3 **19.** 2,157,165 ft^3 **21.** 306.52 = 19.4h; 15.8 m **23.** Sample answer: $5 \times 4 \times 2$ or 40 ft^3 **25.** 6 ft **27.** Sample answer: the volumes are the same; the volume of prism B is $8 \times 4 \times 16$ which can be written as $8 \times 4 \times (2 \times 8) = 8 \times (4 \times 2) \times 8 = 8 \times 8 \times 8$. **29.** 4032

31.

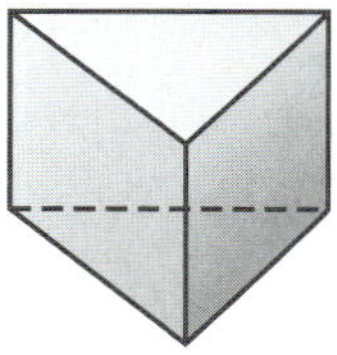

33. rectangle; rectangular prism **35.** 50 mph **37.** Sample answer: $5 \cdot 3^2$ or 45 **39.** Sample answer: $3 \cdot 2^2 \cdot 2$ or 24

Pages 658–661 **Lesson 12-10**

1. 141.4 in^3 **3.** 617.7 ft^3 **5.** about 603.2 cm^3 **7.** 4,071.5 ft^3 **9.** 2,770.9 yd^3 **11.** 35.6 m^3 **13.** 103.4 m^3

15. 288.6 in^3 **17.** 163.4 m^3 **19.** 124,642.7 m^3 **21.** d.
23. a. **25.** 1,413 in^3 **27.** 9 cm **29.** about 40.7 ft
31. Sample answer:

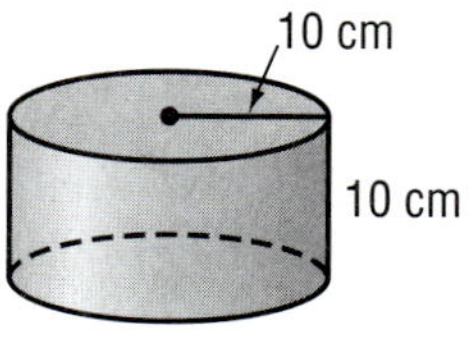

33. 1 to 4 **35.** D
37. 152.9 m^3

39. Sample answer:

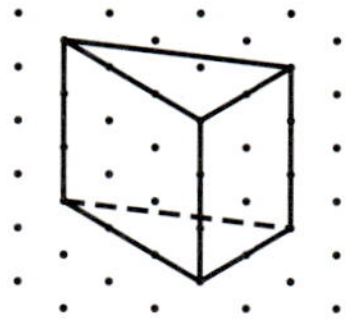

41. $\frac{1}{4}$ **43.** $\frac{5}{12}$

Pages 664–668 Chapter 12 Study Guide and Review

1. rectangular prism **3.** trapezoid **5.** cylinder
7. circle **9.** 2,520 in^2 **11.** 36 ft^2 **13.** 527.3 yd^2
15. 75.4 in. **17.** $26\frac{2}{5}$ ft **19.** $29\frac{6}{7}$ ft **21.** 1,520.5 cm^2
23. 800 cakes **25.** $105 **27.** 67.8 yd^2 **29.** triangle; triangular prism **31.** cylinder **33.** rectangular pyramid

35.

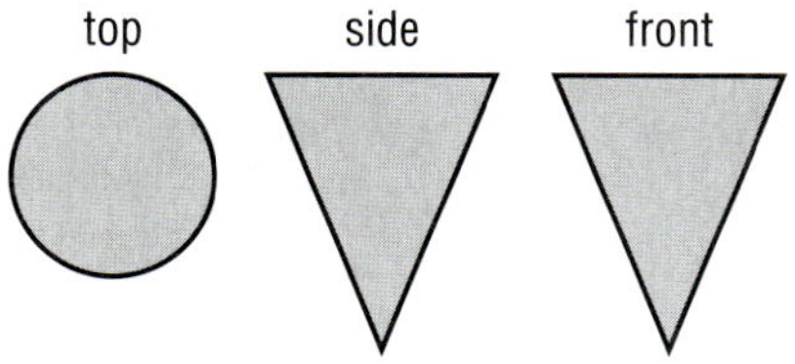

37.

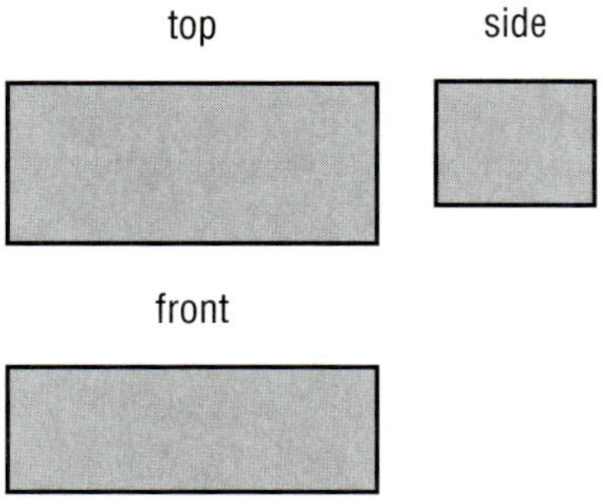

39. 639.6 in^3 **41.** 1,330 ft^3 **43.** 3,728.7 mm^3
45. 942 $in.^3$

Chapter 13 Extending Algebra and Geometry

Page 673 Chapter 13 Getting Ready

1. 16 **3.** 169 **5.** 89 **7.** 225 **9.** 130 yr **11.** 226
13. 42.1 **15.** 527.8

Pages 675–677 Lesson 13-1

1. 6 **3.** 9 **5.** 2.6 **7.** 11.6 **9.** 9.7 cm **11.** 4 **13.** 8
15. 11 **17.** 20 **19.** 2.8 **21.** 9.4 **23.** 23.9 **25.** 52.9
27. 6 **29.** 50 **31.** 81 **33.** 0.7 **35.** 1.7 **37.** 3.8
39. 3.17 cm **43.** Sample answer: 17, 18, 19 **45.** 2
47. 5 **49.** It cannot be written as a fraction. **51.** G
53. 63 in^3 **55.** acute **57.** obtuse **59.** 20 **61.** 85

Pages 681–684 Lesson 13-2

1. 26 mm **3.** 18.5 cm **5.** 4.0 ft **7.** 16.1 m **9.** 14.1 m
11. 5.4 ft **13.** 2.8 yd **15.** 25 in. **17.** 5.6 mi **19.** 72.1 in.
21. 5.3 in. **23.** 7.7 cm **25.** yes **27.** no **29.** 7.2 ft
31. Sample answer: The mirror will not fit horizontally or vertically. However, the diagonal of the doorway measures about 7.2 feet. So, the mirror will fit through the doorway if you tilt it diagonally.
33. about 10.4 in. **35.** Devin; the hypotenuse is 16 cm, not x cm as Jamie assumed. **37.** B **39.** 11.3
41. 1,413 in^3 **43.** 0.45 **45.** 1.24 **47.** 151,200 breaths

Pages 685–686 Lesson 13-3

1. Sample answer: A three-dimensional object allows you to physically change the object. This makes it easier to make the pattern and then solve the problem.
3. 11.25 in. by 9 in. **5.** 47 in. **7.** 6.25 min **9.** 144 ft^2
11. Take the square root followed by addition followed by subtraction; 586 ft

Pages 690–693 Lesson 13-4

1. 108 ft^2 **3.** No; The surface area of the toy box is 48 ft^2. To paint it twice would require enough paint for 48×2 or 96 ft^2. Since 87 $ft^2 < 96$ ft^2, he does not have enough paint. **5.** 314 cm^2 **7.** 833.1 mm^2 **9.** 125.4 in^2 or $124\frac{3}{8}$ in^2 **11.** 234 in^2 **13.** 243.8 ft^2 **15.** 11,150 yd^2
17. 30,791.2 m^2 **19.** 216.82 cm^2 **21.** about 864 ft^2
23. 6 cm^2 **25.** Sample answer: The granulated sugar has greater surface area than a sugar cube.
27. $6.50 **29.** 1,926 cm^2 **31.** B **33.** 248 ft **35.** 8
37. 6 **39.** 351. 9 in^3 **41.** 346.4 m^2 **43.** 1,661.9 km^2

Pages 697–699 Lesson 13-5

1. 88.0 mm^2 **3.** about 471.2 m^2 **5.** 1,215.8 m^2
7. 272.0 mm^2 **9.** 1,120.0 in^2 or $1{,}119\frac{44}{45}$ in^2
11. 61.3 cm^2 **13.** Sample answer: $2 \cdot 3 \cdot 4^2 + 2 \cdot 3 \cdot 4 \cdot 4$ or 192 m^2 **15.** 205.0 in^2 **17.** No; the surface area of the side of the cylinder will double, but the area of the bases will not. **19.** A cylinder with radius 6 cm and height 3 cm has a greater surface area than a cylinder with height 6 cm and radius 3 cm; Sample answer: The first cylinder has a surface area of 339.3 cm^2 while the second cylinder has a surface area of 169.6 cm^2.
21. G **23.** 112 cm^2 **25.** 12.8 in. **27.** 7.2 cm

Pages 700–702 Chapter 13 Study Guide and Review

1. false; right triangle **3.** true **5.** true **7.** false; positive and negative **9.** false; cylinder **11.** 2
13. 7 **15.** 4 **17.** 7.8 **19.** 21.1 **21.** 11 ft **23.** 26.7
25. 6.6 yd **27.** 29.8 ft **29.** 875 in^2 **31.** 202 yd^2
33. 43 ft^2 **35.** 2,261.9 in^2

Photo Credits

Cover (t)Created by Michael Trott with Mathematica. From *Graphica 1*, Copyright ©1999 Wolfram Media, Inc., (b)Scott Berner/Index Stock Imagery; **i** (t)Created by Michael Trott with Mathematica. From *Graphica 1*, Copyright ©1999 Wolfram Media, Inc., (b)Scott Berner/Index Stock Imagery; **iv** Aaron Haupt; **v** Aaron Haupt; **x** Herbert Kehrer/CORBIS; **xi** Ralph White/CORBIS; **xii** John Giustina/Taxi/Getty Images; **xiii** Carolyn Brown/The Image Bank/Getty Images; **xiv** Zigmund Leszczynski/Animals Animals; **xv** Garry Black/Masterfile; **xvi** Tom Brakefield/CORBIS; **xvii** Charles O'Rear/CORBIS; **xviii** Barbara Peacock/Taxi/Getty Images; **xix** Michael Newman/PhotoEdit; **xx** CORBIS; **xxii** Collin Reid/AP/Wide World Photos; **xxv** John D. Wigmore/Index Stock Imagery; **xxvi** Photodisc/Getty Images; **1** Digital Vision/Punchstock; **2** Didrik Johnck/CORBIS; **3** John Evans; **4** (t)Chris Lisle/CORBIS, (b)John Evans; **6** Mike Blake/Reuters/CORBIS; **8** Matt Meadows; **10** (tl)CORBIS/PictureQuest, (tr)Comstock/PictureQuest, (bl)Brand X Pictures/PunchStock, (br)Barbara Penoyar/Getty Images; **12** John Evans; **13** John Evans; **14** John Evans; **16** CORBIS; **17** (l)roadsideamerica.com, (r)Terry Vine/Stone/Getty Images; **18** (tl)W. Perry Conway/CORBIS, (tr)Theo Allofs/CORBIS, (b)PNC/Getty Images; **20–21** Mike Powell/Getty Images; **22** State Preservation Board, Austin, Texas; **26** Jose Luis Pelaez, Inc./Getty Images; **27** Dimitri Lundt/CORBIS; **35** CORBIS; **39** Chuck Savage/CORBIS; **41** (l)Michael Newman/PhotoEdit, (r)David Young-Wolff/PhotoEdit; **42** CMCD/Getty Images; **45** SW Productions/Getty Images; **49** Getty Images; **52** (l)David Young-Wolff/PhotoEdit, (r)Tony Freeman/PhotoEdit; **64** (t)Eric and David Hosking/CORBIS, (b)Noel Hendrickson/Digital Vision; **66** Herbert Kehrer/CORBIS; **78** CORBIS; **80** Jed Jacobsohn/Getty Images; **84** Mark Tomalty/Masterfile; **86** Rob Van Petten/Digital Vision; **90** Hummer/Getty Images; **91** Miriam Silverstein/Animals Animals; **95** Richard Kaylin/Getty Images; **97** Australian Picture Library/CORBIS; **99** (l)Myrleen Ferguson Cate/PhotoEdit, (r)David Young-Wolff/PhotoEdit; **104** NASA/Photo Researchers; **106** (l)Cleve Bryant/PhotoEdit, (r)David Young-Wolff/PhotoEdit; **107** John Evans; **111** Ralph White/CORBIS; **116** NASA; **117** José Fuste Raga/zefa/CORBIS; **126** Carltons/Botanica/Getty Images; **129** Martin Harvey/CORBIS; **135** John Giustina/Taxi/Getty Images; **137** Rob Gage/Taxi/Getty Images; **142** (t)State of Texas, (b)Dave King/Dorling Kindersley; **144** (l)Michael Newman/PhotoEdit, (r)Myrleen Ferguson Cate/PhotoEdit; **148** Getty Images; **151** Masterfile; **154** John Evans; **158** Steve Vidler/SuperStock; **160** (t)Lois Ellen Frank/CORBIS, (bl)Jonathan Nourok/PhotoEdit, (br)Michael Newman/PhotoEdit; **162** John Chumack/Photo Researchers; **165** Jessica Wecker/Photo Researchers; **174** Skyscan/CORBIS; **176** JPL/NASA; **177** Carolyn Brown/The Image Bank/Getty Images; **180** (t)CORBIS, (bl)CORBIS, (br)Dann Tardif/LWA/Getty Images; **185** Roger Ressmeyer/CORBIS; **187** Eddie Adams/CORBIS; **188** David Cannon/Getty Images; **191** Jose Luis Pelaez, Inc./Blenc Images/Getty Images; **194** (l)Ryan McVay/Getty Images, (r)CORBIS; **196** John Evans; **201** Michael Newman/PhotoEdit; **208** David Young-Wolff/PhotoEdit; **213** Brett Froomer/Getty Images; **224–225** Richard Hutchings/PhotoEdit; **226** Gay Bumgarner/Photographer's Choice/Getty Images; **231** Zigmund Leszczynski/Animals Animals; **233** Raymond K. Gehman/National Geographic/Getty Images; **236** KS Studios; **238** Matt Meadows; **241** David Tardif/CORBIS; **243** (l)Seth Kushner/Getty Images, (r)Image Source/SuperStock; **246** Comstock/SuperStock; **251** Doug Martin; **256** Steve Bloom/Taxi/Getty Images; **258** RubberBall/SuperStock; **260** Roy Ooms/Masterfile; **263** CORBIS; **264** Digital Vision/Getty Images; **267** Yiorgos Karahalis/Reuters/CORBIS; **276** Eclipse Studios; **280** Michael Newman/PhotoEdit; **281** Doug Martin; **282** Russell Kightley/Photo Researchers; **286** Tim Hursley/SuperStock; **287** *Thomas Jefferson*, 1776. Charles Willson Peale. Oil on canvas. The Huntington Library, Art Collections, and Botanical Gardens, San Marino, CA/SuperStock; **288** (l)Stockbyte/Getty Images, (r)Michael Newman/PhotoEdit; **292** Aaron Haupt; **295** Getty Images; **302** Garry Black/Masterfile; **303** Joseph Nettis/Photo Researchers; **304** Rob Lewine/CORBIS; **310** Daybreak Imagery/Animals Animals; **314** Aaron Haupt; **316** Darrell Gulin/CORBIS; **318** (l)CORBIS, (r)Barbara Penoyar/Getty Images; **326–327** Nicole Duplaix/Getty Images; **328** Alan Schein/zefa/CORBIS; **331** Elaine Shay; **333** (tl)Tom Brakefield/CORBIS, (tr)David Young-Wolff/PhotoEdit, (b)David Young-Wolff/PhotoEdit; **334** (l)Donna Day/ImageState, (r)Kareem Black/Getty Images; **337** Doug Menuez/Getty Images; **338** Ryan McVay/Stone/Getty Images; **339** Don Emmert/AFP/Getty Images; **342** CORBIS; **348** Doug Martin; **350** Project Exploration; **352** CORBIS; **354** Aaron Haupt; **356** KS Studios; **360** Matt Meadows; **363** Joseph Sohm/CORBIS; **366** Richard Lord/The Image Works; **369** Franz Marc Frei/CORBIS; **373** Stockbyte/Stockbyte Gold/Getty Images; **374** (l)Charlotte Nation/Getty Images, (r)Michael Krasowitz/Getty Images; **382** Wes Thompson/CORBIS; **389** G. Biss/Masterfile; **392** NASA; **394** Donna Ikenberry/Animals Animals; **397** CORBIS; **398** Michael Newman/PhotoEdit; **400** D. Robert & Lorri Franz/CORBIS; **401** (l)Photodisc/First Light, (r)Comstock/SuperStock; **403** John Evans; **407** Alaskastock; **416** Charles O'Rear/CORBIS; **420** (l)RubberBall/ImageState, (r)Barbara Penoyar/Getty Images; **422** KS Studios; **426** Andersen Ross/Getty Images; **438–439** James Richard/Stock Connection/PictureQuest; **440** Jason Knutson/coasterphotos.com; **445** Lorentz Gullachsen/The Image Bank/Getty Images; **446** (l)Catherine Ledner/Getty Images, (r)Amos Morgan/Getty Images; **452** CORBIS; **456** Barbara Peacock/Taxi/Getty Images; **457** Matt Meadows; **459** Brandon D. Cole/CORBIS; **462** CORBIS; **465** Daryl Balfour/Getty Images; **470** Mark Mattock/Taxi/Getty Images; **474** John Evans; **481** Bob Daemmrich/Stock Boston; **485** Diana Healey/Iconica/Getty Images; **490** Andrew J.G. Bell/Eye Ubiquitous/CORBIS; **502** KS Studios; **505** Matt Meadows; **512** Ariel Skelley/CORBIS; **513** Aaron Haupt; **515** Geoff Butler; **517** O'Brien Productions/CORBIS; **520** Michael Newman/PhotoEdit; **521** Andrew Hetherington/TIME Life Pictures/Getty Images; **525** Geoff Butler; **527** (l)Masterfile, (r)Michelle Pedone/zefa/CORBIS; **528** Laura Sifferlin; **532** Michael Newman/PhotoEdit; **536** CORBIS; **548–549** Charles O'Rear/CORBIS; **550** Gerry Ellis/Digital Vision/Getty Images; **559** Jon Feingersh/CORBIS; **567** (l)Damir Frkovic/Masterfile, (r)DeCordova Museum and Sculpture Park; **569** Laura Sifferlin; **572** Vaughn Youtz/ZUMA/CORBIS; **574** Didier Dorval/Masterfile; **575** George W. Hart; **576** (l)Michael Newman/PhotoEdit, (r)Michelle Pedone/zefa/CORBIS; **582** Bill Ross/CORBIS; **586** (l)Ariel Skelley/CORBIS, (r)Aaron Haupt; **588** (l)Jeff Greenberg/PhotoEdit, (r)Christine Osborne/CORBIS; **594** *Horsemen*, 1946. M.C. Escher. Cordon Art-Baarn-Holland. All rights reserved.; **598** R. Sponlein/zefa/CORBIS; **599** (l)Allen Wallace/Photonica/Getty Images, (r)CORBIS; **608** Danny Lehman/CORBIS; **611** Don Farrall/Getty Images; **613** Jules Frazier/Getty Images; **618** Jeremy Woodhouse/Masterfile; **621** Matt Meadows; **622** Ben Wood/CORBIS; **625** (t)Studio Wartenberg/zefa/CORBIS, (c)Circlemakers, (bl)Thinkstock/SuperStock, (br)David Young-Wolff/PhotoEdit; **628** The United States Mint; **630** (t)Alinari Archives/CORBIS, (bl)David Young-Wolff/PhotoEdit, (br)Gary Houlder/CORBIS; **631** CORBIS; **632** Doug Martin; **642** Nicholas Eveleigh/SuperStock; **643** (t)C Squared Studios/Getty Images, (c)Glencoe photo, (b)PhotoLink/Getty Images; **646** Tribune Media Services, Inc.; **648** Chris Bell/Taxi/Getty Images; **649** (tl)CORBIS, (tr)Ryan McVay/Getty Images, (b)CORBIS; **652** Charles Gupton/CORBIS; **655** Keate/Masterfile; **658** (t)Tony Freeman/PhotoEdit, (b)C Squared Studios/Getty Images; **659** Denis Scott/CORBIS; **667** G. Schuster/Photo-AG/zefa/CORBIS; **669** CORBIS; **672** Horizons Companies; **676** Myrleen Ferguson Cate/PhotoEdit; **679** Collin Reid/AP/Wide World Photos; **683** (t)Schlitterbahn Waterparks, (bl)Comstock/SuperStock, (br)Stockbyte/SuperStock; **685** Laura Sifferlin; **692** Melanie Acevedo/Botanica/Getty Images; **706** Eclipse Studios; **TX1** Michael Newman/PhotoEdit; **TX2** Tim Fuller.

Photo Credits

Index

A

B

C

D

G

H

I

K

L

M

Index

N

O

P

Index

Q

R

S

Mathematics Chart

Measurement Conversions

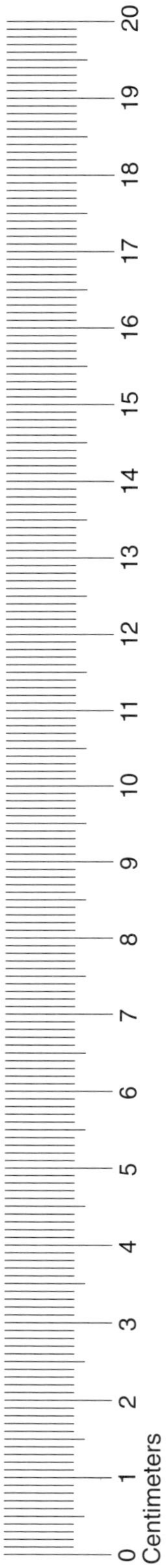

LENGTH

Metric	Customary
1 kilometer = 1000 meters	1 mile = 1760 yards
1 meter = 100 centimeters	1 mile = 5280 feet
1 centimeter = 10 millimeters	1 yard = 3 feet
	1 foot = 12 inches

CAPACITY AND VOLUME

Metric	Customary
1 liter = 1000 milliliters	1 gallon = 4 quarts
	1 gallon = 128 fluid ounces
	1 quart = 2 pints
	1 pint = 2 cups
	1 cup = 8 fluid ounces

MASS AND WEIGHT

Metric	Customary
1 kilogram = 1000 grams	1 ton = 2000 pounds
1 gram = 1000 milligrams	1 pound = 16 ounces

TIME

1 year = 365 days

1 year = 12 months

1 year = 52 weeks

1 week = 7 days

1 day = 24 hours

1 hour = 60 minutes

1 minute = 60 seconds